INTERNATIONAL INSTITUTE OF HUMAN RIGHTS

N°20

CAPTURED IN WAR

LAWFUL INTERNMENT IN ARMED CONFLICT

PRÉFACE
Andrew CLAPHAM

René Cassin Prize

2012

Published by
EDITIONS A. PEDONE AND HART PUBLISHING
PARIS – OXFORD
2013

This work is co-published by Editions Pedone in Paris, France and Hart Publishing Ltd in Oxford, United Kingdom, as the first volume in a new collaboration which brings to an international audience important new works by leading young scholars in the field of human rights. The series, under the editorship of Sébastien Touzé, publishes in English theses which have been awarded the Rene Cassin Prize by the International Institute of Human Rights in Strasbourg.

Published in France by Editions Pedone
13 rue Soufflot – 75005 – Paris
Telephone: +33 (0) 1 43 54 05 97 Fax: +33 (0)46 34 07 60
E-mail: editions-pedone@wanadoo.fr
Website: http://www.pedone.info

Published in the United Kingdom by Hart Publishing Ltd
16C Worcester Place, Oxford, OX1 2JW
Telephone: +44 (0)1865 517530
Fax: +44 (0)1865 510710
E-mail: mail@hartpub.co.uk
Website: http://www.hartpub.co.uk

Published in North America (US and Canada) by
Hart Publishing
c/o International Specialized Book Services
920 NE 58th Avenue, Suite 300
Portland, OR 97213-3786
USA
Tel: +1 503 287 3093 or toll-free: (1) 800 944 6190
Fax: +1 503 280 8832
E-mail: orders@isbs.com
Website: http://www.isbs.com

British Library Cataloguing in Publication Data – Data Available

I.S.B.N. 978-1-84946-530-4

I.S.B.N. 978-2-233-00672-1

PREFACE

Dr Els Debuf has broken new ground in this book on the legal bases for internment during all types of armed conflict. She asks hard questions about where the authority comes from to intern, and she provides carefully considered answers which will be of considerable interest to scholars and authorities working in this field. The huge merit of this work is that it provides fresh insights to contemporary problems related to detention – and it does not simply rehash the existing doctrine. Where Dr Debuf's research leads her to conclude that international law provides no legal basis to intern people, she does not flinch from highlighting the threats to human dignity that this entails. She challenges the international community to fill these gaps in the rule of law and her suggestions deserve to be taken seriously.

The book is based on a realistic appreciation of the fact that an occupying power and all parties to an armed conflict may need to intern those who threaten them. Dr Debuf is, however, careful to separate out members of the armed forces from civilians and take into account the specific situation of those civilians who take a direct part in hostilities. While she details all the national developments regarding the treatment of 'unlawful enemy combatants' and those detained in the 'war on terror', she contrasts these developments with what international law allows, and provides us with a helpful grid to judge the legality of a number of recent practices.

The book has the additional quality of contributing to the ongoing debates surrounding the adequacy of the 1949 Geneva Conventions and their interaction with the more recent developments in international human rights law. Dr Debuf goes beyond the well worn clichés which now bedevil this topic, and provides us with bold conclusions. Dr Debuf (in her words) 'found that some of the "traditional" interpretations of the provisions of the Geneva Conventions were no longer tenable in light of the important normative developments in international law since their adoption, and that a dynamic and teleological interpretation is called for if they are to withstand the test of time.' In particular her interpretation leads to a number of conclusions regarding the obligations on parties to an international armed conflict detaining their own nationals, and protection for prisoners of war who fear for their safety should they be returned to their state of origin after the conflict.

It was a huge pleasure to follow this work as it developed over the years. The original PhD was brilliantly defended at the Graduate Institute and awarded the René Cassin Prize by the Strasbourg-based International Institute of Human Rights in 2012. Dr Debuf is to be congratulated, not only for her for her careful research, but also for presenting us with a vision which will surely be influential for many years to come.

Andrew CLAPHAM
Professor of International Law
Graduate Institute of International and Development Studies
Director Geneva Academy
of International Humanitarian Law and Human Rights

ACKNOWLEDGEMENTS

My sincere thanks go out to Andrew Clapham, whose commitment to the protection of human dignity and whose belief in using the law to achieve that noble aim have always been a source of inspiration. His valuable comments and suggestions have contributed immensely to this book.

Special thanks also to Judge Theodor Meron, Professor Nicolas Michel, Julie Gaudreau, Vida Amirmokri and colleagues at the International Committee of the Red Cross, for stimulating discussions on the subject-matter of this book and on international law more generally, and to Yasmin Naqvi for precious counsel in times of doubt. Michèle Huang and the ICRC Library staff were of great support in the research carried out for this book.

My sincere thanks also go out to the International Institute for Human Rights, for their interest in my work and for including it in their prestigious collection of publications. Special thanks also to the editors and staff at Pedone and Hart Publishing Editions.

I am indebted and grateful to my parents for their unconditional support and for passing on the awareness, values and commitment that undoubtedly influenced the path in life I have chosen to walk.

A path in life I walk in excellent company, that of my husband Stef, whose unconditional love and staunch support have been crucial in completing this project, and whose passion and company on the adventurous paths of life I will always treasure. I dedicate this book to him and to our beautiful daughter Ella-Yaël.

I hope the book will be of use to those who believe in the right of every individual, friend or foe, to human dignity, to liberty and to freedom from arbitrary deprivation thereof, and who, in many different ways, contribute to making those rights a reality for thousands of prisoners around the world.

Els DEBUF
Geneva, 26 December 2012

TABLE OF CONTENTS

PART II: SECURITY INTERNMENT IN SITUATIONS OF INTERNATIONAL ARMED CONFLICT AND OCCUPATION

PART III: SECURITY INTERNMENT IN SITUATIONS OF NON-INTERNATIONAL ARMED CONFLICT

TABLE OF ABBREVIATIONS

GENERAL

ACHR	American Convention on Human Rights
ACHPR	African Charter on Human and Peoples' Rights
AC°HPR	African Commission on Human and Peoples' Rights
ADRDM	American Declaration of the Rights and Duties of Man
AMISOM	African Mission in Somalia
AP I	Additional Protocol I (to the 1949 Geneva Conventions)
AP II	Additional Protocol II (to the 1949 Geneva Conventions)
AU	African Union
CA	Court of Appeal
CA2	common article 2 (of the 1949 Geneva Conventions)
CA3	common article 3 (of the 1949 Geneva Conventions)
CIHL	customary international humanitarian law
CIS	Commonwealth of Independent States
CNDP	Congrès national pour la défense du peuple (Democratic Republic of Congo)
CoE	Council of Europe
CRC	Convention on the Rights of the Child
CRC-OP	Optional Protocol to the CRC on the Involvement of Children in Armed Conflict
DRC	Democratic Republic of the Congo
ECHR	European Convention on Human Rights
ECtHR	European Court of Human Rights
ECOWAS	Economic Community of West-African States
ELN	Ejército de Liberación Nacional (Colombia)
EU	European Union
FARC	Fuerzas Armadas Revolucionarias de Colombia (Colombia)
GC I	Geneva Convention I
GC II	Geneva Convention II
GC III	Geneva Convention III
GC IV	Geneva Convention IV
HR	Hague Regulations
HRC	Human Rights Committee

KFOR	Kosovo Force
IAC	international armed conflict
IAC°HR	Inter-American Commission on Human Rights
IACtHR	Inter-American Court of Human Rights
ICC	International Criminal Court
ICCPR	International Covenant on Civil and Political Rights
ICJ	International Court of Justice
ICRC	International Committee of the Red Cross
ICTR	International Criminal Tribunal for Rwanda
ICTY	International Criminal Tribunal for the Former Yugoslavia
IHL	international humanitarian law
IHRL	international human rights law
ILC	International Law Commission
INTERFET	International Force East Timor
IO	international organization
ISAF	International Security Assistance Force (Afghanistan)
LTTE	Liberation Tigers of Tamil Eelam (Sri Lanka)
MILF	Moro Islamic Liberation Front (Philippines)
MNF-I	Multinational Force – Iraq
MNLF	Moro National Liberation Front (Philippines)
MONUC	Mission de l'Organisation des Nations Unies au Congo
NATO	North-Atlantic Treaty Organization
NIAC	non-international armed conflict
NPA	New People's Army (Philippines)
OHCHR	Office of the High Commissioner for Human Rights
ONUC	Organisation des Nations Unies au Congo
PCA (EECC)	Permanent Court of Arbitration (Ethiopia-Eritrea Claims Commission)
PCIJ	Permanent Court of International Justice
PKK	Partiya Karkerên Kurdistan (Turkey)
POW	prisoner(s) of war
RUF	Revolutionary United Front (Sierra Leone)
SC	Supreme Court
UDHR	Universal Declaration of Human Rights
UK	United Kingdom of Great Britain and Northern Ireland
UN	United Nations
UNCHR	United Nations Commission on Human Rights

UNC-Korea	United Nations Command in Korea
UNGA(R)	United Nations General Assembly (Resolution)
UNHCR	United Nations High Commissioner for Refugees
UNHRC	United Nations Human Rights Council
UNSC(R)	United Nations Security Council (Resolution)
UNSG	United Nations Secretary-General
UNTAET	United Nations Transitional Administration in East-Timor
US	United States of America
VCLT	Vienna Convention on the Law of Treaties
WGAD	Working Group on Arbitrary Detention

JOURNALS

ACDI	Annuaire canadien de droit international
AdV	Archiv des Völkerrechts
AEI	Annales d'études internationales
AFDI	Annuaire français de droit international
AJICL	African Journal of International and Comparative Law
AJIL	American Journal of International Law
Ariz.JICL	Arizona Journal of International and Comparative Law
ASIL Insights	American Society of International Law Insights
AUJILP	American University Journal of International Law and Policy
AULR	American University Law Review
BYIL	British Year Book of International Law
Calif.LR	California Law Review
CEH	Contemporary European History
CJIL	Chinese Journal of International Law
CJTL	Columbia Journal of Transnational Law
Ch.JIL	Chicago Journal of International Law
CHRLR	Columbia Human Rights Law Review
CLR	Columbia Law Review
CWRJIL	Case Western Reserve Journal of International Law
DJCIL	Duke Journal of Comparative and International Law
EHRLR	European Human Rights Law Review
EJIL	European Journal of International Law
FA	Foreign Affairs
FFWA	Fletcher Forum of World Affairs
GJICL	Georgia Journal of International and Comparative Law

GRP	Global Responsibility to Protect
GWLR	George Washington Law Review
GYIL	German Yearbook of International Law
JCLC	Journal of Criminal Law and Criminology
JDI	Journal de droit international
JICJ	Journal of International Criminal Justice
Harv.ILJ	Harvard International Law Journal
HRLR	Human Rights Law Review
HRQ	Human Rights Quarterly
HV	Humanitäres Völkerrecht
ICLQ	International and Comparative Law Quarterly
IJConstit.L	International Journal of Constitutional Law
ILM	International Legal Materials
JCH	Journal of Contemporary History
JCSL	Journal of Conflict and Security Law
JIHLS	Journal of International Humanitarian Legal Studies
LJIL	Leiden Journal of International Law
IA	International Affairs
IAEHRJ	Inter-American and European Human Rights Journal
IJIL	Indian Journal of International Law
ILR	Israel Law Review
ILSA JICL	ILSA Journal of International Comparative Law
IRRC	International Review of the Red Cross
Isr.YHR	Israel Yearbook on Human Rights
LCP	Law and Contemporary Problems
Melb.JIL	Melbourne Journal of International Law
MLR	Military Law Review
MLLWR	Military Law and the Law of War Review
NILQ	Northern Ireland Law Quarterly
NILR	Netherlands International Law Review
Nordic JIL	Nordic Journal of International Law
NYIL	Netherlands Yearbook of International Law
NYUJILP	New York University Journal of International Law and Policy
RBDI	Revue belge de droit international
RGDIP	Revue générale de droit international public
RI	Relations internationales
RIS	Review of International Studies

SALJ	South African Law Journal
SSRN	Social Science Research Network
Stanf.JIL	Stanford Journal of International Law
Virg.JIL	Virginia Journal of International Law
YIIHL	Yearbook of the Institute of International Humanitarian Law
YJIL	Yale Journal of International Law
YLJ	Yale Law Journal
WaS	War and Society
ZaöRV	Zeitschrift für ausländisches öffentliches Recht und Völkerrecht

The essence of the whole corpus of international humanitarian law as well as human rights law lies in the protection of the human dignity of every person, whatever his or her gender. The general principle of respect for human dignity is the basic underpinning and indeed the very raison d'être of international humanitarian law and human rights law; indeed in modern times it has become of such paramount importance as to permeate the whole body of international law.

(ICTY, Furundžija (1998), §183)

INTRODUCTION

The research and analysis in this book deal with a number of legal questions regarding internment in armed conflict. Essentially a security measure designed to neutralize threats emanating from an adverse party to an armed conflict, internment has long since been, and continues to be, a common incident of warfare. In light of this reality, and in order to protect internees from potential abuse at the hands of their captor, internment in armed conflict has become the subject of international legal regulation. The legal protection of captured enemy troops – "prisoners of war" – is one of the earliest manifestations of the international community's endeavour to humanize warfare through legal regulation. From a historical perspective, the international legal regulation of conflict-captivity, especially when compared to other aspects of warfare, is rather recent. However, in light of the rapidly changing nature of both armed conflicts and international law itself, the main international legal instruments regulating internment in armed conflict (the 1949 Geneva Conventions), may seem outdated to some.

Internment in armed conflict has long since been a subject of academic research and analysis. It has mustered renewed interest in recent years, sparked by an increase in international interventions in armed conflict, by the recognition that international human rights law continues to apply in armed conflict, and finally by the public outcry over the United States' internment operations in various armed conflicts and counter-terrorism operations that followed the terrorist attacks against that nation on 11 September 2001.

All these factors have exerted increasing pressure on the existing international legal regulation of internment in armed conflict, which was originally designed to apply in traditional inter-State wars. The international legal framework for internment in armed conflict, the essence of which is laid down in the 1949 Geneva Conventions, has been criticized for being outdated or inadequate at worst, and ambiguous or lacunose at best. In light of such criticism, it is important to examine, and where necessary demonstrate, the continued relevance and adequacy of the existing legal framework for internment in the Geneva Conventions; to identify its shortcomings – be they due to age, scope of application, ambiguity or lacunae – and to propose possible avenues to remedy these shortcomings. With this book, we hope to make a modest contribution to that exercise.

AIM AND SCOPE

The subject of this book raises a myriad of interesting and challenging questions of international law. Initially, we hoped to propose a comprehensive study of the international legal framework for internment in armed conflict, covering all types of armed conflict and including an analysis of both the legal basis and grounds for internment, and procedural and other safeguards designed to prevent arbitrariness and abuse. However, during the research process it became clear that several of the issues connected to this topic are so rich, both in materials for analysis and questions to be explored, that their comprehensive analysis would merit separate studies altogether.

Taking into consideration that most of the recent research and debate on internment in armed conflict have focused on its procedural aspects, we have opted to explore those questions that are, in our opinion, often treated too superficially, namely: who can be interned on the basis of existing international humanitarian law, for what reasons and for how long? By answering these questions, we wish to contribute to the academic efforts aimed at clarifying the international legal framework for internment in armed conflict. Moreover, in the process of answering our specific research questions, we also hope to contribute to a number of other debates in international law, in particular that on the interaction between simultaneously applicable norms of international humanitarian law and international human rights law. Finally, we hope that the answers to our research questions will prove useful for parties to armed conflicts engaging in internment operations (both the authorities in charge of internment operations, and the authorities responsible for internment review) and for international courts and treaty monitoring bodies that may be called upon to assess the lawfulness of internment in a specific context of armed conflict. Taking into account these aims, we have delineated the scope of the research and analysis offered in this book along the following lines.

First, we have purposefully limited our research and analysis to internment on the basis of international humanitarian law. We do not deal with any form of deprivation of liberty that may occur in situations that do not amount to an armed conflict,[1] nor do we seek to determine who may be interned in situations of armed conflict on the basis of domestic legislation. This does not mean, however, that international humanitarian law is the only relevant body of international law for answering our research questions. Indeed, the lawfulness of deprivation of liberty in armed conflict cannot be determined by reference to international humanitarian law alone. Other relevant rules of international law regulating the deprivation of liberty must be taken into account when applying, interpreting, clarifying and developing international humanitarian law. Since the latter is by definition a context-specific body of law, it will be necessary to outline the general legal framework within which it must be read.

[1] The threshold of applicability of international humanitarian law will be discussed in considerable detail in Part I.

Second, the research and analysis presented in this book are concerned with a particular form of deprivation of liberty, namely internment, a legitimate preventive security measure in situations of armed conflict.[2] Other forms of deprivation of liberty are discussed only to the extent relevant for the definition of the general principles governing deprivation of liberty in international law, or to emphasize the distinct features of internment in armed conflict.

Finally, we devote only limited attention to the procedural aspects of internment in armed conflict, the specific safeguards against arbitrary deprivation of liberty, and the rules concerning the treatment of internees and the material conditions of captivity that are prescribed by international law.[3]

We concentrate primarily on two aspects of the broader debate on deprivation of liberty in situations of armed conflict. First, we found it appropriate to outline the general legal framework within which these debates ought to take place. In the quest for rapid practical solutions to important legal challenges that have arisen during recent years, the general normative framework in which these challenges arise has often been overlooked.[4] Second, we have sought to answer our research questions through detailed analysis of existing legal bases for internment in international humanitarian law and of suggestions for expanding those legal bases. Ultimately, we hope our work will contribute to the clarification, and where appropriate, the further development of international humanitarian law as an effective tool in the prevention of unnecessary and arbitrary deprivation of liberty in armed conflict.

Before turning to the presentation of our research and analysis, we will define some of the technical terms that will be used throughout the book, and explain the methodological approach taken in answering the questions it examines.

---

[2] We will come back to the concept of internment in the section on terminology below.

[3] When one discusses the legal protection of persons deprived of liberty, it is important to distinguish between (1) the legal framework that regulates the deprivation of liberty itself and (2) the legal framework that regulates the treatment of persons deprived of liberty and their material conditions of captivity. In this book we are only concerned with the first type of regulation, conformity with which will determine whether a given deprivation of liberty is lawful. Failure to comply with the second type of regulation does not render the deprivation of liberty itself unlawful or arbitrary, but may result in violations of a detainee or internee's other rights under international law.

[4] As Plattner points out: "seule la référence aux outils de droit international public général peut satisfaire la rigueur dans l'analyse que requiert tout particulièrement le domaine du droit international humanitaire" (Plattner, "La portée juridique des déclarations de respect du droit international humanitaire qui émanent de mouvements en lutte dans un conflit armé" (*RBDI* 1984-1985), p. 304).

TERMINOLOGY

"Internment" is a form of deprivation of liberty, initiated or ordered by the executive authorities of a party to an armed conflict or an occupying power, as a preventive security measure and thus without any criminal charge being brought against the person concerned. The concept is reserved for situations of armed conflict[5] and used as a legal term of art in international instruments designed to regulate such situations.[6]

Internment is to a certain extent comparable to the concept of administrative detention in general international law. The term "administrative detention" is commonly used to denote a form of deprivation of liberty that is initiated or ordered by the administrative (i.e. executive) authorities of a State as a preventive measure and thus without any criminal charge being brought against the person concerned.[7] Administrative detention and internment are thus to be distinguished from "detention" or "judicial detention", a form of deprivation of liberty that is initiated or ordered by the judicial authorities of a State for the purpose of preventing, investigating and/or punishing the commission of criminal offences.[8] Rather than using the term "detention" in its generic sense, we will use the term "deprivation of liberty" as an umbrella term for internment, administrative detention, judicial detention and any other form of deprivation of

[5] Sandoz, Swinarski & Zimmerman (eds.), *Commentary on the Additional Protocols of 8 June 1977 to the Geneva Conventions of 12 August 1949* (1987), p. 875.

[6] E.g.: article 21 Geneva Convention (III) Relative to the Treatment of Prisoners of War (1949) (hereinafter "Third Geneva Convention" or "GC III"); articles 41-43, 78 and 79 Geneva Convention (IV) Relative to the Protection of Civilian Persons in Time of War (1949) (hereinafter "Fourth Geneva Convention" or "GC IV"); article 75§3 Protocol Additional to the Geneva Conventions of 12 August 1949, and Relating to the Protection of Victims of International Armed Conflicts (1977) (hereinafter "Additional Protocol I" or "AP I"); articles 2 and 5 Protocol Additional to the Geneva Conventions of 12 August 1949, and Relating to the Protection of Victims of Non-International Armed Conflicts (1977) (hereinafter "Additional Protocol II" or "AP II"). Moreover, the technical term "internment" is generally recognized and used as such in national legislation implementing instruments of international humanitarian law and in military manuals and doctrine, e.g.: UK, *Joint Doctrine Publication 1-10: Prisoners of War, Internees and Detainees* (2006), "Lexicon of Terms and Definitions" pp. 1-2; and France, *Manuel de droit des conflits armés* (2001), p. 38. In the same sense: Pictet, *Commentary to the Third Geneva Convention* (1960), p. 178; Pictet, *Commentary to the Fourth Geneva Convention* (1958), pp. 256 and 368; Sandoz et al., *Commentary AP I and II* (1987), pp. 875 and 1386; Verri, *Dictionary of the International Law of Armed Conflict* (1992), pp. 60-61; and Federal Department of Foreign Affairs of Switzerland, *ABC of International Humanitarian Law* (2009), p. 28.

[7] E.g.: *Report on the Practice of Administrative Detention*, submitted to the UN Sub-Commission on Prevention of Discrimination and Protection of Minorities by Louis Joinet (1990): "Detention is considered 'administrative detention' if *de jure* and/or *de facto*, it has been ordered by the executive and the power of decision rests solely with the administrative or ministerial authority, even if a remedy *a posterior* does exist in the courts against such a decision. The courts are then responsible only for considering the lawfulness of this decision and/or its proper enforcement, but not for taking the decision itself."

[8] In the same sense: Working Group on Arbitrary Detention (WGAD), *Annual Report 1996*, §96; Pictet, *Commentary GC III* (1960), p. 178; Pictet, *Commentary GC IV* (1958), pp. 256 and 368; Pejic, "Procedural Principles and Safeguards for Internment/Administrative Detention in Armed Conflict Other Situations of Violence" (*IRRC* 2005), p. 376.

liberty.[9] This broad term thus covers any compulsory measure, restrictive of an individual's freedom of movement, and resulting in a prohibition for that person to leave the premises where he or she is ordered to remain.[10]

The Geneva Conventions and their Additional Protocols, as well as most commentators of these instruments, use the generic term "Detaining Power" to refer to the party to the conflict that either "interns" or "detains" a given person in relation to that armed conflict. In order to respect the fundamental distinction between internment (a preventive security measure) and judicial detention (on the basis of criminal charges) in situations of armed conflict, and to avoid any confusion, we will refer to the party to the conflict in whose physical custody internees and detainees find themselves respectively as the "Interning Power" and the "Detaining Power."[11]

"Internment" must also be distinguished from the concepts of "capture" and "surrender". These concepts reflect the act through which a person falls into the hands of a party to the conflict, either voluntarily (surrender) or involuntarily (capture).[12] A person's deprivation of liberty starts at the time when he or she is captured or surrenders and thus effectively finds him- or herself in the hands of a party to the conflict[13] without permission to leave the place where he or she is

---

[9] In the same sense: WGAD, *Factsheet No. 26*: "It must [...] be noted that international instruments do not always use the same terminology to refer to deprivations of liberty: they may refer to 'arrest', 'apprehension', 'detention', 'incarceration', 'prison', 'reclusion', 'custody', 'remand', etc. For this reason the Commission on Human Rights [...] opted for the term 'deprivation of liberty', term that eliminates any differences in interpretation between the different terminologies. This terminology was chosen since the objective entrusted to the [Working Group on Arbitrary Detention] relates to the protection of individuals against arbitrary deprivation of freedom in all its forms, and its mandate extends to deprivation of freedom either before, during or after the trial (a term of imprisonment imposed following conviction), as well as deprivation of freedom in the absence of any kind of trial (administrative detention)."

[10] "In order to determine whether someone has been 'deprived of liberty' [...] the starting point must be his concrete situation and account must be taken of a whole range of criteria such as the type, duration, effects and manner of implementation of the measure in question. [...] the difference between deprivation of liberty and restriction upon liberty is merely one of degree or intensity, and not one of nature or substance." ECtHR (Grand Chamber), *Medvedyev and Others v. France* (2010), §73. The definition of the European Court is general enough to serve as a standard definition of "deprivation of liberty"; in the same sense: Kleffner, "Operational Detention and the Treatment of Detainees" in Gill & Fleck, *The Handbook of the International Law of Military Operations* (2010), pp. 465-466.

[11] For the same reasons, the term "Retaining Power" will be used in relation to the retention of medical and religious personnel of the armed forces of the parties to the conflict; *cf. infra* chapter II-2.

[12] In the same sense "detention" must be distinguished from "arrest" and "surrender". The protection of international legal instruments regulating deprivation of liberty starts from the time of arrest, capture or surrender and last until the person's final release. In this sense, see also Council of Europe, *Human Rights Handbook No. 5: The Right to Liberty and Security of the Person. A Guide to the Implementation of Article 5 of the European Convention on Human Rights* (2002), p. 17; Nowak, *U.N. Covenant on Civil and Political Rights - CCPR Commentary* (2005), p. 221.

[13] At that point in time, the person is also *hors de combat* and thus can no longer be the object of attack. E.g.: article 41§§1-2 AP I: "A person who is recognized or who, in the circumstances, should be recognized to *hors de combat* shall not be made the object of attack. A person is *hors de combat* if: (a) he is in the power of an adverse Party; (b) he clearly expresses an intention to surrender; or (c) he has been rendered unconscious or is otherwise incapacitated by wounds or sickness, and therefore

ordered to remain. The authorities representing that party to the conflict must subsequently decide to release, detain or intern that person.[14]

Internment may only be ordered where there is a valid legal basis to do so and the conditions set out in that legal basis are met in the given case. The "legal basis" for internment is the specific legal instrument that prescribes the grounds and procedures in accordance with which internment may be ordered. The "grounds" for internment are the specific reasons for which internment may be ordered and reflect its purpose. The legal basis and the grounds for internment are therefore two distinct notions.[15] We will discuss both concepts in more detail in chapter I-1. For our present purposes two examples may illustrate the difference. In our first example, an Occupying Power interns an inhabitant of an occupied territory because he or she is expected to engage in attacks against the Occupying Power's military infrastructure. The legal *basis* for that internment is the Fourth Geneva Convention, and in particular its article 78, which prescribes the grounds and procedures in accordance with which the internment may be ordered. The lawful *ground* for the internment is that such a measure of control is necessary for imperative reasons of security. Our second example concerns the administrative detention by the immigration services of an international airport of a person without the necessary visa in order to verify his or her claim for asylum. Internment to prevent a person from "effecting an unauthorized entry into the country" is recognized as a lawful *ground* for administratively detaining a person under the European Convention on Human Rights (ECHR), but that Convention itself cannot serve as a legal *basis* for ordering administrative detention on this ground. For such an order to be lawful, it will need to be based on a legal instrument that prescribes the precise reasons and the procedures in accordance with which the detention may be ordered, such as the authority that can make the decision to detain, the duration of the detention, the rights of the detainee during his or her detention, and the competent authorities and procedural requirements for the detainee to challenge the lawfulness of his or her detention. That legal basis will normally be found in domestic legislation.

---

is incapable of defending himself; provided that in any of these cases he abstains from any hostile act and does not attempt to escape." For the scope of application *ratione temporis* of the 1949 Geneva Conventions and their Additional Protocols, *cf. infra* Part II.

[14] As Fischer points out: "Custody [in the sense of internment or detention] of a prisoner of war only commences with an act by a competent state organ" (Fischer, "Prisoners of war" in Fleck, *The Handbook of International Humanitarian Law* (2008), p. 384).

[15] See also International Committee of the Red Cross (ICRC) and Chatham House, *Report of the Expert Meeting on Procedural Safeguards for Security Detention in Non-International Armed Conflict* (2008), p. 866: "The distinction proposed by the ICRC between 'legal basis' and 'permissible grounds' for internment is supported by requirements flowing from general IHRL under which a deprivation of liberty may be ordered on the basis of lawful authority and on specified grounds permitting a restriction of liberty."

METHODOLOGY AND APPROACH

Before we present our research and analysis, we will outline our approach for answering the questions formulated above, as it reflects our views on international law, the specific functions of certain of its branches and the tools for its interpretation and application in practice.

The role of international humanitarian law in the international legal system

International humanitarian law has been defined as a set of "international rules, established by treaties or custom, which are specifically intended to solve humanitarian problems directly arising from international or non-international armed conflicts and which, for humanitarian reasons, limit the right of Parties to a conflict to use the methods and means of warfare of their choice or protect persons and property that are, or may be, affected by conflict."[16]

One may therefore expect to find most if not all the answers to our research questions in that particular body of law. We will see however that this expectation is only partly met by existing international humanitarian law. International humanitarian law does not operate in a legal vacuum though; it is part of the broader international legal system and performs a specific function therein to achieve the system's ultimate goals.

International law is not just a compilation of rules. It is a normative system with a social purpose.[17] Like any other legal system, international law is designed to regulate life and relations in a given community or society, in this case the international community of States, their populations and the individuals that compose them. The role of law in any society is to provide an operational system for securing the community's commonly shared values.[18] When called to apply international law in practice, one must therefore be guided by its ultimate purpose, which is to transform these values into a reality for the members of that community.

One of the international community's commonly shared values is the preservation of human dignity and the protection of fundamental rights and freedoms that inherently belong to any human being. In the preamble of its founding charter, the international community, represented by "the peoples of the United Nations", expresses its determination both to "save succeeding generations from the scourge of war" and to "safeguard fundamental human rights [...] and the dignity and worth of the human person."[19] As a first step on

---

[16] Sandoz et al., *Commentary AP I and II* (1987), p. xxvii.

[17] Our approach to international law is very similar to what Rosalyn Higgins defined as a policy-oriented approach to international law. Several of the terms used to outline our approach here are borrowed from Judge Higgins' writings and teachings, and in particular from her General Course at the Hague Academy of International Law (1993), published as Higgins, *Problems and Process: International Law and How We Use It* (1994).

[18] In the same sense, see also Bianchi, "Ad-hocism and the Rule of Law" (*EJIL* 2002), pp. 265-266.

[19] The text in quotation marks is from the first two paragraphs of the preamble of the United Nations Charter (1945) (hereinafter "UN Charter"). The Charter was drafted and initially adopted by 51 States,

the path to the realization of this pledge, these "united nations" adopted the Universal Declaration of Human Rights[20] and ever since, international human rights law has developed into an inevitably imperfect but quite impressive tool for achieving the goals set out in the Charter.

The preservation of human dignity and the protection of fundamental human rights has increasingly come to occupy the centre stage in the international legal system, reflecting the growing importance accorded by both States and their populations to the values of humanity and human dignity (rather than the mere interests of sovereign princes or nation States). That process often gained momentum in the wake of particularly large-scale or atrocious armed conflicts.[21] The international legal regulation designed to achieve the realization of the values of humanity and human dignity has also evolved significantly and rapidly under the impetus of a human rights movement that came to exert unprecedented influence on international law and politics since the mid-20th century.[22]

The development of international human rights law has had, and continues to have, an impact on both the *interpretation* and the *development* of international humanitarian law. While international humanitarian law has always balanced military imperatives and basic principles of humanity, and while the humanization of warfare started well before the adoption of the first international human rights instruments, the impact of international human rights law has contributed significantly to a process in which that balance is increasingly struck in favour of humanitarian imperatives.[23] It shall be shown particularly in Part II of this book that the focus of what used to be called the law of war has shifted increasingly from merely safeguarding States' or belligerents' interests to the

but has since been adhered to by all member States of the United Nations, which today include all 194 existing States.

[20] Universal Declaration of Human Rights (1948) (hereinafter "UDHR").

[21] See for example the adoption of the UN Charter, the UDHR and the Geneva Conventions shortly after the Second World War; the creation of international criminal tribunals in the wake of the conflicts that led to the break-up of the former Yugoslavia in the early 1990s and the 1994 Rwandan genocide; and the allied military intervention in Kosovo in 1999, meant to prevent or at least put a halt to another genocide. In her course at the Hague Academy, which she taught shortly after the end of the Cold War, Judge Higgins noted that the emphasis of States had become "less on international law as the co-ordination of clashing wills, than on international law as the articulation of a universal interest. That universal interest is exemplified by the common threat to human survival" (Higgins (1994), p. 11).

[22] This "humanization" of the international legal system under the influence of the human rights movement has been aptly described by Theodor Meron in his General Course at the Hague Academy of International Law (2003). Drawing on his earlier work and on his experience as an international legal scholar and practitioner, a revised and expanded version of Judge Meron's course has been published as Meron, *The Humanization of International Law* (2006). For a critical assessment of the advantages and risks inherent in this process as far is international humanitarian law is concerned, see Schmitt, "Military Necessity and Humanity in International Humanitarian Law: Preserving the Delicate Balance" (*Virg.JIL* 2010).

[23] The shift in focus is reflected in the increasing use, since 1949, of the term "international humanitarian law" to refer to what was traditionally known as the "law of war" or the "law of armed conflict"; *cf. infra*, note 325. As Schmitt points out however, while "the label has the marked disadvantage of masking the role military necessity plays in the law governing armed conflict," it also "accurately reflects the trend toward according greater weight to the humanitarian features of the law" (Schmitt (*Virg.JIL* 2010), pp. 805-806).

protection of the individual human beings affected by armed conflict.[24] This process started in the mid-19th century, is reflected in the 1949 Geneva Conventions and their 1977 Additional Protocols, and is ongoing today.

At least since the second half of the 19th century, the specific function of humanitarian law in the international legal system is to regulate the conduct of war and to "[fix] the technical limits at which the necessities of war ought to yield to the requirements of humanity."[25] This specific function is summarized well in the preamble of the Fourth Hague Convention of 1907:

> "Seeing that while seeking means to preserve peace and prevent armed conflicts between nations, it is likewise necessary to bear in mind the case where the appeal to arms has been brought about by events which their care was unable to avert, [the parties to the Convention further developed international humanitarian law,] [a]nimated by the desire to serve, even in this extreme case, the interests of humanity and the ever progressive needs of civilization."

While the drafters of the 1949 Geneva Conventions ultimately rejected the idea of including a preamble setting out these motives, the provisions of the Conventions clearly reflect the purpose of preserving human dignity and protecting fundamental rights and freedoms in armed conflict[26] and protecting

[24] Pictet, *Commentary GC III* (1960), pp. 20 and 23; Pictet, *Commentary GC IV* (1958), p. 21; ICTY, *Tadic* (1995), §97; ICTY, *Furundžija* (1998), §183; ICJ, *Wall Opinion* (2004), §95. In the same sense: Rosas, *The Legal Status of Prisoners of War* (1976), p. 18; Gasser, "International Humanitarian Law and Human Rights Law in Non-International Armed Conflict: Joint Venture or Mutual Exclusion?" (*GYIL* 2002), pp. 151, 155 and 161; Meron (2006), pp. 1-2, 9-15 and 36; Sassòli & Bouvier (2006), *How Does Law Protect in War? Cases, Documents, Teaching Materials on Contemporary Practice in International Humanitarian Law* (2006), pp. 89-90, 108-110, 118-120; and Tomuschat, "Human Rights and International Humanitarian Law" (*EJIL* 2010), pp. 16 and 20. For reasons of legibility of the footnotes, we have abbreviated references to the decisions and opinions of international courts and treaty monitoring bodies; for the full references we refer the reader to the Bibliography, where the abbreviations used in the text of the book are indicated.

[25] Preamble of the Declaration Renouncing the Use, in Time of War, of Explosive Projectiles under 400 Grammes of Weight (1868) (hereinafter "St-Petersburg Declaration"), §1. The signatories of the St-Petersburg Declaration regulated the use of expanding bullets considering that "the progress of civilization should have the effect of alleviating as much as possible the calamities of war [and that] the only legitimate object which States should endeavour to accomplish during war is to weaken the military forces of the enemy [and that suffering unnecessary to achieve that object] would, therefore, be contrary to the laws of humanity" (*Ibidem*, §§2-3 and 6).

[26] The failure to disagree on a text for a Preamble did not concern the ultimate motives of the drafters, which are reflected in many of the Conventions' provisions. It was essentially the inclusion of a reference to the divine origin of man and divinity as the ultimate source of all law that was subject to great controversy; see Pictet, *Commentary GC III* (1960), pp. 12-16 and Pictet, *Commentary GC IV* (1958), pp. 11-14. The text of the draft preambles discussed at the Diplomatic Conference in 1949 referred explicitly to the purpose of preserving both human dignity and fundamental rights and freedoms, a purpose that is reflected in many of the actual provisions of the Conventions. Moreover, the drafters referred back to what they considered to be principles of "universal human law" (Pictet, *Commentary GC IV*, p. 12) in the renowned de Martens clause enshrined in the fourth paragraph of common article 63/62/142/158 GC I-IV (referring to "the obligations which the Parties to the conflict shall remain bound to fulfil by virtue of the principles of the law of nations, as they result from the usages established among civilized peoples, from the laws of humanity and the dictates of public conscience"). Moreover, the text of common article 3 of the Geneva Conventions reflects a number of the principles that featured in the draft preambles discussed at the Conference.

individual human beings "from arbitrary actions on the part of the enemy."[27] Article 72 of the First Additional Protocol to the Geneva Conventions (1977), refers in more explicit terms to that purpose where it states that its rules (and those of the Geneva Conventions it supplements) are *additional* to "other applicable rules of international law relating to the protection of fundamental human rights during international armed conflict." In a similar vein, the Preamble of the Second Additional Protocol to the Geneva Conventions (1977) recalls that while "international instruments relating to human rights offer a basic protection to the human person," the Protocol aims to *improve* that protection for the victims of non-international armed conflicts.[28]

Shortly before the adoption of these two Protocols, Draper summarized the influence of international human rights law on the interpretation and development of international humanitarian law as follows: "the two branches of law have met, are fusing together at some speed, and [...] in a number of practical instances the regime of human rights is setting the general direction and objectives for the revision of the law of war."[29] That general direction given by international human rights law to the revision and development of international humanitarian law is not only visible in the 1977 Protocols, but also in the development of customary international humanitarian law.[30]

Not only has international human rights law come to influence the interpretation and further development of international humanitarian law, it is generally accepted today that both branches of international law *apply simultaneously* in situations of armed conflict.[31] The interplay of international

[27] Pictet, *Commentary GC IV* (1958), p. 10 and in same sense: Pictet, *Commentary GC III* (1960), pp. 14-15.

[28] Preamble of Additional Protocol II, §§2-3.

[29] Draper, "The Relationship between the Human Rights Regime and the Law of Armed Conflict" (*Isr.YHR* 1971), p. 191. In a similar vein, the International Law Commission found in 2006 that the two bodies of law "related to each other as today's reality and tomorrow's promise", International Law Commission, *Fragmentation of International Law: Difficulties Arising from the Diversification and Expansion of International Law* (2006), §105.

[30] See Meron (2006), p. 3, with further references. The impact of international human rights law on the formation of customary international humanitarian law is particularly noticeable in the ICRC's compilation of that body of law, published as Henckaerts & Doswald-Beck (eds.), *Customary International Humanitarian Law* (2005), available and updated online at http://www.icrc.org/customary-ihl/eng/docs/home.

[31] ICJ, *Nuclear Weapons* (1996), §25; ICJ, *Wall Opinion* (2004), §106; ICJ, *DRC v. Uganda* (2005), §§215-216; United Nations Security Council (UNSC), *Resolution 237* (1967), preamble; United Nations General Assembly (UNGA), *Resolution 2675* (1970), §1; Human Rights Committee (HRC), *General Comment 29* (2001), §3; HRC, *General Comment 31* (2004), §10; HRC, *Concluding Observations US* (2006), §10; WGAD, *Annual Report 2005*, §§68-75; WGAD and Special Rapporteurs, *Situation of Detainees at Guantánamo Bay* (2006), §§15-16; IAC°HR, *Abella v. Argentina* (1997), §§158-161; IAC°HR, *Third Report Colombia* (1999), chapter IV, §§8-19 and 153-154; IAC°HR, *Coard v. USA* (1999), §§36-44; IACtHR, *Las Palmeras* (2000), §§32-34; IACtHR, *Bámaca Velásquez v. Guatemala* (2000), §209; ECtHR, *Varnava v. Turkey* (2009), §185. Objections raised by the United States (e.g. IAC°HR, *Coard v. USA* (1999), §35; US, *Additional Response of the United States to Request for Precautionary Measures - Detainees in Guantánamo Bay, Cuba* (2002), §9; and US, *Third Periodic Report of States Parties Due in 2003 (ICCPR)* (2005)) and by Israel (e.g. HRC, *Concluding Observations Israel* (1998), §10, and HRC, *Concluding Observations Israel*

humanitarian and human rights norms in practice has given rise to discussions on the general relationship between these two bodies of law,[32] itself part of the broader debate on the fragmentation of international law and the legal tools that deal with the norm conflicts that may arise from it.[33] Without going into this debate here, it is important to point out the relevance of both bodies of law for the subject of our research analysis, and to apply their respective norms where relevant for answering our research questions.[34] In doing so, we must be guided by their common goal, one of which is the prevention of arbitrary deprivation of liberty, but must also take into account the specific functions of each body of law in the international legal system.

While international humanitarian law and international human rights law seek to achieve a common goal of preserving human dignity, each branch of international law has a specific function in the international legal system.[35] As we have mentioned before, the function of international humanitarian law is to regulate the conduct of war. International human rights law has a distinct,

---

(2003), §11) to the applicability of international human rights law to situations of armed conflict, do not withstand the authoritative decisions of the International Court of Justice, decisions that are supported moreover by what Hampson has called "the overwhelming weight of international legal opinion and state practice" (Hampson, "The Relationship between International Humanitarian Law and Human Rights Law from the Perspective of a Human Rights Treaty Body", (*IRRC*, 2008), p. 551). Nevertheless, it is thought unlikely the US will change its position, which should be articulated in the forthcoming revised US military manual on the law of armed conflict (as remarked by Professor Derek Jinks during a lecture at the Graduate Institute of International and Development Studies on 24 March 2010).

[32] The relationship between IHL and IHRL has been the subject of a considerable amount of case law and of extensive scholarly research and debate. For some of the most important contributions *cf. infra* chapter I-2, section 2.2.2.2.

[33] For some of the most important contributions to this debate, see International Law Commission, *Fragmentation* (2006); Jenks, "The Conflict of Law-Making Treaties" (*BYIL* 1953); Dupuy, "L'unité de l'ordre juridique international" (*Hague Academy Collected Courses* 2002); Koskenniemi & Leino, "Fragmentation of International Law: Postmodern Anxieties?" (*LJIL* 2002); Pauwelyn, *Conflict of Norms in Public International Law: How WTO Law Relates to Other Rules of International Law* (2003); "Symposium: Post-ILC Debate on Fragmentation of International Law" (*FYIL* 2006); Zimmerman, Hoffmann & Goeters (eds.), *Unity and Diversity of International Law* (2006); Wellens & Huesa Vinaixa (eds.), *L'influence des sources sur l'unité et la fragmentation du droit international* (2006); Crawford, "Multilateral Rights and Obligations in International Law" (*Hague Academy Collected Courses* 2006); and Kammerhofer, "Systemic Integration, Legal Theory and the ILC" (*FYIL* forthcoming). With particular attention for international humanitarian and human rights law, see for example Sassòli, "Le droit international humanitaire, une *lex specialis* par rapport aux droits humains?" in Auer, Flückiger & Hottelier (eds.), *Les droits de l'homme et la constitution: Études en l'honneur du Professeur Giorgio Malinverni* (2007); and Prud'homme, "*Lex Specialis*: Oversimplifying a More Complex and Multifaceted Relationship?" (*ILR* 2007) *Cf.* also *infra* chapter I-2, section 2.2.2.2.

[34] We will discuss the interaction of the relevant norms of both bodies of law with regard to internment in armed conflict in chapter I-2 before applying them to this specific subject-matter in Parts II and III.

[35] See also ICTY, *Furundžija* (1998), §183: "The essence of the whole corpus of international humanitarian law as well as human rights law lies in the protection of the human dignity of every person, whatever his or her gender. The general principle of respect for human dignity is the basic underpinning and indeed the very raison d'être of international humanitarian law and human rights law; indeed in modern times it has become of such paramount importance as to permeate the whole body of international law."

broader function in the international legal system: it is designed to protect human beings against the arbitrary and abusive exercise of power by the authorities in whose hands they may find themselves. Contrary to international humanitarian law, which by definition is occasional law, its provisions were not designed specifically to apply in armed conflict but rather to all human beings, at all times and in all circumstances.[36] Provost aptly notes that:

---

[36] The applicability of human rights treaty norms is subject to the jurisdictional clauses of the treaties they belong to, but the general principles are part of customary international law. A particular question arises with regard to the extra-territorial applicability of international human rights treaties. The question is subject to intense debate both before international courts and human rights monitoring bodies and in scholarly work. Nevertheless, the extra-territorial applicability of international human rights treaties where persons are deprived of liberty abroad by a party to such treaties is well-established, see for example: HRC, *Lopez Burgos v. Uruguay* (1981), §12(3); HRC, *General Comment 31* (2004), §10; HRC, *Munaf v. Romania* (2009), §14(2); Committee against Torture (CAT), *Conclusions and Recommendations UK* (2004), §4(b); WGAD & Special Rapporteurs, *Situation of Detainees at Guantánamo Bay* (2006), §11; IAC°HR, *Coard v. USA* (1999), §37; IAC°HR, *Guantánamo* (2002); EC°HR, *Cyprus v. Turkey* (1976), §§282 and 308; ECtHR (Grand Chamber), *Öcalan v. Turkey* (2005), §91; ECtHR (Grand Chamber), *Behrami & Saramati v. France, Germany & Norway* (2007); ECtHR (Grand Chamber), *Medvedyev* (2010), §67; ECtHR, *Al-Saadoon & Mufdhi v. UK* (2010); Council of Europe, Venice Commission, *Opinion on the Possible Need for Further Development of the Geneva Conventions* (2003), §49; Kälin, "The Covenant on Civil and Political Rights and its Relationship with International Humanitarian Law" in University Centre of International Humanitarian Law, *Report of the Expert meeting on the Supervision of Lawfulness of Detention* (2004); Rowe, *The Impact of Human Rights Law on Armed Forces* (2006), p. 152; Droege, "Elective Affinities? Human Rights and Humanitarian Law" (*IRRC* 2008), p. 516; Hampson (*IRRC* 2008), p. 569; Cassel, "International Human Rights Law and Security Detention" (*CWRJIL* 2009), p. 387; and Naert, *International Law Aspects of the EU's Security and Defence Policy, with a Particular Focus on the Law of Armed Conflict and Human Rights* (2010), pp. 556 and 625. For the purposes of this book, it is therefore not necessary to go into the general debate on extra-territorial applicability of human rights treaties; for some of the main contributions – representing different strands of opinion – see for example: ICJ, *Wall Opinion* (2004), §§108-113; HRC, *Lopez Burgos v. Uruguay* (1981); HRC, *Celiberti v. Uruguay* (1981); HRC, *Concluding Observations Cyprus* (1994); HRC, *Concluding Observations Israel* (2003); HRC, *Concluding Observations Belgium* (1998); HRC, *General Comment* 31 (2004); Committee on the Rights of the Child (CRC), *Concluding Observations Israel* (2002); IAC°HR, *Chile Report* (1985), IAC°HR, *Suriname Report* (1985), IAC°HR, *Salas v. USA* (1993); IAC°HR, *Coard v. USA* (1999); ECtHR, *Drozd & Janousek* (1992); ECtHR (Grand Chamber), *Loizidou v. Turkey* (1995); ECtHR (Grand Chamber), *Bankovic* (2001); ECtHR, *Issa v. Turkey* (2004); ECtHR (Grand Chamber), *Ilascu et al. v. Moldova & Russia* (2004); Meron, "Extraterritoriality of Human Rights Treaties" (*AJIL* 1995); Coomans & Kamminga, *Extraterritorial Application of Human Rights Treaties* (2004); Dennis, "Application of Human Rights Treaties Extraterritorially in Times of Armed Conflict and Military Occupation" (*AJIL* 2005); Cerone, "Jurisdiction and Power: The Intersection of Human Rights Law & the Law of Non-International Armed Conflict in an Extraterritorial Context" (*ILR* 2007); Dennis, "Non-Application of Civil and Political Rights Treaties Extraterritorially during Times of International Armed Conflict" (*ILR* 2007); Buyse, "A Legal Minefield – The Territorial Scope of the European Convention" (*IAEHRJ* 2008); Dennis & Surena, "Application of the International Covenant on Civil and Political Rights in Times of Armed Conflict and Military Occupation: The Gap between Legal Theory and State Practice" (*EHRLR* 2008); Gondek, *The Reach of Human Rights in a Globalizing World: Extraterritorial Application of Human Rights Treaties* (2009); Goodwin-Gill, "The Extra-Territorial Reach of Human Rights Obligations: A Brief Perspective on the Link to Jurisdiction" in de Chazournes & Kohen, *International Law and the Quest for its Implementation: Liber Amoricum Vera Gowlland-Debbas* (2010); ICRC and University Centre of International Humanitarian Law, *Report of the Expert Meeting on Multinational Peace Operations* (2003); Hampson, "Human Rights Law, International Humanitarian Law & Situations of Conflict"

"There is an observable tendency in the literature inspired primarily by human rights law to consider humanitarian law as merely a subset of human rights. Conversely, some writers in humanitarian law have argued for an overly rigid differentiation between human rights and humanitarian law, as a defence against the perceived threat to subsume the latter into the former. Comparative analysis ought to be grounded in a deep understanding of both legal systems and an awareness of the differences in the nature and structure of human rights and humanitarian law, as well as an openness to meaningful interaction."[37]

In the wake of atrocities that have marked the history of mankind, modern nation States have – to a certain extent under the pressure of general public opinion[38] but also responding to the general evolution of values and the respective weight attributed to them in today's society – increasingly sought to "humanize" international law, including international humanitarian law.[39] In spite of the formal prohibition of war in contemporary international law,[40] armed conflict continues to be a reality that affects the lives of millions of people around the globe. As a result, international humanitarian law continues to play an important role as one of several tools in mitigating human suffering in situations that put humanity to its harshest test. In order to achieve that purpose, it must take into account the practical constraints on parties to armed conflict and their

(*Tehran conference paper* 2004); Meron (2006); Wilde, "Triggering State Obligations Extraterritorially: The Spatial Test in Certain Human Rights Treaties" (*ILR* 2007); Hampson (*IRRC* 2008); Meredith & Christou, *Not in my Front Yard: Security and Resistance to Responsibility for Extraterritorial State Conduct* (2009); Lock, "Beyond Bosphorus: The European Court of Human Rights' Case Law on the Responsibility of Member States of International Organisations Under the European Convention on Human Rights" (*HRLR* 2010); Miller, "Revisiting Extraterritorial Jurisdiction: A Territorial Justification for Extraterritorial Jurisdiction under the European Convention" (*EJIL* 2010); Naert (2010); Wilde, "Compliance with Human Rights Norms Extraterritorially: 'Human Rights Imperialism'?" in *Liber Amoricum Gowlland-Debbas* (2010); and Kleffner in Gill & Fleck (2010), p. 468 ("Operational detainees [defined as persons deprived of liberty in the context of a military operation, whether for reasons of security or for law enforcement purposes] find themselves 'within the jurisdiction of' the Detaining State. Accordingly, human rights law applies to the relationship between the individual detainee and the detaining authority").

[37] Provost, *International Human Rights and Humanitarian Law* (2002), p. 9.

[38] Meron (2006), pp. 6 and 23.

[39] Already in 1880, the Institute of International Law pointed out that such a humanization of international humanitarian law is also in the interest of the parties to the conflict themselves. The Institute found that its *Manual of the Laws of War on Land* was "stating clearly and codifying the accepted ideas of our age so far as this has appeared allowable and practicable. By so doing, it believes it is rendering a service to military men themselves. In fact so long as the demands of opinion remain indeterminate, belligerents are exposed to painful uncertainty and to endless accusations. A positive set of rules, on the contrary, if they are judicious, serves the interests of belligerents and is far from hindering them, since by preventing the unchaining of passion and savage instincts – which battle always awakens, as much as it awakens courage and manly virtues – it strengthens the discipline which is the strength of armies; it also ennobles their patriotic mission in the eyes of the soldiers by keeping them within the limits of respect due to the rights of humanity" (Institute of International Law, *Manual of the Laws of War on Land* (1880) (hereinafter "Oxford Manual (1880)"), "Preface", §§4-5). See also Schmitt (*Virg.JIL* 2010), pp. 805-806: "International humanitarian law necessarily evolves to reflect the nature of conflict and the values of its participants. Since the nineteenth century, it has moved steadily in the direction of humanity and away from that of military necessity."

[40] Enshrined in article 2§4 UN Charter.

need to achieve military victory; its provisions thus incorporate inevitable choices between the competing interests of military necessity and the principle of humanity. Moreover, the rules that result from these choices must be clear and practical if they are to be implemented by soldiers on the ground. While the concepts of military necessity and humanity are themselves dynamic and the definition of the balance's equilibrium may thus shift over time, a fair balance must continue to be struck between both military and humanitarian imperatives. Failure to do so would prevent international humanitarian law from fulfilling its role in the international legal system.

Our view of international law as a system and of the specific function international humanitarian and human rights law have therein, also shapes our approach to applying its norms: how do we work with the different sources of international legal norms that are relevant to our research questions?

Working with international law to answer our specific research questions

As Judge Higgins has pointed out, international law is a continuous decision-making process.[41] Like those who make international law, those who apply it continuously take decisions when determining the relevant norms to address a specific question and interpreting their content. When establishing or clarifying the normative substance of specific norms of international law, scholars and practitioners ought to take into account not only existing international treaty or customary rules, but also the context in which they were adopted, the context in which they are evolving, the purpose of those norms and that of the international legal system to which they belong[42] and the way these norms have been applied in practice to achieve their purpose. "All of this makes up the fabric of international law."[43] This brings us to the sources of international law that contain answers to our research questions, and the way in which we must interpret their norms.

We will see in Part I that the general principle of legality in international law regarding restrictions of fundamental individual rights and freedoms, and the specific prohibition of arbitrary deprivation of liberty require that any deprivation of liberty be prescribed by law. It is that "law" that must answer the questions we have posed above, and for the purpose of our research that "law" (i.e. the legal basis for a particular form of deprivation of liberty) – at least in situations of international armed conflict and occupation – is an international treaty. In interpreting the provisions of that treaty and applying them in practice, we must also take into account the context in which they were drafted and adopted, the overall purpose of the treaties that contain them, and the subsequent

41 Higgins (1994), p. 2.

42 In this sense, Tomuschat recalls "the necessity never to lose sight of the basic premises of the entire system of modern international law, namely human life and dignity" (Tomuschat (*EJIL* 2010), pp. 15-16).

43 Higgins (1994), p. 10.

developments in the international legal system to which those treaties belong. As the International Court of Justice has pointed out:

> "Mindful as it is of the primary necessity of interpreting an instrument in accordance with the intentions of the parties at the time of its conclusion, the Court is bound to take into account [...] the changes which have occurred in the supervening half-century, and its interpretation cannot remain unaffected by the subsequent development of law [...]. Moreover, an international instrument has to be interpreted and applied within the framework of the entire legal system prevailing at the time of the interpretation. In the domain to which the present proceedings relate [...] as elsewhere, the *corpus iuris gentium* has been considerably enriched, and this the Court, if it is faithfully to discharge its functions, may not ignore."[44]

Article 31§1 of the Vienna Convention on the Law of Treaties (VCLT) formulates the general rule for treaty interpretation as follows:

> "A treaty shall be interpreted in good faith in accordance with the ordinary meaning to be given to the terms of the treaty in their context and in the light of its object and purpose."[45]

There is no hierarchical order in the elements that must be taken into account when interpreting a treaty norm. Its text, context and the object and purpose of the treaty must be interpreted together and in good faith to reveal the norm's substance.[46] Article 31§3 VCLT clarifies further that:

> "There shall be taken into account, together with the context: (a) any subsequent agreement between the parties regarding the interpretation of the treaty or the application of its provisions; (b) any subsequent practice in the application of the treaty which establishes the agreement of the parties regarding its interpretation; (c) any relevant rules of international law applicable in the relations between the parties."[47]

---

[44] ICJ, *Namibia Opinion* (1971), §53. The proceedings in this case concerned non-self-governing treaties and the right to self-determination and independence of peoples.

[45] The Convention was adopted in 1969 and while its article 4 specifies it will not apply retroactively, we agree with the European Court of Human Rights that "its Articles 31 to 33 enunciate in essence generally accepted principles of international law" (ECtHR, *Golder v. UK* (1975), §29. In the same sense: ICJ, *Libya v. Chad* (1994), §41 ("in accordance with customary international law, reflected in Article 31 of the 1969 Vienna Convention on the Law of Treaties"); and ILC, *Fragmentation* (2006), §427. For an overview of State and other international practice, see Villiger, *Customary International Law and Treaties: A Study of their Interactions and Interrelations with Special Consideration of the 1969 Vienna Convention on the Law of Treaties* (1985), pp. 334-343.

[46] See Cheng, *General Principles of Law as Applied by International Courts and Tribunals* (1987), pp. 106 and 114-115: "The law of treaties is closely bound with the principle of good faith, if indeed not based on it [...] The principle that treaty obligations should be fulfilled in good faith and not merely in accordance with the letter of the treaty has long been recognised by international tribunals and is reaffirmed by the United Nations [article 2§2 UN Charter]. [...] Performance of a treaty obligation in good faith means carrying out the substance of this mutual understanding honestly and loyally. [...] treaties ought not to be interpreted exclusively according to their letter, but according to their spirit."

[47] Forowicz rightly points out that "if this rule were to be used systematically by international and domestic courts, the relationship between the various international treaties would certainly become clearer. International law could also be applied in a more coherent and harmonious manner" (Forowicz, *The Reception of International Law in the European Court of Human Rights* (2010), p. 25).

Therefore, when interpreting relevant treaty norms, our primary sources will include the manner in which States have applied and interpreted these norms in practice (*literae* a and b) and other relevant international legal norms that have an impact on their substantive content (*litera* c). For example, when interpreting the internment provisions of the 1949 Geneva Conventions we will take into account the articulation of the prohibition of arbitrary deprivation of liberty in general international law as well as the right to liberty as enshrined in international human rights law.[48] Likewise, when applying the provisions of international human rights treaties relating to the right to liberty in a situation of armed conflict, we must take into account relevant provisions of international humanitarian law.[49] The ultimate purpose of international humanitarian law and its function in the international legal system will guide us throughout, and evolutions in the international legal system's tools to achieve that purpose will at times dictate an interpretation that nuances or overrides the literal meaning of the text of the treaty provisions.[50] Finally, where necessary to confirm the meaning of a specific treaty norm, we will rely on supplementary sources such as the "preparatory work of the treaty and the circumstances of its conclusion"[51] and the decisions of both international and national courts and treaty monitoring bodies regarding the interpretation of such norms.[52]

---

[48] Since it demands the interpreter to take into account the broader legal system in which the treaty functions, the rule in article 31§3(c) is often referred to as the principle of systemic integration (e.g. McLachlan, "The Principle of Systemic Integration and Article 31(3)(c) of the Vienna Convention" (*ICLQ* 2005); p. 280; Villiger, *Commentary on the 1969 Vienna Convention on the Law of Treaties* (2009), p. 432). Article 31§3(c) VCLT (1969) requires us to take into account only those rules of international law that are applicable in the relations between the parties to the treaty we are called upon to interpret. While the Geneva Conventions have been universally ratified, the same is not true for international human rights instruments. Nevertheless, there is a common nucleus of international human rights norms that cuts across the different treaties to which States may be parties and that have attained the status of general customary international law. The normative content of that common nucleus comprises those rules that are relevant to interpret the treaty provisions of the Geneva Conventions that offer answers to our research questions. The text of specific human rights treaties and the case law of the bodies that monitor and adjudicate their respect will nevertheless be useful to illustrate these general rules of international human rights law. Where possible, we have relied on case law that deals with cases of internment in armed conflict.

[49] See for example our discussion of the forcible repatriation of prisoners of war in chapter II-1, section 1.2.3.6.

[50] The humanization of international law and the developments in the international legal system subsequent to the adoption of international humanitarian and human rights law treaties must be taken into account when interpreting their provisions. Without indulging in jurisprudential or scholarly "law-making" (in this sense, see Kammerhofer's critique of "orthodox generalist", "political activist" and "international constitutionalist" legal methodology from a normativist-positivist approach in "Law-Making by Scholarship? The Dark Side of 21st Century International Legal 'Methodology'" (*SSRN* 2010)), international legal practitioners must take into account subsequent developments in international law when applying its norms in contemporary practice. On the impact of the humanization of international law on the rules on treaty interpretation, and for a summary of the debate between proponents of a teleological approach and more traditional schools of treaty interpretation, see Meron (2006), pp. 193-201. More generally on treaty interpretation in contemporary international law, see Villiger (2009), and Fitzmaurice, Elias & Merkouris, *Treaty Interpretation and the Vienna Convention on the Law of Treaties: 30 Years on* (2010).

[51] Article 32 VCLT. Where appropriate we will also refer to expressions of intent during preparatory

Judge Higgins finds that when one adopts a policy-oriented approach to international law, the distinction between *lex lata* and *lex ferenda* becomes less important.[53] Nevertheless, we find, on a number of issues that are central to our research and analysis, the distinction not to be without importance altogether. In order to answer questions identical or similar to those we have raised above, both States and international scholars have attempted to push "the law" in one or the other direction, based on specific policy considerations. But some seem to present their *interpretation* of the law as the law *itself*.[54] We submit that the research and analysis presented in this book take into account both the general objectives of the international legal system as a whole and the evolution of its norms – at times to a point of contradicting the traditional or literal reading of certain treaty rules – but does not for that matter anticipate the development of the law itself.[55]

The interaction between the specific norms of international humanitarian law and international human rights law that regulate internment in armed conflict will be discussed in more detail in the substantive part of this book, reflecting our general view that within the international legal system, international human rights law sets out the general principles regulating deprivation of liberty, while international humanitarian law – at least to a certain extent – gives expression to how these principles must be applied in situations of armed conflict. That view is also reflected in the general structure of the book.

OUTLINE

In the first part of this book we will examine the meaning of the prohibition of arbitrary deprivation of liberty in general international law, based on common principles expressed in treaty and customary international law regarding the right to liberty and on the general international legal framework for restricting fundamental rights and freedoms (chapter I-1). We will see that the individual's right to liberty is not an absolute right but may be restricted where necessary to protect the legitimate interests of the community as a whole; it may be imposed

work and drafting of treaties in order to illustrate either the object and purpose of a particular treaty, or certain States' interpretation of its norms.

[52] Apart from general decisions and opinions on the status and interpretation of certain legal norms, courts and treaty monitoring bodies dealing with individual cases have "a very unique function, in concretizing a given treaty norm" and "[a] case that is satisfactorily solved means hope for all persons in a similar situation, who can invoke the norm and the case law with a reasonable expectation that it will be similarly applied or even further developed. Moreover, a situation that is satisfactorily solved puts everyone on notice, and should contribute to preventing future violations" (Möller & de Zayas, *United Nations Human Rights Committee Case Law 1977-2008* (2009), p. 49).

[53] Higgins (1994), p. 10.

[54] In this regard, Judge Higgins notes that "to remain 'legal' is to ensure that decisions are made by those authorized to do so, with important guiding reliance on past decisions, and with available choices being made on the basis of community interests and for the promotion of common values" (Higgins (1994), p. 9).

[55] Where we propose such developments, we will clearly indicate that they are not more than proposals, or *de lege ferenda* at most.

both as a punitive and a preventive measure to safeguard public order and national security. In order to prevent arbitrariness, however, international law strictly regulates all forms of deprivation of liberty.

We will then identify exceptional situations in which security concerns may require further-reaching restrictions of the right to liberty (chapter I-2). The derogation regime inherent in most international human rights instruments allows States to take exceptional measures, restricting the individual right to liberty to an extent that would normally not be allowed, but is strictly necessary to address specific security concerns that may arise in situations of public emergency. Moreover, the international legal system allows for specific and far-reaching restrictions of the right to liberty to address specific security needs that may arise in situations of armed conflict. The extent to which such additional exceptional measures are lawful is defined by the specific branch of international law designed to regulate armed conflict, namely international humanitarian law. We will first examine the threshold of applicability of that particular body of law, an important exercise since the rules on internment are not identical for situations of international and non-international armed conflict. We will then outline how the rules of international humanitarian law and international human rights law interact as regards the specific form of deprivation of liberty that is internment in armed conflict. That general outline will be the background against which we will seek to answer the questions of who can be interned on the basis of international humanitarian law, for what reasons and for how long. The answers to these questions, as we mentioned, differ for situations of international and non-international armed conflict and must thus be treated separately.

In Part II we will examine the different legal bases for internment that exist today in international humanitarian law. In situations of international armed conflict and occupation, IHL provides for a direct legal basis to intern certain categories of persons. It distinguishes three categories of persons and prescribes the grounds and the procedures in accordance with which persons belonging to each of these categories may be interned, while at the same time limiting the duration of that internment in time. In that sense, international humanitarian law provides us with answers to all three of our research questions. We will explore who may be interned, for what reasons and for how long on the basis of respectively the Third Geneva Convention (prisoners of war, chapter II-1), the first two Geneva Conventions (medical and religious personnel of the armed forces of the parties to the conflict, chapter II-2) and the Fourth Geneva Convention (other protected persons, chapter II-3). We will interpret and clarify where necessary the relevant international humanitarian law norms, as applied in practice and in light of other relevant international law norms and subsequent developments in general international law.

In Part III we will see that international humanitarian law does not itself provide for a legal basis for internment in situations of non-international armed conflict (chapter III-1). It does not prescribe the grounds and procedures in accordance with which internment may be ordered in such situations and thus does not offer satisfactory answers to our research questions. We will see that this is no oversight but rather a deliberate choice by States, who have consistently refused to expand the internment provisions of international humanitarian law for international armed conflict to situations of non-international armed conflict, and have left the adoption of a legal basis for internment in such conflicts entirely to their domestic legal orders.

This lack of a direct legal basis for internment in international humanitarian law is today considered by some as problematic and a gap that needs to be filled. The fact that international humanitarian law does not offer a direct legal basis to intern persons in non-international armed conflict indeed causes legal problems both for non-State parties to such conflicts – whether they be organized armed groups or international organizations – and for States who are parties to such conflicts outside their national territory. We will explore some of the options to address these problems, assess to what extent they may seek guidance in the legal bases for internment in the Geneva Conventions, and propose a way forward that attempts to strike an appropriate balance between the requirements of military necessity and the principle of humanity (chapter III-2).

PART I

THE RIGHT TO LIBERTY AND THE PROHIBITION OF ARBITRARY DEPRIVATION OF LIBERTY IN INTERNATIONAL LAW

CHAPTER I – 1
REQUIREMENTS FOR LAWFUL DEPRIVATION OF LIBERTY UNDER GENERAL INTERNATIONAL LAW

1.1 THE RIGHT TO LIBERTY AND THE PROHIBITION OF ARBITRARY DEPRIVATION OF LIBERTY IN GENERAL INTERNATIONAL LAW

1.1.1. A universally recognized right

The right to liberty, and the corollary prohibition of arbitrary deprivation thereof, is one of the oldest and most well-established individual rights and freedoms, dating as far back in recorded law as the 13th-century Magna Carta. Enshrined in the constitutions of nearly all nation States, it finds its first expression in international law in articles 3 and 9 of the Universal Declaration of Human Rights (UDHR).[56] One of the most fundamental human rights, quintessential to the rule of law more generally,[57] it is enshrined in all subsequent international[58] and regional[59] human rights instruments and a special

---

[56] Articles 3 ("Everyone has the right to life, liberty and security of person") and 9 ("No one shall be subject to arbitrary arrest, detention or exile") UDHR. Actually, the UDHR was preceded by seven months by a regional human rights instrument, notably the American Declaration of the Rights and Duties of Man (ADRDM), adopted by the Organization of American States on 2 May 1948, which already provides that "Every human being has the right to life, liberty and the security of his person" (article 1) and that "No person may be deprived of his liberty except in the cases and according to the procedures established by pre-existing law" (article 25).

[57] *Cf. infra* section 1.2.2.

[58] Article 9§1 of the International Covenant on Civil and Political Rights (1966) (ICCPR): "Everyone has the right to liberty and security of person. No one shall be subjected to arbitrary arrest or detention"; article 37(b) of the Convention on the Rights of the Child (1989) (CRC): "No child shall be deprived of his or her liberty unlawfully or arbitrarily"; article 55§1(d) of the Statute of the International Criminal Court (1998) (ICC Statute): "In respect of an investigation under this Statute, a person [...] shall not be subjected to arbitrary arrest or detention"; article 95 of the United Nations Standard Minimum Rules for the Treatment of Prisoners (1955) (*Standard Minimum Rules*) (through reference to article 9 ICCPR); principle 2 of the United Nations Body of Principles for the Protection of All Persons under Any Form of Detention or Imprisonment (1988) (*Body of Principles*): "Arrest, detention or imprisonment shall only be carried out strictly in accordance with the provisions of the law and by competent officials or persons authorized for that purpose." For the text of the main treaty provisions used in this book, see Annex A.

[59] While most human rights treaties combine the right to liberty and the prohibition of arbitrary detention in their relevant provisions, the European Convention on Human Rights (1950) (ECHR) does not explicitly prohibit arbitrary detention, it focuses on the right to liberty and security of person: "Everyone has the right to liberty and security of person" (article 5§1). The European Court of Human Rights (ECtHR) has clarified however that the very purpose of article 5 ECHR is to protect the individual from arbitrariness (e.g. ECtHR, *Kurt v. Turkey* (1998), §122). The Council of Europe's (CoE) guidelines for the implementation of Article 5 ECHR equally underline that implementation must be in conformity with the overarching obligation not to arbitrarily detain (CoE,

body has been set up within the United Nations human rights system to monitor and supervise its respect and improve the protection of individuals from arbitrary deprivation of liberty worldwide.[60]

The prohibition of arbitrary deprivation of liberty also plays a prominent role in other branches of international law. International refugee law (IRL) limits the power of States to order the administrative detention of refugees and asylum seekers to those exceptional circumstances in which such detention is absolutely

Human Rights Handbook No. 5: The Right to Liberty and Security of the Person: Guide to the Implementation of Article 5 of the European Convention on Human Rights (2002) (hereinafter "*HRH No. 5*"), pp. 12-13). As to other, non-European regional human rights instruments, see articles 1 ("Every human being has the right to life, liberty and the security of his person") and 25 (entitled "Right to protection from arbitrary arrest") ADRDM; Articles 7§1 ("Every person has the right to personal liberty and security") and 7§3 ("No one shall be subjected to arbitrary arrest or imprisonment") of the American Convention on Human Rights (1969) (ACHR); principle 3§1 of the Inter-American Commission on Human Rights' *Principles and Best Practices on the Protection of Persons Deprived of Liberty in the Americas* (2008) ("Every person shall have the right to personal liberty and to be protected against any illegal or arbitrary deprivation of liberty"); article 6 of the African Charter on Human and People's Rights (1981) (ACHPR) ("Every individual shall have the right to liberty and to the security of his person [...] no one may be arbitrarily arrested or detained"); article 14 Arab Charter on Human Rights (2004) (Arab Charter) ("Everyone has the right to liberty and security of person. No one shall be subjected to arbitrary arrest, search or detention without a legal warrant"); article 5 of the Commonwealth of Independent States' Convention on Human Rights and Fundamental Freedoms (1995) (CIS Convention) ("Everyone shall have the right to liberty and security of person"); and article 20 of the Organization of the Islamic Conference's Cairo Declaration on Human Rights in Islam (1990) (Cairo Declaration) ("It is not permitted without legitimate reasons to arrest an individual, or restrict his freedom, to exile or to punish him"). So far, there is no Asian regional human rights instrument or monitoring body. Nevertheless, the Charter of the Association of South East Asian Nations (ASEAN) (2007) includes the respect for, and the promotion and protection of human rights, in the purposes and principles of the organisation (articles 1§7 and 2§2(i) of the Charter), and foresees the creation of an ASEAN human rights body (article 14 ASEAN Charter), the terms of reference of which are currently in the process of being drafted. See also Chalermpalanupap, "10 Facts about ASEAN Human Rights Cooperation" (available on ASEAN's website). To be noted that 6 of the 10 member States of ASEAN are also parties to the ICCPR.

60 The United Nations Working Group on Arbitrary Detention (WGAD) was established by Resolution 1991/42 of the United Nations Commission on Human Rights, an inter-governmental human rights monitoring body established by the United Nations General Assembly, which is the predecessor of today's Human Rights Council. For a description of the mandate and working methods of the WGAD, see WGAD, *Factsheet No. 26* (available on the WGAD's website). The WGAD has excluded situations of international armed conflict and occupation from its mandate, explaining its decision as follows: "The Working Group will not deal with situations of international armed conflict insofar as they are covered by the Geneva Conventions of 12 August 1949 and their Additional Protocols, particularly when the International Committee of the Red Cross (ICRC) has competence" (WGAD, *Opinion No. 33/2006*, quoting from its (revised) methods of work). The Working Group has clarified however that it does esteem to have a mandate where persons interned in relation to situations of international armed conflict and occupation are denied the protection of the Third or Fourth Geneva Convention, and in all cases where the reasons for not dealing with detention in armed conflict (applicability of IHL as *lex specialis* and avoidance of duplication of work with the ICRC) are absent (WGAD, *Annual Report 2005*, §§68-75). Finally, the Working Group esteems not to have a mandate regarding cases of arbitrary deprivation of liberty by non-State actors (WGAD, *Annual Report* 2004, §66). All in all, the analysis of the Working Group with regard to internment on the basis of international humanitarian law is therefore rather limited.

necessary for legitimate purposes. Furthermore, it absolutely prohibits any form of arbitrary deprivation of liberty of both refugees and asylum-seekers.[61]

[61] The prohibition of arbitrary detention is not as such spelled out in the Convention Relating to the Status of Refugees (1951) (UN Refugee Convention). However, the Convention's article 31§2 indicates that the restriction of movement (including deprivation of liberty which is the most extreme of such measures) of refugees and asylum-seekers needs to remain exceptional and may only be resorted to when necessary. Additionally, the Convention's Preamble recalls that the UDHR (which includes the right to liberty and the prohibition of arbitrary deprivation of liberty) applies to all human beings without any discrimination (preambular paragraphs 1 and 2), thus implying that the UDHR also applies to refugees and asylum-seekers. Therefore, whilst the possibility to detain (administratively) in the immigration context is endorsed by both international law and practice, any *arbitrary* arrest or detention remains prohibited. The Human Rights Committee (HRC), the United Nations High Commissioner for Refugees (UNHCR), the WGAD and other human rights courts and treaty monitoring bodies have confirmed that refugees and asylum-seekers continue to benefit from the protection of international and regional human rights treaties (e.g.: HRC, *A. v. Australia* (1997), §§6(1) to 6(5); WGAD, *Deliberation No. 5 on the Situation Regarding Immigrants and Asylum Seekers* (1999); ECtHR, *Amuur v. France* (1996), §§41-43; ECtHR (Grand Chamber), *Saadi v. UK* (2008), §§69-74 (the Courts' majority in *Saadi* found that administrative detention under article 5§1(f) does not need to satisfy a proportionality test, except as regards the duration of the detention, a decision on which 6 out of the 17 judges strongly disagreed, *cf. infra* note 96). The right to liberty and the prohibition of arbitrary arrest or detention is reiterated in article 5§1(a) of the UN Declaration on the Human Rights of Individuals Who Are not Nationals of the Country in which They Live (1985) for all persons who are not nationals of the State in which they are present: "Aliens shall enjoy, in accordance with domestic law and subject to the relevant international obligations of the State in which they are present, the following rights: (a) the right to life and security of person; no alien shall be subjected to arbitrary arrest or detention." The Declaration also reiterates the general human rights protection for aliens in its Preamble: "Recognizing that the protection of human rights and fundamental freedoms provided for in international instruments should also be ensured for individuals who are not nationals of the country in which they live." In its Conclusion No. 44 (XXXVII) (1986), operative paragraph (b), the UNHCR's Executive Committee (EXCOM) "[e]xpressed the opinion that in view of the hardship which it involves, detention should normally be avoided. If necessary, detention may be resorted to only on grounds prescribed by law to verify identity; to determine the elements on which the claim to refugee status or asylum is based; to deal with cases where refugees or asylum-seekers have destroyed their travel and/or identity documents or have used fraudulent documents in order to mislead the authorities of the State in which they intend to claim asylum; or to protect national security or public order"; and in its Conclusion No. 85 (XLIX) (1998), operative paragraph (dd), the EXCOM, after recalling article 31 UN Refugee Convention and reaffirming its Conclusion No. 44, "deplores that many countries continue routinely to detain asylum-seekers (including minors) on an arbitrary basis, for unduly prolonged periods" and "notes that such detention practices are inconsistent with established human rights standards and urges States to explore more actively all feasible alternatives to detention." The UNHCR's *Revised Guidelines on Applicable Criteria and Standards Relating tot the Detention of Asylum-Seekers* (1999) (hereinafter "*Detention of Asylum-Seekers*") reiterate and comment on the conditions placed on detention by article 31 of the UN Refugee Convention; for example its introductory paragraph 5 reads: "For detention of asylum-seekers to be lawful and not arbitrary, it must comply not only with the applicable national law, but with Article 31 of the Convention and international law," and its guideline number 2: "As a general principle asylum-seekers should not be detained." For a good overview of the practice of States, see Goodwin-Gill, "Article 31 of the 1951 Convention Relating to the Status of Refugees: Non-Penalization, Detention, and Protection" in Feller, Türk & Nicholson (eds.), *Refugee Protection in International Law* (2003), pp. 185-252. Finally, at a regional level, the Organization of African Unity's Convention Governing the Specific Aspects of Refugee Problems in Africa (1969) (OAU Refugee Convention) reiterates the applicability of the UN Refugee Convention and complements it on certain aspects, specifically regarding definitions and the specificities of the African context; the same holds true for Central America through the Cartagena Declaration on the International Protection of Refugees in Central America, Mexico and Panama (1984) (Cartagena

Even in times of armed conflict, international humanitarian law (IHL) prescribes that restrictions to the right to liberty must remain exceptional[62] and that arbitrary deprivation of liberty is not only prohibited but amounts to a war crime.[63] A considerable part of international humanitarian law is devoted to the protection of persons deprived of their liberty in relation to armed conflict.[64]

Declaration on Refugees). Both the OUA Refugee Convention and the Cartagena Declaration on Refugees reiterate the applicability of international human rights law to refugees and asylum-seekers.

[62] While not spelled out as such in the 1949 Geneva Conventions (GC) or their 1977 Additional Protocols (AP), the right to liberty and the prohibition of arbitrary deprivation of liberty are part of customary international humanitarian law and must be respected in any armed conflict. Rule 99 of the ICRC's compilation of customary international humanitarian law clearly reiterates that "[a]rbitrary deprivation of liberty is prohibited" (Henckaerts & Doswald-Beck (2005), Vol. I, p. 344). For references to the relevant practice and *opinio juris* on this rule, including military manuals, national legislation, national and international case law and other elements of practice, see Henckaerts & Doswald-Beck (2005), Volume II, pp. 2328-2363 and the ICRC's updated *Customary International Humanitarian Law Database* (ICRC, *CIHL Database*), available online at http://www.icrc.org/customary-ihl/eng/docs/home.

[63] Deprivation of liberty that is arbitrary or otherwise not in conformity with the relevant rules of international humanitarian law is generally referred to as the war crime of unlawful confinement. Article 147 GC IV lists as a grave breach "the unlawful confinement of a protected person", but article 85§4(b) AP I adds that "unjustifiable delay in the repatriation of prisoners of war or civilians" is also a grave breach. The war crime of unlawful confinement of a protected person under GC IV has been defined by the International Criminal Tribunal for the former Yugoslavia (ICTY) as follows: "The Appeals Chamber agrees with the Trial Chamber that the exceptional measure of confinement of a civilian will be lawful only in the conditions prescribed by Article 42, and where the provisions of Article 43 are complied with [footnote 505: This does not preclude the existence of other circumstances which may render confinement of a civilian unlawful, but that question does not now arise for determination by the Appeals Chamber]. Thus the detention or confinement of civilians will be unlawful in the following two circumstances: (i) when a civilian or civilians have been detained in contravention of Article 42 of Geneva Convention IV, i.e. they are detained without reasonable grounds to believe that the security of the Detaining Power makes it absolutely necessary; and (ii) where the procedural safeguards required by Article 43 of Geneva Convention IV are not complied with in respect of detained civilians, even where their initial detention may have been justified" (ICTY, *Delalíc* (2001), §322, confirmed in ICTY, *Kordić & Čerkez* (2004), §73). That any protected person under the Geneva Conventions and Additional Protocol I may be the victim of unlawful confinement is clear from article 85§4(b) AP I and has been confirmed in the ICC Statute: article 8§2(a)(vii) of the Statute lists as a war crime "unlawful deportation or transfer or unlawful confinement" without limiting it, as the Statute of the International Criminal Tribunal for the Former Yugoslavia (1993) (ICTY Statute) does, to persons protected by GC IV). The elements of crime for article 8§2(a)(vii) specify that unlawful confinement can be committed against any person "protected under one or more of the Geneva Conventions of 1949" in international armed conflict, including retained medical and religious personnel and interned prisoners of war, see Dörmann, *Elements of Crime Under the Rome Statute of the International Criminal Court: Sources and Commentary* (2003), pp. 118-123. This rule is now part of customary international humanitarian law (CIHL), see Henckaerts & Doswald-Beck (2005), Vol. I, p. 346. The question whether unlawful confinement is also a war crime when committed in non-international armed conflict (NIAC) is not explicitly settled by international humanitarian or criminal law. The crime is not listed in the ICC Statute's provisions on war crimes in non-international armed conflict. Nevertheless, the war crime provisions of the Statute of the International Criminal Tribunal for Rwanda (1994) (ICTR Statute) (Article 4) and the Statute of the Special Court for Sierra Leone (2000) (SCSL Statute) (article 3) define war crimes in non-international armed conflict as *including but not limited to* violations of common article 3 of the Geneva Conventions. Finally, there is some State practice that indicates that unlawful confinement may be a war crime in NIAC under customary international law (see for example the national legislation of Burundi, Colombia, Georgia, Nicaragua and Niger referred to in Henckaerts &

Finally, imprisonment or other deprivations of liberty in violation of fundamental rules of international law, when committed as part of a widespread or systematic attack directed against a civilian population and with knowledge of that attack, may amount to a crime against humanity and can be prosecuted as such before domestic and international tribunals.[65]

Not only are the right to liberty and the prohibition of arbitrary detention enshrined in all relevant branches and instruments of international law, they are part of customary international law.[66] Moreover, while not yet a settled issue, there are indications that the prohibition of arbitrary deprivation of liberty may be a peremptory norm of international law.[67]

Doswald-Beck (2005), Vol. II, pp. 2329-2337; to be noted that all these countries are or have been confronted with non-international armed conflicts and that their practice is thus particularly relevant).

[64] Out of the substantive provisions of the 1949 Geneva Conventions, 55,6% relate directly to persons deprived of liberty (216 out of 388 articles); for the 1977 Additional Protocols the percentage is 10% (11 out of 109 articles).

[65] Article 7§1 (e) of the ICC Statute; article 5(e) ICTY Statute; article 3(e) ICTR Statute; article 18(j) of the International Law Commission's Draft Code of Crimes against the Peace and Security of Mankind (1996) (ILC, *Draft Code of International Crimes*). On the definition of unlawful confinement as a crime against humanity, see the case law of the ICTY and the ICTR as summarized in Human Rights Watch, *Digest of the Case Law of the ICTY* (2006), pp. 256-258 and Human Rights Watch, *Digest of the Case Law of the ICTR* (2010), pp. 123-124.

[66] See for example: ICJ, *Tehran Hostages Case* (1980), §91 ("wrongfully to deprive human beings of their freedom and to subject them to physical constraint in conditions of hardship is in itself manifestly incompatible with the principles of the Charter of the United Nations"); HRC, *General Comment No. 24* (1994), §8 ("Reservations that offend peremptory norms would not be compatible with the object and purpose of the Covenant. [...] Accordingly, provisions in the Covenant that represent customary international law (and a fortiori when they have the character of peremptory norms) may not be the subject of reservations. Accordingly, a State may not reserve the right to [...] arbitrarily arrest and detain persons"); Henckaerts & Doswald-Beck (2005), Vol. I, p. 346 ("Rule 99: Arbitrary deprivation of liberty is prohibited"); Office of the High Commissioner of Human Rights (OHCHR), *Brief of Amicus Curiae United Nations High Commissioner for Human Rights in Support of Petitioners before the United States Supreme Court in Boumediene et al. v. Bush and al-Odah et al v. USA* (2008) (hereinafter "OHCHR, *Boumediene & al-Odah Brief*"), pp. 1-2 ("The prohibition of prolonged arbitrary detention also constitutes customary international law"); US, *Restatement (Third) of Foreign Relations Law of the United States* (1987), §702 and comments (n) and (11) (according to the Restatement, the prohibition of prolonged arbitrary detention practiced, encouraged or condoned as a matter of State policy is a rule of customary international law and even a peremptory norm of international law (jus cogens)). See also Lillich, "The Growing Importance of Customary International Human Rights Law" (*GJICL* 1995-1996), p. 6 ("a number of the norms found in the Universal Declaration have achieved customary international law status [...] they include the prohibitions against arbitrary detention, [...]"); de Londras, "The Right to Challenge the Lawfulness of Detention: An International Perspective on US Detention of Suspected Terrorists" (*JCSL* 2007), p. 240 ("As well as being protected in specific conventions [...] it is clear that the right to be free from arbitrary detention is a customary international law right"); Droege (*IRRC* 2008), p. 520 ("it is uncontroversial that core human rights such as [...] the prohibition of arbitrary deprivation of liberty [...] form part of customary international law"); and Lubell, *Extraterritorial Use of Force against Non-State Actors* (2010), p. 183 ("The right to freedom from arbitrary detention is not only to be found in all major treaties, but can also be considered one of the human rights that have acquired the status of customary international law.")

[67] Apart from the US *Restatement (Third) on the Foreign Relations Law* referred to above, see also HRC, *General Comment 24* (1994), §8 ("Reservations that offend peremptory norms would not be compatible with the object and purpose of the Covenant. [...] provisions in the Covenant that represent customary international law (and a fortiori when they have the character of peremptory

1.1.2. A right with a comprehensive scope of application

The right to liberty inherently belongs to the individual as a human being: the prohibition of arbitrary deprivation of liberty therefore covers all forms of deprivation of liberty, regardless of their denomination or whether they are ordered on the basis of criminal charges or imposed as part of an administrative procedure. While some substantive aspects of the right to liberty specifically refer to detention in the framework of criminal proceedings, the right as such in all its other aspects applies to all deprivations of liberty, including administrative detention or internment. The right to liberty and the prohibition of arbitrary deprivation of liberty, moreover, apply both in peacetime and during armed conflict, without any distinction on the basis of nationality or citizenship.

This broad scope of application of the right to liberty is apparent from the general terms of its formulation in treaty provisions[68] and has been confirmed by all relevant human rights monitoring mechanisms, as is illustrated by the following examples.

The United Nations Human Rights Committee (HRC), in its General Comment No. 8, dealing with the right to liberty enshrined in the ICCPR, explicitly points out that:

> "paragraph 1 [of Article 9 ICCPR] is applicable to all deprivations of liberty, whether in criminal cases or in other cases [...]. It is true that some provisions of article 9 (part of para. 2 and the whole of para. 3) are only applicable to persons against whom criminal charges are brought. But the rest, and in particular the important guarantee laid down in paragraph 4, i.e. the right to control by a court of the legality of the detention, applies to all persons deprived of their liberty by arrest or detention. [...] Also if so-called preventive detention is used, for reasons of public security, it must be controlled by the same provisions, i.e. it must not be arbitrary, and must be based on grounds and procedures established by law (para.1), information of the reasons must be given (para. 2) and court control of the detention must be available (para. 4) as well as compensation in the case of a breach (para. 5). And if, in addition, criminal charges are brought in such cases, the full protection of article 9(2) and (3), as well as article 14, must also be granted."[69]

The United Nations Human Rights Commission, an intergovernmental body monitoring the human rights situation in UN member States, made it clear that

---

norms) may not be the subject of reservations. Accordingly, a State may not reserve the right to [...] to arbitrarily arrest and detain persons"); and HRC, *General Comment 29* (2001), §11 ("the category of peremptory norms extends beyond the list of non-derogable provisions as given in [article 4§2 ICCPR]. States parties may in no circumstances invoke article 4 of the Covenant as justification for acting in violation of humanitarian law or peremptory norms of international law, for instance [...] through arbitrary deprivations of liberty"). In the same sense: Brownlie, *Principles of International Law* (1998), p. 575 and Naert (2010), p. 626.

[68] *Cf. supra* note 57 and Annex A.

[69] HRC, *General Comment No. 8* (1982), §§ 1 and 4. For a summary of the discussions at the time of drafting, see Nowak, *U.N. Covenant on Civil and Political Rights: CCPR Commentary* (2005), pp. 219-225.

there is no "purpose in treating the question of administrative detention independently, even if, in certain cases, the procedure of administrative detention gives rise to specific abuses."[70] Likewise, the mandate of the Working Group on Arbitrary Detention – set up by the Commission to monitor the respect of the prohibition of arbitrary deprivation of liberty – includes all forms of deprivation of liberty:

> "the objective entrusted [...] to the Group relates to the protection of individuals against arbitrary deprivation of freedom in all its forms, and its mandate extends to deprivation of freedom either before, during or after the trial [...], as well as deprivation of freedom in the absence of any kind of trial (administrative detention). The Group also regarded as forms of detention measures of house arrest and rehabilitation through labour, when they are accompanied by serious restrictions on liberty of movement."[71]

In the same way, the European Court of Human Rights (ECtHR) has made it clear that:

> "Article 5 enshrines a fundamental human right, namely the protection of the individual against arbitrary interference by the State with his or her right to liberty [...]. The text of Article 5 makes it clear that the guarantees it contains apply to 'everyone'."[72]

Moreover, in its Guide to the implementation of Article 5 ECHR, the Council of Europe reiterates that any form of deprivation of liberty falls within the material scope of Article 5, regardless of how the measure is designated by

---

[70] United Nations Commission on Human Rights (UNCHR), *Resolution 1994/32* (1994), 5th preambular paragraph.

[71] WGAD, *Factsheet No. 26*, last paragraph under "Section A. What is meant by deprivation of liberty?" To be noted that the Working Group has, in principle, excluded deprivation of liberty in the context of international armed conflict and occupation and deprivation of liberty by non-State actors from its mandate (*cf. supra* note 59). It has done so respectively for reasons of judicial economy (to avoid duplication with the work of the ICRC) and because the question of human rights obligations of non-State entities remains unsettled in international law (*cf.* also *infra* chapter III-2). This does not mean that these deprivations of liberty fall outside the scope of application of the prohibition on arbitrary deprivation of liberty. As the Group itself points out: "The Working Group decided not to deal with individual communications arising from situations in which [the GC and their AP are] clearly applicable. This was also to avoid duplication of the work done by the ICRC, which in the exercise of its mandate to improve the situation of detainees, by doing all it can to ensure that they are treated with dignity and humanity, might also deal with the status of detainees and the legality of detention" (*Annual Report 2005*, §74); and "The taking of hostages by terrorist groups is undoubtedly a particularly serious form of arbitrary deprivation of liberty, though by non-State actors and thus beyond the confines of the Working Group's mandate" (*Annual Report 2004*, §66).

[72] ECtHR, *A and Others v. UK* (2009), §162. The Court indeed relies on article 5 of the ECHR to deal not only with detention in the framework of criminal proceedings, but also in cases dealing specifically with administrative detention, whether ordered in normal circumstances (e.g. in the immigration context and in the context of military discipline), or in times where a State has validly derogated from its obligations under the Convention for reasons related either to a situation of armed conflict (e.g. the Cyprus, Turkey and Chechnya cases regarding deprivation of liberty) or of terrorist activities (e.g. the Court's case law on the situation in Northern Ireland in the 1970s and 1980s, or in relation to UK legislation adopted in the wake of 9/11). In the same sense: Bingham, "The Rule of Law" (*Sir David Williams Lectures* 2006), pp. 14-15 and 29 (with references to UK case law and parliamentary discussions on the subject).

domestic legislation (arrest, detention, imprisonment, internment, confinement, etc.) or by the authorities responsible for it.[73]

In the case of *Amnesty International and Others v. Sudan*, the African Commission on Human and Peoples' Rights (AC°HPR) has applied article 6 of the African Charter on Human and Peoples' Rights (ACHPR), concerning the right to liberty, to cases of administrative detention or internment under Sudan's decreed emergency powers dealing with non-international armed conflicts in that country.[74]

Likewise, both the Inter-American Commission (IAC°HR) and the Inter-American Court on Human Rights (IACtHR) have applied the provisions of the American Declaration on the Rights and Duties of Man (ADRDM) and the American Convention on Human Rights (ACHR) regarding the right to liberty and the prohibition of arbitrary deprivation of liberty to instances of both administrative detention and internment in armed conflict.[75]

Finally, as the United Nations High Commissioner for Human Rights has pointed out, the right to liberty and the prohibition of arbitrary deprivation of liberty apply to nationals and aliens and to citizens and non-citizens alike:

> "The [...] obligations under the Covenant extend to '*all* individuals within its territory and subject to its jurisdiction ... *without distinction of any kind* ...' ICCPR art. 2§1 [...]. Hence, whatever interpretation might be given the phrase 'all individuals within its territory and subject to its jurisdiction' there can be no suggestion that the protections afforded by Article 9 of the Covenant do not extend to citizens and non-citizens alike."[76]

Thus, all relevant international human rights bodies uphold the broad scope of application of the right to liberty and the prohibition of arbitrary deprivation of liberty. However, and as shall be shown below, this does not prevent the specific circumstances of every case or other relevant norms of international law to be taken into account in the interpretation and implementation of the right, or in an assessment of whether it has been violated in a given case.

1.1.3. A right at the heart of the rule of law

In spite of the clear prohibition under international law and strong condemnation of arbitrary deprivation of liberty by the international community,

---

[73] CoE, *HRH No. 5* (2002), pp. 17-21.

[74] AC°HPR, *Amnesty International and Others v. Sudan* (1999), §§3 and 58-64. For a summary of Sudan's Decree No. 2 of 1989, which granted the extraordinary powers of arrest and detention discussed in this case, see the International Labour Organizations' *National Legislation Database* at http://www.ilo.org.

[75] E.g. IAC°HR, *Coard v. USA* (1999), §45; IAC°HR, *Third Report Colombia* (1999), chapter IV; IAC°HR, *Second Report Peru* (2000) and IAC°HR, *Guantánamo* (2002).

[76] OHCHR, *Boumediene & al-Odah Brief* (2008), p. 14, original emphasis, with reference to relevant decisions of the Human Rights Committee. See also WGAD, *Annual Report 2007*, §46 ("While administrative detention of asylum-seekers and illegal immigrants is not prohibited a priori by international human rights law, it can amount to arbitrary detention if it is not necessary in all circumstances of the case").

the legal protection of persons deprived of their liberty has been and remains at the very core of the challenges faced by international humanitarian and human rights law, and by other branches of international law aiming to protect individuals from the abusive exercise of power by the authorities in whose hands they find themselves. Arbitrary deprivation of liberty unfortunately occurs on a daily basis worldwide and continues to undermine the protection of human rights and the rule of law more generally. It also significantly increases the risk of enforced disappearance,[77] torture and other forms of ill treatment or abuse.[78]

[77] Henckaerts & Doswald-Beck (2005), Vol. I, p. 344 ("both international humanitarian law and human rights law aim to prevent arbitrary detention [...] to prevent disappearance"); United Nations Assistance Mission in Afghanistan (UNAMA), *Arbitrary Detention in Afghanistan: A Call for Action* (2009), Vol. 1, p. 1 ("Arbitrary detentions in many instances lead to violations of other rights, such as [...] enforced disappearances"). Deprivation of liberty is a key element in the definition of enforced disappearances, because many if not all enforced disappearances follow a deprivation of liberty. Article 2 of the International Convention for the Protection of All Persons from Enforced Disappearance (Enforced Disappearance Convention) (2006) defines enforced disappearance as "the arrest, detention, abduction or any other form of deprivation of liberty by agents of the State or by persons or groups of persons acting with the authorization, support or acquiescence of the State, followed by a refusal to acknowledge the deprivation of liberty or by concealment of the fate or whereabouts of the disappeared person, which place such a person outside the protection of the law"; article 2 of the Inter-American Convention on Forced Disappearance of Persons (1994) defines forced disappearance as "the act of depriving a person or persons of his or their freedom, in whatever way, perpetrated by agents of the state or by persons or groups of persons acting with the authorization, support, or acquiescence of the state, followed by an absence of information or a refusal to acknowledge that deprivation of freedom or to give information on the whereabouts of that person, thereby impeding his or her recourse to the applicable legal remedies and procedural guarantees." The risk of disappearance is especially important where the conditions for deprivation of liberty under international law are not met, see e.g. ECtHR, *Kurt v. Turkey* (1998), §124: "Article 5 [ECHR, concerning the right to liberty] must be seen as requiring authorities to take effective measures to safeguard against the risk of disappearance." The Inter-American Commission and Court on Human Rights – based on the experience in the hemisphere they cover – have repeatedly warned against the additional violation of very fundamental human rights that more often than not accompany cases of arbitrary deprivation of liberty, including that of enforced disappearance (e.g. IACtHR, *Bámaca Velásquez v. Guatemala* (2000), §121(f) and §124). On the link between arbitrary deprivation of liberty and enforced disappearance generally, see for example Aeschlimann, "Protection of Detainees: ICRC Action behind Bars" (*IRRC* 2005), pp. 108-109; Rodley & Pollard, *The Treatment of Prisoners under International Law* (2009), pp. 329-332 and 344-347.

[78] E.g.: CoE, *HRH No. 5* (2002), p. 6; ECtHR, *Daoudi v. France* (2009), §§68-70 ("les personnes impliquées dans des faits de terrorisme sont arrêtées et détenues [...] de façon peu prévisible et sans une base légale clairement établie, essentiellement afin d'être interrogées pour obtenir des renseignements, et non dans un but uniquement judiciaire [...] ces personnes, placées en détention sans contrôle des autorités judiciaires ni communication avec l'extérieur (avocat, médecin ou famille), peuvent être soumises à des mauvais traitements, y compris la torture"); UNAMA, *Arbitrary detention in Afghanistan: A call for action* (2009), Vol. 1, p. 1 ("Arbitrary detentions in many instances lead to violations of other rights, such as the prohibition against inhuman or degrading treatment or torture, and enforced disappearances"); Pfanner, "Editorial" (*IRRC* 2005), pp. 5-6; Aeschlimann (*IRRC* 2005), p. 112; Kelman, "The Policy Context of Torture: A Social-Psychological Analysis" (*IRRC* 2005), pp. 123-134; Rodley & Pollard (2009), pp. 450-452. See also generally the reports of the UN Committee Against Torture (CAT) at http://www2.ohchr.org/english/bodies/cat/.

The right to liberty has rightfully been described by the Israeli Supreme Court as a "constitutional right of the first degree and from a practical viewpoint [...] also a condition for realizing other basic rights."[79] In the Final Act of the 1975 Conference on Security and Cooperation in Europe in Helsinki, participating States recognized that respect for human rights and fundamental freedoms "is an essential factor for the peace, justice and well-being necessary to ensure the development of friendly relations and co-operation among themselves as among all States."[80] Likewise, the United Nations High Commissioner for Human Rights has emphasized "[a] State's compliance with its obligations under the Covenant [the ICCPR] and other human rights treaties reflects its basic commitment to the rule of law."[81]

Arbitrary arrest and detention of individuals who exercise their fundamental rights in opposition to the authorities in power also restricts the free exercise of other rights that are crucial for the development and effective functioning of societies construed on the rule of law, such as the right to freedom of expression, movement and association.[82]

In the following section, we will explore how the principle of the rule of law and the principle of legality regarding the restriction of fundamental rights and freedoms are reflected in the right to liberty and the prohibition of arbitrary deprivation thereof. These principles form the background against which we can then examine in more detail the requirements for lawful deprivation of liberty imposed by general international law that are relevant for answering our research questions.

---

[79] Israel, Supreme Court (SC), *A and B. v. Israel* (2008), §28 (with reference to its established case law, including in cases where it seated as the High Court of Justice). See also Israel, SC, *Bargaining Chips Case* (2000), §17: "Liberty and dignity are at the foundation of our social order. They are the ones allowing other fundamental rights. [...] Therefore, the maintenance and protection of individual liberty and dignity constitutes a fundamental value, which extends over the entire legislative corpus."

[80] Organization for Security and Cooperation in Europe (OSCE), *Final Act of the Conference on Security and Cooperation in Europe* (1975), chapter on "Questions Relating to Security in Europe", subtitle "(a) Declaration on Principles Guiding Relations between Participating States", article VII.

[81] OHCHR, *Boumediene & al-Odah Brief* (2008), p. 3.

[82] CoE, *HRH No. 5* (2002), pp. 5-6; UNCHR, *Resolution 1994/32* (1994), §13 (reflecting on the work of the WGAD, the Commission "expresses its concern at the fact that most cases of arbitrary deprivation of liberty are motivated by [the] exercise of the right to freedom of opinion and expression"); WGAD, *Factsheet No. 26*, chapter II; Human Rights First, *Behind the Wire* (2005), pp. 24-25; Waxman, "Administrative Detention: The Integration of Strategy and Legal Process" (*Counterterrorism and American Statutory Law Series* 2008), pp. 19-20; see also generally reports by Human Rights Watch at http://www.hrw.org and by Amnesty International at http://www.amnesty.org.

1.2. THE RULE OF LAW, THE PRINCIPLE OF LEGALITY AND THE RIGHT TO LIBERTY

1.2.1. The right to liberty and the definition of prohibition of arbitrary deprivation of liberty in international law: criteria for assessing the lawfulness of detention and internment

While international treaty law firmly prohibits arbitrary deprivation of liberty, it does not define this concept in precise terms. As we discussed the definition of "deprivation of liberty" above, we will now outline when a given deprivation of liberty is "arbitrary". For the purpose of determining the mandate of the Working Group on Arbitrary Detention, the UN Human Rights Commission has used a pragmatic criterion, considering as arbitrary:

> "those deprivations of liberty which for one reason or another are contrary to relevant international provisions laid down in the Universal Declaration of Human Rights or in the relevant international instruments ratified by States."[83]

The Working Group itself has further elaborated that definition for situations of armed conflict:

> "Arguably, when deprivation of liberty occurs in connection with an armed conflict, the "relevant international standards" referred to in the [Human Rights Commission's resolutions governing the Working Group's mandate] will have to be looked for primarily in the Geneva Conventions of 12 August 1949 and the 1977 Additional Protocols thereto, but also in the Universal Declaration of Human Rights, the International Covenant on Civil and Political Rights and other human rights law instruments."[84]

In the same sense, the ICRC defines arbitrary deprivation of liberty – indirectly through the definition of the war crime of unlawful confinement – as "detention that is not in conformity with the various rules provided by the Geneva Conventions."[85] The ICRC also affirms that internment and administrative detention will be arbitrary "if the reasons for it do not or do no longer exist"[86] or if they continue "despite a final release order"[87] from the body in charge of their review.

It can thus be said that any deprivation of liberty that is not in full conformity with international legal standards regulating that deprivation of liberty will be

[83] UNCHR, *Resolution 1991/41* (1991) as revised by UNCHR *Resolution 1997/50* (1997), summarized in WGAD, *Factsheet No. 26*, Section IV.B, §2.
[84] WGAD, *Annual Report 2005*, §69 (references to the UNCHR's resolutions omitted).
[85] Henckaerts & Doswald-Beck (2005), Vol. I, p. 346. The ICRC's definition of the war crime of unlawful confinement largely coincides with the concept of arbitrary deprivation of liberty used by the WGAD and is included in its compilation of customary international humanitarian law as part of the rule prohibiting arbitrary deprivation of liberty in time of armed conflict.
[86] Pejic (*IRRC* 2005), p. 382. Pejic's article "reflects the ICRC's official position and now guides its operations" (ICRC, *International Humanitarian Law and the Challenges of Contemporary Armed Conflicts* (2007), p. 11).
[87] Pejic (*IRRC* 2005), p. 387.

arbitrary and unlawful. To know whether a given deprivation of liberty (including internment in armed conflict) is lawful under international law, it must therefore be tested against the relevant requirements of the right to liberty as defined by general international (human rights) law. The Universal Declaration of Human Rights provides that:

"Everyone has the right to life, liberty and the security of person"; and that

"No one shall be subjected to arbitrary arrest, detention or exile."[88]

Subsequent human rights instruments elaborate upon these core provisions in similar terms. For the purposes of the present section, we will work with the text of the ICCPR and the ECHR, on the one hand because their wording is representative of that of the other relevant instruments, and on the other hand because they are slightly different in conception, as we will see in more detail below.[89] Their relevant provisions read as follows:

Article 9 ICCPR	Article 5 ECHR
1. Everyone has the right to liberty and security of person. No one shall be subjected to arbitrary arrest or detention. No one shall be deprived of his liberty except on such grounds and in accordance with such procedure as are established by law.	1. Everyone has the right to liberty and security of person. No one shall be deprived of his liberty save in the following cases and in accordance with a procedure prescribed by law: [list of lawful grounds, *cf. infra*]
2. Anyone who is arrested shall be informed, at the time of arrest, of the reasons for his arrest and shall be promptly informed of any charges against him.	2. Everyone who is arrested shall be informed promptly, in a language which he understands, of the reasons for his arrest and of any charge against him.
3. Anyone arrested or detained on a criminal charge shall be brought promptly before a judge or other officer authorized by law to exercise judicial power and shall be entitled to trial within a reasonable time or to release. It shall not be the general rule that persons awaiting trial shall be detained in custody, but release may be subject to guarantees to appear for trial, at any other stage of the judicial proceedings, and, should occasion arise, for execution of the judgement.	3. Everyone arrested or detained in accordance with the provisions of paragraph 1.c of this article shall be brought promptly before a judge or other officer authorised by law to exercise judicial power and shall be entitled to trial within a reasonable time or to release pending trial. Release may be conditioned by guarantees to appear for trial.
4. Anyone who is deprived of his liberty by arrest or detention shall be entitled to take proceedings before a court, in order that that court may decide without delay on the lawfulness of his detention and order his release if the detention is not lawful.	4. Everyone who is deprived of his liberty by arrest or detention shall be entitled to take proceedings by which the lawfulness of his detention shall be decided speedily by a court and his release ordered if the detention is not lawful.
5. Anyone who has been the victim of unlawful arrest or detention shall have an enforceable right to compensation.	5. Everyone who has been the victim of arrest or detention in contravention of the provisions of this article shall have an enforceable right to compensation.

[88] UDHR, articles 3 and 9 respectively.

[89] The definition of the right to liberty in the ACHR, the ACHPR and the Arab Charter on Human Rights is closer to that in the ICCPR, while its definition in the CIS Convention is quasi-identical to that in the ECHR.

The fundamental right to liberty, like the right to life, is so crucial for the preservation of human dignity and for the exercise of all other individual rights and freedoms that deprivation of liberty must always remain an exceptional measure. The text of both article 9 ICCPR and article 5 ECHR (and equivalent provisions in other human rights instruments alike) therefore points to a presumption in favour of liberty. In order to be lawful, any deprivation of liberty must therefore be justified by legitimate needs and must last no longer than absolutely necessary. Liberty must be easily recovered where its deprivation is unlawful. The burden of proof of the lawfulness of detention or internment rests on the detaining or interning authority.[90] As the Council of Europe highlights: "[a]nything less than that would entail an abandonment of the rule of law and a surrender to arbitrary treatment."[91]

We will see in Part II that international humanitarian law specifically reiterates the exceptional nature of deprivation of liberty. In order to protect individuals against arbitrary interference with their fundamental right to liberty, the internment of persons considered to be a military or security threat is only permitted in exceptional circumstances.[92]

For deprivation of liberty to be lawful then, a number of criteria must be met; each designed to prevent unnecessary or arbitrary deprivation of liberty. They must be interpreted narrowly in order to preserve the exceptional character of the

[90] CoE, *HRH No. 5* (2002), pp. 6-9. Under criminal law, the presumption of liberty is also reflected in the principle of *favor rei* (which forms part of the articulation of the principle of legality discussed below): in case of conflicting interpretations of the rule, criminal law supports the construction that favours the accused. Here too, the rationale of the principle is to protect the individual against arbitrariness and abuse of power. As a standard for appraisal of evidence, the principle is known as *in dubio pro reo* (if the evidence leaves doubt, it should be appreciated in favour of the accused). See Cassese, *International Criminal Law* (2003), pp. 156-157. The presumption of liberty and the exceptional character of deprivation thereof are even more stringent in cases of administrative detention and internment, which are inherently preventive and not punitive measures of control. See for example WGAD, *Annual Report 2007*, §51 ("It is necessary to remind all States that illegal immigrants placed in administrative detention are not criminals or suspects. Therefore, detention must be the exception, not the rule. The Working Group considers that taking aliens into custody without a legal basis is totally unjustifiable and amounts to arbitrary detention"). See also Parliamentary Assembly of the Council of Europe (PACE), *Resolution 1707: Detention of Asylum Seekers and Irregular Migrants in Europe* (2010), §3 ("Whilst it is universally accepted that [administrative detention of asylum-seekers and refugees] must be used only as a last resort, it is increasingly used as a first response and also as a deterrent. This results in mass and needless detention. [...] The Assembly reiterates that the grounds for immigration detention are limited [by article 5 ECHR]. Detention should be used only if less intrusive measures have been tried and found insufficient. Consequently, priority should be given to alternatives to detention for the individuals in question. [...] the Assembly calls on member states [...] in which asylum seekers and irregular migrants are detained to comply fully with their obligations under international human rights and refugee law"); and Pejic (*IRRC* 2005), p. 380 ("that internment is an exceptional measure is [...] based on the general principle that personal liberty is the rule, and on the assumption that the criminal justice system is able to deal with persons suspected of representing a danger to State security").

[91] CoE, *HRH No. 5* (2002), p. 9.

[92] According to the ICRC, the presumption of liberty and the exceptional character of deprivation of liberty is one of the general principles for internment in armed conflict and administrative detention in other situations of violence that are required by international human rights and humanitarian law. See Pejic (*IRRC* 2005), p. 380.

measure and to avoid arbitrariness in its implementation.[93] They can be summarized as follows.

First, deprivation of liberty can only be lawful when it is based on a law that properly prescribes the grounds on which it may be ordered and the procedures in accordance with which it may be initiated or continued (§1 of articles 9 ICCPR and 5 ECHR). The requirement of a valid legal basis prescribing lawful grounds is of primary importance to effectively protect individuals against arbitrary deprivation of liberty. The legal basis for deprivation of liberty, i.e. the legal instrument regulating a specific deprivation of liberty, must conform to certain basic qualities to be valid under international law.

Second, the grounds on which the deprivation of liberty is ordered, namely the reasons for which it may be ordered, must reflect valid needs throughout its entire duration and serve a purpose considered legitimate under international law. These two criteria as applied in armed conflict will be studied in depth in Parts II and III and guide the answers to our research questions. We will briefly come back to their general features in sections 1.2.3 and 1.2.4 below.

Third, the right to liberty includes a number of procedural safeguards that are essential in preventing arbitrariness and are therefore inherent in the right to liberty itself. Failure to effectively provide for them will entail a direct violation of the right to liberty (§§2-5 of articles 9 ICCPR and 5 ECHR). These procedural safeguards are required to deprive any person of his or her liberty under both international humanitarian and human rights law and can be summarized as follows:

- the right to be informed of the reasons for deprivation of liberty;
- the right – for persons charged with a criminal offence – to be brought promptly before a competent legal authority to decide on the merits of the charges and the right to be tried within a reasonable lapse of time and to be released pending trial;
- the right to challenge the lawfulness of the deprivation of liberty itself; and
- the right to a remedy and compensation in case of unlawful deprivation of liberty.[94]

---

[93] See for example, ECtHR, *Kurt v. Turkey* (1998), §122: "This insistence on the protection of the individual against any abuse of power is illustrated by the fact that Article 5§1 circumscribes the circumstances in which individuals may be lawfully deprived of their liberty, it being stressed that these circumstances must be given a narrow interpretation having regard to the fact that they constitute exceptions to a most basic guarantee of individual freedom (see, *mutatis mutandis*, ECtHR, *Quinn v. France* (1995), §42)."

[94] Article 9, §§2-5 ICCPR; article 5§§2-5 ECHR; article 25§3 ADRDM; article 7§§4-6 and article 25 ACHR; article 7§1 ACHPR; article 16 Arab Charter; article 5§§2-5 CIS Convention. See also HRC, *General Comment 8* (1982); United Nations, *Body of Principles* (1988), principles 10, 11, 32 and 37; WGAD, *Annual Report 2007*, §§64-69; Council of Europe, *HRH No. 5* (2002), pp. 46-68; IAC°HR, *Principles and Best Practices* (2008), principles 5 to 7; and AC°HPR, *Principles and Guidelines on the Right to a Fair Trial and to Legal Assistance in Africa* (2001). While the 2nd guarantee only concerns detention in the framework of criminal proceedings, the others apply fully to administrative detention and internment, apart from the general references already mentioned, see also in particular

For any deprivation of liberty to be lawful, these safeguards must be accessible to the detainee or internee in question.[95] The criteria for lawful deprivation of liberty must not only be ensured by law but must also be implemented in a way that serves their ultimate purpose and effectively protects individual detainees and internees against arbitrary interference with their right to liberty.

The protection against arbitrariness is the underlying purpose of the right to liberty and the concept of arbitrariness will therefore guide the interpretation of these criteria and the general process for assessing the lawfulness of any deprivation of liberty. The notion of arbitrariness is broader than that of unlawfulness though.[96] Apart from the three rather technical criteria discussed above (legal basis, lawful grounds and basic procedural safeguards against arbitrariness), the evaluation of the arbitrary character of a deprivation of liberty must therefore include elements of appropriateness, justice, predictability, due process of law, proportionality, and respect for the dignity of the human person. Even when a valid legal basis for deprivation of liberty exists, every individual

---

HRC, *General Comment 8* (1982), §§1 and 4; Institute for Human Rights, *Turku Declaration of Minimum Humanitarian Standards* (1990), articles 4 and 11; articles 43 and 78 GC IV; article 75§3 AP I; Henckaerts & Doswald-Beck (2005), Vol. I, pp. 345 and 349-352; Nowak (2005), pp. 228-240; Pejic (*IRRC* 2005), pp. 386 and 388-389; Bingham (*Sir David Williams Lectures* 2006), p. 28; and Cassel (*CWRJIL* 2009), pp. 384-385 (Cassel lists the core requirements of international human rights law for security detention, adding that these also apply in situations of armed conflict, even if they may be modified to some extent by the relevant international humanitarian law).

[95] A number of additional safeguards against arbitrariness must be put in place and failure to do so may in some instances equally render an otherwise lawful detention arbitrary. They include the right to legal assistance and representation, the right to be held in an officially recognized place of detention, the obligation to register persons deprived of liberty and the details of their deprivation of liberty, and the obligation to provide for independent monitoring of the conditions of detention or internment (e.g.: *Standard Minimum Rules* (1955); *Body of Principles* (1988); *Siracusa Principles on the Limitation and Derogation of Provisions in the International Covenant on Civil and Political Rights* (1984); *Turku Declaration* (1990); WGAD, *Annual Report 2005*; AC°HPR, *Principles on Fair Trial and Legal Assistance* (2001); IAC°HR, *Principles and Best Practices* (2008); Delaplace & Pollard, "Visits by Human Rights Mechanisms as a Means of Greater Protection for Persons Deprived of Liberty" (*IRRC* 2005); Pejic (*IRRC* 2005), pp. 384-385 and 388-391). These measures do not only safeguard against arbitrary deprivation of liberty but also against other potential violations of human rights to which persons deprived of liberty are often exposed (*cf. supra* notes 77-78).

[96] See for example Nowak (2005), p. 224: "It is not enough for deprivation of liberty to be provided for by law. The law itself must not be arbitrary, and the enforcement of the law in a given case must not take place arbitrarily." See also the debates during the drafting of article 9§1 ICCPR as referenced in Bossuyt, *Guide to the "Travaux Préparatoires" of the International Covenant on Civil and Political Rights* (1987), pp. 199-202. The ECtHR has consistently held that apart from being in conformity with the law, deprivation of liberty may not be arbitrary, e.g. ECtHR, *Winterwerp v. the Netherlands* (1979), §39: "in a democratic society subscribing to the rule of law [...] no detention that is arbitrary can ever be regarded as 'lawful'"; ECtHR (Grand Chamber), *Çakici v. Turkey* (1999), §104: "[The Court] has repeatedly stressed that any deprivation of liberty must not only have been effected in conformity with the substantive and procedural rules of national law but must equally be in keeping with the very purpose of Article 5, namely to protect the individual from arbitrary detention"; and ECtHR (Grand Chamber), *A and Others v. UK* (2009), §164: "the notion of arbitrariness in Article 5§1 extends beyond lack of conformity with national law, so that a deprivation of liberty may be lawful in terms of domestic law but still arbitrary and thus contrary to the Convention."

deprivation of liberty must be reasonable and necessary in the specific circumstances of the case. It must be carried out in good faith and the actual reasons for depriving a specific person of his or her liberty must fall within the scope of the grounds prescribed by the law. "Necessity" also includes an element of proportionality: the restriction of an individual's right to liberty must be proportionate to the purpose pursued. The duration of the deprivation of liberty must remain within the confines of what is reasonably required for the purpose pursued and is thus also subject to the necessity requirement.[97] Finally, where

[97] Bossuyt (1987) and Nowak (2005) referred to *supra* note 95. See also HRC, *Van Alphen v. the Netherlands* (1990), §5(8): "the drafting history of article 9, paragraph 1, confirms that 'arbitrariness' is not to be equated with 'against the law', but must be interpreted more broadly to include elements of inappropriateness, injustice and lack of predictability [...] this means that remand in custody pursuant to lawful arrest must not only be lawful but reasonable in all the circumstances. Further, remand in custody must be necessary in all the circumstances"; confirmed amongst others in HRC, *Mukong v. Cameroon* (1994), §9(8) and HRC, *A v. Australia* (1997), §9(2). In the same sense: IACtHR, *Gangaram Panday v. Suriname* (1994), §47: "no one may be subjected to arrest or imprisonment for reasons and by methods which, although classified as legal, could be deemed to be incompatible with the respect for the fundamental rights of the individual because, among other things, they are unreasonable, unforeseeable or lacking in proportionality"; confirmed amongst others in IACtHR, *Bámaca Velásquez v. Guatemala* (2000), §139); ECtHR (Grand Chamber), *Saadi v. UK* (2008), §§68-70: "While the Court has not previously formulated a global definition as to what types of conduct on the part of the authorities might constitute "arbitrariness" for the purposes of Article 5§1, key principles have been developed on a case-by-case basis. [...] One general principle established in the case-law is that detention will be 'arbitrary' where, despite complying with the letter of national law, there has been an element of bad faith or deception on the part of the authorities. The condition that there be no arbitrariness further demands that both the order to detain and the execution of the detention must genuinely conform with the purpose of the restrictions permitted by the relevant sub-paragraph of Article 5§1. There must in addition be some relationship between the ground of permitted deprivation of liberty relied on and the place and conditions of detention. The notion of arbitrariness in the contexts of sub-paragraphs (b), (d) and (e) also includes an assessment whether detention was necessary to achieve the stated aim. The detention of an individual is such a serious measure that it is justified only as a last resort where other, less severe measures have been considered and found to be insufficient to safeguard the individual or public interest which might require that the person concerned be detained. The principle of proportionality further dictates that where detention is to secure the fulfilment of an obligation provided by law, a balance must be struck between the importance in a democratic society of securing the immediate fulfilment of the obligation in question, and the importance of the right to liberty. The duration of the detention is a relevant factor in striking such a balance." Note however that the majority of the court found that "the notion of arbitrariness in the context of Article 5 [ECHR] varies to a certain extent depending on the type of detention involved" and in particular that the requirement to demonstrate that the detention can be "reasonably considered necessary, for example to prevent the person concerned from committing an offence or fleeing" need not be fulfilled for deprivation of liberty for purposes defined in article 5§1(a) and (f) ECHR to be lawful (citations from ECtHR (Grand Chamber), *Saadi v. UK* (2008), §§68 and 73). Especially with regard to the administrative detention of asylum-seekers and refugees, the decision is contestable, especially in light of international refugee and asylum law; see in particular the arguments put forth by the UNHRC, third-party intervener in the case (summarized in §§54-57 of the judgment), and the joint dissenting opinion of judges Rozakis, Tulkens, Kovler, Hajiyev, Spielmann and Hirvelä: "As regards detention generally, the requirements of necessity and proportionality oblige the State to furnish relevant and sufficient grounds for the measure taken and to consider other less coercive measures, and also to give reasons why those measures are deemed insufficient to safeguard the private or public interests underlying the deprivation of liberty. Mere administrative expediency or convenience will not suffice. We fail to see what value or higher interest can justify the notion that these fundamental guarantees of

deprivation of liberty occurs in the framework of criminal proceedings, the complete or partial infringement of international standards for fair trial will also render it arbitrary.[98]

The protection of individuals against the arbitrary or abusive exercise of power by the authorities in whose control they are is one of the main purposes of the principle of the rule of law. As Lord Bingham aptly remarked, arbitrariness "is the antithesis of the rule of law."[99] In what follows we will therefore sketch how the principle of the rule of law and the principle of legality of restrictions on fundamental rights and freedoms form the interpretive background for analyzing the right to liberty in international law. The principle of legality in particular will guide our search for answers to our research questions in Parts II and III, both in its formal aspect (restrictions on the right to the liberty must be based on a valid legal basis, i.e. they must be "prescribed by law") and its material aspect (restrictions on the right to liberty may only be ordered on grounds that reflect a legitimate purpose for restricting fundamental rights and freedoms).

1.2.2. The rule of law, the principle of legality and the right to liberty: "nulla custodia sine lege"

The principle of legality is probably best known under its specific articulation in criminal law, where it finds expression in the maxim *nullum crimen sine lege, nulla poena sine lege.* A cornerstone of both domestic and international criminal justice, this rule is enshrined in international law as a general principle of law and a fundamental, non-derogable individual human right.[100] It means that no one can be prosecuted nor punished for a crime that was not explicitly and appropriately prescribed by law at the time of its occurrence, and that no

individual liberty in a State governed by the rule of law cannot or should not apply to the detention of asylum seekers." *Cf.* also *supra* note 60.

[98] The Working Group of Arbitrary Detention considers deprivation of liberty is arbitrary "when the total or partial non-observance of the international norms relating to the right to a fair trial, spelled out in the Universal Declaration of Human Rights and in the relevant international instruments accepted by the States concerned, is of such gravity as to give the deprivation of liberty an arbitrary character" (WGAD, *Factsheet No. 26*, section IV.B, category III).

[99] Bingham (*Sir David Williams Lectures* 2006), p. 10. In his lecture, Lord Bingham defined the core of the principle of the rule of law as follows: "all persons and authorities within the state, whether public or private, should be bound by and entitled to benefit of laws publicly and prospectively promulgated and publicly administered in the courts", adding that the scope of the principle cannot be "adequately understood without examining its implications, which may be conveniently broken down into a series of sub-rules." Lord Bingham identified eight such sub-rules, several of which will be referred to in this chapter.

[100] Article 11§2 UDHR; articles 4§2 and 15 ICCPR; article 40§2(a) CRC; articles 9 and 27§2 ACHR; articles 7 and 15§2 ECHR; article 7§2 ACHPR; article 19(d) Cairo Declaration; articles 4§2, 6 and 15 Arab Charter; and articles 7 and 35§2 CIS Convention. *Nullum crimen sine lege, nulla poena sine lege* is one of the general principles of criminal law (ICC Statute, Part 3 "General Principles of Criminal Law", articles 22 and 23). It remains entirely valid in times of armed conflict, as is explicitly confirmed by international humanitarian law, see article 99§1 GC III; articles 65 and 67 GC IV; article 75§4(c) AP I; article 6§2(c) AP II; and Rules 100-101 of the ICRC's compilation of customary IHL (Henckaerts & Doswald-Beck (2005), Vol. I, pp. 352-372).

punishment other than that prescribed by law for a particular crime at the time of its occurrence can be imposed on the offender.[101]

However, the principle of legality is not restricted to the criminal law sphere. It has a broader scope, to which the maxims *nullum crimen sine lege, nulla poena sine lege* mentioned above and *nulla custodia sine lege* proposed here, only give expression with regard to specific rights.[102] This conclusion is based on the premise that a general principle of legality governs the restriction of individual rights and freedoms in any legal system construed on the basis of the rule of law. The principle dictates that the enjoyment or exercise of individual rights and freedoms cannot be restricted except by law and for legitimate reasons. The dictate reflects the principle of legality in both its formal ("except by law"/"legal certainty") and material ("for legitimate reasons"/"legitimacy") aspects.[103] We will now look at these notions in more detail before demonstrating their role in the articulation and implementation of the right to liberty.

1.2.2.1. The rule of law and the principle of legality with regard to restrictions of fundamental rights and freedoms

Already in its 1935 Advisory Opinion on the *Consistency of Certain Danzig Legislative Decrees with the Constitution of the Free City* (hereinafter "*Danzig Opinion*") the Permanent Court of International Justice (PCIJ) emphasized the direct relationship between the principle of the rule of law and the principle of legality. While *in casu*, the Court was concerned with the particular articulation of the principle of legality in criminal law, it outlined the general normative framework within which *nullum crimen sine lege, nulla poena sine lege* operates: the Court analyzed the "principle that fundamental rights may not be restricted except by law" as part of the broader principle of the "*Rechtsstaat*" or a "State governed by the rule of law".[104] The Court points out two main elements of the rule of law, namely that

[101] For a recent comprehensive study, see Gallant, *The Principle of Legality in International and Comparative Criminal Law* (2009). See also Cassese (2003), pp. 139-158.

[102] Our argument below bears similarity with that made by Gallant (2009), see particularly p. 15: "Legality in criminal law is one manifestation of the more general notion of the rule of law in society."

[103] We use the term "restrictions" for all measures that restrict the enjoyment or exercise of individual rights and freedoms recognized by international law. In this sense, it includes both "limitations" (authorized in normal circumstances) and "derogations" (authorized only in times of public emergency threatening the life of the nation, *cf. infra* chapter I-2). The terms "limitations" and "derogations" are used most commonly to denote these two types of restrictions of the enjoyment or exercise of fundamental rights and freedoms. The ACHR however employs the term "suspension" rather than "derogation" (article 27 ACHR), and the Inter-American Court distinguishes "suppression" of rights and freedoms (i.e. acts that do away with the right or freedom all-together), which are prohibited at all times, from "limitations", "restrictions" and "suspension" of the enjoyment or exercise of rights and freedoms, which may be allowed if certain conditions (including the principles of legality and legitimacy) are met.

[104] The text in quotation marks is from the Permanent Court of International Justice (PCIJ), *Consistency of Certain Danzig Legislative Decrees with the Constitution of the Free City* (1935), p. 54 (original italics).

• all branches of Government (legislative, executive and judiciary) must themselves abide by the law, in particular with fundamental rights and freedoms enshrined in law, which they must not only guarantee, but which also set bounds to their own actions; and that

• restrictions on the full enjoyment and exercise of fundamental rights and freedoms must be provided for by law and may only be imposed in the general and legitimate interests of the community.[105]

As one author points out, in spite of "compelling evidence that adherence to the rule of law is an accepted measure worldwide of government legitimacy [and] notwithstanding its quick and remarkable ascendance as a global ideal [...] the rule of law is an exceedingly elusive notion."[106] Nevertheless, his study of the notion revealed that at least the following elements seem to be inherent to any notion of the rule of law. First, the rule of law aims to restrain government tyranny and therefore subjects government authorities, including sovereigns, the State and its officials, or any other governing authority, to the law. This means that such authorities must themselves abide by "currently valid positive law",[107] but also that their legislative powers are restricted in legal terms.[108] In order to achieve its aims, the principle of the rule of law thus includes the principle of formal legality: "[t]he rule of law in this sense entails public, prospective laws, with the qualities of generality, equality of application, and certainty. [...] Above all, it is about predictability."[109] Finally, the rule of law is opposed to the so-called rule of man, in the sense that law is general, objective and rational, as opposed to the rule of man, dominated by individuals' personal,

[105] The Court's opinion, in relevant part, reads as follows: "The principle according to which the constitutional system of the Free City corresponds to that of a State governed by the rule of law (*Rechtsstaat*) is shown in the first place by the manner in which the Senate must perform its duties. Though it conducts the administration of the State, and issues regulations or otherwise provides for the safety and welfare of the State upon its own authority, it must always, in performing these important functions, keep within the bounds of the Constitution and the law [...]. Danzig's character as a State governed by the rule of law (*Rechtsstaat*) is also and more particularly revealed in Part II [...] of the Constitution, which deals with fundamental rights and duties. [...] All the organs of the State dealt with in Part I of the Constitution [i.e. organs involved in legislation, administration of justice and the conduct of public affairs] are therefore required to guide themselves by these fundamental rights which, at the same time, set bounds to their activities. [...] The Constitution provides that, in the general interests of the community, some of these liberties of the individual may be restricted. But such restrictions can only be imposed by law" (PCIJ, *Danzig Opinion* (1935), pp. 54-55, original italics).

[106] Tamanaha, *On the Rule of Law: History, Politics, Theory* (2004), p. 3. In his valuable contribution to a number of ongoing debates in international law, Tamanaha offers a comprehensive and lucid overview of the historical origins and development of the concept of the rule of law and its contemporary formulation in political and legal theory. Pointing out that no common definition of the concept exists and that both explicit and implicit understandings reveal disagreement on the matter, Tamanaha sets out to identify elements that are (or not) included in contemporary understandings and use of the notion. His book offers excellent background for understanding the principle of legality of restrictions of individual rights and freedoms, reflected in the prohibition of arbitrary deprivation of liberty.

[107] Tamanaha (2004), p. 115.

[108] These restrictions include the obligations of States under general international human rights law and, in times of armed conflict, international humanitarian law.

[109] Tamanaha (2004), p. 119.

subjective and essentially moral opinions. Apart from its institutional implications, which vary according to different conceptions of the rule of law, this is also where the legal profession, and specifically the role of the judiciary, comes into play. It is also where the notion of the rule of law is most vulnerable, in that to at least some extent it denies the fact that those who make the law, interpret and apply it are inevitably men and while professional they can not be expected to cease to be men.[110]

The predominant conception of the rule of law in our area of concern includes – as the PCIJ pointed out – another element, namely the requirement that the law itself is must be in conformity with fundamental rights and freedoms. In this sense, it includes the principle of legality in its material aspect (principle of legitimacy). As we have mentioned before, a primary purpose of the rule of law is to restrain government tyranny and to protect a government's subjects against abusive or arbitrary exercise of power by the authorities in whose hands they happen to find themselves. The recognition and protection of fundamental rights and freedoms reflects this purpose[111] and, it is submitted, forms part and parcel of the concept of the rule of law at the international level, as is reflected in the judgment of the PCIJ and in those of other international tribunals and treaty monitoring bodies.[112] Moreover, the UN Security Council recently recognized that "respect for international humanitarian law is an essential component of the rule of law in conflict situations."[113]

As previously mentioned, international law is a normative system that seeks to realize the values shared by the international community at large. In such a system, the rule of law inevitably subjects the exercise of government to the

---

[110] Tamanaha (2004), pp. 123-124 (the words "man" and "men" are used in the sense of "person", without any distinction being made on the basis of gender). We agree with Judge Higgins though that the process of legal decision-making – be it by the legislative, executive or judicial branch of government or by legal practitioners – is not rendered less "legal" by the fact that it is executed by human beings, see Higgins (1994), pp. 2 and 9: "When [...] decisions are made by authorized persons or organs, in appropriate forums, within the framework of certain established practices and norms, then what occurs is *legal* decision-making" and "[t]o 'remain legal' is not to ignore everything that is not 'rules'. To remain 'legal' is to ensure that decisions are made by those authorized to do so, with important guiding reliance on past decisions, and with available choices being made on the basis of community interests and for the promotion of common values."

[111] While we subscribe to a substantive formulation of the rule of law concept – which we consider to be predominant not only in Western society but in the international community at large as far as individual rights and freedoms are concerned – we recognize that proponents of a purely formal concept of the rule of law exclude substantive legal restrictions from the notion itself and accept that as long as the formal principle of legality is adhered to, an undemocratic State or one that flouts general international law may still be said to adhere to the rule of law. For a summary of both formalist and substantive theories on the rule of law, see Tamanaha (2004), pp. 91-126.

[112] E.g.: IAC°HR, *Second Report Peru* (2000), §242: "The maintenance of and respect for the rule of law depends on three fundamental principles. [...] Finally, the third principle is recognition of fundamental rights. Therefore [a State respecting the rule of law is] a State set up on the principle of the declaration or recognition of the fundamental rights accorded constitutional recognition." See also Bingham (*Sir David Williams Lectures* 2006), pp. 16-20 (where he describes one of the sub-rules of the principle of the rules of law, namely that "the law must afford adequate protection of fundamental human rights").

[113] UNSC, *Statement by the President of the Security Council*, 26 June 2010, §5.

legal rules designed to protect the values of human dignity and individual freedom.[114] In this sense, the United Nations Secretary General has defined the rule of law as follows:

> "The 'rule of law' is a concept at the very heart of the [United Nation's] mission. It refers to *a principle of governance* in which all persons, institutions and entities, public and private, including the State itself, are accountable to *laws that are publicly promulgated, equally enforced and independently adjudicated*, and which are *consistent with international human rights norms and standards*. It requires, as well, measures to ensure adherence to the principles of supremacy of law, equality before the law, accountability to the law, fairness in the application of the law, separation of powers, participation in decision-making, legal certainty, avoidance of arbitrariness and procedural and legal transparency."[115]

1.2.2.2. The principle of legality as formulated in international human rights law

A society based on the rule of law seeks to restrain government tyranny by legally protecting individuals from arbitrary government interference with their life, liberty and freedoms.[116] The principle of legality, inherent in the rule of law, therefore dictates that the enjoyment or exercise of individual rights and freedoms cannot be restricted except by law (hereinafter "principle of formal legality" or "principle of legal certainty") and for legitimate reasons (hereinafter "principle of legitimacy"). Both these principles are expressed in the constitutions of the majority of nation States and are reflected in the international legal framework for the protection of human dignity in international law.[117]

The rule of law and the principle of legality are overarching principles of international human rights law, very much in the same way as they are in most domestic legal systems' provisions regarding fundamental rights and civil liberties.[118] Underlying both domestic and international human rights law is the

---

[114] While the normative substance of international human rights law may be open to disagreement and divergence, the values of human dignity and individual freedom are universally recognized, as is the right to liberty and the prohibition of arbitrary deprivation thereof, *cf. supra* section 1.1.1.

[115] United Nations Secretary-General (UNSG), *The Rule of Law and Transitional Justice in Conflict and Post-Conflict Societies* (2004), §6. On the United Nations' role and activities in promoting the rule of law, see also the UN's *Rule of Law* web-portal at http://www.unrol.org.

[116] See also Tamanaha (2004), in particular pp. 114-119, 129-131, and 137-139.

[117] Including but not limited to international human rights law, international refugee law, international humanitarian law, international criminal law and United Nations law.

[118] E.g.: Preambular paragraph 3 UDHR ("it is essential, if man is not to be compelled to have recourse, as a last resort, to rebellion against tyranny and oppression, that human rights should be protected by the rule of law"); preambular paragraph 6 ECHR ("Being resolved, as the governments of European countries which are like-minded and have a common heritage of political traditions, ideals, freedom and the rule of law, to take the first steps for the collective enforcement of certain of the rights stated in the Universal Declaration"); preambular paragraph 3 of the Statute of the Council of Europe (1949) ("Reaffirming their devotion to the spiritual and moral values which are the common heritage of their peoples and the true source of individual freedom, political liberty and the rule of law, principles which form the basis of all genuine democracy"); preambular paragraph 4 Arab Charter on Human Rights ("believing in the sovereignty of the law and its contribution to the protection of universal and interrelated human rights"); and preambular paragraph 6 CIS Convention

principle that human beings are born free and equal[119] and have a number of inviolable rights[120] that inherently belong to them as human beings.[121]

("Striving for the effective fulfilment of their obligations to protect human rights and fundamental freedoms, in the spirit of the concerting of the efforts [...] for the purpose of asserting ideals of freedom and the rule of law"). The UN's *Rule of Law* web-portal confirms the "concept of the rule of law is embedded in the Charter of the United Nations", citing preambular paragraph 4 and article 1§1 of the Charter ("determined [...] to establish conditions under which justice and respect for the obligations arising from treaties and other sources of international law can be maintained [...] The Purposes of the United Nations are [...] to maintain international peace and security [...] and to bring about by peaceful means, and in conformity with the principles of justice and international law, adjustment of disputes or situations which might lead to a breach of the peace"), to which we would add article 1§3 ("The Purposes of the United Nations are [...] to achieve international co-operation in [...] promoting and encouraging respect for human rights and for fundamental freedoms for all"). For recognition that the rule of law is at the heart of the UN Charter, human rights law instruments adopted under UN auspices, and the international order more generally, see also UNGA, *Declaration on the Principles of International Law concerning Friendly Relations and Co-Operation among States in accordance with the Charter of the United Nations* (1970), preambular paragraph 4: "Bearing in mind also the paramount importance of the Charter of the United Nations for the promotion of the rule of law among nations"; UNGA, *Resolution 60/1* (2005), §§1 and 134: "We, Heads of State and Government [...] Recognizing the need for universal adherence to and implementation of the rule of law at both the national and international levels, we: (*a*) Reaffirm our commitment [...] to an international order based on the rule of law and international law"; UNSG, *Rule of Law Report* (2004): "The 'rule of law' is a concept at the very heart of the [United Nations'] mission"; and UNSC, *Statement of the President* (2010), §§1 and 5: "The Security Council reaffirms its commitment to [...] an international order based on the rule of law and international law. [...] The Security Council recognizes that respect for international humanitarian law is an essential component of the rule of law in conflict situations."

119 E.g.: article 1 UDHR: "All human beings are born free and equal in dignity and rights"; preambular paragraph 4 common to the ICCPR and the International Covenant on Economic, Social and Cultural Rights (ICESCR): "Recognizing [...] in accordance with the [UDHR] the ideal of free human beings"; preambular paragraph 1 ADRDM: "All men are born free and equal in dignity and in rights"; preambular paragraph 1 of the 12th Protocol to the ECHR: "Having regard to the fundamental principle according to which all persons are equal before the law and are entitled to the equal protection of the law"; preambular paragraph 1 Arab Charter: "Based on the faith of the Arab nation in the dignity of the human person [...] affirm the human right to a decent life based on freedom, justice and equality"; article 1(a) Cairo Declaration: "All men are equal in terms of basic human dignity."

120 E.g.: preambular paragraph 1 common to the UDHR, ICCPR, ICESCR, CRC and the Convention against Torture (CAT): "recognition of the inherent dignity and of the equal and inalienable rights of all members of the human family"; preambular paragraph 2 common to the ICCPR, ICESCR and CAT: "these rights derive from the inherent dignity of the human person"; preambular paragraph 2 ACHR: "recognizing that the essential rights of man are not derived from one's being a national of a certain state, but are based upon attributes of the human personality"; principle VII§2 OSCE, *Final Act* (1975): "will promote and encourage the effective exercise of civil, political, economic, social, cultural and other rights and freedoms all of which derive from the inherent dignity of the human person and are essential for his free and full development"; preambular paragraph 5 ACHPR: "fundamental human rights stem from the attributes of human beings"; article 1§4 Arab Charter: "The present Charter seeks [...] To entrench the principle that all human rights are universal, indivisible, interdependent and interrelated."

121 These ideals are part of the universal values attached to the preservation of humanity and human dignity. While the precise definition of these inviolable rights may differ from one culture, country or region to another, the ideal of preserving human dignity is shared by the international community as a whole and is reflected in the general principles of international human rights law and in the rules of international humanitarian law.

In order to realize these principles and to prevent arbitrary or abusive exercise of government power, restrictions on the enjoyment or exercise of fundamental rights and freedoms may only be imposed by law and for legitimate purposes.[122] The principle of legality is thus reflected in the structure of international human rights law's provisions on limitations and derogations: whether a restriction takes the form of a limitation or a derogation, three essential conditions must be fulfilled: (1) the restriction must be authorized by the treaty in which the restricted right or freedom is enshrined (in this sense it is important to note that some rights may never be limited or derogated from[123]); (2) it must be prescribed or established by an applicable law (principle of legal certainty); and (3) it must be necessary for the protection of the general interest or legitimate purpose for which the restriction is authorized (principle of legitimacy).[124] Such legitimate purposes typically include the maintenance of national security and public safety, public order, public health or morals, and respect for the rights and freedoms of others.[125]

---

[122] See also Gallant (2009), p. 21: "legality also protects the individual against the arbitrary power of the political, the prosecutorial, or the judicial departments [...] Legality in criminal law is necessary to the historical conception of the rule of law that seeks to restrain tyranny that arises from the arbitrary application of coercive force. [...] It thus substantively protects life, liberty [and] protects the underlying freedom of the human being". While Gallant is concerned with the principle of legality in criminal law, these statements are as true with regard to the right to liberty, especially taking into account that detention is – apart from the death penalty – the most severe form of punishment in criminal law and may only be imposed where both the crime and the punishment have been prescribed by law.

[123] A small number of rights are absolute in nature, and may not be restricted in any circumstance or for any reason. These absolute rights include at least the prohibition of slavery and servitude, the prohibition of torture, cruel, inhuman or degrading treatment or punishment, and the right to recognition as a person before the law. Apart from those, some other rights are non-derogable (but may be restricted on the basis of international humanitarian law in time of armed conflict), *cf. infra* notes 303 and 305 and accompanying text.

[124] These three conditions flow from the text of the limitation clauses and derogation provisions of international human law treaties (*cf. infra* note 125 and chapter 1-2, section 2.1.1.2) and their interpretation in international practice (see in particular articles 1, 5-6, 10-11, 13 and 15-18 of the *Siracusa Principles* (1984); IACtHR, *The Word "Laws" in Article 30 of the American Convention on Human Rights*, Advisory Opinion (1986); IAC°HR, *Principles and Best Practices* (2008), principle IV; ECtHR, *Sunday Times* (1979), §§46-68 with references in footnotes 288-290. On limitations of human rights in a context of armed conflict, see for example Israel, SC, *A and B v. Israel* (2008), §§ 29-53; generally on restrictions on individual rights and freedoms and the principle of legality, see Svensson-McCarthy, *The International Law of Human Rights and States of Exception, with Special Reference to the Preparatory Works and the Case-Law of the International Monitoring Organs* (1996), in particular pp. 65-122. At least within the European and Inter-American human rights system, the principle of the rule of law and the principle of legality are closely connected to the existence of democratic institutions (the limitation clauses in the ACHR and the ECHR require the purpose of restrictions not only to be legitimate but to be legitimate "in a democratic society"; IACtHR, *Opinion on the Word "Laws"* (1986), §§24-37 (see in particular §32: "there exists an inseparable bond between the principle of legality, democratic institutions and the rule of law") and the overview of Inter-American and European case law in Svensson-Mc-Carthy (1996), in particular pp. 123-193 and 527-530. Proponents of a substantive formulation of the rule of law consider democratic institutions to be an inherent part of the rule of law: for an overview, see Tamanaha (2004), pp. 36-38 and 110-112; for an example, see Bingham (*Sir David Williams Lectures* 2006), p. 35.

[125] See the limitation clauses in article 29§2 UDHR; articles 12§3, 13, 18§3, 19§3, 21 and 22§2

1.2.2.3. The principle of legality and the right to liberty: preventing arbitrariness

While the three conditions for the restriction of fundamental rights and freedoms are generally included *expressis verbis* in human rights treaties with regard to the freedom of expression, movement, association and assembly and the right to privacy, they are less explicit but equally (if not more) important with regard to the rights to life and liberty. The nature of these two rights requires that the restrictions placed upon them should be even more exceptional than in the case of restrictions of other rights; such restrictions must therefore at least be governed by the same conditions. The applicability of the principle of legality to the right to liberty, as we will show here, is reflected in the articulation of the right in international human rights law treaties. To this effect, the case law of international courts and treaty monitoring bodies emphasizes the importance of conformity with the principle of legality and the rule of law in order to prevent arbitrary deprivation of liberty.

Human rights instruments express the principle of legality for the right to liberty and the right to life in different terms as compared with other rights and freedoms. For example, article 6 ICCPR provides, in relevant part, that:

> "Every human being has the inherent right to life. This right shall be *protected by law*. No one shall be *arbitrarily* deprived of his life. In countries which have not abolished the death penalty, sentence of death may be imposed only for the most serious crimes in *accordance with the law in force* at the time of the commission of the crime."[126]

As to the right to liberty, the principle goes back as far as the Magna Carta – one of the earliest human rights instruments (England, 1215):

ICCPR; article 4 ICESCR; articles 12§3, 13§2, 13§4, 15, 16§2, 22§3, 22§6, and 30 ACHR; articles 9§2, 10§2, 11§2 and 18 ECHR; article 2§§3-4 Protocol 4 to the ECHR Securing Certain Rights and Freedoms other than Those already Included in the Convention and the First Protocol thereto (1963) (Protocol 4 ECHR); articles 9§2, 10§1, 11 and 12§2 ACHPR; articles 11§2, 12§2, 22§3, 25§3 and 32 CIS Convention; articles 24§7, 26§2, 30§§1-2, 32§2 and 35§2 Arab Charter. The Cairo Declaration on Human Rights in Islam allows only for those restrictions to the freedom of expression (article 22§a) and of movement (article 12) that are required by Shari'ah (Islamic law). For representative examples of this test being applied by the treaty monitoring bodies for some of these instruments, see IACtHR, *Opinion on the Word "Laws"* (1986), §§18, 22 and 29-31; ECtHR, *Sunday Times* (1979), §§46-68. For guidelines on the interpretation of "necessity" and the notion of general interest in the ICCPR, see *Siracusa Principles* (1984), Part I. For a general overview of the meaning of "national security", "public safety", "public order", "public health" and "public morals" used in limitations clauses, see Kiss, "Permissible Limitations on Rights" in Henkin, *The International Bill of Rights: the Covenant on Civil and Political Rights* (1976), pp. 293-304.

[126] Article 6 ICCPR (emphasis added). Article 2 ECHR, article 4 ACHR, article 4 ACHPR, article 5 Arab Charter, and article 2 CIS Convention are phrased in similar terms, prohibiting arbitrary deprivation of life and subjecting deprivation of life to the principle of legality. Article 2(a) of the Cairo Declaration on Human Rights in Islam prohibits any deprivation of life that is not prescribed by Shari'ah (Islamic law).

"No freemen shall be taken or imprisoned or disseised or exiled or in any way destroyed, nor will we go upon him nor send upon him, except by the *lawful judgment* of his peers or *by the law of the land*."[127]

The principle is also reflected in the articulation of the right to liberty in all international human rights instruments. For example, article 9 ICCPR reads, in relevant parts, as follows:

"No one shall be subjected to *arbitrary* arrest or detention. No one shall be deprived of his liberty except on such grounds and in accordance with such procedures *as are established by law*."[128]

Thus, the text of the treaties subjects deprivation of life and liberty to the principle of legality in both its formal (deprivation of life/liberty must be prescribed by law) and material (prohibition of "arbitrary" deprivation of life/liberty, requirement of necessity for a recognized legitimate purpose) aspects. The ultimate purpose of the prohibition of arbitrary interference with the rights to life and liberty is in line with that of the principle of the rule of law, namely to protect individuals against arbitrary or abusive exercise of power by the authority in whose power they find themselves.

The applicability and the particular importance of the principle of legality where the right to liberty is at stake has been illustrated and emphasized by international courts and treaty monitoring bodies. Let us briefly return to the

---

[127] Article 39 England, *Magna Carta (Great Charter of English Liberty)* (1215) (emphasis added).

[128] Article 9§1 ICCPR (emphasis added). Articles 37 (b) CRC; 55§1(d) ICC Statute; 5§1 ECHR; 14§1 Arab Charter; 6 ACHPR; 25 ADRDM; 7§2 ACHR; and 5§1 CIS Convention are phrased in similar terms. Article 20 of the Cairo Declaration on Human Rights in Islam prohibits deprivation of liberty "without legitimate reason", which one might infer to be reasons allowed under Shari'ah law, as it is for the right to life (article 2§a: "it is prohibited to take away life except for a shari'ah prescribed reason"). The WGAD defines the 1st category of arbitrary detention as deprivation of liberty without a valid legal basis (*WGAD, Factsheet No. 26*); and the principle is also reiterated in the UN's *Body of Principles* (1988), principle 2; the IAC°HR's *Principles and Best Practices* (2008), principle 4; the International Law Association's (ILA) *Paris Minimum Standards of Human Rights Norms in a State of Emergency* (1984), article 4 of Section B and article 5 of Section C; and the *Turku Declaration* (1990), article 11. The principle of legality has also been reaffirmed in international refugee law instruments with regard to the administrative detention of refugees and asylum-seekers, see for example UNGA, *Declaration on the Human Rights of Individuals who Are not Nationals of the Country in which They Live* (1985), article 5§1(a): "no alien shall be subjected to arbitrary arrest or detention; no alien shall be deprived of his or her liberty except on such grounds and in accordance with such procedures as are established by law"; UNHCR, Executive Committee, *Detention of Asylum-Seekers and Refugees: The Framework, the Problem and Recommended Practice* (1999), §§6, 7 and 26(a): "no one should be arbitrarily deprived of his or her liberty. This includes, of course, both refugees and asylum-seekers. [...] The Executive Committee's 1986 Conclusion on Detention of Refugees and Asylum-Seekers sets out the limited accepted bases on which the detention of refugees and asylum-seekers may be justified [...] Governments should ensure that detention of asylum-seekers is resorted to only for reasons recognized as legitimate, consistent with international standards"; UNHCR, *Detention of Asylum-Seekers* (1999), guideline 3: "Detention [...] may exceptionally be resorted to for the reasons set out below as long as this is clearly prescribed by a national law which is in conformity with general norms and principles of international human rights law"; WGAD, *Deliberation No. 5* (1999), principle 6: "The decision [to detain] must be taken by a duly empowered authority with a sufficient level of responsibility and must be founded on criteria of legality established by law."

PCIJ's *Danzig Opinion* in order to illustrate the argument before providing further examples. Before concluding on the specific question it was requested to address,[129] the PCIJ illustrated its vision of the rule of law by outlining what is in essence the principle of legality as applied to the right to personal liberty:[130]

> "The rule that a law is required in order to restrict the liberties provided for in the Constitution therefore involves the consequence that the law itself must define the conditions in which such restrictions of liberty are imposed. If this were not so, i.e. if a law could simply give a judge power to deprive a person of his liberty, without defining the circumstances in which his liberty might be forfeited, it could render entirely nugatory a provision such as that contained in Article 74 of the Constitution [i.e. the right to liberty]. But, as the Court has already explained, the decrees [...] empower a judge to deprive a person of his liberty even for an act not prohibited by the law, provided that he relies on the fundamental idea of a penal law and on sound popular feeling. These decrees therefore transfer to the judge an important function which, owing to its intrinsic character, the Constitution intended to reserve to the law so as to safeguard individual liberty from any arbitrary encroachment on the part of the authorities of the State."[131]

With regard to the penal reform mentioned in this extract, the Court also underlined the rationale behind the exigencies of the rule of law and the principle of legality:

> "Sound popular feeling is a very elusive standard. It was defined by the Agent of the Free City as "*une conviction correspondant aux strictes exigences de la morale.*" This definition covers the whole extra-legal field of what is right and what is wrong according to one's ethical code or religious sentiments. Hence it follows that sound popular feeling may mean different rules of conduct in the minds of those who are to act in accordance therewith. It is for this reason that legislation is necessary in order to lay down the precise limits between *morale* and law."[132]

The Court therefore concluded that the penal reform was not only contrary to the principle of legality in its criminal law aspect (*nullum crimen sine lege, nulla poena sine lege*), but was moreover inconsistent with the broader principle of legality, which requires that the authority to order restrictions of fundamental rights (the Court pointed out specifically the right to liberty, the right to freedom of movement and assembly, and the right to freedom of expression), and the reasons for which they can be imposed, are prescribed by law.

With regard to the right to liberty enshrined in the Universal Declaration of Human Rights and the ICCPR, the importance of the principle of legality was raised in debates during the drafting process of the ICCPR:

[129] Namely whether certain penal legislation reforms undertaken by the Government of the Free City of Danzig in violation of the maxim *nullum crime sine lege, nulla poena sine lege* would violate the Free City's Constitution.

[130] *In casu* detention, imposed by a competent court as a sentence for a criminal offence on the basis of national penal legislation.

[131] PCIJ, *Danzig Opinion* (1935), p. 56.

[132] PCIJ, *Danzig Opinion* (1935), p. 53 (original italics).

"The reason for introducing the criterion of arbitrariness in the second sentence [of §1 of a draft of article 9 ICCPR] was that *legal grounds and procedures or the criterion of legality* set out in the third sentence might themselves be open to question on the grounds of arbitrariness."[133]

Moreover, the Human Rights Committee has found that:

"if so-called preventive detention is used, for reasons of public security, it must be controlled by these same provisions, i.e. it must not be arbitrary, and must be based on grounds and procedures *established by law*".[134] and

"As to [article 9§1 ICCPR] the Committee recalls that the *principle of legality* is violated if an individual is arrested or detained on grounds which are not clearly established in domestic legislation."[135]

The European Court of Human Rights for its part has ruled that:

"a practice of keeping a person in detention without a specific legal basis, but because of a lack of clear rules governing the detainee's situation, with the result that a person may be deprived of his liberty for an unlimited period without judicial authorisation, is incompatible with the *principles of legal certainty* and the protection from arbitrariness, which are *common threads throughout the Convention and the rule of law*"[136]; and

"In laying down that any deprivation of liberty must be effected 'in accordance with a procedure prescribed by law', Article [5§1] primarily requires any arrest or detention to have a legal basis in domestic law. However, these words do not merely refer back to domestic law; *like the expressions 'in accordance with the law' and 'prescribed by law' in the second paragraphs of Article 8 to 11* [limitation clauses for the right to private and family life, freedom of thought, conscience and religion, freedom of expression and of assembly and association], they also relate to the quality of the law, requiring it to be compatible with *the rule of law, a concept inherent in all the Articles of the Convention*"[137]; and

---

[133] Report of the Third Committee to the General Assembly (A/4045, 9 December 1958), §46, reprinted in: Bossuyt (1987), p. 199 (emphasis added). See also §§43-49 of the Report more generally (reprinted in: Bossuyt (1987), pp. 199-202) and Nowak (2005), pp. 223-224.

[134] HRC, *General Comment 8* (1982), §4 (emphasis added).

[135] HRC, *McLawrence v. Jamaica* (1996), §5.5 (emphasis added).

[136] ECtHR, *Jecius v. Lithuania* (2000), §62 (emphasis added), reiterating previous case law (e.g. ECtHR, *Baranowski v. Poland* (2000), §§ 54-57); and confirmed in subsequent cases (e.g. recently by the Court's Grand Chamber in *Mooren v. Germany* (2009), §72). For the conception of the rule of law, the principle of legality and the right to liberty in the European human rights system, see also CoE, *HRH No. 5* (2002), pp. 9-17: "The requirement of lawfulness has been interpreted as referring to both procedure and substance. Moreover, lawfulness is understood to mean that any detention must be in accordance with national law and the European Convention and must not be arbitrary. [...] This designation [arbitrary] would certainly be seen as appropriate when a power is used in circumstances where a deprivation of liberty is not really needed or is designed to achieve an illegal objective. [...] The failure to satisfy this test [legal certainty or formal legality] might also be seen as a requirement to shape the law in such a way as to limit the scope for arbitrary treatment."

[137] ECtHR, *Amuur v. France* (1996), §50. We will come back to the required qualities of a law restricting individual rights and freedoms, and the right to liberty in particular, in section 1.2.3.

> "The [Grand Chamber of the] Court stresses that where deprivation of liberty is concerned it is particularly important that the *general principle of legal certainty* be satisfied."[138]

Article 30 of the American Convention on Human Rights explicitly reiterates that:

> "The restrictions that, pursuant to this Convention, may be placed on the enjoyment or exercise of the rights or freedoms recognized herein may not be applied except in accordance with laws enacted for reasons of general interest and in accordance with the purpose for which such restrictions have been established."

The Inter-American Court of Human Rights has clarified the meaning of the word "law" in this provision in the following manner:

> "The necessary existence of the elements inherent in the concept of law in Article 30 of the Convention leads to the conclusion that, for purposes of the interpretation of this Article, the *concepts of legality and legitimacy* coincide, inasmuch as *only a law* that has been passed by democratically elected and constitutionally legitimate bodies and is tied to the general welfare may restrict the enjoyment or exercise of the rights or freedoms of the individual."[139]

Both the Inter-American Commission and the Inter-American Court of Human Rights have applied the principle of legality to the right to liberty in article 7 ACHR:

> "In the [case concerning the detention of four members of a rebel group in Peru], the detention occurred amid a terrible disruption of public law and order that escalated in 1992 and 1993 with acts of terrorism that left many victims in their wake. In response to these events, the State adopted emergency measures, one of which was to allow those suspected of treason to be detained without a lawful court order. [...] the crime of treason classified under Peru's legal system, violates universally accepted *principles of* international law, of *legality*, [etc.]";[140]

> "The Commission [recalls its earlier considerations with regard to the detention of persons in relation to the armed conflict in Peru on the basis of anti-terrorism legislation] with respect to the lack of a clear definition of the conduct that constitutes terrorism, as the acts that constitute the crime of terrorism are defined and described in Article 2 of Decree Law No. 25,475 with notable imprecision, in very broad language, creating open-ended criminal definitions that rely on very vague terms, contrary to one of the basic principles of modern criminal justice, which is [the principle of legality]"[141]; and

> "Although this is a case of the detention of a guerrilla during an internal conflict [i.e. a member of a rebel group in Guatemala], the detainee should have been ensured the guarantees that exist under the rule of law, and been submitted to

---

[138] ECtHR (Grand Chamber), *Medvedyev* (2010), §80 (emphasis added).

[139] IACtHR, *Opinion on the Word "Laws"* (1986), §37 (emphasis added).

[140] IACtHR, *Castillo Petruzzi et al. v. Peru* (1999), §§109 and 16. The applicants in this case were members of the Movimiento Revolucionario Túpac Amaru (MRTA), a party to the non-international armed conflict that has ravaged in Peru – alternating relatively calm periods with periods of intense violence – since the early 1980's.

[141] IAC°HR, *Second Report Peru* (2000), §81.

a legal proceeding. This Court has already stated that, although the State has the right and obligation to guarantee its security and maintain public order, it must execute its actions 'within limits and according to procedures that preserve both public safety and the fundamental rights of the human person.'"[142]

In a similar vein, the African Commission on Human and Peoples' Rights has found that:

> "According to Article 9 (2) of the Charter, dissemination of opinions may be restricted by law. This does not however mean that national law can set aside the right to express and disseminate one's opinions guaranteed at the international level; this would make the protection of the right to express one's opinion ineffective. To permit national law to take precedence over international law would defeat the purpose of codifying certain rights in international law and indeed, the whole essence of treaty making. [...] The justification of limitations must be strictly proportionate with and absolutely necessary for the advantages which follow. Most important, a limitation may not erode a right such that the right itself becomes illusory";[143] and

> "[Article 6 ACHPR, on the right to liberty] must be interpreted in such a way as to permit arrests only in the exercise of powers *normally granted to the security forces in a democratic society*. In these cases, the wording of this decree allows for individuals to be arrested for vague reasons, and upon suspicion, not proven acts, which conditions are not in conformity with the *spirit of the African Charter*."[144]

The International Convention on Enforced Disappearances stresses the importance of the principle of legality for deprivation of liberty, by reiterating it in the obligations of States parties designed to prevent enforced disappearances. Its article 17§2 prescribes that:

> "Without prejudice to other international obligations of the State Party with regard to the deprivation of liberty, each State Party shall, in its legislation: [e]stablish the conditions under which orders of deprivation of liberty may be given; (b) [i]ndicate those authorities authorized to order the deprivation of liberty."

Individual States have also highlighted the importance of the principle of legality where the right to liberty is at stake. For example, the *Restatement (Third) of Foreign Relations Law of the United States* gives expression to the principle of legality, both in its formal and material aspects in its statement that:

---

[142] IACtHR *Bámaca Velásquez v. Guatemala* (2000), §143, with references to earlier judgments, notably IACtHR, *Durand & Ugarte v. Peru* (2000), §69; IACtHR, *Castillo Petruzzi et al. v. Peru* (1999), §§89 and 204; IACtHR, *Godínez Cruz v. Honduras* (1989), §162; and IACtHR, *Velásquez Rodríguez v. Honduras* (1988), §154. The applicant in *Bámaca Velásquez* was the commander of the Organización del Pueblo en Armas (OPA), a rebel group part of the umbrella organization Unidad Revolucionaria Nacional Guatemalteca (URNG), involved in a non-international armed conflict with the government of Guatemala from 1962 to 1996.

[143] AC°HPR, *Constitutional Rights Project et al. v. Nigeria* (1999), §§40 and 42.

[144] AC°HPR, *Amnesty International and Others v. Sudan* (1999), §59 (emphasis added).

> "Detention is arbitrary if it is not pursuant to law; it may be arbitrary also if 'it is incompatible with the principles of justice or with the dignity of the human person'."[145]

In cases relating to the Israeli conflict with Hezbollah, the Israeli Supreme Court has held that:

> "like all protected human rights, the right to personal liberty is not absolute and a violation of the right is sometimes required in order to protect essential public interests. The balancing formula in this regard is provided in the limitations clause in section 8 of the Basic Law, which states: The rights under this Basic Law may only be violated by a law that befits the values of the State of Israel, is intended for a proper purpose, and to an extent that is not excessive, or in accordance with a law as aforesaid by virtue of an express authorization therein"[146]; and

> "this decision does not make it easier for the country to struggle against those who wish to destroy it. The holding of a detainee who does not pose a threat to national security in administrative detention as a 'bargaining chip' may at times prove an effective means of promoting the security of the State. However, not every effective means is also legal. I cannot but repeat what I have said in a different case: [...] This is the destiny of a democracy – it does not see all means as acceptable, and the ways of its enemies are not always open before it. A democracy must sometimes fight with one hand tied behind its back. Even so, a democracy has the upper hand. The rule of law and the liberty of an individual constitute important components in its understanding of security. At the end of the day, they strengthen its spirit and this strength allows it to overcome its difficulties".[147]

We will see in chapter I-2 that the principle of legality plays an important role in the system of derogations through which international human rights treaties offer States the flexibility to impose additional restrictions on rights and freedoms in order to deal with exceptional situations that threaten the life of the nation or the security of the State and its population. As the Human Rights Committee and the Inter-American Court of Human Rights have stressed:

> "Safeguards related to derogation, as embodied in article 4 of the Covenant, are based on the principles of legality and the rule of law inherent in the Covenant as a whole"[148]; and

> "[The possibility to derogate] does not mean, however, that the suspension of guarantees implies a temporary suspension of the rule of law, nor does it

---

[145] US, *Restatement (Third) of Foreign Relations Law of the United States* (1987), §702 at (h).

[146] Israel, SC, *A and B v. Israel* (2008), §28. The judgment refers to Israeli domestic human rights law, but the argument of the Court can be applied *mutatis mutandis* to the requirements regarding limitations of individual rights and freedoms under international human rights law. In general, the Israeli Supreme Court attaches great importance to the rule of law and the principle of legality of restrictions on individual rights and freedoms, even in the context of armed conflict, see for example the case law on administrative detention referred to *infra* in Part II.

[147] Israel, SC, *Bargaining Chip Case* (2000), §23, reference to previous case law omitted.

[148] HRC, *General Comment 29* (2001), §16.

authorize those in power to act in disregard of the principle of legality by which they are bound at all times."[149]

The fact that the international community adheres to the principle of the rule of law is possibly best demonstrated by its continued commitment to this principle in times of armed conflict.[150] Contrary to the realities of a distant past, where it was accepted that *inter arma enim silent leges* (i.e. in times of war the laws fall silent), the existence of contemporary international humanitarian law subjects the conduct of war to principles and rules that apply to all parties to armed conflicts.[151] The conditions reflecting the principle of legality of restrictions of fundamental rights and freedoms are therefore also visible in the provisions of international humanitarian law, and the conditions for restricting fundamental rights and freedoms on the basis of international humanitarian law mirror those set for limitations and derogations in international human rights law. Restrictions of fundamental rights and freedoms for reasons related to a situation of armed conflict will only be lawful if they are authorized by international humanitarian law, and the manner in which these rights and freedoms may be restricted are prescribed by an established and applicable rule of international humanitarian law. Moreover, to be lawful, such restrictions must serve a purpose that is recognized as legitimate in situations of armed conflict and may not be arbitrary in their design or application (*cf. infra* chapter I-", section 2.2.2). With regard to the right to liberty in particular, we will see in Part III that the 1949 Geneva Conventions do authorize internment, but only for purposes of military necessity and security, and in accordance with strict conditions that are prescribed by the Conventions themselves.[152]

We can thus conclude that international law, in order to prevent arbitrary deprivation of liberty, requires that all restrictions on the right to liberty be ordered on a valid legal basis (principle of legal certainty) and for a legitimate purpose transpiring in lawful grounds for detention or internment (principle of legitimacy). This is so whether the restrictions are imposed through limitations

---

[149] IACtHR, *Habeas Corpus in Emergency Situations, Advisory Opinion* (1987), §24.

[150] See also UNSC, *Statement of the President* (2010), quoted *supra* note 113.

[151] Baroness Hale, in her opinion attached to the UK House of Lord's judgment in *Al-Jedda v. Secretary of State for Defence* (2007), §122 emphasized that persons interned in relation to armed conflicts "are the people most in need of the protection of the rule of law." In the same sense, Justice Scalia remarked in his Dissenting Opinion (he was joined in his dissent by Justice Stevens) in US, Supreme Court (SC), *Hamdi v. Rumsfeld* (2004), p. 27 *in fine*: "The Founders well understood the difficult tradeoff between safety and freedom [in times of war] [...] Many think it not only inevitable but entirely proper that liberty give way to security in times of national crisis – that, at the extremes of military exigency, *inter arma silent leges*. Whatever the general merits of the view that war silences law or modulates its voice, that view has no place in the interpretation and application of a Constitution designed precisely to confront war and, in a manner that accords with democratic principles, to accommodate it."

[152] See also Rule 99 of the ICRC's compilation of customary IHL in Henckaerts & Doswald-Beck (2005), Vol. I, pp. 344 and 348: "Arbitrary deprivation of liberty is prohibited. [...] Detention which goes beyond that provided for by law is a violation of the principle of legality and amounts to arbitrary detention." Recalling that finding, Pejic (*IRRC* 2005), p. 383, lists the principle of legality as one of the general principles that any administrative detention or internment in armed conflict or other situations of violence must conform to.

or derogations allowed under international human rights law or through direct reliance on international humanitarian law. That the legal basis and the grounds for deprivation of liberty are not one and the same thing is demonstrated in the *Medvedyev* case referred to above:

> "The Court notes first of all that it is not disputed that the purpose of the deprivation of liberty to which the applicants were subjected on board the *Winner* while it was being escorted to France was to bring them 'before the competent legal authority' within the meaning of Article 5§1(c) of the Convention [i.e. legitimate purpose/lawful ground]. In this case the Court notes that the parties disagree as to whether the facts of the case had a 'legal basis' under public international law and domestic law [i.e. formal legality/legal certainty/legal basis]."[153]

In what follows, we will examine both requirements in somewhat more detail so as to lay the groundwork for our analysis of the legal basis and grounds for internment in armed conflict in Parts II and III.

1.2.3. The principle of legal certainty: the requirement of a valid legal basis for deprivation of liberty

The first question when assessing the lawfulness of any deprivation of liberty must be whether it was prescribed by law. In other words, one must inquire into the existence of a *legal basis* for the deprivation of liberty. Before turning to questions of whether the deprivation of liberty was carried out for lawful reasons (i.e. on lawful *grounds*) and in conformity with the relevant *procedures* inherent to the right to liberty, one must look at the validity of the actual legal rule prescribing these grounds and procedures. It is the "law" or legal basis that grants the authority to deprive a person of his or her liberty, and at the same time identifies and circumscribes the detaining or interning authorities' powers of detention or internment.

At first glance, the principle of legality in its formal aspect, also referred to as the principle of legal certainty, is rather straightforward. Nevertheless, a closer look – especially when applied in the context of armed conflict or other situations of violence – reveals more potential for controversy. Several questions come to mind. What exactly does it mean that deprivation of liberty must be prescribed by "law"? Must such a law emanate from the legislative branch of government, or can an executive order or administrative provision be considered a "law" for the present purposes? Must the "law" be a written legal instrument, or can it take the form of a common law or customary law? Must it be a domestic law, or can it also be an international law? To answer these questions, we must examine both the basic qualities required of a legal instrument to be "law" (section 1.2.3.2), and the forms such a "law" must take in order to comply with the maxim of *nulla custodia sine lege* (section 1.2.3.3).

---

[153] ECtHR (Grand Chamber), *Medvedyev* (2010), §82.

1.2.3.1. The meaning of the word "law"

Let us briefly recall the exact wording of article 9§1 ICCPR:

> "Everyone has the right to liberty and security of person. No one shall be subjected to arbitrary arrest and detention. No one shall be deprived of his liberty except on such grounds and in accordance with such procedures *as are established by law*."[154]

None of the existing international human rights treaties further defines the word "law" as it appears in the formulation of the right to liberty. However, international practice and the decisions of human rights courts and treaty monitoring bodies allow us to further explore the exact meaning of this word and inform us on the question of the form and qualities a legal instrument must have if it is to qualify as "law" and thus serve as a valid legal basis for a deprivation of liberty.

Before turning to such practice, it is useful to note that the text of international treaties must be interpreted in accordance with the rules of the legal order to which these treaties belong, namely the international legal order. Therefore, when examining the word "law" for our present purposes, we must determine its meaning in international rather than domestic law. Thus, we will have no recourse to the definition of "law" in different domestic legal orders.[155] Moreover, the term "law" as it appears in international human rights treaties must be interpreted in light of the object and purpose of those treaties,[156] but also in light of the nature and origin of the international human rights system. As the Inter-American Court of Human Rights recalled:

> "The meaning of the word 'laws' in the context of a system for the protection of human rights cannot be disassociated from the nature and origin of that system. [...] the protection of human rights must necessarily comprise the concept of the restriction of the exercise of state power. In order to guarantee human rights, it is therefore essential that state actions affecting basic rights not be left to the discretion of the government but, rather, that they be surrounded by a set of guarantees designed to ensure that the inviolable attributes of the individual not be impaired. Perhaps the most important of these guarantees is that restrictions to basic rights only be established by a law [...] there can be no doubt that this is an important obstacle to the arbitrary exercise of power."[157]

While the exercise of interpreting the word "law" must of course be carried out for the specific treaty or treaties applicable in each case, the meaning of the word "law" for the purpose of the principle of legality is generally the same

---

[154] The wording of other human rights treaties does not substantially differ from that of article 9§1 ICCPR, they all refer to the word "law" without further definition. *Cf. supra* and see also Annex A for the text of these provisions.

[155] In the same sense: IACtHR, *Opinion on the Word "Law"* (1986), §§19-20: "The meaning of the word 'laws' must be sought as a term used in an international treaty. It is not, consequently, a question of determining the meaning of the word 'laws' within the context of the domestic law of a State Party."

[156] ECtHR, *Sunday Times* (1979), §48: "the Court must interpret [the Convention's provisions] in a way that [...] is most appropriate in order to realise the aim and the object of the treaty." See also Kiss in Henkin (1981), pp. 293-294, 309.

[157] E.g.: IACtHR, *Opinion on the Word "Laws"* (1986), §§21-22.

throughout the different human rights systems. Where relevant, however, different approaches in specific human rights regimes will be pointed out in what follows.

1.2.3.2. The basic qualities of a "law"

Whether national, international,[158] legislative, executive or customary, the "law" prescribing the grounds and procedure for detention or internment must possess the basic qualities required for any law to satisfy the principle of legal certainty. Serving the ultimate aim of the principle, these qualities reduce the risk of abuse of power and protect individuals from arbitrary interference with their rights. They can be summarized as follows: the "law" must be (a) accessible, (b) possess a degree of precision that allows for sufficient predictability and foreseeability of a potential restriction of the right, and (c) generate adequate and effective protection against arbitrariness.[159]

These requirements apply to the legal basis taken in its entirety, which, as we will see below, can be composed of a primary legal rule and secondary rules adopted to enforce that rule, or case law clarifying its interpretation. It is important that, as a whole, the legal basis relied upon to justify a decision to detain or intern possesses the quality required to satisfy the principle of legality.[160] Let us now examine what these requirements involve.

---

[158] The qualities of "law" as discussed below are applicable to both international and national legal instruments. For examples of cases where a legal basis for deprivation of liberty in international law was subjected to the test of the principle of legality: ECtHR (Grand Chamber), *Medvedyev* (2010) and IAC°HR, *Coard v. USA* (1999). *Cf.* also *infra* section 1.2.3.3.

[159] Relatively little extensive attention is devoted to this issue in international case law regarding deprivation of liberty or other restrictions to rights and freedoms. Tthe notable exception is the European Court of Human Rights, whose case law we will therefore refer to extensively in the current section. Nevertheless, the basic qualities of a "law" restricting fundamental rights or freedoms as discussed below apply throughout the different international and regional human rights systems. In his commentary of the ICCPR, Nowak refers explicitly to the elements of accessibility, precision and foreseeability as inherent in the principle of legality in article 9 ICCPR (Nowak (2005) at p. 224). In her study on limitations to human rights in states of emergency, Svensson-McCarthy comes to the same conclusion: whereas her study of the principle of legality in the UDHR, ICCPR and ACHR does not reveal anything specific on the basic qualities of a "law" restricting human rights, she still concludes that the three qualities mentioned here are part of the general principle of legality in international human rights law (Svensson-McCarthy (1996). This conclusion is also supported by the PCIJ's *Danzig Opinion* quoted above; and by articles 17 and 18 of the *Siracusa Principles* (1984): "Legal rules limiting the exercise of human rights shall be clear and accessible to everyone" and "[a]dequate safeguards and effective remedies shall be provided by law against illegal or abusive imposition or application of limitations on human rights." Finally, we agree with Lord Bingham that the requirement that "the law must be accessible and so far as possible intelligible, clear and predictable" is part of the principle of the rule of law (Bingham (*Sir David Williams Lectures* 2006), pp. 6-9).

[160] For example, in *Silver and Others v. UK* (1983), §88 the ECtHR found that legislation limiting the right to privacy, as supplemented by precise administrative provisions, was sufficiently clear to satisfy the principle of legality. Similarly, in *Steel and Others v. UK* (1998), §55 the Court considered that the concept of breach of the peace as proscribed only quite vaguely by the criminal code had been sufficiently clarified by the courts over the past two decades to allow for any individual to be able to predict which specific behaviour may entail deprivation of liberty on that basis. With regard to the latter judgment, the Council of Europe – in its guide to the implementation

(a.) Accessibility

"Firstly, the law must be adequately accessible: the citizen must be able to have an indication [about the existence and content of the law] that is adequate in the circumstances of the legal rules applicable to a given case."[161]

The accessibility criterion will be met if the legal basis for deprivation of liberty is made reasonably available and known to the public, or at least to the interested parties, by means of an official publication or by public communication.[162]

On the contrary, the accessibility requirement will not be met when the legal basis for deprivation of liberty is either secret, or unpublished, or has been insufficiently brought to the attention of the public concerned. For example, in *Amuur v. France* (1996), the ECtHR had to examine the legality of an unpublished ministerial circular that formed the legal basis for the temporary administrative detention of aliens refused entry into a transit zone. Since the Court did not consider the circular itself to have met the precision requirement (*cf. infra litera* b), the fact that it was also unpublished was mentioned, but not material to deciding the case.[163] In its Guide on the implementation of article 5 ECHR the Council of Europe however clarified that "there is no doubt that there could be other instances where this [the fact that the circular was unpublished] would be the key consideration. In such cases the quality of the content should be insufficient to prevent the inaccessibility of the rule being overlooked and the deprivation of liberty being found to be lawful."[164]

(b.) A degree of precision allowing for sufficient foreseeability and predictability

"Secondly, a norm cannot be regarded as "law" unless it is formulated with sufficient precision to enable the citizen to regulate his conduct: he must be able – if need be with appropriate advice – to foresee, to a degree that is reasonable in the circumstances, the consequences which a given action may entail."[165]

---

of article 5 ECHR – warns however that "such rulings are not an invitation to reject a challenge to a provision's lawfulness on the basis that appropriate precision will ultimately be derived from cases to be decided in the future" (CoE, *HRH No. 5* (2002), p. 16).

[161] ECtHR, *Sunday Times* (1979), §49. The *Sunday Times* case is the leading case on the basic qualities a law restricting individual rights and freedoms must possess to satisfy the principle of legal certainty. While it dealt with a restriction of the freedom of expression, the Court's analysis of the principle of legal certainty has been confirmed in subsequent case law dealing specifically with the right to liberty, see for example *Amuur v. France* (1996), §§ 50-54; *Steel and Others v. UK* (1998), §55; *Baranowski v. Poland* (2000), §§50-57; *Kawka v. Poland* (2001), §§ 48-51; *Medvedyev and Others v. France* (2008), §53; *Grori v. Albania* (2009), §148; and *Medvedyev* (2010), §§ 80-103.

[162] To be noted that an individual's ignorance of a given law, as long as the law is sufficiently accessible, does not render deprivation of liberty on the basis of that law unlawful. In the same sense: Gallant (2009), p. 364.

[163] ECtHR, *Amuur v. France* (1996), §§ 50-54.

[164] CoE, *HRH No. 5* (2002), p. 15.

[165] ECtHR, *Sunday Times* (1979), §49. In the same sense as *Sunday Times*, but with regard to deprivation of liberty, see the cases of the ECtHR referred to *supra* note 160; PCIJ, *Danzig Opinion* (1935), pp. 53 and 57 ("It must be possible for the individual to know, beforehand, whether his acts are lawful or liable to punishment"); IACtHR, *Gangaram Panday v. Suriname* (1994) §47 ("no one

Predictability and foreseeability also require that the legal basis for detention or internment exist and be known to the public at the time when the behaviour that may trigger such deprivation of liberty occurs. As far as detention in the criminal justice framework is concerned this rule is sometimes described as "*nulla poena sine praevia lege.*"[166] The same holds true for administrative detention and for internment in armed conflict.[167]

---

may be subjected to arrest or imprisonment for reasons and by methods which, although classified as legal, could be deemed to be incompatible with the respect for the fundamental rights of the individual because, among other things, they are unreasonable, *unforeseeable* or lacking in proportionality", emphasis added); IACtHR, *Bamaca Velasquez v. Guatemala* (2000), §139 (in the same terms as the *Gangaram Panday* case but applied to internment of a rebel commander in armed conflict); IAC°HR, *Second Report Peru* (2000), §§81-82 (with regard to anti-terrorism legislation used to detain members of organized armed groups in Peru's internal armed conflict, the Commission found the "decree is abstract and vague, and thereby violates the basic principle of legality, [...] whose ultimate objective is the juridical security the individual needs to know precisely what acts and omissions may trigger his or her criminal liability [and imprisonment] [...] [the] notable imprecision, in very broad language, creating open-ended criminal definitions that rely on very vague terms, [is] 'contrary to one of the basic principles of modern criminal justice, which is that the language used to describe the prohibited conduct must be precise so as to leave as little discretionary latitude as possible to those whose function it is to enforce and interpret the law.' [...] This new body of law [i.e. the counter-terrorism legislation at stake] is contrary to universally accepted principles of legality [...] under these laws, merely being suspected of a terrorist act or of in any way collaborating in terrorist acts is sufficient cause to hold someone in prison for long periods, regardless of whether that person actually committed an act classified as terrorism or treason [...] this is a grave threat to the people's juridical security.' The Inter-American Court [...] specified, in this respect, that the right to personal liberty [...] implies not being deprived of physical liberty other than for causes established beforehand by law, indicating that 'no one may be subjected to arrest or imprisonment for reasons and by methods which, although classified as legal, could be deemed to be incompatible with the respect for the fundamental rights of the individual because, among other things, they are unreasonable, unforeseeable or lacking in proportionality'", footnotes omitted); AC°HPR, *Amnesty International and Others v. Sudan* (1999), §59 (in a case concerning a decree allowing for the arrest and detention of anyone "suspected of being a threat to political or economic security" the Commission found that "the wording of this decree allows for individuals to be arrested for vague reasons, and upon suspicion, not proven acts, which conditions are not in conformity with the spirit of the African Charter [and article 6 of the Charter on the right to liberty]"). See also the definition of specificity as a requirement for the principle of legality in international criminal law in Cassese (2003), p. 145: "Under the principle of specificity, criminal rules must be as specific and detailed as possible, so as to clearly indicate to their addressees the conduct prohibited [...] the principle is aimed at ensuring that all those who may fall under the prohibitions of the law know in advance which specific behaviour is allowed and which conduct is instead proscribed. They may thus foresee the consequences of their action and freely choose either to comply with, or instead breach, legal standards of behaviour. Clearly, the more accurate and specific the criminal rule, the greater is the protection accorded to the agent from arbitrary action of either enforcement officials or courts of law."

[166] Gallant (2009), p. 12: "no punishment may be imposed except under previously existing law." Gallant explains that this principle has been challenged in exceptional situations on the view that "[r]adical evil needs to be punished [and the] nature of such evil may not be fully predictable in advance [...] thus criminal law may have some retroactive aspects, but in the rare instances in which this is the case, the system should be clear about what it is doing and why" (*Ibidem*, p. 39) Gallant also warns that "transitional justice – the set of criminal and other legal issues arising from the transition of tyranny or violent societal disintegration to democracy and rule of law [...] can also be abused by new authoritarian regimes" (*Ibidem*, p. 39).

[167] E.g.: ECtHR, *Amuur v. France* (1996), §§52 *in fine* and 54.

The European Court of Human Rights, when reaffirming the principle of legal certainty, has occasionally added an important element of pragmatism to be considered in its application:

> "Those consequences [which a given action may entail] need not be foreseeable with absolute certainty: experience shows this to be unattainable. Again, whilst certainty is highly desirable, it may bring in its train excessive rigidity and the law must be able to keep pace with changing circumstances. Accordingly, many laws are inevitably couched in terms which, to a greater or lesser extent, are vague and whose interpretation and application are questions of practice."[168]

With regard to the right to liberty, this means the legal basis for detention must be sufficiently precise to allow any individual concerned to know what behaviour may lead to what type of deprivation of liberty. Nevertheless, while the law must be precise enough to ensure foreseeability, it must at the same time be sufficiently broad to accommodate the circumstances in which it is to be applied.

Flexibility in adapting to the changing nature of security threats will be of particular importance in situations of armed conflict, which explains the relatively broad terms in which international humanitarian law frames the lawful grounds for internment in armed conflict. For example, article 42 GC IV, applying to foreign nationals in the territory of a party to the conflict, allows parties to an international armed conflict to intern them where "absolutely necessary for the security of the Detaining Power." This ground is not as precise as other grounds for deprivation of liberty may or must be, but is generally accepted to be clear enough to satisfy the principle of legality in the particular situation of armed conflict. While the substance of the meaning of the word "security" has and continues to give rise to discussion (*cf. infra* chapter II-3), article 42 GC IV has until today never been challenged as being insufficiently precise to serve as a legal basis for internment in armed conflict.[169]

---

[168] E.g.: ECtHR, *Sunday Times* (1979), §49. On the theme of the inevitable indeterminacy of language and its impact on the interpretation of the principle of legal certainty, specifically as regards the retroactivity of criminal law, see also Gallant (2009), pp. 31-33 ("The ideal of *lex certa* can never be absolute as a rule [...] The issue here will always be whether the law is certain enough, and what warning to potential offenders is sufficiently clear to guide [the public]" (original italics)) and pp. 362-363. More generally, see also *infra* section 1.2.3.3.

[169] Note that the lack of specificity of the 1929 Geneva Convention relative to the Treatment of Prisoners of War (GC 1929) was used by parties to the Second World War to deny prisoner-of-war status to members of resistance movements and other irregular armed forces, resulting in their arbitrary deprivation of liberty and often ill-treatment. See for example Bugnion, *The International Committee of the Red Cross and the Protection of War Victims* (2003), pp. 192-194. This explains the more elaborate and precise wording of article 4 GC III and the precisions brought by that Convention to the legal basis for prisoner of war internment in earlier conventions (*cf. infra* chapter II-1). Similarly, the lack of any regulation of the protection of civilians in armed conflict, and in particular the lack of a legal basis to intern persons, other than prisoners of war, who posed a threat to the security of the parties to the conflict, resulted in arbitrary deprivation of liberty of (oft innocent and clearly not dangerous) civilians on unprecedented scales during the Second World War and resulted in the Fourth Geneva Convention's strict internment provisions (*cf. infra* chapter II-3).

(c.) Adequate and effective protection against arbitrariness

In the *Klass* case (1978), which concerned a law on secret surveillance for national security reasons that satisfied both the accessibility and foreseeability criteria, the European Court of Human Rights underlined the importance of a third basic quality of a "law" restricting human rights, namely that the law foresees "adequate and effective guarantees against abuse."[170] The European Court places particular emphasis on effective control over a State's interference with an individual's rights as required by the principle of the rule of law. It considered this requirement to be particularly important where "the law bestows on the executive wide discretionary powers, the application whereof is a matter of practice which is susceptible to modification but not to any Parliamentary scrutiny."[171] In the opinion of the Court, judicial control of restrictive measures is one of such safeguards specifically commanded by the principle of the rule of law:

> "The rule of law implies, inter alia, that an interference by the executive authorities with an individual's rights should be subject to an effective control which should normally be assured by the judiciary, at least in the last resort, judicial control offering the best guarantees of independence, impartiality and a proper procedure."[172]

This requirement is reflected both in the exigency that the procedures regulating deprivation of liberty be prescribed by law (principle of legal certainty) and in certain procedural safeguards inherent in the right to liberty (i.e. the right to information and the possibility to challenge the lawfulness of one's detention). The absence of procedural safeguards, including, but not limited, to judicial control, may lead courts to judge a deprivation of liberty unlawful even if it is based on an otherwise valid legal basis and on lawful grounds. These procedural safeguards must be established by a law, which is sufficiently accessible, and precise enough so as to allow individuals to reasonably foresee/predict when and how they may be deprived of their liberty.

1.2.3.3. What form can a "law" take?[173]

While one should not interpret the word "law" by reference to its definition under domestic law, this does not mean that the "law" referred to cannot exist *within* the domestic legal order.[174] On the contrary, the treaty provisions concerning the right to liberty primarily refer to a legal basis in the domestic

[170] ECtHR, *Klass and Others v. Germany* (1978), §50. In the same sense: ECtHR, *Amuur v. France* (1996), §§53-54.
[171] ECtHR, *Silver and Others v. UK* (1983), §90.
[172] ECtHR, *Klass and Others v. Germany* (1978), §55.
[173] For the purposes of the analysis below, we focus on the specific *form* a legal basis for deprivation of liberty can take. Where we say a certain instrument may constitute a valid legal basis for deprivation of liberty, we do this on the assumption that (1) it possesses the basic qualities of "law" as discussed above and (2) the other criteria for lawful deprivation of liberty (*cf. supra* section 1.2.1) are equally fulfilled.
[174] We are concerned here not with the validity of the legal basis in the specific domestic legal order in which it may be found. While the conformity of a legal basis for deprivation of liberty with domestic law may arise before national courts, it is of limited relevance to the validity of that legal basis under international law and therefore beyond the scope of this work.

legal order of the detaining or interning State and most instances of deprivation of liberty are indeed based on domestic legislation. This does not mean, however, that the legal basis for deprivation of liberty can exclusively be found in domestic law. We will see below that such a legal basis can also exist in international law.

(a.) Laws adopted in the domestic legal order

In the domestic legal order, all three branches of government (legislative, executive and judicial) may be involved – to some extent – in the process of lawmaking.[175] But to what extent can they make "laws" that qualifies as such for the purposes of restricting the right to liberty? In this subsection, we will analyze to what extent a legal basis for deprivation of liberty can be enacted by the legislative, executive and judicial branches of government.

(a.1) Legislation

The legal basis for deprivation of liberty is usually a legislative act, i.e. emanating from the legislative branch of government and promulgated by its executive branch. For example, the legal basis for detention in the framework of criminal justice – before, during or after a potential trial – will normally be found in the penal legislation of the detaining State. Where such penal law allows a court to order imprisonment as a punishment for a specific criminal offence, or to order provisional detention before or pending trial, a court order in conformity with that law will constitute a valid legal basis for such detention.[176]

Similarly, administrative detention in the framework of immigration proceedings, for reasons of public and mental health, for reasons of educational supervision or protection of minors and to a certain extent for reasons of public and/or national security (*cf. infra* section 1.2.4) will normally be based on domestic legislation. Where such legislation possesses the basic qualities of a law as discussed above, the principle of legal certainty will also be satisfied.

[175] We work on the assumption that a State functions on the basis of the principle of separation of powers and thus has three independent branches of government: the legislative, executive and judicial branches. The effective independence of these branches may vary from one State to another (and in a few instances even be virtually inexistent) but represents (at least on paper) the general organization of government structure in most if not all modern nation States. Proponents of a substantive conception of the rule of law include the principle of separation of powers and the existence of democratic institutions within the definition of the rule of law; see Tamanaha (2004), pp. 36-38 and 110-112. This is also the conception of the rule of law in the Inter-American (e.g.: IACtHR, *Opinion on the Word "Laws"* (1986), §§ 25, 32-34) and European human rights systems, and within the United Nations (e.g.: UNSG, *Rule of Law Report* (2004), §6). See also the overview of Inter-American and European case law in Svensson-McCarthy (1996), pp. 123-193 and 527-530. In the same sense: Bingham (*Sir David Williams Lectures* 2006), pp. 23-25.

[176] It seems to be uncontroversial that with regard to criminal justice the principle of legality imposes that the "law" establishing the crime/offence and its punishment must emanate from the State's legislative branch (with the exception of common law systems, *cf. infra*). The only exception seems to be related to international crimes defined by international treaties upon which certain international tribunals may rely directly to order the detention of a person accused of such a crime (*cf. infra* note 201). Since detention in the framework of criminal justice is beyond the scope of this book, the issue does not however require further discussion here.

(a.2) Common law

Depending on the domestic legal order, "law" does not necessarily have to be written, or even emanate from the legislative branch of government. It is generally accepted that in common law systems "law" may be unwritten and emanate from the judicial branch of government. Where such a common law possesses the basic qualities of "law" described above, its unwritten nature or judicial origin will not prevent it from being a valid legal basis for restricting the enjoyment or exercise of a fundamental right or freedom such as the right to liberty. In this sense, the European Court of Human Rights has correctly pointed out that:

> "the word "law" in the expression 'prescribed by law' covers not only statute but also unwritten law. Accordingly, the Court does not attach importance here to the fact that contempt of court is a creature of the common law and not of legislation. It would clearly be contrary to the intention of the drafters of the Convention to hold that a restriction imposed by virtue of the common law is not 'prescribed by law' on the sole ground that it is not enunciated in legislation: this would deprive a common-law State which is Party to the Convention of the protection of Article 10 (2) (art. 10-2) and strike at the very roots of that State's legal system."[177]

(a.3) Executive orders

Administrative detention – which by definition falls outside the confines of criminal law enforcement and penal legislation – does not always seem to be based on legislative acts.[178] In some instances, administrative detention seems to be based on orders or decisions that emanate directly from the executive branch of government. This occurs most often in times of emergency or of armed conflict in attempts to justify administrative detention on security grounds (*cf. infra* chapter I-2). The question therefore arises whether a mere executive order or decision prescribing the grounds and procedures for administrative detention can satisfy the principle of legal certainty. Especially in respect of immigration control, it may be argued that the executive institutions dealing with this issue are better placed than members of Parliament to assess the necessity of confining certain individuals for security reasons.

A similar argument can be made in the context of armed conflict, arguing that the military is better placed than the legislature to decide which individuals pose a security threat of a kind that requires their internment. The Inter-American Court of Human Rights nevertheless explicitly rejected the possibility

---

177 ECtHR, *Sunday Times* (1979), §47. Thus, the Court focused on its basic qualities rather than on its form to evaluate whether the legal basis for restricting the right concerned met the test of the principle of legal certainty. In the same sense, see IACtHR, *Opinion on the Word "Laws"* (1986), §20. For the interpretation of the principle of legal certainty in domestic criminal law, and the different approach to it in civil and common law systems: see Cassese (2003), pp. 141-142; Gallant (2009), pp. 13-14 and Svensson-McCarthy (1996), pp. 69-73. Thus, in a common law system, what is important is that the legal basis for deprivation of liberty possesses the basic qualities of a "law", not necessarily that it is part of written, statutory law.

178 Certain countries have adopted legislation to allow them to administratively detain for reasons of national security, or for reasons related to a (non-international) armed conflict (*cf. infra* chapter III-1).

that a legal instrument other than a formal act of parliament could be the legal basis for limiting the enjoyment or exercise of a right enshrined in the American Convention on Human Rights. In an opinion addressing an explicit request on the matter by Uruguay, the Court held that:

> "Within the framework of the protection of human rights, the word 'laws' would not make sense without reference to the concept that such rights cannot be restricted at the sole discretion of governmental authorities. To affirm otherwise would be to recognize in those who govern virtually absolute power over their subjects. On the other hand, the word 'laws' acquires all of its logical and historical meaning if it is regarded as a requirement of the necessary restriction of governmental interference in the area of individual rights and freedoms. The Court concludes that the word 'laws,' used in Article 30, *can have no other meaning than that of formal law, that is, a legal norm passed by the legislature* and promulgated by the Executive Branch, pursuant to the procedure set out in the domestic law of each State."[179]

The Inter-American Commission has confirmed this principle, adding that:

> "Administrative authorities may neither alter the rights and guarantees enshrined in international law, nor limit nor restrict them any further than expressly allowed."[180]

Other human rights bodies have not explicitly addressed the issue.[181] In his Commentary to article 9§1 of the ICCPR, Nowak deduces, however, from the systemic interpretation of all comparable provisions in the Covenant that use the word "law" to delimit permissible limitations of rights that this term:

[179] IACtHR, *Opinion on the Word "Laws"* (1986), § 27 (emphasis added). Article 30 ACHR reads as follows: "The restrictions that, pursuant to this Convention, may be placed on the enjoyment or exercise of the rights or freedoms recognized herein may not be applied except in accordance with *laws* enacted for reasons of general interest and in accordance with the purpose for which such restrictions have been established" (emphasis added). The criteria of article 30 ACHR apply to all provisions in the Convention that use the word "laws" or comparable expressions in referring to restrictions those provisions authorize with regard to the right they provide for (§17). The only exception concerns common law systems, *cf. supra* note 177.

[180] IAC°HR, *Principles and Best Practices* (2008), principle 4: "The judicial or administrative orders and resolutions that are capable of affecting, limiting, or restricting the rights and guarantees of persons deprived of liberty, shall conform to domestic and international law. Administrative authorities may neither alter the rights and guarantees enshrined in international law, nor limit nor restrict them any further than expressly allowed."

[181] We have not found any explicit case law on the matter from the AC°HPR, the HRC or the WGAD. The European Court in *Amuur v. France* (1996) dealt with a purely administrative provision that served as the legal basis for detention, which it found did not satisfy the principle of legal certainty because it was insufficiently precise and did not offer adequate protection against arbitrariness (§§50-54). It is unclear however whether an accessible, precise administrative provision that offered sufficient safeguards against arbitrariness would have been acceptable to the Court. In *Golder v. UK* (1975), the European Court accepted that Prison Rules (which restricted the prisoners' right to correspondence), issued by the Home Secretary (and thus the executive branch of government) were "law" for the purposes of article 5§1 ECHR (at §45), but in its summary of the facts (§17) the Court had specified that "[t]he rules made by the Home Secretary in the exercise of this power are the Prison Rules 1964, which were laid before Parliament and have the status of a Statutory Instrument."

> "is to be understood here [i.e. in article 9§1 ICCPR] in the strict sense of a parliamentary statute or an equivalent, unwritten norm of common law, accessible to all individuals subject to the relevant jurisdiction. Administrative provisions are thus not sufficient."[182]

It is also interesting to note that in the case of *Amuur v. France* before the national courts, a French court held that:

> "the current detention by order of the Minister of Interior [...] is not provided for by any legislation [...] under the legislative and constitutional provisions currently applicable in France, detention may not be ordered by the administrative authorities in cases other than those provided for in [the relevant applicable law, prescribing the grounds and procedures for administrative detention of aliens refused entry into France]. In French law as it stands at present, therefore [...] the applicants must have been considered arbitrarily deprived of their liberty."[183]

The relevant French law was subsequently amended to include the type of detention ordered directly by the Minister of Interior in the Amuur case, but since it was not applicable yet at the time of their detention, it could not be relied upon as a legal basis for their detention.[184]

When confronted with a similar question in a situation of armed conflict the US Supreme Court, pointed out the reasons why deprivation of liberty should only be lawful if ordered on the basis of a legislative act by parliament. It did not decide the matter since *in casu* it found such a legal basis to exist in an act of Congress, but its reasoning is still of interest to us here:

> "The threshold question before us is whether the Executive has the authority to detain citizens who qualify as 'enemy combatants.' [...] 18 U.S.C. §4001(a) [...] states that '[n]o citizen shall be imprisoned or otherwise detained by the United States except pursuant to an Act of Congress.' Congress passed §4001(a) in 1971 as part of a bill to repeal the Emergency Detention Act of 1950, 50 U. S. C. §811 *et seq*., which provided procedures for executive detention, during times of emergency, of individuals deemed likely to engage in espionage or sabotage. Congress was particularly concerned about the possibility that the Act could be used to reprise the Japanese internment camps of World War II. [...] ('The concentration camp implications of the legislation render it abhorrent'). The Government again presses two alternative positions. First, it argues that §4001(a), in light of its legislative history and its location in Title 18, applies only to 'the control of civilian prisons and related detentions,' not to military detentions. [...] Second, it maintains that §4001(a) is satisfied, because Hamdi is being detained 'pursuant to an Act of Congress' – the AUMF. [...] Again, because we conclude that the Government's second assertion is correct, we do not address the first. In other words, for the reasons that follow, we conclude that the AUMF is explicit congressional authorization for the detention of individuals in

---

182 Nowak (2005), p. 224. See also Bossuyt (1987), p. 187.

183 France, Tribunal de Grande Instance de Créteil, Judgment of 31 March 1992, quoted (in translation) in ECtHR, *Amuur v. France* (1996), §12.

184 ECtHR, *Amuur v. France* (1996), §52.

the narrow category we describe (assuming, without deciding, that such authorization is required), and that the AUMF satisfied §4001(a)'s requirement that a detention be 'pursuant to an Act of Congress' (assuming, without deciding, that §4001(a) applies to military detentions)."[185]

These examples shed light on what is common practice in administrative detention. They illustrate the fact that the question of whether an executive act can be the legal basis for detention does not arise very often in its most pure form (i.e. the legal basis invoked being a purely administrative provision enacted by the executive branch of government). In most States, administrative detention is based on legislation (or established common law) that delegates the authority to detain to a department or to a specific member of the executive branch of government, rather than to the judiciary as would be the case for detention on the basis of criminal law. Usually, the law sets out the grounds and procedures that must regulate such detention in general terms and leaves it up to the executive to adopt detailed administrative rules and regulations, implementing the legislation. It is the combination then of the legislation (or common law) and the administrative rules and regulations adopted by the executive that makes up the legal basis for administrative detention. In such cases, the legislation (or common law) by itself may be insufficiently precise to meet the principle of legality, but this is made good by the precisions conveyed by the administrative regulations or executive orders.[186] Likewise, the administrative regulation or executive order by itself may not be "law" for the purpose of the principle of legality, but the specific delegation by parliament of legislative power or authorization to detail the grounds and procedures of administrative detention may make up for this. The system thus leaves a wider margin of discretion to the executive branch, without leaving the restriction of the right to liberty entirely up to the executive authorities.[187]

Where the State relies upon such a combined legal basis for detention, it is necessary to assess on a case-by-case basis whether the principle of legality has

---

[185] US, SC, *Hamdi* (2004), section II of the judgment, §§1 and 3 (the applicant was captured in relation to the armed conflict in Afghanistan). We will come back to both the US internment legislation during WW II and the AUMF in more detail in chapter II-3 below.

[186] On the condition that these regulations be reasonably accessible to the individuals concerned, *cf. supra* section 1.2.3.1 (a).

[187] In a recent case on executive orders allowing the government to freeze the assets of suspected terrorists (which we quote here because the argument is as relevant for restrictions on the right to liberty and the Court itself refers to other cases involving administrative detention to make its arguments), the UK courts ruled that by overstepping the powers delegated to the executive by Parliament, the orders were unlawful: UK, High Court of Justice (HCJ), *Jabar Ahmed and Others v. Her Majesty's Treasury* (2010), §§6 and 75: "The consequences of the Orders that were made in this case are so drastic and so oppressive that we must be just as alert to see that the coercive action that the Treasury have taken really is within the powers that the 1946 Act has given them. Even in the face of the threat of international terrorism, the safety of the people is not the supreme law. We must be just as careful to guard against unrestrained encroachments on personal liberty. [...] the principle of legality, which lies at the heart of the relationship between Parliament and the citizen [requires that f]undamental rights may not be overridden by general words. This can only be done by express language or by necessary implication. So it was not open to the Treasury to use its powers under the general wording of section 1(1) of the 1946 Act to subject individuals to a regime which had these effects."

been satisfied by the legal basis in its entirety, (in both its formal and material aspects) and the other criteria for lawful deprivation of liberty (*cf. supra* 1.2.1).

While very firm on the exigency of a legislative act for limiting the rights and freedoms enshrined in the American Convention on Human Rights, the Inter-American Court does not exclude the possibility of the system described above:

> "The [fact that the enjoyment or exercise of individual rights may not be restricted except by an act of Parliament] does not necessarily negate the possibility of delegations of authority in this area, provided that such delegations are authorized by the Constitution, are exercised within the limits imposed by the Constitution and the delegating law, and that the exercise of the power delegated is subject to effective controls, so that it does not impair nor can it be used to impair the fundamental nature of the rights and freedoms protected by the Convention."[188]

(a.4) Emergency legislation

We will see below that the derogation provisions of international human rights treaties do not explicitly require such measures to be adopted by a legislative act.[189] But a similar form of delegation of legislative power to the executive also underlies the system of *ad hoc* emergency legislation derogating from the right to liberty or other fundamental rights and freedoms. In many if not all States, the constitution or a legislative act grants extraordinary powers (including of arrest and detention) to the executive in times of public emergency, and at the same time circumscribes such powers. For example, the UK's *Civil Contingencies Act* (2004) allows the Queen, the Privy Council or the Prime Minister to enact emergency regulations if there is a serious threat to human welfare or the environment, or in case of war or terrorism.[190] Such emergency regulations:

> "may make provision of any kind that could be made by Act of Parliament or by the exercise of the Royal Prerogative; in particular, regulations may [...] create an offence of (i) failing to comply with a provision of the regulations; (ii) failing to comply with a direction or order given or made under the regulations; (iii) obstructing a person in the performance of a function under or by virtue of the regulations [...] Emergency regulations may not (a) create an offence other than one of the kind described in section 22(3)(i), [...] Emergency regulations may not amend (a) this Part of this Act, or (b) the Human Rights Act".[191]

Another good example of the system is that of Guinea. The constitution authorizes the President to proclaim a state of siege or emergency[192] and a

[188] IACtHR, *Opinion on the Word "Laws"* (1986), §36.

[189] Kiss in Henkin (1981), p. 290. To be noted that the Inter-American Court's opinion referred to above does not deal with derogations from the Convention; it is only concerned with limitations of the enjoyment or exercise of individual rights and freedoms in normal circumstances, see IACtHR, *Opinion on the Word "Laws"* (1986), §§16-17.

[190] UK, *Civil Contingencies Act* (2004), Part II, sections 19-20.

[191] *Ibidem*, sections 22§3, 23§4 and 23§5.

[192] Guinea, *Loi fondamentale* (1992): "Article 74 – L'état de siège, comme l'état d'urgence, est décrété par le Président de la République, après avis du Président de l'Assemblée Nationale et du Président

legislative act circumscribes the executive's power in such situations. The latter expressly provides for the executive's power to administratively detain. While the grounds for such detention are formulated in rather vague terms and left to be detailed by the executive according to the specific situation, the law prescribes a number of safeguards geared at preventing any arbitrary or abusive exercise of these powers:

> "Article 11: Le décret instituant l'état d'urgence peut, par une disposition expresse, conférer à l'autorité administrative compétente le pouvoir de prononcer l'internement administratif des personnes *dont l'activité présente un danger pour la sécurité publique*. Cette mesure peut être prononcée pour un délai maximum d'un mois, renouvelable une seule fois, pour une durée égale. Les personnes ayant fait l'objet d'une telle mesure peuvent demander l'examen de leur situation à la commission consultative de contrôle prévue à l'article 5."[193]

Any executive orders or other types of emergency regulations adopted to allow for administrative detention in situations of public emergency – regardless of whether they are valid under national law – will still need to conform to international human rights law.[194] The prohibition of arbitrariness is absolute.[195] Any law – regardless of its form – that authorizes deprivation of liberty but does not offer adequate protection against arbitrariness does not satisfy the principle of legality. It is useful in this regard to recall also the following concern of the Working Group for Arbitrary Detention:

> "The Working Group [...] recalls that it has continuously considered that states of emergency are a root cause of arbitrary detentions and cautioned against their promulgation. Given the frequency of arbitrary detentions occurring in such situations, it would like to remind Governments that they may only be imposed in strict compliance with the principle of proportionality. Each measure taken thereunder, including the suspension of and restrictions on derogable fundamental rights and freedoms, must also pursue a legitimate goal, be

---

de la Cour Suprême. Ces avis sont publiés au Journal Officiel. Le Président de la République peut prendre, par ordonnance, *toute mesure nécessaire à la défense de l'intégrité du territoire et au rétablissement ou au maintien de l'ordre public*. L'Assemblée Nationale se réunit alors de plein droit, si elle n'est pas en session. Elle ne peut être dissoute. Le décret proclamant l'état de siège ou l'état d'urgence cesse d'être en vigueur après douze jours, à moins que l'Assemblée Nationale, saisie par le Président de la République n'en autorise la prorogation pour un délai qu'elle fixe. Les ordonnances prises en application de l'état de siège et de l'état d'urgence cessent d'être en vigueur à la fin de ceux-ci" (emphasis added).

[193] Guinea, *Loi organique relative à l'état d'urgence et a l'état de siège* (1991) (emphasis added).

[194] See in this sense also UK, High Court of Justice, *H.X.A. v. Home Office* (2009), §4, dealing with administrative detention ordered by the Secretary of State for the purposes of implementing a deportation order: "it was and is unlawful for the defendant, as a public authority, to act in a way incompatible with the claimant's convention rights under, amongst others, Article 5 [ECHR, right to liberty]."

[195] See also the reports on the drafting process of article 9§1 ICCPR as reproduced in Bossuyt (1987), p. 201: "[the prohibition of arbitrary arrest and detention in article 9§1 is] a safeguard against the injustices of States, because it applied not only to laws but also to statutory regulations and to all acts performed by the executive. [...] An arbitrary act was any act which violated justice, reason or legislation, or was done according to someone's will or discretion; or which was capricious, despotic, imperious, tyrannical or uncontrolled."

necessary and appropriate to the goal to be achieved. Whatever the threat, under no circumstances may detention based on emergency legislation last indefinitely. The Working Group attaches particular importance to the existence of effective internal control mechanisms over the legality of detention. It considers the remedy of habeas corpus as one of the most effective means of preventing and combating arbitrary detention. It must not be suspended or rendered impracticable in states of emergency."[196]

Finally, while emergency legislation by definition will be *ad hoc* and focus on the exigencies of the specific situation in which it is adopted, an emergency law that derogates from international human rights law to restrict the enjoyment or exercise of individual rights and freedoms still must be of general applicability in order to qualify as "law".[197] The grounds for deprivation of liberty must be framed in objective and general terms and not single out individuals on an arbitrary or discriminatory basis.[198]

(a.5) Conclusion

Based on the foregoing, it is submitted that under international law a mere executive order or decision prescribing the grounds and procedures for deprivation of liberty in principle does not qualify as a 'law' for the purpose of the principle of legality. However, where these grounds and procedures are prescribed by a combination of a broad legislative act (or common law) and more detailed administrative regulations lawfully adopted by the executive branch and sufficiently clear and accessible, the principle of legal certainty may be satisfied. The further lawfulness of the deprivation of liberty will then depend on whether the grounds and procedures established are lawful and the legal basis as a whole offers adequate and effective protection against arbitrariness and abuse. In the words of Alexandre Kiss:

"In every case, the objective [of the principle of legality, reflected in the words "prescribed by law" in limitation clauses] is to avoid arbitrary restrictions on

[196] E.g.: WGAD, *Annual Report 2007*, §64. We will discuss the conditions for adopting emergency regulations that derogate from the right to liberty in more detail in chapter I-2 below.

[197] E.g.: Abi-Saab, "The Security Council as Legislator and as Executive in its Fights against Terrorism and against Proliferation of Weapons of Mass Destruction: The Question of Legitimacy" in Wolfrum & Röben, *Legitimacy in International Law* (2008), p. 117: "legislation *stricto sensu* signifies the enactment of prospective, general and abstract rules of conduct that bind all the subjects in the unlimited future, whenever the contingencies they provide for obtain."

[198] E.g.: Dinstein, "The Right to Life, Physical Integrity, and Liberty" in Henkin (1981), p. 131: "Of course, what is or is not arbitrary may depend on the context and the circumstances [but] one form of arbitrariness is surely within the prohibition of Article 9 – when the law permitting detention is [...] applicable solely to John Doe and not to others. Article 9 implies that the law governing detention must be of general applicability. The arrest of a given person on legal grounds fitting only the specific occasion is arbitrary – notwithstanding the form of law supporting it – because it is capricious"; and Kiss in Henkin (1981), p. 304, with regard to the words "prescribed by law" in limitation clauses: "the objective is to avoid arbitrary restrictions on rights by requiring that the limitation be established by general rule." The derogation provisions of all but the European Convention on Human Rights explicitly prohibit discriminatory emergency measures (*cf. infra* section 2.1.1.). Such prohibition is nevertheless inherent in the ECHR too, e.g. ECtHR (Grand Chamber), *A and Others v. UK* (2009), §190: "the derogating measures [...] discriminated unjustifiably between nationals and non-nationals."

rights [...] any restriction on recognized rights and freedoms in a state must be by general rule, normally imposed by the legislature; measures taken by the executive authority, such as the police or local administration, are excluded unless authorized by general legislation."[199]

(b.) Laws adopted in the international legal order

So far we have focused on the domestic legal order, but can a legal basis for deprivation of liberty be established directly in international rather than domestic law?

The question has received little to no attention, which is not surprising since most cases of deprivation of liberty will be based on a domestic legal basis. Moreover, in a normal situation, there seems to be little reason to rely on international rather than domestic law to deprive a person of his or her liberty. Correspondingly, there are only very few examples of an international legal instrument authorizing internment and prescribing the grounds and procedures in accordance with which it may be ordered. To our knowledge, only two such examples exist.

(b.1.) International treaties as a legal basis for deprivation of liberty

The first example is in the sphere of international criminal law. Deprivation of liberty in the framework of criminal justice will almost always require a legislative act (or common law), if only to designate the competent authority for ordering an arrest or detention. While detention on the basis of criminal law is not as such within the scope of this book, a small parenthesis on the issue of international crimes is in order to illustrate our point. Whereas these crimes – established by international law – are usually transcribed into domestic law in order to empower the domestic judiciary to prosecute and punish them, an individual can also be tried – and detained in the framework of the proceedings – directly on the basis of international criminal law by an international criminal court or tribunal. It is submitted that the statutes of the different international criminal tribunals that exist today[200] conform to the principle of legality both as expressed in *nulla crimen sine lege, nulla poena sine lege* as in *nulla custodia sine lege*.[201] Detention in the framework of criminal proceedings before a

[199] Kiss in Henkin (1981), pp. 304-305.

[200] We specifically have in mind detention in the framework of criminal proceedings before the ICTY and the ICTR (whose Statutes were however adopted by UN Security Council resolutions rather than by treaty and will be discussed in chapter III-1) and the ICC (whose Statute was adopted as a multilateral treaty to which 114 States are a party at the time of writing). For hybrid tribunals such as the Special Court for Sierra Leone and the Extraordinary Chambers in the Courts of Cambodia, the legal basis for detention in the framework of potential or established criminal proceedings is also hybrid in nature (i.e. a combination of an international agreement between the United Nations and the government of Sierra Leone and Cambodia respectively, and of crimes defined by international treaties and existing national penal legislation).

[201] E.g.: the detention of a person accused and tried by the ICC can be based on the ICC's Statute, which reiterates the prohibition of arbitrary detention in its article 55§1(d) ("In respect of an investigation under this Statute, a person [...] [s]hall not be subjected to arbitrary arrest or detention, and shall not be deprived of his or her liberty except on such grounds and in accordance with such procedures as are established in this Statute"), describes the crimes and penalties in articles 6-9

competent[202] international criminal tribunal therefore finds its legal basis in its internationally adopted statute and rules and procedures as lawfully applied by that tribunal.

The second example concerns us directly and is that of internment[203] on the basis of the Geneva Conventions in situations of international armed conflict and occupation. As we will see in Part II, the Geneva Conventions prescribe the grounds and procedures in accordance with which internment can be ordered in such situations and thus provide for a direct legal basis for deprivation of liberty in international law.[204]

That an international treaty can be the legal basis for a deprivation of liberty is not by itself at variance with the text of international human rights treaties' provisions on the right to liberty. The latter merely require that the grounds and procedures in accordance with which an authority can order the deprivation of liberty be prescribed by law. Nowhere do these treaty provisions exclusively require such grounds and procedures to be based in *domestic* law. Moreover, the text of these treaties must be interpreted in light of their context, which includes "any relevant rules of international law applicable in the relations between the parties."[205] Therefore, the existence of a direct legal basis for deprivation of liberty in international criminal law or international humanitarian law treaties must be taken into account when interpreting the provisions on the right to liberty in international human rights treaties.

While international human rights bodies have interpreted the relevant provisions on the right to liberty as referring primarily to domestic law, they have not excluded the possibility of a legal basis for deprivation of liberty in

---

(*crimen*) and 77-78 (*poena*), and the Court's powers of arrest and detention in articles 57-60 and 91-92 (*custodia*: grounds and procedures for provisional detention). The Statute also prescribes the proceedings in accordance with which the detention must be carried out and provides for the procedural safeguards inherent in the right to liberty, see in particular articles 55, 59-60 (right to information, speedy trial and habeas) and 85 (compensation) ICC Statute.

[202] Whether a specific international court or tribunal is competent to conduct specific criminal proceedings will depend on the scope of its mandate and the jurisdictional provisions of its statute.

[203] Since detention in the framework of criminal proceedings presupposes the designation of a competent court or judicial officer to issue orders of arrest and detention and/or convict a person to a prison sentence, such detention will find its legal basis in the domestic legislation of the detaining State. An occupying power can rely either on the penal laws of the occupied country or issue additional penal legislation in as far as allowed specifically by articles 64 and 68 GC IV. On the legislative powers of an occupying power, see e.g. Sassòli, "Legislation and Maintenance of Public Order and Civil Life by Occupying Powers" (*EJIL* 2005). Whereas internment is by definition ordered by the executive branch of government (and more specifically the military), domestic legislation is not necessary as long as the grounds and procedures in accordance with which it may be ordered are prescribed in a sufficiently precise manner by IHL itself.

[204] To the contrary, but without references or specific arguments explaining or supporting his position, see Arai-Takahashi, *The Law of Occupation: Continuity and Change of International Humanitarian Law, and its Interaction with International Human Rights Law* (2009), p. 490: "In order to implement internment or administrative detention in harmony with Article 78 GC IV, the occupying power must adopt a specific implementing law upon which measures of security detention can be based."

[205] Article 31§3(c) VCLT.

international law. For example, the ECtHR, in a case concerning an arrest and provisional detention of the crew of a ship on the high seas for the purpose of bringing them before a competent court on charges of drug-trafficking has held that:

> "where the 'lawfulness' of detention is in issue, including the question whether 'a procedure prescribed by law' has been followed, the Convention refers essentially to national law but also, where appropriate, to other applicable legal standards, including those which have their source in international law. In all cases it establishes the obligation to conform to the substantive and procedural rules of the laws concerned, but it also requires that any deprivation of liberty be compatible with the purpose of Article 5, namely, to protect the individual from arbitrariness. [...] where deprivation of liberty is concerned it is particularly important that the general principle of legal certainty be satisfied. It is therefore essential that the conditions for deprivation of liberty *under domestic and/or international law* be clearly defined and the law itself be foreseeable in its application, *so that it meets the standard of 'lawfulness' set by the Convention*, a standard which requires that all law be sufficiently precise to avoid all risk of arbitrariness and to allow a citizen – if need be, with appropriate advice – to foresee, to a degree that is reasonable in the circumstances of the case, the consequences which a given action may entail."[206]

Moreover, in practice, detention on the basis of the statutes of international courts and tribunals, or on the basis of the Geneva Conventions in situations of international armed conflict or occupation, has never been challenged on grounds that these treaties did not provide a valid *legal basis* for depriving a person of his or her liberty.[207]

In the case of the Geneva Conventions, where the detaining power by definition will be a State or a State-like entity, this is without prejudice to the fact that in certain countries a domestic legal basis will be required for the deprivation of liberty to be lawful in the domestic legal order.[208] The requirement

---

[206] ECtHR (Grand Chamber), *Medvedyev* (2010), §§79-81 (emphasis added). *In casu* the French authorities claimed to rely both on domestic and on international law (i.e. the United Nations Convention on the Law of the Sea (1982), hereinafter UNCLOS) to detain the ship's crew. The Court examined whether there was a valid legal basis for their detention *either* in French law *or* international law, focusing essentially on whether the legal bases invoked satisfied the requirement of "foreseeability" (i.e. whether the ship's crew could have foreseen their detention on the basis of the law). After discarding the applicability of the French law, the Court examined the international legal basis put forward by France: in the absence of application of the relevant treaties between France and Cambodia (the flag State of the ship), the French government relied upon a diplomatic note in which Cambodia authorized France to "intercept, inspect and take legal action against" the ship concerned. The Court found that the diplomatic note could indeed be of source of international law but that it was in any case not sufficiently precise, since it granted a power only to "intercept, inspect and take legal action against" the ship and did not specifically prescribe the detention of its crew.

[207] In the little case law of human rights bodies on internment in international armed conflict or occupation, both States and the human rights bodies themselves implicitly acknowledged that the Geneva Conventions were the legal basis for such internment. See e.g. EC°HR, *Cyprus v. Turkey* (1976); IAC°HR, *Coard v. USA* (1999); ICTY, *Delalic* (1998) and ICTY, *Delalic* (2001), cases that will be discussed in detail in Part II.

[208] For example, under UK law, the internment of prisoners of war and other persons that may pose a

of a domestic legal basis in such cases does not flow from international law but from domestic law and its relation with international law in a given domestic legal order.[209]

In conclusion, while the general rule seems to be that deprivation of liberty must have a legal basis in domestic law, some exceptions to this rule are generally accepted, at the very least as far as detention by international criminal courts and tribunals and – of specific interest to our research – internment in situations of international armed conflict or occupation are concerned.

(b.2). A legal basis for deprivation liberty in other sources of international law?

In Part III we will have to address the question of whether a legal basis for internment in non-international armed conflict can be found in customary international humanitarian law. This specific question triggers a more general one, which must be examined here: can the legal basis for deprivation of liberty be found in customary law *tout court*?

We have seen above that in common law systems, a common law rule that possesses the basic qualities of a "law" imposing restrictions on the enjoyment or exercise of fundamental rights and freedoms may qualify as a legal basis for deprivation of liberty. The provisions of international human rights treaties have thus been interpreted to accommodate the specificities of common law legal systems. It is submitted that these provisions can be similarly interpreted to accommodate the sources of law specific to the international legal system, such as custom,[210] which is made up of binding legal rules of general application. If such a customary rule possesses the basic qualities of a "law", it should be able to qualify as a valid legal basis for deprivation of liberty. The question is nevertheless a hypothetical one so far, as there are no examples of such a legal basis in international customary law.[211] The only approximate example we have

threat requiring their internment within UK territory will require a domestic legal basis (the GC are not as such part of English law, only those provisions that are formally incorporated into national legislation are). Under UK common law, prisoners of war can be interned on the basis of royal prerogative (i.e. executive order). Persons other than prisoners of war may however be deprived of their liberty on the basis of statutory law alone. During the 1990-1 Gulf War, a number of foreign nationals residing in the UK were therefore interned on the basis of the 1971 Immigration Act rather than directly on the basis of GC IV (internment during World Wars I and II was based on especially adopted emergency legislation). The requirement of a statutory legal basis to intern such persons does not seem to apply extraterritorially though. See Risius, "Prisoners of War in the United Kingdom" in Rowe, *The Gulf War 1990-91 in International and English Law* (1993), pp. 293-295; and Walsh, "Detention and Deportation of Foreign Nationals in the United Kingdom during the Gulf Conflict" in Rowe (1993), pp. 304-319.

209 Thus, as far as international law is concerned, the UK could have interned both prisoners of war and other persons posing a threat during the 1990-1 Gulf War (*cf. supra* note 208) directly on the basis of the Geneva Conventions.

210 E.g. article 38§1(b) of the Statute of the International Court of Justice (1945) (ICJ Statute); Brownlie (1998), pp. 4-11; Harris, *Cases and Materials on International Law* (1998), pp. 23-44, Nguyen, Daillier & Pellet, *Droit international public* (1999), pp. 317-343.

211 The Geneva Conventions being part of customary international law, one could wonder whether internment could be based on the basis of the customary equivalent of the legal bases in the Conventions. The question has never arisen since all States are parties to the Geneva Conventions and

found is that of the ECtHR's judgment in the case of *Drozd and Janousek v. France and Spain*. In that case, the European Court considered a regional customary rule dating back to the Middle Ages – allowing for persons lawfully sentenced to imprisonment in Andorra courts to be detained in France – to have "*sufficient stability and legal force to serve as a basis for the litigious detention*."[212] Nevertheless, the customary international law norm only provided a legal basis to *enforce* in France a deprivation of liberty that had itself a legal basis in domestic law in Andorra.

International legal instruments that are legally binding, and possess the basic qualities required of a "law" to satisfy the principle of legality, cannot therefore be automatically excluded from constituting a potentially valid legal basis for depriving a person of his or her liberty.[213]

One may wonder whether a legal basis to deprive persons of their liberty could exist in other international legal instruments than treaties and custom. We will discuss the question of whether a UN Security Council resolution can serve as a valid legal basis for deprivation of liberty in chapter III-1, but generally any "law" relied upon to deprive a person of his or her liberty may satisfy the principle of formal legality if it is legally binding in the legal order in which it is applied, is of general applicability, and possesses the basic qualities required of a "law" restricting the enjoyment or exercise of fundamental rights and freedoms.

In order to satisfy the principle of legality, a legal basis in customary international law or in other sources of international law will thus have to establish the grounds and procedures in accordance with which deprivation of liberty can be ordered in a manner that is at least as precise as the relevant provisions of the Geneva Conventions and the Statute of the ICC referred to above. Moreover, apart from the principle of formal legality and the principle of legitimacy, the legal basis must also satisfy the other requirements for lawful deprivation of liberty under international human rights law (*cf. supra* section 1.2.1).

can thus rely on its treaty legal bases to intern in situations of international armed conflict and occupation. The only State that has rejected the *de jure* applicability of the GC to such a situation, namely Israel (*cf. infra* note 477), has never claimed or relied upon any legal basis in customary IHL to intern persons who pose a threat, but has relied on domestic legislation to intern them (*cf. infra* Part II).

212 ECtHR, *Drozd and Janousek* (1992), §107 (emphasis added).

213 In the same sense, see Brunnee & Toope, "The Responsibility to Protect and the Use of Force: Building Legality?" (*GRP* 2009), p. 2 of the online version: "legal norms are social norms and as such they are connected to social practice – they must be grounded in shared understandings [but] what distinguishes law from other types of social ordering is not so much form or pedigree, as adherence to specific criteria of legality: generality, promulgation, non-retroactivity, clarity, non-contradiction, not asking the impossible, constancy, and congruence between rules and official action. When norm creation meets these criteria and, third, is matched with norm application that also satisfies the legality requirements, international law will have legitimacy and generate a sense of commitment among those to whom it is addressed."

1.2.4. The principle of legitimacy: the requirement of lawful grounds for deprivation of liberty

The second limb of the principle of legality of restrictions on fundamental rights and freedoms requires that such restrictions only be imposed in the general and legitimate interests of the community and that they are not arbitrary. Lawful grounds for detention or internment are grounds that serve a purpose that is generally accepted by the international community as a legitimate purpose for deprivation of liberty.[214] The international community has defined these legitimate purposes for depriving an individual of his or her liberty in international law.

The European Convention on Human Rights is the only treaty to list these grounds explicitly.[215] Article 5§1 of the Convention states that:

"No one shall be deprived of his liberty save in the following cases [...]:

(a) the lawful detention of a person after conviction by a competent court;

(b) the lawful arrest or detention of a person for non-compliance with the lawful order of a court or in order to secure the fulfilment of any obligation prescribed by law;

(c) the lawful arrest or detention of a person effected for the purpose of bringing him before the competent legal authority on reasonable suspicion of having committed an offence or when it is reasonably considered necessary to prevent his committing an offence or fleeing after having done so;

(d) the detention of a minor by lawful order for the purpose of educational supervision or his lawful detention for the purpose of bringing him before the competent legal authority;

(e) the lawful detention of persons for the prevention of the spreading of infectious diseases, of persons of unsound mind, alcoholics or drug addicts or vagrants;

(f) the lawful arrest or detention of a person to prevent his effecting an unauthorised entry into the country or of a person against whom action is being taken with a view to deportation or extradition."[216]

The list is exhaustive and the grounds therein must be interpreted narrowly:

---

214 The principle of legitimacy refers back directly to the common values of the international society in which the international legal system operates (*cf. supra* Introduction). In the same sense, see Abi-Saab in Wolfrum & Röben (2008), pp. 115-116: "Professor Frowein considers that 'legitimacy … refers not to the lawfulness in the strict sense, but to a higher justification of what is being done by lawful means.' Thus, legitimacy lies at one remove, upstream, from legality, and explains is anchorage or rooting in society. It is not an alternative that can replace legality."

215 Except for the less relied upon CIS Convention, which mirrors to a large extent the provisions of the ECHR and article 5 of which lists the following as lawful grounds for deprivation of liberty: "the lawful detention of a person after conviction by a competent court; the lawful arrest or detention of a person; the lawful detention of a minor for the purpose of referring his case for investigation, sentencing or trial."

216 Article 1 Protocol 4 ECHR explicitly adds that "[n]o one shall be deprived of liberty merely on the ground of inability to fulfil a contractual obligation."

"Article 5 enshrines a fundamental human right, namely the protection of the individual against arbitrary interference by the State with his or her right to liberty. The text of Article 5 makes it clear that the guarantees it contains apply to 'everyone'. Sub-paragraphs (a) to (f) of Article 5§1 contain an exhaustive list of permissible grounds on which persons may be deprived of their liberty and no deprivation of liberty will be lawful unless it falls within one of those grounds";[217]

"The Court notes at the outset the fundamental importance of the guarantees contained in Article 5 for securing the right of individuals in a democracy to be free from arbitrary detention at the hands of the authorities. It is precisely for that reason that the Court has repeatedly stressed in its case-law that any deprivation of liberty must not only have been effected in conformity with the substantive and procedural rules of national law but must equally be in keeping with the very purpose of Article 5, namely to protect the individual from arbitrariness. This insistence on the protection of the individual against any abuse of power is illustrated by the fact that Article 5§1 circumscribes the circumstances in which individuals may be lawfully deprived of their liberty, it being stressed that these circumstances must be given a narrow interpretation having regard to the fact that they constitute exceptions to a most basic guarantee of individual freedom."[218]

The list in the European Convention was discussed by and has inspired the drafters of both the ICCPR and the American Convention on Human Rights,[219] but neither of these Conventions ultimately included an exhaustive list of grounds defining the legitimate purposes for depriving an individual of his or her liberty.[220] The initial discussion of draft article 9§1 ICCPR focused mainly on the grounds for deprivation of liberty and on whether a list like the one in the ECHR should be included in the article.[221] An early draft reproduced the list of the ECHR in almost identical terms, but during the drafting process States proposed to add a number of other grounds to it.[222] In light of the failure to

[217] ECtHR (Grand Chamber), *Al-Jedda v. the United Kingdom* (2011), §99; ECtHR (Grand Chamber), *A and Others v. UK* (2009), §§162-163, with references to ECtHR, *Aksoy v. Turkey* (1996), §76 and ECtHR (Grand Chamber), *Saadi v. Italy* (2008), § 43. See also CoE, *HRH No. 5* (2002), p. 12.

[218] ECtHR, *Kurt v. Turkey* (1998), §122, with references to ECtHR (Grand Chamber), *Chahal v. UK* (1996), §118 and (*mutatis mutandis*) ECtHR, *Quinn v. France* (1995), §42.

[219] The text of article 7 ACHR is largely identical to that of article 9 ICCPR. De Londras points out that "[i]n fact, the ACHR is substantially modelled on the ICCPR", referring to Harris & Livingstone, *The Inter-American System of Human Rights* (1998); see de Londras (*JCSL* 2007), p. 239, note 111.

[220] The drafters of the ECHR were heavily influenced by the provisions of the UDHR and instructed the drafting Committee to pay close attention to the discussions on the draft ICCPR that started as early as 1947. The United Kingdom insisted in both negotiation *fora* on the importance of including a list of exhaustive grounds of detention in the provisions on the right to liberty. Whereas it achieved this in the ECHR, it was ultimately unsuccessful in reaching the same result for the ICCPR. For an overview of the drafting history of article 5 ECHR, see European Commission of Human Rights, *Preparatory Work on Article 5 of the European Convention on Human Rights* (1956).

[221] For an overview of the debates with extensive quotes from various reports of the proceedings, see Bossuyt (1987), pp. 187-202. For a shorter summary, with references to the case law of the HRC and the WGAD, see also Nowak (2005), pp. 216-217, 223 and 225-228.

[222] For a summary, see Bossuyt (1987), pp. 190-191. For our purposes, it is appropriate to point out here that the US proposed to include "detention of enemy aliens" in the list of lawful grounds under the ICCPR

achieve agreement on an exhaustive list at the time, an Australian proposal to replace such a list with a general reminder that *arbitrary* detention is prohibited, found unanimous approval and solved the problem.[223]

The case law of the Human Rights Committee and the Working Group on Arbitrary Detention regarding article 9§1 ICCPR, and the case law of the Inter-American Commission and Court of Human Rights regarding article 7§1 ACHR demonstrate nevertheless that the list of permissible grounds in the ECHR largely reflects the legitimate purposes and permissible grounds under international law under which an authority may deprive a person of his or her liberty. They can be summarized as follows.

1.2.4.1. Legitimate purposes for restricting the right to liberty: lawful grounds[224]

(a.) Deprivation of liberty in the framework of criminal justice and law enforcement

First, in the framework of criminal justice and law enforcement,[225] the following grounds for deprivation of liberty are generally accepted to comply with international law:[226]

• Imprisonment following lawful conviction by a competent court for a criminal offence, for the duration of the sentence;[227]

---

and that China proposed to include the detention of "persons suspected as spies" (*Ibidem*, p. 190).

[223] For an overview of the debates with extensive quotes from various official reports on the proceedings, see Bossuyt (1987), pp. 187-202.

[224] Deprivation of liberty based on these grounds will of course only be lawful if it also meets the other criteria for lawful deprivation of liberty, namely the principle of legal certainty, the inclusion in the legal basis of the procedural safeguards prescribed by international human rights law, and the absence of any arbitrariness in the form, substance or implementation of that law *in casu*.

[225] Including military criminal justice, see for example ECtHR, *Engel and Others v. the Netherlands* (1976); ECtHR, *De Jong and Others v. the Netherlands* (1984); and ECtHR (Grand Chamber), *Hood v. UK* (1999).

[226] Bossuyt (1987), pp. 187-202; Nowak (2005), pp. 225-228 (with reference to relevant case law of the HRC and the WGAD); article 5§1(a), (c) and (f) ECHR; CoE, *HRH No. 5* (2002), pp. 22-40 (with reference to relevant case law of the ECtHR); IAC°HR; *Terrorism and Human Rights* (2002), pp. 89-92 (with reference to relevant case law of the IAC°HR and the IACtHR); article 5§1(a) and (b) of the CIS Convention. See also more generally, Doswald-Beck & Kolb, *Judicial Process and Human Rights: United Nations, European, American and African Systems: Texts and Summaries of International Case-Law* (2004), pp. 59-76 (with reference to relevant case law of the HRC, the ECtHR, the IAC°HR, the IACtHR and the AC°HPR); OHCHR, *Human Rights in the Administration of Justice. A Manual on Human Rights for Judges, Prosecutors and Lawyers* (2003), pp. 172-175 and 191-196; and Jayawickrama, *The Judicial Interpretation of Human Rights Law: National, Regional and International Jurisprudence* (2002) pp. 376-381, 385-396 and pp. 400-404 (with reference to both international and national case law).

[227] Imprisonment beyond the term of the prison sentence is unlawful, e.g.: HRC, *Massiotti v. Uruguay* (1982). Nevertheless, dangerous recidivists may continue to be detained – if the law provides for it – when they are so dangerous to the public as to justify their continued detention. Again, such detention may not go beyond the duration allowed by law; see for example: ECtHR, *M. v. Germany* (2009), §§94-101.

• Provisional detention for the purpose of bringing a person before a competent legal authority on reasonable suspicion of having committed a criminal offence or intending to commit one in the immediate future. Nevertheless, any deprivation of liberty on this ground must be based on reasonable suspicion of a specific offence,[228] which is actually established by the relevant criminal legislation (principle of legality).[229] Moreover, the purpose at the time of the deprivation of liberty must be the instigation of criminal proceedings, even if in the end no such proceedings are brought because the suspicion has been lifted or there is not enough evidence to substantiate the charges.[230] At this pre-trial stage there is no need to *prove* that an offence has actually been or was going to be committed, but the suspicion must still be of a certain quality in order to avoid arbitrary interference with the right to liberty. The threshold here is the "reasonableness" of the suspicion.[231] In light of the

---

[228] This ground cannot be relied upon to justify deprivation of liberty on the basis of a general suspicion of involvement in criminal activity or as a measure to prevent a person from engaging in criminal behaviour in general. E.g.: ECtHR, *Guzzardi v. Italy* (1980), §102; ECtHR, *Ciulla v. Italy* (1989), §40 and ECtHR, *M. v. Germany* (2009), §102. To be noted however that, in most jurisdictions, an attempt to commit a specific criminal offence constitutes an offence in itself.

[229] E.g.: ECtHR, *Lukanov v. Bulgaria* (1997), §43-45.

[230] The ECtHR has repeatedly pointed out that this follows from the plain and natural meaning of article 5 ECHR and the indissoluble link between the grounds enunciated in its §1(c) and the requirement in §3 to bring a person so detained promptly before an authority competent to exercise judicial power and initiate a trial. E.g.: ECtHR, *Lawless v. Ireland* (1961), §14, confirmed amongst others in ECtHR, *Engel and Others v. the Netherlands* (1976), §69; ECtHR, *Ireland v. UK* (1978), §196; ECtHR, *Jecius v. Lithuania* (2000) and ECtHR, *Denizci and Others v. Cyprus* (2001), where the Court established a violation because the actual purpose of deprivation of liberty was not linked to the instigation of criminal proceedings for a specific offence. On the other hand, where no proceedings followed but the Court was satisfied that the purpose of the arrest and detention at the time it occurred was to bring the persons before a competent legal authority as the initial phase of a criminal trial, the Court esteemed article 5 ECHR had not been violated (e.g.: ECtHR, *Brogan and Others v. UK* (1988), §53; ECtHR (Grand Chamber), *Murray v. UK* (1994), §§67-69). This interpretation is fully in line with the purpose of article 5, which is to protect the individual from arbitrary interference with his or her right to liberty. As the European Court has convincingly stated: "if the construction [...] were not correct, anyone suspected of harbouring an intent to commit and offence could be arrested and detained for an unlimited period on the strength merely of an executive decision without its being possible to regard his arrest or detention as a breach of the Convention; whereas such an assumption, with all its implications of arbitrary power, would lead to conclusions repugnant to the fundamental principles of the Convention" (ECtHR, *Lawless* (1961), §14). Therefore, the interpretation of the link between article 5§1 and 5§3 ECHR by the European Court also holds true for the link between article 9§1 and 9§3 ICCPR, article 7§2 and 7§5 ACHR and article 5§1 and 5§3 CIS Convention.

[231] For the meaning of "reasonable suspicion", see for example ECtHR, *Fox, Campbell & Hartley v. UK* (1990), §§32-34: "having a 'reasonable suspicion' presupposes the existence of facts or information which would satisfy an objective observer that the person concerned may have committed the offence. What may be regarded as 'reasonable' will however depend upon all the circumstances. [...] As the Government pointed out, in view of the difficulties inherent in the investigation and prosecution of terrorist-type offences in Northern Ireland, the 'reasonableness' of the suspicion justifying such arrests cannot always be judged according to the same standards as are applied in dealing with conventional crime. Nevertheless, the exigencies of dealing with terrorist crime cannot justify stretching the notion of 'reasonableness' to the point where the essence of the safeguard secured by Article 5 § 1 (c) (art. 5-1-c) is impaired". See also Sir Baker, a retired member of the English judiciary, quoted by the Court in §19: "where the requirement is reasonable suspicion

general presumption of liberty, provisional detention must remain the exception and can only be ordered where it is necessary to prevent an impending crime or to bring its perpetrator to justice.[232]

• Provisional detention for the purpose of preventing flight, interference with the course of justice, or recidivism. Elements of necessity and proportionality in the specific circumstances of each case are of crucial importance to assess any risk of arbitrariness. Moreover, the length of such provisional detention must not be excessive and the possibility of release pending trial must be properly considered;

• Provisional detention pursuant to a lawful request for extradition to another country – as long as the detention is necessary and proportional, and only if the extradition proceedings are conducted with the requisite diligence.

(b.) Administrative detention

While administrative detention should remain exceptional, a number of grounds for such a deprivation of liberty are generally considered to be lawful. As long as the grounds and procedures for such detention are prescribed by law and the other criteria for lawful deprivation of liberty (especially the necessity and proportionality requirements) are met,[233] the following are deemed legitimate purposes that may justify administrative detention:[234]

[as opposed to mere 'suspicion' which is a subjective standard and refers to the personal opinion of the arrestor or detaining authority] it is for the court to judge the reasonableness of the suspicion. It is an objective standard. The facts which raise the suspicion may be looked at by the court to see if they are capable of constituting reasonable cause. Reasonable suspicion is itself a lower standard than evidence necessary to prove a prima facie case. Hearsay may justify reasonable suspicion but may be insufficient for a charge." In the same sense: OHCHR, *Manual* (2003), p. 174.

[232] E.g.: Article 6§1 of the United Nations *Standard Minimum Rules for Non-Custodial Measures* (1990) (also referred to as the "*Tokyo Rules*"): "Pre-trial detention shall be used as a means of last resort in criminal proceedings, with due regard for the investigation of the alleged offence and for the protection of society and the victim." For a concrete and recent example of this rule in practice, see Special Tribunal for Lebanon (STL), *Order on Pre-Trial Detention* (2009), §22 and 33 (footnotes omitted): "Firstly, provisional detention is an exceptional measure, which is only warranted where it proves strictly necessary and under the circumstances set out in the Rules [of Procedure and Evidence of the Tribunal]. [...] it should first be established [...] whether the person is suspected or accused of a crime within the jurisdiction of the Tribunal. Indeed, as the European Court of Human Rights has emphasized '[t]he persistence of reasonable suspicion that the person arrested has committed an offence is a condition sine qua non for the validity of the continued detention'. If that condition is not met, reviewing the other conditions for provisional detention [...] becomes superfluous."

[233] With regard to the ECtHR's position on the requirement of an element of necessity and proportionality (apart from the duration of the detention) for administrative detention under article 5§1(f) ECHR, *cf. supra* notes 60 and 96.

[234] With regard to the ICCPR, see Bossuyt (1987), pp. 187-202; Nowak (2005), pp. 225-228 (with reference to relevant case law of the HRC and the WGAD). With regard to the ECHR, see article 5§1(b), (d), (e) and (f) ECHR; and CoE, *HRH No. 5* (2002), pp. 41-45. With regard to the ADRDM and ACHR, see IAC°HR; *Terrorism and Human Rights* (2002), pp. 89-92 (with reference to relevant case law of the IAC°HR and the IACtHR). See also article 5§1(a) and (b) of the CIS Convention; and article 31§2 UN Refugee Convention. More generally, see Doswald-Beck & Kolb (2004), pp. 59-76 (with reference to relevant case law of the HRC, the ECtHR, the IAC°HR, the IACtHR and the AC°HPR); OHCHR, *Manual* (2003), pp. 173-181; and Jayawickrama (2002) pp. 376-381, 385-396 and pp. 400-404 (with reference to both international and national case law).

• Deprivation of liberty to ensure compliance with the lawful order of a court, or to secure the fulfilment of an obligation prescribed by law.[235] It should be noted that the latter ground cannot be invoked to justify an administrative detention ordered to compel a person to discharge his or general obligation to abide by the law or for the mere purpose of deterrence; the deprivation of liberty in this case must be based on a specific or concrete obligation, such as mandatory military service;[236]

• Reasons of public and mental health may justify the administrative detention of persons of unsound mind, alcoholics, drug addicts or vagrants, or in order to prevent the spread of infectious diseases;

• Deprivation of liberty of minors for the purpose of educational supervision or for the purpose of bringing them before a court in order to secure their removal from a harmful environment;

• Deprivation of liberty for purposes of preventing a person from effecting an unauthorized entry into the country; or for the purposes of lawful deportation, as long as the deportation proceedings are pursued with the required diligence and the deportation can realistically be expected to take place in the near future;[237]

---

[235] These grounds will only be lawful when the fulfilment of the obligation or the compliance with the court order is immediately necessary and when in the specific circumstances of the case there are no alternative means to ensure compliance with the court order or fulfilment of the legal obligation at stake. The duration of the deprivation of liberty will also be taken into account when assessing its potentially arbitrary character.

[236] E.g.: ECtHR, *Engel and Others v. the Netherlands* (1976); ECtHR, *Ciulla v. Italy* (1989).

[237] The UNHCR's Executive Committee, in its *Conclusion No. 7* (1977), §e found that "an expulsion order should only be combined with custody or detention if absolutely necessary for reasons of national security or public order and that such detention should not be unduly prolonged." In the same sense, see also WGAD, *Opinion No. 45/2006* (2006): "due to the lack of prospect for the removal to Somalia, [the applicant's] detention has assumed the character of indefinite detention. Such indefinite detention can only be qualified as 'arbitrary' within the meaning of article 9, paragraph 1 of ICCPR"; WGAD, *Annual Report 2007*, §§51-53: "it is necessary to remind all States that illegal immigrants placed in administrative detention are not criminals or suspects. Therefore, detention must be the exception, not the rule. The Working Group considers that taking aliens into custody without a legal basis is totally unjustifiable and amounts to arbitrary detention"; ECtHR (Grand Chamber), *A and others v. UK* (2009), §§ 162-164: "Article 5§1(f) does not demand that detention be reasonably considered necessary, for example to prevent the individual from committing an offence or fleeing. Any deprivation of liberty under the second limb of Article 5 § 1(f) will be justified, however, only for as long as deportation or extradition proceedings are in progress. If such proceedings are not prosecuted with due diligence, the detention will cease to be permissible under Article 5 § 1(f)"; and *IAC°HR, Terrorism and Human Rights* (2002), pp. 90 and 91 (with reference to relevant case law of the IAC°HR and the IACtHR). The UK High Court of Justice (HCJ) recently ruled that detention pending deportation was only justified to lawfully remove an individual from the UK and not to ensure further detention in the receiving country. The Court ruled that the latter detention would be unlawful (UK, HCJ, *H.X.A.* (2010), §§47-78). In a similar case, the WGAD found that "[r]epresentatives of the Yemeni authorities [held] that the reason for their detention is that their transfer from United States detention was conditional upon them being held in Yemen. [...] No charges have been made by the Government of Yemen against these three men. They have not been informed of any accusation against them, nor have been brought before any judicial authority. No legal procedure has been followed to accuse them. Their deprivation of liberty is, as such, devoid of any legal basis" (WGAD, *Opinion No. 47/2005* (2005), §§12 and 20). For a good general analysis of detention for deportation purposes, see Goodwin-Gill in Feller, Türk & Nicholson (2003), pp. 220-233.

1.2.4.2. Illegitimate purposes for restricting the right to liberty: unlawful grounds

Based on treaty provisions and international case law it is also possible to list grounds generally considered *not* to be lawful for deprivation of liberty, either because they do not serve a purpose that is legitimate in the eyes of the international community for restricting a person's liberty, because they nullify the presumption of liberty, or because they otherwise involve too much of a risk of arbitrariness. They include at least:

• Deprivation of liberty on grounds of inability to fulfil a contractual obligation;[238]

• Deprivation of liberty resulting from the lawful exercise of the freedom of opinion and expression, freedom of thought, conscience and religion, freedom of peaceful assembly and association, freedom of movement, the right to participate in the administration and government of one's country, the right to equality before the law without any discrimination, the right to seek and enjoy asylum from persecution and the specific rights of minority groups;[239]

And of specific interest for our research:

• Deprivation of liberty for the mere purpose of information gathering. Obviously, interrogation often occurs when persons are deprived of liberty, and forms part of normal procedures to conduct a criminal investigation into a suspected offence.[240] By itself however, interrogation without a nexus to a specific offence or threat does not constitute a lawful ground for deprivation of liberty;[241]

---

[238] Article 11 ICCPR; article 1 Protocol 4 ECHR; article 25§2 ADRDM; article 7§7 ACHR; article 18 Arab Charter; and article 8 CIS Convention. Under the ICCPR and the Arab Charter this is a non-derogable right.

[239] E.g.: WGAD, *Factsheet No. 26*, category II of arbitrary detention; HRC, *Jaona v. Madagascar* (1982); HRC, *Ngalula Mpandanjila v. Zaire* (1986), §8(2) and §9: "eight former Zairian parliamentarians and one Zairian businessman [...] were subjected to measures of arrest, banishment or house arrest on account of the publication of an 'open letter' to Zairian President Mobutu. [...] these facts disclose violations of [article 9§1 ICCPR], because the authors were subjected to arbitrary arrest and detention"; HRC, *Mukong v. Cameroon* (1994), §9(7): "The State party has indirectly justified its actions on grounds of national security and/or public order, by arguing that the author's right to freedom of expression was exercised without regard to the country's political context and continued struggle for unity. While the State party has indicated that the restrictions on the author's freedom of expression were provided for by law, it must still be determined whether the measures taken against the author were necessary for the safeguard of national security and/or public order. The Committee considers that it was not necessary to safeguard an alleged vulnerable state of national unity by subjecting the author to arrest, continued detention [...]. It further considers that the legitimate objective of safeguarding and indeed strengthening national unity under difficult political circumstances cannot be achieved by attempting to muzzle advocacy of multi-party democracy, democratic tenets and human rights; in this regard, the question of deciding which measures might meet the 'necessity' test in such situations does not arise"; AC°HPR, *Constitutional Rights Project et al. v. Nigeria* (1999), §51: "To detain persons on account of their political beliefs, especially where no charges are brought against them renders the deprivation of liberty arbitrary"; and AC°HPR, *Jawara v. Gambia* (2000), §65: "The intimidation and arrest or detention of journalists for articles published and questions asked deprives not only the journalists of their rights to freely express and disseminate their opinions, but also the public, of the right to information." For confirmation of this rule in international humanitarian law for situations of armed conflict, *cf. infra* Part II.

[240] Deprivation of liberty however will have to be based on a reasonable suspicion of having committed

• Kidnapping[242] and any form of deprivation of liberty for the sole reason of obtaining an advantage or concession from a third party. The latter would amount to hostage- taking, prohibited under general international law and a crime under both domestic and international law.[243] Hostage-taking is also

---

or being about to commit a specific offence (*cf. supra*); mere interrogation to find out whether the detainee or others about whom he or she may have information, may have committed or plan to commit any criminal offences will not be sufficient. See for example ECtHR, *Brogan and Others v. UK* (1988), §§49-53, the Dissenting Opinion of Judge Pinheiro Farinha at §3, and the Dissenting Opinion of Judges Walsh and Carrillo Salcedo at §§4-5 and 7; see also ECtHR, *Fox, Campbell and Hartley v. UK* (1990), §§19, 32 and 34 and the Joint Dissenting Opinion of Judges Sir Vincent Evans, Bernhardt and Palm; and ECtHR (Grand Chamber), *Murray v. UK* (1994), §§ 50-69, the Joint Dissenting Opinion of Judges Loizou, Morenilla and Makarczyk, and the Partly Dissenting Opinion of Judge Jambrek.

[241] E.g.: HRC, *Monguya Mbenge et al. v. Zaire* (1977), §20: "Oyabi [...] was arrested on 1 September 1977 in order to force him to disclose the whereabouts of Simon Biyanga and [...] was not released from detention until late in 1978 or early in 1979. The State party has not claimed that there was any criminal charge against him. In the view of the Committee, therefore, he was subject to arbitrary arrest and detention contrary to article 9 [ICCPR]"; see also WGAD, *Annual Report 2005*, §§53-59, *Annual Report 2006*, §§ 30-59, *Annual Report 2007*, §§59-68, and the individual cases referred to in these reports (with regard to the system of extra-ordinary renditions practiced under the surveillance of US agents, where most detainees were held and transferred around for the mere purpose of interrogation, the Working Group held that in general there was no legal basis for the deprivation of liberty of these persons which therefore was arbitrary and unlawful). The ECtHR, in *Ireland v. UK* (1978), §196, has found that when "arrest had merely to be 'for the preservation of the peace and maintenance of order' and was sometimes used to interrogate the person concerned about the activities of others [...] Irrespective of whether extrajudicial deprivation of liberty was or was not founded in the majority of cases on suspicions of a kind that would render detention on remand justifiable under the Convention, such detention is permissible under Article [5§1 ECHR] only if it is 'effected for the purpose of bringing [the detainee] before the competent legal authority'." The US Supreme Court, in *Hamdi* (2004), at p. 521 found that "certainly we agree that indefinite detention for the purpose of interrogation is not authorized." See also the UN Special Rapporteur to the Human Rights Council on Counterterrorism (Mr. Martin Scheinin), *Compilation of Good Practices on Legal and Institutional Frameworks and Measures that Ensure Respect for Human Rights by Intelligence Agencies while Countering Terrorism, Including on their Oversight* (2010), good practice 29: "If intelligence services possess powers of arrest and detention they comply with international human rights standards on the rights to liberty." As to the prohibition of internment in armed conflict for mere interrogation purposes, *cf. infra* Part II.

[242] E.g.: HRC, *Lopez Burgos v. Uruguay* (1981), §13; HRC, *Celeberti v. Uruguay* (1981), §11; HRC, *Domukovsky and Others v. Georgia* (1998), §18.2; IACtHR, *Velásquez Rodríguez v. Honduras* (1988), §155; IACtHR, *Godínez Cruz v. Honduras* (1989), §163.

[243] The WGAD has qualified hostage-taking as "undoubtedly a particularly serious form of arbitrary deprivation of liberty." (WGAD, *Annual Report 2004*, §66). The International Convention against the Taking of Hostages (1979) (hereinafter "Hostages Convention"), considers "that the taking of hostages is an offence of grave concern to the international community, and that, in accordance with the provisions of this convention, any person committing an act of hostage taking shall either be prosecuted or extradited", and defines hostage-taking as follows: "[a]ny person who seizes or detains and threatens to kill, to injure or to continue to detain another person (hereinafter referred to as the 'hostage') in order to compel a third party, namely, a State, an international intergovernmental organization, a natural or judicial person, or a group of persons, to do or abstain from doing any act as an explicit or implicit condition for the release of the hostage commits the offence of taking of hostages ('hostage-taking') within the meaning of the Convention. Any person who (a) attempts to commit an act of hostage-taking, or (b) participates as an accomplice of anyone who commits or attempts to commit an act of hostage-taking likewise commits an offence for the purposes of this Convention" (citations from preambular paragraph 4 and article 1 of Convention. The Hostages Convention does not apply in times of armed conflict, since the crime of hostage-taking is already prescribed by the Geneva Conventions and their Additional Protocols (article 12).

explicitly prohibited by international humanitarian law and when committed in armed conflict constitutes a war crime;[244]

• Administrative detention as an alternative to criminal proceedings and thus of a punitive rather than a preventive nature.[245]

Under the ECHR regime, administrative detention of persons who pose a threat to national security is prohibited unless article 5§1 ECHR is lawfully derogated from.[246] The Human Rights Committee has emphasized that should administrative detention be used for reasons of public order and security it must meet all the standards inherent to the right to liberty and the prohibition of arbitrary detention.[247] But it is unclear whether the Committee would find

---

[244] Articles 34 and 147 GC IV; article 75§2(c) AP I; common article 3§1(b) GC; article 4§2(c) AP II; Rule 96 of the ICRC's compilation of customary IHL (Henckaerts & Doswald-Beck (2005), Vol. I, 334-336); article 8§2(a)(viii) and (c)(iii) ICC Statute. None of these treaties defines the word hostage-taking, but Pictet explains that "[t]he modern form, with which this Article is concerned, is the taking of hostages as a means of intimidating the population in order to weaken its spirit of resistance and to prevent breaches of the law and sabotage in order to ensure the security of the Detaining Power" (Pictet, *Commentary GC IV* (1958), p. 230) and that "[t]he taking of hostages is contrary to the modern idea of justice in that it is based on the principle of collective responsibility for crime and strikes at persons who are innocent of the crime which it is intended to prevent or punish" (Pictet, *Commentary GC III* (1960), p. 39). As to its definition as a war crime, the ICC has taken over the definition of the International Hostage Convention and has added that the required act of the third party can also be a condition for the *safety* of the hostage. See also Dörmann (2003), pp. 124-127 and pp. 406-407. The prohibition of hostage-taking applies to all persons, civilians and combatants alike (Henckaerts & Doswald-Beck (2005), Volume I, p. 336 (Rule 96). For a good overview of other treaties and instruments laying down the absolute prohibition of hostage-taking and its status as an international crime, see Henckaerts & Doswald-Beck (2005), Volume I, pp. 334-336 and the State practice referred to in Volume II, pp. 2262-2285 and in the updated *CIHL Database* (2010). For the specific issue of internment ordered for the sole purpose of prisoners-exchange or other negotiations in situations of armed conflict, *cf. infra* chapter II-3.

[245] E.g.: IAC°HR, *Morales Zegarra et al. v. Peru* (1999), §62; Pejic (*IRRC* 2005), p. 381; and *infra* chapter II-3.

[246] E.g.: ECtHR (Grand Chamber), *A and Others v. UK* (2009), §171: "It is, instead, clear from the terms of the derogation notice and Part 4 of the 2001 Act that the applicants were certified and detained because they were suspected of being international terrorists and because it was believed that their presence at liberty in the United Kingdom gave rise to a threat to national security. The Court does not accept the Government's argument that Article 5§1 permits a balance to be struck between the individual's right to liberty and the State's interest in protecting its population from terrorist threat. This argument is inconsistent not only with the Court's jurisprudence under sub-paragraph (f) but also with the principle that paragraphs (a) to (f) amount to an exhaustive list of exceptions and that only a narrow interpretation of these exceptions is compatible with the aims of Article 5. If detention does not fit within the confines of the paragraphs as interpreted by the Court, it cannot be made to fit by an appeal to the need to balance the interests of the State against those of the detainee." See also CoE, *HRH No. 5* (2002), p. 32-33; and UK, HoL, *Al-Jedda* (2007), where Lord Bingham held that internment for security reasons in armed conflict would infringe article 5§1 ECHR in the absence of an exonerating condition, namely either a lawful derogation, or a displacement of 5§1ECHR by a lawful UN Security Council Resolution (§§38-39); and where Lord Carswell added that in such cases the necessity standard in article 5 ECHR should be the same one as that in article 42 and 78 GC IV (§132). On the *Al-Jedda* case, *cf.* also *infra* chapter II-4. See also UK, HCJ, *H.X.A.* (2010), §6: "[i]t is common ground that these exceptions do not include and hence article 5 does not permit internment on security grounds." On the conditions for lawful derogation from the right to liberty, *cf. infra* chapter I-2.

[247] HRC, *General Comment No. 8* (1982), §4: if so-called preventive detention is used, for reasons of public security, it must be controlled by these same provisions, i.e. it must not be arbitrary, and must be based on grounds and procedures established by law (para. 1), information of the reasons must be

administrative detention for reasons of national security that would comply with the safeguards in article 9 ICCPR to be lawful without derogation.[248] It is interesting to note in this sense that the Working Group on Arbitrary Detention has found that administrative detention for preventive purposes of suspected terrorists will be arbitrary unless the detaining power has lawfully derogated from article 9§1 ICCPR.[249] In the same sense, Manfred Nowak, in his Commentary of the ICCPR, finds that "preventive detention of persons beyond the limits permitted by article 5(1) ECHR" would be arbitrary before endorsing the position of the Working Group on Arbitrary Detention.[250] The Inter-American Commission on Human Rights seems to share that opinion.[251]

1.2.4.3. Military necessity: an additional legitimate purpose for restricting the right to liberty in situations of armed conflict

In a background document for an expert meeting on detention in armed conflict, Doswald-Beck wrote that:

> "[h]umanitarian law aims at preventing arbitrary detention by two main means: [by] [p]roviding for permissible grounds of detention based on military necessity [and by] [p]roviding for some supervision of the fact of detention."[252]

International humanitarian law indeed allows for further permissible grounds for administrative detention – or internment, the term of art for such deprivation of liberty in situations of armed conflict – inspired by the concept of military necessity. Doswald-Beck went on to point out that these grounds are:

> "determined by international law and [...] have been chosen by custom and the drafters of the Geneva Conventions on the basis of what is necessary. Conversely what is unnecessary is not or no longer allowed. The major grounds are: a. Prisoners of war: the *categories* of persons that are POWs are carefully defined; and *length of detention* limited to what is really necessary. Both the types of persons chosen and the time of detention allowed are based on *reasonableness* i.e. because the persons are still a potential threat if they join their army again. b. Civilian detainees: the *categories* are aliens in enemy territory and

given (para. 2) and court control of the detention must be available (para. 4) as well as compensation in the case of a breach (para. 5). And if, in addition, criminal charges are brought in such cases, the full protection of article 9 (2) and (3), as well as article 14, must also be granted."

248 In *Cámpora Schweizer v. Uruguay* (1982), §18(1), the Committee found that: "[a]lthough administrative detention may not be objectionable in circumstances where the person concerned constitutes a clear and serious threat to society which cannot be contained in any other manner, the Committee emphasizes that the guarantees enshrined in the following paragraphs of article 9 fully apply in such instances."

249 WGAD, *Annual Report 2002*, §§61-64.

250 Nowak (2005), p. 226.

251 IAC°HR, *Terrorism and Human Rights* (2002), §§124-126.

252 Doswald-Beck, "Background Paper" in *Report of the Expert Meeting on the Supervision of Lawfulness of Detention* (2004), p. 2. She also pointed out that it is the 2nd set of protections (procedural safeguards) that is the "major weakness of the system [...] as the provisions [in IHL] are not as stringent as human rights law" (*Ibidem*) . Doswald-Beck thus seems to suggest – and we agree – that the grounds for internment in international armed conflict and occupation as prescribed by international humanitarian law do not, or at least not to the same extent, present the same problem. We will come back to this argument and the grounds for internment in armed conflict below in Part II.

civilians in occupied territory. The *grounds, including length of detention*, are respectively 'if the security of the Detaining Power makes it absolutely necessary' and 'for imperative reasons of security'."[253]

Much of this book will be devoted to clarifying these grounds, in order to answer the questions of who can be interned, for what reasons and for how long on the basis of international humanitarian law. Whether or not a State needs to derogate from its obligations under international human rights law to rely on these grounds will be discussed below in chapter I-2, section 2.2.2.2.

1.2.5. Conclusions

In order to satisfy the principle of legality, it is not sufficient that detention or internment be in conformity with the domestic law of the detaining or interning State. Restrictions of fundamental rights and freedoms such as the right to liberty must conform to the general principle of legality as understood in international law. In this sense, the European Court has held that:

> "Where the 'lawfulness' of detention is in issue, including the question whether 'a procedure prescribed by law' has been followed, the Convention refers essentially to national law and lays down the obligation to conform to the substantive and procedural rules of national law. *Compliance with national law is not, however, sufficient*: Article 5§1 requires in addition that any deprivation of liberty *should be in keeping with the purpose of protecting the individual from arbitrariness*. It is *a fundamental principle* that no detention which is arbitrary can be compatible with Article 5 § 1 and *the notion of 'arbitrariness' in Article 5 § 1 extends beyond lack of conformity with national law, so that a deprivation of liberty may be lawful in terms of domestic law but still arbitrary and thus contrary to the Convention.*"[254]

Similarly, the African Commission on Human and Peoples' Rights has found that:

> "The Military government has not refuted the allegations of arbitrary arrests and detentions, but has defended its position by stating that, its action must be 'studied and placed in the context of the changed circumstances in The Gambia'. It also claims that it is acting within the confines of legislation 'previously laid down by law', as required by the wordings of Article 6 of the Charter. The Commission in its decision on communication 101/93 laid down a general principle with respect to freedom of association that 'competent authorities should not enact provisions which limit the exercise of this freedom. The competent authorities should not override constitutional provisions or undermine fundamental rights guaranteed by the constitution or international human rights standards'. This principle therefore applies not only to freedom of association but also to all other rights and freedoms. For a State to avail itself of this plea, it must show that such a law is consistent with its obligations under the [African] Charter [on Human and Peoples' Rights]. The Commission finds the arrests and

---

[253] *Ibidem* (original emphasis).

[254] ECtHR (Grand Chamber), *A and Others v. UK* (2009); §164, with reference to ECtHR (Grand Chamber), *Saadi v. UK* (2008), §67 (emphasis added). See also CoE, *HRH No. 5* (2002), pp. 9-17.

incommunicado detention of the aforementioned persons inconsistent with Gambia's obligations under the Charter. They constitute arbitrary deprivation of their liberty and thus a violation of Article 6 of the Charter. Decree No. 3 is, therefore, contrary to the spirit of Article 6."[255]

In order to satisfy the principle of legality as understood in international law, the legal basis for any deprivation of liberty, regardless of its form and whether it is found in domestic or in international law, must possess the basic qualities of "law", necessary to achieve the purpose of avoiding arbitrary or abusive exercise of powers of arrest and detention by the detaining or interning authorities. Apart from being legally binding in the legal order in which it is applied, the law must be accessible, prescribe the grounds and procedures in accordance with which deprivation of liberty can be ordered in a manner that is sufficiently precise to allow individuals concerned to foresee the behaviour that may trigger the deprivation of liberty, and offer adequate protection against arbitrary deprivation of liberty.

Moreover, for the grounds of detention or internment to be lawful under international law they must not only be prescribed by law and sufficiently precise to allow predictability, they must also serve a legitimate purpose recognized as such under international law. The legal grounds invoked for any given detention or internment must indeed reflect the real purpose of that specific deprivation of liberty[256] and must exist both at the time of the initial deprivation of liberty and throughout its entire duration.[257] Finally, the reasons for detaining or interning a person must be necessary and proportionate to achieve the purpose for which the deprivation of liberty is ordered.[258]

[255] AC°HRP, *Jawara v. Gambia* (2000), §§58-59 (Decree No. 3 was adopted shortly after a military coup that took place on 22 July 1994, the ousted Head of State brought the case before the AC°HPR). In the same sense with regard to the ICCPR, see Dinstein in Henkin (1981), p. 131 and Nowak (2005), p. 224.

[256] E.g.: CoE, *HRH No. 5* (2002), p. 24; Nowak (2005), p. 224.

[257] E.g.: ECtHR, *Quinn v. France* (1995), §§42-43; CoE, *HRH No. 5* 82002), p. 10: Nowak (2005), p. 226.

[258] E.g.: IACtHR, *Gangaram Panday v. Suriname* (1994), §47; IACtHR, *Suárez-Rosero v. Ecuador* (1997), §38; IACtHR, *Bámaca Velásquez v. Guatemala* (2000), §139; and Jayawickrama 82002) pp. 379-380.

CHAPTER I – 2
EXCEPTIONAL TIMES AND EXCEPTIONAL MEASURES

We have seen above that the right to liberty is not an absolute right, but may be restricted where necessary for a legitimate purpose. Nevertheless, certain situations may require restrictions of the right to liberty going beyond what is normally allowed under the limitation clause that is part of the right to liberty as enshrined in international human rights instruments. International law is not insensitive to such exceptional situations. It accepts that certain challenges can only be met by seriously restricting individual rights and freedoms. All but one international human rights treaty therefore includes the possibility to derogate from its provisions:

> "In time of public emergency which threatens the life of the nation [...] States Parties to the present Covenant may take measures derogating from their obligations under the present Covenant to the extent strictly required by the exigencies of the situation."[259]

The drafters of these human rights treaties grudgingly accepted that such situations might arise and require severe restrictions on the exercise of human rights for the nation to survive. But they also had in mind the reality of abuse that often results from the exercise of extraordinary powers granted to State authorities. Rather than risking the whole system of rights being suspended because it would not allow some flexibility in situations of real crisis, a system of derogations was finally included in the treaties themselves.[260] Ironically, the emphasis on the risk of abuse, and the importance of keeping emergency measures within the confines of legality voiced so often by the academic and civil society today, were precisely points of concern for many governments at the time of drafting the main international human rights treaties.

International courts and treaty monitoring bodies have recognized the special challenges that may arise from problems such as international terrorism, drug-trafficking or piracy on the high seas. Law enforcement actions meant to counter these threats may pose challenges that are difficult if not impossible to meet

---

[259] Article 4§1 ICCPR. The text of articles 15§1 ECHR, 27§1 ACHR, 35§1 CIS Convention and 4§1 Arab Charter does not substantially differ (*cf. infra* note 270). The ACHPR does not allow its provisions to be derogated from, *cf. infra* note 283 and accompanying text. To be noted that for the present purposes, we only consider human rights treaties that deal with the right to liberty.

[260] For example, the UK put forth such concerns during the drafting sessions of both the ICCPR and the ECHR, for a summary see Nowak (2005), pp. 88-89 and OHCHR, *Manual* (2003), pp. 816-821. In the same sense: IACtHR, *Habeas Opinion* (1987), §21: "rather than adopting a philosophy that favours the suspension of rights, the Convention establishes the contrary principle, namely, that all rights are to be guaranteed and enforced unless very special circumstances justify the suspension of some, and that some rights may never be suspended, however serious the emergency."

without derogating from the right to liberty. Nevertheless, while often legitimate at first, the declaration of a state of emergency and the derogation from fundamental human rights are not without risk.

Derogations under emergency legislation often lead to an erosion of the general human rights protection of the populations affected by them. Based on its vast experience in the matter, the United Nations Working Group on Arbitrary Detention has repeatedly listed the exercise of extraordinary powers of arrest and detention in emergency situations, and the lack of proportionality between these emergencies and the measures adopted to address them, among the root causes of arbitrary deprivation of liberty.[261] Moreover, derogatory measures from the right to liberty are not necessarily more effective in the fight against terrorism, drug-trafficking or piracy as compared to measures taken within the framework of criminal justice and international cooperation that do not require derogation.

The definition of an appropriate balance between national security interests and the protection of individual human rights and freedoms is the subject of much debate and often leads to divergence of opinions. The recent judgment of the Grand Chamber of the European Court of Human Rights in the *Medvedyev* case illustrates the issues at stake well. The case concerned a law enforcement operation by the French authorities on the high seas that resulted in the seizure of a ship and the detention of its crew, whom the authorities suspected of involvement in international drug-trafficking. A combination of facts meant that the French authorities did not dispose of a valid legal basis in either domestic or international law to arrest and detain the crew of the ship on board for the duration of the journey between the place of arrest and the nearest French port (Brest). Moreover, the detainees were only brought before a judge upon arrival in Brest, 13 days after their initial arrest and detention.

The Court did not find a violation of article 5§3 EHCR (prompt judicial oversight), accepting that the wholly exceptional circumstances of carrying out an arrest on the high seas justified the delay in bringing the detainees before a

[261] WGAD, *Annual Report 1995*, §106. See also the consistent confirmation of this fact in the Working Groups' subsequent reports: *Annual Report 2003*, §§54-55 and 58-60, *Annual Report 2004*, §61, *Annual Report 2007*, §64. For examples of the erosive effect of emergency laws and derogations on fundamental human rights, the rule of law and democracy, see O'Boyle, "Emergency Situations and the Protection of Human Rights: A Model Derogation Provision for a Northern Ireland Bill of Rights" (*NILQ* 1977), pp. 160-165; Cole, "Out of the Shadows: Preventive Detention, Suspected Terrorists, and War" (*Calif.LR* 2009), pp. 728-729; Amnesty International (AI), *Syria: 41 Years of the State of Emergency* (2004); and Egyptian Organization of Human Rights, *The Effects of the Emergency Law on the Human Rights Situation in Egypt: 1992-2002* (2003). The emergency legislation in Egypt has been in place since the assassination of former President Sadat in 1981 and is the subject of widespread criticism, see for example AI, *Egypt: Systematic Abuses in the Name of Security* (2007). For an example of the use and abuse of emergency legislation in armed conflict, see Amnesty International's review of Sri Lankan emergency legislation: AI, *Sri Lanka: Security Measures Violate Human Rights* (1995).

judge.[262] It did however find a violation of article 5§1 ECHR (absence of a legal basis to detain), explaining itself in the following terms:[263]

> "However legitimate as it may be, the end does not justify the use of no matter what means [...] The court stresses that where deprivation of liberty is concerned *it is particularly important that the general principle of legal certainty be satisfied.* [...] the Grand Chamber shares the view of the Government and the Chamber that it must be borne in mind that the measures taken by the French authorities against the *Winner* and its crew were taken in the context of France's participation in the effort to combat international trafficking in drugs. [...] Nevertheless, the special nature of the maritime environment relied upon by the Government in the instant case cannot justify an area outside the law where ships' crews are covered by no legal system capable of affording them enjoyment of the rights and guarantees protected by the Convention which the States have undertaken to secure to everyone within their jurisdiction, any more than it can provide offenders with a 'safe haven'. [...] It is regrettable, in the court's view, that the international effort to combat drug trafficking on the high seas is not better coordinated bearing in mind the increasingly global dimensions of the problem. [...] Having regard to the gravity and enormity of the problem posed by illegal drug trafficking, *developments in public international law* [that would provide jurisdiction and a legal basis for detention of suspected drug-traffickers on the highs seas] *would be a significant step in the fight* against illegal trade in narcotics."[264]

The dissenting opinions of the Court's judges illustrate the broader debate on whether special circumstances (*in casu* the fact that arrest and detention takes place on the high seas) and the importance of achieving certain legitimate goals (*in casu* combating international drug-trafficking, but the same question arises for combating terrorism or piracy, or for achieving military victory in armed conflict) should allow for a less strict interpretation of the right to liberty than is normally required. Seven out of fifteen judges in *Medvedyev* disagreed with the majority's finding of a violation of article 5§1 in the absence of a legal basis to detain and found that:

> "it is necessary to be realistic in such exceptional circumstances. [...] When there is sufficient concurring evidence to suspect that a ship on the high seas, thousands of miles from the State thus authorised to board it, is engaged in international trafficking to which all countries want to put a stop, it is without a doubt legitimate not to place as narrow an interpretation on the legal basis as one would inside the territory of the state concerned."[265]

---

[262] Article 5§3 ECHR reads in relevant part: "Everyone arrested or detained in accordance with the provisions of paragraph 1.c of this article shall be brought promptly before a judge or other officer authorised by law to exercise judicial power."

[263] The "recommendations" of the European Court in *Medvedyev* regarding the development of public international law to enable States to detain drug-traffickers on the high seas (as is foreseen by international law on piracy) are of interest in light of cases concerning internment in non-international armed conflict, for which international law does not offer a legal basis either (*cf. infra* Part III).

[264] ECtHR (Grand Chamber), *Medvedyev and Others v. France* (2010), §§49, 80-81 and 101 (emphasis added).

[265] ECtHR (Grand Chamber), *Medvedyev* (2010), Joint Partly Dissenting Opinion of Judges Costa,

The other eight judges – who disagreed for their part with the finding that there was no violation of article 5§3 – commissioned more caution:

> "At the outset, we emphasise that we are as opposed to the scourge inflicted upon society by those involved in illegal drug trafficking as is the majority. Where we differ is in our unwillingness to endorse *unnecessary* abridgements of fundamental human rights in the fight against that scourge. Such abridgements add nothing to the efficacy of the battle against narcotics but subtract, substantially, from the battle against the diminution of human rights protection. [...] We do not exclude the possibility that there may, at times, exist 'wholly exceptional circumstances' which might justify [a departure from the right to liberty beyond what is normally allowed]. [...] [A number of] examples, which are not exhaustive, demonstrate that there were, at least, other possibilities open to the French authorities which, if pursued or even explored, might have enabled them to comply with their Convention obligations. Such alternative measures as outlined herein may be considered as extraordinary or far-reaching but when fundamental human rights are at stake exceptional circumstances may, indeed, call for exceptional measures [...] We could have accepted a dilution of the protection of personal liberty had it been the result of some material impossibility on the part of the authorities [...]. We cannot accept it when the authorities had within their power alternative ways to ensure respect for fundamental rights but chose, rather, to do next to nothing about it."[266]

Tomuschat aptly summed up what is at stake in the debate on balancing national security and human rights: "If so-called 'national security' is elevated to the top of the hierarchy of values, the international human rights system falls apart."[267]

Taking into account this caveat and the concern and caution expressed by the majority of the judges of the European Court in *Medvedyev*, we will now focus on the question of whether and to what extent the right to liberty may be departed from in the context of armed conflict. There are two avenues for imposing measures that effectively derogate from the right to liberty, which we will explore in the two sections of this chapter. First, apart from the general limitations that may be placed on the right to liberty in times of armed conflict, States may adopt emergency legislation that allows them to intern individuals who pose a threat by lawfully derogating from their human rights obligations as provided for in the relevant human rights treaties themselves. Second, the existence of an armed conflict triggers the applicability of a specialized body of international law that regulates the conduct of hostilities between the parties to the conflict and the status and treatment of persons affected by it, including their deprivation of liberty for reasons directly related to the conflict. Where that body of law offers a proper legal basis for internment, States may rely directly on that legal basis to intern persons envisaged by its provisions.

Casadevall, Birsan, Garlicki, Hajiyev, Sikuta and Nicolaou, §10.

[266] ECtHR (Grand Chamber), *Medvedyev* (2010), Joint Partly Dissenting Opinion of Judges Tulkens, Bonello, Zupancic, Fura, Spielmann, Tsotsoria, Power and Poalelungi, §§ 2, 6, 10-11 (original emphasis).

[267] Tomuschat, *Human Rights: Between Idealism and Realism* (2008), p. 67.

2.1. DEROGATION FROM INTERNATIONAL HUMAN RIGHTS LAW IN TIMES OF PUBLIC EMERGENCY

Like any set of international norms, the derogation regimes of international human rights treaties serve a specific purpose in the international legal system. They are designed to afford States legitimate means to face an exceptional situation that cannot be appropriately addressed without resorting to extraordinary measures, and thus allow a swift restoration of order, peace and normal conditions, where human rights can be enjoyed fully by all. As the Human Rights Committee put it, "[t]he restoration of a state of normalcy where the full respect for the Covenant can again be secured must be the predominant objective of a State party derogating from the Covenant."[268] Article 4 ICCPR and its equivalents in other human rights treaties attempt to strike a delicate balance between the protection of individual rights and the system of the rule of law on the one hand, and the protection of collective interests and the needs of the nation as a whole on the other hand.[269] In light of the risks inherent in the granting of extraordinary powers to State authorities, derogations are strictly regulated in international law.[270]

It is not our intention in the present section to examine the question of derogation from human rights law in detail, but rather to highlight those points

[268] HRC, *General Comment 29* (2001), §1. In the same sense, see IACtHR, *Habeas Opinion* (1987), §20.

[269] To be noted that the balance is not just between two abstract competing interests, but needs to take into account the effect of specific derogatory measures on individuals in general (including minorities), its effects on the general protection of individual rights and freedoms over time, and the effectiveness of the measures in achieving both the short- and long-term objectives they are meant to achieve. For a critical view on the appropriateness of a "balancing approach" to human rights in the context of counter-terrorism measures, see Marks & Clapham, *International Human Rights Lexicon* (2005), pp. 356-358 and Moeckli, *Human Rights and Non-Discrimination in the 'War on Terror'* (2008). The following remark is also in point: "The interpretation of the term 'state security' in this context is commonly conceived as a hermeneutical exercise designed to balance between the personal interest in liberty on the one hand, and the collective interest in security on the other hand. This conception, however, may be misleading inasmuch as it gives no weight to the fact that in democratic systems, human rights are not only a personal, but also a national interest" (Ben-Naftali & Gleichgevitch, "Missing in Legal Action: Lebanese Hostages in Israel" (*Harv.ILJ* 2000), p. 221).

[270] Apart from the treaty provisions themselves and the case law of treaty monitoring and enforcement mechanisms (*cf. infra*), the following instruments provide important elements for the interpretation of the conditions for the lawfulness of derogation measures we will discuss in section 2.1.1 below: the reports of the Special Rapporteur to the UN Human Rights Commission on Human Rights and States of Emergency (Mr. Leandro Despouy) (especially his *Final Report* (1997)); *Siracusa Principles* (1984); ILA, *Paris Minimum Standards* (1984)); *Turku Declaration* (1990). For a practical tool, see also OHCHR, *Manual* (2003), chapter 16. Generally on derogation from human rights and the conditions for the lawfulness of such derogations, see Higgins, "Derogations under Human Rights Treaties" (*BYIL* 1976-1977); O'Boyle (*NILQ* 1977); Montealegre, "The Compatibility of a State Party's Derogation under Human Rights Conventions with its Obligations under Protocol II and Common Article 3" (*AULR* 1984); the proceedings of the *Symposium on Limitation and Derogation Provisions in the International Covenant on Civil and Political Rights* (*HRQ* 1985); Svensson-McCarthy (1996); Prémont, Stenersen and Oseredczuk, *Droits intangibles et états d'exception* (1996); McGoldrick, "The Interface between Public Emergency Powers and International Law" (*IJConstit.L* 2004), pp. 380-429; and Nowak (2005), pp. 83-110.

that are relevant for the purposes of our research, notably whether and to what extent the right to liberty may be derogated from in situations of armed conflict.

2.1.1. Conditions for the adoption of derogatory measures under international human rights law

2.1.1.1. A public emergency threatening the life of the nation

First and foremost, derogation is only permissible in truly exceptional circumstances: emergency powers are not necessary, nor permissible, to take legitimate law enforcement measures or to deal with crime as such. Situations permitting derogation are commonly referred to as "states of emergency" or "public emergencies threatening the life of the nation."[271] The European Commission on Human Rights distinguished four criteria required for a state of emergency permitting derogation from the European Convention on Human Rights to exist:[272] (1) the public emergency must be actual and imminent;[273] (2) its effects must involve the whole nation; (3) the continuance of the organized life of the community must be threatened;[274] and (4) the crisis or danger must be exceptional, in that the normal measures or restrictions for the maintenance of public safety, health, and order are plainly inadequate.[275] These criteria have also been used to assess whether a situation justifying derogation exists under the provisions of other human rights treaties.[276] As derogation is only allowed in truly exceptional situations, the criteria must be narrowly construed.[277]

States have a rather wide margin of appreciation in deciding whether an emergency situation of this nature exists, as they are in principle better placed than any international monitoring body to judge the situation in their own

---

[271] The wording differs slightly but not substantially from one treaty to another; see article 4§1 ICCPR ("In time of public emergency which threatens the life of the nation"); article 15§1 ECHR ("In time of war or other public emergency threatening the life of the nation"); article 27§1 ACHR ("In time of war, public danger, or other emergency that threatens the independence or security of a State party"); article 4§1 Arab Charter on Human Rights ("In time of public emergency which threatens the life of the nation"); and article 35§1 CIS Convention ("In time of war or other emergency situation threatening the higher interest of any Contracting Party").

[272] EC°HR, *Denmark, Norway, Sweden and the Netherlands v. Greece* (1969), §§152-165 and 207.

[273] On the notion of imminence, see also the clarifications proffered by the Grand Chamber of the ECtHR in *A and Others v. UK* (2009), §177: "The requirement of imminence cannot be interpreted so narrowly as to require a State to wait for disaster to strike before taking measures to deal with it."

[274] For details on criteria (2) and (3), see also ECtHR (Grand Chamber), *A and Others v. UK* (2009), §179.

[275] The Human Rights Committee has emphasized that "[m]easures derogating from the provisions of the Covenant must be of an exceptional and temporary nature" (HRC, *General Comment 29* (2001), §2); whereas the European Court noted that its "case-law has never, to date, explicitly incorporated the requirement that the emergency be temporary, although the question of the proportionality of the response may be linked to the duration of the emergency" (ECtHR, *A and Others v. UK* (2009), §179).

[276] E.g.: HRC, *General Comment 29* (2001); IAC°HR, *Second Report Peru* (2000), §§69-70; IACtHR, *Zambrano v. Ecuador* (2007), §46. See also *Siracusa Principles* (1984), §39; Nowak (2005), pp. 86, 90-91; and Buergenthal, "To Respect and to Ensure: State Obligations and Permissible Derogations" in Henkin (1981), p. 78.

[277] See also the dissenting opinion of Judges Tulkens *et al.* in ECtHR (Grand Chamber), *Medvedyev* (2010), quoted *supra* note 264 and accompanying text.

country. Even if the judgment of the national authorities (and particularly any decisions on the matter by the judicial branch of government) has considerable weight, it is nevertheless subject to the scrutiny of the monitoring bodies of the treaty they wish to derogate from. States adopting measures derogating from a human rights treaty must demonstrate with sufficient arguments the existence of a situation permitting them to do so.[278]

The question arises then whether the existence of an armed conflict automatically amounts to a public emergency threatening the life of the nation. The text of the European and American Conventions on Human Rights explicitly refer to "war" as a situation permitting derogation.[279] While the term "war" in these provisions does not necessarily have the same meaning as the term "armed conflict" in international humanitarian law,[280] and while the texts of the ICCPR and the Arab Charter do not include either one of these terms, situations of armed conflict were clearly on their drafter's minds when they designed the derogation provisions of all these treaties.[281] A situation of armed conflict – be it international or non-international in nature – is indeed likely[282] to qualify as a public emergency threatening the life of the nation, but it does not do so automatically.[283] The concept of a public emergency threatening the life of the nation and that of armed conflict may overlap to a certain extent, but they are not identical. The four criteria referred to above for a public emergency to exist must be met for any situation of armed conflict to allow a State to avail itself of the derogation provisions of the ICCPR, the ECHR, the ACHR and the Arab Charter on Human Rights.

---

[278] E.g.: HRC, *Landinelli Silva v. Uruguay* (1981), §8(3); HRC, *Salgar de Montejo v. Colombia* (1982), §10(3); ECtHR, *Lawless v. Ireland* (1961), §22; ECtHR, *Aksoy v. Turkey* (1996), §68 and ECtHR (Grand Chamber), *A and Others v. UK* (2009), §173. Note that the existence of a public emergency threatening the life of the nation and that of an armed conflict both depend on the factual situation on the ground and not on an official declaration by the States concerned (see also *infra* section 2.2.1).

[279] See article 15§1 ECHR: "In time of war or other public emergency threatening the life of the nation"; and article 27§1 ACHR: "In time of war, public danger, or other emergency that threatens the independence or security of a State party." In the same sense: article 35§1 CIS Convention: "In time of war or other emergency situation threatening the higher interests of any Contracting Party."

[280] E.g.: Hampson (*Tehran conference paper* 2004), p. 11: "War is a technical legal term. It is not the same as armed conflict. At the time of the adoption of the ECHR in 1950, the term armed conflict was already in use in the Geneva Conventions of 1949. The choice of 'war' was presumably deliberate and designed to apply to international armed conflicts." For the definition of armed conflict, *cf. infra* section 2.2.1.

[281] Since the United Nations had been established with the purpose of preventing it, "war" was not explicitly mentioned in the derogation provision of the ICCPR "in order to prevent giving the impression that the United Nations accepted war" (Nowak (2005), p. 89, with references to the *travaux préparatoires* in notes 22 and 29). In the same sense, e.g.: Buergenthal in Henkins (1981), p. 79; Dinstein, *The Conduct of Hostilities under the Law of International Armed Conflict* (2010), pp. 22.

[282] In the same sense: Solf, "The Status of Combatants in Non-International Armed Conflicts under Domestic Law and Transnational Practice" (*AULR* 1983), p. 296; Pejic (*IRRC* 2005), pp. 379-380; and Rosas (1976), p. 93. See also Canada, *National Defence Act* (1985), article 2 ("'emergency' means an insurrection, riot, invasion, armed conflict or war, whether real or apprehended") and the derogation notices submitted to the UN Secretary-General by Israel, Nicaragua and Azerbaijan referred to *infra* note 307.

[283] In the same sense: Montealegre (*AULR* 1984), pp. 43-44 and Provost (2002), pp. 274-275.

Finally, it is interesting to note that the continent that is arguably most plagued by armed conflict, and by other situations of violence that may require extraordinary measures to bring them under control, has deliberately and consciously chosen not to include any possibility for States to derogate from their obligations in its human rights system. In a case concerning various human rights violations committed in the context of the non-international armed conflict in Chad, the African Commission on Human and Peoples' Rights reconfirmed that:

"The African Charter, unlike other human rights instruments [...], does not allow for states parties to derogate from their treaty obligations during emergency situations. Thus, even a civil war [...] cannot be used as an excuse by the State violating or permitting violations of rights in the African Charter."[284]

The Commission offers the following explanation for the absence of a derogation clause in the African Charter:

"the Charter contains no derogation clause, which can be seen as an expression of the principle that the restriction of human rights is not a solution to national difficulties: the legitimate exercise of human rights does not pose dangers to a democratic state governed by the rule of law."[285]

We have not found any official explanation for the decision taken by the African Union's member States, but it suffices to think of the risks inherent in the adoption of emergency powers pointed out at the outset of this chapter, and of the abuse of emergency powers by more than one government in the continent's history to understand the position taken both in the African Charter and by the African Commission.

In a similar vein, the Inter-American Court of Human Rights has repeatedly invoked the experience of authoritarian rule and armed conflict ravaging 20th-century Latin America and resulting in widespread and systematic abuse against its populations, to remind the risks inherent in allowing for derogation from human rights, and the importance of safeguarding against arbitrariness and abuse.[286]

2.1.1.2. Other conditions for lawful derogation from international human rights

Where a particular situation (including that of armed conflict) does meet the threshold for derogation, the declaration of a public emergency does not provide the authorities with a "*carte blanche*" to exercise any emergency powers they may see fit to deal with that situation. To be lawful the invocation of the

[284] AC°HPR, *Commission Nationale des Droits de l'Homme et des Libertés v. Chad* (1995), §21. See also AC°HPR, *Constitutional Rights Project et al. v. Nigeria* (1999), §41: "In contrast to other international human rights instruments, the African Charter does not contain a derogation clause. Therefore limitations on the rights and freedoms enshrined in the Charter cannot be justified by emergencies or special circumstances. The only legitimate reasons for limitations of the rights and freedoms of the African Charter are found in Article 27(2), that is, that the rights of the Charter 'shall be exercised with due regard to the rights of others, collective security, morality and common interest'."

[285] AC°HRP, *Amnesty International and Others v. Sudan* (1999), §79.

[286] E.g.: IACtHR, *Habeas Opinion* (1987), §§20-21.

derogation regime and the specific derogatory measures taken must still meet a number of other conditions, which can be summarized as follows.[287]

(a.) Legality and respect for the rule of law

Contrary to international humanitarian law, which applies automatically as soon as the threshold of armed conflict is established by the facts on the ground, the derogation regime in international human rights law must be invoked to apply.[288] In practice this usually involves an executive or legislative act, declaring a state of emergency and detailing the specific measures adopted to address the situation. The fact that derogation from certain human rights is allowed does not mean that these rights cease to apply or exist, but rather that their full enjoyment can be temporarily restricted in an extraordinary situation. The principle of legality and the rule of law remain fully applicable in times of armed conflict or other public emergencies threatening the life of the nation,[289] and are of crucial importance to avoid abuse. As a former United Nations High Commissioner for Human Rights recalled: "The strength of our rule of law and human rights norms can only be measured by whether they can resist the temptations to surrender to fear in times of crisis."[290] And the Inter-American Commission on Human Rights in a case concerning emergency powers of arrest and detention to deal with a non-international armed conflict in Peru:

[287] While the lawfulness of every case of derogation measures needs to be assessed not only in the light of the specific circumstances of the case, but also according to the specific criteria imposed by the legal system in which it operates, the list of conditions below are common to the different legal systems and part of a general framework for the evaluation of the validity of the declaration of a state of emergency permitting derogation, and the lawfulness of the measures adopted to address that situation. Apart from the specific provisions of the treaties, the list is based on the decisions of the different treaty monitoring bodies on the matter, and in particular: HRC, *General Comment 29* (2001); IACtHR, *Habeas Opinion* (1987); IAC°HR, *Ascencios Lindo and Others v. Peru* (2000), §§55-57, 63-69 and 83-85; IACtHR, *Durand & Ugarte* (2000), §99; IACtHR, *Zambrano v. Ecuador* (2007); ECtHR, *Lawless v. Ireland* (1961), §§ 22-47; ECtHR, *Brannigan and McBride v. UK* (1993), §§41-74; ECtHR, *Aksoy v. Turkey* (1996), §§68-87; ECtHR (Grand Chamber), *A and Others v. UK* (2009), §§173-190; and the instruments and literature referenced above in note 269.

[288] Hampson (*IRRC* 2008), p. 563. This makes sense as international humanitarian law is a general set of rules, applicable to all situations of armed conflict, while derogation measures are by definition *ad hoc* rules, designed to deal with the challenges that arise from a particular situation at a given time, in a given place, and in given circumstances.

[289] E.g. HRC, *General Comment 29* (2001), §16: "Safeguards related to derogation, as embodied in article 4 of the Covenant, are based on the principles of legality and the rule of law inherent in the Covenant as a whole"; IACtHR, *Habeas Opinion* (1987), §24: "This does not mean, however, that the suspension of guarantees implies a temporary suspension of the rule of law, nor does it authorize those in power to act in disregard of the principle of legality by which they are bound at all times"; IAC°HR, *Ascencios Lindo and Others v. Peru* (2000), §84: "Suspending the need for a court-provided arrest warrant does not mean that public officials have been freed from the legal prerequisites needed to legally decree such a measure"; *Siracusa Principles* (1984), §64: "In a public emergency the rule of law stall still prevails."

[290] Louise Arbour, quoted in Tomuschat (2008), pp. 67-68. Tomuschat rightly points out that this statement "contains in a nutshell the challenge which Western democracies must overcome [in the fight against international terrorism] in order to remain faithful to their basic tenets."

"Suspending the need for a court-provided arrest warrant does not mean that public officials have been freed from the legal prerequisites needed to legally decree such a measure."[291]

(b.) Publicity

In order for derogatory measures to be lawful they must therefore be officially proclaimed so that the affected population will know their impact on the exercise of their human rights. This requirement is essential for satisfying the principle of legality and rule of law and has been emphasized by the ECtHR, the IAC°HR and IACtHR in their reviews of derogation measures under their respective human rights treaties.[292]

The requirement of publicity is to be distinguished from the duty to notify the derogation to the relevant treaty authorities.[293] As Nowak points out in his Commentary to article 4 ICCPR:

> "the derogation of rights [...] constitutes a violation of international law so long as the emergency has not been officially announced by the domestic organ empowered to do so. This legal effect distinguishes the proclamation from the international duty to notify [...] The latter is not a necessary condition that renders lawful the taking of emergency measures, serving instead only international supervision by the other States parties and the Committee. On the other hand,

[291] IAC°HR, *Ascensios Lindo v. Peru* (2000), §84. Since the early 1980's, Peru has known a non-international armed conflict involving mainly two rebel groups, namely the Sendero Luminoso and the smaller Movimiento Revolucionario Túpac Amaru (MRTA). For background on the conflict, see e.g.: IAC°HR, *First Report Peru (1993);* and IAC°HR, *Second Report Peru* (2000).

[292] While only explicitly mentioned in the ICCPR (article 4§1), it is generally accepted that this condition must also be fulfilled for derogations from other human rights treaties to be lawful. E.g. ECtHR, *Lawless v. Ireland* (1961), §37; IACtHR, *Habeas Opinion* (1987), §24 and IAC°HR, *Ascencios Lindo v. Peru* (2000), §76 (the requirement of publicity is inherent in the principle of legality as understood in the Inter-American Human Rights system, *see* IACtHR, *Opinion on the Word "Laws"* (1986) *supra* in chapter I-1).

[293] E.g. article 4§3 ICCPR: "Any State Party to the present Covenant availing itself of the right of derogation shall immediately inform the other States Parties to the present Covenant, through the intermediary of the Secretary-General of the United Nations, of the provisions from which it has derogated and of the reasons by which it was actuated. A further communication shall be made, through the same intermediary, on the date on which it terminates such derogation." Derogations from the ECHR must be notified to the Secretary-General of the Council of Europe (article 15§3 ECHR), derogations from the ACHR to the Secretary-General of the Organization of American States (article 27§3 ACHR), derogations from the Arab Charter to the Secretary-General of the League of Arab States (article 4§3 Arab Charter) and derogations from the CIS Convention to the Executive Secretariat of the Commonwealth of Independent States (articles 35§3 and 39 CIS Convention). Notifications of derogation must be sufficiently clear to allow for a serious assessment of the lawfulness of the derogation measures under the concerned treaty regime. They must be sent as soon as the state of emergency is proclaimed and their addressees must be regularly kept informed of the continuation, extension or termination of the state of emergency and the specific measures adopted to address it. The Human Rights Committee, upon a recommendation made by experts in the *Siracusa Principles* (1984) (§73), has started to request States subject to allegations of serious human rights violations resulting from armed conflict or other situations of violence (e.g. Rwanda, Yugoslavia, Iraq and Peru) to submit specific emergency reports to the Committee for examination of the lawfulness of the derogatory measures adopted.

official proclamation is a condition sine qua non and serves domestic supervision, in particular, the legislative and judicial branches."[294]

(c.) Strict necessity and proportionality

States may take only those measures that are "strictly required by the exigencies of the situation."[295] Again, States are left with a wide margin of discretion as to what specific measures may be required in a given situation, subject to supervision and scrutiny by the competent monitoring and enforcement mechanisms.[296] Necessity and proportionality are at the core of almost every controversy over emergency measures and have given rise to extensive case law, the main traits of which can be summarized as follows.[297]

For one, the territorial, temporal and material scope of the emergency situation, of each derogation measure adopted to address it and their implementation in each individual case must meet the test of strict necessity and proportionality. That test must take into account the circumstances leading to the emergency situation and its duration, the nature of the measures adopted, the nature of the rights affected and the specific circumstances of every case at hand.

Moreover, derogatory measures may only be applied where existing alternatives are insufficient in light of the specific circumstances of the situation and the case concerned. Before derogating from their human rights obligations, States must seriously assess whether the situation cannot be dealt with through the use of normal limitations and restrictions on the exercise of human rights as permitted by the treaty that it wishes to derogate from. It is up to the derogating State in each case to demonstrate precisely and sufficiently what is necessary and why, and how every measure is strictly required by the exigencies of the situation.

In applying the necessity and proportionality test, international human rights bodies have emphasized the importance of accompanying substantive restrictions to human rights with strong and efficient procedural safeguards against abuse and effective remedies for cases where such abuse does occur. We will see below that such procedural safeguards are particularly important where the right to liberty is concerned. Finally, apart from procedural safeguards incorporated into the design of the derogatory measures themselves, derogations from international human rights treaties and their continuous necessity should be subject to regular review by independent organs of the State, such as the legislative and judicial branches of government or independent experts.[298]

---

[294] Nowak (2005), p. 92.

[295] Articles 4§1 ICCPR; 5§1 ECHR; 27§1 ACHR; 4§1 Arab Charter; and 35§3 CIS Convention.

[296] This margin of discretion is less wide however than the one for establishing the existence of a state of emergency permitting derogation. See Hampson (*IRRC* 2008) p. 563, with reference to Higgins (*BYIL* 1976-1977), p. 281.

[297] For references to the case law, *cf. supra* note 287.

[298] See for example the importance attached by the European Court to parliamentary supervision of emergency legislation allowing for internment in Northern-Ireland, e.g. ECtHR, *Lawless v. Ireland* (1961), §37.

(d.) Non-discrimination

While it is acknowledged that the specific nature of an emergency may require the adoption of measures that have a different impact on different groups within a population, they may not intentionally target such groups or discriminate "solely on the ground of race, colour, sex, language, religion or social origin."[299] Differentiations in the application of derogation measures will only be lawful if they pursue a lawful aim and are proportionate and reasonable in light of that purpose in the specific circumstances.

(e.) Consistency with other obligations under international law

Derogation regimes are specific to the treaties in which they are contained and therefore have no impact on the obligations of the derogating State under other sources of international law.[300] What is more, in order to be valid, derogation measures must be in conformity with those other obligations.[301] In situations of armed conflict, the derogating State's obligations under international humanitarian law will be particularly relevant. Other relevant branches of international law may include international refugee law, international criminal law,[302] other human rights obligations than those contained in the treaty from which the State is derogating,[303] and obligations under general international law.[304]

(f.) Non-derogable rights

While derogation regimes are designed to grant States the necessary flexibility to deal with extraordinary situations by placing restrictions on the

---

[299] The text is identical in articles 4§1 ICCPR; 27§1 ACHR; 4§1 Arab Charter and 35§1 CIS Convention. While not explicitly mentioned in article 15§1 ECHR, the European Court has found discriminatory derogation measures to be disproportionate and thus unlawful, see e.g. ECtHR (Grand Chamber), *A and Others v. UK* (2009), §§ 186-190.

[300] The HRC (*General Comment 29* (2001), §10 and note 6) has affirmed that these sources include both treaties and customary international law, and that in order to fulfil the obligation of consistency with other obligations under international law, derogating States should duly take into account the development of international law reflected in expressions of customary law (the Committee explicitly mentions "customary rules of international humanitarian law applicable in international and non-international armed conflicts" and the ICRC's compilation of customary IHL) and in so-called soft-law instruments detailing human rights standards for emergency situations (including the *Siracusa Principles*, the *Paris Minimum Standards* and the *Turku Declaration*).

[301] The text of article 4§1 ICCPR requires that derogatory measures "are not inconsistent with their other obligations under international law." The text of articles 5§1 ECHR, 27§1 ACHR, 4§1 Arab Charter and 35§1 CIS Convention contains quasi-identical wording.

[302] Measures that would amount to international crimes when implemented will obviously be unlawful.

[303] With regard to children it is important to note that no derogation is allowed from the Convention on the Rights of the Child (CRC), a Convention that has been ratified by all but two States (the US and Somalia). Any derogatory measure that affects children will thus be unlawful if not consistent with the derogating State's obligations under the CRC. In the same sense: HRC, *General Comment 29* (2001), §10, note 5.

[304] While the European Court of Human Rights has made it clear that it can and must verify – if necessary *proprio motu* – whether a derogation under the ECHR is consistent with the State's other obligations under international law, its case law seems to indicate – unfortunately – that in the absence of proper submissions on the matter by the applicant, the Court will not go very deeply into the matter, see for example ECtHR, *Lawless v. Ireland* (1961), §§40-41.

exercise of human rights, certain rights cannot be derogated from, even in times of extraordinary threats, including armed conflict. Those rights differ from one treaty regime to another but the following list of non-derogable rights is common to all treaties: the right to life, the prohibition of torture and other forms of cruel, inhuman or degrading treatment, the prohibition of slavery and servitude and the principle of legality in criminal law.[305] The subject of non-derogable rights is one where international law is constantly evolving; we will mention examples regarding the right to liberty below.

Since States are left with a considerable margin of discretion to derogate from human rights where required by extraordinary situations, the conditions for adopting and applying such derogatory measures must be complied with in good faith[306] and serve the ultimate purpose of the derogation regime, i.e. "[t]he restoration of a state of normalcy where the full respect for the Covenant can again be secured."[307]

2.1.2. Scope of lawful derogations from the right to liberty

None of the existing human rights treaties lists the right to liberty as a non-derogable right. Indeed, in practice, the right to liberty is almost always derogated from as soon as a state of emergency is declared, particularly in situations of violence or a threat to State security. States derogating from the right to liberty either establish additional *grounds* for deprivation of liberty (article 9§1 ICCPR) or suspend or relax the *procedural* safeguards inherent in the right to liberty (article 9§§2-5 ICCPR).[308]

---

[305] The ICCPR adds to that list the prohibition of imprisonment for contractual debt, the freedom of movement, the freedom of thought, conscience and religion and the right to recognition as a person before the law. Moreover, the HRC has held that the prohibition of the death penalty in the Second Optional Protocol to the ICCPR Aiming at the Abolition of the Death Penalty (1989) (ICCPR-OP2) is also non-derogable (HRC, *General Comment 29* (2001), §7). Likewise, the prohibition of the death penalty (including in time of war) has been made non-derogable by Protocol No. 13 to the ECHR Concerning the Abolition of the Death Penalty (2002) (Protocol 13 ECHR). The ACHR adds the rights of the family, the right to a name, the rights of the child, the right to a nationality and the right to participate in government, and the judicial guarantees essential for protecting non-derogable rights. Finally, the Arab Charter on Human Rights also considers non-derogable the prohibition of medical or scientific experimentation and of organ transfers without the individual's free informed consent, the right to challenge the lawfulness of one's deprivation of liberty, the prohibition of imprisonment for contractual debt, the principle of *ne bis in idem*, the right to humane treatment in detention, the right to recognition as a person before the law, the right to leave and to return to one's country, the right to political asylum, the right to nationality and the right to freedom of thought, conscience and religion, and the "judicial guarantees required for the protection of [these] rights."

[306] E.g.: *Siracusa Principles* (1984), §62.

[307] HRC, *General Comment 29* (2001), §1. In the same sense: IACtHR, *Habeas Opinion* (1987), §20.

[308] See for example the derogation notices of Azerbaijan (derogation notice of 16 April 1993), Israel (derogation notice of 03 October 1991), Colombia (derogation notices of 25 March 1996 and 18 June 1996), Nepal (derogation notices of 08 March 2002 and 16 February 2005), Peru (derogation notice of 18 March 1983), Russia (derogation notice of 07 April 1993), Sri Lanka (derogation notices of 21 May 1993, 18 May 1993 and 30 May 2000), all available at: http://treaties.un.org/Pages/View Details.aspx?src=TREATY&mtdsg_no=IV-4&chapter=4&lang=en. See also ECtHR, *Lawless v. Ireland* (1961), "The Facts", §17; ECtHR, *Aksoy v. Turkey* (1996), §31; ECtHR (Grand Chamber), *A and Others v. UK* (2009), §11.

Nevertheless, certain derogable rights have a non-derogable core.[309] We have seen above that derogation measures must always conform to the principle of legality and the rule of law, so as to prevent abuse and arbitrariness. The principle of legality, requiring the grounds and procedures for any deprivation of liberty to be prescribed by law, may therefore not be derogated from. Likewise, the prohibition of arbitrary deprivation of liberty, an absolute rule of general international law, remains fully applicable in times of emergency and elements of necessity, proportionality and justice will be taken into account to assess the lawfulness of deprivation of liberty on the basis of emergency legislation. The adoption or application of derogation measures that effectively result in arbitrary interference with the right to liberty can never be lawful.[310]

As mentioned in the introduction to this section, the risk of arbitrary deprivation of liberty is highest in emergency situations.[311] It is therefore important to incorporate into emergency powers of arrest and detention the necessary safeguards to prevent such arbitrariness. The debate on the derogability of certain procedural safeguards, essential to prevent arbitrary interference with non-derogable rights, is at the core of almost all discussions and controversies regarding the expansion of the list of non-derogable rights. While not immediately relevant to answer our research questions, the example of the right to challenge the lawfulness of one's deprivation of liberty merits a brief discussion.[312]

The right to challenge the lawfulness of one's deprivation of liberty – commonly referred to as *habeas corpus* or simply *habeas* – is one of the most efficient means to protect individuals against arbitrary deprivation of liberty. This is even more so in times of emergency when authorities are granted more

---

[309] HRC, *General Comment 29* (2001), §13.

[310] HRC, *General Comment 29* (2001), §11 *in fine*: "States parties may in no circumstances invoke article 4 of the Covenant as justification for acting in violation of humanitarian law or peremptory norms of international law, for instance by taking hostages, [...], through arbitrary deprivations of liberty." Article 20 Cairo Declaration on Human Rights in Islam explicitly prohibits arbitrary detention in times of emergency: "It is not permitted without legitimate reason to arrest an individual, or restrict his freedom, to exile or to punish him. [...] Nor is it permitted to promulgate emergency laws that would provide executive authority for such actions." On the potentially peremptory character of the prohibition of arbitrary deprivation of liberty, *cf. supra* chapter I-1, section 1.1. Some experts have even found the right to liberty to be non-derogable in its entirety see e.g. the *Paris Minimum Standards* (1984), Section C, article 5.

[311] *Cf. supra* note 261 and accompanying text.

[312] The right to *habeas* is at the heart of debates on the procedural safeguards that must be afforded to internees in non-international armed conflict. Moreover, it would be interesting to put the review procedures prescribed for internment in international armed conflict (notably articles 43 and 78 GC IV) to the test of international human rights law and to examine whether the absence of such a review procedure in GC III means internment of prisoners of war in full compliance with GC III would still amount a violation of the (possibly non-derogable) right to *habeas* in international human rights law. While these questions are beyond the scope of our work, it is submitted that the legal bases for internment in the Geneva Conventions offer sufficient protection against arbitrariness when applied with full respect of their provisions and in good faith and that internment in full compliance with the Conventions is not arbitrary and therefore does not violate the right the non-derogable core of the right to liberty under international human rights law, *cf. infra* section 2.2.2.2.

expansive powers of arrest and detention in order to address the threats they are faced with. It is therefore not surprising that a rapidly growing number of domestic and international courts, treaty monitoring bodies, international organizations, legal scholars and practitioners find the right to challenge the lawfulness of one's detention to be so essential to prevent arbitrary deprivation of liberty that it must be considered a non-derogable right. The recently revised Arab Charter on Human Rights is the first human rights treaty to explicitly include this right in the list of non-derogable rights in its article 4 on derogations.[313]

Article 27§2 of the American Convention on Human Rights states that the "judicial guarantees essential for the protection of such [non-derogable] rights" cannot be derogated from. The Inter-American Court of Human Rights has ruled that the "writs of habeas corpus and of 'amparo' are among those judicial remedies that are essential for the protection of various rights whose derogation is prohibited [...] and that serve, moreover, to preserve legality in a democratic society."[314]

With regard to the ICCPR, the Human Rights Committee has found that the right to challenge the lawfulness of one's detention has become a non-derogable right, not only because it is an indispensable safeguard against arbitrary deprivation of liberty but also because it offers essential protection against the violation of non-derogable rights such as the right to life, the prohibition of torture and other forms of cruel, inhuman or degrading treatment and is essential in the prevention of enforced disappearances.[315] The Working Group on Arbitrary Detention has endorsed that position and even found the right to challenge the lawfulness of one's detention to be a peremptory norm of international law.[316]

---

[313] Article 4§2 reads: "In exceptional situations of emergency, no derogation shall be made from [...] article 14, paragraph 6"; article 14§6 states that "[a]nyone who is deprived of his liberty by arrest or detention shall be entitled to petition a competent court in order that it may decide without delay on the lawfulness of his arrest or detention and order his release if the arrest or detention is unlawful.". A similar provision was not yet included in the 1994 version of the Charter (which never entered into force).

[314] IACtHR, *Habeas Opinion* (1987), §42, confirmed in IACtHR, *Judicial Guarantees in States of Emergency, Advisory Opinion* (1987) §31; in IAC°HR, *Principles and Best Practices* (2008), principle 1§4; and in a number of contentious cases, e.g. IAC°HR, *Asencios Lindo v. Peru* (2000), §§ 78-82. The writ of amparo concerns the right to an effective remedy and compensation for violation of one's rights.

[315] HRC, *General Comment 29 (2001)*, §16, with a reference to the Committee's Concluding Observations regarding the suspension of judicial review of administrative detention in Israel (HRC, *Concluding Observations Israel* (1998), §21). See also the *Siracusa Principles* (1984), §70(d), the ILA's *Paris Minimum Standards* (1984), article 5§3; and the *Turku Declaration* (1990), articles 4§3 and 11. In his commentary to article 4 ICCPR, Nowak (2005), refers to the fact during the negotiations of article 4 ICCPR the US and France proposed to include the right to personal liberty or at least parts thereof in the list of non-derogable rights (at p. 94) and confirms the views adopted by the HRC in its *General Comment 29* (2001) (at p. 98); for further details, see also pp. 212 and 226.

[316] WGAD, *Annual Report 2007*, §67: "in addition to those enumerated in article 4, paragraph 2 of the ICCPR, certain other rights are non-derogable even during a state of emergency, such as the right to take proceedings before a court to enable the court to decide without delay on the lawfulness of detention. In the view of the Working Group these guarantees represent peremptory norms of

As we have mentioned before, under the African Charter on Human and Peoples' Rights, no derogations are allowed *tout court*. The non-derogability of the right to liberty and in particular the right to challenge the lawfulness of one's deprivation of liberty has moreover repeatedly been recalled by the African Commission on Human and Peoples' Rights.[317]

The European Court of Human Rights seems to grant more leeway to States excluding the right to *habeas* for certain detainees subject to emergency legislation that derogates from the European Convention, as long as the State can justify this derogation to be strictly necessary for the exigencies of the situation. Nevertheless, while the Court endorsed the justifications to derogate from article 5§4 ECHR put forward by the UK and Turkey in relation respectively to armed conflicts in Northern Ireland and South-East Turkey,[318] the increasingly restrictive measures adopted by some member States in the fight against international terrorism has sparked increased criticism from the Strasbourg judges.[319] It seems therefore that even the case law of the European Court is evolving towards the non-derogability of the right to some form of *habeas*.

International law is clearly evolving on the subject of non-derogable rights and the right to *habeas* is well on its way to find a place in the list of non-derogable rights for all international human rights treaties. This does not necessarily mean that the right to *habeas* must be guaranteed in exactly the same manner as it is when no emergency situation exists or where the emergency measures adopted do not require a derogation from that right.[320] What is essential is that the person deprived of liberty can effectively challenge the lawfulness of his or her detention before an independent and impartial body that has the power to order release when the deprivation of liberty is not, or ceases to be, lawful.[321]

(customary) international law so that they are also binding on States which are not parties to the Covenant." The UN Human Rights Commission, upon recommendation of the WGAD "encourages States [...] to establish a procedure such as habeas corpus or a similar procedure as a personal right not subject to derogation, including during states of emergency" (UNCHR, *Resolution 1994/32* (1994) (adopted without a vote), §16).

[317] See for example AC°HPR, *Amnesty International and Others v. Sudan* (1999), §§58-62 and AC°HPR, *Principles on Fair Trial and Legal Assistance* (2001), section M§2(h).

[318] See for example the case law referenced *supra* in notes 271-275.

[319] E.g.: ECtHR (Grand Chamber), *A and Others v. UK* (2009), §§ 221-224.

[320] For example, the ECtHR in *Lawless v. Ireland* (1961), §37 found the following system of revision of internment in Northern-Ireland to be lawful: "the Offences against the State (Amendment) Act 1940, provided for the establishment of a 'Detention Commission' made up of three members, which the Government did in fact set up, the members being an officer of the Defence Forces and two judges; whereas any person detained under this Act could refer his case to that Commission whose opinion, if favourable to the release of the person concerned, was binding upon the Government; whereas, moreover, the ordinary courts could themselves compel the Detention Commission to carry out its functions." In the same sense: ECtHR, *Klass and Others v. Germany* (1978), §§55-56; ECtHR (Grand Chamber), *A and Others v. UK* (2009), §§202-203 and 219; and, with regard to internment by the UK in Iraq, UK, Court of Appeal, *Al-Jedda v. Secretary of State for Defence* (2010), §§113-114, 148-156.

[321] See also ECtHR (Grand Chamber), *A and Others v. UK* (2009), §§202-211 (summarizing the principles arising from existing case law on the issue); Pejic (*IRRC* 2005), pp. 384-389; and *Report of the Expert Meeting on Security Detention in NIAC* (2008).

The Inter-American Court of Human Rights also found the right to an effective remedy and compensation for violations of human rights (commonly referred to in Latin-America as the writ of amparo) to be an essential judicial guarantee for the protection of both derogable and non-derogable rights.[322] The Human Rights Committee has found the right to an effective remedy to be inherent in the Convention as a whole and thus non-derogable.[323] It is indeed difficult to imagine circumstances in which the suspension of the right to a remedy and compensation for arbitrary deprivation of liberty[324] may be "strictly required by the exigencies of the situation", an essential condition for such a measure to be lawful. Finally, it is useful to recall that the obligation of humane treatment of persons deprived of liberty can never be derogated from.[325]

Any further reference in this book to a "lawful derogation" must be understood as a derogation that fully complies with the conditions discussed in the present section.

2.2. DIRECT RELIANCE UPON INTERNATIONAL HUMANITARIAN LAW IN TIME OF ARMED CONFLICT

International humanitarian law (IHL), also known as the law of armed conflict (LoAC),[326] is a set of "international rules, established by treaties or

---

[322] *Cf. supra* note 313.
[323] HRC, *General Comment 29* (2001), §14. See also *Siracusa Principles* (1984), §§59-60.
[324] E.g. article 9§5 ICCPR: "Anyone who has been the victim of unlawful arrest or detention shall have an enforceable right to compensation." In similar terms: articles 5§5 ECHR; 14§7 Arab Charter; and 5§4 CIS Convention. See also article 25 ACHR and AC°HPR, *Principles on Fair Trial and Legal Assistance* (2001), section C.
[325] The prohibition of torture and other forms of cruel, inhuman or degrading treatment is absolute and is included in all international and regional human rights treaties as a non-derogable right (*cf. supra*); it is also the subject of a number of international and regional subject-specific human rights treaties. Some human rights treaties recall the general obligation to humane treatment explicitly for persons deprived of liberty, taking into account the specific vulnerability of detainees in this respect (*cf. infra*). The right to humane treatment in detention is non-derogable under the Arab Charter on Human Rights (article 4§2 and 20§1). The HRC has stressed that the right to humane treatment of prisoners as laid down by article 10 ICCPR is the reflection of a norm of general international law and as such has to be non-derogable (HRC, *General Comment 29* (2001), §13 (a)). In its *Principles and Best Practices on the Protection of Persons Deprived of Liberty in the Americas* (2008), the IAC°HR has reiterated the principle of humane treatment as one that can never be set aside, not even in situations of war or any other national or international emergency (principle 1§4). The principle is also reiterated in the UN's *Body of Principles* (1988), principle 1; the ILA's *Paris Minimum Standards* (1984), article 5§2(g); and the *Turku Declaration* (1990), article 4§4. Moreover, both treaty law and customary humanitarian law impose humane treatment of persons deprived of their liberty for reasons related to an armed conflict (article 3 common to the Geneva Conventions; article 13 GC III; 27 GC IV; article 75§1 AP I; article 4 AP II; Rule 87 of the ICRC's compilation of customary IHL: Henckaerts & Doswald-Beck (2005), Volume I pp. 306-308 and the references to State practice in *Ibidem*, Volume II pp. 1986-2024, and the ICRC's updated *Customary IHL Database* (2010). As regards the prohibition of torture, it is one of the few recognized peremptory norms of international law and thus can never be derogated from (article 53 VCLT); and has always been part of customary IHL, see Henckaerts & Doswald-Beck (2005), Vol. I, pp. 315-319, with references to State practice summarized in *Ibidem*, Volume II and the ICRC's updated *Customary IHL Database* (2010).
[326] The international law of armed conflict in its broad sense includes three sets of rules: (1) the rules

custom, which are specifically intended to solve humanitarian problems directly arising from international or non-international armed conflicts and which, for humanitarian reasons, limit the right of Parties to a conflict to use the methods and means of warfare of their choice or protect persons and property that are, or may be, affected by conflict."[327]

While a truly context-specific and at times highly specialized body of law, we have already mentioned in the Introduction to this book that international humanitarian law does not exist in a legal vacuum but is part of the general international legal system, where it interacts with other bodies of international law and in particular international human rights law. The international legal system allots to each of its branches a specific function and purpose in order to achieve the goals of the international community, which are based on commonly shared universal values. While international human rights law protects the individual human being from arbitrariness or abuse at all times and in all circumstances, its provisions were not designed to address the specific dangers to humanity that may arise from armed conflict. The regulation of armed conflict is the specific function of international humanitarian law, whose provisions are designed to defend the shared values of the international community in this particularly challenging context.

In order to do so, it must reconcile the competing interests at stake in armed conflict and establish an acceptable compromise based on a balance between the requirements of military necessity on the one hand and, the requirements of humanity on the other hand.[328] Military necessity is generally defined as "the necessity of those measures which are indispensable for securing the ends of

---

regulating the use of force by States or international organizations, also called *jus ad bellum*, or – since the prohibition of the use of force in article 2 of the UN Charter – *jus contra bellum* (note that – except for peoples with a right to self-determination – the use of force by organized armed groups against a State is not regulated by international law and falls within the unique purview of domestic legal orders); (2) the rules regulating the rights and duties of neutral States (the international law of neutrality); and (3) the rules applicable between the parties to an actual armed conflict (*jus in bello*). It is to this third set of rules, the *jus in bello* that we refer to here when using the terms "international humanitarian law" and "law of armed conflict", namely the body of law that contains the rules governing the actual conduct of hostilities and the protection of persons affected by armed conflict.

327 Sandoz et al., *Commentary AP I and II* (1987), p. xxvii. The bulk of contemporary IHL or LoAC is contained in the four Geneva Conventions of 12 August 1949 (Geneva Convention for the Amelioration of the Condition of the Wounded and Sick in Armed Forces in the Field (GC I); Geneva Convention for the Amelioration of the Condition of Wounded, Sick and Shipwrecked Members of Armed Forces at Sea (GC II); Geneva Convention relative to the Treatment of Prisoners of War (GC III); and Geneva Convention relative to the Protection of Civilian Persons in Time of War (GC IV)); their Additional Protocols of 8 June 1977 (Protocol Additional to the Geneva Conventions of 12 August 1949 and Relating to the Protection of Victims of International Armed Conflicts (AP I) and Protocol Additional to the Geneva Conventions of 12 August 1949 and Relating to the Protection of Victims of Non-International Armed Conflicts (AP II); and in customary international humanitarian law. Other treaties further regulate specific issues such as the use of weapons, the protection of cultural property and the definition of war crimes. For a complete list of relevant treaty law, see the ICRC's *Treaty Database*, available at http://www.icrc.org/ihl, and for a comprehensive overview of customary international humanitarian law, see Henckaerts & Doswald-Beck (2005) and the updated ICRC's *CIHL Database* (2010).

328 Sandoz et al., *Commentary AP I and II* (1987), pp. 392-393; Dinstein (2010), pp. 4-5.

war, and which are lawful according to the modern law and usages of war", the only legitimate objective in war being "to weaken the military forces of the enemy";[329] while the requirements of humanity "[forbid] the infliction of suffering, injury, or destruction not actually necessary for the accomplishment of legitimate military purposes."[330] As Rosas points out:

> "the principle of humanity [...] should be understood as meaning certain humanitarian values, which emerge through the evolution of society as some kind of general guidelines for human intercourse. While the concept of military necessity relates to the short-term interests of belligerents in the conduct of war, the concept of [humanity] seems to come close to what may be termed the long-term interests of society."[331]

In striking a delicate balance between the parties' need to ensure security and military victory and the protection of human dignity throughout armed conflict, international humanitarian law thus seeks to minimize human suffering in situations where humanity is put to its harshest test. In order to achieve that purpose, it regulates the conduct of hostilities and the situation of individuals in the power or control of an enemy to protect them against arbitrariness and abuse,[332] but it also defines specific restrictions that may be imposed on

---

[329] Citations respectively from US, *Instructions for the Government of Armies of the United States in the Field* (1983) (Lieber Code), article 14; and St-Petersburg Declaration (1868), preambular paragraph 2. This definition of military necessity (based on a combined reading of the Lieber Code and the preamble of the St-Petersburg Declaration) has been reaffirmed in definitions of the concept in contemporary military manuals, jurisprudence and legal doctrine. For example, the UK's *Manual of the Law of Armed Conflict* (2004) (hereinafter "*LOAC Manual*"), pp. 21-22, section 2(2) defines military necessity as follows: "military necessity permits a state engaged in armed conflict to use only that degree and kind of force, not otherwise prohibited by the law of armed conflict, that is required in order to achieve the legitimate purpose of the conflict, namely the complete or partial submission of the enemy at the earliest possible moment with the minimum expenditure of life and resources", and the IAC°HR, *Third Report Colombia* (1999), §37 finds: "[t]he principle of military necessity justifies those measure of military violence, not forbidden by international law, which are necessary and proportionate to securing the prompt submission of the enemy with the least possible expenditure of human and/or economic resources." Most modern definitions of the principle of military necessity integrate the corollary principle of humanity. For a general overview, see Melzer, *Targeted Killing in International Law* (2008), pp. 282-286.

[330] UK, *LOAC Manual* (2004), p. 23, section 2(4). The IAC°HR, *Third Report Colombia* (1999), §38 finds "The principle of humanity both complements and inherently limits the doctrine of military necessity. This principle prohibits the infliction of suffering, injury or destruction not actually necessary, i.e. proportionate, for the realization of lawful military purposes. Moreover, the principle of humanity also confirms the basic immunity of civilians from being the object of attack in all armed conflicts."

[331] Rosas (1976), p. 25 (original emphasis omitted). The general guidelines for human intercourse that are in the long-term interest of society definitely include the general principles of international human rights law, *cf. infra* section 2.2.2.2.

[332] See also our discussion of the role of IHL in the international legal system in the Introduction. International humanitarian law was not designed however to regulate all aspects of life in time of armed conflict. States are rarely completely paralyzed by the existence of an armed conflict, and even if armed conflicts today have a much greater impact on the every-day life of the population than in previous centuries when wars were mainly fought between standing armies on battlefields situated outside the habitat of normal life, there are a number of activities and issues that go on regardless of the existence of an armed conflict. They continue to be regulated by domestic law, which must conform to international human rights law.

an individual's right to liberty to meet the specific military and security challenges that arise in situations of armed conflict.[333]

We will see in Parts II and III to what extent international humanitarian law itself provides a *legal basis* for imposing such restrictions, and that the situation differs according to the type of armed conflict concerned. It is therefore important to establish the threshold of applicability of international humanitarian law and define the material scope of application of two subsets of its rules, namely that regulating situations of international armed conflicts and occupation and that regulating situations of non-international armed conflict.

2.2.1 Threshold of applicability of international humanitarian law: the existence of an armed conflict

The substantive rules of international humanitarian law are divided in two subsets, which apply to two different types of armed conflict. If a person is interned for reasons related to an armed conflict, it is important therefore to identify which of the two subsets of specific rules in international humanitarian law regulates that internment: that of international armed conflict or that of non-international armed conflict. Moreover, in situations of international armed conflict different provisions prescribe the grounds and procedures for internment in the *territory of* a party to the conflict and for internment in *territory occupied by* a party to the conflict. Therefore, the qualification of a situation as international armed conflict, occupation or non-international armed conflict is important as it determines the specific set of rules that is relevant to answer questions of who may be interned, for what reasons and for how long in a specific situation of armed conflict.

From a humanitarian point of view, many of the needs and problems that arise in non-international armed conflict are similar to those that arise in international armed conflicts. The same is true from an operational military point of view, albeit mainly as regards the rules on the conduct of hostilities. Some have argued that applying the law of international armed conflict in all situations of armed conflict, regardless of their character "avoids confusion on the side of troops and their commanders, as regular armed forces are normally trained for military operations in international armed conflicts and not for law enforcement purposes. Also, the character of an armed conflict is not always clear, sometimes it may even change during operations."[334] For these reasons, the rules for

---

[333] *Cf. infra* section 2.2.2.1.

[334] Greenwood, "Scope of Application of Humanitarian Law" in Fleck (ed.), *The Handbook of International Humanitarian Law* (2008), p. 56. From a purely operational perspective, this is also confirmed in the military doctrine of many States. For example, US military doctrine provides that: "US forces will comply with the Law of War during military operations involving armed conflict, no matter how the conflict may be characterized under international law, and will comply with its principles and spirit during all other operations" (Chairman of the Joint Chiefs of Staff Instruction, *Standing Rules of Engagement for US Forces*, Ref. CJCSI 3121.01A (2000), and other military-doctrinal statements quoted or referred to in Roberts, "The Laws of War and the War on Terror" (*Isr.YHR*, 2002), p. 197, note 6). Such policy considerations have not however prevented the US or

international armed conflicts have increasingly become applicable in situations of non-international armed conflict as a matter of customary law, so much so that some have argued to lift the distinction entirely and have a single body of international humanitarian law apply to all situations of armed conflict,[335] which would have the additional advantage of avoiding political sensitivities, disagreements on the interpretation of the law and practical difficulties related to the qualification of a given situation as international or non-international.

Nevertheless, efforts to establish such a single body of international humanitarian law have always met with strong opposition from States and therefore never materialized. Schindler explains the rejection of a proposal made in the run-up for the 1974-1977 Diplomatic Conference on the Reaffirmation and Development of International Humanitarian Law to adopt a single Additional Protocol to the Geneva Conventions, applicable in all armed conflicts, as follows:

"[S]uch a uniform protocol would not correspond to the current structure of the world community. International law has to take into account that the world is divided into sovereign States, and that these States keep to their sovereignty. They are not willing to put insurgents within their territory on equal terms with the armed forces of enemy States, or members thereof."[336]

It is submitted that the situation is not so different today.[337] While the structure of the world community has changed to a certain extent, particularly with regard to the increased role international and regional organizations play in situations of armed conflict, the attitude of States towards insurgents has not changed to the extent that States would be ready to expand the full application of the law of international armed conflict to all situations of non-international armed conflict. On the contrary, insurgents, today more than ever, are considered criminals – and not even ordinary ones, but particularly dangerous "terrorists" – who must be punished for their violent acts against a State and its population. The distinction between international and non-international armed conflicts

---

other States to object to the applicability *de jure* of the law of international armed conflict to situations that do not reach that threshold.

335 E.g.: ICTY, *Tadíc* (1995), §97; Meron (2006), pp. 31-33 and Crawford, *The Treatment of Combatants and Insurgents under the Law of Armed Conflict* (2010), pp. 2 and 171-173. That single body of law could either be the law applicable to international armed conflict (which it is submitted will never gain the acceptance of the international lawmakers that are States), or those rules that are accepted to apply as a matter of customary law in both situations (which would be unacceptable both from a military point of view, since it would effectively do away with prisoner of war status and combatant privilege and immunity, and from a humanitarian point of view, since it would inevitably result in a lowest common denominator and do away with some of the protective provisions of the law international armed conflict that are not applicable in non-international armed conflict).

336 Schindler, "The Different Types of Armed Conflicts According to the Geneva Conventions and Protocols" (*Hague Academy Collected Courses* 1979), pp. 154-155.

337 In the same sense: *European Union Guidelines on Promoting Compliance with International Humanitarian Law (IHL)* (2005), §§9 and 11: "Different legal regimes apply to [IAC and NIAC]. Rules of customary international law apply to both [IAC and NIAC] but again there are differences between the two regimes."

therefore continues to dominate international humanitarian law, especially with regard to the subject of our research.[338]

While we agree that customary international humanitarian law applicable to the different types of armed conflicts has evolved in many areas to a point of almost uniformity,[339] the subject of our attention here is one of these on which the rules of international humanitarian law applicable in international and non-international armed conflicts remain fundamentally different. The rules on the *treatment* of internees and detainees and on the *material conditions* of deprivation of liberty in armed conflict may be almost identical in both bodies of law; the same is not true for the legal framework defining the lawful *grounds* for internment and *the procedural and other protective mechanisms against arbitrary deprivation of liberty*.[340] In her book *The Treatment of Combatants and Insurgents under the Law of Armed Conflict*, Crawford argues – convincingly for the most part – that the provisions on treatment and conditions of detention, and those on judicial guarantees in criminal proceedings are quasi-identical in the

[338] *Cf. infra* Part III. The distinction has been reaffirmed in article 8 of the ICC Statute. Note however that States who are ready to apply the provisions of the law of international armed conflict, in full or in part, to a situation of non-international armed conflict can do so either by concluding a special agreement to that effect with the adverse party to the conflict, or by unilateral declaration. This possibility is explicitly provided for and encouraged by common article 3 to the Geneva Conventions and thus does not require any further normative development of international humanitarian law. Should States frequently make use of this possibility, their practice would contribute to the further expansion of the law of non-international armed conflict as a matter of customary law. Until today however, very little use has been made of this possibility in practice (*cf. infra* section 2.2.1.4).

[339] See Henckaerts & Doswald-Beck (2005), p. xxix. In this compilation of customary IHL, the ICRC identified 161 customary IHL rules, 143 of which apply both in international and non-international armed conflicts (one could thus conclude that international humanitarian law for international and non-international armed conflicts is identical to as much as 89%). Updates of the 2005 compilation, worked upon by the ICRC in partnership with the British Red Cross, may in the future even show an increase in the number of rules applicable to armed conflicts throughout. See also Meron (2006), pp. 31-33, Sassòli in *Liber Amoricum Malinverni* (2007), p. 378, and generally Crawford (2010). At the time of writing, no such increase has so far taken place, see the ICRC's *Customary IHL Database*, last updated on 12 August 2010.

[340] Of the 16 rules of the ICRC's compilation of customary IHL that are applicable in IAC only (or that apply differently in NIAC), half directly concern the legal framework for internment and the independent monitoring of deprivation of liberty (rules 3, 4, 106, 107 and 108 concerning the definition of armed forces, combatant and prisoner of war status, rule 124 on ICRC access to those deprived of liberty and rule 128 limiting the duration of internment). The other rules concern the law of occupation (rules 41, 51, 129 and 130), the prohibition of reprisals (rules 145-147), the authorization to take war booty (rule 49) and the obligation to return the bodies and belongings of the dead to their next of kin (rule 114). See also Kleffner, "From 'Belligerents' to 'Fighters' and Civilians Directly Participating in Hostilities: On the Principle of Distinction in Non-International Armed Conflicts One Hundred Years after the Second Peace Conference" (*NILR* 2007), p. 321-322: "It is clear from the relevant conventional provisions and customary international humanitarian law that the formal status of "combatant" does not apply in non-international armed conflicts. As such, combatant status and its aforementioned consequences is one of the areas, in which customary international humanitarian law has *not* evolved beyond the dichotomy of international and non-international armed conflicts, despite the imprecise use of the term "combatant" in some texts, which relate to both types of conflicts. [...] Furthermore, those who have directly participated in hostilities in a non-international armed conflict and have been interned or detained are not entitled to treatment as prisoners of war." In the same sense: Lubell (2010), pp. 93 and 102.

customary international humanitarian law applicable to international and non-international armed conflict, and even coincide to a large extent with the provisions of international human rights law.[341] She does not deal however with the *grounds, procedures and supervision of internment*, exactly because this is the area where both bodies of law do not converge.[342] Crawford makes a compelling case for further expanding the applicability of the law of international armed conflict to situations of non-international armed conflict to achieve a "universal combatant status",[343] but it is in our opinion unlikely that States, the ultimate international lawmakers, are ready to take this final but crucial step towards full standardization of the law of armed conflict any time soon.[344]

For our present purposes, it remains therefore important to define the threshold of applicability of international humanitarian law for situations of international armed conflict, occupation and non-international armed conflict. Moreover, in light of recent challenges and debates, a word will also be said about the legal qualification of the so-called war on terrorism and about the impact of an intervention by international armed forces on the qualification of a conflict and the law applicable between the parties to it.

2.2.1.1. The existence of armed conflict: a question of facts on the ground

The existence of a situation of armed conflict or occupation and the commensurate applicability of specific bodies of international humanitarian law do not depend on the legality of the resort to force (regulated by the *jus ad bellum*),[345] the reciprocal application of the law between adverse parties to the

[341] Crawford (2010), pp. 78-152.
[342] Crawford (2010), p. 3.
[343] Crawford (2010), pp. 153-169.
[344] In the same sense: Zegveld, *Accountability of Armed Opposition Groups under International Law* (2002), p. 36: "The strongest argument against the abolition of the distinction [between IAC and NIAC] seems to lie [...] in the premise underlying the Prisoner of War Convention, where it is maintained that members of armed forces fighting in an international conflict may not be subjected to punishment for the mere act of participating in hostilities. States do not, and presumably will not in the future, accept the application of this principle to armed opposition groups." We will explain in chapter III-2 why we think any expansion of the internment provisions of the law of international armed conflict to situations of non-international armed conflict should be based exclusively on the internment provisions of GC IV.
[345] The legitimacy of the reasons for engaging in armed conflict has no impact on either the applicability or the interpretation of international humanitarian law. Whichever theory of "just war" may underpin discussions on the use of force and the authority or legitimacy to use force (*jus ad bellum*), it has no place in the application and interpretation of the norms of the *jus in bello*. See preambular paragraph 5 AP I; Pictet, *Commentary GC IV* (1958), p. 18; Sandoz et al., *Commentary AP I and II* (1987), pp. 28-29 and 37; ICRC, *Current Challenges to the Law of Occupation* (2005); UK, *Manual of the Law of Armed Conflict* (2004) (hereinafter "*LOAC Manual*")), p. 31; ICJ, *Wall Opinion* (2004), §§23 and 90-101; SCSL, *Fofana & Kondewa* (2008), §§ 529-530; and US, Military Tribunal, *List et al.* (1948), pp. 34-76. See also Schindler (*Hague Academy Collected Courses* 1979), p. 131; Greenwood, "The Relationship between *Jus ad Bellum* and *Jus in Bello*" (*RIS* 1983), pp. 221-234; Gasser, *International Humanitarian Law: An Introduction* (1993), p. 22; Kolb, "Sur l'origine du couple terminologique *jus ad bellum/jus in bello*" (*IRRC* 1997), p. 593; Roberts & Guelff (eds.), *Documents on the Laws of War* (2000), p. 1; Bugnion, "Guerre juste, guerre d'agression et droit international humanitaire" (*IRRC* 2002), pp. 523-546; Provost (2002), p. 849; Rona, "Interesting Times for International Humanitarian Law:

conflict,[346] a formal declaration of war or the official recognition of an armed conflict by the parties to it or by the international community at large.[347] They depend on the facts on the ground and on whether these facts qualify as a situation to which international humanitarian law applies.[348] The qualification of

Challenges from the 'War on Terror'" (*FFWA* 2003), pp. 67-68; Jinks, "The Applicability of the Geneva Conventions to the 'Global War on Terrorism'" (*Virg.JIL* 2005-2006), pp. 171-172; Sassòli & Bouvier (2006), pp. 102-108; Walzer, *Arguing about War* (2006), p. 21; Sassòli "*Ius ad Bellum* and *Ius in Bello:* The Separation between the Legality of the Use of Force and Humanitarian Rules to Be Respected in Warfare: Crucial or Outdated?" in Schmitt & Pejic (eds.), *International Law and Armed Conflict: Exploring the Faultlines: Essays in Honour of Yoram Dinstein* (2007); Greenwood in Fleck (2008), p. 51; Bassiouni, "The New Wars and the Crisis of Compliance with the Law of Armed Conflict by Non-State Actors" (*JCLC* 2008), p. 787; Dinstein (2010), p. 3; and Lubell (2010), pp. 7-9 and 91-92. To the contrary – at least for the assessment of proportionality in the conduct of hostilities in asymmetric conflicts against non-State actors, see Benvenisti, "Rethinking the Divide between Jus ad Bellum and Jus in Bello in Warfare against Nonstate Actors" (*YJIL* 2009). For a recent review of the continued relevance of the strict distinction between *jus ad bellum* and *jus in bello*, see Sloane, "The Cost of Conflation: Preserving the Dualism of *Jus ad Bellum* and *Jus in Bello* in the Contemporary Law of War" (*YJIL* 2009).

[346] E.g.: article 60§5 VCLT; Pictet, *Commentary to the First Geneva Convention* (1952), p. 51; and Sandoz et al., *Commentary AP I and II* (1987), pp. 37-38. See also Zorgbibe, *La guerre civile* (1958), p. 187; de Preux, "The Geneva Conventions and Reciprocity" (*IRRC* 1985), pp. 25-26; Kalshoven, "Laws of War" in Bernhardt (ed.), *Encyclopaedia of Public International Law* (2000) Vol. IV, p. 1379; Sassòli, "La 'guerre contre le terrorisme', le droit international humanitaire et le statut de prisonnier de guerre" (*ACDI 2001*), p. 233; Jinks (*Virg.JIL* 2005-2006), pp. 190-195; Sassòli & Bouvier (2006), p. 301; Melzer (2008), pp. 248 and 255; Bassiouni (*JCLC* 2008), p. 787; and Dinstein (2010), pp. 3-4.

[347] Common article 2 GC; Pictet, *Commentary GC III* (1960), pp. 19-23 and 35; Sandoz et al., *Commentary AP I and II* (1987), p. 1351; UK, *LOAC Manual* (2004), p. 28; Institute of International Law (IIL), *The Application of International Humanitarian Law and Fundamental Human Rights, in Armed Conflicts in which Non-State Entities are Parties* (1999), §V *in fine*; ICTR, *Akayesu* (1998), §§603 and 624. See also Schindler (*Hague Academy Collected Courses* 1979), p. 131; Bothe et al. (1982), p. 628; Kwakwa, *The International Law of Armed Conflict: Personal and Material Fields of Application* (1992), pp. 44-46; Risius in Rowe (1993), p. 290; Roberts & Guelff (2000), p. 2; Sassòli (*ACDI* 2001), p. 215; David, *Principes de droit des conflits armés* (2002), pp. 103-110; Provost (2002), pp. 278-284; Jinks, (*Virg.JIL* 2005-2006), pp. 166-168, 172-173, and 186; Melzer (2008), pp. 246-248; Sassòli & Bouvier (2006), pp. 108-109; Greenwood in Fleck (2008), pp. 46-51; and Vité, "Typology of Armed Conflicts in International Humanitarian Law: Legal Concepts and Actual Situations" (*IRRC* 2009), p. 72.

[348] Pictet, *Commentary GC III* (1960), p. 23; Sandoz et al., *Commentary AP I and II* (1987), pp. 506 and 1351; UK, *LOAC Manual* (2004), p. 29; ICTR, *Akayesu* (1998), §603; ICTR, *Rutaganda* (1999), §93; ICTY, *Blaskíc* (2000), §87 (on the role of judges: "Whatever the case, the parties to the conflict may not agree between themselves to change the nature of the conflict, which is established by the facts whose interpretation, where applicable, falls to the Judge"); ICTY, *Kordić and Čerkez* (2001), §339; ICTR, *Bagilishema* (2001), §101; ICTR, *Semanza* (2003), §357; IIL, *Resolution on IHL and Non-State Entities* (1999), § V; ICRC, *Opinion Paper on the Definition of Armed Conflict in International Humanitarian Law* (2008), p. 1. See also Schindler (*Hague Academy Collected Courses* 1979), p. 131; Risius in Rowe (1993), p. 290; Sassòli (*ACDI* 2001), pp. 217 and 229; Moir, *The Law of Internal Armed Conflict* (2002), p. 34; Provost (2002), p. 280; Hampson, (*Tehran conference paper* 2004), p. 2; Jinks, (*Virg.JIL* 2005-6), pp. 166-167, 170-173 and 186; Melzer (2008), pp. 246-247; Sassòli & Bouvier (2006), p. 103; Greenwood in Fleck (2008), p. 47; Vité (*IRRC* 2009), p. 72; Naert (2010), p. 466; and Lubell (2010), pp. 88, 91-92 and 104. But see also the debates at the 1977 Diplomatic Conference and the formal opposition there, summarized well in Forsythe, "Legal Management of Internal War: The 1977 Protocol on Non-International Armed Conflicts" (*AJIL* 1978), p. 285-287. There is no officially recognized body that can make a legally binding determination on the qualification of a situation as armed conflict and the applicability of the

a situation as an international or non-international armed conflict, or as a situation of occupation only has significance for the applicability of international humanitarian law, it does not affect the legal status of the parties to the conflict, the legitimacy of their resort to force or the legal status of a particular territory. International humanitarian law does not purport to affect the legal or political status of the parties to the conflict or the territory in which it takes place,[349]

---

relevant body of law (for an exploration of various options, put forth by military and legal experts consulted by the ICRC on the matter, see ICRC, *Report for the Conference of Government Experts* (1971), Vol. 5, pp. 37-42). The ICRC repeatedly declined proposals to be that authority during negotiations of the Additional Protocols to the Geneva Conventions (*Ibidem*, Vol. 5, p. 42; ICRC, *Report on the Work of the Conference of Government Experts* (1972), §195) and Sandoz et al., *Commentary AP I and II* (1987), p. 56 point out that "[a]s regards the crucial question of the inevitable disputes regarding the qualification of a specific conflict, one must assume that the Parties concerned will carry out their obligations in good faith, and count on the positive influence of all the High Contracting Parties." This being said, the ICRC, along with international courts and tribunals (such as the ICJ, the ICTY/R and the ICC) are generally recognized to be the most authoritative bodies to rule on the applicability of international humanitarian law. The ICJ recently emphasized the special role of the ICRC in this matter: "the Court would observe that the ICRC, whose special position with respect to execution of the Fourth Geneva Convention must be 'recognized and respected at all times' by the parties pursuant to Article 142 of the Convention, has also expressed its opinion on the interpretation to be given to the Convention [regarding the applicability of GC IV to the Israeli-occupied territories]" (ICJ, *Wall Opinion* (2004), §97). In the same sense: UK, *LOAC Manual* (2004), p. 17. For a comprehensive study of the issue, see Provost (2002), pp. 242-246 and 277-337. Provost discards the parties to the conflict, third States and the political organs of international or regional organizations as being capable of emitting a legally binding characterization of a situations as an armed conflict (or a state of emergency for the purposes of derogation from human rights law for that matter). According to Provost, independent bodies such as international courts, the ICRC and the Fact-Finding Commission established by AP I are better placed to do so, but are often limited by the scope of their own jurisdiction or mandate to pronounce on the matter.

[349] Common article 3 GC, *in fine*: "The application of the preceding provisions shall not affect the legal status of the Parties to the conflict"; article 4 AP I: "The application of the Conventions and of this Protocol, as well as the conclusion of the agreements provided for therein, shall not affect the legal status of the Parties to the conflict. Neither the occupation of a territory nor the application of the Conventions and this Protocol shall affect the legal status of the territory in question"; article 5§5 API: "In accordance with Article 4, the designation and acceptance of Protecting Powers for the purpose of applying the Conventions and this Protocol shall not affect the legal status of the Parties to the conflict or of any territory, including occupied territory"; article 3 AP II: "Nothing in this Protocol shall be invoked for the purpose of affecting the sovereignty of a State or the responsibility of the government, by all legitimate means, to maintain or re-establish law and order in the State or to defend the national unity and territorial integrity of the State. Nothing in this Protocol shall be invoked as a justification for intervening, directly or indirectly, for any reason whatever, in the armed conflict or in the internal or external affairs of the High Contracting Party in the territory of which that conflict occurs." See also Pictet, *Commentary GC III* (1960), pp. 43-44; Sandoz et al., *Commentary AP I and II* (1987), pp. 71-74, 87-89 and 1361-1364; Bothe, Partsch & Solf, *New Rules for Victims of Armed Conflict: Commentary on the Two 1977 Additional Protocols to the Geneva Conventions of 1949* (1982), p. 632; and IIL, *Resolution on IHL and Non-State Entities* (1999), §II *in fine*. For confirmation in international case law, see for example IAC°HR, *Third Report Colombia* (1999), §18; and for confirmation in the literature, see Melzer (2008), p. 253; and Sassòli & Bouvier (2006), p. 269, with further references. Similarly, non-recognition as a State or as the legitimate government of a State of the adverse party does not prevent the applicability of the law of international armed conflict if the parties are States under international law, see Schindler (*Hague Academy Collected Courses* 1979), pp. 128-130 and Greenwood in Fleck (2008), p. 51 (e.g. the non-recognition of Israel by the Arab States did not prevent the Geneva Conventions to apply in the Arab-Israeli conflict, and the non-recognition by the US of the Taliban as the legitimate Afghan

it merely seeks to mitigate the effects of war and preserve human dignity throughout its duration. Therefore, the definitions below are legal definitions, in accordance with, and for the sole purpose of determining the applicability of, international humanitarian law.[350] It is however worthwhile to note that the nature of a conflict can evolve over time and the body of law applicable to it will evolve accordingly.[351]

2.2.1.2. International armed conflicts (IAC)

Under contemporary international humanitarian law, there are two types of international armed conflicts, defined as follows:

> "Any difference arising between two States and leading to the intervention of members of the armed forces [or forces assimilated thereunto, pursuant to Article 4 GC III] [...], even if one of the Parties denies the existence of a state of war. It makes no difference how long the conflict lasts, how much slaughter takes place, or how numerous are the participating forces; it suffices for the armed forces of one Power to have captured adversaries falling within the scope of Article 4 [GC III]. Even if there has been no fighting, the fact that persons covered by the Convention are detained is sufficient for its application.

government did not have such an effect either).

[350] It is worthwhile to recall that the protective purpose of IHL requires that its scope of application be interpreted as widely as possible (e.g.: Pictet, *Commentary GC III* (1960), p. 36; Schindler (*Hague Academy Collected Courses* 1979), p. 131; Jinks, (*Virg. JIL* 2005-2006), p. 183; David (2002), p. 122; Greenwood in Fleck (2008), p. 47; and Vité (*IRRC* 2009), p. 72). The absence of precise definitions in the Geneva Conventions intentionally contributes to such a wide application (e.g.: Siotis, *Le droit de la guerre et les conflits armés d'un caractère non-international* (1958), p. 208; David (2002), p. 123; Provost (2002), p. 266; Rona, (*FFWA* 2003), p. 69 note 63; Melzer (2008), p. 252; Greenwood in Fleck (2008), p. 47; Lubell (2010), pp. 100-104. For general case law and literature on qualification of situations of violence and the scope of application of international humanitarian law, see: ICTY, *Tadić* (1995), §§; ICTR, *Akayesu* (1998), §§619-625; ICTR, *Rutaganda*, (1999), §92; ICTR, *Kayishema and Ruzindana* (1999), §171; ICTR, *Musema* (2000), §248; Kalshoven, "Reaffirmation and Development of International Humanitarian Law Applicable in Armed Conflicts: the Diplomatic Conference, Geneva, 1974-1977" (*NYIL* 1977), pp. 18-61; Schindler (*Hague Academy Collected Courses* 1979); Kwakwa (1992); Gasser (1993); Sassòli, "The Legal Qualification of the Conflicts in the Former Yugoslavia: Double Standards or New Horizons for International Humanitarian Law?" in Wang & Lee (eds.), *International Law in the Post Cold War World: Essays in Honour of Li Haopei* (2001); David (2002), pp. 101-239; Provost (2002), pp. 247-267; Tahzib-Lie & Swaak-Goldman "Determining the Threshold for the Application of International Humanitarian Law" in Lijnzaad, Van Sambeek & Tahzib-Lie (eds.), *Making the Voices of Humanity Heard* (2004), pp. 239-254; Sassòli & Bouvier (2006), pp. 108-120, 186-190 and 261-265; Greenwood in Fleck (2008), pp. 45-78; Kolb, *Ius in bello: Le droit international des conflits armés* (2009), pp. 156-199. For the ICRC's position, see its *Opinion Paper on the Definition of Armed Conflict in International Humanitarian Law* (2008).

[351] UK, *LOAC Manual* (2004), p. 17. For example, the invasion of Iraq by a US-led coalition of States on 20 March 2003 triggered an international armed conflict. When the coalition defeated the Iraqi armed forces and established actual control over at least part of the territory, it effectively became an Occupying Power (1 May 2003). When the coalition effectively transferred control of the territory to a transitional Iraqi government on 30 June 2004, the situation became one of non-international armed conflict between the Iraqi State (and the coalition forces whom Iraq requested to stay and assist the government to suppress the ongoing insurgency) and the armed opposition in the country.

The number of persons captured in such circumstances is, of course, immaterial";[352] and

"armed conflicts in which peoples are fighting against colonial domination and alien occupation and against racist regimes in the exercise of their right of self-determination, as enshrined in the Charter of the United Nations and the Declaration on Principles of International Law concerning Friendly Relations and Co-operation among States in accordance with the Charter of the United Nations" ("CAR conflicts").[353]

[352] Pictet, *Commentary GC III* (1960), p. 23, interpreting common article 2 GC, which defines the Conventions' scope of application as follows: " all cases of declared war or of any other armed conflict which may arise between two or more of the High Contracting Parties, even if the state of war is not recognized by one of them." Note that common article 2 GC modified pre-existing law in that it no longer requires a declaration of war for international humanitarian law to apply (Pictet, *Commentary GC III* (1960), pp. 19-23 and p. 35). Pictet's interpretation of common article 2 GC has been explicitly confirmed in international case law (e.g.: ICTY, *Delalić* (1998), §§184 and 208) and is accepted by the majority of legal scholars (e.g.: Schindler, (*Hague Academy Collected Courses* 1979), p. 131 Gasser (1993), pp. 21-23; David (2002), pp. 105-114; International Institute of Humanitarian Law (IIHL), *XXVIIth Round Table on Current Problems of International Humanitarian Law: International Humanitarian Law and Other Legal Regimes: Interplay in Situations of Violence: Summary Report* (2003), p. 3; Quéguiner, "Dix ans après la création du Tribunal pénal pour l'ex-Yougoslavie: Évaluation de l'apport de sa jurisprudence au droit international humanitaire" (*IRRC* 2003), p. 275; Greenwood in Fleck (2008), pp. 46-51); Naert (2010), p. 478. As the definition shows, there is no need for mutual hostilities; a single hostile act by one State against another suffices (Pictet, *Commentary GC III* (1960), p. 23; Pictet, *Commentary GC I* (1952), p. 32; Greenwood – in Fleck (2008), at p. 48 – is more sceptical). Such a hostile act can consist of the actual use of force by at least one State against the armed forces of another State, the military presence or use of force on another State's territory without its consent, or the capture of a member of another State's armed forces. However, the hostile act must explicitly or implicitly demonstrate a belligerent intent. Accidental military presence or use of force does not trigger an international armed conflict: for example a drunken border guard firing at a border post of a neighbouring State outside any planned operation does not by itself trigger the applicability of the GC. Neither does the unintended intrusion by one State's armed forces into the territorial waters of another State, as was the case with a British naval vessel in Iranian territorial waters (however the subsequent capture and internment of seven British soldiers by the Iranian armed forces did trigger the applicability of the GC, these soldiers were prisoners of war (this very short-lived international armed conflict was quickly resolved and did not involve any other use of forces between the parties to it, for an overview of the facts, BBC, "Timeline UK-Iran Stand-Off" (2007). Finally, when a State consents – explicitly or implicitly but clearly and freely – to a military intervention in its territory or otherwise directly affecting its sovereignty, there is no armed conflict (see e.g. International Law Commission, *Eighth Report of the Special Rapporteur on State Responsibility* (1979), §§68-77). However, consent given as a result of the unlawful threat or actual use of force cannot be the basis of a valid consent (*Ibidem*; see also article 52 VCLT). The threat or actual use of force is not unlawful if it respects articles 2§4, 42 and 51 UN Charter.

[353] Article 4§1 AP I. Until today, there is no example in practice where the Protocol has applied to a CAR conflict. This is not surprising since most of the conflicts the article sought to cover had reached their final stages by the time the Protocol was adopted, since most States who continue to be faced with such conflicts did not ratify AP I (e.g. Morocco and Israel, *cf. infra* section 2.2.1.7), and since the UN General Assembly has not recognized any new peoples with a right to self-determination since the adoption of the Protocol. Recognition as a people with a right to self-determination by the international community is an absolute pre-requisite for its armed forces to qualify as a national liberation movement for the purposes of article 1§4 AP I. Its applicability does not flow from auto-proclamation as such; only movements representing a people with a right to self-determination under international law (UN Charter (1945) and UNGA, *Friendly Relations Declaration* (1970)) qualify as parties to an international armed conflict under AP I. Therefore,

It is in these two types of armed conflict that the four Geneva Conventions of 1949, Additional Protocol I (in as far as it is ratified by the States parties to the conflict[354]) and customary IHL of international armed conflict apply, and in these situations alone. Their specific norms regulating internment can only be relied upon or invoked where persons are interned by a party to an international armed conflict or an Occupying Power.[355]

The 1949 Geneva Conventions were clearly drafted and intended to apply only between States.[356] Subsequent departures from this general rule show

---

the FARC and ELN in Colombia, the NPA, MILF and MNLF in the Philippines or the LTTE in Sri Lanka are armed groups party to non-international armed conflict, despite their claim of being national liberation movements (for the full names of the group and the qualification of the conflicts to which they are a party, *cf. infra* section 2.2.1.7 table). Article 1§4 AP I was conceived for the specific context of decolonization, but the conflicts in Kosovo, South Ossetia and Abkhazia have renewed interest for that provision and for the right of peoples to self-determination outside the context of decolonization. In this sense it is worth noting that the ICJ has skilfully avoided addressing the question of whether the right to self-determination applies in such contexts in its *Kosovo Opinion* (2010). For comprehensive studies of the scope of application of art. 1§4 AP I, see Abi-Saab, "Wars of National Liberation in the Geneva Convention and Protocols" (*Hague Academy Collected Courses* 1979), pp. 353-445; Koenig, *Wars of National Liberation and Modern International Humanitarian Law: A Consideration of the Scope of Application of Article I, Para. 4 of Additional Protocol I to the 1949 Geneva Conventions* (1988); and Wilson, *International Law and the Use of Force by National Liberation Movements* (1988). For a more recent work, taking into account new developments in international law and practice and arguing the expansion of article 1§4 AP I to new types of struggle for national liberation (including the cases of Kosovo, South Ossetia and Abkhazia), see Weller, *Escaping the Self-Determination Trap* (2009). For a contrary view, see Provost (2002), pp. 256-257, and the declaration made by Indonesia upon accession to the ICCPR (2006): "With reference to Article 1 of the International Covenant on Civil and Political Rights, the Government of the Republic of Indonesia declares that, consistent with the Declaration on the Granting of Independence to Colonial Countries and Peoples, and the Declaration on Principles of International Law concerning Friendly Relations and Cooperation Among States, and the relevant paragraph of the Vienna Declaration and Program of Action of 1993, the words 'the right of self-determination' appearing in this article do not apply to a section of people within a sovereign independent state and can not be construed as authorizing or encouraging any action which would dismember or impair, totally or in part, the territorial integrity or political unity of sovereign and independent states."

354 Unlike the Geneva Conventions, Additional Protocol I has not been ratified universally. It therefore only applies if ratified by the States parties to the conflict. A large portion of its provisions are customary international humanitarian law, but this is not the case for some of the provisions that are relevant to our subject (most notably, the modified conditions to qualify as a prisoner of war in article 44 AP I have not reached customary status and in this sense do not modify article 4 GC III for States who are not parties to AP I, *cf. infra*). The official and up to date list of States parties to AP I is available on the website of the Swiss Ministry of Foreign Affairs (Switzerland is the depositary State for the Conventions and their Protocols) at http://www.eda.admin.ch.

355 These are not the only instruments of IHL applicable in international armed conflict, but they are the only ones relevant to our subject matter since they are the only ones currently in force that contain provisions regarding the legal framework of deprivation of liberty in armed conflict. To be noted that IHL applies geographically to all territory under the control of a party to the conflict and is not limited to the areas of actual combat or military operations, *cf.* also *infra* section 2.2.1.4 with regard to the geographical scope of application of IHL for non-international armed conflict.

356 Sandoz et al., *Commentary AP I and II* 81987), p. 507; confirmed by the ICTY in *Tadić*, (1995), §70, ruling that an international armed conflict exists "whenever there is resort to armed force between States". This is also clear from the final provisions of the Conventions regarding their signature, ratification and entry into force, and from the provisions on implementation and

however that this does not mean that a non-State entity can never become a party to an international armed conflict. Already before 1949, the doctrine of recognition of belligerency made it possible to transpose a non-international armed conflict into an international armed conflict with the non-State entity becoming a full-fledged party to that conflict. The doctrine has fallen into desuetude and was not integrated into the Geneva Conventions, but theoretically it could still be re-activated.[357] More importantly however, by including CAR conflicts into the definition of international armed conflict (*cf. supra*), Additional Protocol I effectively recognized that certain non-State entities, *in casu* national liberation movements officially representing a people with a right to self-determination under international law, can be a party to an international armed conflict.[358]

Current debates on the definition of an international armed conflict concentrate on whether an international intergovernmental organization – such as the United Nations, the North Atlantic Treaty Organization (NATO), the European Union (EU), the African Union (AU) or the Economic Community of West-African States (ECOWAS) – can *itself* be a party to an armed conflict, and if so whether such a conflict would qualify as an international or a non-international one. We will come back to this debate in section 2.2.1.5 below.[359]

Without becoming a party to the international armed conflict itself, a non-State entity can participate in an international armed conflict *on behalf of* a State party to that international armed conflict, regardless of whether the State party's own

enforcement of the Convention. All these provisions have clearly been drafted upon the understanding that the parties to the Conventions (the "High Contracting Parties" in common article 2 GC) are States. See respectively the Conventions' articles 47/48/127/144 (dissemination); 49/50/129/146 (implementation in domestic law and criminalisation of grave breaches); 56/55/136/151 (signature); 57/56/137/152 (ratification) and 58/57/138/153 (entry into force) and the ICRC Commentary to these provisions (Pictet, *Commentary GC III* (1960), pp. 613-615, 620-625 and 640-644. Nevertheless, these provisions indicate certainly who can be a party to the Geneva Conventions, but this does not exclude the possibility that non-State entities may be a party to a conflict, as is demonstrated by the inclusion of CA3 in the Geneva Conventions, but also by provisions similar to the ones just cited in Protocols I and II, which specifically apply to non-State entities. See for example articles 83/19 (dissemination), 85 (implementation in domestic law and criminalisation of grave breaches), 92/20 (signature), 93/21 (ratification) and 95/23 (entry into force) of AP I/AP II. Art. 96 AP I specifically provides for the possibility of the authority representing a people engaged against a High Contracting (State) Party in an armed conflict as defined in its article 1§4 to make a declaration to the depositary State with the effect of bringing into force the Conventions and the Protocol between that authority and the High Contracting (State) Party in as far as the latter has also ratified the GC and AP I. No similar provision is included in AP II, probably because the non-State parties to the conflicts covered thereby are not recognized as subjects of international law in the same way as those referred to in article 1§4 AP I.

357 *Cf. infra* Part III (NIAC).

358 This expansion of the definition of international armed conflict did not take place without controversy, and it remains subject to disagreement today. Article 1§4 AP I has not (yet) evolved into customary law and it therefore only applies to conflicts where the State party to it has ratified AP I. *Cf.* also *supra* note 354.

359 The only other controversies over the definition of international armed conflicts concern the expansion of article 1§4 AP I to struggles of national liberation outside the decolonization context in which the article was adopted (*cf supra*, note 353); and the question of whether cross-border or transnational armed conflict against non-State entities are international or non-international armed conflict (*cf. infra* section 2.2.1.4).

armed forces intervene in the conflict. This is the case where that non-State entity is *de facto* operating under the international legal responsibility of a State party to the conflict. The general standard for attributing conduct of *private* persons or groups to a State[360] requires that the State have effective control over the actions of that person or that group.[361] Under international humanitarian law, however, members of the armed forces of a party to an international armed conflict are not private citizens, operating outside the official structure of the State,[362] but are at all times *official representatives of the State.*[363] The armed forces of a party to an international armed conflict, as we shall see further on, are defined broadly to include both a State's official armed forces and those military units that – without being incorporated into the regular armed forces of the State – also *belong* to that State party to the conflict.[364] The degree of control required for a military unit to *belong* to a party to the conflict is less stringent than the degree of control required for attribution of private persons or groups' acts to a State, and more along the lines of the overall control test set forth by the ICTY in the *Tadić* case.[365]

---

360 Should the party to the conflict be an international organization rather than a State (*cf. infra*), general international law rules on the responsibility of international organizations will be relevant in determining whether another entity's operations can be attributed to that organization and whether its armed forces belong to the armed forces of that organization. *Cf. infra.* We will discuss the unusual but not illogical idea that a State's armed forces can belong to a non-State party to an IAC or NIAC (an international organization) in section 2.2.1.5 below.

361 Crawford, *The International Law Commission's Articles on State Responsibility* (2002), pp. 110-113. See also ICJ, *Nicaragua v. US* (1986), §115, and ICJ, *Bosnia v. Serbia* (2007), §413.

362 Crawford (2002), p. 110.

363 Sassòli, "State Responsibility for Violations of International Humanitarian Law" (*IRRC* 2002), pp. 401-406.

364 *Cf. infra* chapter II-1, section 1.1.2.1. States are responsible under international law for the acts of both their *de jure* agents (which include their "regular armed forces") and their *de facto* agents (which include their "irregular armed forces"). Both these classes of agents may trigger an international armed conflict if using force against another State, or the fact that they are agents of a State may turn an originally non-international armed conflict into an international one. See Sassòli, (*IRRC* 2002), p. 406; and Melzer (2008), pp. 71-74 and 248-250.

365 This is borne out by article 4§A(2) GC III and article 43 AP I (in the same sense: Mallison & Mallison, "The Juridical Status of Irregular Combatants under the International Humanitarian Law of Armed Conflict" (*CWRJIL* 1977), pp. 50-55). The ICTY (*Tadić* (1999), §§88-145 and in particular §§93-94 and 137), in order to determine whether an organized military group belongs to a party to the conflict starts from the definition of armed forces in article 4 GC III, and demonstrates that "belonging to a party to the conflict" requires a relationship of dependence and allegiance. It then continues to define when an organized armed group belongs to a State party to the conflict by setting an alternative IHL test for attribution of conduct to a State – less stringent than the general test of the law on State responsibility for private persons or groups – namely that of overall control (§137): "control by a State over subordinate armed forces or militias or paramilitary units may be of an overall character (and must comprise more than the mere provision of financial assistance or military equipment or training). This requirement, however, does not go so far as to include the issuing of specific orders by the State, or its direction of each individual operation. Under international law, it is by no means necessary that the controlling authorities should plan all the operations of the units dependent on them, choose their targets, or give specific instructions concerning the conduct of military operations and any alleged violations of international humanitarian law. The control required by international law may be deemed to exist when a State (or, in the context of an armed conflict, the Party to the conflict) has a role in organising, coordinating or planning the military actions of the military group, in addition to financing, training and equipping or providing operational support to that group". Sassòli rightly remarks: "Some would argue that this standard has recently been further

However, where a group does not belong to the armed forces of a party to the conflict as defined by international humanitarian law, they are acting in a private capacity and the degree of control required for the imputation of their acts to a State is that of the general rule on State responsibility, i.e. effective control over the specific acts.

A different situation is that where a non-international armed conflict already exists in State A between that State A and an organized armed group, and a State B either attacks State A for reasons unrelated to that NIAC and thus triggers an IAC; or intervenes militarily in the NIAC to support the organized armed group in its struggle against State A.[366] In the first scenario, the two conflicts – the international one opposing States A and B, and the non-international one opposing State A and the armed group – are completely unrelated and exist in parallel. In the second scenario, the two conflicts are related but still exist – for legal purposes – in parallel, the law of international armed conflicts applying to the relations between State A and State B, and the law of non-international armed conflict applying between State A and the organized armed group. Therefore, while the two scenarios may be factually and politically different, their legal qualification for the purposes of determining the applicable law in the relations between the parties is identical.[367]

2.2.1.3. Occupation: a sub-set of rules applicable in international armed conflict

A special sub-set of international humanitarian law for international armed conflict governs territories that are occupied by one or more of the parties to the conflict. While the general body of international humanitarian law continues to apply, the provisions of the law of occupation deal with issues specifically arising in occupied territory.[368]

---

lowered when the UN Security Council acquiesced in US self-defence against Afghanistan in reaction to the terrorist attacks of 11 September 2001 committed by the non-State Al Qaeda group harboured by the Taliban, the then de facto government of Afghanistan" (he refers to UN Security Council resolutions 1368 (2001) and 1373 (2001) and to Condorelli, "Les attentats du 11 septembre et leurs suites: Où va le droit international?" (*RGDIP* 2001), pp. 838-839). However, Sassòli adds that "[i]t remains to be seen whether this indicates a development, applicable to all primary rules, of the secondary rule and whether the purported new rule is meant to apply to all States and future similar cases — this claim is indispensable for it to be a legal rule" (Sassòli, (*IRRC* 2002), p. 409).

366 This scenario is different from that discussed in the previous paragraph in that State B intervenes in *support* of the armed group but does not *control* the armed group, which does not fight *on behalf of* State B.

367 For examples, see the table in section 2.2.1.7 below.

368 The "law of occupation", i.e. those provisions of IHL of international armed conflict dealing specifically with the administration of occupied territories, is contained in articles 42-56 of the Regulations Concerning the Laws and Customs of War on Land, annexed to the Hague Convention (IV) Respecting the Laws and Customs of War on Land (hereinafter "HR 1907"), articles 47-78 GC IV, articles 3, 14, 18, 63, 66 and 85 API and customary international humanitarian law applicable in occupied territory (see for example rules 41, 51, 129A, 130 of the ICRC's compilation of customary IHL in Henckaerts & Doswald-Beck (2005)). To be noted that there is no gap in the application of the provisions of international humanitarian law between what is sometimes termed the "invasion phase" and the establishment of an effective occupation regime (e.g. Pictet, *Commentary GC IV* (1958), pp. 60; and IAC°HR, *Coard v. USA* (1999), §51). For an overview of the sources of the law

International humanitarian law defines occupation as follows:

"Territory is considered occupied when it is actually placed under the authority of the hostile army [...] even if the said occupation meets with no armed resistance [...] The occupation extends only to the territory where such authority has been established and can be exercised."[369]

Occupation includes an element of military control by the Occupying Power over the occupied territory, to a degree sufficient to trigger the applicability of the law of occupation, a set of rules that are part of the international humanitarian law of international armed conflict.[370] Whether the threshold of actual territorial control has been reached must be established on a case-by-case basis; it is possible, however, to distil a number of general indicators from international case law and the works of scholars in this field, including but not limited to the following:[371]

---

of occupation, see the literature referred to *infra* note 371.

[369] Article 42 HR 1907 and common article 2 GC. Before the adoption of the 1949 Geneva Conventions, international humanitarian law only applied to *belligerent* occupation (see article 42 HR 1907). Common article 2 GC explicitly makes it applicable to *any* occupation, even if it does not meet with any armed resistance. This definition of occupation is now part of customary international law, as has been confirmed in ICJ, *Wall Opinion* (2004), §§78 and 89; ICJ, *DRC v. Uganda* (2005), §172; ICTY, *Kordić & Čerkez* (2001), §338.

[370] A state of occupation does not mean that the international armed conflict that is likely to have preceded it has come to an end. Common article 2 GC includes occupation in the scope of application of the Conventions as a whole. This is particularly important for persons deprived of liberty as is pointed out by Pictet: "This new provision is particularly pertinent for the protection of civilian persons under the Fourth Convention, but its inclusion is none the less appropriate in regard to prisoners of war, since, even in the absence of resistance, the Occupying Power might be tempted to intern all or part of the armed forces of the adversary in the interests of its future security. For that reason it was necessary to ensure that such internees would be treated as prisoners of war throughout their detention" (Pictet, *Commentary GC III* (1960), p. 23); and "[i]n case of war being declared or of armed conflict, the Convention enters into force; the fact that the territory of one or other of the belligerents is later occupied in the course of hostilities does not in any way affect this; the inhabitants of the occupied territory simply become protected persons as they fall into the hands of the Occupying Power. [...] An armistice suspends hostilities and a capitulation ends them, but neither ends the state of war, and any occupation carried out in wartime is covered by paragraph 1. It is, for that matter, when a country is defeated that the need for international protection is most felt. The full application of the Convention under those circumstances is limited in point of time by Article 6" (Pictet, *Commentary GC IV* (1958), pp. 21-22). Moreover, even in the absence of hostilities, occupation by itself constitutes a military intervention against the sovereignty of the occupied State; the occupying and occupied State are thus in a state of international armed conflict and the full body of law regulating such conflict applies (common article 2§2 GC, article 6§3 GC IV and article 3§b AP I). In the same sense, e.g.: ICRC, *Current Challenges to the Law of Occupation* (2005), at 4; Sassòli & Bouvier (2006), p. 189; Melzer (2008), p. 250. To the contrary: US, *Digest of United States Practice in International Law* (2008), p. 169 (insisting that occupation is a legally separate situation from that of international armed conflict, to which only the law of occupation applies).

[371] On the definition of occupation, the scope of application of the law of occupation, the lawfulness of armed resistance to occupation and the legal status of persons involved in such resistance see: ICJ, *Wall Opinion* (2004), §§78, 92 and 95 and ICJ, *DRC v. Uganda* (2005), §§173-178; ICRC, *Current Challenges to the Law of Occupation* (2005); Boyd, "The Applicability of International Law in the Occupied Territories" (*Isr.YHR* 1971); Shamgar, "*The Observance of International Law in the Administered Territories*" (*Isr.YHR* 1971); Mallison & Fabri, "The Juridical Characteristics of Belligerent Occupation and the Resort to Resistance by the Civilian Population: Doctrinal Development and Continuity" (*GWLR*, 1974); Roberts, "What is Military Occupation?" (*BYIL* 1984);

• Authority is usually exercised by virtue of the Occupying Power's effective *factual* control, the legality of that control is irrelevant;

• Authority is no less that of the Occupying Power where the latter has set up a quasi-independent puppet regime that remains under its overall control or similarly exercises its authority through existing local government structures;[372]

• Effective territorial control goes beyond mere military presence in or around the territory; it implies a *substitution* by the armed forces of the Occupying Power of administration powers of the occupied State;[373]

Roberts, "Prolonged Military Occupation; The Israeli-Occupied Territories since 1967" (*AJIL* 1990); Haggenmacher, "L'occupation militaire en droit international: genèse et profil d'une institution juridique" (*RI* 1994), pp. 285-301; Bothe, Michael, "Occupation after Armistice" in: Bernhardt, Rudolf (ed.), *Encyclopedia of Public International Law* (1997); Kretzmer, *The Occupation of Justice: The Supreme Court of Israel and the Occupied Territories* (2002); Benvenisti, *The International Law of Occupation* (2004); Kolb, Porretto & Vité, *L'application du droit international humanitaire et des droits de l'homme aux organisations internationales: Forces de paix et administrations civiles transitoires* (2005), pp. 205-232; College of Europe & ICRC, *Proceedings of the Bruges Colloquium: Current Challenges to the Law of Occupation* (2006); and Dinstein, *The Law of Belligerent Occupation* (2009). The list of indicators summarized below is based on a combined reading of these sources.

372 Roberts, "Military Occupations and the Problem of Transformation: Applying the Laws of War and of Human Rights" (*Tehran Conference paper* 2004), pp. 1-2: "The occupant, including such occupying forces or officers as are mentioned in the conventions, usually exercises authority by virtue of his effective factual control, rather than by virtue of any legal entitlement. That factual authority is nonetheless accorded a degree of recognition in the conventions. [...] There is a clear implication in all of this of a well ordered chain of military command and legal responsibility coming down from the government of the occupying state: and indeed most occupation administrations have such a character." [...] Occupants often attempt to disguise or limit their own role by operating indirectly: either by setting up some kind of quasi-independent puppet regime; or by operating through the existing system of government, which remains in post within occupied territory. However the obligations laid on an occupant remain. Illegal acts committed through the instrumentality of such bodies are a responsibility of the occupying power." In the same sense: ECtHR (Grand Chamber), *Loizidou v. Turkey* (1995), §62: "The obligation to secure, in such an area, the rights and freedoms set out in the Convention derives from the fact of such control whether it be exercised directly, through its armed forces, or through a subordinate local administration"; and ICTY, *Tadić* (1997), §584: "the relationship of de facto organs or agents to the foreign Power includes those circumstances in which the foreign Power 'occupies' or operates in certain territory solely through the acts of local de facto organs or agents." The degree of control necessary to establish occupation through de facto local organs or agents is that of 'overall control', namely where the State "has a role in organising, coordinating or planning the military actions of the military group, in addition to financing, training and equipping or providing operational support to that group" (ICTY, *Tadić* (1999), §137; confirmed for occupation through local structures in ICTY, *Blaškić* (2000), §149; ICTY, *Naletilić & Martinović*, (2003), §§181-188 and 197-202). See also ICRC, *Current Challenges to the Law of Occupation* (2005): "Not every transfer of authority to a local government and subsequent expression of consent to the presence of foreign troops necessarily amounts to the end of occupation. The devolution of governmental authority to a national government must be sufficiently effective. [...] if occupying powers operate indirectly through an existing or newly appointed indigenous government, the law of occupation is likely to continue to apply. The reason for this is evident. Situations must be avoided where the protections to be granted to persons and property under the law of occupation are circumvented. The occupying power cannot discard its obligations by installing a puppet government or by pressuring an existing one to act on its behalf. In all these cases, the occupying power maintains *de facto* – albeit indirectly – full control over the territory."

373 ICJ, *DRC v. Uganda* (2005), §173: "the Court will need to satisfy itself that the Ugandan armed forces in the DRC were not only stationed in particular locations but also that they had substituted their own authority for that of the Congolese Government. In that event, any justification given by

• Annexation does not affect the continued applicability of IHL;[374] and

• A territory is not occupied if the occupied State has given its free and genuine consent to the Occupying Power's exercise of control and authority in the territory.

Recent debates on the definition of occupation for the purposes of the applicability of international humanitarian law have raised the question whether and when the administration of a territory by an international intergovernmental organization like the United Nations or the European Union qualifies as occupation, and thus triggers the applicability of the specific international legal rules regulating such a situation. We will come back to this debate in section 2.2.1.5.

2.2.1.4. Non-international armed conflicts (NIAC)

For the purpose of determining the applicable international humanitarian law, there are two types of non-international armed conflicts, the second one being a specific subset of the first one:

• Situations in which one or more organized armed groups engage in hostilities against a State, or against one or more other organized armed groups; and

• Armed conflicts which "take place in the territory of a High Contracting Party between its armed forces and dissident armed forces or other organized armed groups which, under responsible command, exercise *such control over a part of its territory as to* enable them to carry out sustained and concerted military operations and to implement [the obligations of parties to the conflict contained in AP II]."[375]

Uganda for its occupation would be of no relevance; nor would it be relevant whether or not Uganda had established a structured military administration of the territory occupied" (emphasis added). The Court concluded that Uganda occupied part of the DRC's territory (§178).

[374] Article 47 GC IV.

[375] Article 1§1 AP II (emphasis added). Additional Protocol II has a more restricted and significantly higher threshold of application: armed conflicts between different factions in a country but not involving the armed forces of the State are excluded, and the "dissident armed forces or other organised armed groups" need to have a substantial control over a part of the territory of the State. On the contrary, the terminology in common article 3 of the Geneva Conventions (CA3) was understood to include armed conflict between different groups in one State. During the three-year Diplomatic Conference leading to the adoption of AP II, two main tendencies shaped the debate and consequently the final wording of this article. On the one hand the compromise for the adoption of the Protocol was to be either a broad definition combined with a minimised set of normative rules, or a restrictive definition combined with a more detailed set of norms. On the other hand, States did not want to yield on the issue of internal disturbances and tensions, which remained excluded from the definition of non-international armed conflict. The end result is that the AP II has both a restricted scope of application *and* a minimised set of normative rules. For an analysis of the debates, based on the official documents of the Diplomatic Conference, see Forsyth (*AJIL* 1978); Junod, "Additional Protocol II: History and Scope", (*AULR* 1983); Lysaght, "The Scope of Protocol II and its Relation to Common Article 3 of the Geneva Conventions of 1949 and Other Human Rights Instruments" (*AULR* 1983); and Abi-Saab, "Humanitarian Law and Internal Conflicts: The Evolution of Legal Concern" in Delissen & Tanja (eds.), *Humanitarian Law of Armed Conflict: Challenges Ahead. Essays in Honour of Frits Kalshoven* (1991).

Common article 3 of the Geneva Conventions (CA3 GC) and customary international humanitarian law for non-international armed conflict apply to both types of conflicts.[376] Only in the second type of armed conflict, however, does Additional Protocol II apply as a matter of treaty law.[377]

Moreover, international humanitarian law encourages the parties to non-international armed conflicts to conclude special agreements in order to bring into force all or some of the provisions of the law applicable to international armed conflicts, and in particular the four Geneva Conventions.[378]

The scope of application of common article 3 GC and AP II must be given the widest interpretation possible, and their applicability may not be objected to on the basis of the principle of non-intervention, since their substantive provisions do "not in any way limit the right of a State to put down rebellion, nor [...] increase in the slightest the authority of the rebel party."[379]

It has proven difficult to find agreement on a precise positive definition of non-international armed conflict.[380] The upper threshold is defined in clear terms by the negative definition in CA3 GC as armed conflicts *not of an international*

[376] While it may be less reader-friendly, we prefer the use of the term "non-international armed conflict" (also used in the text of CA3) over the term "internal armed conflict" for two reasons. First, in the absence of a positive definition of the type of armed conflict that triggers the applicability of CA3, the negative definition of non-international armed conflict as including all armed conflicts that are "not international" (and thus covered by CA2 and AP I) better reflects the requirement of a broad interpretation of the material scope of application of the GC and its AP in light of their protective purpose (cf. *supra* and *infra*). Second, the use of the term "internal armed conflict" may give the incorrect impression that only armed conflicts that are confined to the territory of a single State are armed conflicts in the sense of CA3 or AP II (*cf. infra*).

[377] To be noted that the distinction is increasingly moot, since the bulk of the provisions of AP II apply in all non-international armed conflicts as a matter of customary international humanitarian law. E.g.: Henckaerts, "Study on Customary International Humanitarian Law: A Contribution to the Understanding and Respect for the Rule of Law in Armed Conflict" (*IRRC* 2005), p. 188, see also Henckaerts & Doswald-Beck (2005) and the ICRC's updated *Customary IHL Database* (2010).

[378] CA 3 GC: "The Parties to the conflict should further endeavour to bring into force, by means of special agreements, all or part of the other provisions of the present Convention." Examples of such special agreements are those conclude in course of the Balkan conflicts in the early 1990's (extracts reprinted in Sassòli & Bouvier (2006), Vol. I, p. 262 and Vol. II, pp 1761-1769). Moreover, both State and non-State parties to the conflict can also unilaterally declare their intention to respect international humanitarian law for international armed conflicts in part or in full, on the legal value of such declarations, see Plattner (*RBDI* 1984-1985). Note that the conclusion of CA3 agreements or the adoption of unilateral declarations of adherence do not make the conflict an international armed conflict and have no other legal consequences than bringing into the force the selected provisions of international humanitarian law. In the same sense: Sassòli & Bouvier (2006), p. 269.

[379] Pictet, *Commentary GC III* (1960), p. 36: "the scope of application of the Article must be as wide as possible." The Commentary upon stating this, immediately addresses the main concern of States in adopting any law for NIAC at all: "There can be no drawback in this, since the Article in its reduced form, contrary to what might be thought, does not in any way limit the right of a State to put down rebellion, nor does it increase in the slightest the authority of the rebel party." *Cf.* also *supra* note 349 and note 350.

[380] Failure to achieve consensus over its content is another reason for the absence of a precise definition in CA 3 GC (Pictet, *Commentary GC III* (1960), pp. 35-37. For the importance of a sufficiently abstract definition to ensure a wide scope of application to CA3 GC, *cf. supra* note 379, see also ICRC, *Report for the Conference of Government Experts* (1971), Vol. 5, pp. 44-46.

character, which refers back to the positive definition of international armed conflicts in the Conventions' common article 2 (CA 2). Therefore, a conflict that qualifies as an international armed conflict or situation of occupation as defined above cannot be a non-international armed conflict. The definitions of armed conflict in common article 2 and common article 3 to the 1949 Geneva Conventions are mutually exclusive: any armed conflict is either international or non-international, and consequently covered either by CA 2 or by CA 3.[381]

It is the lower threshold of non-international armed conflict that may prove more difficult to establish.[382] For the purposes of the applicability of

[381] This flows from the text of both CA 2 ("any [...] armed conflict which may arise between two or more of the High Contracting Parties") and CA 3 ("armed conflict not of an international character" as defined in CA 2); and from the purpose of those Conventions to regulate all situations of armed conflict. To be noted in this regard that IHL *only* applies to situations of armed conflict as defined in CA2 and CA3 (definitions that have been further developed in articles 1§4 AP I and 1§1 AP II) and not to situations that fall below this threshold, e.g.: ICJ, *Corfu Channel* (1949), p. 22; David (2002). pp. 185-189. In the same sense: EU, *Guidelines on Promoting Compliance with IHL* (2005), §§9-11; Lavoyer, "International Humanitarian Law and Terrorism" in Lijnzaad et al. (2004), p. 262; Quéguiner (*IRRC* 2003), p. 281; Rona (*FFWA* 2003), p. 69; Jinks (*Virg.JIL* 2005-2006), p. 168; Sassòli, "Transnational Armed Groups and International Humanitarian Law" (*HPCR Series* 2006), p. 9; Sassòli & Bouvier (2006), p. 108; Melzer (2008), pp. 268-269. This is also the position the US has taken with regard to the definition of armed conflict in the ILC's *Draft Articles on Effects of Armed Conflict on Treaties* (2008): "we feel strongly that attempting to define the term 'armed conflict,' as in draft article 2(b), is likely to be confusing and counterproductive. The wide variety of views that have been expressed about what the definition should be is evidence of the challenges that such an exercise involves. A better approach would be to make clear that *armed conflict refers to the set of conflicts covered by common articles 2 and 3 of the Geneva Conventions* (i.e., international and non-international armed conflicts)" (US, *Digest of Practice* (2008), p. 169, emphasis added). The ILC in its commentary to draft article 2(b) specifies that its definition of armed conflict) is "for the purposes of the [...] draft articles only. It is not the intention to provide a definition of armed conflict for international law generally" (ILC, *Report of the 60th* Session, Chapter V, "Effects of Armed Conflicts on Treaties" (2008), p. 90). Article 2 of the ILC's *Draft Articles* reads: "'Armed conflict' means a state of war or a conflict which involves armed operations which by their nature or extent are likely to affect the application of treaties between States parties to the armed conflict or between a State party to the armed conflict and a third State, regardless of a formal declaration of war or other declaration by any or all of the parties to the armed conflict."

[382] See for example the IAC°HR in *Abella v. Argentina* (1997), §153 and 155 explaining that what differentiated the events at La Tablada from a situation of internal disturbances was "the concerted nature of the hostile acts undertaken by the attackers, the direct involvement of governmental armed forces, and the nature and the level of the violence attending the events in question [...] an armed attack, i.e., a military operation, against a quintessential military objective – a military base." This reflects the organizational and intensity criteria further discussed below. The scope of application of AP II is formulated in more precise terms (*cf. supra* note 374) and their interpretation has given rise to less debate. However, the degree and nature of territorial control required by its article 1§1 is not always easy to establish in practice. Generally, but taking into account the non-State nature of the party to the conflict, such control is defined by reference to the definition of occupied territory (*cf. supra* note 368 and accompanying text). For the purposes of the analysis in this book, there is no need to distinguish between CA3 and AP2 conflicts since the (very scarce) rules on internment in NIAC are not different according to the type of NIAC in which they apply. Moreover, as the ICRC rightly points out: "Additional Protocol II '*develops and supplements* [CA3] *without modifying its existing conditions of application*' [...]. This means that the restrictive definition is relevant for the application of Protocol II only, but does not extend to the law of NIAC in general" (ICRC, *Opinion paper* (2008), p. 3, original italics). This is also confirmed in article 8§2 ICC Statute (*cf. infra* notes

international humanitarian law, it is important to distinguish situations of armed conflict from situations that fall below that threshold, usually referred to as internal disturbances or tensions.[383] Two criteria must be met for armed violence to be qualified as an *armed conflict*: (a) the non-State party or parties to the conflict must be sufficiently organized, and (b) the hostilities must have reached a certain level of intensity. The following factual indicators are useful for determining whether these two criteria have been met in a given situation at a given time:[384]

390-391 and accompanying text), without prejudice to the fact that the distinction between CA3 and AP II conflicts remains relevant for the definition of war crimes under the Statute.

[383] They are defined in article 1§2 AP II as "situations of internal disturbances and tensions, such as riots, isolated and sporadic acts of violence and other acts of a similar nature, as not being armed conflicts." In the same sense: ICJ, *Nicaragua v. US* (1986), §§115-116 and 219; ICTR, *Akayesu* (1998), §601; and article 8§2(c) and (f) ICC Statute. For further details see Sandoz et al., *Commentary AP I and II* (1987), pp. 1354-1356 (including further definitions for practical use that are part of official ICRC doctrine), and the case law and literature referred to in notes 349 and 384.

[384] They are factual indicators, not cumulative and constitutive elements of the legal definition of a non-international armed conflict. If these or other factual indicators demonstrate that the two cumulative criteria of organisation and intensity are fulfilled, the threshold of armed conflict is met and international humanitarian law applicable. This will need to be done on a case by case basis taking into account the specific circumstances of any given case at any given moment. The list of criteria is based on the text of articles 4 GC III, 43 AP I, 1 AP I; and 1 AP II; article 8§2 ICC Statute; and on the discussions regarding the scope of application of CA 3 GC in the preparatory works of the Conventions and their Additional Protocols (summarized well in Pictet, *Commentary GC III* (1960), pp. 37-38, Sandoz et al., *Commentary AP I and II* (1987), pp. 39-41, 55-56 and 1319-1356); international case law (in particular ICJ, *Nicaragua v. US* (1986), §218; IAC°HR, *Abella v. Argentina* (1997), §§149-156; ICTR, *Akayesu* (1998), §§619-625; ICTR, *Rutaganda* (1999), §93; and ICTY, *Haradinaj* (2008), §§ 39-99, the Trial Chamber in *Haradinaj* reviews the whole case law of the ICTY to examine how the Tribunal has applied the test put forth in the Tadić decision of 1995 (*cf. infra*) to distil and substantiate the factual indicators for the criteria of organisation and intensity to be met, the reviewed case law includes the decisions in the *Delalíc, Milošević, Kordić & Čerkez, Halilović, Limaj et al., Hadžihasanović & Kubura, Martić,* and *Mrskic et al.* cases); the writings of authoritative legal experts (*cf. supra* note 349 and in particular Pinto, "Les règles du droit international concernant la guerre civile" (*Hague Academy Collected Courses* 1965), pp. 524-548; Draper, "The Status of Combatants and the Question of Guerrilla Warfare" (*BYIL* 1971), pp. 209-210; Bothe, "Conflits armés internes et droit international humanitaire" (*RGDIP* 1978); Forsythe (*AJIL* 1978); Gasser, "International and Non-International Armed Conflicts: Case Studies of Afghanistan, Kampuchea and Lebanon" (*AULR* 1982); De Schutter & Van den Wyngaert, "Coping with Non-International Armed Conflicts: The Borderline Between National and International Law" (*GJICL* 1983); Solf (*AULR* 1983); Abi-Saab, "Conflits armés de caractère non-international" in UNESCO/Institut Henry Dunant, *Les dimensions internationales du droit humanitaire* (1986); Cassese, "La guerre civile et le droit international" (*RGDIP* 1986), pp. 553-578; Levie, *The Law of Non-International Armed Conflict* (1987); Abi-Saab (R.) in *Liber Amoricum Kalshoven* (1991); Abi-Saab (G.), "The 1977 Additional Protocols and General International Law: Some Preliminary Reflections" in *Liber Amoricum Kalshoven* (1991); Gasser, "Armed Conflict within the Territory of a State" in Haller et al. (eds.) *Im Dienst an der Gemeinschaft. Festschrift für Dietrich Schindler zum 65. Geburtstag* (1989); Momtaz, "Le droit international humanitaire applicable aux conflits armés non-internationaux" (*Hague Academy Collected Courses* 2001); Moir (2002) pp. 30-52; Institute of International Law, *Resolution on IHL and Non-State Entities* (1999); IIHL, *Report of the San Remo Roundtable* (2003), p. 6; Sassòli (*HPCR Series* 2006), pp. 8-9; Bassiouni (*JCLC* 2008); ICRC, *Opinion Paper* (2008); Rona, "Observations on U.S. Practice Relating to 'Enemy Combatants'" (*Human Rights First paper* 2008), pp. 5-6; Kolb (2009), pp. 171-174; Cullen, *The Concept of Non-International Armed Conflict in International Humanitarian Law* (2010); and Lubell (2010), pp. 107-11; and our own professional experience as an operational legal advisor at the ICRC.

(a.) Organization:[385]

• Existence of a command structure or some kind of hierarchical organization, troops acting under the authority of identified commanders or leaders (permanently based in headquarters or mobile but disposing of sufficient communication means with troops to plan and organise military operations);

• Ability to plan, organize, coordinate and carry out military operations, to define a unified military strategy and to use military tactics;

• Collective character of armed violence (as opposed to a series of acts committed by isolated individuals without co-ordination);

• Existence of disciplinary rules and mechanisms, members generally executing orders of their commanders and being sanctioned for failing to do so;

• Ability to gain access to weapons and other military equipment necessary to carry out military operations;

• Ability to recruit a sufficient number of troops to carry out sustained military operations, and to provide them with basic military training;

• Capacity to respect basic rules of international humanitarian law; inclusion of such rules in the training of recruits and the planning of military operations; proclaimed and/or actual adherence to international humanitarian law by political or military authorities;

• Ability to move around in a determinate territory, or actual control of territory;

• Ability to distinguish in a way that its members are recognizable by the adverse party (uniforms, armlets, headgear, tattoos, etc.);

• Existence of a political authority closely linked to the military structure of the group, and nature of the objectives sought to achieve through armed struggle;

• Nature of the targets of operations (military/official versus civilian/private);

• Ability to speak with one voice on behalf of the group to the adverse party, the population, representatives of international organisations or the media;

• Ability to conduct negotiations or conclude agreements with the adverse party or a neutral intermediary;

• Official or *de facto* recognition of the insurgents as an organized armed group by the State party to the conflict, third States or organisations representing the population or the regional or international community.

---

[385] States' armed forces are presumed to meet the organisational criterion (*cf. infra*, chapter II-1; and ICTY, *Haradinaj*, (2008), §60). Theoretically speaking however, should they in practice fail to meet this test, they would not qualify as a party to the conflict. This may be the case in some so-called "failed States", where in practice there is no State nor any State armed forces. The situation may still be a non-international armed conflict if it takes place between two or more organized armed groups. If however, there are not at least two organized armed groups fighting each other, the threshold of armed conflict will not be reached and international humanitarian law will not apply.

(b.) Intensity:

• Type of forces, weapons and equipment (military versus law enforcement) used by a State party engaged in the hostilities;[386]

• Type of weapons and equipment used by the non-State party to carry out its operations;

• Number and type of State troops engaged in hostilities and nature of their training;

• Number, scale and intensity of armed confrontations;

• Duration of and intervals between armed confrontations;

• Number of casualties (dead, wounded), of persons fleeing zones of combat, and extent of destruction caused by hostilities between the parties;

• Attention or involvement of actors like the UN Security Council, the ICRC and international or regional conflict resolution mechanisms;

• References made by the local authorities or population to zones of combat and intense armed confrontations;

• Capacity of local or national authorities to deal with the humanitarian consequences of the violence; scale of activities of non-governmental or international relief organizations to address these consequences.

• A non-international armed conflict thus exists when the parties to the conflict are clearly identifiable,[387] sufficiently organized as a military force, and when the hostilities are of military nature and have reached a certain level of intensity that distinguish them from sporadic incidents of armed violence.

(c.) Duration: an additional criterion?

In its renown definition of a non-international armed conflict in the *Tadić* case – the only positive definition of such a conflict in international law – the International Criminal Tribunal for the Former Yugoslavia seems to add a third criterion, namely that of the duration of the hostilities. For such an armed conflict to exist, the Tribunal's Trial Chamber in that case considered the hostilities must be of a "protracted" nature:

> "an armed conflict exists whenever there is a resort to armed force between States or *protracted* armed violence between governmental authorities and organised armed groups or between such groups within a State."[388]

---

[386] On the concept of hostilities and the main differences between a hostilities paradigm and a law enforcement paradigm on the use of force, see Melzer (2008), pp. 85-89, 243-245 and 269-278.

[387] The parties must be identifiable both for determining their degree of organization, for the implementation of the fundamental principle of distinction, and for the identification of the bearers of rights and responsibilities under international humanitarian law. Phenomena such as terrorism, drug-trafficking and other cannot be parties to an armed conflict. In the same sense, e.g.: Draper, "The Geneva Conventions of 1949 (*Hague Academy Collected Courses* 1965), p. 63, 90); Jinks, "September 11 and the Laws of War" (*YJIL* 2003); Rona (*FFWA* 2003), p. 60; and Melzer (2008), p. 254. *Cf.* also *infra* section 2.2.1.6.

[388] ICTY, *Tadić* (1995), §70 (emphasis added). The ICTY thus discarded the requirement of territorial control in Additional Protocol II and included armed conflicts not involving government forces.

The Chamber did not however define "protracted" and consequently debates arose about how long armed violence must go on before a situation can be qualified as an "armed conflict".

Two years later, the Inter-American Commission of Human Rights, in the *Abella* case found however that an armed attack by an organized armed group on a governmental military base resulting in intense hostilities lasting for 2 days, triggered, despite its brief duration, the application of common article 3 to the Geneva Conventions.[389]

Another year later, the Statute of the International Criminal Court – a treaty negotiated and adopted by the international community of States at large, even if not ratified universally – endorsed the broad definition given earlier by the ICTY in its definition of non-international armed conflicts *covered by customary international humanitarian law* and included the "protracted" element.[390] For conflicts covered by common Article 3 of the Geneva Conventions *as treaty law* however, the condition of "protracted" armed violence was not withheld in the ICC Statute.[391]

In 2008, the Trial Chamber of the ICTY in the *Haradinaj* case conducted a very useful overview of the Tribunal's case law regarding the criteria that must be met for a non-international armed conflict to exist. Based on how the Tribunal applied the definition of the Trial Chamber in the *Tadić* case to the various conflicts it has been concerned with since, the Trial Chamber rightly concluded that:

> "The criterion of protracted armed violence has [...] been interpreted in practice, including by the *Tadić* Trial Chamber itself, as referring more to the intensity of the armed violence than to its duration."[392]

This interpretation, that duration is a factual indicator for the criterion of intensity rather than a separate constitutive element of a non-international armed conflict, is in our view the correct one. Whereas duration is an important factor with considerable weight, it is not as such a constitutive element of the threshold of armed conflict. If the armed violence is carried out by an organized armed group, planned and controlled rather than spontaneous, and results in short but intense hostilities between that group and a State's armed forces or another organized armed group, the threshold of non-international armed conflict is met.[393] We therefore agree with the Inter-American Commission's qualification

---

389 IAC°HR, *Abella v. Argentina* (1997), §§155-156.

390 While explicitly excluding "internal disturbances and tensions", it defines non-international armed conflicts as: "armed conflicts that take place in the territory of a State when there is protracted armed conflict between governmental authorities and organised armed groups or between such groups" (article 8§2 (f) ICC Statute which applies to the war crimes that are serious violations of the "laws and customs of war" applicable in internal armed conflicts and are listed in its article 8§2 (e)).

391 Article 8§2(c) ICC Statute.

392 ICTY, *Haradinaj* (2008), §49.

393 In the same sense, e.g.: Provost (2002), pp. 266 and 268; IIHL, *Report of the San Remo Roundtable* (2003), p. 6; Quéguiner (*IRRC* 2003), pp. 278-281; Tahzib-Lie & Swaak-Goldman in

of the situation in the *Abella* case. Taking into account the clearly protracted nature of the different conflicts in the Balkans since the early 1990's – the only conflicts that fall within its scope of jurisdiction – the ICTY will not have to pronounce itself further on how short a non-international armed conflict can actually be. It is also unlikely – but not impossible – that a conflict of such short duration will be the subject of a decision by the International Criminal Court any time soon.

(d.) Geographical limits to the definition of NIAC?

Non-international armed conflicts are not defined by geographical boundaries but by the nature of the parties to the conflict.[394] What makes an armed conflict international is that there are at least two adverse State parties (*cf. supra* section 2.2.1.2); conflicts that do not oppose at least two States are by definition non-international in nature.[395] The parties to such a conflict must be organized and identifiable (*cf. supra*). Similarly, a conflict must take place in a sufficiently confined and identifiable territory; but this does not necessarily mean the conflict cannot take place across international borders.[396] For example, a non-international armed conflict opposing a State A and an organized armed group on the territory of A but "spilling over" into the territory of a neighbouring State B remains a non-international armed conflict.[397] Equally so, a conflict may oppose a State A to an organized armed group exclusively present in and operating from the territory of a State B without changing the non-international nature of that armed conflict. Such "exported" non-international armed conflicts will not trigger the parallel application of the law of international armed conflict as long as State B consents to State A engaging with an adverse party on its territory.[398]

Lijnzaad et al. (2004), pp. 247-248; Sassòli *(HPCR Series* 2006), pp. 6-7; Melzer (2008) p. 257; Lubell (2010), p. 106. To the contrary: Jinks (*Virg.JIL* 2005-2006), pp. 185-186.

394 In the same sense, e.g.: ICTR, *Musema*, (2000), §247; Sandoz et al., *Commentary AP I and II* (1987), p. 1319; Sassòli (*HPCR Series* 2006), p. 9; Lubell (2010), pp. 104-108.

395 With the notable exception of CAR conflicts (article §4 AP I). *Cf. supra* note 381 and accompanying text, in the same sense: Lubell (2010), pp. 104-108.

396 In the same sense: Zegveld (2002), p. 136; Sassòli (*HPCR Series* 2006), p. 9; Kälin & Künzli, *The Law of International Human Rights Protection* (2009), p. 151; and Lubell (2010), pp. 104-108.

397 Therefore, article 1 and 7 of the ICTR Statute extend the jurisdiction of the tribunal to prosecute crimes committed in relation to the non-international armed conflict that took place in Rwanda in 1994 to crimes committed in direct relation to that conflict by the parties thereto on the territory of neighbouring countries. Spill-overs have also occurred in the context of the NIAC in Afghanistan (into Pakistan) and in the NIAC opposing Uganda to the Lord Resistance Army (LRA) (*cf. infra* section 2.2.1.7).

398 For example, the conflict opposing Israel and the Hezbollah in 2006 was non-international in nature (opposing Israel and the Hezbollah), even if it took place on Lebanese territory. However, the fact that Lebanon did not consent but on the contrary fiercely objected to Israel's military intervention in its territory – without controlling or even allying itself with the Hezbollah – triggered a parallel international armed conflict between Israel and Lebanon, even if their armed forces did not confront each other in combat. The Israeli government claims the question of the nature of cross-border conflicts is not settled, e.g.: Israel, Ministry of Foreign Affairs (MFA), *The Operation in Gaza: 27 December 2008 – 18 January 2009. Factual and Legal Aspects* (2009), §29: "It is not yet settled which regime applies to cross-border military confrontations between a sovereign State and a

Some authors oppose this interpretation and claim that a non-international armed conflict is by definition confined to the territory of a single State, and that spill-over, cross-border or transnational armed conflicts therefore fall outside the scope of application of the international humanitarian law of non-international armed conflict.[399] Such a restrictive definition of non-international armed conflict certainly fits the type of conflicts that existed at the time of the drafting of the Geneva Conventions and their Additional Protocols, and – at first glance – finds therefore some support in the language of their relevant provisions. Common article 3 contains provisions applicable in "armed conflicts [...] in the territory of one of the High Contracting Parties" and article 1§1 AP II defines the scope of application of the Protocol as " in the territory of a High Contracting Party between its armed forces [...] part of its territory." Pictet's Commentary to CA 3 GC aptly sums up the type of conflicts the drafters had in mind: the article applies to "armed conflicts, with armed forces on either side engaged in hostilities – conflicts, in short, which are in many respects similar to an international war, but take place within the confines of a single country."[400]

But such a restrictive interpretation of the scope of application of the law of non-international armed conflict would not be in line with the object and purpose of these provisions and the treaties they belong to. Pictet himself said in his commentary that CA 3 must be interpreted to allow for a wide scope of application.[401] International humanitarian law seeks to mitigate human suffering by regulating the conduct of *hostilities* wherever they take place and protecting all *persons* directly affected by an armed conflict wherever they may find themselves. This protective purpose imposes a wide interpretation of its scope of application to include all situations of armed conflict.[402] The text in CA 3 GC and in article 1 AP II referring to the territory of one of the "High Contracting

non-State terrorist armed group operating from a separate territory." The Israeli Supreme Court however found the conflict with Hezbollah to be international, e.g. Israel, SC, *Targeted Killings Case* (2006), §§12 and 21. We respectfully disagree with the Court's finding on this issue and submit that it is not in conformity with the provisions of CA2 and CA3 GC. On the Israeli conflicts with Hezbollah and Hamas and the legal basis for the internment of persons captured in relation to these conflicts, *cf. infra* chapter II-3, section 3.2.2.2.

[399] E.g.: Moir (2002), p. 31; Dinstein, Garraway and Schmitt, *The Manual on the Law of Non-International Armed Conflict, with Commentary* (2006), p. 3; and Bartels, "Timelines, Borderlines and Conflicts: The Historical Evolution of the Legal Divide between International and Non-International Armed Conflicts" (*IRRC* 2009), p. 39, note 15.

[400] Pictet, *Commentary GC III* (1960), p. 37 (original emphasis omitted).

[401] Pictet, *Commentary GC III* (1960), p. 36: "the scope of application of the Article must be as wide as possible." *Cf.* also *supra* note 350.

[402] *Cf. supra* note 350. As Kolb rightly points out, the material and personal scope of application of IHL defines its geographically applicability: "L'applicabilité spatiale du droit des conflits armés tourne autour du principe d'effectivité : là où se déroulent des rapports d'hostilités, là s'applique le droit des conflits armés. [...] le droit des conflits armés n'est pas spatialement limité. C'est un droit purement fonctionnel: l'espace couvert par l'application de ses normes découle du rapport d'hostilité ou de neutralité. Autrement dit, le critère matériel induit le critère spatial : *actus regit locus*" (Kolb (2009), p. 218). This broad geographical applicability of IHL is of course restricted by the requirement of a direct nexus between the activity concerned and an ongoing armed conflict. In the same sense: Bassiouni, (*Harv.ILJ* 2002), p. 99; Jinks (*YJIL* 2003), pp. 40-41; Sassòli (*HPCR Series* 2006), p. 9; Lubell (2010), pp. 104-108.

Parties" is therefore not intended to restrict the definition of non-international armed conflict geographically; it serves a different function, namely to restrict the treaty obligations in the Conventions and the Protocol to States who have ratified these treaties. As regards CA 3 GC, this caveat is of no practical relevance today since all States have ratified the Conventions and any non-international armed conflict will thus *per se* occur in the territory of at least one "High Contracting Party."[403] Article 1§1 AP I has not modified the scope of application of CA 3. It merely sets a higher threshold for its provisions to apply by requiring the non-State party to the conflict to control a territory that allows it to implement the provisions of the Protocol. Finally, the applicability of CA 3 to all armed conflicts, regardless of their characterization, reinforces the fact that its scope of application is not limited by geographical criteria.[404] Therefore, the object and purpose of the Conventions and their Additional Protocols do not justify a restrictive interpretation of their provisions as suggested by some. The distinction between international and non-international armed conflicts is not based on any geographical criteria but on the nature and status of the parties to the conflict under international law. The conduct of hostilities directly related to an armed conflict not opposing two States constitute a non-international armed conflict, regardless of whether the hostilities take place within the territorial confines of a single State.[405]

---

[403] See also ICRC, *Opinion Paper* (2008), p. 3: "As the four Geneva Conventions have universally been ratified now, the requirement that the armed conflict must occur "*in the territory of one of the High Contracting Parties*" has lost its importance in practice. Indeed, any armed conflict between governmental armed forces and armed groups or between such groups cannot but take place on the territory of one of the Parties to the Convention"; and Sassòli (*HPCR Series* 2006), pp. 8-9: "common Article 3 refers to conflicts 'occurring in the territory of one of the High Contracting Parties,' whereas Article 1 of Protocol II refers to those 'which take place in the territory of a High Contracting Party.' According to the aim and purpose of IHL, this must be understood as simply recalling that treaties apply only to their state parties. If such wording meant that conflicts opposing states and organized armed groups and spreading over the territory of several states were not 'non-international armed conflicts', there would be a gap in protection, which could not be explained by states' concerns about their sovereignty. Those concerns made the law of non-international armed conflicts more rudimentary. Yet concerns about state sovereignty could not explain why victims of conflicts spilling over the territory of several states should benefit from less protection than those affected by conflicts limited to the territory of only one state [...] even a conflict spreading across borders remains a non-international armed conflict.'" In the same sense: ICTY, *Tadić* (1995), §69; ICTR, *Akayesu* (1998), §635; ICTY, *Blaškić* (2000), §74; Switzerland, Military Court of Cassation (MCC), *Niyonteze* (2001), §3c ; Jinks (*Virg.JIL* 2005-2006), pp. 188-189; Melzer (2008), pp. 257-261; and Geneva Academy of International Humanitarian Law and Human Rights, *Rule of Law in Armed Conflicts*, available at http://www.adh-geneva.ch/RULAC/.

[404] Cerone (*ASIL Insights*, 2006) rightly points out that "this position rests on the logic of the Convention regime in the context of the international legal system. If Common Article 3 would apply even in the context of a purely internal conflict, then *a fortiori* it would apply to a conflict with a transnational dimension, in which the principle of non-intervention would have less force." He also points out that this was confirmed at least implicitly by the US Supreme Court where it found that the transnational conflict opposing the US and Al Qaeda was governed by common article 3 GC (US, SC, *Hamdan* (2006), §548). We do not agree with the Court's final conclusion, but for a different reason, namely that we do not think Al Qaeda globally fulfils the organizational criterion to be a party to an armed conflict (*cf. infra* section 2.2.1.6).

[405] The farther away it takes place from the main battlefield, the more the requirement of a nexus to the armed conflict will weigh into the evaluation of whether a specific act is regulated by

On the basis of the preceding four sub-sections, and for the purposes of determining which body of law is applicable to a given conflict, we may conclude that an armed conflict is either international (opposing at least two States, or a State and a people with an internationally recognized right to self-determination) or non-international (any other situation of armed conflict, opposing at least one State and one organized armed group, or opposing two such groups).[406] This is our point of departure for the next two sections, which deal respectively with the legal qualification of armed conflicts in which international or regional organizations intervene, and the legal qualification of the so-called war on terrorism.

2.2.1.5. Intervention by international organizations in a situation of armed conflict

While not an entirely new phenomenon,[407] the last 10 to 15 years have witnessed an increase of the number of interventions by international organizations in situations of armed conflict.[408] When armed forces deployed

international humanitarian law (without prejudice to the applicability of that law to the non-international armed conflict).

[406] Additional rules to those of IAC apply in occupied territory.

[407] See for example the United Nations Command in Korea (UNC-Korea) (1950-1953) and the United Nations forces in Congo (ONUC) (1960-1963). Following the invasion of the Republic of South Korea (ROK) by the Democratic People's Republic of (North) Korea (DPRK) on 25 June 1950, the UN Security Council called on its member States to "furnish such assistance to the [ROK] as may be necessary to repel the armed attack and to restore international peace and security in the area" (UNSCR 83 (1950), §2). Seeing that several States heeded the call, the Council recommended UN member States "providing military forces and assistance [...] make such forces and other assistance available to a unified command under the United States of America; Requests the United States to designate the commander of such forces; Authorizes the unified command at its discretion to use the United Nations flag in the course of operations against North Korean forces concurrently with the flags of the various nations participating; Requests the United States to provide the Security Council with reports as appropriate on the course of action taken under the command" (UNSCR 84 (1950), §§3-6). A coalition of 15 UN members States and the majority of the armed forces units of the Republic of South Korea (ROK) itself were thus placed under the unified command and control of the United States, to defend the ROK against the DPRK and China. For background, see for example Pak, *Korea and the United Nations* (2000), pp. 75-91; and http://www.globalsecurity.org/military/ops/korea.htm. Certain aspects of the internment operations of the UNC-Korea will be discussed in chapter II-1. Designed as a peacekeeping force, ONUC forces intervened in the Katanga secession war in what is today the Democratic Republic of the Congo (DRC). The UN denied it was a party to the conflict and claimed to be merely assisting the Congolese government in restoring the unity of the country. Nevertheless, Katangese military personnel captured and interned by UN Forces were *de facto* treated as prisoners of war; see Rosas (1976), pp. 152-155, with further references. For background and legal analysis regarding ONUC, see for example Simmonds, *Legal Problems Arising from the United Nations Military Operations in the Congo* (1968).

[408] See for example the UN-mandated and NATO-led Kosovo Force (KFOR, 1999-today); the UN-mandated and Australian-led International Force in East-Timor (INTERFET, 1999-2000); the UN-mandated Mission of the United Nations in Congo (MONUC, 1999-2010; MONUSCO 2010-today); the UN-mandated and NATO-led International Security Assistance Force in Afghanistan (ISAF, 2001-today); the UN-mandated and US-led Multinational Forces in Iraq (MNF-I, 2004-2009); and the AU-mandated African Mission in Somalia (AMISOM, 2007-today). For background information on the mandate, troop-contributing nations and military structure of these forces, see respectively http://www.nato.int/kfor/; http://pandora.nla.gov.au/parchive/2000/S2000-Nov-7/easttimor.defence.gov.au/index.html; http://monuc.unmissions.org/; http://www.isaf.nato.int/;
http://webarchive.nationalarchives.gov.uk/+/http://www.mod.uk/DefenceInternet/FactSheets/OperationsInIr

under the banner of international (or regional) organizations[409] such as the UN, NATO, the EU, the AU or ECOWAS, engage in armed conflict, they may, as a party thereto, also come to capture and intern certain individuals for reasons directly related to the armed conflict.[410] Whether or not an IO or its troop-contributing States are entitled to intern persons on the basis of international humanitarian law will depend on (1) whether they are a party to the conflict, and (2) what type of conflict they are involved in. Hence, the importance of determining who is a party to what type of conflict in case of military intervention under the auspices of an international organization.

That an international organization (IO) *can* be a party to an armed conflict seems to be generally agreed upon.[411] The text of the provisions defining the material scope of application of the Geneva Conventions and their Additional Protocols are indeed sufficiently broad to accommodate this possibility.[412] This being said, the nature and legal consequences of IO participation in armed conflict remain controversial and raise a multitude of questions, which may be regrouped under three different headings.[413] A first set of questions concerns the impact of military intervention by an IO on the qualification of the conflict and the applicable legal framework.[414] A second set of questions relates to the

---

aqKeyFactsFigures.htm; http://www.africa-union.org/root/au/auc/departments/psc/amisom/amisom.htm.

[409] When we refer to international organizations (IO), we mean to cover both the international and the regional inter-governmental organizations mentioned.

[410] Specific examples will be mentioned and discussed where relevant in Parts II and III.

[411] See for example Canada, *Joint Doctrine Manual on the Law of Armed Conflict at the Operational and Tactical Levels* (2001) (hereinafter "*LOAC Manual*"), p. GL-14: "A party to a conflict is a state or other entity engaging in armed conflict"; Institute of International Law (IIL), *Resolution on the Conditions of Application of Humanitarian Rules of Armed Conflict to Hostilities in which United Nations May Be Engaged* (1971), preambular §§3-4 and article 2; IIL, *Conditions of Application of Rules, other than Humanitarian Rules, of Armed Conflict to Hostilities in which United Nations Forces May be Engaged* (1975), preambular §4 and article 2; IIL, *Resolution on the IHL and Non-State Entities* (1999), §II; Simmonds (1968), pp. 173-174 (with references in the same sense to Kotzsch, Bowett and Baxter); Kolb (2009), p. 202 and Naert (2010), *cf. infra* note 414, with further references.

[412] Where the Conventions and Protocols refer to "parties" or "powers", these words may arguably be interpreted to cover international organizations of the type we are concerned with here. As we have seen above, common articles 2 and 3 must, in light of the protective object and purpose of the treaties, be interpreted broadly so as to cover all armed conflicts; *cf. supra* notes 350, 379, 381 and accompanying text. In the same sense: Sandoz et al., *Commentary AP I and II* (1987), pp. 506-508; Kwakwa (1992), pp. 48-49; and Kolb (2009), pp. 202-211. One can wonder to what extent the wording of article 1§4 AP I can be read to include international organizations. Lubell, in his study of the international law applicable to the extraterritorial use of force against non-State actors, finds that "[a]lthough the situations described in Protocol I do indeed open the door for consideration of international armed conflict involving a non-state actor, this is a narrow doorway, clearly defined so as to include only those non-state actors who, by and large, are engaging in a struggle for self-determination and fighting against an oppressor within national boundaries, or under a regime of occupation" (Lubell (2010), p. 96).

[413] Some of these questions are also closely linked to the – not less controversial – debates on the concepts of subjects, persons, actors and participants in international law. For a recent overview of the issues at stake and the different positions taken in the debate, see Portmann, *Legal Personality in International Law* (2010). *Cf.* also *infra* chapter III-1, section 1.3.4.3.

[414] For the purposes of our work, we are only concerned with the applicable international humanitarian law, in order to determine whether or not it can provide an IO or its troop-contributing States with a legal basis to intern.

definition of the obligations under international law of both the IO and its troop-contributing States with regard to their involvement in that armed conflict. Finally, a third set of questions has to do with the determination of international responsibility for violations of international law committed by the armed forces of the IO or its troop-contributing States within the context of the conflict. The legal nature of the relationship between an IO and the States that contribute troops to its military operations, may vary from one IO to another and differ according to the type and structure of each operation, thus adding layers of complexity to all three sets of questions. For the present purposes, we are concerned only with the first set of questions, namely those relating to the identification of the applicable body of international humanitarian law in situations where an IO (or its troop-contributing States) engages or participates in armed conflict or occupation.[415]

In order to qualify any situation of violence as an armed conflict, one needs to be able to identify the *parties* to the conflict and their *nature* (State or non-State parties to the conflict). With regard to IO intervention, the following two elements must be taken into account when determining who is a party to the conflict.[416] First, an IO can only be a separate party to a conflict if it disposes of armed forces, engaging in hostilities, under its operational command.[417] In this regard, it is important to note that IOs in general do not dispose of armed forces of their own but must rely on their member States to place armed forces at the disposal of the organization for a given operation.[418]

---

415 For a good and up to date overview of the obligations and responsibility of international organizations, their member States and troop-contributing States under international humanitarian and human rights law in situations of armed conflict, the different questions that arise, the issues at stake and the different positions in the debates, see Naert (2010), pp. 361-539 and 641-658, with a wealth of further relevant references (the main focus is on the UN, NATO and the EU, other organizations are less discussed). With regard to issues of responsibility, see also ILC, *Articles on State Responsibility* (2001) (hereinafter "ASR"); ILC, *Draft Articles on the Responsibility of International Organizations* (2009) (hereinafter ("DARIO")); and Crawford, Pellet & Olleson (eds.), *The Law of International Responsibility* (2010); with regard to the ECHR, see also Malenovský, "L'enjeu délicat de l'éventuelle adhésion de l'Union européenne à la Convention européenne des droits de l'homme: de graves difficultés dans l'application" (*RGDIP* 2009) and Lock (*HRLR* 2010).

416 IO intervention usually occurs in a pre-existing armed conflict, but it could also trigger an armed conflict by itself. Such would be the case for example where the UNSC, on the basis of chapter VII of the UN Charter, would authorize or decide on the use of force against a State in order to stop it from committing massive human rights violations against its population but without the situation in that State (before the actual intervention) amounting to a situation of armed conflict. Whether or not such an intervention would be lawful under the *jus ad bellum* is beyond the scope of our work, but would have no impact on the qualification of the conflict or the applicability of IHL, *cf. supra* note 345.

417 For our present purposes, we work with the assumption that the IO or its troop-contributing States are indeed involved in hostilities. Where the violence is not of a military nature, or in the case of a NIAC has not reached the required level of intensity, the situation will not qualify as an armed conflict and IHL will not apply. In the same sense, see Naert (2010), pp. 468-473, with further references. Such cases (which constitute the majority of international operations under the auspices of the UN or other IO) are outside the scope of this book (for a good summary and references, see Naert (2010), pp. 468-470, 541-588 and 641-658). Note that the definition of the mandate of the force will be indicative but not decisive for the qualification of the conflict, which will be determined by the facts on the ground, *cf. supra* note 348.

418 To our knowledge, only one IO seems to dispose of its own armed forces, independent of the

This then leads us to the second element: it is *either* the IO *or* the (allied) troop-contributing States that will be the party (or parties) to the conflict, but it cannot be both.[419] This flows from the fact that the armed forces involved will either be under the effective command and control of their national States or under that of the international organization. The fact that it is either the IO or the troop-contributing States that is/are *party* to the conflict does not mean that the IO or troop-contributing States that are not a party to the conflict have no obligations under IHL; they are obliged to ensure respect of IHL under common article 1 GC, and their specific position with regard to the operation will confer additional *responsibility* upon them to ensure respect.[420] Neither does it exclude the possibility of joint responsibility for violations of international law committed during the conflict. In this sense it is important to distinguish between being a party to the conflict (which includes responsibility for the whole of the military operations in connection to that conflict) for the purposes of international humanitarian law, and bearing international responsibility for certain wrongful acts committed in the context of that same conflict. Where the IO is the *party* to the conflict, both the IO and the troop-contributing States may be responsible for violations of IHL committed by the IO's armed forces in the context of the conflict: the IO will be directly responsible for such violations since they are considered to be its own acts; the troop-contributing State may be indirectly responsible for the acts of the IO over which it had a certain degree of influence or control.[421] Where the troop-contributing States are the parties to the conflict, the opposite reasoning can be applied.[422]

---

military structure of its member States and under a permanent unified command directly responsible to the IO, namely the Western European Union's Eurocorps. Until today, however, Eurocorps has only participated in situations of armed conflict as an integral part of a military structure placed under NATO command, but theoretically, it can also operate independently (according to its website such a situation is, however, unlikely to occur). For background on the military structure of the Eurocorps and its participation in international military operations, see http://www.eurocorps.org. A possible further exception could be the AU's African Standby Force (ASF). Our finding is based on the documents detailing its organizational structure (available at http://www.africa-union.org/root/au/AUC/Departments/PSC/Asf/asf.htm). Pending the ASF' full establishment and operationalization it is difficult, however, to be conclusive on whether or not such forces could indeed be qualified as the AU's own armed forces.

[419] Except where the IO disposes of its own armed forces and can thus be one amongst other allied parties to the conflict.

[420] As Naert (2010) points out (at p. 510): "Indeed, it is the general understanding, confirmed in State practice, that forces put at the disposal of international organizations by troop-contributing nations are always to comply with the LOAC obligations of their sending State, even if under the effective command and control of an international organization. This mainly stems from the obligation under [CA1 GC]."

[421] Respectively under articles 3-7 DARIO (direct responsibility of the IO), and under articles 1-2, 11 and 57 ASR, articles 3-4 and 57-61 DARIO (indirect responsibility of the troop-contributing States). In the same sense: IIL, *Resolution on Applicability of IHL to UN Forces* (1971), article 8: "The United Nations is liable for damage which may be caused by its Forces in violation of the humanitarian rules of armed conflict, without prejudice to any possible recourse against the State whose contingent has caused the damage."

[422] Respectively under articles 1-9 and 16-18 ASR (direct responsibility of the troop-contributing States), and under article articles 3-4, 8 and 13-16 DARIO (indirect responsibility of the IO).

The main factor in determining whether it is the IO that is the *party* to the conflict, or the troop-contributing States, will be who exercises effective command and control ("C2" in military parlance) over the operation and the armed forces deployed.[423] When States place armed forces at the disposal of an IO for a particular operation, they transfer at least some degree of command and control over the operation and over their forces to the IO. "Command and control" is not, however, always interpreted in a uniform way, and the degree to which it is transferred to the IO may differ according to the structure of the IO concerned, the nature of the relationship with its member and/or troop-contributing States, and the specific operation in which the troops are deployed.[424] In order to identify who is the party to the conflict and which IHL will apply, the *de facto* reality on the ground will however prevail over any formal agreements on the issue of C2.[425] Apart from C2, additional factors to identify the party to the conflict may be the authority to issue the troops' rules of engagement (ROE),[426] and who is considered the armed forces' commander-in-chief. In conclusion, the definition of armed forces in article 43 AP I is also worth mentioning: "The armed forces of a Party to a conflict consist of all organized armed forces, groups and units which are under a command

[423] The terms of the *mandate* of the deployed forces may give certain indications on who exercises effective command and control, but it is the real situation on the ground that defines who is the party to the conflict. The terms of the mandate are however likely to have an incident on the determination of international responsibility for wrongful acts committed in the course of the conflict.

[424] Generally on C2 in international military operations, see Cathcart, "Command and Control in Military Operations" in Gill & Fleck (2010). For discussion of C2 arrangements in EU, NATO and UN military operations, see Naert (2010), pp. 515-517, with further references in notes 2201-2206. For the impact of the definition of C2 and the degree to which it is transferred to the IO on the *responsibility* of the concerned IO and troop-contributing States, see Naert (2010), pp. 517-526. His overview includes a comprehensive discussion and critique of the controversial ECtHR Grand Chamber's judgment in *Behrami & Saramati* (2007) and the UK House of Lords' judgment in *Al-Jedda v. Secretary of State for Defence* (2007). With regard to C2 in UN and NATO operations, see also Canada, *Joint Doctrine Publication 3.0: Operations* (2010) (hereinafter "*JDP 3.0*"), chapters 3 and 7; NATO, *AJP—3 Allied Joint Operations* (2007). See also AU, *Policy Framework for the Establishment of the African Standby Force and the Military Staff Committee* (2003), Part I, section 2.36: "Multinational brigades raise legal as well as technical command and control issues that need to be resolved prior to deployment. This could be achieved through appropriate AU command and control policies, Letters of Exchange (LOEs), Letters of Intent (LIs) or MOUs. In general, the command of the brigades will need to reflect the multinational nature of the formation, and be combined with a system of rotation of staff appointments, having regard to the capacities, contributions, and professional competence levels in the respective defence forces of Member State."

[425] *Cf. supra* note 348.

[426] ROE are "[d]irectives issued by competent military authority which specify the circumstances and limitations under which forces will initiate and/or continue combat engagement with other forces encountered" (NATO, AAP-6: NATO Glossary of Terms and Definitions (2010), hereinafter "AAP-6", at p. 2-R-10). Where the IO itself issues uniform ROE, this may be an indication of the fact that the IO, rather than its troop-contributing States, is the party to the conflict. The fact that individual troop-contributing States also issue their own ROE is not necessarily counter-indicative in as far as these deviate from the IO's general ROE only to take into account each State's specific obligations under international law (and thus placing additional restrictions on the use of force or other coercive measures by their troops).

responsible *to that Party* for the conduct of *its subordinates*."[427] Where these armed forces have indeed been placed under the effective control and command of an IO, they may then be considered the armed forces of that IO, which will be the party to the conflict. On the contrary, where they remain under effective national command and control, they ought to be considered the armed forces of their national States, who will then be the parties to the conflict.

Considering these elements, and based on the definitions of international armed conflict, occupation, and non-international conflict discussed in subsections 2.2.2.1 to 2.2.2.3, we can then distinguish two sets of possible scenarios.[428]

(a.) The troop-contributing States are the parties to the conflict

In this first set of scenarios (which seems to cover the vast majority of cases), the troop-contributing States are part of a coalition of States, each of which is a party to the conflict.[429] The fact that the coalition has been authorized or mandated by the IO to engage in armed conflict (or acts on its behalf but without having transferred effective command over its troops to the IO) will not have an impact on the qualification of the conflict and the applicable legal framework. The latter will then only depend on the nature of the coalition's adverse party to the conflict: the following scenarios can be distinguished.[430]

(a.1) The coalition is engaged in armed conflict against a State or an NLM

Where the coalition is engaged in an armed conflict against one or more States, the situation will qualify as an international armed conflict under the definition of common article 2 GC, and international humanitarian law for situations of international armed conflict (IAC-IHL) will apply. Examples would include the Korean War (1950-1953), opposing the Republic of (South) Korea, Australia, Belgium, Canada, Colombia, France, Greece, Luxemburg, the Netherlands, New Zealand, the Philippines, South Africa, Thailand, Turkey, the UK and the US to the Democratic People's Republic of (North) Korea and China;[431] the First Gulf War (1990-1991), opposing a very broad US-led coalition of States to Iraq in order to liberate occupied Kuwait;[432] and the first phase of the ongoing conflict in Afghanistan (October 2001-June 2002),

---

[427] Emphasis added.

[428] The list of scenarios is not necessarily exhaustive, further research might put forth other possible scenarios.

[429] If the coalition's armed forces are placed under the exclusive and effective command and control of one State, it could be argued that only that State is a party to the conflict, and that the armed forces of the other troop-contributing States are part of the armed forces of that party to the conflict.

[430] In the same sense: Kleffner in Gill & Fleck (2010), p. 465.

[431] Authorized by UNSCR 83 (1950) and UNSCR 84 (1950), *cf. supra*.

[432] The use of force had been authorized by the UN Security Council before the coalitions' actual deployment, see UNSCR 678 (1990), §2, authorizing "Member States co-operating with the Government of Kuwait, unless Iraq on or before 15 January 1991 fully implements, as set forth in paragraph 1 above, the above-mentioned resolutions, to use all necessary means to uphold and implement resolution 660 (1990) and all subsequent relevant resolutions and to restore international peace and security in the area."

opposing the US, UK, Australia, Canada, Denmark, France, Germany and Norway to Afghanistan.[433]

Where the coalition of States or some of its members occupy all or part of the territory of the State against which they are engaged in armed conflict, the States that exercise the effective control over the territory become Occupying Powers subject to the law of occupation. An example would be the occupation of Iraq, from 1 may 2003 to 30 June 2004, by the UK and the US. Both States recognized their status as Occupying Powers, which was also confirmed by the Security Council.[434]

In the (unlikely) event that a coalition of States, authorized or mandated by an IO, would become engaged in armed conflict against a "people fighting against colonial domination and alien occupation and against racist régimes in the exercise of their right of self-determination as enshrined in the Charter of the United Nations and the Declaration on Principles of International Law concerning Friendly Relations and Co-operation among States in accordance with the Charter of the United Nations",[435] those States that have ratified AP I will be engaged in an international armed conflict against that people.[436] Since article 1§4 AP I is not (yet) part of customary IHL, coalition States that have not ratified AP I would be engaged in a non-international armed conflict. Finally, where the coalition acts without the consent of the State against which the people is fighting in the exercise of its right of self-determination, it will trigger a parallel international armed conflict against that State.

(a.2) The coalition is engaged in armed conflict against a non-State entity

Where the coalition of States is engaged in armed conflict against one or more non-State entities, on the side, or with the consent of, the State in whose territory the conflict takes place, the situation will be one of non-international armed conflict, to which international humanitarian law for situations of non-international armed conflict (NIAC-IHL) will apply. A clear example would be the Multinational Force-Iraq (MNF-I), a US-led coalition of about 40 States (with

---

433 The use of force in self-defence had (implicitly) been authorized by UNSCR 1368 (2001), §3: "*Recognizing* the inherent right of individual or collective self-defence in accordance with the Charter." *Cf.* also *infra* notes 466-467. The armed conflict opposing the coalition States to Afghanistan existed in parallel with the pre-existing non-international armed conflict opposing the Afghan government to the Northern Alliance. As soon as US and UK troops invaded Afghanistan in October 2001, the Northern Alliance and the US-led coalition became allies in the conflict against the Taliban-governed Afghan State.

434 UNSCR 1483 (2003), preambular paragraph 13: "*Noting* the letter of 8 May 2003 from the Permanent Representatives of the United States of America and the United Kingdom of Great Britain and Northern Ireland to the President of the Security Council (S/2003/538) and recognizing the specific authorities, responsibilities, and obligations under applicable international law of these states as occupying powers under unified command (the "Authority")." The other coalition States in Iraq were not Occupying Powers but, like the Occupying Powers themselves, remained bound by general IAC-IHL (*cf. supra* 2.2.2.4).

435 The language is from article 1§4 AP I.

436 In as far as the authority representing that people has taken the appropriate steps under article 96§3 of the Protocol so as to bring both the Geneva Conventions and the Protocol into force.

a vast majority of US troops, but including also troops form Australia, Georgia, South-Korea, Spain, the UK and about 35 other States) that fought alongside the Iraqi government against a number of armed groups party to the non-international armed conflict in Iraq that followed the demise of Saddam Hussein.[437]

(b.) The IO is the party to the conflict

Where the IO, rather than the troop-contributing States, is the party to the conflict, an additional question arises, namely: what is the nature of an IO involved in armed conflict in light of the definitions of armed conflict and occupation in common articles 2 and 3 of the Geneva Conventions? An IO certainly is not a State; but it is not the same type of non-State party to the conflict as an organized armed group either. At least one crucial difference between an organized armed group – at least one that does not represent a people with a right to self-determination under the UN Charter or the Friendly Relations Declaration – and the IOs of the type we are concerned with here, is that the latter have international legal personality, and – on the basis of their respective charters – have the right to engage in armed conflict.[438]

Opinions on the nature of IOs parties to armed conflict and the impact on the qualification of the conflict and the applicable legal framework diverge. At least two schools of thought may be distinguished.[439] For some authors, all armed conflicts in which an IO intervenes are to be considered international armed conflicts, regardless of the nature of the adverse party to the conflict.[440] Vité summarizes this position as follows:

> "To the extent that the operations concerned are decided, defined and carried out by international organizations, they are by nature included in that category. It is of little relevance whether the opposing party is a State or a non-governmental group. In accordance with that doctrinal position, the hypothesis envisaged constitutes an international armed conflict *sui generis*, the particular status of the organization involved being enough to qualify it as such."[441]

---

[437] The MNF-I was established upon the request of the Iraqi government; its mandate was defined by US-Iraqi agreement and endorsed by the United Nations Security Council (UNSCR 1546 (2004), Annex, p. 11). By the end of 2009 all non-US troops had withdrawn and MNF-I's mandate came to an end. It has been replaced by the United States Forces-Iraq, see http://www.usf-iraq.com/, on the basis of US-Iraqi bilateral agreement.

[438] That right will of course be circumscribed by articles 2§4 and 39-51 of the UN Charter.

[439] Further research would be required to come to any conclusions on international practice, but State practice and international courts and treaty monitoring bodies do not seem to converge either. For the moment, the (written or public) debate seems to take place mainly in the literature.

[440] See for example Shraga, "The UN as an Actor Bound by International Humanitarian Law" in Condorelli et al. (eds.), *The United Nations and International Humanitarian Law* (1996), p. 333; Benvenuti, "The Implementation of International Humanitarian Law in the Framework of UN Peace-Keeping" in European Commission Humanitarian Office, *Law in Humanitarian Crises: How Can International Humanitarian Law Be Made Effective in Armed Conflicts?* (1995), pp. 96ff.; Emanuelli, "United Nations Forces and Humanitarian Law' in Condorelli et al. (1996), pp. 357 ff; Kolb, *Droit humanitaire et opérations de paix internationales* (2006), pp. 57 ff; Byron, "Armed Conflicts: International or Non-International?" (*JCSL* 2001), pp. 82-83; Bartelt, *Der rechtliche Rahmen für die neue operative Kapazität der Europäischen Union* (2003), pp. 191-192 and 196.

[441] Vité (*IRRC* 2009), pp. 87-88. According to Vité, this view represents the majority opinion; Naert

Others, including Vité, are of the opinion that:

> "a differentiated application of international humanitarian law must be followed [...] depending on the parties to the conflict in each individual case in the field. The law of international armed conflict must therefore be applicable when international troops clash with government forces. By contrast, if fighting is between those troops and non-governmental groups, it is the law of non-international armed conflict which must prevail. The legal regime applicable in the same conflict thus varies depending on the adversaries present in each situation."[442]

In light of the complexity of the issue, we prefer to reserve our final opinion on the matter, which would require research well beyond the scope of this book. For the first school of thought to be correct though, one would need to prove one of two theses. Either the interpretation of CA2 GC has been modified by "subsequent practice in the application of the treaty which establishes the agreement of the parties regarding its interpretation",[443] or a *sui generis* type of international armed conflict has emerged in customary international law, to which the customary law for international armed conflict applies. We are not convinced that there is sufficient and coherent State practice and *opinio juris* to support either of these theses.[444] We find the argument made by the second school of thought more convincing, but regret that it does not seem to distinguish between situations where the IO is the party to the conflict and situations where it is the troop-contributing States that are the parties to the conflict, while it must be admitted that the question is not settled for the first case, and requires further research and possibly normative development to be conclusive.[445]

Nevertheless, both schools of thought seem to place IOs on the same footing as States, and thus appear to agree that when an IO engages in armed conflict against another State, it will be involved in an international armed conflict.[446]

---

however does not seem to agree (Naert (2010), p. 484, note 2071).

442 Vité (*IRRC* 2009), p. 88, who refers to the following authors in support of his view: McCoubrey & White, *The Blue Helmets: Legal Regulation of United Nations Military Operations* (1996), p. 172 ("there is no reason to think that the involvement of a UN force in a situation of armed conflict will of itself render the conflict 'international' for the purposes of the application of the *jus in bello*"); Condorelli, "Le statut des forces des Nations Unies et le droit international humanitaire", in Emanuelli (ed.), *Les casques bleus: policiers ou combattants?* (1997), p. 110; Tittemore, "Belligerents in Blue Helmets: Applying International Humanitarian Law to United Nations Peace Operations" (*Stanf.JIL*1997), p. 110; Pejic, "Status of Armed Conflicts" in Wilmshurst & Breau (eds.), *Perspectives on the ICRC Study on Customary International Humanitarian Law* (2007), p. 94.

443 Article 31§3(b) VCLT.

444 In the same sense: Naert (2010), p. 483. An expanded reading of CA2 GC, to include armed conflicts in which IO are involved, would, however, possibly meet with less resistance than the expanded reading of CA2 GC in article 1§4 AP I or than proposals to lift the distinction between international and non-international armed conflicts all-together (*cf. supra*).

445 Vité points out that some authors have suggested "that international humanitarian law be revisited with a view to adapting it to the distinctive characteristics of multinational forces" Vité (*IRRC* 2009), p. 88, note 71. He refers , for an attempt to do so, to Kolb (2006), pp. 65 ff.

446 The reason probably is that most authors see the situation as one where both the IO and the troop-contributing States are a party to the conflict, an assumption that in our view is unfounded (*cf. supra*). Somewhat surprisingly, the question of whether an IO can be a party to the conflict

As we have mentioned above, we think the issue merits further research,[447] but since at least on this point there seems to be agreement in the literature, we will work with this assumption. Agreeing with the second school of thought that the qualification of the conflict will then depend on the nature of the adverse party,[448] we can then distinguish the three following scenarios.

(b.1) The IO is engaged in armed conflict against a State

If the IO engages in armed conflict against one or more States, the situation will qualify as an international armed conflict and IAC-IHL will apply. An example would probably include the military intervention carried out by NATO in 1999 against the then Federal Republic of Yugoslavia (Operation Allied Force).[449]

If, for the sake of argument, the coalition of States that fought Taliban-governed Afghanistan alongside the Northern Alliance from October 2001 to June 2002 had been under the effective command and control of NATO, that situation too would have qualified as an international armed conflict, one opposing NATO (rather than the US-led coalition of States) to Afghanistan.

(b.2) The IO is engaged in armed conflict against a non-State entity

If the IO engages in armed conflict with a non-State entity, alongside or with the consent of the State in whose territory the conflict takes place, the situation will be one of non-international armed conflict and be regulated by NIAC-IHL. In this scenario, neither the exact nature of the IO as a party to the conflict, nor the question of whether it is the IO or the troop-contributing States that are the parties to the conflict, has an impact on the qualification of the situation as a non-international armed conflict. Examples would probably include the UN's

---

without its member States or troop-contributing States being a party to that same conflict seems not to have been the subject of analysis so far, with the exception of the EU (Naert (2010), p. 524). Naert points out (at p. 524) that "[p]resumably, this results from a reluctance to acknowledge that international organizations may be a party to an armed conflict even while admitting that they may be bound by some LOAC obligations." As we have mentioned, however, the fact that both the IO and the troop-contributing States have obligations under IHL, and that they may be responsible for violations of IHL both separately and jointly, is a distinct issue from that of determining the nature of the conflict and the applicable legal framework.

[447] If an IO would not be placed on an equal footing as States, it would essentially be a non-State entity, and any armed conflict to which an IO is a party would therefore qualify as a non-international armed conflict, regardless of the State or non-State nature of the adverse party.

[448] The most convincing argument on the issue has in our view been formulated by Naert (2010), pp. 483-486, 491-492, and 506-540.

[449] For examples in the same sense: Kalshoven, *Reflections on the Law of War: Collected Essays* (2007), pp. 920-921; and Naert (2010), pp. 518-519. For examples to the contrary: Kolb, Porretto & Vité (2005), pp. 285-288, who do not find NATO had effective command and control over the operation; and Klein, "The Attribution of Acts to International Organizations" in Crawford et al. (2010), p. 302, who points out, in general, that "[m]ilitary forces deployed in that framework [i.e. under the auspices of NATO] remain subject to national command and control and are not linked to the Organisation by any formal organic tie." If indeed C2 was with the troop-contributing States rather than with NATO, the conflict would nevertheless still be international in nature (scenario (a.1) above). For the purposes of the analysis in this book it is therefore not necessary to settle the question.

military operations in the Congo between 1963 and 1964 (ONUC);[450] the conflict opposing Afghanistan and NATO (ISAF appears to be placed under NATO's effective command and control)[451] to the Islamic Emirate of Afghanistan (comprised of the ousted Taliban and affiliated forces); the non-international armed conflict in the Democratic Republic of the Congo opposing the Congolese government and the UN (MONUC) to a number of armed opposition groups including the *Congrès national pour la défense du people* (CNDP) and the *Forces démocratiques de libération du Rwanda* (FDLR); and the conflict opposing Somalia and AMISOM against *Harakat al-Shabaab al-Mujahideen* (Al-Shabaab). It is unclear whether ECOWAS had the type of command and control that would make it a party to the conflict opposing Liberia and ECOMOG forces[452] against Charles Taylor's National Patriotic Front of Liberia (NPFL) and other rebel groups (1990-1997) and the conflict opposing Sierra Leone and ECOMOG forces against Foday Sankoh's Revolutionary United Front (RUF) (1997-1999).[453]

(b.3) The IO effectively administers all or part of the territory of a State against which it previously was engaged in armed conflict

Finally, the question arises whether a situation where an international organization that has effective control over all or part of the territory of a State and effectively administers such territory, may be qualified *de jure* as an

---

[450] ONUC was established as a subsidiary organ of the UN and national contingent commanders were effectively placed under the direct military command of the UN Commander: "in so far as the conduct of the military operations is concerned it is the Commander who is legally responsible and accountable to the UN Secretary General [...] The significant division of responsibilities between the Commander and the national Commanders can really be found in the *internal* administration or personnel matters of national contingents. [...] the operational responsibility was vested in the Commander appointed by and acting under the orders of the Secretary-General. Thus, the Commander of the Force was not only responsible to the Secretary-General but also (and it is necessary to emphasis this point) independent of the policies and control of any member State. Moreover, the authority of the United Nations in the performance of all functions assigned to the Force and for the deployment and assignment of troops placed at the disposal of ONUC was not qualified by the fact that each national contingent was under the direct command of its national officers, since these in turn received their orders in all operational matters relating to the Force, not from their national Government, but from the Commander of ONUC. However, the Supreme Commander in turn took his orders from the Secretary-General" (Simmonds (1968), pp. 155 and 161-162, original emphasis).

[451] In the opposite case, where the troop-contributing States to ISAF rather than NATO itself would be the party to the conflict, the situation would still qualify as a NIAC. For the purposes of the analysis in this book it is therefore not necessary to settle the question.

[452] ECOWAS Monitoring Group in Liberia (ECOMOG), was composed of troops from Nigeria, Ghana, Guinea, Sierra Leone and Gambia. For background on the operation and the conflict, see Adebajo, *Liberia's Civil War: Nigeria, ECOMOG, and Regional Security in West Africa* (2002).

[453] See for example BBC, "Profile: ECOMOG" (2004): "Ecomog's top brass were answerable to the head of Ecowas. The Ecowas Defence Council was responsible for assessing the situation in a conflict zone and deciding on strategy. On the ground, Ecomog's force commander oversaw military operations. Before 1999 the force commander did not have complete control of the various contingents, whose leaders also answered to military chiefs in their home countries." For background on the conflict in Sierra Leone, see also Koroma, *Crisis and Intervention in Sierra Leone 1997-2003* (2004).

occupation. Two specific operations immediately come to mind,[454] namely the administration of Kosovo (1999-2008) and East-Timor (1999-2002) by the United Nations. Only the civilian component of the administration of Kosovo was directly carried out by the UN (in particular by the United Nations Mission in Kosovo or UNMIK), which "outsourced" the security component to NATO (KFOR).[455] In East-Timor, the United Nations Transitional Administration in East-Timor (UNTAET) was composed of both a civilian and a military component.[456]

The doctrine is divided over whether such situations fall within the definition of occupation.[457] Both States and international organizations have been reluctant

[454] For a comprehensive overview, see Kolb, Porretto & Vité (2005).

[455] UNMIK was established by UNSCR 1244 (1999), §§10-11, in which the Council "Authorizes the Secretary-General [...] to establish an international civil presence in Kosovo in order to provide an interim administration for Kosovo under which the people of Kosovo can enjoy substantial autonomy within the Federal Republic of Yugoslavia, and which will provide transitional administration while establishing and overseeing the development of provisional democratic self-governing institutions to ensure conditions for a peaceful and normal life for all inhabitants of Kosovo; Decides that the main responsibilities of the international civil presence will include: [...] (b) Performing basic civilian administrative functions [...]; (c) [...] the holding of elections; [...] (i) Maintaining civil law and order, including establishing local police forces and meanwhile through the deployment of international police personnel to serve in Kosovo." In the same resolution, the Security Council authorized the establishment of what was to become KFOR, see UNSCR 1244 (1999), §§7 and 9: "Authorizes Member States and relevant international organizations to establish the international security presence in Kosovo [...] with all necessary means to fulfil its responsibilities [...] [which] include: (a) Deterring renewed hostilities, maintaining and where necessary enforcing a ceasefire, and ensuring the withdrawal and preventing the return into Kosovo of Federal and Republic military, police and paramilitary forces [...]; (b) Demilitarizing the Kosovo Liberation Army (KLA) and other armed Kosovo Albanian groups [...]; (d) Ensuring public safety and order until the international civil presence can take responsibility for this task; [...] (h) Ensuring the protection and freedom of movement of itself, the international civil presence, and other international organizations." UNMIK gradually transferred its powers to Kosovo authorities. It still exists (see http://www.unmikonline.org), but has a reduced role since the establishment of the European Union Rule of Law Mission in Kosovo (EULEX), in February 2008, which continues to assist and support the Kosovo authorities in police, judiciary and custom matters (http://www.eulex-kosovo.eu).

[456] In its Resolution 1272 (1999), the UN Security Council "Decides to establish, in accordance with the report of the Secretary-General, a United Nations Transitional Administration in East Timor (UNTAET), which will be endowed with overall responsibility for the administration of East Timor and will be empowered to exercise all legislative and executive authority, including the administration of justice; Decides also that the mandate of UNTAET shall consist of the following elements: (a) To provide security and maintain law and order throughout the territory of East Timor; (b) To establish an effective administration [...];Decides further that [...] its main components will be: (a) A governance and public administration component, including an international police element [...]; (c) A military component, with a strength of up to 8,950 troops [...]; Authorizes UNTAET to take all necessary measures to fulfil its mandate" (UNSCR 1272, §§1-4). UNTAET ceased to exist once the people of East-Timor had exercised its right to self-determination and the independent State of East Timor was established.

[457] For a discussion of the main features of the debate and references to the most important contributions thereto, see Kolb, Porretto & Vité (2005); and (for a short and more recent summary) Naert (2010), pp. 493-499. See also Lijnzaad "How not to Be an Occupying Power: Some Reflections on UN Security Council Resolution 1483 and the Contemporary Law of Occupation" in Lijnzaad et al. (2004); Gasser in Fleck (2008), p. 272; and Cameron & Everly, "Conceptualizing the Administration of Territory by International Actors" (*EJIL* 2010).

to accept this possibility. One likely explanation is that some of the objectives of such operations (including that of UNMIK and UNTAET) are not compatible with the law of occupation itself, which prohibits an Occupying Power from modifying the occupied State's political and legal system.[458] Nevertheless, whether or not States or IOs are willing to accept the possibility is irrelevant in that the applicability of the law of occupation will depend on the facts on the ground.[459] If one accepts then – as the majority of authors does (*cf. supra* (b)) – that an IO engaged in armed conflict against a State (which it is *de jure* if it is has a military presence and/or exercises governmental powers in that State's territory without its consent) is a party to an IAC; it is difficult to understand how it could not be an Occupying Power if the threshold of application set out by article 42 HR 1907 and CA2 GC is met (*cf. supra* 2.2.1.3).

(c.) Conclusions for the purposes of this book

The different issues discussed in this subsection will have an impact on the qualification of an armed conflict to which an IO is or is not a party, and consequently will have an impact on whether or not an IO can lawfully intern persons for reasons related to the armed conflict on the basis of international humanitarian law. One cannot properly answer those questions without taking a position on the issues raised in this subsection, which merit a separate book altogether. We will therefore not devote a specific chapter of this book to internment operations by international organizations. Nevertheless, for the scenarios described under (a) above, questions about the lawfulness of and legal bases for internment are identical to situations where there is no IO intervention, and will thus be answered in Parts II and III. For the scenarios described under (b), the rules discussed in Part II will apply to situations that qualify as IAC or occupation and the rules discussed in Part III will apply to situations that qualify as NIAC.

2.2.1.6. The "war on terrorism"

> "'Wars have typically been fought against proper nouns (Germany, say) for the good reason that proper nouns can surrender and promise not to do it again. Wars against common nouns (poverty, crime, drugs) have been less successful. Such opponents never give up. The war on terrorism, unfortunately, falls into the second category.' Emergency measures put into effect because of the 'war on terrorism' may likewise never end, and governmental officials may justify military actions that have little to do with our immediate security by invoking such a broad description of the latter threat."[460]

Doubtlessly, both domestic and international terrorism may – depending on their nature and scale – constitute emergencies threatening the life of the nation.[461] Moreover, the Security Council has qualified international terrorist acts

[458] Naert (2010), pp. 494-497, with further references.

[459] *Cf. supra* note 348.

[460] Byford, "The Wrong War" (*FA* 2002), p. 34.

[461] Condorelli (*RGDIP* 2001), pp. 831-832. In the same sense, the ECtHR has recognized that several situations qualified by States as domestic terrorism constitute a public emergency threatening the life

like the 9/11 attacks against the United States, and similar acts elsewhere in the world, as a grave "threat to international peace and security" under article 39 of the UN Charter, and has adopted legally binding resolutions requiring States to deal with the threat of such international terrorism.[462] On this basis, States have adopted numerous measures at both the national and international level to effectively search for, arrest, prosecute and detain individuals engaged or suspected to be engaged in international terrorism.[463]

The question of that interests us here, however, is whether the so-called war on international terrorism constitutes an armed conflict, triggering the applicability of international humanitarian law. Put like this, the question oversimplifies the complexity of the issue. The "war on terror" is not a univocal situation, and certainly not a single armed conflict. War in the legal sense of the word is not waged against phenomena like terrorism, poverty, drugs or human trafficking. It is fought between identifiable parties, either States, State-like entities (like national liberation movements or intergovernmental organizations) or organized armed groups.[464]

---

of the nation permitting derogation under article 15 ECHR. For example, it has done so in relation to the situation in Northern Ireland (ECtHR, *Lawless v. Ireland* (1961), §28, subsequently confirmed in ECtHR, *Ireland v. UK* (1978), §205, and *Brannigan & McBride* (1993), §47); and in relation to the actions of the Workers' Party of Kurdistan (PKK) in South-East Turkey (e.g. ECtHR, *Aksoy v. Turkey* (1996), §70). The Court has also accepted the existence of such a threat in the context of international terrorism in the wake of 9/11 (e.g.: ECtHR (Grand Chamber), *A and Others v. UK* (2009), §181).

[462] See the numerous resolutions adopted by the UNSC on counterterrorism, both thematic and country-focused, and including but not limited to the 9/11 attacks, e.g.: UNSC, *Resolution 1368* (2001); and UNSC, *Resolution 1373* (2001), which also creates the UN Counterterrorism Committee. For an overview of the UN's actions against terrorism, see http://www.un.org/terrorism/.

[463] Such measures include the adoption of legislation and regulations to expand the possibility of both administrative detention, and (preventive and punitive) detention in the framework of criminal proceedings. For examples of such legislation and regulations, see United Nations Office on Drugs and Crime (UNODC), *Electronic Legal Resources on International Terrorism*, database available at https://www.unodc.org/tldb/, and the annual reports of the Working Group on Arbitrary Detention.

[464] For this reason we disagree with the current US position that the so-called war on terrorism is a global (or transnational) non-international armed conflict to which CA 3 GC applies (as reflected in US, SC, *Hamdan* (2006), §548 and Koh, "The Obama Administration and International Law" (2010)). Note though that the Supreme Court did not as such say the situation was one of armed conflict, rather it said the conflict cannot be international since Al Qaeda is not a State, and that it is therefore covered by common article 3, only implicitly suggesting it is an armed conflict. According to Abu Musab al-Suri (known as the principal architect of the radical thinking that characterizes "Al Qaeda"), however, "Al Qaeda is not an organization, it is not a group, nor do we want it to be... It is a call, a reference, a methodology" (cited by Wright, "The Master Plan: For the New Theorists of Jihad, Al Qaeda Is just the Beginning", *The New Yorker*, 11 September 2006, at p. 50). Generally on Al Qaeda, see also Lia, Brynjar, *Architect of Global Jihad: The Life of Al-Qaida Strategist Abu Mus'ab al-Suri* (2008). Few authors have explicitly pronounced themselves on whether Al-Qaeda meets the organization criterion. In the same sense as our position, see for example Goldman & Tittemore, "Unprivileged Combatants and the Hostilities in Afghanistan: Their Status and Rights under International Humanitarian and Human Rights Law" (*ASIL Task force on terrorism* 2002), p. 29; Vité (*IRRC* 2009), p. 93; and Lubell (2010), pp. 118-120. To the contrary, see for example Aldrich, "The Taliban, Al Qaeda, and the Determination of Illegal Combatants" (*HV* 2002), p. 203 (implicitly) and Jinks (*Virg.JIL* 2005-2006), p. 187 (more explicit), both of whom esteem Al Qaeda is sufficiently identifiable and organized for there to be a global non-international armed conflict with the US. Cole finds that both the Taliban and Al Qaeda meet

In a political sense, the denomination "war on terrorism" indicates the existence of certain policies; in a practical sense, it seems to serve as an umbrella term for a large and very diverse number of counterterrorism operations. These operations have in some specific instances been carried out within the context of an armed conflict, or may even have triggered one, but they do not, as a whole, constitute a single, worldwide, armed conflict waged between an unidentifiable number of individuals and groups and the international community at large.[465] Some of these operations, involving the use of force between two or more States, are regulated by the law of international armed conflict. Examples are the early phases of the conflicts in Afghanistan (2001-2002) and Iraq (2003-2004).[466] Other operations, involving hostilities of certain intensity between a State and an organized armed group, or between such groups, qualify as a non-international armed conflict to which IHL for NIAC applies. Examples are the ongoing non-international armed conflicts in Afghanistan (2002-today) and Iraq (2004-

the organizational criteria, but finds the NIAC against them is centred in Afghanistan and does not extend worldwide (Cole (*Calif.LR* 2009), pp. 729-730).

[465] The position set out in this paragraph is in line with that of the ICRC (*Official Statement of 21 July 2005 on the Relevance of IHL in the War on Terror*; and *International Humanitarian Law and the Challenges of Contemporary Armed Conflicts* (2003), pp. 7-8); the United Nations (e.g.: WGAD and Special Rapporteurs, *Situation of Detainees at Guantánamo Bay* (2006), §§21, 25-26 and 83); and a great number of legal scholars, such as Condorelli (*RGDIP* 2001); Sassòli (*ACDI* 2001), pp. 217-227 and 229; Aldrich (*HV* 2002), pp. 202-206; McDonald, "Defining the War on Terror and the Status of Detainees: Comments on the Presentation of Judge George Aldrich" (*HV* 2002), p. 207; Goldman & Tittemore (*ASIL Task Force* 2002), pp. 23-30; Roberts (*Isr.YHR* 2002), p. 243; Rona (*FFWA* 2003), pp. 55-74; Condorelli & Naqvi, "The War against Terrorism and Jus in Bello: Are the Geneva Conventions Out of Date?" in Bianchi & Naqvi, *Enforcing International Law Norms against Terrorism* (2004); Lavoyer in Lijnzaad et al. (2004), pp. 256-263; Pejic, "Terrorist Acts and Groups: A Role for International Law?" (*BYIL* 2004); Sassòli, "The Status of Persons Held in Guantánamo under International Humanitarian Law" (*JICJ* 2004), pp. 98-100; Borelli, "Casting Light on the Legal Black Hole: International Law and Detentions Abroad in the 'War on Terror'" (*IRRC* 2005), pp. 45-46; Jinks (*Virg.JIL* 2005-2006), pp. 165-195; Kalshoven (2007), pp. 928-929; Walen & Venzke, "Unconstitutional Detention of Nonresident Aliens: Revisiting the Supreme Court's Treatment of the Law of War in *Hamdi v. Rumsfeld*" (*ZaöRV* 2007), p. 850; Melzer (2008) pp. 262-269; Ojeda, "US Detention of Taliban Fighters: Some Legal Considerations" in: Schmitt (ed.), *The War in Afghanistan: A Legal Analysis* (2009), pp. 358-360; Vité (*IRRC* 2009), pp. 92-93; and Lubell (2010), pp. 112-121. For a good example of the minority view of the so-called "war on terrorism" as a single, global and thus international armed conflict, see Wedgewood, "Personal View: Prisoners of a Different War: The Geneva Convention Applies to Conventional Soldiers, not to the Terrorists Being Held at Camp X-Ray", *Financial Times*, 30 January 2002. For another critical view, see Greenwood, "International Law and the 'War against Terrorism'" (*IA* 2002).

[466] Regardless of whether the 9/11 attacks could be attributed to the *de facto* government of Afghanistan and triggered an armed conflict by themselves, or whether the armed conflict was triggered only by the US-led intervention in Afghanistan (we share Sassòli's analysis of this question in Sassòli (*ACDI* 2001), pp. 217-224, for another interesting contribution, see Lubell (2010), pp. 30-35 and 89-92), the ensuing hostilities opposing the US-led coalition of States and Afghanistan until the military defeat of the Taliban and the installation of a transitional government by the Lloya Jirga on 19 June 2002 qualified as an international armed conflict to which the 1949 Geneva Conventions were fully applicable. Neither the US nor Afghanistan have ratified AP I which was therefore not applicable to the conflict. Similarly, the US-led invasion of Iraq on 20 March 2003 triggered an international armed conflict between that coalition of States and Iraq until the installation of, and transfer of powers to, a transitional Iraqi government on 29 June 2004.

today).[467] Counter-terrorist operations that have no direct link to a specific international or non-international armed conflict are beyond the scope of application of international humanitarian law and must be analyzed under general international human rights law as part of an effort at international cooperation in global law enforcement.[468] Deprivation of liberty in the context of domestic or international counterterrorism operations is regulated by international humanitarian law only when it is ordered for reasons related to a specific armed conflict.[469]

---

[467] The situation in Afghanistan and Iraq, respectively since 20 June 2002 and 30 June 2004, are non-international armed conflicts, opposing respectively Afghanistan and Iraq (and the international forces participating in the conflicts on their behalf) to a number of organized armed groups that challenge their authority.

[468] See for example the arrest, detention and trial of suspected terrorists and members of Al-Qaeda reported in US, Department of Justice, "Assistant Attorney General David Kris speaks at the Brookings Institution" (2010): "Between September 2001 and March 2010, DOJ convicted more than 400 defendants in terrorism-related cases. Some of these convictions involve per se terrorism offenses, while others do not – Al Capone was convicted of tax fraud rather than racketeering, but that doesn't make him any less of a gangster. Of course we have Najibullah Zazi and David Headley, both of whom have pleaded guilty and are awaiting sentencing, and now Faisal Shahzad, but there have been many others over the years, ranging from Ramzi Yousef (the first World Trade center bomber) to the East Africa Embassy bombers, to Richard Reid, to Ahmed Omar Abu Ali, all of whom are now serving life sentences in federal prison. Just in the past year, among others, Wesam al-Delaema was sentenced to 25 years for planting IEDs in Iraq, Syed Harris and Ehsanul Sadequee were sentenced to 13 and 17 years for providing material support to al Qaeda, and Oussama Kassir was sentenced to life in prison for attempting to establish a jihad training camp in the United States. Last year we also arrested two individuals in separate undercover operations after they allegedly tried to blow up buildings in Dallas, Texas and Springfield, Illinois. And there are many others." In the same sense: Cole (*Calif.LR* 2009), pp. 727-729.

[469] Therefore, the persons deprived of liberty in the context of the so-called war on terrorism against the Taliban, Al Qaeda and affiliates fall into five legally distinct categories: (1) Members of the armed forces of a party to the international armed conflicts in Afghanistan (2001-2002) and Iraq (2003-2004) are prisoners of war and could have been interned on the basis of GC III for the duration of these hostilities (*cf. infra* chapter II-1); if individual members of such armed forces forfeited their individual right to be a prisoners of war they could have been interned on the basis of GC IV as long as that was necessary to counter the threat they posed (*cf. infra* chapter II-3); (2) Persons who were not a member of such armed forces but posed a military threat necessitating their deprivation of liberty, could have been interned on the basis of GC IV (*cf. infra* chapter II-3); (3) Persons who did not fall within the scope of application of either GC III or GC IV could not have been interned on the basis of the Conventions; if interned anyway for reasons related to these conflicts (either lawfully on another legal basis, or unlawfully) they would still have enjoyed a number of minimum guarantees under IHL (*cf. infra* chapter II-4). All persons interned on the basis of GC III and GC IV had to be released at the latest at the close of the hostilities that characterized the international armed conflict (in Afghanistan on 19 June 2002 and in Iraq on 29 June 2004) unless their continued detention was justified on a separate lawful legal basis (e.g. on the basis of criminal charges). (4) Persons arrested or captured in relation to a non-international armed conflict (e.g. in Afghanistan since 20 June 2002 until today, in Iraq since 30 June 2004 until today, or in Pakistan since 2003) must be treated by the parties to such conflict in conformity with the relevant international humanitarian law, but there is no direct legal basis to intern them in that body of law and thus they can only be interned on the basis of domestic law (*cf. infra* chapter III-1); (5) Persons arrested or captured in counterterrorism operations elsewhere and without a direct link to the armed conflicts note above, may not be deprived of liberty on the basis of international humanitarian law; the lawfulness of their deprivation of liberty must be examined solely with reference to the relevant international human rights and domestic law (*cf. supra* chapter I-1 and section 2.1 of the present chapter). In the same sense: ICRC, "Operational Update" (2009); UN WGAD & Special Rapporteurs, *Situation of Detainees at Guantánamo Bay* (2006),

Is the war on terrorism a "new" type of armed conflict, conducted on the basis of counterterrorism rather than counterinsurgency doctrines and not regulated by international humanitarian law as it stands? Domestic and international terrorism are not new phenomena. Already in the 1970's and 1980's States were confronted with what was at the time also called a "new" type of conflict called terrorism, to which an important quantity of scholarly work was devoted, without necessarily legally qualifying it as an armed conflict.[470] But even if current forms of international terrorism present new features or challenges, that does not mean that existing international humanitarian law does not apply if specific situations of violence reach the threshold of armed conflict and fall within the scope of application as defined by the text, context and purpose of the Geneva Conventions and AP I.[471]

We agree that international humanitarian law is not intended nor fit to regulate what are essentially law enforcement operations, nor is it intended to regulate the war on terrorism as such since it is not an armed conflict. International humanitarian law is not inadequate to deal with armed conflicts, but it is indeed neither adequate nor the appropriate branch of international law to regulate counterterrorism operations that do not meet the threshold of armed conflict.[472] Recourse to concepts of international humanitarian law does not provide the answer to the complex legal questions that may arise in such operations, just as recourse to military means is in most cases probably unlikely to be the most effective answer to the practical and ideological challenges that international terrorism poses.[473]

2.2.1.7. Conclusions on the threshold of applicability of international humanitarian law

The following table presents an overview of different scenarios of armed conflict and the applicable body of international humanitarian law. It also shows that several armed conflicts may exist in parallel, and that the relations between

§§21-26; Sassòli (*ACDI* 2001), pp. 229-242; Goldman & Tittemore (*ASIL Task Force* 2002), pp. 23-32; McDonald (*ZaöRV* 2002), pp. 207-209; Sassòli (*JICJ* 2004), pp. 100-105; Borelli (*IRRC* 2005), pp. 49-52; Rona (*HRF paper* 2008), p. 6.

470 E.g.: Jenkins, *International Terrorism: A New Mode of Conflict* (1975); Jenkins, "High Technology Terrorism and Surrogate War: The Impact of New Technology on Low-Level Violence" (*Rand Paper Series* 1975); Schamis, *War and Terrorism in International Affairs* (1980); or Bassiouni (*Harv.ILJ* 2002). Kalshoven (2007), at p. 928 assimilates today's war on terrorism to "not just an aggravation but a sort of institutionalised version of the Lockerbie-type terrorist activities of earlier decades."

471 E.g.: Sassòli (*ACDI* 2001), p. 229.

472 In the same sense: Kalshoven (2007), p. 929

473 See Difo, *Ordinary Measures, Extraordinary Results: An Assessment of Foiled Plots since 9/11* (2010), p. 2: "This report analyzes 32 attacks that were thwarted since 9/11 to determine which factors led to the plots' successful disruption. The report finds that in the majority of cases, traditional law enforcement techniques and methods developed prior to 9/11, direct and indirect action by concerned citizens, and international law enforcement cooperation contributed significantly to identifying terrorists and preventing attacks. It also finds that post-9/11 legislation and methods were instrumental in disrupting terror plots in only a relatively small number of cases."

the different parties to a single armed conflict may be regulated by different bodies of international humanitarian law[474] (diversified applicability of IHL).

The table includes a number of examples to which we shall return in Parts II and III in order to illustrate the different questions that arise in our analysis of the legal framework for internment in armed conflict:[475]

Situation	**Applicable law**	**Examples**
State A v. State B	IHL(IAC)	Iran v. Iraq (1980-1988) Ethiopia v. Eritrea (1998-2000)
State A v. NLM	IHL(IAC)	Morocco v. Polisario Front (Western Sahara)[476] (1975-1991) (cf. infra for occupation)
State A v. IO	IHL(IAC)	Serbia v. NATO (1999) ♣
State A v. rebels A[477]	IHL(NIAC)	Colombia v. FARC, ELN (1964-today) Philippines v. NPA (1969-today) Philippines v. MILF, MNLF (1960's-today) Sierra Leone v. RUF (1991-2001) Sri Lanka v. LTTE (1976-2009) Turkey v. PKK (1978-today) UK v. OIRA (1969-1998)

[474] UK, *LOAC Manual* (2004), pp. 16-17.

[475] Legend:

NLM = national liberation movement – to be noted however that it is the authority representing the people with a right to self-determination (= PRD) under international law that is the party to the conflict, and not its armed forces;

IO = international or regional intergovernmental organization that is a party to an armed conflict;

♣ The IO can only be considered a party to the conflict if it has effective command and control over the operations carried out by troops put at its disposal by States (*cf. supra* section 2.2.1.5); the examples in this table are therefore subject to further analysis of whether the IO indeed had such effective command and control;

Rebels A = an organized armed group that has taken up arms against its own State;

Rebels B = an organized armed group that has taken up arms against another State than its own;

IHL(IAC/OCC/NIAC) = IHL applicable in international armed conflict/occupation/non-international armed conflict;

NATO = North Atlantic Treaty Organization; DRC = Democratic Republic of the Congo; MONUC = Mission de l'Organisation des Nations Unies au Congo; MNF-I = Multinational Forces in Iraq (UN mandate); AU = African Union; AMISOM = African Union Mission in Somalia; FARC = Fuerzas Armadas Revolucionarias de Colombia; ELN = Ejercito de Liberación Nacional; NPA = New People's Army; MILF = Moro Islamic Liberation Front; MNLF = Moro National Liberation Front; RUF = Revolutionary United Front; LTTE = Liberation Tigers of Tamil Eelam; PKK = Partiya Karkerên Kurdistan; OIRA = Official Irish Republican Army; LRA = Lord Resistance Army; CNDP = Congres National pour la Défense du Peuple; IEA = Islamic Emirate of Afghanistan (Taliban insurgency in Afghanistan).

[476] The Polisario Front are the armed forces of the Sahrawi Arab Democratic Republic, representing the peoples of Ifni and Spanish Sahara who are recognized as peoples with a right to self-determination by the UN General Assembly in its *Resolution 2229 (XXI)*, 20 December 1966, §1.

[477] Some of the examples mentioned here have displayed varying levels of intensity, resulting in an equally variable applicability of IHL over time: IHL only applied during those intervals where the intensity threshold of armed conflict was reached.

Situation	Applicable law	Examples
State A v. rebels A with spill-over hostilities on territory State B but without B taking part in the conflict	IHL(NIAC)	Afghanistan v. IEA, spill-over to Pakistan (2002-today) Uganda v. LRA, spill-over to the Central-African Republic, Sudan & DRC (2003-today) Colombia v. FARC, spill-over to Venezuela & Ecuador (2004-today)
State A v. dissident armed forces	IHL(NIAC)	Niger (February 2010)
States A and B v. rebels A	IHL(NIAC)	Somalia & Ethiopia v. Islamic Courts Union in Somalia (2006)
State A and IO v. rebels A	IHL(NIAC)	DRC & UN (MONUC) v. various rebel groups in the DRC ♣ Iraq & UN (MNF-I) v. various Iraqi rebel groups (2004-2009) ♣ Afghanistan & NATO v. IAE (2002-today) ♣ Somalia & AU (AMISOM) v. Al-Shabaab (2009-today) ♣
State A v. rebels A and State B	One conflict, but different sets of IHL apply in the relation between the parties to the conflict – diversified applicability IHL: State A v. rebels A: IHL(NIAC); State A v. State B: IHL(IAC)	DRC v. various rebel groups & Uganda, Burundi, Rwanda (1998-2003) Georgia v. South Ossetia & Russia (2008) Georgia v. Abkhazia & Russia (2008)
State A v. rebels A and IO	One conflict, but diversified applicability IHL: State A v. rebels A: IHL(NIAC); State A v. IO: IHL(IAC)	No existing example. Hypothetical: Afghanistan versus Northern-Alliance & NATO (October 2001 – June 2002) ♣
State A v. rebels B with consent State B	IHL(NIAC)	Saudi-Arabia versus Al-Houthi group in Yemen (2009-today) US v. IAE in Pakistan (2008-today)
State A v. rebels B without consent State B	Two separate conflicts: State A v. rebels B: IHL(NIAC); State A v. State B: IHL(IAC)	Israel v. Hezbollah in Lebanon (2006)
State A occupies State B	IHL(IAC+OCC)	USSR v. Afghanistan (1979-1989) Iraq v. Kuwait (1990-1991) US, UK, Australia v. Iraq (2003-2004)

Situation	Applicable law	Examples
State A occupies territory NLM/PRD	IHL(IAC+OCC)	Israeli/Palestinian territories (1948-today)[478] Morocco v. Polisario Front (Western Sahara) (1975-today)
IO administers territory State A	IHL(IAC+OCC)	UN administration of Kosovo (UNMIK/KFOR, 1999-2008) ♣
IO administers territory PRD	IHL(IAC+OCC)	UN administration of Timor Leste (INTERFET, 1999-2000) ♣

2.2.2. Scope of lawful departures from the right to liberty

We have seen above that the right to liberty is not an absolute right, but can be lawfully restricted where necessary to protect a legitimate collective interest or need. International *human rights law* explicitly recognizes the possibility to limit the right to liberty on certain grounds,[479] and allows for farther-reaching restrictions of the right in emergency situations through lawful derogation.[480]

In the present section we will outline how international *humanitarian law* may allow for specific departures from the right to liberty in situations of armed conflict, and how that impacts the applicability and interpretation of the right to liberty as enshrined in international human rights law. We will then look at whether and how international humanitarian law defines who can be interned in armed conflict, for what reasons and for how long, in Parts II and III.

2.2.2.1 Restrictions on the right to liberty specific to situations of armed conflict

In situations of armed conflict, international humanitarian law may prescribe specific restrictions of the right to liberty – which go beyond those allowed under international human rights law – to meet specific military and security challenges that arise from the existence of an armed conflict.[481] Whether it actually *does* prescribe such restrictions differs according to whether the situation is one of international or non-international armed conflict, and will be the subject of our attention in Parts II and III of this book. But that it *can* create such restrictions follows from its specific function in the international legal

[478] The Palestinian people's right to self-determination has been recognized by the UNGA (e.g. *Resolution 58/163* (2003), §1) and by Israel itself in the 1993 Oslo Accords between Israel and the PLO (Palestine Liberation Organization). It has been reconfirmed by the ICJ, *Wall Opinion* (2004), §118 (unanimous). Israel does not consider the GC to be *de jure* applicable to the conflict but accepts most of its provisions to apply as a matter of customary international humanitarian law (e.g. ICJ, *Wall Opinion* (2004), §§90, 93 and 101). The ICJ took note of the Israeli position but found it incompatible with international law and ruled the Conventions are *de jure applicable* to Israel's occupation of the Palestinian territories (§§94-101, unanimous).
[479] *Cf. supra*, chapter I-1, section 1.2.4.
[480] *Cf. supra*, section 2.1.2.
[481] In the absence of armed conflict, military necessity has no place in the balance between individual rights and State interests in general international law. Where an armed conflict exists however, the necessity requirement in the right to liberty must be interpreted to include the concept of military necessity as defined or expressed in the relevant rules of international humanitarian law.

system, which is to regulate the conduct of hostilities and the treatment of individuals who find themselves in enemy hands.

To fulfil its function of "[fixing] the technical limits at which the necessities of war ought to yield to the requirements of humanity",[482] the entire normative framework of international humanitarian law is construed on the permanent quest for a balance between the requirements of military necessity on the one hand, and those of humanity on the other hand. These concepts, which we have defined in general terms earlier,[483] have been the subject of analysis and interpretation mainly in the context of the rules on the conduct of hostilities.[484] Nevertheless, they also inform the rules of international humanitarian law that define who can be interned in relation to the armed conflict, for what reasons and for how long, and thus merit some further attention here.

In the context of the conduct of hostilities, the concept of military necessity reflects what is considered a legitimate purpose for causing injury, death and destruction in the conduct of hostilities: "the only legitimate object which [the parties to the conflict] should endeavour to accomplish during war is to weaken the military forces of the enemy".[485] The principle prohibits any military actions that either do not serve that purpose, or are not necessary to achieve it.

In a similar way, the internment provisions of international humanitarian law reflect what are generally recognized as legitimate purposes for restricting fundamental rights and freedoms in a situation of armed conflict, namely to allow parties to the conflict: (1) to achieve military victory over the enemy; (2) to reasonably minimize their own military losses; or (3) to protect the civilian population under their control or responsibility against direct or indiscriminate attacks by an adverse party to the conflict.[486] The principles of military necessity and humanity thus allow for restrictions of fundamental rights and freedoms that are necessary to achieve these legitimate purposes, and at the same time prohibit restrictions that are not necessary to do so.

In this sense, international humanitarian law allows for a type of deprivation of liberty that is not allowed under general international law outside the context of an

---

[482] Quotation from the opening sentence of the preamble of the St-Petersburg Declaration (1864). On the specific function of international humanitarian law in the international legal system, *cf.* also *supra* Introduction.

[483] *Cf. supra* the introductory paragraphs to section 2.2.

[484] For an overview of the literature and practice on the principle of military necessity in the conduct of hostilities, see Melzer (2008), pp. 278-297.

[485] Preambular paragraph 2 of the St-Petersburg Declaration. We have replaced the word "States" in the preamble with the word "parties to the conflict" to reflect the fact that in contemporary IHL the parties to international armed conflicts may also be non-State entities (*cf. supra* section 2.2.1).

[486] The first two purposes coincide with those defined in the context of the conduct of hostilities (*cf. supra* note 329). The third purpose reflects the fact that parties to the conflict are responsible for the protection of the populations under their control against the effects of hostilities and therefore must be entitled to take such military measures as may be necessary to prevent and repel attacks by an adverse party against that population. To the extent that such measures are necessary to reduce unnecessary loss of civilian life, injury and destruction in armed conflict, they are generally considered to serve a legitimate purpose.

armed conflict – namely internment for reasons of military necessity – and at the same time limits the extent to which parties to the conflict may have recourse to it. The definition of these limits is informed not only by the concept of necessity itself, but also by "certain humanitarian values, which emerge through the evolution of society as some kind of general guidelines for human intercourse."[487] In establishing the balance between military necessity and humanity, international humanitarian law follows and where necessary confirms, the general principles governing deprivation of liberty in international human rights law,[488] but it adapts those principles to the practical realities of armed conflict.

For one, international humanitarian law offers – at least in situations of international armed conflict and occupation – a direct legal basis in international law to intern persons for reasons of military necessity.[489] International humanitarian law itself prescribes the grounds and procedures in accordance with which such internment may be ordered and there is therefore no need to adopt domestic legislation to do so.

We will see in Part II that the lawful grounds for internment[490] in international humanitarian law give expression to the legitimate purposes for restricting fundamental rights and freedoms in situations of armed conflict. They leave a considerable margin of discretion to the parties to the conflict to establish when internment is absolutely necessary for reasons of military necessity, so that they can be applied with due consideration both for the specific dynamics and environment of a particular conflict, and the individual situation of the internee.

Moreover, the procedural requirements for such internment take into account the potential constraints the existence of armed conflict may place on the capacity of the parties to the conflict to fully comply with the procedural requirements for deprivation of liberty under international human rights law. For example, in order to ensure its effectiveness for internees held on the battlefield, the Fourth Geneva Convention prescribes that the initial and periodic review of the lawfulness of their internment may be carried out by either a court or an administrative board, as long as the review body is independent and impartial, has the power to order release where internment is unlawful, and offers an effective possibility for the internee to challenge the lawfulness of his or her internment.[491]

Finally, international humanitarian law reinforces and supplements the protection of persons deprived of liberty in armed conflict. It does so for example

---

[487] Rosas (1976), p. 25.

[488] Such as the principles of legality, necessity, proportionality and in general the prohibition of arbitrary deprivation liberty.

[489] *Cf. supra* chapter I-1, section 1.2.3.3.

[490] We are not speaking here about the *lawfulness* of the use of force, be it collective (which is regulated by the *jus ad bellum*) or individual (such as the use of lethal force in the conduct of hostilities) but about the *reality* of the use of such force in situations of armed conflict and the legitimate need it may trigger to intern persons who pose a threat.

[491] Articles 43 and 78 GC IV. For the basic procedural safeguards required for internment review on the basis of the Fourth Geneva Convention to offer effective protection against arbitrariness, see Pejic (*IRRC* 2005), pp. 384-391.

by strictly regulating their treatment in captivity and the conditions of their detention/internment,[492] by ensuring their evacuation from the battlefield and more generally their protection against the effects of hostilities,[493] and by prescribing rules and setting up institutions to guarantee the right of persons deprived of liberty to correspond with their families and where possible receive visits from their loved ones.[494] It also provides for neutral mechanisms to monitor the compliance with international humanitarian law by the parties to the conflict.[495]

While international humanitarian law allows for specific departures from the general norms regulating deprivation of liberty in international human rights law, it does not give to the parties to the conflict a blanket authorization to adopt any measures they seem fit.[496] The norms regulating deprivation of liberty in both international humanitarian and human rights law aim to prevent arbitrariness; we have seen above that the prohibition of arbitrary deprivation of liberty is part of customary international law and may well qualify as a peremptory norm of international law.[497] It is definitely one of those "elementary considerations of humanity" and "intransgressible principles of customary international law" referred to by the International Court of Justice,[498] violation of which gives rise to both State[499] and individual criminal responsibility under international law.[500]

[492] E.g. articles 28 and 30 GC I; article 37 GC II; 12-108 GC III; articles 5, 37, 76 and 79-131 GC IV; articles 75-77 AP I; article 5 AP II; and Rules 118-127 of the ICRC' compilation of customary IHL: Henckaerts & Doswald-Beck (2005), pp. 428-451.

[493] E.g. articles 19-20 and 23-24 GC III; articles 49, 83 and 88 GC IV; article 5§2(c) AP II and Rule 121 of the ICRC' compilation of customary IHL: Henckaerts & Doswald-Beck (2005), pp. 435-437.

[494] E.g. articles 48§1, 70-76, 122-124 GC III; articles 25, 106-112, 116, 128, 136-141 GC IV; article 32 AP I; article 5§2(b) AP II; and Rules 125-126 of the ICRC's compilation of customary IHL: Henckaerts & Doswald-Beck (2005), pp. 445-449.

[495] International humanitarian law provides for the institution of Protecting Powers (i.e. neutral or other States not party to the conflict) and confers a specific mandate on the International Committee of the Red Cross to monitor the deprivation of liberty of persons in relation to the conflict and the parties' compliance with their obligations under international humanitarian law (articles 8/8/8/9 and 10/10/10/11 GC I-IV, articles 126/143GC III-IV and article 5 AP I). For the specific functions of delegates of such Protecting Powers and the ICRC with regard to detainees and internees, see e.g. articles 56, 58, 62-63, 65-66, 68-69, 71-73, 75, 77-79, 81, 96, 100-101, 104-105, 107 and 120-122 GC III; articles 30, 42-43, 45, 49, 71-72, 74-76, 96-98, 101-105, 109, 111, 123, and 129 GC IV; articles 11§6, 33, and 45 AP I).

[496] See for example the discussions at the 1949 Diplomatic Conference that adopted the four Geneva Conventions of what was to become article 27 GC IV. While article 27§1 recalls the general protection of protected persons under GC IV; its 4th paragraph allows parties to the conflict to "take such measures of control and security in regard to protected persons as may be necessary as a result of the war". The participants in the conference noted however that: "[t]he reservation thus introduced did not, however, restore to Governments the right to take arbitrary action" (*Final Record of the Diplomatic Conference of Geneva of 1949*, Vol. II-A, p. 712).

[497] *Cf. supra* chapter I-1, section 1.1.

[498] ICJ, *Nuclear Weapons* (1996), §79: "It is undoubtedly because a great many rules of humanitarian law applicable in armed conflict are so fundamental to the respect of the human person and reflect "elementary considerations of humanity" as the Court put it in its Judgment of 9 April 1949 in *Corfu Channel* (p. 22), that the Hague and Geneva Conventions have enjoyed a broad accession. Further these fundamental rules are to be observed by all States whether or not they have ratified the conventions that contain them, because they constitute intransgressible principles of international customary law" (original italics).

[499] See articles 2 and 3 of the International Law Commission's *Articles on State Responsibility* (2001)

International humanitarian law thus also places absolute limits on the restrictions of the rights of persons deprived of liberty in armed conflict. Contrary to the right to liberty under international human rights law, the provisions of international humanitarian law regulating deprivation of liberty cannot be derogated from.[501] As this body of law is expressly designed for the very specific situation of armed conflict, and its norms are the result of a careful balance between military necessity and human dignity, there is no margin for invoking the special circumstances presented by a situation of armed conflict to circumvent compliance with its provisions. Not all IHL provisions lay down absolute obligations of result, and in certain instances, a considerable margin of discretion is left to the parties to the conflict to accommodate serious obstacles to full compliance with specific norms.[502] Nevertheless, unless and to the extent exceptions are explicitly allowed for in the Conventions and their Additional Protocols, "military or similar 'necessity' cannot be invoked as a general ground for non-compliance."[503]

The provisions of international humanitarian law regulating deprivation of liberty in armed conflict apply to all persons protected by that body of law, without possibility to derogate from them. They constitute an absolute minimum; any mechanism set up for the detention or internment of individuals in armed conflict that does not meet this minimum is not in conformity with international law.[504] As one author points out with regard to the internment provisions of the Fourth Geneva Convention:

---

published with commentary in Crawford (2002), pp. 81-90. The obligations being owed to the international community as a whole, articles 40-41 and 48 are also relevant, Crawford (2002), pp. 242-253 and 276-280. If the violation can be attributed to an intergovernmental organization party to an armed conflict (*cf. supra*), it will give rise to international responsibility under the rules on the responsibility of international organizations, see articles 3-4, 40 and 48 of the International Law Commission's *Draft Articles on the Responsibility of International Organizations* (2009).

500 E.g. article 8§2(a)(vii) ICC Statute. On unlawful deprivation of liberty as a war crime, *cf. supra* chapter I-1.

501 As recently reaffirmed by Judge Higgins: "the obligations [...] imposed [by international humanitarian law] are (save for their own qualifying provisions) absolute. That is the bedrock of humanitarian law, and those engaged in conflict have always known that it is the price of our hopes for the future that they must, whatever the provocation, fight 'with one hand behind their back' and act in accordance with international law. [...] that factor diminishes relevance of context so far as the obligations of humanitarian law are concerned" (ICJ, *Wall Opinion* (2004), Separate opinion of Judge Higgins, §14). In the same sense: Dinstein (2010), pp. 21-22.

502 E.g. article 5 GC IV, which provides that certain protected persons "shall not be entitled to claim such rights and privileges under the present Convention as would, if exercised in the favour of such individual person, be prejudicial to the security of such State"; or article 126 GC III: "Visits [to prisoners of war by Protecting Powers or the ICRC] may not be prohibited except for reasons of imperative military necessity, and then only as an exceptional and temporary measure".

503 Rosas (1976), p. 115. In the same sense: Sandoz et al., *Commentary AP I and II* (1987), pp. 393 and 399; Cheng (1987), p. 63 ("military operations should be conducted in accordance with the rules and customs of warfare. Acts which are contrary to these rules, although they may be justifiable and advantageous from a military point of view, are considered as unlawful or even criminal"); Dinstein (2010), pp. 21-22.

504 In the same sense, e.g.: Solf (*AULR* 1983), p. 296: "the norms of [CA3 and AP II] are not subject to derogation. [...] article 3 prohibits 'the passing of sentences and carrying out of executions without previous judgment pronounced by a regularly constituted court, affording all the judicial guarantees

"the very function of Articles 5, 27, 42 and 43 [GC IV, i.e. respectively the legal basis to restrict certain rights under the Convention for detainees and internees, and the legal basis to intern protected persons under GC IV] is to account for security threats posed by protected persons [and in doing so] Geneva Convention IV 'fully takes into account the security needs of a state confronted with dangerous people'."[505]

2.2.2.2 Interaction of the rules on internment in IHL with the right to liberty in IHRL

The existence of an armed conflict does not suspend or cancel the applicability of other branches of international law in the relation between the parties to the conflict or in their relation to the individuals in their power.[506] In this sense, of particular relevance to our research project is the continued applicability of international human rights law.[507] Two specific questions require

---

which are recognized as indispensable by civilized peoples.' [...] Article 6 [AP II] provides a respectable catalogue of that these indispensable guarantees are [...] I doubt that there were many military lawyers present when the human rights treaties were drafted, but military lawyers were represented on most delegations at the 1949 and 1977 diplomatic conferences on the Law of Armed Conflict and they did not seem to think that there was any reason to dispense with fair trial standards, even in the heat of a civil war"; Sassòli & Olson, "The Relationship between International Humanitarian and Human Rights Law where it Matters: Admissible Killing and Internment of Fighters in Non-International Armed Conflicts" (*IRRC* 2008), p. 626: "the humanitarian law of international armed conflict – from which no derogation is possible – would set a baseline below which no derogation from the human rights rules could go, as humanitarian law provisions already apply in situations most threatening to a nation"; and Lubell (2010), p. 191: "if international humanitarian law is applicable to a particular situation, then a restriction cannot be placed on a derogable right if it would result in violating an applicable principle of IHL."

[505] Stewart, "Rethinking Guantánamo: Unlawful Confinement as Applied in International Criminal Law" (*JICJ* 2006), p. 20 (footnotes omitted).

[506] See the Resolutions of the Institute of International law, adopted at its 1912 and 1985 sessions (respectively entitled "Règlement concernant les effets de la guerre sur les traités" and "The Effect of Armed Conflicts on Treaties"); the example of UNSC, *Resolution 667* (1990), §3 (on the continuous applicability of the Vienna Conventions on diplomatic and consular relations during armed conflict); and more generally, the work of the International Law Commission on this subject: the Commission identified the topic "Effect of Armed Conflict on Treaties" at its 52nd session in 2000, and upon request of the General Assembly decided to include it in its programme of work and appointed Mr. Ian Brownlie as Special Rapporteur. Mr. Brownlie submitted four reports to the Commission, respectively at its 57th, 58th, 59th, and 60th session (2005-2008). At its 60th session, the Commission adopted, on first reading, a set of 18 draft articles on the effects of armed conflicts on treaties, together with an annex and a set of commentaries. In accordance with its Statute, the Commission transmitted the draft to Governments for comments and observations, with the request that these would be submitted to the Secretary-General by 1 January 2010 (*Ibidem*, §63). Upon the resignation from the Commission of Mr. Brownlie, the Commission, during its 61st session in 2009 appointed Mr. Lucius Caflisch as Special Rapporteur for the topic.

[507] The relationship between IHL and IHRL has been the subject of a considerable amount of case law (see in particular ICJ, *Nicaragua v. US* (1986), §§24-25; ICJ, *Wall Opinion* (2004), §106; ICJ, *DRC v. Uganda* (2005), §§215-216; HRC, *General Comment 31* (2004), §11; ICTY, *Furundžija* (1999), §159; IAC°HR, *Abella v. Argentina* (1997), §§157-171; IAC°HR, *Third Report Colombia* (1999), chapter IV, §§8-19 and 153; IAC°HR, *Coard v. USA* (1999), §§38-43; IACtHR, *Las Palmeras* (2000), §§32-34; IACtHR, *Bámaca Velásquez v. Guatemala* (2000), §§143 and 207-209; EC°HR, *Cyprus v. Turkey* (1976) and ECtHR, *Varnava v. Turkey* (2009), §185. Specifically with regard to deprivation of liberty in armed conflict, see: HRC, *General Comment 29* (2001), §11; WGAD, *Annual Report 2002*, §64; WGAD, *Annual Report 2005*, §§69-75; WGAD & Special

Rapporteurs, *Situation of Detainees at Guantánamo Bay* (2006), §§15-16; Permanent Court of Arbitration (PCA), Ethiopia-Eritrea Claims Commission (EECC), *Civilians Claims, Ethiopia's Claim 5* (2004), §§27-29; and IAC°HR, *Coard v. USA* (1999), §42). The issue has also been the subject of extensive scholarly research and debate. For some of the most important contributions to this debate, see Draper (*Isr.YHR* 1971); Wilhelm, "Problèmes relatifs à la protection de la personne humaine par le droit international dans les conflits armés ne présentant pas un caractère international" (*Hague Academy Collected Courses* 1972), pp. 378-384; Meron, "On the Inadequate Reach of Humanitarian and Human Rights Law and the Need for a New Instrument" (*AJIL* 1983); Montealegre (*AULR* 1983-1984); Solf, "Problems with the Application of Norms Governing Interstate Armed Conflict to Non-International Armed Conflict" (*GJICL* 1983); Cerna, "Human Rights in Armed Conflict: Implementation of International Humanitarian Law Norms by Regional Intergovernmental Human Rights Bodies" in Kalshoven & Sandoz (eds.), *Implementation of International Humanitarian Law* (1989); Doswald-Beck, "International Humanitarian Law: A Means of Protecting Human Rights in Time of Armed Conflict" (*AJICL* 1989); Hampson, "Using International Human Rights Machinery to Enforce the International Law of Armed Conflicts" (*RDPMDG* 1992); Doswald-Beck & Vité, "International Humanitarian Law and Human Rights Law" (*IRRC* 1993); Simma, "From Bilateralism to Community Interest in International Law" (*Hague Academy Collected Courses* 1994); Cançado Trindade, *Tratado de Direito Internacional dos Direitos Humanos (Volume I)* (1997), pp. 269-280; Martin, "Application du droit international humanitaire par la Cour interaméricaine des droits de l'homme" (*IRRC* 2001); Gasser (*GYIL* 2002); Heintze, "The European Court of Human Rights and the Implementation of Human Rights Standards during Armed Conflicts" (*GYIL* 2002); Moir (2002), pp. 193-231; Provost (2002); Ben-Naftali & Shany, "Living in Denial: The Application of Human Rights in the Occupied Territories" (*ILR* 2003-2004); ICRC, *Protection through Complementarity of the Law* (2003); ICRC, *International Humanitarian Law and the Challenges of Contemporary Armed Conflicts* (2003); IIHL, *Report of the San Remo Roundtable* (2003), pp. 8-9; Dinstein (2010), pp. 19-26; Hampson (*Tehran Conference paper* 2004); Heintze, "On the Relationship between Human Rights Law Protection and International Humanitarian Law" (*IRRC* 2004); Watkin, "Controlling the Use of Force: A Role for Human Rights Norms in Contemporary Armed Conflict" (*AJIL* 2004); Hampson & Salama, *Working Paper on the Relationship between Human Rights Law and International Humanitarian Law* (*Subcommission on Human Rights* 2005); Dennis, "Applying Human Rights Law and Humanitarian Law in the Extraterritorial War against Terrorism: Too Little, Too Much, or Just Right? Application of Human Rights Treaties Extraterritorially to Detention of Combatants and Security Internees: Fuzzy Thinking All Around?" (*ILSA JICL* 2006); Green, "The Relations between Human Rights Law and International Humanitarian Law: A Historical Overview" in Breau & Jachec-Neale (eds.), *Testing the Boundaries of International Humanitarian Law* (2006); Krieger, "A Conflict of Norms: The Relationship between Humanitarian Law and Human Rights Law in the ICRC Customary Law Study" (*JCSL* 2006); Meron (2006); Roberts, "Transformative Military Occupation: Applying the Laws of War and Human Rights" (*AJIL* 2006); Rowe (2006); Gross, "Human Proportions: Are Human Rights the Emperor's New Clothes of the International Law of Occupation?" (*EJIL* 2007); ICRC, *International Humanitarian Law and the Challenges of Contemporary Armed Conflicts* (2007); Sassòli in *Liber Amoricum Malinverni* (2007); Hampson (*IRRC* 2008); Orakhelashvili, "The Interaction between Human Rights and Humanitarian Law: Fragmentation, Conflict, Parallelism, or Convergence?" (*EJIL* 2008); Shany, "Human Rights and Humanitarian Law as Competing Legal Paradigms for Fighting Terror" (*Hebrew University of Jerusalem Research Papers* 2009); Arnold & Quenivet, *International Humanitarian Law and Human Rights Law: Towards a Merger in International Law* (2008); Goldman, "History and Action: The Inter-American Human Rights System and the Role of the Inter-American Commission on Human Rights" (*HRQ* 2009); Higgins, *Themes and Theories: Selected Essays, Speeches and Writings in International Law* (2009); Milanović, "Norm Conflicts in International Law: Whither Human Rights?" (*DJCIL 2009*); and Milanović (*JCSL* 2010). See also the numerous contributions in special issues on the subject in the following law reviews: "50th anniversary of the Universal Declaration of Human Rights: Human Rights and International Humanitarian Law" (*IRRC* 1998, especially the contributions of Kolb, Reidy, and Zegveld), "Parallel Applicability of IHR and IHL" (*Israeli Law Review* 2007), especially the contributions by Provost, Prud'homme & Schabas); "Human Rights" (*IRRC* 2008, especially the contributions by Droege, Hampson, and Sassòli & Olson); "Symposium: The Relationship between International Humanitarian Law and International

our attention in this regard: how does the simultaneous applicability of the norms on deprivation of liberty of international humanitarian law and international human rights law influence the interpretation of their norms? And must parties to an armed conflict derogate from their obligations under international human rights law to avail themselves of the legal bases to intern that are provided for by international humanitarian law? [508]

(a.) Coherent and effective interpretation of international norms regarding deprivation of liberty

Article 31§3(c) VCLT provides that the interpretation of a given treaty norm must take into account "any relevant rules of international law applicable in the relations between the parties [to that treaty]."[509] Since international humanitarian law and international human rights law apply simultaneously in armed conflict, this means that the interpretation of the norms on deprivation of liberty of both these bodies of law must take into account equivalent norms in the other body of law. Taking into account the specific functions of each body of law, their respective norms must be interpreted in light of each other to be effective in achieving the common goal of preventing unnecessary and arbitrary deprivation of liberty.

On the one hand, the internment provisions of IHL must be interpreted with due consideration for their equivalent norms in international human rights law. For example, we will see in Part II that the internment provisions of the four Geneva Conventions reflect the same general principles underpinning the right to

Human Rights Law" *JCSL* 2010 (especially the contributions by Bowring, Cryer, Scobbie and Milanovic). Specifically with regard to deprivation of liberty in armed conflict: Goldman & Tittemore (*ASIL Task Force* 2002); Kälin in *Report of the Expert Meeting on the Supervision of Lawfulness of Detention* (*2004*); Jinks, (*Virg.JIL* 2005-2006); Rowe (2006); Sassòli & Olson (*IRRC* 2008); Hampson, "Is Human Rights law of Any Relevance to Military Operations in Afghanistan?" in Schmitt (2009); Olson, "Practical Challenges of Implementing the Complementarity between International Humanitarian and Human Rights Law, Demonstrated by the Procedural Regulation of Internment in Non-International Armed Conflict" (*CWRJIL* 2009); Milanovic (*JCSL* 2010); and Naert (2010).

[508] The relationship between IHL and IHRL is often phrased in terms of *lex specialis* and *lege generali*. For an overview of the possible meaning and functions of this maxim as a tool for norm conflict avoidance and solution, see ILC, *Fragmentation* (2006), pp. 30-65. The best analysis of how this tool may be used as a tool for conflict avoidance and resolution in the relationship between IHL and IHRL remains in our view that of Marco Sassòli, reflected in his "Le droit international humanitaire, une *lex specialis* par rapport aux droits humains?" in *Liber Amoricum Malinverni* (2007). Nevertheless, the tool itself nor the concrete results it produces when applied to norm conflicts between IHL and IHRL is entirely clear: moreover, its usefulness for addressing such conflicts is subject to controversy, for a critical view see for example Prud'homme (*ILR* 2007), pp. 356-395; Milanovic (*JCSL* 2010), pp. 473-476; and Lubell (2010), pp. 239-247. We share much of the criticism with regard to the use of the *lex specialis* principle in the concurrent application of IHL and IHRL norms and will thus not rely on it. In our opinion, the interpretative tools of the VCLT are sufficient to deal with the simultaneous applicability of IHL and IHRL in situations of armed conflict. The proposals made below (especially with regard to IHL as an automatic equivalent to derogation where it explicitly prescribes measures that depart from those allowed under general international law) may produce similar results as certain *lex specialis* approaches, but are consciously made without having recourse to it.

[509] *Cf. supra* the section on methodology in the introduction.

liberty enshrined in international human rights law (discussed in chapter I-1), but adapt their specific content to situations of international armed conflict and occupation to take into account both the additional legitimate purposes for restricting fundamental rights and freedoms in situations of armed conflict, and the practical constraints that may hinder parties to armed conflict to ensure full enjoyment of such rights and freedoms in these situations. Nevertheless, the interpretation of these provisions continues to be guided by the general principles of international human rights law as they evolve over time.[510]

On the other hand, where international humanitarian law provides a direct legal basis for internment, its provisions must be taken into account to assess whether a given case of internment in armed conflict violates the right to liberty under international human rights law.[511] For one, the interpretation of the requirement "prescribed by law" must take into account the fact that a number of legal bases for internment in international armed conflict exist in the Geneva Conventions. Moreover, the interpretation of the requirement of lawful grounds must take into account the additional grounds for internment prescribed by these Conventions. Also, the interpretation of the requirement of *habeas* must take into account the fact that the Conventions explicitly allow for the review of the legality of (initial and continued) internment to be carried out by an independent and impartial administrative body rather than by a court.

Most provisions of international human rights law leave sufficient room for taking into account the norms of international humanitarian law where they

[510] See for example the structure of the internment provisions of GC IV, discussed below in chapter II-3, section 2.1, and summarized aptly by Pictet in his Commentary to the Convention: "The right to personal liberty, and in particular, the right to move about freely, can naturally be made subject in wartime to certain restrictions made necessary by circumstances [...] That right is not, therefore, included among the other absolute rights laid down in the Convention, but that in no way means that it is suspended in a general manner. Quite the contrary: the regulations concerning occupation and those concerning civilian aliens in the territory of a Party to the conflict are based on the idea of the personal freedom of civilians *remaining in general unimpaired*. The right in question is therefore a relative one which the Party to the conflict or the occupying power *may restrict or even suspend within the limits laid down by the Convention*" (Pictet, *Commentary GC IV* (1958), pp. 201-202 (emphasis added)). See also article 38§1 GC IV which provides that "[w]ith the exception of special measures authorized by the present Convention, in particular Articles 27 and 41 thereof, the situation of protected persons shall continue to be regulated, in principle, by the provisions concerning aliens in time of peace." The adoption of articles 27§4 and 38§ GC IV was closely connected and based on a single draft article discussed at the 1949 Diplomatic Conference, which provided that "[t]he situation of protected persons shall continue to be governed, in principle, by the provisions relating to the treatment of aliens in time of peace, subject to such measures of control or security as may be ordered with respect to them, as a result of war" (*Final Record 1949*, Vol. I, p. 119).

[511] For other examples of the interpretation of international human rights norms when applied in situations of armed conflict, see Rowe (2006), pp. 134-158 (the right to life, liberty and fair trial, the prohibition of torture and other forms of inhumane or degrading treatment, the right to property and to freedom of movement in situations of international armed conflict), pp. 158-161 (human rights in occupied territory), and pp. 180-196 (the right to life, liberty and fair trial, the prohibition of torture and other forms of inhumane or degrading treatment, the right to property and to freedom of movement in situations of non-international armed conflict). For an example of interpretation of IHL norms with reference to relevant IHRL norms, see ICTY, *Delalić* (1998), §§452-459 (referring to international human rights law to define the prohibition of torture in IHL).

apply. For example, article 9§1 ICCPR provides that "[n]o one shall be subjected to arbitrary arrest or detention" and that "[n]o one shall be deprived of his liberty except on such grounds and in accordance with such procedure as are established by law." Contrary to the European Convention on Human Rights, article 9§1 ICCPR does not contain an exhaustive list of the lawful grounds for deprivation of liberty. One could therefore argue that the text of the provision itself therefore leaves sufficient room to accommodate at least the grounds for internment prescribed by the Geneva Conventions: where internment is carried out in full compliance with the relevant provisions of these Conventions, it will not be arbitrary and therefore there will not trigger a violation of article 9 ICCPR.

Such was the reasoning of the International Court of Justice with regard to the right to life in article 2 ICCPR ("No one shall be arbitrarily deprived of his life"):

> "The Court observes that the protection of the [ICCPR] does not cease in times of war, [...] In principle, the right not arbitrarily to be deprived of one's life applies also in hostilities. The test of what is an arbitrary deprivation of life, however, then falls to be determined by the applicable *lex specialis*, namely, the law applicable in armed conflict, which is designed to regulate the conduct of hostilities. Thus whether a particular loss of life, through the use of a certain weapon in warfare, is to be considered an arbitrary deprivation of life contrary to Article 6 of the Covenant, can only be decided by reference to the law applicable in armed conflict and not deduced from the terms of the Covenant itself."[512]

The Inter-American Commission on Human Rights has applied the same reasoning with regard to the right to liberty when it has examined the lawfulness of internment in situations of international armed conflict under the provisions of the American Declaration on the Rights and Duties of Man:

> "it would be inconsistent with general principles of law for the Commission to construe and exercise its Charter-based mandate without taking into account other international obligations of member states which may be relevant [footnote refers to article 31§3(c) VCLT]. [...] [I]n a situation of armed conflict, the test for assessing the observance of a particular right, such as the right to liberty, may, under given circumstances, be distinct from that applicable in a time of peace. For that reason, the standard to be applied must be deduced by reference to [international humanitarian law] [footnote refers to ICJ, *Nuclear Weapons* (1996), §25]. The American Declaration is drawn in general terms, and does not include specific provisions relating to its applicability in conflict situations. [...] the Commission determined that the analysis of the petitioners' claims under the Declaration within their factual and legal context requires reference to

[512] ICJ, *Nuclear Weapons* (1996), §25. In the same sense: IAC°HR, *Abella v. Argentina* (1997), §161; IAC°HR, *Third Report Colombia* (1999), chapter IV, §169; UN Human Rights Council, Special Rapporteur on Extrajudicial, Summary or Arbitrary Executions (Mr. Philip Alston), *Study on Targeted Killings* (2010), §29. For an overview of this issue, see the *Report of the Expert Meeting on the Right to Life in Armed Conflicts and Situations of Occupation* (2005); Doswald-Beck, "The Right to Life in Armed Conflict: Does International Humanitarian Law Provide All the Answers?" (*IRRC* 2006), pp. 881-904; Melzer (2008); and Quénivet, "The Right to Life in International Humanitarian Law and Human rights Law" in Arnold & Quénivet (2008), pp. 331-353.

international humanitarian law, which is a source of authoritative guidance and provides the specific normative standards which apply to conflict situations. In the present case, the standards of humanitarian law help to define whether the detention of the petitioners was "arbitrary" or not under the terms of Articles I and XXV of the American Declaration."[513]

The same reasoning can arguably be applied to interpret the right to liberty in the International Covenant on Civil and Political rights, the Convention on the Rights of the Child, the American Convention on Human Rights, the African Convention on Human and Peoples' Rights and the Arab Charter on Human Rights, all of which prohibit arbitrary deprivation of liberty without specifically listing the lawful grounds on which such deprivation of liberty may be based.[514]

On the contrary, the provisions of the European Convention on Human Rights do not leave room for such an interpretation. Article 5§1 ECHR – as we have seen in chapter 1 – lists the lawful grounds for deprivation of liberty in an

---

[513] IAC°HR, *Coard v. USA* (1999), §§40 and 42 (the case concerned internment by US forces in Grenada in 1983 and will be discussed in more detail in chapter II-1). In the same sense, IAC°HR, *Guantánamo* (2002): "In certain circumstances, however, the test for evaluating the observance of a particular right, such as the right to liberty, in a situation of armed conflict may be distinct from that applicable in time of peace. In such situations, international law, including the jurisprudence of this Commission, dictates that it may be necessary to deduce the applicable standard by reference to international humanitarian law"; and WGAD & Special Rapporteurs, *Situation of Detainees at Guantánamo Bay* (2006), §19: "any person having committed a belligerent act in the context of an international armed conflict and having fallen into the hands of one of the parties to the conflict (in this case, the United States) can be held for the duration of hostilities, as long as the detention serves the purpose of preventing combatants from continuing to take up arms against the United States. Indeed, this principle encapsulates a fundamental difference between the laws of war and human rights law with regard to deprivation of liberty. In the context of armed conflicts covered by international humanitarian law, this rule constitutes the *lex specialis* justifying deprivation of liberty which would otherwise, under human rights law as enshrined by article 9 of ICCPR, constitute a violation of the right to personal liberty." While the Inter-American Commission's decisions and the reports of the special rapporteurs to the UN Human Rights Commission are not legally binding, they reflect the opinion of distinguished human rights experts and provide a useful contribution to reflection on this and other subjects. So far these decisions constitute the only international case law referring explicitly to IHL in order to decide on whether a particular deprivation of liberty in armed conflict was arbitrary for the purposes of the right to liberty in international human rights law.

[514] Articles 9§1 ICCPR; 37(b) CRC; 7§§2-3 ACHR; 6 ACHPR and 14§§1-2 of the Arab Charter. The possibility of applying the ICJ's reasoning on the right to life to internment in situations of international armed conflict or occupation has also been confirmed by the participants in the *Report of the San Remo Roundtable* (2003), p. 11; Doswald-Beck in *Report of the Expert Meeting on the Supervision of Lawfulness of Detention* (2004), p. 5; Kälin in *Report of the Expert Meeting on the Supervision of Lawfulness of Detention* (2004), p. 31; Sassòli in *Liber Amoricum Malinverni* (2007), p. 389; Hampson (*IRRC* 2008), p. 564; Cassel (*CWRJIL* 2009), pp. 389-395 and 400-401; Milanovic (*JCSL* 2010), p. 25 of the online version; and Naert (2010), p. 625. Whereas non-international armed conflicts are concerned these same authors – with whom we agree – conclude that in the absence of explicit norms in IHL, the right to liberty must be interpreted without any reference to (non-existing) provisions of IHL, *cf. infra* Part III. Such is also the position of the Inter-American Court of Human Rights (e.g. IACtHR, *Bámaca Velásquez v. Guatemala* (2000), § 143), and that of the United Nations Working Group on Arbitrary Detention and five Special Rapporteurs to the United Nations Human Rights Council, see WGAD Special Rapporteurs, *Situation of Detainees at Guantánamo Bay* (2006), §24: "In the ongoing non-international armed conflicts involving United States forces, the *lex specialis* authorizing detention without respect for the guarantees set forth in article 9 of ICCPR therefore can no longer serve as a basis for that detention."

exhaustive manner and that list does not include internment on the basis of military necessity in armed conflict.[515] Does this mean that the parties to the ECHR must derogate from their obligations under that Convention before they are allowed to lawfully intern in armed conflict on the basis of the internment provisions of the Geneva Conventions? This brings us to the second question that arises from the simultaneous applicability of international humanitarian and human rights law in situations of armed conflict.

(b.) Internment on the basis of international humanitarian law and the question of derogation

Taking into account the fact that international humanitarian law provides, at least in situations of international armed conflict and occupation, a legal basis to intern for reasons of military necessity, the question arises whether the parties to such conflict or an Occupying Power must derogate from their obligations under international human rights law to rely on that basis for their internment operations.

The starting point for the answer to that question must in our view be the fact that international humanitarian law and international human rights law are both part of a single international legal system, and that they both seek to prevent unnecessary and arbitrary deprivation of liberty.[516] To achieve that aim in situations of armed conflict, the Geneva Conventions' internment provisions reflect and adhere to the same basic principles regarding deprivation of liberty as human rights treaties, but take into account the specific features of the situations to which they apply, resulting in a different articulation of the rules on deprivation of liberty than those enshrined in international human rights treaties.[517] These complementary rules do not only confer additional protection on the individuals affected by armed conflict, but also allow the parties to the conflict to restrict fundamental rights and freedoms where "necessary as a result of the war." Logically therefore, where the parties to the conflict rely on a legal basis to intern provided for by international humanitarian law, and fully comply with its provisions, such internment should not at the same time give rise to a violation of the right to liberty under international human rights law.

---

[515] As was recently reconfirmed by the European Court of Human Rights (ECtHR (Grand Chamber), *Al-Jedda* (2011), §107), and also holds true for the CIS Convention, the provisions of which mirror those of the ECHR in an almost identical matter.

[516] In the same sense: Meron, *Human Rights in Internal Strife: Their International Protection* (1987), pp. 18-19 (who cites the prohibition of arbitrary arrest and detention as one of the issues on which IHL and IHRL norms converge).

[517] It is true of course that the Geneva Conventions (the only IHL treaties that provide parties to the conflict with a direct legal basis to intern in armed conflict) were adopted earlier in time than any of the international human rights treaties (the ADRDM and UDHR had been adopted one year earlier but they are non-binding declarations, not treaties). Nevertheless, we have seen in chapter I-1 that the basic principles regulating restrictions of fundamental rights and freedoms predate the adoption of international human rights law treaties and are part of general international law. Moreover, the contemporary interpretation and application of the Geneva Conventions must take into account developments in international law and in the environment in which it operates that have occurred since their adoption. *Cf. supra* note 44 and accompanying text.

We have seen above that the provisions of international human rights law usually leave sufficient room for interpretation to take into account the relevant rules of international humanitarian law, without a need to derogate. Yet, what if this is not the case? We have mentioned the example of the exhaustive list of lawful grounds in article 5§1 ECHR, but the question may arise for other human rights provisions too.[518]

Moreover, when the ICJ and the IAC°HR interpret the word "arbitrary" in the provisions regarding the rights to liberty and life with reference to the rules of IHL, they effectively resort to a broad interpretation of the limitation clauses within the substantive rights to life and liberty. Such an approach runs counter to the principle that limitation clauses must be interpreted strictly, and that "special" or "exceptional" circumstances may justify restrictions which go beyond the permissible limitations but require derogation (and the specific procedural safeguards that come with it).[519] What then is to prevent a similarly broad interpretation of the right to life or the right to liberty in other situations, that do not amount to armed conflict but may – *de facto* – result in similar levels of violence or threats to public order and security?

Another way to approach the question is to accept that international humanitarian law treaties such as the Geneva Conventions – explicitly and intentionally – allow for certain restrictions of the right to liberty that are incompatible with international human rights treaty norms, that they do so as part of a balance struck between military necessity and humanity in the particular situations of armed conflict that fall within their scope of application, and that the parties to these Conventions did not subsequently intend to depart from that intention when they (or at least some of them) drafted and adopted international human rights treaty norms on deprivation of liberty. There indeed does not seem to be any indication that States parties to the ECHR, ICCPR, ACHR, ACHPR or other relevant human rights treaties wished to abrogate the legal bases for internment in the Geneva Conventions when they designed and drafted the right to liberty enshrined within these human rights treaties.[520] Thus, rather than

---

518 For example, the question arises whether the requirement of *habeas* as expressed in the right to liberty in international human rights law leaves sufficient room to take into account the fact that review of internment in international humanitarian law may be carried out by an administrative body rather than by a court. That question is even more complex when one takes into account the fact that the right to habeas is increasingly considered to be a non-derogable right, and a strict interpretation of the term "court" could therefore render it impossible for the parties to an international armed conflict to intern persons in accordance with the Fourth Geneva Convention without violating their obligations under international human rights law.

519 *Cf. supra* chapter I-1.

520 In this sense it may be interesting to mention the US proposal to include "detention of enemy aliens" in a list of lawful grounds that would be lawful under article 9§1 ICCPR. While in the end the drafters of the ICCPR decided not to include such a list in article 9§1 ICCPR (as was done for article 5§1 ECHR), the discussions on what grounds should be included therein do shed some light on what certain States found to be lawful grounds for deprivation of liberty (*cf.* also *supra* note 221). The US proposal to include "detention of enemy aliens" does not seem to have been the object of any further discussion nor of any specific objection (see the extracts from the reports in Bossuyt (1987), pp. 190-202). This may be an indicator of the fact that States would indeed have considered such detention

interpreting the permissible *limitations* on substantive rights and freedoms broadly (as the ICJ and the IAC°HR did with regard to the rights to life and liberty), our approach favours an interpretation of the *derogation* provisions in human rights treaties that recognizes the existence of international humanitarian law and the lawfulness of the exceptional restrictions on fundamental rights and freedoms it has explicitly sanctioned.

Moreover, practice shows that States do not find it necessary to derogate from their obligations under human rights treaties to intern persons on the basis of the Geneva Conventions in situations of international armed conflict and occupation.[521] One possible and, admittedly, likely explanation (at least where

---

(in as far as compatible with their obligations under the Geneva Conventions, which were adopted almost twenty years earlier) to be lawful as such, and thus not requiring any derogation.

[521] Our conclusion is based on an analysis of the derogations notified to the concerned authorities for the ICCPR and the ECHR, as reflected in the UN's and the Council of Europe's online databases (available respectively at http://treaties.un.org, and http://conventions.coe.int, and last verified on 1 October 2010). Our research of these databases – focused on international armed conflicts and occupations in which States parties to the ICCPR and ECHR were involved since their date of ratification – has provided us with the following information (we will examine some of the situations referred to here in more detail in Part II). Neither Afghanistan nor the Soviet Union derogated from the ICCPR during the conflict that opposed the two States from 1979 to1989. Likewise, neither Afghanistan, Australia, Canada, Denmark, France, Germany, Italy, the Netherlands, New Zealand, the UK or the US derogated from the right to liberty under the ICCPR or the ECHR in relation to the international phase of the recent conflict in Afghanistan (2001-2002); the same is true for the conflict that opposed Iraq to the US, UK and other States from 2003 to 2004. The following States have also interned persons on the basis of the Third and Fourth Geneva Conventions without derogating from the right to liberty in the ICCPR or ECHR: the UK and Argentina in the conflict over the Falklands/Malvinas islands in 1982; the US during its military operations in Grenada in 1983; India and Bangladesh in the conflicts with Pakistan in the 1970's (Pakistan is not a party to the ICCPR); Iran and Iraq during the 1980-1988 war; Israel and the Arab States in any of the international armed conflicts opposing them in the Middle East (1948-today); the States parties to the ECHR that participated under the umbrella of the UN in the Korean War from 1950 to 1953; Iraq, Kuwait, the US and the UK during the 1991 Gulf War (Saudi-Arabia, which interned many prisoners of war during that conflict, is not a party to the ICCPR); Angola, Burundi, the Democratic Republic of the Congo (DRC), Namibia, Rwanda, Uganda and Zimbabwe in the DRC (1998-2003); Ethiopia in the conflict opposing it to Eritrea from 1998 to 2000 (Eritrea had not yet ratified the ICCPR at the time); Eritrea and Djibouti in the short border conflict in 2008; Georgia and Russia in the blitz war of August 2008; Russia did not derogate from the ICCPR in relation to the conflict with Moldova over Transdnistria in 1992 (Russia was not yet a party to the ECHR and Moldova was not yet a party to either the ICCPR or the ECHR at the time). Neither Cyprus nor Turkey derogated from the ICCPR or the ECHR to intern on the basis of GC III-IV in Northern-Cyprus (note that Turkey did not consider the ICCPR or the ECHR to apply extra-territorially); Turkey did derogate from the ECHR as far as persons within mainland Turkey were concerned but since it did not specify the articles from which it intended to derogate it is unclear whether it thought it necessary to do so in order to intern persons on the basis of GC III and IV. Similarly, Azerbaijan derogated from the ICCPR (it was not a party to the ECHR yet at the time) to take measures that were necessary as a result of the conflict with Armenia (1988-1994), but it is unclear whether it did so to intern persons on the basis of the Geneva Conventions; Armenia did not derogate from the ICCPR (it was not yet a party to the ECHR at the time). Likewise, Nicaragua derogated from article 9 ICCPR, saying it was obliged to do so following the US involvement in the conflict with the Contras in the 1980s. It is unclear whether Nicaragua thought it necessary to derogate from the ICCPR to intern on the basis of the Geneva Conventions, in its notices of derogation it insisted that article 9§1 was only derogated from for offences against national security and public order.

less recent conflicts are concerned) is that States did not (at the time) consider international human rights law to apply in such situations. But even when States do accept the simultaneous applicability of both bodies of law, which most of them do today (at least since the International Court of Justice and other international courts have settled this question), their practice demonstrates a conviction that there is no need to derogate to intern persons on the basis of the Geneva Conventions as long as the latter are fully complied with.

That conviction seems to be shared by the Inter-American Commission on Human Rights and by an increasing number of legal scholars.[522] In the few relevant cases that have come before it,[523] the Inter-American Commission has not taken issue with the fact that States relied directly on international humanitarian law to justify internment on the basis of the Geneva Conventions, without derogating from article 7 ACHR to do so.[524]

In light of the above, we think it may be argued, on the basis of article 31§3(b) VLCT, that "subsequent practice in the application of the treaty" has established "the agreement of the parties regarding its application", namely that no derogation is required from the relevant human rights treaties to order restrictions of fundamental rights and freedoms that are explicitly prescribed for and regulated by international humanitarian law. If parties to a human rights treaty do not derogate from that treaty when they intern persons directly on the basis of international humanitarian law, then that practice may indeed be

[522] Scholars seem to espouse the fact that internment in full compliance with international humanitarian law in situations of international armed conflict and occupation does not require derogation from the right to liberty (possibly with the exception of the ECHR), see for example Doswald-Beck in *Report of the Expert Meeting on the Supervision of Lawfulness of Detention* (2004), p. 5 (with exception of the right to *habeas*); Kälin in *Report of the Expert Meeting on the Supervision of Lawfulness of Detention* (2004), pp. 31-32; Hampson (*IRRC* 2008), p. 564; Sassòli & Olson (*IRRC* 2008), pp. 617 and 621; Cassel (*CWRJIL* 2009), pp. 389-400; Milanovic (*JCSL* 2010), p. 25 of the online version; and Naert (2010), p. 625. Pejic (*IRRC* 2005) seems to suggest that, in order to intern or administratively detain in international, non-international armed conflicts or other situations of violence, States must derogate from the right to liberty under the ICCPR (see footnotes 2 and 18 and accompanying text), but makes an exception for the internment of prisoners of war, which she suggests is exclusively regulated by GC III (p. 376 and p. 380, footnote 18). Discussion with Pejic clarified however that she does not think derogation from international human rights treaties is necessary to intern on the basis of GC III or GC IV in situations of international armed conflict and occupation. Allan Rosas, in his comprehensive work on prisoners of war, finds that international human rights law applies to prisoners of war in as far as they are within the jurisdiction of the Interning Power for the purpose of the respective human rights treaty, and that the derogation provisions of the ICCPR, ECHR and ACHR must be applied strictly in their regard. He does not discuss or express an opinion on whether or not these instruments must be derogated from in order to avoid prisoner of war internment by States parties to the Conventions to amount to a breach of their human rights obligations (Rosas (1976), pp. 93-94).

[523] See IAC°HR, *Coard v. USA* (1999) and IAC°HR, *Guantánamo* (2002), quoted above. The case law of the Inter-American Commission and Court regarding internment in armed conflict will be discussed in more detail in Parts II and III.

[524] The Human Rights Committee has so far not been called to pronounce on the relationship between the internment provisions of international humanitarian law and article 9 ICCPR. Both the European Commission (in a case concerning Cyprus and Turkey, which we will discuss below) and the European Court of Human Rights (in the *Al-Jedda* case, which we will also discuss below) briefly touched upon the issue, without however clearly deciding it.

understood to establish their agreement that derogation is indeed not necessary in such situations.

Rather than presenting internment as a lawful deprivation of liberty under IHRL (thus not requiring derogation), our approach reflects an acceptance that internment would, in normal times, be an unlawful deprivation of liberty, but is justified in the specific circumstances in which the Geneva Conventions apply. In this sense, the Conventions function in a very similar way as a domestic emergency law, derogating from the right to liberty: the deprivation of liberty is considered to be unlawful in "normal" times but justifiable in certain "exceptional" times and, in such times, thus precludes a violation of the right to liberty. As the Geneva Conventions themselves define the threshold of application for this specific deprivation of liberty to become available, there is neither a need to establish whether or not the situation amounts to a public emergency threatening the life of the nation (the legal bases in the Geneva Conventions may be relied upon when a situation falls within that treaty's material, temporal and personal scope of application) nor a need to demonstrate that the measure is strictly required by the exigencies of that situation (the legal bases' inclusion in the Geneva Conventions reflects the acceptance that internment may be strictly necessary in a situation of armed conflict and moreover defines specific criteria to limit its use to cases where it is indeed necessary). The specific "derogatory measures" allowed for under international humanitarian law thus apply automatically.[525]

For example, in order to intern a prisoner of war, there would be no need to derogate from article 5§1 ECHR since such a "derogation" is inherent in the explicit provisions of the Third Geneva Convention. As long as the internment of the prisoner falls within the scope of application of GC III and the Interning Power fully complies with that Convention's provisions, the internment would be lawful under international law. Similarly, to intern a protected person under GC IV, there would be no need to derogate from the requirement of *habeas* in article 9§4 ICCPR or equivalent provisions in other human rights treaties to justify recourse to an independent and impartial administrative tribunal to review that (initial or continued) internment, since the "derogation" would be inherent in articles 43 and 78 GC IV.[526]

The question of whether derogation from international human rights treaties is necessary to rely on the legal bases for internment provided by the Geneva

[525] In the same sense: one (unnamed) participant in *Report of the Expert Meeting on the Right to Life in Armed Conflicts and Situations of Occupation* (2005), p. 13; and Naert (2010), pp. 573-574. See also the dissenting opinion of Commissioners Sperduti and Trechsel in EC°HR, *Cyprus against Turkey* (1976), which we will discuss in detail below.

[526] This is without prejudice to the answer to the questions raised in note 518 above, which merit further research and analysis. Nevertheless, the approach proposed could possibly offer a solution for the impact of non-derogability of article 9§4 ICCPR (and equivalent norms in other human rights treaties) on the international validity of the review procedures of articles 43 and 78 GC IV. In this sense, it is useful to note that the jurisprudence of international human rights bodies and international criminal tribunals on the lawfulness of internment in international armed conflict does not suggest the need to derogate from international human rights, *cf. infra*.

Conventions has, so far, not come up directly before any international court or treaty monitoring body,[527] with the notable exception of the European Commission on Human Rights, which touched upon it in a case opposing Cyprus and Turkey concerning Turkish military operations in Cyprus following the coup d'Etat that occurred on the island in 1974.[528] While the report of the Commission is somewhat ambiguous, two of the dissenting commissioners adopted a more articulate and straightforward approach, which lends support to the one we proposed above.

The following extracts from the Commission's report concern persons who are either prisoners of war or protected persons under GC IV:

> "309. The Commission considers that the detention of *Greek Cypriot military personnel in Turkey*, which is clearly imputable to Turkey under the Convention, constituted a deprivation of liberty within the meaning of [article 5§1 ECHR]. Since it did not serve any of the purposes enumerated in sub-paragraphs (a) to (f) of this provision, the Commission concludes, by thirteen votes against one, that it was not in conformity with article 5§1 ECHR].
>
> 310. As regards the detention of *Greek Cypriot civilians*, the Commission considers that, in so far as it occurred in Turkey and therefore is imputable to Turkey, it equally constituted a deprivation of liberty within the meaning of article 5§1 ECHR] not serving any of the purposes mentioned in sub-paragraphs (a) to (f) of this provision. The Commission therefore concludes, by thirteen votes against one, that the detention of civilians in Turkey was equally not in conformity with [article 5§1 ECHR].
>
> [...]
>
> 313. The Commission has taken account of the fact that both Cyprus and Turkey are Parties to the (Third) Geneva Convention [...], and that, in connection with the events in the summer of 1974, Turkey in particular assured the International Committee of the Red Cross (ICRC) of its intention to apply the Geneva Conventions and its willingness to grant all necessary facilities for humanitarian action. In fact, ICRC delegates made regular visits to *soldiers and civilians* who had been *granted prisoner-of-war status by the authorities on either side*. [...] Having regard to the above, the Commission has not found it necessary to examine the question of a breach of Art. 5 of the European Convention on Human Rights with regard to *persons accorded the status of prisoners of war*."[529]

With regard to the first two categories of persons, referred to in paragraphs 309 and 310 of the Report, the Commission reserves "the question whether any of the above deprivations of liberty, in particular the detention of military personnel as prisoners-of-war, were justified under Art. 15 of the Convention";[530] a question that, in the opinion of the Commission, does not arise

[527] *Cf. supra* notes 523 and 524.

[528] For the factual background of the case, see EC°HR, *Cyprus against Turkey* (1976), §§6-18.

[529] EC°HR, *Cyprus against Turkey* (1976), §§309, 310 and 313, emphasis added, footnotes omitted.

[530] EC°HR, *Cyprus against Turkey* (1976), §312.

with regard to "persons accorded the status of prisoners of war" by the parties to the conflict and whose internment was monitored by the ICRC.

A number of observations are in place with regard to the Commission's findings. First, the distinction made by the Commission between persons who are and persons who are not "accorded the status of prisoners of war" by the parties to the conflict, and persons who clearly fall within the scope of application of the Third and Fourth Geneva Conventions but were not accorded such status, is unfounded in law. Whether or not a person falls within the personal scope of application of either the Third or the Fourth Geneva Convention is not for the parties to the conflict to decide, but is determined by the Convention's personal scope of application.[531] Second, and of particular interest to us here, the Commission's finding with regard to "persons accorded the status of prisoners of war" (§313) seems to suggest that their protection was sufficiently ensured by the parties' agreement to treat them as prisoners of war[532] and by the ICRC visits so as not require further examination. The Commission's exclusion of those cases from consideration under the derogation provisions of the Convention suggests moreover that the Commission did not find the internment of "persons granted the status of prisoners of war" and benefiting from ICRC visits, to be unlawful under article 5§1 ECHR.

As to the possible lawfulness of the internment of persons referred to in paragraphs 309 and 310 of the report under the European Convention's derogation provisions, the Commission found that the violations of article 5§1 ECHR with regard to these persons were not remedied by a derogation under article 15 ECHR, since Turkey had not communicated a "formal and public of derogation" that was applicable to the persons concerned. Indeed, with regard to persons interned in Northern Cyprus, Turkey did not derogate from its obligations under the ECHR, because it felt it had no obligations under the ECHR outside its own territory.[533] The Commission found that:

> "Art. 15 requires some formal and public act of derogation, such as a declaration of martial law or state of emergency, and that, where no such act has been proclaimed by the High Contracting Party concerned, although it was not in the circumstances prevented from doing so, Art. 15 cannot apply."[534]

However, with regard to persons interned within Turkey proper, Turkey had informed the Secretary-General of the Council of Europe that:

> "The Turkish Government has declared martial law for a duration of one month in the provinces of Ankara, Istanbul, Tekirdag, Izmir, Aydin, Mugla, Kanisa, Kirklareli, Edirne, Canakkale, Balikesir, Adana, Igel and Hatay in conformity

[531] *Cf. infra* Part II.

[532] It not clear on what basis the Commission finds these persons were granted prisoner of war status by the parties to the conflict. The three categories distinguished by the Commission in paragraphs 309-313 of its report are generally referred to as "prisoners and detainees", with a reference to inter-communal agreements that were exclusively concerned with the release and transfer of such "prisoners and detainees." (See paragraphs 296-296 and 303-306 of the Commission's report).

[533] EC°HR, *Cyprus against Turkey* (1976), §526.

[534] *Ibidem*, §527.

with Article 20 of the Constitution. This decision on martial law which was taken due to a situation that may necessitate war, foreseen in paragraph 1 of Article 15 of the European Convention on Human Rights, is communicated hereby in accordance with the third paragraph of the same article of the above-mentioned Convention."[535]

Nevertheless, and without further explanation, the Commission found that:

"the said declaration of martial law cannot, within the conditions prescribed in Art. 15, be extended to cover the treatment of persons brought into Turkey from the northern area of Cyprus."[536]

Two commissioners dissented on the issue of derogation. Their reasoning is in line with the approach we proposed above. First, with regard to the principle of legality and publicity of emergency measures, and the duty to notify the relevant treaty authorities thereof,[537] Commissioners Sperduti and Trechsel found that:

"the obligation [to notify the treaty authorities] should, in principle at least, be seen as an autonomous obligation in the sense that its violation does not affect the valid exercise of the right of derogation flowing from the same article. Having said this, [...] it is scarcely conceivable that they should not receive some form of publicity. [...] A distinction must indeed be drawn between these concrete measures and the acts which authorise and regulate them. Whether laws or ordinances or proclamations are involved, it is inherent in the very nature of these acts that they should be promulgated by means of certain forms of publicity. [...] There may [...] be situations [...] envisaged by domestic or international law as being *situations which, from the moment when they arise, render applicable rules* - of domestic or international law as the case may be - *under which exceptional measures can be taken in the conditions envisaged by them*. One cannot see how one could deduce from Art. 15 that it was necessary to resort to further forms of publicity in relation to these rules. This is notably the case in military occupation of the territory of a foreign state [...] The state of emergency which the establishment of military rule in a foreign territory brings about for the occupying authorities differs from other emergency situations in that *it bears, to a large extent, certain typical characteristics, so that it is sufficient that the military occupation should be known for the state of emergency which it has brought about to be equally known as an inherent phenomenon*. This has allowed the elaboration of *rules of the law of war* concerning the occupation of territories and *covering*, amongst other matters, *the exercise of exceptional powers by* the occupying authorities."[538]

[535] *Ibidem*, §521. Turkey renewed its declaration at several intervals for the duration of one year, after which it informed the Secretary-General that martial law had been lifted in all provinces.
[536] *Ibidem*, §530.
[537] With regard to the difference between the requirement of publicity (a *conditio sine qua non* for the lawfulness of a derogation) and the obligation to notify the relevant treaty authorities of such derogation, *cf. supra* notes 291-293 and accompanying text.
[538] EC°HR, *Cyprus against Turkey* (1976), "Dissenting Opinion of Mr. G. Sperduti, joined by Mr. S. Trechsel on article 15 ECHR", §§3-5, emphasis added.

The dissenting Commissioners said their reasoning with regard to the law of occupation could be developed even further:

"It is to be noted that the rules of international law concerning the treatment of the population in occupied territories [...] are undeniably capable of assisting the *resolution of the question whether the measures taken* by the occupying power *in derogation from the obligations which it should in principle observe* – by virtue of the European Convention – where it exercises (de jure or de facto) its jurisdiction, *are or are not justified according to* the criterion that only measures of derogation *strictly required by the circumstances* are authorised. In fact these rules duly take account of the necessities of the occupying power: *they are inspired by the search for a just balance* between military necessities and the safeguarding of the rights and interests of the civil population. *It follows that respect for these* same rules by a High Contracting Party during the military occupation of the territory of another state, *will in principle assure that that High Contracting Party will not go beyond the limits of the right of derogation* conferred on it by Art. 15 of the Convention."[539]

Finally, with regard to the Commission's finding on "persons accorded the status of prisoners of war" (§313 of the report, *cf. supra*), Commissioners Sperduti and Trechsel resolved that:

"It can be said, in accordance with the above approach, that measures which are in themselves contrary to a provision of the European Convention but which are taken legitimately under the international law applicable to an armed conflict, are to be considered as legitimate measures of derogation from the obligations flowing from the Convention."[540]

State practice is less clear as regards situations of non-international armed conflict. There are several possible explanations for this. For one, we will see in Part III that international humanitarian law applicable in non-international armed conflict does not provide a direct legal basis to intern as the Geneva Conventions do for situations of international armed conflict and occupation,[541] which may explain why States do derogate from the right to liberty in international human rights law to adopt emergency legislation allowing for security internment in such situations.[542] Moreover, many States are reluctant to recognize the existence

[539] *Ibidem*, §6, emphasis added.

[540] *Ibidem*, §7, emphasis added.

[541] In light of the absence of such a legal basis in IHL for non-international armed conflicts, many scholars esteem derogation from international human rights law is necessary to intern or administratively detain in such situations, both with regard to grounds and procedures. See for example Pejic (*IRRC* 2005), pp. 376-380; Hampson (*IRRC* 2008), pp. 562-564; *Report of the Expert Meeting on Security Detention in NIAC* (2008), p. 878 footnote 18; Milanovic (*JCSL* 2010), p. 24-25 of the online version; and Naert (2010), p. 628. Without being explicit, this also seems to be the position of Rowe (2006), pp. 190-192.

[542] An analysis of the derogations notified to the concerned authorities for the ICCPR and the ECHR (as reflected in the UN's and Council of Europe's respective databases, *cf. supra* 520), shows for example that Ireland, Nepal, Sri Lanka, Thailand and the UK (with regard to Northern-Ireland) have derogated from their human rights obligations (article 9 ICCPR and/or article 5 ECHR) to adopt emergency legislation allowing for administrative detention in non-international armed conflict. Several States have derogated from article 9 ICCPR/article 5 ECHR to adopt special legislation restricting the procedural safeguards and judicial guarantees of persons charged with crimes such as

of any internal armed conflict and thus do not avail themselves of the existence of such a conflict to justify any potential derogations from or violations of human rights. Finally, most States seem to rely on domestic criminal legislation to detain persons involved in the conflict.[543] Where detention is based on criminal legislation or on a lawful conviction by a court, there is no need to derogate from any human rights obligations, at least as far as the legal basis and the grounds for the detention are concerned.[544] At least in as far as the European Court of Human Rights is concerned, it seems that derogation will indeed be necessary to intern in situations of non-international armed conflict.[545] It is submitted that – unless an international humanitarian law treaty provides for a direct legal basis to intern in such conflict (which in our opinion it does not to this day) – derogation will also be necessary for other human rights treaties.

In conclusion, it is submitted that where international humanitarian law itself provides a legal basis to intern, and internment effectively complies with the grounds and procedures prescribed thereby, such internment does not require the

---

terrorism, treason, rebellion, or insurrection in relation to non-international armed conflict, namely Argentina, Bolivia, Colombia, Nicaragua, Peru, the Russian Federation, Sri Lanka, Sudan, Turkey (Turkey only derogated from article 5 ECHR, not from article 9 ICCPR), and Uganda. Other States have adopted such legislation (allowing either for administrative detention, or creating special crimes or restricting procedural safeguards and judicial guarantees of persons detained in relation to non-international armed conflict) without derogating from article 9 ICCPR/article 5 ECHR, as is the case for example for Ethiopia, Guatemala, the Philippines, and Spain. To be noted that India has adopted legislation allowing for administrative detention without derogating from article 9 ICCPR, but had, upon its ratification of the ICCPR, submitted the following reservation: "With reference to article 9 of the International Covenant on Civil and Political Rights, the Government of the Republic of India takes the position that the provisions of the article shall be so applied as to be in consonance with the provisions of clauses (3) to (7) of article 22 of the Constitution of India." The provisions of the Constitution referred to in the reservation concern the detention of "enemy aliens" and administrative detention under Indian law. Most of the national legislation passed by the countries mentioned here will be discussed in Part III.

[543] *Cf. infra* Part III.

[544] *Cf. infra* Part III. States parties to non-international armed conflicts *outside* their own territory have so far not derogated from their human rights obligations in order to intern opponents. Troop-contributing nations to KFOR, ISAF and MNF-I for example have not derogated from their obligations under IHRL to intern persons for reasons related to the armed conflict (the conclusion is based on an analysis of the UN's and the Council of Europe's databases on notifications of derogation, *cf. supra* 520). The explanation seems to be that either they do not accept international human rights law to apply extra-territorially (e.g. the US or Israel) or they argue their obligations in international human rights law are overridden by a UN Security Council Resolution on the basis of article 103 UN Charter (e.g. the UK). In light of these explanations, such practice does not tell us anything on these States' opinion on whether derogation from the ICCPR or ECHR is necessary to intern in situations of non-international armed conflict in general.

[545] As summarized well by Hampson (*IRRC* 2008), p. 564 and note 64: "ECtHR, Lawless v. Ireland, 332/57, Judgment of 1 July 1961. It is clear from the reasoning of the Court in Ireland v. UK, 5310/71, ECtHR, Judgment of 18 January 1978, that internment in Northern Ireland would have been unlawful but for the notice of derogation. In Brogan & others v. UK, 11209/84, Judgment of 29 November 1988, the ECtHR found a violation of Article 5 of the Convention on account of the length of detention (rather than the ground). The United Kingdom then submitted a notice of derogation and detention under the same legislation was subsequently found not to violate the Convention, taking account of the derogation, in Brannigan & McBride v. UK, 14553-4/89, ECtHR, Judgment of 24 May 1993."

Interning Power to derogate from the right to liberty to be lawful under international human rights law. Such is the case, as we have seen in chapter I-1, for the legal bases for internment included in the Geneva Conventions. On the contrary, where the legal bases provided for in the Geneva Conventions do not apply – either because a person does not fall within their scope of application, or because internment occurs in a situation of non-international armed conflict – a positive act of derogation from the right to liberty will be necessary for internment similar to that allowed for in situations of international armed conflict or occupation to be lawful under international law, since no "automatic derogation" is included in international humanitarian law.

(c.) Complementarity and the further development of international norms on deprivation of liberty

The mutual influence of international humanitarian law and international human rights law is also noticeable in the development of these norms. Where any further development of their norms on deprivation of liberty in armed conflict should be undertaken, the exigencies of both bodies of law must therefore be taken into account.

For example, any further development of international human rights law should take into account not only the applicability of international humanitarian law in situations of armed conflict but also the fact that that body of law, at least for situations of international armed conflict and occupation, provides the parties to the conflict with a legal basis for internment in armed conflict that adapts the requirements of the general right to liberty to strike a delicate balance between the requirements of both military necessity and humanity.

Similarly, should the international community decide to engage in a further development of common article 3 of the Geneva Conventions and their Second Additional Protocol relative to non-international armed conflicts, it must take into account the exigencies of existing international human rights law (*cf. infra* Part III). Likewise, any future development or revision of the law of international armed conflict should reflect the modifications to this body of law that are the result of developments in international law subsequent to the adoption of the Geneva Conventions and their Additional Protocols (*cf. infra* Part II).

Nevertheless, we agree with Yuval Shany that one must be aware of an important risk that may arise from assessing military operations in armed conflict predominantly pursuant to human rights standards:

> "Human rights law is founded upon a number of fundamental ethoi that profoundly affect the way in which it is interpreted and applied. [...] Significantly, the different points of departures of human rights law and IHL derive not only from differences in ideological inclinations of their forefathers, but also from structural reasons relating to the typical factual and institutional conditions that they are designed to govern. [...] Although human rights law has an important role to play even in the course of a full-scale armed conflict as a harm-mitigating methodology with particular relevance to individualized measures applied during the conflict [...], an attempt to alter the basic attributes

of the "armed conflict" paradigm through the application of human rights law may result in problematic normative-overreaching. In other words, such an attempt may lead to a law-application exercise divorced from the actual conditions and needs of warfare and is likely to attract limited support from important constituencies. As a result, a 'reconfigured armed conflict' paradigm may have only little impact on state conduct."[546]

Schindler noted in 1979 that "[a] separate set of rules for armed conflicts is in fact what States want."[547] While the situation is constantly evolving, that reality does not seem to have changed much today. Apart from the wishes of States, the existence of a special set of rules to complement – and where necessary depart from – the general rules in situations of armed conflict also allows international humanitarian law to effectively fulfil its function in the international legal system, without eroding the general protection afforded by international human rights law in situations that do not meet the threshold of armed conflict. We will have the opportunity to come back to this issue in Part III.

2.2.2.3. Conclusions

Deprivation of liberty, and internment in particular, is a common incident of warfare, and it is generally accepted to be a legitimate measure to neutralize enemy armed forces or other persons who pose a direct threat to the security of the parties to the conflict or their military operations. Nevertheless, *arbitrary* deprivation of liberty remains absolutely prohibited, even in times of armed conflict. Therefore, where international humanitarian law provides for a direct legal basis to intern, it subjects such internment to strict conditions and rules.

The type of deprivation of liberty specific to armed conflict, namely security internment, goes beyond what are considered lawful limitations of the full enjoyment of the right to liberty enshrined in international human rights law. In order to ensure its lawfulness under general international law, the parties to the conflict have two different avenues at their disposal to justify internment measures that depart from the right to liberty beyond what is allowed in normal situations.

On the one hand, if the given situation of armed conflict meets the threshold of a "public emergency threatening the life of the nation", the parties to the conflict may adopt emergency legislation to provide for a legal basis to intern in derogation from the right to liberty. For such derogation to be lawful, it must meet the conditions to derogate set forth in the relevant international human rights treaties.[548] One of these conditions is that the derogation may not be

[546] Shany (*Hebrew University of Jerusalem Research Papers* 2009), pp. 21-23. In a similar vein and with specific regard to the right to life and the conduct of hostilities, see Watkin (*AJIL* 2004), p. 32: "The positive effect that human rights norms can bring to international humanitarian law in respect of targeting will be directly related to how successfully the emphasis on accountability accommodates the differences between the two normative frameworks."

[547] Schindler, "The International Committee of the Red Cross and Human Rights" (*IRRC* 1979), p. 14.

[548] Note that no derogation from the ACHPR is allowed. Derogation from the Charter to intern in armed conflict is therefore not available for the parties to that Charter, *cf. supra* section I-2.1.

inconsistent with other obligations under international law, and in particular international humanitarian law. International humanitarian law thus defines the absolute limits of the extent to which the right to liberty may be derogated from in situations of armed conflict.[549]

On the other hand, international humanitarian law may provide a direct legal basis to intern. International humanitarian law applies automatically in situations of armed conflict, and allows parties to an armed conflict to take certain measures that are derogatory to fundamental rights and freedoms. Where such "derogations" from the right to liberty are explicitly provided for in the applicable international humanitarian law itself, no further derogation from the parties' obligations under international human rights law will be necessary for deprivation of liberty to be lawful under international law.[550] It is submitted that an interpretation of international human rights law in conformity with the Vienna Convention on the Law of Treaties, taking into account the general objectives of the international legal system and the specific objectives of both international humanitarian and human rights law, allows us to conclude that full compliance with an explicit legal basis to intern in international humanitarian law does not amount to arbitrary deprivation of liberty and therefore does not violate the right to liberty as enshrined in international human rights law.[551]

---

[549] See for example: Israel, SC, *A and B v. Israel* (2008), §§9-10: "an Israeli act of legislation [*in casu* the *Incarceration of unlawful combatants law* (2002), effectively implementing article 42 GC IV into Israeli domestic law] should be interpreted in a manner that is consistent, in so far as possible, with the norms of international law to which the State of Israel is committed [...] the arrangements provided in the law should be interpreted in a manner that is as consistent as possible with the international humanitarian law that governs the matter [the provisions of which] will be our interpretive tools and they will assist us in interpreting the provisions of the statute and in evaluating the nature and scope of the power of detention provided in it." The Israeli legislation and case law will be discussed in considerable detail in chapter II-3.

[550] To be noted that automatic derogations from the right to liberty incorporated in IHL are restricted to those that are explicitly prescribed by the applicable internment provisions of IHL. Any further departure from the right to liberty in relation to such internment will require derogation from the Interning Power's human rights obligations. In this sense, the UK House of Lords in *Al-Jedda* (2007) found that a legal basis for internment in a UN Council Resolution that provided for internment on grounds similar to that in article 78 GC IV, qualified the UK's obligations under article 5§1 ECHR, but Baroness Hale of Richmond (§125 of the judgment) pointed out that: "[t]he right is qualified but not displaced. This is an important distinction, insufficiently explored in the all or nothing arguments with which we were presented. We can go no further than the UN has implicitly required us to go in restoring peace and security to a troubled land. The right is qualified only to the extent required or authorised by the resolution. What remains of it thereafter must be observed. This may have both substantive and procedural consequences." It is submitted that the House of Lords would most likely have reached the same conclusion if the UK would have relied directly on article 78 GC IV rather than on the Security Council Resolution. The judgments of the UK courts in this case will be discussed in more detail in Part II.

[551] In the same sense, see Kälin in *Report of the Expert Meeting on the Supervision of Lawfulness of Detention* (2004), pp. 31-32; Rowe (2006), pp. 148-153 and 190-192; Droege (*IRRC* 2008), pp. 521-523 (while she uses the example of the right to life to demonstrate her argument, it suggests she would reach the same conclusion with regard to the right to liberty); Hampson (*IRRC* 2008), pp. 562-572; Cassel (*CWRJIL* 2009), pp. 389-395 and 400-401; *Report of the Expert Meeting on Security Detention in NIAC* (2008); Milanovic (*JCSL* 2010), pp. 24-25 of the online version; and Naert (2010), pp. 625-628. All these authors (and the participants in the expert meeting) do point out the

In Parts II and III, we will examine in which cases international humanitarian law does indeed offer such a direct legal basis to intern persons for reasons of military necessity, and we will attempt to offer comprehensive answers to the questions of who can be interned on the basis of international humanitarian law, for what reasons and for how long.

2.3. CONCLUSIONS TO PART I

To conclude this Part of the book, we would like to come back to the issue of the rule of law, the principle of legality and the right to liberty in armed conflict with a reference to the dissenting opinion of a judge in the UK's House of Lords in a case concerning internment during the Second World War. This opinion, very controversial at the time, has been described 60 years later by Lord Bingham of Cornhill as "a legal morality tale apt for our times", and has much to say not only about internment in armed conflict but also about "the problems of terrorism, public emergencies, threats to national security and the detention of suspects without charge or trial."[552] In short, it is an exemplary case of how exceptional remedies in exceptional times, no matter how well intended or endorsed by the political and judicial elite and even the general public, may carry the risk of eroding fundamental human rights and adherence to the rule of law.

The case concerned the internment of a member of the British Royal Air Force on the basis of an executive order made by the UK Secretary of State pursuant to the infamous Defence Regulation 18B, on grounds that he was "a person of hostile associations" which made his internment necessary in the interests of "the public safety or the defence of the Realm."[553] The internee's lawyers pressed first the Home Office and then the courts for details on the grounds on which their client was considered to be "a person of hostile associations" so as to enable him to challenge the lawfulness of his internment, but without success. In his dissenting opinion, Lord Atkin viewed:

> "with apprehension the attitude of judges who on a mere question of construction [...] when face to face with claims involving the liberty of the subject show themselves more executive minded than the executive. [...] I protest, even if I do it alone, against [an interpretation of the law] with the effect of giving an uncontrolled power of imprisonment to the minister."[554]

Lord Atkin's opinion inspired a leading British legal scholar to comment:

> "Generations of Englishmen have been brought up to regard it as one vital aspect of the Rule of Law (for which, among other things, this country is now fighting the most crucial war in its history), that all persons are equal before the law and that for any unjustified infringement of the liberty of the subject the liability of a

particularity of the ECHR in this regard.

552 Citations are from Bingham, "The Case of Liversidge v. Anderson: The Rule of Law amid the Clash of Arms" (*The International Lawyer* 2009), p. 33.

553 Citations are from the specific order in the case and the Defence Regulation 18B. We will come back to this regulation in more detail in chapter II-3.

554 Quoted in Bingham (*The International Lawyer* 2009).

Minister of State is no whit different from that of a policeman, or indeed, from the meanest of the King's subjects."[555]

And it led Lord Bingham to conclude in 2009 that:

"At one of the lowest moments of our national history, it was no doubt easy to feel that exceptional circumstances called for exceptional remedies, that it was no time for legal niceties, that it was expedient to intern one man that the whole nation perish not, that the safety of the people was the supreme law. But we are entitled to be proud that even in that extreme national emergency there was one voice – eloquent and courageous – which asserted older, nobler, more enduring values: the right of the individual against the state; the duty to govern in accordance with law; the role of the courts as guarantor of legality and individual right; the priceless gift, subject only to constraints by law established, of individual freedom. It would be hard to express these values more shortly, more simply, more memorably than in Atkin's neatly turned Ciceronian allusion, which in closing I venture to repeat:

'In this country, amid the clash of arms, the laws are not silent. They may be changed, but they speak the same language in war as in peace. It has always been one of the pillars of freedom ... that the judges are no respecters of persons and stand between the subject and any attempted encroachments on his liberty by the executive, alert to see that any coercive action is justified in law'."[556]

[555] C.K. Allen, quoted in Bingham (*The International Lawyer* 2009).
[556] Bingham (*The International Lawyer* 2009), p. 38.

PART II

SECURITY INTERNMENT IN SITUATIONS OF INTERNATIONAL ARMED CONFLICT AND OCCUPATION

INTRODUCTION TO PART II

We have seen in Part I that international humanitarian law, as a regime specifically designed to regulate armed conflict, may allow parties to an armed conflict to impose specific restrictions on an individual's right to liberty – restrictions that go beyond what is allowed under international human rights law – in order to meet the specific military and security challenges that may arise from the existence of an armed conflict. In situations of international armed conflict and occupation, it does indeed provide the parties to the conflict with a legal basis to intern persons for reasons of military necessity.

In order to prevent any arbitrary deprivation of liberty, international humanitarian law subjects such internment measures to strict conditions: "[h]umanitarian law aims at preventing arbitrary detention by two main means: [by] [p]roviding for permissible grounds of detention based on military necessity [and by] [p]roviding for some supervision of the fact of detention."[557]

Taking into account the chaos that normally ensues with the outbreak of hostilities, and the impracticalities of relying on domestic law to intern in situations of armed conflict, especially when acting abroad, international humanitarian law creates the basic tool necessary for the parties to the conflict to intern during an armed conflict without the need to fall back on domestic legislation: a legal basis for internment. The universally ratified 1949 Geneva Conventions thus prescribe the grounds and procedures in accordance with which internment can be ordered for reasons of military necessity and offer the parties to the conflict a legal basis for deprivation of liberty additional to those at its disposal under general domestic and international law. The validity in international law of the legal bases in the Geneva Conventions for internment in situations of international armed conflict and occupation is not subject to any serious controversy and has in practice never been challenged.[558]

In situations of international armed conflict and occupation, international humanitarian law therefore provides us with answers to all three of our research questions. The scope of application of the four Geneva Conventions defines who can be interned on the basis of international humanitarian law, and their specific internment provisions prescribe the reasons and duration for which such persons

---

[557] Doswald-Beck in *Report of the Expert Meeting on the Supervision of Lawfulness of Detention* (2004), p. 2.

[558] In the little case law of human rights bodies on internment in situations of international armed conflict and occupation, both States and the human rights bodies themselves implicitly acknowledged that the Geneva Conventions were the legal basis for such internment. See for example EC°HR, *Cyprus v. Turkey* (1976); IAC°HR, *Coard v. USA* (1999); ICTY, *Delalic* (1998); and ICTY, *Delalic* (2001). These cases will be discussed in more detail below.

can be interned. The specific answer to each question will depend on the type of persons concerned. The Geneva Conventions distinguish between three mutually exclusive categories of internees. The definition of each category of internees corresponds to the personal scope of application of the Convention authorizing their internment and is not subject to a person's status for the purposes of the rules on the conduct of hostilities.[559] The internment provisions of international humanitarian law do not distinguish between combatants and non-combatants/civilians, but rather between:

• prisoners of war, who can be interned on the basis of the Third Geneva Convention;

• the medical and religious personnel of the armed forces of the parties to the conflict, who can be interned on the basis of the First and Second Geneva Conventions;

• and other persons, who can be interned on the basis of the Fourth Geneva Convention.

There is no legal basis to intern persons who do not fall within one of these three categories and who thus effectively fall outside the scope of application of the Geneva Conventions, at least not in international law. Should such persons be interned on the basis of domestic law, they remain under the full protection of international human rights law and – if they are interned for reasons related to the armed conflict – are also protected to a certain extent under international humanitarian law.

The balance between military necessity and humanity permeating the entire normative framework of international humanitarian law also informs the definition of who can be interned, for what reasons and for how long on the basis of the Geneva Conventions.[560] We will see that internment on the basis of these Conventions is only allowed if and to the extent it is necessary to achieve one of the purposes recognized as legitimate for restricting fundamental rights and freedoms in armed conflict, namely to allow parties to the conflict: (1) to achieve military victory over the enemy; (2) to reasonably minimize their own military losses; or (3) to protect the civilian population under their control or responsibility against direct or indiscriminate attacks carried out by the armed forces of an adverse party to the conflict. The first three chapters of this Part focus on how the balance between military necessity and the right to liberty is struck for each of the three categories of internees.

The fact that international humanitarian law does provide answers to our three research questions does not mean that other bodies of international law are irrelevant to define who can be interned, for what reasons and for how long on

[559] *Cf. infra* chapter II-3, section 3.2.2.2 for a discussion on the relevance of the rules on targeting for the interpretation or development of the rules on internment in armed conflict.

[560] For the definition of the principles of military necessity and humanity, and the general articulation of the balance between them with regard to deprivation of liberty in armed conflict, *cf. supra* chapter I-2, section 2.2.

the basis of the four Geneva Conventions. The Geneva Conventions do not exist in a legal vacuum, but are part of a broader and continuously evolving international legal system. When interpreting their provisions, we must therefore take into account subsequent developments of international humanitarian law[561] and other relevant rules of international law applicable in the relations between parties to an international armed conflict.[562]

The present part is divided in four substantive chapters, based on the four categories of persons who may *de facto* be interned in situations of international armed conflict and occupation. In chapters II-1 to II-3 we analyze the relevant provisions of the Geneva Conventions for each recognized category of internees in order to define who can be interned on the basis of these Conventions, for what reasons and for how long. The purpose of these chapters is to analyze the scope of application and the grounds for internment in each of these Conventions in sufficient detail to allow authorities on the ground to establish when they may lawfully intern a given person, and to allow review authorities to assess the lawfulness of the internment decisions taken by authorities on the ground.[563] Rather than trying, artificially, to adopt the same structure for each of these three chapters, we have opted to organize each chapter according to the conceptualization and architecture of the specific Geneva Convention concerned. In chapter II-4, we outline the international legal protection proffered upon persons who fall outside the personal scope of application of the Conventions. Chapter II-5 is a concluding chapter in which we summarize the answers to our three research questions for situations of international armed conflict and occupation, and briefly touch upon issues of responsibility and supervision.

[561] The internment provisions of the 1949 Geneva Conventions have been further developed in the Additional Protocols thereto, adopted on 8 June 1977 and in customary international humanitarian law (for a recent compilation by the ICRC, see Henckaerts & Doswald-Beck (2005) and the updated *CIHL Database* (2010).

[562] In particular, but not limited to, international human rights law, *cf. supra* Part I.

[563] The term "review authorities" is used here in a general sense, including: the authorities responsible for status determination in case of doubt on the applicability of a particular Geneva Convention, the authorities in charge of initial and periodical review of internment on the basis of GC IV, and the national and international courts and tribunals that may be called upon to assess the lawfulness of a given case of internment that took place in a situation of international armed conflict or occupation.

CHAPTER II – 1
INTERNMENT ON THE BASIS OF THE THIRD GENEVA CONVENTION: PRISONERS OF WAR

The legal basis for the internment of prisoners of war originates in a longstanding custom allowing State parties to a conflict to intern troops of the adverse party for the duration of the conflict in order to prevent them from returning to the battlefield. It would take until the end of the 19th century however for such internment to be regulated by international treaty law. The 1899 Hague Regulations concerning the Laws and Customs of War on Land confer, for the first time, an internationally recognized legal status upon captured troops – the status of prisoners of war – and include specific regulations for their internment that are aimed to protect them against arbitrary treatment and abuse by the capturing State:[564]

> "The armed forces of the belligerent parties may consist of combatants and non-combatants. In case of capture by the enemy both have a right to be treated as prisoners of war."[565]

The Regulations define the categories of persons entitled to the legal status of prisoner of war (POW) and the protection that goes with it as follows:

> "Article 1. The laws, rights, and duties of war apply not only to armies, but also to militia and volunteer corps fulfilling the following conditions: 1. To be commanded by a person responsible for his subordinates; 2. To have a fixed distinctive emblem recognizable at a distance; 3. To carry arms openly; and 4. To conduct their operations in accordance with the laws and customs of war. In countries where militia or volunteer corps constitute the army, or form part of it, they are included under the denomination 'army.'

[564] Articles 1-20 and 29-31 of the Regulations Concerning the Laws and Customs of War on Land, annexed to Convention (II) with Respect to the Laws and Customs of War on Land (1899) (hereinafter the "Hague Regulations (1899)" or "HR 1899"). Issues concerning prisoners of war were dealt with in various international *fora* and instruments before the adoption of the HR 1899, but these Regulations are the first legally binding instrument of international law that regulated the legal status and protection of prisoners of war. The research and analysis in this book focuses on the challenges in the contemporary legal regime and is thus based on the 1949 Geneva Conventions, their Additional Protocols and subsequent practice. Rather than including a comprehensive overview of the historical background to and evolution of the status and treatment of prisoners of war (and the related concept of combatants) – for which we refer the reader to the important contributions made by Rosas (1976), Levie, *Prisoners of War in International Armed Conflict* (1979) and Draper (*Isr.YHR* 1971) – we will make reference to specific historical documents where directly relevant for clarifying the contemporary legal framework and challenges. For an interesting contribution on the issue of prisoners of war in Islamic law, see Zemmali, *Combattants et prisonniers de guerre en droit islamique et en droit international humanitaire* (1997).

[565] Article 3 HR 1899.

Article 2. The population of a territory which has not been occupied who, on the enemy's approach, spontaneously take up arms to resist the invading troops without having time to organize themselves in accordance with Article 1, shall be regarded as belligerent, if they respect the laws and customs of war."

These provisions have been further developed in subsequent treaties dealing with prisoners of war and will be the subject of the first section of the present chapter.[566]

In contemporary international law, the main legal basis for interning prisoners of war is article 21 of the Third Geneva Convention relative to the Treatment of Prisoners of War, which provides that "[t]he Detaining Power may subject prisoners of war to internment."[567] For one specific category of prisoners of war however, the legal basis is found elsewhere. The legal basis for the mandatory internment by neutral States of members of the armed forces of a party to the conflict who are present on their territory is provided for – in similar terms as that of article 21 GC III – in articles 11 and 24 of respectively the Fifth and the Thirteenth Hague Convention concerning the Rights and Duties of Neutral Powers in Case of War:

> "A neutral Power which receives on its territory troops belonging to the belligerent armies shall intern them, as far as possible, at a distance from the theatre of war. It may keep them in camps and even confine them in fortresses or in places set apart for this purpose. It shall decide whether officers can be left at liberty on giving their parole not to leave the neutral territory without permission."[568]

> "If, notwithstanding the notification of the neutral Power, a belligerent ship of war does not leave a port where it is not entitled to remain, the neutral Power is entitled to take such measures as it considers necessary to render the ship incapable of taking the sea during the war, and the commanding officer of the ship must facilitate the execution of such measures. When a belligerent ship is detained by a neutral Power, the officers and crew are likewise detained. The officers and crew thus detained may be left in the ship or kept either on another vessel or on land, and may be subjected to the measures of restriction which it may appear necessary to impose upon them. A sufficient number of men for looking after the vessel must, however, be always left on board. The officers may be left at liberty on giving their word not to quit the neutral territory without permission."[569]

---

[566] Articles 1 and 2 of the Hague Regulations (1899) were reproduced in articles 1 and 2 of the Regulations Concerning the Laws and Customs of War on Land, annexed to Convention (IV) respecting the Laws and Customs of War on Land (1907) (hereinafter "Hague Regulations (1907)" or "HR 1907") and subsequently expanded upon by articles 1 and 2 of Geneva Convention relative to the Treatment of Prisoners of War (1929) (hereinafter "GC 1929"), article 4 of GC III and articles 43-47 AP I.

[567] In order to define the lawful duration of such internment, article 21 must be read in conjunction with article 118§1 GC III: "Prisoners of war shall be released and repatriated without delay after the cessation of active hostilities."

[568] Article 11 of Convention (V) respecting the Rights and Duties bof Neutral Powers and Persons in Case of War on Land (1907) (hereinafter "HC V (1907)").

[569] Article 24 of Convention (XIII) Concerning the Rights and Duties of Neutral Powers in Naval War (1907) (hereinafter "HC XIII (1907)"). For an interesting account of the origins and development of the provisions in the Hague Conventions V and XIII, see Bugnion, "The Arrival of Bourbaki's Army at Les Verrières" (*IRRC* 1996). For further examples of internment in neutral

The Hague Conventions (V) and (XIII) concerning the Rights and Duties of Neutral Powers in Case of War do not contain any further provisions regulating the internment of prisoners of war. The internment of military internees in neutral territory must conform in full to the regulations for prisoner of war internment in the Third Geneva Convention.[570]

Before analyzing the grounds for and duration of internment on the basis of GC III, which will be the subject of section 2 of the present chapter, it is useful to recall that Convention's scope of application, since only persons who fall within its material and personal scope of application can be interned on the basis of its provisions.

We have seen in Part I that the Geneva Conventions, apart from their common article 3 common, only apply in situations of international armed conflict and occupation.[571] The most important subject of controversy regarding the applicability of GC III, however, remains the question of who exactly is entitled to prisoner of war status in the first place.[572] The personal scope of application of GC III is defined by its article 4, which defines who is a prisoner of war and therefore may be interned on the basis of article 21 GC III. It will be the subject of our attention in the first section of the present chapter, where we will see that the preventive purpose of prisoner of war internment (preventing captured combatants from returning to the battlefield), coupled with the immunity of captured combatants from prosecution for mere participation in hostilities have, time and again, guided the development of the definition of categories of persons legally entitled to prisoner of war status.

---

countries, see also Steiner, *Die Internierung von Armeeangehörigen Kriegführender Mächte in neutralen Staate, insbesondere in der Schweiz während des Weltkrieges 1939/45* (1947); and Ozerden, *Le sort des militaires belligérants, victimes de la guerre, débarqués dans un port neutre, d'après la Convention de Genève* (1971). For an example of internment in neutral territory (*in casu* Switzerland) of (*in casu* Soviet) soldiers captured by a non-State party to an armed conflict (*in casu* the Afghan opposition to Soviet occupation), see Charlotte Car-Gregg, "An Extension of Humanitarian International Law: The Case of Soviet Soldiers Captured by Afghan Liberation Movements, 1982-1986" (*WaS* 1989).

570 Prisoners of war interned in neutral States are entitled to both the legal status and the protection of prisoners of war under GC III. Only the legal basis for their internment – which can be considered as an extension of the legal basis for POW internment in article 21 GC III – is located in the separate Hague Conventions on the Rights and Duties of Neutral Powers. A direct reference to these legal bases is included in article 4§B(2) GC III: "The persons belonging to one of the categories enumerated in the present Article, who have been received by neutral or non-belligerent Powers on their territory and whom these Powers are required to intern under international law, without prejudice to any more favourable treatment which these Powers may choose to give and with the exception of Articles 8, 10, 15, 30, fifth paragraph, 58-67, 92, 126 and, where diplomatic relations exist between the Parties to the conflict and the neutral or non-belligerent Power concerned, those Articles concerning the Protecting Power. Where such diplomatic relations exist, the Parties to a conflict on whom these persons depend shall be allowed to perform towards them the functions of a Protecting Power as provided in the present Convention, without prejudice to the functions which these Parties normally exercise in conformity with diplomatic and consular usage and treaties."

571 For the definition of the material scope of application of the 1949 Geneva Conventions, *cf. supra* chapter I-2.

572 Article 4 GC III gave rise to the lengthiest and substantively most important discussions during the drafting process of the Convention (Pictet, *Commentary GC III* (1960), pp. 7, 53 and 62; Rosas (1976), pp. 293-419) and continues to be subject to controversy today.

1.1. WHO CAN BE INTERNED ON THE BASIS OF GC III? DEFINING "PRISONERS OF WAR"

The purpose of the present section is to define who can be interned on the basis of the Third Geneva Convention.[573] The simple answer to that question is: anyone who is a prisoner of war, which immediately prompts another question, namely: who is a prisoner of war? The simple answer to that second question is: any person who falls within the personal scope of application of the Third Geneva Convention, defined in considerable detail by its article 4. Nevertheless, the question of who is or should be entitled to prisoner of war status and thus the exact scope of application of GC III has been and continues to be one of the most controversial questions concerning prisoner of war internment.

So who is entitled to prisoner of war status and can thus be interned on the basis of the provisions of GC III? Article 4 GC III defines who is entitled to the legal status of prisoner or war. We will analyze its text in light of the object and purpose of the Convention but must also take into account subsequent agreements regarding their interpretation between (the majority of) the parties to that Convention (most notably articles 43 to 47 AP I), other relevant rules of international law applicable between such parties, and subsequent developments in international law.[574]

1.1.1. Prisoners of war, combatants, and the armed forces of the parties to the conflict

Articles 43§2 and 44§1of the First Additional Protocol to the Geneva Conventions stipulate that:

> "Members of the armed forces of a Party to the conflict [...] are combatants, that is to say, they have the right to participate directly in hostilities. [...] Any combatant [...] who falls into the power of an adverse Party shall be a prisoner of war."[575]

[573] This book only deals with internment. For the relevant provisions on *detention* of prisoners of war as a penal or disciplinary sanction that may be imposed during their captivity, see articles 82 to 108 GC III and articles 75 to 77 AP I.

[574] Article 31§3 VCLT: "There shall be taken into account [...] (a) any subsequent agreement between the parties regarding the interpretation of the treaty or the application of its provisions; (b) any subsequent practice in the application of the treaty which establishes the agreement of the parties regarding its interpretation; (c) any relevant rules of international law applicable in the relations between the parties."

[575] Regarding the issue of combatant status, article 43§2 AP I is an improvement over previous texts, both because it explicitly defines the concept of combatant and because it makes explicit what previously was only implicit, namely that combatants have the right to participate directly in hostilities, which is one of the main combatant privileges, the other ones being entitlement (in principle) to prisoner of war status and combatant immunity upon capture. While combatants' entitlement to prisoner of war status is also made explicit in article 43 AP I, their entitlement to immunity from prosecution is not spelled out as such. See also Rosas (1976), p. 307; Sandoz et al., *Commentary AP I and II* (1987), pp. 515-516; Dörmann, "The Legal Situation of 'Unlawful/Unprivileged Combatants'" (*IRRC* 2003), p. 45; Doswald-Beck, "Private Military Companies under International Humanitarian Law" in Chesterman & Lehnardt, *From Mercenaries to Markets: The Rise and Regulation of Private Military Companies* (2007), p. 117.

While the Protocol's section on "Combatant and prisoner-of-war status"[576] was a necessary and welcome complement to the rules of the 1907 Hague Regulations and the 1949 Third Geneva Convention, it has complicated the interpretation of article 4 GC III[577] and possibly added to existing confusions due to a conflation of the concepts of "armed forces", "combatants", and "prisoners of war."

In a distant past, the *de facto* equation of these three terms was almost absolute. Where traditional professional armies confronted each other on isolated battlefields, the equation clearly reflected the facts on the ground, long before any international legal status of combatants or prisoners of war existed. This battleground reality very much shaped the conception of international humanitarian law, or the "laws and customs of war" as was then common parlance for the rules regulating the conduct of hostilities. From the late 19th century, with the first international codification of these rules, the concepts of "combatants" and "civilians" came to occupy centre stage in the rules on the conduct of hostilities. They are the reference points and operative terms of the principle of distinction, at the core of all rules on the conduct of hostilities or so-called "Hague law."[578]

But gradually, the concepts of "armed forces", "combatants" and prisoners of war" ceased to represent a homogeneous group of people.[579] Civilians became more and more involved in military operations and were also increasingly present on or close to the battlefield. Moreover, while certain hostile acts remained lawful under the laws and customs of war, they were considered so dangerous to military operations that those combatants who engaged in it were denied prisoner of war status. While the categories of "armed forces", "combatants" and prisoners of war" continued to overlap to a large extent, not all combatants were entitled to prisoner of war status (e.g. spies)[580] and some persons were entitled to prisoner of war status upon capture despite the fact that they were not combatants (e.g. civilians accompanying the armed forces without being members thereof).[581]

---

[576] Section 2 of Part III entitled "Methods and Means of Warfare, Combatant and Prisoner-of-War Status" comprises five articles, namely articles 43 to 47 AP I.

[577] *Cf. infra* sections 1.1.2 and 1.1.3 for the amendments made by some of the articles of AP I to article 4 GC III.

[578] For an expression of the principle of distinction in treaty law, see article 48 AP I. The ICJ referred to the principle as one of the "cardinal principles [...] constituting the fabric of humanitarian law" (ICJ, *Nuclear Weapons* (1996), §78). See also Henckaerts & Doswald-Beck (2005), Vol. I, pp. 3-24 for its customary nature; and Sassòli & Bouvier (2006), pp. 144-145 and 199-216 with further references to literature and case law.

[579] In the same sense: UK, *LOAC Manual* (2004), section 4§2(1) at p. 38.

[580] Espionage is not an unlawful act of war, but it is long-standing custom that when caught in the act, spies are not entitled to prisoner of war status and may be punished for their acts under the domestic law of their captor. E.g. articles 29-30 HR 1907. See also *infra* section 1.1.3 and chapter II-3, section 3.2.2.2.

[581] E.g.: article 13 HR 1907: "Individuals who follow an army without directly belonging to it, such as newspaper correspondents and reporters, sutlers, contractors, who fall into the enemy's hands, and whom the latter think fit to detain, have a right to be treated as prisoners of war, provided they can produce a certificate from the military authorities of the army they were accompanying"; and article

Reflecting this reality, the Third Geneva Convention does not make any reference to combatant status, combatant privilege or combatant immunity.[582] But the automatic equation of the concepts of armed forces, combatants and prisoners of war did not in as much cease to dominate the minds of troops on the ground, politicians and legal experts.[583] While this is normal to the extent that numerically these three categories of persons are still likely to overlap to great extent, an automatic equation between them may have serious consequences for the correct interpretation and application of international humanitarian law. It is therefore important, from the outset of the present part of the book to distinguish the concept of prisoner of war from the concept of combatant. As we said earlier on, not all prisoners of war are combatants, and not all captured combatants are prisoners of war. What the definitions of both concepts have in common however is a reference to membership in the armed forces of a party to the conflict.

A combatant can be defined as any member of the armed forces of a party to the conflict who has the right – under international humanitarian law – to directly participate in hostilities.[584] The definition of a prisoner of war, for the purposes of the applicability of the Third Geneva Convention (and thus the legal basis to intern) can be summarized as follows: Prisoners of war are (1) members of the armed forces of a party to the conflict (apart from medical and religious personnel), who (2) have not forfeited their entitlement to prisoner of war status, and (3) other specific categories of persons, who are not members of the armed forces of a party to the conflict but are entitled to prisoner of war status upon capture.

---

81 GC 1929: "Persons who follow the armed forces without directly belonging thereto, such as correspondents, newspaper reporters, sutlers, or contractors, who fall into the hands of the enemy, and whom the latter think fit to detain, shall be entitled to be treated as prisoners of war, provided they are in possession of an authorization from the military authorities of the armed forces which they were following." See also *infra* section 1.1.4.

582 Neither do the First and Second Geneva Conventions, whose personal scope of application is defined in identical terms to that of article 4 GC III (see article 13§2 GC I/II). This is of course also due to the fact that these three Conventions were concerned with the *protection* and *treatment* of prisoners of war and the wounded, sick and shipwrecked and not with the conduct of hostilities (See also Sandoz et al., *Commentary AP I and II* (1987), p. 515). Combatant privilege (i.e. the right to participate directly in hostilities) and combatant immunity (i.e. the immunity from prosecution under the domestic law of the adverse party to the conflict for mere participation in hostilities and lawful acts of war) are not necessarily legal terms of art (they do not feature expressly in any rule of IHL), but are commonly used in military and IHL-parlance.

583 It was and continues to be also very much present in the discussions on the definition of POW status, and led to lengthy and lively debates every time expansion of the categories of prisoners of war was negotiated (in 1899 and 1907, in 1949 and again in 1977, *cf. infra*).

584 This definition (as enshrined in article 43§2 API) reflects long-standing customary IHL: all members of the armed forces of a party to the conflict are combatants, except medical and religious personnel, civil defence personnel and mercenaries (Henckaerts & Doswald-Beck (2005), pp. 11-14). It is beyond the scope of our work to define the concept of combatant in more detail; for an overview with further references, see Ipsen, "Combatants and Non-Combatants" in Fleck (2008) and Bellal & Chetail, "The Concept of Combatant under International Humanitarian Law" in Doswald-Beck, Chowdhury & Bhuiyan, *International Humanitarian Law: An Anthology* (2009). We will see in the present section however that the concept cannot be defined by a simple reference to the definition of prisoners of war in article 4 GC III. We will see in Part III, moreover, that the concept of combatant is only relevant in situations of international armed conflict and occupation, since there is no recognized combatant status in the law of non-international armed conflict (*cf. infra* chapter III-1).

The following three sub-sections examine these three elements of the definition of prisoners of war in more detail, so as to allow us to conclude on the personal scope of application of the Third Geneva Convention and thus define who can be lawfully interned on the basis of its provisions. Before we embark on this analysis, a final point is in order. The opening phrase of article 4 GC III specifies that "[p]risoners of war, in the sense of the present Convention, are persons belonging to one of the following categories, who have fallen into the hands of the enemy."[585] The words "who have fallen into the hands of the enemy" were explicitly included in article 4 to avoid prisoners of war to be denied such status or protection for having surrendered, either individually or as part of a mass capitulation.[586] Regardless of *how* a person referred to in article 4 GC III has fallen into the hands of the enemy – be it through arrest, capture, surrender, transfer or in any other way – he or she will be protected by GC III.

1.1.2. The principle: members of the armed forces of a party to the conflict

The first category of prisoners of war consists of certain members of the armed forces of a party to the conflict. But who are members of such forces and what types of organizational units make up "the armed forces of a party to the conflict" in the first place?

1.1.2.1. Definition of the armed forces of a party to the conflict

While both the Hague Regulations and the Third Geneva Convention refer respectively to "armies" and "armed forces of a party to the conflict" in their personal scope of application, they do not further define these terms. Nevertheless, their provisions already indicate that such "armies" or "armed forces" are not limited to the regular armed forces of a State as defined by domestic law, but cover a broader category of troops.[587] The Third Geneva Convention applies (amongst others) to:

---

[585] The term "enemy" refers to any adverse *party* to the conflict, and not necessarily only to its armed forces. Persons who meet the definition of article 4 GC III are prisoners of war, regardless of whether they are held by the civilian or the military authorities of the adverse party. See also Pictet, *Commentary GC III* (1960), p. 50; and Levie (1978), p. 395. The term will be relevant for answering the question whether members of the armed forces of an adverse party to the conflict who are nationals of the State that captured them are prisoners of war and may thus be interned on the basis of its provisions. We will deal with this question in section 1.1.3 below.

[586] For example, the Allied Forces in the Second World War took advantage of the unconditional surrender of Germany and Japan to deny members of their armed forces POW status (Vance, *Encyclopedia of Prisoners of War and Internment* (2006), pp. 107-108). They justified their action by relying on the wording of article 1 GC 1929, which made the Convention applicable to "persons referred to in [articles 1-3 HR 1907], who are *captured* by the enemy." In order to avoid such abuses in the future, the words "who have fallen into the hands of the enemy" were included in article 4 GC III to avoid any potential controversy. See also Pictet, *Commentary GC III* (1960), pp. 50 and 76.

[587] The domestic law of a State may limit the notion of armed forces to its regular land, sea and air forces; but in international humanitarian law the concept is broader than that and includes militias, volunteer corps, police forces, border guards and other, so-called irregular, forces that have either been integrated in the armed forces or engage in combat operations or hostilities on behalf of the party to the conflict (Rosas employs the term "independent" armed forces for the latter, e.g. Rosas (1976), p. 327). The definition under IHL does not have any impact on national legislation regulating

"(1) Members of the armed forces of a Party to the conflict as well as members of militias or volunteer corps forming part of such armed forces.

(2) Members of other militias and members of other volunteer corps, including those of organized resistance movements, belonging to a Party to the conflict and operating in or outside their own territory, even if this territory is occupied, provided that such militias or volunteer corps, including such organized resistance movements, fulfill the following conditions:

(a) that of being commanded by a person responsible for his subordinates;

(b) that of having a fixed distinctive sign recognizable at a distance;

(c) that of carrying arms openly;

(d) that of conducting their operations in accordance with the laws and customs of war.

(3) Members of regular armed forces who profess allegiance to a government or an authority not recognized by the Detaining Power."[588]

Article 43§1 AP I however does include a definition of the concept of armed forces:

"The armed forces of a Party to a conflict consist of all organized armed forces, groups and units which are under a command responsible to that Party for the conduct of its subordinates, even if that Party is represented by a government or an authority not recognized by an adverse Party. Such armed forces shall be subject to an internal disciplinary system which, *inter alia*, shall enforce compliance with the rules of international law applicable in armed conflict."[589]

The definition of article 43§1 AP I does away with the textual distinction in article 4 GC III between "regular" and "irregular" armed forces, reflecting established customary international law,[590] but also accommodates the fact that

who is a member of the regular armed forces of a State; it only serves the purposes of interpreting the relevant rules of IHL.

588 Article 4§A (1)-(3) GC III. Article 1 of the HR1899/1907 stipulates that "[t]he laws, rights, and duties of war apply not only to armies, but also to militia and volunteer corps fulfilling the following conditions [the conditions are the same those in article 4§A(2) GC III]. In countries where militia or volunteer corps constitute the army, or form part of it, they are included under the denomination 'army'."

589 Units of police and other security forces normally tasked with law enforcement functions that are, in the event of armed conflict, incorporated into the armed forces also form part of the armed forces for the purposes of IHL. See Henckaerts & Doswald-Beck (2005), pp. 16-17; and article 43§3 AP I and comments thereto in Sandoz et al., *Commentary AP I and II* (1987), pp. 517-518.

590 For an early indication of such a common understanding of the concept of armed forces, see article 2 of the Institute of International Law's Oxford Manual (1880): "The armed force of a State includes: 1. The army properly so called, including the militia; 2. The national guards, landsturm, free corps, and other bodies which fulfil the three following conditions: (a) That they are under the direction of a responsible chief; (b) That they must have a uniform, or a fixed distinctive emblem recognizable at a distance, and worn by individuals composing such corps; (c) That they carry arms openly; 3. The crews of men-of-war and other military boats; 4. The inhabitants of non-occupied territory, who, on the approach of the enemy, take up arms spontaneously and openly to resist the invading troops, even if they have not had time to organize themselves." Article 43§1 AP I was adopted by consensus (*Official Records of the Diplomatic Conference on the Reaffirmation and Development of International Humanitarian Law Applicable in Armed conflicts, Geneva (1974-1977)*, Vol. VI, p. 111). The Israeli delegation nevertheless asked the record to take note of the fact that, in its opinion, the effective enforcement and compliance with IHL by armed forces in the field is

the Protocol has widened the material scope of application of the Conventions and the Protocol to include wars of national liberation movements.[591]

From the provisions of article 4 GC III and article 43 AP I we can deduce three key elements in the definition of the "armed forces of a party to the conflict" for the purposes of international humanitarian law. First, they regroup groups of armed actors with a certain degree of *organization*. Second, those groups are *military* in nature and tasked with conducting hostilities on behalf of a party to the conflict. Third, such groups only qualify as armed forces if they *belong to a party to the conflict*. Let us have a brief look at each of these three elements.

As to the first element, the ICRC commentary to article 43 AP I explains that:

> "[t]he term "organized" is obviously rather flexible, as there are a large number of degrees of organization. In the first place, this should be interpreted in the sense that the fighting should have a collective character, be conducted under proper control and according to rules, as opposed to individuals operating in isolation with no corresponding preparation or training."[592]

Moreover:

> "A 'responsible' command cannot be conceived of without the persons who make up the command structure being familiar with the law applicable in armed conflict."[593]

"a *conditio sine qua non* for qualification as armed forces" (*Official Records 1974-1977*, Vol. VI, p. 116). We agree that this is indeed how article 43 AP I should be understood as far as the effective compliance is a collective requirement incumbent on the armed forces as a group, but the group's qualification as armed forces is not called into question by incidental non-compliance by its individual members. If the latter nuance were rejected, it would be difficult to find a single armed force in the world that would qualify as "armed forces" for the purposes of international humanitarian law. Article 43 AP I – to the extent that it defines the concept of "armed forces of a party to the conflict" for the purpose of IHL – does not depart from earlier international law (this is without prejudice to the fact that other provisions of AP I do create new legal norms; here we are however only concerned with the concept of "armed forces"). "Members of the armed forces of a party to the conflict" – for the purposes of the definition of prisoners of war – must thus be understood in a broad sense to include the categories in article 4§A(1), (2), (3) and (6) GC III, article 4§B of GC III and in article 43 AP I (on category 4§A(6), *cf. infra*). In the same sense: Rosas (1976), p. 298; Sassòli (*ACDI* 2001), pp. 231 and 233; Henckaerts & Doswald-Beck (2005), Vol. I, pp. 14 and 16; and Doswald-Beck in Chesterman & Lehnardt (2007), pp. 120-121, with further references.

[591] Sandoz et al., *Commentary AP I and II* (1987), pp. 508, 512-513. The Protocol's article 1§4 expands the applicability of the law of international armed conflict and occupation to "armed conflicts in which peoples are fighting against colonial domination and alien occupation and against racist regimes in the exercise of their right to self-determination [under international law]" which by definition makes the authority representing the people a party to the conflict. The armed wing of that Party to the conflict qualifies as "armed forces" under IHL and in this sense, its members are put on an equal footing with those of the State(s) they are fighting against (Mallison & Mallison (*CWRJIL* 1977), p. 41).

[592] Sandoz et al., *Commentary AP I and II* (1987), p. 512. For further indicators of a sufficient degree of military organization, see also the criterion of organization of a non-State party to a conflict in situations of non-international armed conflict *supra* chapter I-2, section 2.2.1.4.

[593] Sandoz et al., *Commentary AP I and II* (1987), p. 512. See also Draper (*Isr.YHR* 1971), pp. 201-202.

The ICRC's Interpretative Guidance on the Notion of Direct Participation in Hostilities requires "a sufficient degree of military organization to conduct hostilities on behalf of a party to the conflict."[594]

Second, these organized formations must *take part in the armed conflict* and thus by definition engage in hostilities. This element sets the armed forces of a party to the conflict apart from other organizations that may engage in violent acts, including against the parties to the conflict, but for reasons unrelated to the conflict, such as organized criminal gangs, local mafias, or transnational terrorist organizations. The second element is closely related to the third in that the armed forces of a party to the conflict are those organized formations that engage in hostilities on behalf of a party to the conflict.

Third, for armed groups and other formations to qualify as armed forces of a party to the conflict, they must *belong to* a party to the conflict:[595]

> "All armed forces, groups and units are necessarily structured and have a hierarchy, as they are subordinate to a command which is responsible to one of the Parties to the conflict for their operations. In other words, all of them are subordinate to a command and to a Party to the conflict, without exception, for it is not permissible for any group to wage a private war."[596]

But how is this requirement of "belonging" to a party to the conflict established in practice? Groups and units officially incorporated in the regular armed forces of a State by definition "belong" to that State party to the conflict. While the requirement of "belonging to a Party to the conflict" is only explicitly included in the treaty references to the so-called irregular armed forces of a party to the conflict,[597] it is clearly implicit in the treaty references to the regular armed forces of the parties to the conflict,[598] and most notably in the expression "armed

---

[594] ICRC, *Interpretative Guidance on the Notion of Direct Participation in Hostilities* (2009) (hereinafter "*Interpretative Guidance*" or "*IGPDH*"), p. 22. The *Interpretative Guidance* is concerned exclusively with the rules on the conduct of hostilities but the concept of "armed forces of a party to the conflict" serves the purposes of all rules of international humanitarian law and must therefore be interpreted in a uniform way. The *Interpretative Guidance* needed to rely on the definition of armed forces to define the concept of "civilian" (as opposed to that of "combatant"), it defined the concept both for situations of international armed conflict and occupation (*IGDPH*, pp. 21-26) and for situations of non-international armed conflict (*IGDPH*, pp. 30-32) as the rule it examined applies in both situations. The present study only needs to rely on the definition of armed forces to define the first sub-category of "prisoners of war." Whereas most members of the armed forces are "combatants", not even all such combatant members of the armed forces are "prisoners of war" (*cf. infra* section 1.1.3). The concept of armed forces has no relevance in the rules on deprivation of liberty in non-international armed conflict, which, contrary to the rules on international armed conflict and occupation, do not distinguish between different categories of detainees or internees, *cf. infra* Part III.

[595] For the definition of a party to an international armed conflict, *cf. supra* note 591 and chapter I-2, section 2.2.1.2. See also Pictet, *Commentary GC III* (1960), p. 57; Sandoz et al., *Commentary to AP I and II* (1987), pp. 506-507 and 512; and Gasser (1993), p. 53.

[596] Sandoz et al., *Commentary to AP I and II* (1987), p. 512.

[597] Article 1 HR 1899/1907, article 13§1(2) GCI/II and article 4§A.2 GC III.

[598] Article 1 HR 1899/1907, article 13§1(1) GC I/II and article 4§A(1) GC III. See also ICRC, *IGDPH* (2009), p. 23.

forces *of* a party to the conflict" in article 4§A(1) and (3) quoted above (emphasis added).

So-called "irregular" armed forces belong to a party to the conflict when a *de facto* relationship exists between those forces and that party to the conflict. The group must belong to a *party* to the conflict, not necessarily to its *regular armed forces*, and thus it must not necessarily be integrated in the normal chain of command of those armed forces.[599] This was clearly the case for organized resistance movements during the Second World War.[600] The ICRC Commentary to article 4 GC III recalls that ever since the 1899 and 1907 Hague Conferences, and contrary to earlier State practice:

> "[such] a de facto relationship [...] is sufficient. It may find expression merely by tacit agreement, if the operations are such as to indicate clearly for which side the resistance organization is fighting."[601]

The affiliation with a party to the conflict may be demonstrated by deliveries of equipment or supplies, military training or other factual indicators, including official or public declarations by the party to the conflict on whose behalf the group is fighting.[602] An organized armed group or unit, engaging in hostilities against a party to the conflict and whose collective behaviour can be attributed to an adverse party to the conflict under the international law of State responsibility

---

[599] I agree on this issue with Doswald-Beck, who makes the point with regard to private contactors that are part of the armed forces of a party to a conflict: "These 'militias and volunteer corps' were meant to be groups that are not necessarily officially authorized by the government and are not part of the formal [in the sense of "regular"] army. [...] and [thus] not subjected to the normal chain of command. Such a condition [...] would therefore exceed what both [GC III and AP I] require for [POW] status" (Doswald-Beck in Chesterman & Lehnardt (2007), p. 121). In the same sense: UK, *LOAC Manual* (2004), section 4§3(3) at p. 39.

[600] See also Meyrowitz, "Le statut des guérilleros dans le droit international" (*JDI 1973*), Vol. 100, p. 901: "il n'y a aucun lien juridique entre le mouvement et la puissance de rattachement. Ni le commandement ni les membres de l'organisation de résistance ne sont soumis au pouvoir disciplinaire de cet État." While the text of article 43 AP I may suggest that a closer link is required ("command responsible to that Party for the conduct of its subordinates"), its drafters did not intend to depart from the wide interpretation of "belonging" under article 4 GC III. The concept of "responsible command" is an indicator of organization rather than belonging; for the latter it is more important that the group or unit "conduct[s] hostilities on behalf and with the agreement of [a party to the conflict]" (ICRC, *IGDPH* (2009), p. 23). In the same sense: Rosas (1976), p. 262. Like article 44 AP I, article 43 must be "without prejudice to the right of any person to be a prisoner of war pursuant to Article 4 of the Third Convention" (article 44§8 AP I).

[601] Pictet, *Commentary GC III* (1960), p. 57.

[602] Pictet, *Commentary GC III* (1960), pp. 57-59. For a more detailed discussion (with references to earlier literature on the subject), see also Rosas (1976), pp. 257-261. Many authors have since confirmed Pictet's and Rosas' interpretation, e.g. Sandoz et al., *Commentary AP I and II* (1987), p. 512; Bothe et al. (1987), p. 234; Dinstein, "Unlawful Combatancy" (*Isr.YHR* 2002), p. 259; Doswald-Beck in Chesterman & Lehnardt (2007), pp. 118-121; and Del Mar, "The Requirement of 'Belonging' under International Humanitarian Law" (*EJIL* 2010), pp. 109-113. Some authors have framed this requirement in terms of "public" versus "private" warfare, reflecting the same general idea, see for example Mallison & Mallison (*CWRJIL* 1977), pp. 50-55 and 72-75 and further references there; and Watkin, "Warriors Without Rights? Combatants, Unprivileged Belligerents, and the Struggle over Legitimacy" (*HPCR Series* 2005), p. 5.

shall also be considered as belonging to the armed forces of that party to the conflict for the purposes of international humanitarian law.[603]

Members of other organized armed groups, even those groups who engage in hostilities against a party to the conflict but without "belonging" to a (adverse) party to that conflict, are not therefore "members of the armed forces of a party to the conflict."[604]

1.1.2.2. Definition of membership in the armed forces of a party to the conflict for the purpose of article 4 GC III

Members of the armed forces of a party to the conflict include all military personnel[605] of such armed forces, regardless of whether they belong to the land, sea or air forces, and regardless of whether they have a combatant or non-combatant function in such armed forces.[606] As long as military personnel with

---

[603] Pictet, *Commentary GC III* (1960), pp. 506-508; Draper (*Isr.YHR* 1971), p. 201; and ICRC, *IGDPH* (2009), p. 23. For the degree of control required, *cf. supra* chapter I-1, section 2.2.1.2 and Del Mar (*EJIL* 2010), pp. 117-123. The same argument could also be made under the (emerging) law of the responsibility of international organizations, *cf. supra* chapter I-2, section 2.2.1.5). To be noted that the relevant rules are not those establishing responsibility, but those determining the attribution of conduct to a State or international organization (articles 4 to 11 of the ILC *Articles on State Responsibility* (2001) and articles 5 to 8 of the ILC *Draft Articles on the Responsibility of International Organizations* (2009)).

[604] Under article 1 of the 1856 Paris Declaration respecting Maritime Law, and established customary international law, "privateering is, and remains, abolished." See also Dinstein (2010), p. 34. Unless members of such armed groups fall into the sub-categories in articles 4§A (4), (5) or (6), they are therefore not prisoners of war. They will not qualify as "combatants" either but rather are to be considered "civilians" for the purposes of the rules on the conduct of hostilities (ICRC, *IGDPH* (2009), pp. 23-24, with reference to relevant case law of the Israeli Supreme Court). Regardless of how they are viewed by their captor – e.g. "as rioters, terrorists, pirates, gangsters, hostage-takers or other organized criminals" (*Ibidem*, p. 24) – they are most likely to qualify as protected persons under GC IV and where they pose a threat to the security of the military operations of a party to the conflict, they may be interned on the basis of articles 42§1 or 78 GC IV (*cf. infra* chapter II-3, section 3.2.2.2).

[605] Article 4 GC III refers to prisoners of war as "persons" belonging to the various categories described in that article and the ICRC Commentary to article 43 AP I says members of the armed forces are "persons" and that the concept of "members of the armed forces [...] does not allow, for example, the use of animals trained to attack, who are incapable of distinguishing between an able-bodied enemy and an enemy who is *hors de combat*" (Sandoz et al., *Commentary AP I and II* (1987), pp. 511-512). It would be interesting to see however – taking into account the threat such animals may pose to the parties to the conflict, but also the emerging idea of animal rights (which would prohibit them being unnecessarily killed) – whether parties to the conflict could lawfully "intern" such animals as animal prisoners of war.

[606] Pictet, *Commentary GC III* (1960), p. 51. See also article 11 of the Project of an International Declaration Concerning the Laws and Customs of War (1874) (hereinafter "Brussels Declaration"); article 3 HR 1899/1907; article 13§1(1)-(3) GC I/II; Sandoz et al., *Commentary AP I and II* (1987), p. 515; and – for its customary nature – Henckaerts & Doswald-Beck (2005), p. 13. This definition of "members of the armed forces of a party to the conflict" is for the purposes of IHL alone, it is independent of the definition of such membership under the domestic law of the party concerned (*cf. supra* note 586). Risius – and scholars he refers to – find that: "The [Third Geneva] Convention does not define what is meant by the phrase 'Members of the armed forces'. [...] Whether a person is a member of a country's armed forces [and thus a prisoner of war] must depend, therefore, on the law and practice of the country concerned, on the basis that 'It would seem to be generally accepted that a State has the exclusive right to determine the method of recruitment in its armed forces [and] to determine the composition of its armed forces, whether they be regular, part-time volunteer or militia

non-exclusive non-combatant functions are trained and can at any moment be called upon to engage in combat, they are considered members of the armed forces of a party to the conflict.[607]

A question may arise as to whether reservists must be considered members of the armed forces, and from what time and for how long. The question actually arose during the 1990-1991 Gulf War:

> "The UK had interned Iraqi students studying in London and kept them as prisoners of war. The reason stated was that the students were registered on a list of Iraqi reserve forces. The British position was criticized because the mere inclusion on a reserve list does not prove membership of the armed forces. Instead, passive and active reservists have to be distinguished."[608]

Risius points out some of the questions that arise, and suggests factual indicators for establishing whether a particular person is an active or passive reservist:

> "What about "ex-regular soldiers with an unexpired reserve liability? Can they be regarded as members of their country's AF, and if so, at all times, or only when called up? What if a reservist receives his call-up papers but decides to ignore them? Authority in this area is lacking, and in the absence of evidence of the law and practice of the state concerned, it is suggested that relevant considerations might include the following: prior military service; reserve liability; the continued use of rank; the receipt of military pay; the receipt of call-up papers; current subjection to military law and discipline; and the individual's own views regarding his status. None of these individually would necessarily be conclusive, but taken together they might point either to military or civilian status."[609]

Another way of establishing whether a particular person is an active or passive reservist is to contact the power on which he or she depends, if necessary through the offices of a Protecting Power or the ICRC.[610] Fischer finds that "[a]s every state determines autonomously the composition of its armed forces, the

troops.'" (Risius in Rowe (1993), pp. 290-291). Such an interpretation of the law however goes against the explicit wording of article 4 GC III and that of article 43§1 AP I. The latter, as we have mentioned before, did not depart from the common understanding of the concept of armed forces under the Hague Regulations 1899/1907 or the 1949 Geneva Conventions and thus was adopted by consensus at the Diplomatic Conference of 1974-1977 (*cf. supra* note 586).

[607] In principle, any member of the armed forces may be called upon to directly participate in combat and therefore normally receives basic combat training. There are only three exceptions to this rule, namely that of medical and religious personnel (*cf. infra* chapter II-2) and those of civil defense personnel and mercenaries (*cf. infra* section 1.1.3). In the same sense: ICRC, *IGDPH*, p. 25: "For the regular armed forces of States, individual membership is generally regulated by domestic law and expressed through formal integration into permanent units distinguishable by uniforms, insignia and equipment. The same applies where armed units of police, border guard, or similar uniformed forces are incorporated into State armed forces [...] regardless of their individual conduct or the function they assume within the armed forces [...] Membership in irregular armed forces [...] generally is not regulated by domestic law and [presumably because of the absence of any known alternative system of formal incorporation, *our addition*] can only be reliably determined on the basis of functional criteria [i.e. that of continuous combat function]."

[608] Fischer, "Protection of Prisoners of War" in Fleck (2008), pp. 383-384.

[609] Risius in Rowe (1993), p. 291.

[610] *Cf.* also *infra* chapter II-5.

commencement and termination of service in the armed forces must be ascertained according to the national law of the state involved",[611] which seems to be the opinion of other academic and governmental experts too.[612] Where an individual falls into the hands of an enemy power on the battlefield or in the company of a unit of the armed forces clearly on active duty should however be presumed on active duty and thus an active member of the armed forces.[613]

An interesting case arose during the conflict opposing Ethiopia and Eritrea at the turn of the century (1998-2000). During that conflict, Eritrea interned a number of Ethiopian nationals whom it said were "former Ethiopian 'Fighters' and members of the Tigrayan People's Liberation Front and Tigrayan Development Authority."[614] The Tigrayan People's Liberation Front (TPLF) was an armed group fighting for Tigrayan self-determination in Ethiopia's Civil War (1974-1993), ultimately ousting the Mengistu government in 1991 as part of the Ethiopian People's Revolutionary Democratic Front (EPRDF).[615] The EPRDF still holds power in Ethiopia today and thus was Ethiopia's government when it engaged in armed conflict with Eritrea.[616] These former members of armed groups involved in the Ethiopian civil war (which also involved armed groups fighting for Eritrean independence) cannot be considered members of the Ethiopian armed forces. The groups of which they were a part did no longer exist. Unless they were members of the Ethiopian armed forces at the time of the conflict between Eritrea and Ethiopia they could not be considered members of the armed forces of a party to the conflict.[617]

Being a member of the armed forces does not automatically mean that one is entitled to either combatant status (e.g. the example of mercenaries, cf. infra section 1.1.3, or that of medical and religious personnel of the armed forces of the parties to the conflict, cf. infra chapter II-2) or prisoner of war status. Not all members of the armed forces of a party to the conflict are prisoners of war when

---

611 Fischer in Fleck (2008), pp. 383-384.

612 See note 86 in Henckaerts & Doswald-Beck (2005), Vol. I, p. 14: "The experts also considered that it may be necessary to consider the legislation of a State in determining when reservists actually become members of the armed forces."

613 The ICRC found that "[f]or the purposes of the principle of distinction [and the rules on targeting], membership in the armed forces ceases [...] when a member disengages from active duty and re-integrates into civilian life, whether due to a full discharge from duty or as a deactivated reservist." ICRC, *IGDPH* (2009), p. 25.

614 PCA (EECC), Civilians Claims, Ethiopia's Claim 5 (2004), §74.

615 During the Ethiopian Civil War in the 1970's and 1980's the group had close links with the Eritrean People's Liberation Front (EPLF), who later fought for Eritrean independence from Ethiopia. After the EPRDF ascended to power in 1991, the two movements, which pursued very different political agendas, grew apart.

616 See Berhe, "The Origins of the Tigray's People's Liberation Front" (*African Affairs* 2004); Vance (2006), pp. 123-124; and Institute for Policy Studies, *The War between Ethiopia and Eritrea* (2005).

617 Nevertheless, they may, because of their past, potentially have posed a threat to Eritrea's security or military operations, and in that case possibly lawfully interned on the basis of GC IV. Without further details, it is impossible to give a definite answer to that question, but it is interesting to note that the Ethiopia-Eritrea Claims Commission set up within the Permanent Court of Arbitration discarded the case from their considerations on claims of *unlawful* internment of Ethiopian nationals by Eritrea on the basis of GC IV: PCA (EECC), *Civilians Claims, Ethiopia's Claim 5* (2004), §74.

they fall into the hands of an enemy party. Which members of the armed forces are prisoners of war upon capture or surrender is the subject of the following sub-section.

1.1.2.3. Identification of those members of the armed forces that are prisoners of war

By the definition of article 4 GC III, the following members of the armed forces of a party to the conflict are – when they fall into the hands of an adverse party to the conflict – prisoners of war and may thus be interned on the basis of the Third Geneva Convention's internment provisions:

"Members of the armed forces of a Party to the conflict as well as members of militias or volunteer corps forming part of such armed forces;" (article 4§1A(1) GC III)

> "Members of other militias and members of other volunteer corps, including those of organized resistance movements, belonging to a Party to the conflict and operating in or outside their own territory, even if this territory is occupied, provided that such militias or volunteer corps, including such organized resistance movements, fulfill the following conditions:
>
> (a) that of being commanded by a person responsible for his subordinates;
>
> (b) that of having a fixed distinctive sign recognizable at a distance;
>
> (c) that of carrying arms openly;
>
> (d) that of conducting their operations in accordance with the laws and customs of war;" (article 4§1A(2) GC III)
>
> "Members of regular armed forces who profess allegiance to a government or an authority not recognized by the Detaining Power;" (article 4§1A(3) GC III)
>
> "Persons belonging, or having belonged, to the armed forces of the occupied country, if the occupying Power considers it necessary by reason of such allegiance to intern them, even though it has originally liberated them while hostilities were going on outside the territory it occupies, in particular where such persons have made an unsuccessful attempt to rejoin the armed forces to which they belong and which are engaged in combat, or where they fail to comply with a summons made to them with a view to internment;" (article 4§1B(1) GC III)
>
> "The persons belonging to one of the categories enumerated in the present Article, who have been received by neutral or non-belligerent Powers on their territory and whom these Powers are required to intern under international law, without prejudice to any more favourable treatment which these Powers may choose to give." (article 4§1B(2) GC III)[618]

Some of these extracts from article 4 GC III merit further comment or explanation.

First, whereas the definition of the *armed forces* of a party to the conflict includes both regular and irregular armed forces, for the purpose of defining *prisoners of war*, article 4 GC III still makes a distinction between regular and

[618] Regarding the obligation of neutral countries to intern members of the armed forces of the parties to the conflict so as to prevent them from returning to the battlefield, *cf.* also *infra* section 1.2.3.4.

irregular armed forces, by imposing conditions on the latter for their members to qualify as prisoners of war.

Article 4§A(2) subjects irregular armed forces to four conditions for their members to be prisoners of war:[619]

> "Members of other militias and members of other volunteer corps, including those of organized resistance movements, belonging to a Party to the conflict and operating in or outside their own territory, even if this territory is occupied, *provided that such militias or volunteer corps, including such organized resistance movements*, fulfill the following conditions:
>
> (a) that of being commanded by a person responsible for his subordinates;
>
> (b) that of having a fixed distinctive sign recognizable at a distance;
>
> (c) that of carrying arms openly;
>
> (d) that of conducting *their* operations in accordance with the laws and customs of war." (emphasis added)

By imposing these conditions, the drafters of the Convention gave expression to their conviction that "the right of waging war and engaging armed combat devolve exclusively upon the armed forces of States and those groups of individuals who, by analogy and concession, have been partially assimilated to such armed forces."[620] As is clear from the text of article 4§A(2) GC III, these conditions must be fulfilled by the group as such (see the emphasized words in the text quoted above) and not by each and every of its individual members.[621] Failure of individual members of the group to comply with these conditions does not disqualify other members of the group to qualify as prisoners of war.[622] Whether the group as such meets the conditions set forth by article 4§A(2) GC III depends "on the general policy of the organization as this is evidenced by its activities, or on the consistent practice of a significant part of its members."[623]

[619] The same conditions are required for their members to be entitled to combatant status, with the ensuing privileges and immunities, e.g.: Bellal & Chetail in Doswald-Beck et al. (2009), p. 63. Generally on these conditions, see Pictet, *Commentary GC III* (1960), pp. 52-61; Draper (*Isr.YHR* 1971), pp. 199-205; Rosas (1976), pp. 338-374 and Levie (1978), pp. 38-54.

[620] Draper (*BYIL* 1971), p. 181. See also *supra* note 603.

[621] See also Rosas (1976), pp. 333, 335-336, 354 and 361; Levie (1978), pp. 45 and 54; Sandoz et al., *Commentary AP I and II* (1987), p. 551; CoE, Venice Commission, *Opinion on the Possible Need for Further Development of the Geneva Conventions* (2003), §21; Henckaerts & Doswald-Beck (2005), p. 15. This does not take away that each individual member is obliged to distinguish him-or herself and otherwise respect international humanitarian law.

[622] Pictet, *Commentary GC III* (1960), p. 59. On the consequences regarding entitlement to prisoner of war status for the individuals who failed to comply with these conditions themselves, *cf. infra* section 1.1.3 and note 682.

[623] Kalshoven, "The Position of Guerrilla Fighters under the Law of War" (*MLLWR* 1972), p. 87 (quoted in Rosas (1976), p. 335). See also Sandoz et al., *Commentary AP I and II* (1987), p. 551, note 24, who summarize part of the debates on this issue during the Diplomatic Conference as follows: "In this respect the following case was mentioned, namely, where it has become clear from statements or instructions emanating from the responsible command of the irregular force or from statements of its members, that the force is not willing or able to respect in its operations the rules and principles of international law applicable in armed conflict. However, the same representative considered that too easily evidence to the contrary might be concluded by following an inductive reasoning, that since some members of the force have violated one or more rules of international law

The conditions are however cumulative and if the group does not fulfil them, its members will not be prisoners of war and thus may not be interned on the basis of the Third Geneva Convention.[624]

These four collective conditions have however, to a certain extent, been reduced to two conditions by article 43§1 AP I. That article no longer requires such groups to ensure their members are visible *at all times* (i.e. to have a fixed distinctive sign recognizable at a distance and to carry arms openly) as is clear from its text:

> "The armed forces of a Party to a conflict consist of all organized armed forces, groups and units which are under a command responsible to that Party for the conduct of its subordinates, even if that Party is represented by a government or an authority not recognized by an adverse Party. Such armed forces shall be subject to an internal disciplinary system which, *inter alia*, shall enforce compliance with the rules of international law applicable in armed conflict."[625]

Article 43§1 AP I was adopted by consensus and is part of customary international humanitarian law.[626] It therefore effectively has amended article 4§1A(2).[627] The other two conditions in article 4§1A(2) – that of a having a responsible command and of conducting operations in conformity with international humanitarian law – remain intact.[628]

The four conditions of article 4§A(2) are not included for the regular armed forces in articles 4§A(1), 4§A(3) or 4§B. In his commentary of article 4, Pictet does not even refer to these conditions as far as these members of regular armed forces are concerned.[629] The reason for this is that it has always been assumed that regular armed forces comply with all four conditions,[630] and the drafters, according to Pictet, "were thus fully justified in considering that there was no

---

applicable in armed conflict, this can be attributed to the whole irregular force as its general policy, even if one has no idea about the actual size of the force" (references to the record of the conference proceedings omitted).

624 It is likely however that they will meet the threshold of articles 42§1 and 78 GC IV and could thus be interned on the basis of and in accordance with the provisions of GC IV, *cf. infra* chapter II-3, section 3.2.2.2.

625 On the consequences for an *individual* members' entitlement to prisoner of war status when he or she fails to distinguish him- or herself, *cf. infra* section 1.1.3.

626 *Cf. supra* note 590.

627 Article 31§3 VCLT, provides that, when interpreting a specific treaty, one must take into account "(a) any subsequent agreement between the parties regarding the interpretation of the treaty or the application of its provisions; [and] (b) any subsequent practice in the application of the treaty which establishes the agreement of the parties regarding its interpretation."

628 As is visible from the text of article 43§1 AP I. See also Sandoz et al., *Commentary AP I and II* (1987), pp. 513 and 525 ("armed forces as such must submit to the rules of international law applicable in armed conflict, this being a constitutive condition for the recognition of such forces", *cf.* also *supra* note 589); Henckaerts & Doswald-Beck (2005), pp. 15-16.

629 He does refer to the conditions in his comments on article 4§A(3) but only to say they are assumed to be fulfilled, like for other regular armed forces, see Pictet, *Commentary GC III* (1960), pp. 51-52, 63, and 68-72.

630 See also Henckaerts & Doswald-Beck (2005), p. 15.

need to specify for such armed forces the requirements states in [article 4§A(2)]."[631]

Does that mean members of the regular armed forces automatically qualify as prisoners of war when they fall into the hands of an enemy Power, regardless of whether these armed forces actually meet these requirements in practice? In other words, can the presumption in article 4§A(1) and (3) and in article 4§B be rebutted, with the consequence that the members of these armed forces would not be prisoners of war?

Sassòli points out the dangers of such an approach:

> "For regular armed forces, however, it would be dangerous to require respect for the laws of war as a precondition for prisoner of war status. In all armed conflicts, the enemy is accused of not complying with IHL, and such accusations are all too often accurate. If IHL violations by regular armed forces were permitted to deprive all their members, independently of their individual behaviour, of prisoner of war status, that status could frequently not perform its protective effect. Historically, the US never invoked such an argument concerning the German Wehrmacht, which cannot be considered to have consistently complied with the laws of war."[632]

Nevertheless, taking into account the text of article 43§1 AP I (which as we saw earlier intentionally did away with the distinction between regular and irregular armed forces of a party to the conflict, reduced the four conditions of article 4§A(2) to two, and effectively amended the text of article 4 GC III in this sense), and the fundamental principle of equal rights and obligations under IHL for all parties to armed conflict,[633] it is submitted that the members of a unit of a regular armed force that clearly does not comply collectively with the conditions of a responsible command and general conduct of operations in conformity with IHL are not prisoners of war.[634] Any objection against that premise would be difficult to sustain unless one accepts that regular armed forces may adopt policies that refute international humanitarian law as a whole and still be considered as any other regular armed force whose members are prisoners of war upon capture. Moreover, where the members of such a unit are not prisoners of war, they are not therefore unprotected by IHL; the provisions of GC IV regulate their situation.[635] Moreover, any member of such a unit that is responsible for

---

[631] Pictet, *Commentary GC III* (1960), p. 63. While Pictet makes this comment specifically with regard to regular armed forces referred to in article 4§A(3), his comment is valid for all regular armed forces, as is clear from the preceding sentence of his comment: "These 'regular' armed forces' [i.e. those in article 4§A(3)] have all the material characteristics and all the attributes of armed forces in the sense of [article 4§A(1)]."

[632] Sassòli (*JICJ* 2004), pp. 102-103.

[633] See Meyrowitz, *Le principe de l'égalité des belligérants devant le droit de la guerre* (1970).

[634] In the same sense, e.g.: Rosas (1976), pp. 328 and 333; Mallison & Mallison (*CWRJIL* 1977), pp. 48 and 74, and Mallison & Mallison, "The Juridical Status of Privileged Combatants under the Geneva Protocol of 1977 Concerning International Conflicts" (*LCP* 1978), pp. 30; Sandoz et al., *Commentary AP I and II* (1987), pp. 511 and 514; Aldrich, (*AJIL* 2002), pp. 895-896; Dinstein (*Isr. YHR* 2002), pp. 255 and 269; and Doswald-Beck in Chesterman & Lehnardt (2007), p. 121.

[635] *Cf. infra* chapter II-3.

committing war crimes, or for ordering such crimes to be committed, must be tried and punished accordingly.[636]

Article 43§1 AP I extends the traditional presumption of compliance for the regular armed forces of a State to all armed forces of the parties to a conflict, a presumption that can thus be rebutted for all. For "regular" armed forces of a State, the presumption of compliance will be very strong,[637] and the contrary will need to be proven beyond doubt for such forces to disqualify as armed forces whose members are entitled to POW status. For "irregular" armed forces, there might in practice be more room for doubt, but the seriousness of the consequences that flow from disqualification as armed forces (notably loss of both combatant and prisoner of war status for all its members) makes that such allegations should not be made lightly and should not be presumed without being properly investigated.

The armed forces referred to in article 4§A(3) GC III only differ from those referred to in article 4§1A(1) in that they profess allegiance to a government or an authority not recognized by their captor: "[t]he distinguishing feature of such armed forces is simply the fact that in the view of their adversary, they are not operating or are no longer operating under the direct authority of a Party to the conflict in accordance with Article 2 of the Convention."[638] In all other aspects they must be considered as regular armed forces of the party to the conflict they belong to. Pictet adds the following useful clarifications:

> "It is not expressly stated that this Government or authority must, as a minimum requirement, be recognized by third States, but this condition is consistent with the spirit of the provision, which was founded on the specific case of the forces of General de Gaulle. It is also necessary that this authority, which is not recognized by the adversary, should either consider itself as representing one of the High Contracting Parties, or declare that it accepts the obligations stipulated in the Convention and wishes to apply them. The present provision naturally covers armed forces which continue operations under the orders of a Government in exile which is not recognized by the adversary, but has been given hospitality by another State. In our view, it also covers armed forces which continue to fight in a 'national redoubt', under the orders of an authority or Government which has its headquarters in that part of the country while the occupying authorities may have recognized a Government, which may or may not support them, in that part of the country occupied by their troops. It is of little consequence whether or not another State is engaged in the same struggle as these 'regular armed forces'. As we have seen, the authors of the Convention deliberately dropped the requirement that such armed forces should be fighting in conjunction with a State recognized as a regular belligerent."[639]

---

[636] Article 146 GC IV.

[637] See also Pfanner, "Military Uniforms and the Law of War" (*IRRC* 2004), p. 115 and Bellal & Chetail in Doswald-Beck et al. (2009), p. 62.

[638] Pictet, *Commentary GC III* (1960), p. 63.

[639] Pictet, *Commentary GC III* (1960), pp. 63-64.

In conclusion, for an individual member of the armed forces of a party to the conflict to be a prisoner of war, he or she must belong to a group or unit – part of these armed forces – that collectively meets the conditions set out in article 4 GC III as amended by article 43§1 AP I. Apart from the specific exclusion clauses we will discuss in section 1.1.3 below, the members of such armed forces may not be denied prisoner of war status. Prisoner of war status has nevertheless been denied to persons who did qualify as such under the provisions of article 4 GC III for a number of other reasons. We will discuss some examples of such unlawful exclusions from prisoner of war status, and in particular the controversy over the allegedly implicit requirement of enemy nationality, in section 1.1.3 below. Before we turn to that section however, a word must be said about the special case of the *levée en masse*.

1.1.2.4. A special case: levée en masse

Article 4§A(6) reflects a customary rule of international humanitarian law where it includes in the definition of prisoners of war:

> "Inhabitants of a non-occupied territory, who on the approach of the enemy spontaneously take up arms to resist the invading forces, without having had time to form themselves into regular armed units, provided they carry arms openly and respect the laws and customs of war."[640]

Participants in what is commonly referred to as a *levée en masse* are not as such members of the armed forces of the party to the conflict (they are by definition not organized into military units or under any military command). They must be distinguished from organized resistance movements who operate in occupied territory and who, subject to the conditions in article 4§A(2), are part of the armed forces of the party to the conflict whose territory is occupied.[641]

Nevertheless, for the duration of the invasion by an adverse party of a so far non-occupied territory, and subject to the conditions stipulated in article 4§A(6), they are placed on an equal footing as members of the armed forces of the party whose territory they attempt to defend and entitled to both combatant[642] and prisoner of war status.[643] We will therefore include them whenever we refer to members of the armed forces of a party to the conflict who are prisoners of war.

---

[640] The equivalent provision of the Hague Regulations 1899/1907 (article 2) reads: "The inhabitants of a territory which has not been occupied, who, on the approach of the enemy, spontaneously take up arms to resist the invading troops without having had time to organize themselves in accordance with Article 1, shall be regarded as belligerents if they carry arms openly and if they respect the laws and customs of war." Similar provisions already figured in article 10 of the Brussels Declaration (1874) and in article 1§4 of the Oxford Manual (1880).

[641] Pictet, *Commentary GC III* (1960), pp. 67-68, reaffirmed in Sandoz et al., *Commentary AP I and II* (1987), pp. 532-533 and by Bellal & Chetail in Doswald-Beck et al. (2009), p. 64. On the transition of a *levée en masse* into an organized resistance movement once the territory is effectively occupied, and the consequence on their member's status as prisoners of war and their (continued) internment, *cf. infra* section 1.2.3.

[642] E.g.: ICRC, *IGDPH* (2009), p. 25; Bellal & Chetail in Doswald-Beck et al. (2009), p. 64.

[643] See also Pictet, *Commentary GC III* (1960), pp. 67-68; Sandoz et al., *Commentary AP I and II* (1987), p. 510; and Henckaerts & Doswald-Beck (2005), Vol. I, pp. 386-387, with references to international practice.

Participants in a *levée en masse*, in order to qualify as combatants and as prisoners of war, must carry their arms openly and respect the law and customs of war. These conditions are reminiscent of those imposed on irregular armed forces for their members to qualify as prisoners of war. In the absence of the other requirements imposed on irregular armed forces – namely responsible command and a distinctive sign – the obligation to carry arms openly takes on

> "special significance and has a more precise meaning than in [article 4§A(2)]; this requirement is in the interest of combatants themselves who must be recognizable in order to qualify for treatment as prisoners of war. They must therefore carry arms *visibly*."[644]

Upon capture or surrender, participants in a *levée en masse* may be interned on the basis of the Third Geneva Convention. The lawfulness of their internment on that basis may however be subject to a possible change in the status of the territory they defend, as we will see in section 1.2.3 of this chapter.

1.1.3. Exception N° 1: members of the armed forces who are not prisoners of war

The preceding section shows us that individual members of the armed forces of a party to the conflict, who as a group conform to the conditions set out in articles 4 GC III and 43§1 AP I are in principle entitled to POW status.[645] There are however a number of exceptions to that rule.[646]

1.1.3.1. Members of the armed forces who fall outside the scope of application of GC III

(a.) Medical and religious personnel

Medical and religious personnel of the armed forces of a party to the conflict, i.e. members of such armed forces who are exclusively assigned to medical and spiritual assistance, have – since the earliest codifications of international humanitarian law – a special status under that law. They must be protected and allowed to carry out their humanitarian functions so crucial to minimize the suffering of combatants on the battlefield and in the rear, and may not be subject to attack.

While they are clearly members of the armed forces, if they fall into the hands of an adverse party to the conflict, they are not prisoners of war and may therefore not be interned on the basis of the Third Geneva Convention.[647] Their

[644] Pictet, *Commentary GC III* (1960), p. 67 (emphasis added), with further references.

[645] Members of such armed forces (except for medical and religious personnel) are in principle also entitled to combatant status (article 43§2 AP I), see for example Bellal & Chetail in Doswald-Beck et al. (2009), pp. 61-68 (with further references).

[646] Article 44§6 AP I notably explains that the definition of prisoners of war in its 1st paragraph is without prejudice to the entitlement of certain civilians to POW status under article 4 GC III.

[647] Article 4§C GC III: "This Article shall in no way affect the status of medical personnel and chaplains as provided for in Article 33 of the present Convention." Article 33 GC III reads in relevant part: "Members of the medical personnel and chaplains while retained by the Detaining Power with a view to assisting prisoners of war, shall not be considered as prisoners of war." Medical and religious personnel of the armed forces of the parties to the conflict are not combatants and have no right to

possible retention based on the medical and spiritual needs of the prisoners of war in the power of the party to the conflict in whose hands they fell, will be the subject of our full attention in chapter II-2.

Some members of the armed forces may forfeit their right to prisoner of war status, on the basis of specific behaviour that is not unlawful as such under international humanitarian law, but that is either so damaging or dangerous to the military capacity of the parties to the conflict or the success of their military operations, or considered so shameful, that it is sanctioned with the loss of entitlement to prisoner of war status and – for some – even loss of combatant status. These categories of persons – namely spies, deserters and defectors, mercenaries, and combatants who fail to distinguish themselves in attack – are not mentioned in article 4 GC III, but are specifically defined by other provisions of international humanitarian law that are relevant for its interpretation.

(b.) Spies

While acts of espionage are not a prohibited method of warfare,[648] they are sanctioned under international humanitarian law "because they are so dangerous, and it is difficult to guard against them."[649] Members of the armed forces who engage in acts of espionage are, if caught in the act, not entitled to prisoner of war status and may be punished for their acts under the domestic law of their captor. They may not, however, be sentenced or convicted for these acts without a fair trial.[650]

Article 46 AP I confirms this customary rule of international humanitarian law,[651] and extends its application to occupied territory:

> "1. Notwithstanding any other provision of the Conventions or of this Protocol, any member of the armed forces of a Party to the conflict who falls into the power of an adverse Party while engaging in espionage shall not have the right to the status of prisoner of war and may be treated as a spy.
>
> 2. A member of the armed forces of a Party to the conflict who, on behalf of that Party and in territory controlled by an adverse Party, gathers or attempts to gather information shall not be considered as engaging in espionage if, while so acting, he is in the uniform of his armed forces.

take part in hostilities (article 43§2 AP I).

[648] E.g.: article 24 HR 1907; Baxter, "So-Called 'Unprivileged Belligerency': Spies, Guerrillas, and Saboteurs" (*BYIL* 1951), p. 330; Sandoz et al., *Commentary AP I and II* (1987), p. 563.

[649] Article 101 Lieber Code (1863).

[650] Article 20 Brussels Declaration (1874); article 25 Oxford Manual (1880); article 30 HR 1907; article 45§3 AP I. The rule is part of customary international humanitarian law (Rule 107 of the ICRC's compilation of customary IHL: Henckaerts & Doswald-Beck (2005), Vol. I, pp, 390-391).

[651] Articles 20-21 Brussels Declaration (1874); articles 23-26 Oxford Manual (1880); article 29-31 HR 1907. See also Sandoz et al., *Commentary AP I and II* (1987), pp. 561-570; and Henckaerts & Doswald-Beck (2005), Vol. I, pp. 389-391 with references to established practice. For more general studies of the legal status and protection of spies under international humanitarian law, see Baxter (*BYIL* 1951); Chadwick, "The Legal Position of Prisoners, Spies and Deserters during World War I" (*MLLWR* 1997); Lafouasse, "L'espionnage en droit international" (*AFDI* 2001); and Ferrell, "No Shirt, no Shoes, no Status: Uniforms, Distinction and Special Operations in International Armed Conflict" (*MLR* 2003).

3. A member of the armed forces of a Party to the conflict who is a resident of territory occupied by an adverse Party and who, on behalf of the Party on which he depends, gathers or attempts to gather information of military value within that territory shall not be considered as engaging in espionage unless he does so through an act of false pretences or deliberately in a clandestine manner. Moreover, such a resident shall not lose his right to the status of prisoner of war and may not be treated as a spy unless he is captured while engaging in espionage.
4. A member of the armed forces of a Party to the conflict who is not a resident of territory occupied by an adverse Party and who has engaged in espionage in that territory shall not lose his right to the status of prisoner of war and may not be treated as a spy unless he is captured before he has rejoined the armed forces to which he belongs."

(c.) Deserters and defectors

Members of the armed forces of a party to the conflict who severe their allegiance to the power they depend on are referred to as deserters and defectors. A further distinction is made on the basis of whether they do so in order to escape their military obligations out of fear for being sent out to the battlefield (deserters) or whether they do so with the intention of joining the ranks of an enemy power (defectors).[652]

When they express their intention to severe allegiance to the power they serve in due time and effectively act upon that intent before they fall into the hands of an adverse party to the conflict, customary international humanitarian leaves the question of whether they are prisoner of war to the discretion of their captor.[653] If that power grants them prisoner of war status, they may be interned, like any other prisoner of war, on the basis of the Third Geneva Convention.[654] In deciding on whether to grant prisoner of war status to a deserter or defector,

[652] Rosas (1976), p. 388 and Sassòli, "The Status, Treatment and Repatriation of Deserters under International Humanitarian Law" (*YIIHL* 1985), pp. 13-18. It is important to point out that this category of persons does not include members of the armed forces who surrendered to the enemy (*cf. supra* note 586 and *infra* section 1.1.3.2(a)). These definitions serve the purposes of international humanitarian law and in particular that of status determination under GC III. It is considerably narrower than the definition of deserters in most military manuals, definitions that may be valid under domestic legislation but are not necessarily in conformity with international humanitarian law. For a detailed discussion of the legal status deserters and defectors under international humanitarian law, see Shapiro, "Repatriation of Deserters" (*BYIL* 1952); Rosas (1976), pp. 388-391; Levie (1978), pp. 76-80; and Sassòli (*YIIHL* 1985). Acts of desertion and defection are usually severely punished under domestic law, e.g. Rosas (1976), p. 383 and Sassòli (*YIIHL* 1985), p. 13.

[653] Pictet, *Commentary GC III* (1960), p. 549; Rosas (1976), pp. 390-392; Sassòli (*YIIHL* 1985), pp. 18-21. Rosas points out that the rule is firmly established for defectors but only relatively so for deserters; we would add that the Interning Power must be guided by the rationale behind prisoner of war internment in deciding on whether or not a deserter or defector should be interned, if it deems such internment necessary, the deserter and defector should indeed be treated as any other prisoner of war).

[654] The fact that they cannot reasonably be expected to rejoin their own ranks will however play a role in whether and for how long they can be so interned (*cf. infra* section 1.2.3.5). Neutral countries are not obliged to intern deserters and may grant them asylum. The same holds true for defectors, unless they are trying to reach enemy territory via the neutral territory (e.g. Sassòli, (*YIIHL* 1985), p. 27, with further references).

the power in whose hands they fell must be guided by the protective purpose of article 4 GC III.[655]

We will deal with the question of deserters and defectors who fall into the hands of the power they owe allegiance to in section 1.1.3.2 below.

(d.) Mercenaries

The rule concerning mercenaries in article 47 AP I is a new rule; it did not exist in international humanitarian law before the adoption of the Protocol.[656] The international community, in light of the use by some States of mercenaries to repress the legitimate struggle of national liberation movements in the 1960's, found mercenarism to be a "shameful" activity[657] and the first paragraph of article 47 AP I therefore provides that "[a] mercenary shall not have the right to be a combatant or a prisoner of war."

Since they are not combatants, they are not entitled to combatant privilege and may be tried and punished for their acts under the domestic law of the power in whose hands they fall. No such conviction or sentence may however be imposed without a fair trial.[658] They may moreover be interned – as long as the conditions for such internment are met – on the basis of the Fourth Geneva Convention (*cf. infra* chapter II-3).

The second paragraph of article 47 defines a mercenary as:

> "any person who: (a) is specially recruited locally or abroad in order to fight in an armed conflict; (b) does, in fact, take a direct part in the hostilities; (c) is motivated to take part in the hostilities essentially by the desire for private gain and, in fact, is promised, by or on behalf of a Party to the conflict, material compensation substantially in excess of that promised or paid to combatants of similar ranks and functions in the armed forces of that Party; (d) is neither a national of a Party to the conflict nor a resident of territory controlled by a Party to the conflict; (e) is not a member of the armed forces of a Party to the conflict; and (f) has not been sent by a State which is not a Party to the conflict on official duty as a member of its armed forces."

---

[655] *Cf. also infra*, section 1.2.3.5. During the 1990-91 Gulf War, the UK treated Iraqi deserters as prisoners of war. Such practice, explains Rowe, was "consistent with the policy of coalition commanders of encouraging desertion among Iraqi forces and is, perhaps, of particular significance where an enemy is comprised mainly of conscripts and is at a distinct military disadvantage to its adversary. These conditions were met in the Gulf War, since the Iraqi forces in Kuwait could make little military response to the coalition bombardment of their positions by air or by land" (Rowe, "Prisoners of War in the Gulf Area" in Rowe (1993), p. 191).

[656] Widely recognized in the meantime, it has come to form part of customary international law, see Henckaerts & Doswald-Beck (2005), pp. 391-395.

[657] Sandoz et al., *Commentary AP I and II* (1987), p. 574. To be noted that mercenarism is not prohibited as such under international humanitarian law, but it is prohibited under at least two instruments of general international law, namely the Convention for the Elimination of Mercenarism in Africa (1977) and the International Convention against the Recruitment, Use, Financing and Training of Mercenaries (1989), *cf.* also *infra* note 666.

[658] Sandoz et al., *Commentary AP I and II* (1987), pp. 575-576; Henckaerts & Doswald-Beck (2005), pp. 391 and 393-395.

While the article was ultimately adopted by consensus, its place in a treaty of international humanitarian law remains controversial and to a certain extent objectionable in that it effectively establishes a distinction between members of the armed forces of a party to the conflict on the basis of the personal reasons that may motivate an individual to join such forces. As the ICRC Commentary to article 47 points out:

> "The Conference, which had shown itself to be fairly liberal [...] regarding the granting of combatant or prisoner-of-war status to members of the armed forces of a Party to the conflict, came to a different conclusion on this matter, at least in principle. Whatever conclusions one could actually draw from an analysis of Article 47, the concession made by this article is not without importance, for it is not the task of humanitarian law to make distinctions based on the motives which induce a particular person to participate in an armed conflict. However, as things stand, it could be said that this was no more and no less than reparation – it could be considered a moral reparation – for past wrongs, and a preventive measure against possible damage in the future. Whatever the facts of the matter, no one, or virtually no one, at first opposed the principle of this provision. Article 47 was adopted by consensus at a plenary meeting. The result of a compromise, it was approved by some unquestioningly, though it was criticized by others, who considered it to be timorous, incomplete or of doubtful orientation. One delegation stated that it did not belong in Protocol I, which has an essentially humanitarian character."[659]

(e.) Combatants who fail to distinguish themselves in attack

The provisions on combatant and prisoner of war status of Additional Protocol I accommodated the expansion of the law of international armed conflict to national liberation wars to ensure that members of the armed forces of national liberation movements representing and exercising a people's right to self-determination would be entitled to both combatant and prisoner of war status.[660] We have seen above that article 43§1 AP I relaxes the conditions for

[659] Sandoz et al., *Commentary AP I and II* (1987), pp. 573-574. For in-depth analysis of the legal status of mercenaries under international law more generally and the controversies over article 47 AP I, see Rosas (1976), pp. 392-401; David, *Mercenaires et volontaires internationaux en droit des gens* (1978); Green, "The Status of Mercenaries in International Law" (*Isr.YHR* 1978); Cassese, "Mercenaries: Lawful Combatants or War Criminals?" (*ZaöRV* 1980); and Boumedra, "International Regulation of the Use of Mercenaries in Armed Conflicts" (*MLLWR* 1981). The concept of mercenaries has gained renewed interest in discussions on the legal status under international law of the personnel of private military and security companies deployed in situations of armed conflict, *cf. infra* note 733.

[660] *Cf. supra* chapter I-2, section 2.2.1.2: so-called Third World countries applied considerable pressure to expand the application of AP I to national liberation movements (resulting in article 1§4 AP I) and to grant combatant and POW status to members of the armed forces of such movements (resulting in articles 43§§1-2 and 44§1 AP I). Other countries supported the relaxation of distinction requirements in situations where guerrilla warfare is the only effective method of combat (resulting article 44§§3-45 AP I). Representatives of national liberation movements were actually brought into the Conference proceedings for drafting the Protocol's provisions on this matter; their input was expected to make the rules realistically feasible to implement in practice and thus offer an incentive for them to comply in general with international humanitarian law. See Sandoz et al., *Commentary to AP I and II* (1987), pp. 521-522; Rosas (1976), pp. 313-325; and Mallison & Mallison (*LCP* 1978), in particular pp. 6, 8, 10 and 22.

armed forces to collectively and generally distinguish themselves at all times by wearing a distinctive sign and carrying arms openly (imposed by article 4 GC III) so as to accommodate the necessity in certain situations to resort to guerrilla warfare and techniques.[661] At the same time article 44§§3-5 – for the purpose of safeguarding the principle of distinction in the conduct of hostilities – subjects their *individual members'* right to prisoner of war status to the condition to distinguish themselves during actual attacks. Its provisions read in relevant part as follows:

> "In order to promote the protection of the civilian population from the effects of hostilities, combatants are obliged to distinguish themselves from the civilian population while they are engaged in an attack or in a military operation preparatory to an attack. Recognizing, however, that there are situations in armed conflicts where, owing to the nature of the hostilities an armed combatant cannot so distinguish himself, he shall retain his status as a combatant, provided that, in such situations, he carries his arms openly: (a) during each military engagement, and (b) during such time as he is visible to the adversary while he is engaged in a military deployment preceding the launching of an attack in which he is to participate. Acts which comply with the requirements of this paragraph shall not be considered as perfidious;" (article 44§3 AP I)
>
> "A combatant who falls into the power of an adverse Party while failing to meet the requirements set forth in the second sentence of paragraph 3 shall forfeit his right to be a prisoner of war, but he shall, nevertheless, be given protections equivalent in all respects to those accorded to prisoners of war by the Third Convention and by this Protocol. This protection includes protections equivalent to those accorded to prisoners of war by the Third Convention in the case where such a person is tried and punished for any offences he has committed;" (article 44§4 AP I)
>
> "Any combatant who falls into the power of an adverse Party while not engaged in an attack or in a military operation preparatory to an attack shall not forfeit his rights to be a combatant and a prisoner of war by virtue of his prior activities." (article 44§5 AP I)

Article 44§5 AP I – which applies to all armed forces of a party to the conflict, whether they be regular or irregular[662] – thus effectively establishes a new ground for denying individual members of the armed forces of a party to an

[661] Guerrilla warfare can be defined as "a form of combat which is often clandestine and sporadic in nature, based on the element of surprise and on the capacity to melt in the local population or in the countryside. This method of combat tends to give [members of the armed forces of national liberation movements] a substantial military advantage, which often compensates for their disadvantage in terms of numbers and equipment. This explains why some States were extremely reluctant to give them any further privileges through the recognition of prisoner-of-war status." (Bellal & Chetail in Doswald-Beck et al. (2009), pp. 64-65). Note however that members of national liberation movements are entitled to prisoner-of-war status not on the basis of paragraphs 3 and 4 of article 44 AP I but on the basis of a combined reading of article 43§2 and article 44§1 AP I.

[662] Article 43§1 AP I. See also Sandoz et al., *Commentary AP I and II* (1987), pp. 511 and 532; Rosas (1976) p. 325 and note 484; Mallison & Mallison (*LCP* 1978), pp. 25-26; and Henckaerts & Doswald-Beck (2005), pp. 385-386 (with references to State practice). This interpretation is also in conformity with the general principle of international humanitarian law on equality of rights and obligations of the parties to the conflict under IHL (*cf. supra* note 632).

international armed conflict the right to be a prisoner of war.[663] To that extent one could wonder whether it is applicable only in the relations between those parties to an international armed conflict that have ratified Additional Protocol I[664] or applies more generally. While the provisions of article 44 AP I were among the most controversial and bitterly disputed innovations of that Protocol,[665] they seem to have become part of customary international humanitarian law and thus apply to all parties to any international armed conflict.[666]

(f.) Consequence of loss of entitlement to prisoner of war status

Spies, deserters, defectors, mercenaries, and combatants who fail to distinguish themselves in attack, forfeit their *right* to be a prisoner of war when they fall into the hands of an enemy power. Whether such persons may be prisoners of war and thus entitled to the full protection of the Third Geneva Convention is therefore left to the discretion of the enemy power in whose hands they are.

A party to the conflict may nevertheless decide to grant a spy, deserter, defector, mercenary or a combatant who fails to distinguish him- or herself in attack prisoner of war status in spite of his or her acts.[667] If granted such status, they are prisoners of war like any other combatant, are entitled to combatant

---

663 E.g. Sandoz et al., *Commentary AP I and II* (1987), p. 540: "The link in time between violation [of paragraphs 3 and 4 of article 44 AP I] and capture must be so close as to permit those making the capture to take note of it themselves. This is the case of *flagrante delicto*. There is no doubt that this is, *mutatis mutandis*, analogous to the situation of the spy, and consequently there is some relationship with the concept of an unprivileged belligerent. Like a spy, the combatant who does not carry his arms openly must be caught in the act for the sanction to be applicable to him. Similarly, like him, the combatant who is captured while he is not committing this breach, does not incur any responsibility for acts which he committed previously. However, it should be noted that in contrast to espionage, which is not prohibited by the law of armed conflict, but is merely made punishable, it is prohibited in the Protocol for a combatant not to carry his arms openly, and in principle the Protocol makes him responsible for this. However, in practical terms the adversary cannot do anything against him as a matter of criminal law unless he has surprised him *flagrante delicto* at the moment of capture. The prohibition exists, but the sanction can only be applied under this condition. A combatant who commits this breach preserves, at least temporarily, his status as a combatant, and his right to prisoner-of-war status" (original italics).

664 A total of 172 States are now party to AP I (last verified on 16 December 2012).

665 E.g. Bothe et al. (1982), pp. 251-256; and Sandoz et al., *Commentary AP I and II* (1987), pp. 521-539.

666 While other provisions of the Protocol have been the subject of objections and would possibly not have attained customary law status so far, article 44§5 does not seem to have been the subject of contrary practice. E.g.: Henckaerts & Doswald-Beck (2005), p. 389.

667 See also Oxford Manual (1880), article 23; Pictet, *Commentary GC III* (1960), p. 51; Rosas (1976), 379-382 and 391-392; Sandoz et al., *Commentary AP I and II* (1987), p. 563; Pfanner (*IRRC* 2004), p. 117 (with examples of State practice). Note however that under article 3 of the Convention for the Elimination of Mercenarism in Africa (1977), parties to that Convention may not grant either combatant or prisoner of war status to a mercenary: "[m]ercenaries shall not enjoy the status of combatants and shall not be entitled to the prisoners of war status." Article 16 (b) of the International Convention against the Recruitment, Use, Financing and Training of Mercenaries (1989) leaves the choice of granting such status to the power in whose hands the mercenary finds himself: "[t]he present Convention shall be applied without prejudice to: [...] [t]he law of armed conflict and international humanitarian law, including the provisions relating to the status of combatant or of prisoner of war." At the time of writing 30 States have ratified the African Convention and 32 States have ratified the International Convention (last verified on 16 December 2012).

immunity and may be interned on the basis of the Third Geneva Convention.[668] Should the power that holds them decide not to grant them prisoner of war status, they do not fall within the personal scope of application of that Convention and the question of whether they may be interned on the basis of international humanitarian law, and if so for what reasons and for how long, will therefore be defined by the relevant provisions of the Fourth Geneva Convention (*cf. infra* chapter II-3).[669]

Finally, it may be worthwhile to note that members of the armed forces of a party to the conflict who thus forfeit their entitlement to prisoner of war status do not in the process lose their combatant status.[670] With the exception of mercenaries, they remain combatants who are entitled to engage in hostilities,[671] but are not entitled to prisoner of war status and combatant immunity upon capture. Such combatants are therefore sometimes called "*unprivileged* combatants" or "*unprivileged* belligerents"[672] (to be distinguished from civilians *unlawfully* participating in hostilities, *cf. infra* chapter II-3).

---

[668] A person entitled to combatant status who upon capture is either entitled to prisoner of war status or is granted such status is entitled to immunity from prosecution for his or her mere participation in hostilities (also referred to as combatant immunity, *cf. supra* section 1.1.1). Note that combatant immunity flows directly from combatant status; prisoners of war who are not entitled to combatant status (i.e. those referred to in article 4§A(4) and (5) GC III) are not immune from prosecution for acts that would amount to participation in hostilities.

[669] E.g.: Sandoz et al., *Commentary AP I and II* (1987), pp. 570 and 575: "The spy who is denied the status of prisoner of war is [...] protected by the Fourth Geneva Convention. [...] Deprived of the status of [...] prisoner of war, a mercenary [...] could fall [within the scope of] the Fourth Convention."

[670] Rosas (1976), p. 336.

[671] For the purpose of the principle of distinction and the rules on the conduct of hostilities that flow from it, they remain combatants and may be the object of attack at all times, e.g.: ICRC, *IGDPH* (2009), p. 22 and note 16: "[Where a member of the armed forces] may not be entitled to combatant privilege [used here in the sense of combatant immunity from prosecution] and prisoner-of-war status after capture, it does not follow that any such person must necessarily be excluded from the category of armed forces and regarded as a civilian for the purpose of the conduct of hostilities. [...] As illustrated by the treatment of spies [...] and of other combatants failing to distinguish themselves as required by IHL [...], loss of entitlement to combatant privilege [used here in the sense of combatant immunity from prosecution] or prisoner-of-war status does not necessarily lead to loss of membership in the armed forces [and thus combatant status for the purposes of the rules on the conduct of hostilities]."

[672] E.g.: Baxter (*BYIL* 1951).

1.1.3.2. Unlawful exclusions of prisoners of war from the scope of application of GC III

The criteria for denying a member of the armed forces prisoner of war status may not be determined arbitrarily; they are defined by international humanitarian law. Apart from the specific exclusion clauses provided for in international humanitarian law and discussed above, no other reason may be therefore be invoked for denying a member of the armed forces of a party to the conflict the right to be a prisoner of war and to benefit from the full protection of the Third Geneva Convention. For the purpose of clarity, and to avoid any confusion, it is useful to discuss some examples.

(a.) Non-combatant members of the armed forces

The definition in international humanitarian law of members of the armed forces – with the exception of medical and religious personnel – includes all military personnel of those armed forces, regardless of their individual function or skills.[673] The fact that a member of the armed forces has never engaged in combat or does not fulfil a combat function in the armed forces he or she depends on, is no lawful reason to exclude that person from the definition of prisoner of war and the scope of application of GC III.[674] Nevertheless, the Power in whose hands they fall is not *obliged* to intern them,[675] and where – in light of their function and skills – their internment for the duration of hostilities is not really necessary, it may (and we will argue below should) decide to either release or repatriate them as soon as practically feasible.[676]

(b.) Surrender

We have seen above that the drafters of the Third Geneva Convention were careful in formulating article 4 GC III in such a way as to avoid any potential controversy over the fact that members of the armed forces of a party to the conflict who surrender (either individually or in the framework of a mass capitulation) are included in its personal scope of application and thus entitled to be prisoners of war. As soon as they have "fallen into the power of the enemy" – whether through capture, surrender, transfer or other ways – persons belonging to the categories listed in article 4 GC III are prisoners of war.[677]

(c.) Recapture after successful or attempted escape from captivity

A prisoner of war who is recaptured after an unsuccessful attempt to escape continues to have the right to be a prisoner of war and to combatant immunity.[678] Members of the armed forces of most if not all States have the legal obligation

---

673 *Cf. supra* section 1.1.2.2.

674 See also Pictet, *Commentary GC III* (1960), *p. 51;* Sandoz et al., *Commentary to AP I and II* (1987), pp. 515-516.

675 For the obligation of neutral Powers to intern members of the armed forces of the parties to the conflict in their territory, *cf. infra* section 1.2.3.4.

676 *Cf. infra* section 1.2.3.5.

677 *Cf. supra* note 586 and accompanying text.

678 See also Pictet, *Commentary GC III* (1960), p. 76.

under domestic law to attempt escape from captivity and rejoin their ranks as soon as possible. Articles 91 and 92 GC III therefore explicitly provide that:

"The escape of a prisoner of war shall be deemed to have succeeded when: (1) he has joined the armed forces of the Power on which he depends, or those of an allied Power; (2) he has left the territory under the control of the Detaining Power, or of an ally of the said Power; (3) he has joined a ship flying the flag of the Power on which he depends, or of an allied Power, in the territorial waters of the Detaining Power, the said ship not being under the control of the last named Power. Prisoners of war who have made good their escape in the sense of this Article and who are recaptured, shall *not be liable to any punishment* in respect of their previous escape." (Article 91 GC III, emphasis added)[679]

"A prisoner of war who attempts to escape and is recaptured before having made good his escape in the sense of Article 91 shall be *liable only to a disciplinary punishment* in respect of this act, even if it is a repeated offence. A prisoner of war who is recaptured shall be handed over without delay to the competent military authority. [...] prisoners of war punished as a result of an unsuccessful escape may be subjected to special surveillance. Such surveillance must not affect the state of their health, must be undergone in a prisoner of war camp, and must not entail the suppression of any of the safeguards granted them by the present Convention." (Article 92 GC III, emphasis added)

(d.) Violations of international humanitarian law

Individual members of the armed forces of the parties to the conflict have an obligation to respect all rules of international humanitarian law.[680] When they commit any violations of those rules, they must be tried and punished accordingly. Individual members of the armed forces who commit grave breaches of international humanitarian law incur individual criminal responsibility under both national and international law for the commission of war crimes. Combatant immunity does not extend to any violations of international humanitarian law or to crimes against humanity. Individual prisoners of war who are suspected of having committed or ordered such crimes,[681] or other violations of international humanitarian law must thus be tried and punished accordingly.[682]

[679] See in this sense also article 28§3 of the Brussels Declaration (1874): "If, after succeeding in escaping, he is again taken prisoner, he is not liable to punishment for his previous acts."

[680] This customary rule of international humanitarian law is explicitly codified in article 44§2 AP I.

[681] Article 129§§1-2 GC III and article 85 AP I. The obligation to try and punish war criminals is part of customary international humanitarian law, see the comments on rules 151 to 155 ("Individuals are criminally responsible for war crimes they commit; Commanders and other superiors are criminally responsible for war crimes committed pursuant to their orders; Commanders and other superiors are criminally responsible for war crimes committed by their subordinates if they knew, or had reason to know, that the subordinates were about to commit or were committing such crimes and did not take all necessary and reasonable measures in their power to prevent their commission, or if such crimes had been committed, to punish the persons responsible; Every combatant has a duty to disobey a manifestly unlawful order; Obeying a superior order does not relieve a subordinate of criminal responsibility if the subordinate knew that the act ordered was unlawful or should have known because of the manifestly unlawful nature of the act ordered"), rule 158 ("States must investigate war crimes allegedly committed by their nationals or armed forces, or on their territory, and, if

They do not, however, cease to be prisoners of war,[683] and their trial, punishment and potential detention must be in conformity with the provisions of the Third Geneva Convention regulating penal proceedings and sanctions against prisoners of war.[684] Contrary to prior practice, article 85 GC III stipulates that "[p]risoners of war prosecuted under the laws of the Detaining Power for acts committed prior to capture shall retain, even if convicted, the benefits of the present Convention." These acts include violations of international humanitarian law,[685] as is reaffirmed by article 44§2 and §5:

> "2. While all combatants are obliged to comply with the rules of international law applicable in armed conflict, violations of these rules shall not deprive a combatant of his right to be a combatant or, if he falls into the power of an adverse Party, of his right to be a prisoner of war, except as provided in paragraphs 3 and 4. [...] 5. Any combatant who falls into the power of an adverse Party while not engaged in an attack or in a military operation preparatory to an attack shall not forfeit his rights to be a combatant and a prisoner of war by virtue of his prior activities."

While the failure to distinguish oneself triggers loss of prisoner of war status under article 44§§3-5 AP I (*cf. supra*), the fact of not wearing one's *uniform* is by itself not sufficient to deny a members of the armed forces belonging to the categories in article 4§A(1) to (3) and article 4§B of GC III of his or her right to be a prisoner of war.[686]

---

appropriate, prosecute the suspects. They must also investigate other war crimes over which they have jurisdiction and, if appropriate, prosecute the suspects") and rules 160-161 ("Statutes of limitation may not apply to war crimes; States must make every effort to cooperate, to the extent possible, with each other in order to facilitate the investigation of war crimes and the prosecution of the suspects"), all in Henckaerts & Doswald-Beck (2005), pp. 551-567, 607-611 and 614-621. See also articles 5 to 8 ICC Statute; articles 4 to 6 of the Convention on the Prevention and Punishment of the Crime of Genocide (1948); and articles 1 to 5 of the Convention on the Non-Applicability of Statutory Limitations to War Crimes and Crimes Against Humanity (1968).

682 Article 129§3 GC III.

683 In the same sense, e.g.: Pictet, *Commentary GC III* (1960), pp. 76 and 413-425; Rosas (1976), pp. 311-312, 338 and 402-405; Levie (1978), pp. 37-38; Sandoz et al., *Commentary AP I and II* (1987), pp. 512-513, 524-526 and 539-540; Rowe in Rowe (1993), p. 193; Sassòli (*ACDI* 2001), p. 233; Aldrich (*AJIL* 2002), p. 896; Dörmann (*IRRC* 2003), p. 45. See also UK, *LOAC Manual* (2004), section 8§3 at p. 143; UK, *JDP 1-10* (2006), p. 1-6: "Lawful enemy combatants who do not comply with the Law of Armed Conflict (LOAC) are nevertheless entitled to full [POW] status". According to Goldman & Tittemore (*ASIL Task Force* 2002), p. 27, this is also consistent with US practice: "the proposition that members of regular armed forces are ineligible for prisoner of war status because some or all of its members have violated the laws of war or other conditions specified in Article 4A(2) is dubious at best and most certainly at odds with U.S. practice in other recent international armed conflicts."

684 Articles 82-108 and 129§4 GC III and article 75§7 AP I. See also the customary rules on fair trials as summarized in Henckaerts & Doswald-Beck (2005), Vol. I, pp. 352-375.

685 And other international crimes: *cf. supra* note 64 and accompanying text.

686 E.g.: Baxter (*BYIL* 1951), p. 343; Rosas (1976), pp. 341, 344-349 and 356; Mallison & Mallison (*CWRJIL* 1977), pp. 56-57; Sandoz et al., *Commentary AP I and II* (1987), pp. 512-513; Aldrich (*AJIL* 2002), pp. 895-896; Goldman & Tittemore (*ASIL Task Force* 2002), p. 13; Dinstein (*Isr.YHR* 2002), p. 256; Pfanner (*IRRC* 2004), pp. 94-140 and Henckaerts & Doswald-Beck (2005), Vol. I, pp. 385-386 (with references to international practice). To the contrary: Levie (1978), p. 44.

(e.) Sabotage

While often mentioned in one breath with spies, the question of whether members of the armed forces of the parties to the conflict who engage in acts of sabotage are, if caught in the act, equally not entitled to prisoner of war status and may be tried and punished for their acts under the domestic law of their captor, is not settled under international law. The term sabotage is not defined in any text of international law. According to Pictet, the term "should be understood to mean acts whose object or effect is to damage or destroy material belonging to the army of occupation or utilized by it."[687]

Acts of sabotage committed by members of the armed forces of a party to the conflict who otherwise qualify for prisoners of war status are not prohibited as such by international humanitarian law. Unless they are in direct violation of another rule of international humanitarian law – because of the nature of their objective or the means and methods employed to carry them out – they cannot therefore be considered unlawful under international law.[688]

Some legal scholars[689] and States[690] have found that saboteurs caught in the act, like spies, are not entitled to prisoner of war status upon capture. It is submitted here that such a position is not in conformity with article 4 GC III, read in the context of other provisions of international humanitarian law and interpreted in light of its object and purpose.

Members of the armed forces of a party to the conflict who engage in acts of sabotage – whether they are lawful or unlawful – are not excluded from prisoner of war status by any rule of treaty or customary international humanitarian

---

[687] Pictet, *Commentary GC IV* (1958), p. 57.

[688] Meyrowitz, "Le statut des saboteurs dans le droit de la guerre" (*MLLWR* 1966), p. 132: "C'est une règle bien établie que les actes de sabotage accomplis par des combattants légitimes [incluant, à part les membres des forces armées régulières, les membres des groupes mentionnées dans l'article 4§A(2) CG III et les participants d'une levée en masse] contre les objectifs licites, dans des circonstances n'impliquant aucune infraction aux lois de la guerre, constituent des actes de guerre permis." On the qualification of lawful and unlawful acts of sabotage, see Meyrowitz (*MLLWR* 1966), pp. 133-155 and 160-164.

[689] Baxter (*BYIL* 1951), pp. 338-342; and Castrén, Oppenheim & Lauterpacht, and Bindschedler-Robert as referred to in Rosas (1976), p. 355 at note 619.

[690] E.g.: Israel, Military Court, *Swarka Case* (1974), referred to in Henckaerts & Doswald-Beck (2005), Vol. II, Part II, p. 2543. The Court found that members of the Egyptian armed forces who infiltrated Israeli territory in civilian attire and launched an attack against a civilian settlement. To be noted that Court based its decision on the fact that the soldiers failed to distinguish themselves during the attack. Failure to distinguish oneself in attack is a lawful ground for denying a member of the armed forces of a party to the conflict prisoner of war status. It is therefore unclear whether the Court considered any saboteur would disqualify for prisoner of war status or only those who, in the process, failed to distinguish themselves in conformity with IHL. Members of the armed forces were also denied prisoner of war status by military courts in Israel, Nigeria, and the UK and their exclusion from prisoner of war status is reflected in a number of military manuals (summaries in Rosas (1976), p. 355 and in Mallison & Mallison (*CWRJIL* 1977), pp. 73-74, the reasoning is much the same as that in the *Swarka* case and all cases concerned members of "irregular armed forces" who were not wearing their uniform and failed to distinguish themselves in attack). As with the Israeli Military Court's decision in *Swarka*, it is unclear however whether saboteurs who distinguish themselves in attack would also be denied prisoner of war status.

law.[691] In this sense, article 4 GC III – contrary to other categories of members of the armed forces explicitly excluded from prisoner of war status – is not qualified by any other rules applicable between the parties to that Convention. Therefore, and taking into account its protective purpose, it must be understood to include members of the armed forces who engage in acts of sabotage. Those who have done so in violation of international humanitarian law may be tried and punished for their acts. As Meyrowitz points out:

> "Lorsque le sabotage illicite est le fait d'un membre des forces armées de l'ennemi, les sanctions pénales sont régies par les dispositions de la IIIe Convention et les règles relatives à la répression des crimes de guerre, et ce quel que soit le lieu de la commission du délit ou celui de la capture."[692]

The argument made by advocates of the exclusion of saboteurs from the definition of prisoners of war generally only concerns acts of sabotage carried out in civilian attire rather than in uniform.[693] We have seen earlier that failure to wear a uniform is by itself no ground for denying a member of the armed forces prisoner of war status. On the other hand, we have also seen that in certain situations, combatants who fail to distinguish themselves in attack may lose their entitlement to prisoner of war status and treatment. Nevertheless, the ground for exclusion in such cases is not the fact that the combatant is a saboteur, but rather that he or she failed to comply with the rules in articles 44§§3-4 AP I.

(f.) Legality of the struggle

When acceding to the 1949 Geneva Conventions in 1973, the government of the then Provisional Revolutionary Government of South Vietnam submitted the following reservation to article 85 G III:

> "The Provisional Revolutionary Government of the Republic of South Viet-Nam declares that prisoners of war prosecuted and convicted for crimes of aggression, crimes of genocide or war crimes, and crimes against humanity in accordance with the principles established by the Nuremberg Tribunal shall not benefit from the provisions of the present Convention."[694]

Article 6 of the Charter of the International Military Tribunal of Nuremberg (IMT) defined crimes against peace – which later came to be called crimes of aggression – as:

> "[the] planning, preparation, initiation or waging of a war of aggression, or a war in violation of international treaties, agreements or assurances, or participation in a common plan or conspiracy for the accomplishment of any of the foregoing."

During the 1974-1977 Diplomatic Conference for the adoption of the Additional Protocols to the Geneva Conventions, the by then Democratic Republic

---

[691] See also Meyrowitz (*MLLWR* 1966), pp. 132 and 165, with reference to relevant State practice; Draper (*Isr.YHR* 1971), pp. 196-198; and Rosas (1976), pp. 355-356.

[692] Meyrowitz (*MLLWR* 1966), p. 165.

[693] *Cf. supra* note 690.

[694] Viet Nam, *Reservations Made upon Accession to the Geneva Conventions by the Provisional Revolutionary Government of the Republic of South Viet-Nam on 3 December 1973*, available in the ICRC's online *Treaty Database*.

of Vietnam proposed not only to insert a provision on international crimes in AP I, but also to exclude from prisoner of war status their perpetrators, including persons who engaged in "wars of aggression" and "crime against peace."[695] While the proposal initially found support from a number of other States, the participants in the Conference rapidly lost interest, "[a]pparently [taking] it for granted that the proposal would be totally unacceptable for a considerable number of states."[696] Indeed, "it would have been impossible to reconcile [such a] proposal with the general function and rationale of present-day international humanitarian law."[697]

We have seen in Part I that the lawfulness of an armed conflict itself has no impact on the applicability or the interpretation of the international humanitarian law that regulates that conflict, and that conversely the applicability of that – by definition neutral – body of law does not affect the legal status of the parties to the conflict or its lawfulness under international law either.[698] Whichever

---

[695] E.g.: *Official Records 1974-1977*, Vol. IV, pp. 177-188 (Annex III: Draft Amendments to Draft Additional Protocol I Submitted by the Democratic Republic of Viet-Nam, CDDH/41, 12 March 1974): "(a) We propose that the following new article covering international crimes related to armed conflicts be inserted immediately after Article 1 of draft Protocol I: 'The High Contracting Parties recognize the following international crimes related to armed conflicts, defined in modern international law since the Judgement of the Nuremburg International Military Tribunal: (1) Wars of aggression, which constitute the ultimate international crime; (2) Crimes against peace; (3) The continued existence of colonial regimes, the practice of apartheid and all forms of racial discrimination; (4) War crimes stricto sensu, i.e., serious violations of the laws and customs of war; (5) The crime of genocide; (6) Crimes against humanity'" (at p. 182); and "in accordance with the spirit of humanity based on justice, we propose that the following article be added [...]: Article 42 (b): (1) All those who commit international crimes related to armed conflicts and who are caught in the act shall not be entitled to prisoner-of-war status. (2) However, the persons referred to in paragraph (1) shall be treated humanely during their detention, shall not be put to death or subject to torture of any kind shall be fed and housed in the conditions normal to a citizen of the Detaining Power, and shall be cared for in the event of sickness or injury. If they are found guilty of grave infringements of the law during their detention they shall have the right to present their defence and they shall be entitled to a fair and proper trial" (at p. 187).

[696] Rosas (1976), p. 404.

[697] Rosas (1976), p. 405.

[698] *Cf. supra* chapter I-2, section 2.1, note 345 and accompanying text. This notwithstanding, any development of international humanitarian law obviously takes place against a political and social background and the important privileges that come with membership in the armed forces of a party to the conflict (in its broad sense) explain why the definition of such membership in binding law has historically taken place against the backdrop of political debates on legitimacy of the struggle in which they took part (e.g. Rosas (1976), pp. 23-140 and Watkin (*HPCR Series* 2005), pp. 13-15). While recognition as a prisoner of war does not affect the legal status of that person other than for the purposes of IHL, nor the political or legal legitimacy of the party to the conflict he or she depends on or the cause for which the conflict is fought, questions of the legitimacy of a particular struggle have always strongly influenced the development of the categories of persons entitled to the legal statuses of combatant and prisoner of war. Almost every time a "new" category of persons was accorded prisoner of war status under IHL, it was the political legitimacy of the actions of such persons in past conflicts or the cause they fought for that led to that recognition. This was the case for the inclusion of organized resistance movements in the wake of the Second World War (article 4§A(2) GC III) and for members of the armed forces of national liberation movements during the decolonization period that followed the adoption of the United Nations Charter and in particular the General Assembly's *Resolution 2105 (XX) on the Implementation of the Declaration on the Granting of Independence to Colonial Countries and Peoples* (1965), §10 of which recognizes the "legitimacy of the struggle by

theory of "just war" underpins discussions on the use of force and the authority to engage in an armed conflict (*jus ad bellum*), it has no place in the interpretation of the norms of the *jus in bello*.[699] Moreover, the creation of an international legal status of prisoner of war reflected the intention of States to separate the status of the men in arms from that of the party on who behalf they (often without choice) fight.[700]

Therefore, a member of the armed forces of an adverse party to the conflict (as defined in article 4 GC III) cannot be denied prisoner of war status on the sole basis that the party on whose behalf he or she fights has engaged in or entered the conflict for illegitimate reasons.[701] As the drafters of Additional Protocol I – after expressing "their conviction that nothing in this Protocol or in the Geneva Conventions of 12 August 1949 can be construed as legitimizing or authorizing any act of aggression or any other use of force inconsistent with the Charter of the United Nations" – reaffirmed:

> "the provisions of the Geneva Conventions of 12 August 1949 and of this Protocol must be fully applied in all circumstances to all persons who are protected by those instruments, without any adverse distinction based on the nature or origin of the armed conflict or on the causes espoused by or attributed to the Parties to the conflict."[702]

While its proposals were rejected at the Diplomatic Conference, the ultimate purpose of the Vietnamese demarches – namely to achieve international condemnation of international crimes and a legally binding obligation on States to try and punish their perpetrators, including those responsible for engaging in armed conflict in violation of the Charter of the United Nations[703] – was achieved to a certain extent by the war crimes provisions in the Geneva Conventions and Additional Protocol I. Further achievements of that purpose were made by the adoption of various instruments of international criminal law that establish individual criminal responsibility not only for war crimes but also for genocide and crimes against humanity.[704] Finally, with regard to the crime of

---

the peoples under colonial rule to exercise their right to self-determination and independence" (articles 43 and 44§1 AP I).

699 *Cf. supra* note 345. Debates on the legitimacy of cause under the *jus ad bellum* and on the authorization under international law of certain States or non-State entities to engage in armed conflict may constitute the political background for the *development* of international treaty law on the definition of prisoners of war, they may not however be used to impede the normal *application or interpretation* of the law as it stands.

700 *Cf. infra* section 1.2 below (note 757 and accompanying text).

701 In the same sense, e.g.: Rosas (1976), pp. 402-405; Mallison & Mallison (*LCP* 1978), pp. 11-12; Sassòli (*ACDI* 2001), pp. 217, 229 and pp. 215-217; Goldman & Tittemore (*ASIL Task Force* 2002), pp. 26-27 (referring to this principle as one of customary international law and "expressly recognized in the US Air Force Pamphlet, which states that it is 'unacceptable' to make the legal protections of victims of conflict, including prisoners of war, 'contingent on the causes of the conflict.' (AFP 110-3, at 1-5)"); and Watkins (*HPCR Series* 2005), p. 8.

702 The text in quotation marks is from the last two paragraphs of the preamble of AP I.

703 This intention is clear from the explanations to the proposed amendments to AP I referred to above and in particular from that submitted in 1974; see *Official Records 1974-1977*, Vol. IV, pp. 177-188.

704 *Cf. supra* note 681.

aggression, the picture has been almost entirely completed in June 2010, when the States party to the Statute of the International Criminal Court inserted therein what is the equivalent in contemporary international law of the IMT's crimes against peace by establishing individual criminal responsibility under the Statute for the crime of aggression, a crime they defined as follows:

> "the planning, preparation, initiation or execution, by a person in a position effectively to exercise control over or to direct the political or military action of a State, of an act of aggression which, by its character, gravity and scale, constitutes a manifest violation of the Charter of the United Nations."[705]

Members of the armed forces of a party to the conflict who are prisoners of war must, like any other person, be tried and punished for any international crimes they are suspected to have committed or ordered before capture, including the crime of aggression as defined in the ICC Statute.[706] They do not however cease for that reason to be prisoners of war and are entitled to benefit from the protection of the Third Geneva Convention until their final release and repatriation.[707]

(g.) Nationality

It is generally accepted that nationality is in principle irrelevant to a person's right to be a prisoner of war.[708] Nevertheless, where that person falls into the hand of his national State or those of its allies while serving in the armed forces of an adverse party to the conflict, the issue is subject to more controversy. Practice has shown that such individuals are often denied prisoner of war status and are tried and punished under domestic law for having taken up arms against their own country.[709] The argument that one cannot be a prisoner of war of one's

---

[705] Article 8bis§1 ICC Statute, inserted into the Statute by Resolution RC/Res.6 of 11 June 2010, adopted by consensus at the 13th plenary meeting of the Review Conference of the Rome Statute held in Kampala, Uganda between 31 May and 11 June 2010.

[706] *Cf. infra* note 1097. To be noted however that, as far as the crime of aggression is concerned, the States parties to the ICC Statute agreed that the inclusion of the crime aggression in the ICC Statute "shall not be interpreted as creating the right or obligation to exercise domestic jurisdiction with respect to an act of aggression committed by another State" (Resolution RC/Res.6 (2010), Annex III, §5).

[707] *Cf. supra* notes 683-685.

[708] E.g.: Rosas (1976), pp. 392-395; Levie (1978), pp. 74-75; Canada, *LOAC Manual* (2001), article 1009§2: "Nationality does not affect entitlement to PW status. This entitlement depends on the country to which the captive's armed force belongs, so that even though the captive's own country is neutral, a national serving with a party to the conflict becomes a PW if captured." In a recent contribution concerning the conflict in Afghanistan, Goldman & Tittemore (*ASIL Task Force* 2002), p. 26 confirm, with references to US military doctrine, that "[i]t is important to note at the outset that the fact that foreigners, including some members of al Qaeda, may have been members of the Taliban's armed forces is, in principle, legally insufficient to deny them or all other members of these regular forces, prisoner of war status. Entitlement to such status has long been recognized as not being dependent on the nationality of the combatant. The U.S. Air Force Pamphlet specifically notes in this regard: 'members of regular armed forces are lawful combatants whether they are ... nationals of the state ... [or] foreigners (including neutrals who have joined the armed forces of a Party to a conflict).'" Note however that where a person meets the definition of a mercenary under article 47§2 AP I, that person will not be entitled to prisoner of war status (article 47§1 AP I, *cf. supra* section 1.1.3.1).

[709] We have examined the definition of desertion and defection and their often severe punishment under domestic criminal legislation above (section 1.1.3.1). Persons who serve in the armed forces of

own national State is based on two assumptions, namely (1) that persons who participate in armed conflict usually do so on behalf of the country whose nationality they have; and (2) that persons who take up arms against their own country break their duty of allegiance to that country and must be treated as traitors. While these assumptions reflect reality to a large extent, they do not take into account the exceptions to what is considered to be the general rule.

Some examples may serve to illustrate the issue. During the Second World War, the 250th Infantry Division of the German land forces – also called the Blue Division, and subsequently the Blue Legion – was composed of former Spanish soldiers (many of them veterans of the Spanish Civil War) and ordinary Spanish citizens who volunteered to serve the German armed forces – driven by anti-communist feelings and as revenge for Stalin's support to the communist forces in the Spanish Civil War – to fight the Soviet Red Army. Around 300 of them were captured on the Eastern Front by Soviet forces. They were interned for the duration of the conflict along with German, Italian and Hungarian prisoners of war, but were not treated as such and at the end of the war the USSR refused to repatriate them to Spain. Only in 1954, following long and tense negotiations, in which the ICRC served as a neutral intermediary, were the surviving prisoners allowed to return to Spain.[710]

Similarly, British Commonwealth prisoners of war and internees in German hands were – voluntarily – recruited into the German armed forces, forming the British Free Corps. Some felt ideological affinities with Nazi Germany; others were motivated by other reasons such as the desire to leave the prisoner camps. Upon capture by Allied Forces, they were denied the benefit of prisoner of war treatment and were tried for treason by their own governments after the war.[711]

Finally, a more recent example is that of John Walker Lindh, a US national who converted to Islam as a teenager and, when the conflict between the US and Afghanistan broke out in 2001, served with the Afghan (Taliban) armed forces. Captured and initially interned by the Northern Alliance, he was transferred to US custody shortly after he revealed his identity, and nationality, to a television reporter.[712] The US did not consider Lindh to be a prisoner of war and indicted

---

an enemy State have also been charged with the crime of treason. For example, the US Code, Title 18, §2381 defines the crime of treason and its punishment as follows: "Whoever, owing allegiance to the United States, levies war against them or adheres to their enemies, giving them aid and comfort within the United States or elsewhere, is guilty of treason and shall suffer death, or shall be imprisoned not less than five years and fined under this title but not less than $10,000; and shall be incapable of holding any office under the United States"; and articles 411-1 and 411-2 of the French penal code stipulate that "Les faits définis par les articles [suivants] constituent la trahison lorsqu'ils sont commis par un Français ou un militaire au service de la France [...] Le fait de livrer à une puissance étrangère, à une organisation étrangère ou sous contrôle étranger ou à leurs agents soit des troupes appartenant aux forces armées françaises [...] est puni de la détention criminelle à perpétuité et de 750000 euros d'amende."

[710] Vance (2006), pp. 44-45 and Kleinfeld & Tambs, *Hitler's Spanish Legion: The Blue Division in Russia* (1979).

[711] Vance (2006), pp. 53-54.

[712] Vance (2006), p. 432.

him in February 2002 on 10 criminal charges,[713] two of which he finally pleaded guilty to (serving in the Taliban army and carrying weapons in doing so), as part of a plea agreement.[714] He was sentenced to 20 years in prison.[715]

Some but not all of the individuals concerned by these examples were members of the armed forces of one party to the conflict who defected to an adverse party in the course of that conflict. We have seen above that defectors are not automatically entitled to be prisoners of war.

But most of the persons concerned by the above examples were no longer or never had been members of the armed forces of their national State, but had, out of ideological conviction, joined the ranks of an enemy power during an international armed conflict. Those members of the Blue Division/Legion and the British Free Corps, and John Walker Lindh were members of the armed forces of respectively Nazi Germany and Afghanistan who fell into the hands of their national State or one of its allies and were not defectors, they were denied prisoner of war status merely on the basis of their nationality.

This leads us to raise the following question: can a member of the armed forces of a party to the conflict (as defined above in section 1.1.2) who cannot be denied his right to be a prisoner of war on the basis of the specific exclusion clauses allowed by international law (*cf. supra* section 1.1.3.1)[716] be lawfully excluded from the scope of application of the Third Geneva Convention on the basis of his or her nationality? It is submitted that this is not the case.

The text of article 4 GC III – contrary to its equivalent in GC IV[717] but in line with other international treaty provisions regarding prisoners of war[718] – does not require an individual to be of enemy nationality, but only to have "fallen into the power of the enemy", the enemy being understood to be any adverse party to the conflict.[719]

What can be deduced from the wording of article 4 GC III and that of articles 43 and 44§1 AP I, as we have seen above,[720] is that the definition of prisoners of war, at least in as far as members of the armed forces are concerned, is first and foremost based on their effective allegiance to an adverse party to the conflict

[713] Conspiracy to murder U.S. nationals, two counts of conspiracy to provide material support & resources to foreign terrorist organizations, two counts of providing material support & resources to foreign terrorist organizations, conspiracy to contribute services to al Qaeda, contributing services to al-Qaeda, conspiracy to supply services to the Taliban, supplying services to the Taliban, and using and carrying firearms and destructive devices during crimes of violence (US, District Court, *USA v. John Philipp Walker Lindh* (Indictment) (2002)).

[714] US, District Court, *USA v. John Philipp Walker Lindh* (Plea Agreement) (2002).

[715] CNN, "Walker Lindh Sentenced to 20 Years" (2002).

[716] The arguments made below are without prejudice to a potential exclusion from the personal scope of application of GC III of the special cases of defectors and mercenaries (*cf. supra* section 1.1.3.1).

[717] On the question of nationality and the personal scope of application of GC IV, *cf. infra* chapter II-3, section 3.1.2.

[718] The text of articles 1 to 3 HR 1899/1907, article 1 GC 1929 and articles 43 and 44§1 AP I do not include a requirement that a prisoner of war be of enemy nationality either.

[719] *Cf. supra* notes 585-586 and accompanying text.

[720] Amply quoted above, the full text of these provisions is also included in Annex A.

(expressed through membership of that party's armed forces), rather than on formal nationality requirements. While in the overwhelming majority of cases nationality is a proper indicator for such allegiance, the examples of the Blue Division/Legion, the British Free Corps and John Walker Lindh demonstrate that it may not always be sufficient to determine whether an individual indeed has fallen into the hands of an "enemy power." This is especially the case where individuals join the armed forces of an adverse party of their national State in armed conflict out of ideological reasons, but also where they have *de facto* ruptured the national link to the State that captured them (for example by having fled that State and settled as a refugee in a third country),[721] or have the nationality of both the power in whose hands they fell (or that of an allied power) and that of the power in whose armed forces they serve.[722]

Where an individual serves the armed forces of a party to the conflict, he or she will clearly be regarded as an enemy by any State engaged in armed conflict against that power whose nationality he or she has. Most certainly, the Spanish soldiers of the Blue Division/Legion, the members of the British Free Corps and John Walker Lindh were regarded as enemies by their respective national or allied States. They clearly had "fallen into the hands of an enemy power."

Moreover, this interpretation is in line with the object and purpose of the Third Geneva Convention, namely to protect members of the armed forces of the parties to the conflict against abuse or arbitrary action when they fall into the hands of a party to that conflict who considers them to be an enemy. And as Rosas points out: "The general spirit of the [3rd Geneva] Convention indicates an intention to afford the individual protection even against his own country."[723]

One could argue that such an interpretation is contrary to the context of article 4 GC III by pointing at other provisions of the Convention that explicitly refer to the fact that a prisoner of war is generally *not* a national of the Interning Power. For example, articles 87 and 100 GC III stipulate that:

> "When fixing the penalty [for a violation of the laws, regulations and orders in force in the armed forces of the Detaining Power, to which prisoners of war are subject during captivity[724]], the courts or authorities of the Detaining Power shall take into consideration, to the widest extent possible, the fact that the accused, not being a national of the Detaining Power, is not bound to it by any duty of allegiance, and that he is in its power as the result of circumstances independent of his own will." (Article 87§2 GC III)

> "The death sentence cannot be pronounced on a prisoner of war unless the attention of the court has, in accordance with Article 87, second paragraph, been particularly called to the fact that since the accused is not a national of the Detaining Power, he is not bound to it by any duty of allegiance, and that he is in

[721] See the example of an Iraqi refugee in Kuwait during the international armed conflict resulting in the occupation of Kuwait by Iraq in 1990 (*cf. infra* chapter II-3, section 3.1.2).
[722] See the example of Hilal Abdul-Razzaq Ali Al-Jedda, a British-Iraqi national interned by UK forces in Iraq (*cf. infra* chapter II-4 where we discuss this case in more detail).
[723] Rosas (1976), p. 480.
[724] Article 82§1 GC III.

its power as a result of circumstances independent of his own will." (Article 100§3 GC III)

Nevertheless, the language of these articles merely reflects the reality that *most* individuals fight on behalf of their country of nationality; it does not take into account however that this is not *always* the case. Most of the members of the Blue Division/Legion and British Free Corps, units that were formally integrated into the German armed forces, owed allegiance to Germany and not to Spain or the UK, in whose armed forces they never served. The same holds true for John Walker Lindh, who was never a member of the armed forces of the US and therefore did not owe them his allegiance. Moreover, while the combatant immunity to which members of the armed forces of a party to the conflict are normally entitled upon capture (with the exception of mercenaries and the medical and religious personnel of the armed forces) covers their participation in hostilities and thus their lawful acts of war, it does not necessarily cover the crime of treason, which punishes behaviour that is not immunized by any rule of international law.

The ICRC's commentary to AP I recognizes the complexity of the situations and finds that:

> "[captured] nationals taking up the cause of the adverse nation, and even giving support to its military action [...] who are subject to security measures must be considered as enemy nationals and treated accordingly. They are not actually bound by a duty of allegiance with respect to the State in whose territory they find themselves or of which they bear the nationality [...] [They are] interned, arrested or prosecuted because of their attitude towards the conflict [and therefore] should have the benefit of all the provisions of the Geneva Conventions; combatants must be treated as prisoners of war, and civilians as protected persons under the fourth Convention."[725]

The authors of that Commentary make the argument for situations of international armed conflict defined in article 1§4 AP I, where it is likely (but not automatically so) that the majority of the members of the armed forces of both parties to the conflict will have the same nationality. In such cases, an interpretation of article 4 GC III as including a nationality requirement (which is actually contrary to the text of the article itself as we have seen earlier on) would effectively mean that the Convention could cease to have any protective effect. Their argument can therefore be applied *mutatis mutandis* to all cases of international armed conflict where individual prisoners of war have the nationality of their Interning Power or that of its allies. Article 4 GC III cannot be said to apply differently in wars of national liberation on the one hand and in other international armed conflicts on the other hand.

Finally, a broad interpretation of the text of article 4 GC III as proposed above – based on the text of article 4 in light of its object and purpose, and on an understanding of the general assumptions underlying the text of some the other provisions of the Convention –finds support in the main case law and the

---

[725] Sandoz et al., *Commentary AP I and II* (1987), p. 867.

majority of scholarly work that addresses this topic in some depth,[726] and is in line with subsequent developments in contemporary international law on the protection of the human person in times of armed conflict.[727]

Therefore, as long as no rule of treaty or customary international law establishes the contrary, the text of article 4 GC III and the object and purpose of the Third Geneva Convention do not allow for any individual to be excluded from the personal scope of application of that Convention on the basis of his or her nationality alone. Prisoners of war who have committed the crime of treason against the power in whose hands they have fallen may be tried and punished for that crime and may be detained during trial or imprisoned upon conviction, but they "retain, even if convicted, the benefits of the [Third Geneva] Convention."[728] Nevertheless, the granting of prisoner of war status of soldiers – regardless of their nationality – who, in the course of an international armed conflict, defect from their armed forces to join an adverse party's ranks and subsequently fall into the hands of the power they initially depended on, is left to the discretion of the latter.

(h.) Waiver of GC III protection

Finally, prisoners of war, legally entitled to the protection of the Third Geneva Convention, cannot by choice or individual decision waive their entitlement to prisoner of war status or the protection of any of the Convention's provisions:

> "Prisoners of war may in no circumstances renounce in part or in entirety the rights secured to them by the present Convention, and by the special agreements referred to in [article 6 GC III], if such there be."[729]

Neither can they be stripped of their status or protection by an agreement to that effect between the parties to conflict:

---

[726] Rosas remains hesitant to depart from the traditional rule, but his arguments leave room for the limited exceptions to the general rule that are the subject of our attention here (Rosas (1976), pp. 383-388). Levie takes a more principled position, identical to ours (Levie (1978), pp. 74-76); and so does Tse, "The Relevancy of Nationality to the Right to Prisoner of War Status" (*CJIL*, 2009), pp. 395-421. Sassòli (*ACDI* 2001), at p. 233, and Dinstein (*Isr.YHR* 2002), at pp. 259-262, underline the general assumptions referred to above, but their positions do not seem to prevent the interpretation of article 4 GC III we propose here. State practice and the little case law on the subject (*Koi*, *Quirin*, *Territo* and *Hamdi* in respectively UK and US courts, and *Delalic* before the ICTY) as discussed in detail by Rosas, Levie, Dinstein and Tse, generally supports – or does at least not invalidate – the arguments made above.

[727] The focus on the protection of the individual (rather than the interests of the States in whose power he or she finds him- or herself) is much stronger in contemporary international law than in the past. The influence of international human rights law on the interpretation and formation of international humanitarian law demonstrates this development in general international law (*cf. supra* Introduction). In particular with regard to prisoners of war, see Pictet, *Commentary GC III* (1960), pp. 20 and 23; Rosas (1976), pp. 387-388; Levie (1978), p. 76 and note 304; and Tse (*CJIL* 2009), pp. 411-416.

[728] Article 85 GC III.

[729] Article 7 GC III.

> "No special agreement [between the parties to the conflict] shall adversely affect the situation of prisoners of war, as defined by the present Convention, nor restrict the rights which it confers upon them."[730]

1.1.4. Exception N° 2: non-members of the armed forces who are prisoners of war

The Third Geneva Convention's definition of prisoners of war does not only include members of the armed forces of a party to the conflict but also two specific categories of other persons, namely:

> "Persons who accompany the armed forces without actually being members thereof, such as civilian members of military aircraft crews, war correspondents, supply contractors, members of labour units or of services responsible for the welfare of the armed forces, provided that they have received authorization from the armed forces which they accompany" (Article 4§A(4) GC III); and

> "Members of crews, including masters, pilots and apprentices, of the merchant marine and the crews of civil aircraft of the Parties to the conflict, who do not benefit by more favourable treatment under any other provisions of international law." (Article 4§A(5) GC III)[731]

Pictet recalls that the list in article 4§A(4) is "only by way of indication" and "the text could therefore cover other categories of persons or services who might be called upon, in similar conditions, to follow the armed forces during any future armed conflict."[732] Article 4§A(4) may therefore be of particular interest with regard to the increased use of private military and security companies that accompany (and sometimes form part of) State armed forces during military operations.[733]

As to the subcategory of persons in article 4§A(5), Pictet points out that:

> "The term 'members of crews' covers only members of the merchant marine who have mustered on a ship, but not those who, after completing their time of service, are on board ship as passengers and still less those who are on leave, for instance in their homes. Fishermen are excluded, since Article 3 of the

---

730 Article 6§2 GC III.

731 The entitlement of such persons to prisoner of war status reflects a long-standing custom, reflected in article 34 Brussels Declaration (1874), articles 21 and 22 Oxford Manual (1880), and article 81 GC 1929.

732 Pictet, *Commentary GC III* (1960), p. 64.

733 The relevance of article 4§A(4) for contemporary international armed conflicts in which the parties to the conflict rely on private military or security companies to accompany or provide certain services to their armed forces on the battlefield is convincingly demonstrated by Doswald-Beck in Chesterman & Lehnardt (2007), pp. 123-124. In the same sense: University Centre for International Humanitarian Law, *Report of the Expert Meeting on Private Military Contractors* (2005), pp. 13-14; Bellal & Chetail in Doswald-Beck et al. (2009), p. 75. On the question of whether and when such private contractors may be the targets of attack, see ICRC, *IGDPH* (2009), pp. 37-40. More generally on the status of private military and security companies under IHL, e.g.: Schmitt, "Humanitarian Law and Direct Participation in Hostilities by Private Contractors or Civilian Employees" (*Ch.JIL* 2005); Cameron, "Private Military Companies: Their Status under International Humanitarian Law and its Impact on their Regulation" (*IRRC* 2006), pp. 573-598; Gillard, "Business Goes to War: Private Military/Security Companies and International Humanitarian Law" (*IRRC* 2006); and Jäger & Kümmel (eds.), *Private Military and Security Companies: Chances, Problems, Pitfalls and Prospects* (2007).

XIth Hague Convention, 1907, stipulates that fishing boats cannot be captured. In some countries, pilots and apprentices are not members of merchant marine crews; the 1949 Convention therefore makes specific reference to them [...]. Lastly, the phrase 'who do not benefit by more favourable treatment under any other provisions of international law' is a reference to Article 6 of the XIth Hague Convention which, as we have seen, provides that merchant seamen may not be made prisoners of War."[734]

Neither one of these categories of persons belongs to the armed forces of the party to the conflict whose forces they may accompany. They are not combatants and thus have neither the right to participate in hostilities nor combatant immunity if they would.[735] Nevertheless, they are entitled to prisoner of war status upon capture or surrender.[736] They may therefore in principle be interned on the basis of the Third Geneva Convention, but the fact that they are not members of the armed forces and have no combatant privileges will need to be taken into account in the decision to intern them and will affect the lawful duration of their internment (*cf. infra* section 1.2.3.5).[737]

1.1.5. Conclusions

Who is a prisoner of war and thus can be interned on the basis of the Third Geneva Convention is defined by the text of article 4 of that Convention, read in light of its object and purpose, and taking into account its understanding and application in practice, subsequent developments in international humanitarian and relevant development in general international law. In defining who is a prisoner of war it is important not to make automatic conclusions on an individual's status as a prisoner of war based on his or her status as a (lawful) combatant. While the persons covered by these two notions overlap to a considerable extent, each concept must be interpreted in light of the purpose it serves. We have seen above that not every combatant will be entitled to prisoner of war status, and that not all prisoners of war are entitled to combatant status. These nuances will also have to be kept in mind when analyzing the lawful

---

[734] Pictet, *Commentary GC III* (1960), p. 66. *Cf.* also *infra* section 1.2.3.5.

[735] These two categories of persons were considered non-combatant members of the armed forces under article 13 HR 1899/1907. Today, they are included in the definition of civilians under article 50 AP I ("A civilian is any person who does not belong to one of the categories of persons referred to in article 4 A (1); (2); (3) and (6) of the Third Convention and in Article 43 of this Protocol") and their entitlement to POW status does not change their civilian status for the purposes of the rules on the conduct of hostilities, even if their proximity to the armed forces of a party to the conflict may expose them to additional dangers.

[736] Their right to be a prisoner of war may not be denied on the basis of their surrender, recapture after escape, their having committed violations of international humanitarian law, the fact that they do or do not carry out combat functions, or their nationality. The same rules apply as to members of the armed forces who are prisoners of war, *cf. supra* section 1.1.3.2.

[737] Generally speaking though, article 4§A(4) and (5) only concerns a marginal number of internees in contemporary international armed conflicts, and the definitions in the article itself are sufficiently clear, they therefore do not require much further explanation here. For more detail, see also Rosas (1976), pp. 302-304 and 375-378; and Levie (1978), pp. 60-66.

grounds for and duration of both prisoner of war internment (*cf. infra* section 1.2) and internment on the basis of GC IV (*cf. infra* chapter II-3).

Prisoners of war include certain but not all members of the armed forces of the parties to the conflict and a number of other persons whom – due to their physical closeness to members of the armed forces on the battlefield – the drafters of the Third Geneva Convention also sought to protect in case of capture or surrender.[738]

In case of doubt,[739] a person captured on the battlefield or while taking part in hostilities will be presumed a prisoner of war until a competent tribunal can determine his or her status.[740] It is beyond the scope of this book to examine the procedural aspects of status determination in any detail, but it is useful to point out the importance of the fact that this procedure must guarantee an effective and objective means of evaluating of whether or not a person is a prisoner of war as

[738] Arguably such protection may indeed have been necessary in the Hague Regulations (which contained no provisions on the treatment and protection of civilian internees), but that there was no real reason to protect them under GC III by including them in the definition of prisoners of war since they would have been protected under GC IV.

[739] The doubt may be raised by the power in whose hands the person fell, the person him-or herself, or the power on which he or she depends. E.g.: article 45§1 AP I; Sandoz et al., *Commentary AP I and II* (1987), pp. 547-550 and 553; Risius in Rowe (1993), p. 296; Naqvi, "Doubtful Prisoner-of-War Status" (*IRRC* 2002), pp. 574-577. Naqvi also correctly points out that: "States should not be able to unilaterally decide that no doubt has arisen for an entire group of captured persons who have taken part in hostilities." In the same sense: CoE, *Venice Commission Opinion* (2003), §§26-28.

[740] Article 5§2 GC III: "Should any doubt arise as to whether persons, having committed a belligerent act and having fallen into the hands of the enemy, belong to any of the categories enumerated in Article 4, such persons shall enjoy the protection of the present Convention until such time as their status has been determined by a competent tribunal" and article 45§1 AP I: "A person who takes part in hostilities and falls into the power of an adverse Party shall be presumed to be a prisoner of war, and therefore shall be protected by the Third Convention, if he claims the status of prisoner of war, or if he appears to be entitled to such status, or if the Party on which he depends claims such status on his behalf by notification to the Detaining Power or to the Protecting Power. Should any doubt arise as to whether any such person is entitled to the status of prisoner of war, he shall continue to have such status and, therefore, to be protected by the Third Convention and this Protocol until such time as his status has been determined by a competent tribunal." See also Sandoz et al., *Commentary AP I and II* (1987), p. 550: "Despite the precautions taken by the drafters of this article, and all the presumptions which were outlined above, it is clear that cases of doubt may occur at the time of capture. There may be doubt regarding the individual capacity of the person concerned to be granted the status of prisoner of war, as well as regarding the status of the armed forces to which he belongs, or claims to belong, which should be organized in accordance with Article 43 *(Armed forces)*. However, one thing is certain, and on this point the provision is quite clear: all persons who are captured and who are not considered either as prisoners of war or as civilians who have not participated in the hostilities, are treated there and then as prisoners of war until such time as their status has been determined by a competent tribunal" (original italics). For a good overview of the provisions in article 5§2 GC III and article 45§1 AP I, of State practice, and the contentious issues, see Naqvi (*IRRC* 2002), pp. 571-595. On the customary nature of article 45§1 AP I, see Naqvi (*IRRC* 2002), pp. 591-593, who concludes that "while the exact provisions of Article 45(1) may be said not to reflect customary law in their entirety, it is submitted that the underlying principle establishing a general presumption of prisoner-of-war status for those participating in hostilities is developing into a customary rule. In addition, the right of a captured person who does not appear to be a prisoner of in many military manuals and is consistent with State practice." In the same sense: CoE, *Venice Commission Opinion* (2003), §§26-28.

defined by article 4 GC III and article 44 AP I.[741] The effectiveness and fairness of this procedure is crucial in the prevention of unlawful or arbitrary deprivation of liberty.[742]

For purposes of easy recognition on the battlefield, and to avoid as much as possible any confusion or errors, article 17§3 GC III obliges parties to the conflict to:

> "furnish the persons under its jurisdiction who are liable to become prisoners of war, with an identity card showing the owner's surname, first names, rank, army, regimental, personal or serial number or equivalent information, and date of birth. The identity card may, furthermore, bear the signature or the fingerprints, or both, of the owner, and may bear, as well, any other information the Party to the conflict may wish to add concerning persons belonging to its armed forces. As far as possible the card shall measure 6.5 x 10 cm and shall be issued in duplicate. The identity card shall be shown by the prisoner of war upon demand, but may in no case be taken away from him."[743]

Nevertheless, should a party to the conflict fail to issue members of the armed forces, persons accompanying its armed forces of otherwise liable to become prisoners of war with such an identity card, or should the concerned person lose that card, this will not have any impact on his or her entitlement to prisoner of war status and the protection of the Third Geneva Convention.[744]

When we use the term "prisoner of war" or "members of the armed forces" entitled to prisoner of war status, this term should be understood in accordance with the present section.

---

[741] On the composition of the "competent tribunal" and the procedural guarantees to ensure an effective and fair status determination, see Pictet, *Commentary GC III* (1960), pp. 77-78; Rosas (1976), pp. 407-408; Genot, "Quelques garanties nouvelles offertes au combattant capturé" (*RBDI* 1977); Levie (1978), pp. 55-59; Sandoz et al., *Commentary AP I and II* (1987), pp. 552-554; Risius in Rowe (1993), pp. 295-297; Naqvi (*IRRC* 2002), pp. 577-584. See also Canada, *Regulations respecting the Determination of the Entitlement of Persons Detained by the Canadian Forces to Prisoner-of-War Status* (1991); UK, *LOAC Manual* (2004), pp. 49 (section 4§12) and 150 (section 8§21); and CoE, *Venice Commission Opinion* (2003), §29.

[742] Such was certainly the intention of the drafters of both article 5§2 GC III and article 45§1 AP I. For example, the commentators of AP I concluded their examination of article 45§1 with the following sentence: "it is obvious that in the present paragraph the authors of the Protocol intended to reduce to a minimum those cases in which a captor could arbitrarily deny the status of prisoner of war to a person who had been apprehended" (Sandoz et al., *Commentary AP I and II* (1987), p. 553). In this sense it is also useful to recall that the prohibition of arbitrary deprivation of liberty is an absolute rule of customary international humanitarian law, applicable to all persons protected by that body of law, including prisoners of war. In the same sense: Henckaerts & Doswald-Beck (2005), Vol. I, pp. 345-346, who also point out the role of the Protecting Powers in this regard: "the Geneva Conventions provide for the appointment of Protecting Powers to try and prevent arbitrary detention." Risius in Rowe (1993), at p. 302, points out in this regard that a Protecting Power could contact the power on which a presumed prisoner of war depends in order to establish whether he or she is a member of its armed forces or not.

[743] See also article 4§A(4) regarding persons who accompany the armed forces of a party to the conflict without being a member thereof and whom these party to the conflict "shall provide with an identity card similar to the annexed model." The model is included in Annex 4 of GC III.

[744] *Final Record 1949*, Vol. II-A, pp. 417-418. See also Pictet, *Commentary GC III* (1960), pp. 64-65.

1.2. ON WHAT GROUNDS AND FOR HOW LONG CAN PRISONERS OF WAR BE INTERNED ON THE BASIS OF GC III?

Article 21 GC III: The Detaining Power may subject prisoners of war to internment.

Article 118 GC III: Prisoners of war shall be released and repatriated without delay after the cessation of active hostilities.

The lawful grounds for internment of prisoners of war are not explicitly defined in article 21 GC III. They are however clearly established in practice and are reflected in the other provisions of the Convention that regulate prisoner of war internment.[745] The lawful duration of internment of prisoners of war is on the contrary clearly prescribed by article 118 GC III, but the interpretation of that article when applied in practice also merits further clarification.

The purpose of the present section is thus to shed light on both the lawful grounds for and duration of prisoner of war internment today, based on a reading of the relevant provisions of the Third Geneva Convention in light of their object and purpose and taking into account their application by the parties to that Convention, other relevant rules of international law applicable in the relations between them, and subsequent developments in international law that bind them all.[746]

1.2.1. Preventing captured combatants from returning to the battlefield

We have seen in the preceding section that the provisions of GC III originate in a longstanding custom of interning enemy troops for the duration of the conflict. The purpose of prisoner of war internment is to prevent captured members of the enemy's armed forces from returning to the battlefield and continue to fight on behalf of the party to the conflict they belong to. That it is lawful to intern prisoners of war on this ground is therefore beyond any controversy,[747] as is reflected in State practice, international and national case law and scholarly works.

---

[745] Other than the possibility to challenge one's qualification as a prisoner of war (*cf. supra* section 1.1.5), the Third Geneva Convention does not provide for a review procedure of continued internment of prisoners of war.

[746] Article 31§3 VCLT: "There shall be taken into account [...] (a) any subsequent agreement between the parties regarding the interpretation of the treaty or the application of its provisions; (b) any subsequent practice in the application of the treaty which establishes the agreement of the parties regarding its interpretation; (c) any relevant rules of international law applicable in the relations between the parties."

[747] Article 21 GC III reflects international custom since the mid-17th century, enshrined also in articles 1-3 HR 1899/1907, *cf. supra* section 1.1. It is therefore not surprising that the drafters of GC III did not devote any attention to the question of lawful grounds for internment of prisoners of war in their discussion of what became article 21 GC III (*Final Record 1949*, Vol. I, pp. 77-78; Vol. II-A, pp. 252-253, 347, 353, 391-392. 472-474, 564, 581; Vol. II-B, pp. 267, 281, all substantive discussions concerned the institution of parole) and that, in his *Commentary to GC III* (1960), Pictet does not discuss the grounds for such internment either.

For example, Canadian military doctrine states that:

"The taking of Prisoners of War (PW) has always been a part of the mechanism of war and their treatment has fluctuated between the barbarous and the honourable. Prisoners are taken not only by reason of man's humanity but also for other more pragmatic reasons. The taking of PW *reduces the enemy's numerical strength and fighting capacity*. The knowledge that the enemy holds friends and colleagues as captives depresses the morale of those remaining free and may even constrain the tactics of their commanders. Finally, PW are an important source of information";[748] and

"The primary reasons for which members of the CF may be called upon to detain individuals in the course of an operation are *to prevent their further participation in a conflict or*, when authorized, to prevent them from *interfering with the military mission*. The reason for captivity is never related to revenge or punishment."[749]

Similarly, UK military doctrine reiterates that:

"It should always be remembered that prisoners of war are not convicted criminals in need of corrective training or punishment. They are members of the armed forces who, until capture, were simply doing their duty."[750]

US military doctrine does not elaborate on the grounds to intern prisoners of war but in the *Coard case* before the IAC°HR, the US maintained that:

"the petitioner's detention and treatment were justified under the 1949 Geneva Convention III, Relative to the Treatment of Prisoners of War [...] *as in furtherance of lawful military objectives*."[751]

The International Military Tribunal in Nuremberg, relying on "principles of general international law on the treatment of prisoners of war", found that:

"Since the eighteenth century these [principles] have gradually been established along the lines that war captivity is neither revenge nor punishment, but solely protective custody, the *only purpose of which is to prevent the prisoners of war from further participation in the war*. This principle was developed in accordance with the view held by all armies that it is contrary to kill or injure helpless people."[752]

---

[748] Canada, *Joint Doctrine Manual: Prisoner of War Handling, Detainees and Interrogation and Tactical Questioning in International Operations* (hereinafter *PWDITQ*) (2004), p. 1-1, article 101 (emphasis added).

[749] Canada, *Code of Conduct for CF Personnel* (2005), p. 2-9 (emphasis added). The *Code of Conduct* applies to all international operations of Canadian Armed Forces, including international armed conflict, occupation and peace-support operations. It does not apply to domestic operations (including non-international armed conflict in Canada) (*Ibidem*, p. 1-1).

[750] UK, *LOAC Manual* (2004), section 8§1(§) at p. 141.

[751] IAC°HR, *Coard v. USA* (1999), §30 (emphasis added). At a later point in the proceedings, the US claimed the petitioners were not prisoners of war but "civilian detainees held briefly for reasons of military necessity" (*Ibidem*, §32). For a discussion of this case, *cf. infra* chapter II-3, section 3.2.2.2 (c).

[752] IMT, *Trial of German Major War Criminals* (1946), p. 48, reprinted in *AJIL* (1947), pp. 228-229 (emphasis added).

Relying on that judgment and other legal authority, the US Supreme Court in *Hamdi* recognized that:

"The purpose of detention [of enemy combatants during the active phase of hostilities] is to *prevent captured individuals from returning to the field of battle and taking up arms once again.*"[753]

The continued lawfulness of this ground for internment of prisoners of war has also been widely recognized in the works of expert scholars. Dinstein for example writes that:

"Being a prisoner of war carries the price tag of denial of liberty, i.e., detention for the duration of the hostilities (which may drag on for many years). However, that detention has *solely one purpose: to preclude the further participation of the prisoner of war in the ongoing hostilities*. The detention is not due to any misgivings about previous reprehensible conduct on the part of the prisoner of war, and he cannot be prosecuted and punished 'simply for having taken part in hostilities'."[754]

And Shields-Delessert writes that under modern international humanitarian law:

"Conquered and disarmed enemies could be captured, but the purpose of making them prisoners was *to preclude them from taking up arms again and to weaken the enemy*. [...] Captivity in war was, therefore, reduced to a temporary deprivation of liberty. The prisoner of war [...] became a living instrument of war to be confined for the duration of hostilities so as to *prevent him from rendering service to his country on the battlefield.*"[755]

1.2.2. No revenge or punishment

Already in 1880, the International Law Association's Manual on the Law of War on Land pointed out that "[t]he confinement of prisoners of war is not in the nature of a penalty for crime (Article 21): neither is it an act of vengeance. It is a temporary detention only, entirely without penal character."[756]

The examples of international practice quoted above confirm that internment is an inherently preventive measure and that the reason for keeping prisoners of war captive may never relate to revenge or punishment. The preventive character of prisoner of war internment is also reflected in the regime established by GC III to govern their treatment in captivity: "a detailed regime making sure that

---

[753] US, SC, *Hamdi* (2004), p. 10 (emphasis added); at p. 12 the Court – who examines the legality of Hamdi's detention on the basis of US domestic law – explains that its "understanding is based on longstanding law-of-war principles."

[754] Dinstein (2010), p. 35, with reference to Rosas (1976), emphasis added.

[755] Shields-Delessert, *Release and Repatriation of Prisoners of War at the End of Active Hostilities: A Study of Article 118, Paragraph 1, of the Third Geneva Convention relative to the Treatment of Prisoners of War* (1977), pp. 29-30 (emphasis added). See also Naqvi (*IRRC* 2002), p. 572; and Sassòli (*JICJ* 2004), p. 103. Automatic internment of prisoners of war for the duration of hostilities seems so generally recognized that most scholars writing about prisoners of war do not examine the grounds for prisoner of war internment, or even the lawfulness of such internment. Neither Levie (1978) nor Rosas (1976) devotes any attention to this issue in their comprehensive analysis of the prisoners of war regime under international humanitarian law.

[756] Oxford Manual (1880), introductory comment to the rules on prisoner of war captivity (articles 61-72).

they are treated not only humanely, but also not as prison inmates – as they are not serving a sentence and have committed no unlawful act."[757]

Combatants who fall into the hands of an enemy power are also entitled to immunity from prosecution and punishment by their captor for their mere participation in hostilities (commonly referred to as combatant immunity, *cf. supra*).[758] That immunity from prosecution does not extend however to disciplinary or criminal proceedings that may be brought against a prisoner of war who has violated disciplinary regulations regulating his or her captivity, or international humanitarian law.[759]

1.2.3. Internment of prisoners of war: military necessity versus the right to liberty

1.2.3.1. Broad authorization to intern but still an element of necessity

While the plain language of articles 21 and 118 GC III suggests that prisoners of war may always automatically be interned for the duration of hostilities, that does not mean that the requirement of necessity to lawfully deprive a person of his or her liberty is entirely absent from the Convention's provisions. The Convention generally strikes the balance between military necessity and the individual prisoner's right to liberty in favour of the first, but at the same time the broad authorization to intern prisoners of war is not entirely unlimited.

That the balance has generally been struck in favour of the Interning Power's military and security concerns is reflected in the fact that the Convention is based on a presumption that the internment of prisoners of war – the majority of whom are members of the armed forces and bound in allegiance to the Power they serve – is always justified on the basis of military necessity.[760] Indeed,

---

[757] Sassòli (*JICJ* 2004), p. 103. The premise on which the entitlement of combatants to prisoner of war status rests is that armed conflicts are fought between States (or national liberation movements in AP I) and not between the individuals that make up their armed forces. The individual soldier – who more often than not is obliged to serve in the military during conflict under domestic law – is not responsible for the actions of the State (or NLM) he belongs to and cannot be punished for merely participating in hostilities.

[758] There are some exceptions to this rule; for example, spies who are caught in the act are not entitled to prisoner of war status and combatant immunity, they may be punished for their acts under the domestic law of their captor (*cf. supra* section 1.1), or interned on the basis of GC IV when it can be reasonably expected they would attempt to rejoin their ranks or further engage in acts of espionage upon release (*cf. infra*, chapter II-3, section 3.2.2.2).

[759] *Cf. supra* section 1.1.3. Every prisoner of war is obliged to respect the lawful disciplinary regulations for captivity put in place by the Interning Power (article 82 GC III). While a prisoner of war may not be held responsible for the actions of the party to the conflict he belongs to, he or she may be held individually responsible for violations of military discipline, serious violations of international humanitarian law and other international crimes articles 49/50/129/146 and 50/51/130/147 GC I-IV; articles 25-28 ICC Statute). For the legal basis for detention in the framework of disciplinary and penal proceedings against a prisoners of war, *cf. supra* note 573.

[760] See in this sense also the wording of article 4§B(1) GC III, regarding the internment of persons belonging, or having belonged to the armed forces of the occupied country. Such persons shall be prisoners of war "if the occupying Power considers it *necessary by reason of such allegiance to intern them*, even though it has originally liberated them while hostilities were going on outside the territory it occupies, *in particular where such persons have made an unsuccessful attempt to rejoin the armed forces* to which they belong and which are engaged in combat, or where they fail to

by interning members of enemy armed forces, their captor prevents them from taking any further part in the hostilities and thus effectively weakens the military capacity of an adverse party to the conflict. There is however no *obligation* to intern prisoners of war,[761] and the specific purpose of such internment also sets limits to the otherwise very broad authority to intern. In other words, the presumption of threat does not always apply. We have seen that internment of prisoners of war is ultimately justified by military necessity.[762] This means that where such necessity is entirely absent, prisoners of war may not lawfully be interned.

1.2.3.2. Legal presumption of threat for members of the armed forces

Before looking at exceptional cases where prisoners of war may not be interned because there is no real military need to do so, it is important to recognize the presumption inherent in GC III that the internment of members of the armed forces of an adverse party to the conflict *per se* accommodates a legitimate military need of the Interning Power.[763] The mere fact of qualifying as such a prisoner of war justifies internment.[764] This presumption stands in stark contrast with the internment provisions of GC IV, which require an individual threat assessment, allow for internment only when it is absolutely necessary to counter such a threat, and demand the decision to intern be reviewed by an independent and impartial authority (*cf. infra*). No such individual threat assessment is required by article 21 GC III, nor does it establish a review procedure similar to that in GC IV.[765]

The presumption in GC III is justified however by the fact that members of the armed forces of a party to the conflict may always be expected to rejoin their ranks and return to the battlefield upon release, because they are legally obliged to do so under the domestic law of the State to whose armed forces they belong.[766] Failure to resume the fight would amount to desertion, a crime usually

comply with a summons made to them with a view to internment" (emphasis added).

761 Article 21§1 GC III says prisoners of war *may* be interned.

762 See also Shields-Delessert (1977), p. 110 and Fisher in Fleck (2008), p. 372.

763 Note that the presumption in GC III only concerns members of armed forces who qualify for POW status and thus fall within the personal scope of application of the Convention. We will deal the issue of presumption of threat posed by members of armed forces who do not qualify as POW below, *cf. infra* chapter II-3, section 3.2.2.2.

764 Article 21 GC III; Sassòli (*JICJ*, 2004), p. 103. If there is a doubt as to whether a person is or is not entitled to POW status, a competent tribunal must proceed to an individual status determination (*cf. supra* section 1.1.5). In the meantime, the presumption of POW status remains in force and the person may thus be interned on the basis of article 21 GC III. Should the tribunal decide that the person is not a prisoner of war, article 21 GC III can no longer serve as a legal basis for his or her continued internment. If the Interning Power finds it necessary to continue to intern the person on the basis of the individual military threat he or she poses, it must resort to the legal bases for internment provided for under GC IV.

765 Article 5 GC III and article 45 AP I provide nevertheless for a procedure to challenge POW status, in itself a safeguard against error and arbitrariness, *cf. supra* section 1.1.5.

766 A duty of allegiance usually binds members of the armed forces to the Power they serve, see Pictet, *Commentary GC III* (1960), p. 547.

punished by the death penalty or life imprisonment.[767] Taking into account that duty of allegiance, the reality of armed conflict and the fact that internment may well be the most humane way to reduce the numerical strength of an enemy and bring the latter to defeat, the balance between the legitimate military and security needs of the Interning Power and the right to liberty of individual prisoners of war has been clearly struck in favour of the first.

Nevertheless, the broad authority to intern prisoners of war is not unlimited. There are a number of exceptional cases where the presumption does or should not apply and where there is thus no real need to intern prisoners of war.

In some cases, the Convention itself explicitly limits the authority to intern prisoners of war. This is the case for seriously wounded and sick prisoners, who must be released and repatriated as soon as their medical condition allows for it. It is also reflected in the strict provisions of the Convention on release and repatriation of prisoners of war at the end of hostilities. In other cases, the Convention clearly encourages parties to the conflict to favour early release and repatriation where possible. The ultimate purpose of internment, and the demands of general international law that deprivation of liberty be kept to a strict necessary minimum, even in armed conflict, lead us to suggest that these implicit encouragements to favour liberty whenever possible, should be reinforced by an interpretation of international humanitarian law that puts the individual's rights not before but at least at the same level as the military needs of the parties to the conflict. The impact of international human rights norms may well have tilted the balance somewhat more to equilibrium.

1.2.3.3. Direct or early release and repatriation on humanitarian grounds

First, prisoners of war who are seriously wounded or sick and are no longer able to participate in hostilities pose no military or security threat and their internment constitutes no definite military advantage. To avoid unnecessary deprivation of liberty, article 109§1 GC III prescribes that they must be released and repatriated as soon as their medical condition allows and their repatriation can be safely organized,[768] unless they themselves object to such repatriation.[769] Prisoners of war eligible for direct repatriation include:

> "(1) Incurably wounded and sick whose mental or physical fitness seems to have been gravely diminished.

[767] E.g.: Rosas (1976), p. 383; Sassòli (*YIIHL* 1985), p. 13.

[768] Seriously wounded and sick prisoners of war who are eligible for direct repatriation, but are also subject to disciplinary punishment, may not be held back on the plea that they have not undergone or completed such punishment (article 115§1 GC III). If they are detained in the framework of criminal proceedings, they may benefit from repatriation before the end of the completion of such proceedings or punishment if the Interning Power consents (article 115§2 GC III).

[769] Article 119§3 GC III: "No sick or injured prisoner of war who is eligible for repatriation under the first paragraph of this Article, may be repatriated against his will during hostilities." This provision must apply to all persons repatriated during the active phase of hostilities, see also Pictet, *Commentary GC III* (1960), pp. 512-513 and Sassòli (*YIIHL* 1985), p. 31. On forcible repatriation at the end of hostilities, *cf. infra* section 1.2.3.5(b).

(2) Wounded and sick who, according to medical opinion, are not likely to recover within one year, whose condition requires treatment and whose mental or physical fitness seems to have been gravely diminished.

(3) Wounded and sick who have recovered, but whose mental or physical fitness seems to have been gravely and permanently diminished."[770]

Should these repatriated prisoners of war recover before the cessation of active hostilities, they may not be employed on active military service (article 117 GC III).[771]

Less seriously wounded and sick prisoners of war should be accommodated in a neutral country. This includes prisoners

"whose recovery may be expected within one year of the date of the wound or the beginning of the illness, if treatment in a neutral country might increase the prospects of a more certain and speedy recovery"; or

"whose mental or physical health, according to medical opinion, is seriously threatened by continued captivity, but whose accommodation in a neutral country might remove such a threat."[772]

The parties to the conflict must do their utmost throughout the duration of hostilities, with the cooperation of the neutral Powers concerned, to conclude agreements to this effect.[773] The Convention also encourages them to seek such a solution for able-bodied prisoners of war who have undergone a long period of captivity.[774]

---

[770] Article 110§1 GC III. For the procedures on determining who may thus be repatriated, see articles 110§3, 112-116 GC III. Generally on repatriation of wounded and sick prisoners of war during hostilities, with references to the debates on the relevant articles in GC III and State practice, see Pictet, *Commentary GC III* (1960), pp. 506-539; Rosas (1976), pp. 471-474; and Levie (1978), pp. 407-416.

[771] Article 117 GC III. The inclusion and interpretation of the word "*active* military service" was the subject of lengthy discussions at the Diplomatic Conference (*Final Record 1949*, Vol. II-A, pp. 291, 295, 316, 365, 374-375, and 573). Pictet notes that "[i]n interpreting this phrase, the spirit of the Convention rather than national legislation should serve as a guide. It is, of course, difficult to give a precise definition, but the expression may be considered as broadly covering any participation, whether direct or indirect, in armed operations against the former Interning Power or its allies. In effect, Article 117 forbids any repatriated person to serve in units which form part of the armed forces but does not prevent their enrolment in unarmed military units engaged solely in auxiliary, complementary or similar work" (Pictet, *Commentary GC III* (1960), p. 539).

[772] Articles 109§2 and 110§2 GC III. See also Hoffer, "L'internement des malades et blessés dans les pays neutres" (*IRRC* 1919); Pictet, *Commentary GC III* (1960), pp. 506-539; Rosas (1976), pp. 474-475; and Levie (1978), pp. 416-417. As to prisoners who are subject to disciplinary punishments or criminal prosecution or imprisonment, article 115§§2-3 referred to above applies *mutatis mutandis*.

[773] Articles 109§2, 110§3, 111-116 GC III; a Model Agreement is annexed to GC III. Where the neutral Power who accommodates wounded or sick prisoners of war is subsequently obliged to repatriate those "whose state of health has deteriorated so as to fulfil the conditions laid down for direct repatriation" or "whose mental or physical powers remain, even after treatment, considerably impaired" (article 109§3 GC III), and they recover before the end of active hostilities, they may not be employed on active military service (article 117 GC III).

[774] Articles 109§2 GC III. For the historical evolution of this rule and the few examples of its application in practice, see Levie (1978), pp. 416-417, who concludes this possibility is unlikely to be used frequently but that "it was proper to include such a provision in the Convention so that it will be available as a basis for a proposal to the belligerents by the Protecting Power or the ICRC should the occasion arise." See also Shields-Delessert (1977), who suggests that able-bodied prisoners of war

1.2.3.4. Parole, exchange, early repatriation and internment in neutral countries

Prisoners of war may be released on parole or promise, in so far as the laws of the Power on which they depend allow for it. Article 21§2 GC III prescribes that such measures "shall be taken particularly in cases where this may contribute to the improvement of their state of health."[775] Obviously, the system of parole or promise can only work where both parties to the conflict and the prisoners of war themselves respect its premise. Non-respect of the terms of parole and promise has contributed to its near disappearance in practice.[776] Nevertheless, it is still an option available to the parties to the conflict and prisoners of war who accept liberty on parole or promise "are bound on their personal honour scrupulously to fulfil, both towards the Power on which they depend and towards the Power which has captured them, the engagements of their paroles or promises" and "the Power on which they depend is bound neither to require nor to accept from them any service incompatible with the parole or promise given."[777] While the obligation on the Power on which he depends is a legal one, the obligation on the paroled prisoner of war is more of a moral nature. If a prisoner of war breaks his parole or promise and takes flight, he does not forfeit his prisoner of war status if recaptured, but he may be tried and sentenced for his offence.[778] Breach of parole or promise or other violations of article 117 GC III ("No repatriated person may be employed on active military service") does not amount to a war crime.[779]

In practice, the non-respect of parole – a condition traditionally also tied to any exchange of prisoners of war between parties to the conflict while hostilities are still ongoing – by "deceitful" or "unreliable" States has brought about not only the decline of the institution of parole, but also the practice of prisoner exchanges before the end the conflict.[780] GC III therefore no longer obliges

who have lost their real military value due to prolonged captivity must be released after a period of maximum two years, even if hostilities have not come to an end (at pp. 108-111 and 114-118). Apart from this, she also suggests that prisoners whom it is not necessary to intern for reasons of military necessity, should be released and repatriated forthwith (*Ibidem*, pp. 108, 110).

775 Prisoners of war can however not be compelled to accept liberty on parole or promise (article 21§2 GC III). Upon the outbreak of hostilities, parties to the conflict must notify one another of their regulations on parole and promise (article 21§3 GC III). On parole and promise, see also Pictet, *Commentary GC III* (1960), pp. 178-182; Rosas (1976), p. 475; and Levie (1978), pp. 398-402.

776 Vance (2006), p. 124.

777 Article 213 GC III. Article 117 GC III would also apply in this case.

778 Contrary to article 12 HR 1907, the drafters of GC III did not wish to go that far (*Final Record 1949*, Vol. II-A, pp. 252-253, 347, 472-474). See also Pictet, *Commentary GC III* (1960), p. 181; Levie (1978), p. 402; Dinstein in Swinarksi (ed.), *Studies and Essays on International Humanitarian Law and Red Cross Principles in Honour of Jean Pictet* (1984), p. 38; and Fischer in Fleck (2008), p. 413 with further reference to de Preux.

779 Pictet, *Commentary GC III* (1960), p. 539 (with references to Bretonnière, Charpentier and Rasmussen) and *cf. supra* note 770. See also Fischer in Fleck (2008), p. 413: "The list of grave breaches in Article 130 GC III does not refer to Article 117 GC III. Neither has a recognition that breaches of Article 117 GC III constitute war crimes emerged in customary law."

780 Fischer in Fleck (2008), p. 414; Levie (1978), pp. 397-398; Vance (2006), p. 124. See also UK, *JDP 1-10.1* (2006), Annex 2E, p. 2E-3: "PW exchange is outside the provisions of GC III and

States to endeavour to conclude agreements on exchange, but where possible, such exchanges are of course allowed and should be encouraged.[781] Like prisoners released on parole, prisoners of war repatriated as the result of an exchange before the cessation of active hostilities may not be employed on military service.[782]

The parties to the conflict may also unilaterally decide to release (with or without parole or promise) or repatriate able-bodied prisoners of war throughout the active phase of hostilities (see also article 109§2 GC III above).[783] Since there is no obligation to release or repatriate able-bodied prisoners of war before the cessation of active hostilities, such early release or repatriation is a matter of policy. And as Risius points out: "Since it is hardly in the interests of a state to supply its enemy with, in effect, reinforcements, the practice of repatriating healthy prisoners of war is rare."[784] This is even more so where States do not respect the conditions of parole or promise or the prohibition in article 117 GC III to employ on active military services prisoners of war who have been repatriated during the active phase of hostilities.

During the Falklands/Malvinas war, Argentina decided to release captured British Marines, presumably on the assumption that article 117 GC III would prohibit the UK from redeploying them. No parole or promise was tied to the release however and the UK – arguing that article 117 GC III only applies to repatriated wounded and sick prisoners of war – saw no legal objection to redeploying its Marines in the ongoing conflict.[785] That argument contradicts both the text and the rationale of GC III. The Convention's provisions on "direct repatriation and accommodation in neutral countries" may deal to a large extent with the wounded and sick, there is nothing in the text of the Convention that

---

although in the past there have been instances of the exchange of PW, man for man, in the course of truces or temporary cessation in hostilities, such instances are likely to be the exception. The UK will not engage in PW exchange without the specific authority of the MOD. When such authority is granted, the exchange is to take place under the supervision of the Protecting Power or the International Committee of the Red Cross (ICRC)."

781 Levie, "Legal Aspects of the Continued Detention of the Pakistani Prisoners of War by India" (*AJIL* 1973), p. 695; Rosas (1976), p. 475. For example, Croatia and Serbia, through the mediation of the ICRC, concluded an agreement to exchange prisoners of war in 1991 (Fischer in Fleck (2008), p. 415 with further references); several prisoner of war exchanges have taken between Israel and its Arab neighbour States in the course of armed conflict between them (see for example Vance (2006), p. 126). Taking or interning prisoners of war for the sole purpose of securing a prisoner exchange is however not allowed, *cf. infra* chapter II-3, section 3.2.2.2.

782 Article 117 GC III.

783 Levie (*AJIL* 1973), p. 695; Rosas (1976), p. 475.

784 Risius in Rowe (1993), p. 292. In the same sense, Shields-Delessert (1977), p. 118; and Levie (1978), pp. 417-418.

785 Risius in Rowe (1993), pp. 425-426 (note 8). The New Zealand delegate at the 1949 Diplomatic Conference held the same position (*Final Record 1949*, Vol. II-A, p. 291). Pictet however recalls that the proponents of article 117 GC III had in mind able-bodied prisoners as much as the wounded and sick (Pictet, *Commentary GC III* (1960), pp. 512-513). See also Dinstein in *Liber Amoricum Pictet* (1984), p. 38: "Article 117 [...] sets forth that no repatriated person may be employed on active military service. This general provision encompasses, *inter alia*, the case of able-bodied prisoners of war repatriated under Article 109."

excludes the application of those provisions to able-bodied prisoners of war. On the contrary, article 109§2 explicitly encourages States to repatriate or accommodate in neutral countries "able-bodied prisoners of war who have undergone a long period of captivity." The inclusion of these concessions to the principle of humanity was balanced for reasons of military necessity by the prohibition to employ repatriated prisoners on active military service. Article 117 GC III applies to all prisoners of war who are repatriated during the active phase of hostilities, and the rationale behind that article demands that it should apply even more strictly to able-bodied prisoners than it does to those prisoners who due to their wounds or ill health are not able to serve in the armed forces any longer.[786]

Finally, we have seen earlier on that neutral States are obliged to intern members of the armed forces of parties to an international armed conflict for the duration of hostilities.[787] Nevertheless, where other measures of control would be adequate to prevent them from returning to the battlefield and continue participating in hostilities, the Interning Power should prefer such measures to that of internment. For example, it could establish a system of daily or weekly registration with a local police office or military base, seize or invalidate the prisoners' travel documents for the duration of hostilities or otherwise ensure that prisoners of war cannot leave the country or engage in hostile activity against an adverse party to the conflict. GC III applies by analogy to prisoners of war interned in neutral territory, but their internment regime should be adapted to the fact that in neutral territory they cannot participate in hostilities and pose a lesser threat.[788]

1.2.3.5. Prisoners of war whose internment is not necessary for military purposes

There may be cases where even able-bodied members of the armed forces to the conflict do not really pose any threat to their Interning Power or do not contribute substantially to the military capacity of the Power they depend on. In such cases, the Interning Power should consider whether there are no alternative measures than internment to deal with these prisoners.

(a.) Deserters and defectors

For example, some members of the armed forces – either before or after their capture or surrender – may want to take the risks inherent in desertion or defection and choose to sever their allegiance to the Power they serve. We have seen above that it is left to the discretion of the Interning Power to grant or refuse deserters and defectors prisoner of war status.[789] If it does grant them such status, it may intern them[790] but it may not subsequently enlist them in its own armed

---

[786] For the rule that prisoners of war may not be repatriated – either during or after hostilities – where they have a well-founded fear to be subject to persecution, ill-treatment, or arbitrary deprivation of life or liberty, *cf. infra* section 1.2.3.6 (b).

[787] *Cf. supra* note 618.

[788] Article 4§B(2) GC III. See also Pictet, *Commentary GC III* (1960), pp. 69-72.

[789] *Cf. supra* section 1.1.3.1.

[790] Any person who has lawfully been granted prisoner of war status may be interned on the basis of article 21 GC III.

forces (article 7 GC III).[791] In taking the decision to intern, the Interning Power should nevertheless take into account that the purpose of prisoner of war internment – i.e. to prevent the prisoner from continuing or resuming the fight on behalf of the party they depend on – is not likely to require internment in such cases. Where a soldier expressed his or her intent to desert or defect and where there is reason to believe such intention is sincere, it is submitted he or she may not be interned but should be released.[792]

(b.) Military personnel assigned to civil defence organizations

Article 67 AP I provides that members of the armed forces and military units of the parties to the conflict, who are permanently assigned to civil defence organizations and exclusively devoted to the specific humanitarian tasks of such organizations, "shall, if they fall into the power of an adverse Party, be prisoners of war."[793] Under the Protocol, civil defence organizations carry out exclusively humanitarian tasks "intended to protect the civilian population against the dangers, and to help it to recover from the immediate effects of hostilities or disasters and also to provide the conditions necessary for its survival."[794] In occupied territory, captured military personnel assigned to civil defence organizations may be employed by the Interning Power on civil defence tasks

[791] The prohibition of renunciation of rights as a prisoner of war covers both mandatory and voluntary enlistment of a prisoner of war into the armed forces of an adverse party (Pictet, *Commentary GC III* (1960), p. 88; Rosas (1976), pp. 389-390; and Sassòli (*YIIHL* 1985), p. 21). If *not* granted POW status, a deserter is a protected person under GC IV (Sassòli (*YIIHL* 1985), pp. 21-22). In that case, he or she may not be interned on the basis of article 21 GC III, but may only be interned on the basis of article 42 or 78 GC IV (*cf. infra*). Already noteworthy here is that GC IV prohibits coercive enlistment of protected persons of the Interning Power (articles 40 and 127 GC IV), but does not prohibit the latter from accepting a deserter's voluntary offer to enlist (Sassòli (*YIIHL* 1985), pp. 22-23, with further reference to the literature, which considers this as a generally accepted rule).

[792] It is generally accepted that deserters may not be forcibly repatriated to the Power they depend on, see Shapiro (*BYIL* 1952), pp. 323-324; Levie (1978), pp. 78-80; Dinstein in *Liber Amoricum Pictet* (1984), p. 41; and Sassòli (*YIIHL* 1985), pp. 33-35. Shapiro (at p. 324) says this "would be both an act of bad faith and an act of inhumanity, and one which customary international law does not require of a belligerent." In our view, deserters who are granted prisoner of war status may not be repatriated against their will if upon return they would face a real risk of persecution, ill-treatment or arbitrary deprivation of life or liberty (*cf. infra* on forcible repatriation of prisoners of war and our interpretation of article 118 GC III). If they are not granted such status, the principle of non-refoulement explicitly enshrined in article 45§4 GC IV, interpreted in light of subsequent developments in international law, also opposes repatriation in cases where such a risk exists.

[793] Article 67§§1-2 AP I.

[794] Article 61§1(a) AP I; the specific tasks civil defence organizations are to carry out are defined as "(i) warning; (ii) evacuation; (iii) management of shelters; (iv) management of blackout measures; (v) rescue; (vi) medical services, including first aid, and religious assistance; (vii) fire-fighting; (viii) detection and marking of danger areas; (ix) decontamination and similar protective measures; (x) provision of emergency accommodation and supplies; (xi) emergency assistance in the restoration and maintenance of order in distressed areas; (xii) emergency repair of indispensable public utilities; (xiii) emergency disposal of the dead; (xiv) assistance in the preservation of objects essential for survival; (xv) complementary activities necessary to carry out any of the tasks mentioned above, including, but not limited to, planning and organization." Article 61§1(b) defines civil defence organizations as "those establishments and other units which are organized or authorized by the competent authorities of a Party to the conflict to perform any of the tasks mentioned under sub-paragraph (a), and which are assigned and devoted exclusively to such tasks."

"in so far as the need arises, provided however that, if such work is dangerous, they volunteer for such tasks."[795]

In light of the fact that such personnel is exclusively assigned to humanitarian tasks aimed to protect and aid the civilian population, and is not entitled to participate in hostilities or commit other harmful acts against the adverse party to the conflict,[796] military personnel belonging to a civil defence organization should be released as soon as possible so they can return to their tasks. In this sense, it is useful to point out that during the drafting of AP I certain States recommended to give military personnel assigned to civil defence organizations the same status as permanent medical military personnel, who are not prisoners of war and may not be interned as such (*cf. infra* chapter II-2). Ultimately, it was the "concern to make a clear distinction between military civil defence personnel and civilian civil defence personnel which led to attributing prisoner-of-war-status to the former."[797]

Where such personnel is needed to provide for the needs of the inhabitants of occupied territory, or where they may nevertheless be expected to participate in hostilities or otherwise present a military threat upon release, they may of course continue to be interned.

(c.) Civilians

Similarly, the question arises whether and to what extent the two categories of civilians entitled to POW status may – like any other prisoner of war – be interned for the duration of hostilities. The answer in principle must be in the affirmative. Since they are prisoners of war, they may be interned on the basis of article 21 GC III. The Convention does not make their early release mandatory for the Interning Power. Their particular status as civilians, and the extent and reasons for their affiliation with the armed forces of a party to the conflict must however be taken into account when establishing the necessity to intern them.

As to persons who accompany the armed forces of a party to the conflict without actually being members thereof (article 4§A(4) GC III), the Power that captures them should take into account, in its decision to intern them, their functions and the potential security threat they may pose to its security or the potential damage they may cause to its military operations. A correct application of the principle of military necessity that underlies the internment provisions of GC III demands that persons referred to in article 4§A(4) GC III should only be

[795] Article 67§2 AP I.

[796] Article 67§1 provides that military personnel assigned to civil defence organizations are entitled to the same protection as civilian members of such organizations "provided that [...] such personnel do not perform any other military duties during the conflict; [...] are clearly distinguishable from the other members of the armed forces by prominently displaying the international distinctive sign of civil defence [...] are equipped only with light individual weapons for the purpose of maintaining order or for self-defence [...]; do not participate directly in hostilities, and do not commit, or are not used to commit, outside their civil defence tasks, acts harmful to the adverse Party; [...] perform their civil defence tasks only within the national territory of their Party."

[797] Sandoz et al., *Commentary to AP I and II* (1987), p. 800, with further references to the relevant extracts from the *Official Records 1974-1977*.

interned where this is necessary to counter any real military threat they may pose.[798] Article 13 HR 1907 (which has not been abrogated by GC III), provides that the individuals who follow an army without directly belonging to it (the list of examples is quasi-identical to that in article 4 GC III), may be interned when the power in whose hands they have fallen "think it expedient to detain" them. The term "expedient" indicates that such persons should only be interned where such internment is necessary to secure the military operations of the Interning Power and its allies. Already before, the International Institute of International Law, in its Manual on the Laws of War on Land, had stipulated that when such individuals fall into the hands of an enemy Power they may only "be detained for such length of time as is warranted by strict military necessity."[799]

The same argument can therefore be made for members of crews of the merchant marine and civil aviation of parties to the armed conflict and who qualify as prisoners of war (article 4§A(5) GC III). In this respect it is also useful to recall article 6 of the Hague Convention (XI) relative to certain Restrictions with regard to the Exercise of the Right of Capture in Naval War (1907), regarding the crews of enemy merchant ships:

> "The captain, officers, and members of the crew, when nationals of the enemy State, are not made prisoners of war, on condition that they make a formal promise in writing, not to undertake, while hostilities last, any service connected with the operations of the war."[800]

On the basis of the object and purpose of GC III, and in light of the relevant provisions of Hague Conventions (IV) and (XI) of 1907 and the right to liberty under general international law, it is submitted that a person referred to in article 4§A(4) and (5) GC III may only be interned on the basis of GC III where he or she poses a threat to the military operations of the Interning Power. In taking the decision to intern or to release on parole, the Interning Power must take into account the functions the person fulfilled and the fact that persons referred to in article 4§A(4) and (5) GC III are not necessarily bound by the laws and regulations on desertion, defection and parole that apply to members of the armed forces they accompany.[801] Where such persons do not pose a real military threat and their internment is not otherwise necessary, direct or early repatriation, where possible and if necessary on parole, must be preferred over internment.

---

[798] In the same sense: Shields-Delessert (1977), pp. 119-122.

[799] Oxford Manual (1880), article 22.

[800] The Convention only applies between the 31 Parties who have ratified it, namely Austria-Hungary, Belgium, Brazil, China, Denmark, El Salvador, Ethiopia, Fiji, Finland, France, Germany, Guatemala, Haiti, Japan, Liberia, Luxembourg, Mexico, the Netherlands, Nicaragua, Norway, Panama, Poland Portugal, Romania, South Africa, Spain, Sweden, Switzerland, Thailand, the UK and the USA (last verified on 16 December 2012).

[801] If these persons are contractually employed, they may also be subject to provisions similar to those in the laws and regulations of parole for members of the armed forces. This may be particularly relevant in the case of private military and security companies' personnel (*cf. supra*, note 732).

(d.) Participants in a levée en masse

Moreover, with regard to participants in a *levée en masse* (article 4§A(6) GC III), they are only entitled to prisoner of war status and thus can only be interned as such for the duration of the invasion phase.[802] Once the Interning Power establishes control over the territory and thus effectively becomes the Occupying Power, interned participants in the *levée en masse* should in principle be released. If the Interning Power has serious and legitimate reasons to think that individual participants in a *levée en masse* may continue to pose a security threat upon release, it may intern them on the basis of article 78 GC IV (*cf. infra*). If however, the spontaneous movement has transformed into an organized resistance movement which continues to operate in the territory now occupied, individuals who may reasonably be expected to join such a movement – in as far as that movement fulfils the conditions in article 4§A(2) – remain prisoners of war and may be interned on the basis of article 21 GC III.[803]

(e.) Child soldiers

In deciding on internment, the special situation of children[804] recruited into the armed forces of a party to the conflict should be taken into account, especially where they have been forcefully recruited.[805] Article 37(b) of the Convention on the Rights of the Child provides that "[t]he arrest, detention or imprisonment of a child [...] shall be used only as a measure of last resort and for the shortest appropriate period of time."[806] While child prisoners of war may be subject to internment on the basis of GC III, the long-term consequences of internment on their personal development and on their education should be taken

[802] In this sense, see also the following comment from Pictet, *Commentary GC III* (1960), p. 68: "It should, however, be emphasized that a mass levy can only be considered to exist during a very short period, i.e. during the actual invasion period."

[803] Pictet, *Commentary GC III* (1960), p. 68: "If resistance continues, the authority commanding the inhabitants who have taken up arms, or the authority to which they profess allegiance, must either replace them by sending regular units, or must incorporate them in its regular forces, Otherwise, the mass levy could not survive the total occupation of the territory which it has tried in vain to defend."

[804] The Convention on the Rights of the Child (CRC) defines the word child as "every human being below the age of eighteen years unless under the law applicable to the child, majority is attained earlier" (article 1 CRC). Article 77§2 AP I obliges parties to an armed conflict to take all feasible measures to ensure that children below the age of 15 are not recruited into their armed forces and do not participate directly in hostilities; the Optional Protocol to the Convention on the Rights of the Child on the Involvement of Children in Armed Conflict (2000) (hereinafter "CRC-OP") raises that age to 18 years old.

[805] Article 77 AP I oblige the parties to the conflict to take into account the special needs of women and children in captivity. Articles 37 and 38 of the Convention on the Rights of the Child also provide for specific rules for children deprived of liberty and more generally affected by armed conflict. On the specific issue of children deprived of liberty in armed conflict, see Happold, "Child Prisoners in War" in Scheipers (ed.), *Prisoners in War* (2010), who rightly points out (at p. 237) that "the rules [...] regulating their treatment when captured by an adverse party to a conflict, are sparse."

[806] In force since 1990, the CRC has been ratified by 193 States (last verified on 16 December 2012). Apart from the 1949 Geneva Conventions, it is the most widely ratified treaty of international law. It explicitly applies in situations of armed conflict (articles 2 and 38). Where the purpose of internment under GC III is to incapacitate the enemy's troops, the CRC however puts the best interest of the child first (article 2§1 CRC).

into account when deciding on whether internment is indeed the most appropriate measure to deal with them or whether other measures should be preferred.[807] In this sense it may also be useful to recall the obligation of States parties to the Optional Protocol to the Convention on the Rights of the Child to "take all feasible measures to ensure that persons within their jurisdiction recruited or used in hostilities contrary to this Protocol are demobilized or otherwise released from service."[808] While this obligation concerns mainly the demobilisation or release from service of one's own child soldiers, the article could also be relied upon to urge parties to the conflict to search for alternative measures to internment to deal with child prisoners of war. Parties to the conflict could seek cooperation from local or international humanitarian organizations to set up demobilization centres for captured child soldiers. Where this would be acceptable for family reasons, accommodation in neutral countries that can ensure their education and cater to their special needs should be preferred over internment.[809]

(f.) Prisoners with intelligence value

Finally, Canadian military doctrine referred to above pointed out that prisoners of war are a useful source of information, and the US has argued before the Inter-American Commission for Human Rights that the persons it briefly interned during the armed conflict with Grenada (1983) were "interrogated for the purpose of securing tactical information essential to the effective conduct of ongoing military operations and the security of US forces' personnel" and that interrogation "of POW's for tactical and security purposes during hostilities is a right clearly recognized and provided for in Article 17th of the Geneva Convention Relative to the Treatment of Prisoners of War."[810]

[807] See in this sense also UNHCR, EXCOM, Conclusion No. 107 (2007), operative paragraph b(xi): "detention can affect the physical and mental well-being of children and heighten their vulnerability, States should refrain from detaining children, and do so only as a measure of last resort and for the shortest appropriate period of time, while considering the best interests of the child." While it is not a party to the CRC, the US for example has asserted its right to hold enemy combatants in armed conflict for the duration of hostilities regardless of their age, but claims to have "a number of policies in place that attempt to limit the length of time a juvenile is held in detention. The average stay of a juvenile in detention is under 12 months. Although this is not true for every case, we do our best to ensure that the overwhelming majority of juveniles in detention are released within the 12-month time frame." (US, *Response to Questions Asked by the Committee on the Rights of the Child* (2008), §§28-35.

[808] Article 6§3 CRC-OP. The Protocol entered into force on 10 February 2002 and has been ratified by 150 parties to date (last verified on 16 December 2012).

[809] Note that article 7 CRC-OP prescribes that "States Parties shall cooperate in the implementation of the present Protocol, including in the prevention of any activity contrary to the Protocol and in the rehabilitation and social reintegration of persons who are victims of acts contrary to this Protocol, including through technical cooperation and financial assistance. Such assistance and cooperation will be undertaken in consultation with concerned States Parties and relevant international organizations. States Parties in a position to do so shall provide such assistance through existing multilateral, bilateral or other programmes, or, inter alia, through a voluntary fund established in accordance with the rules of the General Assembly." Note however that child prisoners of war in occupied territory may not be transferred to any other country but must be interned within the frontiers of the occupied country (article 49 GC IV).

[810] IAC°HR, *Coard v. USA* (1999), §26.

These statements are entirely correct, but it is useful to quote the relevant parts of article 17 GC III in full:

> "Every prisoner of war, when questioned on the subject, is bound to give only his surname, first names and rank, date of birth, and army, regimental, personal or serial number, or failing this, equivalent information. [...] No physical or mental torture, nor any other form of coercion, may be inflicted on prisoners of war to secure from them information of any kind whatever. Prisoners of war who refuse to answer may not be threatened, insulted, or exposed to any unpleasant or disadvantageous treatment of any kind."[811]

The UN Working Group on Arbitrary Detention and five of the Human Rights Council's Special Rapporteurs found that "The indefinite detention of prisoners of war [...] for purposes of continued interrogation is inconsistent with the provisions of the Geneva Conventions",[812] referring to article 17§3 GC III. Article 17 GC III does however not concern the lawful grounds for internment of prisoners of war, nor does it oblige parties to the conflict to release them before the end of hostilities; it merely prohibits the use of force or coercion to obtain information from an internee.[813] In light of the legal presumption that prisoners of war pose a threat justifying their internment for the duration of hostilities, the question of whether prisoners of war may be held for the mere purpose of interrogation does not really arise. Nevertheless, two nuances are in place. First, the repatriation and release of wounded and sick prisoners of war during the active phase of hostilities may not be delayed for the purpose of interrogation where this may further endanger their health.[814] Moreover, once the active phase of hostilities has come to an end, prisoners of war may not continue to be interned for the mere purpose of interrogation.[815]

1.2.3.6. Release and repatriation at the end of active hostilities

Internment of prisoners of war may not be indefinite.[816] Article 118 GC III provides that at the latest they "shall be released and repatriated without delay

---

[811] Article 17§§1 and 4 GC III. On the subject of interrogation of prisoners of war, see Pictet, *Commentary GC III* (1960), pp. 155-164; Rosas (1976), pp. 442-445; Levie (1978), pp. 106-109; and Geiss, "Name, Rank, Date of Birth, Serial Number and the Right to Remain Silent" (*IRRC* 2005).

[812] WGAD and Special Rapporteurs, *Situation of Detainees at Guantánamo Bay* (2006), §23. The Report, which deals explicitly with internment by US Authorities in Guantánamo Bay, noted that "Information obtained from reliable sources and the interviews conducted by the special procedures mandate holders with former Guantánamo Bay detainees confirm, however, that the objective of the ongoing detention is not primarily to prevent combatants from taking up arms against the United States again, but to obtain information and gather intelligence on the Al-Qaida network."

[813] It may be assumed the Report meant to refer to article 17§4 GC III rather than to article 17§3.

[814] Article 109§1 GC III, *cf. supra* section 1.2.3.3.

[815] Article 118 GC III, see also *infra* chapter II-3, section 3.2.2.2.

[816] See in this sense the comment made by Justice O'Connor who delivered the US Supreme Court's judgment in *Hamdi* (2004), p. 14, suggesting that in an "indefinite" war, internment of prisoners of war for the duration of the hostilities may no longer be lawful: "It is a clearly established principle of the law of war that detention may last no longer than active hostilities. [...] we understand Congress' grant of authority to detain for the duration of the relevant conflict, and our understanding is based on long-standing laws-of-war principles. If the practical circumstances of a given conflict are entirely unlike those of the conflicts that informed the development of the law of war, that understanding may

after the cessation of active hostilities."[817] As the Institute of International Law wrote in its Manual on the Law of War on Land: "[t]he reasons justifying detention of the captured enemy exist only during the continuance of the war."[818] Once active hostilities have ceased, the only legitimate reason to intern prisoners of war ceases to exist, since the general military threat posed by the enemy has come to an end and prisoners of war have no battlefield to return to or no hostilities to engage in.[819] The legal basis in international humanitarian law to intern them thus becomes extinct.[820] No new internment measures may be taken beyond that point in time. As to prisoners interned before the cessation of active hostilities, the legal basis to intern them under GC III will remain valid for the period necessary to organise their release and repatriation in accordance with the relevant provisions of the Convention.[821]

While the Convention thus allows for some flexibility for practical purposes,[822] the obligation to release and repatriate prisoners of war "without

unravel. But that is not the situation we face as of this date. Active combat operations against Taliban fighters apparently are ongoing in Afghanistan [...] The United States may detain, for the duration of these hostilities, individuals legitimately determined to be Taliban combatants who "engaged in an armed conflict against the United States."

[817] This is true for all prisoners of war, interned in the territory of the parties to the conflict, in occupied territory and in the territory of neutral powers. Article 24 HC VIII (1907) refers to the detention in neutral territory of belligerent ships and their personnel "as necessary to render the ship incapable of taking the sea *during the war*" (emphasis added). The pertinent provisions of HC V (1907) are silent on the issue of the duration of internment. The text of both Conventions must however be interpreted (in light of their object and purpose and their subsequent development by GC III) in the same sense as article 118 GC III. Therefore, military internees in neutral countries must also be released and repatriated without undue delay after the cessation of active hostilities.

[818] Oxford Manual (1880), introductory comment to article 73.

[819] See also Pictet, *Commentary GC III* (1960), pp. 546-547. See also Shields-Delessert (1977), pp. 47-72, detailing State practice and the negotiation history of GC III to support her conclusion that "[t]he corollary of the idea, developed during the eighteenth century, that captivity is merely a temporary device preventing the prisoner from returning to his own force and reentering the fight, is that he should be freed and returned to his own country once the reasons for his detention cease to exist, *i.e.* once the States fighting each other have laid down their arms" (at p. 47, original emphasis). She also refers to the position taken by the ICRC at the eve of the 1949 Diplomatic Conference: [the view that prisoners of war should be released and repatriated as soon as possible after the cessation of hostilities] was shared by the International Committee of the Red Cross which stressed that the aim of captivity was that of making the enemy helpless and that it should therefore cease as soon as the military situation no longer induced prisoners of war to seek to harm the detaining country, *i.e.* on the cessation of hostilities" (at p. 65, original emphasis).

[820] See also Rowe (2006), p. 152, note 180.

[821] See articles 118 and especially 119 and 122§§ 5 and 9 GC III, referring back in part to the rules on transfers of prisoners of war in articles 46-48 GC III. See also commentaries on these provisions in Pictet, *Commentary GC III* (1960), pp. 253-258, pp. 551-557 and pp. 577-580; Shields-Delessert (1977); Rosas (1976), pp. 426-430 and 470-490; and Levie (1978), pp. 187-194 and pp. 419-420. For a recent confirmation in international case law, see PCA (EECC), *Prisoners of War, Eritrea's Claim 17* (2003), §147.

[822] Article 118 GC III was adopted by majority rather than consensus, precisely because of the insistence of several delegations on the need to take into account material and economic obstacles to immediate release and repatriation of prisoners upon cessation of hostilities. Proposals for the article to explicitly include a "practical" safeguard clause were however rejected in order not to re-open the door for the kind of abusive delays that occurred at the end of the Second World War. In spite of the explicit provisions of article 118 GC III, undue delays in release and repatriation of prisoners of war

delay" after the cessation of active hostilities must be complied with in good faith and not be subject to any undue delay. Lack of reciprocal release and repatriation of prisoners by an adverse party is no justification for holding on to prisoners of war dependent on that power.[823] Lack of a formal agreement on the cessation of hostilities, or the absence of provisions in such an agreement to the effect of releasing and repatriating prisoners of war, does not justify any delays either. Likewise, the Convention encourages parties to the conflict to conclude agreements on the costs of returning their respective prisoners, but the conclusion of such agreements may in no circumstances justify any unreasonable delay.[824] Unjustifiable delay in the release and repatriation of prisoners of war amounts to a war crime, triggering the individual criminal responsibility of the commanders holding decision-making power in the matter.[825]

There is one exception to the obligation to release and repatriate prisoners of war at the end of active hostilities. Article 119§5 GC III provides that prisoners of war awaiting trial or convicted of an indictable offence may continue to be detained beyond the cessation of active hostilities for as long as permissible under the applicable penal law. It is unclear from the text of the law whether article 119§5 extends to war crimes and other international crimes.[826] It is submitted that

have at times continued to be a problem (e.g. during the Korean war in the 1950's, the Indo-Pakistani war in the 1970's and the Iran-Iraq war in the 1980's (for a discussion and summary of these cases, see Rosas (1976), pp. 487 and pp. 489-490, Bretton, "De quelques problèmes du droit de la guerre dans le conflit indo-pakistanais" (*ADFI* 1972) p. 201; Levie (1978), pp. 424-429; and Tavernier, "Combattants et non-combattants: L'expérience de la guerre entre l'Irak et l'Iran" (*RBDI* 1990)). See also PCA (EECC), *Prisoners of War, Eritrea's Claim 17* (2003), §147. The problems did not so much concern the rule as such, but rather the modalities of its implementation in practice (*cf. infra*).

823 See also Shields-Delessert (1977), p. 70 and pp. 129-131; Levie (1978), p. 419; PCA (EECC), *Prisoners of War, Eritrea's Claim 17* (2003), §148; and Fischer in Fleck (2008), p. 414.

824 Article 118§§2-3 GC III. The absence of agreement between co-belligerents or allied forces of different States on the release and repatriation of prisoners of war in their hands will not justify any delay, as each Interning Power is obliged in such case to unilaterally establish and execute a plan of repatriation (article 118§2). The obligations of GC III are incumbent on each Interning Power for the prisoners of war in its hands, without regard for alliances and even joint command and control over military operations. See also Rosas (1976), pp. 488-489; and Fischer in Fleck (2008), p. 414.

825 The 1949 GC only list unlawful confinement of civilians (to be understood as protected persons under GC IV, *cf. infra* chapter II-3, section 3.1) as a grave breach (article 147 GC IV). Article 2(g) ICTY Statute equally limits the war crime of unlawful confinement in this way. Article 85§4 (b) AP I however explicitly lists "unjustifiable delay in the repatriation of prisoners of war or civilians" as a grave breach and the ICC's Statute confirms that the war crime of unlawful confinement applies with regard to all persons protected by the Geneva Conventions, including prisoners of war (article 8§2(vii) ICC Statute. See also Dörmann (2003), p. 122. Internment or detention that continues beyond the time limit imposed by the relevant legal basis (in GC I, II, III or IV) will render an initially lawful deprivation of liberty arbitrary and unlawful, and – if subjected to obtaining something from another party to the conflict – may amount to hostage-taking (Henckaerts " Doswald-Beck (2005), Vol. I, p. 452). More generally on arbitrary and unlawful deprivation of liberty as a war crime, *cf. supra* chapter I-1, section 1.2.4.2.

826 For example, India justified its continued detention of Pakistani prisoners of war after the cessation of hostilities in 1971 claiming they were charged with war crimes (Rosas (1976), pp. 488-489; Bretton (*AFDI* 1972)). For other examples where the Interning Power invoked such an argument, see Levie (1978), pp. 351 and 420 and Sassòli & Bouvier (2006), Vol. II, pp. 1751-1752 (regarding the Balkans conflicts).

such continued detention must also be allowed, as long as it is based on a proper legal basis for pre-trial detention in the framework of commenced criminal proceedings or imposed as a sentence upon conviction. On humanitarian grounds however, persons should be allowed to purge long-term prison sentences in their country of origin on in a country where their family resides.

In practice however, the great majority of prisoners of war are released upon the cessation of active hostilities.[827] While the time limit for the internment of prisoners of war is clearly established in international law and reflects longstanding practice,[828] two issues remain open to some controversy.[829] On the one hand, the exact time of cessation of active hostilities may not always be easy to establish in practice and may thus be subject to disagreement. On the other hand, the text of the law remains ambiguous on whether prisoners of war may be repatriated to their country of origin against their will. Both issues therefore merit clarification.

(a.) Determination of active cessation of hostilities for release and repatriation

Provisions of international humanitarian law pre-dating the 1949 Geneva Conventions set the latest time to release and repatriate prisoners of war at the conclusion of peace, armistice or an agreement on the cessation of hostilities. Practice during the two World Wars showed however that the release and repatriation of prisoners of war suffered important delays well beyond the time where hostilities *de facto* had come to an end, due to the political difficulties in negotiating such agreements. The reasons advanced to justify delays could hardly be reconciled with the object and purpose of the law (HR 1907), but could nevertheless be successfully argued by sticking to a literal reading of its provisions.[830] It follows directly from the purpose of internment of prisoners of war itself – namely to prevent them from returning to the battlefield and resume fighting on behalf of the adverse party – that continued internment beyond the actual cessation of hostilities no longer serves that purpose and should therefore not be allowed.[831] The worrisome practice witnessed during the World Wars was the direct cause for the explicit provisions of article 118 GC III referred to

---

[827] See also Levie (1978), p. 417.

[828] The obligation in article 118 GC III is based on well-established practice since the mid-17th century (at least in Western Europe, see Carr-Greg (*War and Society* 1989) and is part of customary international humanitarian law (see article 73 Oxford Manual (1880); article 20 HR 1899/1907; article 75 GC 1929; Rule 128(A) of the ICRC's compilation of customary IHL: Henckaerts & Doswald-Beck (2005), Vol. I, pp. 452-456). See also Shields-Delessert (1977); pp. 47-72; Rosas (1976), pp. 53-54 and 486-490; Levie (1978), pp. 418-419; and Carr-Greg (*War and Society* 1989), pp. 97-98). GC III explicitly advanced the deadline for release from the end of conflict to the *de facto* cessation of active hostilities, leaving no room for political bargaining on the issue.

[829] They are important to have in mind, since they were the subject of substantive disagreement during the drafting process of the Third Geneva Convention (Pictet, *Commentary GC III* (1960), p. 7).

[830] For examples and further references, see Pictet, *Commentary GC III* (1960), p. 541; Rosas (1976); p. 486; Shields-Delessert (1977), pp. 70-71, 85-88, 90-96 and 102-103; and Levie (1978), p. 418.

[831] Pictet, *Commentary GC III* (1960), p. 541; Shields-Delessert (1977), p. 47; and Levie (1978), pp. 419 and 421 (footnote 133).

above. The results are clearly visible in post-1949 practice,[832] even if the practical aspects of the application of the norm have at times continued to be the subject of disagreement.[833] When such disagreement occurs, it is no longer due to an ambiguity in the law – as it was before 1949 – but rather to the practical difficulty of determining when active hostilities have effectively ceased.

Some contemporary international armed conflicts have been somewhat "on and off", alternating shorter periods of intense military confrontations with longer lulls in hostilities, and with prisoners of war interned throughout. Moreover, even when there is no such alternation, it is not always easy to decide at what point it is reasonable to exclude the renewal of hostilities in the near future.[834] This raises the question of whether each active period of hostilities should be regarded as a separate conflict and prisoners should be released immediately when they end, or whether one should take into account the overall political and military situation to define the duration of a single conflict, and prisoners may be interned until final closure of the conflict. While the overall situation will indeed be indicative of whether hostilities have ceased or not, one must be careful not to fall back on the type of political justifications for delaying release and repatriation of prisoners of war that were the direct reason for the clear language adopted in article 118 GC III.[835] The cessation of active hostilities is an objective test that relies solely on the facts on the ground; it must be made independent of any political agenda the parties to the conflict may have.[836]

Article 118 GC III is not the only provision of IHL that refers to the factual situation on the ground to establish the beginning and end of the rights and obligations of the parties to a conflict.[837] As is the case for these other provisions, compliance with article 118 GC III must be analyzed on a case-by-case basis. Nevertheless, the object and purpose of the norm must guide its application *in casu*: internment of prisoners of war is only justified as long as

---

[832] Rosas (1976), p. 487; Levie (1978), pp. 419-442; Rowe in Rowe (1993), p. 202 (including UK practice and UN Security Council practice); and Vance (2006), p. 336.
[833] *Cf. infra* note 834 and accompanying text.
[834] Rosas (1976), at pp. 487-488, describes the example of the 1967-1973 armed conflict in the Middle East. Other examples include the 1971 Indo-Pakistani war (Shields-Delessert (1977), pp. 102-103); the 1977-1988 conflict between Ethiopia and Somalia (ICRC, *Annual Report 1988*, pp. 25-26), and the 1998-2000 conflict between Ethiopia and Eritrea (PCA (EECC), *Prisoners of War, Eritrea's Claim 17* (2003), §145).
[835] See Rosas (1976), pp. 487-488 and Shield-Delessert (1977), pp. 106-111 (including proposals for a more flexible interpretation of the notion of "cessation of active hostilities" in article 118 GC III to avoid prisoners of war being held indefinitely) and pp. 126-129.
[836] Dinstein, *The Laws of War* (1983), p. 124; and Benvenisti, "Expert Opinion submitted to the Deputy Attorney General (Legislation) before the Foreign Affairs and Defence Committee of the Knesset (2000)", pp. 1-2, referred to in Moodrick-Even Khen, "Unlawful Combatants or Unlawful Legislation? An Analysis of the Imprisonment of Unlawful Combatants Law (2002)" (*Hebrew University of Jerusalem Research Papers* 2006), p. 21. Likewise, Fischer rejects as too subjective and prone to manipulation Schwarzenberger's oft-quoted definition that hostilities have ceased "if neither side expects a resumption of hostilities"; he insists "it is more appropriate to refer to the military circumstances accompanying the cessation of hostilities and to choose an objective approach" (Fischer in Fleck (2008), p. 415).
[837] See for example common article 2 GC and article 6 GC IV (*cf. supra* chapter I-2, section 2.2.1.1).

actual combat operations in which they could participate if released are ongoing, or can reasonably be expected to resurge in the near future.[838] From this purpose, it is possible to deduce a number of indicators that allow us to establish with more precision when active hostilities must be considered to have come to an end. Examples of such indicators include the military defeat of one or more parties to the conflict, the total surrender of one or more parties to the conflict, the absence of actual combat operations for an unusual duration of time (skirmishes could still occur but not as part of a general military strategy), general demobilization of troops, withdrawal of troops from the frontlines, official declarations of cease-fires, deployment of peace-keeping forces to monitor a ceasefire, and statements or communications on the conclusion of cease-fire or armistice agreements.[839] In case of doubt or disagreement on the facts or on the analysis of the situation, the parties to the conflict could refer to a neutral power or institution to help them assess the factual situation on the ground and the intentions of the parties to the conflict.[840] Prolonged negotiations on peace, armistice, or cessation of hostilities, or logistical and financial agreements on prisoner exchange are however explicitly disqualified as justifications for undue delays in release and repatriation (*cf. supra*).

---

[838] See also Shields-Delessert (1977), pp. 107-108: "Although it has been recognized that there are unstable situations in which the danger of a renewal of hostilities is likely, it is not possible to discard the spirit of the Geneva Convention. The underlying fundamental humanitarian principles in the entire Convention require that prisoners of war should not be interned indefinitely. One should not lose sight of the original purpose of captivity [...] as a temporary deprivation of liberty intended to weaken the military potential of the armed forces to whom the prisoner belongs. It would appear, however, that after a certain time spent in captivity, prisoners lose their military value. [...] These views imply that the protracted character of a conflict should be no excuse for retaining prisoners in captivity beyond reasonable time limits." In the same sense: Dinstein in *Liber Amoricum Pictet* (1984), pp. 43-44.

[839] Pictet, *Commentary GC III* (1960), pp. 547; Rosas (1976), pp. 488-489; Levie (1978), pp. 421, 426-429; Risius in Rowe (1993), p. 290; Rowe in Rowe (1993), p. 202; and Fischer in Fleck (2008), p. 415. The fact that a territory continues to be occupied does not necessarily mean that active hostilities have not ceased (*cf. supra* chapter I-2, section 2.2.1.3 and see also Fischer in Fleck (2008), p. 415). For a detailed study of the meaning of the words "cessation of active hostilities" for the purposes of article 118 GC III, see Shields-Delessert (1977), pp. 79-137 and pp. 104-105 in particular for factual indicators that hostilities have come to an end.

[840] The appointment of Protecting Powers (neutral States or the ICRC) in accordance with articles 8/8/8/9 and 10/10/10/11 GC I-IV and article 5 AP I could be useful in this perspective. Levie (1978), at pp. 17-20 and 428 elaborates a proposal to create an independent commission of facts, tasked with ensuring respect of the Geneva Conventions (and by extension their Additional Protocols). The proposal is similar to the idea behind the Independent Fact Finding Commission established under article 90 AP I. Levie explicitly favours recourse to an independent commission of experts (composed of representatives of the Foreign Offices of neutral States and of the ICRC) rather than to the United Nations Security Council (UNSC), since the later is inherently political nature and thus a less adequate forum for independent and impartial fact-finding (Levie (1978), p. 428). Fischer does not discard a potential role for the UN Security Council though (Fischer in Fleck (2008), p. 415). For an example of UNSC intervention in this sense, see UNSC, *Resolution 598* (1987) under Chapter VII of the UN Charter (operative paragraphs 1 and 3), demanding the parties to the Iran-Iraq war to immediately cease hostilities and release and repatriate their prisoners of war in accordance with article 118 GC III. For examples of ICRC intervention as a neutral intermediary regarding the release and repatriation of prisoners of war, see ICRC *Annual Report 1988* (Ethiopia/Somalia), and ICRC, *Annual Report 1990*, pp. 76-77 (Iran/Iraq); ICRC, *Annual Report 1991* (Iraq/Coalition), pp. 100-102.

As was mentioned before, arguments to justify a delay in the release and repatriation of prisoners of war must be made in good faith, and the expectation of a possible renewal of hostilities may not be used as a fig leaf for what really are political or economic reasons to delay the operation, such as retaining prisoners of war as bargaining chips in political negotiations of armistice or peace[841] or as a cheap labour force for post-conflict reconstruction.[842] Economic concerns may actually be an incentive to release and repatriate prisoners of war as soon as possible, as the responsibility for their maintenance and pay remains upon the Interning Power until their final release and repatriation[843] and usually generates important expenses and logistics.

(b.) forcible repatriation of prisoners of war to their country of origin[844]

Article 118 GC III and general State practice demand that prisoners of war be repatriated to their country of origin, i.e. the State on whose behalf they fought in the conflict.[845] Proposals to respect the individual prisoner's will in this matter were expressly rejected by the drafters of the Convention.[846] This general rule remains valid for a number of reasons: (1) repatriation to the country of origin is the restitution of the normal situation of the individual before capture; (2) such repatriation is usually the wish of the majority of prisoners of war who want to return to their homes, families and normal life; and (3) as members of a State's armed forces, individual prisoners of war have a duty of allegiance to the State they serve, compelling them to rejoin their armed forces as soon as released.[847]

---

841 A practice that would amount to hostage-taking, *cf. infra* chapter II-3, section 3.2.2.2.

842 Levie (1978) suggests India's delay in releasing Pakistani prisoners of war after the *de facto* end of the conflict in the early 1970's should at least partly be understood as being part of its efforts to force particular terms of a peace agreement on its defeated Pakistani adversary (at p. 427). He also refers to the "cheap labour" argument as an impermissible reason to delay release and repatriation of prisoners of war (at p. 429). The issue of release and repatriation of prisoners of war is also discussed, with reference to the final agreement signed between India, Pakistan and Bangladesh in 1974 (*ILM* 1974), pp. 501-505, see also Bretton (*AFDI* 1972) and Shields-Delessert (1977), p. 127. Generally, see Shields-Delessert (1977), pp. 132-133; and Fischer in Fleck (2008), p. 414.

843 Articles 5§1, 15 and 66 GC III.

844 This section deals with forcible repatriation of prisoners of war at the end of hostilities. Prisoners of war who are repatriated during the active phase of hostilities may never be repatriated against their will. Article 109§3 GC III applies to all prisoners of war repatriated before the end of hostilities, see also Pictet, *Commentary GC III* (1960), pp. 512-513 and Sassòli (*YIIHL* 1985), p. 31.

845 See in this sense the following extract from the report of the Conference of Government Experts of 1947, preparatory to the 1949 Diplomatic Conference: "As regards the practical aspect of repatriation, it was considered that [...] repatriation should be to the home countries of PW" (ICRC, *Report of the Conference of Government Experts 1947*, at p. 243). It is membership in a particular State's armed forces, and not nationality of that State, that determines the "country of origin" for the purposes of article 118 GC III. In the same sense: Shields-Delessert (1977), p. 138.

846 *Final Record 1949*, Vol. II-A, p. 462; Pictet, *Commentary GC III* (1960), p. 542; Rosas (1976), pp. 480-484; Shields-Delessert (1977), pp. 68-69; and Levie (1978), p. 423.

847 For example, the Canadian *National Defence Act* (article 76) considers guilty of a service offence punishable with life imprisonment "[e]very person who (*a*) by want of due precaution, or through disobedience of orders or wilful neglect of duty, is made a prisoner of war, (*b*) having been made a prisoner of war, fails to rejoin Her Majesty's service when able to do so, or (*c*) having been made a prisoner of war, serves with or aids the enemy."

However, the question arises whether a prisoner of war who fears for his life, liberty or physical integrity upon return to his country of origin may be forcibly repatriated if such a risk indeed exists. Such an exceptional situation may arise for example when the political situation in the prisoners' country of origin has changed to the extent that certain groups of persons – to which the prisoner belongs – have become the subject of persecution after the end of the conflict. Moreover, certain State armies do not take lightly to combatants who were captured or have surrendered instead of dying in combat.[848] An interpretation of article 118 GC III in light of the object and purpose of the Geneva Conventions, subsequent normative developments in general international law, evolutions in State practice and international case law supports a negative answer to the question of forcible repatriation in such cases.[849]

First and foremost, the object and purpose of the Convention is to protect prisoners of war from arbitrary action at the hands of the enemy and to preserve their human dignity.[850] If the life and/or human dignity of a prisoner of war are put at serious risk by repatriation, article 118 GC III cannot be interpreted in a fashion that would sanction a forcible return.[851]

---

848 For example, a US soldier found guilty of "shameful surrender" is punishable with the death penalty (US, *Uniform Code of Military Justice*, article 899§2). See also *infra* with regard to the almost certain death that awaited Chinese and North-Korean prisoners of war upon repatriation to their home country.

849 See also Pictet, *Commentary GC III* (1960), pp. 542-549; Rosas (1976), pp. 478-486; Levie (1978), pp. 421-426; Meron (2006), pp. 42-45; Rowe (2006), pp. 144-145; Sassòli in *Liber Amoricum Malinverni* (2007), p. 392; Sassòli & Bouvier (2006), Vol. I, p. 159. Shields-Delessert, in her detailed study of article 118 GC III, published in 1977, concludes that article 118 GC III does not allow to take into account the prisoner's refusal to return, and imposes an unconditional obligation on the Interning Power to repatriate prisoners of war to their country of origin (at p. 174). Nevertheless, our argument – that this general rule is subject to at least one exception in cases where the prisoner faces a real risk of persecution, ill-treatment, or arbitrary deprivation of life or liberty upon return to that country – is not incompatible with the provisions of the GC itself and even if it would be, the subsequent developments in international law and practice have by now (more than 40 years after Shields-Delessert wrote her study) either amended or superseded article 118 GC III in order to include such an exception. On the basis of her study and arguments (and especially her thoughts on the possible impact of international human rights law), we think it likely that Shields-Delessert herself would come to the same conclusion today.

850 As we have mentioned in the Introduction, the object and purpose of the Convention is not explicitly expressed in the treaty (which does not have a preamble stating the motives of its drafters). A draft preamble discussed in great detail by the Committee in charge of GC III read, in part, as follows: "Respect for the personality and dignity of human beings constitutes a universal principle which is binding even in the absence of any contractual undertaking. Such a principle demands that, in time of war, all those not actively engaged in the hostilities and all those placed *hors de combat* by reason of sickness, wounds, capture, or any other circumstance, shall be given due respect and have protection from the effects of war." No preamble was ultimately included in any of the Geneva Conventions, but the essential humanist and protective purposes for which the Conventions were drawn up was not subject to disagreement and are reflected in their provisions; for examples, see Pictet, *Commentary GC III*, pp. 14-16.

851 In the same sense: Kunz, "Die koreanische Kriegsgefangenenfrage" (*AdV* 1954), p. 420. According to Kunz, such an interpretation does not depart either from the text or the spirit of the Convention.

Secondly, while it is true that exceptions to the rule of repatriation to the country of origin were rejected by the drafters of article 118 GC III, they seem to have had in mind mainly situations in which the prisoner refuses repatriation for personal, economic or political-ideological reasons, or to escape prosecution and punishment for ordinary criminal offences committed in their country of origin before their enrolment in the armed forces and deployment to the battlefield. These situations are very different than those where a prisoner of war refuses repatriation for fear for his or her life, liberty or physical integrity. From the debates in 1949, it is not clear that States wanted to exclude the possibility to refuse repatriation in such cases.[852] To the contrary, Pictet highlights that the Convention aims to protect prisoners against pressure or propaganda by the Interning Power aimed at convincing them to refuse repatriation, which may fit the post-conflict political discourse of the Interning Power (e.g. to invoke the cruelty of its enemy to justify the fact of having gone to war in the first place).[853]

Subsequent State and other international practice support the interpretation that such was indeed not the intention, and that prisoners who feared for their life or limb in their country of origin could not be forcibly repatriated. The following examples are not intended to be exhaustive, but are particularly relevant in light of the important numbers of prisoners of war captured and interned by the parties to the conflict, and the clarification in State practice on the nature of the obligation to repatriate under article 118 GC III.

Only three years after the adoption of the Geneva Conventions, the UN General Assembly affirmed that "force shall not be used against prisoners of war to prevent or effect their return to their homelands."[854] The resolution was

---

[852] See also Sassòli (*YIIHL* 1985), pp. 31-32, with reference to Garcia-Mora, *International Law and Asylum as a Human Right* (1956), p. 114; and to Shields-Delessert (1977), pp. 168-172. This was also the position of the UN Command in Korea in 1952 (Shields-Delessert (1977), p. 162, see also *infra*). The issue was already the subject of debate during the 1947 *Conference of Government Experts*, as is clear from the report on the Conference (at p. 245): "The ICRC also drew attention to the distressing cases of PW repatriated against their will (which sometimes led to suicide), and of PW anxious to be sent home to another country than their country of origin, usually for family or residential reasons. The Commission did not think it possible to make exceptions in view of these special cases, owing to the difficulties they would involve, particularly in countries with strict immigration laws. *While recommending that these particular situations should be settled by the Governments concerned*, the Commission decided to maintain the general principle of repatriation of all PW nationals of a given country to that country" (emphasis added). For the discussions on what eventually became article 118 GC III during the Diplomatic Conference itself, see *Final Record 1949*, Vol. I, p. 96, Vol. II-A, pp. 295-296, 324, 337-338, 449-454, 462, 525-527, 573-574, 599, and Vol. II-B, pp. 316-318. For a summary of the debates, see Rosas (1976), pp. 482 and 485-486 and Levie (1978), p. 424; and for a detailed scrutiny, see Shields-Delessert (1977), pp. 167-175.

[853] Pictet, *Commentary GC III* (1960), pp. 548-549; see also Mayda, "The Korean Repatriation Problem and International Law" (*AJIL* 1953), p. 433 and Charmatz & Wit, "Repatriation of Prisoners of War and the 1949 Geneva Convention" (*YLJ* 1953), pp. 402-405. For examples of such "political struggle over prisoners of war", see Rosas (1976), pp. 434-439.

[854] UNGA, *Resolution 610 (VII)* (1952), §2. It had adopted a similar position previously in relation to the Greek civil war (1946-1949) and WW II, see Levie, (1978), p. 425. Note that GC III had not entered into force between the parties to the Korean conflict at the time and that any conclusions drawn from that experience could not at that time offer a conclusive interpretation of article 118 GC III. These conclusions are nevertheless useful for the present purposes in that they have been

adopted in course of the armistice negotiations in the Korean War, where the exact meaning of article 118 GC III was the subject of disagreement.[855] China and North Korea argued it obliged the Interning Power to repatriate all prisoners of war, if need be forcibly, while the UN Command in Korea opined it merely required the repatriation of those prisoners of war willing to return and could not oblige a Interning Power to repatriate prisoners likely to face political persecution upon their return.[856] The General Assembly found the latter position to be "in accordance with [GC III]" and "the well-established principles and practice of international law" and following an agreement reached between the parties to the conflict, important numbers of prisoners of war were not forcibly repatriated.[857] The following submissions by the UN Command and the French representative in the UN General Assembly at the time support our argument that the object and purpose of GC III do not allow an interpretation of article 118 GC III that would result in the forcible repatriation of a prisoner of war, especially where the latter would be at risk of political persecution or arbitrary deprivation of life:

> "There is no specific provision in the Third Geneva Convention regarding prisoners of war who do not desire repatriation at the end of hostilities. But nothing in the letter and the spirit of the Convention requires forcible repatriation. [...] Forcible repatriation introduces an element foreign to and not implied by the normal conception of repatriation. A detailed study of the Convention "irresistibly" leads to the conclusion that it has been drawn up to protect individual rights."[858]

> "It would be a distortion of both aim and scope of the provisions of the Geneva convention to turn the inalienable right of all prisoners to repatriation, into an obligation to use force or violence in order to repatriate them against their will. That principle could not be extended in such a way as to defeat its own purpose."[859]

Attempts to deal with the fate of non-repatriated prisoners of war were made, but with little success (*cf. infra*). To avoid the problem of forced repatriation, Allied forces, conscious of the consequences some prisoners might face when returned home, are even said to have organized a mass flight of North Korean prisoners of war.[860]

confirmed in subsequent State practice on the application of article 118. In this sense, they set into motion a trend towards a prohibition of forcible repatriation of prisoners of war who are at risk of political persecution, ill-treatment or arbitrary deprivation of liberty, a trend that has been confirmed in recent State practice but also by developments in general international law (which gives expression to the *opinio juris* of States).

855 For a summary of the main arguments and the debates, see Charmatz & Wit (*YLJ* 1953); Mayda (*AJIL* 1953); Levie (1978), pp. 424-425, with further references to abundant literature there; and Rosas (1976), pp. 478-480.

856 Rowe in Rowe (1993), pp. 202-203. For a more detailed account, see Shields-Delessert (1977), pp. 157-163.

857 UNGA, *Resolution 610 (VII)* (1952), §1.

858 Position of the UN Command in Korea, as summarized in Shields-Delessert (1977), pp. 162-163.

859 Position of France in the UN General Assembly, as summarized in Shields-Delessert (1977), p. 163.

860 Kunz (*AdV* 1954), pp. 416-417: "Von den anti-kommunistischen Kriegsgefangenen brachen auf alliierter Seite 27 000 aus. Das U.N. Command gab zu, dass diese Aktion von Südkorea im geheimen geplant und sorgfältig vorbereitet war; die südkoreanischen Wachen in den alliierten

Probably in light of the experience of the Korean War, South Korea included the following paragraph in a declaration made at the time of its ratification of Additional Protocol I to the Geneva Conventions (1982):

> "in relation to paragraph 4 (b) of Article 85 of Protocol I, a party detaining prisoners of war may not repatriate its prisoners agreeably [sic] to their openly and freely expressed will, which shall not be regarded as unjustifiable delay in the repatriation of prisoners of war constituting a grave breach of this Protocol".[861]

The US Department of Defence, in its official report to Congress on the conduct of the 1990-91 Gulf War outlined its position on the issue as follows:

> "Article 118 [GC III] establishes a POW's right to be repatriated. In conflicts since the [GC III] adoption, *this principle has become conditional*: *Each POW must consent to repatriation rather than being forced to return*. This proved to be the case after hostilities in this war ended."[862]

It further explained how the issue was dealt with in practice and what alternative solution was adopted for those prisoners of war who refused to be repatriated:

> "In March, Coalition forces and Iraqi military representatives signed an agreement for the repatriation of prisoners of war, to be conducted under ICRC auspices. [...] No EPW [enemy prisoner of war] was forcibly repatriated. Coalition forces identified to the ICRC those Iraqi EPWs not desiring repatriation. Once an Iraqi EPW scheduled for repatriation reached the repatriation site, the ICRC reconfirmed his willingness to be repatriated. Those who indicated they no longer desired to return to Iraq were returned to the custody of the detaining power. On 4 March, Iraq released the first group of 10 Coalition prisoners of war, six of whom were US personnel. The United States simultaneously released 294 Iraqi EPWs for repatriation to Iraq. Of the 294, 10 refused repatriation at the repatriation site and were returned to US custody. Iraq and the Coalition forces continued repatriation actions through August 1991, at which time 13,318 Iraqi EPWs who refused repatriation remained under Saudi control. On 5 August 1991, Iraqi EPWs still refusing repatriation were reclassified as refugees by the United States (in coordination with Saudi Arabia and the ICRC), concluding application of [GC III]. When US custody of Iraqi EPWs ended, ICRC officials informed the 800th Military Police Brigade (PW) that the treatment of Iraqi EPWs by US forces was the best compliance with

---

Kriegsgefangenenlagern setzten der Massenflucht kein Hindernis entgegen. [...] Es wurde zwar versprochen, Maßnahmen für die Wiederergreifung der geflohenen Kriegsgefangenen zu treffen, zugleich aber mitgeteilt, dass diese praktisch erfolglos bleiben würden, da jene Kriegsgefangenen bereits unter der Zivilbevölkerung Südkoreas, die ihnen jede Hilfe gewährte, verschwunden wären" (our English summary: about 27.000 anti-communist POW broke out of an allied prisoner camp, without encountering any resistance from the South-Korean guards; while the allied forces undertook to search for them, they conceded there was little chance for succeeding in this endeavour as the prisoners had vanished quickly into the civilian population); Vance (2006), pp. 226-228; Rosas (1976), p. 479.

[861] The declaration is available in the ICRC's online *Treaty Database*.

[862] US, DoD, *Final Report to Congress on the Conduct of the Persian Gulf War* (1992), p. 707 (emphasis added).

> [GC III] by any nation in any conflict in history. Coalition measures to comply with [GC III] had no adverse effect on planning and executing military operations; if anything, by encouraging the surrender of Iraqi military personnel, they improved those operations."[863]

Likewise, the UK did not forcibly repatriate Iraqi prisoners of war who expressed an unwillingness to return:

> "Whilst in the Maryhill prisoners-of-war camp, three Iraqi prisoners of war expressed a wish not to be repatriated to Iraq at the end of hostilities. They were interviewed by a British Army lawyer who explained to them the procedure that would be adopted by the International Committee of the Red Cross representatives when they were transferred to the Saudi authorities, via a US prisoner-of-war camp. On transfer to the US the names of these three individuals were notified to the International Committee of the Red Cross. Subsequently, representatives of the International Committee of the Red Cross interviewed all Iraqi prisoners of war who expressed an unwillingness to return to Iraq and took the view that they should be considered as refugees and warned them of the difficulty in finding a country of asylum. On 26 April King Fahd of Saudi Arabia offered to 'take in 50,000 Iraqi refugees and prisoners of war including army deserters.'"[864]

Moreover, it is now official UK military doctrine not to repatriate prisoners of war against their will.[865]

The Eritrea Ethiopia Claims Commission set up in the Permanent Court of Arbitration, with regard to prisoners of war, found that "there must be adequate procedures to ensure that individuals are not repatriated against their will."[866] And in the Dayton peace agreement for Bosnia-Herzegovina, Bosnia-Herzegovina, Croatia and the Federal Republic of Yugoslavia agreed that "the Parties shall take no reprisals against any prisoner or his/her family in the event that a prisoner refuses to be transferred" and tasked the ICRC "to privately interview each prisoner [...] prior to his or her release for the purpose of implementing and monitoring the [release and repatriation] plan, *including determination of the onward destination of each prisoner*."[867]

Academic and other legal experts, based on both research and experience, have confirmed that there is no legal obligation on parties to a conflict to forcibly

---

[863] US, DoD, *Final Report to Congress on the Conduct of the Persian Gulf War* (1992), pp. 705-708. On the release and repatriation operation of Iraqi POW, see also ICRC, *Annual Report 1991*, pp. 100-102.

[864] Rowe in Rowe (1993), p. 203, with references to *ICRC Bulletin no. 184* (May 1991) and articles in *The Times* of 27 April 1991 and 25 February 1992; Risius in Rowe (1993), p. 301: "Despite the unqualified nature of Article 118 GC III, the duty to repatriate prisoners of war at the conclusion of active hostilities should accordingly not be regarded as absolute. This was accepted by the Ministry of Defence, and steps were taken to devise a procedure which would ensure a proper balance between the duty to repatriate and the each prisoner's own wishes."

[865] UK, *JDP 1-10.1* (2006), §297 at p. 2-26.

[866] PCA (EECC), *Prisoners of War, Eritrea's Claim 17* (2003), §§143-163 (in part 8 on delayed repatriation of prisoners of war) and in particular §147 *in fine*.

[867] Article 9 of the General Framework Agreement for Peace in Bosnia-Herzegovina (1995), "Annex 1A: Military Aspects of the Peace Settlement" (*ILM* 1996), p. 99.

repatriate prisoners of war.[868] Where prisoners object to repatriation, and especially where such refusal is based on a well-founded fear of persecution, they may not be forcibly repatriated to their country of origin.

Fischer claims that State practice on the issue is inconsistent, but his only reference is to a study dating from 1952.[869] State and other international practice since that time have continued to evolve and come to consolidate the position taken by the ICRC since before 1949 and by the UN in the wake of the Korean war, namely that article 118 GC III does not oblige a party to the conflict to forcibly repatriate prisoners of war who fear for their life or limb upon return to their country of origin. On the contrary, general international law has come to prohibit States from forcibly returning or transferring any person to a State where it may reasonably expect that that person will be subject to persecution, arbitrary deprivation of life or liberty, torture or other forms of inhuman, cruel and degrading treatment.[870]

---

868 Shapiro (*BYIL* 1952), p. 324; Baxter, "Asylum to Prisoners of War" (*BYIL* 1953), pp. 489-498; Pictet, *Commentary GC III* (1960), p. 546; Rosas (1976), p. 481; Dinstein in *Liber Amoricum Pictet* (1984), p. 41; Sassòli (*YIIHL* 1985), pp. 33-35; Risius in Rowe (1993), p. 301; Rowe in Rowe (1993), pp. 202-203; Meron, "The Humanization of Humanitarian Law" (*AJIL* 2000), p. 253; Rowe (2006), p. 145 ("It is accepted that, despite the mandatory language of Article 118 [GC III], a State is under no legal obligation forcibly to repatriate prisoners of war"); Gillard, "There's No Place like Home: States' Obligations in Relation to Transfers of Persons" (*IRRC* 2008), p. 710. In the older literature, one finds authors who disagreed with this conclusion (Rosas (1976), p. 507 mentions Draper (*The Red Cross Conventions*, (1958), p. 69) and Greenspan (*The Modern Law of Warfare* (1959), pp. 612-613). Note that those authors who are reticent or disagree on allowing for any exceptions to the general rule of repatriation in article 118 GC III are motivated essentially by concerns about abuse by the Interning Power, rather than by a rejection of the general principle of modern international law that no person may be returned to a country where he or she would be at risk of torture, ill-treatment, or arbitrary deprivation of life or liberty, see for example Rosas (1976), pp. 483-484. Sassòli (*YIIHL* 1985), p. 35, comes to the same conclusion.

869 Fischer in Fleck (2008), p. 416, he refers to Sassòli (*YIIHL* 1985), p. 32 but Sassòli himself refers to Shapiro (*BYIL* 1952). In the article Fleck refers to, Sassòli added however that State practice also showed that prisoners of war who opposed repatriation, often regarded as deserters by the Power they depend on, were usually not repatriated unless the Power they depended on would grant them an amnesty (Sassòli (*YIIHL* 1985), pp. 32-33 with reference to Shapiro (*BYIL* 1952) and other more recent literature); see also Levie (1978), p. 421 and Shields-Delessert (1977), pp. 185-192). In 1985, Sassòli summed up State practice and the scholarly debate on the article 118 GC III as follows: "one can say there is no internationally recognized rule of customary law which *prohibits* the repatriation of prisoners of war who refuse to be repatriated for fear of persecution. At the same time, there is no rule either in treaty law or in customary law which *compels* States to repatriate by force prisoners of war who refuse to be repatriated for fear of persecution in their own country" (Sassòli (*YIIHL* 1985), p. 33, original italics). On the same issue, Levie, writing in 1978, said it remained to be seen whether the practice of Korean War would be repeated in future conflicts (Levie (1978), p. 426). The examples from the more recent Gulf War and the Ethiopia-Eritrea conflict referred to above and the impact of recent developments in international human rights and refugee law show a consolidation of the practice that initiated shortly after the adoption of the 1949 Geneva Conventions.

870 This is the direct consequence of the evolution of general international law on this matter, which has superseded the 1949 IHL norms on the issue. In the same sense: Rosas (1976), at p. 484: "[a]n exception [i.e. an exception to forced repatriation of prisoners of war] should apparently be provided for situations when it is obvious that the prisoner would face consequences in his own country that would mean flagrant violations of basic human rights [...]. However, it is not necessary, nor even desirable, to find the basis for such an exception in the provisions of the Third Convention alone. Instead, it seems possible to base the exception on general human rights law, it being

While recognizing and defending the rationale behind the general obligation to repatriate prisoners of war at the end of active hostilities, the ICRC has always referred to "general principles of international law for the protection of the human being" to justify exceptions[871] to this general rule where "there are serious reasons for fearing that a prisoner of war who is himself opposed to being repatriated may, after his repatriation, be the subject of unjust measures affecting his life or liberty, especially on grounds of race, social class, religion or political views."[872] These "general principles of international law" include what has become known as the principle of non-refoulement, precluding States from expelling, extraditing or otherwise returning a person to another State, where there are substantial grounds to believe that the person would be subject to torture, cruel, inhuman or degrading treatment, arbitrary deprivation of life or liberty on the account of his or her particular characteristics, such as ethnicity, nationality, religion or political opinion.[873]

Like the absolute prohibitions of torture and other forms of inhuman, cruel and degrading treatment and of arbitrary deprivation of life or liberty,[874] the corollary prohibition of return or expulsion in any manner, to a country where the individual be subject to such treatment, constitutes a peremptory norm of international law.[875]

---

understood that the latter would on this point override article 118 of the Third Convention. [...] It is also possible to contend that in such exceptional cases there is not only a right, but also a duty not to repatriate the prisoners in question." And Meron (2006), p. 45: "[p]ractice informed by human rights has in fact recast Article 118". It is also generally accepted that deserters may not be repatriated against their will when they will face persecution, ill-treatment or arbitrary deprivation of their life or liberty (Sassòli (*YIIHL* 1985), pp. 33 and 35-36 with further references there).

[871] To be noted that under article 109§3 GC III, wounded & sick prisoners of war who are eligible for repatriation during the hostilities, may not be so returned against their will. While this rule also applies to able-bodied prisoners of war (they may be more at risk upon repatriation while hostilities are ongoing), it does not solve the question of repatriation at the end of active hostilities.

[872] Pictet, *Commentary GC III* (1960), p. 547. The ICRC has consistently invoked the principle of *non-refoulement* in its operations as a neutral intermediary between parties to a conflict for the repatriation of prisoners of war or other persons deprived of liberty in relation to the conflict. See for example its *Annual Report 1989*, p. 87 (Iran/Iraq), *Annual Report 1991*, p. 100 (1990-1 Gulf War), *Annual Report 2006*, p. 97 and *Annual Report 2007*, p. 102 (Ethiopia/Eritrea).

[873] For an extensive analysis of the principle of *non-refoulement* in international law, see Gillard (*IRRC* 2008); and Lauterpacht & Bethlehem, "The Scope and Content of the Principle of *Non-Refoulement*: Opinion" in Feller, Türk & Nicholson (2003). Specifically with regard to persons deprived of their liberty, see also Rodley & Pollard (2009), pp. 166-179. The UN WGAD has found that the principle of non-refoulement includes situations where an individual is at risk of arbitrary deprivation of liberty in the country of destination (WGAD, *Annual Report 2006*, §§47-48). For the impact of the ECtHR's judgment on the merits in *Al-Saadoon & Mufdhi v. UK* (2010), *cf. infra*.

[874] See article 33 of the 1951 UN Refugee Convention; article 3 of the Convention Against Torture (CAT); common article 3 of the Geneva Conventions; articles 3, 5 and 9 UDHR; articles 6, 7 and 9 ICCPR; articles 4, 6 and 7 ACHR; articles 2, 3 and 5 ECHR; articles 4, 5 and 6 ACHPR; articles 2-3 and 20 Cairo Declaration on Human Rights in Islam; articles 5, 8 and 13 Arab Charter on Human Rights; and articles 2, 3 and 5 CIS Convention for their most relevant expression for present purposes. On the peremptory character of the prohibitions, see HRC, *General Comment 20* (1992), §§3 and 9 (with regard to torture and other forms of ill-treatment); and ICJ, *Nicaragua v. US* (1986), §§218-220 (with regard common article 3). With regard to arbitrary deprivation of liberty: HRC, *General Comment 29* (2001), §§11-15; WGAD; *Annual Report 2007*, §67; Brownlie (1998), p. 575; Rodley & Pollard (2009), p. 478; and Naert (2010), p. 626, *cf.* also *supra* chapter I-1.

[875] HRC, *General Comment 20* (1992), §9; Sassòli (*YIIHL* 1985), p. 34 (with reference to judgments

The absolute and peremptory character of these norms dictates their equal application to prisoners of war.[876] Sassòli has even found that if any normative conflict of these norms would exist with article 118 GC III under a strict interpretation, it must be resolved in favour of the hierarchically higher norm: *lex superior* (non-refoulement) *derogat lex inferior* (article 118 GC III).[877]

In this context, an interesting and important question arises regarding prisoners of war who upon return to their country of origin are likely to face the death penalty, as a punishment for defection, desertion or any other offence they may have committed in the course of the conflict under their domestic criminal law. The death penalty as such is not (yet) prohibited in international humanitarian law.[878] While many States have abolished the death penalty or imposed a moratorium on its execution, in others it remains in place, and particularly for serious crimes such as war treason, defection or desertion.[879]

---

from the Swiss Federal Tribunal); Lauterpacht & Bethlehem in Feller, Türk & Nicholson (2003), §§252-253; Sassòli in *Liber Amoricum Malinverni* (2007), p. 392; Gillard (*IRRC* 2008).

[876] In the same sense: Sassòli (*YIIHL* 1985), pp. 34-36; Rowe (2006), p. 145. Even Shields-Delessert (1977), at p. 196 concedes that international human rights instruments, "by proclaiming the right for a human person to 'life, liberty' and 'security', the right not to 'be subjected to torture or to cruel, inhumane or degrading treatment or punishment', the right 'to leave any country, including his own and to return to his country' and specifically providing for the right 'to seek and enjoy in other countries asylum from persecution' would appear to limit the unconditional right a State has to the repatriation of all its prisoners."

[877] Sassòli in *Liber Amoricum Malinverni* (2007), p. 392: "Entretemps, le principe de non-refoulement est toutefois reconnu comme règle du *jus cogens*, et doit prévaloir en tant que *lex superior* sur l'obligation de rapatrier du DIH, qui est interétatique et n'appartient pas, contrairement à bien d'autres règles du DIH, au *jus cogens*."

[878] It is to a certain extent officially sanctioned as a penalty for particularly serious crimes (see article 100 GC III and article 686§2-4 GC IV). Articles 76§3 AP I, 77§5 API and 6§4 AP II however prohibit the execution of the death penalty on pregnant women and mothers with dependent children and prohibits its imposition on children who were less than 18 years old when the offence punishable with the death penalty was committed.

[879] Two thirds of the world's nations have abolished the death penalty entirely, others retain if for particularly serious crimes. Only about 35 States still resort to the death penalty today. The international community has adopted four international treaties specifically providing for the abolition of the death penalty, one universal and three regional ones. The UN General Assembly has called for a moratorium on the use of the death penalty (*Resolution 62/149* (2007) and *Resolution 63/168* (2008)). Regional inter-governmental organizations and human rights bodies have called for a moratorium on executions as a step towards global abolition of the death penalty (e.g. African Commission on Human and Peoples' Rights, *Resolution Calling on State Parties to the African Charter on Human and Peoples' Rights to Observe the Moratorium on the Death Penalty* (2008); OSCE, *Resolution on a Moratorium on the Death Penalty and towards its Abolition* (2009). Under articles 2 and 15 ECHR, the death penalty was still authorized as a sentence following a fair trial for a serious crime, and in times of war or other public emergencies threatening the life of the nation. On 1 July 2003, Protocol No. 13 to the ECHR (2002) entered into force, effectively amending those articles and making the prohibition of the death penalty absolute (article 1 prohibits the death penalty in all circumstances, articles 2 and 3 explicitly provide that the prohibition is not subject to either derogation or reservation). The ECHR, as modified by Protocol No. 13, now effectively precludes States from extraditing, transferring or returning a person to any State where he or she may face the death penalty (ECtHR (Grand Chamber), *Al-Saadoon & Mufdhi v. UK* (2010), §123). For facts and figures on the death penalty in State practice, see the UN Secretary-General's quinquennial reports of the status of the death penalty (the most recent is that of 18 December 2009, entitled *Capital Punishment and Implementation of the Safeguards Guaranteeing Protection of the Rights of those Facing the Death Penalty* (2009)); and http://www.amnesty.org/en/death-penalty.

The question whether a party to an armed conflict may forcibly repatriate prisoners of war, who would face the death penalty upon their return, cannot always be answered in the negative. First, the general principle of non-refoulement only prohibits return where there is a risk of *arbitrary* deprivation of life. On this basis one could argue that the principle only precludes repatriation of prisoners of war where there is a substantial risk that the death penalty is imposed without previous judgment pronounced by a regularly constituted court affording essential judicial guarantees.[880] But there are arguments that could justify non-repatriation even where the death penalty would not be arbitrarily imposed. The manner in which the death penalty is executed may amount to cruel, inhuman or degrading treatment, and it is generally accepted that exposure to the psychological agony prisoners suffer when awaiting execution, also amount to such treatment. Finally, it can be argued that the death penalty itself amounts to cruel and inhuman treatment, and that a prisoner of war, risking such penalty upon return to his country of origin, may therefore not be forcibly repatriated.

At least where States parties to the European Convention on Human Rights are concerned, the question has been settled by the Grand Chamber of the European Court of Human Rights in its judgment in the case of *Al-Saadoon & Mufdhi v. UK* (2010). The case concerned two "security internees" held by the UK in Iraq between 2003 and 2009:

> "All but two of the Member States have now signed Protocol No. 13 [which abolishes the death penalty in all circumstances] and all but three of the States which have signed have ratified it. These figures, together with consistent State practice in observing the moratorium on capital punishment, are strongly indicative that Article 2 has been amended so as to prohibit the death penalty in all circumstances. Against this background, the Court does not consider that the wording of the second sentence of Article 2§1 continues to act as a bar to its interpreting the words "inhuman or degrading treatment or punishment" in Article 3 as including the death penalty [...]. Article 3, which prohibits in absolute terms torture and inhuman or degrading treatment or punishment, enshrines one of the fundamental values of democratic societies. It makes no provision for exceptions and no derogation from it is permissible under Article 15, even in the event of a public emergency threatening the life of the nation. As the prohibition of torture and of inhuman or degrading treatment or punishment is absolute, irrespective of the victim's conduct, the nature of any offence allegedly committed by the applicant is therefore irrelevant for the purposes of Article 3 [...]. The Court further reiterates that expulsion by a Contracting State may give rise to an issue under Article 3, and hence engage the responsibility of that State under the Convention, where substantial grounds have been shown for believing that the person concerned, if deported, faces a real risk of being subjected to treatment contrary to Article 3. In such a case Article 3 implies an obligation not to deport the person in question to that country [...].

[880] The language is taken from CA3§1(d), as an expression of elementary considerations of humanity (*cf. supra*).

Similarly, Article 2 of the Convention and Article 1 of Protocol No. 13 prohibit the extradition or deportation of an individual to another State where substantial grounds have been shown for believing that he or she would face a real risk of being subjected to the death penalty there".[881]

The case concerned two Iraqis captured by the UK in Iraq in 2003 and interned by the UK until their transfer to Iraqi authorities. The Court did not pronounce on whether the applicants were prisoners of war (the UK had classified them as "security internees"), but the wording of the judgment indicates that the prohibition to return an individual to his or country of origin where he or she may be subject to the death penalty, applies regardless of the status the individuals concerned may have under international humanitarian law.[882]

The evolution in the practice of Council of Europe member States and the reasoning of the European Court in this case reflect rapidly evolving international State practice and it can be expected that other international and regional human rights bodies will follow suit when presented with similar cases. It also shows that even in sensitive domains of national security and in situations of armed conflict, the balance between national security and individual rights and freedoms can be redefined by international practice and effectively amend explicit treaty provisions in light of the evolution of both international legal norms and State practice.[883]

In light of the above, it is safe to conclude that that there is at least one exception to the general obligation to repatriate prisoners of war under article 118 GC III.[884] Both the text of the Convention, interpreted in light of its object and purpose, and in light of subsequent developments in international law and in

---

[881] ECtHR (Grand Chamber), *Al-Saadoon & Mufdhi v. UK* (2010), §120-123 (original italics, references to previous case law omitted). Note that States who have abolished or have undertaken to abolish the death penalty in all circumstances (without further qualification regarding situations of armed conflict) may not themselves impose the death penalty on persons deprived of liberty in such situations, even where specifically allowed by IHL. In the same sense: Rowe (2006), p. 145 and Naert (2010), p. 627.

[882] For an overview of the evolution of the ECtHR's case law on this matter and similar evolutions in the case law of other universal and regional human rights bodies, see Gillard (*IRRC* 2008). That such an evolution was already noticeable in the Western States' attitude towards the forcible repatriation of North-Korean and Chinese POW in 1953 (cf. supra) has been correctly pointed out by Kunz: "Es besteht weiter keine Zweifel, dass die Alliierten den Kriegsgefangenen gegenüber, die als Deserteure gekommen waren, verpflichtet fühlten, sie nicht durch Repatriierung dem Tod auszuliefern." (Kunz (*AdV* 1954), p. 420) (our English summary: the allied forces without a doubt felt obliged not to repatriate POW who had deserted the communist forces and would meet with certain death upon their repatriation).

[883] In this sense, any future development of international humanitarian law should explicitly mention the prohibition to repatriate prisoners of war who have expressed a well-founded fear of persecution, ill-treatment, or arbitrary deprivation of life or liberty. Proposals to revise the text of article 118 GC III to better reflect the limits on the duty to repatriate prisoners of war, have been made since the early 1950's, see e.g. Gutteridge, "The Repatriation of Prisoners of War" (*ICLQ* 1953), pp. 207 and 216; Kunz (*AdV* 1954), pp. 422-423 and Kunz, "The Laws of War" (*AJIL* 1956), pp. 313-337. See also Shields-Delessert (1977), pp. 198-203.

[884] Other exceptions could be the subject of agreements between the parties to the conflict, aimed at granting the request of certain prisoners of war not to be repatriated. However, there are also risks inherent in such practice, risks that led the drafters of article 118 GC III to reject exceptions to the rule (*cf. infra*).

State practice, and the general principle of non-refoulement, demand that in situations where there are substantial grounds to believe that a prisoner of war faces the threat of being subject to persecution, ill-treatment or arbitrary deprivation of life or liberty in his country of origin, he or she may not be repatriated to that country against his or her will. The Interning Power must seriously assess the existence of such a risk on an individual basis and the concerned prisoner must be duly informed and heard.

A refusal to repatriate an individual prisoner of war is not at the complete discretion of the Interning Power. It is lawful only where such refusal has been voluntarily expressed by the prisoner him- or herself. No propaganda, pressure or disinformation may be employed to instil unfounded fears prompting prisoners of war to refuse repatriation. Prisoners should have access to adequate information on potential risks entailed in repatriation to their country of origin, if need be through a supervisory body or a neutral intermediary. It is important to recall that the language in article 118 GC III was not incidental, and ultimately aimed to protect prisoners of war against abusive behaviour by the Interning Power, who could dissimulate economic and political reasons to refuse or delay repatriation by relying on an alleged refusal of repatriation by the prisoners of war themselves.[885] Therefore, an individual's refusal to repatriate must be handled with the utmost care.

Verification of the sincerity of a prisoner's refusal to be repatriated, by a Protecting Power, the ICRC or another neutral and independent institution, will be crucial in this sense.[886]

At the end of the Korean War, the parties to the conflict agreed to organize screenings on both sides and identify prisoners of war who did not want to be repatriated. Almost 15,000 Chinese and 8,000 North Korean prisoners of war refused to return to their respective countries of origin; at least twenty-one US soldiers and one British marine preferred to stay in Communist China. On the proposal of the UN General Assembly, a Neutral Nations Repatriation Commission (NNRC) composed of India, Sweden, Switzerland, Poland and Czechoslovakia was set up to take over custody of non-repatriated prisoners and find another solution for their release.[887] The prisoners became, as one author has put it, "hotly contested symbols of ideological illegitimacy in the Cold War

[885] For example, a representative of the Soviet Union at the Diplomatic Conference in 1949 opposed the Austrian proposal to give prisoners of war the "option of not returning to their country if they so desire" and stressed: "a prisoner of war might not be able to express himself with complete freedom when he was in captivity. Furthermore, this new provision might give rise to the exercise of undue pressure on the part of the Detaining Power." The US shared this opinion, and the UK, apparently for similar reasons, also opposed the Austrian proposal (*Final Record 1949*, Vol. II-A, p. 462). For the main traits of the debate, *cf. supra* notes 845 and 853 and accompanying text.

[886] On the monitoring functions of Protecting Powers and the ICRC, *cf. infra* chapter II-5, section 5.2. In the same sense, Baxter (*BYIL* 1953), pp. 495-496; Shields-Delessert (1977), p. 192-203; Dinstein, "Refugees and the Law of Armed Conflicts" (*Isr.YHR* 1982), p. 102; (Sassòli (*YIIHL* 1985), p. 35; Fischer in Fleck (2008), p. 416.

[887] UNGA, *Resolution 610 (VII)* (1952). On the NNRC in general, see also Baxter (*BYIL* 1953), pp. 490-495 (who also discusses previous examples of such commissions being set up).

struggle",[888] and because each side suspected the other of having coerced its prisoners into refusal to repatriate, the NNRC was to organize sessions where prisoners of war "could receive 'explanations' from their original commands in the presence of neutral observers."[889] Few such sessions were organized in practice however and only 15 percent of the prisoners of war were actually heard by the NNRC, which suffered organizational but also internal political problems: the Commission was "neutral in name only, with Sweden and Switzerland favoring the UN position while Poland and Czechoslovakia backed the Chinese and North Koreans. Only the Indian delegation made any genuine attempt at neutrality, and even they were overly dependent on the UN for logistical support."[890] Finally, after six months of only very limited success, the NNRC returned the remaining prisoners of war to their captors and ceased to exist.[891]

In light of this and other experiences, Fischer and Gasser underline the important role ICRC delegates – representing a neutral, independent and impartial humanitarian organization, mandated by the international community to ensure protection and assistance of victims of armed conflict and compliance with international humanitarian law – can and have to play in this domain:

> "They alone are in a position to determine whether prisoners of war prefer to remain in the state of the detaining power, or in another state, rather than returning to their home country. In this respect the detaining power's duty to repatriate under Article 118 GC III cannot be limited. The duty is absolute. In individual cases exceptions can be made for humanitarian reasons if the life of the prisoner of war might be endangered by the repatriation. However, this goal can only be achieved on a case-by-case basis taking into account the supervision of the ICRC."[892]

Finally, refusal to repatriate should not result in continued internment.[893] We have seen above that the legal basis to intern prisoners of war after the end of active hostilities becomes extinct and that non-repatriated prisoners of war must be released, unless there is another valid legal basis for their continued deprivation of liberty. It is generally accepted that an Interning Power may grant asylum to prisoners of war who refuse to be repatriated.[894] After the Gulf War, the US,

[888] Vance (2006), p. 286.
[889] Vance (2006), p. 287.
[890] Vance (2006), p. 287.
[891] Vance (2006), pp. 286-287, with further references there and at p. 107. On this issue see also Baxter, (*BYIL* 1953), pp. 490-495; and Rosas (1976), p. 479.
[892] Fischer in Fleck (2008), p. 416, with reference to Gasser, "Das Humanitäre Völkerrecht" in Haug (ed.), *Menschlichkeit für Alle* (1991), p. 538.
[893] See also Baxter (*BYIL* 1953), p. 495.
[894] Baxter (*BYIL* 1953), p. 489; Sassòli (*YIIHL* 1985), pp. 23-24. Rosas (1976), at p. 484) concedes that it may to a certain extent be argued that GC III abolished the right to asylum for prisoners of war. But even if this were so, he maintains an exception should be made for cases where "it is obvious that the prisoner would face consequences in his own country that would mean flagrant violations of basic human rights. [...] In this case the institution of asylum may, of course, be of some relevance." In this sense it is also worth noting that the right to asylum is enshrined for everyone in article 14 UDHR ("Everyone has the right to seek and to enjoy in other countries asylum from persecution"). There seems to be no valid reason why prisoners of war should be excluded from this

UK and Saudi Arabia thus refused to repatriate Iraqi prisoners of war who refused to return to Iraq for fear or persecution and granted them asylum as refugees. Where more appropriate, non-repatriated prisoners of war may also be transferred to another country where they would not have to fear for their life or limb.

1.3. CONCLUSIONS ON PRISONERS OF WAR INTERNMENT

Only persons entitled to prisoner of war status may be interned on the basis of article 21 GC III.[895]

Most but not all members of the armed forces of a party to the conflict, and some specific categories of other persons, are entitled to prisoner of war status as long as the armed forces they belong to have a responsible command and a disciplinary system that ensure the forces' effective compliance with international humanitarian law on the ground. Individual members of the armed forces may forfeit their right to be a prisoner of war if they engage in espionage or mercenarism, desert or defect, or fail to distinguish themselves as required by international humanitarian law. Prisoners of war cannot be denied such status and protection of the Third Geneva Convention solely for having the nationality of the capturing State or its allies; in cases of double nationality or *de facto* rupture of the nationality link, the material allegiance to the party to the conflict in whose armed forces they serve will prevail. Individual prisoners of war who have committed war crimes or other international crimes must be tired and punished for their act but do not cease to be prisoners of war and continue to benefit from the protection of the Third Geneva Convention until their final release and repatriation.

In cases of doubt as to whether an individual member of the armed forces is a prisoner of war or not, he or she shall be treated as such until his status is determined by a competent tribunal.[896]

Prisoners of war may in principle be subject to automatic internment for the duration of hostilities, but there are some exceptions to this general rule where an individual prisoner does not really pose a military threat or his internment does not effectively weaken the military capacity of an adverse party to the conflict. The Third Geneva Convention must in this sense be interpreted in light of its

---

right (in the same sense, e.g.: Charmatz & Wit (*AJIL* 1953), pp. 407-408). Sassòli also notes that a person who qualifies as a refugee for the purposes of the 1951 International Refugee Convention or its 1967 Protocol benefits also from the principle of non-refoulement enshrined in article 33 of that Convention and may not be repatriated by either the Interning Power or a neutral country (Sassòli (1985), p. 24).

[895] According to at least one author (Rosas (1976), p. 379-382), the categories of prisoners of war in article 4 GC III are however not exhaustive, and parties to a conflict may – unilaterally or by agreement – decide to expand POW status to other persons. *Cf.* also *supra* note 667 and accompanying text.

[896] Article 5§2 GC III and article 45§1 AP I. If the person fell into the hands of the enemy while committing a belligerent act, he or she is presumed a prisoner of war – and may be interned on the basis of article 21 GC III – until final status determination by the tribunal. *Cf. supra* section 1.1.5.

own object and purpose but also in conformity with other relevant rules of international law.

Nevertheless, articles 21 and 118 GC III effectively establish a legal presumption that prisoners of war (or at least those who are members of the armed forces of a party to the conflict and the participants in a *levée en masse*) are a threat to the security of their Interning Power. While that presumption does not apply to all prisoners of war, it does still apply to the great majority of them. It continues to be justified by the fact that members of the armed forces of a State are under a legal obligation to serve the Power they depend on, an obligation that includes the duty to resist capture and to rejoin their ranks and reengage in the fight as soon as they can escape or are released. Taking into account that duty, and the fact that most States sanction it with very severe punishments, including the death penalty, it may be presumed that such persons upon release will pose a threat to the security of the Interning Power and its capacity to win the war.

Members of the armed forces and participants in a *levée en masse* are not the only persons who participate in hostilities or otherwise pose a serious security threat to the parties to the conflict. Moreover, not all members of the armed forces are prisoners of war. Actually, we have seen that some of what are considered the most dangerous members of armed forces are not entitled to POW status, for example spies, saboteurs and mercenaries. Finally, members of organized armed groups that do not meet the group requirements for their members to be prisoners of war do not necessarily pose a lesser threat than their counterparts who are entitled to such status.

International humanitarian law allows parties to the conflict to counter the threat such persons pose by allowing for a similar but more restricted system of internment on the basis of GC IV. In order to avoid unnecessary or arbitrary deprivation of liberty and abuse, both the grounds for internment and the procedural safeguards in GC IV are stricter than those for prisoners of war. Before discussing the lawful grounds for internment on the basis of GC IV in chapter II-3, we will however first look at a category of persons who are members of the armed forces of the parties to the conflict but are entitled to a special status under international humanitarian law, including as regards the possibility of interning them. Their exceptional internment can be ordered on the basis of the first two Geneva Conventions of 1949.

CHAPTER II – 2

INTERNMENT ON THE BASIS OF THE FIRST AND SECOND GENEVA CONVENTIONS: RETENTION OF MEDICAL AND RELIGIOUS PERSONNEL OF THE ARMED FORCES OF THE PARTIES TO THE CONFLICT

Article 28 GC I/37 GC II: Medical and religious personnel shall be retained only in so far as the state of health, the spiritual needs and the number of prisoners of war require.

Before turning our attention from the Third Geneva Convention to the lawful grounds for internment under the Fourth Geneva Convention, a word must be said about the retention of medical and religious personnel of the armed forces of the parties to the conflict.[897]

Medical and religious personnel of the armed forces must be distinguished from other non-combatant members of these forces. They have enjoyed a special status since the earliest times of international humanitarian law, based on the exclusively humanitarian nature of their function, and their professional and vocational neutrality.[898] That special legal status – which has developed "with rare consistency and continuity" and "has not been fundamentally altered since 1864"[899] – brings with it a special protection under international humanitarian law, established in a set of specific rules enshrined in the First, Second and Third Geneva Conventions.[900]

---

[897] For the definition of the "armed forces of the parties to the conflict", *cf. supra* chapter II-1, section 1.1.2.1.

[898] Ipsen in Fleck (2008), pp. 101-103; Kumar, "Religious Personnel" in Fleck (2008), p. 420. Already in 1864, the Geneva Convention for the Amelioration of the Condition of the Wounded in Armies in the Field (articles 1-2) established the neutrality of medical and religious personnel for the purposes of the conflict. Their neutrality and special status were reaffirmed by the Institute of International Law in articles 12 to 18 of its Oxford Manual on the War on Land (1880) and in articles 28 GC I and 36-37 and 39 GC II. See also Pictet, *Commentary GC I* (1952), p. 244 and *Commentary GC II* (1952), pp. 206 and 222; de La Pradelle, "De la neutralité du personnel sanitaire" (*IRRC* 1955); and Meuli, "De la neutralité du personnel sanitaire au cours des hostilités" (*IRRC* 1956).

[899] Ipsen in Fleck (2008), p. 102. As the issue of the legal framework for the retention of medical and religious personnel of armed forces is rather straightforward and uncontroversial, we will limit ourselves to the relevant legal provisions as comprehensively commented upon in Pictet's Commentaries to GC I and GC II (which offer a good overview of the historical background and evolution of the norms and their content in contemporary IHL).

[900] For a good overview of the main rules concerning the status and protection of religious personnel, see Kumar in Fleck (2008), pp. 419-432 and Lunze, "Serving God and Caesar: Religious Personnel and their Protection in Armed Conflict" (*IRRC* 2004), pp. 69-91. For medical personnel, see Pictet,

Medical and religious personnel of the armed forces of a party to the conflict – unlike other combatant and non-combatant members of such forces – may not be interned for the duration of hostilities. We have seen above that captured medical and religious personnel are not prisoners of war; they can therefore not be interned on the basis of article 21 GC III.[901]

As protected persons under the first two Geneva Conventions, they are excluded from the scope of application of the Fourth Geneva Convention, and can thus not be interned on the basis of that Convention's internment provisions either.[902] Contrary to other members of the armed forces, medical and religious personnel are not allowed to engage in active combat activities, and must exclusively devote themselves to their humanitarian functions. They therefore do not pose a security or military threat to the adverse party that would justify internment. While their services without doubt may strengthen the military capacity of the adversary's armed forces, the balance is in this case clearly and absolutely struck in favour of the principle of humanity. The right to adequate medical care and spiritual assistance are essential features of human dignity, which inspired a substantial part of contemporary IHL.[903] These rights cannot effectively be ensured unless the medical and religious personnel of the armed forces are allowed to stay with their troops and carry out their functions at all times.

There are however circumstances in which medical and religious personnel of the adverse party's armed forces may be retained[904] by the adverse party – inspired by the same considerations of humanity – namely when and for as long as is necessary to provide the prisoners of war in the hands of that adverse party

---

"The Medical Profession and International Humanitarian Law" (*IRRC* 1985). Needless to say that where medical or religious personnel overstep their exclusively medical or religious functions, and engage in combat, they will lose their special protective status and may be treated like other members of the armed forces of an adverse party (e.g.: UK, *LOAC Manual* (2004), section 4§2(3) at p. 38). Their treatment should be the same as that of auxiliary medical and religious personnel of the armed forces (*cf. infra*). Medical and religious personnel who do not belong to the armed forces of a party to the conflict, including crews of coastal rescue craft and coastal installations who may be called to come to the assistance of wounded, sick and shipwrecked soldiers at sea, benefit from similar special protection (under GC IV, as complemented by AP I). Since they are protected under GC IV rather than GC III, the present section does not apply to them (See also Pictet, *Commentary GC II* (1952), pp. 205-206; Levie (1978), pp. 73-74).

901 Article 28§2 GC I, articles 36-37 and 39§5 GC II. For a good summary of the debates on this issue at the 1949 Diplomatic Conference, see Pictet, *Commentary GC I* (1952), pp. 238-240. *Cf. supra* chapter II-1, section 1.1.3.1.

902 Article 4§4 GC IV, *cf. infra* chapter II-3, section 3.1.

903 *Cf. supra* Introduction. The first IHL treaty (the 1864 Geneva Convention) dealt exclusively with the protection of wounded, sick and shipwrecked soldiers and the personnel that comes to their aid. The status and protection of medical and religious personnel – military and civilian – has been strengthened in various IHL instruments IHL ever since. *Cf. supra*, note 899.

904 To mark the difference with the internment of prisoners of war for the duration of hostilities, the Conventions employ the term "retention" for the internment of medical and religious personnel if and for as long as necessary to accommodate the medical and spiritual needs of interned and detained prisoners of war. While their "retention" is a form of deprivation of liberty identical to internment, we will respect the use of the word "retention" in the Conventions, which is also that used in practice. For reasons of coherence, we will refer to the Power that retains medical and religious personnel as the "Retaining Power" rather than the "Interning Power".

with the medical and religious services they are entitled to. The legal basis for their retention is found in the First and Second Geneva Conventions; they prescribe which medical and religious personnel may be retained and on what grounds, when they fall into the hands of an adverse party, and which personnel may not be so retained.[905]

On land, permanent medical and religious personnel of the armed forces and medical personnel of recognized aid societies subject to the military law and regulations of the party to which they belong,[906] who fall into the hands of the

[905] Pictet (*Commentary GC I* (1952), p. 242) reminds us that the wording "fall into the hands of the adverse Party" implies that the capture of medical personnel must be a matter of chance and depend upon fluctuations at the battle front; for it is hardly conceivable that a belligerent should deliberately try to capture such personnel. An organized "medical hunt" would certainly be a sorry sight and completely contrary to the spirit of the Geneva Convention. On the other hand one can well imagine a fighting unit coming upon a group of medical personnel and leaving them to carry on their duties, and the medical staff, for their part, not taking in flight when enemy forces draw near." To be noted that the provisions of GC I to III also apply to medical and religious personnel of the armed forces of a party to the conflict received and interned in the territory of a neutral power (article 4 GC I and article 5 GC II; while not explicitly confirmed for the relevant provisions of GC III, the same rule can be deduced from article 4§B(2) GC III and article 15 HC (V) 1907).

[906] Permanent medical and religious personnel of the armed forces is "[m]edical personnel exclusively engaged in the search for, or the collection, transport or treatment of the wounded or sick, or in the prevention of disease, staff exclusively engaged in the administration of medical units and establishments, as well as chaplains attached to the armed forces", medical personnel of recognized aid societies subject to the military law and regulations of the party to which they belong are defined in article 26 GC I as "[t]he staff of National Red Cross Societies and that of other Voluntary Aid Societies, duly recognized and authorized by their Governments, who may be employed on the same duties as the personnel named in Article 24, are placed on the same footing as the personnel named in the said Article, provided that the staff of such societies are subject to military laws and regulations." Article 8 AP I expands that definition and defines "medical personnel" as "those persons assigned, by a Party to the conflict, exclusively to the medical purposes enumerated under sub-paragraph e) ["namely the search for, collection, transportation, diagnosis or treatment -- including first-aid treatment -- of the wounded, sick and shipwrecked, or for the prevention of disease"] or to the administration of medical units ["establishments and other units, whether military or civilian, organized for [such] medical purposes", including "for example, hospitals and other similar units, blood transfusion centres, preventive medicine centres and institutes, medical depots and the medical and pharmaceutical stores of such units. Medical units may be fixed or mobile, permanent or temporary"] or to the operation or administration of medical transports. [...] The term includes: i) medical personnel of a Party to the conflict, whether military or civilian, including those described in the First and Second Conventions, and those assigned to civil defence organizations; ii) medical personnel of national Red Cross (Red Crescent, Red Lion and Sun) Societies and other national voluntary aid societies duly recognized and authorized by a Party to the conflict; iii) medical personnel of medical units or medical transports described in Article 9, paragraph 2 [namely those "made available to a Party to the conflict for humanitarian purposes: (a) by a neutral or other State which is not a Party to that conflict; (b) by a recognized and authorized aid society of such a State; (c) by an impartial international humanitarian organization."]." It defines "religious personnel" as "military or civilian persons, such as chaplains, who are exclusively engaged in the work of their ministry and attached: i) to the armed forces of a Party to the conflict; ii) to medical units or medical transports of a Party to the conflict; iii) to medical units or medical transports described in Article 9, paragraph 2 [namely those "made available to a Party to the conflict for humanitarian purposes: (a) by a neutral or other State which is not a Party to that conflict; (b) by a recognized and authorized aid society of such a State; (c) by an impartial international humanitarian organization."]; or iv) to civil defence organizations of a Party to the conflict." For the purposes of article 8 AP I ""medical transportation" means the conveyance by land, water or air of the wounded, sick, shipwrecked, medical personnel, religious personnel, medical equipment or medical supplies protected by the Conventions and by this

adverse Party, "shall be retained *only in so far as the state of health, the spiritual needs and the number of prisoners of war require*."[907] Auxiliary medical personnel of the armed forces however "shall be prisoners of war but shall be employed on their medical duties in so far as the need arises."[908]

At sea, "[t]he religious, medical and hospital personnel of hospital ships and their crews [...] may not be captured during the time they are in the service of the hospital ship, whether or not there are wounded and sick on board."[909] This rule is justified by the absolute protection in maritime warfare conferred to hospital ships by the Conventions: "a hospital ship could no longer carry out its duties if it were deprived of its personnel and crew, for those men constitute, so to speak, an integral part of the ship. [...] The protection which the [...] Convention affords to hospital ships would become illusory."[910]

Other permanent medical, religious and hospital personnel at sea may "if they fall into the hands of the enemy, [...] continue to carry out their duties as long as this is necessary for the care of the wounded and sick. They shall afterwards be sent back as soon as the Commander-in-Chief, under whose authority they are, considers it practicable" unless "it proves necessary to retain some of this personnel *owing to the medical or spiritual needs of prisoners of war*."[911]

Protocol; "medical transports" means any means of transportation, whether military or civilian, permanent or temporary, assigned exclusively to medical transportation and under the control of a competent authority of a Party to the conflict; "medical vehicles" means any medical transports by land; "medical ships and craft" means any medical transports by water; "medical aircraft" means any medical transports by air." Finally, for the purposes of article 8 AP I "permanent" medical and religious personnel are "those assigned exclusively to medical purposes for an indeterminate period" whereas "temporary medical and religious personnel are "those devoted exclusively to medical purposes for limited periods during the whole of such periods." In our text, we refer to both these categories as "permanent" personnel, in the sense of persons that are exclusively assigned to such functions, as opposed to auxiliary personnel defined in article 29 GC I referred to below.

907 Article 28§1 GC I (emphasis added). The personnel of aid societies (referred to in article 26 GC I) may only be retained at their own express wish, see article 1§2 *Model Agreement (Retention)*, *cf. infra* note 914.

908 Article 29 GC I. Auxiliary medical personnel are "[m]embers of the armed forces specially trained for employment, should the need arise, as hospital orderlies, nurses or auxiliary stretcher-bearers, in the search for or the collection, transport or treatment of the wounded and sick shall likewise be respected and protected if they are carrying out these duties at the time when they come into contact with the enemy or fall into his hands" (article 25 GC I). As prisoners of war they may be interned for the duration of the hostilities, since such personnel is primarily combatant personnel and only assigned to medical or religious duties on a subsidiary basis. Article 29 GC I ensures however that their special training be put to use in so far as the need arises.

909 Article 36 GC II. Note that article 36 GC II only covers the personnel necessary for the hospital ship to function properly. Any additional medical personnel the ship is authorized to transport (pursuant to article 35§5 GC II) is covered by article 37 GC II. For further details, see also Pictet, *Commentary GC II* (1952), pp. 203-206.

910 Pictet, *Commentary GC II* (1952), p. 204. Therefore, the crew, as long as they are in the service of the hospital ship, may not even be retained when they leave their ship temporarily or to land, or when there are no wounded or sick on board for the ship "must be ready to put to sea at any moment" (*Ibidem*).

911 Article 37 GC II (emphasis added). Article 37 also covers medical personnel of the merchant marine (Pictet, *Commentary GC II* (1952), pp. 207-208).

The provisions concerning personnel of medical aircraft are similar to those that apply at sea. The personnel of medical aircraft "may not be captured during the time they are in the service of the medical aircraft, whether or not there are wounded and sick on board." Other medical personnel on board aircrafts forced to land may "continue to carry out their duties as long as this is necessary for the care of the wounded and sick. They shall afterwards be sent back as soon as the Commander-in-Chief, under whose authority they are, considers it practicable" unless "it proves necessary to retain some of this personnel *owing to the medical or spiritual needs of prisoners of war*."[912]

The negative formulation of the grounds for retention in all these provisions (medical and religious personnel may *not* be retained *unless* or *only if* necessary owing to the medical and spiritual need of prisoners of war) is deliberate and reflects the fact that retention of medical and religious personnel of the armed forces – in contrast to the internment of prisoners of war – is to be the exception and never the rule.[913] Pictet insists on this again in his commentary:

> "in order that a belligerent may retain a proportion of the medical personnel and chaplains who have fallen into his power, one essential condition must be fulfilled: he must have in his charge prisoners of war whose state of health and spiritual needs 'require' or render 'indispensable' the presence of such personnel. Retention must be justified by a real and pressing need."[914]

How many medical and religious personnel may be retained will therefore be calculated on the basis of the number of prisoners of war the Retaining Power holds and on their medical and spiritual needs. The parties to the conflict may

---

[912] Article 39§5 *juncto* articles 36-37 GC II (emphasis added). Medical aircraft is defined in article 39§1 GC II as "aircraft exclusively employed for the removal of the wounded, sick and shipwrecked, and for the transport of medical personnel and equipment." Whereas article 37 GC II covers medical personnel of the merchant marine, article 39 does not cover any medical personnel that may be attached to civil aviation services (Pictet, *Commentary GC II* (1952), p. 209).

[913] The ICRC, in its commentary to the *Model Agreement (Retention)* referred to *infra* in note 914, fears retention may occur on a regular basis in future conflicts but recalls that "It is clear, however, from the very terms of Article 28 (paragraphs 1 and 2) and from the whole system proposed [...] that retention should only be considered as a complementary measure to those taken by the Detaining Power itself for the health of the prisoners."

[914] Pictet, *Commentary GC I* (1952), pp. 240-241. See also *Ibidem*, pp. 260-261: "The repatriation of medical personnel, traditionally a principle of the Geneva Convention, remains [...] the essential rule. Retention is only a secondary possibility. Medical personnel must always, as a matter of principle, be in a position to carry on their particular work. To hinder them in this by holding doctors idle while they might be saving the lives of patients in their own country, would be gravely at variance with the Geneva Convention and the very idea of the Red Cross. [...] The provisions spring as a whole from the central idea that sick and wounded soldiers form a single group, and must be cared for as well as possible, whether they are with their own forces or in enemy hands. All the preliminary discussions [to the adoption of the GC] were dominated by the desire to maintain a just balance between the needs of the wounded on the battlefield and those of prisoners of war. [...] The system of retention will not, we must repeat, give the good results expected of it, unless the principle of repatriation is also scrupulously observed. It is at this price that the new provisions will take on their full value and that the Convention as a whole will retain its high moral significance." See also the ICRC's comments to article 11 *Model Agreement (Retention)*: "the only reason justifying the retention of medical personnel is the need which prisoners may have of their care" and "the ultimate object aimed at is purely and simply the amelioration of the conditions of captivity of sick and wounded prisoners."

agree to adopt a fix percentage of medical and religious personnel deemed necessary to tend to a defined number of prisoners of war. Upon request of the Diplomatic Conference, the ICRC drafted a Model Agreement dealing with the issue in full.[915] In the absence of any agreement, the Retaining Power:

> "will determine the percentage in the light of common sense, equity and experience. The maximum which may be allowed, but in no circumstances exceeded, is the staff necessary to meet the real needs of a camp without calling upon personnel of the detaining forces. Should the Power of Origin consider the proportion fixed excessive, it may open negotiations with the Detaining Power and call upon the good services of the Protecting Power or the International Committee of the Red Cross."[916]

Since auxiliary medical personnel of an enemy's armed forces held by the Retaining Power "shall be employed on their medical duties, in so far as the need arises", the questions arises whether their number should be taken into account to establish the extent to which permanent medical personnel of enemy armed forces can be retained. In the absence of an established rule, the question is left to the discretion of the parties to the conflict. It is to be kept in mind however that often:

> "auxiliary personnel are only trained to act as stretcher-bearers or auxiliary medical orderlies, so that their presence in camps could at most justify the repatriation of permanent personnel of the same class, not of fully qualified personnel. Besides, there is unlikely to be a constant need for stretcher-bearers in the camps, so that the problem will probably be limited in practice to the case of auxiliary medical orderlies. If some of them are able to fill the necessary posts satisfactorily and permanently, the Detaining Power should admittedly consider freeing a corresponding number of the permanent medical orderlies retained under Article 28. Such an attitude would be in full accordance with the spirit and general principles of the Convention."[917]

Moreover, medical personnel attached to the navy, specialized and accustomed to performing their functions at sea, are often fewer in number than their colleagues attached to the armed forces on land. Therefore, when a Retaining Power has the choice, it should retain medical personnel of the armed on land rather than those attached to the navy, who should be left to work at sea.[918]

As Pictet points out in this commentary to article 28 GC I:

---

[915] Article 31§2 GC I, articles 37§3 and 39§5 GC II. Upon request of the Diplomatic Conference (*Final Record 1949*, Vol. I, p. 361), the ICRC produced a *Model Agreement Relating to the Retention of Medical Personnel and Chaplains (Model Agreement (Retention))*, which it published, with comments, in *IRRC* (1955), pp. 7-21. In drafting the model agreement, the ICRC relied on its own experience, that of various army medical services, the International Committee of Military Medicine and Pharmacy, and other organizations with relevant experience.

[916] Pictet, *Commentary GC I* (1952), p. 241.

[917] Pictet, *Commentary GC I* (1952), pp. 259-260. A rule to this effect is also included in article 7§2 *Model Agreement (Retention)*.

[918] Pictet, *Commentary GC II* (1952), p. 210; adding: "Similarly, it would be unsatisfactory if medical personnel attached to the merchant marine were retained in order to help care for prisoners of war belonging to the armed forces. Wherever possible, they should therefore be assigned only to caring for merchant seamen in the hands of the adverse Party."

> "It is not possible to read into the text of the Convention that retention is permissible only when the Detaining Power holds prisoners of the same nationality. The text with which we are dealing speaks of "prisoners of war" in general. [[919]] Furthermore, paragraph 2 of Article 28 [GC I] lays down that retained medical personnel are to carry out their duties "on behalf of prisoners of war, 'preferably' those of armed forces to which they themselves belong". The implication clearly is that, when a belligerent holds prisoners who are nationals of different countries, he shall as far as possible allocate retained medical personnel on a basis of nationality. But a belligerent who held a surplus of personnel of any one nationality might be justified in retaining them, should circumstances so demand, to care for prisoners of a different nationality. Such a solution is obviously an abnormal one, and should only be adopted as an exceptional and temporary measure; we must not forget that it was decided to make provision for the retention of medical personnel, largely because it was thought desirable that prisoners should be cared for by their own countrymen, speaking the same language and using methods of treatment to which the prisoners were accustomed. It would seem in any event that the eventuality considered will rarely occur in practice, since medical personnel are nearly always captured at the same time as combatants."[920]

Nevertheless, the exceptional authorization to retain medical and religious personnel of the enemy's armed forces does not relieve the Interning Power of its obligations under GC III towards the prisoners of war in its power. Pictet thus rightly adds that:

> "A Detaining Power must not be able to use the fact that the retention of a portion of the opposing party's medical and religious personnel is authorized, as a pretext for avoiding its own obligations or as justification for a dereliction on its part; it may not, for example, find in the retention of enemy medical personnel a reason for not making available such of its own personnel as may be necessary. Retention, as the new Convention regards it, must remain a supplementary measure taken for the good of the prisoners themselves and to assist the Detaining Power. The latter continues to be fully responsible for the prisoners of war who have fallen into its hands."[921]

If and for as long as they are so retained, medical and religious personnel are entitled, as a minimum, to the benefits and the full protection accorded under the Third Geneva Convention to the prisoners of war they are called upon to assist.[922] Moreover, they must be given the necessary facilities to exercise their

---

[919] The same holds true for articles 37 and 39 GC II.

[920] Pictet, *Commentary GC I* (1952), p. 241 and 247 (with reference to the debates on the issue during the Diplomatic Conference); Levie (1978), p. 136. For this reason, article 1 of the *Model Agreement (Retention)* obliges rather than recommends (as the Convention does) to attach retained personnel to the prisoners of war of their own armed forces.

[921] Pictet, *Commentary GC I* (1952), p. 258. See also the ICRC's comments on the *Model Agreement (Retention)*.

[922] Article 33 GC III, article 28§§2-4 GC I and articles 37§3 and 39§5 GC II. See also Pictet, *Commentary GC I* (1952), pp. 243 and 252-258. Pictet highlights that the Retaining Power can "apply to retained medical personnel only those provisions of the Prisoners of War Convention that are manifestly to their advantage", and summarizes the applicability of GC III provisions as follows:

functions and accomplish the mission for which they are retained, namely to provide for adequate medical care and religious ministration to the prisoners of war they tend to.[923] They must carry out their functions in accordance with the military laws and regulations of the Retaining Power, but may not be compelled to carry out tasks that are incompatible with their exclusive medical or religious function or with their professional ethics.[924]

As soon as their services are no longer required to adequately assist the medical and spiritual needs of the prisoners of war in the power of the Power that holds them, retained medical and religious personnel must be returned to the party to the conflict to whose armed forces they belong.[925] Such return may be delayed if the Retaining Power has serious reasons to believe that retained medical or religious personnel were, "at the time of capture, able to collect information of tactical or strategic value which they will communicate to their own army command on their return", but this does not mean they can be retained forever, as any information of military value they may have been able to collect will very soon be out of date.[926] As long as the need to retain medical and religious personnel of an adverse party's armed forces persists, the Retaining Power must try to make arrangements for relieving them from time to time.[927]

"[i]n matters where special provisions relating to retained personnel and similar provisions relating to prisoners of war both apply, the first-named always take precedence.
In matters regulated only by provisions designed for prisoners of war, it is necessary to take into consideration certain consequences of the special position and duties of retained personnel." Article 11 of the *Model Agreement (Retention)* provides that "[i]n general, the provisions of the Third Convention [...] shall always be applied in a such manner as to allow such personnel to carry out their medical duties in all circumstances and under the best possible conditions", and the ICRC comments on that article by saying that "should difficulties arise with regard to the application of these rules, the solution most favourable to the accomplishment of this mission should always be sought, since the ultimate object aimed at is purely and simply the amelioration of the conditions of captivity of sick and wounded prisoners" (these comments may be applied *mutatis mutandis* to religious personnel). We agree with Pictet (*Commentary GC I* (1952), p. 260) that when called upon to act in a professional capacity, auxiliary medical personnel of the enemy's armed forces – like their fellow prisoners of war who are physicians, surgeons, dentists, nurses or medical orderlies but are not as such employed by the armed forces to which they belong – should benefit from article 32 GC III and receive the same treatment as retained permanent medical personnel. A similar provision to article 32 GC III exists for prisoners of war who are ministers of religion without holding such function in the armed forces they belong to (article 36 GC III).

[923] Article 28§2 GC I; articles 30§§1-2, 33§§2-3 and 35 GC III. See also Pictet, *Commentary GC I* (1952), pp. 246-252; and Pictet, *Commentary GC II* (1952), pp. 209-211, 219-223 and 231-232.

[924] Article 28§2 GC I; articles 37 and 39§5 GC II; articles 33§2 and 35 GC III. See also Pictet, *Commentary GC I* (1952), p. 246; and Pictet, *Commentary GC III* (1960), pp. 219 and 231.

[925] Article 30 GC I; articles 37§3 and 39§5 GC II. See also Pictet, *Commentary GC I* (1952), pp. 261-264.

[926] Pictet, *Commentary GC I* (1952), p. 262. Medical and religious personnel who, during their retention, overstep their exclusively medical or religious functions and abuse of their privileged status to engage in activities that would effectively amount to espionage or sabotage do not enjoy immunity from prosecution for such acts on the basis of the Retaining Power's relevant domestic law and may be preventively detained for the purposes of such proceedings and imprisoned upon conviction. Shields-Delessert (1977) suggests that medical and religious personnel should only be retained for a maximum of six months after capture (p. 124).

[927] Article 28§3 GC I, articles 37§3 and 39§5 GC II; article 33§3 GC III. Pictet, *Commentary GC I* (1952), at p. 257 notes however that the Diplomatic Conference did not consider it could make such arrangements compulsory, since security considerations are bound to create difficulties. He recalls

In selecting retained personnel that can be returned, the chronological order of their capture and their state of health must be taken into account.[928] Finally, if still retained at the time of cessation of active hostilities, retained medical and religious personnel must be released and repatriated with all prisoners of war.[929]

"that on the one occasion when relief on a partial scale was found possible during the last World War, the home country of the medical officers concerned was itself occupied by the Detaining Power." See also Levie, (1978), pp. 72-73. Upon request of the Diplomatic Conference (*Final Record 1949*, Vol. I, p. 361), the ICRC designed a *Model Agreement Relating to the Relief of Medical Personnel and Chaplains*, published, with comments in *IRRC* (1955). The ICRC noted that such relief operations are difficult to regulate in a general manner due to their "special character, highly technical and often varying to the regions and nationalities concerned." The agreement lays down principles applicable in all cases and provides for the setting up of special *ad hoc* Commissions to solve practical problems.

[928] Article 31§1 GC I; articles 37§3 and 39§5 GC II.

[929] Unless more advantageous provisions apply, retained medical and religious personnel are entitled to the protection of GC III, including its article 118 as discussed in chapter II-1, section 1.2.3.6.

CHAPTER II – 3
INTERNMENT ON THE BASIS OF THE FOURTH GENEVA CONVENTION: PROTECTED PERSONS

We have seen in chapter II-1 that members of the armed forces of a party to the conflict and participants in a *levée en masse* are legally presumed to pose a threat to any adverse party to the conflict. In contemporary armed conflict however, they are often not the only persons who participate in hostilities or otherwise pose a serious threat to the security or military operations of the parties to the conflict. Moreover, we have also seen that not all members of the armed forces of the parties to the conflict are prisoners of war, and that some of what are considered the most dangerous elements of such armed forces do not fall within the personal scope of application of GC III and thus cannot be interned on that basis.

Whereas prisoners of war have been the subject of numerous bilateral agreements and international treaties throughout modern history, the Fourth Geneva Convention is the first multilateral treaty dealing with the internment of civilians and other persons who do not qualify as prisoners of war but find themselves in the power of an enemy State.[930] As observed by Rosas:

> "it was a general rule during the eighteenth and nineteenth centuries not to detain the great bulk of the civilian population. In so far as civilians were detained or their freedom of movement restricted they were not covered by any specific legal status distinct from that of prisoners of war. At the Hague Conference of 1907 it was generally considered forbidden to intern or expel *en masse* enemy civilians residing in the territory of the adversary, although a provision to this effect was not inserted in the Hague Regulations."[931]

The mass internment of civilians in World Wars I and II, made the ICRC's efforts to regulate deprivation of liberty of persons other than prisoners of war – efforts initiated during the inter-bellum – a must for all participants in the 1949 Diplomatic Conference that lead to the adoption of the Geneva Conventions.[932] In order to avoid unnecessary or arbitrary deprivation of liberty and other abuses witnessed during recent conflicts, the Fourth Geneva Convention established a

---

930 For the relevant pre-1949 developments, *cf. infra* section 3.2.

931 Rosas (1976), p. 79.

932 See Wilson, "Treatment of Civilian Alien Enemies" (*AJIL* 1943); Baxter (*BYIL* 1951), p. 326; and Stibbe, "The Internment of Civilians by Belligerent States during the First World War and the Response of the International Committee of the Red Cross" (*JCH* 2006).

similar but more restricted system of internment as compared to that applicable to prisoners of war.

In the first section of this chapter, we will examine the Convention's scope of application in order to define who exactly can be interned on the basis of its provisions. We will then discuss the lawful grounds for, and duration of internment on the basis of GC IV in considerable detail in section two. But before doing so, a particular feature of the Fourth Geneva Convention needs to be highlighted.

Contrary to the first three Geneva Conventions,[933] the Fourth Geneva Convention includes a specific set rules regulating the particular situation of occupation. We have seen above that these rules do not constitute an alternative or a separate legal regime to that of international armed conflict, but are rather a subset of the rules on international armed conflict, addressing particular issues that may arise when one of the parties to such a conflict occupies all or part of the territory of an adverse party.[934]

The Fourth Geneva Convention therefore contains two separate legal bases for the internment of protected persons. Articles 41 to 43 GC IV define for what reasons and in accordance with which procedures protected persons can be interned in the territory of a party to the conflict that is under its own effective control. Article 78 GC IV prescribes the grounds and procedures for internment of protected persons in occupied territory. These legal bases are exhaustive and article 79 GC IV explicitly recalls that:

> "[t]he Parties to the conflict shall not intern protected persons, except in accordance with the provisions of Articles 41, 42 and 43, 68 and 78."[935]

---

[933] The internment of prisoners of war and the retention of medical and religious personnel of the armed forces of the parties to the conflict is regulated respectively by GC III (*supra* chapter II-1) and by GC I-II (*supra* chapter II-2), without any distinction on the basis of whether these persons find themselves within a party to the conflict's own territory, in territory occupied by a party to the conflict, or in the territory of a neutral power.

[934] *Cf. supra* chapter I-2, section 2.2.1.3.

[935] Article 68 GC IV is special in that it also allows for internment but as an alternative – lighter – penal sanction for minor offences against the Interning Power: "Protected persons who commit an offence which is solely intended to harm he Occupying Power, but which does not constitute an attempt to the life or limb of the occupying forces or administration, nor a grave collective danger, nor seriously damage the property of the occupying forces of administration or the installations used by them, shall be liable to internment or simple imprisonment, provided the duration of such internment or imprisonment is proportionate to the offence committed. Furthermore, internment or imprisonment shall, for such offences, be the only measure adopted for depriving protected persons of liberty. The courts provided for under Article 66 of the present Convention may at their discretion convert a sentence of imprisonment to one of internment for the same period." Internment in the sense of article 68 is not a measure of preventive security detention. Rather, it is a penalty for minor offences, an alternative to "imprisonment" which involves a stricter regime of deprivation of liberty that is reserved for convicted criminals. See also Pictet, *Commentary GC IV* (1958), pp. 343-344: "Internment is a preventive administrative measure and cannot be considered a penal sanction. It is nevertheless mentioned here under the same head as simple imprisonment, because the authors of the Convention wished to make it possible for the military courts of the Occupying Power to give persons guilty of minor offences the benefit of the conditions of internment provided for in Articles 79 et sqq. The provision was a humane one and was intended to draw a distinction between such offenders and common criminals." Since this book is limited to

Article 78 GC IV takes into account certain specificities of internment in occupied territory. Apart from the procedural aspects, the substance of its provisions is quasi-identical to that of articles 41 to 43 GC IV. The personal scope of application of the provisions in the Convention's section on occupied territories is slightly wider than that of the provisions applicable to the rules applicable in the own territory of the parties to the conflict. Rather than treating the two regimes separately and risk a great amount of repetition, we will examine the legal bases for internment in both sets of rules together and point out the specificities of the occupation regime where relevant.

3.1. WHO CAN BE INTERNED ON THE BASIS OF GC IV? DEFINING "PROTECTED PERSONS"

We have seen in Part I that the Geneva Conventions, apart from their common article 3 common, only apply in situations of international armed conflict and occupation.[936] The purpose of the present section is to define who can be interned on the basis of the Fourth Geneva Convention,[937] which leads us to the question of who are "protected persons" under GC IV.[938]

Article 4 GC IV defines both who is, and who is not, a "protected person" under GC IV:

> "[1] Persons protected by the Convention are those who, at a given moment and in any manner whatsoever, find themselves, in case of a conflict or occupation, in the hands of a Party to the conflict or Occupying Power of which they are not nationals.
>
> [2] Nationals of a State which is not bound by the Convention are not protected by it. Nationals of a neutral State who find themselves in the territory of a belligerent State, and nationals of a co-belligerent State, shall not be regarded as protected persons while the State of which they are nationals has normal diplomatic representation in the State in whose hands they are.
>
> [3] The provisions of Part II are, however, wider in application, as defined in Article 13.

---

internment in the proper sense of the word, namely as a preventive security measure, article 68 GC IV will not be the object of further analysis.

[936] For the definition of the material scope of application of the 1949 Geneva Conventions, *cf. supra* chapter I-2, section 2.2.1.

[937] This book only deals with internment. For the relevant provisions on deprivation of liberty as a penal or disciplinary sanction imposed on persons protected under GC IV, see articles 37 and 64-77 GC IV and articles 75 to 77 AP I. To be noted that an Occupying Power may adopt additional penal legislation to that of the occupied territory it administers and thus need not necessarily rely on internment to address threats to its security or that of the population of the occupied territory.

[938] The term "protected person" does not confer any legal *status* on an individual, but it has become common shorthand for all persons who fall within the scope of application of GC IV. In its broader sense, it covers all persons protected by the Geneva Conventions and their Additional Protocols, meaning all persons protected by international humanitarian law. In the present chapter, it will be used – as it is in GC IV – in its more restricted sense of persons within the personal scope of application of GC IV.

[4] Persons protected by the Geneva Convention for the Amelioration of the Condition of the Wounded and Sick in Armed Forces in the Field of August 12, 1949, or by the Geneva Convention for the Amelioration of the Condition of Wounded, Sick and Shipwrecked Members of Armed Forces at Sea of August 12, 1949, or by the Geneva Convention relative to the Treatment of Prisoners of War of August 12, 1949, shall not be considered as protected persons within the meaning of the present Convention."[939]

In the following two sub-sections, we will analyze the text of article 4, in its context and in light of the object and purpose of the Fourth Geneva Convention. Where relevant, subsequent developments in international law applicable between the parties to that Convention will also be taken into account. Finally, where necessary, we will resort to subsidiary means of interpretation such as the *travaux préparatoires* of the Convention, international case law and the writings of distinguished scholars in order to clarify the meaning of its provisions in contemporary international humanitarian law.[940]

We will discuss the definition of protected persons in article 4 GC IV by addressing the two main controversies that surround it. First, we will examine whether so-called unlawful or unprivileged combatants are included in its scope of application. Second, we will examine whether its exclusion clause on the basis of nationality must be interpreted strictly or rather broadly, and how that interpretation has evolved under the influence of developments in international law subsequent to the adoption of the Fourth Geneva Convention.

3.1.1. Protected persons: unprivileged combatants and civilians alike

The title of the Fourth Geneva Convention is misleading and may lead to confusion as to its personal scope of application.[941] Labelled *Geneva Convention relative to the Protection of Civilian Persons in Time of War*, it may suggest to cover only (peaceful) civilians, as opposed to combatants, the majority of which are the subject of Geneva Conventions I to III. This may in turn lead to believe that persons who are not entitled to the protection of GC I to III, but who actively take part in hostilities on behalf of a party to the conflict, must also be excluded from the personal scope of application of this so-called *Civilians* Convention.

[939] The scope of application of Part II of GC IV, entitled "General protection of populations against certain consequences of war" as defined in article 13 includes: "the whole of the populations of the countries in conflict, without any adverse distinction based, in particular, on race, nationality, religion or political opinion." Its provisions deal with civilian hospitals, safety and neutralized zones, the protection of the wounded and sick, medical staff, infrastructure and transportation, the consignment of medical supplies, food and clothing, measures relating to child welfare, and the maintenance and reestablishment of family links. They are of little to no relevance to the subject of this research and do not therefore have an impact on the definition of who can be interned on the basis of GC IV.

[940] Article 31§3 VCLT: "There shall be taken into account [...] (a) any subsequent agreement between the parties regarding the interpretation of the treaty or the application of its provisions; (b) any subsequent practice in the application of the treaty which establishes the agreement of the parties regarding its interpretation; (c) any relevant rules of international law applicable in the relations between the parties."

[941] For the use of the word "civilian" in the body of the text of the Convention, *cf. infra* note 962.

The problem with the Convention's title's use of the word "civilian" is that the concept of "civilian" is a legal term of art that belongs to the sphere of the rules on the conduct of hostilities.[942] Together with the concept of "combatant" it makes up the reference point for the principle of distinction, the cornerstone of all rules on the conduct of hostilities and in particular those on lawful targeting.[943] In this sense, "civilians" are defined in article 50 AP I as all those who are not combatants and thus are not members of the armed forces of a party to the conflict.[944] For the purposes of the principle of distinction, these concepts are mutually exclusive: one is either a combatant or a civilian, and cannot be both at the same time.[945]

These concepts are however without relevance for the interpretation of the personal scope of application of either GC III or IV, which contain precise provisions defining who is a "prisoner of war" and who is a "protected person under GC IV."[946] Each of these definitions includes persons who – for the purposes of the rules on the conduct of hostilities – are either combatants or civilians and – contrary to an intuitive understanding of the Conventions' scope of application – no automatic equations exist between the concepts of combatant and prisoner of war, or between those of civilian and protected person under GC IV. We have seen in chapter II-1 that not all combatants are prisoners of war, not all prisoners of war are combatants, and that certain civilians are prisoners of war. The present sub-section will demonstrate that not all protected persons under GC IV are civilians but that some of them could qualify – for the purpose of the conduct of hostilities – as (either lawful or unlawful) combatants.

While article 4 GC IV does not distinguish between protected persons on the basis of their status under the rules on the conduct of hostilities, it may be useful – for our present persons – to distinguish the following four groups of persons falling within its scope of application:[947]

---

[942] This is to some extent quite surprising in that the principal purpose of the Fourth Geneva Convention, adopted in the wake of the two World Wars, was the protection of civilians in enemy hands from arbitrary action and abuse, rather than their protection against the effects of the actual conduct of hostilities (Pictet, *Commentary GC IV* (1958), pp. 10-11). Nevertheless, the formulation of the Convention's title and the common reference to GC IV as the "Civilians Convention" are understandable in that the great majority of persons the Convention aimed to protect, and in actual practice covers, are indeed civilians for the purpose of the rules on the conduct of hostilities. This given may not distract us however from the fact the Convention's personal scope of application (or definition of persons under its protection) is broader and also includes persons who – for the purposes of the conduct of hostilities – are not civilians, or are civilians who have, temporarily, lost their immunity from attack.

[943] On the concept of "combatant" and the principle of distinction, *cf. supra* chapter II-1, section 1.1.1.

[944] Article 50 AP I reads in relevant part: "A civilian is any person who does not belong to one of the categories of persons referred to in Article 4 A (1), (2), (3) and (6) of the Third Convention and in Article 43 of this Protocol." The articles of GC III and AP I referred to in this definition define who is a member of the armed forces of a party to the conflict and is thus entitled, in principle, to combatant status (with the ensuing privileges and immunities), *cf. supra* chapter II-1, section 1.1.1.

[945] E.g.: ICRC, *IGDPH* (2009), pp. 20-21; Dinstein (2010), p. 35; Lubell (2010), pp. 143-145.

[946] In the same sense: Lubell (2010), pp. 136-145.

[947] These distinctions have no legal value; they are only intended to facilitate our response to arguments that so-called unlawful or unprivileged combatants are excluded from the personal scope of application of GC IV, which would only be applicable to civilians.

• Peaceful civilians, i.e. individuals who are not members of the armed forces of a party to the conflict and do not participate in hostilities (except those who are prisoners of war under the definition of article 4 GC III, *cf. supra* chapter II-1, section 1.1.4);

• Civilians who participate directly in hostilities, i.e. individuals who are not members of the armed forces of any party to the conflict but participate directly in the hostilities between the parties to that conflict;

• Members of armed groups engaged in hostilities against a party to the conflict or an Occupying Power, and participants in a levée en masse, who – as a group – do not qualify as armed forces of a party to the conflict or do not fulfil the conditions for their members to be prisoners of war (*cf. supra* chapter II-1, section 1.1.2); and

• Members of the armed forces of a party to the conflict who have forfeited their individual right to prisoner of war status, may thus lawfully be excluded from the personal scope of application of GC III, and have not been granted prisoner of war status by the power in whose hands they fell (*cf. supra* chapter II-1, section 1.1.3).

The latter three groups of persons are sometimes – and to a variable extent – referred to as "unlawful combatants/belligerents"[948] or "unprivileged combatants/belligerents",[949] and have been the subject of intense debate both in the past and over recent years.[950] While they are not legal terms of art, these

[948] E.g.: Dinstein (2010), pp. 34-39. The concept has also been used in some legislation and military doctrine, e.g. Israel, *Incarceration of Unlawful Combatants Law* (2002), article 2: ""unlawful combatant" means a person who has participated either directly or indirectly in hostile acts against the State of Israel or is a member of a force perpetrating hostile acts against the State of Israel, where the conditions prescribed in Article 4 of the Third Geneva Convention of 12th August 1949 with respect to prisoners-of-war and granting prisoner-of-war status in international humanitarian law, do not apply to him"; Canada, *LOAC Manual* (2001), pp. GL-18 to GL-19: "Unlawful combatants are persons who engage in hostilities but are not legally entitled to do so under the LOAC. Unlawful combatants include: civilians who take a direct part in hostilities (other than as part of a levee en masse; mercenaries; and spies who engage in hostilities while not in the uniform of their armed forces."

[949] E.g.: Baxter (*BYIL* 1951), p. 323. See also Canada, *PWDITQ* (2004), pp. 1B-1 and 1B-2: Annex B is entitled "Direction for the detention of civilians and unlawful belligerents other than prisoners of war" and the first category of detainees covered by that Annex is defined as: "Belligerents, including armed civilians, who commit a hostile act, demonstrate hostile intent or otherwise obstruct friendly forces in the conduct of operations"; and US, *Operational Law Handbook* (2010), p. 16: "Unprivileged belligerents may include spies, saboteurs, or civilians who are participating in the hostilities or who otherwise engage in unauthorized attacks or other combatant acts. Unprivileged belligerents (a/k/a unlawful combatants) are not entitled to POW status and may be prosecuted under the domestic law of the captor."

[950] Rogers, in order to avoid calling them either combatants or civilians refers to them as "unqualified participants in hostilities" (Rogers, "Combatant Status" in Wilmshurst & Breau, *Perspectives on the ICRC Study on Customary International Humanitarian Law* (2007), p. 113). For some of the main contributions to the debate on unlawful, unprivileged or unqualified combatants, belligerents or participants, see Baxter (*BYIL* 1951); Draper (*Isr.YHR* 1971); Kalshoven (*MLLWR* 1972); Mallison & Mallison (*CWRJIL* 1977); Mallison & Mallison (*LCP* 1978); Dinstein (*Isr.YHR* 2002); Goldman & Tittemore (*ASIL Task Force* 2002); Greenwood (*IA* 2002); Dörmann (*IRRC* 2003); CoE, *Venice Commission Opinion* (2003); Dinstein (2010), pp. 33-39; Sassòli (*JICJ* 2004); Watkin (*HPCR Series* 2005); Rogers in Wilmshurst & Breau (2007); Ipsen in Fleck (2008); Dinstein (2010), pp. 33-39; and

labels may prove useful to the military on the ground for the purposes of targeting.[951] The label "unlawful combatants" in that sense would fit the 2nd and 3rd groups of persons in the sense that these persons participate in hostilities without being authorized to do so under international humanitarian law.[952] The 4th group is then composed of persons who are "lawful but unprivileged combatants": as members of the armed forces they are entitled to participate in hostilities, but they have forfeited their individual right to be a prisoner of war because of specific types of behaviour. The latter group typically includes spies and combatants who fail to distinguish themselves properly in attack. Whatever the practical usefulness of labels such as unlawful or unprivileged combatants for the rules on targeting on the ground, they are not legal terms of art in international humanitarian law, and therefore inappropriate for interpreting its provisions.[953] Their direct connotation to the rules on the conduct of hostilities makes them even less appropriate for interpreting the personal scope of application of either GC III or GC IV.

Since neither one of these four groups of persons are prisoners of war upon arrest, capture or surrender, they cannot be interned on the basis of article 21 GC III. If they qualify as protected persons under GC IV, their internment – if necessary – can be ordered on the basis of articles 42 and 78 of that Convention. That the first group of persons (peaceful civilians) are protected persons under GC IV is uncontroversial. As to the other three groups of persons, it is useful – in light of the persistent controversies in legal doctrine – to demonstrate that they do indeed fall within the personal scope of application of the Fourth Geneva Convention, regardless of their status under the rules of the conduct of hostilities.[954]

Lubell (2010), pp. 136-146.

[951] We agree with Lubell (2010), p. 146 that "States may use a variety of rhetorical devices within domestic polices and laws, but the actions taken on the basis of these policies and laws must conform to the applicable international law. This is true whether it is in relation to targeting or detention. For example, while Israel has a law on detention of unlawful combatants, the key question regardless of the use of the term, is whether the resulting acts of detention adhere to appropriate international law, such as the laws on administrative detention of civilians during conflict. In other words, whilst the view taken here is that the use of 'unlawful combatant' should be avoided as it is not a category defined in international law, the focus of scrutiny should be on the actual practice of states which use it."

[952] Only members of the armed forces of the parties to the conflict are – in principle – combatants and have the right to participate in hostilities (article 43§2 AP I), *cf. supra* chapter II-1, section 1.1.

[953] In the same sense: CoE, *Venice Commission Opinion* (2003), §§4 and 44-48; Lubell (2010), p.144. Labels such as "unlawful combatant" or "unlawful belligerent" have at times been abused to re-introduce questions about the legality or legitimacy of the use of force and of the causes a party to a conflict may adhere to, for the purpose of excluding persons fighting on that party's behalf from the protection of international law all-together (the most recent example is that of the qualification of members of the Afghan armed forces by the US as "enemy combatants" not entitled to prisoner of war status or any protection under the Geneva Conventions; e.g. Steyn, "Guantánamo Bay: The Legal Black Hole" (*ICLQ* 2004). This is an additional reason to avoid the use of such labels in discussions on the legal status and protection of such persons under international law. See the references with regard to legitimacy of cause above (notes 698-700); see also Rosas (1976), pp. 312-316.

[954] To be noted that traditionally such persons were not entitled to any protection under international humanitarian law, since most of them were excluded from the protection as prisoners of war and their was – until 1949 – no international treaty law that regulated the protection (and internment) of persons

3.1.1.1. The text of article 4 GC IV

First, we must look at the text of article 4 GC IV, which reads in relevant part:

> "Persons protected by the Convention are those who, at a given moment and in any manner whatsoever, find themselves, in case of a conflict or occupation, in the hands of a Party to the conflict or Occupying Power [...] Persons protected by [Geneva Convention I, II or III], shall not be considered as protected persons within the meaning of the present Convention." (article 4§1 and 4§4 GC IV)

As we can see, the text of article 4 does not limit the Convention's application to "civilians" or even "persons not participating in hostilities". On the contrary, its wording – "persons [...] who [...] in any manner whatsoever [are] in the hands of a Party to the conflict or Occupying Power" – is broad enough to include all four groups of persons we discussed above.[955] Moreover, since none of these persons are protected persons within the meaning of Geneva Conventions I, II or III, they do not fall into the category of persons explicitly excluded from the scope of application of GC IV by the last sentence of article 4 GC IV.[956]

Thus, the text of article 4 does not exclude[957] so-called unlawful or unprivileged combatants from the scope of application of GC IV.[958] This question was not absent from the minds of the drafters of GC IV, as is illustrated by the preparatory works of that Convention.[959] Pictet points out that:

> "The words 'at a given moment in any manner whatsoever' were intended to ensure that all situations and cases were covered. The articles refer [...] even,

other than prisoners of war. E.g.: Baxter (*BYIL* 1951), pp. 327-327.

[955] The definition of "protected persons" under GC IV is not restricted to persons interned on the basis of its provisions. As internees are concerned however, the words "in the hands of" must be understood in the same sense as the words "fallen into the power of the enemy" in article 4 GC III to include both persons who have been arrested or captured and persons who have, individually or collectively, surrendered; *cf. supra* chapter II-1, section 1.1.

[956] The 4th group of persons described above (members of the armed forces of a party to the conflict who have forfeited their individual right to be a prisoner of war) would still be protected under GC I or II in case they are wounded, sick or ship-wrecked. These Conventions do not contain any provisions on their possible deprivation of liberty however, which is regulated exclusively by GC III and IV. Therefore, when they are subsequently interned, they are in fact not (sufficiently) protected under GC I or II and can therefore not be excluded from the scope of application of GC IV. Finally, we have seen in chapter II-1 that the personal scope of application of GC I and GC II is quasi-identical to that of GC III and they therefore risk to fall outside their scope of application in any case.

[957] We will discuss any potential exclusion on the basis of nationality in the next section, as it concerns all protected persons under GC IV and not only so-called unlawful or unprivileged combatants.

[958] In the same sense, see e.g. Dörmann (*IRRC* 2003), p. 50; CoE, *Venice Commission Opinion* (2003), §§30-31.

[959] Under the rules of treaty interpretation, recourse may be had to the preparatory works of a treaty as a subsidiary means of interpretation "in order to confirm the meaning resulting from the application of article 31 [i.e. the ordinary meaning to be given to the terms of the treaty in their context and in the light of its object and purpose]" (article 32 VCLT). In light of the controversies over the inclusion of so-called unlawful or unprivileged combatants in the scope of application of GC IV and the possible confusion that may flow from the Convention's title, it is useful to illustrate that the text of article 4 GC IV clearly reflects the intention of its drafters not to exclude this categories of persons from the protection of GC IV.

> it may be, to spies or saboteurs. [...] The definition of protected persons in paragraph 1 [of article 4 GC IV] is a very broad one which includes members of the armed forces - fit for service, wounded, sick or shipwrecked – who fall into enemy hands. The treatment which such persons are to receive is laid down in special Conventions to which the provision refers. They must be treated as prescribed in the texts which concern them. But if, for some reason, prisoner of war status – to take one example – were denied to them, they would become protected persons under the present Convention. [A heated debate broke out over article 5 GC IV] because the Convention had adopted a definition of protected persons which covered those who committed hostile acts without being members of the regular combatant forces."[960]

And Sassòli highlights that:

> "The ICRC had first suggested referring to 'persons who take no active part in hostilities'. The XVIIth International Red Cross Conference objected that '[t]his phrasing did not, however, cover those who commit hostile acts whilst not being regular combatants, such as *saboteurs* and *franc-tireurs*.' This problem was reported to the Diplomatic Conference, which therefore adopted the present wording [of article 4 GC IV]."[961]

Other relevant provisions of the Fourth Geneva Convention and Additional Protocol I confirm this reading of the text of article 4 GC IV.

3.1.1.2. The context of article 4 GC IV

First, for our present purposes – namely who may and who may not be interned on the basis of GC IV – it is important to point out first that the Convention's provisions on who can be interned and for what reasons (articles 41-43 and 78 GC IV), do not use the word "civilian" but rather the term "protected persons" as defined in article 4 GC IV.[962]

Moreover, the 2nd paragraph of article 110 GC IV, concerned with the exemption from postal and transport charges for correspondence and relief parcels for internees, explicitly alludes to the fact that not only civilians can be interned on the basis of GC IV:

> "the exemption provided by the Universal Postal Convention of 1947 and by the agreements of the Universal Postal Union in favour of *civilians* of enemy nationality detained in camps or civilian prisons, *shall be extended to the other interned persons protected by the present Convention.* The countries not

960 Pictet, *Commentary GC IV* 8 (1958), pp. 47, 50 and 52. We will discuss article 5 GC IV in more detail below.

961 Sassòli (*JICJ* 2004), p. 101, original italics.

962 Actually, the word "civilian" is only used 27 times in GC IV: once in the title, once in the first paragraph of the Preamble which reiterates that title, once in relation to humanitarian organizations with relief operations for civilians (article 10), once in relation to neutralized zones for the protection of all persons not or no longer taking part in hostilities (article 15), twelve times in relation to civilian hospitals, civilian wounded and sick and civilian medical and religious personnel (articles 18 to 23), twice with regard to the obligation of humane treatment of protected persons for both civilian and military agents of the party in whose hands they are (articles 32 and 144), seven times with regard to the Occupying Power's responsibility to protect and provide for the needs of the civilian population in occupied territory (articles 49, 55, 57 and 63) and twice more in article 110 GC IV, *cf. infra*.

signatory to the above-mentioned agreements shall be bound to grant freedom from charges in the same circumstances." (emphasis added)

Also relevant here is article 45§3 AP I, which stipulates that:

"Any person who has taken part in hostilities, who is not entitled to prisoner-of-war status and who does not benefit from more favourable treatment in accordance with the Fourth Convention shall have the right at all times to the protection of Article 75 of this Protocol."

The language of article 45§3 AP I clearly takes into account that some persons who have directly participated in hostilities are indeed protected persons under GC IV. Otherwise "the formulation 'who does not benefit from more favourable treatment in accordance with the Fourth Geneva Convention' would be meaningless."[963] Moreover, article 45§3 AP I contains another implicit confirmation of our reading of article GC IV where it concludes that:

"In occupied territory, any such person, unless he is held as a spy, shall also be entitled, notwithstanding Article 5 of the Fourth Convention, to his rights of communication under that Convention."

Which brings us to article 5 GC IV – entitled "derogations" – which reads in relevant part as follows:

"Where, in the territory of a Party to the conflict, the latter is satisfied that an individual protected person is definitely suspected of or engaged in activities hostile to the security of the State, such individual person shall not be entitled to claim *such rights and privileges* under the present Convention as would, if exercised in the favour of such individual person, be *prejudicial to the security* of such State.

Where in occupied territory an individual protected person is detained as a spy or saboteur, or as a person under definite suspicion of activity hostile to the security of the Occupying Power, such person shall, in those cases *where absolute military security so requires*, be regarded as having forfeited *rights of communication* under the present Convention.

In each case, such persons shall nevertheless be treated with humanity, and in case of trial, shall not be deprived of the *rights of fair and regular trial prescribed by the present Convention.* They shall also be granted the *full* rights and privileges of a protected person under the present Convention at the earliest date consistent with the security of the State or Occupying Power, as the case may be." (our emphasis, both italics and underlining)

Article 5 allows for derogation from certain rights under the Convention for persons engaging in espionage,[964] sabotage or other activities hostile to the

[963] Dörmann (*IRRC* 2003), p. 51. In the same sense: CoE, *Venice Commission Opinion* (2003), §41.

[964] We have seen in chapter II-1 that members of the armed forces who engage in acts of espionage and are caught in the act or before they rejoin their ranks are not entitled to be prisoners of war. If their captor does not grant them such status, they are not protected by the Third Geneva Convention and thus are protected persons under GC IV; e.g. Sandoz et al., *Commentary AP I and II* (1987), p. 570: "The spy who is denied the status of prisoner of war is a [...] protected by the Fourth Convention (except that in occupied territory [he] may lose his rights of communication (Article 5)), and by Article 75 [AP I]." In the same sense, mercenaries – a typical example of so-called unlawful combatants (they are not entitled

security of a party to the conflict, or an Occupying Power (words underlined in the text of provision quoted above), demonstrating that these persons are indeed protected under GC IV.[965] Persons involved in such activity – like any other protected person under GC IV – may not only be punished for their acts under the domestic legislation of the State in who hands they fall; some of their rights as protected persons under the Fourth Geneva Convention may also be restricted when necessary for military or security reasons.

The provisions of article 5 GC IV – when read superficially – could create the impression that the persons mentioned therein are to be excluded from the scope of application of the Convention as a whole.[966] But the precise wording of the article itself (in italics in the text of the provision quoted above) contradicts such a conclusion: in the territory of a party to the conflict, only "such rights and privileges as would be prejudicial to the security of the State" may be suspended, and they must be restored "at the earliest date consistent with the security of the State." Likewise, in occupied territory the "rights of communication" of spies, saboteurs and persons suspected of hostile activity may be suspended; rights that must also be restored "at the earliest date consistent with the security of the Occupying Power." And in any case: persons against whom such restrictions are imposed "shall not be deprived of the rights of fair and regular trial prescribed by the Convention."[967] As Pictet points out:

> "It may [...] seem rather surprising that a humanitarian Convention should tend to protect spies, saboteurs or irregular combatants. Those who take part in the struggle while not belonging to the armed forces are acting deliberately outside the laws of warfare. Surely they know the dangers to which they are exposing themselves. It might therefore have been simpler to exclude them from the benefits of the Convention, if such a course had been possible, but the terms espionage, sabotage, terrorism, banditry and intelligence with the enemy, have so often been used lightly, and applied to such trivial offences, that it was not advisable to leave the accused at the mercy of those detaining them."[968]

If spies, saboteurs or so-called unlawful or unprivileged combatants were not protected under GC IV, there would be no need to include an article which allows an Interning Power to derogate from some of their rights under the Convention where this is necessary for military or security reasons.[969]

---

to combatant status and thus not entitled to participate in hostilities, article 47§1 AP I) – are protected persons under GC IV; e.g. Sandoz et al., *Commentary AP I and II* (1987), p. 575: "Deprived of the status of combatant and prisoner of war, a mercenary is a civilian [in the sense of a protected person under GC IV] who could fall under Article 5 of the Fourth Convention."

965 In the same sense: Pictet, *Commentary GC IV* (1958), p. 55; Dörmann (*IRRC* 2003), p. 50; CoE, *Venice Commission Opinion* (2003), §43.

966 For such an interpretation, see for example Canada, *LOAC Manual* (2001), section 1104.

967 Sandoz et al., *Commentary to AP I and II* (1987), p. 870, concerning "persons who, on the basis of Article 5 of the fourth Convention, are deprived of certain rights laid down by that Convention during detention" note that "[t]here can be no doubt that Article 75 constitutes a minimum standard which does not allow for any exceptions. Such persons must regain all the rights and privileges laid down by the Convention as soon as circumstances permit." In the same sense: Dörmann (*IRRC* 2003), pp. 66-71.

968 Pictet, *Commentary GC IV* (1958), p. 53.

969 In this sense, see also Gehring, "Loss of Civilian Protections under the Fourth Geneva Convention

Article 5 does not limit the personal scope of application of GC IV; it authorizes derogations where military necessity or security so requires, derogations that must be lifted as soon as the reasons justifying them cease to exist. As long as such derogations are in force, all other provisions of the Convention with regards to persons subject to them must be complied with.[970] The argument that so-called unlawful or unprivileged combatants are excluded from the personal scope of application of GC IV is therefore not in conformity with the text of the Convention itself, in that it would render the existence of article 5 GC IV completely unnecessary.

3.1.1.3. The object and purpose of GC IV

The purpose of the Fourth Geneva Convention – like that of the other Geneva Conventions and their Additional Protocols – is to protect individuals who face a genuine risk of abuse or arbitrary action at the hands of a party to the conflict who perceives them as belonging to the enemy. The text of article 4 GC IV, read in light of the protective purpose of the Convention and that of international humanitarian law more generally, may thus not be interpreted in a manner that a person genuinely so at risk falls outside the scope of application of the Geneva Conventions as a whole. Therefore, a person who falls into the hands of an enemy power who deprives him or her of his or her liberty either is a prisoner of war, retained medical or religious personnel, or a protected person under GC IV. In the oft-quoted words of Pictet:

> "[Article 4§4 GC IV confirms] a general principle which is embodied in all four Geneva Conventions of 1949. Every person in enemy hands must have some status under international law: he is either a prisoner of war and, as such, covered by the Third Convention, a civilian [in the sense of protected person] covered by the Fourth Convention, or again, a member of the medical personnel of the armed forces who is covered by the First Convention. *There is no* intermediate status; nobody in enemy hands can be outside the law. We feel that that is a satisfactory solution - not only satisfying to the mind, but also, and above all, satisfactory from the humanitarian point of view."[971]

The above interpretation of article GC IV and the fact that there is no gap between GC III and GC IV is also supported by State practice,[972] international case

---

and Protocol I" (*MLLWR* 1980), p. 79: "several delegations [to the 1949 Diplomatic Conference] stated that, in cases involving spies, saboteurs or *unprivileged combatants*, there should be some derogations permitted *from the rights normally accorded protected persons*. Otherwise those rights could be used to the disadvantage of the detaining state. *To satisfy this concern, article 5 was adopted*. It permits denial of certain rights [...] when exercise of the rights denied would be prejudicial to the security of the territorial state or occupying power" (footnotes omitted, emphasis added). As Gehring indicates, the interpretation of article 5 GC IV above also finds support in the preparatory works of that article; for a good summary thereof, see Jinks, "The Declining Significance of POW Status" (*Harv.ILJ* 2004), pp. 383-384.

970 Pictet, *Commentary GC IV* (1958), pp. 52-53, 56 and 57-58. In the same sense: CoE, *Venice Commission Opinion* (2003), §43 and §§45-46.

971 Pictet, *Commentary GC IV* (1958), p. 51.

972 See for example UK, *LOAC Manual* (2004); pp. 44 and 48 (including references to UK practice); UK, *JDP 1-10* (2006), Chapter 1, Section 2; US, *Army Field Manual, FM 27-10 The Law of Land*

law,[973] and the majority of academic experts who have addressed the issue.[974] As to the minority of scholars who continue to reject the idea that so-called

---

Warfare (1956), §73 ("If a person is determined by a competent tribunal, acting in conformity with Article 5, *GPW*, not to fall within any of the categories listed in Article 4, [GC III] he is not entitled to be treated as a prisoner of war. He is, however, a "protected person" within the meaning of Article 4, [GC IV])", §247 ("Subject to qualifications set forth in paragraph 248 [re: article 5 GC IV], those protected by [GC IV] also include all persons who have engaged in hostile or belligerent conduct but who are not entitled to treatment as prisoners of war"); US, *Army Regulation 190-8: Enemy Prisoners of War, Retained Personnel, Civilian Internees and Other Detainees* (1997), which mentions spies and saboteurs under the chapter on civilian internees, protected by GC IV (and subject to the derogations of its article 5) ; US, *Annex A to Army Directive No. 381-46 (1967), "Criteria for Classification and disposition of Detainees"* (1967), article 2 (confirms the mutual exclusiveness of POW (including members of "irregular armed forces" captured while engaged in "combat or a belligerent act under arms") and non-POW (including under "civil defendants" members of irregular armed forces who are suspected of "being a spy, saboteur or terrorist" or who do not engage in "combat or a belligerent act under arms"); but departing from its general practice and doctrine, US *Joint Doctrine Publication 3-63 on Detainee Operations* (2005) establishes "[i]n reference to the Global War on Terror [...] an additional classification of detainees who, through their own conduct, are not entitled to the privileges and protection of the Geneva Conventions [and] when detained, are classified as enemy combatants" (to be noted that the US in the meantime considers the global war on terror to be a NIAC and thus the classification of "enemy combatant" should no longer be understood to create a fourth category of internees in IAC. We will come back to the notion of enemy combatant in the so-called war on terror in more detail below in section 3.2.2); Canada, *LOAC Manual* (2001), section 1104 erroneously interprets article 5 GC IV as an exclusion clause to the definition of protected under GC IV, but Canada's *Joint Doctrine Manual on Prisoner of War Handling, Detainees and Interrogation & Tactical Questioning in International Operations* (2004) establish equal treatment for interned and detained "civilians and unlawful belligerents" (Annex B).

[973] E.g.: ICTY, *Delalić* (1998), §271; IAC°HR, *Coard v. USA* (1999), §§31 and 51; Israel, SC, *Targeted Killings Case* (2006), §§26-28. To US Supreme Court's decision in *Ex Parte Quirin* (1942), often relied upon to exclude so-called unlawful combatants from the scope of application of international humanitarian law as a whole – is not really relevant for the interpretation of article 4 GC IV. It pre-dates the 1949 Geneva Conventions and thus, where it concluded that members of enemy armed forces engaged in sabotage are not entitled to prisoner of war status and thus were not protected by international humanitarian law, it could not take into account the fact the protection that GC IV would confer on persons not entitled to prisoner of war status.

[974] Draper (*Isr.YHR* 1971), p. 197; Kalshoven (*MLLWR* 1972), p. 71; Mallison & Mallison (*LCP* 1978), p. 5; Bothe et al. (1982), pp. 261-263; Risius in Rowe (1993), p. 290; McCoubrey, *International Humanitarian Law: Modern Developments in the Limitation of Warfare* (1998), p. 137; Ben-Naftali & Gleichgevitch (*Harv.ILJ* 2000), pp. 243-244; Sassòli (*ACDI* 2001), pp. 230-231 and 240; Aldrich (*AJIL* 2002), p. 893 and note 12; Aldrich (*HV* 2002), p. 203 and note 4; David (2002), p. 436; Gasser, "Acts of Terror, 'Terrorism' and International Humanitarian Law" (*IRRC* 2002), p. 566; Naqvi (*IRRC* 2002), p. 581 and note 46; Dörmann (*IRRC* 2003), pp. 45-72; IIHL, *Report of the San Remo Roundtable* (2003), pp. 10-11; CoE, *Venice Commission Opinion* (2003), §§9, 15, 30, and 40-48; Murphy, Prisoner of War Status and the Question of Guantánamo Bay Detainees (*HRLR* 2003), p. 267; Condorelli & Naqvi, "The War against Terrorism and *Jus in Bello*: Are the Geneva Conventions Out of Date?" in Bianchi (2004), p. 35; Jinks (*Harv.JIL* 2004), pp. 367 and 380-409; Pejic (*BYIL* 2004), pp. 79-80; Sassòli (*JICJ* 2004), pp. 100-102; Cassese, "On whether Israel's Targeted Killings of Palestinian Terrorists is Consonant with International Humanitarian Law", Expert opinion submitted to the Israeli Supreme Court in the *Targeted Killings Case* (2006), §§7, 22 and 26; Doswald-Beck in Chesterman & Lehnardt (2007), pp. 124-125; Rogers in Wilmshurst & Breau (2007), pp. 115 and 125; Walen & Venzke (*ZaöRV* 2007), p. 854; Ipsen in Fleck (2008), p. 83; Rona (*HRF Paper* 2008), p. 7; Goodman, "The Detention of Civilians in Armed Conflict" (*AJIL* 2009), p. 53 and note 25; and Lubell (2010), pp. 144-146. Some authors find the question is unsettled, but do not reject the interpretation above entirely. Dinstein, for example, does not explicitly say unlawful combatants are protected persons under GC IV, but his references to their

unlawful or unprivileged combatants are protected persons under GC IV,[975] and some of the domestic case law they rely on, Dörmann correctly points out that:

> "Despite the clear indications in the wording of GC IV, some legal commentators seemingly do not recognize the applicability of GC IV to unlawful combatants at all. However, they do not give any legal reasoning for their position. It is merely asserted that GC IV does not cover unlawful combatants; an analysis of its Article 4 is not provided. When these authorities refer to case law (in particular *ex parte Quirin*), it is case law that predates GC IV. Considering that the issue was simply not specifically regulated in any instrument of international humanitarian law before the adoption of GC IV, this approach is somewhat doubtful. More recent case law correctly adopts a rather different view [...] In 1949, GC IV was adopted in the knowledge of the problems associated with unlawful combatants [...] It is therefore in our view hardly defendable to maintain that unlawful combatants were generally excluded from the scope of application of GC IV, contrary to the rather comprehensive wording of its Article 4. The same would be true of claims that there is coexisting customary international law which comprehensively covers unlawful combatants and would constitute a sort of *lex specialis*. [...] In this connection it should also be recalled that the drafters of [AP I] apparently had an understanding of the scope of application of GC IV which would include at least certain types of unlawful combatants."[976]

3.1.1.4. The potential of GC IV to adequately deal with protected persons who pose a security threat

The main reasons advanced to exclude so-called unlawful or unprivileged combatants from prisoner of war status actually support our argument that they

rights and especially article 5 GC IV suggest he might agree with the majority opinion (Dinstein (2004), pp. 29-33 and Dinstein (2010), pp. 35-38). Goldman & Tittemore do not devote any attention nor take a final position on the issue, but refer to Baxter (1951) to say that "automatic" protection under GC IV for persons who do not qualify as POW is "problematic" (Goldman & Tittemore (*ASIL Task Force* 2002), note 108 at p. 33). In a similar vain, Roberts does not reject the possibility of protection under GC IV, but finds it "doubtful" (Roberts (*Isr.YHR* 2002), pp. 225 and 229-230). Watkin on the one hands sees unlawful or unprivileged combatants as "a subset of civilians" as opposed to combatants, but then follows Baxter's position on their exclusion from GC IV, while acknowledging at the same time that protection under GC IV would be a better approach (Watkin, "Combatants, Unprivileged Belligerents and Conflicts in the 21st Century" (*HPCR Background Paper* 2003), pp. 4-5 and 18). Finally, it is worth noting that some of the older literature raises doubts as to whether persons captured in the "zone of operations" (i.e. where active combat is ongoing) as opposed to territory under the control of a party to a conflict or of an Occupying Power, qualify as protected persons under GC IV, see for example e.g. Baxter, (*BYIL* 1951), p. 328; Draper, (*Isr.YHR* 1971), p. 197; and Rosas (1976), p. 411. We agree with Jinks – based on our analysis of the relevant provisions of GC IV and AP I above – that a correct reading of articles 4 and 5 GC IV should be able to dissipate that doubt (Jinks (*Harv.ILJ* 2004), pp. 393-397).

975 E.g.: Baxter (*BYIL* 1951), pp. 328 and 332 (it is interesting to note however that Baxter was the principal author of the 1956 US *Army Field Manual*, which explicitly classifies unlawful and unprivileged combatants as protected persons under GC IV, *cf. supra*); Detter de Lupis, *The Law of War* (2000), p. 136; Greenwood (*IA* 2002), p. 316; and Green, *The Contemporary Law of Armed Conflict* (2008), pp. 129 and 225.

976 Dörmann (*IRRC* 2003), pp. 59-60 (original italics). While his article only covers our sub-categories 2 and 3, Dörmann's argument and conclusion applies also to our sub-category 4. In the same sense: Rona (*HRF Paper* 2008), p. 9.

should qualify as protected persons under GC IV. On the one hand States are reluctant to grant prisoner of war status in these cases because they say this would bar them from prosecuting and punishing the unlawful behaviour of such "combatants".[977] On the other hand, those who wish to deny them the protection of GC IV nonetheless feel they may be interned since they pose an obvious military threat. At the same time most accept that such persons should for the rest be entitled to treatment in captivity and conditions of detention that are very similar if not identical to that in GC III. All these concerns are addressed by the GC IV.

For one, protected persons who are not entitled to combatant immunity[978] may be prosecuted and punished for their mere participation in hostilities or for any specific criminal offence under the domestic legislation of the captor or the Occupying Power.[979]

Moreover, the Fourth Geneva Convention allows for protected persons who pose a direct military of security threat (which would definitely include the actual commission of belligerent acts or participation in hostilities, *cf. infra* section 3.2.2.2) to be interned without criminal charges, and for as long as necessary to counter that threat.

Also, when such persons have or are suspected to engage in hostile activities against the Interning or Detaining Power, the exact type of restrictions on their rights that may be necessary for military or security reasons are explicitly allowed for under the derogation provisions of article 5 GC VI.[980]

As Sassòli has pointed out: "The Fourth Convention has not been drafted by professional do-gooders or professors, but by experienced diplomats and military leaders, fully taking into account the security needs of a state confronted with dangerous people."[981] Therefore, it seems to us difficult to sustain the argument that for reasons of military necessity, so-called unlawful combatants or unprivileged belligerents should be excluded from the scope of application of GC IV.[982]

---

977 E.g.: Baxter (*BYIL* 1951), pp. 329-333 and 343; Cassese (*Expert Opinion Israel* 2006), §§23-25 and 28.

978 Which will be the case for virtually all so-called unlawful (e.g. civilians directly participating in hostilities, mercenaries,) or unprivileged (e.g. spies or combatants who failed to properly distinguish themselves in attack) combatants. Only members of the armed forces have combatant privilege and immunity (article 43§2 AP I), see also Dörmann (*IRRC* 2003), pp. 45-46, and Dinstein (2010), p. 37; and *supra* chapter II-1.

979 For an analysis of what criminal offences they may be prosecuted and punished for, see for example Baxter (*BYIL* 1951), p. 328; Dinstein (2010), p. 37; and Rogers in Wilmshurst & Breau (2007), pp. 120-126.

980 In the same sense: CoE, *Venice Commission Opinion* (2003), §§45-46.

981 Sassòli (*JICJ* 2004), p.104.

982 In the same sense, see also CoE, *Venice Commission Opinion* (2003), §§47-48: "This state of the law [i.e. unlawful or unprivileged combatants falling within the scope of application of GC IV] is appropriate, particularly in the light of the new forms of terrorism, which have recently emerged [...] The comprehensive system of the Geneva Conventions, which leaves no room for persons to fall into a legal void between GC III and GC IV, has a well-founded humanitarian rationale, and it is sufficiently flexible to accommodate legitimate security concerns, in particular as they arise from the new forms of international terrorism."

Finally, the rules on treatment and conditions of detention of internees in GC IV are almost identical to those for prisoners of war under GC III, but do not include the privileges prisoners of war are entitled to on the basis of membership in the armed forces of a party to the conflict.[983]

3.1.1.5. Conclusion

In conclusion, so-called unprivileged combatants (e.g. spies or combatants who fail to distinguish themselves as required by GC III and AP I), and so-called unlawful combatants (e.g. mercenaries, members of armed groups that do not qualify as armed forces of a Party to the conflict, and other persons who directly participate in hostilities without being entitled to do so), are protected persons under GC IV and may be interned – where necessary – on the basis of articles 41 to 43 GC IV (in the territory of a party to the conflict) or article 78 GC IV (in occupied territory). Moreover, some of their rights under the Convention may be restricted – where necessary for military or security reasons – in accordance with article 5 GC IV. Finally, they may be prosecuted, punished and imprisoned for any criminal offence they may have committed (including acts that would qualify as participation in hostilities) on the basis of the domestic legislation of their captor or penal legislation adopted by an Occupying Power in conformity with article 64 GC IV (*cf. infra*).

The Fourth Geneva Convention does not distinguish between different categories of persons on the basis of their status for the rules on the conduct of hostilities. The only distinction it makes is between protected persons who are in the territory of a party to the conflict and those who find themselves in occupied territory. Even so, with regard to internment, the provisions for both are quasi-identical. To avoid any confusion, it is therefore better to use the Convention's own terms to define who falls within its scope of application, namely that of "protected persons" rather than "civilians" or "civilian internees".[984]

The exclusion of individuals from the personal scope of application of GC IV – or of any other of the four Conventions or their Additional Protocols for that matter – may not be implied, but is only lawful when based on explicit exclusion clauses either in their provisions or in established customary international law. As far as the Fourth Geneva Convention is concerned, the only existing basis for exclusion from its personal scope of application is contained in paragraphs 2 and 3 of article 4 GC IV, to which we will turn our attention now.

3.1.2. Protected persons: the nationality requirement in article 4 GC IV

In the present section, we will discuss the nationality requirement in the Fourth Geneva Convention's definition of protected persons. According to article 4 GC IV a State's own nationals, or that of an allied or neutral State, do

---

[983] E.g.: articles 43-44 on the treatment of prisoners of war in accordance with their military rank; or article 60 on their continued payment in captivity.

[984] Again, the use of the terms "civilians" or "civilian internees" may lead to the – incorrect – belief that all persons interned on the basis of GC IV are civilians for the purposes of the conduct of hostilities.

not fall into the personal scope of application of the Fourth Geneva Convention. In this section, we will explain why in our view the nationality requirement in article 4 GC IV must be interpreted in a nuanced manner if it is to give the Convention's provisions their full effect and let them achieve their ultimate purpose, namely to protect all persons who find themselves in the hands of a party to a conflict that regards them as enemies against arbitrariness and abuse. Aware that the arguments go against predominant scholarly opinion, we will try to offer a number of elements in response to anticipated criticism.

3.1.2.1. A nuanced reading of article 4 to achieve the Convention's protective purpose

In what follows, we do not mean to propose an interpretation of the Convention that does away with the criterion of nationality, which, as we will see, remains an important limit on the scope of application of the Convention. We only propose to read that requirement in a nuanced manner, taking into account the reality of contemporary armed conflicts and developments in international law subsequent to the adoption of the article, so as to permit the Convention's provisions to continue to cover all those in need of its protection today.

(a.) The text of article 4 GC IV: indications of whom the Convention seeks to protect

Article 4 GC IV defines the personal scope of application of the Convention as follows:

> "Persons protected by the Convention are those who, at a given moment and in any manner whatsoever, find themselves, in case of a conflict or occupation, in the hands of a Party to the conflict or Occupying Power of which they are not nationals.
>
> Nationals of a State which is not bound by the Convention are not protected by it.
>
> Nationals of a neutral State who find themselves in the territory of a belligerent State, and nationals of a co-belligerent State, shall not be regarded as protected persons while the State of which they are nationals has normal diplomatic representation in the State in whose hands they are.
>
> Persons protected by [Geneva Convention I, II or II], shall not be considered as protected persons within the meaning of the present Convention."

The definition combines inclusive elements (single underlining) with exclusive elements (double underlining) aiming conjunctively to extend the Convention's application to all persons in need of its protection and at the same time limit it to only those persons who need its protection. Let us briefly look at each of these elements in turn to understand whom exactly the Convention sought to protect.

> "In the hands of" is intentionally broad language that seeks to include all persons present on the territory under the control of a party to the conflict, since they may face a real risk of arbitrary action, and thus need the protection of the Convention. It clearly includes persons in the physical custody of the Controlling

Power,[985] such as detainees and internees.[986] As is the case with prisoners of war under the protection of the Third Geneva Convention, the words "find themselves" cover those who either forcibly or voluntarily came to find themselves in the hands of the Controlling Power. This is reinforced by the wording "in any manner whatsoever", reflecting the intention of the drafters to cover all persons in actual need of protection against arbitrariness at the hands of the Controlling Power.[987]

Based on the same rationale of protection, the Convention logically excludes from its scope of application persons not considered to be at risk.[988]

First, it restricts its scope of application to persons in the hands of a "Party to the conflict or Occupying Power". Indeed, persons who are in the hands of a neutral State should by definition not be regarded by that State as enemies and thus are thus unlikely to be exposed to any risk of abusive or arbitrary action for reasons related to the armed conflict.

Second, the Convention excludes a good number of persons from its personal scope of application on the basis of their nationality. The Convention does not apply to the Controlling Power's own nationals,[989] nationals of co-belligerent (or allied) States with normal diplomatic representation in the territory of the Controlling Power, and nationals of neutral States with normal diplomatic representation in the Controlling Power in as far as these persons are present on the latter's territory. "Normal diplomatic representation" means a diplomatic representation that is functioning essentially as it would in peacetime: it must be able to offer effective diplomatic protection to its nationals at the hands of the Controlling Power, thus implying the accreditation of at least one diplomat to the Ministry of Foreign Affairs of the Controlling Power, who is effectively in a position to make official representations on behalf of his nationals, and whose

---

985 The term Controlling Power is used here as shorthand for the terms "a Party to the conflict or Occupying Power" in whose hands a protected person finds him- or herself.

986 Pictet, *Commentary GC IV* (1958), p. 47: "It is not merely a question of being in enemy hands directly, as a prisoner is."

987 Pictet, *Commentary GC IV* (1958), pp. 47-49.

988 The exclusion of nationals from a State who is not a party to the Fourth Geneva Convention has become merely theoretical since all States are parties to the Geneva Conventions today (the list of States parties to the Geneva Conventions is available on the website of the Swiss Ministry of Foreign Affairs at http://www.eda.admin.ch). Moreover, the fact that most of the Convention's provisions are part of customary IHL makes them applicable to all parties to all international armed conflicts. For their applicability to the conflicts where the United Nations is a party to the conflict, see Institute of International Law, *Resolution on the Applicability of IHL to UN Forces* (1971), article 2§2(b).

989 It is important to note that the inhabitants of an occupied territory do not become nationals of the Occupying Power, regardless of any territorial claims made by the Occupying Power regarding that territory; e.g.: Meron, "Prisoners of War, Civilians and Diplomats in the Gulf Crisis" (*AJIL* 1991), p. 105-106. See also article 47 GC IV: "Protected persons who are in occupied territory shall not be deprived, in any case or in any manner whatsoever, of the benefits of the present Convention by any change introduced, as the result of the occupation of a territory, into the institutions or government of the said territory, nor by any agreement concluded between the authorities of the occupied territories and the Occupying Power, nor by any annexation by the latter of the whole or part of the occupied territory."

representations are effectively followed by acceptable replies and results from the Controlling Power.[990]

Applied to internees, the text of article 4 thus excludes from the scope of application of GC IV persons who have the nationality of the Interning Power, or that of its allies or of a neutral State with whom the Interning Powers maintains normal diplomatic relations.[991]

(b.) The context of article 4: understanding the reasons behind the exclusion clause

Despite the clear wording in article 4, the Convention itself provides for an exception to this general regime, reflecting a "very special case, based on the position [...] people have taken up with regard to their own country":[992] Article 44 GC IV deals with refugees; it provides that a

> "Detaining Power shall not treat as enemy aliens exclusively on the basis of their nationality *de jure* of an enemy State, refugees who do not, in fact, enjoy the protection of any government."

Similarly, according to article 70 GC IV, nationals of an Occupying Power who – before the outbreak of armed conflict – sought refuge in the territory of a State subsequently occupied by their own State are protected persons regardless of their nationality.

For example, an Iraqi refugee present in Kuwait at the time of Iraq's invasion of that country (1990), who found himself in the hands of Iraqi forces during the conflict or the resulting occupation of Kuwait by Iraq, is a protected person under GC IV. The ICRC's Commentary on articles 44 and 70 GC IV is particularly enlightening for the purposes of our arguments below (on the interpretation of GC IV in light of its object and purpose) and merits to be quoted extensively:

> "When the country in which they [refugees] have taken refuge is involved in a war with their country of origin, *they become enemy aliens*, since they are citizens of an enemy Power. *Their position, however, is a special one*, for they are expatriates who have no longer any connection with their State of origin and do not enjoy the assistance of a Protecting Power. On the other hand, they have not established any permanent connection with the country which has granted

[990] Pictet, *Commentary GC IV* (1958), p. 49. See also articles 3§1(b) and 45(c) of the Vienna Convention on Diplomatic Relations (1961). Generally on diplomatic protection, see the ILC's *Draft Articles on Diplomatic Protection* (2006), article 1 of which defines diplomatic protection as follows: "diplomatic protection consists of the invocation by a State, through diplomatic action or other means of peaceful settlement, of the responsibility of another State for an injury caused by an internationally wrongful act of that State to a natural or legal person that is a national of the former State with a view to the implementation of such responsibility." As to the diplomats themselves, they are protected persons under GC IV, and in addition benefit from other international laws and customs that are specifically applicable to them. If the latter's provisions are more favourable they override the provisions of GC IV (Pictet, *Commentary GC IV* (1958), p. 51; Meron (*AJIL* 1991), p. 108-109).

[991] The definition of protected persons in occupied territory differs slightly on this point, *cf. infra* section 3.1.3.

[992] Pictet, *Commentary GC IV* (1958), p. 46.

them asylum. Consequently they do not enjoy the protection of any government. During the Second World War the number of refugees living in the territory of the belligerents was greater than ever before. Various belligerent countries made allowances for this state of affairs by introducing laws exempting such persons from measures taken against enemy aliens. [...] The Convention does not define the term refugee. It merely notes the fact that certain persons do not 'enjoy the protection of any government': if a protected person who is in law a national of an enemy State is in actual fact without any diplomatic protection (whether because he has broken with his country's government or because he does not wish to claim its protection), this provision applies to that person. The clause should be interpreted in this broad sense, in accordance with the spirit of the Convention. [...] *The purely formal criterion of nationality must therefore be adjusted*, for it rests on an essentially legal and technical conception, and the *strict application of such a criterion would be in contradiction to human reality and contrary to justice and morality*. When the Convention stipulates that the position of an enemy alien must not be considered solely in the light of his legal nationality, it *in fact invites belligerents to take into consideration a whole set of circumstances which may reveal what might be called the "spiritual affinity" or "ideological allegiance" of a protected person*. A State must decide whether the application of security measures is justified or not on the basis of these data and not by applying the superficial criterion of nationality. [...][[993]] *In view of the complexity of the problem and the variety of cases which may occur in practice, the Conference had to confine itself* to laying down general rules of a sufficiently flexible character, leaving a great deal to the discretion of governments. In the absence of more detailed rules, which it did not appear either possible or advisable to lay down, it is to be hoped that belligerents will apply this Article in the broadest humanitarian spirit, in order that the maximum use may be made of the resources it offers for the protection of refugees."[994]

---

[993] Part of the left out text reads: "As has been very rightly stressed [with reference to *Final Record 1949*, Vol. III, pp. 122-123], there is justification for the assumption that nationals who enjoy the protection of their government and of its agent, the Protecting Power, sympathise with the cause of their country and may represent a danger to the safety of the country where they are living. In the case of refugees, on the other hand, the contrary is to be presumed; the term refugee tends to imply that the persons concerned are opposed to the political system in force in their home country and have no reason to promote its success in any manner whatsoever. The Article does not give refugees an absolute right to exemption from security measures. It is only an urgent recommendation to belligerents. The status of refugees does not of itself give anyone a right to immunity. It does not prevent the adoption of security measures, internment for example. There may conceivably be among the refugees people whose political convictions or activities represent a danger to the security of the State, which would then be entitled to resort to the necessary control measures to the same extent and subject to the same conditions as for any person protected under the Convention [with a reference to *Final Record 1949*, Vol. II-B, pp. 411-413, and Vol. III, pp. 122-123]."

[994] Pictet, *Commentary GC IV* (1958), pp. 264-265 (emphasis added). The quotation is from the Commentary on article 44. The main arguments are reiterated explicitly in the Commentary on article 70, *Ibidem*, p. 350: "The clause should be compared with Article 44, which also deals with the position of refugees. [...] The commentary on Article 44 showed the meaning attached to the word "refugee" in the Convention. Refugees are people who have left their home country to seek refuge on alien soil as a result of political events or under the threat of persecution. They are thus in actual fact without the protection normally afforded by the State to which they belonged, but are not yet entitled to the legal protection of the State which has given them refuge."

While articles 44 and 70 GC IV are limited to the specific category of refugees, as defined by the Convention,[995] they are proof of the drafters' recognition of the risks of arbitrariness and abuse run by persons who find themselves in the hands of the State of which they are nationals, but whose "spiritual affinity" or "ideological allegiance" with another party to the conflict effectively places them outside the protection of that government. When drafting article 4 GC IV, States assumed that a person's loyalty in armed conflict would generally lie with his or her national State, and that the nationals of allied or neutral States would benefit from the protection of their country of origin. The exceptions provided for in article 4 itself (*cf. supra* on the requirement of normal diplomatic relations) and in articles 44 and 70 GC IV (refugees) however also demonstrate an awareness that this was only an assumption and that it did not always reflect reality. The protective purpose of the Convention and the logic of the definition of its personal scope of application, impose that persons who do not benefit from the effective protection of any government, should not be automatically deprived of the Convention's protection on the sole basis of their nationality, but must be considered protected persons under GC IV. As Pictet noted in his commentary of GC IV, the practice of States during World War II supports the logic behind this exception to the general rule on nationality.[996] That logic has also been confirmed and reinforced in the provisions of Additional Protocol I.

On the one hand, article 73 AP I reinforces articles 44 and 70 of GC IV by asserting that all refugees and stateless persons are protected by the Fourth Geneva Convention, "in all circumstances and without any adverse distinction."[997] On the other hand, in the type of conflicts covered by article 1§4 AP I, most if not all persons affected by the conflict will be in the power of a State of which it has the nationality. A literal interpretation of article 4 GC IV would lead to the absurd result that virtually no one affected by such conflicts would benefit from the provisions of Convention; nationality cannot be the sole basis for excluding them from the protection of the Convention, since this would mean the latter would virtually cease to apply at all.[998]

[995] It is important to note that the definition of refugees under the Geneva Conventions is broader than that of the 1951 International Refugee Convention. See Pictet, *Commentary GC IV* (1958), pp. 263-264 and 350: "Several instruments of international law [...] have defined the term refugee. The definitions in question are valid for the particular purposes of law for which they were formulated, but are too technical and too limited in scope to meet the requirements of the Geneva Conventions" [...] [who define refugees as persons] "in actual fact without the protection normally afforded by the State to which they belonged, but [...] not yet entitled to the legal protection of the State which has given them refuge."

[996] Pictet, *Commentary GC IV* (1958), p. 263. See also Wilson (*AJIL* 1943), p. 30.

[997] See also Sandoz et al., *Commentary AP I and II* (1987), at pp. 845-855, who highlight that the Protocol expanded the definition of refugees under the Convention to include refugees as defined by other instruments of international law accepted by the parties concerned, regardless of whether they have binding force or not ("all instruments containing a definition of refugees or stateless persons are relevant") and by relevant national legislation.

[998] Sandoz et al., *Commentary AP I and II* (1987), p. 867.

(c.) The object and purpose of the Fourth Geneva Convention: protecting persons in enemy hands

The discussion on refugees already demonstrates that in interpreting article 4 GC IV to determine whether a given individual falls within the scope of application of the Convention or not, one may not lose sight of the ultimate object and purpose of the Convention, which is to protect individual human beings against specific risks of abusive and arbitrary actions they may face in the context of armed conflict when they fall into the hands of a party to the conflict who considers them as enemies: persons whose loyalty or affinity lies with an adverse party to that conflict.[999] In this sense, it is useful to recall that proposals to exclude spies, saboteurs and so-called unlawful or unprivileged combatants from the Convention's scope of application were rejected because:

> "It might [...] have been simpler to exclude them from the benefits of the Convention [...] but the terms espionage, sabotage, terrorism, banditry and intelligence with the enemy, have so often been used lightly, and applied to such trivial offences, that it was *not advisable to leave the accused at the mercy of those detaining them*."[1000]

Those risks will most likely be exacerbated when the individual has the same nationality as his captor or interning power and will be considered a traitor.

In classic inter-State conflicts, nationality was and continues to be a *prima facie* indicator of where an individual's allegiance or loyalty lies. Nevertheless, the protective purpose of the Convention requires us to interpret its provisions – including article 4 – in a nuanced way, taking into account the potential risk a given individual may run in the hands of a party to the conflict that considers him or her an enemy, regardless of nationality. Moreover, a number of developments, both in society and in international law, that have an immediate impact on the issue must be taken into account when defining who is and who is not a protected person under GC IV today.

(d.) The circumstances of the conclusion of GC IV and subsequent developments in society and in international law: the need for dynamic interpretation in order to achieve the Convention's purpose

The Geneva Conventions were adopted in 1949, at a time where abuses witnessed in recent conflicts, and in particular the horrors of World War II profoundly shocked the international community and led to a series of important changes in the conception and normative substance of international law. In the wake of World War II, the international community adopted the United Nations Charter (1945), which prohibits the use of force in international relations; the Geneva Conventions (1949), meant to strengthen and expand the capacity of international humanitarian law to minimize human suffering in times of war; and the Universal Declaration of Human Rights (1948), which laid the groundwork

[999] Pictet, *Commentary GC IV* (1958), p. 75.

[1000] Pictet, *Commentary GC IV* (1958), p. 53. In the same sense (based on an analysis of the preparatory works of the Convention): Jinks (*Harv.ILJ* 2004), pp. 383-384.

for the development of a whole new body of international law, specifically aimed to protect individual human beings against an arbitrary and abusive exercise of power at the hands of their own government.

But the late 1940's were still the early days of contemporary international law.[1001] In spite of the adoption of the Universal Declaration of Human Rights only 9 months earlier (the first international instrument directly seeking to regulate the relation between a State and its citizens), and in spite of the adoption of common article 3 of the Geneva Conventions (the first international treaty norm directly regulating non-international armed conflict), the definition of the personal scope of application of the Fourth Geneva Convention still reflects the important role the principle of non-intervention continued to play in international relations. The restriction of the scope of application of GC IV on the basis of nationality – apart from reflecting the generally valid assumption that a State does not consider its own nationals as enemies and its nationals are therefore not at risk in its hands because of the mere existence of an armed conflict – also obliged that cornerstone of traditional international law.[1002]

The following reflection by Pictet, made only a few years after the adoption of the Fourth Geneva Convention, is interesting to note here:

> "Satisfactory as they may be, the results achieved [by GC IV] are not yet complete; for the Convention, we must remember, does not apply to the relations of a State with its own 'nationals'. It conforms to the traditional conception of international law. A person is only a legal subject within a State and the provisions concerning the protection of civilians in time of war take no account of disputes which may exist between the State and its own citizens. That is a serious matter, in view of the arbitrary action of certain governments during the last world war. [...] It is possible that a doctrine which is today only beginning to take shape may acquire authority in international law tomorrow and one day provide the basis for establishing the rights of the individual in relation to the State of which he is a 'citizen'. The Universal Declaration of Human Rights is doubtless as yet only a 'common standard of achievement for all peoples and all nations', but just as the protection afforded by the humanitarian Conventions applied first to the wounded and sick on the battlefield, and was then extended to prisoners of war and finally to civilians (with the exception of nationals), it may well end by covering the 'citizens' of a country themselves, and so embody in law the original guiding idea of the Red Cross, that suffering should be relieved wherever it exists, without political considerations of any kind, in the name of the respect due to the human person. Two important Expert Conferences convened by the International Committee of the Red Cross and composed of persons eminent in international law or in the Red Cross movement have already stated that that is their view. It is to be hoped that governments will concur in the conclusions of the experts and consider that it is in the interests of humanity and in accordance with the requirements of civilization that humanitarian safeguards

[1001] *Cf. supra* Introduction.

[1002] Pictet, *Commentary GC IV* (1958), p. 46.

– in particular those defined in the present Convention – should apply to people with whom their own government is in dispute for political or social reasons."[1003]

Pictet's hope did materialize, slowly but surely, in the decades following the adoption of the Convention, and governments indeed heeded the call for a progressive humanization of international law.[1004] The process set in motion by the adoption of the UDHR and common article 3 of the Geneva Conventions quickly gathered considerable speed and the substantive scope of the traditional principle of non-intervention was significantly reduced in the second half of the 20th century, with the adoption of an important number of widely ratified treaties in the spheres of peoples' right to self-determination, individual and collective human rights, the protection of refugees and asylum-seekers, and the repression of international crimes.[1005]

Today, international law imposes important legal limits on the authority of States to restrict an individual's fundamental rights and freedoms, including his or her right to liberty, both in times of peace and in times of war, and regardless of his or her nationality.[1006] The principle of non-intervention, as it was understood by the drafters of the Fourth Geneva Convention in 1949 can therefore no longer stand in the way of an interpretation of article 4 GC IV that takes it beyond the ordinary meaning of its provisions in order to take into account subsequent developments both in international law and in the features of contemporary armed conflicts, and to ensure its continued effectiveness in protecting all those at particular risk of abuse or arbitrariness in times of armed conflict.

Another important factor to consider when reading the provisions regarding nationality in article 4 GC IV is that it relies on the assumption that a Party to the conflict or an Occupying Power will not regard its own nationals, that of co-belligerent States and that of neutral States as enemies, and they therefore do not *need* the protection of the Convention. The provisions of article 44 and 70 GC IV demonstrate the drafter's awareness that this assumption does not always reflect reality. Nevertheless, not only refugees, but also other persons may, because of their ethnic, religious, political or ideological affinity with an adverse party to the conflict, be considered enemies by their own national State.[1007] An interpretation of

---

1003 Pictet, *Commentary GC IV* (1958), pp. 372-373 (footnotes omitted).

1004 *Cf. supra* notes 38-39 and accompanying text.

1005 This is without prejudice to the continued relevance of the principle of non-intervention by States in the internal affairs of a third State, which remains a cornerstone of international law. The scope of this principle (which is much wider than the extent to which international law can affect a State's legal relationship with its citizens or nationals) has however evolved, and there are today more exceptions to this principle than was the case until the mid-20th century. See for example Institute of International Law, *La détermination du domaine réservé et ses effets* (1954), article 1§2: "L'étendue de ce domaine dépend du droit international et varie suivant son développement"; Brownlie (1998), pp. 295-296 (on the gradual erosion of the reserved domain); and Meron (2006), pp. 247-306 (on the impact in the law on State responsibility) and 497-527 (on the humanitarian and human rights factors in multilateral sanctions and interventions).

1006 *Cf. supra* Part I.

1007 This is also demonstrated by the domestic legislation of certain States in determining "enemy character" in time of armed conflict. As Weis points out: "each belligerent State is free to apply – without prejudice to existing treaty obligations – its own laws for determining enemy character. [...]

article 4 GC IV that relies on the text of that provision alone may in certain cases defy the Convention's object and purpose for the exact same reason underpinning the exception made for refugees in articles 44 and 70 GC IV: in such cases, a strict application of the nationality requirement in article 4 would effectively exclude persons in need of the Convention's protection from its personal scope of application. The assumption of the drafters of article 4 GC IV in such cases does not always reflect reality, and today it does so less and less. The explanations for this phenomenon are manifold and not entirely new.[1008]

First, emigration and other population movements result in an increasing number of persons being expatriate and/or having multiple nationalities. In the Iraq-Kuwait example mentioned above, the child of an Iraqi refugee in Kuwait with a Kuwaiti mother would most likely have had both Kuwaiti and Iraqi nationality and thus be a national of both parties to the conflict. It is submitted that that person would most likely be as much at risk at the hands of Iraq as any other Kuwaiti would have been, in spite of his Iraqi nationality. Furthermore, as an Iraqi in Kuwait, possibly with more affinity with Kuwait than with the Iraqi government that caused his or her father to flee his native country, he or she might be considered more of an enemy worth of punishment than a non-Iraqi Kuwaiti. Another, real, example is that of Hilal Abdul-Razzaq Ali Al-Jedda. Born in Iraq but granted asylum and permanent leave in the UK in 1994, Al-Jedda was captured by US forces in Iraq in 2003 and transferred into UK custody there. A dual British-Iraqi national, he was treated as an enemy national and interned by UK forces in Iraq, but was still denied the protection of GC IV by the UK courts because of his British nationality.[1009]

Second, an increasing number of persons, for reasons of "spiritual affinity or ideological allegiance", reside abroad or even travel to the territory of a party engaged in armed conflict with their national State to actively participate in hostilities on behalf of that party. For example, John Walker Lindh and David

Moreover, nationals of a neutral State acquire enemy character if they have in some way, identified themselves by their conduct with the enemy, e.g. by joining his armed forces: they have become 'assimilated to enemy nationals'. This applies even to belligerent's own subjects" (Weis, *Nationality and Statelessness in International Law* (1979), pp. 9 and 12). See also Brownlie, "The Relations of Nationality in Public International Law" (*BYIL* 1963), pp. 347-348: "it is common for legislation and judicial decisions to create functional nationality whereby parts of national law are applied to aliens on the basis of allegiance, residence and other connexions [...] Thus legislation in many countries has defined the enemy alien in functional terms and without dependence on the 'technical' nationality of the country in question. [...] From the functional approach it follows that stateless persons may be classified as 'neutrals', and further, that a dual national may be held by one of the States concerned to be an enemy. [...] Hence functional rules may concentrate on a system of evidence and not primarily on 'effectiveness.' In time of war any link may give cause for concern and quantum of links is less important."

1008 Some of these reasons existed and were invoked by scholars even before 1949 to justify a definition of protected persons not exclusively based on nationality. See for example Wilson's premonitory thoughts (*AJIL* 1943), p. 30: "Even the term "enemy" tends to cause undue hardships if applied without discrimination. Ideological cleavage in the twentieth century has unquestionably caused a mere nationality test for determining "enemy" character to be less adequate than in past wars. The possibilities of dual nationality, and denaturalization for reasons of lack of loyalty, are present."

1009 UK, HoL, *Al-Jedda* (2007), §32 confirming on this issue the Judgment of the Court of Appeal in the same case (UK, Court of Appeal, *Al-Jedda* (2006), §40.

Hicks, respectively a US and an Australian citizen, converted to Islam and travelled to Afghanistan, where they fought alongside the Taliban against the US and its allies in 2001. Both were initially captured by the Northern Alliance but were transferred into US custody. Lindh was subsequently tried and convicted to 20 years imprisonment in the US; Hicks was transferred to Guantánamo Bay where he spent five years before being tried and convicted to seven years imprisonment, after which he was repatriated to Australia to serve what was left of his sentence.[1010]

Third, some armed conflicts are fought by or with the participation of rather broad coalitions of States, therefore expanding the potential number of persons who are nationals of co-belligerent States. Examples are again Iraq and Afghanistan, but also the Democratic Republic of the Congo.[1011]

Finally, the authorization or mandate to engage or participate in international armed conflicts and occupations that States may receive from international intergovernmental organizations, challenges the notion of neutral States in such conflicts.[1012] For example, would a national of Albania – a member State of NATO that did not have troops on the ground in Afghanistan during the international phase of the conflict – be a national of a neutral State when he fell into the hands of the Taliban?[1013] Similarly, would a national of a UN member State without troops on the ground in East-Timor be a national of a neutral State in the hands of INTERFET, the United Nations mandated troops that effectively administered East-Timor in 1999? These hypothetical cases demonstrate that the issue of nationality may not always be as simple as it seems.

[1010] On Lindh, *cf. supra* notes 711-714 and accompanying text; on Hicks, see BBC, David Hicks: 'Australian Taleban'", 20 May 2007. A similar case is that of Mamdouh Habib, a dual Egyptian-Australian citizen who was captured by US forces in Afghanistan on 5 October 2001, transferred to Pakistan, subsequently to Egypt, then back into US custody in Afghanistan, and finally to Guantánamo Bay in May 2002. Habib was ultimately released without charge and repatriated to Australia on 28 January 2005. Australia has so far denied the applicability of the Geneva Conventions to Habib, on the basis of his nationality. For more background on this case, see: Australia, Federal Court, *Habib v. Commonwealth of Australia* (2010). The Court in this case did not find it necessary to address the question of the applicability of the GC nor of Mr. Habib's status under those Conventions: "Mr Habib alleges that he was entitled to protection either under the Third or the Fourth Geneva Convention because there were wars or armed conflicts taking place and because he was necessarily either a prisoner of war or a civilian. The Commonwealth has previously denied the applicability of the Conventions to Mr Habib. The thicket of difficult issues arising from that denial – whether there was an armed conflict, whether Mr Habib as a national of a US ally is entitled to their protection and whether he was an enemy combatant rather than a civilian or prisoner of war – do not presently fall for consideration. For a summary of the judgment, see Tully, "Australian Court Permits Damages Claim for Torture by Former Guantánamo Bay Detainee to Proceed" (*ASIL Insights* 2010).

[1011] Several neighbouring States (e.g. Uganda, Burundi, Rwanda and others) have intervened in the various non-international armed conflicts that ravage the Democratic Republic of the Congo, *cf. supra* chapter I-2, section 2.2.1.7.

[1012] Moreover, with regard to neutral States, Neff, in his *The Rights and Duties of Neutrals: A General History* (2000), has found that the question of whether nationality of a neutral State automatically confers neutral status upon a person remains unresolved.

[1013] For the specific contributions of NATO member States to the International Security Assistance Force in Afghanistan, see http://www.isaf.nato.int/troop-numbers-and-contributions/index.php.

The combination of these four – and possibly other – factors, results in there being an increasingly important number of persons who, in the event of armed conflict, may find themselves in the power of an adverse party to the conflict, but have that party's nationality or the nationality of a co-belligerent or neutral State with normal diplomatic relations with that party to the conflict. Under a strict interpretation of article 4, none of the persons in the examples above, would qualify as protected persons. It is however undeniable that at least some of them will be considered "enemies" by the State in whose hands they are, regardless of their nationality. Some of them may have participated in actual hostilities against their national State or its allies, but without necessarily being entitled to prisoner of war status under the Third Geneva Convention. They therefore do not benefit from that Convention's protection upon capture.[1014]

An overly restrictive interpretation of article 4 GC IV, resulting in their simultaneous exclusion from the scope of application of the Fourth Geneva Convention contradicts the object and purpose of that Convention and of international humanitarian law more generally, on account of both the principle of military necessity (providing a legal basis in international humanitarian law for the internment of persons who participate in hostilities or otherwise pose a direct security threat) and the principle of humanity (ensuring protection of persons at risk of arbitrary action or abuse in the hands of the enemy).

In the end, establishing where the allegiance of such persons lies and whether they enjoy effective diplomatic protection by any government, may no longer be possible to determine on the basis of their nationality (or nationalities) alone. Other relevant factors must be taken into account, such as ethnicity, religion, ideology or political affiliation or sympathies.[1015]

(e.) Case law and literature: conservatism or insufficient attention to the problems caused by a strict interpretation of article 4 GC IV?

The problems raised above – where persons who have the same nationality as the Controlling Power but are regarded by the latter as enemies because of their affinity or allegiance with an adverse party to the conflict – affect only a minority of actual cases in practice. This is possibly the reason why only scant attention is paid to the protection problems that arise from a strict application of article 4 GC IV in their regard. It also partly explains why there is little case law on the subject.

Nevertheless, the little existing case law where judges addressed the question directly demonstrates that – despite important developments in international law over the last half-century – the issue remains subject to controversy. Two

[1014] On the contrary, persons who *are* entitled to POW status under GC III or are granted such status by the Power in whose hands they fell are not protected persons under GC IV (article 4§4 GC IV, *cf. supra*). Should that Power wish to intern them, it can do so on the basis of article 21 GC III or of the relevant provisions of the Hague Conventions on the Rights and Duties of Neutral Powers in War discussed in chapter II-1.

[1015] These factors were already mentioned in Pictet's *Commentary to GC IV* (1958) (on article 44), *cf. supra*.

examples may illustrate the choice to be made between a dynamic, purposeful interpretation of article 4 GC IV allowing the Convention to fulfil its protective purpose, and a strict textual interpretation reminiscent of the traditional concept of non-intervention of international law in the relationship between a State and its citizens.

The ICTY has abandoned a strictly literal interpretation of article 4 GC IV in favour of a dynamic and teleological interpretation that allows, in certain cases, to replace the nationality factor in the definition of protected persons in the Fourth Geneva Convention with those of ethnicity and allegiance, considered more appropriate in the context of ethnic conflicts like those that ravaged the Balkans in the 1990's.[1016] The Tribunal's reasoning can be summarized by the following extracts of its judgments:

> "The Commentary to the Fourth Geneva Convention charges us not to forget that "the Conventions have been drawn up first and foremost to protect individuals, and not to serve State interests", and thus it is the view of this Trial Chamber that their protections should be applied to as broad a category of persons as possible. [...] The law must be applied to the reality of the situation before us and thus, [...] insofar as they were not protected by any of the other Geneva Conventions, [persons interned on the basis of their ethnic identity] must be considered to have been 'protected persons' within the meaning of the Fourth Geneva Convention, as they were clearly regarded by the [interning] authorities as belonging to the opposing party in an armed conflict and as posing a threat to the [interning] State. [...] [T]he complexity of many modem conflicts [does] not, perhaps, [reflect] the paradigm envisaged in 1949. In order to retain the relevance and effectiveness of the norms of the Geneva Conventions, it is necessary to adopt the approach here taken [...] [i]n interpreting the law, our goal should be to avoid paralyzing the legal process as much as possible and, in the case of humanitarian conventions, to enable them to serve their protective goals."[1017]

> "This legal approach, hinging on substantial relations more than on formal bonds, becomes all the more important in present-day international armed conflicts. [...] [N]ot only the text and the drafting history of the Convention but also, and more importantly, the Convention's object and purpose suggest that allegiance to a Party to the conflict and, correspondingly, control by this Party over persons in a given territory, may be regarded as the crucial test";[1018] and thus

[1016] The ICTY extended the definition of protected persons to individuals who had the same nationality as the Power in whose hands they were but were nevertheless considered by that Power to be enemies on the basis of their ethnic identity, which they shared with an adverse party to the conflict. E.g.: ICTY, *Tadíc* (1999), §§164-169 reversing a Trial Chamber's finding that Bosnian Muslims in the hands of Bosnian Serbs were not protected persons under GC IV because they had the same (Bosnian) nationality as the power in whose hands they were (ICTY, *Tadíc* (1997), §§ 584-608), and endorsing the reasoning of the Trial Chamber in *Delalíc* (1998), §§263-266. In the same sense: ICTY, *Aleksovski* (2000), §151; and ICTY, *Delalíc* (2001), §84.

[1017] ICTY, *Delalíc* (1998), §§ 263-266.

[1018] ICTY, *Tadíc* (1999), §166.

"in certain circumstances, Article 4 may be given a wider construction so that a person may be accorded protected status, notwithstanding the fact that he is of the same nationality as his captors;[1019] and

"[t]he nationality of the victims for the purpose of the application of Geneva Convention IV should not be determined on the basis of formal national characterisations, but rather upon an analysis of the substantial relations, taking into consideration the different ethnicity of the victims and the perpetrators, and their bonds with the foreign intervening State."[1020]

To the contrary, UK courts have found that a dual British-Iraqi national in the custody of UK forces in Iraq did not qualify as a protected person under article 4 GC IV. On the basis of a strict textual reading of article 4§1 GC IV, they found that Hilal Abdul-Razzaq Ali Al-Jedda did not fall within the personal scope of application of that Convention since he was a British citizen.[1021] Mr. Al-Jedda appealed the House of Lord's judgment against him before the European Court of Human Rights.[1022] It would have been interesting to see whether that Court would argue along the same lines as the ICTY if it had been called upon to decide on whether M. Al-Jedda was or was not a protected person under GC IV. However, the Court did not address that question in its judgment in the case.[1023]

During the early stages of the 1990-91 Gulf War, Meron qualified the exclusion of persons in real need of the Convention's protection from the personal scope of application of GC IV merely on the basis their nationality (and without regard for the question of whether they are regarded as enemies by the Controlling Power) as an important, and at times nonsensical, deficiency in international humanitarian law.[1024] Moreover, it led him and others to suggest that the ICTY – in the context of the Balkan conflicts – should develop an expanded reading of article 4 GC IV to take into account the challenges of contemporary armed conflict and the anomalies arising from a strict application of its terms,[1025] which the Tribunal, as we just saw, did.

[1019] ICTY, *Aleksovski* (2000), §151.

[1020] ICTY, *Delalic* (2001), §84.

[1021] UK, HoL, *Al-Jedda* (2007), §32 confirming on this issue the Judgment of the Court of Appeal in the same case (UK, CA, *Al-Jedda* (2006), §40).

[1022] ECtHR (Registry), *Al-Jedda v. the United Kingdom*, Application No. 27021/08, communicated on 17 February 2009.

[1023] The case raised important questions about the attributability of the deprivation of liberty to the UK, whose presence in Iraq at the time was part of a UN-mandated international operation (*cf. infra* footnote 1416 and accompanying text). Even though the Court did find Mr. Al-Jedda's deprivation of liberty was attributable to the UK and thus found the ECHR to be applicable to the case, it did not address the question of whether Mr. Al-Jedda was a protected person under GC IV. Actually, the Court seems to call into question whether GC IV applied at all to Mr. Al-Jedda's case, his capture and internment having taken place at a time where there no longer was an international armed conflict in Iraq and the UK had ceased to be an Occupying Power (ECtHR (Grand Chamber), *Al-Jedda* (2011), §107), a point on which we would agree with the Court, *cf. infra* chapter II-4, section 4.3.

[1024] Meron (*AJIL* 1991), p. 107.

[1025] E.g. Meron, "Crimes and Accountability in Shakespeare" (*AJIL* 1998), pp. 238-242; and Greenwood, "International Humanitarian Law and the *Tadic* Case" (*EJIL* 1996), pp. 273-274.

While the judgment of the ICTY is debatable in some aspects and has been the subject of criticism,[1026] its interpretation of the nationality requirement in article 4 GC IV is in our view predicated on a correct reading of that article in light of the object and purpose of the Convention and international humanitarian law more generally. The Tribunal's reading of article 4 GC IV has attracted a critical response from some authors, but these authors do not address the arguments – some reminiscent of those of the Tribunal – we have made above.[1027]

Most recent surveys of the definition of protected persons under GC IV pay only scant attention to the potential problems of a strict application of the nationality requirements in article 4. Admittedly, most of these writings have focused – in light of the US administration's denial of the applicability of the Geneva Conventions to persons it held and continues to hold in relation to the international armed conflict in Afghanistan – on demonstrating the applicability of the Fourth Geneva Convention to so-called unlawful or unprivileged combatants (*cf. supra*). For their purpose, it may indeed have been sufficient to remind the reader of the general exception on the basis of nationality explicitly provided for in article 4 GC IV.[1028]

We are inclined to think however, that the writings of at least some of these scholars do not *per se* run counter the arguments we have made above. The writings of some authors also support our arguments.[1029] Nevertheless, still others may disagree with our arguments in full. We will therefore try to anticipate some points of critique and offer additional elements in response.

3.1.2.2. Anticipation of criticism

The interpretation allows for exceptions to the rule that go beyond those originally intended and explicitly provided for by the Convention – The Convention's drafters were indeed adamant about their refusal to allow for exceptions to the nationality rule. This was partly so because of their attachment to the principle that international law should not regulate the relationship between a State and its nationals, a principle that in the sphere of protecting individual rights and freedom and human dignity is no longer valid today. Moreover, the drafters themselves recognized that exceptions to the rule must be made in cases where "based on the position [...] people have taken up with regard to their own country"[1030] they may find themselves at serious risk when they fall into their own country's hands. Such an exception is explicitly provided for in the Convention concerning refugees (in the broad sense of the word adopted by the Convention). At the same time the drafters realized the

[1026] For a critical review of the judgment, see for example Sassòli & Olson, "The Judgment of the ICTY Appeals Chamber on the Merits in the Tadić Case" (*IRRC* 2000), pp. 733-769.
[1027] E.g.: Sassòli & Olson (*IRRC* 2000), p. 4 of the online version. See also the arguments of the defence in ICTY, *Delalic* (2001), §§ 64-65.
[1028] E.g.: Dörmann (*IRRC* 2003), p. 48; Doswald-Beck in Chesterman & Lehnardt (2007), p. 125; Gasser, "Protection of the Civilian Population" in Fleck (2008), p. 319.
[1029] E.g.: Provost (2002), pp. 39-40; Arai-Takahashi (2009), p. 306; Meron (2006), pp. 34-35.
[1030] Pictet, *Commentary GC IV* (1958), p. 46, quoted *supra* notes 992 and 1002.

complexity of the issue and chose therefore not to deal with in full in the Convention.[1031] This leaves room for an interpretation based on the same logic as the one concerning refugees to deal with – equally exceptional – cases that are both complex but real and where a strict application of article 4 would go against the protective purpose of the Convention and international law more generally.

(a.) *The ICTY's case law concerns a specific type of conflict, its arguments cannot be extrapolated to any other type of conflict*[1032] – It is, in our opinion, not the nature of the conflict that imposes the exceptions we have proposed above, but rather the nature of the relationship between an individual and the party to the conflict in whose power he or she finds him- or herself. Where that relation is perceived by the State in terms of enmity – be it on the basis of allegiance, ethnicity, religion, political or ideological affinity with an adverse party to the conflict – and results in a potential risk of abuse or arbitrary action against the individual, the Convention must apply. At least where security measures are taken against such persons, the relationship must be assessed on an individual, case-by-case basis. Nationality will remain the main standard for making an initial assessment on whether or not an individual is a protected person, and where there is no potential protection problem, there is no need to depart from it. Exceptions must be interpreted strictly enough so as not to render the Convention applicable to every individual, as this is not the purpose of the Convention or of international humanitarian law, which seeks to protect only those directly affected by the armed conflict. However, in cases of potential risk of abuse or arbitrary action because of a person's allegiance, ethnic, spiritual, political, ideological or other affinity with an adverse party to the conflict, the formal nationality of the individual should not lead to his or her automatic exclusion from the Convention's protection. In such "very special" cases, an exception should be read into the Convention's provisions in light of its object and purpose.

(b.) *Persons who side with the enemy are liable of treason and are thus at the mercy of their national State upon capture or arrest*[1033] – It is useful to recall here that the Convention's provisions do not in any way prevent a State from prosecuting and punishing protected persons, even its own nationals, for any violations of national or international law. The Fourth Geneva Convention does not confer any prosecutorial immunity on the persons that fall within its scope of application, it only reiterates the fundamental guarantees of fair trial a person must be granted in accordance with international law.[1034] Moreover, the

---

[1031] Pictet, *Commentary GC IV* (1958), p. 47, quoted *supra* notes 986-987.

[1032] E.g.: Kolb (2009), p. 366. Rowe on the contrary seems to be open – in order to avoid a protective gap – to apply the reasoning of the ICTY to the case of persons detained by the US in relation to the international armed conflict in Afghanistan and who are nationals of States with whom the US has normal diplomatic relations, see Rowe (2006), p. 152, note 177.

[1033] Kolb (2009), p. 366.

[1034] See in particular articles 71-76 and 126 GC IV, article 75§§3-4 and §§7-8 AP I, and Rules 100-103 of the ICRC's compilation of customary IHL (Henckaerts & Doswald-Beck (2005), Vol. I, pp. 352-375). But see also articles 10 UDHR, 14 ICCPR, 6 ECHR, 28 ADRDM, 8 ACHR, 7 ACHPR, and 16 Arab Charter on Human Rights.

applicability of the Convention means that where that State does not or cannot press criminal charges due to domestic legal constraints, but considers the person poses a real threat to its security and military operations, it can intern that person on the legal bases provided for by the Fourth Geneva Convention (article 42 and 78 GC IV, cf. infra). The latter would not be possible if the person disqualified as a protected person for then the Convention would not be applicable in his or her regard.

(c.) *The proposed interpretation of article 4 is difficult to apply in the heat of combat or in the theatre of operations* – This argument has been raised specifically with regard to the ICTY's replacement of the nationality standard with one of allegiance or ethnicity in cases where the latter is a better indicator of the risks individuals may run in the hands of their captor.[1035] We find it hard to believe though that during the Balkans conflicts the determination of allegiance on the basis of ethnicity was that difficult, even when operations were still ongoing. It was crystal clear that persons interned in the Omarska, Keraterm and Trnopolje camps run by Serb forces in Prijedor and in the Čelebići camp run by Bosnian military authorities in Konjic, were interned on the basis of their ethnic identity and presumed allegiance to an adverse party to the conflict.[1036] Moreover, criteria of allegiance like ethnicity are not necessarily more difficult to ascertain than the criterion of nationality, especially in some of the cases to our concern here (multiple nationalities, clear indications of allegiance, and so forth).

Additionally, persons who have been deprived of their liberty are by definition *hors de combat*. The decision to intern or detain takes place *after* the moment of surrender or capture and *away* from the battlefield. Such a decision – to be lawful – must in any case be based on an individual assessment of the threat a person poses. At that point in time, there should surely be sufficient time to allow for an assessment of whether or not the person concerned is a protected person under GC IV, including by verifying his or her origins and allegiance. If it cannot be

---

[1035] Sassòli & Olson (*IRRC* 2000), p. 4 of the online version.

[1036] See also ICTY, *Delalić* (1998), §265: "it is clear that the victims [...] were arrested and detained mainly on the basis of their Serb identity. As such, [...] they were clearly regarded by the Bosnian authorities as belonging to the opposing party in an armed conflict and posing a threat to the Bosnian State" (on the internment of ethnic Serbs by Bosnian authorities in Čelebići camp); ICTY, *Tadić* (1999), §167 confirms the Trial Chamber's finding (ICTY, *Tadić* (1997), § 608) that the victims, Muslim Bosnians in the hands of the Bosnian Serb authorities (Republica Srpska) who were *de facto* organs of their ethnically related Federal Republic of Yugoslavia (Serbia and Montenegro), were in the hands of a Power of which they are not nationals and thus qualified as protected persons under GC IV (on the internment of Muslims and ethnic Croats by Serb authorities in Prijedor; for a description of some of the facts, see ICTY, *Tadić* (1997), §§ 154, 163, 176, 178, 182). See also ICTY, *Blaskić* (2000), §128-129: "The disintegration of Yugoslavia occurred along "ethnic" lines. Ethnicity became more important than nationality in determining loyalties or commitments", and §§130-131: "Croatia's policy towards the Bosnian Croats placed more emphasis on their ethnic background than on their nationality. [...] the fact that the people identified more with ethnicity than formal nationality when expressing their loyalty. [...] and the Bosnian Croat officials considered the Bosnian Muslims and Serbs to be people of another nationality or another people altogether. [...] The supporters of the HVO [Croatian Defence Council, the armed forces of the self-proclaimed Croatian Republic of Bosnia-Herzegovina] were in no doubt that Croatia was their ally and that the Bosnian Muslims were their adversaries."

established that the individual concerned is a protected person under GC IV, the Convention cannot be relied upon as a legal basis to intern that person.

(d.) *It is doubtful whether States will be ready to consider their own nationals who side with the enemy as protected persons*[1037] – Where the interpretation of a particular provision in a particular case is the only one that effectively achieves the object and purpose of the Convention, the provision should be applied as thus interpreted. To quote Pictet: "It must not be forgotten that the Conventions have been drawn up first and foremost to protect individuals, and not to serve State interests."[1038] Moreover, we have seen above that GC IV does not prevent a State from punishing its own nationals for treason or other offences under its domestic legislation. Finally, a State may even have an interest in accepting the application of GC IV to such nationals as protected persons, since that Convention also allows for their internment when they pose a military or security threat (*cf. infra*).

(e.) *The decision on whether a person is protected under GC IV cannot be altered ex-post facto during a criminal trial (on unlawful confinement of protected persons)* – This argument was put forward by Sassòli and Olson with regard to the trial of Duško Tadić on the charge of unlawful confinement of protected persons under GC IV in the Prijedor area.[1039] We fully agree with the authors on the importance of the non-retroactivity of penal laws, including the definition of a crime (in casu unlawful confinement of protected persons under GC IV). We would like to add however the following thoughts. If the authorities in Prijedor had interpreted the Fourth Geneva Convention in good faith, that interpretation should have resulted in the protection of persons whom they clearly considered to be enemy aliens on the basis of their ethnic affinity with an adverse Party to the conflict. Where a criminal tribunal finds that the interning authorities wrongly interpreted GC IV at the time of its application, we see no obstacle in that tribunal correcting the authorities' reading in a later trial.

3.1.2.3. Conclusions on nationality

While nationality remains the main indicator for assessing whether a given individual is a protected person under GC IV, no one should be excluded from the personal scope of application of that Convention where he or she is clearly considered an enemy by the Controlling Power based on his or her ethnic, religious, political, ideological or other affinities with an adverse party to the conflict. The Convention's provisions on refugees must be taken into account where relevant, and additional exceptions to the general rule in article 4 GC IV must be made where necessary to give full effect to the Convention's provisions in light of its ultimate object and purpose. Any other interpretation would result in a serious gap in conventional protection of persons directly affected by armed conflict, a gap which the drafters did not intend to create.[1040]

[1037] Sassòli & Olson (*IRRC* 2000), p. 4 of the version online.

[1038] Pictet, *Commentary GC IV* (1958), p. 21.

[1039] Sassòli & Olson (*IRRC* 2000), p. 4 of the version online.

[1040] In the same sense (with regard to the intentions of the drafters): Kolb (2009), p. 366. Note that

Admittedly, the nuanced reading of the definition of protected persons in article 4 GC IV may not always be easily applicable by soldiers on the ground. The evaluation of whether a given individual, who has the nationality of the Controlling Power or that of a co-belligerent or neutral State, is a protected person must in such cases be made on a case-by-case basis. In principle there should not be many such cases, but they are likely to be complex. This may be one of the reasons why UK military doctrine provides that:

"In all cases where a British national falls into the hands of UK Armed Forces operating abroad, legal and policy advice should be sought through the chain of command at the earliest possible opportunity, commensurate with mission accomplishment and the safety of the force. Close liaison with the [Ministry of Defence] and other Government Departments is required in relation to the handling of any British national captured by British forces overseas."[1041]

3.1.3. Protected persons in occupied territory

The personal scope of application of GC IV is slightly wider in occupied territory than it is in the territory of the parties to the conflict. Let us briefly recall the text of paragraph 2 of article 4 GC IV:

> "Nationals of a neutral State who find themselves in the territory of a belligerent State, and nationals of a co-belligerent State, shall not be regarded as protected persons while the State of which they are nationals has normal diplomatic representation *in the State in whose hands they are*." (emphasis added)

> Pictet explains:

> "Paragraph 2 [...] defines the position of nationals of neutral States; in occupied territory they are protected persons and the Convention is applicable to them; its application in this case does not depend on the existence or non-existence of normal diplomatic representation. On the other hand, nationals of a neutral State in the territory of a Party to the conflict are only protected persons if their State of origin has no normal diplomatic representation in the State in whose hands they are. This seems to be a legitimate distinction. In the territory of the belligerent States the position of neutrals is still governed by any treaties concerning the legal status of aliens and their diplomatic representatives can take steps to protect them. In occupied territory, on the other hand, the diplomatic representatives of neutral States, even assuming that they remain there, *are not accredited to the Occupying Power* but only to the occupied Power. This *makes it more difficult for them to make representations to the Occupying Power*. In such cases diplomatic representations are usually made by the neutral State's diplomatic representatives in the occupying State, and not by those in the occupied territory. It should moreover be noted that the Occupying Power is not bound by the treaties concerning the legal status of aliens which may exist. The existence of such situations, often of a complicated nature, gave rise to the idea of granting

persons who fall outside the personal scope of application of GC IV are not without protection under international law, *cf. infra* chapter II-4.

[1041] UK, *JDP 1-10* (2006), chapter 4, section 413.

neutral nationals in occupied territory the status of protected persons within the meaning of the Convention."[1042]

It is also useful to remind Pictet's explanation of "normal diplomatic representation":

"According to the Rapporteur of Committee III normal diplomatic representation is 'that which functions in peace time comprising at least one diplomatic representative accredited to a Ministry of Foreign Affairs'. This definition has some value, but does not seem adequate; the words 'accredited to' (in the French version of the Report: *trouvant audience auprès de*) must at all events be understood in the widest sense, as implying that the representations made by the diplomatic representative will be followed by results and that satisfactory replies will be given to him. *It would also seem essential for the representatives in question to have sufficient liberty of action and liberty of movement to be able to visit their fellow-countrymen and come to their help when circumstances so require.*"[1043]

The distinction between nationals of neutral States in occupied territory and those in the territory of the party to the conflict in whose hands they are indeed seems legitimate in that the diplomatic representatives of their State of origin in the occupied territory are not accredited to the Occupying Power and thus cannot make normal representations to that Power, and their diplomatic representatives accredited to the Occupying Power, being by definition in the latter's territory, cannot "visit their fellow-countrymen and come to their help when circumstances so require."

It is surprising therefore that nationals of a co-belligerent State in occupied territory are not protected persons as long as their State or origin has normal diplomatic representation in the territory of the Power in whose hands they are, namely the occupying State. As is the case for neutral States, the diplomatic representatives of the co-belligerent State in the occupied territory are not accredited to the Occupying Power and thus cannot make normal representations to that Power and their diplomatic representatives accredited to the Occupying Power, being by definition in the latter's territory, cannot "visit their fellow-countrymen and come to their help when circumstances so require."

In this sense, it seems illogical that nationals of neutral States in occupied territory are protected persons but that national of co-belligerent States in occupied territory are not. Gasser concludes that nationals of neutral States in occupied territory, whose State of origin has normal diplomatic representation in the territory of the Occupying Power should also be excluded from the personal scope of application.[1044] One could also argue the opposite and say that nationals of co-belligerent States in occupied territory should be protected persons regardless of their State's diplomatic representation in the territory of the Occupying Power, as is the case for nationals of neutral States. Pictet seems to explain the distinction in occupied territory between nationals of neutral and co-

---

[1042] Pictet, *Commentary GC IV* (1958), pp. 48-49 (emphasis added).
[1043] Pictet, *Commentary GC IV* (1958), p. 49 (emphasis added).
[1044] Gasser in Fleck (2008), p. 272.

belligerent States by the fact that the drafters of the Convention "assumed [...] that the nationals of co-belligerent States, that is to say, of allies, do not need protection under the Convention."[1045]

We have seen above that such an assumption explains – at least partly – the reason why article 4 GC IV excludes certain categories of persons on the basis of their nationality in the first place. We have also seen that that assumption may prove to be wrong, and that in such cases persons who are nationals of the Power in whose hands they find themselves – whether that be in occupied territory or in that Power's own territory – may be in need of the protection of the Convention regardless of their nationality. In such cases, the Convention's protective purpose requires a nuanced reading of article 4 GC IV so as to allow the Conventions to effectively fulfil that purpose for all persons in need.[1046]

3.2. ON WHAT GROUNDS AND FOR HOW LONG CAN PROTECTED PERSONS BE INTERNED ON THE BASIS OF GC IV?

Article 42§1 GC IV: The internment or placing in assigned residence of protected persons may be ordered only if the security of the Detaining Power makes it absolutely necessary.

Article 42§2 GC IV: If any person, acting through the representative of the Protecting Power, voluntarily demands internment, and if his situation renders this step necessary, he shall be interned by the Power in whose hands he may be.

Article 78 GC IV: If the Occupying Power considers it necessary, for imperative reasons of security, to take safety measures concerning protected persons, it may, at the most, subject them to assigned residence or to internment.

Before the adoption of the Fourth Geneva Convention, no international treaty or custom provided for the internment of persons other than prisoners of war and the medical and religious personnel of armed forces.[1047] Until the early 20th century it was not only "a cardinal principle of the law of war that military operations must be confined to the armed forces and that the civilian population must enjoy complete immunity", but also a factual reality that few civilians were directly affected by hostilities or in a position to pose a military threat to the belligerents.[1048] It is interesting to note – as Pictet does – that the drafters of the

[1045] Pictet, *Commentary GC IV* (1958), p. 49.
[1046] In the same sense: Arai-Takahashi (2009), pp. 305-306.
[1047] The 1907 Hague Regulations were the first to have some provisions concerning the protection of civilians in armed conflict (articles 42-56) but its provisions concern only occupied territory and do not contain a legal basis for internment, *cf. infra* Chapter II-4, section 4.3.
[1048] Pictet, *Commentary GC IV* (1958), p. 3.

1907 Hague Regulations (only 7 years before the outbreak of World War I) decided "not to include a provision to the effect that the nationals of belligerents residing in the territory of an adverse party should not be interned, considering that this principle *went without saying*."[1049]

The First World War demonstrated the contrary, with large numbers of such "enemy nationals" being interned upon the outbreak of hostilities.[1050] Notwithstanding this reality, immediate post-war efforts by the ICRC for the adoption of a convention regulating the protection of civilians in armed conflict did not – at a time of unfettered belief in future peace – meet with any success. A Draft International Convention on the Condition and Protection of Civilians of Enemy Nationality who are on Territory Belonging to or Occupied by a Belligerent was however adopted by the International Conference of the Red Cross in 1934. It was submitted to a Diplomatic Conference, to which States reacted only slowly, still firmly believing that war would no more be upon them. The advent of the Second World War shattered that belief and prevented the Draft Convention from being adopted in time to protect the millions of "enemy" civilians who came to bear the brunt of violence in that conflict.[1051]

The horrors inflicted upon civilians during the Second World War are the immediate background against which the revision of the law of armed conflict – since then more often referred to as international *humanitarian* law – at the 1949 Diplomatic Conference must be read. The internment of civilians on a massive scale by both Allied and Axis Forces ultimately convinced States that the principle of non-internment of "enemy" civilians no longer went without saying but needed explicit confirmation in the Fourth Geneva Convention: the legal basis for such internment needed to be explicitly prescribed and limited in the international treaty norms that would govern future conflicts.

The Fourth Geneva Convention contains two separate legal bases for internment, depending on whether the internment takes place in the territory of a party to the conflict or in occupied territory. The legal basis for internment of persons other than prisoners of war in the territory of a party to the conflict is article 42 of the Fourth Geneva Convention; in occupied territory the legal basis is article 78 of the same Convention. These legal bases are exhaustive; article 79 GC IV explicitly provides that:

1049 Pictet, *Commentary GC IV* (1958), p. 3 (emphasis added).

1050 See for example ICRC, Rapport général du Comité international de la Croix-Rouge sur son activité de 1912 à 1920 (1921), pp. 129-176.

1051 Pictet, Commentary GC IV (1958), pp. 4-6; Seeger, *Le statut personnel des étrangers ennemis et la Convention de Genève du 12 août 1949 relative à la protection des civils* (1958); ICRC, *Rapport du Comité international de la Croix-Rouge sur son activité pendant la seconde guerre mondiale (1er septembre 1939 -30 juin 1947* (1948), pp. 591-709. For historical overviews and factual information on the internment of enemy aliens during World War II, see for example Cesarani & Kushner, *The Internment of Aliens in Twentieth Century Britain* (1993); the documents of the US Commission of Wartime Relocation and Internment of Civilians; the Wartime Internment web-portal of the National Archives of Australia; Archer, *The Internment of Western Civilians under the Japanese 1941-145: A Patchwork of Internment* (2004); Pautsch, "Prisoners of War and Internees in the Second World War: A Survey of Some Recent Publications" (*CEH* 2006); and Vance (2006).

"The Parties to the conflict shall not intern protected persons, except in accordance with the provisions of Articles 41, 42 and 43, 68 and 78."[1052]

In the present section we will examine the lawful grounds for the internment of civilians and other persons who do not qualify as prisoners or war as prescribed by contemporary international humanitarian law.[1053] In doing so, it is important to keep in mind that while the internment of prisoners of war for the duration of active hostilities is a generally accepted consequence resulting from their status, the contrary is true for persons who do not qualify as such: their internment is generally prohibited and can only be imposed exceptionally, on a case-by-case basis, where military necessity or the security of the Interning Power render such a deprivation of liberty inevitable.

3.2.1. Essential features of internment on the basis of GC IV

In what follows we will examine the lawful grounds for internment prescribed by the Fourth Geneva Convention. It is worthwhile to recall that this Convention can only serve to intern individuals who fall within the scope of application of that Convention. We have discussed the concept of protected persons under GC IV above and will not come back to it here, since it is relevant only for determining the applicability of the legal regime to specific individuals and thus identify whether GC IV can be the legal basis for their internment. It does not have any impact on the substance of the rules on internment in GC IV.[1054] Once the applicability of the Convention is established – and only then – the individual can be lawfully interned on the basis of the Fourth Convention, in accordance with the grounds and procedures prescribed therein.

The Fourth Geneva Convention prescribes three lawful grounds (and accompanying procedures) for internment.[1055] Articles 42 and 78 GC IV prescribe the lawful grounds for internment of protected persons in respectively the territory of the parties to the conflict (article 42) and occupied territory (article 78)(emphasis added):

> Article 42§1: "The internment or placing in assigned residence of protected persons may be ordered only *if the security of the Detaining Power makes it absolutely necessary.*"

[1052] On article 68, *cf. supra* note 934.

[1053] Articles 41 to 43 and 78 GC IV concern both internment and assigned residence. The focus of this book is on internment, but the analysis of these provisions is applicable *mutatis mutandis* to measures of assigned residence. On the difference between these two measures, *cf. infra* note 1085.

[1054] The material and personal scope of application of GC IV with regard to internees can be summarized as follows: the person is interned (i) by a party to an international armed conflict, (ii) either in its own territory or in territory occupied by it, (iii) for reasons related to the conflict and (iv) is a protected person in accordance with article 4 GC IV (for the interpretation of article 4, see our detailed analysis *supra* in section 3.1). Only in such cases does the Convention apply and can its norms regulating internment be taken into account to assess the lawfulness of the deprivation of liberty under international law. Where the Convention does not apply, individuals cannot be deprived of their liberty on the basis of its provisions, and a legal basis for their detention or internment must exist in applicable domestic or other international law.

[1055] On article 68, *cf. supra* note 934.

> Article 42§2: "If any person, acting through the representatives of the Protecting Power, *voluntarily* demands internment *and* if his situation renders this step *necessary*, he shall be interned by the Power in whose hands he may be."
>
> Article 78: "If the Occupying Power considers it *necessary, for imperative reasons of security*, to take safety measures concerning protected persons, it may, at the most, subject them to assigned residence or to internment."

We will examine these grounds in considerable detail, but before doing so – and in order to fully understand them – it is necessary to situate articles 42 and 78 within the broader framework regulating the restriction of rights of protected persons under GC IV.

3.2.1.1. Measures of control and security as may be necessary as a result of the war

The internment provisions of the Fourth Geneva Convention are contained in its Part III, which regulates the status and treatment of the persons the Convention aims to protect. The first provision of Part III, article 27, is "the central point in relation to which all its other provisions must be considered [...] proclaiming as it does the principles on which the whole of [the Convention] is founded."[1056] Article 27 reflects the balance inherent in all international humanitarian law between the principles of military necessity and humanity. Its first three paragraphs recall a number of absolute rights and prohibitions concerning the human person, while its last paragraph accommodates the principle of military necessity:

> "Protected persons are entitled, in all circumstances, to respect for their persons, their honour, their family rights, their religious convictions and practices, and their manners and customs. They shall at all times be humanely treated, and shall be protected especially against all acts of violence or threats thereof and against insults and public curiosity.
>
> Women shall be especially protected against any attack on their honour, in particular against rape, enforced prostitution, or any form of indecent assault.
>
> Without prejudice to the provisions relating to their state of health, age and sex, all protected persons shall be treated with the same consideration by the Party to the conflict in whose power they are, without any adverse distinction based, in particular, on race, religion or political opinion.
>
> However, the Parties to the conflict may take such measures of control and security in regard to protected persons as may be necessary as a result of the war." (emphasis added)

The first three paragraphs of the article concern areas where the principle of humanity always takes precedence over the principle of military necessity. The rights therein are formulated as absolute rights, from which departure is not allowed, no matter what military or security considerations or requirements would call for it. The last paragraph, however, concerns areas where such considerations and requirements may be taken into account and allows the

---

[1056] Pictet, *Commentary GC IV* (1958), pp. 199-201.

parties to the conflict to take "such measures of control and security as may be necessary as a result of the war."[1057]

Article 27§4 does not however constitute a blanket authorization to take whatever measures may be dictated by military or security needs. This was already pointed out during the Diplomatic Conference in 1949: "The reservation thus introduced did not, however, restore to Governments the right to take arbitrary action."[1058] Moreover, the use of the definite article in the phrase "necessary as a result of the war" indicates that any control and security measures imposed upon protected persons must be necessary in the context of the particular conflict during which they are adopted. The automatic repetition of "necessary" measures adopted in previous conflicts is thus not allowed: in deciding upon such measures, the specific context, conflict dynamics and available alternatives must be taken into account.

The provisions of Part III of GC IV set out the limits imposed on the general allowance made for military necessity in article 27§4. The first section of Part III contains provisions common to the territories of the parties to the conflict and occupied territories, such as the prohibitions of coercion, torture, collective penalties and hostage-taking. Sections II and III set further limits concerning nationals of adverse parties to the conflict in the territory of these parties (e.g. regarding their means of existence, employment, the possibility to leave the territory but also the situation of those already imprisoned or detained for offences committed before the outbreak of hostilities) and the inhabitants of occupied territories (e.g. the prohibition of deportation and the administration of the territory). Finally, Section IV sets out the comprehensive and detailed regulations for the treatment of internees and the material conditions for their internment.

Pictet's Commentary to article 27 GC IV underscores that the provisions in its first three paragraphs – along with the other provisions of Section I – must be read as "rules considered to constitute the 'basis of universal human law'"[1059] and thus supports the continued validity of international human rights law even

---

[1057] The US insisted on the inclusion of the 4th paragraph in this provision (it was originally included rather in draft article 35/final article 38 GC IV) qualifying the 3rd paragraph which prohibits discrimination on the basis of political opinion in order to allow for a distinction to be made "between those enemy aliens who were actively hostile on political grounds and those who did not possess such extreme views. For example, out of 300,000 Germans living in the United States during the last war, only 4,000 were National Socialists and had to be interned. The United States Government had no desire to limit the freedom of the 296,000; but it could not restrain the 4,000 without making distinctions based on political opinions" (*Final Record 1949*, Vol. II-A, p. 713). It is submitted that there is no need for the 4th paragraph qualifying as such the 3rd paragraph, since a person cannot be interned merely on the basis of his or her political opinions without presenting a real threat to the security of the Interning Power (*cf. infra*). Any discrimination based upon a person's political opinions, without these opinions materializing into a real threat to the security of the Interning Power, remains therefore prohibited.

[1058] *Final Record 1949*, Vol. II-A, p. 712.

[1059] Pictet, *Commentary GC IV* (1958), p. 200, with reference to the Universal Declaration of Human Rights (adopted only 7 months before the Conventions) and to some of the early works on the relation between the two bodies of law. On the relation and interaction between international humanitarian and human rights law, *cf. supra* chapter I-2, section 2.2.2.2.

in situations of international armed conflict and occupation. As is the case in the latter body of law, the right to liberty in international humanitarian law is not such an absolute right, but is open to the restrictions referred to in article 27§4:

> "The right to personal liberty, and in particular, the right to move about freely, can naturally be made subject in wartime to certain restrictions made necessary by circumstances [...] That right is not, therefore, included among the other absolute rights laid down in the Convention, but that in no wise means that it is suspended in a general manner. Quite the contrary: the regulations concerning occupation and those concerning civilian aliens in the territory of a Party to the conflict are based on the idea of the personal freedom of civilians remaining in general unimpaired. The right in question is therefore a relative one which the Party to the conflict or the occupying power may restrict or even suspend within the limits laid down by the Convention."[1060]

Articles 41 to 43, 64, 68 and 78 of the Convention lay down these limits on departures from the right to liberty that are allowed under article 27§4.[1061] Apart from deprivation of liberty for criminal offences under applicable penal legislation,[1062] the parties to the conflict or the Occupying Power "may not have recourse to any other measure of control more severe than that of assigned residence or internment" on the grounds prescribed by the Convention.[1063] The procedures for such internment, prescribed by articles 43 and 78 GC IV,[1064]

[1060] Pictet, *Commentary GC IV* (1958), pp. 201-202 (emphasis added). See also ICTY, *Delalić* (1998), §565.

[1061] Pictet, *Commentary GC IV*, p. 367: "All three provisions [article 41, 42 and 78] are based on the general reservation permitting 'such measures and of control and security as may be necessary as a result of the war.' (Article 27, fourth paragraph)." Articles 64 and 68 define the limits of the legislative powers of an Occupying Power regarding deprivation of liberty in the framework of criminal justice.

[1062] Such deprivation of liberty (or detention, since it is ordered in the framework of criminal proceedings) is lawful when carried out in full compliance with articles 37-38 (aliens in the territory of a party to the conflict) and articles 64-75 (in occupied territory) GC IV. Article 38§1 sets forth an important principle in this matter, worth recalling here: "With the exception of special measures authorized by the present Convention, in particular by Articles 27 and 41 thereof, the situation of protected persons shall continue to be regulated by the provisions concerning aliens in time of peace." This means that detention measures in the framework of criminal proceedings – except where the Convention specifically and explicitly departs from it – must, in order to be lawful, also fully conform to the relevant norms of international human rights law.

[1063] Article 41 GC IV. Article 78 contains similar wording: "If the Occupying Power considers it necessary [...] to take safety measures concerning protected persons, it may, at the most, subject them to assigned residence or to internment."

[1064] Article 43 GC IV: "Any protected person who has been interned or placed in assigned residence shall be entitled to have such action reconsidered as soon as possible by an appropriate court or administrative board designated by the Detaining Power for that purpose. If the internment or placing in assigned residence is maintained, the court or administrative board shall periodically, and at least twice yearly, give consideration to his or her case, with a view to the favourable amendment of the initial decision, if circumstances permit. Unless the protected persons concerned object, the Detaining Power shall, as rapidly as possible, give the Protecting Power the names of any protected persons who have been interned or subjected to assigned residence, or who have been released from internment or assigned residence. The decisions of the courts or boards mentioned in the first paragraph of the present Article shall also, subject to the same conditions, be notified as rapidly as possible to the Protecting Power"; article 78§2 GC IV: "Decisions regarding such assigned residence or internment shall be made according to a regular procedure to be prescribed by the Occupying Power in accordance with the provisions of the present Convention. This procedure shall include the right of appeal for the parties

and the independent monitoring mechanisms established by the Convention[1065] are intended to ensure that the parties to the conflict do not overstep these limits.[1066] Our focus here is on the lawful grounds for and duration of internment on the basis of GC IV.[1067]

Now that we have set out the Fourth Convention's general framework for restricting individual rights and freedoms as may be necessary as a result of the war, we will study the general requirements flowing from this framework before examining the specific distinctive features of the three lawful grounds for internment it prescribes.

3.2.1.2. An exceptional measure designed to avoid abuse

While the right to liberty is not an absolute right and may be restricted where "necessary as a result of the war", that does not mean it may be suspended or restricted in a general manner. International humanitarian law allows for restrictions to the right to liberty that go beyond what is allowed under IHRL in normal circumstances, but its provisions regulating such deprivation of liberty are "based on the idea of the personal freedom of civilians remaining in general unimpaired."[1068] Internment can only be ordered in exceptional circumstances.

The Fourth Geneva Convention stresses the exceptional character of internment by allowing it only when "absolutely" or "imperatively" necessary (cf. supra text of articles 42 and 78 GC IV), and by making it subject to strict conditions. There are several reasons for this. For one, the majority of persons protected by the Convention are civilians who are not allowed to, and in the majority do not, participate in hostilities or otherwise pose a military or security threat to the Interning Power. Moreover, internment – even more so than detention in the context of criminal proceedings, which is subject to judicial oversight and other guarantees against abuse and arbitrariness – is a particularly harsh restriction of the right to liberty. But most importantly, history has shown

concerned. Appeals shall be decided with the least possible delay. In the event of the decision being upheld, it shall be subject to periodical review, if possible every six months, by a competent body set up by the said Power." See also Pictet, *Commentary GC IV* (1958), pp. 260-262 and 368-369; Henckaerts & Doswald-Beck (2005), Vol. I, pp. 345-346 and Pejic (*IRRC* 2005), pp. 384-389.

[1065] The specific monitoring mechanisms foreseen by the Geneva Conventions are the institution of Protecting Powers and the International Committee of the Red Cross (e.g. articles 11, 30, 61, 76 and 143 GC IV). *Cf.* also *infra* chapter II-5, section 5.2.

[1066] Pictet, *Commentary GC IV* (1958), p. 260.

[1067] Other relevant provisions in Part III of GC IV reiterate the general obligation of humane treatment of article 27§1 specifically for persons deprived of liberty (articles 37 and 76) and regulate the general internment regime, including material conditions of deprivation of liberty, camp management, and relations with the exterior (Part III, Section IV "Regulations for the treatment of internees" is to a large extent identical to the regime established by GC III for prisoners of war). These provisions have been further developed and complemented by Additional Protocol I, in particular its articles 11, 72, and 75-77.

[1068] Pictet, *Commentary GC IV* (1958), p. 202 (*cf. supra* article 27§4 GC IV). See also for example Israel, SC, *Marab* (2003), §20: "Moreover, it must always be kept in mind that detention without the establishment of criminal responsibility should only occur in unique and exceptional cases. The general rule is one of liberty. Detention is the exception. The general rule is one of freedom. Confinement is an exception."

that it renders the internees, who are virtually at the mercy of authorities who by definition consider them "enemies", extremely vulnerable to abuses such as torture and other forms of cruel, inhuman or degrading treatment, arbitrary deprivation of life, or enforced disappearance.[1069] Pictet's commentary to article 27§1 GC IV refers back to the specific experiences of the Second World War to illustrate this vulnerability, which directly inspired the strict regulations of internment under GC IV:

> "The experience of the Second World War has shown in tragic fashion that under such conditions there is a particularly great danger of offences against the human person. That is why the Convention, conscious of the danger, only accepts internment and assigned residence as measures to be adopted in the last extremity, and makes them subject to strict rules (Articles 41 to 43 and Article 78); and why, furthermore, it lays down in great detail (Articles 79 to 135 – treatment of internees) standards of treatment designed to ensure that the human person is respected under the circumstances where it appears to be in greatest danger."[1070]

Unfortunately, the strict provisions in GC IV have not always been able to prevent the mass internment of civilians in recent conflicts like the ones that ravaged the Balkans in the early 1990s. The mass internment of civilians in the former Yugoslavia, mainly on the basis of their ethnicity,[1071] and other heinous crimes committed in the course of these conflicts prompted the international community to create the first international criminal tribunal to prosecute and punish serious violations of international law committed in armed conflict. The International Criminal Tribunal for the Former Yugoslavia (ICTY) recalls the words of Pictet's Commentary to GC IV regarding the exceptional character of internment measures, before proceeding to examine the various instances of unlawful internment on the basis of GC IV (we will come back to those in our discussion of article 42§1 GC IV below):

> "[T]he relevant norms of international humanitarian law have been developed such that only absolute necessity, based on the requirements of State security, can justify recourse to these measures, and only then if security cannot be safeguarded by other, less severe means. [...] The drafters of the Fourth Geneva

[1069] *Cf. supra* chapter I-1; Aeschlimann (*IRRC*, 2005), pp. 83-84; ICTY, *Delalić* (1998), §571; WGAD, *Annual Report 2006*, §48 *in fine*. The notion of exceptionality attached to any lawful deprivation of liberty in international human rights law is even more compounding in situations of armed conflict where the risk of abuse against persons deprived of liberty is seriously increased by the characteristics and dynamics of violence, enmity and vengeance. For examples of such abuses against internees in armed conflict, see Cesarani & Kushner (1993) (specifically on internment in the UK during WW I, II and Gulf War); Rodley & Pollard (2009), pp. 8-16; the *Tadić*, *Delalić*, *Blaškić* and *Kordić & Čerkez cases* before the ICTY; http://www.amnesty.org/en/detention; and http://www.apt.ch.

[1070] Pictet, *Commentary GC IV* (1958), p. 207 (emphasis added). See also the report of the Committee in charge of the negotiation of GC IV to the Plenary Assembly at the 1949 Diplomatic Conference with regard to the security measures allowed for under article 27§4 (which include internment): "Obviously, however, this reservation does not re-establish arbitrary governmental power, it deals *only with such persons as really constitute a danger for the security of the State*" (*Final Record 1949*, Vol. II-A, p. 821, emphasis added).

[1071] See the examples referred to *supra* in note 1035. See also ICTY, *Delalić* (1998), §570, with reference to Pictet, *Commentary GC IV* (1958), p. 207.

Convention, conscious of these dangers, only permitted internment and assigned residence as a last resort, and makes them subject to strict rules (articles 41 to 43 and article 78)."[1072]

3.2.1.3. Absolute/imperative necessity: proportionality and alternatives

Article 42§1 GC IV says internment for security reasons is only lawful when "absolutely necessary", article 42§2 GC IV allows for voluntary internment where the situation of the applicant "renders this step necessary", and article 78 GC IV allows for internment in occupied territory only for "imperative reasons" of security.[1073] That threshold of absolute or imperative necessity will only be met when an internment measure is based on a correct proportionality calculus and is imposed as a last resort.

The interpretation of the term absolute or imperative necessity can be described as "a hermeneutical exercise designed to balance between the personal interest in liberty on the one hand, and the collective interest in security on the other hand."[1074] In other words, when ordering internment, a proportionate balance must be struck between the individual's fundamental right to liberty and the consequences of internment on his or her personal situation on the one hand, and the Interning Power's right to take such measures of control and security as are necessary as a result of an ongoing armed conflict on the other hand. The balance is a delicate one to strike, and must at all times be made in good faith.

"Absolute" or "imperative" necessity means that internment may not be ordered where it is simply convenient, expedient or advantageous.[1075] Contrary to

[1072] ICTY, *Delalić* (1998), §§571-572 (emphasis added). The *Delalić* case is the leading case in the ICTY's jurisprudence on the interpretation of article 42 GC IV. The Trial Chamber's legal findings on the internment of protected persons on the basis of GC IV have been confirmed and reinforced on appeal and in subsequent case law of the tribunal.

[1073] In cases of voluntary internment it is the internee's own security that is at stake and not the security of the Interning Power or the inhabitants of an occupied territory. In what follows we will focus rather on the balance inherent in the requirements of absolute/imperative necessity in articles 42§1 and 78 GC IV. This does not mean however that a balance must not be struck when deciding to grant or reject a request for voluntary internment. In the latter case the security needs of the applicant and the internment capacity of the Interning Power must be balanced and alternative measures should also be preferred over internment. Finally, the decision to grant or reject such an application must be taken on an individual basis and reviewed in light of changing circumstances. On voluntary internment, *cf. infra*, section 3.2.3.

[1074] Ben-Naftali & Gleichgevitch (*Harv.ILJ* 2000), p. 221. The authors' comment related to grounds for internment prescribed by the Israeli *Emergency Powers (Detention) Law* (1979) (hereinafter "*EPDL*"), a law that effectively implements article 42§1 GC IV into Israeli domestic law. The phrase reflects precisely the kind of balance that is at stake in article 42§1 GC IV itself (and in article 78 GC IV for that matter), and we hope therefore that the authors would not object to our using it here.

[1075] *Report of the Expert Meeting on Security Detention in NIAC* (2008), p. 866: "The experts were of the view that "imperative reasons of security" seems to constitute a permissible ground for internment taking into account the specific circumstances and given the available alternatives. Internment that is merely convenient or useful for the interning power, or internment for the sole purpose of information gathering, or undertaken in order to facilitate the exchange of detainees or negotiations is not lawful" (the examples raised by the experts will be discussed in more detail below). See also Shraga, "UN Peacekeeping Operations: Applicability of International Humanitarian Law and Responsibility for Operations-Related Damage" (*AJIL* 2000), pp. 410-411: "'operational necessity' [which the author, former head of the UN's Legal Office, describes as the equivalent of "military necessity" in peacekeeping operations, legitimizing 'what would otherwise be unlawful']

prisoners of war, persons protected under GC IV may not be interned merely because their internment gives the Interning Power a military advantage, such as being able to use them as guides, for intelligence purposes, or to weaken the enemy's military capacity. Internment on the basis of articles 42§1 and 78 GC IV is only allowed where the individual internee poses a military or security *threat*, and where his or her internment is *unavoidable* to meet that threat.[1076]

In this sense, the ICTY has held that:

"the involuntary confinement of a civilian where the security of the Detaining Power does not make this *absolutely necessary* will be unlawful [...] As observed in the ICRC Commentary, the measure of confinement of civilians is an 'exceptionally severe' measure, and it is for that reason that the *threshold for its imposition is high* – it must, on the express terms of Article 42, be 'absolutely necessary'."[1077]

Determining whether the threshold of absolute/imperative necessity is met inevitably involves an exercise in proportionality. We have seen in Part I that proportionality is a *leitmotiv* for any restriction of fundamental individual rights and freedoms to be lawful. Articles 42 and 78 GC add an element to the proportionality test under general international law for a specific deprivation of liberty (namely security internment) authorized by the Convention in situations of international armed conflict and occupation, notably legitimate military or security needs. Nevertheless, such needs must still be weighed against the drastic restrictions of an individual's fundamental right to liberty.

In this sense, the Israeli Supreme Court found that internment is a very serious violation of the right to liberty, but may be justified where the internee poses a very serious threat to the security of the State or its population. In assessing the constitutionality (and conformity with IHL) of the Israeli implementing legislation for article 42§1 GC IV, the Court has submitted that law to a proportionality test composed of three subsets:

"the first is the *rational connection test* that requires the legislative measure that violates the constitutional right to correspond to the purpose that the law is intended to realize; the second is the *least harmful measure test*, which requires the legislation to violate the constitutional right to the smallest degree possible while achieving the purpose of the law; and the third is the *test of proportionality*

---

must meet four cumulative conditions: the force commander, who holds the discretionary power to decide on the operational necessity of any given measure, must be convinced that an operational necessity exists; that the measure itself *is strictly necessary and not just a matter of mere convenience or expediency*; that it is part of an overarching operational plan and not the result of a rash individual action; and that the damage inflicted will be proportional to what is strictly necessary to achieve the operational goal" (emphasis added).

1076 See for example, Lord Carswell in UK, HoL, *Al-Jedda* (2007), §130: "Internment without trial is so antithetical to the rule of law as understood in a democratic society that recourse to it requires to be carefully scrutinised by the courts of that society. There are, regrettably, circumstances in which the threat to the necessary stability of the state is so great that in order to maintain that stability the use of internment is *unavoidable*" (emphasis added).

1077 ICTY, *Delalić* (2001), §§320 and 330, confirmed in ICTY, *Kordić & Čerkez* (2001), §282.

> *in the narrow sense*, according to which the violation of the constitutional right must be commensurate with the social benefit arising from it."[1078]

Moreover, each individual decision to intern must be proportionate. The Israeli Court again:

> "it must always be kept in mind that detention without the establishment of criminal responsibility should only occur in unique and exceptional cases. The general rule is one of liberty. Detention is the exception. The general rule is one of freedom. Confinement is an exception. [...] There is no authority to detain arbitrarily. [...] The fundamental principles which are most important to the matter at hand are those regarding the duty of each public authority to act *reasonably and proportionately, while properly balancing between individual liberty and public necessity.*"[1079]

Proportionality cannot be fixed in absolute or general terms but must take into account the specific circumstances of each case and the importance of the rights and needs at stake. This is why it is impossible to define what "absolute" or "imperative" necessity exactly means.[1080] Nevertheless, we will see below in our examination of the lawful grounds for security internment that not all military or security needs justify internment. The internment of certain persons may be *useful* for protecting ones own troops, it may be advantageous and even *necessary*, but as long as it is not *absolutely* necessary, it will not be lawful. What is certain however is that "absolute" or "imperative" necessity means that there are no alternative, less restrictive measures available that could adequately counter the threat posed by the individual internee.

Pictet reiterates this crucial issue in his commentaries with regard to both articles 42 and 78 GC IV, which lay down the reasons for which internment of "enemy aliens" may be ordered, and highlights that the parties to the conflict can only have recourse to such exceptional measures as a last resort:

> "Earlier Articles [i.e. article 27§4 GC IV] referred to "measures of control" without giving any further details; the present text picks out two of them –

[1078] Israel, SC, *A and B v. Israel* (2008), §31. The Supreme Court's test is "for determining the proportionality of an act of legislation that violates a constitutional human right", but since the law under the Court's scrutiny *de facto* implements the legal basis for internment in articles 42§1 and 78 GC IV, it is interesting for our present purposes to see how the Court subjects the general balance struck by the Israeli authorities to a proportionality test influenced not only by IHL but also by (domestic) human rights law. In the same sense: Israel, SC, *Salem Said* (2008), §§ 19 and 27.

[1079] Israel, SC, *Marab* (2003), §20 (emphasis added).

[1080] See *Report of the Expert Meeting on Security Detention in NIAC* (2008), p. 865: "The majority of operational experts argued that whilst it is easy to provide examples that clearly pass or fail the 'imperative reasons of security' test, the borderline cases pose significant challenges as there is neither a concrete definition nor practical guidelines on what the concept of 'imperative reasons of security' exactly means. State practice is of limited help, as it is difficult to establish an exhaustive list of specific activities that would in all circumstances fall within or outside the legal standard." And *Ibidem*, p. 864: "In such cases, much depends on the specific context of the military operation at hand, on the available alternatives and – as argued by many – on a certain amount of 'common sense'."

> assigned residence and internment – as being the most severe to which the detaining State may resort *when other measures have proved inadequate*."[1081]
>
> "The Convention *stresses the exceptional character* of measures of internment and assigned residence by making their application subject to *strict conditions*; its object in doing this is to put an end to an abuse which occurred during the Second World War. All too often the mere fact of being an enemy subject was regarded as justifying internment. Henceforward *only absolute necessity*, based on the requirements of state security, can justify recourse to these two measures, and *only then if security cannot be safeguarded by other, less severe means.* All considerations not on this basis are strictly excluded."[1082]
>
> "In occupied territories the internment of protected persons should be *even more exceptional* than it is inside the territory of the Parties to the conflict [...] That is why Article 78 speaks of *imperative* reasons of security."[1083]

Pictet thus underlines that the parties to the conflict can only resort to assigned residence or internment "when other measures have proved inadequate."

In the same sense, Canadian military doctrine prescribes that:

> "detention of civilians, hostile forces or belligerents shall be in accordance with the principles of necessity and proportionality" and therefore that "detention of hostile forces/belligerents who obstruct friendly forces is permitted, but *only after appropriate non-forcible attempts to negate such obstruction have failed*".[1084]

The Israeli Supreme Court has also consistently held that in order to establish whether security internment is lawful

> "it is necessary to examine less harmful alternatives and to verify that the restriction of the detainee's liberty is proportionate to the danger he poses."[1085]

That internment is a means of last resort does not necessarily mean that all other available measures must in each case be exhausted before a decision to intern can be taken. But it does mean that alternative measures must be

---

1081 Pictet, *Commentary GC IV* (1958), p. 256 (emphasis added). See also the text of article 41§1 GC IV: "Should the power in whose hands protected persons may consider the measures *of control mentioned in the present Convention to be inadequate*, it may not have recourse to any other measure of control more severe than that of assigned residence or internment, in accordance with the provisions of Articles 42 and 43" (emphasis added).

1082 Pictet, *Commentary GC IV* (1958), p. 258 (emphasis added).

1083 Pictet, *Commentary GC IV* (1958), p. 367 (emphasis added).

1084 Canada, *PWDITQ* (2004), p. 1B-5 (emphasis added). Baroness Hale, in the UK House of Lord's judgment in *Al-Jedda* (2007), §128, found internment was not "necessary for imperative reasons of security" in Iraq where the internee, a UK national, could have been repatriated to the UK and thus cease to pose a threat *in Iraq*. While we do not agree with the Baroness' reasoning in this case on all aspects, it goes to show that internment really must be a last resort and does not meet the threshold of necessity if other, less restrictive means, are available.

1085 As summarized in B'Tselem, Without Trial: Administrative Detention of Palestinians by Israel and the Internment of Unlawful Combatants Law (2009), p. 13. See for example Israel, HCJ, Sajadiya v. Minister of Defence, No. 253/88, quoted by B'Tselem: "The detention is intended to thwart a security danger resulting from acts that the detainee is liable to commit, where it is not reasonably possible to prevent them by taking regular legal measures (a criminal proceeding) or by an administrative measure that results in less serious harm [to the detainee's right to liberty]."

considered and evaluated before doing so.[1086] The Convention does not list the type of control and security measures that are allowed under article 27§4 where necessary, but Pictet lists a number of examples, "ranging from comparatively mild restrictions such as the duty of registering with and reporting periodically to the police authorities, the carrying of identity cards or special papers, or a ban on the carrying of arms, to harsher provisions such as a prohibition on any change in place of residence without permission, prohibition of access to certain areas [or] restrictions of movement."[1087] In cases where alternative measures could sufficiently meet the threat posed by an individual person, they must be preferred over his or her internment.

Since internment of protected persons is only lawful for as long as it is necessary to meet the threat they pose, it must also mean that throughout the entire period of internment such alternative measures must be re-evaluated in order to decide whether continuing to intern a person is absolutely necessary, or whether the threat he or she poses can be sufficiently neutralized through other, less severe measures of control. The evaluation of available alternatives must therefore be considered at the time of the decision to intern and throughout the period of internment by the interning authority – usually situated at theatre level – and not only by the authorities in charge of the initial and periodic review of the lawfulness and continued necessity of the internment.[1088]

3.1.2.4. Internment is a preventive measure, never a punishment for past acts

Internment is by definition a preventive measure: its purpose is to prevent a security threat emanating from an individual person from materializing. It is not designed to punish a person for past behaviour that may have put the security or military operations of the Interning Power at risk. We have seen in chapter II-1 that the internment of prisoners of war may never be a form of revenge or punishment for their participation in hostilities or any crimes they may have committed. The same holds true for persons who do not qualify as prisoners of war.[1089] While the latter may be prosecuted and punished even for their mere participation in hostilities, and in the framework of such criminal proceedings

[1086] See also Gasser in Fleck (2008), pp. 319-320: "Internment is a drastic restriction of personal freedom. It is permitted only as *ultima ratio*, i.e. only if security requirements cannot be satisfied by less severe measures, such as, e.g., the obligation to register with the police or assigned residence" and "[i]n exercising their discretion [the parties to the conflict] must take into account the personal situation of the person concerned. Internment may be ordered only as a last resort, if other measures are not sufficient." To be noted that assigned residence is not always a less severe measure than internment but where it is, we agree with Gasser that it should be preferred over internment.

[1087] Pictet, *Commentary GC IV* (1958), p. 207.

[1088] We will refer to the "interning authority" as the person or persons in charge of the actual decisions to intern specific persons; and to the "review authority" as the body in charge of the review of the lawfulness and continued necessity of internment as prescribed by articles 43 and 78 GC IV. These authorities are normally situated at theatre level and are not the same authorities as those who set out operational directives for internment (usually the joint force commanders through the adoption of standard operating procedures) on the basis of the more general policy set out at the general level (usually the joint army services and the executive department in charge of defence matters).

[1089] Pictet, *Commentary GC IV* (1958), p. 343: "Internment is a preventive administrative measure and cannot be considered a penal sanction."

may be placed in preventive pre-trial detention or imprisoned upon conviction, they may not be interned on that basis.[1090]

The first conclusion that flows from the preventive character of internment measures is that they may never be imposed merely as an alternative for criminal proceedings, not even where such proceedings are fraught with practical problems preventing them from being brought to a conclusion.

In this sense, the ICRC, experts and legal scholars have recalled that:

"Internment/administrative detention is a measure of control aimed at dealing with persons who pose a real threat to State security, currently or in the future, in situations of armed conflict, or to State security or public order in non-conflict situations; it is not a measure that is meant to replace criminal proceedings";[1091]

"it is of crucial importance that internment not be used as an (disguised) alternative to criminal proceedings. Internment is conceived and implemented as a preventive measure and therefore may not be used to punish a person for earlier criminal acts. [...] Given that it is a preventive measure, internment should not be used as an alternative to criminal proceedings";[1092]

"Administrative detention must have a preventive nature, that is, must be resorted to not as a penalty for an offence committed in the past but as a measure denying the suspect the possibility of committing an offence in the future. [...] True, it happens that administrative detentions are inflicted on persons who are suspected of having committed offences in the past, when there is not sufficient evidence to bring about their conviction by a court of law, or where proof of their guilt beyond reasonable doubt requires the disclosure of intelligence sources (especially the exposure of secret agents whom the occupant does not wish to endanger or whose clandestine operation he is unwilling to discontinue). Yet, even in such instances, the reason for the internment (at least in theory) is not punishment (without due process of law) for the offence committed in the past, but apprehension lest similar acts be committed in the future."[1093]

1090 See for example our reference to the Canadian *Code of Conduct infra* notes 1235-1237; Rudman & Qupty, "The Emergency Powers (Detention) Law: Israel's Courts Have a Mission – Should they Choose to Accept it?" (*CHRLR* 1990), p. 493; Gasser in Fleck (2008), p. 320. See also Israel, HCJ, *Nasrallah v. Commander of Military Forces in the West Bank* (1988) at 271, summarized in B'Tselem (2009), p. 13 (no English version of the judgment is public available): "according to the Supreme Court justices, it may only be used as a *forward-looking preventive* measure against a person who poses an individual threat and *may not be used as punishment* for past acts" (emphasis added); and Israel, HCJ, *Ajuri* (2002), §24: "the basis for exercising the discretion for assigning residence is the consideration of *preventing* a danger presented by a person whose place of residence is being assigned" (emphasis added, the rules on internment and assigned residence in articles 42§1 and 78 GC IV apply *mutatis mutandis*).

1091 As reflected in Pejic (*IRRC* 2005), p. 381.

1092 Report of the Expert Meeting on Security Detention in NIAC (2008), pp. 865-866.

1093 Dinstein, "The International Law of Belligerent Occupation and Human Rights" (*Isr.YHR* 1978), p. 125. See also Israel, *Instructions of the Attorney General 21.927* (1982), quoted in Rudman & Qupty (1990), p. 493: "Under his instructions, 'a person *[could] not be administratively detained as a punishment* for an act prejudicial to state security or public security.' Such punishment would 'only be imposed by a court in the ordinary judicial proceedings'" (original emphasis and brackets). See also Ben-Naftali & Gleichgevitch (*Harv.ILJ* 2000), p. 216: "Indeed, the concept of the Cartesian man, capable of making up his own mind and therefore, responsible for his own deeds, is the basic premise of all human rights and is thus implicit in all relevant legal pronouncements [reference is made to articles

The question may arise whether an Interning Power that has both sufficient evidence to commence criminal proceedings against an individual and sufficient evidence to establish a future security threat, has a choice between criminal prosecution and internment or must always favour the first over the latter. While in the majority of cases the answer will have to be in the affirmative, there may also be instances where this is not the case. In any case, the provisions of article 27§4, 42§1 and 78 GC IV, and relevant international human rights law must guide that choice.

First, under article 27§4 the parties to the conflict are obliged, when adopting measures of security and control that may be necessary as a result of the war, to adopt those measures that will have the least possible impact on the individual's right to liberty.

Second, articles 42§1 and 78 GC IV set a high threshold for internment: it may only be ordered when it is absolutely/imperatively necessary in light of other available measures that could adequately meet that threat. It is clear that deprivation of liberty within the framework of criminal proceedings and security internment equally restrict the individual's right to liberty in terms of confinement. Nevertheless, there are two important differences between the two regimes that may influence the assessment of which one is more severe than the other. On the one hand, internment may only last as long as the reasons justifying it exist and at most until the cessation of active hostilities. Criminal prosecution may result in imprisonment that may last much longer than security internment, and a prison sentence may extend beyond the end of the conflict. Moreover, the internment regime in international humanitarian law is generally less invasive of individual rights and freedoms than a normal criminal detention regime and internees are generally subject to fewer restrictions on their freedom of movement. On the other hand, not all procedural safeguards and judicial guarantees related to detention in the framework of criminal proceedings are required for the review and supervision of security internment.

In each case, the decision-making authorities and any supervisory instances reviewing such decisions, will have to take into account which of the two measures is more restrictive to the right to liberty of the individual concerned and prefer the less restrictive over the more severe measure. In most cases, preference must be given to criminal prosecution. As the ICRC, international experts and legal scholars have pointed out:

> "A person who is suspected of having committed a criminal offence, whether in armed conflict or other situations of violence, has the right to benefit from the additional stringent judicial guarantees provided for in humanitarian and/or human rights law for criminal suspects, which include the right to be tried by a regularly constituted, independent and impartial court. Unless internment/administrative

---

14, 17 and 26 ICCPR, articles 10-12 UDHR, and to UNGA/Res. 217 (III) 1948]. This principle of personal liability is so entrenched that even a state of war does not permit a deviation therefrom [sic], as is evidenced in Article 33 [GC IV] [Article 33 provides: 'No protected person may be punished for an offence he or she has not personally committed']."

detention and penal repression are organized as strictly separate regimes there is a danger that internment might be used as a substandard system of penal repression in the hands of the executive power, bypassing the one sanctioned by a country's legislature and courts. The rights of criminal suspects would thus be gravely undermined";[1094]

"If a person is held solely on suspicion of involvement in criminal activity his or her deprivation of liberty will only be permitted if it is in accordance with the applicable criminal law procedure and relevant human rights law";[1095]

"When a person is suspected of having already committed an offence, he should be prosecuted before a competent court."[1096]

Finally, where the person is suspected of war crimes or crimes against humanity, the Interning Power does not have any choice, but is under an absolute obligation to prosecute and punish.[1097]

An individual's past acts or behaviour may be indicative for assessing his or her future threat level and thus whether the internment of that person may be absolutely necessary to counter that threat.[1098] While an Interning Power may take into account the past behaviour of a potential internee to assess whether he or she poses a threat that requires internment, such past behaviour may never be the only basis on which a decision to intern is finally taken. In this sense, the Israeli Supreme Court has consistently held that:

"Indeed, the purpose of administrative detention is to prevent anticipated future threats to the security of the state, and naturally we can learn of these threats from tangible evidence concerning the detainee's acts in the past [...]. Notwithstanding, for the purposes of long-term [internment], adequate administrative evidence is required, and a single piece of evidence with regard to an isolated act carried out in the distant past is insufficient."[1099]

Finally, an individual person may not be interned as punishment for the acts of other persons, or as a general deterrent to prevent the commission of criminal

---

1094 As reflected in Pejic (*IRRC* 2005), p. 381.

1095 *Report of the Expert Meeting on Security Detention in NIAC* (2008), p. 865.

1096 Dinstein (*Isr.YHR* 1978), pp. 125-126. According to B'Tselem, the Israeli High court of Justice in *Sajadiya v. Minister of Defense* (1988) also held that internment "may not be used unless it is not possible to prevent the said danger by a criminal proceeding or by an administrative measure that causes less harm of human rights" (B'Tselem (2009), p. 13, no English version of the judgment is public available).

1097 Common articles 49/50/129/146 and 50/51/130/147 GC I-IV; article 85 AP I; article 1 Convention on the Prevention and Punishment of the Crime of Genocide (1948); preambular paragraph 5 ICC Statute (1998).

1098 *Report of the Expert Meeting on Security Detention in NIAC* (2008), p. 865: "as internment is based on the threat posed by an individual, his or her past activities may well be an important factor in assessing whether the individual constitutes or may constitute a significant enough threat to the security of the interning Power to justify internment."

1099 Israel, SC, *A and B v. Israel* (2008), §22 (references to previous case law omitted). See also the Fact Sheet on administrative detention published by the Israeli Ministry of Foreign Affairs (2003), referring to the decision of a military court regarding the petitioner's claim that she was being interned for acts she had already committed and served prison sentences for: "the past of the petitioner cannot be used in itself, as a ground upon which an administrative detention order may be made" (no English version of the judgment referred to is public available).

acts by other, related persons. For example, the Israeli Supreme Court in *Ajuri* has held that:

> "an essential condition for being able to assign the place of residence of a person under art. 78 of the Fourth Geneva Convention is that the person himself constitutes a danger, and that assigning his place of residence will aid in averting that danger. It follows that [...] The place of residence of an innocent person who does not himself present a danger may not be assigned, merely because assigning his place of residence will deter others. Likewise, one may not assign the place of residence of an innocent family member who did not collaborate with anyone, or of a family member who is not innocent but does not present a danger to the area. This is the case even if assigning the place of residence of a family member may deter other terrorists from carrying out acts of terror."[1100]

In both such cases the internment measure would amount to collective punishment, expressly prohibited by international humanitarian law.[1101]

3.1.2.5. Ensure exceptionality, necessity and proportionality: individual decisions

In order to reduce the risk of arbitrary deprivation of liberty, collective punishments, and the risk of other violations of other fundamental rights and freedoms to which internees may be exposed, and because the proportionality assessment inherent in the threshold of "absolute" or "imperative" necessity must take into account the specific circumstances of each case, decisions as to whether the threshold for internment is met must be taken on an individual case-by-case basis.

Contrary to the regime applicable to prisoners of war, the grounds for internment in GC IV are not based on status or on any legal presumption of threat that may come with it. On the contrary, they are based on the individual military or security threat an individual person may pose. Prisoners of war – the large majority of which will be members of the armed forces of a party to the conflict[1102] and thus entitled to participate in hostilities – pose a recognized collective threat to the security of the adverse party, and preventing their resumption of hostilities after capture is accepted as constituting a military need justifying a departure from the right to individual liberty. All prisoners of war may in principle be interned; exceptions are made for reasons of humanity or where their return to the battlefield is unlikely or can otherwise be prevented. We have already seen above that the reasoning under GC IV is exactly the opposite: persons not qualifying as prisoners of war – protected persons under GC IV – may in principle not be interned, and only a limited number of exceptions to this rule, dictated by military necessity, are allowed.[1103]

1100 Israel, HCJ, *Ajuri* (2002), §24 with further references to previous case law of the Court (emphasis added, the rules on internment and assigned residence in articles 42§1 and 78 GC IV apply *mutatis mutandis*).

1101 Article 50 HR1907; article 87§3 GC III; article 33 GC IV; articles 75§2(d) and 75§4(b) AP I; article 4§2(b) AP II.

1102 For the definition of prisoners of war, *cf. supra* chapter II-1.

1103 This different basic approach also explains why POW internment can be the subject of a collective

This general rule failed to be included explicitly in the text of the Convention however. During the 1949 Diplomatic Conference some States deemed it necessary not to rule out some very exceptional circumstances in which mass internment may be unavoidable. While the proposal to include a sentence saying that each decision of internment must be taken individually garnered substantial support during the negotiations, it was ultimately not retained in order to allow for such exceptional circumstances, at the "outbreak of war", in cases where a decision to intern on an individual basis would be "impractical":

> "[I]n a time of great emergency, as when a country is threatened with invasion, the government may feel compelled to act immediately to prevent potential hostile action by enemy aliens. All agree that there should be a careful reconsideration of such cases to correct arbitrary or hasty action. This purpose is achieved fully by Article 40 [current article 43 GC IV] without endangering the security of States."[1104]

The fact that, in the territory of the parties to the conflict, the impending outbreak of war may exceptionally justify an initial decision to intern enemy aliens on a collective basis, does not detract from the general rule, which requires that in all other situations, decisions to intern must be taken on a case-by-case basis and an individual threat-assessment.[1105]

This general rule is inherent in the Convention's provisions on internment and its general framework for permitted restrictions of individual rights. We have already discussed (with regard to article 27§4) the different approach to the right to liberty in the Third and Fourth Geneva Conventions and the fact that restrictions to the right to liberty on the basis of GC IV are only allowed on an exceptional and individual basis. Article 5 GC IV also demonstrates this by requiring that derogations from individual rights that internees may have under the Convention may only be made on an individual, and not on a collective,

decision whereas internment on the basis of GC IV must be based on an individual threat assessment, and why the review procedures for the lawfulness and continued necessity of internment are different under both Conventions.

1104 *Final Record 1949*, Vol. II-A, p. 757 and Vol. III p. 126 respectively. The Conference was split on the issue: the phrase was inserted and deleted several times into the text during negotiations and drafting but ultimately retained by the Committee in charge of GC IV by a vote of 15 to 13 with 8 abstentions. It was only upon the renewed insistence of the US in the Plenary Assembly that the phrase was ultimately deleted, by 20 votes to 12, with 6 abstentions. *Final Record 1949*, Vol. II-A, pp. 658, 756-758, 825-826 and 854; Vol. II-B, p. 411; Vol. III, p. 126. See also Pictet, *Commentary to GC IV* (1958) (commentary on article 42§1), p. 256: "[T]he Diplomatic Conference discussed at great length whether the provision should be amended to state that any decision concerning assigned residence or internment 'should be taken individually'. The proposal was rejected, on the ground that there might be situations -- a threat of invasion for example -- which would force a government to act without delay to prevent hostile acts, and to take measures against certain categories without always finding it possible to consider individual cases. The safeguards provided in Article 43 seem adequate to reduce the risk of arbitrary decisions." If the safeguards in article 43 GC IV are to be sufficient to correct such 'hasty action' where necessary, the initial review provided for in article 43§1 must be made available as soon as possible and may not *per se* be postponed for 6 months. See also *infra* notes 1120-1121 and accompanying text.

1105 See also Sassòli (*JICJ* 2004), p. 104. Also note that in occupied territory no exceptions to this rule are allowed, *cf. infra* II-3, section 3.2.4.

basis.[1106] Finally, article 132§1 GC IV, which provides that "[e]ach interned person shall be released by the Interning Power as soon as the reasons which necessitated his internment no longer exist", also shows that internment decisions must be taken on an individual basis.

Individual threat assessments are indispensable to ensure that internment is only ordered in exceptional cases and only where absolutely necessary in the circumstances of each specific case. As Pejic rightly points out:

> "This does not mean that a detaining authority cannot intern a large number of persons, but that both the initial decision on internment and any subsequent decision to maintain it, including the reasons for internment, must be taken with respect to each individual involved."[1107]

The principle that internment measures must be taken on an individual and not on a collective basis has been reaffirmed in more explicit terms in the case law of the ICTY. The images of some internment camps set up during the Balkans conflicts clearly brought back memories of some of the concentration camps of the Second World War mentioned in the Commentary to GC IV quoted above. In the leading case on the interpretation of article 42 GC IV, the ICTY's Trial Chamber stressed that:

> "[I]nternment and assigned residence, whether in the occupying power's national territory or in the occupied territory, are exceptional measures to be taken only after *careful consideration of each individual case*. Such measures are *never to be taken on a collective basis*." [1108]

[1106] Article 5 GC IV in relevant part reads as follows: "Where, in the territory of a Party to the conflict, the latter is satisfied that an *individual* protected person is definitely suspected of or engaged in activities hostile to the security of the State, such *individual* person shall not be entitled to claim such rights and privileges under the present Convention as would, if exercised in the favour of such *individual* person, be prejudicial to the security of such State. Where in occupied territory an *individual* protected person is detained as a spy or saboteur, or as a person under definite suspicion of activity hostile to the security of the Occupying Power, such person shall, in those cases where absolute military security so requires, be regarded as having forfeited rights of communication under the present Convention" (emphasis added). Pictet recalls that "[d]uring the discussions at the Diplomatic Conference several speakers emphasized the importance of these words ["...that an individual protected person is..."]. The suspicion must not rest on a whole class of people; collective measures cannot be taken under this Article; there must be grounds justifying action in each individual case" (Pictet, *Commentary GC IV* (1958), p. 55). See also Gehring (*MLLWR* 1980), p. 81: "Article 5 [...] is concerned with protected persons as individuals. There can be no collective action under article 5" (Gehring says "article 5, Protocol I" but this is clearly a slip-up taking into account the surrounding text and the reference to Pictet's Commentary on article 5 GC IV).

[1107] Pejic (*IRRC* 2005), pp. 381-382. She adds that "*en bloc*, non-individual detention of a whole category of persons could in no way be considered a proportional response, regardless of what the circumstances of the emergency concerned might be. The idea of collective measures of any kind is antithetical to the rules, spirit and purpose of human rights law" (original italics) and highlights furthermore that such *en bloc*, non-individual internment of enemy nationals "would amount to, and violate the general prohibition of, 'collective punishments' under Article 75 (2) (d) of Additional Protocol I."

[1108] ICTY, *Delalić* (1998), §578. The Chamber reiterates this again in §583 ("the confinement of civilians during armed conflict may be permissible in limited cases, but has in any event to be in compliance with the provisions of articles 42 and 43 of Geneva Convention IV. The security of the State concerned might require the internment of civilians and, furthermore, the decision of whether a civilian

Other trial chambers confirmed this reading and so did the Appeals Chamber, whose judges also addressed an argument of the defence reminiscent of the exception to the rule contemplated during the negotiations in 1949 quoted above:

"It is perfectly clear from the provisions of Geneva Convention IV referred to above that there is *no such blanket power* to detain the entire civilian population of a party to the conflict in such circumstances, but that *there must be an assessment that each civilian taken into detention poses a particular risk to the security of the State*. [...] It was contended by Delalić that detention in the present case was justified under international law because '[t]he government is clearly entitled to some reasonable time to determine which of the detainees is a danger to the State's security'. Although the Appeals Chamber accepts this proposition, it does not share the view apparently taken by Delalić as to what is a 'reasonable time' for this purpose. The *reasonableness of this period is not a matter solely to be assessed by the detaining power*. The Appeals Chamber recalls that Article 43 of Geneva Convention IV provides that the decision to take measures of detention against civilians must be 'reconsidered *as soon as possible* by an appropriate court or administrative board.' Read in this light, the reasonable time which is to be afforded to a detaining power to ascertain whether detained civilians pose a security risk must be *the minimum time necessary to make enquiries to determine whether a view that they pose a security risk has any objective foundation.*"[1109]

In the one case concerning internment in international armed conflict dealt with by the Inter-American Commission of Human Rights, the Commission held that:

"The applicable provisions of the Fourth Geneva Convention provide the authorities substantial discretion in making the initial determination, *on a case by*

constitutes a threat to the security of the State is largely left to its discretion. However, it must be borne in mind that the measure of internment for reasons of security is an exceptional one and can never be taken on a collective basis") and §1134 ("the Chamber is convinced that a significant number of civilians were detained in the Celebici prison-camp although there existed no serious and legitimate reason to conclude that they seriously prejudiced the security of the Interning power. To the contrary, it appears that the confinement of civilians in the Celebici prison-camp was a collective measure aimed at a specific group of persons, based mainly on their ethnic background, and not a legitimate security measure." The Trial Chamber in *Delalić* referred also to Gehring (*MLLWR* 1980) (footnote to the judgment's §578). Gehring himself also makes the link with the First and Second World War, see for example pp. 85-86: "Internment and assigned residence, whether in the occupying power's national territory or in occupied territory, are "exceptional" measures to be taken only after careful consideration of each individual case. Such measures are never to be taken on a collective basis. The strict limitations of these articles are a direct reaction to the abuses which occurred during World Wars I and II and which diametrically changed the previous custom that "nationals of a belligerent residing within the territory of the adverse party were not to be interned." Gehring refers to Pictet's reminders of the abuses committed during the Second World War, which we have quoted above, adding that "[i]n the nineteenth century treatment of resident enemy civilians in the event of war was a frequent subject for bilateral agreements", with a reference to Wilson's abovementioned article in the *BYIL* (1943), p. 30, 32-33.

1109 ICTY, *Delalić* (2001), §§ 327 and 328 (footnotes omitted, emphasis added). The initial statement of the Trial Chamber in *Delalić* (1998) (§578) was also repeated by the Trial Chamber in *Kordić & Čerkez* (2001), §285.

case basis, that a protected person poses a threat to its security, and the record provides no basis to controvert the security rationale asserted in this case."[1110]

The Israeli Supreme Court has also consistently emphasized that administrative detention (including internment on the basis of articles 42 and 78 GC IV) can only be ordered on an individual basis, framing this requirement as a core principle both in its own legal system and in international humanitarian and human rights law:

> "It is one of the first principles of our legal system that administrative detention is conditional upon the existence of a ground for detention that derives from the *individual* threat of the detainee to the security of the state. This was discussed by President Barak when he said that: '[In order that there may be a ground for detention] it is necessary that the circumstances of the detention are such that they give rise with regard to [the detainee] – *with regard to him personally and not with regard to someone else* – to a concern of a risk to security, whether because he was found in the combat area when he was actually fighting or carrying out terrorist acts, or because there is a concern that he is involved in fighting or terrorism' (*Marab v. IDF Commander in Judaea and Samaria*, at page 367). The *requirement of an individual threat* for the purposes of placing someone in administrative detention is *an essential part of the protection of the constitutional right to dignity and personal liberty*. [...] its purpose is to prevent the tangible risk *presented by the acts of the detainee* to the security of the state. *It is this risk that justifies* the use of the unusual measure of administrative detention that violates human liberty (see and cf. *Ajuri v. IDF Commander in West Bank*, at pages 370-372, and the references cited there). It should be noted that the individual threat to the security of the state represented by the detainee is *also required by the principles of international humanitarian law*. Thus, for example, in his interpretation of articles 42 and 78 of the Fourth Geneva Convention Pictet emphasizes that the state should make use of the measure of detention only when it has serious and legitimate reasons to believe that *the person concerned* endangers its security. In his interpretation Pictet discusses the membership of organizations whose goal is to harm the security of the state as a ground for recognizing a threat, but he *emphasizes the supreme principle that the threat is determined in accordance with the individual activity of that person*. In Pictet's words: 'To justify recourse to such measures, the state must have good reason to think that the person concerned, by his activities, knowledge or qualifications, represents a real threat to its present or future security'. *No one before us disputes* that the provisions of the Internment of Unlawful Combatants Law *should be interpreted in accordance with the aforesaid principle*, which make administrative detention conditional upon proving the *existence of a ground that establishes an individual threat.*"[1111]

[1110] IAC°HR, *Coard v. USA* (1999), §53 (emphasis added).

[1111] Israel, SC, *A and B v. Israel* (2008), §§18-19 (emphasis added). The case concerned the internment of two inhabitants of the Gaza Strip, allegedly members of Hezbollah, in Israel on the basis of the *Incarceration of Unlawful Combatants Law* (2002), *cf. infra*. The *Marab* (2003) and *Ajuri* (2002) cases referred to in the judgment concern internment in the occupied Palestinian territories. The argument of the Court with regard to human rights provisions in Israeli constitutional law is valid *per analogiam* with regard to equivalent provisions of international human rights law (*in*

And thus, the Court affirmed in a later case concerning the same law, "according to the guiding rule, the detainee must pose a *personal threat* for this definition to be met."[1112]

The little directly relevant case law thus reaffirms the general rule that both at the time of the initial decision to intern and throughout the entire period of internment,[1113] the threat posed by an individual and the necessity to intern that individual in order to counter that threat must be established on an individual case-by-case basis and that, in principle, no collective internment measures are allowed.

3.1.2.6. Necessity and proportionality: limits on the duration of internment

For continued internment to be lawful, the threshold of absolute or imperative necessity must be met throughout its whole duration. Not only may internment only be ordered when absolutely necessary, article 132§1 GC IV prescribes that:

> "Each interned person shall be released by the Detaining Power as soon as the reasons which necessitated his internment no longer exist."

For the ICRC, this rule is one of the most important principles governing internment:

> "this form of deprivation of liberty must cease as soon as the individual ceases to pose a real threat to State security, meaning that deprivation of liberty on such grounds cannot be indefinite. In view of the rapid progression of events in armed conflict, a person considered to be a threat today might not pose the same threat after a change of circumstances on the ground. In other words, the longer internment lasts, the greater the onus on a detaining authority to prove that the reasons for it remain valid. The rationale of the principle is thus to facilitate the release of a person as soon as the reasons justifying the curtailment of liberty no longer exist."[1114]

The ICRC's observation that both the threat level and the necessity to intern a given person may evolve while the person is interned and its statement that

---

casu article 9 ICCPR). Note that while the Israeli government formally objects to the applicability of IHRL in situations of armed conflict and occupation (*cf. supra* 31) – which may explain the absence of any reference to the ICCPR in this judgment – it does consider its constitutional human rights provisions to apply to the persons within its jurisdiction or under its effective control within Israel proper (Israel, SC, *A and B v. Israel* (2008), §27). The Supreme Court however increasingly relies on the ICCPR in cases concerning internment and other security measures in the occupied territories.

1112 Israel, SC, *Salem Said* (2008), §21 (original emphasis). The case concerned the internment of a Palestinian from Gaza, allegedly member of the Popular Resistance Committees, on the basis of the *Incarceration of Unlawful Combatants Law* (2002), *cf. infra*.

1113 See also, Israel, SC, *Salem Said* (2008), §30: "The extreme means of detention [...] places a special duty *both on the competent authority and on the court in making the judicial review* to carefully examine, from time to time, the extent of the justification for continuation of the detention, while exercising restraint in use of the detention means and limiting it to situations in which real security needs require it."

1114 As reflected in Pejic (*IRRC* 2005), p. 382. As we mentioned before, this article reflects the official position of the ICRC (ICRC, *International Humanitarian Law and the Challenges of Contemporary Armed Conflicts* (2007), p. 11 and Annex 1).

"the longer internment lasts, the greater the onus on a detaining authority to prove that the reasons for it remain valid" echoes relevant case law of the Israeli Supreme Court:

> "An administrative detention cannot continue endlessly. As the period of detention is increasingly prolonged, more required considerations are required to justify the further extension of the detention. As time passes, the measure of administrative detention becomes so burdensome as to cease being proportional. Indeed, even once the authority is given to violate liberty through a detention warrant, the use of such authority must be proportional. It cannot reach the 'breaking point' beyond which administrative detention is no longer proportional. The exact location of the breaking point varies according to the circumstances, depending on the importance of object that administrative detention seeks to fulfil; it is all conditional on the probability of attaining the object by means of detention and the compatibility of administrative detention to the attaining of the object; it is all linked with the existence of alternative, less harmful means of accomplishing the goal; It all derives from the severity of the infringement upon individual liberty compared with the worthy purpose being sought. Indeed, we are dealing with a set of considerations that vary from one case to another and from one time to the next."[1115]

The periodic review procedure prescribed by articles 43 and 78 GC IV is of course an essential tool in ensuring that the obligation for the Interning Power in article 132§1 GC IV will be met. As Pictet underlines:

> "The main point [of periodic review] is that no protected person should be kept in assigned residence or in an internment camp for a longer time than the security of the Detaining State demands."[1116]

Nevertheless, the establishment of a periodic review procedure does not relieve the interning authority itself from the obligation to evaluate the continued need for internment of any individual internee it holds. As the ICTY has found:

> "Clearly, the [review] procedures established in Geneva Convention IV itself are a minimum and the fundamental consideration must be that no civilian should be kept in assigned residence or in an internment camp for a longer time than the security of the detaining party absolutely demands."[1117]

Whether the threshold for internment on the basis of GC IV is met must be evaluated from the moment the initial decision to intern is taken throughout the whole period of its duration, and by all decision-makers involved, meaning both the interning authority and the authorities in charge of initial and periodic review.

The initial decision to intern will usually be taken as soon as the captured or arrested individual is evacuated to an area at theatre level where an authority

---

[1115] Israel, SC, *Bargaining Chips Case* (2005), §25; see also Israel, SC, *A and B v. Israel* (2008), §46.

[1116] Pictet, *Commentary GC IV* (1958), p. 261. See also Gasser in Fleck (2008), p. 322: "As civilians can be interned only for as long as security considerations so require [...] the detention must be ended and the internees released as soon as the motive for internment ceases to exist. [...] The periodical review of decisions regarding internment by the responsible court or administrative body [...] serves to ensure that the release is ordered when necessary, even without being requested by the concerned person."

[1117] ICTY, *Delalić* (1998), §§581-582 and 578. In the same sense: ICTY, *Kordić & Čerkez* (2001), §288.

who will make the decision to intern or to release is present.[1118] That decision will be based on the circumstances of the capture or arrest and any other information available at the time.[1119] It will need to be reviewed as soon as possible by the appropriate review authority but apart from this procedural safeguard,[1120] the obligation remains on the interning authority to release individuals whose internment is not or no longer absolutely necessary to meet a real and serious security threat. The interning authority's discretion to intern "is not exercised once and for all but is "iterative": if the decision is to detain, that decision must be kept under constant review with the necessity test continuously reapplied as evidence emerges."[1121]

[1118] See *Report of the Expert Meeting on Security Detention in NIAC* (2008), p. 866: "The decision to intern must be taken on an individual basis and at a sufficiently high level of command to ensure an adequate assessment of the threat and of the necessity to intern." For example, in Israel, the decision to intern is taken by a high-ranking military official (e.g.: under the *Emergency Powers (Detention) Law* (1979), the decision belongs to the Minister of Defence, and partially to the Chief of General Staff; under the *Incarceration of Unlawful Combatants Law* (2002), the decision belongs to the Chief of General Staff who can delegate his powers to a major-general (see also Israel, SC, *Salem Said* (2008), §3: *in casu* the internment order was made by the Head of the Israeli Defence Forces Operations Department, a major-general, "based on a well-founded intelligence opinion"), and can only be taken after a military legal counsel has confirmed "that the information on which it is based has been corroborated by a reliable source. In many cases two or more such sources are required." In the same sense: Israel, MoJ, *Factsheet: The Legal Framework for the Use of Administrative Detention as a Means of Combating Terrorism* (2003), p. 4. The Canadian *PWDITQ* (2004), Annex B: "Direction for the detention of civilians unlawful belligerents other than prisoners of war", article B006, likewise requires internment decisions to be taken "by a responsible commander, legal advice must be sought to intern anyone longer than 24 hours and the "chain of command is to be informed verbally of all detentions by the fastest possible means."

[1119] Persons captured on the battlefield will normally be presumed prisoners of war and may be interned on the basis of article 21 GC III (*cf. supra* II-2). Their internment will be regulated by GC III. In case of doubt as to their eligibility to POW status, the matter will be referred to and decided by a competent tribunal. If the case is decided in the positive, their internment will continue to be governed by GC III. If the tribunal decides they are not prisoners of war, they must be presumed protected persons under GC IV and if they really are they can only be interned if the conditions of article 42 or 78 GC IV are met. Should they not qualify as protected persons under GC IV either, their internment will only be possible on the basis of applicable domestic law.

[1120] See also Pictet, *Commentary GC IV* (1958), p. 260 (article 43§1 right of appeal): "The safeguard provided here is an *a posteriori* arrangement. It has been seen that the Convention leaves a great deal to the discretion of the State of residence in the matter of the original internment or placing in assigned residence. On the other hand decisions to take such measures may be reconsidered after a very short time."

[1121] The quote is from New Zealand's High Court, dealing with a case of administrative detention for immigration purposes, but the statement aptly formulates the continuous obligation for an interning authority in armed conflict to update and corroborate evidence of the security threat poses by individual internees and to release them as soon as it is no longer absolutely necessary to intern them. (New Zealand, High Court, *Refugee Council of New Zealand Inc. and the Human Rights Foundation of Aotearoa New Zealand Inc. and D. v. Attorney-General* (2002), §203 quoted in Goodwin-Gill in Feller, Türk & Nicholson (2003), p. 230). In the same sense with regard to armed conflict: Waxman, "Detention as Targeting: Standards of Certainty and Detention of Suspected Terrorists" (*CLR* 2008), pp. 1409-1410.

It will therefore be important for the interning authority to corroborate and update the information that has led to the initial decision to intern on a continuous basis.[1122] As the Israeli Supreme Court points out:

> "The significance of the requirement that there is clear and convincing evidence [to intern] is that importance should be attached to the quantity and quality of the evidence against the detainee *and the degree to which the relevant intelligence information against him is up to date.*"[1123]

Corroboration of intelligence leading to internment is especially important in the early phases of conflict and in settings where cultural and language differences may render the collection of accurate intelligence more difficult. Moreover, as was pointed out in an expert meeting on security internment in armed conflict:

> "in some contexts intelligence informing a decision to intern is often obtained from informants who exaggerate or provide untruthful information in order to settle personal or communal scores (the 'vendetta problem'). It was accepted that this was especially likely in the early stages of a conflict where the tactical level human intelligence network is likely to be fragmentary."[1124]

The accuracy of information on which an individual threat assessment is based is not only crucial for the internment process to be lawful and for effective review to be possible, but is also important for internment to contribute efficiently to broader military operations. US military doctrine stresses that "[o]nce the capture of individuals has occurred, the proper identification and classification of those personnel remain critical to the overall intelligence and detainee identification effort."[1125] The UN's Special Rapporteur on Counterterrorism has found it to be good practice for intelligence agencies to "conduct regular assessments of the relevance and accuracy of the personal data which they hold. They are legally required to delete or update any information which is assessed to be inaccurate, or no longer relevant to their mandate, the work of oversight institutions or possible legal proceedings."[1126]

[1122] It will also be important to allow the internee to address and if necessary rebut the facts on which the internment decision relies.

[1123] See also Israel, SC, *A and B v. Israel* (2008), §22 (emphasis added).

[1124] *Report of the Expert Meeting on Security Detention in NIAC* (2008), p. 874. See also *Ibidem*, p. 866: "Experts stressed the importance of the continuous updating and verification of information that resulted in a threat assessment leading to internment. [...] The less the information is corroborated, the less certain is the continuing threat posed by an individual and thus the less justifiable is the continued internment. What must be avoided is that initial information on the existence of a threat (unless very clear and specific) remains in an internee's file without being corroborated or further updated."

[1125] US, *JDP 3-63* (2005), p. IV-1.

[1126] UN Human Rights Council, Special Rapporteur on Counterterrorism, *Good Practices Intelligence Agencies* (2010), p. 22. The Special Rapporteur adds a word of caution that is particularly important (*Ibidem*, pp. 22-23): "While intelligence services are ordinarily obliged to delete data which is no longer relevant to their mandate, it is important that this is not to the detriment of the work of oversight bodies or possible legal proceedings. Information held by intelligence services may constitute evidence in legal proceedings that have significant implications for the individuals concerned; the availability of such material may be important for guaranteeing due process rights. Therefore, it is good practice for intelligence services to be obliged to retain all records in cases (including original transcripts and operational notes) which may lead to legal proceedings, and that the deletion of any such information to

In any event, the absolute time limit on any security internment on the basis of GC IV is laid down in article 133§1 GC IV: "Internment shall cease as soon as possible after the close of hostilities." As Gasser points out, the text of article 133 makes clear that this is an absolute obligation.[1127] Nevertheless, until their final release (and repatriation where relevant), internees continue to benefit from the protection of the Convention.[1128] As is the case for the first three Geneva Conventions, article 6§4 GC IV prescribes that:

> "Protected persons whose release, repatriation or re-establishment may take place after [the convention has ceased to apply] shall meanwhile continue to benefit by the present Convention."

Contrary to the general rule applicable for prisoners of war, the Convention does not oblige the Interning Power to repatriate internees to their country of origin, should that issue arise. Moreover, the principle of non-refoulement is explicitly included in article 45 GC IV:

> "In no circumstances shall a protected person be transferred to a country where he or she may have reason to fear persecution for his or her political opinions or religious beliefs."

On the basis of that article, read in light of the developments in general international law we have discussed above, persons interned on the basis of GC IV may not be forcibly repatriated to a country where they may be subject to persecution, ill-treatment, or arbitrary deprivation of life or liberty:

> "Aliens repatriated from the territory of a party to the conflict must have their wishes taken into consideration, in that they shall not be transferred to a country in which they may fear persecution. [...] Any refusal to be transferred to a specific country must at all times be respected if a person must expect serious persecution; this principle is rooted in the general rules of international humanitarian law and of human rights law [...] Upon the return of occupied territory to the original country, a solution must be found, justified by human rights considerations, for those persons who would face serious persecution if transferred to the authorities of that country."[1129]

---

be supervised by an external institution."

[1127] Gasser in Fleck (2008), p. 323. Before the IAC°HR in *Coard v. USA* (1999) (at §§22 and 26), the US argued that the period of internment "coincided with ... the 'hostilities phase' of the operation (i.e. from 25 October to 2 November) when the US military was engaged in putting down armed resistance from enemy forces [...] after the fighting ceased (on about 27 October) [the internees] were turned over to the Caribbean Peacekeeping Force (CPF)." The only exception to the rule is contained in article 133§2 GC IV: "Internees in the territory of a Party to the conflict, against whom penal proceedings are pending for offences not exclusively subject to disciplinary penalties, may be detained until the close of such proceedings and, if circumstances require, until the completion of the penalty. The same shall apply to internees who have been previously sentenced to a punishment depriving them of liberty." The same exception applies to prisoners of war; we therefore refer the reader to our comments on article 119§5 GC III above, which can be applied *mutatis mutandis* to article 133§2 GC IV. See also Pictet, *Commentary GC IV* (1958), pp. 515-516.

[1128] Therefore, regardless of whether their continued internment is lawful or unlawful in light of article 133 GC IV, internees continued to be protected by Fourth Geneva Convention until their final release.

[1129] Gasser in Fleck (2008), p. 323.

Contrary to the other Geneva Conventions, the Fourth Geneva Conventions explicitly prescribes the time at which the Convention ceases to apply. Article 6§2 GC IV prescribes that:

> "In the territory of Parties to the conflict, the application of the present Convention shall cease on the general close of military operations."[1130]

As soon as the Convention ceases to apply, the legal bases for internment contained therein can no longer be relied upon to deprive a person of his or her liberty. Therefore, no new internment can be ordered on the basis of articles 42 and 78 GC IV after the Convention has ceased to apply.[1131]

3.1.2.7. Conclusions

In order to avoid unnecessary and unlawful restrictions of an individual's right to liberty, and taking into account the increased vulnerability of persons deprived of liberty to violations of such fundamental and absolute rights as the right to life and the prohibitions of torture, ill-treatment and enforced disappearances, the Fourth Geneva Convention only allows for security internment in exceptional circumstances.[1132] Where it is authorized, international humanitarian law confines the extent to which the general right to liberty may be restricted or derogated from in very strict terms. Internment may only be ordered on an individual case-by-case basis, where and for as long as the Interning Power's military or security situation makes it absolutely necessary.

In light of the above, the internment provisions in GC IV – which we have quoted at the outset and will discuss in detail below – must be interpreted narrowly. A strict interpretation of the rules regulating internment in armed conflict imposes itself to satisfy both the text and the spirit of the Convention and "the principles of the law of nations, as they result from the usages established among civilized peoples, from the laws of humanity, and the dictates of the public conscience."[1133] Finally, the simultaneous applicability of international human rights law in armed conflict will certainly impose a stricter interpretation of the balance between military necessity and humanity than what was deemed proportionate at the time the Conventions were adopted.[1134]

1130 "'Military operations' means the movements, manoeuvres and actions of any sort, carried out by the armed forces with a view to combat. 'The general close of military operations' [...] may be deemed in principle to be at the lime of a general armistice, capitulation or just when the occupation of the whole territory of a Party is completed, accompanied by the effective cessation of all hostilities, without the necessity of a legal instrument of any kind. When there are several States on one side or the other, the general close of military operations could mean the complete cessation of hostilities between all belligerents, at least in a particular theatre of war." (Sandoz et al., *Commentary AP I And II* (1987), pp. 67-68). In occupied territory, the end of applicability of GC IV is defined differently: *cf. infra* section 3.2.4.

1131 Pictet, *Commentary GC IV* (1958), p. 61.

1132 The ICRC puts forth the exceptional character of the measure as the first of its general principles for internment and administrative detention, see Pejic (*IRRC* 2005), p. 380.

1133 As required by the renowned de Martens clause, here quoted from the preamble of the HR 1907.

1134 *Cf. supra* I-2, section 2.2.2.2 for the interaction of IHL and IHRL in the legal framework for internment in armed conflict.

In what follows, we study the two grounds for internment on the basis of GC IV. In the first section, we deal with "security internment", authorized both in the territory of the parties to the conflict (Article 42§1 GC IV) and in occupied territory (Article 78 GC IV). Second, we examine the less common ground of voluntary internment (Article 42§2 GC IV). Finally, we highlight some particular aspects of the grounds for internment in occupied territory.

3.2.2. Security internment

The most commonly used ground for the internment of persons other than prisoners of war is prescribed in articles 42§1 and 78 GC IV. The provisions are slightly differently worded, but give expression to the same idea: protected persons who pose a serious military or security threat to the Power in whose hands they are, may be interned where that is absolutely necessary:

> Article 42§1 GC IV: The internment or placing in assigned residence of protected persons may be ordered only if the security of the Detaining Power makes it absolutely necessary.
>
> Article 78 GC IV: If the Occupying Power considers it necessary, for imperative reasons of security, to take safety measures concerning protected persons, it may, at the most, subject them to assigned residence or to internment.

The expressions "absolutely necessary for the security of the Detaining Power" and "necessary for imperative reasons of security" are not further defined. The record of the Diplomatic Conference shows that while the original draft language of article 42§1 (internment not permitted "unless the security of the Detaining Power imperatively demands") was changed to the present text ("only if the security of the Detaining Power makes it absolutely necessary"), this was not the subject of any meaningful debate.[1135] The concept of "imperative reasons of security" in article 78 GC IV was not subject to any debate during the Diplomatic Conference either.[1136] The delegates apparently assumed the threshold in both articles 42§1 and 78 GC IV was sufficiently clear and could in any case not be usefully defined in more detail (since the exact meaning in practice depends very much on the specific circumstances of each case).[1137]

In his commentary of article 42 GC IV, Pictet lists the more obvious examples of behaviour that directly threatens security (subversive activity, espionage, sabotage) but is compelled to conclude that a precise definition was deemed impossible and undesirable:

[1135] *Final Record 1949*, Vol. II-A, pp. 659, 721, 809 and 826 and 854; Vol. II-B, pp. 192 and 411.
[1136] *Final Record 1949*, Vol. I-A, pp. 675, 721, 772-773, 790, 801-802, 835-836 and 860; Vol. II-b, pp. 156, 196 and 440-441.
[1137] *Cf.* also *supra* note 1079.

"It did not seem possible to define the expression 'security of the State' in a more concrete fashion. It is thus very largely left to Governments to decide the measure of activity prejudicial to the internal or external security of the State which justifies internment or assigned residence."[1138]

In order to determine the parameters of the war crime of unlawful confinement of civilians the ICTY surveyed the applicable law on internment under GC IV and reached the same conclusion:

"'Security' remains as vague here as in earlier articles, and the expression does not appear susceptible to more concrete definition. The measure of activity deemed prejudicial to the internal or external security of the State which justifies internment or assigned residence is left largely to the authorities of that State itself."[1139]

The ICTY also found however that the Fourth Geneva Convention, as commented upon by Pictet, gives sufficiently clear guidance as to what would amount to unlawful internment:

"The offence of unlawful confinement of a civilian, a grave breach of the Geneva Conventions which is recognised under Article 2(g) of the Statute of the Tribunal, is not further defined in the Statute. As found by the Trial Chamber, however, clear guidance can be found in the provisions of Geneva Convention IV. The Appeals Chamber agrees with the Trial Chamber that the exceptional measure of confinement of a civilian will be lawful only in the conditions prescribed by Article 42, and where the provisions of Article 43 are complied with. Thus the detention or confinement of civilians will be unlawful in the following two circumstances:

(i) when a civilian or civilians have been detained in contravention of Article 42 of Geneva Convention IV, i.e. they are detained without reasonable grounds to believe that the security of the Detaining Power makes it absolutely necessary; and

(ii) where the procedural safeguards required by Article 43 of Geneva Convention IV are not complied with in respect of detained civilians, even where their initial detention may have been justified."[1140]

Nevertheless, in order to define the war crime of unlawful confinement of civilians the Tribunal only needed to interpret articles 42§1 and 78 GC IV. Whilst its case law is useful to determine what are *unlawful* grounds for internment, it only gives us scant hints of what are *lawful* grounds to intern protected persons on the basis of GC IV. In spite of the clear directions given by the Convention itself, it may still be useful to clarify the substantive threshold for security internment for two reasons. On the one hand, it may be useful to further define the meaning of articles 42§1 and 78 GC IV for persons involved in the decision-making and review processes of internment measures.[1141] On the other hand,

[1138] Pictet, *Commentary GC IV* (1958), pp. 257.

[1139] ICTY, *Delalić* (1998), §574, confirmed in ICTY, *Kordić & Čerkez* (2001), §§ 282-289.

[1140] ICTY, *Delalić* (2001), §320, see also *Kordić & Čerkez* (2001), §289.

[1141] In the wake of the scandals surrounding "legal blackholes" such as the internment facility at the US naval base in Guantánamo and (to a lesser extent) the Bagram Theatre Internment Facility in Afghanistan, there is increased pressure to define in more concrete terms the legitimate reasons for

should any efforts to develop additional legal norms for internment in non-international armed conflict be inspired by the legal framework for internment in GC IV, it is important to have a clear understanding of the substance of that framework.

The absence of further guidance in the text or the drafting history of the rules leaves us with two possible avenues for clarifying the kind of threat that justifies security internment. Since the ultimate decision is within the discretion of States, it is useful to see whether and how States have elaborated specific instructions for their troops in the field as to who may be interned on the basis of articles 42§1 and 78 GC IV. Nevertheless, such instructions are rarely publicly available and in their general operational directives on internment, States' military doctrine is much less developed on the issue of internment on the basis of GC IV than it is on the issue of internment of prisoners of war on the basis of GC III. While it does not offer comprehensive answers to all our questions, we have examined the little State practice available to establish what is clear and what possibly needs to be clarified. Moreover, the available case law on internment on the basis of articles 42§1 and 78 GC IV also helps establish the boundaries of lawful and unlawful security internment in armed conflict. Finally, some of the other provisions of GC IV are also useful to establish the threshold and limits of lawful internment on the basis of articles 42§1 and 78 GC IV.

In order to interpret articles 42§1 and 78 GC IV, the ICTY's Trial Chamber in the *Delalić* case relied upon the text of article 5 GC IV, which authorizes parties to the conflict to derogate from certain Convention rights in exceptional circumstances.[1142] The required threshold for such derogations is defined in wording similar to that in articles 42§1 and 78 GC IV:

> "Where, in the territory of a Party to the conflict, the latter is satisfied that an individual protected person is *definitely suspected of or engaged in activities hostile to the security of the State*, such individual person shall not be entitled to claim such rights and privileges under the present Convention as would, if exercised in the favour of such individual person, *be prejudicial to the security of such State*."

Where in occupied territory an individual protected person is detained *as a spy or saboteur, or as a person under definite suspicion of activity hostile to the security of the Occupying Power*, such person shall, in those cases *where absolute military security so requires*, be regarded as having forfeited rights of communication under the present Convention." (emphasis added)

The Trial Chamber seemed to view security internment as envisaged in articles 42§1 and 78 GC IV as one of the measures allowed by article 5 GC IV. This is in our view not a correct interpretation of article 5. Rather, both derogations on the basis of article 5 and internment on the basis of articles

holding persons without trial in the context of armed conflict. Moreover, the Conventions' provisions, dating from 1949, must also be read in light of subsequent developments in both international law and practice, and especially the norms of international human rights law and their impact on the normative framework regulating internment in armed conflict.

[1142] ICTY, *Delalić* (1998), §§ 566-567.

42§1/78 GC IV are specific measures that may be authorized in light of the general allowance for military necessity made in article 27§4 GC IV.[1143] Article 5 allows for exceptional derogations from rights granted to protected persons under GC IV. While the threshold for such derogations to be lawful is indeed very similar to that in articles 42§1 and 78 GC IV to intern protected persons, article 5 GC IV cannot serve as a legal basis for internment.[1144] This is also how the Appeals Chamber in the *Delalić* case seemed to view the relation between these provisions:

> "This provision [article 5 GC IV] reinforces the principle behind Article 42, that restrictions on the rights of civilian protected persons, such as deprivation of their liberty by confinement, are permissible only where there are reasonable grounds to believe that the security of the State is at risk."[1145]

With this caveat in mind, the similarity of the wording defining the threshold for limitation of Convention rights in article 5 and that for security internment on the basis of articles 42§1 and 78 indeed makes that article useful for interpreting certain aspects of the legal bases for internment.

Based on the available State practice and case law, we will try to list examples of both lawful and unlawful grounds for internment on the basis of GC IV. Such a list was initiated – albeit very modestly – by Pictet in his Commentary to articles 42 and 78 GC IV. In what follows, we will update and complete it in light of international practice and case law. We will first look at whose security may justify internment. Next, we will deal with the different reasons that in past and present times have been put forward to justify security internment on the basis of GC IV. In light of our previous discussions on the requirements of exceptionality, necessity and individuality, we will then go through these reasons in an order going from wide and collective criteria, to more narrow and individual criteria, and evaluate their lawfulness as grounds for internment on the basis of articles 42§1 and 78 GC IV.

3.2.2.1. Whose security?

Article 42§1 GC IV only allows internment where it is "absolutely necessary for the security of the Detaining Power." There are two ways of interpreting this provision with regard to the question of whose security must be threatened to justify internment. On the one hand, one could argue that the security "of the Detaining Power" only refers to the security of that power's armed forces and military infrastructure, and does not extend to the civilian population under its control or responsibility.

[1143] *Cf. supra* section 3.2.1. The ICTY also recognizes this, see ICTY, *Delalić* (1998), §§ 565 and 569.

[1144] Note that article 79 GC IV (*cf. supra* note 934) lists the legal bases for internment in GC IV in an exhaustive manner and does not include article 5 GC IV. The wording of article 5, especially that in its §2, also suggests the persons affected by it are already detained or interned on the basis of the provisions in GC IV that prescribe the grounds and procedures for such deprivation of liberty. See also Pictet, *Commentary GC IV* (1958), pp. 52-56: (wrapped up in the following phrase:) "As we see, the Article refers mainly to the relations of the *detained* person with the outside world, and that is the sphere in which restrictions will doubtless be applied."

[1145] ICTY, *Delalić* (2001), §321.

This is indeed one way in which Pictet's commentary to article 42§1 – which reflects the discussions at the Diplomatic Conference in 1949 – could be understood:

> "It did not seem possible to define the expression "security *of the State*" in a more concrete fashion. It is thus very largely left to Governments to decide the measure of activity prejudicial to the *internal or external security of the State* which justifies internment or assigned residence. [...] To justify recourse to such measures the State must have good reason to think that the person concerned [...] represents a real threat to *its* present or future security. [...] Henceforward only absolute necessity, based on the requirements of *state* security, can justify recourse to these two measures."[1146]

The ICTY has followed Pictet's reasoning in interpreting article 42§1 GC IV:

> "Subversive activity carried on inside the territory of a *party to the conflict*, or actions which are of direct assistance to an opposing party, *may threaten the security of the former*, which may, *therefore*, intern people or place them in assigned residence if it has serious and legitimate reasons to think that they may seriously prejudice *its security* by means such as sabotage or espionage. On the other hand, the mere fact that a person is a national of, or aligned with, an enemy party cannot be considered as *threatening the security of the opposing party* where he is living and is *not, therefore*, a valid reason for interning him or placing him in assigned residence. To justify recourse to such measures, the party must have good reason to think that the person concerned [...] represents a real threat to *its* present or future security."[1147]

Another interpretation of article 42§1 GC IV (and of article 78 GC IV), however, includes the security of the population of the Interning Power (or that under the effective control and thus responsibility of an Occupying Power) as within the security of that Interning Power. Pictet's reference to "State security" and the ICTY's reference to "the security of the opposing party to the conflict" may also be understood in this broader sense.

In our opinion, the latter interpretation is more in line with the purposes for restrictions on fundamental rights and freedoms that are recognized under international law as legitimate in situations of armed conflict. We have seen in chapter I-2 that international law – in order to fulfill its function of regulating armed conflict – recognizes additional legitimate purposes for restricting fundamental rights and freedoms in a situation of armed conflict, so as to allow parties to the conflict not only to achieve military victory over the enemy and to reasonably minimize their own military losses, but also to protect the civilian

---

[1146] Pictet, *Commentary GC IV* (1958), pp. 257-258 (emphasis added). See also *Final Record 1949*, Vol. I, p. 120; Vol. II-A, pp. 658-659, 721, 756-758, 809, 825-826, 854; Vol. II-B, pp. 192, 411; Vol. III, pp. 127-128.

[1147] ICTY, *Delalić* (1998), §§576-577 (emphasis added). See also Israel, SC, *Salem Said* (2008), §19: "The threat to *state* security is a significant condition forming the basis of the grounds for internment" (emphasis added).

population under their control or responsibility against direct or indiscriminate attacks by an adverse party to the conflict.[1148]

Nevertheless, a direct link between the reasons for internment and the armed conflict remains needed. The requirement of a nexus with that armed conflict is what sets internment on the basis of article 42§1 and 78 GC IV apart from other forms of deprivation of liberty that may be ordered, even in times of armed conflict, on the basis of domestic law. The internment of persons other than prisoners of war is the most severe measure that – in the words of article 27§4 GC IV – "may be necessary *as a result of the war*" (emphasis added). For internment to be lawful, the reasons justifying it must therefore by definition be linked to ongoing hostilities and military operations.

For example, criminal acts that may be facilitated by or otherwise flow from the general state of insecurity and chaos generated by armed conflict, but that are carried out for private gain and unrelated to the hostilities between the parties to the conflict as such, do not justify internment. Criminal behaviour that is motivated by reasons unrelated to the armed conflict, even if it is directed against the parties to the conflict or their populations, is not as such a lawful ground for internment. Apart from the fact that such behaviour does not necessarily threaten the security of the Interning Power, there are other means to address such threats, including deprivation of liberty within the criminal justice system.[1149] Persons protected by GC IV, even when they are members of an adverse party's armed forces, are not immune from such criminal prosecution.

The requirement of a nexus with the conflict is also reflected in the ultimate limit placed on the duration of security internment: where internees have not been released before, their internment "shall cease as soon as possible after the close of hostilities."[1150] Once hostilities have come to an end, internment by definition ceases to be a measure "necessary as a result of the war" and articles 42§1 and 78 GC IV can therefore no longer serve as a legal basis for deprivation of liberty.[1151]

Thus, internment may not be ordered on the basis of article 42§1 or 78 GC IV as an alternative to criminal proceedings or as a general deterrent in the maintenance of law and order and general public security. Internment may however be ordered on the basis of these provisions where it is absolutely/imperatively necessary to protect the civilian population from direct or indiscriminate attacks by an adverse party to the conflict.[1152]

[1148] *Cf. supra* chapter I-2, section 2.2.2.

[1149] Where local criminal legislation is not sufficient to assure the protection of the population or the security of the Interning Power, an Occupying Power may adopt additional legislation on the basis of article 64§2 GC IV. It is also in this sense that article 68 GC IV must be understood: article 68 GC IV allows for internment as an *alternative punishment* for minor offences against the Interning Power that do not threaten the life or limb of its personnel (*cf. supra*, note 935).

[1150] Article 133§1 GC IV; *cf. supra* section 3.2.1.

[1151] See in this sense also the temporal limits placed on the use of article 78 GC IV, *cf. infra* section 3.2.4.4.

[1152] This is also how article 42§1 and 78 GC IV have been interpreted consistently in Israeli

3.2.2.2. Persons posing a security threat: what does it mean?

A protected person may be interned where his present or future acts or behaviour threaten the security of the Interning Power or its military operations. But when does a person pose such a security threat? In what follows we will look at different examples used or discussed in international practice and case law on articles 42§1 and 78 GC IV and examine whether they would fall within the scope of the lawful ground for internment contained therein.

(a.) Nationals of an enemy power or protected persons otherwise related to an adverse party to the conflict

While in a distant past it may have been deemed legitimate to regard the whole population of a nation with whom one was at war as enemies, the modern law of armed conflict is based on a clear distinction between the parties to the conflict, on the one hand, and their general population on the other hand. The preamble of the 1868 St Petersburg Declaration recalled that "the only legitimate object which States should endeavour to accomplish during war is to weaken the military forces of the enemy" and the Institute of International Law, in its renowned Oxford Manual for the Law of War on Land elaborated on this rule by adding that it "implies a distinction between the individuals who compose the "armed force" of a State and its other 'ressortissants'." The Manual includes a specific provision stating that "[i]t is forbidden to maltreat inoffensive populations."[1153]

Pictet reminds us that the lack of a specific treaty protecting civilians against the effects of war before the adoption of GC IV in 1949 could be explained by the fact that it was "a cardinal principle of the law of war that military operations must be confined to the armed forces and that the civilian population must enjoy complete immunity."[1154] The principle was so well-established that he rightly found it interesting to note that:

> "the Hague Conference of 1907 decided not to include a provision to the effect that the nationals of a belligerent residing in the territory of the adverse Party should not be interned, considering that that principle went without saying."

In his Commentary to article 42§1 GC IV, after reminding the reader of the massive violations of this principle during the First and Second World Wars, Pictet found it therefore necessary to explicitly state that:

> "the mere fact that a person is a subject of an enemy Power *cannot be considered as threatening the security of the country where he is living*; it is *not therefore a*

legislation and jurisprudence. See article 2(a) *EPDL* (1979) ("Where the Minister of Defense has reasonable cause to believe that reasons of *state security or public security* require that a particular person be detained"); article 3(a) *IUCL* (2002) ("Where the Chief of General Staff has reasonable cause to believe that a person being held by the State authorities is an unlawful combatant and that his release will harm *State security*")(emphasis added); and the overview of Israeli case law in Rudman & Qupty (*CHRLR* 1990), pp. 480-483, 492-497 and 504-508; and Israel, SC, *A and B v. Israel* (2008), §§30 and 49.

[1153] St-Petersburg Declaration (1868), preamble; Institute of International Law, *Oxford Manual* (1880), articles 1 and 7 respectively.

[1154] Pictet, *Commentary GC IV* (1958), p. 3.

valid reason for interning him or placing him in assigned residence. To justify recourse to such measures the State must have good reason to think that the person concerned, by his activities, knowledge or qualifications, represents a real threat to its present or future security."[1155]

Pictet's restatement of the rule has subsequently been confirmed in international practice. In 1980 the US Congress established the *Commission of Wartime Relocation and Internment of Civilians*. Congress mandated that Commission to review the facts and circumstances surrounding the mass internment in the US of Japanese Americans and Aleuts during World War II, and to assess the impact these measures had on the affected populations.[1156] The Commission's findings and recommendations resulted in the adoption of an Act of Congress, officially condemning internment that was based essentially on enemy nationality or origins:

> "The Congress recognizes that [...] a grave injustice was done by the evacuation, relocation, and internment of civilians during World War II [...] these actions were carried out without adequate security reasons and without any acts of espionage or sabotage documented by the Commission, and were *motivated largely by racial prejudice*, wartime hysteria, and a failure of political leadership. [...] For these fundamental violations of the basic civil liberties and constitutional rights of these individuals of Japanese ancestry, the Congress apologizes on behalf of the Nation."[1157]

Despite the fact that the rule was firmly established in international law, internment of so-called "enemy" civilians occurred again on a massive scale during the conflicts that led to the break-up of the Former Socialist Republic of Yugoslavia in the early 1990's.[1158] The ICTY, in dealing with cases regarding internee camps holding thousands of "enemy civilians", has been compelled to reiterate Pictet's words quoted above and to stress that internment of protected persons on the mere basis of their ethnic affiliation with the adverse party to the conflict is prohibited and amounts to the war crime of unlawful confinement. For example, in the *Delalić* case, dealing with internment of ethnic Serbs by Bosnian authorities:

> "The Trial Chamber does not deem it necessary to decide whether all of the persons detained in the Čelebići prison-camp were to be considered as "peaceful" civilians, not constituting any threat to the security of the detaining forces. [...] To the contrary, it appears that the confinement of civilians in the Čelebići prison-camp was *a collective measure aimed at a specific group of persons, based mainly on*

[1155] Pictet, *Commentary GC IV* (1958), p. 258 (emphasis added).

[1156] The Commission's documents are available at: http://www.lexisnexis.com/documents/academic/upa_cis/1729_USCommWarRelocInternPt1.pdf.

[1157] US, *Act on Restitution for World War II Internment of Japanese-Americans and Aleuts* (1988), section 1989a (emphasis added). Note that the Act does not refer to any rules of international humanitarian law. It could not have, since at the time the internment occurred the existing treaty law did not yet contain any rules on the internment of so-called enemy aliens.

[1158] Before that, about 30.000 ethnic Persians and Kurdish-Iranians, and about 25.000 other Iranian citizens of Arab origin, residing in Iraq, were interned there – clearly on the basis of their nationality or ethnic affiliation with the adverse party – during the 1980-1988 Iran-Iraq war. See Vance (2006), p. 208.

their ethnic background, and not a legitimate security measure. As stated above, *the mere fact that a person is a national of, or aligned with, an enemy party cannot be considered as threatening the security of the opposing party where he is living*, and is not, therefore, a valid reason for interning him."[1159]

"In the Appeals Chamber's view, there is no necessary inconsistency between the Trial Chamber's finding that the Bosnian Serbs were regarded by the Bosnian authorities as belonging to the opposing party in an armed conflict and the finding that some of them could not reasonably be regarded as presenting a threat to the detaining power's security. To hold the contrary would suggest that, whenever the armed forces of a State are engaged in armed conflict, the entire civilian population of that State is necessarily a threat to security and therefore may be detained. *It is perfectly clear from the provisions of Geneva Convention IV referred to above that there is no such blanket power to detain the entire civilian population of a party to the conflict in such circumstances*, but that there must be an assessment that each civilian taken into detention poses a particular risk to the security of the State. This is reflected in the ICRC Commentary to Article 42 of Geneva Convention IV [...] Thus the Appeals Chamber agrees with the conclusion reached by the Trial Chamber that *"the mere fact that a person is a national of, or aligned with, an enemy party cannot be considered as threatening the security of the opposing party where he is living, and is not, therefore, a valid reason for interning him."*[1160]

The Permanent Court of Arbitration's Eritrea-Ethiopia Claims Commission (EECC), in a Partial Award regarding the mass internment of Ethiopian nationals residing in Eritrea at the outbreak of the conflict (and in many cases for the duration thereof), found that Eritrea violated article 42 GC IV:

"While the evidence is limited, it suggests that Ethiopians were hurriedly rounded up in some areas but not in others; the risk of detention seems to have been heavily influenced by geography. [...] The evidence does not disclose any process, formal or informal, by which detainees could secure review of their status. [...] Taking into account the high standard for forcible internment indicated by Article 42 of Geneva Convention IV, the Commission believes that it was incumbent upon Eritrea to show some substantial basis for abruptly seizing and holding several thousand Ethiopians in detention, particularly as they were detained under harsh conditions. Eritrea failed to show that its mass detentions of Ethiopians during and after May 2000 satisfied the requirements of Article 42 of Geneva Convention IV as being "absolutely necessary" for its security."[1161]

[1159] ICTY, *Delalić* (1998), §1134 (footnotes referring to witness statements and other case documents omitted, emphasis added).

[1160] ICTY, *Delalić* (2001), §327 (footnotes omitted, emphasis added). For other examples, see the judgments of the ICTY's Trial Chambers in *Kordić & Čerkez* (2001), §§285, 773 and 802 and *Blaškić* (2000), §§ 130-131 with regard to the internment of Bosnian Muslims by Bosnian Croat authorities; and the judgment of the Trial Chamber in *Tadić* (1997), §§151-154 with regard to the internment of ethnic Croatians and Bosnian Muslims by the authorities of the *Republica Srpska* (to be noted that Tadić was not charged with unlawful confinement, the focus of the Prosecution's case regarding the internment camps was rather on the murder, sexual assault and various forms of ill-treatment inflicted upon the internees).

[1161] PCA (EECC), *Civilians Claims, Ethiopia's Claim No. 5* (2004), §§102-104.

It is in order to avoid such abuses that article 42§1 GC IV requires that a decision to intern be taken on an individual case-by-case basis and only where the individual him- or herself poses a real security threat that makes internment absolutely necessary.[1162]

(b.) Eligibility for mobilisation or possible enrolment in the enemy's armed forces

In 1934, the 15th International Conference of the Red Cross in Tokyo adopted a Draft International Convention on the Condition and Protection of Civilians of Enemy Nationality Who are on Territory Belonging to or Occupied by a Belligerent, which it submitted for adoption to a Diplomatic Conference that never took place because of the outbreak of World War II.[1163] Article 4 of that Draft Convention listed the following two lawful grounds for preventing enemy civilians in the territory of a party to the conflict to leave that territory at the outbreak of hostilities:

> "a) Those who are eligible for immediate mobilisation or mobilisation within a year, under the laws of their country of origin or of the country of residence;
>
> b) those whose departure may reasonably be opposed on grounds involving the security of the Detaining Power."[1164]

For those civilians who remained in the territory, article 15 of the Draft Convention prescribed the following grounds to intern them:

> "a) where civilians eligible for mobilisation under the conditions set forth in Article 4 (a) of the present Convention are concerned;
>
> b) where the security of the Detaining Power is involved;
>
> c) where the situation of the enemy civilians renders it necessary."[1165]

[1162] At the outbreak of the First Gulf War (1991), the UK government ordered the internment of about 75 Iraqi civilians on the suspicion that they might pose a security risk. Some were released upon consideration of their case, but the majority was held until the end of the conflict. It is unclear what motivated their continued internment and their cases have not been the object of any (publicly available) review. See Vance (2006), p. 169, see also Risius in Rowe (1993), pp. 289-303; and Walsh in Rowe (1993), pp. 304-332.

[1163] *Cf. supra* note 1050.

[1164] Article 4 of the Draft International Convention on the Condition and Protection of Civilians of Enemy Nationality Who are on Territory Belonging to or Occupied by a Belligerent (1934) (Draft Tokyo Convention). Article 2 of the Tokyo draft established the principle that all civilians who are nationals of an adverse party could leave the territory of the party to the conflict in which they were residing at the outbreak of hostilities: "Subject to the provisions of Article 4, enemy civilians who may desire to leave the territory at the outset of military operations shall be granted, as rapidly as possible, the necessary authorizations, as well as all facilities compatible with such operations." A similar system is provided for in article 35 GC IV, which prescribes that enemy aliens in the territory of the parties to the conflict must be given permission to leave, unless their departure is "contrary to the national interests of the State". Contrary to article 15 of the 1934 draft, article 35 GC IV does not provide a legal basis to intern persons who are eligible for mobilisation, it only allows the parties to the conflict to oppose the departure of such persons from the territory in which they find themselves. Nevertheless, like any other protected person under GC IV, those who are prevented to leave may be interned on the basis of article 42 if the threshold for internment laid down by that provision is met.

[1165] Article 15 Draft Tokyo Convention. Note also the draft's article 14: "As a general rule, the compulsory residence of enemy civilians in a specified district shall be preferred to their internment. In particular, those who are established in the territory of the belligerent shall, subject to the security of

Litera (c) refers to voluntary internment and has been included, in an amended form, in article 42§2 GC IV (*cf. infra*). *Literae* (a) and (b) reflect the International Conference's conception of security internment at the time.

Taking into account the experience of the Second World War, at its 1948 session in Stockholm the International Conference adopted a new draft Convention for the Protection of Civilian Persons in Time of War, which served as the basis for negotiations at the 1949 Diplomatic Conference. Article 39 of the Stockholm draft, which was to become article 42 GC IV reads as follows:

> "The internment of protected persons in fenced camps may not be ordered unless the security of the Detaining Power imperatively demands. Should any person, acting through the representatives of the Protecting Power, voluntarily ask to be interned because his or her situation renders that course necessary, the said person shall be interned by the Power in whose hands he or she may be."

One cannot but notice that the mere eligibility for immediate or future mobilisation had been dropped from the new draft's provisions on internment, and that the requirement of imperative necessity was introduced. The massive internment of able-bodied enemy civilians during World War II must be the explanation for this. In the course of the Diplomatic Conference no proposals were submitted to reintroduce the ground prescribed for by article 15 (a) of the Tokyo Draft, and Pictet's commentary explicitly mentions that:

> "[t]he fact that a man is of military age should not necessarily be considered as justifying the application of these measures, unless there is a danger of him being able to join the enemy armed forces."[1166]

This rule has also been reconfirmed by the ICTY. For example, in the *Kordić & Čerkez* case (concerning the internment of Bosnian Muslims by Bosnian Croat authorities), the Trial Chamber found the accused guilty of the war crime of unlawful confinement of civilians, for having interned individuals, amongst other reasons, merely because they were men of military age and thus able to fight.[1167]

The EECC held that the internment of about 85 Eritrean exchange students in Ethiopia, who were rounded up and interned at the outbreak of the conflict (and some almost until the end of hostilities), was lawful on the basis of article 35 GC IV:

> "The record indicates that *the students were of military age and that some had received military training in Eritrea.* Ethiopia contended that their internment was justified under Article 35, paragraph 1, of Geneva Convention IV. Under that provision, nationals of an enemy state have the right to leave a belligerent's

---

the State, be thus restricted."

[1166] Pictet, *Commentary GC IV* (1958), p. 258.

[1167] The evidence on which that conviction was based included the following: "Čerkez told Colonel Morsink of ECMM, that he had people in his prison (males since *he considered every male as somebody able to fight*): the women and children he had released." (ICTY, *Kordić & Čerkez* (2001), §788, emphasis added). In its survey of the applicable law, the Trial Chamber in *Kordić & Čerkez* agreed with the judgment of the Trial Chamber in *Delalić* (1998), §577, that the fact that a man is "of military age should not necessarily be considered as justifying the application of these measures [internment and assigned residence on the basis of article 42 GC IV]" (ICTY, *Kordić & Čerkez* (2001), §284).

territory 'unless their departure is contrary to the national interests of the state.' The Handbook of Humanitarian Law explains that '[t]his reference to the national interest of the state of residence is intended above all to enable the state to prohibit residents suitable for military service from leaving.' Leslie Green similarly describes Article 35 as allowing a belligerent to prevent 'the departure of those likely to be of assistance to the adverse party in its war efforts.' The evidence in this and other claims before the Commission indicates that some movement of civilians between the two countries continued during the war. Ethiopia could reasonably have feared that the students – and other *Eritreans of military age, particularly those with military training* – might have returned to Eritrea and joined the Eritrean forces if left at large. Their internment was consistent with Article 35, paragraph 1, of Geneva Convention IV."[1168]

While the Commission rightly inferred from the sources it consulted that article 35 GC IV would allow States to prevent protected persons who are nationals of an enemy State from leaving their territory where there is a serious risk that they would – willingly or forcibly – join the enemy's armed forces, it wrongly concluded that this article automatically allowed for their internment. So-called enemy aliens who are obliged to remain in the territory of the Party to the conflict in which they were present at the outbreak of the conflict, may only be interned on the basis of article 42§1 GC IV. That article requires the interning authority to establish that there is a real risk in each case that the individual concerned would join the enemy's armed forces if left in liberty.[1169] Moreover, internment may only be ordered if other, alternative measures of control or security would be inadequate, *in casu*, to counter the risk of them joining the enemy's forces.

It may be useful to recall that article 42 GC IV applies to persons who are present in the territory of the State who wishes to intern them. While the latter may theoretically be eligible for mobilisation by their national (enemy) State, in practice they are most likely to find themselves in the practical impossibility of actually joining that enemy's armed forces. Take for example a young Iraqi man studying in the US at the outbreak of the First Gulf War (1990). He would most likely be eligible for mobilisation by Iraq in the armed conflict that opposes his country of origin to the US-led coalition that intervened to liberate Iraqi-occupied Kuwait.[1170] However, in practice it would be impossible for that man to join the Iraqi armed forces without leaving US territory. In this case, it is very likely that a less restrictive measure of control than internment could counter the potential security threat the Iraqi student potentially poses. First, it is possible and even likely that the student would have no wish to leave the US and join the Iraqi armed forces. If this were the case, there would be no need to adopt any

[1168] PCA (EECC), *Civilians Claims, Eritrea's Claims 15, 16, 23 & 27–32* (2004), §§115-118 (footnotes omitted).

[1169] They could also be interned on the basis of article 42§2 GC IV where their voluntarily requested internment renders that step necessary (*cf. infra*).

[1170] Note that persons who are already active members of the enemy's armed forces at the outbreak of the conflict (e.g. members of a visiting military delegation) would be prisoners of war and could be interned on the basis of GC III.

control measures. If however such a risk existed, the authorities would be allowed, under article 35 GC IV to deny the Iraqi student's right to leave US territory since such a departure would obviously be "contrary to the national interests of the State."[1171] Whether the US could also intern such an individual would depend on whether his joining the Iraqi armed forces is a real and serious possibility in the prevailing circumstances at the time, and whether other, less severe restrictions such as registration, travel restrictions and regular presentation at a local police station, would be inadequate to curtail that possibility.

Article 42§1 GC IV prescribes that the internment of a person who may and is likely to effectively join an enemy's armed forces can only be ordered if it is absolutely necessary to counter that threat. An individual's eligibility for mobilisation in the armed forces of an adverse party to the conflict, or the mere theoretical possibility of his or her enrolment in the enemy's armed forces, is not sufficient to qualify as a real security threat. It is only when there is an actual risk that the individual concerned is able and willing to join the enemy's armed forces or is at real risk of being forcibly recruited into such forces, and in the absence of less restrictive measures of control that could adequately prevent this risk from materializing, that he or she may be deemed to pose a security threat justifying internment.

(c.) Members of the armed forces of a party to the conflict who are not prisoners of war

We have seen above that some members of the armed forces of a party to the conflict are not entitled to prisoner of war status. It may be useful to recall here that the armed forces of a party to the conflict include all organized armed forces, groups and units engaging in hostilities on behalf of a party to the conflict.[1172] For their members to be prisoners of war these groups and units must be commanded by a person responsible for the conduct of his or her subordinates, conduct their operations in conformity with international humanitarian law, and enforce respect of that body of law by their members.[1173] Members of groups or units that belong to the armed forces of a party to the

---

[1171] Article 35 GC IV: "All protected persons who may desire to leave the territory at the outset of, or during a conflict, shall be entitled to do so, unless their departure is contrary to the national interests of the State. The applications of such persons to leave shall be decided in accordance with regularly established procedures and the decision shall be taken as rapidly as possible. Those persons permitted to leave may provide themselves with the necessary funds for their journey and take with them a reasonable amount of their effects and articles of personal use. If any such person is refused permission to leave the territory, he shall be entitled to have such refusal reconsidered as soon as possible by an appropriate court or administrative board designated by the Detaining Power for that purpose. Upon request, representatives of the Protecting Power shall, unless reasons of security prevent it, or the persons concerned object, be furnished with the reasons for refusal of any request for permission to leave the territory and be given, as expeditiously as possible, the names of all persons who have been denied permission to leave."

[1172] *Cf. supra* chapter II-1, section 1.1.2.1. As to other organized armed groups that may be active in a zone of conflict but are not part of the armed forces of a party to the conflict, *cf. infra* (d).

[1173] *Cf. supra* chapter II-1, section 1.1.2.3.

conflict but do not, as a group, meet those conditions are not prisoners of war. Moreover, individual members of the armed forces of a party to the conflict may forfeit their entitlement to prisoner of war status; they include: mercenaries, spies, deserters and defectors and individual combatants who failed to distinguish themselves in attack. When they fall into the hands of an adverse party to the conflict they are not automatically entitled to prisoner of war status, and whether or not they be granted such status is left to the discretion of the Interning Power.[1174]

Since these members of the armed forces of the parties to the conflict are not prisoners of war, they do not fall within the scope of application of the Third Geneva Convention and may not be interned on the basis of article 21 GC III. They are however protected persons under the Fourth Geneva Convention,[1175] which means they may be interned in the territory of a party to the conflict on the basis of article 42, or in occupied territory on the basis of article 78 GC IV, as long as the threshold of those provisions is met.

As *members of the armed forces* of a party to the conflict – regardless of the fact they are not *prisoners of war* – these individuals owe allegiance to the Power they depend on, and under the domestic law of that Power they are usually obliged upon capture to try to escape and rejoin their ranks as soon as possible. If they fail to do so, they will usually be guilty of desertion, defection, treason or other criminal offences that are punishable with long-term imprisonment if not the death penalty. Personal allegiance to the Power they depend on and the prospect of harsh punishment if they fail to escape and rejoin their ranks, means they will almost certainly engage in activities that would pose a serious threat to the security of the Interning Power if they would be released or subjected to control measures that fall short of confinement. While the Interning Power cannot rely on the legal presumption of threat that applies to members of the armed forces who qualify as prisoners of war, there is little doubt that in most cases the first threshold for internment in articles 42§1 and 78 GC IV (security threat) will be met.[1176] A few examples may illustrate this.

[1174] *Cf. supra* chapter II-1, section 1.1.3.1.

[1175] *Cf. supra* section 3.1.1.

[1176] The ICRC's *Interpretative Guidance on the Notion of Direct Participation under International Humanitarian Law* (*IGDPH*) (2009) finds that membership in the armed forces of a party to the conflict other than its formal, regular armed forces (for whom it can be defined on the basis of formal incorporation regulated by the party's domestic law, *cf. supra* chapter II-1, section 1.1.2.2) is defined on a functional basis. The *Interpretative Guidance* defines the concept of "continuous combat function" – for the purposes of the rules on targeting – as follows: "the decisive criterion for individual membership [in "irregular" armed forces of a party to the conflict] is whether a person assumes a continuous function for the group involving his or her direct participation in hostilities (hereafter 'continuous combat function'). Continuous combat function does not imply *de jure* entitlement to combatant privilege [i.e. POW status and immunity from prosecution for mere participation in hostilities]. Rather, it distinguishes members of the [irregular armed forces of a party to an armed conflict] from civilians who directly participate in hostilities on a merely spontaneous, sporadic, or unorganized basis, or who assume exclusively political, administrative or other non-combat functions" (ICRC, *IGDPH* (2009), pp. 25, 31 and 33-34). The *Interpretative Guidance* explicitly states that its interpretation of IHL therein is only for the purposes of the rules on targeting

• *US-Grenada 1983* – The Inter-American Commission on Human Rights in *Coard v. USA* was called to assess the lawfulness of the US internment of a number of individuals captured in the international armed conflict that followed the US intervention in Grenada, an intervention aimed to restore the legitimate government that had been violently overthrown by dissident members of Grenada's armed forces. Neither the petitioners nor the Commission pronounced on whether the captured individuals, some of whom clearly belonged to the enemy armed forces, qualified as prisoners of war:

> "As a factual matter [...] certain petitioners were then members of an entity known as the Revolutionary Military Council (hereinafter "RMC"), and had previously been officers in the People's Revolutionary Army. [...] Notwithstanding the membership of those petitioners in the RMC, the *State considers that they did not meet the terms of Article 4 of the Third Geneva Convention* which define POW status, and maintains that the petitioners were civilians briefly detained for reasons of military necessity. The petitioners themselves took no position on the question. [Some of the petitioners] *were involved in the command and control structure of an armed force*. However, neither party briefed whether that armed force met the requisites to fall within the coverage of the Third Geneva Convention or not."[1177]

The Commission – in the absence of protest by the petitioners concerned and sufficient evidence to pronounce itself on POW status – accepted the US' position that all individuals were held as "civilian detainees" and proceeded its analysis of the lawfulness of their internment on the basis of GC IV. In its conclusion on the grounds for internment, the Commission "found nothing in the record to refute the security justification presented by the United States."[1178] The case not only illustrates that members of enemy armed forces who do *not* qualify as prisoners of war are protected persons under GC IV, but also that they clearly present the kind of threat to the "security of the Detaining Power" that

and not for the purposes of either status determination or deprivation of liberty (pp. 7, 11 and 13). Nevertheless, since it may be expected that States will rely on this concept for internment purposes also, it is useful to recall here that functional membership in the armed forces of a party to the conflict, may be a useful indication of a person's threat level but is not by itself sufficient to justify internment on the basis of GC IV.

[1177] IAC°HR, *Coard v. USA* (1999), §§ 49-50. Earlier on in the proceedings, the US had advanced a different position regarding the status of petitioners and the legal basis for interning them. At some point (before claiming all internees were civilians and that in any case their status was of little relevance to the case since they had all been given *treatment* as prisoners of war), the US stated that "[g]iven petitioners' Central Committee party and other prominent political position in Grenada, and *their status in the command and control structure of the armed opposition to U.S. and Caribbean forces*, the petitioners' detention and treatment were justified under the 1949 Geneva Convention III, Relative to Treatment of Prisoners of War ('Geneva Convention III'), as in furtherance of lawful military objectives." (*Response of the United States Government to Report 13/95 on Case 10.951 (Grenada)*, p. 4, quoted in IAC°HR, *Coard v. USA* (1999), Concurring Vote and Opinion of Commissioner Bicudo, §40 (emphasis added)). A thorough analysis of the question would most likely have resulted in the conclusion that at least those petitioners who held positions in the command and control structure of the RMC qualified as prisoners of war and could thus indeed have been interned on the basis of article 21 GC III.

[1178] IAC°HR, *Coard v. USA* (1999), §60. The Commission held the internment to be unlawful for non-compliance with the procedures prescribed by article 43/78 GC IV.

article 42§1 GC IV is meant to address.[1179] It also demonstrates that judges are likely to take into account membership in enemy armed forces for determining a person's individual threat-potential to an extent passing very close to that of a collective threat assessment.[1180]

• *Former Yugoslavia 1990's* – The ICTY has hinted in a similar way to the acceptance of membership in enemy armed forces as a strong factual indicator that an individual poses a security threat justifying internment on the basis of article 42§1 GCIV. For example, the Tribunal discarded the following reasons for internment from its findings on unlawful confinement of protected persons under GC IV:

> "[Article 42§1 GC IV] may permit a Party to intern people or place them in assigned residence – but only if it has a serious and legitimate reason to think that they are *members of a subversive organization...*"[1181] "The [...] Defence case is that Kaonik was a military prison throughout the war. In January several hundred Muslim men were detained, those over 50 being released the next day and most after 10 days. *Sometimes detainees were members of MOS [Muslim Armed Forces, part of the Bosnian armed forces]*: some were civilians and some were armed *members of the TO [Territorial Defence Units, replaced by or resisting Croatian take-over and under the control of the Bosnian army] who posed a security threat* and were arrested pre-emptively."[1182]

1179 One can wonder at what point dissident armed forces that prevail in a *coup d'état* become – for the purposes of IHL – the armed forces of the State. By the time of the US invasion, the RMC was firmly in power and in control of the armed forces. Therefore, members of these armed forces, upon capture by the adverse party to the conflict, would most likely have qualified as prisoners of war. This seems to have been the initial position of the US in the case, but when pressed to take an official stance the US declared the individuals concerned did not qualify as POW under article 4 GC III. It is possible that initially – as was the case with regard to the Taliban in Afghanistan – the US sought to argue that the RCM not being the legitimate or recognized government of Grenada, the RMC members could not qualify as POW. Such argument is however legally erroneous (article 4§A(3) GC III, *cf. supra* chapter II-1, section 1.1) and has not been pursued any further by the US authorities in either the Grenada or Afghan context.

1180 While the Commission did not go into this discussion (it found the internment to be unlawful for lack of compliance with the review procedures prescribed by GC IV and paid only scant attention to the lawful grounds for internment under the Convention), it is useful to recall here that *mere* membership of enemy armed forces – while strong evidence of a potential threat – would however not suffice to meet the threshold required by articles 42§1 and 78 GC IV. In order to meet that threshold, it must be shown that the individual member him-or herself poses a threat to the Interning Power, *cf. infra*.

1181 ICTY, *Kordić & Čerkez* (2001), §284 (original emphasis deleted, our emphasis added). The case concerned the internment of Bosnian Muslims by Bosnian Croatian (but Croatia-controlled) authorities and armed forces.

1182 ICTY, *Kordić & Čerkez* (2001), §776 (emphasis added). The MOS and the TO were organized armed groups (controlled by the Bosnian army) fighting the (Croatia-controlled) Bosnian Croatian armed forces (e.g. §§ 466, 499-500, 636 and 719 and Annex 3B (Glossary) of the Judgment). Most likely, members of the MOS and TO would have qualified as prisoners of war (article 4§A(2) GC III *juncto* article 43§1 AP I), but the Defence did not make that argument and the Tribunal did not need to rule on this. Nevertheless, the Tribunal did hint at the fact that internment of members of the armed forces of a party to the conflict who are protected persons under GC IV and pose a security threat would potentially have been lawful. Nevertheless, since the majority of internees clearly were not members of the armed forces and did not pose any threat, the tribunal found the war crime of unlawful confinement was sufficiently established.

"In light of [the] evidence, the Trial Chamber cannot accept the Defence's contention that all persons detained in the [Bosnian] Celebici prison-camp were *members of an armed rebellion against* the Bosnian authorities."[1183]

• *US-Afghanistan 2001-2002* – In the international armed conflict opposing the US and its allies to Afghanistan, captured members of Afghanistan's armed forces were entitled to prisoner of war status under article 4§A(1) GC III and could therefore have been interned on the basis of article 21 GC III. That is true both for the Taliban and for any foreign fighter who was incorporated into Afghanistan's armed forces.[1184] So-called al-Qaeda and other non-Afghan fighters that fought alongside and on behalf of Afghanistan's armed forces, without being incorporated therein, would also have qualified for POW status if they were organized in military units fulfilling the requirements of article 4§A(2) GC III.[1185] They too could have been interned on the basis of article 21 GC III. For those individual members of the Afghan armed forces who did not qualify for prisoner or war status, the only available legal basis to intern them would have been article 42§1 GC IV.[1186] The mere fact of their *de facto* membership of the enemy's armed forces would surely have indicated that these persons posed a potential security threat to the US and coalition forces in Afghanistan at the time. It is also highly likely that this potential threat – their almost certain return to the battlefield to engage in hostile acts against the US and its allies in order to defend Taliban-governed Afghanistan – could have been established in each individual case and would therefore have rendered their internment "absolutely necessary for the security of the Detaining Power" as long as the active hostilities continued.[1187]

Nevertheless, in order to intern members of the armed forces of a party to the conflict who are not prisoners of war, the interning authority must also establish that the second threshold for internment on the basis of these provisions is met (lack of alternative measures that can adequately counter the threat). Mercenaries, spies and combatants who failed to distinguish themselves in attack are, under the domestic law of most States, punishable with long-term

[1183] ICTY, *Delalić* (1998), § 1134. The case concerned the internment of ethnic Serbs by Bosnian authorities.

[1184] *Cf. supra* II-1, section 1.1.2. In the same sense: Sassòli (*ACDI* 2001), pp. 231-233.

[1185] As modified by article 43§1 AP I, *cf. supra* II-1, section 1.1.2. In the same sense: Sassòli (*ACDI* 2001), pp. 233-234. The US authorities – without recognizing that members of the Taliban or al-Qaeda were entitled to POW status – seem to have relied on this general principle that members of enemy armed forces may be interned as prisoners of war in establishing the standard for internment of what is calls "unlawful enemy combatants"; see for example: US, *JDP 3-63* (2006), pp. I-3 or I-4: "For purposes of the war on terrorism, the term unlawful enemy combatant is defined to include, but is not limited to, an individual who is *part of* or supporting Taliban or al Qaeda *forces* or affiliated *forces that are engaged in hostilities against* the United States or its coalition partners" (emphasis added).

[1186] *Cf. supra* section 3.1.1.

[1187] At the time the international armed conflict came to an end, by the reversal of the Taliban government and the instalment of an interim Afghan government by the Lloya Jirga on 19 June 2002, the legal basis in article 42§1 GC IV would nevertheless have become extinct. Any continued internment of members of enemy armed forces (be they interned on the basis of GC III or GC IV) beyond that date would have had to rely on a different legal basis (*cf. infra* Part III).

imprisonment if not death. Their protected status under GC IV does not give them any immunity from such prosecution. Parties to the conflict who capture such persons may therefore subject them to criminal prosecution and keep them in preventive pre-trial detention for the duration of these proceedings on the basis of domestic criminal law. Where such proceedings are possible, these individuals may not be interned, since their pre-trial detention and imprisonment of conviction would *de facto* already deprive them of their liberty and make internment unnecessary. Only where such proceedings cannot be brought or they cannot be preventively detained on the basis of the applicable criminal legislation, may they be interned on the basis of articles 42§1 or 78 GC IV. It is difficult however to imagine any cases where the evidence available to the Interning Power that justifies denial of prisoner of war status would not be sufficient to try and punish a person for his or her crimes.

(d.) Membership of organizations whose object is to cause disturbances

Members of organized armed groups engaging in hostile acts against the Interning Power but not belonging to a party to the conflict or not qualifying as armed forces as defined above[1188] will, by definition, not be prisoners of war. Their members may however be expected to pose the type of security threat that could justify internment on the basis of articles 42§1 and 78 GC IV. Such groups would surely fit the description of "organizations whose object is to cause disturbances" mentioned by Pictet in his commentary on article 42§1 GC IV:

> "a belligerent may intern people or place them in assigned residence if it has serious and legitimate reason to think that they are members of organizations whose object is to cause disturbances."[1189]

Pictet is however careful to add that mere membership in such an organization is not sufficient to order internment:

> "To justify recourse to such measures the State must have good reason to think that the person concerned, by his activities, knowledge or qualifications, represents a real threat to its present or future security."[1190]

If the interning authority can establish the fact that an individual member of such a group represents such a threat and that alternative measures of control could not counter it, they may then lawfully intern that person on the basis of articles 42§1 and 78 GC IV.

In this context, it is useful to briefly discuss the *Israeli Incarceration of Unlawful Combatants Law* (hereinafter *"Unlawful Combatants Law" or "IUCL")* and the Israeli Supreme Court's case law evaluating its conformity

[1188] The fact that they either do not belong to a party to the armed conflict or do not meet the criteria of article 43§1 AP I to qualify as armed forces, is what distinguishes these groups from the armed forces of a party to the conflict. See also ICRC, *IGDPH* (2009), pp. 23-24 with notes 24 to 28.

[1189] Pictet, *Commentary GC IV* (1958), p. 258. Pictet does not further define the concept of "organizations whose object is to cause disturbances" and it does not feature in any provision of international humanitarian law or in any military or IHL dictionaries. So far, it has not been relied upon by courts dealing with cases of alleged unlawful internment in armed conflict.

[1190] Pictet, *Commentary GC IV* (1958), p. 258.

with Israeli domestic and international humanitarian law.[1191] The *IUCL* is "intended to regulate the incarceration of unlawful combatants not entitled to prisoner-of-war status, in a manner conforming with the obligations of the State of Israel under the provisions of international humanitarian law."[1192] The relevant provisions of international humanitarian law in the case of the *IUCL* are articles 27§4 and 41 to 43 GC IV.[1193]

[1191] The full text of the law is included in Annex B. The Israeli parliament adopted the *IUCL* against the backdrop of the Supreme Court's judgment in the *Bargaining Chips Case* (2000), which we will discuss in more detail below. In a nutshell: the *IUCL* was adopted to complement the *Emergency Powers (Detention) Law* of 1979 (*EPDL*), the domestic legal basis for interning enemy aliens in Israel proper. The Supreme Court had held that on the basis of that law, Lebanese nationals could not be interned for the sole purpose of using them as bargaining chips in negotiations for the release of captured IDF soldiers held by Hezbollah (*cf. infra*). For a detailed description and analysis of the background and legislative history of the *IUCL*, see SC, *A and B v. Israel* (2008); Moodrick-Even Khen (*Hebrew University of Jerusalem Research Papers* 2006); and B'Tselem (2009). In the present chapter we will only examine the *IUCL* and its interpretation by the Supreme Court in as far as it reflects Israeli State practice on the lawful grounds for interning so-called unlawful combatants who do not qualify for prisoner of war status.

[1192] Article 1 *IUCL* (2002). The law does not specify whether it applies both in international and non-international armed conflict. Note however that the Israeli government has suggested that IHL norms regulating internment of unlawful combatants are identical in international and non-international armed conflict. See for example Israel, Ministry of Foreign Affairs (MFA), *The Operation in Gaza* (2009), §§29-30: "It is not yet settled which regime applies to cross-border military confrontations between a sovereign State and a non-State terrorist armed group operating from a separate territory. In this case, the Gaza Strip is neither a State nor a territory occupied or controlled by Israel. In these *sui generis* circumstances, Israel as a matter of policy applies to its military operations in Gaza the rules of armed conflict governing both international and non-international armed conflicts. At the end of the day, classification of the armed conflict between Hamas and Israel as international or non-international in the current context is largely of theoretical concern, as many similar norms and principles govern both types of conflicts" (Israel, MFA, *The Operation in Gaza* (2009), §§29-30). In fact, the report only concerns the use of force employed by the Israeli Defence Forces (IDF) in its 2008-2009 operation. Whereas its statement about the uniformity of rules on the conduct of hostilities under the law of international and non-international armed conflict is to a large extent correct, it fails to recognize the difference between the two bodies of law regarding deprivation of liberty. The Israeli Supreme Court has found the conflict between Israel and Hezbollah to be international in nature (Israel, HCJ, *Targeted killings Case* (2006), §§12 and 21). It has not pronounced itself on whether it considers the armed conflict with Hamas and affiliated armed groups in the Gaza strip to be international or non-international in nature. Nevertheless, it seems to suggest implicitly that any cross-border conflict is international in nature: "with regard to the presumption of conformity to international humanitarian law [... and the declared purpose of the IUCL to conform to that law...] [t]he premise in this context is that an international armed conflicts prevails between the State of Israel and the terrorist organizations that operate outside Israel" (Israel, SC, *A and B v. Israel* (2008), §6).

[1193] Israel does not consider the GC to be *de jure* applicable to the conflict but accepts most of its provisions to apply as a matter of customary international humanitarian law (*cf. supra* note 477). Note also that the Israeli Supreme Court interpreted the *IUCL* to be applicable to "terrorist organizations that operate outside Israel" (and not to organizations operating in Israel proper or in the occupied Palestinian territories). Such organizations would include at least the Lebanon-based Hezbollah (Israel, SC, *A and B v. Israel* (2008), §§ 3, 6, 9 and 11). They would also include Hamas and the Popular Resistance Committees, based in the Gaza strip (which Israel, since its unilateral withdrawal from the territory in September 2005, no longer considers as occupied territory) (Israel, SC, *Salem Said v. State of Israel* (2008), §§6 and 18, and Israel, MFA, *The Operation in Gaza* (2009), §§29-30). They would possibly include other organized armed groups engaged in hostilities against Israel and based outside the borders of Israel proper (no case law so far has been found regarding groups other than those mentioned above). Earlier versions of the law excluded citizens and residents of Israel and the Palestinian occupied

Article 2 of the law defines "unlawful combatants" as follows:

"[i]n this Law [...] 'unlawful combatant' means a person who has participated either directly or indirectly in hostile acts against the State of Israel or is a member of a force perpetrating hostile acts against the State of Israel, where the conditions prescribed in Article 4 of the Third Geneva Convention of 12th August 1949 with respect to prisoners-of-war and granting prisoner-of-war status in international humanitarian law, do not apply to him."

Article 3 of the *IUCL* prescribes that:

"[w]here the Chief of General Staff has reasonable cause to believe that a person being held by the State authorities is an unlawful combatant *and* that *his* release will harm State security, he may issue an order under his hand, directing that such person be incarcerated at a place to be determined (hereinafter referred to as "an incarceration order"); an incarceration order shall include the grounds for incarceration, without prejudicing State security requirements." (emphasis added)

Read alone, articles 2 and 3 do not necessarily go beyond what is authorized under article 42§1 GC IV: while they define who is an unlawful combatant based on an individual's past participation in hostilities or on membership in an armed group engaged in hostilities against Israel, the interning authority (the Chief of General Staff) must still ascertain that the release of the individual concerned "will harm State security."[1194] This means that internment may only be ordered where a person, on the basis of his activities or his membership in a particular organization, can be expected to engage in hostile acts against the State of Israel in the future. This is also how the Supreme Court has interpreted the *IUCL*:

"the definition of 'unlawful combatant' in section 2 of the law [...] should be interpreted with reference to the security purpose of the law and in accordance with the constitutional principles and international humanitarian law that we discussed above, *which require the proof of an individual threat as a ground for administrative detention.* [...] With regard to the second limb that concerns a person who is 'a member of a force carrying out hostilities against the State of Israel,' here too we require an interpretation that is consistent with the purpose of the law and the constitutional principles and international humanitarian law that we discussed above: on the one hand it is *insufficient to show any tenuous connection with a terrorist organization* in order to be included within the cycle

territories from its scope of application, but this exclusion was ultimately not retained. While the Supreme Court in *A and B v. Israel* (2008), §11 seemed to suggest that the law could not apply to residents of the occupied Palestinian territories ("With regard to the inhabitants of the territory (Judaea and Samaria) that is under the effective control of the State of Israel [...] the administrative detention of these inhabitants should be carried out pursuant to the security legislation that applies in the territories and not by virtue of the Internment of Unlawful Combatants Law"); in *Salem Said* (2008), §18 the Court said the question "remains as requiring study." In any case, whether the law would cover internment authorized by article 42§1 or by article 78 GC IV, the substantive questions and their answers would not change.

1194 This is in any case how the text of the law must be interpreted for it to conform, as it purports, to international humanitarian law. Note that the definition of unlawful combatant as a person "who *has* participat*ed* either directly or indirectly in hostile acts against the State of Israel" may not be interpreted as allowing internment as punishment for past acts (*cf. supra*). A person who has committed such acts in the past may only be lawfully interned if he or she can be reasonably expected to continue to engage in such acts in the future.

of hostilities in the broad meaning of this concept. On the other hand, in order to establish a ground for detention with regard to someone who is a member of an active terrorist organization whose self-declared goal is to fight unceasingly against the State of Israel, it is not necessary for that person to take a direct or indirect part in the hostilities themselves, and it is possible that his connection and contribution to the organization will be expressed in other ways that are sufficient to include him in the cycle of hostilities in its broad sense, in such a way that his detention will be justified under the law. Thus we see that for the purpose of detention under the law at issue, the state is liable to prove with administrative proofs that the detainee is an 'unlawful combatant' with the meaning that we discussed, namely that the detainee took a direct or indirect part that involved a contribution to the fighting – a part that is not negligible or marginal – in the hostilities against the State of Israel, or that the detainee belongs to an organization that is carrying out hostilities, in which case we should consider the detainee's connection and the nature of his contribution to the cycle of hostilities of the organization in the broad sense of this concept."[1195]

One of the problems with the *IUCL,* however, is that the obligation to base a decision to intern on the individual threat posed by the person concerned, is effectively annulled by the legal presumption established by article 7 of the law:

"For the purposes of this Law, a person who is a member of a force perpetrating hostile acts against the State of Israel or who has participated in hostile acts of such a force, either directly or indirectly, shall be deemed to be a person whose release would harm State security as long as the hostile acts *of such force* against the State of Israel have not yet ceased, unless proved otherwise."

The appellants in *A and B v. Israel* – the first case of persons interned on the basis of the *IUCL* to reach the Supreme Court and the leading case on its interpretation – claimed that the presumption in article 7 "makes it unnecessary to prove an individual threat from the detainee and that this is inconsistent with constitutional principles and international humanitarian law." We agree with their argument, but the Israeli Supreme Court rejected their claim, stating that the law *did* require the interning authority to prove an individual security threat:

"It should be noted that providing the conditions of the definition of an 'unlawful combatant' in the aforesaid sense naturally includes *proof of an individual threat that derives from the type of involvement in the organization.* It should also be noted that only after the state has proved that the detainee satisfies the conditions of the statutory definition of 'unlawful combatant' can the state make use of the probative presumption set out in section 7 of the law, according to which the release of the detainee will harm state security as long as the contrary has not been proved. It is therefore clear that section 7 of the law does not negate the duty imposed on the state to prove the threat represented by the detainee, which derives from the type of involvement in the relevant organization that is required in order to prove him to be an 'unlawful combatant' under section 2 of the law. In view of this, we are drawn to the conclusion that the argument that the law includes no requirement of an individual threat goes too far and should be rejected."[1196]

[1195] Israel, SC, *A and B v. Israel* (2008), §21 (emphasis added).
[1196] Israel, SC, *A and B v. Israel* (2008), §21 (emphasis added).

We cannot agree with the Court's conclusion on article 7, especially since that article places the burden of proof on the internee rather than on the interning power, which is contrary to articles 27§4 and 42§1 GC IV.[1197] The Israeli government nevertheless declared before the Court that *de facto* it never relies upon the presumption in article 7 *IUCL*, that it had not relied upon that presumption in the appellants' case and that "as a rule, the state acts in order to present a broad and detailed basis in evidence with regard to the threat presented by the detainees."[1198] In light of these declarations, and in light of its interpretation of the provisions of the *IUCL* to include an individual threat assessment, the Court found that:

> "no question arises *in this case* as to whether the aforesaid presumption reduces the requirement of proving the individual threat needed for detention under the law, and whether this violates the constitutional right to liberty and the principles of international humanitarian law excessively. We can therefore leave these questions undecided".[1199]

Apart from the presumption in article 7, the *IUCL* contains another probative presumption in that:

> "[a] determination of the Minister of Defense, by a certificate under his hand, that a particular force is perpetrating hostile acts against the State of Israel or that hostile acts of such force against the State of Israel have ceased or have not yet ceased, shall serve as proof in any legal proceedings, unless proved otherwise." (article 8 *IUCL*)

The appellants in *A and B v. Israel* (2008) claimed that this presumption "places the burden of proof on the detainee in a matter which he will never be able to refute, since it is a matter that is subject to the discretion of the Minister of Defence." Indeed, such a probative presumption would therefore contravene articles 27§4 and 42§1 GC IV. Again, the Israeli government declared that in practice it has never relied solely upon such determinations and that it had not done so *in casu* either, and the Supreme Court found it therefore unnecessary to decide the issue raised by the appellants.[1200]

A later case shows however that the courts that review internment on the basis of the *IUCL* do rely on the probative presumptions in articles 7 and 8. The case of *A and B v. Israel* concerned alleged members of the Hezbollah, an organization for which there is no possible doubt that it is engaged in hostilities against the State of Israel. A later case, *Salem Said v. State of Israel*, concerned however the Popular Resistance Committees ("PRC"), a Palestinian

[1197] In the same sense: ICTY, *Krnojelac* (2002), §123: "A party seeking to rely upon Article 42 of the Geneva Convention IV must show with respect to each individual who has been deprived of his liberty reasonable grounds for concluding that that individual constituted a threat to the security of the depriving party. There was no consideration given to the individual circumstances of any of the non-Serb detainees by those carrying out the detentions." It is also contrary to international human rights law, see for example CoE, *HRH No. 5* (2002), pp. 8-10.
[1198] Israel, SC, *A and B v. Israel* (2008), §24.
[1199] Israel, SC, *A and B v. Israel* (2008), §24 (emphasis added).
[1200] Israel, SC, *A and B v. Israel* (2008), §25.

organization based in the Gaza strip. In that case, the authorities and the review court had relied upon a certificate of the Minister of Defence declaring the PRC to be an organization engaged in hostilities against the State of Israel (article 8 *IUCL*), on the presumption that as a member of that group the internee was presumed to be an unlawful combatant (article 7 *IUCL*), and on evidence that showed the person also posed a personal threat and that his release would harm the security of the State. On appeal before the Supreme Court, Said advanced the claim that the probative presumptions in articles 7 and 8 *IUCL* were unlawful because they effectively made it impossible for him to refute the presumption that the PRC was an organization engaged in hostilities against the State of Israel and that if released he personally would pose a security threat justifying internment.[1201]

The Israeli government objected to that claim by stating that the Supreme Court in *A and B v. Israel* had already found the presumptions to be lawful (which is not exactly correct, *cf. supra*: the Court decided that *in casu* they had not been relied upon and therefore it could leave the general issue undecided) and that "even without considering the presumption in section 7 in this case, the appellant poses an *individual* threat, and that this reason alone is sufficient to justify his continued internment."[1202] The Supreme Court in *Salem Said* recalled that it had left the question undecided in *A and B v. Israel*, but did not go on to pronounce itself on the matter either.[1203]

The question of the legality of the presumptions in articles 7 and 8 *IUCL* therefore remains unresolved under Israeli law. Under international humanitarian law it is important to note that the decision to intern on the basis of article 42§1 or 78 GC IV must be based on the fact that a specific individual – regardless of his past acts or his membership in an organized armed group engaged in hostilities against the Interning Power – poses a threat to the present or future security of the Interning Power. Such an individual threat assessment must be made by the interning authority, and may not be presumed, even if such

[1201] Israel, SC, *Salem Said* (2008), §§9-10. The appellant also claimed that while he may have engaged in a single hostile act against the State of Israel in the past, the duration of his internment had resulted in him no longer posing a danger to the security of the State upon release (*Ibidem*).

[1202] Israel, SC, *Salem Said* (2008), §11 (original emphasis).

[1203] Israel, SC, *Salem Said* (2008), §§25 and 34: since the review court had not relied on the presumptions in article 7 and 8 *IUCL* alone, but had found it established that the person posed an individual threat to State security, the Supreme Court found that the internment order had been lawfully issued. The appellant had not appealed that decision and therefore the Supreme Court found the legality of the internment "was established in a conclusive decision" and that there was no reason to reopen that decision in the case before it. The arguments were also made again on appeal before the Supreme Court by three other internees against a court confirmation of their internment order issued on the basis of the *IUCL*. While the proceedings were still pending, two of the appellants were released in an exchange deal with Hezbollah in 2004 and the third appellant was released and authorized to leave Israel. In spite of the fact that all three appellants had insisted the case be continued despite their release (because it raised important issues regarding the *IUCL* more generally and in order to substantiate a future claim for compensation for unlawful deprivation of liberty), the Supreme Court, after stating that at the time of judgment not a single person was held on the basis of the *IUCL*, dismissed their appeals as being moot (Israel, SC, *Obeid et al. v. State of Israel* (2005), §§5-6).

presumption would be rebuttable. A presumption of threat may be authorized for members of the armed forces of a party to a conflict who qualify as prisoners of war (*cf. supra*), it is not lawful under the provisions of the Fourth Geneva Convention, which apply to persons who do not qualify as prisoners of war, like the unlawful combatants covered by the *IUCL*. In order to meet its purpose of complying with international humanitarian law, the probative presumptions in articles 7 and 8 of the *IUCL* would therefore have to be annulled.

Finally, the *IUCL* itself provides that "[c]riminal proceedings may be initiated against an unlawful combatant under the provisions of any law." It adds however that an unlawful combatant may be interned even if such criminal proceedings have been initiated.[1204] It is submitted that internment in such cases may only be ordered if the institution of criminal proceedings would not allow for pre-trial detention of the person concerned, or if a conviction does not result in imprisonment. This conclusion is based on the general principle that internment may only be ordered where there are no alternative measures that can adequately counter a present or future security threat. Deprivation of liberty in the framework of criminal proceedings makes internment *per se* unnecessary, since the person is already deprived of liberty. If a person does not qualify for pre-trial detention, is convicted of a penalty that does not involve deprivation of liberty, or has already purged the prison sentence imposed, that person may be interned only if he or she continues to pose a threat to the present or future security of the Interning Power.

The US has adopted a similar approach to that of the Israeli *IUCL* to intern persons in its so-called war on terrorism, both in Guantánamo Bay and in Afghanistan. We will discuss their approach in more detail below.

To conclude on both membership in enemy armed forces (sub-section c) and membership in an organized armed group that engages in hostile acts against the Interning Power (sub-section d), we can summarize our reading of the international legal framework for the internment of so-called unprivileged and unlawful combatants[1205] as follows. We do not agree with those who argue that unprivileged and unlawful combatants are "subject to *automatic* detention"[1206] for the duration of hostilities. In the absence of the legal presumption inherent in GC III for prisoners of war, and on the basis of the general principles of internment on the basis of GC IV, such an automatic decision carries a risk of arbitrariness that renders it unlawful under international humanitarian law. Such individuals may be prosecuted, preventively detained and punished for their

[1204] Article 9 (a) and 9(b) respectively.

[1205] *Cf. supra* section 3.1.1.

[1206] Dinstein, (2010), p. 36 (emphasis added). In the same sense, see Waxman (*CLR* 2008) and Goodman (*AJIL* 2009). For a discussion of the status of so-called unlawful or unprivileged combatants (in a wider sense) under international humanitarian law, *cf. supra* section 3.1.1. Our position (like that of the Israeli Supreme Court and many of the experts who opined the law to be at variance with IHL) is that such persons, regardless of the label, are protected persons in the sense of GC IV ("a sub-category of civilians" in the words of the Israeli Supreme Court, *A and B. v. Israel* (2008), §14; see also Israel, HCJ, *Targeted Killings Case* (2006), §26). For a more detailed discussion, *cf. supra* section 3.1.1.

unlawful acts on the basis of the Interning Power's criminal legislation. Where criminal proceedings are impossible or would not result in deprivation of liberty, these individuals may almost always be interned on the basis of articles 42§1 or 78 GC IV since the conditions in those articles – the individual posing an *individual* security threat and their internment being *absolutely necessary* to counter that threat – are very likely to be fulfilled. While membership in these cases may constitute very strong evidence that an individual poses the kind of security threat of the kind envisaged in article 42§1 GC IV, it cannot, however, constitute by itself a *de jure* presumption that the threat will materialize if the person is not interned.

Apart from organized armed groups engaging in activities that seriously endanger the security of the Interning Power or the population the latter is obliged to protect, Pictet's notion of "organizations whose object is to cause disturbances" could possibly include a political or other organization that incites the population to sabotage or otherwise harm enemy armed forces. The inherently political rather than military nature of such groups means their members cannot be reasonably expected to engage in actual hostilities. In any case, regardless of which type of organization can be considered to be an organization whose object is to cause disturbances, it is clear that membership in such an organization will never be sufficient by itself to intern an individual if the State fails to establish in addition that "the person concerned, by his activities, knowledge or qualifications, represents a real threat to its present or future security."[1207]

(e.) Internment for the purposes of exchange ("bargaining chips")

The exchange of internees during the active phase of hostilities is not prohibited as such by international humanitarian law.[1208] What is prohibited, though, is to capture and intern persons for the mere purpose of negotiating such an exchange. In more than one armed conflict, enemy civilians have been deprived of their liberty, both by private persons and State authorities, for the sole purpose of negotiating their release in exchange for that of persons captured by the adversary.[1209] The term "bargaining chips" – commonly used to designate such persons – was coined by the Israeli Supreme Court in what is probably the

---

1207 Pictet, *Commentary GC IV* (1958), p. 258. *Cf.* also *infra* sub-section (j).

1208 While some rare examples still occurred during the two World Wars, there are hardly any noteworthy incidences since the adoption of the Geneva Conventions (notable exceptions occurred in the Israeli-Arab wars where Israel at times concluded agreements with both Lebanon and Syria to exchange both prisoners of war and civilian internees). This may partly be explained by the fact that internment of enemy civilians on the basis of mere nationality is now formally prohibited and there are thus less internees to be exchanged. However, in contemporary armed conflict "it has proven difficult enough to secure the release of POWs and internees at the conclusion of hostilities, let alone negotiate prisoner exchanges while conflicts are still in progress" (Vance (2006), pp. 125-126).

1209 For example, during the Russia-Georgia conflict in the summer of 2008, there were numerous reports of ethnic South-Ossetians seized and held by both private persons and State authorities in Georgia, whose release was subsequently proposed in exchange for ethnic Georgians held (also privately or officially) in South-Ossetia (the information is based on our recollection of Georgian radio and TV reports of that time).

earliest and most well-known judgment on this issue. The case concerned a number of Lebanese nationals interned on the basis of the *Emergency Powers (Detention) Law*, which regulates internment of enemy aliens in Israel proper. At the time the case was brought, Israel was considering withdrawal from occupied Southern Lebanon and the internees were by that time held solely for negotiating the release of captured IDF soldiers (or their bodies) with the Hezbollah. As the most commonly used reference in the matter, correctly highlighting the relevant issues at stake, the Supreme Court's final judgment in the case merits to be quoted extensively:

> "This balance [between individual liberty and national security] assumes [...] that it is permissible in a democratic country that stands for liberty and security to administratively detain an individual who personally poses a risk to national security. However, this option cannot not be extended to include the detention to an individual who does not personally pose a threat to national security and rather is held as 'a bargaining chip'. The ground for this stance is twofold: First, the injury of administrative detention to the liberty and dignity of an individual who does present a threat to national security is severe as it infringes upon individual liberty — a liberty protected in Israel on a constitutional level — without a trial taking place or a sentence rendered. Nevertheless, it is tolerable since it constitutes the lesser evil. In contrast, the infringement on individual liberty and dignity through administrative detention of a person who personally poses no threat to the national security so severe, that it precludes the interpreter from assuming the law was intended to inflict such injury. I have already pointed out the harmful effect caused by administrative detention [...]: 'Administrative detention infringes upon individual liberty. When the detention takes place under circumstances in which the detainee is used as a 'bargaining chip', it effectively violates human dignity since *the detainee is transformed into attain* [sic] *a means of an end and is not the object by itself.* In these circumstances, detention harms the autonomy of the will, and of one being the master of his/her actions and responsible the consequence of for those actions [sic]. The detention of Appellants is but *a situation in which the key to their jail cell is not in their hands, but in the hands of others*. This is a difficult situation' [...] Indeed, the transition from the administrative detention of a person who poses a danger to national security to the administration detention of a person who does not pose a danger to national security is not a *quantitative* one. Rather it is a *qualitative* one. The State detains, using the executive branch, a person who has committed no offense and who presents no danger; his only sin being a bargaining chip. The violation of human liberty and dignity is so profound so as to be intolerable in a country which supports liberty and dignity, even if premised on considerations of national security. My colleague, Justice M. Cheshin has already indicated that [...] the fundamental concept is 'every man will suffer for his own iniquity and every man will die for his own sins… there shall be no punishment without first prohibiting and there shall no striking but the perpetrator himself.' A similar approach should be applied to administrative detention. Every man will suffer for his own iniquity and every man shall be in administrative detention for his own sins. *There shall be no detaining people but their own actions pose a threat to national security*. [...] the violation of basic human rights by administrative detention of a person who poses no danger for the sake of serving

as a bargaining chip *is so acute as to necessitate an express provision* in the Detention Act extending the application of the Act to people who pose no threat to national security, a provision whose legality would have to be reviewed, of course, according to the standards of the Basic Law, could lead the interpreter of the law to the conclusion that the law was intended to allow this type of administrative detention. Indeed, a comparative examination demonstrates, so it seems, that *no state in the Western hemisphere practices administrative detention on persons who personally do not present any threat to national security.*"[1210]

The Supreme Court was very firm in its decision:

"It is forbidden to place in administrative detention a person who poses no threat for the sole purpose of serving as a 'bargaining chip' [...] In the absence of any other ground for detention, Petitioners are to be released from detention and arrangements be made to release them forthwith for their release [sic] and return them to Lebanon."[1211]

The Court also underlined that its final decision was not taken lightly, in that it effectively reversed its previous position that Lebanese nationals could be lawfully interned for the sole purpose of serving as bargaining chips in negotiations with Hezbollah to secure the return of captured IDF soldiers.[1212]

1210 Israel, SC, *Bargaining Chips Case* (2000), §19 (references to previous case law and footnotes omitted, emphasis added).

1211 Israel, SC, *Bargaining Chips Case* (2000), §21, 26. For a detailed analysis of the case, see Gross, "Human Rights, Terrorism and the Problem of Administrative Detention in Israel: Does a Democracy have the Right to hold Terrorists as Bargaining Chips?" (*Ariz.JICL* 2001). Following the Supreme Court's judgment in this case, 13 Lebanese internees held as bargaining chips were released, but Obeid and al-Durani (who had brought the case before the Court) continued to be interned on the basis of the *Emergency Powers (Detention) Law* (1979) as the authorities succeeded to convince the relevant judicial authorities that they presented a security risk to the State of Israel that justified their continued internment (BBC, "Israel to Release Lebanese Prisoners", 18 April 2000). In *A and B v. Israel* (2008), the appellants claimed that the *IUCL* (*cf. supra*) was intended to provide a legal basis for internment of persons as bargaining chips. The Supreme Court rejected that claim saying that the text of the law, its legislative history and its declared purpose to conform to IHL show that the law was "not intended to allow hostages to be held as 'bargaining chips' for the purpose of obtaining the release of Israeli captives and missing servicemen being held in enemy territory" (§6). While this indeed does not seem to be official purpose of the law – which would render it unlawful as such – if remains that the *IUCL* may not be used to justify an internment that would effectively amount to hostage-taking.

1212 Israel, SC, *Anonymous (Lebanese Citizens) v. Minister of Defence* [10/94]; for a summary and critique of that earlier judgment (which has been censored and is not available in English), see Ben-Naftali & Gleichgevitch (2000). The different positions within the Court at that time are also briefly summarized in the *Bargaining Chips Case* (2000) at §§3-4. Judge Barak, who wrote the majority opinion in both instances, explained his change of mind on the issue to considerable length, underlining the importance of the matter: "First, this conclusion contradicts the one I reached in the decision constituting the subject of these proceedings, meaning that I changed my mind. Indeed, ever since the rendering of the first decision, and throughout these proceedings, I have not ceased examining myself whether my position was justly rooted in the law. I am not one who perceives the finality of the decision as evidence of its correctness. Each of us might err. Our professional integrity obliges us to admit our mistakes if we are so convinced that we indeed made them. 'Between truth and consistency, truth is preferable.' Those words were spoken in respect to the power of the Supreme Court to deviate from its own precedents. [...] At the same time, those words apply to all judges who struggle with themselves and examine their ruling. In our toughest hours, when we are examining ourselves, the Northern Star that should guide us shows is exposing the truth [sic], which leads us to the fulfilment of justice within the realm of law. We cannot entrench ourselves in

Moreover, the then minority opinion that such internment would effectively amount to hostage-taking, was adopted on appeal by the majority of the judges of the Court's full bench: "the detention of [...] people as *hostages*, a term encompassing the holding of persons as bargaining chips, is prohibited under international law."[1213]

The Court's findings in this case have been accepted and confirmed since by the Israeli government and have also been reaffirmed in its subsequent case law.[1214]

---

prejudice. We must be ready to admit our mistakes. Self re-examination in the case before us is not easy. Balancing is not a mechanical endeavor. I sympathize with my friends who continue to argue the Detention Law also applies to a detainee who serves as a 'bargaining chip' without posing any threat to national security. I cannot at this time join their opinion" (Israel, SC, *Bargaining Chips Case* (2000), §22, references to previous case law and footnotes omitted).

[1213] Israel, SC, *Bargaining Chips Case* (2000), §20 (original emphasis). For the record, it deserves mention that in the past, hostage-taking was an accepted tool of diplomacy between warring nations, who, voluntarily, put diplomats or other persons with a high social status at the disposal of an adverse party, as a guarantee for the fulfilment of an agreement or obligation. This practice was an essential feature of warfare since the time of ancient Egypt until the end of the 18th century, when it started to decline. It disappeared entirely by the mid-20th century, due to changes in both the conception of sovereignty and the nature of armed conflicts, but also under the influence of developments in international humanitarian law and the advent of international human rights law (Herrmann & Palmieri, "A Haunting figure: The Hostage through the Ages" (*IRRC* 2005), pp. 137-139; Wayne, "Hostages or Prisoners of War: War Crimes at Dinner" (*MLR* 1995), pp. 243-245). Article 54 of the Lieber Code, adopted in 1863, already stated that "[h]ostages are rare in the present age." By the mid-19th century, civilian hostage-taking had become more common practice among parties to armed conflict. These hostages were used to compel the adversary to halt its military advance, to serve as human shields for troops or military objectives, to influence military morale and terrorize the public opinion of the adverse party, or as a form of reprisal (Herrmann & Palmieri (*IRRC* 2005), pp. 140-145; Wayne (*MLR* 1995), pp. 245-250). Until 1949, the taking of civilian hostages by an Occupying Power was still allowed in exceptional circumstances. Article 19 of the Draft Tokyo Convention (1934), which was never ratified, stipulated that: "The High Contracting Parties further undertake to observe the following provisions: a) In the event of it appearing, in an exceptional case, indispensable for an occupying Power to take hostages, the latter shall always be treated humanely. Under no pretext shall they be put to death or submitted to corporal punishments". Article 11 of the same Draft Convention however unequivocally prohibited hostage-taking in the territory of the parties to the conflict. The prohibition of hostage-taking in time of armed conflict became absolute with the adoption of the Geneva Conventions, bringing "positive law into line with the principles of justice and humanity" (Pictet, *Commentary GC IV* (1958), p. 231). Common article 3 of these Conventions prohibits the taking of hostages among persons *hors de combat*; and article 34 GC IV confirms explicitly that the taking of hostages among persons protected by GC IV, whether it be in the territory of the parties to the conflict or in occupied territory, is prohibited. For the prohibition of hostage-taking in general international law and its qualification as a war crime when committed in armed conflict, *cf. supra* notes 242-243 in chapter I-1.

[1214] See for example Israel, MoJ, *Factsheet on Administrative Detention* (2003) under its heading "Detention as a means of prevention" refers to the SC judgment saying that the Minister of Defence does "not have the authority to place a person in administrative detention when that person does not pose a threat to national security and is being held as a "bargaining chip" for the sole purpose of providing leverage for the exchange of kidnapped IDF soldiers." For reaffirmation by the Supreme Court itself, see its judgment in *A and B v. Israel* (2008), §6. The Court's confirmation of the rule in that case is all the more interesting and relevant since it dealt with a law that was enacted as a direct result from the Court's finding in the *Bargaining Chips Case* (2000), and allegedly engineered to get around the Court's findings in that case (*cf. infra*).

The unlawfulness of interning individuals for the sole purpose of using them as leverage in negotiations with the adverse party, and the finding that such internment would amount to hostage-taking has further been confirmed in the case law of the ICTY.[1215] For example, in the *Delalić* case, the Tribunal accepted the following evidence as constitutive of the crime of unlawful confinement:

> "she was informed that she was detained in the Čelebići prison-camp until her husband was found, that is, she was detained as a kind of a hostage."[1216]

In both the *Blaškić* and the *Kordić & Čerkez* cases, the Tribunal held that interning persons as bargaining chips for any kind of negotiations would not only be unlawful but would also amount to hostage-taking. It also underlined that this would be so regardless of whether there was any other – potentially lawful – ground to intern the persons concerned:

> "The parties did not contest that to be characterised as hostages the detainees must have been used to obtain some advantage or to ensure that a belligerent, other person or other group of persons enter into some undertaking. [...] The indictment states that from January 1993 to January 1994 Bosnian Muslim civilians were taken hostage by the HVO and used both in prisoner exchanges and in order to bring to a halt Bosnian military operations against the HVO. The accused thus allegedly committed [the war crime of hostage-taking]. [...] In the opinion of the Defence [...] the detention of Bosnian Muslim civilians was justified on security and safety grounds. A lawful act of this type could not therefore be characterised as taking of hostages. [...] Although not all were necessarily civilians, all were persons placed *hors de combat*. Moreover, the Trial Chamber is of the opinion that, in this instance, detention could in no way be deemed lawful because its main purpose was to compel the ABiH [i.e. the Bosnian armed forces] to halt is advance. The [war crime of hostage-taking] are hereby constituted."[1217]

In the context of the ongoing international armed conflict between Azerbaijan and Armenia, the Human Rights Committee has confirmed that deprivation of liberty for the sole purpose of bargaining amounts to hostage-taking:

> "The Committee deeply deplores the events which have occurred recently in Azerbaijan in the context of the armed conflict and have involved numerous violations of the rights guaranteed by the Covenant. There have been reports of

---

[1215] It is also been confirmed by the ICRC, as is reflected in Pejic (*IRRC* 2005), p. 380, note 20 (under the heading *Internment as an exceptional measure*): "Similarly, interning or administratively detaining persons for the purpose of using them as "bargaining chips" is also not justifiable as a reason for internment. Such deprivation of liberty would in fact amount to hostage-taking, which is prohibited."

[1216] ICTY, *Delalić* (1998), §1132.

[1217] ICTY, *Blaškić* (2000), §§ 187 and 701-709. In the *Kordić & Čerkez* case, where the defence held a similar line as that in *Blaškić*, the Tribunal relied on its findings in *Blaškić* to conclude that the following was evidence of the double crime of unlawful confinement and hostage-taking: "Čerkez received the witness in a friendly manner and said that not a hair would be hurt on the son's head – the son had been taken for the purposes of exchange [...] Čerkez told him that the ABiH had broken through the front line at Dubravica: the witness had to ring the 3rd Corps Commander and say that there were 2,223 prisoners and that if the Muslim advance continued on Vitez he would order the killing of the prisoners. The witness did so and the Commander agreed to halt the advance" (ICTY, *Kordić & Čerkez* (2001), §§307, 744 and 788).

cases of [...] arbitrary detention. The practice of *hostage-taking* as a retaliatory measure or *for bargaining purposes* also seems widespread."[1218]

A final note must be made on Justice Cheshin's claim – in his dissenting opinion attached to the Israeli Supreme Court's judgment in the *Bargaining chips case* – that members of an enemy's armed forces cannot be victims of hostage-taking (and therefore in his opinion the petitioners *in casu* could be interned for the purposes of exchange):

> "Nor are Petitioners 'hostages', not according to the accepted definition in international law or any other definition. [...] we have never heard of those belonging to warring parties and [...] captured by the enemy being 'hostages' as they are kept until the end of the end of the hostilities or until a conclusion of repatriation agreement. Indeed, the same way that detention of Prisoners of War is viewed as a detention for a legitimate and appropriate purpose – thus, they are not depicted as 'hostages' or 'bargaining chips' – so are, in comparison, *Hezbollah* fighters are detained for a legitimate and appropriate purpose, namely, national security. Petitioners exhibit none of the signs of 'hostages' and not even 'bargaining chips'. In any case, we know that they are neither 'hostages' nor 'bargaining chips'. It should be remembered that Petitioners are not naïve villagers who were taken by force to a foreign land. Granted that they were not but common soldiers in the ranks of the *Hezbollah*, they nonetheless pledged themselves to be enemy combatants and therefore are neither 'hostages' nor 'bargaining chips'."[1219]

While contradicted by the majority of the Israeli Supreme Court, and rightly so, the argument made by Justice Cheshin is closely related to the question of whether prisoners of war can ever be victims of hostage-taking as defined by international law.[1220] While that question must be answered in the affirmative,

---

1218 HRC, *Concluding Observations: Azerbaijan* (1994), §8 (emphasis added).

1219 Israel, SC, *Bargaining Chips Case* (2000), Opinion of Justice Cheshin, §7 (original italics).

1220 Actually, as is visible in the extract of his opinion quoted above, Justice Cheshin's position seems to be based entirely on the rationale of POW internment (*cf. supra* chapter I-2), even if the Justice clearly does not consider members of the Hezbollah to qualify for such status. Justice Cheshin refers to Ben-Naftali & Gleichgevitch (*Harv.ILJ* 2000) who suggested there could be a legal basis to intern the appellants in the case in international humanitarian law. These authors rightly point out that if such persons could qualify as POW, they could be interned on the basis of GC III (at pp. 245-246). However, they also argue that even those who do not meet the criteria of article 4 GC III for qualifying as POW but who could qualify as such under AP I (to which Israel is not a party and therefore does not apply) could be interned for the duration of active hostilities "by analogy" (at p. 248). This argument runs counter to the explicit provisions and the object and purpose of GC IV, which Ben-Naftali & Gleichgevitch accept is the relevant regime applying to persons who are not entitled to POW status (at pp. 243-244): if the individuals concerned are not POW under the law applicable to the specific conflict in which they are held (their possible qualification as combatants under AP I is irrelevant since, in the absence of ratification by Israel and Lebanon, the Protocol does not apply *in casu*), they can only be interned on the basis of GC IV (*in casu* there is no doubt they would qualify as protected persons under article 4 GC IV). GC IV does not contain a legal basis to intern analogous to the one that exists for POW. The legal bases to intern persons who fall within the scope of application of GC IV are exhaustively contained in articles 41-43 and 78 GC IV (article 79 GC IV, *cf. supra*); they only allow internment of persons who pose an individual threat to the security of the Interning Power, where no other, less restrictive, measures to meet that threat are available, and their internment is absolutely necessary to counter the threat.

the answer is also somewhat more nuanced than with regard to protected persons under GC IV, and therefore merits some further analysis.

We have seen in chapter II-1 that prisoners of war may be lawfully interned on the basis of article 21 GC III regardless of whether they *de facto* pose an individual threat, and that they may, in principle, be interned without further review for the duration of active hostilities.[1221] This is where the crucial difference between the internment regimes in GC III and GC IV lies: whereas collective internment measures are lawful under GC III, they are not under GC IV. This important conceptual distinction explains the differences between the lawful grounds and procedures prescribed by each of these Conventions.

While articles 21 and 118 GC III specifically allow for the internment of prisoners of war until the cessation of active hostilities, the issue of prisoner of war exchange during the active phase of hostilities is not regulated by international humanitarian law.[1222] Negotiations on the exchange of prisoners of war (i.e. persons who qualify as such under article 4 GC III) between parties to the conflict are not *per se* prohibited during the active phase of hostilities and they have occurred in practice without the objection of hostage-taking being raised.[1223] On the contrary, negotiations on a prisoner exchange once active hostilities have ceased may not unduly delay the immediate release and repatriation of prisoners of war prescribed by article 118 GC III since the legal basis for their internment expires at the time of the active cessation of hostilities (*cf. supra* II-1, section 1.2.3.6). If negotiations between the parties to the conflict unduly delay the release and repatriation of prisoners of war at the close of hostilities, the situation of the prisoners could therefore amount to hostage-taking. Finally, prisoners of war will be considered as victims of hostage-taking when their life or physical integrity, rather than their liberty, is used in negotiations or unilateral demands to obtain an exchange or any other – military – advantage from an adverse party. For example, where a party to the conflict threatens to kill, torture or mutilate its prisoners of war if its adversary does not release the prisoners it holds, halts a military advance or withdraws from certain areas – the situation clearly amounts to hostage-taking, regardless of the fact that these prisoners are lawfully interned on the basis of article 21 GC III.

The claim that the war crime of hostage-taking does not apply where the alleged victims are prisoners of war is therefore unfounded. Both combatants and civilians, both prisoners of war and protected persons under GC IV, and more generally, all persons held as hostages in any armed conflict (international or non-international) can be the victim of this serious crime. This is also reflected in the drafting history of the Third Geneva Convention:

[1221] For the necessary nuance, *cf. supra* chapter II-1, section 1.2.3.

[1222] As demonstrated by Levie (1978) at pp. 397-398, concluding that: "During the twentieth century exchange has practically disappeared as an institution of the law of war. It is not mentioned in any of the general conventions with which we are concerned, including the 1949 Convention."

[1223] *Cf. supra*, note 780 for prisoner exchanges in the Arab-Israeli context. See also Fawkes (BBC), "Prisoner Swap at Russian Checkpoint" (2008), on an exchange of prisoners of war during the Russia-Georgia conflict in 2008.

"The Coordination Committee drew attention to the fact that Article 31 of the Civilians Convention: 'The taking of hostages is prohibited', had no counterpart in the Prisoners of War Convention. Mr. GARDNER (United Kingdom) said that the treatment of prisoners of war was so completely covered in the Prisoners of War Convention, that it was impossible to imagine circumstances in which hostages could be taken without infringing one or more of the existing Articles. The suggested addition would therefore have no practical justification. The Committee decided to take no action on the observation of the Coordination Committee."[1224]

The prohibition of hostage-taking reflects international practice and forms part of customary international humanitarian law.[1225] It was recently reaffirmed by the ICTY in a decision concerning Radovan Karadžić's submission that "under customary international law, the crime of hostage-taking is limited, in the context of international armed conflict, to the taking of civilians."[1226] The Tribunal refuted Radovan Karadžić's claim, both on the basis of GC III itself and on the basis of the prohibition of hostage-taking in common article 3 GC, applicable without distinction on the basis of the status of a person or the nature of the armed conflict:

"First, the Appeals Chamber considers that the prohibition of hostage-taking cannot be considered as extraneous to the Third Geneva Convention. The protection of POWs is covered by an extensive net of provisions within the Third Geneva Convention which, read together, lead to the conclusion that any conduct of hostage-taking involving POWs could not but be in violation of the Third Geneva Convention. [...] The main point confirming the relevance of the prohibition of hostage-taking under the Third Geneva Convention is the very existence of common Article 3, which expresses the shared principles which govern the Conventions and establishes [...] the "taking of hostages", is prohibited "with respect to the above-mentioned persons", that is "[p]ersons taking no active part in the hostilities, including members of the armed forces who have laid down their arms and those placed 'hors de combat' [...]".[...] The well-established jurisprudence of the Tribunal has repeatedly affirmed that the body proper of the Geneva Conventions cannot be interpreted in such a way as to afford lesser protection to individuals than that which is afforded by common Article 3. [...] the lex specialis argument is inevitably irrelevant, as the Third Geneva Convention must be interpreted in light of common Article 3. [...] The Appeals Chamber considers that the Appellant fails to provide any sensible argument suggesting an exception to, or limitation on, the prohibition on hostage-taking for a particular category of persons in a particular type of conflict. [...] The value of common Article 3 as a "*minimum* yardstick" of protections

---

[1224] *Final Record 1949*, Vol. II-A, pp. 399-400.

[1225] Rule 96 of the ICRC's compilation of customary IHL ("The taking of hostages is prohibited") applies "both in international and non-international armed conflict" and "to the taking of any person protected by the Geneva Conventions", combatants and civilians alike, see Henckaerts & Doswald-Beck (2005), Vol. I, pp. 334-336, with references to State and other international practice. For the definition and prohibition of hostage-taking in international law more generally, *cf. supra* chapter I-1.

[1226] ICTY, *Karadžić* (2009), §6. Until then, the Tribunal had never been called upon to pronounce itself on the question whether the internment of prisoners of war could ever qualify as hostage-taking.

applicable regardless of the nature of the conflict necessarily implies that the protections enshrined therein must be applied in full and cannot be applied in part. The prohibition of hostage-taking shares the very same scope of application with the remaining rules enshrined in common Article 3."[1227]

To conclude, the prospect of a prisoner-exchange (real or perceived) is not a lawful ground to intern persons in armed conflict. Moreover, even where another lawful ground to intern exists, on the basis of either GC III or GC IV, internment will become unlawful when in reality it is ordered or continued solely for the purposes of such a prisoner exchange. Apart from a prisoner exchange lawfully negotiated in the active phase of hostilities, any release of prisoners of war made subject to obtaining some advantage or to ensure that a belligerent, other person or other group of persons enter into some undertaking, will render their initially lawful internment on the basis of article 21 GC III unlawful, and amounts to hostage-taking. Persons interned on the basis of articles 42 or 78 GC IV may only be held when they, individually, pose a real security threat to the Interning Power that makes their internment absolutely necessary. When in reality they are held for the mere purpose of negotiating a prisoner exchange or obtaining any other military advantage, their internment will amount to hostage-taking and thus be unlawful. Those who order such internment will be liable for the war crimes of both hostage-taking and unlawful confinement.

So far, we have examined the conformity with IHL of criteria that have been used in practice to translate the ground for internment prescribed by article 42§1 GC IV in more concrete terms and are of a strong – and in most cases excessive – collective nature. Apart from the special case of unprivileged combatants (i.e. members of the armed forces of a party to the conflict who do not qualify for POW status under article 4 GC IV), the fulfilment of these collective criteria cannot by itself mean that the threshold required by article 42§1 GC IV is met. Internment as "bargaining chips" is not necessarily based on a collective threat assessment, but cannot justify internment on the basis of GC IV either. For one, it does not rely on an individual threat posed by the internee but on his or her value in a potential prisoner exchange. Moreover, it effectively amounts to hostage-taking, which is the subject of an absolute prohibition in both international human rights and humanitarian law.

Whereas some of the collective criteria discussed above may prove useful to identify persons who *potentially* pose a security threat, to justify actual recourse to internment on the basis of GC IV, the Interning Power "must have good reason to think that the person concerned, by his activities, knowledge or qualifications, represents a real threat to its present or future security."[1228] With that proviso attached, Pictet gives the following examples of persons posing a security threat:

[1227] ICTY, *Karadžić* (2009), §§ 21-26 (original italics). We referred to the Tribunal's case law on the applicability of CA3 in all types of armed conflict and on the definition of the war crime of hostage-taking above (*cf. supra* note 243).
[1228] Pictet, *Commentary GC IV* (1958), p. 258.

"Subversive activity carried on inside the territory of a Party to the conflict or actions which are of direct assistance to an enemy Power both threaten the security of the country; a belligerent may intern people or place them in assigned residence if it has serious and legitimate reason to think that they are members of organizations whose object is to cause disturbances, or that they may seriously prejudice its security by other means, such as sabotage or espionage. [...] To justify recourse to such measures the State must have good reason to think that the person concerned, by his activities, knowledge or qualifications, represents a real threat to its present or future security." [1229]

Taking Pictet's list as a starting point, we will now try to concretize which "activities, knowledge or qualifications" may present a threat to State security that could justify internment.

(f.) Subversive activity and actions of direct assistance to an enemy Power

According to Pictet, "[s]ubversive activity carried on inside the territory of a Party to the conflict or actions which are of direct assistance to an enemy Power both threaten the security of the country."[1230]

Whether or not a specific activity can be considered the kind of security threat that warrants preventive internment has to be established on a case-by-case basis. Nevertheless, some guidance can be found in the general principles underlying the Convention's internment provisions (*cf. supra* section 3.2.1). On the basis of these principles, a number of acts may *ab initio* be excluded from the notion of "actions that are of direct assistance to an enemy power" for the purposes of interpreting articles 42§1 and 78 GC IV. First, a security threat justifying internment must be directly related to an ongoing armed conflict (nexus). Ordinary criminal behaviour, not directly related to the conflict is not a lawful ground for internment, even if it is directed against the parties to the conflict or their populations. Persons who commit or are expected to commit such acts may be subject to criminal charges (and lawful preventive detention within the framework of such proceedings). Second, the inherently preventive character of internment excludes any deprivation of liberty as a form of punishment for past acts or behaviour.

Moreover, the general principles for internment on the basis of GC IV must also guide the interpretation of the notions of "subversive activity" and "actions of direct assistance to an enemy power". Examples of these two notions will in practice often overlap, but are not necessarily identical. We will therefore treat them separately, looking at how these notions have been applied in practice by States and international tribunals. The little practice available also confirms Pictet's conclusion that these are the type of activities that justify internment on the basis of articles 42§1 and 78 GC IV. Finally, the notions of "subversive

---

[1229] Pictet, *Commentary to GC IV* (1958), p. 258.

[1230] In his commentary to article 5§1 GC IV, Pictet rightly points out that the idea of activities prejudicial or hostile to the security of the State is very hard to define in concrete terms (Pictet, *Commentary GC IV* (1958), p. 58). There is no definition of subversion or subversive activity or of "actions of direct assistance to an enemy power" in Verri's *Dictionary of the International Law of Armed Conflict* (1992).

activity" and "actions of direct assistance to an enemy power" in practice also overlap substantially with the notion of "direct participation in hostilities" ("DPH"), a central concept in the rules on targeting that is increasingly used to establish a standard for internment of so-called unprivileged or unlawful combatants. While still emerging, we will try to point out the risks inherent in an unqualified "DPH-approach" to internment.

(f.1). Subversive activity

NATO's standardized terminology defines subversion as:

> "[a]ction designed to weaken the military, economic or political strength of a nation by undermining the morale, loyalty or reliability of its citizens."[1231]

US military terminology, generally in line with NATO's, is a bit more specific:

> "[Subversion:] Actions designed to undermine the military, economic, psychological, or political strength or morale of a governing authority. (JP 3-24)
>
> [Subversive activity:] Anyone lending aid, comfort, and moral support to individuals, groups, or organizations that advocate the overthrow of incumbent governments by force and violence is subversive and is engaged in subversive activity. All *wilful acts that are intended to be detrimental to the best interests of the government* and that do not fall into the categories of treason, sedition, sabotage, or espionage will be placed in the category of subversive activity.
>
> [Subversive political action:] A planned series of activities designed to accomplish political objectives by influencing, dominating, or displacing individuals or groups who are so placed as to affect the decisions and actions of another government."[1232]

It is important to note that these are general definitions that do not serve the purpose of interpreting the Geneva Conventions or articles 42§1 and 78 GC IV in particular. The concept of subversion in operational military terminology is not limited to activities that occur in armed conflict alone and includes political and propaganda activities. For this reason it is of limited use to clarify Pictet's use of the term in his commentary on article 42§1 GC IV. The US definition of subversion refers to its Joint Doctrine 3-24 on Counter-Insurgency Operations, which maybe brings us closer to what we are looking for here. The JP 3-24 effectively transposes the general idea of subversion into what could be subversive activity in the context of an armed conflict: JP 3-24 defines insurgency as: "[t]he organized use of subversion and violence by a group or movement that seeks to overthrow or force change of a governing authority."[1233] It is very likely that insurgent or rebellious acts, carried out in the context of an armed conflict, are what Pictet had in mind when he said that persons who engage in "subversive activity" pose a threat to the security of the Interning Power for the purposes of article 42§1 and 78 GC IV.

[1231] NATO, *AAP-6* (2010), p. 2-S-14.
[1232] US, DoD, The Dictionary of Military Terms (2010), p. 447.
[1233] US, Joint Doctrine Publication 3-24: Counterinsurgency Operations (2009) (JDP 3-24), p. GL-6.

For the purposes of interpreting these articles, it is therefore appropriate to narrow down the general definition of subversion/subversive activity to actions carried out in the territory of a party to the conflict and designed to weaken that party's military strength or capacity. Such a definition is more in line with the fact that internment is only allowed where a direct nexus to an ongoing armed conflict exists and aims to prevent real military or security threats, and with the basic rule that internment for mere political activity is not allowed (*cf. infra*). In as far as the notion of "subversive activity" overlaps with the notion of "actions of direct assistance to an enemy power", the examples from practice we give in the following sub-section also support the narrow definition of subversive activity we have proposed here.

(f.2.). Actions of direct assistance to an enemy Power: examples from international practice

It is submitted that for the purpose of interpreting articles 42§1 and 78 GC IV, Pictet's reference to "actions of direct assistance to an enemy Power" include both actions that directly threaten the security of the Interning Power and actions that directly contribute to the military operations of an adverse party to the conflict directed against that Interning Power.[1234] The concept is rather straightforward and should in most cases not be difficult to apply in practice. Examples are nevertheless always useful, and we have therefore sought guidance in States' operational guidelines on internment in international armed conflict, as they could give us more concrete indications as to which activities amount to the kind of threat that may justify internment. There is not much to rely on though, since most military manuals and doctrine do not go beyond reiterating the text of articles 42§1 and 78 GC IV and do not further specify which acts would meet the threshold established by these articles.

The *Code of Conduct* for Canadian armed forces involved in armed conflict explains that:

> "[t]he primary reasons for which members of the [Canadian Armed Forces] may be called upon to detain individuals in the course of an operation are to prevent their further *participation in a conflict* or, when authorized, to prevent them from *interfering with the military mission.*"[1235]

Canadian military doctrine on detainee operations recognizes, with regard to "civilians and unlawful belligerents other than prisoners of war" that it "may be necessary" to detain them when they:

[1234] Actions that directly harm an ally of the Interning Power in the armed conflict will also justify internment on the basis of articles 42§1 and 78 GC IV.

[1235] Canada, *Code of Conduct* (2005), p. 2-9 (emphasis added). To be noted that the *Code of Conduct* applies in "all military operations other than Canadian domestic operations." Such military operations include "operations where Canada is a party to an armed conflict as well as to peace support operations." (Section 1 at p. 1-1). The Canadian *Geneva Conventions Act* (1985, last amended in 2008) does not provide any detail on lawful grounds for internment but focuses rather on criminal prosecution of prisoners of war and civilian internees (Part II, articles 4 to 8). Canada's *LOAC Manual* (2001) does not spell out the grounds for internment other than through reiterating he text of articles 43-43 and 78 GC IV without further comment (chapter 11, sections 1125 and 1223).

> "a. carry out *armed attacks* against friendly forces; b. are members of any military or para-military group or organisation whether or not they are actually engaged in attacks against friendly forces, *and who carry personal weapons, or man weapon systems*; [or] *spontaneously take up arms against* friendly forces."[1236]

The manual further underlines that Canadian policy is to keep internment to an absolute minimum, which means that Canadian Forces (CF)

> "will not detain persons other than PW and CF detainees except when absolutely necessary to do so. The CF will only detain civilians when they pose a threat to CF personnel or mission success, or to prevent them from further participation in a conflict."[1237]

Canadian practice therefore demonstrates that the internment of persons who have already or are expected to take part in hostilities is lawful, but that these decisions may not be taken automatically, and must remain limited to cases where it is absolutely necessary.

The US Army Field Manual's chapter on prisoners of war has a brief section devoted to persons who do *not* qualify as such, and is thus of interest to us here.[1238] Apart from spies (*cf. infra*) and other members of enemy armed forces who do not qualify as prisoners of war (*cf. supra*), the section also covers persons who "commit *hostile acts about or behind the lines of the enemy*". The Manual explains that:

> "[s]uch acts include, but are not limited to, sabotage, destruction of communications facilities, intentional misleading of troops by guides, liberation of prisoners of war, and other acts not [qualifying as either espionage or aiding the enemy]."[1239]

The same section includes persons who are "aiding the enemy", a criminal offence under article 104 of the US *Uniform Code of Military Justice* (*UCMJ*) that applies to:

> "[a]ny person who (1) aids or attempts to aid, the enemy with arms, ammunition, supplies, money, or other thing; or (2) without proper authority, knowingly harbors or protects or gives intelligence to, or communicates or corresponds with or holds any intercourse with the enemy, either directly or indirectly".

The Army Field Manual adds that:

1236 Canada, *PWDITQ* (2004), pp. 1B-1 to 1B-2 (emphasis added).

1237 Canada, *PWDITQ* (2004), p. 1B-3. "CF" stands for Canadian (Armed) Forces, "PW" for prisoners of war. The manual does not contain other provisions that give further guidance as to how the grounds for internment in articles 42§1 and 78 GC IV must be interpreted.

1238 The Manual itself underlines that such persons are by definition protected under GC IV: "If a person is determined by a competent tribunal, acting in conformity with [article 5 GC III], not to fall within any of the categories listed in Article 4, *GPW*, he is not entitled to be treated as a prisoner of war. He is, however, a "protected person" within the meaning of [article 4 GC IV]" (US, *Army Field Manual* (1956), Chapter 3, article 73).

1239 US, *Army Field Manual* (1956), Chapter 3, section II, § 81 (emphasis added). The original text reads as follows: "and other acts not falling within Articles 104 and 106 of the Uniform Code of Military Justice and Article 29 of the Hague Regulations." Articles 104 and 106 of the *Uniform Code of Military Justice* (1950, as amended) (*UCMJ*) and article 29 HR 1907 concern persons aiding the enemy and spies.

"In time of war, the rule of the above article is general in its application to all persons whether or not otherwise subject to military law and without regard to citizenship or military or civil status, who give aid to an enemy government or persons adhering to it."[1240]

The section of the US Army Field Manual on persons other than prisoners of war does not explicitly deal with their internment though.[1241] Rather, it provides that persons covered by it are punishable with "the extreme penalty of death because of the danger inherent in their conduct."[1242] This shows that persons who have committed hostile or belligerent acts before their arrest or capture will most likely be detained in the framework of criminal proceedings and the question of internment should therefore not even arise.[1243] Nevertheless, since these acts are considered dangerous enough as to warrant the death penalty, it is reasonable to conclude that in cases where they have not yet materialized, or where criminal proceedings cannot take place for lack of proof, the threat may also warrant internment. The example of the offence of "aiding the enemy" also shows that persons posing a security threat are not necessarily confined to those who directly participate in hostilities, but include persons who in a different manner are of direct assistance to the enemy. That does not mean that all acts listed as constituting the US offence of "aiding the enemy" amount to *direct* assistance to the enemy power though.[1244] For example, while the "little old lady in Switzerland"[1245] who donates money to a charity that indirectly finances an armed group may – under US criminal law – be "aiding the enemy", she can clearly not be considered to pose the kind of security threat that justifies internment on the basis of articles 42§1 and 78 GC IV. Moreover, any threat of financing the enemy – other than the direct and important financing of its military operations – can surely be met by other less restrictive measures of control than internment, such as freezing financial assets or limiting financial transactions of suspected persons.

1240 US, *Army Field Manual* (1956), Chapter 3, Section II, article 79.

1241 In its section on internment of persons protected by GC IV, the Manual simply reproduces the text of articles 42 and 78 GC IV, without adding further indications or examples of persons who pose a security threat (US, *Army Field Manual* (1956), Chapter 5, section IV, §281 and chapter 6, section VIII, §433 respectively). The same holds true for US, *Army Regulation 190-8* (1997), which provides operational guidelines for the handling of prisoners of war, civilian internees and other detainees (US, *Army Regulation 190-8* (1997), pp. 18-19, section 5-1 *litera* b.) and US, *JDP 3-63* (2005), neither one of which provides concrete guidance as to what type of activity would qualify as a security threat justifying internment.

1242 US, *Army Field Manual* (1956), Chapter 3, section II, § 82, which specifies that "[l]esser penalties may, however, be imposed." The same penalties apply to spies and persons "aiding the enemy" (articles 104, 106 *UCMJ* (1950, as amended)).

1243 See for an example of such a criminal prosecution resulting in a conviction: "New Yorker in London Gets Prison for al-Qaida Help", *Miami Herald Online*, June 2010.

1244 Most acts therein would however amount to either espionage or other "actions of direct assistance to the enemy power."

1245 The term was used by a US District Court judge when questioning Department of Justice lawyers on the definition of "enemy combatant" employed by the administration to determine who could be interned on the basis of the *Authorization to Use Military Force (AUMF) Act* of 2001. See Frieden, "U.S. Grilled over Terror Policies", *CNN International*, 2 December 2004.

A Department of Defence (DoD) Factsheet on internees held by the US in Guantánamo Bay – at least some of which would qualify as protected persons under GC IV (*cf. supra*) – claims the purpose of their deprivation of liberty is

> "to *prevent combatants from continuing to fight* against the U.S. and its allies. [...] Enemy combatant is defined as an individual who was part of or supporting Taliban or al Qaeda forces, or associated forces that are engaged in hostilities against the United States or its coalition partners. This includes *any person who has committed a belligerent act or has directly supported hostilities in aid of enemy armed forces.*"[1246]

While there are many legal problems with the internment of persons in the Guantánamo Bay internment facility, the *official* reason for holding persons – as defined in the DoD's Factsheet – is in line with the lawful grounds for internment of persons captured or arrested in relation to an international armed conflict (as for example the first phase of the conflict in Afghanistan).[1247] Preventing confirmed members of enemy armed forces to continue fighting is a lawful ground to intern on the basis of article 21 GC III for those who qualify as prisoners of war (*cf. supra*). Moreover, persons who do not qualify as prisoners of war but can be reasonably expected to commit "belligerent acts" or "directly support hostilities in aid of enemy armed forces" pose the kind of security threat that is likely to allow for internment on the basis of articles 42§1 and 78 GC IV.

As we mentioned earlier on, most military doctrine and operational guidelines on the internment of persons other than prisoners of war merely reproduce the text of articles 41-43 and 78 GC IV, without further specifying what they mean.[1248] In order to ensure both efficient and lawful internment operations, more specific instructions as to who can be interned as a security threat are likely to be articulated in the Rules of Engagement (ROE) adopted for each specific theatre of operations. Unfortunately, such documents are not readily available for academic or other research.[1249] Still, while it is certainly

---

[1246] US, DoD, *Factsheet: Guantánamo Detainee Process*, still in force and available on DoD's Detainee Affairs website (last verified on 16 December 2012).

[1247] It is not within the scope of our discussions to dress a comprehensive overview of the legal problems with the internment of individuals at the US Naval Base in Guantánamo Bay. The issues have been the subject of an impressive amount of literature and some of them have been or still are the subject of legal proceedings in the US and elsewhere. For our present purposes (identifying the lawful grounds for internment on the basis of GC IV) the following points may be made. First, available information demonstrates that the ultimate purpose of internment of persons who were part of or supported the Taliban, Al-Qaeda and affiliated forces or had participated in hostilities against the US and its coalition partners, was (1) to try them for their acts of for their membership in such groups, and (2) to interrogate them for the purpose of preventing future terrorist acts against the US or its allies in the so-called "war on terrorism". We have seen above that internment may not be an alternative to criminal proceedings or detention in the framework of such proceedings. Where there was sufficient evidence to prosecute, the individuals should have been tried and detained in accordance with the relevant criminal legislation. Moreover, internment for the mere purpose of interrogation or intelligence value, where the person otherwise does not pose a threat to the security of the Interning Power, is not allowed in either international humanitarian or international human rights law (*cf. infra*).

[1248] E.g.: UK, Joint Military Doctrine Publication 1-10.2: Internees (2006) (JDP 1-10.2), articles 101 and 281-282).

[1249] For the purposes of predictability and foreseeability, it may be warranted to issue public statements

wise to give detailed instructions to troops on the ground in order to prevent unnecessary or unlawful internment, each actual decision to intern must be taken on an individual basis, taking into account not only the person's past or expected behaviour but also the specific dynamics of the conflict, the factual circumstances at the time and the availability of alternative measures of control. Such decision usually belongs to a high-ranking officer, who normally will consult with his legal advisor.[1250]

The ICTY has confirmed – albeit only implicitly – that belligerent acts and direct participation in acts of resistance or hostilities against the Interning Power may be lawful grounds to deprive persons protected by the Fourth Geneva Convention of their liberty:

> "The evidence before the Trial Chamber indicates that a number of the civilians detained in the Celebici prison-camp at the time of their capture were *in possession of weapons which could have been used, or were in fact used, against the forces of* Bosnia and Herzegovina in the Konjic area. It is difficult to ascertain precisely how many of those detained in the Celebici prison-camp *in this way participated in acts of resistance against* the TO, HVO and MUP forces and, therefore, arguably could have been lawfully detained. According to several witnesses, 100 to 105 detainees admitted in interviews conducted after their detention that they were *in possession of weapons and that they participated actively in the defence of their villages.* (...) Various other witnesses who had been detained in the prison-camp testified that they had not *participated in any military activity*, and posed no genuine threat to the forces that occupied the area."[1251]

---

that include specific examples of behaviour considered to justify internment in a specific context. Not only may such publicly available information deter hostile or otherwise dangerous behaviour, it may help clarify the legal basis relied upon by an Interning Power in cases where courts are called upon to review the legality of its internment decisions.

1250 See for example: US, *Army Regulation 190-8* (1997), pp. 18-19, section 5-1 *litera* makes the order to intern dependent on the condition that "[i]nternment has been *determined by competent U.S. Military authority to be necessary for imperative reasons of security to the United States Armed Forces*" (emphasis added). See also USA, *JDP 3-63* (2005), p. IV-1: "*Tactical commanders* must exercise discretion when determining whether an individual poses a credible threat or possesses sufficient information requiring evacuation and detention." Another example can be found in Canada, *PWDITQ* (2004), pp. 1B-3 to 1B-4: "The authority to detain civilians is to be established by ROE. [...] It is the responsibility of the CF forces to hand the detainee over to the appropriate civil authority at the earliest opportunity unless the *Commander* of the UN/NATO/Coalition Force has directed that the detainee should continue to be held. Under such circumstances the detainee should only be released on direction from the *Force Commander*. [...] The release of a detainee will be dependent on the judgment of the *senior soldier* present. He may at any time during the proceedings decided that there is no longer a requirement to hold the detainee and may release him/her. Once the detainee has been handed over to the Civil Police/CF MP they assume the right to release the detainee. Legal advice is to be sought prior to the release of detainees" (emphasis added). The summary of the detainee process at p. 1B-6 shows that internment decisions must be reviewed (or even ordered) by a Military Police officer immediately after capture or arrest, within 48 hours by the *Force Commander and his legal officer*, and then weekly by the *Force Commander*, or where relevant by the host nation or UN/NATO/Coalition commander. Articles 3(a) and 11 of the Israeli *Incarceration of Unlawful Combatants Law* (2002) reserve the decision to intern on the basis of that law to the Chief of General Staff of the Israeli armed forces, who can delegate this power to an officer with the rank of major-general (*cf.* also *supra* note 1117).

1251 ICTY, *Delalić* (1998), §1131 and 1133 (emphasis added). To be noted, for the purpose of completeness, that such persons could clearly be detained on criminal charges for their possession of

From the little practice available, we can draw two conclusions. First, there is no doubt that a person who may reasonably be expected to engage in actions of direct assistance to an enemy power represents a real threat to the security of the Interning Power, and may be interned if no alternative measure can prevent that threat from materializing. Second, when translating the concept of security threat in articles 42§1 and 78 GC IV into practice, at least some States seem to rely to a certain extent on the notion of direct participation in hostilities (hereinafter "DPH").[1252] It is true that practical examples of the two notions substantially overlap, which explains why the notion of "participation in hostilities" (whether it be direct or indirect) has been increasingly used to determine the lawful grounds for internment in both international and non-international armed conflict.[1253] Before we discuss the "DPH-approach to internment", two important preliminary points must be made.

First, the notion of "actions of direct assistance to an enemy power" is broader than the notion of "direct participation in hostilities". As we will see below, the proponents of what we have called the "DPH-approach to internment" do not disavow this. On the contrary, they usually include indirect participants in hostilities in the category of persons that may be interned on the basis of GC IV.

Second, only actions that are of "direct" assistance to an enemy power qualify as a security threat for the purposes of articles 42§1 and 78 GC IV. Participation in the general war effort or propaganda or other political activity in favour of an adverse party do not meet the threshold for internment established in these provisions. As the ICTY pointed out in the *Delalić* case:

> "What appears to be included [...] is, above all, espionage, sabotage and intelligence activities for the enemy forces or enemy nationals. The clause cannot simply refer to an individual's political attitude towards the State. [...] there is no requirement that the particular activity in question must be judged as criminal under national a law [...] Clearly, a civilian cannot shoot a passing soldier, secrete a bomb in the enemy encampment, or otherwise directly and intentionally harm his enemy [...] However, all of these acts involve material, direct harm to the adversary, rather than merely granting support to the forces of the party which with the civilian is aligned."[1254]

---

weapons or participation in hostilities or acts of violence against the armed forces, but that in order to intern them the Interning Power must have serious and legitimate reasons to think that they present a threat to its present or future security and their internment is absolutely necessary to counter that threat. If so, they could only be lawfully interned as long as they continue to pose such a real threat (*cf. infra*).

[1252] We have not found any publicly available Israeli military doctrine, but the reliance on the notion of participation in hostilities is visible in Israel's legislation and case law regarding internment in armed conflict.

[1253] States and scholars who have attempted to establish a standard for detention by relying on the rules on targeting, do not distinguish between international and non-international armed conflicts. Their arguments rely on a direct application by analogy of the provisions of IHL for international armed conflicts in non-international armed conflict. We will argue in Part III that this assumption may be logical but is legally wrong, at least as the law stands today. Since their argument entirely relies on the law of international armed conflict, we find it more useful to address their "DPH-approach to internment" here.

[1254] ICTY, *Delalić* (1998), §§ 567-568. The text reflects the Trial Chamber's interpretation of article 5

(f.3). The "DPH-approach to internment": guidance from the rules on targeting?

Ever since the terrorist attacks against the US on 9 September 2001, the ensuing armed conflicts in Afghanistan and Iraq and the broader "war on terrorism" have sparked intense debates on the definition of an acceptable standard for interning persons arrested or captured in relation to these conflicts.[1255] At the same time, these "wars" have strongly influenced an already intense debate on the exact meaning of the words "direct participation of hostilities" in the rules on the conduct of hostilities. Neither one of these debates are entirely new, but they have intensified and taken new turns in the context of ongoing warfare and "law-fare" in Afghanistan and Iraq, and in the context of counter-terrorism operations around the world.

As is inevitable when debates on two closely related issues occur simultaneously and within the same (political, military, judicial, academic and non-governmental) circles, participants in the debate have at times borrowed concepts and arguments from one debate to push forward solutions in the other. While not without any merit, such endeavours are not without risk either. That risk is substantial where fundamental differences in the architecture of the rules governing these two similar, but ultimately distinct, issues are insufficiently taken into account.

What we have termed a "DPH-approach to internment" is at the time of writing only emerging. While the debate on the notion of DPH in the rules on the conduct of hostilities has advanced significantly over recent years, the debate on the utility of the notion for interpreting the rules on internment is only in an inchoate stage. In the present section, we will summarize the few existing examples of such a "DPH-approach to internment", assess the conformity of the arguments it relies upon with existing international law, and demonstrate the inherent risk of arbitrariness in an unqualified adoption of this approach to define the lawful grounds for internment in armed conflict of persons who do not qualify as prisoners of war. Before doing so, it is useful to recall the rules on targeting that are being relied upon by the proponents of the approach and the role of the notion of "direct participation in hostilities" therein.

(f.3.1). The rules on targeting and the notion of "direct participation in hostilities"

The rules on the conduct of hostilities are construed around the fundamental principle of distinction between combatants and civilians: only the first are legitimate military targets and may therefore be the object of direct attack. There is however one exception to this general rule: article 51 AP I provides that

---

GC IV, but it reflects the Tribunal's view of the meaning of Pictet's notion of "actions of direct assistance to an enemy power". *Cf. supra* notes 1142-1144 and accompanying text.

[1255] The qualification of the war on terrorism, and of the different stages in the Afghan and Iraqi conflicts is subject to some controversy. We have discussed the main points of contention and presented our position on the issue in chapter I-2, section 2.2.1.6 above. For our present purposes, what is of interest is the interpretation by proponents of the DPH-approach of the internment regime in GC IV, which they apply either directly or by analogy to all security internees in armed conflict.

civilians (defined as any person who does not belong to one of the categories of persons in article 4§A(1), (2), (3) and (6) GC III and article 43 AP I) may not be the object of attack "unless and for such time as they take a direct part in hostilities."[1256] This provision was adopted – in light of the reality of contemporary armed conflict, which has witnessed a trend of increased civilian participation in hostilities – to accommodate the need to redefine, within IHL treaty law, the balance between military necessity and the otherwise absolute prohibition to attack civilians.[1257]

Ever since the adoption of this rule, the need to clarify the precise meaning of the notion of "direct participation in hostilities" became more acute on the ground. In order to address that need, the ICRC and the TMC Asser Institute engaged in a five-year process of extensive consultations with legal experts from government, military, academic and non-governmental circles, which resulted in the publication by the ICRC of an *Interpretative Guidance on the Notion of Direct Participation in Hostilities under International Humanitarian Law.*[1258]

The *Interpretative Guidance* reflects the ICRC's official interpretation of the rule on civilians' loss of protection from attack, including its official legal reading of what type of behaviour amounts to direct participation in hostilities. It defines "hostilities" as the collective resort by parties to the conflict to means and methods of injuring the enemy, and "participation" as individual involvement in these hostilities.[1259] The crux of the matter then is to distinguish "direct" participation in hostilities from "indirect" or non-participation in hostilities.[1260] The *Interpretative Guidance* draws that (sometimes fine) line of distinction as follows:

> "The notion of direct participation in hostilities refers to specific acts carried out by individuals as part of the conduct of hostilities between the parties to an armed conflict. In order to qualify as direct participation in hostilities a specific act must meet the following cumulative criteria: (i) the act must be likely to adversely affect the military operations or military capacity of a party to an armed conflict,

---

[1256] Articles 50 and 51 AP I. The same rule is enshrined in 13§3 AP II. The rule is generally accepted to be part of customary IHL in both international and non-international armed conflict, see: Henckaerts & Doswald-Beck (2005), Rule 6, summarized in Vol. I, pp. 19-24, with references to international practice in Vol. II, pp. 107-133 and the updated *Customary IHL Database* (2010).

[1257] See the ICRC President's foreword to the *IGDPH* (2009), at pp. 4-5.

[1258] Both the *Interpretative Guidance* and the documents from the expert process are available at http://www.icrc.org/web/eng/siteeng0.nsf/html/direct-participation-article-020709. The expert meetings and the *Interpretative Guidance* also address two other questions that are indispensable to interpret articles 51 AP I and 13 AP II, namely (1) who is considered a civilian for the purposes of the of the principle of distinction? and (2) what modalities govern the loss of protection against direct attack? The *Interpretative Guidance* adopts a definition of membership of enemy armed forces that includes, for the purposes of the rules on the conduct of hostilities, persons who occupy a "continuous combat function" in the irregular armed forces of a State or in an organized armed group party to an armed conflict (ICRC, *IGDPH* (2009), pp. 31-36), a concept which we will come back to below.

[1259] ICRC, *IGDPH* (2009), p. 43.

[1260] The distinction was first developed by the UN Human Rights Commissions' Special Rapporteur for El Salvador (Mr. José Antonio Pastor Ridruejo) in his *Final Report on the Situation of Human Rights in El Salvador* to the Commission on Human *Rights (1*985), §32; and has also been used by the IAC°HR in its *Third Report Colombia* (1999), chapter IV, §§ 53-57.

> or alternatively to inflict death, injury, or destruction on persons or objects protected against direct attack (threshold of harm), and (ii) there must be a direct causal link between the act and the harm likely to result either from that act, or from a coordinated military operation of which the act constitutes an integral part (direct causation), and (iii) the act must be specifically designed to directly cause the required threshold of harm in support of a party to the conflict and to the detriment of another (belligerent nexus). Measures preparatory to the execution of a specific act of direct participation in hostilities, as well as the deployment to and the return from the location of its execution, constitute an integral part of that act."[1261]

It is with this definition of "direct participation in hostilities" that we will work here.[1262] For the purpose of the rules on the conduct of hostilities, it is not necessary to further define the notion of "indirect participation in hostilities", since any action that does not meet the threshold outlined above will not result in the perpetrator's loss of protection from attack.

The *Interpretative Guidance* further underlines that the notion of "direct participation in hostilities" has the same meaning in both international and non-international armed conflict,[1263] and does not refer to a person's status, function, or affiliation, but rather to his or her engagement in specific hostile acts.[1264] For our present purposes it is important to highlight from the outset that the ICRC has stressed that the *Interpretative Guidance*:

> "interprets the notion for the purposes of the conduct of hostilities only. Thus, apart from providing guidance on when and for how long a person is considered to have lost protection from direct attack, it does not address the consequences of direct participation in hostilities once he or she finds himself or

---

1261 ICRC, *IGDPH* (2009), pp. 16-17.

1262 While the *Interpretative Guidance* has been acclaimed as an important and certainly unprecedented contribution to the debate, not all its conclusions are entirely uncontroversial. For a good summary of the main criticism and a response by the author of the document, see the special issue of the *New York University Journal of International Law and Policy* (2010), with contributions from Boothby, "'And for Such Time as': The Time Dimension to Direct Participation in Hostilities"; Hays Parks, "Part IX of the ICRC 'Direct Participation in Hostilities' Study: No Mandate, No Expertise, and Legally Incorrect"; Melzer, "Keeping the Balance between Military Necessity and Humanity: A Response to Four Critiques of the ICRC's Interpretative Guidance on the Notion of Direct Participation in Hostilities"; Schmitt, "Deconstructing Direct Participation in Hostilities: The Constitutive Elements"; and Watkin, "Opportunity Lost: Organized Armed Groups and the ICRC 'Direct Participation in Hostilities' Interpretative Guidance." See also Schmitt (*Virg.JIL* 2010), pp. 831-837.

1263 ICRC, *IGDPH* (2009), pp. 44-45, with the proviso that "this does not exclude that some of the consequences, particularly with regard to immunity from prosecution for having participated directly in hostilities, may be regulated differently for the various categories of persons involved in international and non-international armed conflicts."

1264 ICRC, *IGDPH* (2009), p. 44. To illustrate its point, the *Interpretative Guidance* recalls that "[i]n treaty IHL, individual conduct that constitute part of the hostilities is described as direct participation in hostilities, regardless of whether the individual is a civilian or a member of the armed forces [as defined in articles 43§2, 51§3 and 67§1(e) AP I and article 13§3 AP II]. Whether individuals directly participate in hostilities on a spontaneous, sporadic, or unorganized basis or as part of a continuous function assumed for an organized armed force or group belonging to a party to the conflict may be decisive for their status as civilians, but has no influence on the scope of conduct that constitutes direct participation in hostilities."

herself in the adversary's hands. Other rules of international humanitarian law then govern"; and that

"its conclusions are not intended to serve as a basis for interpreting IHL regulating the status, rights and protections of persons outside the conduct of hostilities, such as those deprived of their liberty."[1265]

(f.3.2). Examples of the "DPH-approach" to internment

The following are examples of approaches relying essentially on the rules on targeting to define the standard for lawful security internment of persons other than prisoners of war. In essence, proponents of such approaches claim that persons who have directly participated in hostilities or who are members of groups that engage in hostilities against the Interning Power may be subject to automatic internment, and, according to some, for the duration of hostilities.

- *Examples from State practice*

At the time of writing, two examples of State practice reflect the DPH-approach to internment. Both examples define the standard for lawful internment of persons other than prisoners of war on the basis of (1) the person's participation in hostilities against the Interning Power, or (2) the person's membership in an organized armed group engaged in hostilities against the Interning Power.

The Israeli *Incarceration of Unlawful Combatants Law* (2002) (*IUCL*) allows for the internment of "unlawful combatants." It defines unlawful combatant as a person who is not prisoner of war but who either:

"has participated either directly or indirectly in hostile acts against the State of Israel" or

"is a member of a force perpetrating hostile acts against the State of Israel."[1266]

The *Authorization of the Use of Military Force* (*AUMF*) *Act* adopted by Congress in the wake of the 9/11 authorizes the President of the United States:

"to use all necessary and appropriate force against those nations, organizations, or persons he determines planned, authorized, committed, or aided the terrorist attacks that occurred on September 11, 2001, or harbored such organizations or persons, in order to prevent any future acts of international terrorism against the United States by such nations, organizations or persons."[1267]

The US Supreme Court has held that "necessary and appropriate force" includes "the power to detain combatants subject to such force."[1268] The standard for internment adopted by the US in Guantánamo and Afghanistan has evolved over time, but keeps revolving around the same essential concepts. According to the current US administration, the *AUMF*, informed by the laws of war, allows

[1265] ICRC, *IGDPH* (2009), pp. 7 and 11 respectively.
[1266] Israel, *IUCL* (2002), article 2. The full text of the law is reproduced in Annex B.
[1267] US, *AUMF* (2001), article 1.
[1268] US, SC, *Hamdi* (2004), p. 519.

the internment for the duration of hostilities of persons who do not qualify as prisoners of war but who:

> "planned, authorized, committed, or aided the terrorist attacks that occurred on September 11, 2001" or "harbored those responsible for those attacks"; or
>
> "were part of, or substantially supported, Taliban or al-Qaida forces or associated forces that are engaged in hostilities against the United States or its coalition partners, including any person who has committed a belligerent act, or has directly supported hostilities, in aid of such enemy armed forces." [1269]

We have dealt with the membership standard above. In the present section, the reliance on the notion of participation in hostilities as a standard for internment is of interest. Both Israeli and US practice are essentially based on the argument that a person who has participated in hostilities against the Interning Power (and its allies in the case of the US) may be subject to internment for the duration of hostilities. Nevertheless, the fact that the membership and the participation-in-hostilities approaches go hand in hand is illustrated by the following remarks from the US State Department's chief legal advisor:

> "Some commentators have criticized our decision to detain certain individuals based on their membership in a non-state armed group. But as those of you who follow the Guantánamo habeas litigation know, we have defended this position based on the AUMF, as informed by the text, structure, and history of the Geneva Conventions and other sources of the laws of war. Moreover, while the various judges who have considered these arguments have taken issue with certain points, they have accepted the overall proposition that individuals who are part of an organized armed group like al-Qaeda can be subject to law of war detention for the duration of the current conflict. In sum, we have based our authority to detain not on conclusory labels, like 'enemy combatant,' but on whether the factual record in the particular case meets the legal standard. This includes, but is not limited to, whether an individual joined with or became part of al-Qaeda or Taliban forces or associated forces, which can be demonstrated by relevant evidence of formal or functional membership, which may include an oath of loyalty, training with al-Qaeda, or taking positions with enemy forces. Often these factors operate in combination. While we disagree with the International Committee of the Red Cross on some of the particulars, our general approach of looking at "functional" membership in an armed group has been endorsed not only by the federal courts, but also is consistent with the approach taken in the targeting context by the ICRC in its recent study on Direct Participation in Hostilities (DPH)."[1270]

[1269] US, DoD standard of detention at Bagram internment facility in Afghanistan (quoted in *Wahid et al. v. Gates et al.*, Petition for Writ of Habeas Corpus (2010), §38). The DoD standards reflect the definition of enemy belligerent in the US *Military Commissions Act* (2009), Title XVIII, section 948a(7): "The term 'unprivileged enemy belligerent' means an individual (other than a privileged belligerent) who ''(A) has engaged in hostilities against the United States or its coalition partners; ''(B) has purposefully and materially supported hostilities against the United States or its coalition partners; or ''(C) was a part of al Qaeda at the time of the alleged offense under this chapter."

[1270] Koh, "The Obama Administration and International Law" (2010). The membership approach has also been followed by the US courts; for a summary of the leading cases see Patel, "Who Can Be Detained in 'the War on Terror'?" (*ASIL Insights* 2009), p. 2. For a recent example concerning conflict

Irrespective of how the issue is presented, the Israeli and US approaches to the internment of so-called unlawful combatants are clearly based on the idea that a person who can be killed according to the rules on targeting may, automatically, also be interned for the duration of hostilities. By relying on a DPH-approach to internment, both Israel and the US effectively import the rules on internment of the Third Geneva Convention into the Fourth Geneva Convention. We will now examine the work of two scholars who have attempted to rhyme this approach with existing (or allegedly emerging) rules of international humanitarian law regarding internment in armed conflict.[1271]

• *Waxman: detention as targeting*

In an article aptly entitled "Detention as Targeting", Matthew Waxman seeks to answer the question of the lawful grounds for internment in the conflict that opposes the US to Al-Qaeda. Waxman correctly points out that neither the law of war[1272] nor US criminal law provides an answer to that question. In order to fill that gap and answer the question, he proposes a methodology for further developing either international or domestic US law in a way that is "derived from basic law of war principles", and he claims that:

> "in looking to the law of war as a possible starting point, one should focus not on *detention law* – the body of international humanitarian law primarily concerned with the treatment conditions under which captured enemy fighters are held [...] but on *targeting* law."[1273]

Waxman's arguments can be summarized as follows: (1) the authorization to use force against an individual includes an authorization to intern that person, but such force may only be used when necessary; (2) to determine what is necessary, a balance must be struck between military necessity on the one hand and an individual's right to life or liberty on the other hand; (3) in the absence of a standard in IHL to determine who can be interned, lawmakers could look for inspiration in the standard in IHL that determines who can be lawfully targeted in the conduct of hostilities.

---

in Afghanistan, see US, District Court, *Shawali Khan v. Obama et al.* (2010), as referred to in Stemple, "Federal Judge Allows Indefinite Detention of Guantánamo Detainee", *Jurist*, 7 September 2010 (the decision itself was not yet publicly available at the time of writing).

1271 Both Waxman and Goodman attempt to define the lawful grounds for interning suspected terrorists in the so-called war on terrorism. Apart from our critique below, we have two problems with the authors' point of departure to answer that question. First, we do not agree with the position that the global "war on terrorism" is an armed conflict as such; the reliance upon IHL to determine who may be detained in that "war" is therefore *ab initio* misguided (*cf. supra* chapter I-2, section 2.2.1.6). Second, in as far the situation in any specific theatre in the "war on terrorism" amounts to non-international armed conflict, we disagree with their suggestion that the internment provisions of the Geneva Conventions may serve as a legal basis for internment *per analogiam*, since that suggestion negates one of the most fundamental principles of the rule of law, namely the principle of legality (*cf. supra* chapter I-1 and *infra* chapter III-1). Waxman does seems to recognize this, as the purpose of his analysis is to explore the utility of seeking guidance in the rules on targeting for further developing international humanitarian law where it lacks a legal basis to intern.

1272 Waxman (*CLR* 2008), p. 1379.

1273 Waxman (*CLR* 2008), pp. 1367-1368 (original emphasis).

The problem with that argument is twofold. First, it starts from the controversial premise that detention is a form of targeting,[1274] and therefore part of the means and methods of conducting hostilities. As we will demonstrate below, this is not a correct presentation of the law.[1275] Second, Waxman disregards the fact that international humanitarian law *does* establish a standard to determine the grounds on which a person who does not qualify as a prisoner of war may be interned, and thus *does* provide answers to his questions.[1276] These grounds are prescribed by article 42§1 GC IV as far as the territory of the Interning Power is concerned and by article 78 GC IV for internment in occupied territory. There is therefore *a priori* no need to look at the rules on targeting to define that standard.

• *Goodman and the rules on targeting: a license to kill, a license to detain?*

In an article entitled "The Detention of Civilians in Armed Conflict", Ryan Goodman essentially seeks to answer the same question Waxman raised in his "Detention as Targeting."[1277] Goodman is more explicit in outlining some of the arguments that also seem to underpin Waxman's proposed methodology to fill the perceived gap in IHL, and the US and Israeli standards for internment referred to above. We will therefore present and discuss his work in more detail. While we agree with Goodman that "the confusion surrounding the current and future direction of U.S. detention policy stems in significant part from [...] misconceptions or misuses of [international humanitarian] law", and that many of its opponents rejected that policy all-out "without acknowledging the existing legal authority to detain the same individuals regardless of nomenclature", we do not share his analysis of the legal regime governing internment in armed conflict, nor his analysis of how that regime relates to the rules on targeting.

Goodman summarizes his analysis (which also includes military commission trials) in a matrix entitled "Actions permitted by international law":[1278]

[1274] Waxman (*CLR* 2008), pp. 1386 and 1394: "a decision to detain someone suspected of being an enemy combatant closely resembles a targeting exercise: It is a judgment that the individual is part of an enemy military organization and therefore subject to the application of military force, in this case physical incapacitation. [...] After all, the problem of differentiating enemy terrorist fighters from among the surrounding civilian population is really a problem of targeting: Is the individual an enemy fighter (i.e. a military target) and therefore subject to attack with force (i.e. capture and detention)?" Waxman's analysis is clearly based on the – erroneous – conception that all combatants are prisoners of war and *vice versa*, and on the corollary misconception that any "combatant" can be lawfully interned for the duration of hostilities (*cf. supra* chapter II-1, section 1.1.1).

[1275] In the same sense: Lubell (2010), p. 145.

[1276] We agree with Waxman that existing IHL does not offer these answers for situations of NIAC. Nevertheless, when exploring how to define internment standards for such situations, it would still make more sense to seek guidance in the internment rules of IHL in IAC than in its targeting rules. And the internment provisions of the Geneva Conventions are not – as Waxman seems to suggest – only concerned with the treatment in captivity, but also prescribe who can be interned on the basis of IHL, for what reasons and for how long.

[1277] Goodman (*AJIL* 2009). Contrary to Waxman, whose analysis is intended to feed into debate and reflection on further development of international humanitarian law or US domestic law, Goodman suggests his arguments reflect IHL as it stands.

[1278] Goodman (*AJIL* 2009), p. 56 (modifications are for format purposes and do not affect the substance).

SUBJECTS	COERCIVE MEASURES		
	I. TARGETING	II. MILITARY TRIAL	III. DETENTION
A. Members of regular/irregular armed forces that meet GC III or AP I criteria	(1) YES	(2) YES	(3) YES
B. Direct participants in hostilities ("unlawful combatants")	(4) YES	(5) YES	(6) YES
C. Indirect participants in hostilities (imperative security threats)	(7) NO	(8) NO?	(9) YES
D. Nonparticipants in hostilities ("innocent civilians")	(10) NO	(11) NO?	(12) NO

Our unease with Goodman's interpretation, or at least presentation of some of the substantive rules on internment (column III), originates in a more fundamental disagreement with some of the premises it relies upon. These can be summarized as follows: (1) "The central question is whether IHL prohibits the preventive detention of civilians who pose a security threat on account of their direct or indirect participation in hostilities"; the answer to that question is no, because (2) "it would be absurd to accept an interpretation of IHL that results in a state's possessing the legal authority to kill actor *X* on purpose but lacking the legal authority to detain actor *X*"; and because (3) "if the law permits a state to subject *lawful* combatants to measure *Y*, the law a fortiori permits states to subject *unlawful* combatants to that same measure."[1279] On the basis of these premises, Goodman establishes "macro-connections" between the cells in the matrix above: if the answer in cells 1 and 4 are yes, the answers in cells 6 and 9 must also be yes; and if the answer in cells 1 and 3 are yes, then the answers in cells 4 and 6 must also be yes. These macro-connections result in conclusions on the rules on internment that fail to take into account the substance of these rules themselves and fail to nuance the answers to the question in column III.

(f.3.3). Critique of the "DPH-approach" to internment

We have a number of problems with the DPH-approach to internment as reflected in the above four examples. They concern both the premises on which the approach is being construed and the interpretation of the international norms on internment in armed conflict of persons other than prisoners of war (namely articles 42§1 and 78 GC IV).

We will not discuss column II since it has no direct relevance for our subject-matter. For the same reason, we will discuss column I only in as far as it relates, according to Goodman, to column III. We work on the assumption that the title of the 3rd column ("Detention"), refers only to security internment as permitted by GC IV and not to detention in the framework of criminal proceedings (which seems to be the subject of column II).

1279 The quotes are from Goodman (*AJIL* 2009), pp. 49, 55 and 56 (original italics).

• *The nature of IHL and the articulation of the central question*

First, we respectfully disagree, for reasons discussed in the introduction to this book and in its chapter I-2, with Goodman's articulation of the nature of IHL and its relation with international human rights law. For Goodman and other proponents of a DPH-approach to internment, IHL's permissive rules (like the ones that authorize the use of lethal force and internment) reflect to what extent States have restricted their – otherwise unrestricted – scope of lawful action in armed conflict. For this reason, it is considered that measures dictated by military necessity that are not explicitly prohibited in IHL, cannot but be in conformity with international law.[1280] In our view, IHL's permissive rules rather define to what extent States can depart in situations of armed conflict from the general regime of applicable international law, leads of course to the opposite conclusion: what is prohibited by that general regime (notably by the norms of IHRL) and not clearly authorized by IHL remains prohibited under international law.[1281] Therefore, the ultimate question is not whether IHL *prohibits* the internment of persons other than prisoners of war, but rather whether IHL *allows* for such internment, and whether it provides a valid legal basis clearly prescribing its grounds and procedures. The answer to that last question varies depending on the type of armed conflict in which the issue arises and the degree to which the person concerned poses a threat to the security of the Interning Power. Only when that question can be answered in the affirmative can we conclude that IHL not only *authorizes,* but also *provides a legal basis* for, a particular form of internment in armed conflict.[1282]

• *The different structure of the normative frameworks for targeting and internment*

The rules on targeting and internment have two important things in common – at least they do in situations of international armed conflict and occupation.[1283]

First, both aim to protect the civilian population from the effects of hostilities, while at the same time allowing parties to the conflict to neutralize

---

[1280] Goodman (*AJIL* 2009), particularly at pp. 50 and 56-57. Goodman recognizes that international human rights law "might complicate [his account of IHL]" but does not explain how, nor does he integrate any human rights norms in his analysis, possibly because he considers them to only "impose obligations on the exercise of state power domestically and not extraterritorially" (Goodman (*AJIL* 2009), p. 50 and footnote 9), a position that in our view can no longer be defended today (*cf. supra* note 36).

[1281] *Cf. supra* chapter I-2, section 2.2.2.2. In the same sense, see Meron (2006), p. 27: "The [Martens] Clause [...] supports the argument that what is not prohibited by treaty [IHL] may not necessarily be lawful."

[1282] We have seen in the present part that internment is explicitly authorized by IHL in situations of international armed conflict and occupation, but we will see in Part III that this is not (yet) the case for situations of non-international armed conflict.

[1283] While article 51§3 AP I has an identical counterpart in article 13§3 AP II (*cf. supra* notes 593, 1255 and 1257), articles 41-43 and 78 GC IV do not have such a counterpart in IHL for non-international armed conflict (*cf. supra* note 1252 and accompanying text; for more detail on the absence of combatant and prisoner of war status and the resulting absence of a direct legal basis in IHL to intern members of the armed forces of non-State parties to non-international armed conflict *cf. infra* chapter III-1).

persons posing a direct threat. In order to achieve that goal, the rules strike a balance between an individual's right to life or liberty and the legitimate military and security needs of the parties to the conflict.

Second, to accommodate the two most essential requirements of military necessity – defeating the enemy and protecting one's own forces from defeat – the two sets of rules allow parties to an armed conflict to depart from general international law on the right to life and the right to liberty (as required by military necessity), and define the extent to which such departure is allowed (according to the limits imposed by the principle of humanity). In this sense both the rules on targeting and those on internment define lawful exceptions to general human rights norms in situations of (international) armed conflict and occupation. Article 51 AP I reaffirms the principle that civilians may not be the object of direct attack, but accommodates essential military and security needs by suspending that protection when and for such time as civilians take a direct part in hostilities. Articles 27§4, 42§1 and 78 GC IV reaffirm the principle that persons other than prisoners of war may not be deprived of liberty except on criminal charges, but authorizes their internment when and for as long as it is absolutely necessary to counter any military or security threat they may pose.[1284]

Despite these similarities, the structure and substance of the two legal regimes are fundamentally different. These differences reflect the different starting points of each regime. The use of lethal force against persons who directly participate in hostilities, civilians and combatants alike, is generally allowed in order to place them *hors de combat*. Internment, however, aims to prevent a person who is already *hors de combat* from posing a threat to the Interning Power's future security. The internment of persons other than prisoners of war is therefore only permitted in exceptional circumstances. While in some cases this may not seem *logical*, this is how the law, as it stands today is designed. The attempts to establish lawful grounds for internment by reliance on the rules on targeting fail to recognize this fundamentally different conception of the two sets of rules, resulting in an insufficiently nuanced presentation of these rules in the matrix reproduced above.

To illustrate his views of the structure of the rules on internment, as informed by the rules on targeting, Goodman distinguishes the following four categories of individuals: "(A) regular armed forces and irregular armed forces that meet the criteria of the Third Geneva Convention or Additional Protocol I; (B) direct

[1284] The balance struck by articles 51 AP I, 13 AP II and articles 42§1 and 78 GC IV is inherent in those rules and cannot be readjusted in favour of military or security concerns that go beyond those already taken into account. It is submitted however that – at least as international armed conflict and occupation are concerned – the lawful grounds for internment are sufficiently broad to accommodate all legitimate military and security needs. As Sassòli rightly points out: international humanitarian law "has not been drafted by professional do-gooders or professors, but by experienced diplomats and military leaders, fully taking into account the security needs of a state confronted with dangerous people" (Sassòli (*JICJ* 2004), p. 104). The same holds true for treaties of international human rights law, they have been drafted and adopted not by human rights activists but by States, taking into account the need in any democratic society to strike an appropriate balance between national security and collective interests on the one hand and individual rights and freedoms on the other hand.

participants in hostilities; (C) civilians who are indirect participants in hostilities; and (D) civilians who are nonparticipants in hostilities."[1285] While the rules on the conduct of hostilities indeed distinguish rather neatly between categories A and B on the one hand and categories C and D on the other hand, the Geneva Conventions' provisions on internment only distinguish between prisoners of war (Goodman's category A), whose internment is regulated by GC III, and persons other than prisoners of war (including Goodman's categories B, C and D), whose internment is invariably regulated by GC IV.[1286] As a result of Goodman's classification and the macro-connections he establishes between them (based on the postulates we will discuss in sections c.3 and c.4 below), the conclusions in cells 4 and 6 lack the nuance that is necessary to prevent arbitrary deprivations of life and of liberty.[1287] That lack of nuance in the presentation of the rules on targeting and the rules on internment stems directly from the reliance on two controversial "postulates of IHL", to which we will turn our attention now.[1288] Goodman claims that any interpretation of IHL that contravenes these general postulates should be considered suspect or implausible. We respectfully submit that none of these postulates[1289] – framed in absolute terms and applied as they are to the rules on internment in IHL – reflect either generally accepted interpretations or firmly established norms of international law.[1290]

[1285] Goodman (*AJIL* 2009), p. 51; see also the matrix reproduced above.

[1286] With the exception of medical and religious personnel of the armed forces of the parties to the conflict, who enjoy a special status in international humanitarian law, *cf. supra* chapter II.2.

[1287] To properly nuance the conclusion in cell 4, category B should be split up in two sub-categories. Persons who occupy a continuous combat function in an organized armed group that fights on behalf of a party to the conflict but does not meet the criteria in article 4§A(2) GC III or article 43 AP I, may be lawfully targeted at all times, the answer in cell 4.1 would thus be "yes". On the contrary, civilians who directly participate in hostilities but do not occupy such a continuous combat function in an organized armed group that fights on behalf of a party to the conflict may only be lawfully targeted for as long as their specific act of participation in hostilities lasts. The answer in cell 4.2. would therefore be "yes, for as long as the specific instance of direct participation in hostilities lasts." See also ICRC, *IGDPH* (2009), pp. 70-73 and *infra* our conclusions on the DPH-approach to internment.

[1288] For the formulation of these postulates by Goodman, *cf. supra* note 1279 and accompanying text.

[1289] Apart from the ones discussed in sections c.3 and c-4 below, Goodman (*AJIL* 2009) advances two other postulates to justify the conclusions in his matrix. We will not discuss the postulate that "it is not illogical for a state to have the power to kill actor *X* deliberately, but to lack the power to prosecute actor *X*" (at pp. 56-57) since it does not have any bearing on the subject-matter of our research; it is however the only postulate with which we fully agree. To justify the applicability of his matrix in both international and non-international armed conflicts Goodman says it is uncontroversial that: "if states are permitted to exercise a power in international armed conflict (e.g. to detain civilians), states *a fortiori* are permitted to exercise that power in noninternational [sic] armed conflict." We disagree with this postulate for two reasons. First, we do not agree with Goodman's views on the nature of IHL (what is not prohibited is allowed) (*cf. supra* notes 1278-1279 and accompanying text). Second, we do not agree with the methodology of legal analogy applied to fill a perceived gap in the law of non-international armed conflict regarding a legal basis for internment (*cf. infra* chapter III-1).

[1290] In light of the almost complete convergence of the rules on the conduct of hostilities in international and non-international armed conflict, Goodman's postulates may well be less controversial as far as these rules are concerned.

• *Does a license to kill automatically include a license to intern?*

Proponents of a DPH-approach to internment claim that it would be absurd if international humanitarian law authorized the parties to the conflict to kill a person but did not authorize to intern that same person. In essence, they argue that the license to kill – allegedly granted by the rules on targeting in IHL – *a fortiori* includes a license to intern.[1291]

We agree that a State may *capture* any person it may lawfully kill – including a civilian directly participating in hostilities – but disagree that it can therefore automatically *intern* any such person. While this is without doubt the logic behind articles 21 and 118 GC III and the postulate therefore holds true for persons in category A, the same logic does not lie behind GC IV, which apply to categories B, C and D, and that logic is reflected in its internment provisions: under GC IV internment is the exception rather than the rule, and may never be automatic.

The postulate seems to draw at least partly on the concept of self-defence in the face of an imminent threat. If a soldier may kill a person to defend himself or his comrades, surely he may intern that same person for the duration of hostilities? The right to self-defence in the face of an imminent threat allows a soldier to put a person directly participating in hostilities *hors de combat.* At the time a decision to intern is taken however, the person subject to that decision is already *hors de combat* – through surrender, capture or arrest – and his or her participation in hostilities has thus by definition come to an end.[1292] From that moment onwards, the person has fallen into the hands of an enemy power and is protected by GC IV.[1293] As we have seen above, and Goodman points out himself elsewhere, the status of these persons as "civilians" or more appositely "protected persons under GC IV" is not affected by their participation in hostilities, that participation only suspends their protection from direct attack for as long as it lasts.[1294] Once a person is effectively captured and put *hors de combat,* he poses no imminent threat and the question of self-defence no longer arises.[1295] At that time, a careful analysis must be made as to whether the State

[1291] Some scholars also contest the fact that IHL give the parties to the conflict a "license to kill", see e.g. Melzer (2008), pp. 286-289.

[1292] See for example Pictet, *Commentary GC I* (1952), p. 259: "troops are most often *captured* nowadays in large groups, following encircling operations. When a body of troops is *surrounded in this manner and disarmed, it is sent behind the lines, where the sorting out process begins*" (emphasis added).

[1293] Unless the person is protected under GC III, namely where he or she can be lawfully *presumed* to be a prisoner of war, and until a tribunal in accordance with article 5 GC III has determined his or her final status. Both Conventions apply as soon as a person has fallen into the hands of the enemy, and not only as from the time of their internment; *cf. supra* II-1, section 1.1 and chapter II-3, section 3.1.

[1294] ICRC, *IGDPH* (2009), pp. 11 and 13; Goodman (*AJIL* 2009), p. 53. Note however that according to the ICRC's *IGDPH*, persons who occupy a continuous combat function in an organized armed group fighting on behalf of a party to the conflict are not – at least not where for the purposes of the rules on targeting – civilians and may therefore be subject to attack at all times. Note however that membership in the armed forces of a party to the conflict does not automatically mean the person is also a prisoner of war, *cf. supra* chapter II-1.

[1295] In the same sense: Gehring (*MLLWR* 1980), p. 63: "Once a civilian is captured, his hostile acts

has serious and legitimate reasons to think that that particular person represents a real threat to its present or future security, and that no other, less restrictive measures of control could adequately meet that threat.[1296]

Goodman himself accepts that there may be exceptions to his general rule. Unfortunately he does not do so in an unequivocally affirmative manner, he only mentions in a footnote that "[t]here may be an exception to this rule if (1) an individual's mere membership in the armed forces renders her a legitimate target, and (2) mere membership is insufficient and an additional inquiry into the nature and the scale of the individual's contribution is required for detention."[1297] He notes however that both of these propositions have been qualified.

As to the first proposition, he recalls an ICTY ruling that "membership of the armed forces can be a strong indication that the victim is directly participating in hostilities, it is not an indicator which in and of itself is sufficient to establish this."[1298] On the other hand, the ICRC in its *Interpretative Guidance* adopts a broad definition of armed forces for the purposes of hostilities and considers persons who occupy a continuous combat function in organized armed groups that fight on behalf of a party to the conflict to be members of their armed forces. While the ICRC explicitly stated that the conclusions in the *IGDPH* are not intended to serve the interpretation of the rules on status or on internment, the *Interpretative Guidance* seems to have led at least the US State Department's legal advisor to believe that persons who occupy such a continuous combat function may – just like members of armed forces who qualify for prisoner of war status – be interned for the duration of hostilities.[1299] We respectfully disagree with the US legal advisor's position, but he and other proponents of the DPH-approach to internment may be expected to continue to push their arguments forward.

As to the second proposition – that mere membership in armed forces is insufficient and that the individual must pose an individual threat to qualify for internment on the basis of GC IV – Goodman recognizes that it has indeed been upheld by the Israeli Supreme Court in *A and B v. Israel* (2008), a case we have dealt with extensively above.[1300] In that same case, the Court made an important observation, confirming the different conception of the rules on targeting, which

---

cease. No longer is there any compelling requirement for immediate action; his submission has been achieved."

[1296] Waxman highlights the temporal dimension inherent in detention that makes it different from targeting, but suggests this can be made good by insisting on periodic review of internment (Waxman (*CLR* 2008), pp. 1406-1429). It would be useful to add to his analysis and recommendations the fact that contrary to most targeting decisions, the decision to intern is not taken in the heat of combat nor by the individual soldier on the battlefield; and the need for a continued review of the necessity of the internment to be carried out by the interning authorities themselves (and not only the review authorities), *cf. supra* section 3.2.1.6.

[1297] Goodman (*AJIL* 2009), note 41 at pp. 55-56

[1298] ICTY, *Halilović* (2005), §34.

[1299] *Cf. supra* note 1269 and accompanying text.

[1300] Israel, SC, *A and B v. Israel* (2008), §21, quoted in full above (*cf. supra* note 1194).

it had dealt with in the *Targeted Killings case* (2006); and the rules on internment, which were at stake in the case of *A and B v. Israel* case (2008):

> "it should be emphasized that *prima facie* the statutory definition of 'unlawful combatant' [in the *Incarceration of Unlawful Combatants Law*] applies to a broader group of people than the group of 'unlawful combatants' discussed in [the *Targeted Killings case*], in view of the difference in the measures under discussion: the judgment in [the *Targeted Killings case*] considered the legality of the measure of a military operation intended to cause the death of an 'unlawful combatant.' According to international law, it is permitted to attack an 'unlawful combatant' only during the period of time when he is taking a *direct* part in the hostilities. By contrast, the Internment of Unlawful Combatants Law addresses the measure of internment. [...] our reference to the judgment in [the *Targeted Killings case*] was not intended to indicate that an identical issue was considered in that case. Its purpose was to support the finding that the term 'unlawful combatants' in the law under discussion does not create a separate category of treatment from the viewpoint of international humanitarian law, but constitutes a sub-group of the category of 'civilians.'"[1301]

It is unfortunate that Goodman does not endorse the position of the Israeli Supreme Court on the fact that membership of an organization engaged in hostilities is not sufficient to meet the threshold for internment in articles 42§1 and 78 GC IV. That position is not an "absurd" interpretation of IHL; rather it nuances his general postulate in a way that renders it more conform with existing international humanitarian law.

• *Lawful and unlawful combatants: de* lex lata *et de* lege ferenda

In order to justify the conclusions in cells 4 and 6 of his matrix, Goodman puts forward the postulate that "if the law permits a state to subject *lawful* combatants to measure *Y*, the law a fortiori permits states to subject *unlawful* combatants to that same measure." Again, the postulate is based on logic rather than on international humanitarian law itself.

While the postulate may hold true to a large extent for the rules on targeting (if cell 1 is positive, cell 4 will also be positive),[1302] it does not reflect the fundamental distinction in the rules on internment between prisoners of war and persons who do not qualify as such: whereas cell 3 will almost always be positive (*cf. supra*: subject to a very limited number of exceptions, articles 21 and 118 GC III explicitly allow for the internment of prisoners of war for the duration of the hostilities), the same is not true for cell 6. Cell 6 applies to persons who participate directly in hostilities but do not meet the criteria in GC III or AP I to qualify as prisoners of war. These persons by definition are not within the scope of application of GC III but in that of GC IV. The internment provisions of the Fourth Geneva Convention do not allow for the automatic internment for the duration of hostilities that is allowed for prisoners of war under GC III. Articles 42§1 and

---

[1301] Israel, SC, *A and B v. Israel* (2008), §12.

[1302] Goodman (*AJIL* 2009), p. 56. See however our reservations on such an automatic conclusion for all persons in Goodman's category B, as expressed *supra* in note 1286.

78 GC IV require that the interning authority establishes that the individual person concerned represents a threat to its present or future security, that no alternative measure can counter that threat, and that the person be released as soon as the reasons for his or her internment cease to exist. We have seen above that membership in the armed forces (as defined broadly *supra* chapter II-1, section 1.1.2.1) may be strong evidence for establishing a security threat, but is not by itself sufficient to justify internment on the basis of article 42§1 or 78 GC IV.

There may be arguments to support a claim that the law *should* allow parties to the conflict to deal with lawful and so-called unlawful combatants alike. Indeed, military personnel on the ground – far from political considerations – often do not distinguish between lawful and unlawful combatants. Nevertheless the law as it stands *does not* allow parties to the conflict to intern so-called unlawful combatants on the same basis as it may intern prisoners of war. Goodman's proposition that the State may treat lawful and unlawful combatants alike may, at the most, be *de lege ferenda* but it is definitely not *lex lata* today.[1303]

Moreover, in our view most States are not willing to assimilate unlawful combatants to lawful combatants. With some minor exceptions, so-called lawful combatants are entitled to prisoner of war status and combatant immunity upon capture.[1304] While an expansion of GC III to unlawful combatants would most likely make sense on the ground, it is highly unlikely that States would be ready to amend IHL in this sense. If States continue to insist that members of organized armed groups fighting on behalf of a party to the conflict who occupy a continuous combat function in such a group are *unlawful* combatants and not prisoners of war, it means that they confirm the law as it stands today.

• *Lawful grounds for internment: guidance from the rules on internment*

One of the main problems with the emerging DPH-approach to internment is that it starts from the assumption that the rules on internment do not provide answers to the question it seeks to answer, namely on what grounds persons other than prisoners of war may be interned.[1305] By making that assumption, proponents of the approach seem to ignore the fact that articles 42§1 and 78 GC IV do define those grounds: persons who by their activities, knowledge or

[1303] Even for it to be *de lege ferenda*, there does not so far seem to be much practice to support such a claim.

[1304] Admittedly, combatant immunity does not flow from prisoner of war status itself, but rather from combatant status. This is demonstrated by the fact that there are prisoners of war (namely those referred to in article 4§A(4) and (5) GC III) who are not entitled to combatant immunity because they are not entitled to combatant status. Nevertheless, in light of the sheer majority of prisoners of war also being combatants (as members of the armed forces of a party to the conflict), the entitlement of (so-called lawful) combatants to both combatant immunity and prisoner of war status upon capture makes that the two concepts are closely connected in States' minds (even if clearly separated in law) and has always greatly affected any debates on enlarging the definition of prisoners of war for the purposes of the Third Geneva Convention (*cf. supra* chapter II-1).

[1305] To the extent that such an argument applies to IHL for NIAC alone, it is indeed correct. Nevertheless, any guidance to identify lawful grounds for internment in NIAC should be sought in the internment provisions of IHL for IAC rather than in its rules on the conduct of hostilities. *Cf. infra* Part III.

qualifications represent a real threat to the security of the Interning Power, may be subject to internment for as long as they pose such a threat and no alternative measures are available to counter that threat (*cf. supra*).

In most cases of "unlawful combatants", it should not be difficult to meet that threshold. A person who may reasonably be expected to engage in acts that would amount to direct participation in hostilities as defined in the rules on targeting represents a security threat in the sense of articles 42§1 and 78 GC IV. Membership in enemy armed forces or in other organized armed groups engaged in hostilities against the Interning Power is strong evidence for establishing that the person represents such a threat. And if criminal proceedings are not a viable option or do not allow for preventive detention, it should not be difficult to establish that there are no alternative measures of control that can counter the threat.

In light of the grounds for internment prescribed by articles 42§1 and 78 GC IV, there is *a priori* no need to seek guidance in the rules on targeting to determine who may be interned on the basis of that Convention.

• *Inherent risks in a DPH-approach to internment*

Before we conclude, let us point out some of the risks inherent in a DPH-approach to internment. First, it places a strong emphasis on both the past behaviour of a potential internee and on his or her membership in an armed group. While these are indeed strong indicators of the potential threat a person may pose, they should not be presented as by themselves sufficient to order internment.

Second, as far as persons who do not qualify as prisoners of war are concerned, no automatic conclusions may be drawn from their classification under the rules on targeting to determine whether they may be subject to internment. If we consider Goodman's matrix again, and the postulates it relies upon, it seems difficult to avoid the matrix being used to develop policies that effectively do away with some of the essential features of internment on the basis of GC IV. Both decision-makers and those who review internment decisions may be tempted to conclude that the relationships between the different cells of the matrix – or as Goodman calls them "the macroconnections between classes of individuals and coercive measures" – are automatic.[1306] This

[1306] Waxman recognizes this risk indeed exists and must be taken into account when designing a legal basis to intern in IHL for NIAC: "I note at this point, though, that conceiving of detention as targeting and detention of innocents along with terrorists as 'collateral damage' might dangerously be used to justify mass detentions. Although using a proportionality analysis to help justify detaining everyone in the vicinity might make sense in extreme cases of, for example, an unidentified terrorist believed to have a suitcase nuclear bomb in a crowded neighborhood, a targeting approach generally would not justify overbroad detention practices. First, proportionality is only one of a number of legal rules that should constrain detention; detentions themselves require some independent legal basis, in this case either a belief that a particular individual is an enemy combatant or some other authority. In this regard detentions differ from other military targeting in that detaining individuals not believed to be legitimate military targets is off limits, absent other legal grounds for doing so, whereas in many conventional targeting contexts it is lawful to intentionally strike known civilians along with military targets so long as proportionality is satisfied. Second [...], targeting rules require

risk is exacerbated by the fact that only two of the 12 cells in the matrix are accompanied by a question mark, leaving the reader to think that the others are a matter of uncontroversial law.

The lack of nuance in the DPH-approach to internment is dangerous in that it invites decision-makers and review bodies to effectively install legal presumptions of the kind that are contrary to the text and the spirit of the Fourth Geneva Convention. We have seen examples of this risk materializing in both the Israeli *IUCL* (*cf. supra* on the legal presumption in article 7 of the law) and the US standard for internment in Guantánamo and Afghanistan.[1307]

Nuance in the interpretation of the rules on internment is however crucial in ensuring a correct application of the existing legal norms and to achieve their ultimate purpose, namely to prevent parties to armed conflict from arbitrarily or unnecessarily depriving a person of his or her liberty.

(f.3.4). Conclusions on the "DPH-approach" to internment

In his exploration of the utility of rules on targeting to inform future rules on internment Waxman points out the need to refine the rules on targeting when applying them to internment.[1308] While the exercise is an interesting and useful one, we disagree with Waxman where he concludes that the rules on targeting are indeed the best place to seek answers to the questions has poses. It is submitted here that seeking guidance in the rules on targeting to define who can be interned, for what reasons and for how long on the basis of international humanitarian law, is both inappropriate and unnecessary in situations of international armed conflict and occupation.[1309]

Recognizing the usefulness of a matrix of the kind Goodman proposes, which sums up the different kinds of measures parties to the conflict may impose on individuals, we have tried to adapt his model to reflect some of the essential nuances that must accompany it. Based on the rules on internment in international humanitarian law, we have introduced additional categories of persons in the subject-column. Moreover, for reasons of clarity, we have added a column concerning the possibility to detain persons in the framework of criminal proceedings, as a distinct measure from internment.[1310] Finally, we have

comparative analysis of more precise means of achieving an objective with lower civilian injury, which in most cases would exclude mass detention" (Waxman (*CLR* 2008), p. 1398 and note 117).

1307 Lubell has pointed out the risk that inevitably arises from the ICRC's use of the concept of "continuous combat function" to define membership of the armed forces of the parties to the conflict, which he finds "may have inadvertent repercussions on the debates over post-capture status" (Lubell (2010), p. 155). *Cf.* also *infra* chapter III-2. That this risk has already materialized is clear from the remarks made by the US Department of State chief legal advisor referred to *supra* note 1270.

1308 E.g. Waxman (*CLR* 2008), p. 1402.

1309 We will see in Part III that it equally inappropriate and unnecessary in situations of NIAC.

1310 We have left the column on military trials aside as it does not have any impact on the conclusions on internment. Finally, it is important to note that the matrix reflects the rules of international humanitarian law for international armed conflict and that we do not agree that these rules, as the law stands today, apply in non-international armed conflict. We will propose a matrix wrapping up the rules in NIAC in Part III.

modified some of the macro-connections between the cells to reflect both the rules on targeting and the rules on internment in international humanitarian law as it stands today. The result looks like this:

SUBJECTS	**COERCIVE MEASURES**			
	I. TARGETING	**II. CAPTURE/ARREST**	**III. DETENTION ON CRIMINAL CHARGES**	**IV. INTERNMENT**
A. Members of regular/irregular armed forces that meet GC III or AP I criteria ("POW")	AT ALL TIMES	YES	ONLY FOR WAR CRIMES & CRIMES AGAINST HUMANITY	YES
B. Civilians who are entitled to POW status	NO	YES	ONLY FOR WAR CRIMES & CRIMES AGAINST HUMANITY	YES
C. Members of regular/irregular armed forces that do *not* meet GC III or AP I criteria ("unprivileged combatants" and persons with "continuous combat function")	AT ALL TIMES	YES	YES	YES (UNLESS "DEMOBILIZED")
D. Persons directly who have or are directly participating in hostilities ("actual DPH")	FOR DURATION DPH	YES	YES	NO (UNLESS FUTURE THREAT)
E. Persons for whom there is reasonable & legitimate reason to think they will DPH in the future ("security threat")	ONLY WHEN & FOR DURATION DPH	YES	NO	YES
F. Persons for whom there is reasonable & legitimate reason to think they will otherwise pose a threat to the Detaining Power in the future ("security threat")	NO	YES	NO	YES

G. Persons who have not and are not expected to participate I hostilities and do not otherwise pose as threat ("innocent civilians")	NO	NO (UNLESS FOR COMMON CRMINAL OFFENCE)	NO (UNLESS FOR COMMON CRIMINAL OFFENCE)	NO

(g.) Espionage and sabotage

Whether or not they are members of enemy armed forces, persons who are expected to engage in espionage or sabotage may clearly be interned on the basis of GC IV. Pictet's commentary says as much where he notes that:

> "a belligerent may intern people or place them in assigned residence if it has serious and legitimate reason to think that [...] they may seriously prejudice its security by other means, *such as sabotage or espionage.*"[1311]

The US Army Regulation 190-8 also includes "spies and saboteurs" in the list of grounds for lawful internment of persons other than prisoners of war.[1312]

The *Dictionary of the International Law of Armed Conflict* defines espionage – for the purposes of international humanitarian law – as follows:

> "Efforts made in territory under enemy control by a party to the conflict to collect all information on the enemy that may be useful to the conduct of war in general and to that of hostilities in particular. Espionage as international law understands it is clandestine and takes place under false pretences. The collection of information by members of the armed forces wearing their own uniforms is not espionage, but intelligence activities."[1313]

Espionage by definition serves intelligence purposes, but it is important to note that not all intelligence activities amount to espionage, and that it is only the latter that is presumed so serious a threat as to be mentioned as an obvious example of a security threat justifying internment. The *Dictionary of the International Law of Armed Conflict* defines intelligence activities as:

1311 Pictet, *Commentary GC IV* (1958), p. 258.

1312 US, *Army Regulation 190-8* (1997), pp. 18-19, section 5-1 *litera* e. The US *Army Field Manual* (1956), in article 76 specifies that the sanctions for espionage apply to "persons of all classes, whether military or civilian, without regard to citizenship or sex" but apply "only where the acts are committed in time of war."

1313 Verri (1992), p. 47. Verri's definition reflects the definition of espionage in contemporary IHL, which has evolved since the definition contained in article 23 HR 1907, see Pictet *Commentary GC IV* (1958), p. 57 and Sandoz et al., *Commentary to AP I And II* (1987), pp. 565-567. Verri's definition is in line with state practice as reflected in military doctrine, see for example US, DoD, *Military Dictionary* (2010), p. 160; Canada, *LOAC Manual* (2001), p. GL-6; France, *Manuel de droit des conflits armés* (2000), pp. 31-32. NATO's common glossary (AAP-6) does not contain a definition of espionage. Verri concludes his definition of espionage with a reference to the understanding of the term in its broader sense, disconnected from individual behavior or specific acts: "The word espionage is also applied to the collection by States, in peacetime as well as in time of war, of political and military information regarding each other." For the purposes of status determination and internment, only the definition of the specific individual act committed in relation to a specific armed conflict is directly relevant.

"any attempt to obtain, study or use any kind of information on the enemy in order to assess his situation and the options open to him."[1314]

Acts of espionage are restricted to specific actions carried out in time of armed conflict, in territory under the control of a party to that conflict, in a clandestine manner, with the intention of harming the adverse party and designed to obtain information of military value in order to transfer or communicate it to the enemy.[1315]

As to sabotage, the *Dictionary of the International Law of Armed Conflict* contains a more extensive definition. It describes sabotage as:

"Action taken to destroy or damage material, works or installations that by their nature or purpose add to the efficiency of the enemy's armed forces. [...] Sabotage is generally the work of individuals or small formations operating in enemy-controlled territory and taking advantage of clandestinity, surprise, and ruses of war. It is generally carried out with great precision and therefore does not usually harm the civilian population. The targets of sabotage must form part of the enemy's material infrastructure, that is, they must be military objectives."[1316]

Espionage and sabotage – while as such not prohibited in international humanitarian law and generally recognized as lawful acts of war when committed by the armed forces of a party to the conflict – are considered so serious a threat to State security and military operations as to trigger individual disqualification from POW status for members of the armed forces of a party to the conflict (*cf. supra* chapter II-2, section 1.1.3.1). Therefore, a person who can be expected to engage in such activities against the Interning Power in the near

---

[1314] Verri (1992), p. 60.

[1315] See also Pictet *Commentary GC IV* (1958), p. 57 and Sandoz et al., *Commentary to AP I And II* (1987), pp. 565-567, which are in line with state practice (see the examples referred to above notes 1311 and 1312). To be noted that Verri's definition is limited to members of the armed forces of party to the conflict (see the words "by a party to the conflict" in the first line). This may be understandable in that the definition of a spy for the purposes of IHL is mainly important to decide on whether a member of the armed forces of a party to the conflict is entitled to POW status or not (*cf. supra* II-1, section 1.1.3.1). For our present purposes, acts of espionage committed by non-members of such forces, but *on behalf of* a party to the conflict and in a similar, clandestine manner, would also be indicative (even if not decisive unless repetition can be expected) for the spy qualifying as a person posing a threat to the present or future security of the Interning Power. We have mentioned above that US military doctrine for example explicitly says the definition of espionage applies to civilians and military alike. Note however that where a professional spy, i.e. a member of the enemy's armed forces, can be presumed to continue his or her activities if released, such presumption does not exist where non-members of the armed forces commit such acts; in the latter case the Interning Power will need to have serious and legitimate reasons to think that the captured person will continue to present a real security threat upon release.

[1316] Verri (1992), p. 101. See also Pictet, *Commentary GC IV* (1958), p. 57: "The term "sabotage" should be understood to mean acts whose object or effect is to damage or destroy material belonging to the army of occupation or utilized by it." These definitions are also in line with general State practice, see for example US, DoD, *Military Dictionary* (2010), p. 407; Canada, *LOAC Manual* (2001), p. GL-17; France, *Manuel de droit des conflits armés* (2000), 67. NATO AAP-6 (2010) has no definition of sabotage. Whether sabotage is lawful or not is irrelevant for determining the lawful grounds for internment. It will only be important to determine whether a specific act of sabotage can be criminally prosecuted and punished or not. For a summary, see Verri (1992), p. 101; for a more detailed account, see Meyrowitz (*MLLWR* 1966), pp. 133-155 and 160-164.

future, regardless of his or her original status, will qualify as presenting a security threat requiring internment.

It is useful to recall however that not just any potential spy or saboteur may be interned on the basis of article 42§1 GC IV. First of all, Pictet himself underlined that acts of espionage and sabotage are means that "*may* seriously prejudice its security."[1317] Only when such specific acts actually *would* prejudice security can they be taken into account for establishing a lawful ground for internment. Secondly, as in all cases of internment on this basis, it must be established that there is a real risk that the individual *person in casu* will engage in such prejudicial activities, and that, in light of available alternative measures, his or her internment is absolutely necessary to neutralize that risk.

While espionage and sabotage are not unlawful under international humanitarian law and certainly not war crimes, they amount to criminal offences in most domestic legislations. Spies are not entitled to prisoner of war status and do not enjoy immunity from prosecution under such domestic laws, which usually punish this serious act against State security with imprisonment.[1318] Two options are therefore open to deal with spies: they can be prosecuted and punished for their crimes, or they can be interned where there is a real risk that they will engage in future acts of espionage against the Interning Power. Where criminal proceedings are possible and allow for pre-trial detention or result in a prison sentence, they must be preferred over internment.

Finally, the Interning/Detaining power can restrict the communication rights of interned or detained spies and saboteurs in accordance with article 5 GC IV, so as to prevent them from continuing to engage in or report on such activities from within their place of internment or detention.

(h.) Knowledge and qualifications that result in a person posing a security threat

Pictet explains that security internment is also authorized where the Interning Power has "good reason to think that the person concerned, by his [...] *knowledge or qualifications*, represents a real threat to its present or future security."[1319] The ICTY took over the expression without any further explanation of what it means.[1320] No definition of these terms features in IHL or military dictionaries, most likely because they are not really military concepts to start with. Pictet distinguishes the possession of "knowledge or qualifications" from "activities", which suggests that it is the information or technical skills a person possesses, rather than his or her actions, that represent a threat. In this sense "knowledge" may refer to a person's awareness of information of military value,

[1317] Pictet, *Commentary GC IV* (1958), p. 258.

[1318] Note that spies and saboteurs captured in occupied territory may not be transferred to the territory of the Occupying Power or any other territory to face trial, since this would amount to unlawful deportation under article 49 GC IV. With regard to saboteurs' right to prisoner of war status, *cf. supra* chapter II-1, section 1.1.3.2.

[1319] Pictet, *Commentary GC IV* (1958), p. 258.

[1320] ICTY, *Delalić* (1998), §577.

without him or her being a spy. The difference is that unlike a spy, this person does not necessarily act in a clandestine manner, nor actively seeks to collect information for the purpose of harming the Interning Power by transmitting or communicating it to the enemy.

The (online) *Oxford English Dictionary* (OED) and *Petit Robert* (PR) define the words as follows:

• Qualification (OED): "A quality or accomplishment which qualifies or fits a person for a certain position or function; (now esp.) the completion of a course or training programme which confers the status of a recognized practitioner of a profession or activity ; A necessary condition, imposed by law or custom, which must be satisfied before a certain right can be acquired or exercised, an office held, etc."

• Knowledge (OED): "The fact of knowing a thing, state, etc., or (in general sense) a person; acquaintance; familiarity gained by experience; Acquaintance with a fact; perception, or certain information of, a fact or matter; state of being aware or informed."

• Qualification (PR): Qualification professionnelle: ensemble des aptitudes et des connaissances acquises d'un travailleur pour l'exercice d'une activité de production. Qualifié: Qui satisfait aux conditions requises, a qualité ou compétence (pour faire qqch.)."

• Connaissance (PR): ce qui est connu; ce que l'on sait, pour l'avoir appris; savoir, science."

While these general definitions may be useful as a starting point, for the purposes of establishing whether a person poses a security threat justifying internment, the words must be understood in the particular context of armed conflict: there must be a direct link between a person's knowledge or qualifications and the alleged military or security threat he or she poses. In Pictet's words: "the State must have good reason to think that the person concerned, *by* his [...] knowledge or qualifications, *represents a real threat to* its present or future security."[1321]

Knowledge or qualifications justifying a person's internment must therefore be of a nature that generates such a threat. The fact that a person possesses knowledge or qualifications that may be *useful* for understanding a context or one's enemy, or otherwise *useful* for military or security purposes is not sufficient. Therefore, it will be the knowledge a person possesses *about* rather than *useful to* the Interning Power that could justify internment. Likewise, it will be qualifications that are likely to be used *against* the security of the Interning Power rather than those that could be *useful for* its own offensive actions that could justify internment. A person can only be interned where he or she poses a military or security *threat*, not where he or she is a military or security *asset* to the Interning Power. As a preventive measure, specifically designed to avoid a

[1321] Pictet, *Commentary GC IV* (1958), p. 258 (emphasis added).

military or security threat, internment is by definition a *defensive* operation, not an *offensive* one.

For example, where a person has crucial knowledge of the vulnerabilities in the Interning Power's defence system and may be expected to – voluntarily or under pressure or coercion – share that knowledge with an adverse Party to the conflict, he or she may be considered a security threat and subjected to internment where no alternative measures could adequately meet that threat.[1322] Likewise, where a person has knowledge or qualifications that are crucial for the enemy to carry out a specific military operations against the Interning Power, the person may be interned if necessary to prevent that operation from materializing or succeeding.

This does not necessarily mean that the knowledge or qualifications that may justify internment are *per se* of a military nature; they could be general such as a specific language skill, scientific qualification or a thorough understanding of a particular region or culture. For example, a person who by his qualifications represents a real threat to the security of the Interning Power, could be someone who has scientific qualifications that would permit an adverse party to construct an offensive weapon that the latter could be expected to use to the detriment of the Interning Power's security. Say for example in a conflict between State A and State B, that State A has the resources to construct an offensive weapon that would inflict serious damage on the military capacity of State B, but lacks qualified staff to actually construct the weapon. State B would be allowed – if other less restrictive measures are inadequate – to intern such qualified persons present in its territory if it can be reasonably expected that they would either put themselves at the disposal of State A to build the weapon, or are at real risk of being compelled by State A to do so.

Neither does it mean that they must necessarily be used on behalf of or in favour of an adverse party to the conflict; it suffices to establish that the person can be reasonably expected to use the knowledge or qualifications in a concrete manner against the security of the Interning Power.

Finally, it does not mean that a person's knowledge or qualifications of an inherently military or security nature automatically suffice to intern him or her. For example, it is not because an individual has undergone extensive military training or is familiar with military intelligence technology that he or she *per se* can be expected to use this knowledge or qualifications against the security of the Interning Power. Again, what makes the person a security threat is not the knowledge or qualifications as such, but the fact that it can be reasonably expected that the person will use them against the security of the Interning Power.

A partial equivalent of the word "knowledge" in military parlance could be the concept of "intelligence". In the context of armed conflict, "intelligence" generally refers to information of a military nature. The following operational definitions from military doctrine may be enlightening. It must be kept in mind

[1322] The example was suggested by Goodman (*AJIL* 2009), p. 55 in note 37.

however that these are general definitions, not drawn up for the specific purpose of establishing who poses a security threat justifying internment. On the contrary, they are formulated mainly from a perspective of what is *useful* or *necessary* intelligence to be collected by one's own forces to carry out specific military operations. Nevertheless, they also give an indication of potentially *damaging* information to party's military security. The following definitions are from US and NATO military doctrine:

> "[intelligence:] The product resulting from the collection, processing, integration, evaluation, analysis, and interpretation of available information concerning foreign nations, hostile or potentially hostile forces or elements, or areas of actual or potential operations."[1323]
>
> "[general military intelligence:] Intelligence concerning the (1) military capabilities of foreign countries or organizations or (2) topics affecting potential US or multinational military operations, relating to the following subjects: armed forces capabilities, including order of battle, organization, training, tactics, doctrine, strategy, and other factors bearing on military strength and effectiveness; area and terrain intelligence, including urban areas, coasts and landing beaches, and meteorological, oceanographic, and geological intelligence; transportation in all modes; military materiel production and support industries; military and civilian communications systems; military economics, including foreign military assistance; insurgency and terrorism; military-political-sociological intelligence; location, identification, and description of military-related installations; government control; escape and evasion; and threats and forecasts. (Excludes scientific and technical intelligence)."[1324]
>
> "[combat intelligence:] That knowledge of the enemy, weather, and geographical features required by a commander in the planning and conduct of combat operations."[1325]
>
> "[military intelligence:] Intelligence on any foreign military or military-related situation or activity which is significant to military policymaking or the planning and conduct of military operations and activities."[1326]
>
> "[operational intelligence:] Intelligence that is required for planning and conducting campaigns and major operations to accomplish strategic objectives within theaters or operational areas."[1327]
>
> "[tactical intelligence:] Intelligence required for the planning and conduct of tactical operations."[1328]

1323 US, DoD, *Military Dictionary* (2010), p. 230. The definition is almost identical to the one in NATO's AAP-6 (2010), p. 2-I-6.

1324 US, DoD, *Military Dictionary* (2010), pp. 191-192. NATO's AAP-6 (2010) does not have an equivalent entry.

1325 US ,DoD, *Military Dictionary* (2010), p. 82. NATO's AAP-6 (2010) does not have an equivalent entry.

1326 US, DoD, *Military Dictionary* (2010), p. 295. NATO's AAP-6 (2010) does not have an equivalent entry.

1327 US, DoD *Military Dictionary* (2010), p. 340. NATO's AAP-6 (2010) (p. 2-O-3) defines it as "intelligence required for the planning and conduct of campaigns at the operations level."

1328 US, DoD, *Military Dictionary* (2010), p. 457. NATO's AAP-6 (2010) (p. 2-T-2) defines it as "intelligence required for the planning and execution of operations at the tactical level."

Canadian military doctrine describes "intelligence" as follows:

> "Intelligence is an essential component of military capability that is fundamental to the planning and conduct of joint operations and activities. Intelligence is data, information, and knowledge of a broad range of factors including: the physical environment; weather; demographics and culture of the operational area; the activities, capabilities, and intentions of an actual or potential threat; or any other non-friendly entity or situation about which the CF is concerned. The purpose of intelligence is to allow the commander to gain an accurate understanding of the threat and of the operating environment."[1329]

French military doctrine defines intelligence in accordance with NATO standardized terminology:

> "Renseignement (activité de) (en anglais : intelligence activity) 'Renseignement : résultat de l'exploitation des renseignements bruts, concernant les nations étrangères, les forces armées ennemies ou pouvant le devenir, les zones où des opérations sont effectivement menées ou pourraient l'être. Le terme s'applique aussi aux activités d'élaboration du renseignement et aux organismes qui s'y consacrent.' (AAP 6, glossaire OTAN de termes et définitions d'usage militaire)."[1330]

Again, it must be stressed that an individual who possesses information that could qualify as military intelligence cannot automatically be considered a security threat. In order to intern such a person on the basis of article 42§1 GC IV it must be established that the individual can be reasonably expected to use this information against the security of the Interning Power, and that no alternative, less restrictive measures can adequately prevent him or her from doing so.

(i.) Internment for the purpose of interrogation

We have seen in Part I that internment for the mere purpose of interrogation or intelligence-gathering is prohibited under general international law.[1331] This general rule is not different in times of armed conflict:[1332] security internment can only be ordered if the individual internee concerned poses a security threat. In the absence of such a threat internment is not absolutely necessary for the security of the Interning Power and would therefore be unlawful.

A party to a conflict may *want* to hold on to an individual protected person, whether a civilian or an "unprivileged combatant", for the purpose of interrogation. Whilst persons protected under GC IV can of course be questioned upon arrest or capture and during captivity, their internment cannot be ordered for the mere purpose of interrogation alone.[1333] Persons who possess useful

---

[1329] Canada, *JDP 3.0* (2010), p. 1-9.

[1330] France, *Manuel de droit des conflits armés* (2001), p. 61.

[1331] *Cf. supra* chapter I-1, section 1.2.4.2.

[1332] In the same sense: Arai-Takahashi (2009), p. 485; Goodman (*AJIL* 2009), p. 55; Goodman, "Rationales for Detention: Security Threats and Intelligence Value" in Schmitt (2009), pp. 375-379; Pejic (*IRRC* 2005), p. 380.

[1333] Before the Inter-American Commission on Human Rights in the *Coard* case, the United States – without necessarily relying on their intelligence value to intern some of the petitioners in the case, asserted that interrogation "for tactical and security purposes during hostilities is a right clearly

information for the conduct of military operations may be a military or security *asset*, but they are not by definition a security *threat*. Whilst their internment may be *useful* for military or security purposes, that does not make it *absolutely necessary to* counter an identified security *threat*. In this sense they must be distinguished from the category of persons discussed above, who by their knowledge or qualifications represent a real threat to the security of the Interning Power.

In the wake of the terrorist attacks that took place on US soil on 11 September 2001, the US authorities in Guantánamo Bay, Iraq and Afghanistan have relied on the "intelligence value" of individuals held in relation to the so-called "war on terrorism" to justify internment or deny release.[1334] The authorities and some scholars argued that internment for mere intelligence purposes was not unlawful. Ryan Goodman has aptly summarized their arguments:

> "Three arguments might be raised to support the legality of US practice. First, the Geneva Conventions contain no express prohibition on the use of detention for intelligence-gathering purposes. Second, detention is permitted if obtaining the relevant information serves an imperative security interest. Third, if a State has the authority to detain an individual until the cessation of hostilities, the State has the prerogative to release her earlier if she provides valuable intelligence information."[1335]

There are however important problems with all three arguments, and as Goodman points out, they are contradicted by the provisions of international humanitarian law itself and by an important number of legal authorities, including the US Supreme Court.[1336]

The first argument – that IHL does not expressly prohibit internment for intelligence purposes – does not stand up against the fact that the legal bases for internment in international armed conflict are regulated exhaustively in the Geneva Conventions. The only legal bases for the internment of persons not qualifying prisoners of war, including so-called "unprivileged combatants", are to be found in the Fourth Geneva Convention, article 79 of which explicitly

recognized and provided for in Article 17th of the Geneva Convention Relative to the Treatment of Prisoners of War" (*cf. supra* note 809). Indeed, international humanitarian law does not prohibit a party to the conflict to interrogate prisoners of war or even internees in its power, but it does not authorize internment for that sole purpose. It may also be useful to recall at this point that any form of coercion to obtain information from a protected person is absolutely prohibited by article 31 GC IV (the same holds true for prisoners of war, see article 17§4 GC III).

1334 For a summary, see Goodman in Schmitt (2009), pp. 375-377, with further references, amongst others, to the US Army's Counterinsurgency Field Manual (2006), Department of Defence fact sheets and orders concerning the internment facility in Guantánamo Bay, official statements by the US President and Department of Defence officials, trial documents in the *Padilla* and *al-Marri* cases, and articles by other US scholars.

1335 Goodman in Schmitt (2009), p. 377.

1336 We have discussed the qualification of the "war on terrorism" for the purposes of the applicability of international humanitarian law above; here we will, for the sake of argument, work with the – simplified and partially incorrect – assumption by the authorities that all internees concerned were deprived of their liberty in relation to an international armed conflict.

states that "[t]he Parties to the conflict shall not intern protected persons, except in accordance with the provisions of Articles 41, 42, 43, 68 and 78."

The second argument – that detention for the purpose of interrogation is permitted where it serves an imperative security interest – contradicts the principle that persons other than prisoners of war can only be interned where such internment is absolutely/imperatively necessary to counter a military or security *threat* posed by the person concerned. As we have discussed above, mere *usefulness* of the internment for military operations or other security *interests* do not satisfy that threshold.

The third argument finally is irrelevant where persons who do not qualify as prisoners of war are concerned, since they can only be interned if and for as long as they pose a real individual threat to the security of the Interning Power, and not for the duration of the conflict. Only prisoners of war can be interned on the basis of articles 21 and 118 GC III until the cessation of active hostilities.[1337] Article 132 GC IV requires that internees shall be released "as soon as the reasons which necessitated his internment [in accordance with articles 42 and 78 GC IV] no longer exist."

Regardless of whether internment for intelligence purposes is lawful under US law, it is definitely not lawful under international (humanitarian and human rights) law.

Thus, the ICRC's position on the basic principles of internment and administrative detention affirms that:

> "internment or administrative detention for the sole purpose of intelligence gathering, without the person involved otherwise presenting a real threat to State security, cannot be justified."[1338]

Similarly, the participants in an expert meeting on security internment organized under the auspices of the ICRC and Chatham House, were unanimous in their opinion that:

> "What is clear is that internment must be necessary for security reasons, and not just convenient or useful for the interning power. A concrete example is that internment for the sole purpose of obtaining intelligence is impermissible."[1339]

Specifically with regard to Guantánamo – but valid for all persons interned in relation to an armed conflict – the United Nations Working Group on Arbitrary Detention and five of the UN Human Rights Council's Special Rapporteurs, found that:

> "The indefinite detention of prisoners of war and civilian internees for purposes of continued interrogation is inconsistent with the provisions of the Geneva Conventions."[1340]

1337 For the internment of prisoners of war for interrogation purposes, *cf. supra* II-1, section 1.2.3.5.

1338 As reflected in Pejic (*IRRC* 2005), p. 380.

1339 *Report of the Expert Meeting on Security Detention in NIAC (2008)*, p. 865. Note that some of the experts in that meeting had direct operational experience in ongoing armed conflicts of a complex nature.

The Human Rights Council's Special Rapporteur on Counterterrorism, in a recent report on good practices for the respect of international human rights law by intelligence agencies, stressed that: "[i]ntelligence services are not permitted to deprive persons of their liberty simply for the purpose of intelligence collection."[1341]

(j.) Political opinions and action in favour of an adverse party to the conflict

We have seen in Part I that deprivation of liberty resulting from the lawful exercise of the freedom of opinion and expression, the freedom of thought, conscience and religion, and the freedom of peaceful assembly and association amounts to arbitrary deprivation of liberty and is unlawful.[1342] Indeed, holding or expressing a political opinion or an ideological affinity can never be a lawful ground to deprive any person of his or her liberty.

International humanitarian law does not allow any departure from this rule in times of armed conflict. While political support and propaganda may be crucial assets for the parties to any given armed conflict, a person's political or ideological affinities or support for an adverse party to the conflict cannot as such qualify him or her as a security threat justifying internment. Moreover, it is hard to imagine a case where there are no other, less restrictive measures that can adequately counter any threat emanating from political propaganda or incitement to violence.[1343] Therefore, as long as they cannot be reasonably expected to translate into actual behaviour that would pose a serious security threat to the Interning Power, a person's political or ideological affinities or support for an adverse party to the conflict will not be sufficient to satisfy the threshold of articles 42§1 and 78 GC IV.

Pictet says as much in his commentary to article 5 GC IV, which has been confirmed in the case law of the ICTY:

[1340] WGAD and Special Rapporteurs, *Situation of Detainees at Guantánamo Bay* (2006), §23. The Working Group on Arbitrary Detention has also consistently raised concerns over the US' rendition programmes in the war on terrorism, where many internees were held and transferred around the world for the mere purpose of interrogation (*cf. supra* chapter I-1, section 1.2.4.2).

[1341] UNHRC, Special Rapporteur on Counterterrorism, *Good Practices Intelligence Agencies* (2010), p. 25.

[1342] *Cf. supra* chapter I-1, note 238.

[1343] The rights to freedom of thought, opinion and expression and to freedom of peaceful assembly and association can be lawfully limited, and under specific conditions derogated from, where necessary to protect a legitimate collective interest (*cf. supra* chapter I-2). Such measures should be sufficient to deal with any exercise of these rights and freedoms that has a negative impact on the conduct of military operations, without there being a need to intern anyone. While internment (or administrative detention) on these grounds is not lawful under international law, detention in the framework of criminal proceedings may in very serious cases be an option to deprive of their liberty persons who have exercised their fundamental rights and freedoms in an unlawful manner. For examples of criminalization of incitement to violence and terrorist acts drawn from State practice, and their scrutiny by international human rights bodies, see United Nations Office on Drugs and Crime (UNODC), *Digest of Terrorist Cases* (2010), pp. 38-46 (it is not within the scope of this book to evaluate the lawfulness of the measures discussed in the Digest).

"The clause [activities prejudicial or hostile to the security of the State] cannot refer to a political attitude towards the State, so long as that attitude is not translated into action."[1344]

The Ethiopia-Eritrea Claims Commission, set up within the Permanent Court of Arbitration, also discarded the following evidence as justifying internment:

"Eritrea maintained that its actions were justified under Article 42 of Geneva Convention IV, which allows internment or assigned residence "if the security of the Detaining Power makes it absolutely necessary." It contended at the hearing that many Ethiopians were confined because *their celebrations following Ethiopian victories or other conduct marked them as endangering security*. [...] Eritrea failed to show that its mass detentions of Ethiopians during and after May 2000 satisfied the requirements of Article 42 of Geneva Convention IV as being "absolutely necessary" for its security."[1345]

Israeli case law on the issue has been divided in the past. Whereas some lower courts found that mere political activity or even "forcing without violence the opinions of a section of the public upon another section of the public" does not constitute a security threat justifying internment, the Supreme Court rejected the position of the lower courts, finding that the fact that a person's "activities were of a political nature does not change their destructive characteristics" and that "non-physical action can be much more damaging than physical terrorist action."[1346] However, when the Attorney-General published directives on the implementation of the law regulating administrative detention in Israel proper, he reaffirmed that expressing an opinion, regardless of how extreme, would not be "by itself sufficient grounds for administrative detention."[1347] Further statements from the Israeli authorities, especially when read in light of the Supreme Court's more recent case law on both the *Emergency Powers (Detention) Law* and the *Incarceration of Unlawful Combatants Law* discussed above, suggest mere political opinions or activity or even membership in a political organization would not by themselves qualify as a security threat justifying internment:

"It is clear therefore, that an administrative detention order will never be lawful where it is made on the basis of the *non-violent exercise of a person's right to freedom of expression and association*."[1348]

[1344] Pictet, *Commentary GC IV* (1958), p. 56; ICTY, *Delalić* (1998), §567; ICTY, *Kordić & Čerkez* (2001), §280. See also Goodman (*AJIL* 2009), p. 54.

[1345] PCA (EECC), *Civilians Claims, Ethiopia's Claim 5* (2004), §§101 and 104 (emphasis added).

[1346] Israeli case law concerning internment on the basis of the *Emergency Powers (Detention) Law* 1979 (most of it unpublished) as summarized by Rudman & Qupty (*CHRLR* 1990), pp. 480-482 and 494-495. The quotes in the text are respectively from Haifa district Court, *Bat'hish v. Minister of Defence*, A.D. 18/82 and Supreme Court, *Husseini v. State of Israel*, A.A.D. 1/87.

[1347] Rudman & Qupty (*CHRLR* 1990), p. 492, quoting from the *Instructions of the Attorney General 21.927* (1982).

[1348] Israel, MoJ, Fact Sheet on Administrative Detention (2003), p. 3.

(k.) Religious convictions, opinions or practice

A person's religious convictions or opinions can never be a lawful ground for deprivation of liberty.[1349] International humanitarian law does not depart from this rule, rather to the contrary. The first sentence of Article 27§1 – laying down absolute rights (*cf. supra*) – reads:

> "Protected persons are entitled, in all circumstances, to respect for their persons, their honour, their family rights, their religious convictions and practices, and their manners and customs."

Pictet comments with regard to religious convictions and practices:

> "The principle of freedom of thought is the basis of the great movement for the Rights of Man which invaded and transformed politics and law. It is therefore inscribed at the beginning of the traditional proclamations of essential rights and fundamental liberties. The right to respect for religious convictions is part of freedom of conscience and freedom of thought in general. It implies freedom to believe or not to believe, and freedom to change from one religion or conviction to another. This safeguard relates to any system of philosophical or religious beliefs. Religious freedom is closely connected with the idea of freedom to practise religion through religious observances, services and rites. Protected persons in the territory of a Party to the conflict or in occupied territory must be able to practise their religion freely, without any restrictions other than those necessary for the maintenance of public law and morals."[1350]

Article 75§1 AP I explicitly reaffirms that parties to an armed conflict "shall respect the person, honour, convictions and religious practices of all." Sandoz, Swinarski and Zimmerman comment:

> "As regards respect for the person, honour and religious convictions and practices, this wording was used already in the Geneva Conventions (Articles 14 and 34, Third Convention; Article 27, fourth Convention). However, as pointed out in the commentary on Article 27 of the fourth Convention, respect for "religious convictions and practices" should be understood in a broad sense. It covers all philosophical and ethical convictions. We know that in some armies there are nowadays, in addition to chaplains, counsellors on moral matters to whom members of the armed forces can go for assistance. This should be seen as an example of the modern tendency of individuals to look for a moral code also outside religion."[1351]

They conclude by underlining that "respect for convictions implies that a person professing any particular convictions cannot be arrested or imprisoned for this reason alone."[1352]

[1349] *Cf. supra* chapter I-1.
[1350] Pictet, *Commentary GC IV* (1958), p. 203.
[1351] Sandoz et al., *Commentary AP I and II* (1987), p. 871.
[1352] Sandoz et al., *Commentary AP I and II* (1987), p. 871.

3.2.3. Voluntary internment

A less common, but equally lawful ground to intern a protected person, is where such internment is necessary for that person's own security (as opposed to the interest of State security as is provided for in article 42§1 GC IV). Article 42§2 GC IV defines this ground as follows:

> "If any person, acting through the representatives of the Protecting Power, voluntarily demands internment and if his situation renders this step necessary, he shall be interned by the Power in whose hands he may be."

For voluntary internment on the basis of article 42§2 GC IV to be lawful, it must thus fulfil three cumulative conditions: (1) the internment must be requested by the person concerned; (2) the request must be made through a Protecting Power (or in its absence through the ICRC); and (3) the internment must be warranted by the situation of the person concerned. The first two conditions are designed to ensure that the request to intern is not made lightly, but also that internment is not ordered on the false pretext that it was requested by the internee him-or herself.

It is difficult to establish in a general manner when the third condition will be fulfilled; this will have to be evaluated on a case-by-case basis by the decision-making authority. Examples rendering internment necessary include situations where the applicant lacks sufficient resources to provide for his or her basic needs; or where his or her life or physical integrity is threatened by hostile actions committed by the general public.[1353] It is however worthwhile to recall a comment from the Committee charged at the 1949 Diplomatic Conference with drafting GC IV. In its report to the Plenary Assembly, regarding what ultimately became article 42§2 of that Convention, the Committee explained:

> "[w]e preferred to provide for two conditions, that the person voluntarily requests internment, and that his situation makes internment necessary. The subjective reasons for the request are therefore without importance; the *objective conditions become the determining factor*."[1354]

Where these three conditions are fulfilled, the applicant has an absolute right to be interned.[1355]

Cases of voluntary internment are not very common, and there is little practice or case law on the subject. Most military manuals and operational guidelines do not even mention voluntary internment. There are a few exceptions though.

1353 Pictet, *Commentary GC IV* (1958), pp. 258-259.

1354 *Final Record 1949*, Vol. II-A, p. 826 (emphasis added). The original draft read: "Should any person, acting through the representatives of the Protecting Power, voluntarily ask to be interned because his or her situation renders that course necessary, the said person shall be interned by the Power in whose hands he or she may be" (*Final Record 1949*, Vol. I, p. 120). The Committee's concern was reflected in the new draft it submitted to the Plenary Assembly (*Final Record 1949*, Vol. II-A, p. 854) and which was adopted with no further amendments.

1355 Pictet, *Commentary GC IV* (1958), p. 259. Where the 2nd or 3rd condition is not met, the authorities are free to decide whether they accept or reject the request for internment (*Ibidem*).

US military doctrine provides us with another example of a situation where the personal situation of an internee may render internment – in this case of his or her children – necessary. *US Army Regulation 190-8* provides that:

> "requests by the CI [civilian internee, i.e. any person interned on the basis of GC IV] for the compassionate internment of their dependent children who are at liberty without parental care in the occupied territory will normally be granted when both parents or the only surviving parent is interned."[1356]

The text refers explicitly to occupied territory, but in the absence of other solutions (such as public child care, which may not be available in the occupied territory), the same compassionate internment of an internee's dependent children may be justified on the basis of article 42§2 GC IV, which applies to persons interned in the territory of the parties to the conflict.

In what seems to be a departure from the rule in article 42§2 GC IV, the Canadian Manual for handling persons deprived of liberty in international operations provides that:

> "[t]here is no requirement for CF forces to take into voluntary detention any personnel who have not been engaged in armed conflict with the CF. Such activity may be seen as offering protection to fractional elements, with all the possibilities under ROE which that entails, and may give rise to allegations of partiality on the part of the CF force."[1357]

In order to conform to article 42§2 GC IV, this rule should be interpreted to allow for an exception where the situation of the applicant – especially regarding his physical and mental integrity and personal security – makes his or her internment necessary. Whatever military disadvantages may flow from such internment may not be relied upon to deny a protected person his or her right to voluntary internment under article 42§2 GC IV.

Available case law underscores the importance of establishing the genuinely voluntary character of protective internment on the basis of article 42§2 GC IV. For example, the Ethiopia-Eritrea Claims Commission found that:

> "Eritrea also contended that some Ethiopians were held to *protect them from hostile public opinion*, allegedly inflamed by Ethiopians' provocative celebrations following Ethiopian victories. Indeed, Eritrea contended that some Ethiopians asked to be taken into protective custody. There was little evidence supporting this contention, and the Commission doubts that many persons *requested* internment."[1358]

In his defence before the ICTY, a brigade commander of the Croatian Defence Council, relied upon a similar argument as the one made by Eritrea to deny accusations that civilians under his authority were interned unlawfully. Without necessarily claiming civilians had requested such protective internment themselves, Mario Čerkez argued that "the internment of civilians in wartime may be necessary and justified *in order to safeguard the civilian population*

[1356] US, *Army Regulation 190-8* (1997), p. 19, section 5-1 *litera* d.
[1357] Canada, *PWDTIQ* (2004), p. 1B-1.
[1358] PCA (EECC), Civilians Claims, Ethiopia Claim No. 5 (2004), §103.

living in a combat zone", an argument which was rejected by the Tribunal.[1359] Apart from the fact that such internment does not fulfil the 1st condition for internment on the basis of article 42§2 GC IV, the 3rd condition does not seem to be met either, in that there are other measures of control, less restrictive than internment, that are adequate to protect the civilian population from the effects of hostilities, such as sealing off combat areas, setting up check-points, imposing curfews or other restrictions of movement. It is highly unlikely that internment or even assigned residence may be the only available measure to adequately safeguard civilians from the effects of hostilities.

3.2.4. Specificities of internment in occupied territory

The legal framework for the internment of protected persons in occupied territory is to a large extent identical to the one applicable in the territory of the parties to an international armed conflict. Article 78 GC IV, the equivalent in occupied territory of articles 41 to 43 GC IV,[1360] prescribes the lawful grounds for internment as follows:

> "If the Occupying Power considers it necessary, for imperative reasons of security, to take safety measures concerning protected persons, it may, at the most, subject them to assigned residence or to internment."

The wording is only slightly different than that in article 42, and the lawful grounds for internment on the basis of article 78 GC IV are essentially the same: the expression "imperative reasons of security" must be understood to include (1) voluntary internment of persons whose situations renders this necessary, and (2) security internment of persons who pose a security threat that can only be adequately met by subjecting the person to internment.[1361]

[1359] ICTY, *Kordić and Čerkez* (2001), §§ 278 and 291 respectively (emphasis added).

[1360] Pictet only dedicates two pages of his *Commentary to GC IV* (1958) to article 78 GC IV, mainly referring the reader to his earlier comments on articles 41-43 GC IV for details on its interpretation (pp. 367-369). He recalls that article 78, like articles 41 to 43, is based on article 27§4 allowing for "such measures of control and security as may be necessary as a result of the war." In occupied territory, the only permissible "security measures envisaged are 'assigned residence' and 'internment', which have already been considered in detail in connection with Articles 41 and 42." In his commentary on article 79 GC IV (p. 371), Pictet confirms that article 78 "provides the same safeguards as those laid down in Articles 41, 42 and 43 for aliens in the territory of a Party to the conflict, with the one difference that the six-monthly review of decisions concerning internment, which is compulsory in the case of internees in the actual territory of a belligerent, is optional in occupied territory." Pictet highlights one other important difference regarding security internees in occupied territory, namely that they may not be deported or transferred to the territory of the Occupying Power or that of another country (article 49 GC IV) and can "therefore only be interned, or placed in assigned residence, within the frontiers of the occupied country itself" (Pictet, *Commentary GC IV* (1958), p. 368).

[1361] As is the case with article 42§1 GC IV, the expression "imperative reasons of security" is not further defined in the Convention and the decision of the exact level of the threshold is largely left to the discretion of the Interning Power. For the same reasons, the concept was not subject to any insightful debate during the Diplomatic Conference either, the delegates apparently assumed the threshold was sufficiently clear and could in any case not be usefully defined in more detail (since their exact meaning in practice depends very much on the specific circumstances of each case). See *Final Records 1949*, Vol. I-A, pp. 675, 721, 772-773, 790, 801-802, 835-836 and 860; Vol. II-b, pp. 156, 196 and 440-441.

Article 78 GC IV does not explicitly refer to voluntary internment, but there is no reason why this should not be a lawful ground for internment in occupied territory.[1362] Where a protected person qualifies for voluntary internment under the provisions of article 42§2 GC IV, his internment must be understood to qualify as internment "for imperative reasons of security" under article 78 GC IV. Moreover, in light of the obligation of the Occupying Power to ensure public order and the safety of the inhabitants of occupied territory,[1363] protective custody requested by the inhabitant of and occupied territory must be granted where imperative for the applicant's personal security.

As to security internment under article 78 GC IV, it must be interpreted in the same manner as security internment under article 42§1 GC IV. We therefore refer the reader to section 3.2.2 above for its interpretation,[1364] while pointing out a few relevant differences or specificities regarding internment in occupied territory here.

3.2.4.1. Exceptional character of internment in occupied territory

As is the case for article 42§1 GC IV, personal liberty is the general rule, and internment may only be ordered in exceptional circumstances where a real and imperative security threat makes such a measure absolutely necessary.[1365]

Pictet notes moreover that "[i]n occupied territories the internment of protected persons should be *even more exceptional* than it is inside the territory of the Parties to the conflict [...] That is why Article 78 speaks of *imperative* reasons of security."[1366]

While in very exceptional circumstances, at the outbreak of hostilities, internment on a collective basis may be lawful in the territory of the Interning Power,[1367] such exceptional circumstances cannot occur in occupied territory, and therefore no similar exception to the general rule is allowed: "there can be *no question* of taking collective measures: each case must be decided separately."[1368]

[1362] In the same sense: Arai-Takahashi (2009), p. 484.

[1363] Article 43 HR 1907; article 64 GC IV. See also ICJ, *DRC v. Uganda* (2005), §178.

[1364] As Pictet himself notes that the security measures envisaged in article 78 GC IV are "'assigned residence' and 'internment', which have already been considered in detail in connection with Articles 41 and 42" (Pictet, *Commentary GC IV* (1958), p. 368), his comments on article 42 GC IV may be applied *mutatis mutandis* to the interpretation of article 78. International practice does not distinguish much between security internment in occupied territory and in the territory of the parties to the conflict either, and the practice discussed above is therefore also relevant for interpreting article 78, taking into account the relative stability that may reign in occupied territory, which may impact the proportionality calculus in favour of the internee. Finally, as we have pointed out in our discussion of article 42§1 GC IV, each decision to intern and review of that decision must take into account the specific circumstances of each individual case. See also ICTY, *Delalić* (1998), §578.

[1365] Article 27§4 and article 42§1 GC IV.

[1366] Pictet, *Commentary GC IV* (1958), p. 367. In the same vein, restrictions on the basis of article 5 GC IV are subject to more stringent conditions in occupied territory than in the territory of the parties to the conflict (Pictet, *Commentary GC IV* (1958), p. 57). See also Arai-Takahashi (2009), p. 490, note 29, who confirms the threshold in article 78 GC IV is higher than the one in article 42§1 GC IV.

[1367] *Cf. supra* section 3.2.1.5.

[1368] Pictet, *Commentary GC IV* (1958), p. 367 (emphasis added).

The rule has been consistently recalled in the case law of the Israeli Supreme Court. Much of that case law has been referred to above, but another example may be useful to highlight the very exceptional character of internment in occupied territory. For instance, the Israeli government officially endorsed the following ruling from the Supreme Court:

> "The denial of liberty not on the basis of a decision of a judicial authority is, by its very nature, a far-reaching and highly severe step, which the law permits only when circumstances exist in which it is necessary for imperative grounds of security. Proper discretion, which must be employed prior to issuance of the order, relates also to the question of whether the decision on the detention reflects in each concrete case the appropriate balance between a security necessity for which no other reasonable solution can be found, and the fundamental principle according to which a person's liberty must be respected."[1369]

3.2.4.2. Whose security?

Whereas article 42§1 GC IV speaks of the security "of the Detaining Power", article 78 GC IV does not specify whose security may justify internment.[1370] Should the concept be interpreted more broadly in article 78 GC IV? We have mentioned before that the *travaux préparatoires* of the Conventions do not enlighten us on the difference in wording used in articles 42 and 78 GC IV. The question then arises whether in occupied territory security internment may additionally be ordered as a preventive measure against persons who pose a threat to *general* security. Or, to put the question more precisely, can an Occupying Power resort to internment as a law enforcement measure based on its general obligation to "restore, and ensure, as far as possible, public order and safety" (article 43 HR 1907)?[1371]

Article 43 HR 1907 lays down a general rule concerning the legislative powers of an Occupying Power, allowing it to take such measures as are necessary to maintain public order and safety. Article 64§2 GC IV further clarifies and elaborates on article 43 HR by prescribing that the Occupying Power may:

> "subject the population of the occupied territory to provisions which are *essential to* enable the Occupying Power to fulfil its obligations under the present

[1369] Israel, HCJ, *Sajadiya v. Minister of Defence* as quoted in Israel, MoJ, *Fact Sheet on Administrative Detention* (2003), p. 5 (no English version of the judgment is publicly available). We have referred to the *Marab* case – the leading case in Israeli law on mass detentions in occupied territory – above, *cf. supra* notes 1067 and 1078 and accompanying text.

[1370] The security of the Occupying Power may require it to intern members of organized resistance movements operating in the occupied territory. Where they qualify for POW status under article 4§A(2) GC III, they may be interned for the duration of hostilities in accordance with the Third Geneva Convention (*cf. supra* chapter II-1). If they do not qualify for POW status, they may be interned on the basis of article 78 GC IV, which in such cases must be interpreted in the same manner as article 42§1 GC IV (*cf. supra* section 3.2.2.2).

[1371] See also ICJ, *DRC v. Uganda* (2005), §178: "This obligation comprise[s] the duty to secure respect for the applicable rules of international human rights law and international humanitarian law, to protect the inhabitants of the occupied territory against acts of violence, and not to tolerate such violence by any third party."

> Convention, to maintain the orderly government of the territory, and to ensure the security of the Occupying Power, of the members and property of the occupying forces or administration, and likewise of the establishments and lines of communication used by them." (emphasis added)

According to Sassòli and Benvenisti, the legislative powers of the Occupying Power in article 64§2 are not limited to the adoption of additional penal legislation but must be understood in "a broader sense and allow an occupying power to subject the local population to any (penal, civil, administrative, etc.) laws essential for the purposes it exhaustively enumerates", which include the maintenance of public order.[1372] Sassòli rightly points out that "[t]he most traditional way of restoring public order is criminal prosecution of those who breach it", but that GC IV also offers the "occupying power the additional option of subjecting persons, under various procedural safeguards, to assigned residence or internment 'for imperative reasons of security'." In his view, "this security is not only that of the occupying forces, but, due to the obligation to restore and maintain public order, also that of the inhabitants of the territory."[1373] While the argument makes sense, we cannot agree with it, and this for various reasons.

For one, we disagree with Sassòli and Benvenisti's broad reading of article 64§2 GC I. As Pictet has pointed out:

> "Unlike the articles which come before it [including article 64], Article 78 relates to people who have not been guilty of any infringement of the penal provisions enacted by the Occupying Power, but that Power may, for reasons of its own, consider them dangerous to its security and is consequently entitled to restrict their freedom of action."[1374]

In this sense, it may also be noted that articles 64 to 75 GC IV come under the heading "Penal legislation/procedure", whereas article 78 GC IV is entitled "Security measures." This may also be why Pictet seems to favor a stricter reading of article 64§2 allowing only for additional *penal* legislation.[1375]

But more importantly, article 79 GC IV explicitly states that "[t]he Parties to the conflict shall *not* intern protected persons, *except in accordance with* the provisions of Articles 41, 42, 43, 68 and 78." This exhaustive list of legal bases for internment in situations of international armed conflict and occupation thus leaves no room for the adoption of other legal bases for internment on the basis of article 64§4 GC IV. Clearly, the adoption of internment legislation by an Occupying Power on the basis of article 64§2 is not allowed.[1376]

[1372] Sassòli (*EJIL* 2005), pp. 669-670, with reference to Benvenisti, *The International Law of Occupation* (1993), p. 101. On article 64§2 GC IV, see also Schwenk, "Legislative Power of the Military Occupant under Article 43, Hague Regulations" (*YLJ* 1944-1945).

[1373] All citations from Sassòli (*EJIL* 2005), p. 655 (footnotes omitted).

[1374] Pictet, *Commentary GC IV* (1958), p. 368.

[1375] Pictet, *Commentary GC IV* (1958), pp. 335-337. In the same sense: Gasser in Fleck (2008), pp. 303-305.

[1376] Note that article 68§2 GC IV only authorizes internment as an alternative *sanction* for certain offences committed against the Interning Power, it does not however substitute criminal *proceedings* to determine the person's guilt and the type of sanction that is appropriate as a punishment (*cf. supra* note 934).

Even if Sassòli's view were correct, any internment measures based on article 64§2 GC IV would still require the adoption of legislation by the Occupying Power; article 78 GC IV cannot in such cases be the direct legal basis to intern.[1377] Where such legislation is incompatible with the right to liberty under international human rights law, derogation from the applicable human rights treaties will be necessary (as such derogation is not directly incorporated in IHL as is the case for article 78 GC IV).[1378]

3.2.4.3. Security internment versus detention in the framework of criminal proceedings

Security internment in occupied territory should be all the more exceptional than in the territory of the parties to the conflict precisely because the Occupying Power is expressly authorized under international humanitarian law to adopt such penal legislation as is essential to "to maintain the orderly government of the territory, and to ensure the security of the Occupying Power, of the members and property of the occupying forces or administration, and likewise of the establishments and lines of communication used by them."[1379]

Nevertheless, it is interesting to note that where the text of the Stockholm draft of GC IV provided that internment could only be ordered "with respect to persons against whom no specific charge can be preferred", that language was deleted by the Diplomatic Conference "in order to leave an Occupying Power freedom to intern a person against whom it would have been possible to prefer a charge."[1380] This indeed leaves an Occupying Power with a choice in cases where the person concerned has both committed criminal offences in the past and continues to be a threat to the present or future security of the Occupying Power or the population it is obliged to protect. It does not however do away with the requirement that in order to intern rather than prosecute, the person must pose a future threat. We have seen above that internment is an inherently preventive measure and may never be ordered as a punishment for past acts. We agree therefore with the position of the Israeli human rights organization B'Tselem that "when a person is suspected of having committed a criminal offence, claims that relevant evidence cannot be revealed or that sufficient proof is lacking to prosecute him cannot justify administrative detention",[1381] unless of course the person also poses a future threat to security that makes internment imperative.

[1377] In the same sense: Sassòli (*EJIL* 2005), p. 655. We agree with Sassòli that the adoption of legislation – if indeed it were authorized by article 64§2 GC IV (which we have shown it does not) – would be necessary to order internment (or more aptly in this context administrative detention) as a law enforcement measure based on the general obligation of an Occupying Power to maintain public order and safety. Where internment is however ordered for reasons directly related to ongoing hostilities or military operations in relation to the armed conflict, article 78 GC IV can serve as a direct legal basis for such internment, and does not require the adoption of additional legislation (*cf. supra* chapter I-1, section 1.2.3.3).

[1378] *Cf. supra* chapter I-2, section 2.2.2.2.

[1379] Article 64§2 GC IV.

[1380] *Final Records 1949*, Vol. II-A, p. 835.

[1381] B'Tselem (2009), p. 8.

In the same sense, Dinstein highlights:

"Administrative detention must have a preventive nature, that is, must be resorted to not as a penalty for an offence committed in the past but as a measures denying the suspect the possibility of committing an offence in the future. When a person suspected of having already committed an offence, he should be prosecuted before a competent court. True, it happens that administrative detentions are inflicted on persons who are suspected of having committed offences in the past, when there is not sufficient evidence to bring about their conviction by a court of law, or where proof of their guilt beyond reasonable doubt requires the disclosure of intelligence sources (especially the exposure of secret agents whom the occupant does not wish to endanger or whose clandestine operation he is unwilling to discontinue). Yet, even in such instances, the reason for the internment (at least in theory) is not punishment (without due process of law) for the offence committed in the past, but apprehension lest similar acts be committed in the future."[1382]

To be lawful, the real reason (not just in theory) for internment must be that the person poses an imperative threat to security that renders his or her internment absolutely necessary. Pejic aptly summarizes the importance of keeping to a strict distinction between security internment and preventive or punitive detention in the framework of criminal proceedings:

"Internment/administrative detention is a measure of control aimed at dealing with persons who pose a real threat to State security, currently or in the future, in situations of armed conflict, or to State security or public order in non-conflict situations; it is not a measure that is meant to replace criminal proceedings. A person who is suspected of having committed a criminal offence, whether in armed conflict or other situations of violence, has the right to benefit from the additional stringent judicial guarantees provided for in humanitarian and/or human rights law for criminal suspects, which include the right to be tried by a regularly constituted, independent and impartial court. Unless internment/administrative detention and penal repression are organized as strictly separate regimes there is a danger that internment might be used as a substandard system of penal repression in the hands of the executive power, bypassing the one sanctioned by a country's legislature and courts. The rights of criminal suspects would thus be gravely undermined."[1383]

3.2.4.4. Temporal limits to the use of article 78 GC IV as a legal basis to intern

Whereas the Convention ceases to apply in the territory of the parties to the conflict as soon as military operations have come to a general close, article 6§3 GC IV prescribes that:

"In the case of occupied territory, the application of the present Convention shall cease one year after the general close of military operations; however, the Occupying Power shall be bound, for the duration of the occupation, to the extent that such Power exercises the functions of government in such territory, by the

[1382] Dinstein (*Isr.YHR* 1978), pp. 125-126.
[1383] Pejic (*IRRC* 2005), p. 381.

provisions of the following Articles of the present Convention: 1 to 12, 27, 29 to 34, 47, 49, 51, 52, 53, 59, 61 to 77, 143."

Under the Hague Regulations, the law of international armed conflict and its specific rules on occupation applied until the occupation came to an end. The original draft for the Fourth Geneva Convention confirmed that practice.[1384] At the 1949 Diplomatic Conference however, the decision was made to limit the applicability of the Convention in time because:

> "if the occupation were to continue for a very long time after the general cessation of hostilities, a time would doubtless come when the application of the Convention was *no longer justified*, especially if most of the governmental and administrative duties carried out at one time by the Occupying Power had been handed over to the authorities of the occupied territory. [...] The solution appears to be a reasonable one. One year after the close of hostilities, the authorities of the occupied State will almost always have regained their freedom of action to some extent; communications with the outside world having been re-established, world public opinion will, moreover, have some effect. Furthermore, two cases of an occupation being prolonged after the cessation of hostilities can be envisaged. When the occupied Power is victorious, the territory will obviously be freed before one year has passed; on the other hand, if the Occupying Power is victorious, the occupation may last more than a year, but *as hostilities have ceased, stringent measures against the civilian population will no longer be justified*."[1385]

Taking into account the reality of prolonged occupation, the Convention then goes on to list obligations by which the Occupying Power continues to be bound in so far as it continues to exercise government functions. The selected obligations confirm the rationale behind the limitation in time of the Convention's applicability: apart from the obligations to ensure the protection of the inhabitants of the occupied territory from arbitrary action or abuse in the hands of an enemy power (articles 1-12, 27, 29-34, 47, 49, 53, 59, 61-63, 143), they include the obligations inherent in the continued exercise of government functions by the Occupying Power (articles 51-52 and 64-77). Provisions "closely connected with military operations",[1386] including those regarding internment, are excluded. The selection thus reflects the fact that since hostilities have come to an end, "stringent measures against the civilian population [such as internment or assigned residence] will no longer be justified."[1387]

Indeed, of the internment provisions of the Convention, only article 143 GC IV – which prescribes supervision by the Protecting Powers or the ICRC of the

---

[1384] *Final Record 1949*, Vol. I, p. 114: "The present Convention shall apply from the outset of any conflict covered by Article 2. The application thereof shall cease on the close of hostilities or of occupation, except as regards protected persons whose release, repatriation or re-establishment may take place subsequently and who, until such operations are terminated, shall continue to benefit by the present Convention."

[1385] Pictet, *Commentary GC IV* (1958), pp. 62-63 (emphasis added).

[1386] Pictet, *Commentary GC IV* (1958), p. 63. Military operations in this sense "means the movements, manoeuvres and actions of any sort, carried out by the armed forces with a view to combat." (Sandoz et al., *Commentary AP I and II* (1987), p. 67) *Cf.* also *supra* section 3.2.1.6.

[1387] Pictet, *Commentary GC IV* (1958), p. 63.

parties to the conflict's respect and application of the Convention – continues to apply beyond the one-year time period.[1388] This is explained by the fact that that provision is a general one and while it has specific relevance for the protection of internees, it obliges parties to the conflict to give unimpeded access to the Protecting Power and the ICRC "to all places where protected persons are", including places of detention and labor camps; and by the fact that the provisions of the Convention regarding labor (articles 50-51 GC IV) and regarding detention in the framework of criminal proceedings and the administration of justice (articles 64-77 GC IV) continue to apply until the end of the occupation.

The other internment provisions of the Convention, including the legal basis to intern protected persons where "necessary for imperative reasons of security" (article 78 GC IV), cease to apply one year after the general close of military operations. This means that no person can be interned in the occupied territory on the basis of international humanitarian law after that time.[1389] As we mentioned earlier, since the hostilities have come to an end, such stringent security measures, legitimate only for reasons of military necessity, will no longer be justified. The rationale behind the exclusion of the internment provisions from article 6§3 GC IV is the same as that behind the decision *not* to provide for a one-year waiting period for the Convention to cease to apply in the territory of the parties to the conflict:

> "Committee III had laid down that in the territory of the Parties to the conflict the Convention would not cease to apply until one year after the general close of military operations. The United Kingdom Delegation proposed in plenary session that this waiting period should be dropped. The British amendment was adopted by 17 votes to 14, with 12 abstentions. It has doubtless certain advantages, but also certain drawbacks, for in the period following the close of military operations conditions are still fairly unsettled and the passions roused by war are still aflame. Hence the necessity for clear rules safeguarding protected persons, most of whom are of course enemy nationals. It was argued, however, that while the maintenance in force of the Convention would certainly *protect* foreign nationals in the territory of the Parties to the conflict, *it would* at the same time *provide grounds for prolonging any security measures applied to them, such as assigned residence or internment. But such restrictions of personal liberty are only justified by the existence of an armed struggle*. Viewed from that angle, the solution adopted was a happy one; *it means at any rate that there can be no question after hostilities have ended, of applying restrictive measures of this kind to enemy nationals who have*

[1388] To be noted that article 143§3 GC IV, which prescribes that such access "may not be prohibited except for reasons of imperative military necessity" may no longer be a valid basis of prohibiting or restricting such access when military operations have come to a general close. Again, where there are no ongoing hostilities or military operations, there can be no "military necessity". See also Pictet, *Commentary GC IV* (1958), pp. 576-577.

[1389] For persons interned before that time, article 78 GC IV remains a valid legal basis to intern only for as long as is necessary to organize the release and resettlement or repatriation of the internees in accordance with articles 133 and 134 GC IV. These internees also continue to benefit from the full protection of the Convention until their final release and resettlement or repatriation. Article 6§4 GC IV and *supra* section 3.2.1.6.

> *not been subjected to them before.* This remark only applies, incidentally, to security measures and not to the normal administration of justice."[1390]

The "normal administration of justice" clearly includes detention on criminal charges and imprisonment upon conviction. This explains why the provisions regulating the administration of justice and maintenance of public order in occupied territory (articles 64-77 GC IV) continue to apply in as far as the Occupying Power exercises these government functions. It does not however include security internment for reasons of military necessity. Deprivation of liberty for reasons of military necessity is considered legitimate in international humanitarian law only in as far as hostilities and military operations are ongoing; it is not considered legitimate as a measure of mere law enforcement where such hostilities or military operations have come to an end, and even less so one year later.

In this sense, it also worthwhile to recall that on the basis of article 64§2 GC IV, the Occupying Power can adopt legislation that is

> "essential to enable [it] to fulfill its obligations [under the Convention], to maintain the orderly government of the territory, and to ensure the security of the Occupying Power, of the members and property of the occupying forces or administration, and likewise of the establishments and lines of communication used by them."[1391]

To the extent and for as long as the Occupying Power continues to exercise government functions beyond the one-year time limit in article 6§2 GC IV, it may either rely on legislation in force in the occupied territory (article 64§1 GC IV) or make use of the legislative powers granted by article 64§2 to take such law enforcement measures as are necessary to maintain public order and safety and the security of its troops and equipment.

A final word needs to be said about article 3(b) AP I, which prescribes that "the application of the Conventions and of this Protocol shall cease [...] in the case of occupied territories, on the termination of the occupation". As the commentators of the Protocol point out:

> "This sub-paragraph takes up [...] various aspects of the provisions relating to the end of the application of [GC I, III and IV]. It replaces these provisions and its main effect is to extend the application in occupied territory beyond what is laid down in the fourth Convention."[1392]

The commentators go on to explain:

> "The extension of the application up to the termination of occupation, as laid down in this sub-paragraph (b), actually takes up again the draft which the Diplomatic Conference in 1949 rejected. However good the reasons advanced against this solution at that time may have been, despite the possible extension of the application for some articles as just mentioned, and despite the existence in Article 6 of the fourth Convention of a clause corresponding to that to be studied below under the next heading [regarding the continued protection of the

[1390] Pictet, *Commentary GC IV* (1958), pp. 61-62 (emphasis added).
[1391] Article 64§2 GC IV.
[1392] Sandoz et al., *Commentary AP I and II* (1987), p. 67.

Convention for protected persons until their final release and resettlement or repatriation], obvious progress has been made and any future controversy regarding the exact moment of the general close of military operations will be pointless."[1393]

It remains unclear whether article 3(b) AP I has become part of customary international law and thus can bind parties to the Geneva Conventions who have not ratified AP I.[1394] In this sense, it is interesting to note however that the ICJ, in its advisory opinion on the wall constructed by Israel on parts of the occupied Palestinian territories, did not make any mention of article 3(b) AP I when it found that:

"Since the military operations leading to the occupation of the West Bank in 1967 ended a long time ago, only those Articles of the Fourth Geneva Convention referred to in Article 6, paragraph 3, remain applicable in that occupied territory."[1395]

Regardless of whether article 3(b) AP I has become customary or not, for our present purposes it is important to understand that its purpose in expanding the application *ratione temporis* of the Convention beyond what was provided for by the Fourth Geneva Convention was protective in nature, as is clear from the commentator's explanation for this expansion. Therefore, and in light of the general principles underlying internment on the basis of GC IV, especially those regarding exceptionality and necessity, it is submitted that the legal basis to intern protected persons in occupied territory for reasons of military necessity (article 78 GC IV) will only be a valid legal basis to intern such persons for maximum one year after military operations have come to a general close. A UK Court of Appeal apparently came to the same conclusion and for the same reasons:

"The concept of internment for imperative reasons of security is a very familiar one in international law. It creates a high threshold test, and it is available in the ordinary way to a belligerent power both during a war and for up to a year during any period of occupation that follows the end of the war."[1396]

[1393] Sandoz et al., *Commentary AP I and II* (1987), p. 68.

[1394] The ICRC did not seem to find the issue conclusive enough to be integrated into its compilation of customary IHL, see Henckaerts & Doswald-Beck (2005), and the ICRC's updated *CIHL Database* (2010).

[1395] ICJ, *Wall Opinion* (2004), §125. The General Assembly's request for the advisory opinion of the Court considered both GC IV and AP I are applicable in the occupied Palestinian territories (UNGA, *Resolution ES-10/14* (2003), preambular §8). Israel however has not ratified AP I and while the ICJ relied on both treaty and customary international humanitarian law, it made no reference to article 3(b) AP I in its application of article 6§3 GC IV to the case before it. No reference is made to this issue in the separate and dissenting opinions of the judges of the Court either. This may be an indication that neither the Court nor its judges consider that article to be part of customary international humanitarian law.

[1396] UK, CA, *Al-Jedda* (2006), §85. This is one of the few instances where the Court in this case interpreted the scope of application of GC IV correctly. For a critique of other aspects of the judgment regarding this question, *cf. supra* note 721 and *cf. infra* chapter II-4, section 4.3.

3.3. CONCLUSIONS ON INTERNMENT ON THE BASIS OF GC IV

We have seen in chapters II-1 and II-2 that most but not all members of the armed forces of the parties to an international armed conflict may be interned by an adverse party to that conflict on the basis of the internment provisions of the first three Geneva Conventions. Parties to the conflict who find it necessary to intern a person who does not fall within the personal scope of application of these Conventions can only do so on the basis of international humanitarian law if that person qualifies as a protected person under the Fourth Geneva Convention.

Our analysis of the concept of protected person in section 3.1 of the present chapter demonstrates that the Fourth Geneva Convention's personal scope of application does not distinguish individuals based on their status under the rules on the conduct of hostilities. It does not distinguish between members and non-members of armed forces or between "combatants" and "civilians". The definition of protected persons under GC IV includes any person who is neither a prisoner of war nor a member of the medical and religious personnel of the armed forces of a party to the conflict.

The Convention *a priori* excludes from its personal scope of application persons who are nationals of the power in whose hands they are, or nationals of an ally of that power or of a neutral State with whom that power maintains normal diplomatic relations. Such persons are excluded from the Convention's scope of application on the assumption that they are unlikely to be regarded as enemies by the power in whose hands they find themselves and thus are not in need of the Convention's protection. Nevertheless, where that assumption does not reflect reality, and a person finds him- or herself in the hands of a party to the conflict who regards that person as an enemy belonging to or siding with an adverse party to the conflict, it is submitted that the nationality requirement in article 4 GC IV must be read in a nuanced way, and interpreted in a manner that effectively allows the Convention to achieve its protective purpose.

The Convention's provisions, including those regulating internment – do make one distinction between two categories of protected persons: those who are in the territory of the party to the conflict in whose hands they find themselves, and those who find themselves in occupied territory. Nevertheless, we have seen that, in as far as the lawful grounds for and duration of internment are concerned, there are no substantial differences between these two categories of persons.

There are only two such lawful grounds: either the individual concerned, for reasons of personal security, voluntarily demands internment and such internment is indeed necessary to safeguard his or her security; or the individual concerned present a military or security threat that cannot be countered but by his or her internment. In section 3.2 of this chapter, we have analyzed these grounds in considerable detail. It is hoped that the analysis and examples given will facilitate the task of both decision-makers on the ground and courts or other bodies called upon to evaluate the lawfulness of such decisions under international law, in interpreting and applying the internment provisions of GC IV in practice.

The analysis of the grounds for internment in GC IV will also guide our reflection in Part III on what could be lawful grounds to intern in situations of non-international armed conflict. While existing international humanitarian law applicable to such conflict does not include a legal basis to intern equivalent to those that are enshrined in the Geneva Conventions, there is an ongoing debate on how internment in such situations is or should be regulated by international law. Participants in that debate clearly seek guidance in the provisions of the Geneva Conventions, and it is in this context that the so-called "DPH-approach" to internment has emerged. We chose to discuss this approach in the present Part rather than in Part III since it is essentially based on an interpretation of international humanitarian law applicable in international armed conflict and occupation. The risks inherent in that approach, which in our view are even greater when applied to situations of non-international armed conflict, will also guide our analysis and proposals to address the question of who can be interned, for what reasons and for how long in non-international armed conflict in Part III.

But before we move on to situations of non-international armed conflict, we must finalize our analysis of the issue of internment in situations of international armed conflict and occupation by examining whether there is a legal basis in international humanitarian law to intern persons who fall outside the personal scope of application of the Geneva Conventions and their Additional Protocol I.

CHAPTER II – 4
INTERNMENT OF PERSONS WHO ARE NOT PROTECTED BY THE GENEVA CONVENTIONS

4.1. NO LEGAL BASIS TO INTERN IN THE GENEVA CONVENTIONS OR ADDITIONAL PROTOCOL I

The 1949 Geneva Conventions, as developed further by Additional Protocol I and in customary international humanitarian law, apply to all persons affected by situations of international armed conflict and occupation. Their respective personal scopes of application are mutually exclusive and in principle, any person affected by international armed conflict or occupation should be protected by at least one of the Conventions.

Nevertheless, there may be a limited number of persons who fall outside the scope of application of any of the Conventions, not on the basis of status or behaviour, but on the basis of nationality. Persons who are not prisoners of war or do not belong to the medical and religious personnel of the armed forces of the parties to the conflict, and at the same time do not qualify as "protected persons" under the Fourth Geneva Convention because of their nationality or because of the existence of normal diplomatic relations between the party to the conflict in whose hands they have fallen and the State of their nationality, may indeed fall outside the scope of application of the Conventions as a whole.

The object and purpose of the Geneva Conventions require that the provisions defining their scope of application be interpreted broadly, dynamically and effectively so as to protect the greatest number of persons actually affected by a situation of armed conflict.[1397] Our proposed reading of the nationality requirements in article 4 GC III and article 4 GC IV aims to interpret these provisions in conformity with subsequent developments in general international law, in order to achieve the Conventions' protective purpose by reducing the number of persons that could fall outside of their personal scope of application and be left without adequate protection under international law, and to accommodate some of the contemporary features of armed conflicts, most notably the fact that nationality and allegiance do not always form an automatic pair.

Where a person is deprived of his or her liberty for reasons related to an international armed conflict or a situation of occupation still – in spite of our proposed reading of article 4 GC III and article 4 GC IV – falls outside the

---

[1397] *Cf. supra* notes 349 and 378.

personal scope of application of either Convention,[1398] the Geneva Conventions may obviously not be relied upon to justify that deprivation of liberty. One cannot rely on a treaty to justify an action in a case to which that treaty does not apply. The legal basis for internment of such persons will have to be found in the domestic legal order of the interning State or, hypothetically, in another applicable instrument of international law.[1399] Regardless of the domestic or international nature of that legal basis, it will have to satisfy both the general principle of legality of restrictions on fundamental rights and freedoms and the specific criteria of the right to liberty under international human rights law discussed in Part I.[1400]

Nevertheless, the fact that a person is deprived of liberty for reasons related to an international armed conflict or occupation on the basis of another legal instrument than the Geneva Conventions does not mean this person does not benefit from any international legal protection. Any such person remains under the protection of international human rights law and of a limited number of provisions of international humanitarian law, specifically designed to ensure a minimum of protection to persons that fall outside its personal scope of application.

4.2. PROTECTION IN CAPTIVITY: INTERNATIONAL HUMANITARIAN AND HUMAN RIGHTS LAW

> "[I]t could not be intended by the High Contracting Parties that the cases not provided for should, for want of a written provision, be left to the arbitrary judgment of the military commanders.
>
> Until a more complete code of the laws of war is issued, the High Contracting Parties think it right to declare that in cases not included in the Regulations adopted by them, populations and belligerents remain under the protection and empire of the principles of international law, as they result from the usages established between civilized nations, from the laws of humanity, and the requirements of the public conscience".[1401]

[1398] We leave aside medical and religious personnel of the armed forces to the conflict, whose retention is regulated by GC I-II but whose treatment in captivity must conform to GC III (article 33 GC III; article 28§§2-4 GC I; and articles 37§3 39§5 GC II). For the purposes of the present chapter, such personnel may be assumed to be included in the category of persons protected by GC III.

[1399] So far, no such instrument exists, *cf.* also *infra* section 4.3. On the contrary, (preventive criminal) detention of persons charged with war crimes, genocide or crimes against humanity may be possible in accordance with the Statute of an international criminal tribunal or court, *cf. supra* chapter I-1, section 1.2.3.3.

[1400] Derogations may be possible (*cf. supra* chapter I-2), but there can be no reliance on the internment provisions of IHL as so-called *lex specialis* since they do not apply (*cf.* also *infra* section 4.2.2).

[1401] Preamble of Hague Regulations (1899), §8, commonly referred to as the "Martens clause" and reiterated in preamble Hague Regulations (1907), in articles 63§4 GC I, 62§4 GC II, 142§4 GC III, and 158§4 GC IV, in article 1§2 AP I, and in the preamble of AP II.

4.2.1. Protection under international humanitarian law

Persons who do not benefit from the protection of either the Third or the Fourth Geneva Convention remain protected by article 75 AP I, the substance of which is generally accepted to reflect customary international law.[1402] The first paragraph of article 75 AP I reads:

> "[i]n so far as they are affected by [international armed conflict or occupation], persons who are in the power of a Party to the conflict and who do not benefit from more favourable treatment under the Conventions or under this Protocol shall be treated humanely in all circumstances and shall enjoy, as a minimum, the protection provided by this Article without any adverse distinction."

As a provision of international humanitarian law, the personal scope of application of article 75 AP I is limited to persons *affected by a situation of international armed conflict or occupation*. It therefore does not apply to persons deprived of liberty for reasons unrelated to such conflict.[1403] Article 75 is a safety net that applies only to persons who do not benefit more favourable treatment under the Geneva Conventions and AP I, whether in full or in part.[1404] But it applies to such persons without any adverse distinction, including on the basis of nationality:

[1402] The substantive provisions of article 75 AP I are well reflected in Rules 87-105 of the ICRC's compilation of customary IHL: Henckaerts & Doswald-Beck (2005), Vol. I, pp. 299-383; see also CoE, *Venice Commission Opinion* (2003), §51. The US, who has not ratified AP I and strongly objects to the customary nature of some of its rules, does accept article 75 AP I to reflect customary international humanitarian law. As the US Supreme Court pointed out in *Hamdan* (2006), pp. 70-71: "[with regard to essential judicial guarantees] recognized by customary international law. Many of these are described in Article 75 of Protocol I to the Geneva Conventions of 1949, adopted in 1977 (Protocol I). Although the United States declined to ratify Protocol I, its objections were not to Article 75 thereof. [...] the principles, articulated in Article 75 and indisputably part of the customary international law, that an accused must, absent disruptive conduct or consent, be present for his trial and must be privy to the evidence against him." See also the affirmations of the customary nature of the provisions of article 75 AP I by various legal advisors of the US Department of State and included in the Department of State's Digest of US practice in international law, for example: Matheson, "The US Position on the Relation of Customary International Law to the 1977 Protocols Additional to the 1949 Geneva Conventions, Remarks before Session One of the Humanitarian Law Conference" (*AUJILP* 1987), pp. 426; Taft, "The Law of Armed Conflict after 9/11: Some Salient Features. Remarks at the Symposium on Current Pressures on International Humanitarian Law" (*YJIL* 2003), p. 322; and US, *Digest of Practice* (2002), pp. 972-973: "In commentary on the military commissions [...] Legal Adviser of the U.S. State Department William H. Taft, IV, [...] concluded that the new procedures provided protections consistent with those set out in the 1949 Geneva Conventions, *the customary principles found in article 75 (Fundamental Guarantees) of Additional Protocol I* to the Geneva Conventions, and the International Covenant on Civil and Political Rights" (emphasis added). On the customary nature of article 75 AP I, see also Aldrich (*AJIL* 2002), p. 893; IAC°HR, *Terrorism and Human Rights* (2002), §76; Dörmann (*IRRC* 2003), p. 70; Dinstein (2004), p. 33; WGAD and Special Rapporteurs, *Situation of Detainees at Guantánamo Bay* (2006), §9.

[1403] It does however clearly apply to persons deprived of liberty for being suspected or convicted of war crimes and crimes against humanity committed in the course of that conflict, and to security internees where their internment is for reasons related to the armed conflict (nexus). See Sandoz et al., *Commentary to AP I and II* (1987), p. 867.

[1404] Sandoz et al., *Commentary AP I and II* (1987), pp. 867-868. See also article 45§3 AP I: "Any person who has taken part in hostilities, who is not entitled to prisoner-of-war status and who does not benefit from more favourable treatment in accordance with the Fourth Convention shall have the right at all times to the protection of Article 75 of this Protocol. In occupied territory, any such

"It may justifiably be considered that the wording of this paragraph covers persons in the power of any Party to the conflict, even that of which the individual is a national."[1405]

Article 75 AP I prescribes that all persons deprived of liberty in relation to a situation of international armed conflict or occupation must at all times be treated humanely, are entitled to essential procedural safeguards and (when tried for a criminal offence) essential judicial guarantees to assure a fair trial:

"2. The following acts are and shall remain prohibited at any time and in any place whatsoever, whether committed by civilian or by military agents: (a) violence to the life, health, or physical or mental well-being of persons, in particular: (i) murder; (ii) torture of all kinds, whether physical or mental; (iii) corporal punishment; and (iv) mutilation; (b) outrages upon personal dignity, in particular humiliating and degrading treatment, enforced prostitution and any form of indecent assault; (c) the taking of hostages; (d) collective punishments; and (e) threats to commit any of the foregoing acts.

3. Any person arrested, detained or interned for actions related to the armed conflict shall be informed promptly, in a language he understands, of the reasons why these measures have been taken. Except in cases of arrest or detention for penal offences, such persons shall be released with the minimum delay possible and in any event as soon as the circumstances justifying the arrest, detention or internment have ceased to exist.

4. No sentence may be passed and no penalty may be executed on a person found guilty of a penal offence related to the armed conflict except pursuant to a conviction pronounced by an impartial and regularly constituted court respecting the generally recognized principles of regular judicial procedure, which include the following: (a) the procedure shall provide for an accused to be informed without delay of the particulars of the offence alleged against him and shall afford the accused before and during his trial all necessary rights and means of defence; (b) no one shall be convicted of an offence except on the basis of individual penal responsibility; (c) no one shall be accused or convicted of a criminal offence on account of any act or omission which did not constitute a criminal offence under the national or international law to which he was subject at the time when it was committed; nor shall a heavier penalty be imposed than that which was applicable at the time when the criminal offence was committed; if, after the commission of the offence, provision is made by law for the imposition of a lighter penalty, the offender shall benefit thereby; (d) anyone charged with an offence is presumed innocent until proved guilty according to law; (e) anyone charged with an offence shall have the right to be tried in his presence;

---

person, unless he is held as a spy, shall also be entitled, notwithstanding Article 5 of the Fourth Convention, to his rights of communication under that Convention."

[1405] Sandoz et al., *Commentary AP I and II* 81987), pp. 868-869. In the same sense: Bothe et al. (1982), p. 458. The question of the applicability of article 75 AP I to persons who have the same nationality as the State in whose power they find themselves was subject to disagreement at the Diplomatic Conference. We fully agree however with the conclusion reached by the commentators. The protective object and purpose of the Protocol, and in particular that of article 75 AP I – which intends to set minimum fundamental guarantees to be respected at all times and in all places and thus must be interpreted as broadly as possible – further supports that conclusion.

(f) no one shall be compelled to testify against himself or to confess guilt; (g) anyone charged with an offence shall have the right to examine, or have examined, the witnesses against him and to obtain the attendance and examination of witnesses on his behalf under the same conditions as witnesses against him; (h) no one shall be prosecuted or punished by the same Party for an offence in respect of which a final judgement acquitting or convicting that person has been previously pronounced under the same law and judicial procedure; (i) anyone prosecuted for an offence shall have the right to have the judgement pronounced publicly; and (j) a convicted person shall be advised on conviction of his judicial and other remedies and of the time-limits within which they may be exercised.

5. Women whose liberty has been restricted for reasons related to the armed conflict shall be held in quarters separated from men's quarters. They shall be under the immediate supervision of women. Nevertheless, in cases where families are detained or interned, they shall, whenever possible, be held in the same place and accommodated as family units.

6. Persons who are arrested, detained or interned for reasons related to the armed conflict shall enjoy the protection provided by this Article until their final release, repatriation or re-establishment, even after the end of the armed conflict.

7. In order to avoid any doubt concerning the prosecution and trial of persons accused of war crimes or crimes against humanity, the following principles shall apply: (a) persons who are accused of such crimes should be submitted for the purpose of prosecution and trial in accordance with the applicable rules of international law; and (b) any such persons who do not benefit from more favourable treatment under the Conventions or this Protocol shall be accorded the treatment provided by this Article, whether or not the crimes of which they are accused constitute grave breaches of the Conventions or of this Protocol."

The second paragraph of article 75 AP I reproduces in almost identical terms the text of the first paragraph of common article 3 of the Geneva Conventions, violations of which are prohibited "at any time and any place whatsoever". Common article 3 of the Geneva Conventions applies – as a matter of treaty law – only to situations of non-international armed conflict. The article's provisions are however considered to be an absolute minimum, a "mini-convention", applicable to all types of armed conflicts, and even in times of peace. In the words of the International Court of Justice:

"Article 3 which is common to all four Geneva Conventions of 12 August 1949 defines certain rules to be applied in the armed conflicts of a non-international character. There is no doubt that, in the event of international armed conflicts, these rules also constitute a minimum yardstick, in addition to the more elaborate rules which are also to apply to international conflicts; and they are rules which, in the Court's opinion, reflect what the Court in 1949 called "elementary considerations of humanity" (Corfu Channel, Merits)."[1406]

[1406] ICJ, *Nicaragua v. US* (1986), §218. The relevant passage of the Court's judgment in *Corfu Channel* reads: "Such obligations are based, not on the Hague Convention of 1907 [...], which is applicable in time of war, but on certain general and well-recognized principles, namely: elementary considerations of humanity, even more exacting in peace than in war" (ICJ, *Corfu Channel* (1949), p. 22). For the applicability of CA3 in international armed conflicts and situations of occupation,

The ICRC Commentary to common article 3 explicitly recalls that:

"The value of the provision is not limited to the field dealt with in Article 3. Representing, as it does, the minimum which must be applied in the least determinate of conflicts, its terms must *a fortiori* be respected in the case of international conflicts proper, when all the provisions of the Convention are applicable. For "the greater obligation includes the lesser", as one might say. [...] It makes it absolutely clear that the object of the Convention is a purely humanitarian one [...] and that it merely ensures respect for the few essential rules of humanity which all civilized nations consider as valid everywhere and under all circumstances and as being above and outside war itself."[1407]

The provisions of common article 3 therefore protect – as a matter of customary international law – all persons affected by armed conflict, regardless of the qualification of the conflict or the legal status of the persons concerned.[1408] They demand that:

"(1) Persons taking no active part in the hostilities, including members of armed forces who have laid down their arms and those placed 'hors de combat' by sickness, wounds, detention, or any other cause, shall in all circumstances be treated humanely, without any adverse distinction founded on race, colour, religion or faith, sex, birth or wealth, or any other similar criteria. To this end, the following acts are and shall remain prohibited at any time and in any place whatsoever with respect to the above-mentioned persons: (a) violence to life and person, in particular murder of all kinds, mutilation, cruel treatment and torture; (b) taking of hostages; (c) outrages upon personal dignity, in particular humiliating and degrading treatment; (d) the passing of sentences and the carrying out of executions without previous judgment pronounced by a regularly constituted court, affording all the judicial guarantees which are recognized as indispensable by civilized peoples. (2) The wounded and sick shall be collected and cared for."

Finally, persons who fall outside the personal scope of application of the 1949 Geneva Conventions and their Additional Protocol I remain protected by the relevant provisions of customary international humanitarian law.[1409]

---

see also ICTY, *Tadíc* (1995), §87; IAC°HR, *Abella v. Argentina* (1997), §§155-156; ICTR, *Akayesu* (1998), §601; ICTY, *Delalíc* (2001), §143. For an example of State practice, see US, Department of Defence, *Directive 2310.01* (2006), §4(2): "All persons subject to this Directive shall observe the requirements of the law of war, and shall apply, without regard to a detainees' legal status, at a minimum the standards articulated in Common Article 3 to the Geneva Conventions of 1949 [...] Of note, certain categories of detainees, such as [prisoners of war, civilian internees and retained personnel interned on the basis of GC I-IV] enjoy protections under the law of war in addition to the minimum standards prescribed in Common Article 3."

[1407] Pictet, *Commentary GC IV* (1958), pp. 38 and 44. In the same sense: Pictet, *Commentary GC IV* (1958), p. 14, and Pictet, *Commentary GC III* (1960), p. 16.

[1408] In the same sense: ICTY, *Tadíc* (1995), §616; IAC°HR, *Abella v. Argentina* (1997), §§176 and 189; Council of Europe, *Venice Commission Opinion* (2003), §40. For a more critical, but not necessarily contrary, view: Dinstein (2010), pp. 38-39.

[1409] See in particular Rules 87-105 (fundamental guarantees, reflected to a large extent in the provisions of article 3 common to the GC and article 75 AP I) and Rules 118-128 (persons deprived of liberty) of the ICRC's compilation of customary IHL: Henckaerts & Doswald-Beck (2005), Vol. I, pp. 299-383 and pp. 428-546. See also Dörmann (*IRRC* 2003), pp. 66-71 and – more specifically with regard to the legal framework for internment – the ICRC position on procedural principles and

The importance of the protections afforded under these provisions of international humanitarian law is that they are recognized as a set of absolute minimum rules that may never be derogated from, even in times of armed conflict. Nationality is of no relevance for a person's entitlement to protection under article 75 AP I, common article 3 GC or the relevant provisions of customary international humanitarian law.

4.2.2. Protection under international human rights law

Paragraph 8 of article 75 AP I explicitly provides that:

> "No provision of this Article may be construed as limiting or infringing any other more favourable provision granting greater protection, under any applicable rules of international law, to persons covered by paragraph 1."

Such other "applicable rules of international law" clearly and primarily include the rules of international human rights law. As we have seen above, international human rights law continues to apply alongside international humanitarian law in all situations of armed conflict.[1410] It continues to function as the general legal regime protecting all individuals both in peace-time and in times of armed conflict.

While the application of international human rights norms in situations of armed conflict must take into account relevant rules of international humanitarian law, their application or interpretation may not be affected by those rules that are not applicable to the case at hand. Therefore, only the rules of international humanitarian law referred to above[1411] will be relevant for applying and interpreting the relevant rules of international human rights law applicable to persons interned for reasons related to a conflict but who do not fall within the scope of application of the Geneva Conventions and Additional Protocol I.[1412]

safeguards for internment and administrative detention in armed conflict and other situations of violence as reflected in Pejic (*IRRC* 2005), pp. 375-391.

[1410] The applicability of a given norm of international human rights law will depend on whether the internee is within the jurisdiction of a party to that treaty (*cf. supra* note 36). Nationality and affiliation with a party to the armed conflict are however irrelevant for the determining the applicability of the provisions on the right to liberty in international human rights law, as has been reaffirmed in CoE, *Venice commission Opinion* (2003), §49.

[1411] Article 75 AP I, CA 3 GC, and the rules of customary IHL referred to in note 1408 above.

[1412] These rules include the relevant provisions of the UDHR (1948), the ICCPR (1966), the CAT (1984), the CRC (1989), the International Convention on Enforced Disappearances (2006); those of the ECHR (1950), the AMDRDM (1948), the ACHR (1969), the Inter-American Convention on Forced Disappearances (1994), the ACHPR (1982), the Arab Charter on Human Rights (2004), the Cairo Declaration on Human Rights in Islam (1990), and the CIS Convention on Human Rights and Fundamental Freedoms (1995); and the relevant decisions, opinions and judgments of the international courts and treaty monitoring bodies charged with their application and supervision. Also relevant are so-called soft-law instruments, such as the UN's *Standard Minimum Rules* (1955); the UN's *Code of Conduct for Law Enforcement Officials* (1979); the UN's *Body of Principles* (1988); the AC°HPR's *Principles on Fair Trial and Legal Assistance* (2001); the IAC°HR's *Principles and Best Practices* (2008); the *Siracusa Principles* (1984); the ILA's *Paris Minimum Standards* (1984); and the *Turku Declaration* (1990). *Cf. supra* Part I.

The relevance of international human rights law is not limited to the category of persons covered by article 75 AP I; its pertinence and importance in armed conflict has been underlined since the earliest codifications on international humanitarian law and has been demonstrated in Part I and in chapters 1 to 3 of the present part. For the category of persons we are concerned with here however, international human rights law plays a more prominent role – explicitly recognized under international humanitarian law[1413] – than for persons interned on the basis of the Geneva Conventions, which contain detailed rules regulating their internment. Where applied to a person who is interned in a situation of international armed conflict or occupation but does not fall within the scope of the Geneva Conventions and Additional Protocol I, article 75§8 AP I requires that a more protective applicable human rights norm takes precedence over the minimum protections offered by IHL.

4.3. A LEGAL BASIS TO INTERN IN THE 1907 HAGUE REGULATIONS?

While persons who fall outside the personal scope of application of the 1949 Geneva Conventions benefit from a minimum set of protections under international humanitarian law and the full protection of international human rights law, these protective regimes do not provide parties to an international armed conflict or an Occupying Power with a *legal basis* to intern them for security reasons. Where such internment is necessary, its legal basis will thus have to be provided by the domestic legislation of the Interning Power.[1414]

Nevertheless, the Geneva Conventions and their Additional Protocols are not the only instruments of international humanitarian law in force today. In particular, some have argued that persons in occupied territory who do not fall within the personal scope of application of the Geneva Conventions may be interned on the basis of article 43 of the 1907 Hague Regulations, which reads as follows:

> "The authority of the legitimate power having in fact passed into the hands of the occupant, the latter shall take all the measures in his power to restore, and ensure, as far as possible, public order and safety, while respecting, unless absolutely prevented, the laws in force in the country."

[1413] See preambular paragraph 9/8 of the HR 1899/1907 ("Until a more complete code of the laws of war has been issued [...] in cases not included in the Regulations adopted by them, the inhabitants and the belligerents remain under the protection and the rule of the principles of the law of nations, as they result from the usages established among civilized peoples, from the laws of humanity, and the dictates of the public conscience"); articles 63§4/62§4/142§4/158§4 GC I-IV ("The denunciation [of the GC] shall have effect only in respect of the denouncing Power. It shall in no way impair the obligations which the Parties to the conflict shall remain bound to fulfil by virtue of the principles of the law of nations, as they result from the usages established among civilized peoples, from the laws of humanity and the dictates of the public conscience"); and article 72 AP I ("The provisions of this Section [which includes article 75 AP I] are additional to [...] as well as to other applicable rules of international law relating to the protection of fundamental human rights during international armed conflict").

[1414] We will discuss some of the other options available to States in chapter III-1.

Such an argument was notably made by the UK government, in a case concerning Hilal Abdul-Razzaq Ali Al-Jedda, a dual British-Iraqi national interned by UK forces in Iraq from 10 October 2004 until 30 December 2007.[1415] UK troops in Iraq were, at the time, part of the Multinational Force in Iraq (MNF-I), which upon request of the Iraqi government and with a UN Security Council mandate assisted the Iraqi government in establishing peace and stability in post-occupation Iraq, which continues to be ravaged by non-international armed conflict.[1416]

The government's argument with regard to article 43 HR met with the approval of UK domestic courts. The Court of Appeal, after disqualifying Mr. Al-Jedda as a protected person under GC IV on the basis of his British nationality, found that:

> "This does not mean that he could not have been lawfully detained in Iraq pursuant to the powers and obligations vested in the occupying powers under Article 43 of the Hague Regulations. [...] Article 43 of the Hague Regulations [...] empowers an occupying power to intern anyone it considers to be an immediate threat to security within the occupied territory, whatever their nationality. [...] Article 43 of the Hague Regulations merely embodies the rule of customary international law that such a military commander is bound to take all the measures in his power to restore and ensure, as far as possible, public order and safety, and internment for imperative reasons of security is a tool available in his armoury for achieving that aim. What Geneva IV does is to prescribe the circumstances in which this power is to be used and exercised in relation to the people protected by that convention."[1417]

The House of Lords, on appeal, did not come back on the arguments made by the Court of Appeal, but did suggest – without specifying on which legal basis – that an Occupying Power may lawfully intern persons who are not protected persons under GC IV but pose "a serious threat to the safety of the public or the Occupying power."[1418] It is unfortunate that the House of Lords did not address

---

[1415] ECtHR, *Al-Jedda v. UK* (Statement of Facts) (2009): "On 10 October 2004 the applicant was arrested by United States troops accompanied by Iraqi national guards and British soldiers. He was informed that he was suspected of membership of a terrorist group involved in weapons smuggling and explosive attacks in Iraq; allegations which the applicant denies. He was taken to the Sha'aibah Divisional Temporary Detention Facility in Basra, a detention centre run by British forces and held there until 30 December 2007."

[1416] The US-led MNF-I was in place as from 15 May 2004. It was mandated to assist Iraq in establishing security, peace and stability by UNSC *Resolution 1546* (2004). British troops ended their combat operations as part of MNF-I on 30 April 2009 and UK troops had fully withdrawn by 28 July 2009 (BBC, "UK Troops in Iraq Moved to Kuwait", 28 July 2009). The mandate of MNF-I expired on 31 December 2009; the remainder of the force was reorganized into the United States Forces-Iraq (USF-I) in charge of Operation New Dawn from 1 January 2010 until 31 December 2011.

[1417] UK, CA, *Al-Jedda* (2006), §§40 and 47.

[1418] UK, HoL, *Al-Jedda* (2007), §32: "First, it appears to me that during the period when the UK was an occupying power (from the cessation of hostilities on 1 May 2003 to the transfer of power to the Iraqi Interim Government on 28 June 2004) it was obliged, in the area which it effectively occupied, to take necessary measures to protect the safety of the public and its own safety. Article 43 of the Hague Regulations 1907 provides [...]. This provision is supplemented by certain provisions of the Fourth Geneva Convention. Articles 41, 42 and 78 of that convention, so far as material, provide [...] These three articles are designed to circumscribe the sanctions which may be applied to protected

the issue in more detail, since the Court of Appeal's interpretation of article 43 of the 1907 Hague Regulations is in our opinion clearly wrong.

First of all, at the time Mr. Al-Jedda was arrested and subsequently interned by the UK forces in Iraq, the occupation had already come to an end and the international law of occupation (codified in the 1907 Hague Regulations and the Fourth Geneva Convention) had thus ceased to apply. Neither the Fourth Geneva Convention nor the 1907 Hague Regulations were therefore applicable to the internment of Mr- Al-Jedda by the British forces.[1419] The Court, however, justified its reliance on article 43 HR 1907 on the basis of article 6 of these same Regulations,[1420] which provides that:

> "In the case of occupied territory, the application of the present Convention shall cease one year after the general close of military operations, however, the Occupying Power shall be bound, for the duration of the occupation, to the extent that such Power exercises the functions of government in such territory, by the provisions of the following Articles of the Convention: 1 to 12, 27, 29 to 34, 47, 49, 51, 52, 53, 59, 61 to 77, 143."

However, the "general close of military operations" in Iraq took place on 1 May 2003, and Mr. Al-Jedda's was captured and interned on 10 October 2004, which is more than one year after the close of those operations. Moreover, following the Occupying Powers' transfer of sovereign authority and government functions in Iraq to the newly established Iraqi government on 28 June 2004, the occupation had come to an end.[1421] The US & UK had thus ceased to exercise government functions in Iraq before Mr. Al-Jedda was interned. Finally, even if Mr. Al-Jedda would have been interned in the one-year lapse of time mentioned by article 6, the text of that article demonstrates that article 43 – the alleged legal

---

persons, and they have no direct application to the appellant, who is not a protected person. But they show plainly that there is a power to intern persons who are not protected persons, and it would seem to me that if the occupying power considers it necessary to detain a person who is judged to be a serious threat to the safety of the public or the occupying power there must be an obligation to detain such person: see ICJ, *DRC v. Uganda* (2005)], para 178. This is a matter of some importance, since although the appellant was not detained during the period of the occupation, both the evidence and the language of UNSCR 1546 (2004) and the later resolutions strongly suggest that the intention was to continue the pre-existing security regime and not to change it. There is not said to have been such an improvement in local security conditions as would have justified any relaxation." ICJ, *DRC v. Uganda* (2005), §178 reads: "As [an Occupying Power, Uganda] was under an obligation, according to Article 43 of the Hague Regulations of 1907, to take all the measures in its power to restore, and ensure, as far as possible, public order and safety in the occupied area, while respecting, unless absolutely prevented, the laws in force in the DRC. This obligation comprised the duty to secure respect for the applicable rules of international human rights law and international humanitarian law, to protect the inhabitants of the occupied territory against acts of violence, and not to tolerate such violence by any third party."

1419 As was recognized by the House of Lords on appeal, see HoL, *Al-Jedda* (2007), §32 ("the appellant was not detained during the period of the occupation"); and by the European Court of Human Rights, see ECtHR (Grand Chamber), *Al-Jedda* (2011), §107 ("The Court notes in this respect that paragraph 2 of the Resolution [1546 of the UN Security Council] clearly stated that the occupation was to end by 30 June 2004."). On the temporal limits on internment in occupied territory, *cf.* also *supra* chapter II-3, section 3.2.4.4.

1420 UK, CA, *Al-Jedda* (2006), §42.

1421 BBC, "Timeline: Iraq after Saddam", 20 March 2007.

basis for internment in occupied territory – is not included in the provisions that continue to apply after the general close of military operations. Even if it were a valid legal basis to intern before, it could no longer be relied upon after that time.

But the judgment does raise an important question: can article 43 HR constitute a separate legal basis to intern persons in occupied territory who are not protected under GC IV? In our opinion that question must also be answered in the negative, and this for a number of reasons.

First of all, article 43 HR authorizes, and indeed even obliges an Occupying Power to "take all the measures in his power to restore, and ensure, as far as possible, public order and safety, while respecting, unless absolutely prevented, the laws in force in the country." It does not however prescribe the grounds and procedures in accordance with which it can deprive persons of their liberty in order to do so. The provision may reflect an Occupying Power's inherent right to intern persons in occupied territory where this is absolutely necessary to establish public order and safety, but it does not by itself satisfy the principle of legality and thus cannot be a valid legal basis for any internment.[1422]

In support of its argument, the Court of Appeal relied on the duty of the inhabitants of an occupied territory to obey the martial laws the Occupying Power may issue in order to restore peace and maintain security in the territory under its control.[1423] Apart from the fact that the UK at the time of Mr. Al-Jedda's internment no longer was an Occupying Power in Iraq, there are two additional problems with this argument. On the one hand, article 43 aims to authorize an Occupying Power to enforce local criminal legislation – and if necessary adopt additional penal legislation – for the purpose of restoring and maintaining order, and the prevention and punishment of criminal behaviour in the territory under its control. It is that specific legislation that will be the legal basis for detaining persons for offences, not article 43 HR itself. On the other hand, even if article 43 HR were to recognize an Occupying Power's inherent right to intern persons who otherwise pose a serious

[1422] On the existence of an inherent right to intern in armed conflict, *cf. infra* chapter III-1. To be noted also that the European Court of Human Rights, in its judgment in the *Al-Jedda* case, correctly, pointed out that "under international humanitarian law internment is to be viewed *not as an obligation* on the Occupying Power but as a measure of last resort" (ECtHR (Grand Chamber), *Al-Jedda* (2011), §107, emphasis added).

[1423] UK, CA, *Al-Jedda* (2006), §§37-47. The Court of Appeal quotes from the 1947 edition of *Oppenheim's International Law* ("An occupant having military authority over the territory, the inhabitants are under his Martial Law, and have to render obedience to his commands. Their duty to obey does not, of course, arise from their own Municipal Law, nor from International Law, but from the Martial Law of the occupant to which they are subjected") and from a post-World War II US Military Tribunal decision in *List et al.* (1948) ("The status of an occupant of the territory of the enemy having being achieved, international law places the responsibility upon the commanding general of preserving order, punishing crime, and protecting lives and property within the occupied territory. His power in accomplishing these ends is as great as his responsibility. But he is definitely limited by recognised rules of international law"). Both references however pre-date the 1949 Geneva Conventions and thus provide limited authority to interpret the provisions of the 1907 HR as supplemented by the Conventions. Moreover, the argument does in any case not hold, in that article 43 HR by itself does not satisfy the principle of legality nor the other requirements for lawful deprivation of liberty as it fails to determine the grounds and procedures in accordance with which internment may be ordered.

threat to its security or that of the population it is obliged to protect, here too, additional legislation would need to be adopted to prescribe the grounds and procedures for such internment. As said earlier on, article 43 HR does not by itself satisfy the principle of legality for deprivation of liberty in contemporary international law.[1424] Article 43 HR has been supplemented in 1949 by articles 64-68 GC IV for criminal detention and by article 78 GC IV for internment, the latter article setting out both the permissible ground for internment of civilians in occupied territory (imperative reasons of security) and the procedures regulating such internment (regular review by an administrative board set up for that specific purpose). That is why these articles can serve as a direct legal basis for deprivation of liberty, in contrast to article 43 HR, which does not meet those criteria.

Finally, and without prejudice to their continued applicability and relevance for the interpretation of the Conventions' provisions, the 1907 Hague Regulations cannot be relied upon as an alternative legal regime to that of the Geneva Conventions, since such an interpretation would lead to the absurd result that there are two types of international armed conflict and occupation, those covered by the 1949 Geneva Conventions, and those covered by the 1907 Hague Regulations. According to Pictet's comments on article 154 GC IV, which deals with the relationship between the 1907 HR and GC IV:

> "in the Fourth Convention some of the provisions of the Regulations which deal with civilians have been omitted or amended. [...] Generally speaking, however, it might rightly be claimed that the Convention as a whole determines the treatment of civilians in time of war so that in that connection, with the few exceptions discussed later, the new provisions have entirely replaced the 1907 Regulations."[1425]

The exceptions Pictet mentions include article 43, but in our view this does not have any impact on the question of the legal basis for internment of protected persons in occupied territory, as the grounds and procedures for such internment were not prescribed by any provision of the HR and thus could not have been omitted from GC IV. On the contrary, article 78 GC IV establishes, for the first time, such a legal basis in international law, adding an additional measure to those allowed under article 43 HR by explicitly authorizing security internment of protected persons and prescribing the grounds and procedures on which it may take place.

[1424] The article lays down the general rule limiting the *legislative* powers of an Occupying power by indicating to what extent it may change existing legislation or adopt new legislation in order to fulfil its obligations as the *de facto* authority in the territory. It thus gives indications as to what legislative action may be taken but does not offer by itself a legal basis to arrest and detain or intern persons threatening public order and safety or trespassing penal legislation (in the same sense: Sassòli (*EJIL* 2005), pp. 665-667); and Sassòli & Bouvier (2006), p. 195). Moreover, the obligation in article 43 HR to maintain public order and safety is subject to the limitations set by international human rights law for any measure of law enforcement, *cf. supra* chapter I-1.

[1425] Pictet, *Commentary GC IV* (1958), p. 614. Article 154 GC IV prescribes that "[i]n the relations between the Powers who are bound by [HC (II) 1899 and/or HC (IV) 1907], and who are parties to the [GC IV], this last Convention shall be supplementary to Sections II and III of [HR 1899 and/or HR 1907]."

For these reasons, article 43 of the 1907 Hague Regulations does not offer a separate legal basis to intern any person for reasons related to an international armed conflict or occupation.[1426] Where a person falls outside the personal scope of application of the 1949 Geneva Conventions, his or her internment may only be based on domestic legislation that satisfies the requirements of international human rights law.

[1426] In the present chapter we are concerned with persons who fall outside the personal scope of application of common article 2 of the Geneva Conventions. Nevertheless, we would advance the same arguments regarding article 43 HR 1907 and its inability to serve as a legal basis for internment to counter a claim that persons who come *within* the personal scope of application of these Conventions. Moreover, in as far as protected persons under GC IV are concerned, such a claim would not withstand the text of article 79 GC IV, which explicitly excludes the possibility to intern a protection on any other legal basis than those provided for in the Convention and discussed in chapter II-3.

Chapter II – 5

Conclusions on Internment in Situations of International Armed Conflict and Occupation

Parties to an international armed conflict and Occupying Powers may deprive individuals of their liberty for preventive purposes where this is necessary for reasons directly related to the situation of armed conflict or occupation. Rather than requiring the parties to the conflict or the Occupying Power to adopt domestic legislation for this purpose, the Geneva Conventions of 1949 put at their disposal a number of legal bases to intern for reasons of military necessity directly in international treaty law.

In order to prevent arbitrary deprivation of liberty, these treaties strictly regulate who can be interned, for what reasons, and for how long. Moreover, the treaties prescribe a number of procedural and other safeguards that are geared to prevent unnecessary, erroneous or arbitrary deprivation of liberty. Not all the procedural safeguards that are mandatory for deprivation of liberty to be lawful under general international law are incorporated into the legal bases for internment in the Geneva Conventions. Procedural safeguards for deprivation of liberty that are required under general international law have been adapted by the drafters of the Conventions to accommodate the practical realities of international armed conflict and occupation. Nevertheless, to compensate for this reduced procedural protection, the Conventions prescribe supervision by independent institutions to ensure that internment does not go beyond what is necessary to serve the legitimate purposes for which it is allowed, and conforms to the strict conditions and rules prescribed by the Conventions. We will come back to these supervisory mechanisms in the second section of this chapter.

5.1. Answers to our Research Questions and Conclusions from Part II

In the preceding chapters we have analyzed the legal bases to intern in the Geneva Conventions in order to answer the three questions that are the subject of this research. For that purpose, we have examined the text of each legal basis to intern, in its context and in light of the object and purpose of the treaty it is part of. Together with the context, as prescribed by the Vienna Convention on the Law of Treaties, we have taken into account relevant provisions of Additional Protocol I and relevant rules of customary international humanitarian law, State practice, and other relevant rules of international law applicable in the relations between the parties to the Conventions. Finally, we have been guided throughout by the general purposes of the international legal system and the specific functions performed therein by international humanitarian law and international human rights law. Taking into account the object and purpose of the Conventions and the relevant developments in international law and practice since their adoption, we have proposed an interpretation of their provisions that sometimes goes beyond the ordinary meaning of their original text.

The answers to our research questions that result from our analysis demonstrate that the lawful grounds and duration prescribed by the Conventions reflect the balance struck in those treaties between the requirements of military necessity and the principle of humanity, which requires restrictions to the individual's fundamental right to liberty to be both exceptional and justified by a purpose recognized as legitimate in the international legal system. We have seen that the concept of military necessity is an integral part of the definition of the lawful grounds and duration for the internment of each category of persons covered by the Conventions. In conformity with the relevant norms of general international law, the grounds for internment are "based on needs, in particular security needs."[1427] Military necessity in this sense reflects not only the legitimate need to achieve military victory, but also the need to comply with obligations imposed on the parties to the conflict by international humanitarian law.

The grounds for internment in GC III reflect the general assumption that prisoners of war – by majority members of the armed forces of the parties to the conflict, bound to the party they serve by allegiance – pose a direct threat to the security and military operations of the Interning Power that justifies their internment for the duration of the hostilities in order to prevent them from returning to the battlefield or otherwise resume their combat functions in the armed forces of the power they serve. Where the internment of prisoners of war is not necessary to neutralize any military threat they pose, they must be released and/or repatriated.

GC I and II allow for the internment (or "retention") of medical and religious personnel of the armed forces of the parties to the conflict in as far as is necessary to allow an Interning Power to fulfil its own obligations to provide for the medical and spiritual needs of the prisoners of war it holds in captivity.

Persons who fall within the personal scope of application of GC IV may also be interned where necessary as a result of the armed conflict. On the one hand, individuals may be interned on a voluntary basis where their personal security situation resulting from the conflict renders such a measure necessary. On the other hand, the parties to the conflict may intern individuals where and for as long as absolutely necessary to counter the direct military or security threat they pose to the Interning Power or its military operations, or to protect the population under its control or responsibility against the direct effects of hostilities.

[1427] Henckaerts & Doswald-Beck (2005), Vol. I, p. 344, see also p. 345: "The grounds [for deprivation of liberty for reasons related to the armed conflict] have been limited to valid needs, as evidenced by the list above [i.e. the list of legal bases for deprivation of liberty in GC I-IV]."

The legal bases for internment in the Geneva Conventions thus accommodate the valid security needs of parties to an international armed conflict and Occupying powers, and strike a proper balance between the requirements of military necessity and the right to liberty that inherently belongs to any human being.[1428] The Conventions are specifically designed to apply in such situations and were drawn up with the participation of military experts. It is submitted that they take into account sufficiently any security need that may arise in situations of international armed conflict and occupation. Further restrictions of the right to liberty would be unlawful under both international humanitarian law and general international law. The formulation of the grounds for internment in the Geneva Conventions is sufficiently flexible to take into account the specific features of any situation of international armed conflict and occupation.

Indeed, the internment provisions of the Geneva Conventions leave a considerable margin of discretion to the parties to the conflict to establish when and for how long internment is absolutely necessary for reasons of military necessity. Contrary to other provisions of international humanitarian law that strike the balance between military necessity and humanity in an absolute and final manner, such as the prohibition of torture and other forms of ill-treatment, the Conventions' provisions on internment incorporate the concept of military necessity in their definition of the reasons for which a person can be interned in armed conflict. In doing so, they allow the provisions to be applied with due consideration both for the specific dynamics and environment of a particular conflict (and the specific legitimate military requirements they generate) and the individual situation of internees (i.e. the impact of internment on the enjoyment of their fundamental human rights).

This type of provisions – that refer to the concept of military necessity in the formulation of the rule – "simply [reflect] the fact that the required balance of interests cannot be anticipated in a positive rule for every conceivable situation that might arise in a situation of armed conflict."[1429] They do not however suggest that any derogation from the rule is allowed;[1430] "the parties to the conflict can only invoke [military necessity] to the extent that it is provided for."[1431]

The use of the adverbs "absolutely" or "imperatively" in articles 42 and 78 GC IV strongly reaffirms that "when military necessity is weighed [against the requirements that flow from the principle of humanity], this has to be done with great care."[1432] The lawful grounds for internment in the four Geneva

[1428] The present conclusions only concern the aspects of the legal bases for internment in the Geneva Conventions that are the subject of this book, namely the grounds and duration of internment. We are inclined to think that the procedural aspects of those legal bases, coupled with the specific supervisory mechanisms prescribed by the Conventions, also adequately strike the balance between military necessity and humanity in situations of international armed conflict and occupation, but the issue certainly merits further research and analysis.

[1429] Melzer (2008), p. 281.

[1430] *Ibidem*.

[1431] Sandoz et al., *Commentary AP I and II* (1987), p. 393.

[1432] Dinstein (2004), pp. 19-20. In the 2009 edition of the same book (at pp. 7-8) Dinstein reformulates this comment as follows: "Each of these adverbs or adjectives is devised to stress that military necessity

Conventions leave the parties to the conflict with a considerable margin of discretion to decide when and for how long the internment of a given person is absolutely necessary for reasons of military necessity. With that margin of discretion comes the obligation to apply the provisions in good faith, within the boundaries set by the legitimate purposes for internment and by the specific obligations on the Interning Power under the provisions of the Conventions:

> "it is important that generals and all combatants who have to interpret matters left to their discretion as a result of recourse to military necessity, do so wisely. Good faith is not a virtue which is the exclusive attribute of the interpreters of the law, but is also imposed on those who enjoy a certain degree of freedom of action in the field, even though the heat of battle does not favour an objective view of things. [...] This concept [i.e military necessity] can, in exceptional cases, and only in those where it has been explicitly provided for, justify a certain degree of freedom of judgment, though it can never justify a [restriction of a person's right to liberty that] exceeds the level which is strictly necessary to ensure the success of a particular operation in a particular case.[1433]

Moreover, where an Interning Power claims the internment of a given person, or any delay in his or her release, is necessary for reasons of military necessity or security, the burden of proof for that claim rests on the Interning Power.[1434]

Finally, both the concepts of military necessity and humanity, and the acceptable compromise or balance between the competing interests they represent, evolve over time. When they are used to define who can be interned in armed conflict, for what reasons and for how long, their interpretation must take into account developments in society and in international law subsequent to their adoption.

---

has to be mulled over attentively and not acted upon flippantly." In both editions he refers to Rauch's "Le concept de nécessité militaire dans le droit de la guerre" (*MLLWR* 1980), pp. 216-218.

[1433] E.g.: Sandoz et al., *Commentary AP I and II* (1987), pp. 395-396. We have replaced the words "a degree of violence" with the words "a restriction of a person's right to liberty" in the last sentence of the quotation. In the same sense, see Cheng (1987), pp. 65-66 and 68: "While [under the principle of military necessity] a large discretion is thus left to the State, this must not be abused. Indeed, destruction not justified by military necessity or wanton devastation has long been condemned by international tribunals and is now even regarded as a war crime. [...] In every case, the State must [...] so far as circumstances permit, take every care to safeguard the interests of private individuals, to respect the human personality and to protect the spiritual values of humanity." Sandoz et al and Cheng's remarks on good faith in the quoted texts were made in the context of the rules on the conduct of hostilities, but they are as valid in the context of internment.

[1434] In the same sense: Hampson, "Military necessity" in Dworkin, Gutman & Rieff (eds.), *Crimes of War 2.0: What the Public Should Know* (2007): "In some cases, there is a presumption that certain actions are unlawful; it was not possible to prohibit them in absolute terms but they are unlawful unless justified by 'imperative military necessity.' This qualification of 'absolutely necessary' or 'for reasons of imperative military necessity' puts a significant burden of proof on those invoking the exception. Examples include the Fourth Geneva Convention, which restricts the internment of protected persons." It is submitted that the burden of proof of the necessity of internment lies on the Interning Power for prisoners of war, retained medical and religious personnel and protected persons under GC IV alike. Nevertheless, where prisoners of war are concerned, the Interning Power will only need to prove necessity where the legal presumption of threat is rebutted.

Apart from those grounds explicitly prescribed by the legal bases for internment in the Geneva Conventions, international humanitarian law does not recognize any other lawful grounds for internment.[1435] Moreover, IHL reaffirms the unlawfulness of a number of grounds for deprivation of liberty, even in times of armed conflict. For example, internment for the mere purpose of interrogation or intelligence-gathering is not allowed. No one may ever be subject to internment for purposes of revenge, collective punishment or punishment for past behaviour; internment may not be imposed as an alternative to criminal proceedings. Persons suspected of war crimes or crimes against humanity may not be subject to internment but must be prosecuted and if proven guilty punished in accordance with relevant domestic and international criminal law. Internment for the sole purpose of negotiating a prisoner exchange is never lawful and amounts to hostage-taking. No one may ever be interned solely on the basis of his or her nationality, ethnic or other similar affiliation with an adverse party to the conflict. Likewise, no one may ever be interned for his or her religious convictions or practice, or for holding or lawfully expressing his or her political and other opinions.

Finally, any form of administrative detention the parties to the conflict may wish to impose on a person within their jurisdiction who falls outside the personal scope of application of the Geneva Conventions (as expanded by Additional Protocol I), will require the adoption of a legal instrument that can serve as the legal basis for such detention and will have to conform to the provisions of general international human rights law. International humanitarian law may only be relied upon to depart from these provisions where that body of law explicitly provides for a legal basis to intern and where the individual internee comes within the personal scope of application of the Geneva Conventions.

5.2. RESPONSIBILITY FOR LAWFUL INTERNMENT AND INDEPENDENT SUPERVISION

The Interning Power is responsible for the lawfulness of the internment of the persons that are in its hands.[1436] As a party to an international armed conflict or as an Occupying Power, it must respect and ensure respect for the Geneva Conventions, Additional Protocol I (where applicable), and customary international humanitarian law as a whole.[1437] The text of the Conventions

[1435] E.g.: Pictet, *Commentary GC IV* (1958), p. 258: "only absolute necessity, based on the requirements of state security, can justify recourse to these two measures, and only then if security cannot be safeguarded by other, less severe means. All considerations not on this basis are strictly excluded." In the same sense: Gasser in Fleck (2008), p. 320. Similarly, the ICTY, in *Delalić* (1998), at §581, held that "[t]he judicial or administrative body reviewing the decision of a party to a conflict to detain an individual must bear in mind that such measures of detention should only be taken if absolutely necessary for reasons of security. Thus, if these measures were inspired by other considerations, the reviewing body would be bound to vacate them" (confirmed in ICTY, *Delalić* (2001), §322 and ICTY, *Kordić & Čerkez* (2001), §291).

[1436] Article 12 GC III.

[1437] Common article 1 GC: "The High Contracting Parties undertake to respect and to ensure respect

explicitly reiterates the Interning Power's responsibility for compliance with international humanitarian law with regard to prisoners of war and other internees:

> "Prisoners of war are in the hands of the enemy Power, but not of the individuals or military units who have captured them. Irrespective of the individual responsibilities that may exist, the Detaining Power is responsible for the treatment given them"; and

> "The Party to the conflict in whose hands protected persons may be, is responsible for the treatment accorded to them by its agents, irrespective of any individual responsibility which may be incurred."[1438]

Where the Interning Power is a State or an international organization, any violation of the rules on internment in international humanitarian law will entail its responsibility in accordance with the relevant rules on responsibility under general international law.[1439]

This responsibility for prisoners of war and other internees commences as soon as the person falls into the hands of the Interning Power, be it by capture, arrest, surrender, or transfer. It only comes to an end upon the internee's final release and repatriation. In case of transfer of a prisoner of war or other internee to another party to the conflict, or to a neutral power, the initial Interning Power keeps a residual obligation towards the transferee:

> "Prisoners of war may only be transferred by the Detaining Power to a Power which is a party to the Convention and after the Detaining Power has satisfied itself of the willingness and ability of such transferee Power to apply the Convention. When prisoners of war are transferred under such circumstances, responsibility for the application of the Convention rests on the Power accepting them while they are in its custody. Nevertheless, if that Power fails to carry out the provisions of the Convention in any important respect, the Power by whom the prisoners of war were transferred shall, upon being notified by the Protecting Power, take effective measures to correct the situation or shall request the return of the prisoners of war. Such requests must be complied with";[1440] and

> "Protected persons may be transferred by the Detaining Power only to a Power which is a party to the present Convention and after the Detaining Power has satisfied itself of the willingness and ability of such transferee Power to apply the present Convention. If protected persons are transferred under such circumstances, responsibility for the application of the present Convention rests

---

for the present Convention in all circumstances."

[1438] Article 29 GC IV. See also ICTY, *Tadic* (1997), §584.

[1439] A detailed analysis of the question of responsibility is beyond the scope of this book. For States, see the ILC's *Articles on State Responsibility* (2001), and Sassòli (*IRRC* 2002). For international organizations, see the ILC's *Draft Articles on the Responsibility of International Organizations* (2009), and for the UN in particular Shraga (*AJIL* 2000). Generally on responsibility, see Crawford et al. (2010). To be noted that while there can only be one Interning Power for the purposes of IHL, specific violations of international law can in some cases give rise to the joint international responsibility of coalition States and/or an international organization. Nevertheless, the main responsibility for compliance with IHL lies with the Interning Power itself (*cf. supra* section 2.2.1.5).

[1440] Article 12§§2-3 GC III.

on the Power accepting them, while they are in its custody. Nevertheless, if that Power fails to carry out the provisions of the present Convention in any important respect, the Power by which the protected persons were transferred shall, upon being so notified by the Protecting Power, take effective measures to correct the situation or shall request the return of the protected persons. Such request must be complied with."[1441]

Apart from the Interning Power's responsibility, the individual persons responsible for taking decisions regarding the internment, release and repatriation of specific persons protected under the Geneva Conventions or their Additional Protocol I, will be liable for the war crime of unlawful confinement if their decisions result in a grave breach of the internment provisions of the Geneva Conventions.[1442]

The responsibility of the parties to the conflict and the individuals they mandate to take decisions on internment on the basis of international humanitarian law thus entails an obligation to respect all relevant rules of international law regarding such internment, and their legal responsibility in case of violations of the rules that are attributable to them.

In order to ensure effective compliance with international law and prevent unnecessary or arbitrary deprivation of liberty in situations of international armed conflict and occupation, the Geneva Conventions set up neutral and independent monitoring mechanisms, designed specifically to supervise the application of the Conventions and their Additional Protocol.[1443] Two specific institutions have been mandated by the parties to the Geneva Conventions to carry out this supervision, namely Protecting Powers appointed by the parties to a given international armed conflict or occupation,[1444] and the International Committee of the Red Cross (ICRC).[1445]

[1441] Article 45§3 GC IV. A detailed analysis of transfer obligations is beyond the scope of this book. For a good overview of some of the issues, see WGAD, *Annual Report 2006*, §§ 30-58; Gillard (*IRRC* 2008); and Naert (2010), pp. 628-629, with further references. See also UK, *LOAC Manual* (2004), p. 154 and Canada, *PWDITQ* (2004), pp. 1-7 and 1A-1 to 1-3.

[1442] On the prohibition of arbitrary deprivation of liberty and the war crime of unlawful confinement, *cf. supra* chapter I-1.

[1443] The specific mandates conferred upon the Protecting Powers and the ICRC in the Conventions are without prejudice to other institutions that may be charged with monitoring compliance with other international obligations of the parties to the conflict. In this regard, the United Nations Working Group on Arbitrary Detention and the European Committee for the Prevention of Torture (ECPT) are worth particular mention. In order to avoid duplication, both these institutions only carry out their functions in regard to persons interned on the basis of the Geneva Conventions where the ICRC is unable to carry out its conventional mandate under those Conventions: *cf. supra* note 59 for the WGAD, see article 17§3 of the European Convention for the Prevention of Torture and Inhuman or Degrading Treatment or Punishment for the ECPT.

[1444] A Protecting Power is a neutral or other State not a Party to the conflict which has been designated by a Party to the conflict and accepted by the adverse Party and has agreed to carry out the functions assigned to a Protecting Power under the Conventions and their Additional Protocols (article 2(c) AP I).

[1445] The International Committee of the Red Cross is an independent humanitarian organization founded in Geneva in 1863 and formally recognized in the Geneva Conventions and by the International Conferences of the Red Cross, whose exclusively humanitarian mission is to protect the lives and dignity of victims of armed conflict and other situations of violence and to provide them

Articles 126 GC III and 143 GC IV explicitly charge the Protecting Powers and the ICRC with the supervision of the application and compliance with the Convention, and for that purpose enclose a right of access and visit to persons interned on the basis of the Geneva Conventions. The text of these articles provides that:

> "Representatives or delegates of the Protecting Powers shall have permission to go to all places where prisoners of war may be, particularly to places of internment, imprisonment and labour, and shall have access to all premises occupied by prisoners of war; they shall also be allowed to go to the places of departure, passage and arrival of prisoners who are being transferred. They shall be able to interview the prisoners, and in particular the prisoners' representatives, without witnesses, either personally or through an interpreter. Representatives and delegates of the Protecting Powers shall have full liberty to select the places they wish to visit. The duration and frequency of these visits shall not be restricted. Visits may not be prohibited except for reasons of imperative military necessity, and then only as an exceptional and temporary measure. The Detaining Power and the Power on which the said prisoners of war depend may agree, if necessary, that compatriots of these prisoners of war be permitted to participate in the visits. The delegates of the International Committee of the Red Cross shall enjoy the same prerogatives. The appointment of such delegates shall be submitted to the approval of the Power detaining the prisoners of war to be visited."[1446]

The Ethiopia-Eritrea Claims Commission has stressed that "access to POWs by the ICRC [is an] essential part of the regime for protecting POWs".[1447] And Gasser has reaffirmed that: "The purpose of [ICRC] visits is to check that the provisions of GC IV are observed by the detaining power and to deal with any personal requests by the internees requiring the involvement of a neutral institution."[1448]

The Protecting Powers and the ICRC must be informed of the internment, transfer, escape, death in captivity and release and repatriation of all persons interned on the basis of the Geneva Conventions, and of the location of internment camps and labour detachments.[1449] Moreover, individual internees have the right to communicate with and submit applications through the Protecting Power and the ICRC regarding the respect of the Convention and their

---

with assistance (ICRC, "Mandate and Mission Statement", at http://www.icrc.org/Web/Eng/siteeng0.nsf/htmlall/section_mandate?OpenDocument).

[1446] Article 126 GC III. The text of article 143 GC IV does not substantially differ from that of article 126 GC III. Note that medical and religious personnel of the armed forces retained on the basis of articles 28-29 GC I and 37, 39-40 GC II are entitled to the protection of GC III for the duration until their release and repatriation, *cf. supra* chapter II-2. The ICRC's right of visit and private interviews with prisoners of war and other internees is part of customary IHL, see PCA (EECC), *Prisoners of War, Ethiopia's Claim No. 4* (2003), §61; Henckaerts & Doswald-Beck (2005), Vol. I, pp. 442-445; and the references to international practice compiled in the ICRC's updated *Customary IHL Database* (2010).

[1447] PCA (EECC), *Prisoners of War, Ethiopia's Claim No. 4* (2003), §61.

[1448] Gasser in Fleck (2008), p. 322.

[1449] Articles 4§B(2), 12, 23, 56, 94,120-121, 122 GC III and articles 43§2, 45, 49§4, 83, 96, 105, 129, 131 and 136 GC IV.

conditions of captivity.[1450] As Pictet points out, such "[t]hese measures provide an effective safeguard against arbitrary action on the part of the Detaining Power."[1451]

Finally, in case of disagreement between the parties to the conflict on the application and interpretation of the Conventions, the Protecting Powers and the ICRC are tasked to lend their good offices to the parties to settle the disagreement. In this sense, the Conventions prescribe that:

> "In cases where they deem it advisable in the interest of protected persons, particularly in cases of disagreement between the Parties to the conflict as to the application or interpretation of the provisions of the present Convention, the protecting Powers shall lend their good offices with a view to settling the disagreement. For this purpose, each of the Protecting Powers may, either at the invitation of one Party or on its own initiative, propose to the Parties to the conflict a meeting of their representatives, and in particular of the authorities responsible for prisoners of war, possibly on neutral territory suitably chosen. The Parties to the conflict shall be bound to give effect to the proposals made to them for this purpose. The Protecting Powers may, if necessary, propose for approval by the Parties to the conflict a person belonging to a neutral Power, or delegated by the International Committee of the Red Cross, who shall be invited to take part in such a meeting."[1452]

In the same sense, we have seen in the preceding chapters that the Protecting Powers and in particular the ICRC may also assist the parties to the conflict with legal advice and/or serve as a neutral intermediary where necessary or appropriate to:[1453]

• Determine the applicability of the Conventions and Protocols to a given conflict;[1454]

• Determine whether a given armed group or unit qualifies as part of the armed forces of a party to the conflict;[1455]

[1450] Articles 78, 79 and 81§3 GC III, and articles 101 to 104 GC IV.

[1451] Pictet, *Commentary GC IV* (1958), p. 262. Pictet makes this comment in relation to article 43§2 GC IV, but it is as appropriate with regard to the other measures referred to here, all of which are intended to prevent arbitrariness and abuse and ensure compliance with IHL.

[1452] Common article 11/11/11/12 GC I-IV.

[1453] Supplement with refs to Levie, pp. 87, 255-292, 307-311, State practice and other refs in old draft chapter VI.

[1454] *Cf. supra* chapter I-2, section 2.2.1.2, note 347. See also the ICJ's reaffirmation of the special role of the ICRC in this matter in its *Wall Opinion* (2004) at §97: "the Court would observe that the ICRC, whose special position with respect to execution of the Fourth Geneva Convention must be "recognized and respected at all times" by the parties pursuant to Article 142 of the Convention, has also expressed its opinion on the interpretation to be given to the Convention [regarding the applicability of the GC to the Israeli-occupied Palestinian territories]." In the same sense: EU, *Guidelines on Promoting Compliance with IHL* (2005), §15(a): "In order to enable effective action, situations where IHL may apply must be identified without delay. The responsible EU bodies [...] should monitor situations within their areas of responsibility where IHL may be applicable, drawing on advice, as necessary, regarding IHL and its applicability. [...] Consultations and exchange with knowledgeable actors, including the ICRC [...] should be considered when appropriate."

[1455] *Cf. supra* chapter II-1, sections 1.1.2 and 1.1.5.

• Determine whether a given person falls within the personal scope of application of one of the Conventions and thus can be interned on the basis of its provisions;[1456]

• Transmit an individual protected person's application for voluntary internment to the parties to the conflict;[1457]

• Notify a transferring power of any problems with non-compliance of the Conventions or their Additional Protocol I with regard to transferred internees for the purposes of the transferring power's post-transfer responsibilities;[1458]

• Serve on the Mixed Medical Commissions set up to take decisions on repatriation or accommodation in neutral countries of wounded and sick prisoners of war;[1459]

• Serve as an intermediary in negotiations between parties to the conflict regarding the numbers of medical and religious personnel of the armed forces of these parties that may be retained by an adverse party, and regarding the relief of such personnel;[1460]

• Determine the point at which active hostilities have ceased and prisoners of war and other internees must be released and repatriated;[1461]

• Verify the refusal of individual POW/internees to be repatriated to their country of origin or that of the power they depend on;[1462]

• Or any other task the parties to the conflict require assistance with or wish to rely on the Protecting Power or ICRC for in order to fulfil their obligations under international law.

[1456] *Cf. supra* chapter II-1, section 1.1.5.
[1457] Article 42§2 GC IV; *cf. supra* chapter II-3, section 3.2.3.
[1458] Article 12§§2-3 GC III, and article 45§3 GC IV; *cf. supra.*
[1459] *Cf.* article 112§1 GC III: "Upon the outbreak of hostilities, Mixed Medical Commissions shall be appointed to examine sick and wounded prisoners of war, and to make all appropriate decisions regarding them"; and Annex II to the Convention, articles 1, 2, 11 and 12 of which prescribe that: "The Mixed Medical Commissions [...] shall be composed of three members, two of whom shall belong to a neutral country, the third being appointed by the Detaining Power. One of the neutral members shall take the chair.□[...] The two neutral members shall be appointed by the [ICRC], acting in agreement with the Protecting Power, at the request of the Detaining Power. [...] The decisions made by the Mixed Medical Commissions in each specific case shall be communicated, during the month following their visit, to the Detaining Power, the Protecting Power and the [ICRC]. [...] The Detaining Power shall be required to carry out the decisions of the Mixed Medical Commissions within three months of the time when it receives due notification of such decisions."
[1460] *Cf. supra* chapter II-2; see also Articles 11-12 *Model Agreement Relating to the Relief of Medical Personnel and Chaplains* (1955).
[1461] *Cf. supra* chapter II, 1, section 1.2.3.6 (a).
[1462] *Cf. supra* chapter II, 1, section 1.2.3.6 (b).

PART III

SECURITY INTERNMENT IN SITUATIONS OF NON-INTERNATIONAL ARMED CONFLICT

INTRODUCTION TO PART III

Taking into account the fact that non-international armed conflicts today far outnumber international armed conflicts, the dearth of treaty international humanitarian law rules applicable to such situations may be worrisome. The paucity of treaty IHL for situations of non-international armed conflict is however compensated to a large extent by the existence of an impressive and continuously growing body of customary international humanitarian law, effectively narrowing the normative gap between the law of international armed conflict (IAC-IHL) and that of non-international armed conflict (NIAC-IHL).[1463] Moreover, persons affected by non-international armed conflict remain – despite the applicability of IHL – under the full protection of international human rights law.

Nevertheless, human rights obligations, and the right to liberty in particular, may be derogated from in situations of public emergency threatening the life of the nation, a threshold that most non-international armed conflict are likely to reach. Moreover, as far as the legal framework for the internment of persons who pose a military or security threat are concerned, international humanitarian law applicable to situations of non-international armed conflict, in stark contrast with that applicable in situations of international armed conflict and occupation, remains utterly silent.

In the present chapter we will demonstrate that neither treaty nor customary international humanitarian law provides for a legal basis to intern persons who pose a military or security threat in situations of non-international armed conflict (chapter III-1). We will also explore some of the options that are available to States to remedy this gap in international humanitarian law, and argue that the most preferable of these options is a normative development of international humanitarian law itself. Under the latter option, international humanitarian law would provide for a direct legal basis to intern persons who pose a serious military or security threat where such internment indeed is necessary to achieve a legitimate purpose for restricting fundamental rights and freedoms in situations of armed conflict, and would at the same time regulate such internment and

[1463] In this sense, it is worth mentioning that both common article 3 GC and AP II contain a number of provisions regarding the treatment of persons deprived of liberty, their material conditions of captivity and the essential judicial guarantees that must be respected for persons charged with criminal offences. Moreover, the provisions on treatment of persons deprived of liberty, their material conditions of captivity and their relations with the exterior contained in the Geneva Conventions and Additional Protocol I have largely become applicable to situations of non-international armed conflicts as a matter of customary IHL, *cf. supra* notes 492 and 1409.

establish adequate protections against unnecessary or arbitrary deprivation of liberty, and other related forms of abuse.

On the basis of the research and analysis in the first two parts of this book, we will then make a number of substantive recommendations for such a normative development of IHL. These recommendations are necessarily limited to issues that fall within the scope of this book, and concern the legal basis, lawful grounds and duration of internment in situations of armed conflict.

CHAPTER III – 1

THE ABSENCE OF A LEGAL BASIS FOR INTERNMENT IN INTERNATIONAL HUMANITARIAN LAW

1.1. THE ISSUE OF STATUS IN SITUATIONS OF NON-INTERNATIONAL ARMED CONFLICT

Contrary to situations of international armed conflict and occupation, international humanitarian law is utterly silent on the question of who can be interned, for what reasons, for how long and in accordance with which procedures in a situation of non-international armed conflict. The absence in NIAC-IHL of a legal basis to intern equivalent to those in the Geneva Conventions for situations of international armed conflict and occupation is no accident; it is closely connected to the refusal of States to confer either combatant or prisoner of war status on members of organized armed groups engaged in armed conflict against a State. Moreover, the idea that rebels or insurgents could be considered anything else than ordinary criminals was, and continues to be, one of the main reasons advanced by States for not expanding the scope of application of the full body of international humanitarian law to situations of non-international armed conflict.[1464]

1.1.1. Combatant and POW status as a major obstacle in the formation of NIAC-IHL

Traditionally, the law of armed conflict only related to intra-State conflicts and did not regulate non-international armed conflicts at all. Even if it was accepted that they could be as exacting as international armed conflicts, such

[1464] For a good historical overview (with references to relevant legal and academic sources) of the international legal regulation of non-international armed conflicts, including the different variants of the doctrine of recognition of belligerency and other initiatives to expand the applicability of the law of international armed conflict to non-international armed conflicts, see for example Institute of International Law, *Règlement sur la responsabilité des États à raison des dommages soufferts par des étrangers en cas d'émeute, d'insurrection ou de guerre civile* (1900); O'Rourke, "Recognition of Belligerency in the Spanish Civil War" (*AJIL* 1937); Lauterpacht, *Recognition and International Law* (1947), pp. 175-278; Siordet, *The Geneva Conventions and Civil War* (1950); Siotis (1958); Zorgbibe (1958); Pictet, *Commentary GC IV* (1958), pp. 26-44; Castrén, *Civil War* (1966); Draper (*BYIL* 1971); Forsyth (*AJIL* 1978); Draper, "Humanitarian Law and Internal Armed Conflicts" (*GJICL* 1983), pp. 253-277; Abi-Saab, *Droit humanitaire et conflits internes. Origines et évolution de la réglementation internationale* (1986); Sandoz et al., *Commentary AP I and II* (1987), pp. 1319-1336; Moir (2002), pp. 1-29; Rosas (1976), pp. 277-281; Perna, *The Formation of the Treaty Law of Non-International Armed Conflict* (2006) and Cullen (2010). The short summary below is based on a combined reading of these sources, the official records of the 1949 and 1974-1977 Diplomatic Conferences and the compilation of extracts of these official records per article in Levie (1987), pp. 3-9, 93-106 and 205-241. Specific references will be included where particularly relevant.

conflicts were deemed to be part of the internal affairs of the States in which they occurred and their regulation was consequently left exclusively to the realm of the domestic law of those States. While the application of the law of international armed conflict to civil war was at times favoured by international scholars[1465] and had been actively promoted by the International Red Cross Movement,[1466] no international legal regulation of non-international armed conflict was in place before the adoption of the 1949 Geneva Conventions.

Several factors explain this situation. For one, according to the predominant political and legal opinion before 1945, the realm of international law in general did not and should not extend beyond intra-State relations; the internal affairs of sovereign States were to remain within the exclusive domain of their domestic legal order.[1467] Moreover, States were wary to commit to any international legislative framework that might, either *de jure* or *de facto*, undermine their monopoly over the legitimate use of force, or that might confer any international legitimization on individuals or groups that took up arms against legitimate governments.[1468] Finally, States refused to grant rebels or insurgents any form of combatant immunity under international law, an immunity that would effectively prevent their prosecution and punishment under domestic criminal law for having taken up arms against the State.[1469]

While few States would advance the first of these reasons to deny the relevance of international law in regulating non-international armed conflict today,[1470] the other concerns –directly related to the idea of conferring combatant

---

[1465] E.g.: de Vattel, *Le droit des gens ou principes du droit naturel* (1758), book III, chapter XVIII, p. 238; Bernard, *A Historical Account of the Neutrality of Great Britain during the American Civil War* (1870), pp. 115-116.

[1466] For the efforts of the International Committee of the Red Cross and the International Red Cross Movement with regard to the international regulation of non-international armed conflicts, see in particular the resolutions of the 10th (Geneva 1921) and 16th (London 1938) International Conferences of the Red Cross, published in the *Handbook of the International Red Cross and Red Crescent Movement* (2008), at pp. 1139-1142; the relevant provisions of the draft International Conventions for the Protection of War Victims, adopted by the 17th International Conference of the Red Cross (1948) and submitted to the 1949 Diplomatic Conference as the basis for its work (*Final Records 1949*, Vol. I, pp. 45-143); and the ICRC's *Report for the Conference of Government Experts* (1971), Vol. 5. On the historical role the ICRC and the International Conference of the Red Cross have played in the formation of NIAC-IHL, see also Bugnion (2003), pp. 71-80, 248-249, 258-262, 283-296, 319-321 and 330-344.

[1467] For the traditional conception of international law and the gradual transformation of some of its precepts in contemporary international history, see for example Shaw, *International Law* (1997), pp. 20-53; and Nguyen, Daillier & Pellet (1999), pp. 49-104 and 319-327.

[1468] States were not (and still are not today) ready to endorse any "right to rebel" against the legitimate government of a sovereign State. On the close link between issues of legitimacy and the expansion of IAC-IHL (including combatant and prisoner of war status) to situations of non-international armed conflict, *cf. supra* note 698 and cf. *infra* note 1480.

[1469] Until the adoption of AP I, the only exception to this principle was the doctrine of recognition of belligerency, according to which the law of international armed conflict came into full play following the recognition of the insurgents as belligerents. The doctrine had nevertheless largely fallen into desuetude by the end of the 19th century and its formal integration into the 1949 Geneva Conventions was rejected from the outset. *Cf. supra* note 1464 and *cf. infra* note 1476.

[1470] On the expansion of international law to the relationship between a State and its citizens,

or prisoner of war status upon members of rebel or insurgent groups – have not subsided and explain the consistent refusal of States to formally lift the distinction between international and non-international armed conflict and expand the application of the full body of international humanitarian law to all situations of armed conflict.[1471]

Despite a clear will to offer some international legal protection to the victims of civil war,[1472] the Diplomatic Conference of Geneva of 1949 explicitly rejected proposals to expand the scope of applicability of the Conventions as a whole to situations of non-international armed conflict.[1473] Combatant privileges and prisoner of war status proved to be the major obstacles for expanding the scope of application of the Conventions to non-international armed conflicts, where the adverse party was composed of what States considered to be ordinary criminals, possibly posing a threat to the survival of the State or its legitimate government.[1474]

---

cf. supra Introduction. Moreover, while the UN Charter formally enshrines the principles of sovereignty and of non-intervention (article 2§7 UN Charter), it does not do so without providing for an exception: "The principle of respect for the sovereignty of Member States and of non-interference in their internal affairs is, however, subject to an exception when international peace and security are threatened. In fact, if armed action undertaken by a State in its own territory endangers international peace, it is no longer only an internal matter. That is why the same Article [2§7 UN Charter] specifies in fine that recognition of national jurisdiction 'shall not prejudice the application of enforcement measures under Chapter VII'" (Sandoz et al., *Commentary AP I and II* (1987), p. 1323). On the transformation of the concept of sovereignty in contemporary international law, see for example Schreuer, "The Waning of the Sovereign State: Towards a New Paradigm for International Law?" (*EJIL* 1993); Henkin, "Human Rights and State Sovereignty" (*GJICL* 1995-1996); Schachter, "The Decline of the Nation-State and Implications for International Law" (*CJTL* 1997); Brownlie (1998), pp. 289-297 and 557-558; Meron (2006), pp. 92-93.

1471 Some States have also advanced a practical obstacle against lifting the distinction between IAC-IHL and NIAC-IHL. According to these States, armed groups, who by definition have no recognized legislative powers, cannot, even if they would want to, comply with all the obligations laid down by IAC-IHL. Nevertheless, this fact has not prevented States from expanding the application of IAC-IHL to armed conflicts where at least one of the parties to the conflict is a national liberation movement (article 1§4 AP I) or from arguing its applicability to international organizations (*cf. supra* chapter I-2, section 2.2.1.5). Moreover, some weak or so-called "failed" States will also have difficulties complying with all obligations laid down by IAC-IHL, which has led no one to argue that they are not bound by IAC-IHL when involved in armed conflict against another State. The true nature of the objection thus seems to be political rather than practical in nature and ultimately turns on issues of legitimacy rather than capacity.

1472 In the early drafting process of the Geneva Conventions, proposals were made to limit the applicability of common article 3 GC to "civil wars", which were internal conflicts that bore close resemblance to intra-State wars and were recognized as such. Putting the threshold this high would nevertheless have come down to integrating the doctrine of recognition of belligerency into the GC and make common article 3 superfluous (since it was accepted that in situations of recognition of belligerency the whole of IAC-IHL applied). Note that classic international law distinguished between rebellion, insurgency and belligerency according to the scale and intensity of the conflict (Moir (2002), pp. 4-5). That distinction was abandoned in 1949 in favour of the term "non-international armed conflict" which covered all situations of armed conflict that were not international in nature. *Cf. supra* chapter I-2, section 2.2.1.4 or the short summary in Cullen (2010), pp. 5-24.

1473 *Final Records 1949*, Vol. II-A, pp. 322 and 465, and Vol. II-B, pp. 44, 49-50 and 76-77.

1474 ICRC, *Report on the Conference of Government Experts* (1947), pp. 8-9; *Final Record 1949*, Vol. II-B, pp. 9-15, 34-35, 40-48, 75-79, 82-84, 90, 93-95, 97-102 and 325-339.

Nevertheless, the adoption of common article 3 of the Geneva Conventions (CA3) announced a new era, in which such conflicts are no longer exclusively governed by domestic law but are also subject to international regulation.[1475] Moreover, while the formal integration of the doctrine of recognition of belligerency into the Conventions was rejected from the outset,[1476] CA3§3 provides instead that:

> "[t]he Parties to the conflict should further endeavour to bring into force, by means of special agreements, all or part of the other provisions of the present Convention."[1477]

Even the very limited provisions of CA3 conclude with a safeguard clause to the effect that their application "shall not affect the legal status of the Parties to the conflict." This clause, without which the adoption of the article would probably not have materialized, was meant to address concerns that the applicability or application of CA3 would confer any kind of recognition or legitimacy upon rebels or insurgents, or would bar States from prosecuting and punishing them for having taken up arms.

Against the backdrop of the decolonization process that took place during the second half of the 20th century, and under strong pressure from so-called Third-World countries, the First Additional Protocol to the Geneva Conventions, adopted in 1977, expanded the full body of the law of international armed conflict to one particular type of non-international armed conflict: so-called wars of national liberation.[1478] Accordingly, and on certain conditions, the Protocol confers both combatant and prisoner of war status to members of the armed forces of national liberation movements fighting against colonial domination, alien occupation and racist regimes in the exercise of a people's right to self-

---

[1475] The first two paragraphs of common article 3 GC provide that in situations of "armed conflict not of an international character occurring in the territory of one of the High Contracting Parties, each Party to the conflict shall be bound to apply, as a minimum, the following provisions: (1) Persons taking no active part in the hostilities, including members of armed forces who have laid down their arms and those placed 'hors de combat' by sickness, wounds, detention, or any other cause, shall in all circumstances be treated humanely, without any adverse distinction founded on race, colour, religion or faith, sex, birth or wealth, or any other similar criteria. To this end, the following acts are and shall remain prohibited at any time and in any place whatsoever with respect to the above-mentioned persons: (a) violence to life and person, in particular murder of all kinds, mutilation, cruel treatment and torture; (b) taking of hostages; (c) outrages upon personal dignity, in particular humiliating and degrading treatment; (d) the passing of sentences and the carrying out of executions without previous judgment pronounced by a regularly constituted court, affording all the judicial guarantees which are recognized as indispensable by civilized peoples. (2) The wounded and sick shall be collected and cared for. An impartial humanitarian body, such as the International Committee of the Red Cross, may offer its services to the Parties to the conflict."

[1476] E.g.: *Final Record 1949*, Vol. II-B, pp. 11-13, 42, 46-50, 76-77, 124-125, 241, 325-336 and 515.

[1477] See for example the special agreements concluded in the course of the Balkan conflicts in the early 1990's (for extracts of these agreements, see Sassòli & Bouvier (2006), Vol. I, p. 262 and Vol. II, pp 1761-1769).

[1478] On the history, scope of application and contemporary relevance of AP I as applicable to CAR-conflicts, *cf. supra* I-2, section 2.2.1.2.

determination.[1479] Nevertheless, these provisions were adopted with considerable difficulty[1480] and continue to be the subject of controversy today.[1481]

Like in 1949, proposals to expand the law of international armed conflict not only to wars of national liberation but to all types of non-international armed conflict were categorically rejected. Again, the idea of conferring combatant and prisoner of war status upon rebels and insurgents was one of the main obstacles.[1482] Despite the purely humanitarian provisions of AP II and the care

---

[1479] It is precisely the fact that CA3 prevents insurgents from claiming either combatant or prisoner of war status, and the privileges and immunities that come with it, that contributed to an important number of countries pushing for the inclusion of wars of national liberation in the scope of application of IAC-IHL (Draper (*BYIL* 1971), pp. 212-213).

[1480] On the recognition of combatant and prisoner of war status on the basis of articles 43 to 47 AP I, *cf. supra* chapter II-1. Apart from the records of the conference proceedings (*Official Records 1974-1977*, Vols. 5-15), see also the debates preceding that Conference in the United Nations General Assembly, and in particular UNGA, *Resolution 1514 (XV)* (1960), §2 (reaffirming the right of peoples to self-determination); UNGA, *Resolution 2105 (XX)* (1965), §10 (recognizing the legitimacy of the struggle of peoples exercising their right to self-determination), UNGA, *Resolution 2621 (XXV)* (1970), §3(6)(a) ("All freedom fighters under detention shall be treated in accordance with [GC III]") and UNGA, *Resolution 3103 (XXVIII)* (1973). The latter resolution, entitled "Basic Principles of the Legal Status of the Combatants Struggling against Colonial and Alien Domination and Racist Regimes", clearly demonstrates the link made by States between the legitimate cause of a conflict, the full applicability of IAC-IHL and the granting of combatant and POW status to the armed forces of a non-state party to the conflict: "1. The struggle of peoples under colonial and alien domination and racist régimes for the implementation of their right to self-determination and independence is legitimate and in full accordance with international law. [...] 3. The armed conflicts involving the struggle of peoples against colonial and alien domination and racist regimes are to be regarded as international armed conflicts in the sense of the 1949 Geneva Conventions, and the legal status envisaged to apply to the combatants in the 949 Geneva Conventions and other international instruments is to apply to the persons engaged in armed struggle against colonial and alien domination and racist regimes. 4. The combatants struggling against colonial and alien domination and racist regimes captured as prisoners are to be accorded the status of prisoners of war and their treatment should be in accordance with [GC III]". For an analysis of the debates – both in the United Nations General Assembly and during the 1974-1977 Diplomatic Conference – leading to the expansion by Additional Protocol I of the law of international armed conflict to wars of national liberation, see Abi-Saab (*Hague Academy Collected Courses* 1979); Barberis, "Nouvelles questions concernant la personnalité juridique internationale" (*Hague Academy Collected Courses* 1983); Calogeropoulos-Stratis, *Le droit des peuples à disposer d'eux-mêmes* (1973); Cassese, "War of National Liberation and Humanitarian Law" in *Liber Amoricum Pictet* (1984); Gros Espiell, *The Right to Self-Determination: Implementation of United Nations' Resolutions*, (1979); Sandoz et al., *Commentary AP I and II* 81987), pp. 41-56; Mallison & Mallison (*LCP* 1978); and Schindler (*Hague Academy Collected Courses* 1979). *Cf.* also *supra* chapter I-2, section 2.2.1.2.

[1481] *Cf. supra* chapter II-1.1.

[1482] To be noted that many of the Third-World countries who strongly pushed or the inclusion of wars of national liberation into the definition of international armed conflict in AP I, felt very strongly and negatively about an expansion of the rules of international humanitarian law to other non-international armed conflicts, an expansion of the law that found more support from Western and socialist States. This led some to accuse those Third World States of "selective humanitarianism": "Norway, which had voted with those in favour of defining international war to include anticolonial, anti-occupation, and anti-foreign domination wars, chided the states formerly aligned with it. To Norway, the problem was not the nongovernmental character of at least one of the parties in an internal war but rather the attitude of many Third World states. These states were ready for broad humanitarian protection for national liberation movements, and the Norwegian spokesman 'could see no objective element which would make the application of draft Protocol II more difficult ... for

taken to strike out any references to the concept of "combatant" or even "parties to the conflict",[1483] States insisted on the inclusion of an explicit reminder of the following principles in the text of the Protocol:

> "1. Nothing in this Protocol shall be invoked for the purpose of affecting the sovereignty of a State or the responsibility of the government, by all legitimate means, to maintain or re-establish law and order in the State or to defend the national unity and territorial integrity of the State.
>
> 2. Nothing in this Protocol shall be invoked as a justification for intervening, directly or indirectly, for any reason whatever, in the armed conflict or in the internal or external affairs of the High Contracting Party in the territory of which that conflict occurs."[1484]

There have been no further developments of treaty international humanitarian law since 1977, and even if many of the rules of international armed conflict have come to apply in non-international armed conflicts as a matter of customary international humanitarian law, there is still no combatant or prisoner of war status in non-international armed conflict today.[1485] Kleffner therefore rightly concludes that:

> "combatant status and its aforementioned consequences [i.e. combatant privilege, combatant immunity and POW status and treatment] is one of the areas, in which international humanitarian law has *not* evolved beyond the dichotomy of international and non-international armed conflicts".[1486]

---

dissident forces than the application of the whole of the 1949 Geneva Conventions and draft Protocol I by national liberation movements.' He was 'forced to the conclusion that the problem was not lack of material possibilities concerning the dissident armed forces concerned, but lack of political readiness on the part of certain delegations.' Even some Third World delegations were critical of their colleagues, as demonstrated by an Egyptian statement: 'Selective humanitarianism could not exist. The principle underlying draft Protocol II was the same as that which had prompted the effort to extend protection in international armed conflicts" (Forsythe (*AJIL* 1978), p. 279). See also Forsythe (*AJIL* 1978), pp. 277-283; Rosas (1976), pp. 313-326; Sandoz et al., *Commentary AP I and II* (1987), pp. 41-56; and Levie (1987), pp. 39, 50-54.

[1483] E.g. Sandoz et al. *Commentary AP I and II* (1987), p. 1335: "all the elements considered to contain any possibility at all of being interpreted in the sense of a recognition of insurgent parties were deleted. [...] Such extreme caution also led to the deletion of the term 'parties to the conflict' throughout the draft."

[1484] Article 3 AP II.

[1485] In the same sense: Cassese, "The Status of Rebels under the 1977 Geneva Protocol on Non-International Armed Conflicts" (*ICLQ* 1981), p. 417, note 2; Bothe et al. (1982), p. 646; Solf (*AULR* 1983), pp. 54-55; IAC°HR, *Terrorism and Human Rights* (2002), p. 59; Moir (2002), pp. 60 and 65; Dörmann (*IRRC* 2003), pp. 47-48; Cerone (*ASIL Insight* 2006), p. 2; Dinstein, Garraway & Schmitt, *San Remo Manual* (2006), p. 40; Rowe (2006), p. 168; Doswald-Beck in Chesterman & Lehnardt (2007), pp. 126 and 129; Rona (*HRF Paper* 2008), p. 7; Rogers in Wilmshurst & Breau (2007), pp. 125-126; Bassiouni (*JCLC* 2008), p. 729; Sassòli & Olson (*IRRC* 2008), p. 606; Bellal & Chetail in Doswald-Beck et al. (2009), p. 57; Tomuschat (*EJIL* 2010), p. 21; Lubell (2010), pp. 93, 102, 137-138 and 154; and UN Human Rights Council, Special Rapporteur on Extrajudicial Killings and Summary Executions, *Study on Targeted Killings* (2010), §58. See also Henckaerts & Doswald-Beck (2005), Vol. I, p. 11: "Combatant status [...] exists only in international armed conflicts." The customary IHL rules on combatant and POW status are therefore only applicable in international armed conflict (Henckaerts & Doswald-Beck (2005), Vol. I, pp. 384-395).

[1486] Kleffner (*NILR* 2007), p. 321 (original emphasis).

1.1.2. Main reasons for the rejection of combatant and POW status in NIAC-IHL

The short summary of the history of NIAC-IHL above demonstrates that the absence of combatant and prisoner of war status, and the resulting absence of a legal basis for internment in non-international armed conflict is no accident, but reflects the firm intentions of States not to confer any legal status on members of the armed forces of organized armed groups that are parties to an armed conflict, and to leave the decision of who can be interned in non-international armed conflict, and how, entirely to domestic law.

The main reasons for the continued refusal to grant any legal status to members of organized armed groups that are a party to a non-international armed conflict have not changed much over time and are mostly political in nature.[1487] The most important reason lies in States' reluctance to confer *any* form of recognition, legitimization or status upon rebels or insurgents, or to place them on an equal footing with their own armed forces. In spite of the specific safeguard clauses included to this effect in both CA3 and AP II, this continues to be a major concern for many governments, and especially those who face important domestic political opposition or internal violence. States are unwilling to grant, in a general manner, either combatant privilege (i.e. the right to participate in hostilities) or combatant immunity (i.e. immunity from prosecution under domestic law for such lawful participation in hostilities) to their own citizens or foreign nationals who seek political change through violent means, seek to overthrow the government, or seek to achieve territorial secession. To grant rebels or insurgents such legal status, they claim, would go against the principle of the preservation of State sovereignty, and might even hamper or undermine government actions to maintain public order and security and defend the existing structure of the State. If only for this reason, it remains unrealistic today to expect States to confer either combatant status or prisoner of war status to any member of the armed forces of an organized armed group it faces in a non-international armed conflict.[1488] As the commentators of the 1977 Additional Protocols point out:

[1487] Apart from the references in note 1463 above, see in particular: Pictet, *Commentary GC III* (1960), pp. 28-35; Sandoz et al., *Commentary AP I and II* (1987), pp. 46-56 and 1329-1336; and Levie (1987), pp. 3-9, 21-106 and 205-241. See also Draper (*BYIL* 1971), pp. 207-213; Bond, "Application of the Law of War to Internal Conflicts" (*GJICL* 1973), pp. 367-371; Rosas (1976), pp. 288-290; Forsythe (*AJIL* 1978), pp. 278-293; Cassese (*ICLQ* 1981), p. 417-423; De Schutter & Van den Wyngaert (*GJICL* 1983), pp. 280-282 and 284-285; Draper (*GJICL* 1983), pp. 254-268 and 271-274; Solf (*AULR* 1983), pp. 59; Solf, (*GJICL* 1983), pp. 291-292; Goldman, "International Humanitarian Law and the Armed Conflict in El Salvador and Nicaragua" (*AUJILP* 1987), pp. 545-547; Kleffner, (*NILR* 2007), pp. 322-323; Bassiouni (*JCLC* 2008), pp. 731-737 and 781-782; Rona (*HRF Paper* 2008), pp. 7-8; and Bellal & Chetail in Doswald-Beck et l. (2009), pp. 57-58. Our short summary of the reasons for denying combatant and POW status in NIAC is based on a combined reading of these sources and the official records of the 1949 and 1974-1977 Diplomatic Conferences; further references will be included where particularly relevant.

[1488] We have seen in chapter II-1 that the concepts of combatant status and prisoner of war status have traditionally been so intertwined that it seems difficult to imagine an expansion of international humanitarian law that confers prisoner of war status on persons who are members of the armed forces of a party to the conflict without at the same time conferring combatant status upon them.

"In general it seems unrealistic to establish combatant status for persons who have participated in hostilities and have been captured in non-international armed conflicts. In fact, such status would be incompatible, first, with respect for the principle of sovereignty of States, and secondly, with national legislation which makes rebellion a crime. On the other hand, a trend emerged among the experts in favour of granting captured insurgents not so much a treatment sui generis, but a treatment in accordance with the requirements of humanitarian law, identical for all persons deprived of their liberty for reasons related to the conflict. Such a solution would make it possible to avoid a reference to Article 4 of the Third Convention or to Protocol I."[1489]

Indeed, the recognition of combatant status for members of the armed forces of an organized armed group under international humanitarian law would effectively entail their immunity from criminal prosecution or punishment on the basis of domestic law for their mere participation in hostilities. States did not (and the majority of them still does not) wish to waive in advance their right to prosecute and punish those who have taken up arms against the government or the State. Where such immunity would indeed be desirable for political purposes, they claim, States can still rely on article 6 AP II to grant an amnesty to those who complied with international humanitarian law in their conduct of hostilities.[1490]

Moreover, many States feared that in the absence of such a criminal deterrent, the applicability of international humanitarian law could incite domestic opposition groups to resort to arms to achieve the political or social change they aspire to, and could more easily trigger political or military support to such groups by third States.[1491] Also, some States have expressed the concern that criminal organizations might claim to be a party to a non-international armed conflict in order to escape punishment for their crimes by presenting them as lawful acts of war.[1492]

Furthermore, we already mentioned that States have always been reluctant to accept any international supervision or interference in their internal affairs. In this sense, it is worth noting that granting their opponents in a non-international armed conflict prisoner of war status would trigger an automatic right for the International Committee of the Red Cross to visit these prisoners, and monitor the conformity of their internment with the relevant provisions of the Third

Technically however, there is no obstacle to such an expansion (since combatant immunity does not flow from prisoner of war status but from combatant status). From a humanitarian point of view, the treatment of prisoners of war is not more favourable to the internee than the treatment of persons protected under GC IV.

[1489] Sandoz et al., *Commentary AP I and II* (1987), p. 1332.

[1490] Article 6§5 AP II: "At the end of hostilities, the authorities in power shall endeavour to grant the broadest possible amnesty to persons who have participated in the armed conflict, or those deprived of their liberty for reasons related to the armed conflict, whether they are interned or detained."

[1491] See for example *Final Records 1949*, Vol. II-B, p. 11. See also *supra* the specific safeguard clause on non-intervention in article 3§2 AP II, and Clapham (2006), pp. 46-53.

[1492] E.g.: Pictet's comment on the negotiation of CA3 in *Commentary GC IV* (1958), p. 31.

Geneva Convention.[1493] In non-international armed conflict the Committee so far has only been granted the right to propose its services in this area, a proposal the parties to the conflict are not obliged to accept.[1494]

Finally, since at the time most if not all non-international armed conflicts took place within the territory of a single State, States did not see any real need to rely on international law to deprive a person of his or her liberty as they could rely on the full spectrum of their domestic law to take such measures.[1495] We will see in the following section that in practice States indeed rely on their domestic law for depriving persons of their liberty for reasons related to a non-international armed conflict, a solution that is however not available to other, non-State, parties to such conflicts.

The consistent refusal of States to lift the distinction between IAC and NIAC and to adopt a single body of IHL for all types of armed conflict, the denial of combatant and prisoner of war status to members of the armed forces of organized armed groups party to non-international armed conflicts, and the fact that States can rely upon their domestic law to deprive such persons of their liberty, have thus resulted in the absence of a legal basis to intern in international treaty humanitarian law for situations of non-international armed conflict.

1.2. IS THERE A GAP IN INTERNATIONAL HUMANITARIAN LAW? AND IS THERE A NEED TO FILL IT?

It is not really surprising that States saw no need to include a legal basis to intern in NIAC-IHL since they normally can rely on their domestic legislation to arrest and detain members of organized armed groups that engage in armed conflict within their territory. The mere fact of engaging in armed conflict against a State is usually a criminal offence (rebellion, insurgency, sedition or subversion), punishable with long-term imprisonment or even death, in the

---

[1493] Article 126 GC III and Rule 124A of the ICRC's compilation of customary IHL: Henckaerts & Doswald-Beck (2005), Vol. I, pp. 442-443.

[1494] CA3§2 and CIHL Rule 124B of the ICRC's compilation of customary IHL: Henckaerts & Doswald-Beck (2005), pp. 443-445. The ICRC's right of initiative is implicit in article 18§2 AP II (e.g.: Sandoz et al., *Commentary AP I and II* (1987), p. 1480: "Article 18, paragraph 2, does not in any way reduce the ICRC's right of initiative, as laid down in common Article 3 since the conditions of application of the latter remain unchanged [referring to article 1§1 AP II]. Consequently, the ICRC continues to be entitled to offer its services to each party without such a step being considered as interference in the internal affairs of the State or as infringing its sovereignty, whether or not the offer is accepted"; but proposals to make ICRC visits or any other form of independent supervision mandatory, or at least include an explicit reference to them in article 5 AP II were objected to by States who insisted on the principles of sovereignty and non-intervention and were ultimately struck from the text of article 5. See the compilation of extracts from the conference proceedings in Levie (1987), pp. 206-207, 211-216, 219, 221, 223, 227, 230, 237, 239, and 241.

[1495] *Cf. infra* section 1.2. While it is not apparent at first sight from the reports on the drafting history of either the 1949 Geneva Conventions or their 1977 Additional Protocols, or from the commentaries thereof, it seems that States were also reluctant to establish a legal basis to intern along the lines of that in GC III for fear of effectively granting rebels a legal basis to intern members of the State's armed forces for the duration of the conflict.

domestic legal order. In the absence of combatant immunity under international humanitarian law, members of the armed forces of a non-State party to a non-international armed conflict can thus not only be prosecuted and punished but also detained on the basis of domestic criminal law.

Moreover, we have seen in Part I that administrative detention is not *per se* unlawful under international law and that a State can adopt – within its domestic legal order – a legal basis to administratively detain certain persons as a preventive measure, as long as such detention serves a legitimate purpose and is not arbitrary.[1496] Any domestic legal basis to deprive a person of his or her liberty for reasons related to the conflict must of course conform to the requirements of international human rights law. Nevertheless, we have also seen that some extra latitude is given to States where the situation reaches the threshold of a public emergency threatening the life of the nation. Emergency legislation may derogate from the right to liberty and internment of members of organized armed groups parties to the conflict may in such situations qualify as a measure strictly required by the exigencies of the situation.

Actually, most States who face a non-international armed conflict at home rely exclusively on their domestic criminal legislation to deprive their opponents of their liberty, either for crimes against the State such as rebellion, sedition, subversion or insurgency or for specific hostile acts, such as murder, kidnapping or destruction of property.[1497] Moreover, States have increasingly relied on legislation criminalizing varying offences qualified as terrorist acts or terrorism to charge and detain rebels or insurgents in non-international armed conflict.[1498]

[1496] The adoption of such administrative detention laws will usually (and in the case of the ECHR always) require derogation from the State's obligations under international human rights law (*cf. supra* notes 246-250 and accompanying text, and chapter I-2, section 2.1).

[1497] For example, India's *Unlawful Activities (Prevention) Act* creates the criminal offences of "unlawful activity", membership of unlawful associations, and other related offences, which are punishable with imprisonment. It defines unlawful activity in relation to an individual or an association as "any action taken by such individual or association (whether by committing an act or by words, either spoken or written, or by signs or by visible representation or otherwise), (i) which is intended, or supports any claim, to bring about, on any ground whatsoever, the cession of a part of the territory of India or the secession of a part of the territory of India from the Union, or which incites any individual or group of individuals to bring about such cession or secession; (ii) which disclaims, questions, disrupts or is intended to disrupt the sovereignty and territorial integrity of India." Article 4§3 of India's *Armed Forces (Special Powers) Act* (1958) moreover grants special powers of arrest to the armed forces in the States of Arunachal Pradesh, Assam, Manipur, Meghalaya, Mizoram, Nagaland and Tripura (particularly affected by armed conflict) against "any person who has committed a cognisable offence or against whom a reasonable suspicion exists that he has committed or is about to commit a cognisable offence and may use such force as may be necessary to effect the arrest." Where the armed forces carry out such an arrest, they may however not detain the person, who "shall be made over to the officer-in-charge of the nearest police station with the least possible delay, together with a report of the circumstances occasioning the arrest" (article 5). In Colombia members of the FARC, ELN or other armed groups are detained on the basis of criminal charges such as rebellion, sedition, murder, kidnapping or conspiracy to commit crimes (as defined in articles 125-126, 130, 186, 187, 268-271 and 323 *Código Penal* (2000)). In Peru, persons have been detained for reasons related to the armed conflict on charges of treason on the basis of *Decree No. 25,659* (1992), see IAC°HR, *Second Report Peru* (2000), §64.

[1498] See for example India's *Unlawful Activities (Prevention) Amendment Bill* (2002), which amends

Given the available tools in the criminal law system of most States, there is in the majority of cases no need for administrative detention or internment. Where such a need is nevertheless felt, States have relied on emergency legislation to intern suspected rebels or insurgents in order to prevent them from engaging in hostilities.[1499]

---

the 1967 *Unlawful Activities (Prevention) Act* to include terrorist acts and membership of terrorist organizations; defining terrorist acts as "any act with intent to threaten or likely to threaten the unity, integrity, security or sovereignty of India or with intent to strike terror or likely to strike terror in the people or any section of the people in India or in any foreign country, *(a)* by using bombs, dynamite or other explosive substances or inflammable substances or firearms or other lethal weapons or poisonous or noxious gases or other chemicals or by any other substances (whether biological radioactive, nuclear or otherwise) of a hazardous nature or by any other means of whatever nature to cause or likely to cause (*i*) death of, or injuries to, any person or persons; or (*ii*) loss of, or damage to, or destruction of, property; or (*iii*) disruption of any supplies or services essential to the life of the community in India or in any foreign country; or (*iv*) damage or destruction of any property in India or in a foreign country used or intended to be used for the defence of India or in connection with any other purposes of the Government of India, any State Government or any of their agencies; or (*b*) overawes by means of criminal force or the show of criminal force or attempts to do so or causes death of any public functionary or attempts to cause death of any public functionary; or (*c*) detains, kidnaps or abducts any person and threatens to kill or injure such person or does any other act in order to compel the Government of India, any State Government or the Government of a foreign country or any other person to do or abstain from doing any act." See also Turkey, *Law to Fight Terrorism* (1991); Peru, *Decree-Law No. 25,475* (1992) (as referred to in IAC°HR, *Second Report Peru* (2000), §64); Spain (articles 572-580 *Código Penal* (1995), for an example of convictions of ETA members on this basis, see Anon., "Martitegi adiestraba desde Francia a un nuevo comando", *El País*, 19 April 2009, and Carmella, "Spain Court Sentences Former Basque Separatist Leader for Promoting Terrorism", *Jurist*, 3 March 2010); Sri Lanka, *Emergency Regulation No. 7* (2006); Philippines, *Human Security Act* (2007) (which incorporates into the crime of terrorism the crime of rebellion or insurrection already provided for in article 134 of the Revised Penal Code); the Russian Federation (for a discussion of its use of terrorism legislation in relation to the Chechen conflict, see Renz, "The Status and Treatment of Detainees in Russia's Chechen Campaigns" in Scheipers (2009)); and Ethiopia (HRW, *Analysis of Ethiopia's Draft Anti-Terrorism Law* (2009), the law was passed without taking into account the recommendations made by HRW, see Ehret, "Ethiopia Lawmakers Pass Controversial New Anti-Terrorism Law", *Jurist*, 9 July 2009).

[1499] For example, Sri Lanka's *Prevention of Terrorism (Temporary Provisions) Act* (1979) allows for administrative detention for up to 18 months, and under *Emergency Regulation No. 1* (2005), article 19§1, persons "acting in any manner prejudicial to the national security or to the maintenance of public order, or to the maintenance of essential services" may also be administratively detained for up to 18 months. Pakistan's *Anti-Terrorism (Amendment) Ordinance* (2002), §3 includes in the 1997 Anti-Terrorism Act the following provision "Power to arrest and detain suspected persons. (1) Government if satisfied that with a view to prevent any person whose name is included in the list referred to section 11EE, it is necessary so to do, may, by order in writing, direct to arrest and detain, in such custody as may be specified, such person for such period as may be specified in the order, and Government if satisfied that for the aforesaid reasons it is necessary so to do, may, extend from time to time the period of such detention for a total period not exceeding twelve months". See also Ireland, *Offences Against the State (Amendment) Act* (1940); UK, *Prevention of Terrorism (Temporary Provisions) Act* (1984) (quoted in ECtHR, *Brannigan and McBride v. UK* (1993), §§16-17; Turkey, *Emergency Decree 285* of 10 July 1989 (referred to in ECtHR, *Aksoy v. Turkey* (1996), §§26 and 43; Thailand (through Emergency Decree, martial law and the *Internal Security Act*, see the summary in International Crisis Group, *Southern Thailand: Moving Towards Political Solutions?* (2009), pp. 10-13). Apart from the criminal legislation referred to above, India has also established sweeping administrative detention powers, upon which it at times relies in the context of the non-international armed conflicts within the country. Under its *Jammu and Kashmir Public Safety Act* (1978) local (civil) government authorities may order administrative detention "with a view to

Nevertheless, the need for a legal basis in international humanitarian law may exist for non-State parties to non-international armed conflicts. Neither organized armed groups nor international organizations can rely on "domestic law" to deprive a person of his or her liberty.[1500] Organized armed groups, subject to the law of the country in which they operate, cannot deprive persons of their liberty on the basis of domestic law as this would amount to a form of private detention and thus most certainly a criminal offence.[1501] Moreover, they do not have the legislative power required to enact any law within their domestic legal order.[1502] The same holds true for international organizations. Should they be a party to an armed conflict, they have in principle no legislative power to enact a legal basis for internment either.[1503] Nevertheless, in the latter case,

---

[prevent a person] from acting in any manner prejudicial to [...] the security of the State or the maintenance of the public order" for a period of up to two years (articles 8§2, 8§3(b) and 18§1(b) of the Act). The act explains that ""acting in any manner prejudicial to the maintenance of public order" means (i) promoting, propagating, or attempting to create, feelings of enmity or hatred or disharmony on grounds of religion, race, caste, community, or region; (ii) making preparations for using, or attempting its use, or using, or instigating, inciting, or otherwise abetting the use of force where such preparation, using, attempting, instigating, inciting, provoking or abetting, disturbs or is likely to disturb public order; (iii) attempting to commit, or committing, or instigating, inciting, provoking or otherwise abetting the commission of mischief within the meaning of section 425 of the Ranbir Penal Code where the commission of such mischief disturbs, or is likely to disturb public order; (iv) attempting to commit, or committing, or instigating, inciting, provoking or otherwise abetting the commission of an offence punishable with death or imprisonment for life or imprisonment for a term extending to seven years or more, where the commission of such offence disturbs, or is likely to disturb public order." In a similar vein, the *National Security Act* (1980), applicable to the rest of the Indian territory, gives the central and State government authorities the power to administratively detain, for a period of maximum one year, "with a view to [prevent a person] from acting in any manner prejudicial to the defence of India, the relations of India with foreign powers, or the security of India [...] [or] with a view to preventing him from acting in any manner prejudicial to the security of the State or from acting in any manner prejudicial to the maintenance of Public order" (articles 3 and 13).

1500 The exercise of powers of arrest and detention or internment on the basis of domestic law is in general reserved to designate State organs.

1501 For example, in Colombia, detention of members of the armed forces by the FARC or ELN is referred to as "secuestro" (kidnapping), a criminal offence under Colombian law (articles 268-271 *Código Penal* (2000)). See IAC°HR, *Third Report Colombia* (1999), chapter IV, §§120-121.

1502 Nevertheless, several armed groups in non-international armed conflicts have claimed to intern and treat captured members of the armed forces of their opponent as prisoners of war (see for example FARC (Colombia), "Beligerancia", pp. 7-8; FARC, "Comunicado" (2003); New Peoples Army (NPA) (Philippines), "NPA Releases POW S/Sgt. Arguelles, Jr. on Humanitarian Grounds" (2010); or Partiya Karkerên Kurdistan (PKK) (Turkey), "PKK Statement to the United Nations" (1995), articles 1 and 3. See also Rosas (1976), pp. pp. 146-152, 160-166, 196-202, and 213-218; and Veuthey (1983), pp. 48-51 and 197-215). National liberation movements in conflicts that meet the threshold of article 1§4 AP I could rely directly on the legal bases in GC I- IV to intern members of the armed forces of the State party to the conflict or persons who pose a threat to their security or military operations.

1503 Without necessarily addressing the question of the legal basis for internment in international military operations, the Danish Government has launched an initiative aimed at establishing guidelines for a multilateral approach to detainee- and internee- handling in such operations so as to ensure the troop-contributing States' compliance with their international obligations and to address some of the legal challenges that have arisen out of previous and ongoing operations. For documentation and information on this initiative, see Denmark, MFA, "The Copenhagen Process on the Handling of Detainees in International Military Operations" (*MLLWR* 2007); Denmark, MFA,

they could be granted powers of arrest and detention on the basis of the domestic legislation of the host nation, which would remedy their need for a legal basis to intern in international law.[1504] Nevertheless, there may be instances in which that host nation is not willing to confer such powers on the organization or where its domestic legal system does not provide a legal basis to deprive a person of liberty other than on the basis of criminal law.[1505]

States parties to a non-international armed conflict abroad may also encounter difficulties to rely on domestic law to detain or intern persons arrested or captured on the battlefield.[1506] Their own domestic legislation may not always have an extra-territorial scope of application, and even where it does, the principles of sovereignty and non-intervention prohibit a State from exercising its powers of arrest and detention in the territory of another State without the latter's consent.

These problems have recently led to claims of an implicit or customary legal basis to intern in NIAC-IHL (based on an inherent right in IHL to intern in any situation of armed conflict), and suggestions that parties to a non-international armed conflict could rely on the legal bases to intern in the Geneva Conventions by analogy, to justify internment. In the following section we will explore these emerging arguments and their validity under existing international law.[1507]

"Non-Paper on Legal Framework and Aspects of Detention" (*MLLWR* 2007); Oswald, "Detention in Military Operations: Some Military, Political and Legal Aspects" (*MLLWR* 2007); Denmark, MFA, "The Handling of Detainees in International Military Operations", discussion paper for the Copenhagen Conference (2009); and Winkler, "The Copenhagen Process on Detainees: A Necessity" (*Nordic JIL* 2010).

1504 See for example the powers of arrest, detention and internment granted to the MNF-I in Iraq through an agreement between the US and Iraq, endorsed by the UN Security Council (see UNSCR 1546 (2004), with the annexed letters of agreement). These powers of arrest, detention and internment are based on pre-existing Iraqi domestic legislation (Memorandum No. 3 of 18 June 2003, revised on 27 June 2004 was adopted by the Coalition Provisional Authority during the occupation phase of the conflict, it remained in force as part of Iraqi domestic legislation once the occupation had ended, and this for such time as the Iraqi Government did not abrogate it, see article 26 of the Transitional Administrative Law of 8 March 2004). For a short overview of the legal framework for MNF-I detention and internment operations, see ECtHR (Grand Chamber), *Al-Saadoon and Mufdhi v. UK* (2010), §§9-38.

1505 For example, Afghanistan does not dispose of any administrative detention or internment law, and could thus not, even if it wanted to, grant internment powers on the basis of domestic law to NATO's forces in Afghanistan.

1506 See also Hampson in Schmitt (2009), p. 497, who finds the absence of a legal basis to intern in NIAC-IHL "is not surprising, since the underlying assumption is that the fighting is occurring in the territory of one State and the grounds for detention would be expected to be regulated by domestic law of that State. This is most likely to be a problem where States are involved in an extraterritorial non-international armed conflict." This is also one of the reasons why IHL applicable to IAC and OCC (by definition including an extra-territorial aspect) *does* provide for a legal basis to intern and detain, see also Rona (*HRF Paper* 2008); p. 7: "The IHL of international armed conflict, as contained in the 3rd and 4th Geneva Conventions, governs the power to detain and the right to challenge the detention in such conflicts because the involvement of two or more sovereigns at war renders the application of domestic law impracticable. On the other hand, where the IHL of non-international armed conflict applies, there is no such impracticability."

1507 The text below includes only few references to examples where some of the arguments have been hinted at in either case law or scholarly works. The claims and arguments that are the subject of our

1.3. CLAIMS OF AN INHERENT RIGHT TO INTERN IN ARMED CONFLICT

Capture and detention of enemy forces is a common incident of warfare in any type of armed conflict.[1508] International humanitarian law – taking into account that reality – does therefore not *prohibit* either detention (on criminal charges) or internment (as a measure to prevent individuals from engaging in hostilities).[1509] Indeed, it seems to be generally accepted that internment for reasons of military necessity serves a legitimate purpose in situations of armed conflict, namely that of allowing parties to an armed conflict to weaken the military capacity of the adverse party and to protect their own forces or population against enemy attacks, without neutralizing the adversary's forces by killing or maiming them to effectively prevent them from returning to the battlefield. If parties to an armed conflict are required by international humanitarian law to capture rather than kill their enemy, they must surely be allowed to keep that same enemy in captivity for as long as he or she might be expected to engage in hostilities?[1510]

attention in the present section have emerged in recent debates on the issue of internment in non-international armed conflict in the press, during expert meetings and in the legal blogosphere. So far however, and with the exception of Goodman's article discussed in chapter II, section 3.2.2.2, they have not been the subject of any (published) in-depth analysis or discussion by national or international courts or treaty monitoring bodies or by legal scholars and practitioners.

[1508] E.g.: Dinstein in Henkin (1981), p. 137 ("the right to liberty [is] subject to derogation because [it is] both significant and germane to the conduct of hostilities on the front and to the exigencies of the situation in the rear"); Goodman (*AJIL* 2009), pp. 57-58 ("U.S. practice in coalition and other military campaigns [...] has essentially treated civilian detention as an incident of waging war, as has the practice of U.S. allies, enemies and other states in historical and contemporary [international] conflicts"); HRF, *Fixing Bagram: Strengthening Detention Reforms to Align with U.S. Strategic Priorities* (2009), p. 3 ("We are mindful that [the US, NATO and the Afghan government are] engaged in armed conflict with insurgent groups in Afghanistan and that detention is an element of armed conflict"); and Winkler, (*Nordic JIL* 2010), p. 497 ("Conference participants [in the Copenhagen Process on the Handling of Detainees in International Military Operations] agreed that it should be fully recognised that detentions are necessary and legitimate means to ensure the fulfilment of the aims in international military operations"). See also US, Department of Justice, *Brief for the Respondents in Boumediene* (2008): "Petitioners cite [...] certain rules of engagement governing the targeting of civilians in war zones for violent attack. But the capture and detention of enemy combatants is a fundamental incident of warfare"; and US, SC, *Hamdi* (2004), pp. 10 and 12 of the online version: "The capture and detention of lawful combatants and the capture, detention and trial of unlawful combatants, by 'universal agreement and practice' are 'important incident[s] of war' [with a reference to previous case law of the Court in *Ex Parte Quirin*, which dealt with a situation of international armed conflict] [...] It is of no moment that the AUMF does not use specific language of detention. Because detention to prevent a combatant's return to the battlefield is a fundamental incident of waging war, in permitting the use of 'necessary and appropriate force' Congress has clearly and unmistakably authorized detention in the narrow circumstances considered here."

[1509] See for example IAC°HR, *Third Report Colombia* (1999), chapter IV, §§121, 122 and 132; Cole (*Calif.LR* 2007), p. 732; and Goodman in Schmitt (2009), p. 374.

[1510] See for example Goodman (*AJIL* 2009), p. 55: "it would be absurd to accept an interpretation of IHL that results in a state's possessing the legal authority to kill actor X on purpose but lacking the legal authority to detain actor X". On claims that deprivation of liberty is a coercive measure similar to the use of lethal force and that therefore any person who can be targeted with lethal force may be automatically be interned for the duration of hostilities, *cf. supra* chapter II-3, section 3.2.2.2.

All these arguments make perfect sense and we accept that, as a matter of logic, international humanitarian law should allow parties to the conflict to intern persons who pose a direct military threat and cannot otherwise be prevented from engaging in hostilities against the Interning Power, and thus should provide the parties to the conflict with a valid legal basis to do so. But it is well-known – to the frustration of many an international lawyer – that the fact that law *should* do something does not always mean it actually *does*.

1.3.1. Article 5 AP II: an implicit legal basis to intern in treaty IHL?

Does the explicit mention of detention and internment in common article 3 of the Geneva Conventions and in article 5 of the Second Additional Protocol thereto support claims that international humanitarian law for non-international armed conflict includes an inherent right to intern and thus possibly provides an implicit legal basis to carry out such internment? We think not.[1511]

That internment *de facto* occurs in situations of non-international armed conflict is not denied here. Internment has and continues to be used – lawfully (on the basis of domestic law) and unlawfully (without any legal basis) – in situations of non-international armed conflict.[1512] Both CA3 and AP II indeed recognize this *factual given*, by regulating, at least to some extent, the *treatment* of persons who are interned. Indeed, common article 3 of the Geneva Conventions aims to protect all "[p]ersons taking no active part in hostilities, including members of armed forces who have laid down their arms and those placed *hors de combat* by sickness, wounds, detention, or any other cause",[1513] and Additional Protocol II to these Conventions seeks to elaborate on that protection by providing for a minimal legal protection of persons interned or detained for reasons related to the armed conflict.[1514]

[1511] There are no references to such an inherent right in the negotiation history of either CA3 or AP II, and we have seen earlier that their negotiation history rather shows that States meant to leave this question to the domestic legal order of the State affected by the conflict to respond.

[1512] E.g. Koh, "The Obama Administration and International Law" (2010): "detention of enemy belligerents to prevent them from returning to hostilities is a well-recognized feature of the conduct of armed conflict, as the drafters of Common Article 3 and Additional Protocol II recognized."

[1513] Original italics. The term "detention" in common article 3 is used in its generic sense and must be interpreted to include all forms of deprivation of liberty, regardless of their denomination in domestic law. Detention in this sense includes detention for the purposes of criminal justice, administrative detention or internment, and assigned residence.

[1514] See for example articles 5§1 ("In addition to the [fundamental guarantees of humane treatment laid down in article 4 AP II], the following provisions shall be respected as a minimum with regard to persons deprived of their liberty for reasons related to the armed conflict, whether they are interned or detained [...]") and 6§5 ("At the end of hostilities, the authorities in power shall endeavour to grant the broadest possible amnesty to persons who [were] deprived of their liberty for reasons related to the armed conflict, whether they are interned or detained") AP II. Moreover, article 2 AP II defines the personal scope of application of the Protocol intentionally using very broad terms regarding deprivation or restrictions of the liberty so as to cover all types of detention, internment or assigned residence: "This Protocol shall be applied without any adverse distinction [...] to all persons affected by an armed conflict as defined [by the Protocol]. At the end of the armed conflict, all the persons who have been deprived of their liberty or whose liberty has been restricted for reasons related to such conflict, as well as those deprived of their liberty or whose liberty is restricted after

Nevertheless, for an implicit legal basis to detain or intern to exist (if this would be valid at all, *cf. infra* 1.3.2), it should at least be possible to deduce from it the grounds and procedures in accordance with which a person can be deprived of his or her liberty. However, neither CA3 nor AP II defines who can be interned or detained in non-international armed conflict, for what reasons, in accordance with what procedures, and for how long.[1515] Moreover, neither one of these provisions prescribes any other effective safeguards against arbitrary deprivation of liberty.[1516] This is not surprising, since the *purpose* of these provisions is to protect internees rather than to establish the legal framework for their internment. This is apparent from the text of article 5 AP II itself, which in relevant part reads as follows:

> "In addition to [the fundamental guarantees of humane treatment laid down in article 4 AP II[1517]], the following provisions shall be respected as a minimum with regard to persons deprived of their liberty for reasons related to the armed conflict, whether they are interned or detained:
>
> (a) the *wounded and the sick* shall be treated in accordance with Article 7[[1518]]; (b) [internees and detainees] shall, to the same extent as the local civilian population, be provided with *food and drinking water* and be afforded safeguards as regards *health and hygiene* and *protection against the rigours of the climate and the dangers of the armed conflict*; (c) they shall be allowed to receive individual or collective *relief*; (d) they shall be allowed to practise their *religion* and, if requested and appropriate, to receive spiritual assistance from persons, such as chaplains, performing religious functions; (e) they shall, if made to *work*, have the benefit of working conditions and safeguards similar to those enjoyed by the local civilian population.

---

the conflict for the same reasons, shall enjoy the protection of Articles 5 and 6 until the end of such deprivation or restriction of liberty."

[1515] Dörmann in *Report of the Expert Meeting on the Supervision of Lawfulness of Detention* (2004), p. 15; Doswald-Beck in *Report of the Expert Meeting on the Supervision of Lawfulness of Detention* (2004), p. 3; Sassòli (*JICJ* 2004), p. 105; Doswald-Beck in Chesterman & Lehnardt (2007), p. 127; Sassòli & Olson (*IRRC* 2008), p. 618; Sassòli, "The International Legal Framework for Stability Operations: When May International Forces Attack or Detain Someone in Afghanistan?" in Schmitt (2009), p. 444; Deeks, "Administrative Detention in Armed Conflict" (*CWRJIL* 2009), pp. 404, 413-414; Olson (*CWRJIL* 2009), pp. 440-441.

[1516] Doswald-Beck in Chesterman & Lehnardt (2007), p. 127; Dörmann in *Report of the Expert Meeting on the Supervision of Lawfulness of Detention* (2004), p. 15: "There are no specific supervisory mechanisms provided for non-international armed conflicts except that the ICRC is allowed to offer its services." We have seen above that while States must consider such offer of services in good faith, they are not obliged to accept it and that proposals to include such an independent monitoring system were rejected during the 1977 Diplomatic Conference.

[1517] Article 4 AP II prescribes that all persons affected by armed conflict, without any distinction, and including those whose liberty has been restricted must be respected and treated humanely; it prohibits quarter, murder and other forms of arbitrary deprivation of life, collective punishments, hostage-taking, acts of terrorism, torture and other forms of inhuman, degrading or cruel treatment, rape, slavery, pillage and threats to commit any of these acts. Moreover, it provides obligations regarding the specific care and aid children affected by armed conflict require.

[1518] Article 7 AP II prescribes respect, protection and humane treatment, without any distinction other than on medical grounds, of the wounded, sick and shipwrecked, who "shall receive, to the fullest extent practicable and with the least possible delay, the medical care and attention required by their condition."

Those who are responsible for the internment or detention [...] shall also, within the limits of their capabilities, respect the following provisions [...]: (a) except when men and women of a family are accommodated together, *women* shall be held in quarters separated from those of men and shall be under the immediate supervision of women; (b) they shall be allowed to send and receive *letters and cards*, the number of which may be limited by competent authority if it deems necessary; (c) places of internment and detention shall not be located close to the combat zone. [Internees and detainees] shall be evacuated when the places where they are interned or detained become particularly exposed to danger arising out of the armed conflict, if their evacuation can be carried out under adequate conditions of *safety*; (d) they shall have the benefit of *medical* examinations; (e) their *physical or mental health and integrity* shall not be endangered by any unjustified act or omission. Accordingly, it is prohibited to subject [internees and detainees] to any medical procedure which is not indicated by the state of health of the person concerned, and which is not consistent with the generally accepted medical standards applied to free persons under similar medical circumstances."[1519]

That article 5 AP II was intended to *protect* detainees and internees rather than to prescribe who could be lawfully interned and for what reasons, is also clear from the negotiation history of the Protocol as such (*cf. supra*) and of article 5 in particular:

"[Article 2, defining the personal field of application of the AP II in general] uses the terms "deprived of [...] liberty" and "whose liberty has been restricted" to ensure that there is no gap in *protection*. In fact, these terms cover all possible situations, from release subject to police supervision (such as house arrest or assigned residence, for example), to imprisonment. [...] The expression "persons whose liberty has been restricted" [in the heading of article 5 AP II] was chosen in preference to more specific words such a "prisoners" or "detainees" to take into account the full extent of the article's scope of application, which covers all detainees and persons whose liberty has been restricted for reasons related to the conflict, *without granting them a special status*. [...] The *purpose of this article* is to ensure that *conditions of detention* for persons whose liberty has been restricted for reasons related to the conflict *will be reasonable*. The obligations laid down are concrete measures which must guarantee them *humane treatment in the particular situation* they find themselves [and] express the *basic standard to which anyone* whose liberty has been restricted for reasons related to the conflict *is entitled*, i.e., combatants who have fallen into the power of the adverse party as well as civilians. The term "deprived of their liberty for reasons related to the armed conflict" is taken from Article 2 [...]. Protocol II, *following the example of common Article 3, does not grant a special status to* members of the armed forces or armed groups who have fallen into enemy hands. *They are not legally prisoners of war* entitled to special protection; *this is why it is so important that the rules laid down in this article establish minimum guarantees* [for their treatment in captivity and for their protection]."[1520]

1519 Article 5§§1-2 AP II (emphasis added).

1520 Sandoz et al., *Commentary AP I and II* (1987), pp. 1360, 1384-1386 (emphasis added). For the text of the proceedings, see *Official Records 1974-1977*, or the more user-friendly compilation of relevant extracts per article in Levie (1987), pp. 3-9, 93-106 and 205-241.

The fact that IHL regulates the treatment in, and conditions of, captivity of persons held in relation to the conflict does not say anything about the lawfulness of that captivity as such.[1521] Both in common article 3 GC and in Additional Protocol II, NIAC-IHL seeks to protect detainees and internees regardless of whether their detention or internment as such is lawful.[1522] That does not mean however, they include an implicit legal basis to intern.[1523] As Sassòli aptly summarizes:

> "Conventional IHL applicable to non-international armed conflict prescribes how persons deprived of liberty for reasons related to the armed conflict must be *treated* and it prescribes judicial guarantees for those who are prosecuted for [offences] relating to the conflict (such as individual non-State actor participation in the conflict, which always constitutes a crime under the domestic law of the State affected by the conflict),[1524] but it does not clarify under which circumstances and by which procedures a person may be interned for security reasons."[1525]

[1521] Likewise, the internment regime established in GC III (articles 22-77) and GC IV (articles 79-116) does not address the question of who can be interned, for what reasons, for how long and in accordance with which procedures either. But contrary to NIAC-IHL, the Geneva Conventions do explicitly address this question too (articles 21/118 GC III and 27/42/78/132 GC IV, *cf. supra* Part II) and can therefore serve as a direct legal basis to intern the persons they apply to.

[1522] Moreover, to a large extent the rules on the treatment and conditions of detention of the Third and Fourth Geneva Conventions (which are to a large extent identical) have become part of customary international humanitarian law applicable in non-international armed conflict. In the ICRC's compilation of customary IHL, the 19 rules laying down fundamental guarantees (including humane treatment) for persons affected by armed conflict are identical for both IAC and NIAC; of the 11 rules specific rules regarding the protection and conditions of detention of persons deprived of liberty, only those relative to ICRC access and to release and repatriation differ for situations of IAC and NIAC (Henckaerts & Doswald-Beck (2005), Vol. I, pp. 299-383 and 428-456). For a recent study of the convergence between IAC-IHL and NIAC-IHL on the treatment and conditions of detention of internees and detainees in armed conflict, see also Crawford (2010), pp. 78-117.

[1523] See also Heller, "Detention in NIAC", *Opinio Juris*, 20 September 2010: "Most importantly, *nothing in conventional IHL explicitly authorizes detaining anyone in NIAC.* Common Article 3 and the Second Additional Protocol impose restrictions on how detainees can be treated; they do not authorize detention itself" (original emphasis).

[1524] Common article 3 GC prohibits "the passing of sentences and the carrying out of executions without previous judgment pronounced by a regularly constituted court, affording all the judicial guarantees which are recognized as indispensable by civilized peoples" and article 6§2 AP II clarifies that such "essential guarantees of independence and impartiality" include in particular "(a) the procedure shall provide for an accused to be informed without delay of the particulars of the offence alleged against him and shall afford the accused before and during his trial all necessary rights and means of defence; (b) no one shall be convicted of an offence except on the basis of individual penal responsibility; (c) no one shall be held guilty of any criminal offence on account of any act or omission which did not constitute a criminal offence, under the law, at the time when it was committed; nor shall a heavier penalty be imposed than that which was applicable at the time when the criminal offence was committed; if, after the commission of the offence, provision is made by law for the imposition of a lighter penalty, the offender shall benefit thereby; (d) anyone charged with an offence is presumed innocent until proved guilty according to law; (e) anyone charged with an offence shall have the right to be tried in his presence; (f) no one shall be compelled to testify against himself or to confess guilt."

[1525] Sassòli in Schmitt (2009), p. 444 (emphasis added).

Thus, while common article 3 GC and Additional Protocol II recognize the *fact* that people *are* detained and interned for reasons related to the conflict and provide for a minimal protection of persons so deprived of their liberty, neither one of them can by itself serve as a legal basis for such detention or internment.[1526]

1.3.2. A legal basis to intern in customary IHL?

It is clear from the above that article 5 AP II does not implicitly authorize or give a legal basis for internment. Moreover, such an implicit restriction of the right to liberty would flout the principle of legality as expressed in international human rights law and could therefore not be a valid legal basis for deprivation of liberty.[1527] But can it be argued that a legal basis for internment in non-

[1526] In the same sense: WGAD, *Annual Report 2005*, §72 ("With specific regard to deprivation of liberty, [GC III and IV] provide for the legal status of prisoner of war and of civilian internee, respectively. The treaty-based [IHL] governing non-international armed conflict [CA3 and AP II], on the other hand, only contains provisions concerning the humane treatment of persons detained and the fairness of criminal prosecutions against them, but does not speak to the legal basis itself of deprivation of liberty"); Dörmann in *Report of the Expert Meeting on the Supervision of Lawfulness of Detention* (2004), p. 15 ("International humanitarian law applicable to non-international armed conflicts contains no provisions requiring certain grounds for detention/internment nor are there any procedures defined to check the need for such detention (there are only some rules on the treatment of persons detained, including the right to receive and send letters and rules to ensure a fair trial"); Doswald-Beck in Chesterman & Lehnardt (2007), p. 127 ("Both [CA3 and AP II] provide for basic protective treatment of anyone captured [...] Neither document addresses the issue of detention for security purposes without a criminal procedure being envisaged. The applicable law, therefore, is that of human rights"); Rona (*HRF Paper* 2008), p. 7 ("In non-international armed conflict, civilians [who engage in hostilities against the state or against each other] may also be detained, but the legal basis for detention is found in domestic, not international law"); Hampson in Schmitt (2009), p. 497 ("The law of international armed conflict itself provides for legal authority for detention under [GC III and IV] in international armed conflicts. There is no equivalent provision in relation to non-international armed conflicts. [AP II] recognizes that people may be detained and provides guarantees for such detainees but it does not itself authorize detention"); Deeks (*CWRJIL* 2009), pp. 413-414 ("[CA3 and AP II provide] address the treatment of those detained for reasons related to the armed conflict, but do not contain rules regarding the detention process. [...] IHL treaty law applicable in [NIAC] provides no legal basis for internment"); Lubell (2010), pp. 163 and 186; and Heller (*Opinio Juris* 2010) ("Common Article 3 and the Second Additional Protocol impose restrictions on how detainees can be treated; they do not authorize detention itself"). To the contrary: Kleffner in Gill & Fleck (2010), p. 471: "The law of non-international armed conflict is less explicit in stipulating the legal basis for operational detention than the law of international armed conflicts. However, a generic power to that effect is implicit in Common Article 3 [...] [and] Articles 5 and 6 of Additional Protocol II." See also Pejic (*IRRC* 2005), p. 377, who states that internment is "clearly a measure that can be taken in non-international armed conflict, as evidenced by the language of [AP II], which mentions internment in Articles 5 and 6 respectively, but likewise does not give details of how it is to be organized." Discussion with the author further clarified that in her view "both customary and treaty IHL contain an inherent power to intern and may thus be said to provide a legal basis for internment in NIAC." She bases her position on "the fact internment is a form of deprivation of liberty which is an inevitable and lawful incidence of armed conflict and that Additional Protocol II refers explicitly to internment in Articles 5 and 6." The citations are from an interview with Pejic on 21 August 2010.

[1527] The ECtHR, in a case concerning the right to privacy and in particular the interference with prisoners' correspondence under article 8 ECHR, held that "The restrictive formulation used [...] ('There shall be no interference ... except such as ...') leaves no room for the concept of implied

international armed conflict exists in customary international humanitarian law? We have seen in Part I that a customary international law norm certainly qualifies as a "law" in the international legal order, and that it can therefore not *ab initio* be excluded as a potential source for a legal basis to deprive a person of his or her liberty. Nevertheless, three factors lead us to answer the question in the negative today.

First, should any such customary legal basis to intern indeed exist, it can only have emerged very recently. In 1949 and 1977, the large majority of States still rejected any proposals to establish a legal basis to intern in non-international armed conflict in international humanitarian law and affirmed that the adoption of such a legal basis must be left to the domestic legal order of the State affected by such a conflict. Moreover, the ICRC's compilation of the rules of customary international humanitarian law, which was published in 2005 and based on a comprehensive review of State practice, did not find a legal basis to intern to exist in customary law applicable to non-international armed conflicts.[1528] We have doubts that a clear legal basis to intern in non-international armed conflicts could have emerged since then.[1529] Not because customary law cannot materialize rapidly or even instantly,[1530] but because international practice and *opinio juris* witnessed during the past years on the issue of internment in non-international armed conflict seems to be either inexistent or at most contradictory. Which brings us to the other reasons for which we do not think a legal basis to intern exists in customary NIAC-IHL.

Indeed, if customary law were to provide the legal basis for internment in non-international armed conflict, it would have to possess the basic qualities for any "law" to serve as a legal basis for deprivation of liberty. On the one hand, this means it would have to prescribe the grounds on which internment can be ordered in sufficiently precise terms to allow individuals involved in or affected by non-international armed conflict to know which behaviour could trigger their lawful internment by the parties to the conflict. Admittedly, this may not be where the

---

limitations" (ECtHR, *Golder v. UK* (1975), §44). Article 8§2 ECHR provides that "There shall be no interference by a public authority with the exercise of this right except such as is in accordance with the law and is necessary in a democratic society in the interests of national security, public safety or the economic well-being of the country, for the prevention of disorder or crime, for the protection of health or morals, or for the protection of the rights and freedoms of others." Article 8§2 subjects limitations to the right to privacy to the principle of formal legality and only for legitimate purposes, which it lists exhaustively. The Court's reasoning can thus also be applied with regard to the right to liberty in article 5§1 ECHR, which is phrased in similar terms: "No one shall be deprived of his liberty save in the following cases and in accordance with a procedure prescribed by law [listing exhaustively the legitimate purposes for deprivation of liberty]" (for the text of article 5§1 ECHR, *cf. supra* chapter I, or see Annex A).

[1528] Henckaerts & Doswald-Beck (2005), Vol. I, pp. 347-352.

[1529] Note that the ICRC's update of its *CIHL Database* on 12 August 2010 does not mention any evolution in practice that could have changed its conclusions on this issue.

[1530] See Cheng, "United Nations Resolutions on Outer Space: 'Instant' International Customary Law?" (*IJIL* 1965), pp. 23-48; or Barboza, "State Crimes: A Decaffeinated Coffee", in Boisson de Chazournes & Gowlland-Debbas (eds.), *The International Legal system in Quest of Equity and Universality: Liber Amoricum Georges Abi-Saab* (2001), pp. 357-376.

most important obstacle to the formation of a customary legal basis for internment lies. There are at least some indications of practice that the grounds prescribed by articles 42 and 78 GC IV would also be lawful grounds to intern in non-international armed conflict, and there seems to be general acceptance that this would indeed serve a legitimate purpose for restricting the right to liberty where the circumstances meet the threshold of armed conflict.[1531] On the other hand, there is much less agreement or even potential for agreement, on the procedural safeguards applicable to such internment. Even if most will agree there is a *need* for such safeguards, there is no established practice and *opinio juris* that sufficiently describes *what* these procedures would entail.[1532] In the absence of clarity on these issues, it cannot be said that customary international law defines the procedures applicable to internment in non-international armed conflict, or that this source of international law offers a legal basis adequately protecting the internees against arbitrary interference with their fundamental right to liberty.[1533]

Finally, there does not seem to be any actual practice where States party to a non-international armed conflict have relied on customary international humanitarian law as a legal basis to intern in non-international armed conflict, or claimed they could potentially do so.[1534] On the contrary, States that have

[1531] This is not to say that customary international humanitarian law can already be said to prescribe such grounds in a sufficiently precise manner. Hampson for example seems to suggest that there is no sufficiently established or coherent practice to conclude this (Hampson (*IRRC* 2008), pp. 560-561, 565 and note 64). Nevertheless, we did find some indications on what could be lawful grounds for internment in NIAC in recent international practice, and they do all seem to point in a similar direction, namely that of the grounds for internment in GC IV (*cf. infra* chapter III-2.

[1532] See for example Sassòli & Olson (*IRRC* 2008), p. 603: "state practice [concerning review procedures for internment] is clearly contradictory in non-international armed conflicts." For an important effort to define minimum procedural safeguards for administrative detention and internment in armed conflict and other situations of violence, inspired by both IAC-IHL and IHRL, see Pejic (*IRRC* 2005), pp. 384-391, and – as a further step in an ongoing process at the ICRC to clarify questions regarding internment in non-international armed conflict – the *Report of the Expert Meeting on Security Detention in NIAC* (2008).

[1533] In the same sense: Olson (*CWRJIL* 2009), p. 452, note 64: "Customary IHL applicable to non-international armed conflict appears not to provide the legal basis [with reference to the ICRC's compilation of customary IHL: Henckaerts & Doswald-Beck (2005)]. However, specific inquiry into the existence of customary IHL regulating this matter would be worthwhile." *Cf.* also *supra* note 1528.

[1534] Possibly with the exception of internment by States in some of the national wars of liberation that took place in the context of the decolonization process before the adoption of AP I. See for example the Biaffran conflict in Nigeria and the French-Algerian conflict in the late 1950's and 1960's, as summarized in Rosas (1976), pp. 196-202 and 149-152. Note however that these States did not as such claim to rely on a legal basis to intern in customary international humanitarian law (or any other source of law for that matter). Their practice may thus be more an indication of their belief in an inherent right to intern in armed conflict, rather than constitute *opinio juris* on the existence of a legal basis to intern in NIAC in customary IHL. Apart from these examples, the following States faced with non-international armed conflict have (to our knowledge) not claimed a legal basis to intern in NIAC to exist in customary IHL, but have rather relied on domestic legislation to detain or intern persons for reasons related to this conflict: Afghanistan, Argentina, Bolivia, the Central-African Republic, Colombia, the Democratic Republic of the Congo, El Salvador, Ethiopia, Georgia, Guatemala, India, Indonesia, Ivory Coast, Iraq, Ireland, Mali, Myanmar, Nicaragua, Niger, Nepal, Pakistan, Peru, the Philippines, the Russian Federation, Spain, Sri Lanka, Sudan, Thailand, Turkey, Uganda, the United Kingdom, and Yemen. Our conclusions are based on an analysis of these States' practice as reflected in their domestic legislation and case law; international case law; reports of

claimed any legal basis to intern in non-international armed conflict have done so by reference to domestic legislation.[1535] Even in the ongoing non-international armed conflicts in Afghanistan and Iraq, troop-contributing States in the multinational forces that participate in these conflicts alongside the Afghan and Iraqi governments, have not relied on (either treaty or customary) international humanitarian law to intern persons who pose a threat to their security or that of their military operations. For example, the US administration recently clarified that its internment of persons both on its naval base in Guantánamo Bay, Cuba and in the Bagram Theatre Internment Facility in Afghanistan are based on US domestic law:

> "we are resting our detention authority [in Guantánamo Bay] *on a domestic statute* – the 2001 Authorization for Use of Military Force (AUMF) – as informed by the principles of the laws of war. Our detention authority in Afghanistan comes from the same source."[1536]

UK military doctrine on military operations abroad finds that:

> "During hostilities not amounting to International Armed Conflict, UK Forces can expect to deal with 2 classes of captured or detained persons: a. Internees. UK Forces operating abroad may have a power to intern civilians *under the host nation's law* where they pose an imperative threat to the security of the force; such power may derive *from the host state's own domestic law or from a UN Security Council Resolution.* b. Criminal Detainees. UK Armed Forces operating abroad may have the power (*derived from the host state's own domestic law*) to participate in the arrest of criminal suspects, or may assist the host nation's authorised personnel in the arrest of persons. In the case of criminal suspects or indicted persons, they should be handed over to the appropriate local authorities at the earliest opportunity, provided that there is no reason to believe that they will suffer torture or summary execution";[1537]
>
> "The rules for the internment of civilians apply: [...] During operations not amounting to International Armed Conflict to those civilians interned by UK armed forces under *internment powers granted to UK forces by the Host Nation (HN)*. In these circumstances, civilians may only be interned by UK forces where they pose a serious threat to the security of the force. It should be noted that during operations not amounting to International Armed Conflict (LOAC), civilians who are held by UK armed forces because they are suspected of having committed a criminal offence are not internees but 'detainees.'"[1538]

In its submission to the European Court of Human Rights on the merits of the *Al-Saadoon & Mufdhi* case, which concerned the UK's internment of two Iraqi nationals in the post-occupation phase in Iraq, the UK government stated that in its opinion:

---

treaty monitoring bodies; reports by Human Rights Watch, the International Commission of Jurists, and the International Crisis Group, and on our own professional experience.

1535 *Cf. supra* notes 1497-1499 and 1503.

1536 Koh, "The Obama Administration and International Law" (2010), emphasis added.

1537 UK, *JDP 1-10* (2006), section 113 (emphasis added).

1538 UK, *JDP 1-10.2* (2006), section 101 (emphasis added).

> "[i]t followed from Iraq's sovereignty that the United Kingdom was not entitled to intern or detain Iraqi nationals on Iraq's territory except as permitted by Iraq or otherwise authorised by a binding UNSCR."[1539]

In casu the applicants, who during the occupation phase had been interned directly on the basis of article 78 GC IV, continued to be interned once the occupation had come to an end (and the situation became one of non-international armed conflict), no longer on the basis of GC IV but on the basis of legislation adopted by the Occupying Powers, which had remained in force as part of Iraqi domestic law after the transfer of authority from the Occupying Power to an Iraqi Interim Government.[1540]

1.3.3. Using the legal bases to intern in the Geneva Conventions by analogy?

The absence of a legal basis to intern in both treaty and customary NIAC-IHL has led some scholars to suggest that the legal bases for internment in the Geneva Conventions could be relied upon by analogy as a legal basis to intern at least members of the armed forces of the adverse party or persons otherwise posing a threat to military operations and security in situations of non-international armed conflict.[1541]

Regardless of the fact that the legal bases in the Geneva Conventions may be of useful guidance to define lawful grounds and procedures for internment in NIAC in a domestic or international legal instrument,[1542] they cannot themselves serve as the legal basis for interning persons to whom their provisions do not apply. The principle of legality opposes any deprivation of liberty by analogy on a legal basis designed to deprive a person of his or her liberty in circumstances that do not apply to the specific internee or detainee concerned.

This is clearly recognized where deprivation of liberty on the basis of criminal law is concerned. As Cassese points out:

> "courts normally refrain from applying international criminal law by analogy, that is, they do not extend the scope and purport of a criminal rule to a matter that is unregulated by law (*analogia legis*). [...] The same principle applies in international law. There the ban on analogy derives from the general prohibition of analogical application of *treaties*, stemming from the principle of respect for State sovereignty. [...] in the specific field on international criminal law the prohibition of analogy has a different rationale: the need to protect individuals

[1539] ECtHR (Grand Chamber), *Al-Saadoon & Mufdhi v. UK* (2010), §111.

[1540] Just before transferring its powers to the Iraqi government, the Coalition Provisional Authority (representing the Occupying powers) adopted *CPA Memorandum No. 3 (Revised)*, the first paragraph of which provided that "the ongoing process of security internee management in accordance with the relevant and appropriate standards set out in the Fourth Geneva Convention which shall be applied by the MNF as a matter of policy in accordance with its mandate" and section 6 of which prescribed the grounds and procedures in accordance with which such internment could be resorted to. In accordance with the Transitional Administrative Law adopted by the Governing Iraqi Council in preparation of the transfer of authority, *CPA Memorandum No. 3 (Revised)* remained in force. *Cf.* also *supra* note 1503.

[1541] E.g.: Goodman (*AJIL* 2009).

[1542] *Cf. infra* chapter III-2.

from arbitrary behaviour of States or courts [...] To satisfy this requirement, analogy is prohibited with regard to both treaty and customary rules. Such rules [...] may not be applied by analogy to classes of acts that are unregulated by law. [...] a prohibition closely bound up with that of analogy is the ban on broad or *extensive* interpretation of international criminal rules, and the consequent duty for States, courts, and other relevant officials and individuals to resort to *strict interpretation*. This principle entails that one is not allowed to broaden surreptitiously, by way of interpretation, the content of criminal rules, so as to make them applicable to instances not specifically envisaged by the rules."[1543]

We have seen in Part I that both the maxims *nullum crimen, nulla poena sine lege* and *nulla custodia sine lege* are expressions of the broader principle of legality of restrictions of fundamental rights and freedoms, aiming to protect individuals from the arbitrary or abusive exercise of power by the authorities in whose hands they happen to find themselves. The ban on analogy in criminal law therefore applies in a similar way to deprivation of liberty, and even more so in the particular case of administrative detention or internment, where the persons deprived of liberty are at an even greater risk of arbitrariness than those detained on the basis of criminal legislation. The legal basis for internment in a context-specific treaty may therefore not be applied by analogy in a context other than that regulated by the treaty; and an Interning Power may not, by way of application or interpretation, extend the legal basis for internment in that treaty to situations not specifically envisaged in its scope of application. This is even more so where other international legal instruments regulate these situations and where their drafters explicitly rejected provisions similar to those of the treaty applied by analogy.[1544]

The United Nations Working Group on Arbitrary Detention and five Special Rapporteurs to the United Human Rights Council therefore rejected the possibility to intern persons in non-international armed conflict, by analogy, on the legal bases for internment provided for in the law of international armed conflict and occupation:

"The Chairperson of the Working Group and the Special Rapporteur note that, while United States Armed Forces continue to be engaged in combat operations in Afghanistan as well as in other countries, they are not currently engaged in an international armed conflict between two Parties to the Third and Fourth Geneva

[1543] Cassese (2003), pp. 153-154 (original emphasis). In the same sense, the IAC°HR found in the case of *Castillo Petruzzi et al. v. Peru*, where members of a non-state party to the non-international armed conflict in Peru were tried and convicted by military courts for treason, that "the principle of *nullum crimen nulla poena sine lege praevia* is the cornerstone of a government of laws and a basic principle of criminal law. When coupled with the principles of legal certainty and juridical security, a range of principles follow that serve to reinforce it: [...] the principle prohibiting the use of analogy in criminal law [...] the principle prohibiting ambiguity in the law" (IAC°HR, quoted in IACtHR, *Castillo Petruzzi et al. v. Peru* (1999), §114). See also PCIJ, *Danzig Opinion* (1935), p. 51: "*Nullum crimen sine lege*, and *Nulla poena sine lege*. The law alone determines and defines an offence. The law alone decrees the penalty. A penalty cannot be inflicted in a given case if it is not decreed by the law in respect of that case. A penalty decreed by law for a particular case cannot be inflicted in another case. In other words, criminal laws may not be applied by analogy."

[1544] *Cf. supra* section 1.1 and *infra* note 1552.

Conventions. In the ongoing non-international armed conflicts involving United States forces, the *lex specialis* authorizing detention without respect for the guarantees set forth in article 9 of ICCPR therefore can no longer serve as a basis for that detention."[1545]

Sassòli comes to the same conclusion and adds additional reasons for it:

"[La Troisième Convention de Genève] ne peut toutefois pas être appliquée par analogie à d'autres cas de détention de personnes qui ne sont pas des prisonniers de guerre et qui ne bénéficient donc ni de mécanismes de supervision plus appropriés aux spécificités d'un conflit armé (p. ex. les visites du CICR), ni d'un statut entraînant un régime et un traitement détaillés. [...] Contrairement à ce que soutient l'administration américaine, [les soi-disant combattants ennemis à Guantanamo] ne peuvent pas êtres détenus par analogie à ce qui est admissible pour les prisonniers de guerre (et sous réserve des règles sur les internés civils, au cas où ils tombent sous la Convention IV et bénéficient des garanties qui y sont prévues). En bonne logique, la même chose doit valoir pour des rebelles détenus dans le cadre d'un conflit armé non international [...] [v]u qu'ils ne sont pas des prisonniers de guerre et que le DIH des conflits armés non internationaux ne règles pas les raisons admissibles d'une détention."[1546]

The inclusion of the legal basis for the internment of prisoners of war in the Third Geneva Convention stems from the idea that members of the armed forces of the parties to an international armed conflict – who make up the large majority of prisoners of war – are also entitled to combatant status,[1547] and are thus immune from prosecution for their mere participation in hostilities. The flipside of combatant immunity upon capture is the fact that, as prisoners of war, they may be interned for the duration of hostilities without any form of process or review, in order to neutralize the direct threat to military operations they presumably pose (*cf. supra* chapter II-1). This severe restriction of the right to liberty of combatants is thus compensated by immunity from prosecution and punishment for lawful acts of war on the basis of the domestic law of the Interning Power.[1548] The *de jure applicability* of the Third Geneva Convention in non-international armed conflict (and thus its legal basis to intern prisoners of war) can be brought about by the conclusion of a special agreement extending the application of GC III to members of the armed forces of the parties to the conflict – and possibly also by an unilateral declaration by a State to grant members of the opposition armed forces prisoner of war status and the full

[1545] WGAD & Special Rapporteurs, *Situation of Detainees at Guantánamo Bay* (2006), §24.

[1546] Sassòli in *Liber Amoricum Malinverni* (2007), p. 387.

[1547] Article 43 AP I. On the relationship between the concepts of membership in the armed forces of a party to the conflict, combatant status and prisoner of war status, *cf. supra* chapter II-1.

[1548] ICRC, *Report for the Conference of Government Experts* (1971), Vol. 5, p. 56: "Article 3, de lege lata, which provides fundamental legal guarantees, does not deal at all with the problem of legal penalties which may be inflicted on combatants for the sole fact of having fought. Indeed, the Parties to the conflict, and particularly the authorities in power, can punish enemy combatants who have fallen into their hands even to the extent of capital punishment, because they have transgressed national law. This situation is diametrically opposed to that of persons engaged in international armed conflicts, to whom customary law grants immunity for having taken part in the hostilities. The Third Geneva Convention is based on this principle." In the same sense: Cole (*Calif.LR* 2007), p. 730.

protection of GC III – [1549] but should then also include the combatant immunity from prosecution implied therein.[1550] States may not have recourse to selective analogy any more than they should have recourse to "selective humanitarianism."[1551]

Finally, any application of the legal bases to intern in the Geneva Conventions to a situation of non-international armed conflict would go against the clear intentions of the drafters of both CA3 and AP II not to expand this part of the Conventions to situations of non-international armed conflict. Moreover, it is interesting to note in this regard that even the Working Party in charge of the definition of the scope of application of common article 3 during the 1949 Diplomatic Conference "abandoned the idea of an application by analogy – which was considered dangerous, because it permitted too much freedom of interpretation."[1552]

Even if an *analogia legis* were permissible under international law, there still would be at least one important problem with actually relying directly on the Geneva Conventions to intern in situations of non-international armed conflict. We have seen in Part II that a different legal basis for internment exists in those Conventions according to whether a person qualifies as a prisoner of war (GC III),

---

[1549] E.g.: Goldman (*AUJILP* 1987), p. 545; Sassòli & Bouvier (2006), p. 262; Rogers in Wilmshurst & Breau (2007), p. 125; Sassòli in Schmitt (2009), p. 445. For an example of the conclusion of such special agreements, see those concluded during the Balkan conflicts (in Sassòli & Bouvier (2006), pp. 1761-1769). For an example of a unilateral decision to apply, at least parts of, the Geneva Conventions in a non-international armed conflict, see the *Operational Code of Conduct for the Nigerian Army*, adopted during the Biaffran secessionist conflict. Extracts from the code have been published in Sassòli & Bouvier (2006), pp. 1137-1138, and the Nigerian Government's decisions regarding the application *de facto* of certain provisions of the GC have been discussed in some detail in Rosas (1976), pp. 196-202 and 277. The Nigerian Government did not go as far as effectively applying the doctrine of recognition of belligerency, but it did accord prisoner of war *treatment* to captured rebels and at the end of conflict decreed a general *amnesty* for those who had been "misled into rebellion" (quoted by Rosas at p. 201).

[1550] In the same sense: Goldman (*AUJILP* 1987), p. 545. This assumption also finds support in the few examples of State practice (see the examples of the Balkan and Biaffran conflicts referred to above). Most agreements and unilateral declarations however concern the treatment and conditions of captivity of so-called prisoners of war in non-international armed conflict, and carefully steer away from the issue of POW and combatant status, *cf. infra* note 1597.

[1551] The term was coined by Georges Abi-Saab, member of the Egyptian delegation to the 1974-177 Diplomatic Conference (*cf. supra* note 1481). While it was used in a different context, the idea behind it is the same. Abi-Saab used the term to describe the insistence on maintaining the distinction in IHL between international and non-international armed conflicts: "Mr. Abi-Saab (Arab Republic of Egypt) said that there could be no such thing as 'selective humanitarianism', which was a contradiction in terms. The drive and motivation which prompted the effort to develop the law [i.e. IHL as codified by the GC] and extend protection applied equally to the victims of international and non-international armed conflicts", quoted in Levie (1987), p. 50. The Norwegian representative referred to the term in his expression of his Government's "firm conviction that the need for protection of war victims was the same, irrespective of the political or legal classification of the conflict in question", quoted in Levie (1987), p. 54. A selective application of the rules of international armed conflict in non-international armed conflict – intended to expand the internment powers of States without conferring the inherently attached protection of the individual internees in their power – is not only dangerous for the coherence and clarity of the law, but also substantially increases the already important risks of arbitrariness and abuse in situations of non-international armed conflict.

[1552] *Final Records 1949*, Vol. II-B, p. 76. *Cf.* also *supra* note 1511.

a member of the medical and religious personnel of the armed forces of a party to the conflict (GC I-II) or as a protected person under GC IV. These (partially) status-based categories of persons have no equivalent in NIAC-IHL, which intentionally sought to avoid distinguishing different categories of internees or detainees so as not to grant anyone a specific legal status.[1553] As a consequence, "the law of non-international armed conflicts is deprived of the reference point for making that distinction between different categories of persons."[1554]

1.3.4. The specific situation of non-State parties to armed conflict

Some will say that the absence of a legal basis in NIAC-IHL effectively leaves non-State parties with no legal basis to intern in non-international armed conflict at all.[1555] We do not disagree. Rather on the contrary, we believe that this may be one of the (less publicly expressed) reasons for which States reject to expand the applicability of the internment provisions of the Geneva Conventions to situations of non-international armed conflict. The fact that non-State parties to non-international armed conflict – be they organized armed groups or international organizations – have no legal capacity to procure a formal legal basis to intern raises three important questions, which we will address in what follows.[1556]

1553 See for example the explanation by the ICRC representative on draft article 5 AP II, in Levie (1987), p. 210: "draft Protocol II did not establish any particular category of protected persons; consequently the purpose of [article 5 AP II] was to cover all persons without distinction, both civilian and military, whose liberty had been restricted for reasons in relation to the armed conflict." See also Sandoz et al., *Commentary to AP I and II* (1987), p. 1384: "The expression 'persons whose liberty has been restricted' [in the heading of article 5 AP II] was chosen in preference to more specific words such a 'prisoners' or 'detainees' to take into account the full extent of the article's scope of application, which covers all detainees and persons whose liberty has been restricted for reasons related to the conflict, *without granting them a special status*" (emphasis added).

1554 Kleffner (*NILR* 2007), p. 323. In the same sense: Doswald-Beck in Chesterman & Lehnardt (2007), p. 129; Sassòli & Olson (*IRRC* 2008), pp. 624-625; Sassòli in Schmitt (2009), p. 445; Denmark, MFA, *Discussion Paper* (2009), p. 32; and Lubell (2010), pp. 136-137. The concept of civilians in IAC-IHL is defined negatively by reference to the concept of "combatants." In the absence of that reference point, there is therefore no "civilian status" equivalent to that in IAC-IHL in the NIAC-IHL either. Walen & Venzke (*ZaöRV* 2007) correctly point out that most of the detainees captured in the so-called war on terror do not qualify for the legal status of combatants since they have not been captured or are not detained in for reasons related to an international armed conflict (at pp. 852-854). Nevertheless, these authors apply the negative definition of civilians in AP I (all persons who are not combatants) to conclude that persons *detained* in the so-called war on terror are "civilians" and that their detention therefore must be regulated by the provisions of GC IV. While we agree with the authors that the GC IV regime can inspire reflection on what should be lawful grounds in NIAC (*cf. infra* chapter III-2), it is regrettable that the authors do not acknowledge that the legal status of "civilian" does not have any relevance for the purposes of detention or internment in IAC (GC IV covers not "civilians" but "protected persons", which may include both unprivileged combatants and civilians, *cf. supra* chapter II-3), and even less so in NIAC.

1555 Indeed, it is unlikely that States would create such a legal basis in their domestic law or in a UNSC resolution, at least where organized armed groups are concerned; see also *Report of the Expert Meeting on Security Detention in NIAC* (2008), p. 868: "Domestic law or a UNSC resolution has never included a direct legal basis for a non-State actor to intern (or otherwise deprive of liberty for that matter) any person in a NIAC."

1556 See also Sassòli & Olson (*IRRC* 2008), pp. 622-623; Olson (*CWRJIL* 2009), pp. 450-456 and

1.3.4.1. Asymmetrical obligations under international humanitarian law?

Does the absence of a direct legal basis for internment in NIAC-IHL mean that there is an asymmetry in the legal obligations between different parties to the conflict, contrary to the principle of equality of arms inherent in IHL? The answer to that question is no. The absence of such a direct legal basis does indeed mean that there is an asymmetry in the legal obligations of the different parties to the conflict, but not in as far as international humanitarian law is concerned.

Under the rules of NIAC-IHL every party to the conflict may have an inherent right to intern, but neither one of those parties disposes of a direct legal basis in international humanitarian law to do so. As the participants in an expert meeting on internment in non-international armed conflict pointed out: "treaty IHL does not offer an explicit legal basis for *any* of the parties to a NIAC."[1557]

Under domestic law, there exists an asymmetry in favour of States parties to NIAC in the sense that they can adopt a legal basis to intern in the domestic legal order and can thus avoid a violation of both domestic law and international human rights law, while non-State parties to the conflict do not have a recognized legal capacity to do so.[1558] On the other hand, under international human rights law, States parties to the conflict have more exacting obligations than their non-State counterparts, who are not – or at least not to the same extent – bound by IHRL. We will come back to this latter issue in a moment.

Nevertheless, where IHL offers a direct legal basis to intern, as is the case for international armed conflicts in the Geneva Conventions, that legal basis is available for all parties to that conflict, regardless of whether they are States. For example, a national liberation movement, party to a conflict that falls within the scope of application defined by article 1§4 AP I, may rely directly on the legal bases included in the Geneva Conventions to intern persons who pose a threat. In the same way, where IHL does *not* include such a direct legal basis to intern – as is the case for situations of non-international armed conflict – all parties to the conflict, States and non-State parties alike, will have to seek such a legal basis elsewhere.

1.3.4.2. Internment by non-State parties to a conflict: a violation of international humanitarian law?

Does the absence of a legal basis to intern in NIAC-IHL mean that members of non-State parties to NIAC who intern members of the armed forces of an

---

Report of the Expert Meeting on Security Detention in NIAC (2008), p. 868.

[1557] *Report of the Expert Meeting on Security Detention in NIAC* (2008), p. 868 (emphasis added).

[1558] The imbalance between the parties to the conflict in the domestic legal order is however likely to have negative implications for the respect of IHL by non-State parties to the conflict, who (in the absence of combatant immunity) may not find there to be any real incentive (other than a moral one) to comply with IHL when they capture their opponents (see also Kleffner (*NILR* 2007), pp. 322-323, who makes the same argument with regard to lawful targeting by non-State parties to NIAC). A further development of NIAC-IHL along the lines proposed below may create such an incentive, without necessarily conferring any combatant status on members of non-State parties to NIAC.

adverse State party to the conflict (or other persons who pose a threat to their security or military operations) violate IHL and commit a war crime? It does not. First, we saw earlier on that NIAC-IHL does not prohibit security internment in non-international armed conflict. Some experts have even found that:

> "As a party to an armed conflict a non-State armed group also has an inherent authorization to intern. This is a direct consequence of the principle of equality of rights and obligations of the parties under IHL and has to be the starting point of the discussion. As equality of belligerents provides an incentive for non-State actors to respect IHL, it would be unhelpful to depart from this principle in the context of internment."[1559]

Where a party to the conflict, regardless of whether it is a State or a non-State party, has recourse to security internment, it does not *per se* violate any rule of international humanitarian law. If the internment is not arbitrary, it may still be punishable under domestic criminal law, but it will not violate NIAC-IHL or amount to the war crime of unlawful confinement.[1560] The case law of the Inter-American Commission of Human Rights, and the works of an increasing number of legal scholars and military experts, support this conclusion:

> "Many of the statistics do not specify, for example, whether the detention of combatants by the armed dissident groups are included in calculating kidnapping numbers. Such detentions generally would not constitute violations of international humanitarian law so long as the detainees do not become hostages and are not mistreated. [...] The Commission deems it necessary to clarify why it does not condemn, as violative of international law, the acts of armed dissident groups in capturing members of the Army and security forces where the captives are not converted into hostages. [...] International humanitarian law does not prohibit the capture of combatants. It simply treats such captures as a situation of deprivation of liberty which may, in practice, occur in armed conflict. International humanitarian law then proceeds to impose obligations on the captors to treat captives humanely, with respect and dignity. Violence to the life, health and physical or mental well-being of the captives is expressly and absolutely prohibited. Humanitarian law does not prevent the State from prosecuting and sanctioning under domestic law the individuals responsible for the capture and detention of its troops."[1561]

> "[T]he participants considered the question of the possible right that rebel groups could have, in the context of non-international armed conflicts, to detain individuals by virtue of international human rights law or IHL. Neither of these bodies of law offers a clear legal basis in this regard. [...] Nevertheless, some experts stressed that Articles 5 and 6 of Protocol II do not explicitly prohibit armed groups from detaining individuals but seem rather to describe the detention regime to be applied by all parties to the conflict."[1562]

> "[T]his means that – under IHL – a non-State armed group cannot be penalized for interning persons as long as the internment is otherwise in accordance with

---

[1559] *Report of the Expert Meeting on Security Detention in NIAC* (2008), p. 868.
[1560] For the definition of the war crime of unlawful confinement, *cf. supra* chapter I-1.
[1561] IAC°HR, *Third Report on Colombia* (1999), chapter IV, §§121, 131-132.
[1562] IIHL, *Report of the San Remo Roundtable* (2003), p. 11 and note 27.

IHL. This does not, however, mean that such behaviour cannot be penalized under the domestic law of the relevant State."[1563]

1.3.4.3. Internment by non-State parties to a conflict: a violation of international human rights law?

Does the absence of a legal basis in international humanitarian treaty law mean that non-State parties who resort to security internment of members of the armed forces of a State party to the conflict violate international human rights law? We do not think so either. It remains unsettled whether and to what extent non-State entities are legally bound by international human rights law, an issue that is increasingly subject to debate in the legal literature.[1564] Regardless of the final outcome, however, the answer to our question in our view remains the same. Before making that argument, we will set out our current views on some of the issues that are part of the debate.[1565]

[1563] *Report of the Expert Meeting on Security Detention in NIAC* (2008), p. 868. As we have indicated at the beginning of section 1.3, the existence of an inherent right in IHL to intern in armed conflict is not free from controversy itself (Heller points out that the conclusion of the Expert Meeting that an inherent right to intern is consistent with the spirit of IHL is "itself a contestable conclusion", Heller (*Opinio Juris* 2010)). We agree with the participants in the Expert Meeting's conclusion that if any inherent right to intern indeed exists in (customary) IHL, it would be a right for all parties to the conflict, in full conformity with the principle of equality of arms. Nevertheless, as we have pointed out before, it is doubtful whether States indeed intended to create such a right.

[1564] See for example Special Rapporteur on Terrorism and Human Rights (Ms. Kalliopi K. Koufa), *Final Report* (2004) (hereinafter "*Koufa Report*"), §§54 and 73: "Notwithstanding the adverse consequences for the enjoyment of human rights of all acts, methods and practices of terrorism, the exact meaning, scope, pertinence and legal implications of an assertion that terrorists and other non-State actors are bound by human rights law and may be held accountable for violating it remain very controversial. [...] While able to agree fully that non-State actors who carry out acts identified as crimes under national or international criminal law are accountable under criminal law, she is unable to support fully suggestions that non-State actors are directly accountable under human rights law, even when the crime (such as slavery) is also identified as a human rights violation. In any case, she cannot resolve this question within the confines of this report. [...] therefore recommends that further stocktaking on the issue of direct application of human rights law to non-State actors be carried out." With regard to the more general questions of the place and status of non-State actors in international law, Bianchi points out that the "difficulty of providing sound answers to [the various questions that arise] may be one of the reasons why international legal scholarship has carefully avoided dealing with the issue of non-state actors in a systematic way" and that it is "extraordinary to realize how little attention the theoretical discourse about non-state actors has drawn" (Bianchi (ed.), *Non-State Actors and International Law* (2009), p. xiii). For some of the main contributions to the debate on non-State actors' human rights obligations in armed conflict, see Rodley, "Can Armed Opposition Groups Violate Human Rights Standards?" in Mahoney & Mahoney, *Human Rights in the Twenty-First Century* (1993); Zegveld (2002), pp. 148-152; Tomuschat, "The Applicability of Human Rights Law to Insurgent Movements" in Fischer et al. (et al.), *Crisis Management and Humanitarian Protection: Festschrift für Dieter Fleck* (2004); Alston, *Non-State Actors and Human Rights* (2005); Clapham, *Human Rights Obligations of Non-State Actors* (2006); Clapham, "Human Rights Obligations of Non-State Actors in Conflict Situations" (*IRRC* 2006); Sivakumaran, "Courts of Armed Opposition Groups: Fair Trials or Summary Justice?" (*JICJ* 2009); and Clapham, "The Rights and Responsibilities of Armed Non-State Actors: The Legal Landscape & Issues Surrounding Engagement" (*SSRN* 2010); all with further references.

[1565] An in-depth study of the issue is beyond the scope of this book but for our present purposes we may offer our general ideas thereon. Where we speak of obligations under IHRL treaties, our reflection is restricted to those treaties that enshrine the right to liberty (*cf. supra* chapter I-1), and is

In our view, non-State entities have, in general, no direct legal obligations under international human rights treaties.[1566] International humanitarian law specifically imposes legal obligations on non-State entities that are parties to an armed conflict;[1567] and its rules are specifically intended to create legal obligations for non-State entities.[1568] Most international human rights treaties, however, only imposes legal obligations on States.[1569] For example, article 2§1 ICCPR provides that "[e]ach State Party to the present Covenant undertakes to respect and to ensure to all individuals within its territory and subject to its jurisdiction the rights recognized in the present Covenant"[1570] and, as Zegveld points out, the provisions of human rights treaties "presume the existence of a government, or at least, an entity exercising governmental functions."[1571] Nevertheless, in areas where a non-State party to an armed conflict is the de facto government authority, is effectively exercising governmental functions,

---

without prejudice to the question of non-State entities' obligations under other international human rights treaties, which are outside the purview of our analysis in this book.

1566 To the contrary: Clapham (*IRRC* 2006), pp. 499-508, 511-513 and 523; Fleck, "Humanitarian Protection Against Non-State Actors" in Frowein et al., *Verhandeln für den Frieden – Negotiating for Peace: Liber Amoricum Tono Eitel* (2003), p. 79; International Law Institute, *Resolution on IHL and Non-State Entities* (1999), article IV.

1567 CA3 GC contains obligations for "each Party to the conflict" (which by definition includes the non-State parties to such conflict). The same is true for AP II; article 19 of the 1954 Hague Convention for the Protection of Cultural Property in the Event of Armed Conflict; the 1980 Convention on Prohibitions or Restrictions on the Use of Certain Conventional Weapons Which May Be Deemed to be Excessively Injurious or to Have Indiscriminate Effects and the Protocols thereto (amended article 1); the 1993 Convention on the Prohibition of the Development, Production, Stockpiling and Use of Chemical Weapons and on Their Destruction; and customary IHL applicable to non-international armed conflicts.

1568 In the same sense, e.g.: Cassese (*ICLQ* 1981), pp. 424-429; Meron (1987), p. 39; Sandoz et al., *Commentary AP I and II* (1987), p. 1345; Zegveld (2002), p. 152; Sassòli (*HPCR Series* 2006); p. 12. While there is no agreement in the legal literature over *how* these non-State entities are bound by a treaty to which they are not a party (see Cassese (*ICLQ* 1981); Meron (1987), pp. 38-40; Bothe et al. (1982), pp. Sandoz et al., *Commentary to AP I and II* (1987), p. 1345; Zegveld (2002), pp. 135-148; and Moir (2002), pp. 52-58 and 96-99; all with further references), the idea that organized armed groups *are* legally bound by international humanitarian law treaties is uncontested by States, international organizations or these organized armed groups themselves (see SCSL, *Norman* (2004), §22; Cassese (*ICLQ* 1981), pp. 422-426; Sandoz et al., *Commentary to AP I and II* (1987), p. 1345; International Law Institute, *Resolution on IHL and Non-State Entities* (1999), article II; Moir (2002), p. 52; Zegveld (2002), p. 151; Clapham (*IRRC* 2006), pp. 495 and 498).

1569 An exception may be article 4§1 of the 2000 Optional Protocol to the Convention on the Rights of the Child on the Involvement of Children in Armed Conflict. In the same sense: Zegveld (2002), p. 148 ("Human rights treaties bind in principle only the state in its relation with individuals living under its jurisdiction. The purpose of these norms is to check abuse of state power"); Moir (2002), p. 194 ("human rights obligations are binding on governments only, and the law has not yet reached the stage whereby, during internal armed conflict, insurgents are bound to observe the human rights of government forces, let alone those of opposing insurgents [...] except, of course, to the extent that these obligations coincide with humanitarian law"); and *Koufa Report* (2004), §73 quoted above.

1570 The ICCPR is taken as a representative example (similar provisions are included in articles 1-2 ACHR; 1 ECHR; 1 ACHPR and 3 and 44 Arab Charter. To be noted that articles 27-29 ACHPR also place specific duties on individuals; and that official talks on the accession of the EU to the ECHR have started in July 2010, see CoE, "EU Accession to the European Convention on Human Rights" (2010).

1571 Zegveld (2002), p. 152. This is also clear from the wording of (most of) the provisions of the ICCPR and similar human rights treaties.

and the State is therefore no longer capable of exercising those functions, we would agree that the non-State, de facto government does become bound by international human rights law.[1572]

Moreover, the international community increasingly seems to expect or even demand that non-State parties to armed conflict respect the basic principles of international human rights law and ensure that the fundamental human rights of persons within their power are respected.[1573] In the Preamble of the UDHR, the General Assembly:

> "[p]roclaims this Universal Declaration of Human Rights as a common standard of achievement for all peoples and all nations, to the end that every individual and every organ of society, keeping this Declaration constantly in mind, shall strive by teaching and education to promote respect for these rights and freedoms and by progressive measures, national and international, to secure their universal and effective recognition and observance, both among the peoples of Member States themselves and among the peoples of territories under their jurisdiction." (emphasis added)

Moreover, article 5 ICCPR warns that:

> "Nothing in the present Covenant may be interpreted as implying for any State, group or person any right to engage in any activity or perform any act aimed at the destruction of any of the rights and freedoms recognized herein or at their limitation to a greater extent than is provided for in the present Covenant."[1574]

We agree therefore with Alston, who, in his report as Special Rapporteur on Extrajudicial, Summary or Arbitrary Executions on the situation in Sri Lanka, found that:

[1572] In this sense, see e.g. UNSG, *Situation of Human Rights the Democratic Republic of the Congo* (2002), §83 ("The Democratic Republic of the Congo and MLC, as de facto authorities, must respect the sovereignty of the Democratic Republic of the Congo, halt the human rights violations and secure better protection of vulnerable groups"); and UN Security Council Resolution 1417 (2002), §4 ("*reiterates* that it holds the Rassemblement Congolais pour la Démocratie-Goma, as the de facto authority, responsible to bring to an end all extrajudicial executions, human rights violations and arbitrary harassment of civilians in Kisangani, and all other areas under RCD-Goma's control"). A number of authors also accept that non-State actors that are the *de facto* authority in a region, may be bound by international human rights law, see for example Zegveld (2002), pp. 149 and 151-152; Rodley in Mahoney & Mahoney (1993), p. 313; Tomuschat in *Liber Amoricum Fleck* (2004), pp. 587-588; and Cahin, "The Responsibility of Other Entities: Armed Bands and Criminal Groups" in Crawford, Pellet & Olleson, *The Law of International Responsibility* (2010), p. 339. Apart from Tomuschat, these authors find this is only *de lege ferenda*. Examples of such factual situations are in any case limited, but would include (apart from the Congolese groups mentioned in the UN reports cited above) the situation of the Liberation Tigers of Tamil Eelam (LTTE) in Sri Lanka (until their effective defeat in the summer of 2009), that of the Sudan People's Liberation Army/Movement (SPLM/A) in Sudan, that of the National Democratic Front of the Philippines/New People's Army (NDFP/NPA) in the Philippines, and that of the *Forces Nouvelles* in Ivory Coast.

[1573] In this sense, some authors have pointed out the increasing number of UN Security Council resolutions and statements or resolutions of other international bodies that directly address non-State parties to non-international armed conflicts and demand that they respect fundamental human rights. See for example Zegveld (2002), pp. 149-151; *Koufa Report* (2004), §§61-63; Clapham (*IRRC* 2006), pp. 500-508; and Nasu, "Status of Rebels in Non-International Armed Conflict" in Doswald-Beck et al. (2009), pp. 257-260).

[1574] Similar safeguards can be found in articles 29 ACHR and 17 ECHR.

"Human rights law affirms that both the Government and the LTTE [...] must respect the rights of every person in Sri Lanka. Human rights norms operate on three levels – as the rights of individuals, as obligations assumed by States, and as legitimate expectations of the international community. The Government has assumed the binding legal obligation to respect and ensure the rights recognized in the [ICCPR]. As a non-state actor, the LTTE does not have legal obligations under ICCPR, but it remains subject to the demand of the international community, first expressed in the Universal Declaration of Human Rights, that every organ of society respect and promote human rights. [...] The LTTE and other armed groups must accept that insofar as they aspire to represent a people before the world, the international community will evaluate their conduct according to the Universal Declaration's 'common standard of achievement'."[1575]

Rather than having as of today the same legal obligations under IHRL as States, non-State parties to armed conflicts must therefore be aware of the expectations the international community has towards them with regard to their respect for fundamental human rights principles, and the possible actions the international community may take in their regard when they fail to meet these expectations.

Regardless of the position one finally takes in the – still evolving – debate over the human rights obligations of non-State actors, the question we have asked at the outset of this subsection must be answered in the negative. If one takes the position that non-State entities have no obligations under IHRL, then these non-State entities can obviously not violate them.[1576] But even if one takes the position that non-State parties to an armed conflict indeed have obligations under international human rights law, the question should still be answered in the negative. If international human rights law is to apply to armed groups – or to other non-State entities for that matter[1577] – the application and interpretation of its rules will need to take into account their specific character as a non-State entity. In particular, international human rights courts or monitoring bodies will need to take into account that non-State entities have no (internationally recognized) legislative capacity, or at least not to the same extent or in the same manner as States.[1578] Therefore, when applying human rights norms to a case of

1575 Special Rapporteur on Extrajudicial, Summary or Arbitrary Executions (Mr. Philip Alston), *Mission to Sri Lanka* (2006), §§25 and 27(emphasis added). In the same sense: Commission for Historical Clarification, *Guatemala: Memory of Silence* (1999), §127; Special Rapporteur on Extrajudicial, Summary or Arbitrary Executions, Special Rapporteur on the Right of Everyone to the Enjoyment of the Highest Attainable Standard of Physical and Mental Health, Representative of the Secretary-General on Human Rights of Internally Displaced Persons, and Special Rapporteur on Adequate Housing as a Component of the Right to an Adequate Standard of Living, *Mission to Lebanon* (2006), §19; Greenwood in Fleck (2008), p. 76.

1576 See in this sense Olson (*CWRJIL* 2009), pp. 450-451.

1577 One could think of international organizations that participate in NIAC, *cf. supra* chapter 1-2, section 2.2.1.5.

1578 In the same sense: Sassòli, "Taking Armed Groups Seriously: Ways to Improve Their Compliance with International Humanitarian Law" (*JIHLS* 2010, forthcoming): "Neither Human Rights nor IHL applicable to non-international armed conflicts provide a specific legal basis for internment – while a legal basis for any detention is required by Human Rights. While a State can provide for such a basis in its domestic law, how is the non-State actor to do this? [...] As a deprivation of liberty by a non-State party to an armed conflict, the emphasis in the interpretation of the requirement that the grounds and procedures for deprivation of liberty be "prescribed by law" will have to be on the basic qualities of such a "law" rather than on its form (cf. supra chapter I-1, section 1.2.3).[1579] Where a regulation or order made by a non-State party to an armed conflict possesses the basic qualities of a law (taking into account the structure of that party and the particular context of the armed conflict it is engaged in), it must be able to serve as a valid legal basis for internment.[1580] As Sivakumaran points out:

> "it should be kept in mind that '[i]f humanitarian considerations dominate to the exclusion of the capacity of the insurgents ... then the proposed rules are divorced from reality.' Rules that are inherently beyond the reach of armed groups and which they have no hope of meeting serve little purpose";[1581] and
>
> "to read references to law [in international legal obligations] as including the 'law' of the armed group is simply to interpret the wording of a specific provision in light of the particular setting in which it is applied. This is by no means revolutionary."[1582]

Therefore, it is submitted that a non-State party to a non-international armed conflict will not violate international law if it (1) interns members of the armed forces of an adverse party to the conflict or other persons who pose a direct threat to its security and military operations where and for as long as their internment is absolutely necessary to prevent them from returning to hostilities or stop posing such a threat; (2) respects the principle of legality in its material aspect by clearly prescribing, in a regulation emanating from the appropriate authority,[1583] the grounds and procedures in accordance with which such persons can be interned, in a sufficiently accessible and precise way so as to allow those concerned to foresee the possibility of their internment, and by establishing adequate safeguards to prevent both arbitrary deprivation of liberty and abuse in captivity;[1584] and (3) the internment does not otherwise amount to an arbitrary deprivation of liberty. In other words, where the absence of an act of formal

---

minimum, Human Rights obligations should be translated to fit the reality of armed groups and adapted to what they are actually able to respect."

1579 We have seen in chapter I-1, section 1.2.3 that human rights courts and treaty monitoring bodies have already had recourse to such a teleological interpretation of the principle of legal certainty to accommodate the specific characteristics of common law systems and the international legal system.

1580 To be noted that the legal basis will of course only be lawful if the other criteria for a valid legal basis for deprivation of liberty are also met (*cf. supra* chapter I-1, sections 1.2.1 and 1.2.4). Our argument here bears similarity with those made by Sivakumaran with regard to the establishment of courts by non-State parties to armed conflict, see Sivakumaran (*JICJ* 2009), pp. 498-500, 503 and 507-511.

1581 Sivakumaran (*JICJ* 2009), p. 501, the quotation within the text is from Draper (*GJICL* 1983), p. 264.

1582 Sivakumaran (*JICJ* 2009), p. 508.

1583 If the non-State party has a clearly identified legislative organ, or political representation, the adoption of such regulations or orders should emanate from those organs (or at least be subject to its scrutiny) rather than from its military branch.

1584 Note that Gallant does not treat this issue in his book on the principle of legality in criminal law, even though he points out that the obligation to respect the principle exists in CA3 and AP II and that those rules apply to non-state parties to NIAC as they do to state parties to such conflicts. See Gallant (2009), p. 208.

domestic legislation is not a matter of unwillingness but of legal incapacity, and is the only element lacking in the organization of internment operations by a non-State party to a non-international armed conflict, and where the risk of arbitrariness is sufficiently reduced by adequate safeguards, internment by a non-State party in order to prevent persons from engaging in hostilities against it should not be deemed violative of international law.[1585]

1.3.4.4. Unequal obligations for State and non-State parties to a conflict?

Finally, in light of the above, one may ask the question whether all of this means that international human rights law imposes different obligations on non-State parties to non-international armed conflict as compared to State parties to such conflict. The answer must be affirmative, at least in as far as the formal aspect of the principle of legality is concerned: in that matter States have more stringent obligations under international law than non-State parties. "One may claim" as Sassòli and Olson rightly point out that "this is unfair, as States would need to abide by additional obligations than non-State actors in a non-international armed conflict. This is true at the international law level, where States are traditionally the legal actors, but it would only be true of the rules to which States obligated themselves. Also, it must not be forgotten that non-State actors remain bound by domestic law."[1586] Indeed, the asymmetry under international human rights law is counterbalanced by the asymmetry in domestic law, which clearly tilts in favour of the State parties to the conflict. Finally, the asymmetry does not "favour" any of the parties to the conflict, but rather takes into account their different legal status and capacity in the international legal order.

As far as international humanitarian law is concerned, however, States and non-State parties to the conflict have the same obligations towards internees. They must respect and ensure respect for all obligations towards internees prescribed by CA3 and by articles 4-6 AP II, as complemented by customary international humanitarian and human rights law: they must ensure their humane treatment and decent conditions of captivity.[1587] Moreover, internment may not

---

[1585] In the same sense: IAC°HR, *Third Report on Colombia* (1999), chapter IV, §§131-132. Again, this does not prevent the internment from being a criminal offence under domestic law, *cf. supra* notes 1560-1561 and accompanying text. Where appropriate to facilitate future peace or a process of reconciliation, an amnesty on the basis of article 6§2 AP II could be granted to individuals who interned in conformity with international humanitarian law (which would not be possible if internment by non-State parties to an armed conflict were to be a war crime). Finally, internment by a non-State party to an armed conflict that meets the proposed criteria, does not qualify as hostage-taking, be it for the purposes of the 1979 Hostages Convention, or for the purposes of international humanitarian law. Apart from the fact that the 1979 Hostages Convention does not apply to situations of armed conflict, hostage-taking by definition implies an element of threatening to "kill, injure or continue to detain" a person to compel a third party "to act or refrain from acting as an explicit or implicit condition for the safety or the release of such person or persons" (ICC, *Elements of Crimes* (2002), pp. 18-19 and 36). *Cf.* also *supra* notes 243-244.

[1586] Sassòli & Olson (*IRRC* 2008), p. 625.

[1587] The fact that internees must be treated humanely and that the conditions of their internment must meet standards that are quasi-identical to those required for internees in international armed conflict or occupation, is now generally accepted and part of customary international law applicable to both IAC and NIAC (*cf. supra* note 492). One notable exception is the right of internees to the assistance,

in any way be arbitrary, and the legal basis for internment must possess the basic qualities required of a law restricting individual rights and freedoms. Finally, the question of "whether a non-state actor may establish a court [in order to try persons suspected of criminal offences or to supervise their detention, or in order to allow detainees and internees to challenge the lawfulness of their detention/internment] remains controversial."[1588] In this regard, Pejic observes, and we agree, that:

> "Insofar as armed groups involved in non-international armed conflicts deprive persons of liberty in practice – regardless of the lawfulness of such conduct – they are bound by the applicable treaty-based and customary rules of international humanitarian law governing non-international armed conflicts summarized in this text [on the principles and procedural safeguards for administrative detention and internment in armed conflict and other situations of violence]. Where practically feasible, the other principles and safeguards set forth below [and which draw directly on international human rights law] should also be applied as a means of ensuring the protection of persons deprived of their liberty."[1589]

1.4. CONCLUSIONS AND OPTIONS

1.4.1. Conclusion: no legal basis for internment in existing international humanitarian law

Most of the arguments in favour of including a legal basis to intern at least members of armed forces of the parties to a non-international armed conflict in IHL make perfect sense. Moreover, preventing a person from engaging in hostilities against the Interning Power or its population would – according to the spirit and basic principles of international humanitarian law – indeed fall within the legitimate purposes for depriving a person of his or her liberty in any situation of armed conflict. Finally, the obligations regarding the treatment and conditions of captivity of internees and detainees are quasi-identical in both international and non-international armed conflict.

---

visits and monitoring of internment conditions by a Protecting Power and the ICRC. We have seen above that the ICRC only has a right to propose its services in this matter in situations that do not meet the threshold of common article 2 GC, and that States are not legally obliged to accept such an offer of services. In 1971, military experts had pointed out to the ICRC that "the time has not yet come when the right to act automatically in cases of non-international conflict can be given to a body, whatever it may be", mainly because of certain States' clinging to the principle of sovereignty (see ICRC, *Report for the Conference of Government Experts* (1971), Vol. 5, p. 74). Taking into account the ongoing erosion of that principle in light of humanitarian concerns shared by the international community as a whole, one may hope a renewed proposal in the future would grant either the ICRC or another neutral, impartial and humanitarian body, a right to assist internees in non-international armed conflict and make representations to the Interning Power on their behalf, as is the case in international armed conflicts.

[1588] Sassòli & Olson (*IRRC* 2008), p. 622, with reference to Somer, "Jungle Justice: Passing Sentence on the Equality of Belligerents in Non-International Armed Conflict" (*IRRC* 2007). For a good overview of the issues at stake, see also Sivakumaran (*JICJ* 2009).

[1589] Pejic (*IRRC* 2005), p. 376. In the same sense: Sivakumaran (*JICJ* 2009).

It is exactly this sense of logic and humanitarian concern that has propelled proposals to either expand the scope of application of the Geneva Conventions to all situations of armed conflict regardless of their international or internal nature, or to confer combatant or at least prisoner of war status to members of the armed forces of non-State parties to a non-international armed conflict.[1590] The inclusion of a direct legal basis to intern persons who pose a military threat in treaty NIAC-IHL – as was done for situations of international armed conflict and occupation – would indeed have been a logical choice. Nevertheless, it was not the choice made by the drafters of common article 3 or Additional Protocol II. So far, all such proposals have been consistently rejected by the large majority of States and failed to materialize in either treaty or customary international humanitarian law.

The absence of an express prohibition to intern, or the possible existence of an inherent right to intern in non-international armed conflict, does not by itself provide the Interning Power with a legal basis prescribing the grounds and procedures in accordance with which a specific individual may indeed be interned.[1591] For the internment not to amount to arbitrary deprivation of liberty, these grounds and procedures must be prescribed by law. Moreover, it must be accompanied by at least those procedural safeguards that are inherent in the right to liberty itself. States have created the necessary tools in IHL to exercise any "inherent right to intern" they may have in situations of international armed conflict and occupation by including a proper legal basis to intern directly in treaty IHL. They chose not to do so for situations of non-international armed conflict, but to leave the definition of the grounds and procedures for detention and internment in NIAC entirely up to the domestic law of States affected by such conflicts.[1592] Where international humanitarian law for non-international armed conflict fundamentally differs from that regulating international armed conflict and occupation is in the fact that it does not prescribe either the grounds for security internment, or the essential procedural safeguards that must accompany such deprivation of liberty, and therefore, "[i]n non-international

[1590] *Cf. supra* section 1.1. For an example of a recent plea for a "universal combatant [and POW] status": Crawford (2010), pp. 153-169.

[1591] For example, whereas in the *Expert Meeting on Security Detention in NIAC* "[t]here was prevailing agreement that any party to a NIAC has an inherent power or "qualified right" to intern persons captured", the participants also found that "[i]nternment is an exceptional measure that can only be ordered on certain grounds that must be stipulated in the legal basis for internment" (*Report of the Expert Meeting on Security Detention in NIAC* (2008), p. 864).

[1592] Any domestic legislation adopted to this effect must of course conform with IHRL, and may never result in arbitrary deprivation of liberty. In the same sense, e.g. Deeks (*CWRJIL* 2009), pp. 404, 413; Draper (*BYIL* 1971), p. 207; Doswald-Beck in *Report of the Expert Meeting on the Supervision of Lawfulness of Detention* (2004), p. 3; Doswald-Beck in Chesterman & Lehnardt (2007), p. 127; Dörmann in *Report of the Expert Meeting on the Supervision of Lawfulness of Detention* (2004), p. 15; Rogers in Wilmshurst & Breau (2007), p. 25; Rona (*HRF Paper* 2008), pp. 7-8; Sassòli (*JICJ* 2004), p. 105; Sassòli & Olson (*IRRC* 2008), p. 618; Sassòli in Schmitt (2009), p. 444; Denmark, MFA, *Discussion Paper* (2009), p. 32; and Lubell (2010), pp. 163 and 186.

armed conflicts, IHL cannot possibly be seen as a sufficient legal basis for detaining anyone."[1593]

Scholars and other experts have thus highlighted the need for such a legal basis to be found elsewhere:

> "IHL of non-international armed conflicts indicates that internment occurs in non-international armed conflict, but it contains no indication of how it is to be regulated. Such regulation is necessary so that internment can practically take place."[1594]

> "One of the most important legal challenges posed by internment in NIAC is that there is no explicit legal basis for this type of deprivation of liberty in any branch of international law."[1595]

In the current state of affairs, States seem to be left with only one option to lawfully intern in situations of non-international armed conflict, which is to adopt a legal basis for such internment in their domestic law. Nevertheless, there may be other options that could possibly remedy – to a varying extent – the problems mentioned above.

1.4.2. Other options?

Apart from adopting ad hoc emergency legislation in their domestic legal order, State parties to non-international armed conflicts may possibly have a number of other options to establish a legal basis to intern persons who pose a direct threat to their security and their military operations.[1596] We will briefly outline these options, before examining the option of the development of NIAC-IHL in more detail.[1597]

[1593] Sassòli (*JICJ* 2004), p. 105. In the same sense: Rona (*HRF Paper* 2008), p. 7; Olson (*CWRJIL* 2009), p. 452; Deeks (*CWRJIL* 2009), p. 452; and Hampson in Schmitt (2009), p. 497.

[1594] Sassòli in Schmitt (2009), p. 444.

[1595] *Report of the Expert Meeting on Security Detention in NIAC* (2008), p. 862.

[1596] Note that self-defence cannot be a legal *basis* to deprive anyone of his or her liberty. See also *Report of the Expert Meeting on Security Detention in NIAC* (2008), p. 867: "While some States have invoked the jus ad bellum concept of self-defence as a legal basis for internment, there was general consensus that such invocation is troublesome – if not outright invalid – under international law. For almost all experts it was clear that self-defence in its jus ad bellum sense does not constitute a legal basis for internment in NIAC."

[1597] The various possible options can only be outlined here; they certainly merit further research and analysis, but this is beyond the scope of our present work. Our research and analysis in this book focuses on the questions of who can be interned, for what reasons and for how long, *on the basis of international humanitarian law*. Therefore, only the option of a legal basis within that body of law will be explored. The other options, especially that of the potential legislative powers of the Security Council in this domain – which raises many fundamental questions that are much broader than its power to enact a legal basis to intern in NIAC – merit a separate study all-together. Nevertheless, any of the options mentioned in the present section should meet the international law requirements for a valid legal basis to deprive persons of their liberty discussed in Part I of this book. Finally, it needs to be noted that the options explored in this section – except for the further development of IHL – are not available in situations of international armed conflict and occupation, which regulates internment of persons for reasons related to the conflict in an exhaustive manner (*cf. supra* Part II).

1.4.2.1. Ad hoc expansion of the Geneva Conventions' applicability to a specific conflict

We have seen above that States could conclude special agreements with their adversaries in a given non-international armed conflict to formally extend the application of the Geneva Conventions to that conflict, as is provided for in, and encouraged by, common article 3 of these Conventions.[1598]

Moreover, States could unilaterally declare the Conventions to apply to a particular situation of non-international armed conflict (a modern version of recognition of belligerency). Such an agreement or declaration would effectively make the legal bases for internment in the Geneva Conventions available to the parties to that non-international armed conflict, much in the same way as has been done by international treaty law (through article 1§4 AP I) for wars of national liberation.

1.4.2.2. Delegation of domestic internment powers to a third State or an international organization

Where States participate in a non-international armed conflict abroad, they could conclude a bilateral agreement with the host State that grants them internment powers on the basis of that host State's domestic law. Alternatively, the host State could grant such powers to another State or even an international organization directly within its domestic law.[1599]

[1598] See for example the agreements concluded to this effect during the conflicts in the Balkans, in Sassòli & Bouvier (2006), Vol. II, pp. 1761-1769. In the Nigerian Biaffran secessionist conflict, the parties, short of concluding an actual agreement, both shared their intention to apply the four Geneva Conventions with the ICRC, see ICRC, *Rapport d'activités extérieures* (*IRRC* 1967), pp. 461-465. Most CA3 agreements do *not* deal with the question of prisoners of war however, see for example Mozambique, *Mozambique National Resistance – RENAMO Joint Declaration with the Government of Mozambique on the Guiding Principles of Humanitarian Assistance* (1992); Philippines, *Comprehensive Agreement on Respect for Human Rights and International Humanitarian Law between the Government of the Republic of the Philippines and the National Democratic Front of the Philippines* (1998); Philippines, *Agreement on the Civilian Protection Component of the International Monitoring Team* (2009); or Sudan, *Agreement between the Government of the Republic of Sudan and the Sudan People's Liberation Movement to Protect Non-Combatant Civilians and Civilian Facilities from Military Attack* (2002).

[1599] *Cf. supra* note 1540. Such a solution was recommended – on the basis of policy considerations – to the US in the Afghan context by Human Rights First, *Fixing Bagram* (2009), pp. 4 and 9: "the Afghan government should either confer detention authority upon the Untied States through its domestic legislation or by way of a *public* U.S.-Afghan security agreement. Either must set forth grounds and procedures for detention in accordance with international law. [Such a solution moreover] would bolster U.S. support for Afghan sovereignty and advance U.S. strategy to progressively devolve responsibility for detentions to the Afghan government. The implementation of such legislation or an agreement regularizing U.S. detention would also advance the credibility of U.S. military actions in the exes of Afghans, thus supporting U.S. counterinsurgency goals in Afghanistan [...] any agreement or legislation should be approved by the Afghan National Assembly in accordance with [...] the Afghan Constitution" (original emphasis). This option has also been retained in UK military doctrine (*cf. supra* note 1537). The participants in the 2008 *Expert Meeting on Security Detention in NIAC* found however that: "Given the lack of clarity of international law and the novel scenario of MNF-NIAC in which the MNF [i.e. multinational force] interns persons who pose a security threat, instruments of a more operational nature have been relied on to deal with the issue on the ground. While some troop-contributing States have argued that a legal basis for

1.4.2.3. UN Security Council resolutions

Where the host State is unable or unwilling to conclude such an agreement or adopt such a law, or where its domestic law does not provide for a legal basis to intern those who pose a direct military threat, States could possibly have recourse to the UN Security Council and request it to adopt a resolution under Chapter VII of the UN Charter, which – much like a State can adopt emergency legislation providing a legal basis to intern in derogation from the right to liberty under international human rights law – prescribes the grounds and procedures in accordance with which a particular State or group of States may intern persons for reasons related to the conflict. At least two questions arise in this regard.

The first is whether the Security Council has the legal capacity to enact a legal basis for deprivation of liberty. Without going into the broader debate on the legislative powers of the Security Council,[1600] it is useful to point out that it seems to have effectively done so when it adopted the statutes of the ICTY and the ICTR, both of which include provisions that serve as the only legal basis for these tribunals to preventively detain a person against whom the prosecutor has pressed charges (before, during and after trial) and to sentence such persons to imprisonment upon conviction.[1601] The legal basis for provisional detention and

internment may be provided for in bilateral agreements concluded with a host State, the validity of that argument was challenged by participants to the meeting. Moreover, it remains unclear whether in such a case, the host State, the troop-contributing state or both would need to derogate from their IHRL obligations to allow for internment. Bilateral agreements could take the form of a Status of Forces Agreement ("SOFA"). Some experts argued that SOFAs are not a direct source of law, but rather agreements on the extent to which the domestic law of the host State covers actions of the sending States' forces. Others argued that, as bilateral treaties, SOFAs may create rights and obligations between the contracting parties, but that the latter are still subject to their obligations under general international law (including IHL and IHRL). It was accepted that, in common with bilateral agreements, a SOFA could not be used to circumvent States' international obligations, and that although a SOFA is not an ideal legal vehicle for internment in NIAC it may have some utility as long as its provisions regarding internment are in accordance with international law. Therefore, for it to constitute an adequate legal basis for internment, the grounds and the procedure must not only be made explicit, but must also conform to the relevant IHL and IHRL." Finally, the experts found that "[n]ational standard operating procedures ("SOP") [although they] must always reflect the law [are] not a source of law and therefore cannot provide the lawful authority or legal basis for internment. While [they] may specify the procedures or outline the practical implementation of internment, SOPs need to rely on another, pre-existing lawful authority providing a legal basis for internment (e.g. domestic law, explicit UNSCR, etc.)" *Report of the Expert Meeting on Security Detention in NIAC* (2008), pp. 869-870.

1600 Questions regarding the existence, extent and modalities of any legislative powers the UN Security Council may have, are beyond the scope of this book. For an overview of the main issues and references to the literature, see Boyle & Chinkin, *The Making of International Law* (2007), pp. 109-115 and 229-233. See also Abi-Saab in Wolfrum & Röben (2008), who finds – and argues convincingly – that the Security Council cannot legislate in the legal sense of the word "as neither the text nor the context of the Charter allows for such a possibility" (Abi-Saab at p. 120).

1601 Articles 19, 24 and 27 ICTY Statute (the Statute was adopted by and is annexed to UNSCR 827 (1993); and articles 18, 23 and 26 ICTR Statute (the Statute was adopted by and is annexed to UNSCR 955 (1994). Both resolutions were adopted under Chapter VII of the UN Charter. Each Tribunal subsequently further developed the rules governing such detention, see ICTY, *Rules Governing the Detention of Persons Awaiting Trial or Appeal before the Tribunal or otherwise Detained on the Authority of the Tribunal* (1994); ICTR, *Rules Governing the Detention of Persons Awaiting Trial or Appeal before the Tribunal or otherwise Detained on the Authority of the Tribunal*

imprisonment by the Tribunals has so far not been challenged as a valid legal basis to deprive these persons of their liberty.[1602]

(1998). *Cf.* also *supra* chapter I-1, section 1.2.3.3.

1602 Challenges to the legality of an arrest or detention at the behest of the Tribunals have been made (1) with regard to the legality of an *arrest* by abduction or by luring an individual into a territory where the arrest could be carried, or the legality of the *transfer* of an individual into the custody of the Tribunal (e.g. the ICTY's judgments concerning Dokmanović, Todorović, Milošević and Nikolić discussed in Naqvi (2010), pp. 342-346); and (2) with regard to *procedural* aspects of the arrest and/or detention carried out by States cooperating with the Tribunal (e.g. ICTR, *Kajelijeli* (2005), §§208-223; and the ICTR's decisions in the *Barayagwiza* cases discussed in Naqvi (2010), pp. 348-349). In what resembles most closely to a challenge of the validity of the legal bases to arrest and detain enshrined in the ICTY Statute, Duško Tadić challenged the *jurisdiction* of the ICTY on the basis that the ICTY was not "a tribunal which has been established y law" as is required under article 14§1 ICCPR, article 6§1 ECHR and article 8§1 ACHR (ICTY, *Tadić* (1995), §41). According to Tadić's defence, "established by law" must be interpreted as meaning "established by a legislature" and the ICTY "is the product of a 'mere executive order' and not of a 'decision making process under democratic control, necessary to create a judicial organisation in a democratic society'" (ICTY, *Tadić* (1995), §43). While the ICTY's Appeal Chamber agreed that this is how the requirement has been interpreted by the ECtHR, the Chamber found that this interpretation only applies in the domestic and not in the international legal order (in light of the fact that the United Nations has no legislature). The Appeals Chamber found that the requirement of "established by law" must, in the international legal order, be interpreted as meaning that an international court or tribunal must be established "in accordance with the rule of law [...] it must be established in accordance with the proper international standards; it must provide all the guarantees of fairness, justice and even-handedness, in full conformity with internationally recognized human rights instruments." The Chamber then found that the ICTY Statute and Rules of Procedure and Evidence ensured that this was indeed the case, that the UN's "representative" organ, namely the General Assembly, had "repeatedly approved and endorsed" the establishment of the ICTY, and that it could therefore conclude that the ICTY was "established by law" (ICTY, *Tadić* (1995), §§45-47). It is likely that the Tribunal, faced with a challenge regarding the validity of the legal basis to detain enshrined within its Statute (under IHRL, the grounds and procedures for deprivation of liberty must be "prescribed by law", *cf. supra* chapter I-1), would have argued along the same lines. In the *Talić* case, both the accused and the Tribunal clearly found that the legal basis to preventively detain the accused, enshrined in article 19§2 of its Statute ("Upon confirmation of an indictment, the judge may, at the request of the Prosecutor, issue such orders and warrants for the arrest, detention, surrender or transfer of persons, and any other orders as may be required for the conduct of the trial"), was a valid legal basis in the sense of article 9§1 ICCPR. Talić was detained on the basis of an indictment that was subsequently amended. He then claimed that the *amended* indictment did not specifically provide again for his detention (ICTY, *Talić* (2000), §18). The Tribunal found that: "There can be no quarrel with the terms of article [9§1 ICCPR], and it is true that the amended indictment remains the only legal basis for the proceedings against Talić – in the sense that it (and it alone) contains the statement of the charges against him. But it requires a very large (and impermissible) leap in logic to accept that there is presently no basis in the Tribunal's 'procedures (…) established by law' for his present detention. The procedures [...] are that the judge who confirms an indictment may issue a warrant for the arrest of the accused [reference to article 19§2 Statute and Rule 47(H)(i) of the Rules of Procedure and Evidence]. [...] Upon transfer of the accused to the seat of the Tribunal, he 'shall be detained', and, once detained, he may not be released except upon an order of a Trial Chamber. According to the Tribunal's 'procedures (…) established by law', therefore, the only actions by the Tribunal which are necessary to justify the detention of the accused are the review and confirmation of the indictment and the issue of the arrest warrant. Article 19.2 of the Tribunal's Statute makes it clear that it is the review and the confirmation of the indictment which justifies the issue of the arrest warrant. Thereafter, [...] once the accused is arrested, he remains in custody and then detention until released by an order of a Trial Chamber, as Rule 65(A) provides. [...] The replacement of [the] original redacted indictment with an amended indictment has had no effect upon the operation of [...] that order for detention" (ICTY, *Talić* (2000), §§19-21, references to the Statute and the Rules of Procedure, and original emphasis omitted).

Two other Security Council resolutions are sometimes invoked as the legal basis for internment in non-international armed conflict, namely Resolution 1386 (2001), establishing the mandate of the NATO-led International Security Assistance Force (ISAF) in Afghanistan, and Resolution 1546 (2004), which establishes the mandate of the US-led Multinational Forces in Iraq (MNF-I).[1603] Troop-contributing nations in ISAF and MNF-I have so far not relied on these resolutions as a legal basis for internment in either Afghanistan or Iraq,[1604] but the resolutions are often referred to in debates regarding the legal basis for internment by multinational forces in non-international armed conflict and are thus worth mentioning.

In Resolution 1386 (2001), the Security Council:

> "1. *Authorizes* [...] the establishment for 6 months of an International Security Assistance Force to assist the Afghan Interim Authority in the maintenance of security in Kabul and its surrounding areas, so that the Afghan Interim Authority as well as the personnel of the United Nations can operate in a secure environment; [and] 3. *Authorizes* the Member States participating in the International Security Assistance Force to take *all necessary measures to fulfil its mandate.*" (emphasis added)

The US-Iraqi agreement regarding the mandate of the MNF-I, annexed to Security Council's Resolution 1546 (2004),[1605] is more specific:

> "Under the agreed arrangement, the MNF stands ready to continue to undertake a broad range of tasks to contribute to the maintenance of security and to ensure force protection. These include activities necessary to counter ongoing security threats posed by forces seeking to influence Iraq's political future through violence. This will include combat operations against members of these groups, *internment where this is necessary for imperative reasons of security*, and the continued search for and securing of weapons that threaten Iraq's security." (emphasis added)

Should the Security Council indeed have the power to legislate on grounds and procedures for internment in non-international armed conflict (which we doubt, but cannot exclude *ab initio*), a second question arises and concerns the specificity of the language that would need to be inserted in such a resolution for it to constitute a valid legal basis for internment. Most (but not all) will agree that the language of Resolution 1386 (2001) is insufficient; the possibility of internment is not even mentioned in that resolution. There is somewhat more willingness, amongst legal scholars, to accept that the language in the annexes to

---

[1603] Both resolutions have been adopted under Chapter VII of the UN Charter.

[1604] *Cf. supra* section 1.1, chapter II-3, section 3.2.2.2, chapter II-4, section 4.3.

[1605] In the Resolution's operative paragraphs 9 and 10, the Security Council "*[n]otes* that the presence of the multinational force in Iraq is at the request of the incoming Interim Government of Iraq and therefore *reaffirms* the authorization for the multinational force under unified command established under resolution 1511 (2003), having regard to the letters annexed to this resolution; *Decides* that the multinational force shall have the authority to take all necessary measures to contribute to the maintenance of security and stability in Iraq in accordance with the letters annexed to this resolution expressing, inter alia, the Iraqi request for the continued presence of the multinational force and setting out its tasks" (original emphasis).

Resolution 1546 (2004) may be sufficient. During an expert meeting on internment in non-international armed conflict:

> "experts agreed that a United Nations Security Council Resolution (hereafter "UNSCR") under Chapter VII of the Charter could possibly constitute a legal basis for internment when the measure of internment and the permissible grounds for it are explicitly mentioned in the resolution. Some experts argued that the "all necessary measures" phrase commonly used in Chapter VII resolutions can constitute a legal basis for internment by multinational forces taking part in an armed conflict. However, other experts argued that the phrase is too vague to provide a legal basis for internment, i.e. to be interpreted as giving lawful authority. Human rights bodies are also unlikely to accept the latter but have made no pronouncements on the matter thus far. It was concluded that a Chapter VII UNSCR could possibly provide the legal basis for internment in NIAC. There was, however, no agreement on the level of specificity required of the language of such a resolution."[1606]

Hampson for her part finds that: "[i]t would be possible for [a UN Security Council Resolution under chapter VII] to fill in the gap in a non-international armed conflict. It could provide for authority to detain and specify the grounds on which a person could be detained."[1607] Nevertheless, she rejects the argument that a phrase along the lines of "all necessary means for the fulfilment of the [UN mandate]" would be sufficiently precise:

> "There are particular reasons why the authority to detain must be specific – to comply with respect for human rights law, which is required by virtue of the preambular paragraph [of the UN Security Council Resolution concerning the conflict in Afghanistan and authorizing ISAF to use "all necessary means" to fulfil its security mandate in Afghanistan]." [1608]

Sassòli goes a step further and finds that the wording of UN Security Council Resolution 1546, is also insufficient:

> "UN Security Council Resolution 1546, authorizing 'internment where ... necessary for imperative reasons of security' [...] is not explicit enough to be considered a mandate to UN member States not to provide such internees with the procedural guarantees that they are obliged to offer under IHRL [...] the UN Security Council Resolutions concerning Afghanistan [which do not mention internment but merely state the multinational forces may take "all necessary measures" to fulfil their security mandate in Afghanistan] contain no language similar to that of Resolution 1546 which could be claimed to govern the admissible reasons of detention."[1609]

Kleffner finds that:

> "a mandate 'to use all necessary means' to achieve the assigned tasks logically encompasses operational detention as one such means, if indeed necessary.

[1606] *Report of the Expert Meeting on Security Detention in NIAC* (2008), pp 868-869.

[1607] Hampson in Schmitt (2009), pp. 502-506. In the same sense: Naert (2010), p. 613.

[1608] Hampson in Schmitt (2009), pp. 502-506. In the same sense: Naert (2010), p. 613, and ECtHR (Grand Chamber), *Al-Jedda* (2011), §§102-109.

[1609] Sassòli in Schmitt (2009), p. 439, and ECtHR (Grand Chamber), *Al-Jedda* (2011), §§102-109.

As such a mandate is generally interpreted and applied to include the ultimate means, the use of potentially deadly force, it may logically also include the lesser means of operational detention. [...] This would not apply, however, to any obligations of States under peremptory law (jus cogens), and the general commitment under the Charter, to promote 'universal respect for, and observance of, human rights and fundamental freedoms for all without distinction as to race, sex, language, or religion' is to be considered also in this context. Hence it may hardly be assumed that a Security Council mandate 'to use all necessary means' could provide a legal basis for operational detentions that would not be clearly available under other rules of law. A consistent practice of the Council goes in the opposite direction: strict adherence to human rights law and humanitarian law is stipulated even in the fight against terrorism."[1610]

In his article, Kleffner fails to make the distinction between legal basis and lawful grounds for deprivation of liberty. He speaks of "legal basis" in both senses. In the passage quoted here, he seems however to refer rather to lawful grounds and his argument must thus be understood in the sense that the Security Council (if it could legislate at all, a point that Kleffner does not touch upon) could not prescribe other grounds for internment than those "clearly available under other rules of law." This would mean that any legal basis for deprivation of liberty the Security Council would enact would have to limit the lawful grounds for such deprivation of liberty to those that are allowed for under international human rights law.[1611]

We hope that the analysis in Part I of this book has demonstrated that the language in either of these resolutions would be insufficient to meet the principle of legality, and that neither of them could therefore serve as a legal basis for internment. Any such legal basis must prescribe both the grounds and the procedures in accordance with which internment may be ordered, ensure the essential procedural safeguards inherent in the right to liberty are available to internees,[1612] and must possess at least the basic qualities of a "law". Regardless of whether Security Council resolutions can be "law" in the formal sense, any "law" prescribing restrictions on fundamental rights and freedoms (such as the right to liberty) must be sufficiently precise so as to allow persons potentially affected by it to foresee the application of the restriction in their regard, and the "law" itself must offer adequate protection against arbitrariness.[1613]

Thus, whereas we do not fully discard the possibility that a bilateral agreement between an intervening State and a host nation, or a UN Security Council Resolution under Chapter VII[1614] – both of which have binding force of

[1610] Kleffner in Gill & Fleck (2010), p. 470. With regard to Kleffner's claim that the permission to use of force logically includes permission to detain, see our fundamental disagreement with this position as expressed in chapter II-3, section 3.2.2.2.

[1611] The lawful grounds for internment in international armed conflict would not be "clearly available" since that body of law does not apply to situations of non-international armed conflict.

[1612] *Cf. supra* chapter I-1, section 1.2.1.

[1613] *Cf. supra* chapter I-1, section 1.2.3.2.

[1614] The Danish government finds it to be "common ground that the legality requirement may be satisfied either by national or international law, or even a Security Council resolution" (Denmark, MFA,

law in the international legal order – could possibly satisfy the principle of legality in its formal aspect and thus provide a legal basis for internment in NIAC,[1615] each of these options remains subject to the prohibition of arbitrary deprivation of liberty and will only be valid if it meets the requirements for lawful deprivation of liberty under international human rights law discussed in chapter I-1. In the absence of a legal basis in IHL equivalent to those in the Geneva Conventions, any legal basis to intern in non-international armed conflict – be it domestic or international in nature – may not depart from the right to liberty as enshrined in international human rights treaties, save through (lawful) derogation by the Interning Power.

1.4.2.4. Development of international humanitarian law for non-international armed conflict

A final option remains, namely that of creating a legal basis to intern directly in international humanitarian law, as has already been done for situations of international armed conflict and occupation, including CAR conflicts (article 1§4 AP I). On the whole, this is in our opinion the preferable option, and this for a number of reasons.[1616]

For one, the adoption and abuse of domestic emergency legislation derogating from the right to liberty, and the failure to abrogate it when the alleged emergency has ceased to exist, has proved to be one of the root causes of arbitrary deprivation of liberty worldwide. If directly provided for in IHL, the legal basis to intern for reasons of military necessity will be available only in

---

Discussion Paper (2009), p. 34). It relies mainly on the UK House of Lords' ruling in *Al-Jedda* (2007), where the majority of the Law Lords accepted that a UNSC resolution could potentially satisfy the legality requirement in article 5§1 ECHR. While we do not entirely disagree with the Danish government's finding as such, we think it is important to specify that any such law, be it national or international or even a Security Council resolution, must satisfy both the principle of legality and the criteria for lawful deprivation of liberty prescribed by IHRL in order to serve as a valid legal basis for internment (or any other form of deprivation of liberty). This also seems to be the view of the European Court of Human Rights in its judgment in *Al-Jedda*. While its reasoning on this point is rather summary, the Court does clearly convey that while it does not as such reject the *possibility* of a Security Council resolution (or in the case at hand a bilateral agreement between a host State and an intervening State) constituting a valid legal basis for internment, such an instrument would still need to be in accordance with international human rights law, i.e. to be sufficiently precise and explicit in the prescription of the grounds and procedures for internment (ECtHR (Grand Chamber), *Al-Jedda* (2011), §§ 102-109). In the absence of a valid legal basis for the interment of Mr. Al-Jedda by UK forces in Iraq, the Court found a violation of Article 5§1 ECHR (ECtHR (Grand Chamber), *Al-Jedda* (2011), §§ 109-110).

[1615] The same is not true for situations of international armed conflict and occupation, where the Geneva Conventions prescribe, exhaustively, the grounds and procedures for internment and detention for reasons related to the armed conflict (*cf. supra* Part II).

[1616] Note that our efforts to clarify the legal framework for internment in IHL and our recommendations as to what should guide any process of further development of IHL should not be understood as an unreserved promotion of IHL as providing the only appropriate guidance for designing a legal framework to intern in armed conflict. The relevance of the relevant norms of IHRL has been made clear throughout this book, and is even stronger in non-international armed conflict than in international armed conflict, as in situations of non-international armed conflict most persons in need of protection will be in the hands of their own State.

situations that indeed meet the threshold of armed conflict and be safer from abuse in situations that do not reach that threshold.[1617]

What is more, were international humanitarian law to prescribe the grounds and procedures for internment in non-international armed conflict and offer adequate protection against arbitrariness and abuse – much like the Geneva Conventions already do for situations of international armed conflict and occupation – a party to a non-international armed conflict may no longer need to derogate from its international human rights obligations to lawfully order security internment in non-international armed conflict.[1618]

Moreover, any ad hoc solutions – like the adoption of domestic emergency legislation, bilateral agreements with a host nation, or a UN Security Council – will need to be negotiated at the time hostilities have already broken out. Their negotiation is likely to be very time-consuming,[1619] and the result may be inappropriate and/or untimely to respond to the military and security needs of troops on the ground. Moreover, their result is also likely to be insufficient to satisfy the Interning Power's international human rights obligations.[1620] A direct legal basis in NIAC-IHL, as is the case for situations of international armed conflict and occupation, would make the negotiation and adoption of such *ad hoc* instruments unnecessary.[1621]

Furthermore, a legal basis to intern in NIAC-IHL would also provide multinational forces participating in non-international armed conflict abroad with

---

[1617] See in this sense also the concern expressed by the WGAD, *Annual Report 2007*, §59: "another issue of concern for the Working Group remains the continuing tendency towards deprivation of liberty by States abusing states of emergency or derogation, invoking special powers specific to states of emergency without formal declaration, having recourse to military, special or emergency courts, not observing the principle of proportionality between the severity of the measures taken and the situation concerned, and employing vague definitions of offences allegedly designed to protect State security and combat terrorism."

[1618] *Cf. supra* chapter I-2, section 2.2.2.2.

[1619] Moreover, political factors or sensitivities, even those unrelated to the actual situation of armed conflict, may delay or even block their adoption altogether.

[1620] The ECtHR has pointed out that an *ad hoc* legal basis deprive a person of his or her liberty is unlikely to meet the principle of legal certainty, see ECtHR, *Medvedyev v. France* (2010), §100: "the intervention of the French authorities on the basis of an *ad hoc* agreement cannot reasonably be said to have been "foreseeable" within the meaning of the Court's case-law, even with the help of appropriate advice. In any event the Court considers that the foreseeability, for an offender, of prosecution [...] should not be confused with the foreseeability of the law pleaded as the basis for the intervention. Otherwise any activity considered criminal under domestic law would release the States from their obligation to pass laws having the requisite qualities, particularly with regard to Article 5§1 of the Convention and, in so doing, deprive that provision of its substance." *In casu*, the deprivation of liberty was ordered and executed in the framework of criminal proceedings (namely for drug-trafficking), but the reasoning of the Court with regard to article 5§1 ECHR can be applied *mutatis mutandis* with regard to any deprivation of liberty, including administrative detention or internment. *Cf. supra* chapter I-1.

[1621] On the need for general, rather than *ad hoc* solutions, see also Winkler (*Nordic JIL* 2010), p. 496: "it was realised [by participants in the Copenhagen Process on the Handling of Detainees in International Military Operations] that both the challenges on the ground in regard to the specific handling of detainees and the described legal challenges may only be addressed horizontally. A case-by-case approach varying from operation to operation would only add to the challenges."

a pre-existing and uniform legal basis to intern, which in turn should facilitate coordination and cooperation in their internment and detention operations, as well as avoiding the need for ad hoc solutions. As Winkler points out:

> "It is not satisfactory – either legally, politically or operationally – that the handling of detainees today to a large extent is left to ad hoc solutions thought up by individual troop-contributing States and that the plight of the individual detainee may depend on which State he was detained by. [...] the framework for the handling of detainees will thus vary according to the arrangements of the apprehending State. This is not a satisfactory situation, and the Danish government therefore at an early stage began considering how to ensure a multilateral approach to these challenges."[1622]

Also, the existence of a direct legal basis to intern in international humanitarian law for non-international armed conflicts would effectively provide both State and non-State parties (such as international organizations and organized armed groups) to non-international armed conflicts with the legal basis to intern that is lacking in existing NIAC-IHL. The availability of such a legal basis would confirm the generally accepted inherent right to intern in armed conflict and provide parties to non-international armed conflicts, States and non-State entities alike, with the tool to exercise that right. The existence of a legal basis to intern in international humanitarian law (establishing a strict legal framework for and providing for the protection of internees and supervision of the lawfulness of their internment) may also significantly reduce the risk of arbitrary deprivation of liberty and should counter any claims that tend to justify the use of lethal force in the absence of a legal basis to intern a person considered a military threat upon capture.[1623] It is submitted, as will be demonstrated in chapter III-2 below, that the creation of such a legal basis to intern does not, and should not, have any consequences on questions of prisoner of war status or combatant status and the privileges and immunities inherent therein.

Finally, the adoption of a multilateral treaty, by the international community as a whole and away from the emotions and tribulations of any particular armed conflict, is likely to result in a more balanced and widely accepted solution to the practical and legal challenges that arise from the state of the law as it stands today. Moreover, it would allow for adopting general rather than ad hoc rules and thus have a better chance of satisfying the certainty and predictability criteria required by the principles of legality and the rule of law.[1624] Striking a balance

---

[1622] Winkler (*Nordic JIL* 2010), pp. 491 and 496, with reference to the Danish-propelled Copenhagen Process on the Handling of Detainees in International Military Operations, *cf. supra* note 1502. In the same sense: Deeks (*CWRJIL* 2009), p. 434.

[1623] A similar argument is made by Sivakumaran with regard to the possibility for organized armed groups to set up courts to try persons who have committed offences of either criminal law or IHL, see Sivakumaran (*JICJ* 2009), pp. 509-510: "Without trials, summary executions, a practice already prevalent in armed conflicts, including those in which armed groups have established their own courts, may become the norm."

[1624] *Cf. supra* chapter I-1, section 1.2.2. On the dangers of *ad hoc* decisions by the Security Council for the rule of law, see also Bianchi, "Ad-hocism and the Rule of Law" (*EJIL* 2002), pp. 269-272. In this regard, the following extracts from the Security Council's Statement of 21 July 2010 are also

between military necessity and humanity, between the needs of parties to a conflict to achieve military victory and the rights and freedoms of individuals involved in or otherwise affected by that conflict, is precisely the function international humanitarian law has been allotted in the international legal system. While it is far from the only body of international law capable of protecting the human person, it probably remains the most efficient body of law to achieve that goal in situations of armed conflict.

worth noting: "The Security Council reaffirms its commitment to [...] an international order based on the rule law and international law, which is essential for peaceful coexistence and cooperation amongst States in addressing common challenges, thus contributing to the maintenance of international peace and security. [...] The Security Council recognizes that respect for international humanitarian law is an essential component of the rule of law in conflict situations."

CHAPTER III – 2

RECOMMENDATIONS FOR A NORMATIVE DEVELOPMENT OF INTERNATIONAL HUMANITARIAN LAW

Deprivation of liberty of persons who pose a threat to the security and military operations of the parties to the conflict is a recurrent incident of armed conflict, and both the logic and the spirit of international humanitarian law indicate that the parties to a conflict should be allowed to intern such persons in any situation of armed conflict. The argument that the requirement to "capture rather than kill" should be accompanied by an adequate legal basis to intern persons who pose a direct threat to the security or military operations of the parties to the conflict is only one – but a particularly strong – argument in favour of further development of NIAC-IHL in this area.[1625] Moreover, a proper legal basis to intern should also contribute significantly to efforts of reducing the risk of unnecessary and arbitrary deprivation of liberty and other, related, violations of international law.

We have outlined the options that may be available to remedy the practical and legal challenges that arise from the absence of a legal basis for internment in existing NIAC-IHL in the preceding chapter, and argued that a further normative development of NIAC-IHL is the most preferable amongst these options. On the basis of our research and analysis in Parts I and II, we would like to conclude this part of the book with some recommendations as to how an international legal framework for internment in non-international armed conflict could be designed, at least in as far as the grounds and duration of such internment are concerned. The recommendations are made in view of our proposal to further develop treaty IHL in NIAC so as to include a legal basis for internment, but may also prove useful for parties to armed conflicts who are bound to adopt *ad hoc* solutions to remedy the current absence of a legal basis for internment in international law, and for courts and treaty monitoring bodies that may be called upon to assess the validity of such *ad hoc* solutions under international law.

As a number of experts from academic, government, military and non-governmental circles have pointed out:

> "One of the most important legal challenges posed by internment in NIAC is that there is no explicit legal basis for this type of deprivation of liberty in any branch of international law. At the same time, in reality both States and non-State armed groups detain individuals for security reasons in NIAC and do so outside the framework of criminal proceedings. The legal basis for internment, the grounds and procedural safeguards applicable are questions of urgent concern to both

[1625] We have discussed other arguments in favour of such development in the preceding chapter.

policy and operational military personnel, the academic community, international think tanks, NGO's and others."[1626]

These questions therefore certainly merit answers. The research and analysis presented in book aims to contribute to the debate, at least in as far as the legal basis and grounds for internment are concerned.[1627] On the basis of the research and analysis in Parts I and II, we will in the following sections (1) briefly recall the main characteristics a *legal basis* to deprive persons of their liberty must fulfil to be valid under international law (section 2.1), and (2) propose a definition of the lawful *grounds (and duration)* for internment in situations of non-international armed conflict (section 2.2).

2.1. BASIC QUALITIES OF A VALID LEGAL BASIS TO INTERN IN NON-INTERNATIONAL ARMED CONFLICT

We have expressed our preference on the form of a legal basis for internment in situations of non-international armed conflict in chapter III-1. Whatever the form of the instrument ultimately adopted to serve as a legal basis for internment in NIAC however, it will have to offer adequate protection from arbitrary deprivation of liberty to be valid under international law. It will therefore have to satisfy the principle of legality (*nulla custodia sine lege*) in both its formal (principle of legal certainty) and material (principle of legitimacy) aspects.

[1626] *Report of the Expert Meeting on Security Detention in NIAC* (2008), pp. 862-863.

[1627] The definition of appropriate procedural safeguards for internment in NIAC is outside of the scope of this book. So is the definition of other safeguards against arbitrariness and abuse, such as the establishment of independent monitoring mechanisms, the obligation to register of internees and record all relevant information relating to their internment until their final release, the regulation of transfer of internees from one Interning Power to another, the regulation of internees' relations with the exterior (in particular with their family), and provisions concerning the responsibility for compliance with international law. With regard to the procedural safeguards for internment, the main bone of contention will undoubtedly be the nature of the body that must review, initially and periodically, the necessity and lawfulness of internment. Some will argue on the basis of IHRL that the review of the lawfulness of internment must be carried out by a court, and argue that "[t]he rule of law implies, inter alia, that an interference by the executive authorities with an individual's rights should be subject to an effective control which should normally be assured by the judiciary, at least in the last resort, judicial control offering the best guarantees of independence, impartiality and a proper procedure" (ECtHR, *Klass and Others v. Germany* (1978), §55). Others will be ready to concede that where impossible to establish court review of internment, the review body may resemble those envisaged in article 42 and 78 GC IV and need not be a court as long as it is independent and impartial and has effective power to order the release of persons unlawfully or arbitrarily interned (e.g. Pejic (*IRRC* 2005), pp. 386-387; and *Report of the Expert Meeting on Security Detention in NIAC* (2008), pp. 877-880). A possible way out of this dilemma is to include a general requirement that parties to the conflict must provide for internment review by a court, and add a qualifying clause stating that where the establishment of such a court, or the exercise of its functions, is legally or practically impossible, internment review may be entrusted to an independent and impartial body with full powers to release persons unlawfully or arbitrarily interned (note in this sense the combination of obligations of result and obligations of means in article 5 AP II quoted *supra* in section 1.3.1, note 1518) and Sandoz et al., *Commentary AP I and II* (1987), pp. 1385-1394).

First of all, the instrument as a whole must be sufficiently accessible and precise to enable persons potentially affected by it to foresee, to a reasonable degree, in which circumstances they may be subject to internment by the parties to a non-international armed conflict (legal certainty).[1628] The scope of application of the legal instrument that is to serve as a legal basis for internment must therefore be defined in sufficiently precise terms as to identify when, where and to whom it applies. Moreover, the grounds and procedures in accordance with which internment may be ordered on that basis must be prescribed in sufficiently precise terms as to enable potential subjects to foresee the possibility of their internment, and to allow the competent authorities to conduct a proper review of its lawfulness.

Second, the grounds for internment prescribed by the law must reflect valid needs and serve a purpose internationally recognized as legitimate for restricting fundamental rights and freedoms in situations of armed conflict (legitimacy).[1629] Moreover, where such grounds are prescribed by an instrument of general application (e.g. additional treaty IHL) rather than on an *ad hoc* basis, they must not only be sufficiently precise to allow for predictability, but also be sufficiently flexible to adapt to the variable realities of present and future armed conflicts. Where a large margin of discretion is left to the executive authorities or the military to order internment, the scope and limits of such discretion should be included in the legal basis itself.[1630] Therefore, if it is not possible to be very precise on the grounds, the legal basis should at least stress the exceptional nature of internment and could list grounds that would *not* meet the necessary threshold for internment in armed conflict.[1631]

Finally, the legal instrument serving as a legal basis for internment must establish adequate and efficient protection against arbitrary application of the law and any form of abuse that could result from it. Apart from prescribing the grounds and decision-making procedures for internment,[1632] it must include at least those procedural safeguards that are inherent in the right to liberty under

[1628] *Cf. supra* chapter I-1, section 1.2.3. See also Bingham (*Sir David Williams Lectures* 2006), p. 10.

[1629] *Cf. supra* chapter I-1, section 1.2.4 and chapter I-2, section 2.2.2.

[1630] ECtHR, *Silver and Others v. UK* (1983), §88: "A law [restricting fundamental rights and freedoms] which confers a discretion must indicate the scope of that discretion."

[1631] The proposal of a definition of lawful grounds for internment in non-international armed conflict in section 2.2.3 below opts for a positive definition of permissible grounds in precise terms. If such a proposal would not be acceptable, any broad language of such lawful grounds should be accompanied by a list of unlawful grounds for internment, based on those discussed in chapter I-1, section 1.2.4 and in chapter II-3, section 3.2.2.2.

[1632] Decisions on internment must be made by persons with a sufficient level of responsibility within the armed forces of the party to the conflict, and where possible and necessary with the assistance of their legal advisors. See the examples of Israeli and Canadian practice *supra* note 1249. Similarly, within KFOR, on-site force commanders could order internment for up to 18 hours and multinational brigade commanders could intern a person up to 72 hours. Continued internment beyond the initial 72 hours required a decision by the general force commander (COMKFOR) (COMKFOR Directive 42, issued on 9 October 2001, as referred to by Deeks (*CWRJIL* 2009), p. 417. Likewise, decisions on internment within INTERFET were the responsibility of COMINTERFET or his designated delegate (Deeks (*CWRJIL* 2009), pp. 419-420).

international law. Moreover, other, more practical, safeguards must be established to minimize the risk of arbitrary deprivation of liberty and other violations of international humanitarian and human rights law.[1633]

2.2. LAWFUL GROUNDS FOR INTERNMENT IN NON-INTERNATIONAL ARMED CONFLICT

Lawful grounds for deprivation of liberty are those that reflect valid needs and serve a purpose recognized as legitimate by the international community.[1634] In the context of an armed conflict, the rules of general international law (international human rights law in particular) regarding deprivation of liberty do not cease to apply. Nevertheless, international humanitarian law recognizes a legitimate purpose to impose restrictions on fundamental rights and freedoms that would not be recognized as such in situations that do not reach the threshold of armed conflict. Without prejudice to rights and prohibitions that are absolute and may never be departed from, even in situations of armed conflict, international humanitarian law defines to what extent parties to an armed conflict may adopt measures of security and control that are absolutely necessary to:

(1) achieve military victory over the enemy;

(2) reasonably minimize their own military losses; or

(3) protect the civilian population under its control or responsibility against direct or indiscriminate attacks by an adverse party to the conflict.[1635]

These are the only purposes that may justify deprivation of liberty on the basis of international humanitarian law, and the grounds for internment prescribed by that body of law must therefore reflect valid needs to achieve these purposes.[1636] In order to define lawful grounds for internment in non-international armed conflict (*infra* section 2.2.2), it is therefore useful to look at how these grounds are defined in the only other body of law that recognizes the above purposes as legitimate, namely international humanitarian law applicable to situations of international armed conflict and occupation (*infra* section 2.2.1.1). Taking into account the specific nature of non-international armed conflict, and the refusal by States to grant any form of recognition or status to members of the armed forces of non-State parties to the conflict, such inspiration should be sought in the provisions of the Fourth Geneva Convention of 1949 (*infra* section 2.2.1.2).

[1633] *Cf. supra* chapter I-1, section 1.2.1 and chapter I-2, section 2.1.

[1634] Cf. supra chapter I-1, section 1.2.4.

[1635] *Cf. supra* chapter I-2, section 2.2.2.1 and chapter II-5, section 5.1.

[1636] The function of IHL in the international legal system is to regulate the incidents of situations of armed conflict. The definition of lawful grounds for deprivation of liberty that serves other purposes recognized as legitimate under international law (such as the maintenance of public order and security, the preservation of national security, or the prevention and punishment of criminal offences) is not within the ambit of international humanitarian law and falls exclusively into the domain of international human rights, refugee or criminal law (*cf. supra* chapter I-2, section 2.2.2.2).

2.2.1. Inspiration from other bodies of international law

2.2.1.1. International humanitarian law for international armed conflict and occupation versus international human rights law

Our preference for seeking guidance in international humanitarian law for international armed conflicts and occupation (IAC-IHL), rather than in international human rights law, is based on a number of considerations.

For one, international human rights law is not designed specifically to regulate armed conflict. While it remains *applicable* in situations of armed conflict, it is *designed* to protect the individual against arbitrary interference with his or her fundamental rights and freedoms in peacetime.[1637] It does not therefore offer much concrete guidance for defining the lawful grounds for internment in a situation of armed conflict.[1638]

Moreover, the grounds for internment must reflect legitimate purposes to restrict the fundamental right to liberty. Arbitrary deprivation of liberty is prohibited in both international humanitarian and human rights law, but what is arbitrary will depend on the context in which the deprivation of liberty takes place. The purpose of internment in armed conflict is dictated by both the reality of armed conflict and the balance between military necessity and humanity sought by international humanitarian law; it is not recognized in international law as a legitimate purpose for restricting a person's right to liberty in situations that do not reach the threshold of armed conflict.[1639] In order to accommodate the principle of military necessity, the lawful grounds for deprivation of liberty under international human rights law would have to be interpreted broadly, and to a point where such interpretation is likely to result in an erosion of the general human rights protection of persons who are still far too often at risk of arbitrary deprivation of liberty for reasons unrelated to the existence (past or present) of any armed conflict.[1640] We have seen at the outset of this book that arbitrary deprivation of liberty is a commonly used tool to repress domestic political, social or other opposition, or to extend authoritarian rule. Moreover, in recent years, the conceptualization by some States of the fight against international terrorism as an armed conflict, and the consequent reliance on concepts drawn from the law of (international) armed conflict; has resulted in a gradual and ongoing erosion of fundamental rights and freedoms around the world. The definition of lawful grounds for administrative detention or for restricting the procedural safeguards or judicial guarantees of persons detained on criminal

[1637] IAC°HR, *Coard v. USA* (1999), §39; IAC°HR, *Third Report Colombia* (1999), chapter IV, §10; Wilhelm (*Hague Academy Collected Courses* 1972), p. 382; Gasser (*GYIL* 2002), p. 157; Sassòli in *Liber Amoricum Malinverni* (2007), p. 375.

[1638] Treaty IHRL is silent on internment in armed conflict. Where international human rights bodies have, exceptionally, addressed internment in armed conflict (regardless of whether they did so on the basis of IHL or IHRL), their decisions or opinions will be mentioned and duly taken into account.

[1639] *Cf. supra* chapter I-1, section 1.2.4.

[1640] Frequent or long-term use of emergency powers and derogations often leads to an erosion of the rule of law and general human rights protection in and beyond any armed conflict. *Cf. supra* note 260.

charges, by reference to vague, undefined and controversial notions such as "terrorism"[1641] or "threats to national security"[1642] inevitably contribute to an erosion of international human rights protection in situations that do not amount to armed conflict.[1643]

Furthermore, the grounds for internment in the Fourth Geneva Convention are "battlefield-tested [...] and offer an operationally-sustainable standard" for internment,[1644] not only in situations of international armed conflict and occupation but also in other situations that would qualify as non-international armed conflict and where States so far have relied on *ad hoc* solutions to intern.[1645]

Also, the advantage of seeking guidance for defining the grounds for internment in non-international armed conflict in IAC-IHL is that this would result in the same (or at least very similar) set of lawful grounds in situations of international and non-international armed conflict. The lawful grounds for internment in international armed conflict and occupation are already part of a well-established legal framework and practice, have been disseminated widely and integrated in military training of armed forces, and are therefore generally

1641 Acts of terrorism are criminal offences in both domestic and international criminal law. Persons suspected of involvement in such acts must therefore be the subject of a criminal investigation and where appropriate must be charged, tried and punished in conformity with criminal law. Where a person commits a terrorist act, or threatens to commit such act in a situation of non-international armed conflict, he or she commits a war crime, and must be charged, tried and if guilty punished for such acts. The obligation to do so is enshrined in both international humanitarian and international criminal law (e.g. articles 4§2(d) and 13§2 AP II; rule 2 CIHL; direct attacks against the civilian population or civilian objects are war crimes, e.g. article 8§2(e)(i)-(iv) ICC Statute). There is therefore no justifiable reason to intern or administratively detain suspects of terrorist acts. The processing of such suspects through the criminal justice system – to punish them for any offences they have committed or to prevent them from committing such offences in the future – has proved an effective measure to curb terrorism in the past, and continues to do so (*cf. supra* note 467).

1642 Used increasingly to justify the administrative detention or the deportation of refugees, asylum-seekers and irregular immigrants, the use of concepts such as "terrorism" and "national security" has led to a general erosion of the protection offered to these persons by international human rights and refugee law. The same effect is inevitable if administrative detention is officially endorsed in anti-terrorism legislation with a very broad scope of application that draws on concepts of international humanitarian law to regulate situations that do not meet the threshold of armed conflict. That some legal experts in the US draw on legal terms of art in IHL in their proposals for the design of new US anti-terrorism legislation is therefore deplorable and worrisome, see for example Goldsmith & Katyal, "The Terrorists' Court", *New York Times*, 11 July 2007, or Wittes & Peppard, "Designing Detention: A Model Law for Terrorist Incapacitation" (*Brookings Paper* 2009). For a critique from within the US, see for example Cole (*Calif.LR* 2007), pp. 725-740.

1643 In the same sense: Deeks (*CWRJIL* 2009), p. 434-435: "One disadvantage to uniform rules [on administrative detention/internment in situations of armed conflict and other situations of violence] is that a state's need for detention arguably is greater in armed conflict than during [other] 'states of emergency.' Uniform rules might inadvertently increase a state's ability and willingness to conduct administrative detention outside of armed conflict, even though a state is generally better able to use standard law enforcement tools (which may help surmount the need for particular security detentions) in those situations."

1644 Deeks (*CWRJIL* 2009), p. 405. We do not however agree with Deeks that the *procedures* in GC IV necessarily "strike the proper balance between national security and personal liberty." Moreover, as we will see below, we think it is necessary to prescribe the grounds for internment in non-international armed conflict in a more precise manner than the Fourth Geneva Convention does.

1645 *Cf. infra* section 2.2.2.

well-known and understood. Grounds for internment that are inspired by those in IAC-IHL would therefore be easier to apply by troops on the ground, as they would offer quasi-uniform standards to decide who can be interned, for what reasons and for how long in armed conflict. This may facilitate internment operations in situations where the nature of the situation evolves over time from one of international armed conflict, occupation or non-international armed conflict, and internment operations of multinational forces whose troop-contributing States may have varying obligations under international human rights law. Where troops on the ground, commanders, and review bodies have a clear and simple set of instructions as to whom they can intern, for what reasons and for how long, the risk of mistakes, abuse or innovative interpretation of ambiguous or complicated legal obligations will be reduced to a significant extent.

Finally, as long as the international legal order has not moved to a point where the full protection of international human rights law would be universally accepted, both in substance and in scope of application, and would clearly bind all potential parties to an armed conflict, States and non-State entities alike, international humanitarian law continues to play an important role in the regulation of internment for reasons related to an armed conflict.

2.2.1.2. The full spectrum of legal bases in the Geneva Conventions versus exclusive guidance from the Fourth Geneva Convention

Past proposals to expand the application of the Geneva Conventions, either as a whole, or with regard to their internment provisions, to situations of non-international armed conflict have met with strong objections from States, mainly for fear of granting combatant and prisoner of war status (including combatant immunity upon capture) to members of organized armed groups. It is submitted that recent proposals to achieve a "universal combatant status"[1646] for the armed forces of all parties to all types of armed conflict would meet with the same protests. The Canadian delegation to the 1974-77 Diplomatic Conference that adopted AP II warned that:

> "Nothing in the Protocol should suggest that dissidents must be treated legally other than as rebels. To move in the direction of recognizing the military activities of the rebels as having some degree of legitimacy, is to invite the expectation or even demand for Prisoner-of-War status in capture."[1647]

It is highly likely that States will voice a similar warning during any future diplomatic conference seeking to further regulate non-international armed conflicts. States are not more willing today than they were 33 years ago to grant *any* legal status or immunity to persons whom they consider criminals at best, terrorists at worst. Proposals that seek to transpose the status-based internment provisions of the Third Geneva Convention to situations of non-international armed conflict are therefore bound, in our opinion, to fail.[1648] Nevertheless,

---

[1646] E.g. Crawford (2010), pp. 153-169.

[1647] Draft amendment concerning Protocol II as a whole submitted by the Canadian Delegation, 4 April 1975 (CDDH/212; IV, 1919) quoted in Levie (1987), p .9.

[1648] In the same sense: Lubell (2010), p. 150.

to achieve the essentially humanitarian purpose of such proposals, there is no need to grant rebels or insurgents either combatant or prisoner of war status, or to seek guidance for their internment in the provisions of GC III.[1649]

First, the provisions on the *treatment of internees* and their *conditions of captivity* in the Third and Fourth Geneva Conventions are quasi-identical, and have already become part of customary international law applicable to both international and non-international armed conflicts.[1650]

Moreover, for a State to be allowed to intern members of organized armed groups party to a non-international armed conflict or persons who can otherwise be expected to engage in the hostilities, there is no need to rely on the *grounds* for internment in the Third Geneva Convention as they can be interned on grounds that are inspired by the internment provisions of the Fourth Geneva Convention.[1651] We have seen in our analysis of articles 42§1 and 78 GC IV that factual indications of membership in the armed forces of a party to the conflict, or of expected direct participation in hostilities, will be of considerable weight in establishing that a person poses a direct threat to the security or the military operations of the Interning Power. If such indications indeed exist, but there is no possibility to press criminal charges, it will moreover not be very difficult to demonstrate that their internment is absolutely necessary to counter that threat.[1652]

At the same time, the grounds for lawful internment in the Fourth Geneva Convention are not status-based or membership-based (contrary to GC III). The internment provisions of the Fourth Geneva Convention do not distinguish between members of the armed forces of a party to the conflict and other persons. As long as a given individual poses a direct threat to the security and military operations of the Interning Power, and his or her internment is absolutely necessary to counter that threat, he or she may be interned on the basis of GC IV. Seeking guidance in GC IV allows us to avoid any concerns with regard to granting any status or legitimacy to members of organized armed groups and thus neutralizes the main objection of States to any further development in the law in this matter. In this sense, our proposed approach is similar to that preferred by States during the negotiations of articles 2, 5 and 6 of Additional Protocol II:

> "[Additional Protocol II] uses the terms "deprived of [...] liberty" and "whose liberty has been restricted" [whether they be interned or detained] to ensure that there is no gap in *protection*. In fact, these terms [were] chosen [...] to take into account the full extent of the article's scope of application, which covers all detainees and persons whose liberty has been restricted for reasons related to the

---

1649 In the same sense: Zegveld (2002), p. 38.

1650 *Cf. supra* note 339-340.

1651 *Cf. supra* chapter II-3.2.2.2 (c) and (d).

1652 *Ibidem*. We have also seen that so-called "unprivileged combatants", "unlawful combatants", and any other person who may be expected to participate in hostilities or otherwise pose a direct threat to the security and military operations of the Interning Power and who is not entitled to POW status falls within the scope of application of GC IV and may thus be interned on the basis of its articles 42§1 and 78 (*cf. supra* chapter II-3, section 3.1.1.

conflict, *without granting them a special status.* [...] The obligations laid down are concrete measures which must guarantee them *humane treatment in the particular situation* they find themselves [and] express the *basic standard to which anyone* whose liberty has been restricted for reasons related to the conflict *is entitled,* i.e., combatants who have fallen into the power of the adverse party as well as civilians. [... Additional Protocol II], *following the example of common Article 3, does not grant a special status to* members of the armed forces or armed groups who have fallen into enemy hands. *They are not legally prisoners of war* entitled to special protection; *this is why it is so important that the rules laid down in this article establish minimum guarantees* [for their treatment in captivity and for their protection]."[1653]

Furthermore, an expansion of the internment provisions of GC III to situations of non-international armed conflict, especially in the absence of recognition of combatant status, would run up against the difficult question of how to determine who may be interned on those grounds. A definition of the grounds for internment in NIAC inspired by those in GC IV does not refer to membership and does not therefore require a definition of who is a member of the armed forces of a party to the conflict (for the purposes of internment), a definition that would be unavoidable if one sought to transpose the GC III regime into NIAC-IHL and at the same time respect the principle of legality.[1654] Some may suggest that the "continuous combat function" criterion suggested by the ICRC for the definition of legitimate military targets under the rules of conduct of hostilities may be useful in this sense.[1655] We disagree, for the reasons

[1653] Sandoz et al., *Commentary AP I and II* (1987), pp. 1360, 1384-1386 (emphasis added). For the text of the proceedings, see *Official Records 1974-1977*, or the more user-friendly compilation of relevant extracts per article in Levie (1987), pp. 3-9, 93-106 and 205-241. See in this sense also the observation of the military and legal experts consulted by the ICRC in the run-up to the negotiations of AP II: "Th[e] particular question of treatment of the combatant in cases of non-international armed conflict is part of the larger pattern of the status and treatment of the combatant in all armed conflicts, and of the application of [article 4 GC III] which specifies the persons having a right to the status of prisoner of war. [...] By way of general conclusion to this question, some of [the experts] emphasized that it was not so much the legal status that was important from the humanitarian point of view, as certain fundamental guarantees with reference to the treatment of captured combatants. *Ameliorating the plight of these persons, in particular in the non-international armed conflict, could only be sought by leaving the legal status out of account,* and by seeking, instead, practical guarantees covering the humane treatment of these persons" (ICRC, *Report for the Conference of Government Experts* (1971), Vol. 5, pp. 62-64, emphasis added).

[1654] A mere reference to "members of the armed forces of a party to the conflict" would not satisfy the principle. Neither would a reference to "enemy combatants" (e.g. Waxman (*CLR* 2008), pp. 1388, 1394, 1407, 1410), "participants in hostilities" (e.g. Sassòli & Olson (*IRRC* 2008), p. 617), "fighters" (e.g. Dinstein, Garraway & Schmitt, *San Remo Manual* (2006), section 1.1.2), or "persons who directly participate in hostilities" (e.g. Crawford (2010), pp. 154 and 161). On the risks of what we have called a "DPH-approach" to internment (be it based on membership (continuous combat function) or on direct participation in hostilities itself), *cf. supra* chapter II-3, section 3.2.2.2.

[1655] Lubell (2010), p. 153 points out that: "despite the insistence at the start of the Guidance document that it only concerns the conduct of hostilities and does not relate to questions of post-capture status, once the ICRC proposes formulations according to which members of armed groups 'cease to be civilians', it is hard to imagine that these will not be used to advance theories that the ICRC may not have wished to see." We have seen in chapter II-3 above that some have indeed already started to refer to the concept of continuous combat function in relation to the determination of internment policy.

mentioned in Part II: while there is substantial overlap, no automatic parallels can be drawn between who can be a legitimate target of attack for the purposes of the conduct of hostilities and who can be interned for security reasons in armed conflict.[1656]

If a State party to a NIAC should in a given place and time want to grant a form of combatant immunity to rebels, insurgents, or other persons who participate in hostilities – be it to give an incentive to a non-State party to the conflict to comply with IHL or to facilitate future peace and reconciliation – it can still do so by granting an amnesty under its domestic law, as is not only suggested, but encouraged by article 6§5 AP II.[1657]

Last but not least, the internment provisions of GC IV are more in line with the requirements of international human rights law regarding deprivation of liberty than those of GC III. We have seen in chapter II-3 that internment on the basis of GC IV must be exceptional rather than automatic, may only be ordered on an individual rather than on a collective (membership-oriented) basis, and even then only as a last resort, and may last only as long as is absolutely necessary for the security reasons that initially justified it. Moreover, we have seen in Part I that the prohibition of deprivation of liberty without any form of *habeas* has become almost absolute and may not be derogated from in full in situations of non-international armed conflict. All in all, internment provisions inspired by those of the Third Geneva Convention are unlikely to be endorsed or accepted by international human rights bodies or even national courts, because they depart from the right to liberty to a much further oextent than those of GC IV.

For all these reasons, when defining who can be interned on the basis of IHL, for what reasons and for how long, in situations of non-international armed conflict, we think it is appropriate to seek guidance from the internment provisions in the Fourth Geneva Convention. In doing so, it is submitted, it should be possible to satisfy the exigencies of both international humanitarian law and international human rights law, and achieve the objective of the international legal system to prevent arbitrary deprivation of liberty in all circumstances.

2.2.2. Definition of lawful grounds for internment in non-international armed conflict

On the basis of our research and analysis in Parts I[1658] and II, and the few indications of State and non-State practice, we propose the following grounds for internment in non-international armed conflict:

[1656] In the same sense: Lubell (2010), p. 153.

[1657] In the same sense: Zegveld (2002), p. 38. Such amnesties have for example been granted to facilitate a return to peace in the non-international armed conflicts in Angola (1994) and Sierra Leone (1996). For a discussion, see Naqvi, *Impediments to Exercising Jurisdiction over International Crimes* (2010), pp. 82-84.

[1658] "Imperative reasons of security", the formulation in article 78 GC IV, which has increasingly been referred to as a lawful ground for internment in non-international armed conflict, is too vague to meet the legality test required under international human rights law in situations of non-international armed conflict. The grounds for internment in non-international armed conflict must be more precise and reflect the specific purposes such internment is meant to serve.

1. The parties to the conflict shall not intern any person, except where, on the basis of available and reliable information, that person's internment is

(a) absolutely necessary to prevent a person who can be reasonably expected to engage in hostilities from doing so, or to neutralize or significantly reduce the direct threat he or she may pose to the armed forces or the military operations of the Interning Power;

(b) absolutely necessary to prevent an adverse party to the conflict from carrying out direct or indiscriminate attacks against the civilian population or members of relief societies that come to their aid, against objects or infrastructure indispensable to the survival of the civilian population, or against works or installations containing dangerous forces, where such attacks may cause a severe threat to the life, integrity or security of the civilian population; or

(4) absolutely necessary for the protection of a person who, through the representatives of a Protecting Power or the International Committee of the Red Cross, voluntarily demands internment by a party to the conflict.

2. Medical and religious personnel of the armed forces of the parties to the conflict may only be retained in as far as, and for as long as, is necessary to tend to the medical or spiritual needs of persons deprived of persons interned for the reasons listed in the first paragraph of this article. Medical and religious personnel whose retention is not indispensable to accommodate these needs shall be immediately returned to the party they belong to, or at the latest as soon as the security situation on the ground makes such a return possible.

3. All decisions regarding initial or continued internment must be taken on an individual basis. Internment may only be ordered as a last resort, where other less restrictive measures of control could not adequately meet the potential threat, and where the person cannot be deprived of his or her liberty on the basis of penal legislation and subject to judicial control.

4. Any person interned for the reasons listed above, shall be released as soon as the reasons that necessitate his or her internment have ceased to exist or other, less restrictive measures of control could adequately achieve the purpose for which he or she is interned. Where a person is released from internment before the cessation of active hostilities, the Interning Power shall take the necessary measures to ensure their safe return to their last place of residence.

5. As soon as active hostilities have ceased, all internees must be released immediately. The Interning Power shall ensure the safe return of all internees to their last place of residence.

The proposal is based on our analysis of the lawful grounds for internment under the Fourth Geneva Convention in Part II,[1659] and of the general

[1659] And on GC I and GC II as regards the medical and religious personnel of the armed forces of the parties to the conflict. Such personnel enjoys a special status and protection under international humanitarian law, both in situations of IAC and NIAC (*cf. supra* chapter II-2) and the definition of the grounds for their retention provided for by GC I and II is as adequate for situations of NIAC as it is for situations of IAC.

requirements of international human rights law discussed in Part I. It is submitted that this is a workable definition of lawful grounds for internment in non-international armed conflict and that it finds support in emerging practice.

UK military doctrine, for example, provides that:

"During hostilities not amounting to International Armed Conflict, [...] UK Forces operating abroad may have a power to intern civilians under the host nation's law where they pose an *imperative threat to the security of the force*;"[1660] and that

"The rules for the internment of civilians apply: [...] During operations not amounting to International Armed Conflict to those civilians interned by UK armed forces under internment powers granted to UK forces by the Host Nation (HN). In these circumstances, civilians may only be interned by UK forces where they pose *a serious threat to the security of the force*."[1661]

The Danish government for its part has found that:

"while the legal basis for detention is not always obvious in non-international armed conflicts, it is common ground that some form of temporary detention may be *imperative for reasons of security*."[1662]

Article 78 GC IV has also been relied upon to define grounds for internment in situations where UN-mandated international forces were deployed to ensure security in a territory administered by an international organization, or to assist a State in its efforts to deal with a non-international armed conflict. Such recourse to the grounds in article 78 GC IV seems to have met with the approval of the Security Council. Both the NATO-led Kosovo Force (KFOR)[1663] and the Australian-led International Forces for East Timor (INTERFET)[1664] adopted regulations allowing them to intern persons on grounds that mirrored those provided for in the Fourth Geneva Convention. For example, KFOR's Detention Directive 42 provides that a person may be interned where:

"he constitutes a *threat to KFOR* or *to a safe and secure environment in Kosovo*, if the civilian authorities in Kosovo are unable or unwilling to take responsibility for the matter, and if the person's detention is *necessary because the threat cannot be reasonably be addressed by lesser means*. When those criteria are met, 'COMKFOR authority to detain will only be used as a last resort. [...]

[1660] UK, *JDP 1-10* (2006), section 113 (emphasis added).

[1661] UK, *JDP 1-10.2* (2006), section 101 (emphasis added).

[1662] Denmark, MFA, *Copenhagen Background Document* (2009), p. 35 (emphasis added).

[1663] KFOR was deployed in June 1999 and is still present in Kosovo today. Its mandate derives from UNSCR 1244 (1999) and a Military-Technical Agreement concluded between NATO and the Federal Republic of Yugoslavia and Serbia shortly after. For information on the command, structure, mandate and activities of the force, see http://www.nato.int/cps/en/natolive/topics_48818.htm.

[1664] INTERFET was deployed in September 1999 and handed over the command over military operations to the United Nations Transitional Administration in East-Timor (UNTAET) in February 2000. Its mandate derived from UNSCR 1264 (1999), §3: "to restore peace and security in East Timor, to protect and support UNAMET [the United Nations Mission in East-Timor] in carrying out its tasks and, within force capabilities, to facilitate humanitarian assistance operations, and authorizes the States participating in the multinational force to take all necessary measures to fulfil this mandate." For further information on the force, see http://pandora.nla.gov.au/parchive/2000/S2000-Nov-7/easttimor.defence.gov.au/index.html.

> 'COMKFOR will continue to use the authority to detain but only in cases where this is absolutely necessary. [...] The fact that a person may have information of intelligence value by itself is not a basis for detention."[1665]

Similarly, the Australian INTERFET commander issued an Ordinance that permitted INTERFET "to detain [...] individuals [...] who posed a 'security risk'" and the internment regime for such persons was designed essentially along the lines of that provided for in GC IV.[1666]

Whereas the Multinational Forces in Iraq (MNF-I) were technically granted internment powers on the basis of Iraqi domestic law (endorsed subsequently by an agreement between the US and Iraq), these powers were also endorsed by the UN Security Council. Article 6§1 of the (Revised) Memorandum No. 3 (2004) describes a "security internee" as:

> "Any person who is detained by a national contingent of the MNF *for imperative reasons of security* in accordance with the mandate set out in UNSCR 1546."[1667]

And the agreed mandate for MNF-I, as endorsed in by the Security Council, provides for MNF-I:

> "to contribute to the maintenance of security in Iraq, including by preventing and deterring terrorism and protecting the territory of Iraq. The goal of the MNF will be to help the Iraqi people to complete the political transition and will permit the United Nations and the international community to work to facilitate Iraq's reconstruction. [...] Under the agreed arrangement, the MNF stands ready to continue to undertake a broad range of tasks to contribute to the *maintenance of security* and to ensure *force protection*. These include activities necessary to counter ongoing security threats posed by forces seeking to influence Iraq's political future through violence. This will include combat operations against members of these groups, *internment where this is necessary for imperative reasons of security*, and the continued search for and securing of weapons that threaten Iraq's security."[1668]

The case law of international human rights bodies, called upon to evaluate the lawfulness under international law of specific cases of security internment in situations of non-international armed conflict, also supports the definition of lawful grounds for internment proposed above.

For example, the European Court of Human Rights found internment on the ground that a "person is engaged in activities which [...] are prejudicial to the

---

[1665] A referred to in Deeks (*CWRJIL* 2009), p. 417 (KFOR Detention Directive 42 is not publicly available).

[1666] As referred to in Deeks (*CWRJIL* 2009), p. 419. Oswald, at the time legal advisor to the Australian armed forces and part of the team that designed the internment and detention regulations for INTERFET, has commented that the INTERFET's internment provisions were designed on the basis of the system provided for in the law of occupation as contained in GC IV, see Oswald, "The Law on Military Occupation: Answering the Challenges of Detention during Contemporary Peace Operations?" (*Melb.JIL* 2007), pp. 311-326.

[1667] Iraq, Coalition Provisional Authority, *Revised Memorandum No. 3* (2004), article 6§1. The memorandum is part of Iraqi domestic law until abrogation by the Iraqi Government (*cf. supra* note 1539 and accompanying text).

[1668] UNSC, *Resolution 1546* (2004), Annex, pp. 10-11 (emphasis added).

preservation of public peace and order or to the security of the State" to be a measure "strictly required by the exigencies of the situation [*in casu* clearly amounting to non-international armed conflict]" to satisfy the conditions for a derogation from article 5§1 ECHR.[1669]

In more explicit terms, the Inter-American Commission on Human Rights has found that:

> "The Commission deems it necessary to clarify why it does not condemn, as violative of international law, the acts of armed dissident groups in capturing members of the Army and security forces where the captives are not converted into hostages. As noted above, international humanitarian law prohibits the taking of hostages and the detention or internment of *civilians other than for imperative reasons of security*. International humanitarian law does not prohibit the capture of *combatants*. It simply treats such captures as a situation of deprivation of liberty which may, in practice, occur in armed conflict. International humanitarian law then proceeds to impose obligations on the captors to treat captives humanely, with respect and dignity. [...] Humanitarian law does not [however] prevent the State from prosecuting and sanctioning under domestic law the individuals responsible for the capture and detention of its troops."[1670]

Dingwall has concluded, on the basis of an analysis of the ICTY's case law that "confinement of civilians in internal armed conflict is unlawful when civilians are detained without reasonable grounds to believe that the *security of the Detaining Power makes it absolutely necessary*."[1671]

Finally, international legal scholarship is increasingly inclined to refer to the grounds in articles 42 and 78 GC IV to propose definitions of what could be lawful grounds for internment in non-international armed conflict. Some have merely suggested this implicitly;[1672] others have been more explicit.

[1669] ECtHR, *Lawless v. UK* (1961), §§ 12 and 36.

[1670] IAC°HR, *Third Report on Colombia* (1999), chapter IV, §§131-132, emphasis added (*in casu*, the Commission used the word "combatants" to refer to members of the Colombian army and security forces engaged in hostilities against the FARC, ELN and other organized armed groups involved in the conflict in its territory); confirmed in IAC°HR, *Terrorism and Human Rights* (2002), p. 97: "International humanitarian law applicable to non-international armed conflicts similarly does not prohibit the capture and detention of persons who take an active part in hostilities, but prohibits the detention or internment of civilians except where necessary for imperative reasons of security. Where circumstances justifying the detention of combatants or civilians exist, common Article 3 and Articles 4 and 5 of Additional Protocol II subject the treatment of persons deprived of their liberty for reasons related to the armed conflict to minimum standards of humane treatment and protection."

[1671] Dingwall, "Unlawful Confinement as a War Crime: The Jurisprudence of the Yugoslav Tribunal and the Common Core of International Humanitarian Law Applicable to Contemporary Armed Conflicts" (*JCSL* 2004), p. 144, emphasis added. Dingwall's argument is based only on a Trial Chamber judgment in one case (i.e. the *Naletilić & Martinović* case), but in light of the general case law of the ICTY, it is fair to conclude that the ICTY defines unlawful confinement as a war crime in identical terms in both IAC and NIAC.

[1672] E.g.: Pejic (*IRRC* 2005), p. 376; Sassòli & Olson (*IRRC* 2008), p. 624; Olson (*CWRJIL* 2009), p. 439; Ojeda in Schmitt (2009), p. 365, most of whom have been or are legal advisors in the ICRC. Moreover, the essence of Pejic's article "reflects the ICRC's official position and now guides its operations" (ICRC, *International Humanitarian Law and the Challenges of Contemporary Armed Conflicts* (2007), p. 11). In the same sense, see also Israel, Court of Appeal, *A and B v. Israel*,

For example, the drafters of the 1990 *Turku Declaration*, intended to provide minimum standards to be applied in all situations of armed conflict, and even in situations of armed violence that do not reach the threshold of armed conflict,[1673] provides that:

> "If it is considered *necessary for imperative reasons of security* to subject any person to assigned residence, internment or administrative detention, such decisions shall be subject to a regular procedure prescribed by law affording all the judicial guarantees which are recognized as indispensable by the international community, including the right of appeal or to a periodical review."[1674]

Sassòli finds that "[i]nternment of *enemy fighters* would [...] certainly be admissible [...] under [article 9§1 of] the ICCPR, while the jury is still out for [article 5§1 of] the ECHR."[1675]

Oswald is of the opinion that internationally mandated forces that participate in non-international armed conflicts may intern persons who pose a direct threat to their security, that of the civilian population under their responsibility, or to their military operations, on grounds comparable to those in article 78 GC IV:

> "In these cases, 'such measures can only be ordered for *real and imperative reasons of security*; their exceptional character must be preserved'."[1676]

Finally, participants in the 2008 *Expert Meeting on Security Detention in NIAC* found that:

> "The most recurrent ground invoked for internment in NIAC – and probably the only permissible ground – is that of '*imperative reasons of security*'. The term is borrowed from the text of article 78 of GC IV – where it constitutes the ground for internment in situations of occupation; other legal provisions in different bodies of law are phrased in similar terms to reflect the same concept. The word 'imperative' refers back to the 'necessity' concept and the 'reasons of security' refers to the type of ground allowing for the extraordinary measure of internment. It seems to be clear that this ground is acceptable under IHL, even in NIAC. However, it would probably not be acceptable under IHRL due to the lack of specificity."[1677]

---

referred to in Shany (*Hebrew University of Jerusalem Research Papers* 2009), p. 19; Zegveld (2002), pp. 65-66; Walen & Venzke (*ZaöRV* 2007), pp. 855-862; Goodman (*AJIL* 2009, pp. 53-57); Olson (*CWRJIL* 2009), pp. 454-455; and Deeks (*CWRJIL* 2009), pp. 405 and 433-436. We do not agree however with some of these authors' claim that the balance struck in GC IV can also guide the interpretation of IHRL in situations that do *not* meet the threshold of non-international armed conflict, such as the so-called war on terror.

[1673] Its article 1 establishes that the declaration "affirms minimum humanitarian standards which are applicable in all situations, including internal violence, disturbances, tensions, and public emergency, and which cannot be derogated from under any circumstances."

[1674] *Turku Declaration* (1990), article 11 (emphasis added).

[1675] Sassòli in Schmitt (2009), p. 448 (emphasis added).

[1676] Oswald (*Melb.JIL* 2007), pp. 320-321 (emphasis added). Oswald also favours the inclusion of the ground for voluntary internment in article 42§1 GC IV, which he said "has been usefully applied during the INTERFET's deployment in East Timor [...] may arise where, for example, a person is a member of a local minority and is fearful of how the majority might deal with him if they found out his status."

[1677] *Report of the Expert Meeting on Security Detention in NIAC* (2008), p. 864 (emphasis added).

> "In the discussion, participants coalesced around a two-tiered test to assess whether an individual presents a sufficient threat to allow his or her internment. The first element of the test is whether, on the basis of his or her activity (which as such is not necessarily criminally prosecutable), it is "highly likely" or "certain" (the threshold is unclear) that he or she will commit further acts that are harmful (directly and/or indirectly, the threshold is unclear [note 14: Some experts indicated that on the ground, their *militaries looked for inspiration to art. 78 GC IV*]) to the Interning Power and/or to those whom the Interning Power is mandated to assist or protect, such as the host nation, the civilian population or public order (the threshold is again unclear). The second element of the test is whether internment is necessary to neutralize the threat posed. *It was stressed that if the interpretation of "imperative reasons of security" as the permissible ground for internment is too wide, there is a risk of abuse.* The security threat must be assessed on an individual basis and the decision to intern (as distinct from the decision to capture) must be taken at a sufficiently high level of command to allow for an adequate assessment of both the threat and the necessity to intern in light of the context and available alternatives."[1678]

It is precisely to address concerns under international human rights law over the vagueness of the terms "imperative reasons of security" that we have proposed more precisely defined grounds for internment in non-international armed conflict, inspired by those in articles 42 and 78 GC IV but reflecting their exact meaning in more precise terms.

2.2.3. Conclusions

We have demonstrated in this chapter that there is ample source of inspiration for defining the lawful grounds for internment in non-international armed conflict in the internment provisions of the Fourth Geneva Convention. There is therefore no need, as has been suggested by some scholars, to go and look for such inspiration in the rules of international humanitarian law on targeting.[1679]

As is the case for international armed conflict and occupation, the definition of who can be the lawful target of direct attack, and who can be interned are not necessarily the same. In situations of non-international armed conflict as in situations of international armed conflict, direct attack is permitted against members of the armed forces of a party to the conflict and against non-members of such armed forces for as long as they directly participate in hostilities.[1680] Existing international humanitarian law does not however provide any legal basis to intern persons who pose a military or security threat in situations of non-international armed conflict. If we were to amend Goodman's table of lawful coercive measures – discussed in chapter II-3 – on the basis of existing international humanitarian law for non-international armed conflict, it would look as follows:

[1678] *Report of the Expert Meeting on Security Detention in NIAC* (2008), pp. 865-866 (emphasis added).
[1679] For a discussion and critique of their arguments, *cf. supra* chapter II-3, section 3.2.2.2.
[1680] See article 13 AP II, and ICRC, *IGDPH* (2009), pp. 27-36 and pp. 70-73.

SUBJECTS	**COERCIVE MEASURES**			
	I. TARGETING/DIRECT ATTACK	**II. CAPTURE/ARREST TO NEUTRALIZE A THREAT OR TO BRING BEFORE A COURT FOR PARTICIATION IN HOSTILTIES**	**III. DETENTION ON CRIMINAL CHARGES UNDER DOMESTIC LAW FOR PARTICIPATION IN HOSTILITIES**	**IV. INTERNMENT ON THE BASIS OF IHL**
A. Members of State armed forces and persons who occupy a continuous combat function in the armed forces of a non-State party to the conflict	YES, AT ALL TIMES	YES	YES	NO
B. Persons other than those in category A who *are* participating directly in hostilities ("ongoing DPH")	YES, FOR DURATION OF DPH	YES	N / A	N / A
C. Persons other than those in category A who *have* directly participated in hostilities ("past DPH")	NO	YES	YES	NO
D. Other persons	NO	N / A	N / A	NO

Should NIAC-IHL be the subject of further treaty development along the lines proposed above, the table would look quite differently:

SUBJECTS	**COERCIVE MEASURES**			
	I. TARGETING/DIRECT ATTACK	**II. CAPTURE/ARREST TO NEUTRALIZE A THREAT OR TO BRING BEFORE A COURT FOR PARTICIATION IN HOSTILTIIES**	**III. DETENTION ON CRIMINAL CHARGES UNDER DOMESTIC LAW FOR PAST PARTICIPATION IN HOSTILITIES**	**IV. INTERNMENT ON THE BASIS OF IHL**
A. Members of State armed forces and persons who occupy a continuous combat function in the armed forces of a non-State party to the conflict	YES, AT ALL TIMES	YES	YES	YES
B. Persons other than those in category A who *are* directly participating in hostilities ("ongoing DPH")	YES, FOR DURATION DPH	YES	N / A	N / A
C. Persons other than those in category A who *have* participated directly in hostilities ("past DPH")	NO	YES	YES	NO, UNLESS THEY ALSO PRESENT A FUTURE THREAT AND CRIMINAL PROSECUTION AND DETENTION FOR THEIR PAST ACTS IS IMPOSSIBLE
E. Persons other than those in category A for whom there is reasonable & legitimate reason to think they *will* DPH in the future ("military threat")	NO	YES	YES, IF REASONABLE SUSPICION THAT ABOUT TO COMMIT A CRIMINAL OFFENCE	YES, UNLESS CRIMINAL PROSECUTION (AND PREVENTIVE DETENTION) IS AVAILABLE

F. Persons other than those in category A for whom there is reasonable & legitimate reason to think they *will* otherwise pose a threat in the future ("military threat")	NO	YES	NO, UNLESS REASONABLE SUSPICION THAT ABOUT TO COMMIT A CRIMINAL OFFENCE	YES, UNLESS CRIMINAL PROSECUTION (AND PREVENTIVE DETENTION) IS AVAILABLE
G. Persons who have not and are not expected to participate in hostilities and do not otherwise pose a military threat ("innocent civilians")	NO	N / A	N / A	NO

Ultimately, however, it will be up to States to decide whether or not they wish to engage in a further development of NIAC-IHL in order to remedy the existing gap in international humanitarian law. Should they choose to do so, we hope our proposals in this chapter may contribute to the debate, which promises to be as intense, if not more, as those that took place in 1949 and 1977.

CONCLUSIONS

Internment has long since been and continues to be an inherent and common incident of warfare. While very intrusive on an individual's fundamental right to liberty, it may at times be justified and even unavoidable. What is important – in order to prevent unnecessary or arbitrary internment (and the violations of other human rights that often go with it) – is to provide for a strict regulation of its use by defining who may be interned, on what grounds, in accordance with what procedures, and for how long. International law does not prohibit deprivation of liberty, nor does it prohibit internment in armed conflict. Rather, international law prohibits any form of *arbitrary* deprivation of liberty and sets out a number of specific criteria that any measure depriving a person of his or her liberty must meet to be lawful. By regulating internment in armed conflict, international law intends to restrict such deprivation of liberty to what is necessary and proportionate in light of the circumstances, and to prevent the arbitrary use of internment by the parties to an armed conflict. For such regulation to be effective, the international legal framework for internment in armed conflict must be as realistic, comprehensive and unambiguous as possible.

* * *

The late 20th and early 21st century have witnessed a fair amount of discontent, in military, political, legal and humanitarian circles, with the existing international legal framework for internment in armed conflict; and calls have been made for its clarification, modification, and modernization. Moreover, questions concerning the specific interaction of simultaneously applicable norms of international law have added relatively new layers to the research and analysis of that legal framework.

From a military perspective, one may perceive a number of weaknesses that result either from a lack of explicit provisions within existing treaty international humanitarian law, or from the rapidly changing features of contemporary armed conflict. Moreover, within military circles, a certain uneasiness or even suspicion persists with regard to the possible (negative) impact of international human rights law – a branch of international law oft considered too restrictive to take into account the realities of armed conflict – on the delicate balance between military necessity and humanity that is inherent in international humanitarian law. From a humanitarian perspective, one may consider international humanitarian law's capacity to provide adequate legal protection for internees to be too weak in light of modern standards. Indeed, one may find the system is out of date in that most of its provisions pre-date international human rights treaties, and that it fails to take into account important developments in international law since their adoption. From a legal perspective, the simultaneous applicability of international humanitarian and international human rights law to situations of armed conflict may be beyond serious controversy, but many questions about the interaction between their specific norms remain to be answered or are still unfolding.

These tensions demonstrate to what extent the function of international humanitarian law in the international legal system is a delicate one, in that it must seek an acceptable compromise between the legitimate requirements of military necessity in war and the longer-term interests in preserving "certain humanitarian values, which emerge through the evolution of society as some kind of general guidelines for human intercourse."[1681] Bearing in mind these tensions and the concerns raised, the academic must bring to the debate a thorough research and analysis of the existing legal framework for internment in armed conflict and the impact thereon of other relevant norms of international law. This allows for an informed assessment of whether or not that framework is capable of accommodating new features of armed conflict and developments in international law that have come about since its inception, and enables the identification of possible ways to accommodate the challenges facing the system. This endeavour may facilitate a demystification of some of the perceived tensions and concerns about the legal framework and elucidate the interaction between specific norms of international law on the subject.

1.1. CONCLUSIONS DRAWN FROM THE ANALYSIS OF THE INTERNATIONAL LEGAL FRAMEWORK FOR DEPRIVATION OF LIBERTY

An analysis of the legal framework for internment in armed conflict as it stands today cannot be limited to an isolated reading and interpretation of the specific internment provisions of the 1949 Geneva Conventions and their Additional Protocols of 1977. While these provisions are indeed at the centre of the analysis, they must be understood within the broader international legal system they are a part of. The legal framework for internment in armed conflict is construed on the basis of a number of general norms of international law, is detailed in international humanitarian law, but is also governed by other applicable bodies of international law, including, but not limited to, international human rights law.

As mentioned in the introduction, we found it important to dwell on the general international legal framework for deprivation of liberty before examining the specific framework for internment in armed conflict. This part of the analysis (contained in chapter I-1) brought us to two important conclusions on the subject-matter of this book. On the one hand, it confirmed that there are a number of different criteria a legal framework for deprivation of liberty must

[1681] Rosas (1976), p. 25 (original emphasis omitted).

meet, and revealed that each of these, equally important, criteria raise a number of issues when applied to internment in armed conflict. They are thus worthy of thorough research and detailed analysis, especially if one is to take into account the applicability of international human rights law in armed conflict and its impact on the interpretation of the specific internment provisions of international humanitarian law. These findings further defined the structure of argument and the scope of the book and led us to focus on the legal basis, lawful grounds and lawful duration of internment in armed conflict.

On the other hand, the analysis of the international legal framework for deprivation of liberty, and in particular the general principles governing the restriction of fundamental rights and freedoms, shed light on a criterion for lawful deprivation of liberty that is often overlooked in discussions of the requirements under international law for the lawfulness of internment in armed conflict, namely the requirement of a *legal basis*: a valid legal instrument that regulates a specific form of deprivation of liberty. Indeed, while often taken for granted and thus paid only scant attention, this requirement is the primary legal safeguard against arbitrary deprivation of liberty.[1682]

The requirement of a valid legal basis for restricting fundamental rights and freedoms flows directly from the principle of legality, a cornerstone of the broader principle of the rule of law. A proper legal basis ensures the legal certainty (clarity, precision and foreseeability) and the legitimacy of purpose that are key to protecting individuals and communities from unnecessary or arbitrary interference with their fundamental rights and freedoms, and to upholding the rule of law.[1683] Taking into account that, in principle, the legal basis for deprivation of liberty is to be found in domestic law, it was important therefore to examine whether it could also exist directly in international law. Concluding that it could, we then needed to demonstrate whether or not a legal basis for internment in armed conflict was included in existing international humanitarian law. Our analysis in parts II and III of the book demonstrates that the question can be answered in the positive as regards situations of international armed conflict and occupation, but must be answered in the negative as regards situations of non-international armed conflict.

The lack of a legal basis to intern within international humanitarian law applicable to non-international armed conflict itself may be regrettable, and even nonsensical to some, but we have demonstrated that this is the reality of the law as it stands today. That international humanitarian law *should* include such

[1682] Many authors, when using the term "legal basis" actually refer to the lawful *grounds* for deprivation of liberty. We have seen in Part I however that the two notions are distinct criteria for lawful deprivation of liberty and reflect two different aspects of the principle of legality. The requirement of a legal *basis* (i.e. a law or legal instrument) flows from the principle of legality in its formal aspect (the principle of legal certainty), whereas the requirement of lawful grounds for deprivation of liberty flows from the principle of legality in its material sense (the principle of legitimacy).

[1683] The validity of a legal basis for deprivation of liberty is evaluated on the basis of both its form and normative substance (which apart from lawful grounds must also include a number of procedural and other safeguards to prevent arbitrariness and abuse), *cf. supra* chapter I-1.

a legal basis does not mean it *does*, but certainly pleads in favour of a normative development of that body of law. Whatever solution is adopted to fill the gap in international humanitarian law – be it *ad hoc* or permanent, within domestic law (direct or delegated) or international law – it must conform to the requirements of the principle of legality and to those of the right to liberty under international human rights law if it is to offer adequate protection against unnecessary or arbitrary deprivation of liberty.

1.2. CONCLUSIONS DRAWN FROM THE EXISTING INTERNATIONAL LEGAL FRAMEWORK FOR INTERNMENT IN ARMED CONFLICT

When one tries to reconcile two competing interests, as international humanitarian law must do with military and humanitarian imperatives, a *quid pro quo* between them becomes necessary. In our quest for answers to the three research questions formulated at the outset of the book – namely who can be interned on the basis of international humanitarian law, for what reasons and for how long – we therefore first sought to unravel the intrinsic compromise that underlies the wording of the specific internment provisions in the 1949 Geneva Conventions.[1684] Based on an understanding of the compromise found in 1949, and guided by State practice, we then examined whether, to what extent, and how developments since 1949 have a bearing on the interpretation of these norms today.

The research presented in Part II demonstrates that the key elements in the definition of the lawful grounds and duration of internment in situations of international armed conflict and occupation, are necessity (as opposed to convenience or usefulness) and a nexus with the armed conflict (only those deprivations of liberty that are necessary *as a result of* the armed conflict are lawful).

Necessity resulting from armed conflict is broader than what is commonly referred to as military necessity, which – if interpreted narrowly – would only justify internment where absolutely necessary to achieve military victory or avoid military defeat. Necessity resulting from armed conflict in our context must be understood as the necessity to achieve a purpose that is considered a legitimate one for restricting fundamental rights and freedoms in situations of armed conflict. Apart from the need to achieve military victory and avoid defeat – which justifies internment of persons posing a threat to the security or to the military operations of the parties to the conflict[1685] – internment may, as we

[1684] The 1977 Additional Protocols to the Geneva Conventions do not include provisions that regulate who can be interned in armed conflict and for what reasons.

[1685] It is the concept of military necessity that underlies arguments that there is an "inherent right" to intern in armed conflict. These arguments reflect the general recognition that parties to armed conflicts may, for reasons directly related to the armed conflict, impose certain restrictions on the right to liberty that would not be allowed in situations that do no meet that threshold. We have seen however that the potential existence of such an "inherent right" does not itself provide the parties to the conflict with a valid legal basis to intern, but may justify the adoption of such a legal basis in a future development of

have seen throughout Part II, also be necessary for a party to the conflict to fulfil its obligations towards combatants and civilians within its power, obligations that are essentially based on humanitarian considerations rather than military strategy or tactics. For example, the retention of medical and religious personnel of the armed forces of an adverse party to the conflict is lawful where necessary to tend to the medical and spiritual needs of captured and interned prisoners of war. In that case, the humanitarian needs of the prisoners of war prevail over the right to liberty of the medical and religious personnel. Similarly, internment is lawful where necessary to ensure the safety of a protected person who voluntarily requests to be interned, and is thus based on humanitarian rather than military needs. Moreover, internment may be necessary to protect the civilian population within the power of a party to the conflict from attacks by enemy forces. Finally, the internment of prisoners of war is a measure that is inspired by the necessity for the parties to the conflict to neutralize members of enemy armed forces so as to prevent them from engaging in hostilities, but also by the necessity of providing a (more humane) alternative to killing or maiming combatants in order to neutralize them.

This articulation of the lawful grounds and duration of internment in terms of necessity is indicative of a balance being struck between the parties' need to intern and the individual's fundamental right to liberty, implying therefore an element of proportionality. We have seen that the required threshold of necessity varies in function of the categories of persons that may be interned and their relation to, or function within, the armed forces of the parties to the conflict. The scales of the balance need not necessarily be in equilibrium, but rather reflect an acceptable compromise in the eyes of the international community. Since the balance is based on the respective weight of the interests of the parties to the conflict to win their wars and the long-term interests of society in upholding certain human values and protecting human dignity, the proportionality calculus is inevitably subject to evolution and the balance may shift over time. What was considered an appropriate balance in 1949 may no longer be considered as such today. Whilst the principle of humanity or the concept of humanitarian considerations cannot be reduced to the sum-total of individual and collective human rights, the development of international human rights law reflects certain evolutions in the values of the international society and the importance attached to fundamental rights and freedoms therein, evolutions that are also reflected in State practice of internment in armed conflict.[1686] The advent of international human rights law therefore undeniably has an impact on the interpretation of the concept of necessity inherent in the definition of the lawful grounds for and duration of internment in armed conflict.

---

international humanitarian law governing situations of non-international armed conflict.

[1686] See for example our discussion on the forcible repatriation of prisoners of war in chapter II-1.

International human rights law does not deny the fact that deprivation of liberty, including internment in armed conflict, may be necessary, but it adds the weight of an individual internee's human right to liberty to the scales of the balance. Taking into account the relevant norms of international human rights law in the interpretation of the legal bases for internment in the Geneva Conventions allows us to fine-tune and adjust the balance struck in 1949 to take into account the evolutions in the values and interests of the international community. For example, an interpretation of article 21 of the Third Geneva Convention in light of the object and purpose of the treaty and in light of subsequent developments in international law and practice, demands that certain prisoners of war, whose internment is not or no longer really *necessary* in order to weaken the military capacity of the power they depend on or in order to avoid damage to the military capacity or operations of the Interning Power, should be released and/or repatriated rather than interned for the entire duration of hostilities.

The research for Part III of the book, concerning the legal framework for internment in situations of non-international armed conflict, produced rather different conclusions and laid bare some of the gaps in existing international humanitarian law regarding internment in armed conflict.

The first conclusion to result from the analysis in Part III is that neither treaty nor customary international humanitarian law contains a legal basis to intern anyone in situations of non-international armed conflict. This does not mean that internment does not occur in such situations, nor does it mean that internment may not be justified. And it certainly does not mean that such internment is not *regulated* by international law. Common article 3 to the Geneva Conventions, Additional Protocol II, customary international humanitarian law and international human rights law regulate the treatment and conditions of captivity owed to internees in non-international armed conflict by their Interning Power. International human rights law moreover regulates who can be interned, on what basis, on what grounds, and for how long, and it imposes a number of procedural safeguards against erroneous, unnecessary or arbitrary deprivation of liberty. Contrary to situations of international armed conflict and occupation though, international humanitarian law does not itself include a legal basis for internment in non-international armed conflict, and thus does not define any exceptions to the general rules for deprivation of liberty that may be permitted in such situations. Existing international humanitarian law for non-international armed conflict therefore offers no concrete guidance on whether, and if so to what extent, such exceptions are indeed allowed under international law; nor does it offer the parties to non-international armed conflict the same legal tools to intern it offers to parties to international armed conflicts and Occupying Powers.

This situation begs the question of whether the absence in international humanitarian law applicable to non-international armed conflict of a legal basis for internment is a weakness or gap in the system that is in need of a remedy. One also wonders why the possibility of such a weakness or gap has not worried States parties to non-international armed conflict until quite recently.

Both questions are partly answered by the fact that in the majority of non-international armed conflicts, the State party does not *need* to rely on international humanitarian law to deprive persons of their liberty for reasons related to the armed conflict since it can rely on its domestic criminal law to *detain* them. Nevertheless, we have also seen that the absence of a legal basis to intern in international humanitarian law may effectively deprive certain parties to non-international armed conflicts of a legal basis to intern at all. The issue arises mainly for the non-State parties to such conflicts (organized armed groups and international organizations) and for State parties to non-international armed conflicts abroad.

In order to effectively prevent unnecessary or arbitrary deprivation of liberty in situations of non-international armed conflict, the legal framework for internment should not only be well-established (preferably in international law) but should also take into account both the practical realities of armed conflict and the different nature and legal capacity of the parties to such conflicts. While a number of other options may be open to remedy the absence of a legal basis to intern in international humanitarian law, we have argued that the development of new treaty international humanitarian law is therefore the preferable one. The current prevalence of non-international armed conflicts, the lacunae in the body of international law that specifically regulates such situations, and the derogability of the right to liberty in all but one international human rights treaty, plead in favour of a normative development of international humanitarian law. Its lack of a legal basis to intern in situations of non-international armed conflict in our view hampers international humanitarian law's capacity to effectively fulfil its function in the international legal system: it leaves more room for arbitrariness and abuse, since the parties to such conflicts may either not be bound by the regulation in international human rights law or may derogate from their obligations under that body of law. Moreover, the lack of a direct legal basis to intern in international humanitarian law inevitably requires parties to non-international armed conflicts to fall back on other, time-consuming, and possibly unattainable, legal options to intern. It thus indirectly paves the way for *ad hoc*, improvised practical solutions that cannot satisfy the principle of legality that is at the heart of the rule of law.

There may thus be a need for new rules, but there is no need to reinvent the wheel. In order to define who may be interned in situations of non-international armed conflict, for what reasons and for how long, it is neither appropriate nor necessary to seek guidance – as some have proposed – in the rules on the conduct of hostilities and in particular those on targeting. The rules on targeting are part of the regulation of the use of force *in bello*, they define in particular which objects and persons may be the subject of direct attack. Targeting rules thus permit to establish the legitimacy of a target for attack, by defining which persons may be neutralized through the use of force. The rules on internment do not regulate the use of force, neither in offence nor in defence. As far as persons who pose a direct military or security threat are concerned, the rules on internment define when and for how long such persons may be preventively neutralized *without* the use of force. Moreover, the categories of persons who may be subject to the use of force are more restrictive than the categories of persons who may be subject to internment. Our comparative analysis of the purpose and structure of targeting and internment rules in chapter II-3 shows that any definition by analogy of the lawful grounds and duration of the use of either coercive measure is both inappropriate and dangerous.

Neither is it necessary to seek guidance in the rules on targeting to define the lawful grounds and duration of internment in non-international armed conflict. As we have explained in chapter III-1, we are convinced that guidance is indeed to be sought in humanitarian law applicable to situations of international armed conflict and occupation, since this is the only body of international law that offers concrete and battlefield-tested directions as to what are permissible restrictions of the right to liberty for reasons related to armed conflict. Chapter III-2 further shows that the most appropriate subset of internment provisions to look at is that provided for in the Fourth Geneva Convention, since its provisions allow for the internment of both persons who are members of the armed forces of a party to the conflict without being entitled to prisoner of war (and in some cases even combatant) status, and persons who may not be members of such armed forces but nevertheless pose a threat to the security or military operations of the Interning Power or to the security of the population the latter is responsible for. As to the medical and religious personnel of the armed of the parties to the conflict, the relevant provisions of the First and Second Geneva Conventions offer adequate guidance as to the reasons and duration for which they may be retained.[1687]

Therefore, should States consider it appropriate to engage in further normative development of international humanitarian law, we would, on the basis of the research and analysis in this book, formulate two recommendations. First, in case the international community is ready to adopt new treaty rules of international humanitarian law applicable to non-international armed conflict,[1688] we would suggest they include a legal basis to intern that is designed essentially along the lines of the internment provisions of the Fourth Geneva Convention, but takes into account the higher standards required by contemporary

[1687] As we have pointed out throughout the book, the fact of seeking guidance in the concrete internment provisions of the Fourth Geneva Convention (or the First and Second Geneva Conventions as far as medical and religious personnel is concerned) does not mean that the development of internment provisions for situations of non-international armed conflict must not be guided by general international law and in particular international human rights law. As much as the contemporary interpretation of existing internment provisions in international humanitarian law is directly influenced by the developments in international human rights law, the development of new rules must take into account these developments too. As the ICRC's President recently pointed out: "It is essential that any development or clarification of humanitarian law avoids all unnecessary overlapping with existing rules of human rights law. Any risk of undermining these rules must be avoided" (ICRC, "Strengthening Legal Protection of Victims of Armed Conflicts" (2010), p. 2).

[1688] In this regard, see the invitation of the ICRC's President to make suggestions for "new legal ways for dealing exhaustively with the subject of protection for persons deprived of liberty during non-international armed conflict" (ICRC, "Strengthening Legal Protection of Victims of Armed Conflicts" (2010), pp. 2 and 4), and the subsequent adoption of Resolution (I), *Strenghthering Legal Protection for Victims of Armed Conflicts* at the 31st International Conference of the Red Cross and Red Crescent in December 2011.

international human rights law when defining the appropriate balance between the necessity of internment that may result from the existence of a non-international armed conflict and the individual internee's fundamental right to liberty. Second, should the international community engage in any clarification or propose any development of the internment rules applicable in situations of international armed conflict and occupation,[1689] we would suggest to clarify or amend the following provisions to take into account or better reflect the new features of armed conflict and developments in international law that have come about since their adoption:

Clarify that (at least the duration of) the internment of deserters, defectors, persons referred to in article 4§A(4) and (5) of the Third Geneva Convention, participants in a *levée en masse*, and children should be limited according to what is necessary to counter the threat they may pose to the security or military operations of the Interning Power or to the protection of the civilian population under its responsibility against the direct effects of hostilities (*cf. supra* chapter II-1.2.3.5);

Clarify that article 118 of the Third Geneva Convention is without prejudice to the principle of non-refoulement, and that no prisoner of war may be repatriated to his country of origin where there are substantial grounds to believe that he or she would be subject to torture, cruel, inhuman or degrading treatment, or to arbitrary deprivation of life or liberty on account of his or her ethnicity, nationality, religious or political convictions, or behaviour as a member of the armed forces during the armed conflict (*cf. supra* chapter II-1.2.3.6);

Clarify that persons who are in the hands of a party to the armed conflict that perceives them as enemies may not be excluded from the scope of application of the Fourth Geneva Convention merely on the ground that they have the same nationality as the Interning Power or one of its allies (*cf. supra* chapter II-3.1.2);

Clarify or amend as necessary articles 5 of the Third and articles 43 and 78 of the Fourth Geneva Conventions to bring the procedural safeguards provided therein in line with contemporary standards of international law.

1.3. CONCLUSIONS REGARDING THE RELATIONSHIP BETWEEN INTERNATIONAL HUMANITARIAN AND HUMAN RIGHTS LAW

While the applicability of international human rights law to situations of armed conflict is now beyond serious controversy, many questions remain as to how their simultaneous applicability affects the interpretation of each of their individual norms. Working with both sets of international legal rules to analyze, and clarify where necessary, the specific internment provisions of the 1949 Geneva Conventions, was one of the particular challenges we had to deal with in writing this book.

[1689] In order to avoid a differentiated interpretation of the applicable rules between different parties to the conflict, any proposed development or amendment of the internment provisions in the (universally ratified) Geneva Conventions should be adopted by consensus.

Based on our research and analysis, we have come to the following conclusions regarding the relationship between the two bodies of law. First, it is important to take into account the different functions of international humanitarian law and international human rights law within the international legal system when interpreting their respective provisions in light of each other; doing so allows one to avoid or dispel many apparent conflicts between their norms. Second, while the provisions regarding the right to liberty in international human rights treaties set out general criteria for lawful deprivation of liberty, the internment provisions of the Geneva Conventions provide directly for a legal basis to intern certain persons in situations of international armed conflict and occupation. That legal basis defines in more precise terms who can be interned, on what grounds, and for how long in these specific situations, and in doing so, it takes into account the practical realities of armed conflict. When the threshold of application of these Conventions is met, the legal bases for internment – agreed upon by the international community as a whole[1690] – automatically become available to the parties to that conflict and therefore do not require derogation from the right to liberty in international human rights treaties to prevent the Interning Power from violating its obligations under those treaties. Finally, while the interpretation of the right to liberty in international human rights law must take into account existing norms of international humanitarian law to assess the lawfulness of internment in armed conflict, it would be dangerous (and incorrect) to claim that international humanitarian law has or should have any influence on the definition of lawful deprivation of liberty in situations that do not reach the threshold of armed conflict.

In our analysis of the specific internment provisions in the Geneva Conventions and their Additional Protocols, we sought to bring to light the concrete impact of the applicability of international human rights law on the interpretation of these norms. Throughout this endeavour, we found that the specific norms regarding deprivation of liberty of both bodies of law seek to achieve the same goal, namely to prevent erroneous, unnecessary or arbitrary deprivation of liberty. This commonality of purpose facilitates reconciliation of their seemingly different takes on the legitimate purposes for restricting the right to liberty and on the lawful duration of internment, a preventive and thus inherently temporary measure. On the other hand, we also found that some of the "traditional" interpretations of the provisions of the Geneva Conventions were no longer tenable in light of the important normative developments in international law since their adoption, and that a dynamic and teleological interpretation is called for if they are to withstand the test of time. Ultimately, we found that a systemic and dynamic interpretation of the relevant norms in light of their common purpose not only allowed us to formulate clear and acceptable answers to our specific research questions but also demonstrates that the concurrent application of the provisions of international humanitarian law and

[1690] The Geneva Conventions are universally ratified and considered to represent customary international law.

international human rights law can effectively result in a realistic and protective international regulation of the legal framework for internment in armed conflict and can thus be an effective tool to prevent arbitrary deprivation of liberty in such trying and often chaotic situations.

1.4. AVENUES FOR FURTHER RESEARCH

As we mentioned before, the subject matter of this book raises a multitude of legal questions, the totality of which could not be addressed in a satisfactory manner in a single manuscript. Two particular aspects of the legal framework for internment in armed conflict have not been dealt with in much detail, but undoubtedly merit further research and analysis.

For one, the concrete impact of developments in international human rights law on the interpretation of the procedural safeguards against erroneous, unnecessary or arbitrary deprivation of liberty prescribed by the Geneva Conventions for situations of international armed conflict and occupation, deserves comprehensive research and analysis.

Second, the definition of what are appropriate and effective procedural and other safeguards against erroneous, unnecessary or arbitrary deprivation of liberty with regard to internment in situations of non-international armed conflict continues to be subject to controversy. In particular, the question of whether the lawfulness of such internment should be reviewed, both initially and periodically, by a court, or whether such review could be carried out by an administrative (and possibly military) board continues to be the subject of intense debate and promises to be a difficult hurdle, should any normative development of international humanitarian law in this area indeed take place. Another sensitive issue is the establishment of independent monitoring mechanisms with a right to access to internees and a right to make representations on their behalf to the Interning Power. In our opinion, any normative development of international humanitarian law applicable to non-international armed conflict should include, as a minimum, provisions to this intent that are equivalent to those existing in the Third and Fourth Geneva Conventions (right to access and representation of Protecting Powers and the ICRC). While there is probably considerable support for such a suggestion amongst States, the potential for success in this matter is – in light of the discussions on this subject during the negotiations of Additional Protocol II to the Geneva Conventions and the persistent dismissal by certain countries affected by non-international armed conflict of the ICRC's offers of services in this domain – not to be taken for granted. Both issues – review and monitoring – would benefit from further research that will demonstrate to what extent procedural and monitoring safeguards for internment in non-international armed conflict may be designed on the basis of those prescribed in the Fourth Geneva Convention, or whether they would need to be substantially revised in light of subsequent developments in international human rights law. It is submitted that such research would also provide the potential drafters of new treaty rules for non-international armed conflict with clear indications as to how the options before them would be restricted by their obligations under international human rights law.

Furthermore, a number of questions arise from the possibility that an international organization, rather than its troop-contributing States, may be a party to an armed conflict and may thus, where necessary as a result of that conflict, need to resort to internment.[1691] We have discussed the impact of this possibility on the legal qualification of the conflict and the applicable body of international humanitarian law. While that question itself requires further research to come to a definite conclusion, we have identified the different possible outcomes and their impact on the legal framework for internment in chapter I-2. Nevertheless, we remain convinced that further research is required to conclude on whether an international organization can be a party to the armed conflict itself (i.e. to the exclusion of its troop-contributing States) and, if so, in what capacity it would participate in that conflict (i.e. as a State-like or non-State entity). The outcome of that debate will have a direct impact on the legal framework for internment in such a conflict. First, it will determine whether and which legal bases are available for the international organization to intern persons who pose a threat. Where the situation qualifies as an international armed conflict and the international organization is a party to it, it can rely directly on the legal bases for internment discussed in Part II; where the situation qualifies as a non-international armed conflict, the international organization, like any other party to the conflict, will not dispose of a legal basis to intern in international humanitarian law itself. Second, whether it is the international organization or the troop-contributing States that are the party to the conflict will have an impact on the identification of the Interning Power and thus on the nature of their respective responsibility for the lawfulness of the internment and the treatment of the internees.[1692] Third, where the international organization is considered a party to an international armed conflict, a number of problems will arise with regard to the implementation of the Third Geneva Convention. That Convention is intended to apply to States and a number of its provisions make the treatment of prisoners of war in the hands of the Interning Power

[1691] We have demonstrated in chapter I-2 that in situations where it is the troop-contributing States themselves who are a party to the conflict, the law is clear on the qualification of the conflict and the determination of the applicable body of international humanitarian law. As far as the legal framework for internment is concerned, no specific questions arise in such situations from the fact that the deployment of these troops was mandated by an international organization.

[1692] While both the international organization and the troop-contributing States may incur international legal responsibility for unlawful internment or for violations of the rules on the treatment and conditions of captivity of internees, the Interning Power has direct obligations, while allied States or an international organization only have indirect or secondary obligations. These indirect or secondary obligations are based either on common article 1 to the Geneva Conventions or, for allied States, on the article 12 of the Third and article 45 of the Fourth Geneva Conventions regarding the transfer of protected persons between allied parties to the conflict. See also UK, *LOAC Manual* (2004), p. 153: "Even in the case of multinational forces, where arrangements for handling prisoners of war are administered by several allied states, the original capturing power retains an obligation in respect of prisoners of war [under article 12 GC III]. This also applies where the forces are acting under the command of the United Nations."

depend on the applicable legal standards in the interning State.[1693] Finally, the qualification of the conflict as international or non-international will also have an impact on the legal status of the members of the international armed forces, both in combat and upon capture by an adverse party, and thus determine to what extent they may themselves be interned on the basis of international humanitarian law.[1694] The questions outlined in chapter I-2 regarding the applicable body of international humanitarian law to situations in which an international organization is a party to the conflict therefore merit careful research and analysis before one can formulate specific answers to questions regarding the legal framework for the internment operations of such international organizations, and assess the potential need for additional legal rules to regulate them.

* * *

The research and analysis presented in this book is our personal contribution to two specific contemporary debates in international law, namely, that on the adequacy of the existing legal framework for internment in armed conflict, and that on the concrete consequences of the simultaneous applicability of international humanitarian and international human rights law to situations of armed conflict. The issues at stake in these two debates are closely related. Indeed, the regulation of internment in armed conflict is one of the areas where the relationship between international humanitarian and human rights law really matters.[1695] Undeniably, the definition of the concrete interaction of the norms on deprivation of liberty in both bodies of law has a direct impact on both the needs and obligations of the Interning Power, and the personal situation of any individual internee. According to how these norms interact, international law may or may not be capable to accommodate the Interning Power's legitimate need to preventively deprive certain persons of their liberty in order to neutralize the potential threat they pose. The interpretation of these same norms in light of each other will also define the specific legal restraints placed on the Interning Power when it exercises its power to intern. Finally, and most importantly, the precise articulation of the interaction between the internment provisions of international humanitarian law and the right to liberty under international human rights law determines not only when, why and for how long an individual may lawfully be interned, but also how efficient the international legal system is in

[1693] See for example the penal and disciplinary sanctions regime provided for in articles 82 to 98 and the regulations concerning judicial proceedings against prisoners of war (articles 99-108), both of which refer back to the legislation and judicial infrastructure of the interning State. Moreover, the transfer provisions of both the Third and the Fourth Geneva Conventions (*cf. supra* note 1691) explicitly provide that an internee can only be transferred to "a Power which is a party to the Convention." This would effectively preclude the possibility of a troop-contributing State having captured a person transferring him or her into the custody of an international organization (so far no international or regional organization is a party to the Geneva Conventions).

[1694] An issue also highlighted by McCoubrey & White (1996), pp. 166-168.

[1695] The expression is borrowed from Sassòli & Olson (*IRRC* 2008), p. 599 (title): "The Relationship between International Humanitarian and Human Rights Law where it Matters: Admissible Killing and Internment of Fighters in Non-International Armed Conflicts."

protecting individuals against prevent erroneous, unnecessary and arbitrary deprivation of liberty in armed conflict.

We heeded the calls emanating from different actors concerned with the issue of internment in armed conflict for the clarification and modernization of the existing legal framework for internment in armed conflict. In our effort to provide answers to some of the questions raised, we bore in mind both the practical realities of armed conflict and the significant developments in international law that have secured an individual's right to liberty as one of the most fundamental attributes of any human being, and as one of the cornerstones of a society construed on the rule of law. We often felt we were walking a fine line and gradually came to a deeper understanding of just how important and difficult it is at times to get the balance right.

The research and analysis in this book demonstrates that while some of the internment provisions of existing international humanitarian law may be ambiguous, incomplete, or even outdated, the general structure of the framework and the basic principles it relies upon are clear and well established. We have shown that a dynamic and systemic interpretation of the relevant norms of both international humanitarian and international human rights law allows one to clarify the existing international legal framework for internment as it stands today and to propose normative developments where necessary to remedy its weaknesses. We feel therefore confident to conclude that a combined reading of the general principles of international law regarding the restriction of fundamental rights and freedoms, the specific requirements of the right to liberty under international human rights law, and the existing legal framework for internment in international humanitarian law, forms a solid basis to construe answers to both old and newer questions and to define, and redefine where necessary, the "limits at which the necessities of war ought to yield to the requirements of humanity."[1696]

[1696] St-Petersburg Declaration (1864), preamble.

ANNEXES

ANNEX A
MAIN TREATY PROVISIONS

INTERNATIONAL HUMAN RIGHTS LAW

Universal Declaration of Human Rights (1948) – Articles 3 and 9

Art. 3: Everyone has the right to life, liberty and the security of person.

Art. 9: No one shall be subjected to arbitrary arrest, detention or exile.

European Convention on Human Rights (1950) – Article 5, paragraph 1

Everyone has the right to liberty and security of person. No one shall be deprived of his liberty save in the following cases and in accordance with a procedure prescribed by law:

a) the lawful detention of a person after conviction by a competent court;

b) the lawful arrest or detention of a person for non-compliance with the lawful order of a court or in order to secure the fulfilment of any obligation prescribed by law;

c) the lawful arrest or detention of a person effected for the purpose of bringing him before the competent legal authority on reasonable suspicion of having committed an offence or when it is reasonably considered necessary to prevent his committing an offence or fleeing after having done so;

d) the detention of a minor by lawful order for the purpose of educational supervision or his lawful detention for the purpose of bringing him before the competent legal authority;

e) the lawful detention of persons for the prevention of the spreading of infectious diseases, of persons of unsound mind, alcoholics or drug addicts or vagrants;

f) the lawful arrest or detention of a person to prevent his effecting an unauthorised entry into the country or of a person against whom action is being taken with a view to deportation or extradition.

International Covenant on Civil and Political Rights (1966) – Article 9, paragraph 1

Everyone has the right to liberty and security of person. No one shall be subjected to arbitrary arrest or detention. No one shall be deprived of his liberty except on such grounds and in accordance with such procedure as are established by law.

American Convention on Human Rights (1969) – Article 7, paragraphs 1 to 3

1. Every person has the right to personal liberty and security.

2. No one shall be deprived of his physical liberty except for the reasons and under the conditions established beforehand by the constitution of the State Party concerned or by a law established pursuant thereto.

3. No one shall be subject to arbitrary arrest or imprisonment.

African Charter on Human and Peoples' Rights (1982) – Article 6

Every individual shall have the right to liberty and to the security of his person. No one may be deprived of his freedom except for reasons and conditions previously laid down by law. In particular, no one may be arbitrarily arrested or detained.

Convention on the Rights of the Child (1989) – Article 37(b)

No child shall be deprived of his or her liberty unlawfully or arbitrarily. The arrest, detention or imprisonment of a child shall be in conformity with the law and shall be used only as a measure of last resort and for the shortest appropriate period of time.

INTERNATIONAL HUMANITARIAN LAW

Hague Regulations (1907) – Article 43

The authority of the legitimate power having in fact passed into the hands of the occupant, the latter shall take all the measures in his power to restore, and ensure, as far as possible, public order and safety, while respecting, unless absolutely prevented, the laws in force in the country.

Geneva Conventions I-IV (1949) (common articles)

Article 2 (Application of the Convention)

In addition to the provisions which shall be implemented in peacetime, the present Convention shall apply to all cases of declared war or of any other armed conflict which may arise between two or more of the High Contracting Parties, even if the state of war is not recognized by one of them.

The Convention shall also apply to all cases of partial or total occupation of the territory of a High Contracting Party, even if the said occupation meets with no armed resistance.

Although one of the Powers in conflict may not be a party to the present Convention, the Powers who are parties thereto shall remain bound by it in their mutual relations. They shall furthermore be bound by the Convention in relation to the said Power, if the latter accepts and applies the provisions thereof.

Article 3 (Conflicts not of an international character)

In the case of armed conflict not of an international character occurring in the territory of one of the High Contracting Parties, each Party to the conflict shall be bound to apply, as a minimum, the following provisions:

(1) Persons taking no active part in the hostilities, including members of armed forces who have laid down their arms and those placed 'hors de combat' by sickness, wounds, detention, or any other cause, shall in all circumstances be treated humanely, without any adverse distinction founded on race, colour, religion or faith, sex, birth or wealth, or any other similar criteria. To this end, the following acts are and shall remain prohibited at any time and in any place whatsoever with respect to the above-mentioned persons: (a) violence to life and person, in particular murder of all kinds, mutilation, cruel treatment and torture; (b) taking of hostages; (c) outrages upon personal dignity, in particular humiliating and degrading treatment; (d) the passing of sentences and the carrying out of executions without previous judgment pronounced by a regularly constituted court, affording all the judicial guarantees which are recognized as indispensable by civilized peoples.

(2) The wounded and sick shall be collected and cared for.

An impartial humanitarian body, such as the International Committee of the Red Cross, may offer its services to the Parties to the conflict.

The Parties to the conflict should further endeavour to bring into force, by means of special agreements, all or part of the other provisions of the present Convention.

The application of the preceding provisions shall not affect the legal status of the Parties to the conflict.

Geneva Convention III (1949)

Article 4 (Prisoners of war)

A. Prisoners of war, in the sense of the present Convention, are persons belonging to one of the following categories, who have fallen into the power of the enemy:

(1) Members of the armed forces of a Party to the conflict as well as members of militias or volunteer corps forming part of such armed forces.

(2) Members of other militias and members of other volunteer corps, incuding those of organized resistance movements, belonging to a Party to the conflict and operating in or outside their own territory, even if this territory is occupied, provided that such militias or volunteer corps, including such organized resistance movements, fulfil the following conditions:

(a) that of being commanded by a person responsible for his subordinates;

(b) that of having a fixed distinctive sign recognizable at a distance;

(c) that of carrying arms openly;

(d) that of conducting their operations in accordance with the laws and customs of war.

(3) Members of regular armed forces who profess allegiance to a government or an authority not recognized by the Detaining Power.

(4) Persons who accompany the armed forces without actually being members thereof, such as civilian members of military aircraft crews, war correspondents, supply contractors, members of labour units or of services responsible for the welfare of the armed forces, provided that they have received authorization from the armed forces which they accompany, who shall provide them for that purpose with an identity card similar to the annexed model.

(5) Members of crews, including masters, pilots and apprentices, of the merchant marine and the crews of civil aircraft of the Parties to the conflict, who do not benefit by more favourable treatment under any other provisions of international law.

(6) Inhabitants of a non-occupied territory, who on the approach of the enemy spontaneously take up arms to resist the invading forces, without having had time to form themselves into regular armed units, provided they carry arms openly and respect the laws and customs of war.

B. The following shall likewise be treated as prisoners of war under the present Convention:

(1) Persons belonging, or having belonged, to the armed forces of the occupied country, if the occupying Power considers it necessary by reason of such allegiance to intern them, even though it has originally liberated them while hostilities were going on outside the territory it occupies, in particular where such persons have made an unsuccessful attempt to rejoin the armed forces to which they belong and which are engaged in combat, or where they fail to comply with a summons made to them with a view to internment.

(2) The persons belonging to one of the categories enumerated in the present Article, who have been received by neutral or non-belligerent Powers on their territory and whom these Powers are required to intern under international law, without prejudice to any more favourable treatment which these Powers may choose to give and with the exception of

Articles 8, 10, 15, 30, fifth paragraph, 58-67, 92, 126 and, where diplomatic relations exist between the Parties to the conflict and the neutral or non-belligerent Power concerned, those Articles concerning the Protecting Power. Where such diplomatic relations exist, the Parties to a conflict on whom these persons depend shall be allowed to perform towards them the functions of a Protecting Power as provided in the present Convention, without prejudice to the functions which these Parties normally exercise in conformity with diplomatic and consular usage and treaties.

C. This Article shall in no way affect the status of medical personnel and chaplains as provided for in Article 33 of the present Convention.

Article 21 (Restriction of liberty of movement)

The Detaining Power may subject prisoners of war to internment. It may impose on them the obligation of not leaving, beyond certain limits, the camp where they are interned, or if the said camp is fenced in, of not going outside its perimeter. Subject to the provisions of the present Convention relative to penal and disciplinary sanctions, prisoners of war may not be held in close confinement except where necessary to safeguard their health and then only during the continuation of the circumstances which make such confinement necessary.

Prisoners of war may be partially or wholly released on parole or promise, in so far as is allowed by the laws of the Power on which they depend. Such measures shall be taken particularly in cases where this may contribute to the improvement of their state of health. No prisoner of war shall be compelled to accept liberty on parole or promise.

Upon the outbreak of hostilities, each Party to the conflict shall notify the adverse Party of the laws and regulations allowing or forbidding its own nationals to accept liberty on parole or promise. Prisoners of war who are paroled or who have given their promise in conformity with the laws and regulations so notified, are bound on their personal honour scrupulously to fulfil, both towards the Power on which they depend and towards the power which has captured them, the engagements of their paroles or promises. In such cases, the Power on which they depend is bound neither to require nor to accept from them any service incompatible with the parole or promise given.

Article 118 (Release and repatriation)

Prisoners of war shall be released and repatriated without delay after the cessation of active hostilities.

In the absence of stipulations to the above effect in any agreement concluded between the Parties to the conflict with a view to the cessation of hostilities, or failing any such agreement, each of the Detaining Powers shall itself establish and execute without delay a plan of repatriation in conformity with the principle laid down in the foregoing paragraph.

In either case, the measures adopted shall be brought to the knowledge of the prisoners of war.

The costs of repatriation of prisoners of war shall in all cases be equitably apportioned between the Detaining Power and the Power on which the prisoners depend. This apportionment shall be carried out on the following basis:

(a) If the two Powers are contiguous, the Power on which the prisoners of war depend shall bear the costs of repatriation from the frontiers of the Detaining Power.

(b) If the two Powers are not contiguous, the Detaining Power shall bear the costs of transport of prisoners of war over its own territory as far as its frontier or its port of embarkation nearest to the territory of the Power on which the prisoners of war depend. The Parties concerned shall agree between themselves as to the equitable apportionment of the remaining costs of the repatriation. The conclusion of this agreement shall in no circumstances justify any delay in the repatriation of the prisoners of war.

Geneva Convention IV (1949)

Article 4 (Definition of Protected Persons)

Persons protected by the Convention are those who, at a given moment and in any manner whatsoever, find themselves, in case of a conflict or occupation, in the hands of a Party to the conflict or Occupying Power of which they are not nationals.

Nationals of a State which is not bound by the Convention are not protected by it. Nationals of a neutral State who find themselves in the territory of a belligerent State, and nationals of a co-belligerent State, shall not be regarded as protected persons while the State of which they are nationals has normal diplomatic representation in the State in whose hands they are.

The provisions of Part II are, however, wider in application, as defined in Article 13.

Persons protected by the Geneva Convention for the Amelioration of the Condition of the Wounded and Sick in Armed Forces in the Field of August 12, 1949, or by the Geneva Convention for the Amelioration of the Condition of Wounded, Sick and Shipwrecked Members of Armed Forces at Sea of August 12, 1949, or by the Geneva Convention relative to the Treatment of Prisoners of War of August 12, 1949, shall not be considered as protected persons within the meaning of the present Convention.

Article 5 (Derogations)

Where, in the territory of a Party to the conflict, the latter is satisfied that an individual protected person is definitely suspected of or engaged in activities hostile to the security of the State, such individual person shall not be entitled to claim such rights and privileges under the present Convention as would, if exercised in the favour of such individual person, be prejudicial to the security of such State.

Where in occupied territory an individual protected person is detained as a spy or saboteur, or as a person under definite suspicion of activity hostile to the security of the Occupying Power, such person shall, in those cases where absolute military security so requires, be regarded as having forfeited rights of communication under the present Convention.

In each case, such persons shall nevertheless be treated with humanity, and in case of trial, shall not be deprived of the rights of fair and regular trial prescribed by the present Convention. They shall also be granted the full rights and privileges of a protected person under the present Convention at the earliest date consistent with the security of the State or Occupying Power, as the case may be.

Article 27 (General observations), paragraphs 1 and 4

Protected persons are entitled, in all circumstances, to respect for their persons, their honour, their family rights, their religious convictions and practices, and their manners and customs. They shall at all times be humanely treated, and shall be protected especially against all acts of violence or threats thereof and against insults and public curiosity.

However, the Parties to the conflict may take such measures of control and security in regard to protected persons as may be necessary as a result of the war.

Article 41 (Assigned residence. Internment)

Should the Power in whose hands protected persons may be consider the measures of control mentioned in the present Convention to be inadequate, it may not have recourse to any other measure of control more severe than that of assigned residence or internment, in accordance with the provisions of Articles 42 and 43.

In applying the provisions of Article 39, second paragraph, to the cases of persons required to leave their usual places of residence by virtue of a decision placing them in assigned residence elsewhere, the Detaining Power shall be guided as closely as possible by the standards of welfare set forth in Part III, Section IV of this Convention.

Article 42 (Grounds for internment or assigned residence. Voluntary internment)

The internment or placing in assigned residence of protected persons may be ordered only if the security of the Detaining Power makes it absolutely necessary.

If any person, acting through the representatives of the Protecting Power, voluntarily demands internment and if his situation renders this step necessary, he shall be interned by the Power in whose hands he may be.

Article 43 (Procedure)

Any protected person who has been interned or placed in assigned residence shall be entitled to have such action reconsidered as soon as possible by an appropriate court or administrative board designated by the Detaining Power for that purpose. If the internment or placing in assigned residence is maintained, the court or administrative board shall periodically, and at least twice yearly, give consideration to his or her case, with a view to the favourable amendment of the initial decision, if circumstances permit.

Unless the protected persons concerned object, the Detaining Power shall, as rapidly as possible, give the Protecting Power the names of any protected persons who have been interned or subjected to assigned residence, or who have been released from internment or assigned residence. The decisions of the courts or boards mentioned in the first paragraph of the present Article shall also, subject to the same conditions, be notified as rapidly as possible to the Protecting Power.

Article 78 (Security measures. Internment and assigned residence. Right of appeal)

If the Occupying Power considers it necessary, for imperative reasons of security, to take safety measures concerning protected persons, it may, at the most, subject them to assigned residence or to internment.

Decisions regarding such assigned residence or internment shall be made according to a regular procedure to be prescribed by the Occupying Power in accordance with the provisions of the present Convention. This procedure shall include the right of appeal for the parties concerned. Appeals shall be decided with the least possible delay. In the event of the decision being upheld, it shall be subject to periodical review, if possible every six months, by a competent body set up by the said Power.

Protected persons made subject to assigned residence and thus required to leave their homes shall enjoy the full benefit of Article 39 of the present Convention.

Article 79 (Cases of internment and applicable provisions)

The Parties to the Conflict shall not intern protected persons, except in accordance with the provisions of Articles 41, 42, 43, 68 and 78."

Article 132 (Release and repatriation – During hostilities or occupation)

Each interned person shall be released by the Detaining Power as soon as the reasons which necessitated his internment no longer exist.

The Parties to the conflict shall, moreover, endeavour during the course of hostilities, to conclude agreements for the release, the repatriation, the return to places of residence or the accommodation in a neutral country of certain classes of internees, in particular children, pregnant women and mothers with infants and young children, wounded and sick, and internees who have been detained for a long time.

Article 133 (Release and repatriation – After the close of hostilities)

Internment shall cease as soon as possible after the close of hostilities.

Internees in the territory of a Party to the conflict, against whom penal proceedings are pending for offences not exclusively subject to disciplinary penalties, may be detained until the close of such proceedings and, if circumstances require, until the completion of the penalty. The same shall apply to internees who have been previously sentenced to a punishment depriving them of liberty.

By agreement between the Detaining Power and the Powers concerned, committees may be set up after the close of hostilities, or of the occupation of territories, to search for dispersed internees.

Additional Protocol I (1977)

Article 43 (Armed forces)

1. The armed forces of a Party to a conflict consist of all organized armed forces, groups and units which are under a command responsible to that Party for the conduct of its subordinates, even if that Party is represented by a government or an authority not recognized by an adverse Party. Such armed forces shall be subject to an internal disciplinary system which, 'inter alia', shall enforce compliance with the rules of international law applicable in armed conflict.

2. Members of the armed forces of a Party to a conflict (other than medical personnel and chaplains covered by Article 33 of the Third Convention) are combatants, that is to say, they have the right to participate directly in hostilities.

3. Whenever a Party to a conflict incorporates a paramilitary or armed law enforcement agency into its armed forces it shall so notify the other Parties to the conflict.

Article 44 (Combatants and prisoners of war)

1. Any combatant, as defined in Article 43, who falls into the power of an adverse Party shall be a prisoner of war.

2. While all combatants are obliged to comply with the rules of international law applicable in armed conflict, violations of these rules shall not deprive a combatant of his right to be a combatant or, if he falls into the power of an adverse Party, of his right to be a prisoner of war, except as provided in paragraphs 3 and 4.

3. In order to promote the protection of the civilian population from the effects of hostilities, combatants are obliged to distinguish themselves from the civilian population while they are engaged in an attack or in a military operation preparatory to an attack. Recognizing, however, that there are situations in armed conflicts where, owing to the nature of the hostilities an armed combatant cannot so distinguish himself, he shall retain his status as a combatant, provided that, in such situations, he carries his arms openly:

(a) during each military engagement, and

(b) during such time as he is visible to the adversary while he is engaged in a military deployment preceding the launching of an attack in which he is to participate.

Acts which comply with the requirements of this paragraph shall not be considered as perfidious within the meaning of Article 37, paragraph 1 (c.

4. A combatant who falls into the power of an adverse Party while failing to meet the requirements set forth in the second sentence of paragraph 3 shall forfeit his right to be a prisoner of war, but he shall, nevertheless, be given protections equivalent in all respects to those accorded to prisoners of war by the Third Convention and by this Protocol. This protection includes protections equivalent to those accorded to prisoners of war by the Third Convention in the case where such a person is tried and punished for any offences he has committed.

5. Any combatant who falls into the power of an adverse Party while not engaged in an attack or in a military operation preparatory to an attack shall not forfeit his rights to be a combatant and a prisoner of war by virtue of his prior activities.

6. This Article is without prejudice to the right of any person to be a prisoner of war pursuant to Article 4 of the Third Convention.

7. This Article is not intended to change the generally accepted practice of States with respect to the wearing of the uniform by combatants assigned to the regular, uniformed armed units of a Party to the conflict.

8. In addition to the categories of persons mentioned in Article 13 of the First and Second Conventions, all members of the armed forces of a Party to the conflict, as defined in Article 43 of this Protocol, shall be entitled to protection under those Conventions if they are wounded or sick or, in the case of the Second Convention, shipwrecked at sea or in other waters.

Article 45 (Protection of persons who have taken part in hostilities)

1. A person who takes part in hostilities and falls into the power of an adverse Party shall be presumed to be a prisoner of war, and therefore shall be protected by the Third Convention, if he claims the status of prisoner of war, or if he appears to be entitled to such status, or if the Party on which he depends claims such status on his behalf by notification to the detaining Power or to the Protecting Power. Should any doubt arise as to whether any such person is entitled to the status of prisoner of war, he shall continue to have such status and, therefore, to be protected by the Third Convention and this Protocol until such time as his status has been determined by a competent tribunal.

2. If a person who has fallen into the power of an adverse Party is not held as a prisoner of war and is to be tried by that Party for an offence arising out of the hostilities, he shall have the right to assert his entitlement to prisoner-of-war status before a judicial tribunal and to have that question adjudicated. Whenever possible under the applicable procedure, this adjudication shall occur before the trial for the offence. The representatives of the Protecting Power shall be entitled to attend the proceedings in which that question is adjudicated, unless, exceptionally, the proceedings are held ' in camera ' in the interest of State security. In such a case the detaining Power shall advise the Protecting Power accordingly.

3. Any person who has taken part in hostilities, who is not entitled to prisoner-of-war status and who does not benefit from more favourable treatment in accordance with the Fourth Convention shall have the right at all times to the protection of Article 75 of this Protocol. In occupied territory, any such person, unless he is held as a spy, shall also be entitled, notwithstanding Article 5 of the Fourth Convention, to his rights of communication under that Convention.

Article 50 (Definition of civilians and civilian population)

1. A civilian is any person who does not belong to one of the categories of persons referred to in Article 4 A (1), (2), (3) and (6) of the Third Convention and in Article 43 of this Protocol. In case of doubt whether a person is a civilian, that person shall be considered to be a civilian.

2. The civilian population comprises all persons who are civilians.

3. The presence within the civilian population of individuals who do not come within the definition of civilians does not deprive the population of its civilian character.

Article 51 (Protection of the civilian population), paragraphs 1 to 3

1. The civilian population and individual civilians shall enjoy general protection against dangers arising from military operations. To give effect to this protection, the following rules, which are additional to other applicable rules of international law, shall be observed in all circumstances.

2. The civilian population as such, as well as individual civilians, shall not be the object of attack. Acts or threats of violence the primary purpose of which is to spread terror among the civilian population are prohibited.

3. Civilians shall enjoy the protection afforded by this Section, unless and for such time as they take a direct part in hostilities.

Article 75 (Fundamental guarantees), paragraphs 1,3 and 6

1. In so far as they are affected by a situation referred to in Article 1 of this Protocol, persons who are in the power of a Party to the conflict and who do not benefit from more favourable treatment under the Conventions or under this Protocol shall be treated humanely in all circumstances and shall enjoy, as a minimum, the protection provided by this Article without any adverse distinction based upon race, colour, sex, language, religion or belief, political or other opinion, national or social origin, wealth, birth or other status, or on any other similar criteria. Each Party shall respect the person, honour, convictions and religious practices of all such persons.

3. Any person arrested, detained or interned for actions related to the armed conflict shall be informed promptly, in a language he understands, of the reasons why these measures have been taken. Except in cases of arrest or detention for penal offences, such persons shall be released with the minimum delay possible and in any event as soon as the circumstances justifying the arrest, detention or internment have ceased to exist.

6. Persons who are arrested, detained or interned for reasons related to the armed conflict shall enjoy the protection provided by this Article until their final release, repatriation or re-establishment, even after the end of the armed conflict.

Additional Protocol II (1977)

Article 5 (Persons whose liberty has been restricted)

1. In addition to the provisions of Article 4, the following provisions shall be respected as a minimum with regard to persons deprived of their liberty for reasons related to the armed conflict, whether they are interned or detained: (a) the wounded and the sick shall be treated in accordance with Article 7; (b) the persons referred to in this paragraph shall, to the same extent as the local civilian population, be provided with food and drinking water and be afforded safeguards as regards health and hygiene and protection against the rigours of the climate and the dangers of the armed conflict; (c) they shall be allowed to receive individual or collective relief; (d) they shall be allowed

to practise their religion and, if requested and appropriate, to receive spiritual assistance from persons, such as chaplains, performing religious functions; (e) they shall, if made to work, have the benefit of working conditions and safeguards similar to those enjoyed by the local civilian population.

2. Those who are responsible for the internment or detention of the persons referred to in paragraph 1 shall also, within the limits of their capabilities, respect the following provisions relating to such persons: (a) except when men and women of a family are accommodated together, women shall be held in quarters separated from those of men and shall be under the immediate supervision of women; (b) they shall be allowed to send and receive letters and cards, the number of which may be limited by competent authority if it deems necessary; (c) places of internment and detention shall not be located close to the combat zone. The persons referred to in paragraph 1 shall be evacuated when the places where they are interned or detained become particularly exposed to danger arising out of the armed conflict, if their evacuation can be carried out under adequate conditions of safety; (d) they shall have the benefit of medical examinations; (e) their physical or mental health and integrity shall not be endangered by any unjustified act or omission. Accordingly, it is prohibited to subject the persons described in this Article to any medical procedure which is not indicated by the state of health of the person concerned, and which is not consistent with the generally accepted medical standards applied to free persons under similar medical circumstances.

3. Persons who are not covered by paragraph 1 but whose liberty has been restricted in any way whatsoever for reasons related to the armed conflict shall be treated humanely in accordance with Article 4 and with paragraphs 1 (a), (c) and (d), and 2 (b) of this Article.

4. If it is decided to release persons deprived of their liberty, necessary measures to ensure their safety shall be taken by those so deciding.

INTERNATIONAL CRIMINAL LAW

ICC Statute (1998) – Article 8, paragraph 2(a)(vii)

For the purpose of this Statute, "war crimes" means:

(a) Grave breaches of the Geneva Conventions of 12 August 1949, namely, any of the following acts against persons or property protected under the provisions of the relevant Geneva Convention:

(vii) Unlawful deportation or transfer or unlawful confinement.

ICC Preparatory Commission, Elements of Crime (2000) - Article 8, paragraph 2(a)(vii)

Elements

1. The perpetrator confined or continued to confine one or more persons to a certain location.

2. Such person or persons were protected under one or more of the Geneva Conventions of 1949.

3. The perpetrator was aware of the factual circumstances that established that protected status.

4. The conduct took place in the context of and was associated with an international armed conflict.

5. The perpetrator was aware of factual circumstances that established the existence of an armed conflict.

Annex B
Israel,
Incarceration of Unlawful Combatants Law
(5762-2002)

Object

1. This Law is intended to regulate the incarceration of unlawful combatants not entitled to prisoner-of-war status, in a manner conforming with the obligations of the State of Israel under the provisions of international humanitarian law.

Definitions

2. In this Law -

"the Chief of General Staff" means the Chief of the General Staff of the Israel Defense Forces;

"unlawful combatant" means a person who has participated either directly or indirectly in hostile acts against the State of Israel or is a member of a force perpetrating hostile acts against the State of Israel, where the conditions prescribed in Article 4 of the Third Geneva Convention of 12th August 1949 with respect to prisoners-of-war and granting prisoner-of-war status in international humanitarian law, do not apply to him;

"prisoner" means a person incarcerated by virtue of an order issued by the Chief of General Staff pursuant to the provisions of this Law.

Incarceration of unlawful combatant

3. (a) Where the Chief of General Staff has reasonable cause to believe that a person being held by the State authorities is an unlawful combatant and that his release will harm State security, he may issue an order under his hand, directing that such person be incarcerated at a place to be determined (hereinafter referred to as "an incarceration order"); an incarceration order shall include the grounds for incarceration, without prejudicing State security requirements.

(b) An incarceration order may be granted in the absence of the person held by the State authorities.

(c) An incarceration order shall be brought to the attention of the prisoner at the earliest possible date and he shall be given the opportunity to put his submissions in respect of the order before an officer of at least the rank of lieutenant-colonel to be appointed by the Chief of General Staff; the submissions of the prisoner shall be recorded by the officer and shall be brought before the Chief of General Staff; where the Chief of General Staff finds, after reviewing the submissions of the prisoner, that the conditions prescribed in subsection (a) have not been fulfilled, he shall quash the incarceration order.

QUASHING AN INCARCERATION ORDER

4. Where the Chief of General Staff is of the opinion, at any time after the grant of the incarceration order, that the conditions prescribed in section 3(a) have not been fulfilled, or there are special grounds justifying the release of the prisoner, he shall order the quashing of the incarceration order.

JUDICIAL REVIEW

5. (a) A prisoner shall be brought before a judge of the District Court no later than fourteen days after the date of granting the incarceration order; where the judge of the District Court finds that the conditions prescribed in section 3(a) have not been fulfilled he shall quash the incarceration order.

(b) Where the prisoner is not brought before the District Court and where a hearing has not commenced before it within fourteen days of the date of granting the incarceration order, the prisoner shall be released, unless there exists another ground for his detention under the provisions of any law.

(c) Once every six months from the date of issue of an order under section 3(a) the prisoner shall be brought before a judge of the District Court; where the Court finds that his release will not harm State security or that there are special grounds justifying his release, it shall quash the incarceration order.

(d) A decision of the District Court under this section is subject to appeal within thirty days to the Supreme Court, a single judge of which shall hear the appeal; the Supreme Court shall have all the powers vested in the District Court under this Law.

(e) It shall be permissible to depart from the laws of evidence in proceedings under this Law, for reasons to be recorded; the court may admit evidence, even in the absence of the prisoner or his legal representative, or not disclose such evidence to the aforesaid if, after having reviewed the evidence or heard the submissions, even in the absence of the prisoner or his legal representative, it is convinced that disclosure of the evidence to the prisoner or his legal representative is likely to harm State security or public security; this provision shall not derogate from any right not to give evidence under Chapter Three of the Evidence Ordinance [New Version], 5731-1971[1].

(f) The hearing in proceedings under this Law shall be conducted in camera, unless the court has provided otherwise in this matter.

RIGHT OF PRISONER TO MEET WITH LAWYER

6. (a) The prisoner may meet with a lawyer at the earliest possible date on which such a meeting may be held without harming State security requirements, but no later than seven days prior to his being brought before a judge of the District Court, in accordance with the provisions of section 5(a).

(b) The Minister of Justice may, by order, confine the right of representation in the proceedings under this Law to a person authorized to act as defence counsel in the military courts under an unrestricted authorization, pursuant to the provisions of section 318(c) of the Military Justice Law, 5715- 1955[2].

PRESUMPTION

7. For the purposes of this Law, a person who is a member of a force perpetrating hostile acts against the State of Israel or who has participated in hostile acts of such a force, either directly or indirectly, shall be deemed to be a person whose release would

harm State security as long as the hostile acts of such force against the State of Israel have not yet ceased, unless proved otherwise.

DETERMINATION REGARDING HOSTILE ACTS

8. A determination of the Minister of Defense, by a certificate under his hand, that a particular force is perpetrating hostile acts against the State of Israel or that hostile acts of such force against the State of Israel have ceased or have not yet ceased, shall serve as proof in any legal proceedings, unless proved otherwise.

CRIMINAL PROCEEDINGS

9. (a) Criminal proceedings may be initiated against an unlawful combatant under the provisions of any law.

(b) The Chief of General Staff may make an order for the detention of an unlawful combatant under section 3, even if criminal proceedings have been initiated against him under the provisions of any law.

CONDITIONS OF INCARCERATION

10. (a) A prisoner shall be held under proper conditions which shall not impair his health or dignity.

(b) The conditions for incarceration of prisoners shall be prescribed by the Minister of Defense by regulations.

VESTING OF POWERS

11. The Chief of General Staff may delegate his powers under this Law to any officer of the rank of major-general, as he shall determine.

TRANSITIONAL PROVISIONS

12. (a) The provisions of this Law shall also apply to an unlawful combatant held by the State authorities on the day of its commencement.

(b) As long as regulations are not enacted pursuant to section 10(b), the Emergency Powers (Detention) (Conditions of Internment under Administrative Detention) Regulations, 5741-19814 shall apply to the incarceration of prisoners.

IMPLEMENTATION AND REGULATIONS

13. (a) The Minister of Defense is charged with the implementation of this Law.

(b) The Minister of Justice may enact rules of court for proceedings pursuant to this Law.

BIBLIOGRAPHY

For the reader's convenience, the abbreviation of much-used references used in the text of the book is cited in square brackets following the full bibliographic reference.

INTERNATIONAL LEGAL INSTRUMENTS

Treaties[1697]

International treaties

- Declaration respecting Maritime Law, Paris, 16 April 1856
- Convention for the Amelioration of the Condition of the Wounded in Armies in the Field, Geneva, 22 August 1864 [GC (1864)]
- Declaration Renouncing the Use, in Time of War, of Explosive Projectiles under 400 Grammes of Weight, Saint-Petersburg, 29 November - 11 December 1868 [St-Petersburg Declaration]
- Convention (II) with Respect to the Laws and Customs of War on Land, and its annex: Regulations Concerning the Laws and Customs of War on Land, The Hague, 29 July 1899 [Hague Regulations (1899)] [HR 1899]
- Convention (IV) respecting the Laws and Customs of Wars on Land, and its annex: Regulations concerning the Laws and Customs of War on Land, The Hague, 18 October 1907 [Hague Regulations (1907)] [HR 1907]
- Convention (V) respecting the Rights and Duties of Neutral Powers and Persons in Case of War on Land, The Hague, 18 October 1907 [HC V (1907)]
- Convention (XI) relative to Certain Restrictions with Regard to the Exercise of the Right of Capture in Naval War, The Hague, 18 October 1907 [HC XI (1907)]
- Convention (XIII) Concerning the Rights and Duties of Neutral Powers in Naval War, The Hague, 18 October 1907 [HC XIII (1907)]
- Convention relative to the Treatment of Prisoners of War, Geneva, 27 July 1929 [GC 1929]
- Agreement for the Prosecution and Punishment of the Major War Criminals of the European Axis, and Charter of the International Military Tribunal, London, 8 August 1945 [IMT Charter]
- Charter of the United Nations, San Francisco, 26 June 1945 [UN Charter]
- Statute of the International Court of Justice, annexed to the UN Charter, San Fransisco, 26 June 1945 [ICJ Statute]

[1697] The text and the status of ratification, accession, reservations, declarations and derogations for all treaties adopted under the auspices of the United Nations are available at http://treaties.un.org/pages/ParticipationStatus.aspx. The text and the status of ratification, accession, reservations, declarations and derogations for most of the other treaties are availabalbe at http://www.icrc.org/ihl.

- Convention on the Prevention and Punishment of the Crime of Genocide, Paris, 9 December 1948 [Genocide Convention]
- Geneva Convention (I) for the Amelioration of the Condition of the Wounded and Sick in Armed Forces in the Field, Geneva, 12 August 1949 [First Geneva Convention] [GC I]
- Geneva Convention (II) for the Amelioration of the Condition of the Wounded, Sick and Shipwrecked Members of Armed Forces at Sea, Geneva, 12 August 1949 [Second Geneva Convention] [GC II]
- Geneva Convention (III) relative to the Treatment of Prisoners of War, Geneva, 12 August 1949 [Third Geneva Convention] [GC III]
- Geneva Convention (IV) relative to the Protection of Civilian Persons in Time of War, Geneva, 12 August 1949 [Fourth Geneva Convention] [GC IV]
- Convention Relating to the Status of Refugees, Geneva, 28 July 1951 [UN Refugee Convention]
- Convention for the Protection of Cultural Property in the Event of Armed Conflict, The Hague, 14 May 1954
- Vienna Convention on Diplomatic Relations, Vienna, 18 April 1961
- International Covenant on Civil and Political Rights, New York, 16 December 1966 [ICCPR]
- International Covenant on Economic, Social and Cultural Rights, New York, 16 December 1966 [ICESCR]
- Protocol Relating to the Status of Refugees, New York, 31 January 1967
- Vienna Convention on the Law of Treaties, Vienna, 23 May 1969 [VCLT]
- Convention on the Non-Applicability of Statutory Limitations to War Crimes and Crimes against Humanity, New York, 26 November 1968
- Protocol Additional to the Geneva Conventions of 12 August 1949, and Relating to the Protection of Victims of International Armed Conflicts (Protocol I), Geneva, 8 June 1977 [Additional Protocol I] [AP I]
- Protocol Additional to the Geneva Conventions of 12 August 1949, and Relating to the Protection of Victims of Non-International Armed Conflicts (Protocol II), Geneva, 8 June 1977 [Additional Protocol II] [AP II]
- International Convention against the Taking of Hostages, New York, 17 December 1979 [Hostages Convention]
- Convention on Prohibitions or Restrictions on the Use of Certain Conventional Weapons which May Be Deemed to be Excessively Injurious or to Have Indiscriminate Effects, Geneva, 10 October 1980, as amended by the Final Declaration of the Second Review Conference of the States Parties, Geneva, 21 December 2001
- United Nations Convention on the Law of the Sea, Montego Bay, 10 December 1982 [UNCLOS]
- Convention against Torture and Other Cruel, Inhumane or Degrading Treatment or Punishment, New York, 10 December 1984 [CAT]
- Convention on the Rights of the Child, New York, 20 November 1989 [CRC]
- International Convention against the Recruitment, Use, Financing and Training of Mercenaries, New York, 4 December 1989 [Mercenaries Convention]

- Second Optional Protocol to the International Covenant on Civil and Political Rights, Aiming at the Abolition of the Death Penalty, New York, 15 December 1989 [ICCPR-OP2]
- Convention on the Prohibition of the Development, Production, Stockpiling and Use of Chemical Weapons and on their Destruction, Paris, 13 January 1993
- Rome Statute of the International Criminal Court, Rome, 17 July 1998 [ICC Statute][1698]
- Optional Protocol to the Convention on the Rights of the Child on the Involvement of Children in Armed Conflict, New York, 25 May 2000 [CRC-OP]
- International Convention for the Protection of all Persons from Enforced Disappearance, New York, 20 December 2006 [Enforced Disappearance Convention]

Regional treaties

- Statute of the Council of Europe, London, 5 May 1949
- Convention for the Protection of Human Rights and Fundamental Freedoms (as amended), Rome, 4 November 1950 [European Convention on Human Rights] [ECHR]
- Protocol No. 4 to the Convention for the Protection of Human Rights and Fundamental Freedoms Securing Certain Rights and Freedoms Other than those already Included in the Convention and in the First Protocol thereto, Strasbourg, 16 September 1963 [Protocol 4 ECHR]
- Convention Governing the Specific Aspects of Refugee Problems in Africa, Addis Ababa, 10 September 1969 [OAU Refugee Convention]
- American Convention on Human Rights, San José, 22 November 1969 [American Convention on Human Rights] [ACHR]
- Convention for the Elimination of Mercenarism in Africa, Libreville, 3 July 1977 [OAU Mercenarism Convention (1977)]
- African Charter on Human and Peoples' Rights, Banjul, 27 June 1981 [ACHPR]

Inter-American Convention to Prevent and Punish Torture, Cartagena de Indias, 9 December 1985
- European Convention for the Prevention of Torture and Inhumane or Degrading Treatment or Punishment, Strasbourg, 26 November 1987 [ECPT]
- Inter-American Convention on Forced Disappearances of Persons, Belem do Para, 9 June 1994
- Arab Charter on Human Rights (original), adopted by the League of Arab States, 15 September 1994
- Commonwealth of Independent States (CIS) Convention on Human Rights and Fundamental Freedoms, Minsk, 26 May 1995 [CIS Convention]
- Protocol No. 13 to the Convention for the Protection of Human Rights and Fundamental Freedoms Concerning the Abolition of the Death Penalty in all Circumstances, Vilnius, 3 May 2002 [Protocol 13 ECHR]
- Arab Charter on Human Rights (revised), adopted by the League of Arab States, Tunis, 22 May 2004 [Arab Charter]
- Charter of the Association of Southeast Asian Nations, Singapore, 20 November 2007, available at http://www.aseansec.org/publications/ASEAN-Charter.pdf [ASEAN Charter]

[1698] The list of State parties to the ICC is available at http://www.icc-cpi.int/Menus/ASP/states+parties/.

Other international legal instruments

International instruments

- Project of an International Declaration Concerning the Laws and Customs of War, Brussels, 27 August 1874 [Brussels Declaration]
- Affirmation of the Principles of International Law Recognized by the Charter of the Nürmberg Tribunal, United Nations General Assembly Resolution 95 (I), 11 December 1946
- Universal Declaration of Human Rights, UN General Assembly Resolution 217A (III), 10 December 1948 [UDHR]
- Standard Minimum Rules for the Treatment of Prisoners, adopted by the First United Nations Congress on the Prevention of Crime and the Treatment of Offenders, Geneva, 30 August 1955 [*Standard Minimum Rules*]
- Declaration on the Granting of Independence to Colonial Countries and Peoples, UN General Assembly Resolution 1514 (XV), 14 December 1960
- Human Rights in Armed Conflict, Resolution 23, adopted by the International Conference on Human Rights, Tehran, 12 May 1968
- Declaration on Principles of International Law concerning Friendly Relations and Cooperation among States in Accordance with the Charter of the United Nations, UN General Assembly Resolution 2625, 24 October 1970 [UNGA, *Friendly Relations Declaration*]
- Basic Principles of the Legal Status of the Combatants Struggling against Colonial and Alien Domination and Racist Regimes, UN General Assembly Resolution 3103 (XXVIII), 12 December 1973
- Code of Conduct for Law Enforcement Officials, UN General Assembly Resolution 34/169, 17 December 1979 [UN Code of Conduct]
- Declaration on the Human Rights of Individuals who Are not Nationals of the Country in which they Live, UN General Assembly Resolution 40/144, 13 December 1985
- Body of Principles for the Protection of all Persons under any Form of Detention or Imprisonment, UN General Assembly Resolution 43/173, 9 December 1988 [UN, *Body of Principles*]
- Standard Minimum Rules for Non-Custodial Measures ("Tokyo Rules"), UN General Assembly Resolution 45/110, 14 December 1990
- Statute of the International Criminal Tribunal for the Prosecution of Persons Responsible for Serious Violations of International Humanitarian Law Committed in the Territory of the Former Yugoslavia since 1991, annexed to Security Council Resolution 827, 25 May 1993 [ICTY Statute]
- Statute of the International Criminal Tribunal for the Prosecution of Persons Responsible for Genocide and Other Serious Violations of International Humanitarian Law Committed in the Territory of Rwanda and by Rwandan Citizens Responsible for Genocide and Other such Violations Committed in the Territory of Neighbouring States, between 1 January 1994 and 31 December 1994, annexed to Security Council Resolution 955, 6 November 1994 [ICTR Statute]
- General Framework Agreement for Peace in Bosnia-Herzegovina, initialled in Dayton on 21 November 1995 and signed in Paris on 14 December 1995, published in *International Legal Materials*, Vol. 35, 1996, pp. 89-169

- Statute of the Special Court for Sierra Leone, annexed to Security Council Resolution 1315, 14 August 2000 [SCSL Statute]
- Elements of Crime, adopted by the Assembly of State Parties to the International Criminal Court, New York, 3-10 September 2002 [ICC, *Elements of Crime*]
- Resolution RC/Res.6 of 11 June 2010, adopted at the 13th plenary meeting of the Review Conference of the Rome Statute, Kampala, 31 May - 11 June 2010

Regional instruments

- American Declaration of the Rights and Duties of Man, adopted by the Organization of American States, Bogotá, 2 May 1948 [ADRDM]
- Final Act of the Conference on Security and Cooperation in Europe, adopted by the Organization for Security and Cooperation in Europe, Helsinki, 1 August 1975 [OSCE, *Final Act* (1975)]
- Cartagena Declaration on Refugees, adopted by the Colloquium on the International Protection of Refugees in Central America, Mexico and Panama held in Cartagena, 22 November 1984 [Cartagena Declaration on Refugees]
- Cairo Declaration on Human Rights in Islam, adopted by the Organization of the Islamic Conference, Cairo, 5 August 1990 [Cairo Declaration]

UNITED NATIONS DOCUMENTS[1699]

Security Council[1700]

- Resolution 83, Complaint of Aggression upon the Republic of Korea, 27 June 1950
- Resolution 84, Complaint of Aggression upon the Republic of Korea, 7 July 1950
- Resolution 237, *Situation in the Middle East*, 14 June 1967
- Resolution 598, *Iraq-Islamic Republic of Iran*, 20 July 1987
- Resolution 667, *Iraq-Kuwait*, 16 September 1990
- Resolution 678, *Iraq-Kuwait*, 29 November 1990
- Resolution 1244, *Situation Relating to Kosovo*, 10 June 1999
- Resolution 1264, *Situation in East Timor*, 15 September 1999
- Resolution 1272, *Situation in East Timor*, 25 October 1999
- Resolution 1368, Threats to International Peace and Security Caused by Terrorist Acts, 12 September 2001
- Resolution 1373, Threats to International Peace and Security Caused by Terrorist Acts, 28 September 2001
- Resolution 1417, The Situation in the Democratic Republic of the Congo, 14 June 2002
- Resolution 1483, *Situation in Iraq*, 22 May 2003
- Resolution 1546, *Situation in Iraq*, 8 June 2004
- Statement by the President of the Security Council, 26 June 2010, UN Doc. S/PRST/2010/11

1699 United Nations documents are available at http://www.un.org/en/documents/.

1700 Security Council resolutions are available at http://www.un.org/Docs/sc/unsc_resolutions.html.

General Assembly[1701]

- Resolution 610 (VII), Korea: Reports of the United Nations Commission for the Unification and Rehabilitation of Korea, 3 December 1952
- Resolution 2105 (XX), Implementation of the Declaration on the Granting of Independence to Colonial Countries and Peoples, 20 December 1965
- Resolution 2229 (XXI), *Question of Ifni and Spanish Sahara*, 20 December 1966
- Resolution 2444 (XXIII), *Respect for Human Rights in Armed Conflicts*, 19 December 1968
- Resolution 2621 (XXV), Programme of Action for the Full Implementation of the Declaration on the Granting of Independence to Colonial Countries and Peoples, 12 October 1970
- Resolution 2675 (XXV), Basic Principles for the Protection of Civilian Populations in Armed Conflicts, 9 December 1970
- Resolution 58/163, Right of the Palestinian People to Self-Determination, 22 December 2003
- Resolution ES-10/14, Illegal Israeli Actions in Occupied East Jerusalem and the Rest of the Occupied Palestinian Territory, 12 December 2003 (Emergency Session)
- Resolution 60/1, *World Summit Outcome*, 16 September 2005
- Resolutions 62/149, Moratorium on the Use of the Death Penalty, 18 December 2007
- Resolution 63/168, Moratorium on the Use of the Death Penalty, 18 December 2008

Secretary-General

- Observance by United Nations Forces of International Humanitarian Law, Secretary-General's Bulletin, 6 August 1999, UN Doc. ST/SGB/1999/13 [UNSG, IHL Bulletin]
- Situation of Human Rights in the Democratic Republic of the Congo: Note by the Secretary-General, 29 September 2002, UN Doc. A/57/437
- The Rule of Law and Transitional Justice in Conflict and Post-Conflict Societies: Report of the Secretary-General, 23 August 2004, UN Doc. S/2004/616 [UNSG, *Rule of Law Report* (2004)]
- Capital Punishment and Implementation of the Safeguards Guaranteeing Protection of the Rights of those Facing the Death Penalty: Report of the Secretary General, 18 December 2009, UN Doc. E/2010/10 [UNSG, *Death Penalty Report* (2009)]

Commission on Human Rights (UNCHR) and Human Rights Council (UNHRCouncil)[1702]

Resolutions

- Resolution 1991/42, *Question of Arbitrary Detention*, 5 March 1991, UN doc. E/CN.4/1991/22
- Resolution 1994/32, *Question of Arbitrary Detention*, 4 March 1994, UN Doc. E/CN.4/RES/1994/32
- Resolution 1997/50, *Question of Arbitrary Detention*, 15 April 1997, UN Doc. E/CN.4/RES/1997/50

[1701] General Assembly resolutions are available at http://www.un.org/documents/resga.htm.

[1702] The Commission on Human Right's resolutions concerning arbitrary detention are available at http://ap.ohchr.org/documents/dpage_e.aspx?m=117; all Human Rights Council documents are available at http://www2.ohchr.org/english/bodies/hrcouncil/. All other documents are available at http://documents.un.org/.

Sub-Commission reports and documents

- Sub-Commission on Prevention of Discrimination and Protection of Minorities, Siracusa Principles on the Limitation and Derogation of Provisions in the International Covenant on Civil and Political Rights, 28 September 1984, UN Doc. E/CN.4/1984/4 [Siracusa Principles (1984)]
- Sub-Commission on Prevention of Discrimination and Protection of Minorities, Report on the Practice of Administrative Detention, by Louis Joinet, 1990, UN Doc. E/CN.4/Sub.2/1990/29
- Sub-Commission on the Promotion and Protection of Human Rights, Working Paper on the Relationship between Human Rights Law and International Humanitarian Law, by Françoise Hampson and Ibrahim Salama, 21 June 2005, UN Doc. E/CN.4/Sub.2/2005/14 [Hampson & Salama (Subcommission on Human Rights 2005)]

Special Rapporteurs

- Special Rapporteur for El Salvador (Mr. José Antonio Pastor Ridruejo), *Final Report on the Situation of Human Rights in El Salvador* (1985), 1 February 1985, UN Doc. E/CN.4/1985/18
- Special Rapporteur on Human Rights and States of Emergency (Mr. Leandro Despouy), *Final Report*, 9 June 1997, UN Doc. E/CN.4/Sub.2/1997/19/Add. 1
- Special Rapporteur on Terrorism and Human Rights (Ms. Kalliopi K. Koufa), *Final Report*, 25 June 2004, UN Doc. E/CN.4/Sub.2/2004/40
- Special Rapporteur on Extrajudicial, Summary or Arbitrary Executions (Mr. Philip Alston), *Mission to Sri Lanka (28 November to 6 December 2005)*, 27 March 2006, UN Doc. E/CN.4/2006/53/Add.5
- Special Rapporteur on Extrajudicial, Summary or Arbitrary Executions (Mr. Philip Alston), Special Rapporteur on the Right of Everyone to the Enjoyment of the Highest Attainable Standard of Physical and Mental Health (Mr. Paul Hunt), Representative of the Secretary-General on Human Rights of Internally Displaced Persons (Mr. Walter Kälin), and Special Rapporteur on Adequate Housing as a Component of the Right to an Adequate Standard of Living (Mr. Miloon Kothari), *Mission to Lebanon (7-14 September 2006)*, 2 October 2006, UN Doc. A/HRC/2/7
- Special Rapporteur on the Promotion and Protection of Human Rights and Fundamental Freedoms while Countering Terrorism (Mr. Martin Scheinin), *Compilation of Good Practices on Legal and Institutional Frameworks and Measures that Ensure Respect for Human Rights by Intelligence Agencies while Countering Terrorism, including on their Oversight*, 10 May 2010, UN Doc. A/HRC/14/46 [HRCouncil, Special Rapporteur on Counterterrorism, *Good Practices Intelligence Agencies*]
- Special Rapporteur on Extrajudicial, Summary or Arbitrary Executions (Mr. Philip Alston), *Study on Targeted Killings*, 28 May 2010, UN Doc. A/HRC/14/24/Add.6 [HRCouncil, Special Rapporteur on Counterterrorism, *Targeted Killings*]

International Law Commission (ILC)[1703]

- Principles of International Law Recognized in the Charter of the Nürnberg Tribunal and in the Judgment of the Tribunal, adopted by the ILC at its 2nd session (1950), *ILC Report*, A/1316 (A/5/12), 1950, part III, §§ 95-127
- State Responsibility, Eighth Report of the Special Rapporteur (Mr. Roberto Ago), adopted by the ILC at its 31st session (1979), *ILC Report*, A/34/10, (F), 1979, chapter III(A)(4), §69 [*Eighth Report of the Special Rapporteur on State Responsibility*]
- Draft Code of Crimes against the Peace and Security of Mankind, adopted by the ILC at its 48th session (1996), UN Doc. A/CN.4/L.532 [ILC, *Draft Code of International Crimes*]
- Articles on Responsibility of States for Internationally Wrongful Acts, adopted by the ILC at its 53rd session (2001), UN Doc. A/56/10 [ILC, *Articles on State Responsibility*]
- Conclusion of the Work of the Study Group on the Fragmentation of International Law: Difficulties Arising from the Diversification and Expansion of International Law, adopted by the ILC at its 58th session (2006), UN Doc. A/CN.4/L.682/Add.1 [ILC, *Fragmentation*]
- Draft Articles on Diplomatic Protection, adopted by the ILC at its 58th session (2006), UN Doc. A/61/10 [ILC, *Draft Articles on Diplomatic Protection*]
- Effects of Armed Conflicts on Treaties, adopted by the ILC at its 60th session (2008), *ILC Report* (2008), chapter V, UN Doc. Supp. 10 (A/63/10) [ILC, *Draft Articles on Effects of Armed Conflicts on Treaties*]
- Draft Articles on the Responsibility of International Organizations, adopted by the ILC at its 61st session (2009), UN Doc. A/64/10 [ILC, *Draft Articles on the Responsibility of International Organizations*]

United Nations High Commissioner for Refugees (UNHCR)

Executive Committee[1704]

- Conclusion No. 7 (XXVIII), *Expulsion*, 12 October 1977
- Conclusion No. 44 (XXXVII), *Detention of Refugees and Asylum-Seekers*, 13 October 1986
- Conclusion No. 85 (XLIX), *Conclusion on International Protection*, 9 October 1998
- Detention of Asylum-Seekers and Refugees: The Framework, the Problem and Recommended Practice, Decision of 4 June 1999
- Conclusion No. 107 (LVIII), *Children at Risk*, 5 October 2007

High Commissioner

- Revised Guidelines on Applicable Criteria and Standards Relating to the Detention of Asylum-Seekers, 26 February 1999, available at

[1703] The work of the International Law Commission is available at http://www.un.org/law/ilc/index.htm.

[1704] The UNHCR's Executive Committee's conclusions are compiled in UNHCR, *Compilation of Conclusions Adopted by the Executive Committee on the International Protection of Refugees: 1975-2004 (Conclusion No. 1-101)*, Geneva, UNHCR, 2005, available at http://www.unhcr.org/41b041534.html. The decision on detention of asylum-seekers and refugees is available at http://www.unhcr.org/cgi-bin/texis/vtx/search

http://www.unhcr.org/refworld/docid/3c2b3f844.html [UNHCR, *Detention of Asylum-Seekers*]

Office of the United Nations High Commissioner for Human Rights (OHCHR)

- Human Rights in the Administration of Justice: A Manual on Human Rights for Judges, Prosecutors and Lawyers, 2003, available at http://www.ohchr.org/Documents/Publications/training9Titleen.pdf [OHCHR, *Manual* (2003)]
- Brief of *Amicus Curiae* in Support of Petitioners before the United States Supreme Court in *Boumediene et al. v. Bush* and *al-Odah et al v. USA*, 24 August 2007, available at http://www.mayerbrown.com/public_docs/probono_Amicus_Brief_UNHCHR.pdf [OHCHR, *Boumediene & al-Odah Brief*]

Other UN documents

- Commission for Historical Clarification, *Guatemala: Memory of Silence*, Executive summary, conclusions and recommendations of the Commission annexed to UN Doc. A/53/928, 27 April 1999
- United Nations Assistance Mission in Afghanistan (UNAMA), Arbitrary Detention in Afghanistan: A Call For Action, Vol. II, A Practical Guide to Understanding and Combating Arbitrary Detention Practices in Afghanistan, January 2009, available at http://www.unhcr.org/refworld/docid/49d07fc42.html
- United Nations Office on Drugs and Crime (UNODC), *Digest of Terrorist Cases*, January 2010, available at http://www.unodc.org/documents/terrorism/09-86635_Ebook_English.pdf [UNODC, *Digest* (2010)]

INTERNATIONAL MOVEMENT OF THE RED CROSS AND RED CRESCENT DOCUMENTS

Documents, minutes and reports from diplomatic conferences

- Report on the Work of the Conference of Government Experts for the Study of the Conventions for the Protection of War Victims, Geneva, International Committee of the Red Cross (ICRC), 1947 [*Report on the Conference of Government Experts 1947*]
- Final Record of the Diplomatic Conference of Geneva of 1949, Bern, Federal Political Department, 1951, 4 vols. [*Final Record 1949*] [*FR 1949*]
- Report submitted by the International Committee of the Red Cross to the Conference of Government Experts on the Reaffirmation and Development of International Humanitarian Law Applicable in Armed Conflicts, Geneva, 24 May 12 June 1971, Geneva, ICRC, January 1971, 7 vols. [*Report for the Conference of Government Experts 1971*]
- Report on the Work of the Conference of Government Experts on the Reaffirmation and Development of International Humanitarian Law Applicable in Armed Conflict, Geneva, ICRC, 1972, 2 vols. [*Report on the Conference of Government Experts 1972*]
- Official Records of the Diplomatic Conference on the Reaffirmation and Development of International Humanitarian Law Applicable in Armed Conflicts, Geneva (1974-1977), Bern, Federal Political Department, 1978 [*Official Records 1974-1977*] [*OR 1974-1977*]

Documents of the International Conference of the Red Cross and Red Crescent

- Resolution (XIV), *Civil War*, adopted by the International Conference at its 10th session in Geneva, 1921, reprinted in: *Handbook of the International Red Cross and Red Crescent Movement*, 14th ed., Geneva, ICRC and International Federation of Red Cross and Red Crescent Societies (IFRCS), 2008, pp. 1139-1141
- Draft International Convention on the Condition and Protection of Civilians of Enemy Nationality who are on Territory Belonging to or Occupied by a Belligerent, approved by the 15th International Conference in Tokyo, 1934, availble at http://www.icrc.org/ihl.nsf/FULL/320?OpenDocument [Draft Tokyo Convention (1934)]
- Resolution (XIV), *Role and Activity of the Red Cross in Time of Civil War*, adopted by the International Conference at its 16th session in London, 1938, reprinted in: *Handbook of the International Red Cross and Red Crescent Movement*, 14th ed., Geneva, ICRC and IFRCS, 2008, pp. 1141-1142
- Draft International Conventions for the Protection of War Victims, approved by the 17th International Conference in Stockholm, 1948, reprinted in: *Final Record of the Diplomatic Conference of Geneva of 1949*, Bern, Federal Political Department, 1951, pp. 45-143
- Statutes of the International Red Cross and Red Crescent Movement, adopted by the 25th International Conference in Geneva, 1986 (amended in 1995 and 2006), available at http://www.icrc.org/Web/eng/siteeng0.nsf/htmlall/statutes-movement-220506/$File/Statutes-EN-A5.pdf [Statutes of the International Red Cross Movement]

Documents from the International Committee of the Red Cross (ICRC)

Reports of activities

- Rapport général du Comité International de la Croix-Rouge sur son activité de 1912 à 1920, Geneva, ICRC, 1921
- Rapport du Comité International de la Croix-Rouge sur son activité pendant la Seconde Guerre mondiale (1er septembre 1939 - 30 juin 1947), Geneva, ICRC, 1948
- Rapport d'activités extérieures, *International Review of the Red Cross*, Vol. 38, No. 586, 1967, pp. 461-465
- Annual Report 1988, Geneva, ICRC, 1989
- Annual Report 1989, Geneva, ICRC, 1990
- Annual Report 1990, Geneva, ICRC, 1991
- Annual Report 1991, Geneva, ICRC, 1992
- Annual Report 2006, Geneva, ICRC, 2007
- Annual Report 2007, Geneva, ICRC, 2008
- Operational Update, 26 October 2009, available at http://www.icrc.org/Web/Eng/siteeng0.nsf/html/united-states-detention

Other ICRC documents

- Model Agreement Relating to the Retention of Medical Personnel and Chaplains, *International Review of the Red Cross*, Vol. 26, No. 433, 1955, pp. 7-21 [ICRC, *Model Agreement (Retention)*]
- Model Agreement Relating to the Relief of Medical and Personnel and Chaplains, *International Review of the Red Cross*, Vol. 26, No. 433, 1955, pp. 22-31 [ICRC, *Model Agreement (Relief)*]

- "Protection through Complementarity of the Law", address by Dr. Jakob Kellenberger, President of the ICRC at the 27th Annual Round Table on Current Problems of International Humanitarian Law, entitled "International Humanitarian Law and Other Legal Regimes: Interplay in Situations of Violence" and organized by the International Institute of Humanitarian Law in co-operation with the ICRC, San Remo, 4-6 September 2003, available at http://www.icrc.org/web/eng/siteeng0.nsf/html/5RFGAZ
- International Humanitarian Law and the Challenges of Contemporary Armed Conflicts, report prepared for the 28th International Conference of Red Cross and Red Crescent, December 2003, available at http://www.cicr.org/Web/eng/siteeng0.nsf/htmlall/5XRDCC/$File/IHLcontemp_armedconflicts_FINAL_ANG.pdf [ICRC, *International Humanitarian Law and the Challenges of Contemporary Armed Conflicts* (2003)]
- "Relevance of IHL in the War on Terror", official statement of 21 July 2005, available at http://www.icrc.org/web/eng/siteeng0.nsf/html/tWrighterrorism-ihl-210705?OpenDocument
- "Current Challenges to the Law of Occupation", speech delivered by Prof. Daniel Thürer, Member of the ICRC, 6th Bruges Colloquium, 20-21 October 2005, reprinted in: College of Europe, *Collegium*, No. 34, Autumn 2006, pp. 9-25, and available at http://www.icrc.org/web/eng/siteeng0.nsf/html/occupation-statement-211105 [ICRC, *Current Challenges to the Law of Occupation* (2005)]
- International Humanitarian Law and the Challenges of Contemporary Armed Conflicts, background document prepared for the 30th International Conference of the Red Cross and the Red Crescent, November 2007, available at http://www.icrc.org/Web/eng/siteeng0.nsf/htmlall/ihl-30-international-conference-101207/$File/IHL-challenges-30th-International-Conference-ENG.pdf [ICRC, *International Humanitarian Law and the Challenges of Contemporary Armed Conflicts* (2007)]
- How is the Term "Armed Conflict" Defined in International Humanitarian Law?, opinion paper, March 2008, available at http://www.icrc.org/web/eng/siteeng0.nsf/htmlall/armed-conflict-article-170308/$file/Opinion-paper-armed-conflict.pdf [ICRC, *Opinion Paper* (2008)]
- Interpretative Guidance on the Notion of Direct Participation in Hostilities under International Humanitarian Law, 26 February 2009, available at http://www.icrc.org/Web/eng/siteeng0.nsf/htmlall/review-872-p991/$File/irrc-872-reports-documents.pdf [ICRC, *Interpretative Guidance*] [ICRC, *IGDPH* (2009)]
- "Strengthening Legal Protection of Victims of Armed Conflicts", speech delivered by Dr. Jakob Kellenberger, President of the ICRC, 21 September 2010, available at http://www.icrc.org/web/eng/siteeng0.nsf/htmlall/ihl-development-statement-210910

DOCUMENTS FROM REGIONAL ORGANIZATIONS

Council of Europe (CoE)

- Preparatory Work on Article 5 of the European Convention on Human Rights, European Commission of Human Rights, 8 August 1956, available at http://echr.coe.int/NR/rdonlyres/F49018BA-57B7-4A4B-9E31-0E0876966E30/0/ECHRTravauxART5DH5610EN1674958.pdf
- Human Rights Handbook No. 5: The Right to Liberty and Security of the Person. A Guide to the Implementation of Article 5 of the European Convention on Human Rights, Strasbourg, Directorate General of Human Rights of the Council of Europe, 2002 [CoE, *HRH No. 5* (2002)]

- Opinion on the Possible Need for Further Development of the Geneva Conventions, adopted by the European Commission for Democracy through Law (Venice Commission), at its 57th plenary session, held in Venice on 12 and 13 December 2003, available at www.venice.coe.int/docs/2003/CDL-AD(2003)018-e.asp [CoE, *Venice Commission Opinion* (2003)]
- Resolution 1707: Detention of Asylum Seekers and Irregular Migrants in Europe, Parliamentary Assembly, 28 January 2010, available at http://assembly.coe.int/Mainf.asp?link=/Documents/AdoptedText/ta10/ERES1707.htm
- "EU Accession to the European Convention on Human Rights", statement on the Council of Europe's website, updated September 2010, available at http://www.coe.int/t/dc/files/themes/eu_and_coe/default_EN.asp

European Union (EU)

- European Union Guidelines on Promoting Compliance with International Humanitarian Law (IHL), 2005/C 327/04, *Official Journal of the European Union*, 23 December 2005 [EU, *Guidelines on Promoting Compliance with IHL* (2005)]

Organization for Security and Cooperation in Europe (OSCE)

- Resolution on a Moratorium on the Death Penalty and towards its Abolition, Parliamentary Assembly, 3 July 2009, available at http://www.osce.org/documents/odihr/2009/10/40003_en.pdf

North Atlantic Treaty Organization (NATO)

- NATO Standardization Agency (NSA), *AJP-3 (2007): Allied Joint Operations*, 2007 (so far no unclassified version is publicly available) [NATO, *AJP-3* (2007)]
- NATO Standardization Agency (NSA), *AAP-6 (2010): NATO Glossary of Terms and Definitions (English and French)*, 2010, available at http://www.nato.int/docu/stanag/aap006/aap-6-2010.pdf [NATO, *AAP-6* (2010)]

Organization of American States (OAS)

- Principles and Best Practices on the Protection of Persons Deprived of Liberty in the Americas, Inter-American Commission on Human Rights, March 2008, available at http://www.cidh.org/basicos/English/Basic21.a.Principles%20and%20Best%20Practices%20PDL.htm [IAC°HR, Principles and Best Practices (2008)]

Organization of African Unity (OAU) and African Union (AU)

- Principles and Guidelines on the Right to a Fair Trial and to Legal Assistance in Africa, African Commission on Human and Peoples' Rights, 2001, available at http://www.afrimap.org/english/images/treaty/ACHPR_Principles&Guidelines_FairTrial.pdf [AC°HPR, Principles on Fair Trial and Legal Assistance (2001)]
- Policy Framework for the Establishment of the African Standby Force and the Military Staff Committee, adopted by the Third Meeting of African Chiefs of Defense Staff, Addis Abeba, 15-16 May 2003, available at http://www.africa-union.org/root/au/AUC/Departments/PSC/Asf/Documents.htm
- Resolution Calling on State Parties to the African Charter on Human and Peoples' Rights to Observe the Moratorium on the Death Penalty, African Commission on Human and People's Rights, 24 November 2008, available at http://www.achpr.org/english/resolutions/resolution136_en.htm

NATIONAL LEGISLATION, MILITARY MANUALS AND OTHER OFFICIAL DOCUMENTS

National legislation

Canada, *National Defence Act*, R.S.C. 1985, c. N-5, available at http://laws.justice.gc.ca/en/ShowFullDoc/cs/N-5//20081017/en?co...h_domain=cs&showall=L&statuteyear=all&lengthannual=50&length=50

__, *Geneva Conventions Act*, R.S., 1985, c. G-3, as amended in 2008, available at http://laws.justice.gc.ca/en/ShowFullDoc/cs/G-3//20080718/en?co...h_domain=cs&showall=L&statuteyear=all&lengthannual=50&length=50

__, *Regulations respecting the Determination of the Entitlement of Persons Detained by the Canadian Forces to Prisoner-of-War Status*, 25 January 1991, SOR/91-134, available at http://www.canlii.org/en/ca/laws/regu/sor-91-134/latest/sor-91-134.html

Colombia, *Ley N° 599, Código Penal*, 24 July 2000, available at http://www.unhcr.org/refworld/docid/3dbd1fd94.html [Colombia, *Código Penal* (2000)]

France, *Code pénal (version consolidée au 13 octobre 2010)*, available at http://www.legifrance.gouv.fr/affichCode.do?cidTexte=LEGITEXT000006070719&dateTexte=20101024

Guinea, *Loi organique L/1991/016 du 23 décembre 1991 relative à l'état d'urgence et à l'état de siège*, available at http://www.unhcr.org/refworld/docid/3ae6b524c.html

__, *Loi fondamentale*, 1 March 1992, available at http://www.unhcr.org/refworld/docid/3ae6b5738.html

India, *Constitution*, 6 November 1949, as amended and modified up to 1 December 2007, available at http://lawmin.nic.in/coi/coiason29july08.pdf

__, *The Armed Forces (Special Powers) Act*, Act No. 28 of 1958, 11 September 1958, available at http://www.satp.org/satporgtp/countries/india/document/actandordinances/armed_forces_special_power_act_1958.htm

__, *The Unlawful Activities (Prevention) Act*, Act No. 37 of 1967, 30 December 1967, available at http://www.satp.org/satporgtp/countries/india/document/actandordinances/the_unlawful_activities_act1967.htm

__, *Jammu and Kashmir Public Safety Act*, Act No. 6 of 1978, available at http://www.unhcr.org/refworld/docid/3ae6b52014.html

__, *The National Security Act*, 27 December 1980, available at http://www.satp.org/satporgtp/countries/india/document/actandordinances/NationalSecurityact.htm

__, *The Unlawful Activities (Prevention) Amendment Bill*, Bill No. 76-C of 2008, 17 December 2008, available at http://www.satp.org/satporgtp/countries/india/document/papers/76-c.htm

Ireland, *Offences against the State (Amendment) Act*, 9 February 1940, available at http://www.irishstatutebook.ie/1940/en/act/pub/0002/index.html

Israel, *Emergency Powers (Detention) Law*, 1979, available at http://www.btselem.org/English/Legal_Documents/1979_Emergency_Powers_Law_Detention.pdf [Israel, *EPDL* (1979)]

__, *Incarceration of Unlawful Combatants Law*, 2002, available at http://www.jewishvirtuallibrary.org/jsource/Politics/IncarcerationLaw.pdf [Israel, *IUCL* (2002)]

__, *Order regarding Administrative Detention (Temporary Provision) No. 1591*, as amended (2007), quoted in relevant part in B'Tselem, *Without Trial* (2009), *cf. infra* NGO Reports

Pakistan, *Anti-Terrorism (Amendment) Ordinance*, 18 November 2002, available at https://www.unodc.org/tldb/showDocument.do?documentUid=2300&edit_btn=SEARCH&q=administrative%20detention

Philippines, *Republic Act No. 9372: An Act to Secure the State and Protect our People from Terrorism*, Human Security Act, 19 February 2007, available at http://www.senate.gov.ph/republic_acts/ra%209372.pdf [Philippines, *Human Security Act* (2007)]

Spain, *Ley Organica 10/1995 Código Penal*, 23 November 1995 (as amended), available at http://www.unifr.ch/ddp1/derechopenal/legislacion/l_20100407_01.pdf [Spain, *Código Penal* (1995)]

Sri Lanka, *Prevention of Terrorism (Temporary Provisions) Act*, Act No. 48 of 1979, 20 July 1979, available at http://www.satp.org/satporgtp/countries/shrilanka/document/actsandordinance/prevention_of_terrorism.htm

__, *Emergency (Miscellaneous Provisions and Powers) Regulation No. 1 of 2005*, August 2005, available at http://www.unhcr.org/refworld/docid/471712342.html [Sri Lanka, *Emergency Regulation No. 1* (2005)]

__, *Emergency (Prevention and Prohibition of Terrorism and Specified Terrorist Activities) Regulations No. 7*, 6 December 2006, Gazette of the Democratic Socialist Republic of Sri Lanka - Extraordinary Edition No. 1474/5, 6 December 2006, also available at http://www.unhcr.org/refworld/docid/45af76a62.html [Sri Lanka, *Emergency Regulation No. 7* (2006)]

Turkey, *Law to Fight Terrorism*, Act No. 3713, *Official Gazette*, 12 April 1991, also available at https://www.unodc.org/tldb/showDocument.do?documentUid=1525&country=TUR

United Kingdom (UK), England, *Magna Carta (Great Charter of English Liberty)*, granted by King John, Runnymede, 12 June 1215, available at http://www1.umn.edu/humanrts/education/magnacarta.html

__, *Civil Contingencies Act*, 2004, available at http://www.legislation.gov.uk/ukpga/2004/36/contents

United States of America (US), US Code, Title 18, Crimes and Criminal Procedure, available at http://www.law.cornell.edu/uscode/html/uscode18/usc_sup_01_18.html [US, *Criminal Code*]

__, *Uniform Code of Military Justice*, US Code, Title X, Subtitle A, Part II, Chapter 47, 5 May 1950 (as amended), available at http://www.law.cornell.edu/uscode/10/stApIIch47.html [US, *UCMJ* (1950)]

__, *Act on Restitution for World War II Internment of Japanese-Americans and Aleuts*, US Code, Title 50, Appendix "War and National Defense", 10 August 1980 http://www.law.cornell.edu/uscode/html/uscode50a/usc_sup_05_50.html

__, Coalition Provisional Authority (Iraq), *Memorandum No. 3*, 2003, on file with author

__, Coalition Provisional Authority (Iraq), *Revised Memorandum No. 3*, 27 June 2004, available at

http://www.iraqcoalition.org/regulations/20040627_CPAMEMO_3_Criminal_Procedures__Rev_.pdf

__, *Authorization of the Use of Military Force*, 18 September 2008, available at

http://news.findlaw.com/wp/docs/terrorism/sjres23.es.html [US, *AUMF* (2001)]

__, *Military Commissions Act*, 2009, available at

http://www.defense.gov/news/2009%20MCA%20Pub%20%20Law%20111-84.pdf [US, *MCA* (2009)]

Military manuals, directives and regulations

Canada, *Joint Doctrine Manual on the Law of Armed Conflict at the Operational and Tactical Levels* (2001), B-GJ-005-104/FP-021, 2001, available at http://www.cfd-cdf.forces.gc.ca/sites/page-eng.asp?page=3560 [Canada, *LOAC Manual* (2001)]

__, *Joint Doctrine Manual: Prisoner of War Handling, Detainees and Interrogation and Tactical Questioning in International Operations*, B-GJ-005-110/FP-020, 2004, available at http://www.cfd-cdf.forces.gc.ca/sites/page-eng.asp?page=3560 [*PWDITQ* (2004)]

__, *Code of Conduct for CF Personnel*, B-GJ-005-104/FP-023, 2005, available at http://www.cfd-cdf.forces.gc.ca/sites/page-eng.asp?page=3560

__, Chief of the Defence Staff, *Joint Doctrine Publication 3.0: Operations*, B-GJ-005-300/FP-000, 2010, available at http://www.cfd-cdf.forces.gc.ca/sites/page-eng.asp?page=3560 [Canada, *JDP 3.0* (2010)]

France, *Manuel de droit des conflits armés*, 2001, available at

http://213.139.102.176/sga/enjeux_defense/droit_et_defense/manuel_de_droit_des_conflits_armes

UK, *The Manual of the Law of Armed Conflict*, Oxford, Oxford University Press, 2004 [UK, *LOAC Manual* (2004)]

__, *Joint Doctrine Publication 1-10, Prisoners of War, Internees and Detainees* (2006), available at

http://www.mod.uk/DefenceInternet/MicroSite/DCDC/OurPublications/JDWP/JointDoctrinePublicationjdp110PrisonersOfWarInterneesAndDetainees.htm [UK, *JDP 1-10* (2006)]

US, *Instructions for the Government of Armies of the United States in the Field (Lieber Code)*, 24 April 1863, available at http://avalon.law.yale.edu/19th_century/lieber.asp [US, Lieber Code (1863)]

__, *Army Field Manual FM 27-10: The Law of Land Warfare*, 18 July 1956, as amended, available at http://www.apd.army.mil/ [US, *Army Field Manual* (1956)]

__, *Annex A to Army Directive No. 381-46 of 27.12.1967, "Criteria for Classification and Disposition of Detainees", American Journal of International Law*, Vol. 62, No. 3, 1968, pp. 766-768 [US, *Army Directive Vietnam* (1967)]

__, *Army Regulation 190-8 – Enemy Prisoners of War, Retained Personnel, Civilian Internees and Other Detainees*, 1 October 1997, available at http://www.apd.army.mil/ [US, *Army Regulation 190-8* (1997)]

__, Joint Chiefs of Staff, *Joint Doctrine Publication 3-63: Detainee Operations*, 23 March 2005, available at

www.hrw.org/campaigns/torture/jointdoctrine/jointdoctrine040705.pdf [US, *JDP 3-63* (2005)]

__, Department of Defence, *Directive 2310.01*, 5 September 2006, available at http://www.dtic.mil/whs/directives/corres/pdf/231001p.pdf

__, Joint Chiefs of Staff, *Joint Doctrine Publication 3-24: Counterinsurgency Operations*, 5 October 2009, available at http://www.dtic.mil/doctrine/new_pubs/jp3_24.pdf [US, *JDP 3-24* (2009)]

__, Department of Defence, *The Dictionary of Military Terms*, 12 April 2001, as amended through April 2010, available at http://www.dtic.mil/doctrine/dod_dictionary/ [US, *Military Dictionary* (2010)]

__, The Judge Advocate General's Legal Center & School, *Operational Law Handbook*, 2010, available at http://www.loc.gov/rr/frd/Military_Law/pdf/operational-law-handbook_2010.pdf

Other official State documents

Denmark, Ministry of Foreign Affairs, "The Copenhagen Process on the Handling of Detainees in International Military Operations", Military Law and Law of War Review, Vol. 46, Nos. 3-4, 2007, pp. 363-366

__, Ministry of Foreign Affairs, "Non-Paper on Legal Framework and Aspects of Detention", *Military Law and Law of War Review*, Vol. 46, No. 3-4, 2007, pp. 367-386

__, "The Handling of Detainees in International Military Operations", discussion paper for the Copenhagen Conference (15-16 June 2009), on file with author [Denmark, MFA, *Discussion Paper* (2009)]

Indonesia, *Declaration Made upon Accession to the ICCPR* (2006), available at http://treaties.un.org/Pages/Treaties.aspx?id=4&subid=A&lang=en, in chapter I-2

Israel, *Instructions of the Attorney General 21.927* (1982), issued by Attorney General Yitzhak Zamir on 15 December 1982, quoted in relevant part in Rudman & Qupty (*CHRLR* 1990), *cf. infra* Literature

__, Ministry of Justice, *Fact Sheet: The Legal Framework for the Use of Administrative Detention as a Means of Combating Terrorism*, March 2003, available at http://www.hamoked.org.il/items/90_eng.pdf [Israel, MoJ, *Fact Sheet Administrative Detention* (2003)]

__, Ministry of Foreign Affairs, *The Operation in Gaza: 27 December 2008 – 18 January 2009. Factual and Legal Aspects*, July 2009, available at http://www.mfa.gov.il/NR/rdonlyres/E89E699D-A435-491B-B2D0-017675DAFEF7/0/GazaOperationwLinks.pdf [Israel, MFA, *The Operation in Gaza* (2009)]

Mozambique, *Mozambique National Resistance – RENAMO Joint Declaration with the Government of Mozambique on the Guiding Principles of Humanitarian Assistance*, 16 July 1992, available at http://www.genevacall.org/resources/testi-reference-materials/testi-nsa-states/nsa-states-mar00.pdf

Philippines, *Comprehensive Agreement on Respect for Human Rights and International Humanitarian Law between the Government of the Republic of the Philippines and the National Democratic Front of the Philippines*, The Hague, 16 March 1998, available at http://www.philsol.nl/A03a/CARHRIHL-mar98.htm

Philippines, *Agreement on the Civilian Protection Component of the International Monitoring Team*, Kampala, 27 October 2009 (agreement between the Government of the Republic of the Philippines and the Moro Islamic Liberation Front (MILF), available at http://www.scribd.com/doc/21700037/GRP-MILF-Agreement-on-Civilian-Protection-Component

South Korea, *Declaration upon Accession to Additional Protocol*, 15 January 1982, available at
http://www.icrc.org/ihl.nsf/a/cd8f2df28f824b75c1256402003fb477?opendocument

Sudan, *Agreement between the Government of the Republic of Sudan and the Sudan People's Liberation Movement to Protect Non-Combatant Civilians and Civilian Facilities from Military Attack*, 10 March 2002, available at
http://www.vigilsd.org/resolut/agreemsd.htm#Agreement%20between%20the%20Government%20of%20the%20Republic

Switzerland, Federal Department of Foreign Affairs, *ABC of International Humanitarian Law* (2009), available at
http://www.eda.admin.ch/etc/medialib/downloads/edazen/doc/publi/publi2.Par.0015.File.tmp/HVR_ENG.pdf

UK, Ministry of Defence, *Delivering Security in a Changing World. Future Capabilities, presented to Parliament by the Secretary of State for Defence by command of Her Majesty*, July 2004, available at http://www.mod.uk/NR/rdonlyres/147C7A19-8554-4DAE-9F88-6FBAD2D973F9/0/cm6269_future_capabilities.pdf

US, *Commission of Wartime Relocation and Internment of Civilians*, all documents available at
http://www.lexisnexis.com/documents/academic/upa_cis/1729_USCommWarRelocInternPt1.pdf

__, American Law Institute, *Restatement of the Law Third: The Foreign Relations Law of the United States*, St-Paul, American Law Institute Publishers, 1987, also available at http://www.ali.org/ali_old/foreign.htm [US, *Restatement (Third) of Foreign Relations Law of the United States* (1987)]

__, Department of Defense, *Final Report to Congress on the Conduct of the Persian Gulf War*, 10 April 1992, available at http://www.ndu.edu/library/epubs/cpgw.pdf

__, *Additional Response of the United States to Request for Precautionary Measures - Detainees in Guantanamo Bay, Cuba*, 15 July 2002, available at
http://www.state.gov/s/l/38642.htm

__, Department of State, *Digest of United States Practice in International Law* (2002), available at http://www.state.gov/documents/organization/139638.pdf [US, *Digest of Practice* (2002)]

__, *Third Periodic Reports of States Parties Due in 2003 (ICCPR)*, 28 November 2005, UN Doc. CCPR/C/USA/3, available at http://daccess-dds-ny.un.org/doc/UNDOC/GEN/G05/452/68/PDF/G0545268.pdf?OpenElement

__, Department of Defense, "Fact Sheet: Guantanamo Detainee Process", last update on 2 October 2007, still in force and available on the DoD's Detainee Affairs website at http://www.defense.gov/news/Sep2005/d20050908process.pdf [US, DoD, *Fact Sheet: Guantanamo Detainee Process*]

__, Department of Justice, *Lakhdar Boumediene et al. v. George W. Bush et al.*, Brief for the Respondents, *October 2007*, available at
http://www.justice.gov/osg/briefs/2007/3mer/2mer/2006-1195.mer.aa.html [US, *Government Brief in Boumediene* (2007)]

__, *Response to Questions Asked by the Committee on the Rights of the Child*, 13 May 2008, available at http://2001-2009.state.gov/g/drl/rls/105437.html

__, Department of State, *Digest of United States Practice in International Law* (2008), available at http://www.state.gov/documents/organization/138513.pdf [US, *Digest of Practice* (2008)]

__, "The Obama Administration and International Law" (2010), keynote speech by Harold Koh (Legal advisor of the US State Department) at the Annual Meeting of the American Society of International Law on 25.03.2010, available at http://www.state.gov/s/l/releases/remarks/139119.htm [Koh, "The Obama Administration and International Law" (2010)]

__, Department of Justice, "Assistant Attorney General David Kris Speaks at the Brookings Institution, Washington D.C., Friday, June 11, 2010", available at http://www.justice.gov/nsd/opa/pr/speeches/2010/nsd-speech-100611.html

Viet Nam, *Reservations Made upon Accession to the Geneva Conventions of 12 August 1949 on 3 December 1973 by the Provisional Revolutionary Government of the Republic of South Viet-Nam*, available at www.icrc.org/ihl.nsf/NORM/3092893761F8178BC1256402003F9940?OpenDocument

CASES AND OPINIONS OF INTERNATIONAL COURTS AND TREATY MONITORING BODIES

Permanent Court of Arbitration (PCA) - Eritrea-Ethiopia Claims Commission[1705]

- *Prisoners of War, Ethiopia's Claim 4*, Partial Award, 1 July 2003
- *Prisoners of War, Eritrea's Claim 17*, Partial Award, 1 July 2003
- *Civilians Claims, Ethiopia's Claim 5*, Partial Award, 17 December 2004
- *Civilians Claims, Eritrea's Claims 15, 16, 23 & 27-32*, Partial Award, 17 December 2004

Permanent Court of International Justice (PCIJ)[1706]

- *Consistency of Certain Danzig Legislative Decrees with the Constitution of the Free City*, Advisory Opinion of 4 December 1935 [PCIJ, *Danzig Opinion* (1935)]

International Court of Justice (ICJ)[1707]

Contentious cases

- *Corfu Channel Case (United Kingdom of Great-Britain and Northern Ireland v. Albania)*, Judgment of 9 April 1949 [ICJ, *Corfu Channel* (1949)]
- *Trial of Pakistani Prisoners of War, Interim Protection*, Order of 13 July 1973
- *United States Diplomatic and Consular Staff in Tehran*, Judgment of 24 May 1980 [ICJ, *Tehran Hostages case* (1980)]
- *Certain Military and Paramilitary Activities in and against Nicaragua (Nicaragua v. United States of America)*, Judgment (Merits) of 27 June 1986 [ICJ, *Nicaragua v. US* (1986)]
- *Case concerning the Territorial Dispute between the Libyan Arab Jamahiriya and Chad*, Judgment of 3 February 1994 [ICJ, *Libya v. Chad* (1994)]

[1705] All documents are available at http://www.pca-cpa.org/showpage.asp?pag_id=1151.
[1706] All judgments and opinions of the PCIJ are available at http://www.icj-cij.org/pcij/index.php?p1=9.
[1707] All judgments and opinions of the ICJ are available at www.icj-cij.org.

- *Armed Activities on the Territory of the Congo (Democratic Republic of the Congo v. Uganda)*, Judgment of 19 December 2005 [ICJ, *DRC v. Uganda* (2005)]
- *Application of the Convention on the Prevention and Punishment of the Crime of Genocide (Bosnia and Herzegovina v. Serbia and Montenegro)*, Judgment of 26 February 2007 [ICJ, *Bosnia v. Serbia* (2007)]

Advisory opinions

- *Advisory Opinion on the Legal Consequences for States of the Continued Presence of South Africa in Namibia (South West Africa) notwithstanding Security Council Resolution 276* (1970), Advisory Opinion of 21 June 1971 [ICJ, *Namibia Opinion* (1971)]
- *Legality of the Threat or Use of Nuclear Weapons*, Advisory Opinion of 8 July 1996 [ICJ, *Nuclear Weapons* (1996)]
- *Legal Consequences of the Construction of a Wall in the Occupied Palestinian Territory*, Advisory Opinion of 9 July 2004 [ICJ, *Wall Opinion* (2004)]
- *Advisory Opinion on the Unilateral Declaration of Independence for Kosovo*, Advisory Opinion of 22 July 2010 [ICJ, *Kosovo Opinion* (2010)]

International Military Tribunal (IMT)

- *Trial of German Major War Criminals*, Judgment and Sentence, 30 September and 1 October 1946 (Cmd 6964, HMSO London), reprinted in: *American Journal of International Law*, Vol. 41, 1947, pp. 172-333

International Criminal Tribunal for the Former Yugoslavia (ICTY)[1708]

Rules and regulations

- Rules Governing the Detention of Persons Awaiting Trial or Appeal before the Tribunal or otherwise Detained on the Authority of the Tribunal, 5 May 1994 [ICTY, *Rules of Detention* (1994)]

Contentious cases

- *Prosecutor v. Duško Tadíc a/k/a "Dule"*, IT-94-AR72, Appeals Chamber, Decision on the Defence Motion for Interlocutory Appeal on Jurisdiction, 2 October 1995 [ICTY, *Tadíc* (1995)]
- *Prosecutor v. Ivica Rajíc*, IT-95-12-R61, Review of the Indictment Pursuant to Rule 61 of the Rules of Procedure and Evidence, Trial Chamber, 13 September 1996 [ICTY, *Rajíc* (1996)]
- *Prosecutor v. Duško Tadíc a/k/a "Dule"*, IT-94-1-T, Trial Chamber, Judgment of 7 May 1997 [ICTY, *Tadíc* (1997)]
- *Prosecutor v. Zejnil Delalíc, Zdravko Mucić a/k/a "Pavo", Hazim* Delić *and Esad* Landžo *a/k/a "Zenga" ("Čelebići case")*, IT-96-21-T, Trial Chamber, Judgment of 16 November 1998 [ICTY, *Delalíc* (1998)]
- *Prosecutor v. Anto Furundžija*, IT-95-17/1-T, Trial Chamber, Judgment of 10 December 1998 [ICTY, *Furundžija* (1998)]
- *Prosecutor v. Duško Tadíc a/k/a "Dule"*, IT-94-1-A, Appeals Chamber, Judgment of 15 July 1999 [ICTY, *Tadíc* (1999)]

[1708] All document, judgments and decisions of the ICTY are available at www.icty.org.

- *Prosecutor v. Zoran Kuprekíc et al.*, IT-95-16-T, Trial Chamber, Judgment of 14 January 2000 [ICTY, *Kuprekíc* (2000)]
- *Prosecutor v. Radoslav Brđanin and Momir Talić*, IT-99-36-PT, Trial Chamber II, Decision on Motions by Momir Talić (1) to Dismiss the Indictment, (2) for Release, and (3) for Leave to Reply to Response of Prosecution to Motion for Release, Decision of 1 February 2000 [ICTY, *Talić* (2000)]
- *Prosecutor v. Tihomir Blaškić*, IT-95-14-T, Trial Chamber, Judgment of 3 March 2000 [ICTY, *Blaskíc* (2000)]
- *Prosecutor v. Zlatko Aleksovski*, IT-95-14/1-A, Appeals Chamber, Judgment of 24 March 2000 [ICTY, Aleksovski (2000)]
- *Prosecutor v. Zejnil Delalíc, Zdravko Mucić a/k/a "Pavo", Hazim* Delić *and Esad* Landžo *a/k/a "Zenga" ("Čelebići case")*, IT-96-21-A, Appeals Chamber, Judgment of 20 February 2001 [ICTY, *Delalíc* (2001)]
- *Prosecutor v. Dario Kordić & Mario Čerkez*, IT-95-14/2-T, Trial Chamber, Judgment of 26 February 2001 [ICTY, *Kordić & Čerkez* (2001)]
- *Prosecutor v. Milorad Krnojelac*, IT-97-25-T, Trial Chamber II, Judgment of 15 March 2002 [ICTY, *Krnojelac* (2002)]
- *Prosecutor v. Mladen Naletilić a/k/a "Tuta" and Vinko Martinović a/k/* "Štela", IT-98-34-T, Trial Chamber, Judgment of 31 March 2003 [ICTY, *Naletilić & Martinović*, (2003)]
- *Prosecutor v. Dario Kordić & Mario Čerkez*, IT-95-14/2-A, Appeals Chamber, Judgment of 17 December 2004 [ICTY, *Kordić & Čerkez* (2004)]
- *Prosecutor v. Sefer Halilović*, IT-01-48-T, Trial Chamber, Judgment of 16 November 2005 [ICTY, *Halilović* (2005)]
- *Prosecutor v. Ramush Haradinaj, Idriz Balaj and Lahi Brahimaj*, IT-04-84-T, Trial Chamber I, Judgment of 3 April 2008 [ICTY, *Haradinaj* (2008)]
- *Prosecutor v. Mile Mrkšić and Veselin Šljivančanin*, IT-95-13/1-A, Appeals Chamber, Judgment of 5 May 2009 [ICTY, *Mrkšić & Šljivančanin* (2009)]
- *Prosecutor v. Radovan Karadžić*, IT-95-5/18-AR72.5, Appeals Chamber, Decision on Appeal of Trial Chamber's Decision on Prliminary Motion to Dismiss Count 11 of the Indictment, 9 July 2009 [ICTY, *Karadžić* (2009)]

International Criminal Tribunal for Rwanda (ICTR)[1709]

Rules and regulations

- Rules Governing the Detention of Persons Awaiting Trial or Appeal before the Tribunal or otherwise Detained on the Authority of the Tribunal, 5 June 1998 [ICTR, *Rules of Detention* (1998)]

Contentious cases

- *Prosecutor v. Jean-Paul Akayesu*, ICTR-96-4-T, Trial Chamber, Judgment of 2 September 1998 [ICTR, *Akayesu* (1998)]
- *Prosecutor v. Georges Anderson Nderubumwe Rutaganda*, ICTR-96-3, Trial Chamber I, Judgment of 6 December 1999 [ICTR, *Rutaganda* (1999)]

[1709] All judgments and decisions of the ICTR are available at http://69.94.11.53/default.htm.

- *Prosecutor v. Clément Kayishema and Obed Ruzindana*, ICTR-95-1-T, Trial Chamber II, Judgment of 21 May 1999 [ICTR, *Kayishema & Ruzindana* (1999)]
- *Prosecutor v. Alfred Musema*, ICTR-96-13-A, Trial Chamber I, Judgment of 27 January 2000 [ICTR, *Musema* (2000)]
- *Prosecutor v. Bagilishema*, ICTR-95-1A-T, Trial Chamber I, Judgment of 7 June 2001 [ICTR, *Bagilishema* (2001)]
- *Prosecutor v. Laurent Semanza*, ICTR-97-20-T, Trial Chamber III, Judgment of 15 May 2003 [ICTR, *Semanza* (2003)]
- *Prosecutor v. Juvénal Kajelijeli*, ICTR-98-44A-A, Appeals Chamber, Judgment of 23 May 2005 [ICTR, *Kajelijeli* (2005)]

Special Court for Sierra Leone (SCSL)[1710]

- *Prosecutor v. Sam Hinga Norman*, SCSL-2004-14-AR72(E), Appeals Chamber, Decision on Preliminary Motion Based on Lack of Jurisdiction (Child Recruitement), Decision of 31 May 2004 [SCSL, *Norman* (2004)]
- *Prosecutor v. Moinina Fofana and Allieu Kondewa,* SCSL-04-14-A, Appeals Chamber, Judgment of 28 May 2008 [SCSL, *Fofana & Kondewa* (2008)]
- *Prosecutor v. Issa Hassan Sesay, Morris Kallon and Augistine Gbao*, SCSL-04-15-A, Appeals Chamber, Judgment of 26 October 2009 [SCSL, *Sesay et al.* (2008)]

Special Tribunal for Lebanon (STL)[1711]

- *Case No. CH/PTJ/2009/06, Pre-Trial Judge, Order Regarding the Detention of Persons Detained in Lebanon in Connection with the Case of the Attack against Prime Minister Rafiq Hariri and Others*, 29 April 2009 [STL, *Order on Pre-Trial Detention* (2009)]

United Nations Human Rights Committee (HRC)[1712]

General comments

- General Comment No. 8: Right to Liberty and Security of Persons (Article 9), 30 June 1982, UN Doc. A/37/40 [HRC, *General Comment 8* (1982)]
- General Comment No. 20: Prohibition of Torture, or Other Cruel, Inhuman or Degrading Treatment or Punishment (Article 7), 10 March 1992, UN Doc. A/47/40(supp.) [HRC, *General Comment 20* (1992)]
- General Comment No. 24: Issues Relating to Reservations Made upon Ratification or Accession to the Covenant or the Optional Protocols thereto, or in Relation to Declarations under Article 41 of the Covenant, 4 November 1994, UN Doc. CCPR/C/21/Rev.1/Add.6 [HRC, *General Comment 24* (1994)]
- General Comment No. 29: Derogations during a State of Emergency (Article 4), 24 July 2001, UN Doc. CCPR/C/21/Rev.1/Add.11 [HRC, *General Comment 29* (2001)]
- General Comment No. 31: The Nature of the General Legal Obligation Imposed on States Parties to the Covenant, 29 March 2004, UN Doc. CCPR/C/21/Rev.1/Add. 13 [HRC, *General Comment 31* (2004)]

[1710] All judgments and decisions of the SCSL are available at http://www.sc-sl.org.
[1711] All decisions of the STL are available at http://www.stl-tsl.org/.
[1712] The Committee's general comments are available at http://www2.ohchr.org/english/bodies/hrc/comments.htm; all other documents are available at http://tb.ohchr.org/default.aspx.

Concluding observations in consideration of reports submitted by States parties

- Azerbaijan, 27 July 1994, UN Doc. CCPR/C/79/Add.38
- Cyprus, 21 September 1994, UN Doc. CCPR/C/79/Add.39
- Israel, 28 July 1998, UN Doc. CCPR/C/79/Add.93
- Belgium, 19 November 1998, UN Doc. CCPR/C/79/Add.99
- Israel, 5 August 2003, UN Doc. CCPR/CO/78/ISR
- United States of America, 27 July 2006, UN Doc. CCPR/C/USA/CO/3/Rev.1

Views and opinions on individual communications

- *Salgar de Montejo v. Colombia,* Comm. No. 64/1979, 24 March 1982, UN Doc. CCPR/C/OP/1
- *Landinelli Silva v. Uruguay*, Comm. No. 34/1978, 8 April 1981, UN Doc. CCPR/C/12/D/34/1978
- *Lilian Celeberti de Casariego v. Uruguay*, Comm. No. 56/1979, 29 July 1981, UN Doc. CCPR/C/13/D/56/1979 [HRC, *Celeberti v. Uruguay* (1981)]
- *Sergio Euben Lopez Burgos v. Uruguay*, Comm. No. 52/1979, 29 July 1981, UN Doc. CCPR/C/13/D/52/1979 [HRC, *Lopez Burgos v. Uruguay* (1981)]
- *Massiotti v. Uruguay,* Comm. No. 25/1978, 26 July 1982, UN Doc. CCPR/C/16/D/25/1978
- *Cámpora Schweizer v. Uruguay,* Comm. No. 66/1980, 12 October 1982, UN Doc. CCPR/C/17/D/66/1980
- *Monguya Mbenge et al. v. Zaire,* Comm. No. 16/1977, 25 March 1983, UN Doc. CCPR/C/OP/2
- *Jaona v. Madagascar*, Comm. No. 132/1982, 1 April 1985, UN Doc. CCPR/C/24/D/132/1982
- *Ngalula Mpandanjila v. Zaire,* Comm. No. 138/1983, 26 March 1986, UN Doc. CCPR/C/27/D/138/1983
- *Van Alphen v. the Netherlands,* Comm. No. 305/1988, 23 July 1990, UN Doc. CCPR/C/39/D/305/1988
- *Mukong v. Cameroon,* Comm. No. 458/1991, 21 July 1994, UN Doc. CCPR/C/51/D/458/1991
- *McLawrence v. Jamaica,* Comm. No. 702/1996, 29 September 1997, U.N. Doc. CCPR/C/60/D/702/1996
- *A. v. Australia*, Comm. No. 560/1993, 3 April 1997, UN Doc. CCPR/C/D/560/1993
- *Domukovsky and Others v. Georgia,* Comm. Nos. 623/1995, 624/1995, 626/1995, 627/1995, 6 April 1998, UN Doc. CCPR/C/62/D/623/1995, CCPR/C/62/D/624/1995, CCPR/C/62/D/626/1995, CCPR/C/62/D/627/1995 [HRC, *Domukovsky and Others v. Georgia* (1998)]
- *Mohammad Munaf v. Romania,* Comm. No. 1539/2006, 30 July 2009, UN Doc. CCPR/C/96/D/1539/2006 [HRC, *Munaf v. Romania* (2009)]

Working Group on Arbitrary Detention (WGAD)[1713]

Annual Reports

- Report of the Working Group on Arbitrary Detention, 15 December 1995, UN Doc. E/CN.4/1996/40 [WGAD, *Annual Report 1995*]
- Report of the Working Group on Arbitrary Detention, 17 December 1996, UN Doc. E/CN.4/1997/4, [WGAD, *Annual Report 1996*]
- Report of the Working Group on Arbitrary Detention, 16 December 2002, UN Doc. E/CN.4/2003/8 [WGAD, *Annual Report 2002*]
- Report of the Working Group on Arbitrary Detention, 15 December 2003, UN Doc. E/CN.4/2004/3 [WGAD, *Annual Report 2003*]
- Report of the Working Group on Arbitrary Detention, 1 December 2004, UN Doc. E/CN.4/2005/6, [WGAD, *Annual Report* 2004]
- Report of the Working Group on Arbitrary Detention, 12 December 2005, UN Doc. E/CN.4/2006/7 [WGAD, *Annual Report 2005*]
- Report of the Working Group on Arbitrary Detention, 9 January 2007, UN Doc. A/HRC/4/40 [WGAD, *Annual Report 2006*]
- Report of the Working Group on Arbitrary Detention, 10 January 2008, UN Doc. A/HRC/7/4 [WGAD, *Annual Report 2007*]

Opinions and views on individual communications

- Opinion No. 47/2005 (Yemen, concerning Messrs. Walid Muhammad Shahir Muhammad al-Qadasi; Salah Nasser Salim`Ali and Muhammad Faraj Ahmed Bashmilah), 30 November 2005, UN Doc. A/HRC/4/40/Add.1 [WGAD, *Opinion No. 47/2005* (2005)]
- Opinion No. 33/2006 (Iraq and United States of America, concerning Mr. Tariq Aziz), 17 November 2006, UN Doc. A/HRC/7/4/Add.1 [WGAD, *Opinion No. 33/2006* (2006)]
- Opinion No. 45/2006 (United Kingdom of Great Britain and Northern Ireland, concerning Mr. Mustafa Abdi), 24 November 2006, UN Doc. A/HRC/7/4/Add.1 [WGAD, *Opinion No. 45/2006* (2006)]

Other documents and reports

- Factsheet No. 26, available at http://www.ohchr.org/Documents/Publications/FactSheet26en.pdf
- Deliberation No. 5 on the Situation regarding Immigrants and Asylum Seekers, 28 December 1999, UN Doc. E/CN.4/2000/4, Annex II [WGAD, *Deliberation No. 5* (1999)]
- Report of the Chairperson-Rapporteur of the Working Group on Arbitrary Detention (Mrs. Leila Zerrougui), the Special Rapporteur on the Independence of Judges and Lawyers (Mr. Leandro Despouy), the Special Rapporteur on Torture and Other Cruel, Inhuman or Degrading Treatment or Punishment (Mr. Manfred Nowak), the Special Rapporteur on Freedom of Religion or Belief (Mr. Asma Jahangir), and the Special Rapporteur on the Right of Everyone to the Enjoyment of the Highest Attainable Standard of Physical and Mental Health (Mr. Paul Hunt), 27 February 2006, UN Doc. E/CN.4/2006/120 [WGAD and Special Rapporteurs, *Situation of Detainees at Guantánamo Bay* (2006)]

[1713] The annual reports and the opinions and views on individual communications of the WGAD are available at http://www2.ohchr.org/english/issues/detention/annual.htm.

United Nations Committee against Torture (CAT)[1714]

- Conclusions and Recommendations: United Kingdom of Great Britain and Northern Ireland, Crown Dependencies and Overseas Territories, 18 November 2004, UN Doc. CAT/C/CR/33/3

United Nations Committee on the Rights of the Child (CRC)[1715]

- Concluding Observations: Israel, 9 October 2002, UN Doc. CRC/C/15/Add.195

CASES AND OPINIONS OF REGIONAL COURTS AND TREATY MONITORING BODIES

African Commission on Human and Peoples' Rights (AC°HPR)[1716]

- *Commission Nationale des Droits de l'Homme et des Libertés v. Chad*, Comm. No. 74/92, Decision of October 1995
- *Constitutional Rights Project, Civil Liberties Organisation and Media Rights Agenda v. Nigeria*, Comm. Nos. 140/94, 141/94 and 145/95, Decision of 15 November 1999 [AC°HPR, Constitutional Rights Project et al. v. Nigeria (1999)]
- *Amnesty International, Comité Loosli Bachelard, Lawyers Committed for Human Rights, and Association of Members of the Episcopal Conference of East Africa v. Sudan*, Comm. Nos. 48/90, 50/91, 52/91, 89/93, Decision of 1999 [AC°HPR, *Amnesty International and Others v. Sudan* (1999)]
- *Sir Dawda K Jawara v. the Gambia*, Comm. Nos. 147/95 and 149/96, Decision of 11 May 2000

European Commission of Human Rights (EC°HR)

- *Denmark, Norway, Sweden and the Netherlands v. Greece (Greek case)*, Report of 5 November 1969, Yearbook, Vol. 12, 1969
- *Cyprus v. Turkey*, Applications Nos. 9780/74 and 6950/75, Report of 10 July 1976, available at http://cyprus-conflict.org/index.html

European Court of Human Rights (ECtHR)[1717]

- *Lawless v. Ireland*, Judgment of 1 July 1961
- *Golder v. the United Kingdom*, Judgment of 21 February 1975
- *Engel and Others v. the Netherlands*, Judgment of 8 June 1976
- *Ireland v. the United Kingdom*, Judgment of 18 January 1978
- *Klass and Others v. Germany*, Judgment of 6 September 1978
- *Sunday Times v. the United Kingdom*, Judgment of 26 April 1979 [ECtHR, *Sunday Times* (1979)]
- *Winterwerp v. the Netherlands*, Judgment of 24 October 1979

[1714] Documents related to the work of the CAT are available at http://www2.ohchr.org/english/bodies/cat/.
[1715] Documents related to the work of the CRC are available at http://www2.ohchr.org/english/bodies/crc/.
[1716] All decisions of the AC°HPR on communications are available at http://www.achpr.org/english/_info/Decision_Countries.html.
[1717] All decisions, judgments and documents related to cases before the ECtHR are available at http://cmiskp.echr.coe.int/tkp197/search.asp?skin=hudoc-en.

- *Guzzardi v. Italy*, Judgment of 6 November 1980
- *Silver and Others v. the United Kingdom*, Judgment of 25 March 1983
- *De Jong, Baljet and Van der Brink v. the Netherlands*, Judgment of 22 May 1984
- *Brogan and Others v. the United Kingdom*, Judgment of 19 November 1988
- *Ciulla v. Italy*, Judgment of 22 February 1989
- *Fox, Campbell and Hartley v. the United Kingdom*, Judgment of 30 August 1990
- *Drozd and Janousek v. France and Spain*, Judgment of 26 June 1992
- *Brannigan and McBride v. the United Kingdom*, Judgment of 26 May 1993
- *Murray v. the United Kingdom*, Judgment of 28 October 1994 (Grand Chamber)
- *Quinn v. France*, Judgment of 22 March 1995
- *Loizidou v. Turkey*, Judgment (Preliminary Objections) of 23 March 1995 (Grand Chamber)
- *Amuur v. France*, Judgment of 26 June 1996
- *Chahal v. the United Kingdom*, Judgment of 15 November 1996 (Grand Chamber)
- *Aksoy v. Turkey*, Judgment of 18 December 1996
- *Lukanov v. Bulgaria*, Judgment of 20 March 1997
- *Kurt v. Turkey*, Judgment of 25 May 1998
- *Steel and Others v. the United Kingdom*, Judgment of 23 September 1998
- *Hood v. the United Kingdom*, Judgment of 18 February 1999 (Grand Chamber)
- *Çakici v. Turkey*, Judgment of 8 July 1999 (Grand Chamber)
- *Baranowski v. Poland*, Judgment of 28 March 2000
- *Jecius v. Lithuania*, Judgment of 31 July 2000
- *Kawka v. Poland*, Judgment of 9 January 2001
- *Denizci and Others v. Cyprus*, Judgment of 23 May 2001
- *Bankovic and Others v. Belgium, the Czech Republic, Denmark, France, Germany, Greece, Hungary, Iceland, Italy, Luxembourg, the Netherlands, Norway, Poland, Portugal, Spain, Turkey and the United Kingdom*, Decision (Admissibility) of 12 December 2001 (Grand Chamber) [ECtHR, *Bankovic* (2001)]
- *Ilascu and Others v. Moldova and Russia*, Judgment of 8 July 2004 (Grand Chamber)
- *Issa v. Turkey*, Judgment of 16 November 2004
- *Öcalan v. Turkey*, Judgment of 12 May 2005 (Grand Chamber)
- *Behrami and Behrami v. France and Saramati v. France, Germany and Norway*, Decision (Admissibility) of 2 May 2007 (Grand Chamber) [ECtHR (Grand Chamber), *Behrami & Saramati v. France, Germany & Norway* (2007)]
- *Saadi v. the United Kingdom*, Judgment of 29 January 2008 (Grand Chamber)
- *Saadi v. Italy*, Judgment of 28 February 2008 (Grand Chamber)
- *Medvedyev and Others v. France*, Judgment of 10 July 2008
- *A. and Others v. the United Kingdom*, Judgment of 19 February 2009 (Grand Chamber)
- *Al-Saadoon and Mufdhi v. the United Kingdom*, Decision (Admissibility) of 30 June 2009
- *Grori v. Albania*, Judgment of 7 July 2009
- *Mooren v. Germany*, Judgment of 9 July 2009 (Grand Chamber)
- *Varnava and Others v. Turkey*, Judgment of 18 September 2009
- *Daoudi v. France*, Judgment of 3 December 2009
- *M. v. Germany*, Judgment of 17 December 2009

- *Al-Saadoon and Mufdhi v. the United Kingdom*, Judgment of 2 March 2010 (Grand Chamber)
- *Medvedyev and Others v. France*, Judgment of 29 March 2010 (Grand Chamber) [ECtHR (Grand Chamber, *Medvedyev* (2010)]
- *Al-Jedda v. UK*, Application No. 27021/08, communicated on 17 February 2009
- *Al-Jedda v. UK*, Statement of Facts and Questions to the Parties, 12 January 2009, available in the Court's Communicated Cases Collection at http://cmiskp.echr.coe.int/tkp197/search.asp?skin=hudoc-en [ECtHR, *Al-Jedda v. UK* (Statement of Facts) (2009)]
- *Al-Jedda v. UK*, Judgment of 7 July 2011 (Grand Chamber) [ECtHR (Grand Chamber, *Al-Jedda* (2011)]

Inter-American Commission on Human Rights (IAC°HR)[1718]

Individual cases

- *Salas and Others v. USA*, Case 10.573, Report No. 31/93, 14 October 1993
- *Abella v. Argentina*, Case 11.137, Report No. 55/97, 18 November 1997
- *Morales Zegarra et al. v. Peru*, Case 10.827, Report No. 57/99, 13 April 1999
- *Coard et al. v. USA*, Case 10.951, Report No. 109/99, 29 September 1999
- *Ascencios Lindo and Others v. Peru*, Case 11.182, Report No. 49/00, 13 April 2000
- *Detainees at Guantánamo Bay, Cuba*, Decision on Request for Precautionary Measures, 13 March 2002 [IAC°HR, *Guantánamo* (2002)]

Reports

- *Report on the Situation of Human Rights in Chile*, 9 September 1985 [IAC°HR, *Chile Report* (1985)]
- *Second Report on the Human Rights Situation in Suriname*, 2 October 1985 [IAC°HR, *Suriname Report* (1985)]
- *Report on the Situation of Human Rights in Peru*, 12 March 1993 [IAC°HR, *First Report Peru* (1993)]
- *Third Report on the Human Rights Situation in Colombia*, 26 février 1999 [IAC°HR, *Third Report Colombia* (1999)]
- *Second Report on the Situation of Human Rights in Peru*, 2 June 2000 [IAC°HR, Second *Report Peru* (2000)]
- *Report on Terrorism and Human Rights*, 22 October 2002 [IAC°HR, *Terrorism and Human Rights* (2002)]

Inter-American Court of Human Rights (IACtHR)[1719]

Contentious cases

- *Velásquez Rodríguez v. Honduras*, Judgment of 29 July 1988
- *Godínez-Cruz v. Honduras*, Judgment of 20 January 1989
- *Gangaram Panday v. Suriname*, Judgment of 21 January 1994
- *Suárez-Rosero v. Ecuador*, Judgment of 12 November 1997

[1718] The decisions and reports of the IAC°HR are available at http://www.cidh.oas.org/DefaultE.htm.
[1719] The judgments, decisions and opinions of the IACtHR are available at http://www.corteidh.or.cr.

- *Castillo-Petruzzi et al. v. Peru*, Judgment of 30 May 1999
- *Las Palmeras v. Colombia*, Judgment (Preliminary objections) of 4 February 2000
- *Durand and Ugarte v. Peru*, Judgment of 16 August 2000
- *Bámaca Velásquez v. Guatemala*, Judgment of 25 November 2000
- *Zambrano-Vélez et al. v. Ecuador*, Judgment of 4 July 2007

Advisory opinions

- *The Word "Laws" in Article 30 of the American Convention on Human Rights*, Advisory Opinion OC-6/86 of 9 May 1986 [IACtHR, *Opinion on the Word "Laws"* (1986)]
- *Habeas Corpus in Emergency Situations (Arts 27(2), 25(1) and 7(6) American Convention on Human Rights)*, Advisory Opinion OC-8/87 of 30 January 1987 [IACtHR, *Habeas Opinion* (1987)]
- *Judicial Guarantees in States of Emergency* (Arts 27(2), 25 and 8 American Convention on Human Rights), Advisory Opinion OC-9/87 of 6 October 1987 [IACtHR, *Judicial Guarantees Opinion* (1987)]

NATIONAL CASE LAW

Australia, Federal Court, *Mamdouh Habib v. Commonwealth of Australia*, Order on a Motion to Disallow the Case to Proceed, 25 February 2010, available at http://www.austlii.edu.au/au/cases/cth/FCAFC/2010/12.txt/cgi-bin/download.cgi/download/ au/cases/cth/FCAFC/2010/12.rtf [Australia, Federal Court, Habib (2010)]

Israel, Supreme Court, sitting as a Court of Appeals, *Anonymous (Lebanese citizens) v. Minister of Defence*, FCrA 7048/97, Judgment of 12 April 2000, available at www.oxfordlawreports.com [Israel, SC, *Bargaining Chips Case* (2000)]

__, Supreme Court, sitting as the High Court of Justice, *Kipah Mahmad Afmed Ajuri et al. v. IDF Commander in West Bank et al.*, and *Amtasaar Muhammed Ahmed Ajuri et al. v. IDF Commander in Judeae and Samaria*, HCJ 7015/02 and HCJ 7019/02, Judgment of 3 September 2002, available at www.oxfordlawreports.com [Israel, SC, *Ajuri* (2002)]

__, Supreme Court, sitting as the High Court of Justice, *Iad Ashak Mahmud Marab et al. v. IDF Commander in the West Bank et al.*, HCJ 3239/02, Judgment of 5 February 2003, available at www.oxfordlawreports.com [Israel, SC, *Marab* (2003)]

__, Supreme Court, sitting as the Court of Criminal Appeals, *Sheikh Abd al Qarim Obeid, Mustafa Dib Mari Dirani and Fawzi Muhammad Mustafa Ayub v. State of Israel*, CrimA 3660/03 and CrimA 3675/03, Judgment of 8 September 2005 available at http://elyon1.court.gov.il [Israel, SC, *Obeid et al.* (2005)]

__, Supreme Court, sitting as the High Court of Justice, *The Public Committee against Torture in Israel and Palestinian Society for the Protection of Human Rights and the Environment v. the Government of Israel et al.*, HCJ 769/02, Judgment of 14 December 2006, available at http://elyon1.court.gov.il and at www.oxfordlawreports.com [Israel, SC, *Targeted Killings Case* (2006)]

__, Supreme Court, sitting as the Court of Criminal Appeals, *A and B v. State of Israel*, CrimA 6659/06, CrimA 1757/07, CrimA 8228/07, and CrimA 3261/08, Judgment of 11 June 2008, available at http://elyon1.court.gov.il and at www.oxfordlawreports.com [Israel, SC, *A and B. v. Israel* (2008)]

__, Supreme Court, sitting as the Court of Criminal Appeals, *Khaled Ali Salem Said v. State of Israel*, CrimA 7446/08, Judgment of 7 November 2008, available at http://www.icrc.org/ihl-nat.nsf/46707c419d6bdfa24125673e00508145/cc23f3a54571b9efc12575c300545d81!OpenDocument[Israel, SC, *Salem Said* (2008)]

New Zealand, High Court, *Refugee Council of New Zealand Inc. and the Human Rights Foundation of Aotearoa New Zealand Inc. and D. v. Attorney-General*, Case No. M1881-AS01, Supplementary Judgment of 27 June 2002, available at http://www.humanrights.co.nz/

Switzerland, Tribunal militaire de cassation, *Niyonteze*, Judgment of 27 April 2001, *Arrêts du Tribunal militaire de cassation*, Vol. 12, No. 21, 2001, available at http://www.vbs.admin.ch/internet/vbs/fr/home/documentation/oa009/oa009n.parsys.0004.downloadList.00041.DownloadFile.tmp/entscheid021.pdf [Switzerland, Military Court of Cassation, *Niyonteze* (2001)]

UK, Court of Appeal, *R (on the application of Hilal Abdul-Razzaq Ali Al-Jedda) v. Secretary of State for Defence*, Case No. C1/2005/2251, Judgment of 29 March 2006, available at http://www.publicinterestlawyers.co.uk/cases/cases.php?id=35 [UK, CA, *Al-Jedda* (2006)]

__, House of Lords, *R (on the application of Al-Jedda) (Appellant) (FC) v. Secretary of State for Defence*, Judgment of 12 December 2007, available at http://www.publications.parliament.uk/pa/ld200708/ldjudgmt/jd071212/jedda-1.htm [UK, HoL, *Al-Jedda* (2007)]

__, High Court of Justice, *H.X.A. v. Home Office*, Case No. HQ06X3572, Judgment of 21 May 2010 2009, available at http://www.bailii.org/ew/cases/EWHC/QB/2010/1177.html [UK, HCJ, *H.X.A* (2010)]

__, Supreme Court, *Her Majesty's Treasury (Respondent) v. Mohammed Jabar Ahmed and Others (FC) (Appellants), Her Majesty's Treasury (Respondent) v. Mohammed al-Ghabra (FC) (Appellant), and R (on the application of Hani El Sayed Sabaei Youssef) (Respondent) v. Her Majesty's Treasury (Appellant)*, Judgment of 27 January 2010, available at http://www.supremecourt.gov.uk/docs/uksc_2009_0016_judgment.pdf [UK, HCJ, *Jabar* (2010)]

__, Court of Appeal, *Hilal Abdul-Razzaq Ali Al-Jedda v. Secretary of State for Defence*, Case No. A2/2009/1844, Judgment of 8 July 2010, available at http://www.bailii.org/ew/cases/EWCA/Civ/2010/758.html [UK, CA, *Al-Jedda* (2010)]

US, Supreme Court, *Ex Parte Quirin*, Judgment of 31 July 1942, available at http://www.law.cornell.edu/supct/html/historics/USSC_CR_0317_0001_ZO.html [US, SC, *Ex Parte Quirin* (1942)]

__, Military Tribunal, *The Hostages Trial: Trial of Wilhelm List and Others (Case No. 47)*, United Nations War Crimes Commission, *Law Reports of Trials of War Criminals*, Vol. VIII, 1949, pp. 34-76 [US, Military Tribunal, *List et al.* (1948)]

__, District Court, Eastern District of Virginia, *USA v. John Philipp Walker Lindh*, Grand Jury Indictment, 5 February 2002, available at http://news.findlaw.com/hdocs/docs/lindh/uswlindh020502cmp.html [US, District Court, *Walker Lindh* (Indictment) (2002)]

__, District Court, Eastern District of Virginia, *USA v. John Philipp Walker Lindh*, Plea Agreement, 15 July 2002, available at http://news.findlaw.com/hdocs/docs/lindh/uslindh71502pleaag.pdf [US, District Court, *Walker Lindh* (Plea Agreement) (2002)]

__, Supreme Court, *Hamdi et al. v. Rumsfeld, Secretary of Defense et al.*, Judgment of 28 June 2004, available at http://www.law.cornell.edu/supct/html/03-6696.ZS.html [US, SC, *Hamdi* (2004)]

__, Supreme Court, *Hamdan v. Rumsfeld, Secretary of Defense et al.*, Judgment of 29 June 2006, available at http://www.law.cornell.edu/supct/html/05-184.ZS.html [US, SC, *Hamdan* (2006)]

__, Supreme Court, *Boumediene et al. v. Bush, President of the United States et al.*, Judgment of 12 June 2008, available at http://www.scotusblog.com/wp-content/uploads/2008/06/06-1195.pdf [US, SC, *Boumediene* (2008)]

__, Court of Appeals for the Fourth Circuit, *Ali Saleh Kahlah Al-Marri & Mark A. Berman v. John Pucciarelli*, Opinion on Rehearing En Banc, 15 July 2008, available at http://pacer.ca4.uscourts.gov/opinion.pdf/067427A.P.pdf [US, Court of Appeals, *Al-Marri* (2008)]

__, District Court, District of Columbia, *Falen Gherebi et al. v. Obama et al.*, Memorandum Opinion, 22 April 2009, available at https://ecf.dcd.uscourts.gov/cgi-bin/show_public_doc?2008cv2019-87 [US, District Court, *Gherebi et al.* (2009)]

__, District Court, District of Columbia, *Adel Hamlily et al. v. Barack H. Obama et al.*, Memorandum Opinion, 19 May 2009, available at http://www.scotusblog.com/wp-content/uploads/2009/05/bates-on-detention-power-5-19-09.pdf [US, District Court, *Hamlily* (2009)]

__, *Haji Abdul Wahid et al. v. Gates, Secretary of Defense et al.*, Petition for Writ of Habeas Corpus, 26 February 2010, submitted on behalf of the petitioners by the American Civil Liberties Union, available at http://www.aclu.org/national-security/wahid-et-al-v-gates-et-al-habeas-petition

DOCUMENTS FROM NON-STATE PARTIES TO ARMED CONFLICTS

Ejercito de Liberación Nacional (ELN, Colombia), *Código de Guerra*, 1996, on file with author

___, "Mensaje de año nuevo: con el pueblo vamos a construir la convención nacional y a enfrentar el Plan Colombia", 30 December 2000, available at http://www.ideaspaz.org/secciones/publicaciones/download_boletines/boletindepaz01.htm

___, "Resolver y humanizar el conflicto colombiano", 6 December 2009, available at http://www.eln-voces.com/index2.php?option=com_content&do_pdf=1&id=637.

Fuerzas Armadas Revolucionarias de Colombia – Ejercito del Pueblo (FARC-EP, Colombia), *Beligerancia*, unknown date, available at http://www.abpnoticias.com/boletin_temporal/contenido/libros/Beligerancia__FARC-EP.pdf

___, Estado Mayor Central, "Comunicado", 24 February 2003, available at http://www.ideaspaz.org/secciones/publicaciones/download_boletines/boletindepaz01.htm

___, Carta abierta de las FARC-EP a los gobiernos del mundo, 7 September 2007, available at http://www.conbolivar.org/index.php?option=com_content&task=view&id=108&Itemid=33

National Democratic Front of the Philippines (NDFP, Philippines), "NDFP Declaration of Adherence to International Humanitarian Law", 15 August 1991, available at http://home.casema.nl/ndf/

____, "NDFP Declaration of Undertaking to Apply the Geneva Conventions of 1949 and Protocol I of 1977", 5 July 1996, available at http://home.casema.nl/ndf/, and at http://www.hartford-hwp.com/archives/54a/036.html

New Peoples Army (NPA, Philippines), "NPA Releases POW S/Sgt. Arguelles, Jr. on Humanitarian Grounds", 21 July 2010, available at http://ndfp.net/joomla/index.php?option=com_content&task=view&id=870&Itemid=53

Partiya Karkerên Kurdistan (PKK, Turkey), "PKK Statement to the United Nations", 24 January 1995, available at http://www.hartford-hwp.com/archives/51/009.html

LITERATURE

Abi-Saab, Georges, "Wars of National Liberation and the Laws of War", *Annales d'études internationales*, Vol. 3, 1972, pp. 93-117 [Abi-Saab (*AEI* 1972)]

___, "Wars of National Liberation in the Geneva Conventions and Protocols", *Collected Courses of the Hague Academy of International Law*, Vol. 165, 1979-IV, pp. 353-448 [Abi-Saab (*Hague Academy Collected Courses* 1979)]

___, "The Specificities of Humanitarian Law" in: Swinarski, Christophe (ed.), *Studies and Essays on International Humanitarian Law and Red Cross Principles in Honour of Jean Pictet*, Geneva/The Hague, International Committee of the Red Cross/Martinus Nijhoff Publishers, 1984, pp. 265-280 [Abi-Saab in *Liber Amoricum* Pictet (1984)]

__, "Conflits armés non internationaux" in: UNESCO/Institut Henry-Dunant, *Les dimensions internationales du droit humanitaire*, Paris/Geneva, UNESCO/Institut Henry-Dunant, 1986, pp. 251-277 [Abi-Saab in *Les dimensions internationales* (1986)]

__, "'Humanité' et 'communauté internationale' dans la dialectique du droit international" in: *Humanité et droit international. Mélanges René-Jean Dupuy*, Paris, Pedone, 1991, pp. 1-12 [Abi-Saab in *Liber Amoricum Dupuy* (1991)]

___, "The 1977 Additional Protocols and General International Law: Some Preliminary Reflections" in: Delissen, Astrid J.M. and Tanja, Gerard J. (eds.), *Humanitarian Law of Armed Conflict: Challenges ahead. Essays in Honour of Frits Kalshoven*, The Hague, T.M.C. Asser Institute, 1991, pp. 115-126 [Abi-Saab in *Liber Amoricum Kalshoven* (1991)]

___, "The Security Council as Legislator and as Executive in its Fights against Terrorism and against Proliferation of Weapons of Mass Destruction: The Question of Legitimacy" in: Wolfrum, Rüdiger and Röben, Völker, *Legitimacy in International Law*, Heidelberg, Max-Planck-Institut für ausländisches öffentliches Recht und Völkerrecht, 2008, pp. 155-168 [Abi-Saab in Wolfrum & Röben (2008)]

Abi-Saab, Rosemary, *Droit humanitaire et conflits internes. Origines et évolution de la réglementation internationale*, Geneva/Paris, Institut Henry-Dunant/Pedone, 1986 [Abi-Saab (1986)]

___, "Humanitarian Law and Internal Conflicts: The Evolution of Legal Concern" in: Delissen, Astrid J.M. and Tanja, Gerard J. (eds.), *Humanitarian Law of Armed Conflict: Challenges ahead. Essays in Honour of Frits Kalshoven*, The Hague, T.M.C. Asser Institute, 1991, pp. 209-223 [Abi-Saab in *Liber Amoricum Kalshoven* (1991)]

___, "Les 'principes généraux' du droit humanitaire selon la Cour internationale de Justice", *International Review of the Red Cross*, Vol. 69, No. 256, 1987, pp. 381-389 [Abi-Saab (*IRRC* 1987)]

Abresh, William, "A Human Rights Law of Internal Armed Conflict: The European Court of Human Rights in Chechnya", *European Journal of International Law*, Vol. 16, No. 4, 2005, pp. 741-767 [Abresh (*EJIL* 2005)]

Adebajo, Adekeye, *Liberia's Civil War: Nigeria, ECOMOG, and Regional Security in West Africa*, Colorado/London, Lynne Rienner Publications, 2002 [Adebajo (2002)]

Aeschlimann, Alain, "Protection of Detainees: ICRC Action behind Bars", *International Review of the Red Cross*, Vol. 87, No. 857, 2005, pp. 83-122 [Aeschlimann (*IRRC* 2005)]

Aldrich, George H., "Why the United States of America Should Ratify Additional Protocol I" in: Delissen, Astrid J.M. and Tanja, Gerard J. (eds.), *Humanitarian Law of Armed Conflict: Challenges ahead. Essays in Honour of Frits Kalshoven*, The Hague, T.M.C. Asser Institute, 1991, pp. 127-144 [Aldrich in *Liber Amoricum Kalshoven*]

___, "The Taliban, al Qaeda, and the Determination of Illegal Combatants", *Humanitäres Völkerrecht*, Vol. 15, No. 4, 2002, pp. 202-206 [Aldrich (*HV* 2002)]

___, "The Taliban, al Qaeda, and the Determination of Illegal Combatants", *American Journal of International Law*, Vol. 96, No. 4, 2002, pp. 891-898 [Aldrich (*AJIL* 2002)]

Alston, Philip (ed.), *Non-State Actors and Human Rights, Oxford, Oxford University Press, 2006* [Alston (2006)]

American Bar Association, "American Bar Association Task Force on Terrorism and the Law, Report and Recommendations on Military Commissions", without date, on file with author [ABA, *Military Commissions Report*]

Andreu Guzmán, Federico, *Fuero militar y derecho internacional*, Bogotá, Comisión Internacional de Juristas/Comisión Colombiana de Juristas, 2003 [Andreu Guzmán (2003)]

Arai-Takahashi, Yutaka, *The Law of Occupation: Continuity and Change of International Humanitarian Law, and its Interaction with International Human Rights Law*, Leiden/Boston, Martinus Nijhoff Publishers, 2009 [Arai-Takahashi (2009)]

Archer, Bernice, *The Internment of Western Civilians under the Japanese 1941-1945: A Patchwork of Internment*, London/New York, Routledge/Curzon, 2004 [Archer (2004)]

Arnold, Roberta and Quénivet, Noëlle (eds.), *International Humanitarian Law and Human Rights Law: Towards a Merger in International Law*, Leiden, Martinus Nijhoff Publishers, 2008 [Arnold & Quénivet (2008)]

Ascensio, Hervé; Decaux, Emmanuel and Pellet, Alain (dir.), *Droit international pénal*, Paris, Pedone, 2000 [Ascensio, Decaux & Pellet (2000)], (new edition 2012).

Barberis, Julio A., "Nouvelles questions concernant la personnalité juridique internationale", *Collected Courses of the Hague Academy of International Law*, Vol. 179, 1983-I, pp. 145-304 [Barberis (*Hague Academy Collected Courses* 1983)]

Barboza, "State Crimes: A Decaffeinated Coffee" in: Boisson de Chazournes, Laurence and Gowlland-Debbas, Vera (eds.), *The International Legal System in Quest of Equity and Universality: Liber Amoricum Georges Abi-Saab*, The Hague, Martinus Nijhoff Publishers, 2001, pp. 357-376 [Barberis in *Liber Amoricum Abi-Saab* (2001)]

Bartels, Rogier, "Timelines, Borderlines and Conflicts: The Historical Evolution of the Legal Divide between International and Non-International Armed Conflicts", *International Review of the Red Cross*, Vol. 91, No. 873, 2009, pp. 35-67 [Bartels (*IRRC* 2009)]

Bartelt, Sandra, *Der rechtliche Rahmen für die neue operative Kapazität der Europäischen Union*, Münster, LIT Verlag, 2003 [Bartelt (2003)]

Bassiouni, Cherif M. (ed.), *International Criminal Law*, New York, Transnational Publishers, 1999 [Bassiouni (1999)]

___, "Legal Controls of International Terrorism: A Policy-Oriented Perspective", *Harvard International Law Journal*, Vol. 43, 2002, pp. 83-104 [Bassiouni (*HILJ* 2002)]

___, "The New Wars and the Crisis of Compliance with the Law of Armed Conflict by Non-State Actors", *The Journal of Criminal Law & Criminology*, Vol. 98, No. 3, 2008, pp. 711-810 [Bassiouni (*JCLC* 2008)]

Baxter, Richard R., "So-Called 'Unprivileged Belligerency': Spies, Guerrillas, and Saboteurs", *British Year Book of International Law*, Vol. 28, 1951, pp. 323-345 [Baxter (*BYIL* 1951)]

___, "Asylum to Prisoners of War", *British Year Book of International Law*, Vol. 30, 1953, pp. 489-498 [Baxter (*BYIL* 1953)]

___, "The Privy Council on the Qualifications of Belligerents. A Comment", *American Journal of International Law*, Vol. 63, No. 2, 1969, pp. 290-296 [Baxter (*AJIL* 1969)]

___, "*Ius in Bello Interno*: The Present and Future Law" in: Moore, John N. (ed.), *Law and Civil War in the Modern World*, Baltimore, Johns Hopkins University Press, 1974, pp. 518-536 [Baxter in Moore (1974)]

___, "The Duties of Combatants and the Conduct of Hostilities (Law of The Hague)" in: Henry Dunant Institute and UNESCO (eds.), *International Dimensions of Humanitarian Law*, Paris/Geneva/Dordrecht, UNSECO/Henry Dunant Institute/Martinus Nijhoff Publishers, 1988, pp. 93-133 [Baxter in *International Dimensions of International Law* (1988)]

Bedjaoui, Mohammed, *Law and the Algerian Revolution*, Brussels, International Association of Democratic Lawyers, 1961 [Bedjaoui (1961)]

Bellal, Annyssa and Chetail, Vincent, "The Concept of Combatant under International Humanitarian Law" in: Doswald-Beck, Louise; Chowdhury, Azizur Rahman and Bhuiyan, Jahid Hossain (eds.), *International Humanitarian Law: An Anthology*, Nagpur, LexisNexis & Butterworths Wadhwa, 2009, pp. 57-77 [Bellal & Chetail in Doswald-Beck et al. (2009)]

Bellinger, John B. (III) and Haynes, William J. (II), "A US Government Response to the International Committee of the Red Cross Study *Customary International Humanitarian Law*", *International Review of the Red Cross*, Vol. 89, No. 866, 2007, pp. 443-471 [Bellinger & Haynes (*IRRC* 2007)]

Ben-Naftali, Orna and Gleichgevitch, Sean S., "Missing in Legal Action: Lebanese Hostages in Israel", *Harvard International Law Journal*, Vol. 41, No. 1, 2000, pp. 185-252 [Ben-Naftali & Gleichgevitch (*Harv.ILJ* 2000)]

___ **and Shany, Yuval**, "Living in Denial: The Application of Human Rights in the Occupied Territories", *Israel Law Review*, Vol. 37, No. 1, 2003-2004, pp. 17-118 [Ben-Naftali & Shany (*ILR* 2003-2004)]

Bennoune, Karima, "'To Respect and to Ensure': Reconciling International Human Rights Obligations in a Time of Terror", *ASIL Proceedings*, Vol. 97, 2003, pp. 23-27 [Bennoune (*ASIL Proceedings* 2003)]

Benvenisti, Eyal, *The International Law of Occupation*, Princeton, Princeton University Press, 2004 [Benvenisti (2004)]

___, "Rethinking the Divide between *Jus ad Bellum* and *Jus in Bello* in Warfare against Nonstate Actors", *Yale Journal of International Law*, Vol. 34, No. 2, 2009, pp. 541-548 [Benvenisti, (*YJIL* 2009)]

Benvenuti, Paolo, "The Implementation of International Humanitarian Law in the Framework of UN Peace-Keeping'" in: European Commission Humanitarian Office, *Law in Humanitarian Crises: How Can International Humanitarian Law Be Made Effective in Armed Conflicts?*, Luxembourg, Office for the Official Publications of the European Communities, 1995, Vol. I, pp. 83-119 [Benvenuti (1995)]

Berhe, Aregawi, "The Origins of the Tigray's People's Liberation Front", *African Affairs*, Vol. 103, No. 413, 2004, pp. 569-592 [Berhe (*African Affairs* 2004)]

Bernard, Mountague, *A Historical Account of the Neutrality of Great Britain during the American Civil War*, London, Longmans, 1870 [Bernard (1870)]

Best, George, *War and Law since 1945*, Oxford, Clarendon Press, 1994 [Best (1994)]

Bianchi, Andrea, "Ad-hocism and the Rule of Law", *European Journal of International Law*, Vol. 13, No. 1, 2002, pp. 263-272 [Bianchi (*EJIL* 2002)]

___ (ed.), *Enforcing International Law Norms against Terrorism*, London, Hart Publishing, 2004 [Bianchi (2004)]

___, *Non-State Actors and International Law*, Farnham, Ashgate, 2009 [Bianchi (2009)]

Bingham, Tom, "The Rule of Law" (Sixth Sir David Williams Lecture), Cambridge, Cambridge University, Centre for Public Law, 16 November 2006, available at http://www.cpl.law.cam.ac.uk/past_activities/the_rt_hon_lord_bingham_the_rule_of_la w.php [Bingham (*Sir David Williams Lectures* 2006)]

___, "The Case of *Liversidge v. Anderson*: The Rule of Law amid the Clash of Arms", *The International Lawyer*, Vol. 4, No. 1, 2009, pp. 33-38 [Bingham (*The International Lawyer* 2009)]

___, *The Rule of Law*, London, Penguin Books, 2010 [Bingham (2010)]

Bishop, Joseph W. Jr., "Law in the Control of Terrorism and Insurrection: The British Laboratory Experience", *Law and Contemporary Problems*, Vol. 42, 1978, pp. 140-201 [Bishop (*LCP* 1978)]

Boisson de Chazournes, Laurence and Condorelli, Luigi, "Common Article 1 of the Geneva Conventions Revisited: Protecting Collective Interests", *International Review of the Red Cross*, Vol. 82, No. 837, 2000, pp. 67-87 [de Chazournes & Condorelli (*IRRC* 2000)]

Bond, James E., "Application of the Law of War to Internal Conflicts", *Georgia Journal of International and Comparative Law*, Vol. 3, No. 2, 1973, pp. 345-384 [Bond (*GJICL* 1983)]

Boothby, Bill, "'And for such Time as': The Time Dimension to Direct Participation in Hostilities", *New York University Journal of International Law and Policy*, Vol. 42, No. 3, 2010, pp. 741-768 [Boothby (*NYUJILP* 2010)]

Bordwell, Percy, *The Law of War between Belligerents*, Chicago, Callaghan and Co., 1908 [Bordwell (1908)]

Borelli, Silvia, "Casting Light on the Legal Black Hole: International Law and Detentions abroad in the 'War on Terror'", *International Review of the Red Cross*, Vol. 87, No. 857, 2005, pp. 39-68 [Borelli (*IRRC* 2005)]

Bossuyt, Marc J., *Guide to the "Travaux Préparatoires" of the International Covenant on Civil and Political Rights*, Dordrecht/Boston, Martinus Nijhoff Publishers, 1987 [Bossuyt (1987)]

Bothe, Michael, "Conflits armés internes et droit international humanitaire", *Revue générale de droit international public*, Vol. 82, 1978, pp. 82-102 [Bothe (*RGDIP* 1978)]

___, "Article 3 and Protocol II: Case Studies of Nigeria and El Salvador", *American University Law Review*, Vol. 31, 1982, pp. 899-909 [Bothe (*AULR* 1982)]

___; Partsch, Karl J. and Solf, Waldemar, *New Rules for Victims of Armed Conflicts: Commentary on the Two 1977 Protocols Additional to the Geneva Conventions of 1949*, The Hague, Martinus Nijhoff, 1982 [Bothe et al. (1982)]

Bothe, Michael, "Occupation after Armistice" in: Beinhardt, Rudolf (ed.), *Encyclopedia of Public International Law*, Amsterdam, Elsevier, 1997, pp. 761-768 [Bothe in Beinhardt (1997)]

Boumedra, Tahar, "International Regulation of the Use of Mercenaries in Armed Conflicts", *Military Law and Law of War Review*, Vol. 20, Nos. 1-2, 1981, pp. 35-87 [Boumedra (*MLLWR* 1981)]

Bowring, Bill, "Fragmentation, Lex Specialis and the Tensions in the Jurisprudence of the European Court of Human Rights, *Journal of Conflict & Security Law*, Vol. 14, No. 3, 2009, pp. 485-498 [Bowring (*JCSL* 2009)]

Boyd, Stephen M., "The Applicability of International Law in the Occupied Territories", *Israel Yearbook on Human Rights*, Vol. 1, 1971, pp. 258-261 [Boyd (*Isr.YHR* 1971)]

Boyle, Alan E. and Chinkin, Christine M., *The Making of International Law*, Oxford, Oxford University Press, 2007 [Boyle & Chinkin (2007)]

Bretton, Philippe, "De quelques problèmes du droit de la guerre dans le conflit indo-pakistanais", *Annuaire français de droit international*, Vol. 18, 1972, pp. 201-224 [Bretton (*AFDI* 1972)]

___, "L'incidence des guerres contemporaines sur la réaffirmation et le développement du droit international humanitaire applicable dans les conflits armés internationaux et non internationaux", *Journal du droit international*, Vol. 105, 1978, pp. 208-271 [Bretton (*JDI* 1978)]

Brownlie, Ian, "The Relations of Nationality in Public International Law", *British Year Book of International Law*, Vol. 39, 1963, pp. 284-364 [Brownlie (*BYIL* 1963)]

___, *Principles of International Law*, 5th ed., Oxford, Oxford University Press, 1998 [Brownlie (1998)]

Brunnee, Jutta and Toope, Stephen J., "The Responsibility to Protect and the Use of Force: Building Legality?", *Global Responsibility to Protect*, Vol. 2, No. 3, 2010, pp. 191-212, available online at http://ssrn.com/abstract=1551296 [Brunnee & Toope (*GRP* 2010)]

Buergenthal, Thomas, "To Respect and to Ensure: State Obligations and Permissible Derogations" in: Henkin, Louis, *The International Bill of Rights: The Covenant on Civil and Political Rights*, New York, Columbia University Press, 1981, pp. 72-91 [Buergenthal in Henkin (1981)]

Bugnion, François, "The Arrival of Bourbaki's Army at Les Verrières", *International Review of the Red Cross*, Vol. 78, No. 818, 1996, pp. 181-193 [Bugnion (*IRRC* 1996)]

___, "Guerre juste, guerre d'agression et droit international humanitaire", *International Review of the Red Cross*, Vol. 84, No. 847, 2002, pp. 523-546 [Bugnion (*IRRC* 2002)]

___, *The International Committee of the Red Cross and the Protection of War Victims*, Geneva/Oxford, International Committee of the Red Cross/MacMillan, 2003 [Bugnion (2003)]

Buyse, Antoine, "A Legal Minefield – The Territorial Scope of the European Convention", *Inter-American and European Human Rights Journal*, Vol. 1, No. 2, 2008, pp. 269-296 [Buyse (*IAEHRJ* 2008)]

Byford, Grenville, "The Wrong War", *Foreign Affairs*, Vol. 81, No. 4, 2002, pp. 34-43 [Byford (*FA* 2002)]

Byron, Christine, "Armed Conflicts: International or Non-International?", *Journal of Conflict and Security Law*, Vol. 6, No. 1, pp. 63-90 [Byron (*JCSL* 2001)]

Cahin, Gérard, "The Responsibility of Other Entities: Armed Bands and Criminal Groups" in Crawford, James; Pellet, Alain and Olleson, Simon (eds.), *The Law of International Responsibility*, Oxford, Oxford University Press, 2010, pp. 331-341 [Cahin in Crawford et al. (2010)]

Calogeropoulos-Stratis, Spiros, *Le droit des peuples à disposer d'eux-mêmes*, Brussels, Bruylant, 1973 [Calogeropoulos-Stratis (1973)]

Cameron, Lindsey, "Private Military Companies: Their Status under International Humanitarian Law and its Impact on their Regulation", *International Review of the Red Cross*, Vol. 88, No. 863, 2006, pp. 573-598 [Cameron (*IRRC* 2006)]

___ **and Everly, Rebecca**, "Conceptualizing the Administration of Territory by International Actors", *European Journal of International Law*, Vol. 21, No. 1, 2010, pp. 221-244 [Cameron & Everly (*EJIL* 2010)]

Cançado Trindade, Antônio Augusto, "Desarollo de la relaciones entre el derecho humanitario y la protección internacional de los derechos humanos en su amplía dimension", *Revista del Instituto Interamericano de Derechos Humanos*, Vol. 16, 1992, pp. 39-74 [Cançado Trindade (*RIIDH* 1992)]

___, *Tratado de direito internacional dos direitos humanos*, Porto Alegre, Sergio Antonio Fabris, 1997 [Cançado Trindade (1997)]

Carr-Greg, Charlotte, "An Extension of Humanitarian International Law: The Case of Soviet Soldiers Captured by Afghan Liberation Movements, 1982-1986", *War and Society* (University of New South Wales), Vol. 7, 1989, pp. 95-105 [Carr-Gregg *(WaS* 1989)]

Cassel, Douglas, "Pretrial and Preventive Detention of Suspected Terrorists: Options and Constraints under International Law", *The Journal of Criminal Law & Criminology*, Vol. 98, No. 3, 2008, pp. 811-852 [Cassel (*JCLC* 2008)]

___, "International Human Rights Law and Security Detention", *Case Western Reserve Journal of International Law*, Vol. 40, No. 3, 2009, pp. 383-401 [Cassel (*CWRJIL* 2009)]

Cassese, Antonio (ed.), *The New Humanitarian Law of Armed Conflict*, Naples, Editoriale Scientifica, 1979 [Cassese (1979)]

___, "Mercenaries: Lawful Combatants or War Criminals?", *Zeitschrift für ausländisches öffentliches Recht und Völkerrecht*, Vol. 40, 1980, pp. 1-30 [Cassese (*ZaöRV* 1980)]

___, "The Status of Rebels under the 1977 Geneva Protocol on Non-International Armed Conflicts", *International and Comparative Law Quarterly*, Vol. 30, 1981, pp. 416-439 [Cassese (*ICLQ* 1981)]

___, "Wars of National Liberation and Humanitarian Law" in: Swinarski, Christophe (ed.), *Studies and Essays on International Humanitarian Law and Red Cross Principles in Honour of Jean Pictet*, Geneva/The Hague, International Committee of the Red Cross/Martinus Nijhoff Publishers, 1984, pp. 313-324 [Cassese in *Liber Amoricum Pictet* (1984)]

___, "The Geneva Protocols of 1977 on the Humanitarian Law of Armed Conflict and Customary International Law", *UCLA Pacific Basin Law Journal*, Vol. 3, 1984, pp. 55-118 [Cassese (*UCLA* 1984)]

___, "La guerre civile et le droit international", *Revue générale de droit international public*, Vol. 90, No. 3, 1986, pp. 553-578 [Cassese (*RGDIP* 1986)]

___, *International Law*, Oxford, Oxford University Press, 2001 [Cassese (2001)]

___, *International Criminal Law*, Oxford, Oxford University Press, 2003 [Cassese (2003)]

___, "On whether Israel's Targeted Killings of Palestinian Terrorists is Consonant with International Humanitarian Law", expert opinion submitted to the Israeli Supreme Court in *Case No. 769/02*, Judgment of 13 December 2006, available at http://www.stoptorture.org.il/files/cassese.pdf [Cassese (*Expert opinion Israel* 2006)]

Castrén, Erik, *Civil War*, Helsinki, Suomalainen Tiedeakatemia, 1966 [Castrén (1966)]

Cathcart, Blaise, "Command and Control in Military Operations" in: Gill, Terry D. and Fleck, Dieter (eds.), *The Handbook of the International Law of Military Operations*, New York, Oxford University Press, 2010, pp. 235-244 [Cathcart in Gill & Fleck (2010)]

Cerna, Christina Monica, "Human Rights in Armed Conflict: Implementation of International Humanitarian Law Norms by Regional Intergovernmental Human Rights Bodies" in: Kalshoven, Frits and Sandoz, Yves (eds.), *Implementation of International Humanitarian Law*, The Hague, Martinus Nijhoff, 1989, pp. 31-67 [Cerna in Kalshoven & Sandoz (1989)]

Cerone, John, P., "Status of Detainees in Non-International Armed Conflict, and their Protection in the Course of Criminal Proceedings: The Case of *Hamdan v. Rumsfeld*", *ASIL Insights*, Vol. 10, No. 17, 2006 [Cerone (*ASIL Insights* 2006)]

___, "Jurisdiction and Power: The Intersection of Human Rights Law & the Law of Non-International Armed Conflict in an Extraterritorial Context", *Israel Law Review*, Vol. 40, No. 2, 2007, pp. 72-128 [Cerone (*ILR* 2007)]

Cesarani, David and Kushner, Tony (eds.), *The Internment of Aliens in Twentieth Century Britain*, London, Frank Cass, 1993 [Cesarani & Kushner (1993)]

Chadwick, Elizabeth, "The Legal Position of Prisoners, Spies and Deserters during World War I", *Military Law and Law of War Review*, Vol. 36, Nos. 3-4, 1997, pp. 73-113 [Chadwick (*MLLWR* 1997)]

Chalermpalanupap, Termsak, "10 Facts about ASEAN Human Rights Cooperation", available on the website of the ASEAN Secretariat at http://www.aseansec.org/HLP-OtherDoc-1.pdf

Charmatz, Jan P. and Wit, Harold M., "Repatriation of Prisoners of War and the 1949 Geneva Convention", *Yale Law Journal*, Vol. 62, No. 3, 1953, pp. 391-415 [Charmatz & Wit (*YLJ* 1953)]

Chaumont, Charles, "La recherche d'un critère pour l'intégration de la guérilla au droit international humanitaire contemporain" in: *Mélanges offerts à Charles Rousseau. La communauté internationale*, Paris, Pedone, 1974, pp. 43-61 [Chaumont (1974)]

Cheng, Bin, *General Principles of Law as Applied by International Courts and Tribunals*, Cambridge, Grotius Publications, 1987 (reprint, first published by Stevens & Sons in 1953) [Cheng (1987)]

___, "United Nations Resolutions on Outer Space: 'Instant' International Customary Law?", *Indian Journal of International Law*, Vol. 5, 1965, pp. 23-48 [Cheng (*IJIL* 1965)]

Chetail, Vincent, "The Fundamental Principles of Humanitarian Law through the Case Law of the International Court of Justice", *Refugee Survey Quarterly*, Vol. 21, No. 3, 2002, pp. 199-211 [Chetail (*RSQ* 2002)]

Chubin, Shahram and Green, Jerrold D., *Terrorism and Asymmetric Conflict in Southwest Asia: Conference Proceedings*, Santa Monica/Arlington/Pittsburgh, RAND, 2002, available at http://www.rand.org/pubs/conf_proceedings/CF181/CF181.pdf [Chubin & Green (2002)]

Clapham, Andrew, *Human Rights Obligations of Non-State Actors*, Oxford, Oxford University Press, 2006 [Clapham (2006)]

___, "Human Rights Obligations of Non-State Actors in Conflict Situations", *International Review of the Red Cross*, Vol. 88, No. 863, 2006, pp. 491-523 [Clapham (*IRRC* 2006)]

___, "The Subject of Subjects and the Attribution of Attribution" in: Boisson de Chazournes, Laurence, and Kohen, Marcelo G., *International Law and the Quest for its Implementation/Le droit international et la quête de sa mise en œuvre: Liber Amicorum Vera Gowlland-Debbas*, Leiden, Brill, 2010, pp. 45-58 [Clapham in *Liber Amoricum Gowlland-Debbas* (2010)]

___, "The Rights and Responsibilities of Armed Non-State Actors: The Legal Landscape & Issues Surrounding Engagement", draft paper for the *Ownership of Norms Project – Toward a Better Protection of Civilians in Armed Conflicts*, February 2010, available at SSRN: http://ssrn.com/abstract=1569636 [Clapham (SSRN 2010)]

Cockayne, James, "Islam and International Humanitarian Law: From a Clash to a Conversation between Civilizations", *International Review of the Red Cross*, Vol. 84, No. 847, 2002, pp. 597-626 [Cockayne (*IRRC* 2002)]

Cole, David, "Out of the Shadows: Preventive Detention, Suspected Terrorists, and War", *California Law Review*, Vol. 97, No. 3, 2009, pp. 693-750 [Cole (*Calif.LR* 2009)]

College of Europe and International Committee of the Red Cross, *Proceedings of the Bruges Colloquium. Current Challenges to the Law of Occupation*, Bruges, College of Europe, *Collegium*, No. 34, Autumn 2006, available at http://www.coleurop.be/file/content/publications/pdf/Collegium%2034.pdf [College of Europe (2006)]

Condorelli, Luigi; La Rosa, Anne-Marie and Scherrer, Sylvie (eds.), *The United Nations and International Humanitarian Law*, Paris, Pedone, 1996 [Condorelli et al. (1996)]

Condorelli, Luigi, "Le statut des forces des Nations Unies et le droit international humanitaire", in: Emanuelli, Claude (dir.), *Les casques bleus: policiers ou combattants?*, Montreal, Wilson & Lafleur, 1997, pp. 87-113 [Condorelli in Emanuelli (1997)]

___, "Les attentats du 11 septembre et leurs suites: Où va le droit international?", *Revue générale de droit international public*, Vol. 105, No. 4, 2001, pp. 829-848 [Condorelli (*RGDIP* 2001)]

___ **and Naqvi, Yasmin Q.**, "The War against Terrorism and *Jus in Bello*: Are the Geneva Conventions Out of Date?" in: Bianchi, Andrea and Naqvi, Yasmin Q. (eds.), *Enforcing International Law Norms against Terrorism*, Oxford, Hart, 2004, pp. 25-37 [Condorelli & Naqvi in Bianchi (2004)]

Coomans, Fons and Kamminga, Menno T. (eds.), *Extraterritorial Application of Human Rights Treaties*, Antwerp, Intersentia, 2004 [Coomans & Kamminga (2004)]

Crawford, Emily, *The Treatment of Combatants and Insurgents under the Law of Armed Conflict*, New York, Oxford University Press, 2010 [Crawford (2010)]

Crawford, James, *The International Law Commission's Articles on State Responsibility: Introduction, Text and Commentaries,* Cambridge, Cambridge University Press, 2002 [Crawford (2002)]

___, "Multilateral Rights and Obligations in International Law", *Collected Courses of the Hague Academy of International Law*, Vol. 319, 2006, pp. 325-482 [Crawford (2006)]

___; **Pellet, Alain and Olleson, Simon** (eds.), *The Law of International Responsibility*, Oxford, Oxford University Press, 2010 [Crawford, Pellet & Olleson (2010)]

Crozier, Brian, *The Rebels*, London, Chatto & Windus, 1960 [Crozier (1960)]

Cryer, Robert, "The Interplay of Human Rights and Humanitarian Law: The Approach of the ICTY", *Journal of Conflict & Security Law*, Vol. 14, No. 3, 2009, pp. 511-527 [Cryer (*JCSL* 2009)]

Cullen, Anthony, *The Concept of Non-International Armed Conflict in International Humanitarian Law*, New York, Cambridge University Press, 2010 [Cullen (2010)]

D'Amato, Anthony, "Human Rights as Part of Customary International Law: A Plea for Change of Paradigms", *Georgia Journal of International and Comparative Law*, Vol. 25, No. 1, 1995-1996, pp. 47-98 [D'Amato (*GJICL* 1995-1996)]

David, Eric, *Mercenaires et volontaires internationaux en droit des gens*, Brussels, Éditions de l'Université de Bruxelles, 1978 [David (1978)]

___, *Principes de droit des conflits armés*, 3rd ed., Brussels, Bruylant, 2002 [David (2002)]

Deeks, Ashley S., "Administrative Detention in Armed Conflict", *Case Western Reserve Journal of International Law*, Vol. 40, No. 3, 2009, pp. 403-436 [Deeks (*CWRJIL* 2009)]

Del Mar, Katherine, "The Requirement of 'Belonging' under International Humanitarian Law", *European Journal of International Law*, Vol. 21, No. 1, 2010, pp. 105-124 [Del Mar (*EJIL* 2010)]

Delaplace, Edouard and Pollard, Matt, "Visits by Human Rights Mechanisms as a Means of Greater Protection for Persons Deprived of Liberty", *International Review of the Red Cross*, Vol. 87, No. 857, 2005, pp. 69-82 [Delaplace & Pollard (*IRRC* 2005)]

Delissen, Astrid J.M. and Tanja, Gerard J. (eds.), *Humanitarian Law of Armed Conflict: Challenges ahead. Essays in Honour of Frits Kalshoven*, Dordrecht, Martinus Nijhoff, 1991 [Delissen & Tanja (1991)]

Dennis, Michael J. and Surena, Andre M., "Application of the International Covenant on Civil and Political Rights in Times of Armed Conflict and Military Occupation: The Gap between Legal Theory and State Practice", *European Human Rights Law Review*, No. 6, 2008, pp. 714–731 [Dennis & Surena (*EHRLR* 2007)]

Dennis, Michael J., "Application of Human Rights Treaties Extraterritorially in Times of Armed Conflict and Military Occupation", *American Journal of International Law*, Vol. 99, No. 1, 2005, pp. 119-141 [Dennis (*AJIL* 2005)]

___, "Applying Human Rights Law and Humanitarian Law in the Extraterritorial War against Terrorism: Too Little, too Much, or just Right? Application of Human Rights Treaties Extraterritorially to Detention of Combatants and Security Internees: Fuzzy Thinking All Around?", *ILSA Journal of International & Comparative Law*, Vol. 12, 2006, pp. 459-480 [Dennis (*ILSA JICL* 2006)]

___, "Non-Application of Civil and Political Rights Treaties Extraterritorially during Times of International Armed Conflict", *Israel Law Review*, Vol. 40, No. 2, 2007, pp. 453-502 [Dennis (*ILR* 2007)]

Dershowitz, Alan, "The Laws of War Weren't Written for this War", *Wall Street Journal*, 12 February 2004 [Dershowitz (*WSJ* 2004)]

De Schutter, Bart and Van den Wyngaert, Christine, "Coping with Non-International Armed Conflicts: The Borderline between National and International Law", *Georgia Journal of International and Comparative Law*, Vol. 13 (supp.), 1983, pp. 279-290 [De Schutter & Van den Wyngaert (*GJICL* 1983)]

Detter de Lupis, Ingrid, *The Law of War*, 2nd ed., Cambridge, Cambridge University Press, 2000 [Detter (2000)]

Dhokalia, Ramaa Prasad, "Civil Wars and International Law", *Indian Journal of International Law*, Vol. 11, 1971, pp. 219-250 [Dhokalia (*IJIL* 1971)]

Difo, Germain, *Ordinary Measures, Extraordinary Results: An Assessment of Foiled Plots since 9/11*, Washington D.C., American Security Project, 21 May 2010, report available at http://americansecurityproject.org/wp-content/uploads/2010/09/Foiled-Plots.pdf [Difo (2010)]

Dingwall, Joanna, "Unlawful Confinement as a War Crime: The Jurisprudence of the Yugoslav Tribunal and the Common Core of International Humanitarian Law Applicable to Contemporary Armed Conflicts", *Journal of Conflict & Security Law*, Vol. 9, No. 2, 2004, pp. 133-179 [Dingwall (*JCSL* 2004)]

Dinstein, Yoram, "The International Law of Belligerent Occupation and Human Rights", *Israel Yearbook on Human Rights*, Vol. 8, 1978, pp. 104-143 [Dinstein (*Isr.YHR* 1978)]

___, "The Right to Life, Physical Integrity, and Liberty" in: Henkin, Louis, *The International Bill of Rights: The Covenant on Civil and Political Rights*, New York, Colombia University Press, 1981, pp. 114-137 [Dinstein in Henkin (1981)]

___, "Refugees and the Law of Armed Conflicts", *Israel Yearbook on Human Rights*, Vol. 12, 1982, pp. 94-109 [Dinstein (*Isr.YHR* 1982))]

___, *The Laws of War*, Tel-Aviv, Shoken, 1983 [Dinstein (1983)]

___, "The Release of Prisoners of War" in: Swinarski, Christophe (ed.), *Studies and Essays on International Humanitarian Law and Red Cross Principles in Honour of Jean Pictet*, Geneva/The Hague, International Committee of the Red Cross/Martinus Nijhoff Publishers, 1984, pp. 37-45 [Dinstein in *Liber Amoricum Pictet* (1984)]

___, "Human Rights in Armed Conflict: International Humanitarian Law" in: Meron, Theodor (ed.), *Human Rights in International Law: Legal and Policy Issues*, Oxford, Clarendon Press, 1984, Vol. 2, pp. 345-368 [Dinstein in Meron (1984)]

___, "The Distinction between Unlawful Combatants and War Criminals", in: Dinstein, Yoram (ed.), *International Law at a Time of Perplexity. Essays in Honour of Shabtai Rosenne*, Dordrecht, Martinus Nijhoff Publishers, 1989, pp. 103-116 [Dinstein in *Liber Amoricum Rosenne* (1989)]

___, "Unlawful Combatancy", *Israel Yearbook on Human Rights*, Vol. 32, 2002, pp. 247-270 [Dinstein (*Isr.YHR* 2002)]

___, "*Jus in Bello* Issues Arising in the Hostilities in Iraq in 2003", *Israel Yearbook on Human Rights*, Vol. 34, 2004, pp. 1-14 [Dinstein (*Isr.YHR* 2004)]

___, *The Conduct of Hostilities under the Law of International Armed Conflict*, Cambridge, Cambridge University Press, 2004 [Dinstein (2004)]

___; **Garraway, Charles and Schmitt, Michael N.**, *The Manual on the Law of Non-International Armed Conflict, with Commentary*, San Remo, International Institute of Humanitarian Law, 2006, available at http://www.dur.ac.uk/resources/law/NIACManualIYBHR15th.pdf [Dinstein, Garraway & Schmitt (*San Remo Manual* 2006)]

Dinstein, Yoram, *The Law of Belligerent Occupation*, Cambridge, Cambridge University Press, 2009 [Dinstein (2009)]

___, *The Conduct of Hostilities under the Law of International Armed Conflict*, 2nd ed., Cambridge, Cambridge University Press, 2010 [Dinstein (2010)]

Dörmann, Knut, *Elements of Crime under the Rome Statute of the International Criminal Court. Sources and Commentary*, Geneva/Cambridge, International Committee of the Red Cross/Cambridge University Press, 2003 [Dörmann (2003)]

___, "The Legal Situation of 'Unlawful/Unprivileged Combatants'", *International Review of the Red Cross*, Vol. 85, No. 849, 2003, pp. 45-73 [Dörmann (*IRRC* 2003)]

Doswald-Beck, Louise, "International Humanitarian Law: A Means of Protecting Human Rights in Time of Armed Conflict", *African Journal of International and Comparative Law*, Vol. 1, No. 4, 1989, pp. 595-620 [Doswald-Beck (*AJICL* 1989)]

___ **and Vité, Sylvain**, "International Humanitarian Law and Human Rights Law", *International Review of the Red Cross*, Vol. 76, No. 293, 1993, pp. 94-119 [Doswald-Beck & Vité (*IRRC 1993*)]

___ **and Kolb, Robert**, *Judicial Process and Human Rights: United Nations, European, American and African Systems: Texts and Summaries of International Case-Law*, Kehl/Arlington, N.P. Engel, 2004 [Doswald-Beck & Kolb (2004)]

Doswald-Beck, Louise, "The Right to Life in Armed Conflict: Does International Humanitarian Law Provide all the Answers?", *International Review of the Red Cross*, Vol. 88, No. 864, 2006, pp. 881-904 [Doswald-Beck (*IRRC* 2006)]

___, "Private Military Companies under International Humanitarian Law" in: Chesterman, Simon and Lehnardt, Chia (eds.), *From Mercenaries to Markets: The Rise and Regulation of Private Military Companies*, New York, Oxford University Press, 2007, pp. 115-138 [Doswald-Beck in Chesterman & Lehnardt (2007)]

Draper, Gerald I.A.D., *The Red Cross Conventions*, London, Stevens, 1958 [Draper (1958)]

___, "The Geneva Conventions of 1949", *Collected Courses of the Hague Academy of International Law*, Vol. 114, 1965-I, pp. 59-165 [Draper (*Hague Academy Collected Courses* 1965)]

___, "The Relationship between the Human Rights Regime and the Law of Armed Conflict", *Israel Yearbook on Human Rights*, Vol. 1, 1971, pp. 191-207 [Draper (*Isr.YHR* 1971)]

___, "Humanitarian Law and Internal Armed Conflicts", *Georgia Journal of International and Comparative Law*, Vol. 13, 1983, pp. 253-278 [Draper (*GJICL* 1983)]

___, "The Status of Combatants and the Question of Guerrilla Warfare", *British Year Book of International Law*, Vol. 45, 1971, pp. 173-218 [Draper (*BYIL* 1971)]

Droege, Cordula, "Elective Affinities? Human Rights and Humanitarian Law", *International Review of the Red Cross*, Vol. 90, No. 871, 2008, pp. 501-548 [Droege (*IRRC* 2008)]

Dugard, John, "SWAPO: The *Jus ad Bellum* and the *Jus in Bello*", *South African Law Journal*, Vol. 93, 1976, pp. 144-158 [Dugard (*SALJ* 1976)]

___, "The Treatment of Rebels in Conflicts of a Disputed Character" in: Delissen, Astrid J.M. and Tanja, Gerard J. (eds.), *Humanitarian Law of Armed Conflict: Challenges ahead. Essays in Honour of Frits Kalshoven*, The Hague, T.M.C. Asser Institute, 1991, pp. 447-464 [Dugard in *Liber Amoricum Kalshoven* (1991)]

Dupuy, Pierre-Marie, *L'unité de l'ordre juridique international: Cours général de droit international public* (2000), *Collected Courses of the Hague Academy of International Law*, Vol. 297, 2002, pp. 9-490 [Dupuy (2002)]

Durham, Helen and McCormack, Timothy (eds.), *The Changing Face of Conflict and the Efficacy of International Humanitarian Law*, The Hague, Kluwer Law International, 1999 [Durham & McCormack (1999)]

Dworkin, Anthony, "The Yemen Strike: The War on Terror Goes Global" in: Crimes of War Project, 14 November 2002, available at www.crimesofwar.org/onnews/news-yemen.html [Dworkin (*Crimes of War* 2002)]

Eide, Asbjørn; Rosas, Allan and Meron, Theodor, "Combating Lawlessness in Gray Zone Conflicts through Minimum Humanitarian Standards", *American Journal of International Law*, Vol. 89, No. 1, 1995, pp. 215-222 [Eide, Rosas & Meron (*AJIL* 1995)]

Emanuelli, Claude, "United Nations Forces and Humanitarian Law" in: Condorelli, Luigi; La Rosa, Anne-Marie and Scherrer, Sylvie (eds), *The United Nations and International Humanitarian Law*, Paris, Pedone, 1996, pp. 345-370 [Emanuelli in Condorelli et al. (1996)]

Ewumbue-Monono, Churchill, "Respect for International Humanitarian Law by Non-State Actors in Africa", *International Review of the Red Cross*, Vol. 88, No. 864, 2006, pp. 905-924 [Ewumbue-Monono (*IRRC* 2006)]

Falk, Richard A., "Janus Tormented: The International Law of Internal War" in: Rosenau, James, N. (ed.), *International Aspects of Civil Strife*, Princeton, Princeton University Press, 1964, pp. 185-ff [Falk in Rosenau (1964)]

___, *The International Law of Civil War*, Baltimore, Johns Hopkins Press, 1971 [Falk (1971)]

Ferrell, William H., "No Shirt, no Shoes, no Status: Uniforms, Distinction and Special Operations in International Armed Conflict", *Military Law Review*, Vol. 178, 2003, pp. 94-140 [Ferrell (*MLR* 2003)]

Fischer, Horst, "Protection of Prisoners of War" in: Fleck, Dieter (ed.), *The Handbook of International Humanitarian Law*, Oxford, Oxford University Press, 2008, pp. 367-418 [Fischer in Fleck (2008)]

Fitzmaurice, Malgosia; Elias, Olufemi and Merkouris, Panos (eds.), *Treaty Interpretation and the Vienna Convention on the Law of Treaties: 30 Years on*, Leiden, Martinus Nijhoff Publishers, 2010 [Fitzmaurice, Elias & Merkouris 2010]

Fleck, Dieter (ed.), *The Handbook of the Law of Visiting Forces*, Oxford, Oxford University Press, 2001 [Fleck (2001)]

___, "Humanitarian Protection against Non-State Actors" in: Frowein, Jochen; Scharioth, Klaus; Winkelman, Ingo and Wolfrum, Rüdiger (eds.), *Verhandeln für den Frieden – Negotiating for Peace. Liber Amoricum Tono Eitel*, Berlin, Springer, 2003, pp. 69-94 [Fleck in *Liber Amoricum Eitel* (2003)]

___ (ed.), *The Handbook of International Humanitarian Law*, 2nd ed., Oxford, Oxford University Press, 2008 [Fleck (2008)]

Fletcher, George P., "Black Hole in Guantánamo Bay", *Journal of International Criminal Justice*, Vol. 2, 2004, pp. 121-132 [Fletcher (*JICJ* 2004)]

Forowicz, Magdalena, *The Reception of International Law in the European Court of Human Rights*, New York, Oxford University Press, 2010 [Forowicz (2010)]

Forsythe, David P., "Legal Management of Internal War: The 1977 Protocol on Non-International Armed Conflicts", *American Journal of International Law*, Vol. 72, No. 2, 1978, pp. 272-295 [Forsythe (*AJIL* 1978)]

Fox, Hazel and Meyer, Michael A. (eds.), *Armed Conflict and the New Law, Vol. II: Effecting Compliance*, London, British Institute of International and Comparative Law, 1993 [Fox & Meyer (1993)]

Freeman, Mark, "International Law and Internal Armed Conflicts: Clarifying the Interplay between Human Rights and Humanitarian Protections", *The Journal of Humanitarian Assistance*, 24 May 2000, available at www.jha.ac//articles/a059.htm [Freeman (*JHA* 2000)]

___, *Human Rights: An Interdisciplinary Approach*, Cambridge, Polity Press, 2002 [Freeman (2002)]

Friedrich, Werner, *Die Völkerrechtliche Stellung von Söldnertruppe im Kriege*, Bad Honnef, Bock & Herchen Verlag, 1978 [Friedrich (1978)]

Gaeta, Paula, "May Necessity Be Available as a Defence for Torture in the Interrogation of Suspected Terrorists?", *Journal of International Criminal Justice*, Vol. 2, 2004, pp. 785-794 [Gaeta (*JICJ* 2004)]

Gall, Carlotta and De Waal, Thomas, *Chechnya*, New York, New York University Press, 2000 [Gall & De Waal (2000)]

Gallant, Kenneth S., *The Principle of Legality in International and Comparative Criminal Law*, Cambridge, Cambridge University Press, 2009 [Gallant (2009)]

Garcia-Mora, Manuel R., *International Law and Asylum as a Human Right*, Washington, Public Affairs Press, 1956 [Garcia-Mora (1956)]

Garner, James W., "Recognition of Belligerency", *American Journal of International Law*, Vol. 32, No. 1, 1938, pp. 106-113 [Garner (*AJIL* 1938)]

Gasser, Hans-Peter, "International Non-International Armed Conflicts: Case Studies of Afghanistan, Kampuchea and Lebanon", *American University Law Review*, Vol. 31, 1982, pp. 911-925 [Gasser (*AULR* 1982)]

___, "Armed Conflict within the Territory of a State" in: Haller, Walter, Alfred Kölz et al. (eds.), *Im Dienst an der Gemeinschaft. Festschrift für Dietrich Schindler zum 65. Geburtstag*, Basel, Helbing under Lichtenhahn, 1989, pp. 225-240 [Gasser in *Liber Amoricum Schindler* (1989)]

___, *International Humanitarian Law: An Introduction*, separate print from: Haug, Hans (ed.), *Humanity for All: The International Red Cross and Red Crescent Movement*, Geneva/Bern, Institut Henry-Dunant/Paul Haupt, 1993 [Gasser (1993)]

___, "Acts of Terror, 'Terrorism' and International Humanitarian Law", *International Review of the Red Cross*, Vol. 84, No. 847, 2002, pp. 547-570 [Gasser (*IRRC* 2002)]

___, "International Humanitarian Law and Human Rights Law in Non-International Armed Conflict: Joint Venture or Mutual Exclusion?", *German Yearbook of International Law*, Vol. 45, 2002, pp. 149-162 [Gasser (*GYIL* 2002)]

___, "Protection of the Civilian Population" in: Fleck, Dieter (ed.), *The Handbook of International Humanitarian Law*, Oxford, Oxford University Press, 2008, pp. 237-323 [Gasser in Fleck (2008)]

Gehring, Robert W., "Loss of Civilian Protections under the Fourth Geneva Convention and Protocol I", *Military Law and Law of War Review*, Vol. 19, Nos. 1-2, 1980, pp. 11-48 [Gehring (*MLLWR* 1980)]

Geiss, Robin, "Name, Rank, Date of Birth, Serial Number and the Right to Remain Silent", *International Review of the Red Cross*, Vol. 87, No. 860, 2005, pp. 721-736 [Geiss (*IRRC* 2005)]

Genot, Guy, "Quelques garanties nouvelles offertes au combattant capturé", *Revue belge de droit international*, Vol. 13, Nos. 1-2, 1977 [Genot (*RBDI* 1977)]

Gillard, Emmanuela-Chiara, "Business Goes to War: Private Military/Security Companies and International Humanitarian Law", *International Review of the Red Cross*, Vol. 88, No. 863, 2006, pp. 525-572 [Gillard (*IRRC 2006*)]

___, "There's no Place like Home: States' Obligations in Relation to Transfers of Persons", *International Review of the Red Cross*, Vol. 90, No. 871, 2008, pp. 703-750 [Gillard (*IRRC 2008*)]

Goldman, Robert Kogod, "International Humanitarian Law and the Armed Conflict in El Salvador and Nicaragua", *American University Journal of International Law and Policy*, Vol. 2, No. 2, 1987, pp. 539-578 [Goldman (*AUJILP* 1987)]

___ **and Tittemore, Brian D.**, "Unprivileged Combatants and the Hostilities in Afghanistan: Their Status and Rights under International Humanitarian and Human Rights Llaw", *ASIL Task Force on Terrorism*, December 2002, available at www.asil.org/taskforce/goldman.pdf [Goldman & Tittemore (*ASIL Task Force* 2002)]

Goldman, Robert Kogod, "History and Action: The Inter-American Human Rights System and the Role of the Inter-American Commission on Human Rights", *Human Rights Quarterly*, Vol. 31, No. 4, 2009, pp. 856-887 [Goldman (*HRQ* 2009)]

Gondek, Michal, *The Reach of Human Rights in a Globalizing World: Extraterritorial Application of Human Rights Treaties*, Antwerp, Intersentia, 2009 [Gondek (2009)]

Goodman, Ryan, "Rationales for Detention: Security Threats and Intelligence Value" in: Schmitt, Michael N. (ed.), *The War in Afghanistan: A Legal Analysis*, Newport, Naval War College, *International Law Studies*, Vol. 85, 2009, pp. 371-838 [Goodman in Schmitt (2009)]

___, "The Detention of Civilians in Armed Conflict", *American Journal of International Law*, Vol. 103, No. 1, 2009, pp. 48-74 [Goodman (*AJIL* 2009)]

Goodwin-Gill, Guy S., "Article 31 of the 1951 Convention Relating to the Status of Refugees: Non-Penalization, Detention, and Protection" in: Feller, Erika; Türk, Volker and Nicholson, Frances (eds.), *Refugee Protection in International Law*, Cambridge, Cambridge University Press, 2003, pp. 185-252 [Goodwin-Gill in Feller, Türk & Nicholson (2003)]

___, "The Extra-Territorial Reach of Human Rights Obligations: A Brief Perspective on the Link to Jurisdiction" in: Boisson de Chazournes, Laurence and Kohen, Marcelo G., *International Law and the Quest for its Implementation/Le droit international et la quête de sa mise en oeuvre. Liber Amicorum Vera Gowlland-Debbas*, Leiden, Brill, 2010, pp. 293-308 [Goodwin-Gill in *Liber Amoricum Gowlland-Debbas* (2010)]

Gray, Colin S., "Thinking Asymmetrically in Times of Terror", *US Army War College Quarterly*, Spring 2002, available at http://www.army.mil/usawc/Parameters/02Spring/gray.htm [Gray (*USACQ* 2002)]

Green, Leslie C., "The Status of Mercenaries in International Law", *Israel Yearbook on Human Rights*, Vol. 8, 1978, pp. 9-62 [Green (*Isr.YHR* 1978)]

___, "Human Rights and the Law of Armed Conflict", *Israel Yearbook on Human Rights*, Vol. 10, 1980, pp. 9-37 [Green (*Isr.YHR* 1980)]

___, "The Relations between Human Rights Law and International Humanitarian Law: A Historical Overview" in: Breau, Susan Carolyn and Jachec-Neale, Agnieszka (eds.), *Testing the Boundaries of International Humanitarian Law*, London, British Institute of International and Comparative Law, 2006, pp. 49-84 [Green in Breau & Jachec-Neale (2006)]

___, *The Contemporary Law of Armed Conflict*, 3rd ed., Manchester, Manchester University Press, 2008 [Green (2008)]

Greenspan, Morris, *The Modern Law of Warfare*, Berkeley and Los Angeles, University of California Press, 1959 [Greenspan (1959)]

Greenwood, Christopher J., "The Relationship between *Jus ad Bellum* and *Jus in Bello*", *Review of International Studies*, Vol. 9, No. 4, 1983, pp. 221-234 [Greenwood (*RIS* 1983)]

___, "Customary Law Status of the 1977 Geneva Protocols" in: Delissen, Astrid J.M. and Tanja, Gerard J. (eds.), *Humanitarian Law of Armed Conflict: Challenges ahead. Essays in Honour of Frits Kalshoven*, The Hague, T.M.C. Asser Institute, 1991, pp. 93-114 [Greenwood in *Liber Amoricum Kalshoven* (1991)]

___, "International Humanitarian Law and the *Tadíc* Case", *European Journal of International Law*, Vol. 7, No. 2, 1996, pp. 265-283 [Greenwood (*EJIL* 1996)]

___, "International Law and the 'War against Terrorism'", *International Affairs*, Vol. 78, No. 2, 2002, pp. 301-317 [Greenwood (*International Affairs* 2002)]

___, "Historical Development and Legal Basis" in: Fleck, Dieter (ed.), *The Handbook of International Humanitarian Law*, Oxford, Oxford University Press, 2008, pp. 1-44 [Greenwood in Fleck (2008)]

___, "Scope of Application of Humanitarian Law" in: Fleck, Dieter (ed.), *The Handbook of International Humanitarian Law*, Oxford, Oxford University Press, 2008, pp. 45-78 [Greenwood in Fleck (2008)]

Gros Espiell, Hector, *The Right to Self-Determination: Implementation of United Nations' Resolutions*, UN Doc. E/CN.4/Sub.2/405/Rev.1, New York, United Nations, 1980 [Gros Espiell (1980)]

Gross, Aeyal M., "Human Proportions: Are Human Rights the Emperor's New Clothes of the International Law of Occupation?", *European Journal of International Law*, Vol. 18, No. 1, 2007, pp. 1-35 [Gross (*EJIL* 2007)]

Gross, Emmanuel, "Human Rights, Terrorism and the Problem of Administrative Detention in Israel: Does a Democracy Have the Right to Hold Terrorists as Bargaining Chips?", *Arizona Journal of International and Comparative Law*, Vol. 183, No. 2, 2001, pp. 721-791 [Gross (*Ariz.JICL* 2001)]

Guillaume, Gilbert, "Terrorisme et droit international", *Collected Courses of the Hague Academy of International Law*, Vol. 215, 1989-II, pp. 287-416 [Guillaume (*Hague Academy Collected Courses* (1989)]

Guillory, Michael E., "Civilianizing the Force: Is the United States Crossing the Rubicon? – Role of Civilians under the Laws of Armed Conflict, *Air Force Law Review*, 2001, available at
www.findarticles.com/p/articles/mi_m6007/is_2001_Spring/ai_92044661/print
[Gullory (*AFLR* 2001)]

Gutteridge, J.A.C., "The Repatriation of Prisoners of War", *International and Comparative Law Quarterly*, Vol. 2, No. 2, 1953, pp. 207-216 [Gutteridge (*ICLQ* 1953)]

Haggenmacher, Peter, "L'occupation militaire en droit international : genèse et profil d'une institution juridique", *Relations Internationales*, Vol. 79, 1994, pp. 285-301 [Haggenmacher (*RI* 1994)]

Hampson, Françoise Jane, "Human Rights and Humanitarian Law in Internal Conflicts" in: Meyer, Michael A. (ed.), *Armed Conflicts and the New Law: Aspects of the 1977 Protocols and 1981 Weapons Convention*, London, British Institute of International and Comparative Law, 1989, pp. 55-80 [Hampson in Meyer (1989)]

___, "Using International Human Rights Machinery to Enforce the International Law of Armed Conflicts", *Military Law and Law of War Review*, Vol. 31, Nos. 1-4, 1992, pp. 117-142 [Hampson (*MLLWR* 1992)]

___, "Human Rights Law, International Humanitarian Law & Situations of Conflict", paper for the University of Tehran's *Colloquium on the Interplay between International Humanitarian Law and International Human Rights Law: Global and Regional Perspectives*, Tehran, 13-14 April 2004, on file with author [Hampson (*Tehran Conference Paper* 2004)]

___, "Military Necessity" in: Dworkin, Anthony; Gutman, Roy and Rieff, David (eds.), *Crimes of War 2.0: What the Public Should Know*, revised and updated edition, New York, W.W. Norton & Company, 2007, extract available at http://www.crimesofwar.org/thebook/military-necessity.html [Hampson in Dworkin (2007)]

___, "The Relationship between International Humanitarian Law and Human Rights Law from the Perspective of a Human Rights Treaty Body", *International Review of the Red Cross*, Vol. 90, No. 871, 2008, pp. 549-572 [Hampson (*IRRC* 2008)]

___, "Is Human Rights Law of any Relevance to Military Operations in Afghanistan?" in: Schmitt, Michael N. (ed.), *The War in Afghanistan: A legal Analysis*, Newport, Naval War College, *International Law Studies*, Vol. 85, 2009, pp. 357-370 [Hampson in Schmitt (2009)]

Hannard, Cindy (ed.), *Actes du Colloque de Bruges : Défis contemporains en droit international humanitaire, 27-28 octobre 2000*, Bruges/Geneva, Collège d'Europe/International Committee of the Red Cross, 2000 [Hannard (2000)]

Happold, Matthew, "Child Prisoners in War" in: Scheipers, Sybille (ed.), *Prisoners in War*, Oxford, Oxford University Press, 2010, pp. 237-250 [Happold in Scheipers (2010)]

Harris, David J., *Cases and Materials on International Law*, 5th ed., London, Sweet & Maxwell, 1998 [Harris (1998)]

Hays Parks, W., "Part IX of the ICRC 'Direct Participation in Hostilities' Study: No Mandate, no Expertise, and Legally Incorrect", *New York University Journal of International Law and Policy*, Vol. 42, No. 3, 2010, pp. 769-830 [Hays Parks (*NYUJILP* 2010)]

Heintze, Hans-Joachim, "The European Court of Human Rights and the Implementation of Human Rights Standards during Armed Conflicts", *German Yearbook of International Law*, Vol. 45, 2002, pp. 60-81 [Heintze (*GYIL* 2002)]

___, "On the Relationship between Human Rights Law Protection and International Humanitarian Law", *International Review of the Red Cross*, Vol. 86, No. 856, 2004, pp. 789-814 [Heintze (*IRRC* 2004)]

Henckaerts, Jean-Marie, "Study on Customary International Humanitarian Law: A Contribution to the Understanding and Respect for the Rule of Law in Armed Conflict", *International Review of the Red Cross*, Vol. 87, No. 857, 2005, pp. 175-197 [Henckaerts (*IRRC* 2005)]

___ **and Doswald-Beck, Louise** (eds.), *Customary International Humanitarian Law*, Geneva/Cambridge, International Committee of the Red Cross/Cambridge University Press, 2005, updated (12 August 2010) and available at http://www.icrc.org/customary-ihl/eng/docs/home [Henckaerts & Doswald-Beck (2005)]

Henckaerts, Jean-Marie, "Customary International Humanitarian Law: A Response to US Comments", *International Review of the Red Cross*, Vol. 89, No. 866, 2007, pp. 473-488 [Henckaerts (*IRRC* 2007)]

Henkin, Louis, "Human Rights and State Sovereignty", *Georgia Journal of International and Comparative Law*, Vol. 25, No. 1, 1995-1996, pp. 31-46 [Henkin (*GJICL* 1995-1996)]

Henzelin, Marc, "L'intervention en Iraq et le droit international", *Cahiers internationaux CEDIN Paris I/Centre de droit international ULB*, No. 19, 2004, pp. 171-182 [Henzelin (*Cahiers internationaux* 2004)]

Herrmann, Irène and Palmieri, Daniel, "Les nouveaux conflits: Une modernité archaïque?", *International Review of the Red Cross*, Vol. 85, No. 849, 2003, pp. 23-44 [Herrmann & Palmieri (*IRRC* 2003)]

___, "A Haunting Figure: The Hostage through the Ages", *International Review of the Red Cross*, Vol. 87, No. 857, 2005, pp. 135-145 [Herrmann & Palmieri (*IRRC* 2005)]

Higgins, Rosalyn, "Derogations under Human Rights Treaties" in *British Year Book of International Law*, Vol. 48, 1976-1977, pp. 281-320 [Higgins (*BYIL* 1976-1977)]

___, *Problems and Process: International Law and how we Use it*, Oxford, Clarendon Press, 1994 [Higgins (1994)]

___, *Themes and Theories. Selected Essays, Speeches and Writings in International Law*, Oxford, Oxford University Press, 2009 [Higgins (2009)]

Higham, Robin D.S. (ed.), *Civil Wars in the Twentieth Century*, Lexington, Kentucky University Press, 1972 [Higham (1972)]

Hill, John, "Royal Nepalese Army Adapts to Counterinsurgency Role", *Jane's Intelligence Review*, Vol. 16, 2004, pp. 22-27 [Hill (*Jane's Intelligence Review* (2004)]

Hoffer, Henri-P., "L'internement des malades et blessés dans les pays neutres", *International Review of the Red Cross*, No. 2, 1919, pp. 159-171 [Hoffer (*IRRC* 1919)]

Hofmann, Rainer, "International Humanitarian Law and the Law of Refugees and Internally Displaced Persons" in: *Law in Humanitarian Crises. Le droit face au crises humanitaires*, Luxemburg, Office for Official Publications of the European Communities, 1995, pp. 249-310 [Hofmann (1995)]

Institute of International Law, *Manual of the Laws of War on Land*, Oxford, 9 September 1880 [Oxford Manual (1880)]

___, *Règlement sur la responsabilité des États à raison des dommages soufferts par des étrangers en cas d'émeute, d'insurrection ou de guerre civile*, adopted at its 1900 session in Neuchâtel, available at http://www.idi-iil.org/ [IIL, *Règlement guerre civile* (1900)]

___, *Droits et devoirs des Puissances étrangères, au cas de mouvement insurrectionnel, envers les gouvernements établis et reconnus qui sont aux prises avec l'insurrection*, adopted at its 1900 session in Neuchâtel, available at http://www.idi-iil.org/ [IIL, *Puissances neutres et guerre civile* (1900)]

___, *Règlement concernant les effets de la guerre sur les traités*, resolution adopted at its 1912 session in Christiania, available at http://www.idi-iil.org/ [IIL, *Règlement concernant les effets de la guerre sur les traités* (1912)]

___, *La détermination du domaine réservé et ses effets*, resolution adopted at its 1954 session in Aix-en-Provence, available at http://www.idi-iil.org/ [IIL, *Resolution on "domaine reservé"* (1954)]

___, *Conditions of Application of Humanitarian Rules of Armed Conflict to Hostilities in which United Nations May Be Engaged*, adopted at its 1971 session in Zagreb, available at http://www.idi-iil.org/ [IIL, *Resolution on the Applicability of IHL to UN Forces* (1971)]

___, *Conditions of Application of Rules, other than Humanitarian Rules, of Armed Conflict to Hostilities in which United Nations Forces May be Engaged*, adopted at its 1975 session in Wiesbaden, available at http://www.idi-iil.org/

___, *Effects of Armed Conflicts on Treaties*, adopted at its 1985 session in Helsinki, available at http://www.idi-iil.org/ [IIL, *Resolution on the Effects of Armed Conflicts on Treaties* (1985)]

___, *The Application of International Humanitarian Law and Fundamental Human Rights in Armed Conflicts in which Non-State Entities Are Parties*, adopted at its 1999 session in Berlin, available at http://www.idi-iil.org/ [IIL, *Resolution on IHL and Non-State Entities* (1999)]

Institute for Policy Studies, *The War between Ethiopia and Eritrea*, 11 October 2005, available at http://www.ips-dc.org/reports/the_war_between_ethiopia_and_eritrea

International Institute of Humanitarian Law (San Remo), "Règles du droit international humanitaire relatives à la conduite des hostilities dans les conflits armés non internationaux", *International Review of the Red Cross*, Vol. 72, No. 785, 1990, pp. 415-442 [IIHL (*IRRC* 1990)]

___, *XXVIIth Round Table on Current Problems of International Humanitarian Law: International Humanitarian Law and Other Legal Regimes: Interplay in Situations of Violence – Summary Report*, 2003, available at [IIHL, *Report of the San Remo Roundtable* (2003)]

International Law Association, *Paris Minimum Standards of Human Rights Norms in a State of Emergency*, adopted by the 61st Conference of the International Law Association, Paris, 26 August - 1 September 1984, *Reports of Conferences*, Vol. 61, 1984, and reprinted with an introduction by Lillich, Richard in: *American Journal of International Law*, Vol. 79, No. 4, 1985, pp. 1073-1081 [ILA, *Paris Minimum Standards* (1984)]

Ipsen, Knut, "Combatants and Non-Combatants" in: Fleck, Dieter (ed.), *The Handbook of International Humanitarian Law*, Oxford, Oxford University Press, 2008, pp. 79-118 [Ipsen in Fleck (2008)]

Jäger, Thomas and Kümmel, Gerhard (eds.), *Private Military and Security Companies. Chances, Problems, Pitfalls and Prospects*, Wiesbaden, VS Verlag, 2007 [Jäger & Kümmel (2007)]

Jayawickrama, Nihal, *The Judicial Application of Human Rights Law: National, Regional and International Jurisprudence*, Cambridge, Cambridge University Press, 2002 [Jayawickrama (2002)]

Jenkins, Brian Michael, *International Terrorism: A New Mode of Conflict*, research paper for the California Seminar on Arms Control and Foreign Policy, Santa Monica, Crescent Publications, 1975 [Jenkins (1975)]

___, "High Technology Terrorism and Surrogate War: The Impact of New Technology on Low-Level Violence", *The Rand Paper Series*, No. P-5541, Santa Monica, The Rand Corporation, January 1975, available at http://www.rand.org/pubs/papers/2006/P5339.pdf [Jenkins (*Rand Paper Series* 1975)]

Jenks, Wilfred C., "The Conflict of Law-Making Treaties", *British Year Book of International Law*, Vol. 30, 1953, pp. 401-453 [Jenks (*BYIL* 1953)]

Jinks, Derek, "September 11 and the Laws of War", *Yale Journal of International Law*, Vol. 28, No. 1, 2003, pp. 1-50 [Jinks (*YJIL* 2003)]

___, "The Temporal Scope of Application of International Humanitarian Law in Contemporary Armed Conflicts", Harvard University, Program on Humanitarian Policy and Conflict Research, background paper for the informal High-Level Expert Meeting on the Reaffirmation and Development of International Humanitarian Law, Cambridge 27-29 January 2003, available at http://insct.syr.edu/uploadedFiles/insct/uploadedfiles/PDFs/Jinks,%20Derek.Temporal%20Scope%20of%20IHL%20in%20Contemporary%20Conflicts.pdf [Jinks (*HPCR Paper* 2003)]

___, "The Declining Significance of POW Status", *Harvard International Law Journal*, Vol. 45, No. 2, 2004, pp. 367-442 [Jinks (*Harv.ILJ* 2004)]

___, "The Applicability of the Geneva Conventions to the 'Global War on Terrorism'", *Virginia Journal of International Law*, Vol. 46, No. 1, 2005-2006, pp. 165-196 [Jinks (*VJIL* 2005-2006)]

Junod, Sylvie, "Additional Protocol II: History and Scope", *American University Law Review*, Vol. 33, No. 1, 1983, pp. 29-40 [Junod (*AULR* 1983)]

Kälin, Walter and Künzli, Jörg, *The Law of International Human Rights Protection*, Oxford, Oxford University Press, 2009 [Kälin & Künzli (2009)]

Kalshoven, Frits, "The Position of Guerrilla Fighters under the Law of War", *Military Law and Law of War Review*, Vol. 11, 1972, pp. 55-90 [Kalshoven (*MLLWR* 1972)]

___, "Reaffirmation and Development of International Humanitarian Law Applicable in Armed Conflicts: the Diplomatic Conference, Geneva, 1974-1977", *Netherlands Yearbook of International Law*, Vol. 3, 1977, pp. 18-61 [Kalshoven (*NYIL* 1977]

___, *Constraints on the Waging of War*, Geneva, International Committee of the Red Cross, 1987 [Kalshoven (1987)]

___, "Laws of War" in: Bernhardt, Rudolf (ed.), *Encyclopaedia of Public International Law*, Vol. IV, 2000, p. 1379 [Kalshoven in Bernhardt (2000)]

___, *Reflections on the Law of War: Collected Essays*, Leiden/Boston, Martinus Nijhoff Publishers, 2007 [Kalshoven (2007)]

Kammerhofer, Jörg, "Systemic Integration, Legal Theory and the ILC", *Finnish Yearbook of International Law* (Forthcoming), paper available at http://ssrn.com/abstract=1534086 (12 January 2010) [Kammerhofer (*FYIL* forthcoming)]

___, "Orthodox Generalists and Political Activists in International Legal Scholarship" in: Happold, Matthew (ed.), *International Law in a Multipolar World*, 2010 (forthcoming), paper available at http://ssrn.com/abstract=1551343 (15 February 2010) [Kammerhofer in Happold (2010)]

___, "Non-State Actors from the Perspective of the Pure Theory of Law" in: d'Aspremont, Jean (ed.), *Participants in the International Legal System: Theoretical Perspectives*, 2010 (forthcoming), paper available at http://ssrn.com/abstract=1570107 (23 March 2010) [Kammerhofer in d'Aspremont (2010)]

___, "Law-making by Scholarship? The Dark Side of 21st Century International Legal 'Methodology'", available at http://ssrn.com/abstract=1631510 (28 June 2010) [Kammerhofer (SSRN 2010)]

Kelman, Herbert C., "The Policy Context of Torture: A Social-Psychological Analysis", *International Review of the Red Cross*, Vol. 87, No. 857, 2005, pp. 123-134 [Kelman (*IRRC* 2005)]

Kessler, Birgit, "The Duty to 'Ensure Respect' under Common Article 1 of the Geneva Conventions: Its Implications on International and Non-International Armed Conflicts", *German Yearbook of International Law*, Vol. 44, 2001, pp. 498-516 [Kessler (*GYIL* 2001)]

Kirgis, Frederic L., "United States Charges and Proceedings against Two Guantánamo Detainees for Conspiracy to Commit Crimes Associated with Armed Conflict", *ASIL Insights*, March 2004, available at www.asil.org/insights [Kirgis (*ASIL Insights* 2004)]

Kirk-Green, Anthony H.M., *Crisis and Conflict in Nigeria: A documentary Sourcebook*, London, Oxford University Press, 1971 [Kirk-Green (1971)]

Kirk-McDonald, Gabrielle, "Contributions of the International Criminal Tribunals to the Development of Substantive International Humanitarian Law" in: Yee, Sienho and Tieya, Wang (eds.), *International Law in the Post-Cold War Period: Essays in Memory of Li Haopei*, London/New York, Routledge, 2001, pp. 446-472 [Kirk-McDonald in *Liber Amoricum Li Haopei* (2001)]

Kiss, Alexandre Charles, "Permissible Limitations on Rights" in: Henkin, Louis (ed.), *The International Bill of Rights: The Covenant on Civil and Political Rights*, New York, Colombia University Press, 1981, pp. 290-310 [Kiss in Henkin (1981)]

Klabbers, Jan, "Rebel with a Cause? Terrorists and Humanitarian Law", *European Journal of International Law*, Vol. 14, No. 2, 2003, pp. 299-312 [Klabbers (*EJIL* 2003)]

Kleffner, Jann K., "From 'Belligerents' to 'Fighters' and Civilians Directly Participating in Hostilities – On the Principle of Distinction in Non-International Armed Conflicts One Hundred Years after the Second Peace Conference", *Netherlands International Law Review*, Vol. 54, 2007, pp. 315-336. [Kleffner (*NILR* 2007)]

___, "Operational Detention and The Treatment of Detainees" in: Gill, Terry D. and Fleck, Dieter (eds.), *The Handbook of the International Law of Military Operations*, New York, Oxford University Press, 2010, pp. 465-479 [Kleffner in Gill & Fleck (2010)]

Klein, Pierre, "The Attribution of Acts to International Organizations" in Crawford, James; Pellet, Alain and Olleson, Simon (eds.), *The Law of International Responsibility*, Oxford, Oxford University Press, 2010, pp. 297-315 [Klein in Crawford et al. (2010)]

Kleinfeld, Gerald and Tambs, Lewis, *Hitler's Spanish Legion: The Blue Division in Russia*, Carbondale, Southern University Press, 1979 [Kleinfeld & Tambs (1979)]

Koenig, Christian, *Wars of National Liberation and Modern International Humanitarian Law. A Consideration of the Scope of Application of Article I, para. 4 of Additional*

Protocol I to the 1949 Geneva Conventions, Frankfurt, Peter Lang, Europaïsche Hochschulschriften, Vol. 752, 1988 [Koenig (1988)]

Kolb, Robert, "Sur l'origine du couple terminologique *jus ad bellum/jus in bello*", *International Review of the Red Cross*, Vol. 78, No. 827, 1997 [Kolb (*IRRC* 1997)]

___, "The Relationship between International Humanitarian Law and Human Rights Law: A Brief History of the 1948 Universal Declaration of Human Rights and the 1949 Geneva Conventions", *International Review of the Red Cross*, Vol. 79, No. 831, 1998, pp. 513-529 [Kolb (*IRRC* 1998)]

___, "The Jurisprudence of the European Court of Human Rights on Detention and Fair Trial in Criminal Matters from 1992 to the End of 1998", *Human Rights Law Journal*, Vol. 21, 2000, pp. 348-373 [Kolb (*HRLJ* 2000)]

___, "The Jurisprudence of the European Court of Human Rights on Detention and Fair Trial in Criminal Matters: Addenda 1999-2000", *Human Rights Law Journal*, Vol. 22, 2001, pp. 351-363 [Kolb (*HRLJ* 2001)]

___; **Porretto, Gabriele and Vité, Sylvain** (eds.), *L'application du droit international humanitaire et des droits de l'homme aux organisations internationales : Forces de paix et administrations civiles transitoires*, Brussels, Bruylant, 2005 [Kolb, Porretto & Vité (2005)]

Kolb, Robert, *Droit humanitaire et opérations de paix internationales*, Brussels, Bruylant, 2006 [Kolb (2006)]

___, *Ius in bello : Le droit international des conflits armés*, Basel, Helbing Lichtenhahn, 2009 [Kolb (2009)]

Koroma, **Abdul Karim**, *Crisis and Intervention in Sierra Leone 1997-2003*, Freetown/London, Andromeda Publications, 2004 [Koroma (2004)]

Koskenniemi, Martti and Leino, Päivi, "Fragmentation of International Law: Postmodern Anxieties?", *Leiden Journal of International Law*, Vol. 15, No. 3, 2002, pp. 553-579 [Koskenniemi & Leino (*LJIL* 2002)]

Kretzmer, David, *The Occupation of Justice: The Supreme Court of Israel and the Occupied Territories*, Albany, State University of New York Press, 2002 [Kretzmer (2002)]

Krieger, Heike, "A Conflict of Norms: The Relationship between Humanitarian Law and Human Rights Law in the ICRC Customary Law Study", *Journal of Conflict and Security Law*, Vol. 11, No. 2, 2006, pp. 265-291 [Krieger (*JCSL* 2006)]

Kumar, Nilendra, "Religious Personnel" in: Fleck, Dieter (ed.), *The Handbook of International Humanitarian Law*, Oxford, Oxford University Press, 2008, pp. 419-432 [Kumar in Fleck (2008)]

Kunz, Josef L., "Die koreanische Kriegsgefangenenfrage", *Archiv des Völkerrechts*, Vol. 4, No. 4, 1954, pp. 408-423 [Kunz (*AdV* 1954)]

___, "The Laws of War", *American Journal of International Law*, Vol. 50, No. 2, 1956, pp. 313-337 [Kunz (*AJIL* 1956)]

Kunze, Thomas, *Die Völkerrechtliche Stellung Bewaffneter Kämpfer in Nicht-Internationalen Konflikten*, Ph.D. thesis, Bayerischen Julius-Maximilians-Universität, 1976 [Kunze (1976)]

Kwakwa, Edward K., *The International Law of Armed Conflict: Personal and Material Fields of Application*, Dordrecht/Boston/London, Kluwer Academic Publishers, 1992 [Kwakwa (1992)]

La Pradelle, Paul de, "De la neutralité du personnel sanitaire", *International Review of the Red Cross*, Vol. 37, No. 439, 1955, pp. 434-442 [de La Pradelle (*IRRC* 1955)]

Lafouasse, Fabien, "L'espionage en droit international", *Annuaire français de droit international*, Vol. 47, 2001, pp. 63-136 [Lafouasse (*AFDI* 2001)]

Lapidoth, Ruth, "Qui a droit au statut de prisonnier de guerre?", extract from *Revue générale de droit international public*, January-March 1978, reprinted by Pedone, Paris, 1978 [Lapidoth (1978)]

Lauterpacht, Elihu and Bethlehem, Daniel, "The Scope and Content of the Principle of *Non-Refoulement*: Opinion" in Feller, Erika; Türk, Volker and Nicholson, Frances (eds.), *Refugee Protection in International Law: UNHCR's Global Consultations on International Protection*, 2003, also available at http://www.unhcr.org/419c75ce4.html [Lauterpacht & Betlehem in Feller, Türk & Nicholson (2003)]

Lauterpacht, Hersch, *Recognition in International Law*, Cambridge, Cambridge University Press, 1947 [Lauterpacht (1947)]

___, "The Subjects of International Law" in: Lauterpacht, Elihu (ed.), *International Law: Being the Collected Papers of Hersch Lauterpacht, Vol. I: The General Works*, Cambridge, Cambridge University Press, 1970-2004, pp. 136-150 [Lauterpacht in Lauterpacht (1970)]

Lavoyer, Jean-Philippe, "International Humanitarian Law and Terrorism" in: Lijnzaad, Liesbeth; Sambeek, Johana van and Tahzib-Lie, Bahia (eds.), *Making the Voice of Humanity Heard: Essays on Humanitarian Assistance and International Humanitarian Law in Honour of HRH Princess Margriet of the Netherlands*, Leiden, Nijhoff, 2004, pp. 255-270 [Lavoyer in Lijnzaad et al. (2004)]

Levie, Howard S., "Legal Aspects of the Continued Detention of the Pakistani Prisoners of War by India", *American Journal of International Law*, Vol. 67, No. 4, 1973, pp. 693-710 [Levie (*AJIL* 1973)]

___, *Prisoners of War in International Armed Conflict*, Newport, Naval War College, *International Law Studies*, Vol. 59, 1978 [Levie (1978)]

___, *The Law of Non-International Armed Conflict. Protocol II to the 1949 Geneva Conventions*, Dordrecht/Boston/Lancaster, Martinus Nijhoff, 1987 [Levie (1987)]

___, "The 1977 Protocol I and the United States", *St. Louis University Law Journal*, Vol. 38, No. 2, 1993-1994, pp. 469-484 [Levie (*St. Louis ULJ* 1993-1994)]

Lia, Brynjar, *Architect of Global Jihad: The Life of Al-Qaida Strategist Abu Mus'ab al-Suri*, New York, Columbia University Press, 2008 [Lia (2008)]

Lijnzaad, Liesbeth, "How not to Be an Occupying Power: Some Reflections on UN Security Council Resolution 1483 and the Contemporary Law of Occupation" in: Lijnzaad, Liesbeth; Sambeek, Johanna van and Tahzib-Lie, Bahia (eds.), *Making the Voice of Humanity Heard: Essays on Humanitarian Assistance and International Humanitarian Law in Honour of HRH Princess Margriet of the Netherlands*, Leiden, Nijhoff, 2004, pp. 291-305 [Lijnzaad in Lijnzaad et al. (2004)]

Lillich, Richard B., "The Growing Importance of Customary International Human Rights Law", *Georgia Journal of International and Comparative Law*, Vol. 25, No. 1, 1995-1996, pp. 1-30 [Lillich (*GJICL* 1995-1996)]

Lock, Tobias, "Beyond Bosphorus: The European Court of Human Rights' Case Law on the Responsibility of Member States of International Organisations under the European Convention on Human Rights", *Human Rights Law Review*, Vol. 10, No. 3, 2010, pp. 529-545, also available at http://ssrn.com/abstract=1603937 [Lock (*HRLR* 2010)]

Londras, Fiona de, "The Right to Challenge the Lawfulness of Detention: An International Perspective on US Detention of Suspected Terrorists", *Journal of Conflict & Security Law*, Vol. 12, No. 2, 2007, pp. 223-260 [de Londras (*JCSL* 2007)]

Luard, Evan D.T. (ed.), *The International Regulation of Civil Wars*, London, Thames and Hudson, 1972 [Luard (1972)]

Lubell, Noam, *Extraterritorial Use of Force against Non-State Actors*, Oxford, Oxford University Press, 2010 [Lubell (2010)]

Lunze, Stefan, "Serving God and Caesar: Religious Personnel and their Protection in Armed Conflict", *International Reiview of the Red Cross*, Vol. 86, No. 853, 2004, pp. 69-91 [Lunze (*IRRC* 2004)]

Lysaght Charles, "The Scope of Protocol II and its Relation to Common Article 3 of the Geneva Conventions of 1949 and Other Human Rights Instruments", *American University Law Review*, Vol. 33, No. 1, 1983, pp. 9-27 [Lysaght (*AULR* 1983)]

Maaß, Rainald, *Der Söldner und seine kriegsvölkerrechtliche Rechtsstellung als Kombattant und Kriegsgefangener*, Bochum, Universitätsverlag Brockmeyer, 1990 [Maaß (1990)]

Mailler, Annette, *De la distinction des combattants et des non-combattants comme base du droit de guerre*, Paris, Pedone, 1916 [Mailler (1916)]

Malenovský, Jiří, "L'enjeu délicat de l'éventuelle adhésion de l'Union européenne à la Convention européenne des droits de l'homme : de graves difficultés dans l'application", *Revue générale de droit international public*, Vol. 113, No. 4, 2009, pp. 753-784 [Malenovsky (*RGDIP* 2009)]

Mallein, Jean, *La situation juridique des combattants dans les conflits armés non internationaux*, Ph.D. thesis, University of Grenoble, 1978 [Mallein (1978)]

Mallison, Thomas W. and Jabri, R.A., "The Juridical Characteristics of Belligerent Occupation and the Resort to Resistance by the Civilian Population: Doctrinal Development and Continuity", *George Washington Law Review*, Vol. 42, 1974, pp. 185-221 [Mallison & Jabri (*GWLR* 1974)]

Mallison, Thomas W. and Mallison, Sally V., "The Juridical Status of Irregular Combatants under the International Humanitarian Law of Armed Conflict", *Case Western Reserve Journal of International Law*, Vol. 9, No. 1, 1977, pp. 39-78 [Mallison & Mallison (*CWRJIL* 1977)]

___, "The Juridical Status of Privileged Combatants under the Geneva Protocol of 1977 concerning International Conflicts", *Law and Contemporary Problems*, Vol. 42, 1978, pp. 4-35 [Mallison & Mallison (*LCP* 1978)]

Marks, Susan and Clapham, Andrew, *International Human Rights Lexicon*, Oxford, Oxford University Press, 2005 [Marks & Clapham (2005)]

Martin, Fanny, "Application du droit international humanitaire par la Cour interaméricaine des droits de l'homme", *International Review of the Red Cross*, Vol. 83, No. 844, 2001, pp. 1037-1066 [Martin (*IRRC* 2001)]

Matheson, Michael J., "The US Position on the Relation of Customary International Law to the 1977 Protocols Additional to the 1949 Geneva Conventions, Remarks before Session One of the Humanitarian Law Conference", *American University Journal of International Law and Policy*, Vol. 2, No. 2, 1987, pp. 419-431 [Matheson (*AUJILP* 1987)]

Mayda, Jaro, "The Korean Repatriation Problem and International Law", *American Journal of International Law*, Vol. 47, No. 3, 1953, pp. 414-438 [Mayda (*AJIL* 1953)]

McCoubrey, Hilaire, *International Humanitarian Law. The Regulation of Armed Conflicts*, Aldershot, Dartmouth, 1990 [McCoubrey (1990)]

__ **and White, Nigel D.**, *International Law and Armed Conflict*, Aldershot, Dartmouth, 1992 [McCoubrey & White (1992)]

___, *The Blue Helmets: Legal Regulation of United Nations Military Operations*, Aldershot, Dartmouth, 1996 [McCoubrey & White (1996)]

McCoubrey, Hilaire, *International Humanitarian Law: Modern Developments in the Limitation of Warfare*, 2nd ed., Aldershot, Dartmouth, 1998 [McCoubrey (1988)]

McDonald, Avril, "Defining the War on Terror and the Status of Detainees: Comments on the Presentation of Judge George Aldrich", *Humanitäres Völkerrecht*, Vol. 15, No. 4, 2002, pp. 206-209 [McDonald (*HV* 2002)]

McDonald, Neil and Sullivan, Scott, "Rational Interpretation in Irrational Times: The Third Geneva Convention and the 'War on Terror'", *Harvard International Law Journal*, Vol. 44, 2003, pp. 301-315 [McDonald & Sullivan (*HILJ* 2003)]

McGoldrick, Dominic, "The Interface between Public Emergency Powers and International Law", *International Journal of Constitutional Law*, Vol. 2, No. 2, 2004, pp. 380-429 [McGoldrick (*IJConstit.L* 2004)]

McLachlan, Campbell, "The Principle of Systemic Integration and Article 31(3)(c) of the Vienna Convention", *International and Comparative Law Quarterly*, Vol. 54, No. 2, 2005, pp. 279-320 [McLachlan (*ICLQ* 2005)]

Mégret, Frédéric, "'War'? Legal Semantics and the Move to Violence", *European Journal of International Law*, Vol. 13, No. 2, 2002, pp. 361-199 [Mégret (*EJIL* 2002)]

Melzer, Nils, *Targeted Killing in International Law*, Oxford, Oxford University Press, 2008, [Melzer (2008)]

___, "Keeping the Balance between Military Necessity and Humanity: A Response to Four Critiques of the ICRC's Interpretative Guidance on the Notion of Direct Participation in Hostilities", *New York University Journal of International Law and Policy*, Vol. 42, No. 3, 2010, pp. 831-916 [Melzer (*NYUJILP* 2010)]

Meredith, Catherine and Christou, Theodora, *Not in my Front Yard: Security and Resistance to Responsibility for Extraterritorial State Conduct*, Nijmegen, Wolf Legal Publishers, 2009 [Meredith & Christou (2009)]

Meron, Theodor, "Applicability of Multilateral Conventions to Occupied Territories", *American Journal of International Law*, Vol. 72, No. 3, 1978, pp. 542-557 [Meron (*AJIL* 1978)]

___, "West Bank and Gaza: Human Rights and Humanitarian Law in the Period of Transition", *Israel Yearbook on Human Rights*, Vol. 9, 1979, pp. 106-120 [Meron (*Isr.YHR* 1979)]

___, "On the Inadequate Reach of Humanitarian and Human Rights Law and the Need for a New Instrument", *American Journal of International Law*, Vol. 77, No. 3, 1983, pp. 589-606 [Meron (*AJIL* 1983]

___ (ed.), *Human Rights in International Law: Legal and Policy Issues*, Oxford, Clarendon Press, 1984 [Meron (1984)]

___, *Human Rights in Internal Strife: Their International Protection*, Cambridge, Grotius Publications, 1987 [Meron (1987)]

___, *Human Rights and Humanitarian Norms as Customary Law*, Oxford, Clarendon Press, 1989 [Meron (1989)]

___, "Protected Persons under the Fourth Geneva Convention" in: Eide, Asbjørn and Helgesen, Jan (eds.), *The Future of Human Rights Protection in a Changing World: Fifty Years since the Four Freedoms Address. Essays in Honour of Torkel Opsahl*, Oslo, Norwegian University Press, 1991, pp. 155-162 [Meron in *Liber Amoricum Opsahl* (1991)]

___, "Prisoners of War, Civilians and Diplomats in the Gulf Crisis", *American Journal of International Law*, Vol. 85, No. 1, 1991, pp. 104-109 [Meron (*AJIL* 1991)]

___, "Extraterritoriality of Human Rights Treaties", *American Journal of International Law*, Vol. 89, No. 1, 1995, pp. 78-82 [Meron (*AJIL* 1995)]

___, "Crimes and Accountability in Shakespeare", *American Journal of International Law*, Vol. 92, No. 1, 1998, pp. 1-40 [Meron (*AJIL* 1998)]

___, "The Humanization of Humanitarian Law", *American Journal of International Law*, Vol. 94, No. 2, 2000, pp. 239-278 [Meron (AJIL 2000)]

___, "International Law in the Age of Human Rights: General Course on Public International Law", *Collected Courses of the Hague Academy of International Law*, Vol. 301, 2003-I, pp. 9-490 [Meron (*Hague Academy Collected Courses* 2003)]

___, *The Humanization of International Law*, Leiden/Boston, Martinus Nijhoff Publishers, 2006 [Meron (2006)]

Meuli, Hans, "De la neutralité du personnel sanitaire au cours des hostilités", *International Review of the Red Cross*, Vol. 38, No. 451, 1956, pp. 377-394 [Meuli (*IRRC* 1956)]

Meurant, Jacques, "Humanitarian Law and Human Rights Law: Alike yet Distinct", *International Review of the Red Cross*, Vol. 76, 1993, pp. 89-93 [Meurant (*IRRC* 1993)]

Meyrowitz, Henri, "Le statut des saboteurs dans le droit de la guerre", *Military Law and Law of War Review*, Vol. 5, No. 1, 1966, pp. 121-178 [Meyrowitz (*MLLWR* 1966)]

___, *Le principe de l'égalité des belligérants devant le droit de la guerre*, Paris, Pedone, 1970 [Meyrowitz (1970)]

___, "Le statut des guérilleros dans le droit international", *Journal de droit international*, Vol. 107, 1973, pp. 875-923 [Meyrowitz (*JDI* 1973)]

Milanović, Marko, "Norm Conflicts in International Law: Whither Human Rights?", *Duke Journal of Comparative & International Law*, Vol. 20, No. 1, 2009, pp. 69-131 [Milanović (*DJCIL* 2009)]

___, "A Norm Conflict Perspective on the Relationship between International Humanitarian Law and Human Rights Law", *Journal of Conflict & Security Law*, Vol. 14, No. 3, 2010, pp. 459-483 [Milanović (*JCSL* 2010)]

Miller, Sarah, "Revisiting Extraterritorial Jurisdiction: A Territorial Justification for Extraterritorial Jurisdiction under the European Convention", *European Journal of International Law*, Vol. 20, No. 4, 2010, pp. 1223-1246 [Miller (*EJIL* 2010)]

Moeckli, Daniel, *Human Rights and Non-Discrimination in the 'War on Terror'*, Oxford, Oxford University Press, 2008 [Moeckli (2008)]

Moir, Lindsay, *The Law of Internal Armed Conflict*, Cambridge, Cambridge University Press, 2002 [Moir (2002)]

Möller, Jakob Th. and Zayas, Alfred de, *United Nations Human Rights Committee Case Law 1977-2008*, Kehl am Rhein, N.P. Engel, 2009 [Möller & de Zayas (2009)]

Momtaz, Djachid, "Le droit international humanitaire applicable aux conflits armés non internationaux", *Collected Courses of the Hague Academy of International Law*, Vol. 292, 2001, pp. 9-146 [Momtaz, *Hague Academy Collected Courses* (2001)]

Montealegre, Hernan, "The Compatibility of a State Party's Derogation under Human Rights Conventions with its Obligations under Protocol II and Common Article 3", *American University Law Review*, Vol. 33, No. 1, 1983-1984, pp. 41-51 [Montealegre (*AULR* 1984)]

Moodrick-Even Khen, Hilly, "Unlawful Combatants or Unlawful Legislation? An Analysis of the Imprisonment of Unlawful Combatants Law", Israel Democracy Institute, Jerusalem, 2005, Hebrew University International Law Research Paper No. 03-06, available at http://ssrn.com/abstract=902934 [Moodrick-Even Khen (*Hebrew University of Jerusalem Research Papers* 2006)]

Munkler, Herfried, "The Wars of the 21st Century", *International Review of the Red Cross*, Vol. 85, No. 849, 2003, pp. 7-21 [Munkler (*IRRC* 2003)]

Murphy, Ray, "Prisoner of War Status and the Question of Guantánamo Bay Detainees", *Human Rights Law Review*, Vol. 3, No. 2, 2003, pp. 257-278 [Murphy (*HRLR* 2003)]

Naert, Frederik, *International Law Aspects of the EU's Security and Defence Policy, with a Particular Focus on the Law of Armed Conflict and Human Rights*, Antwerp, Intersentia, 2010 [Naert (2010)]

Naqvi, Yasmin, "Doubtful Prisoner-of-War Status", *International Review of the Red Cross*, Vol. 85, No. 847, 2002, pp. 571-595 [Naqvi (*IRRC* 2002)]

___, *Impediments to Exercising Jurisdiction over International Crimes*, The Hague, T.M.C. Asser Press, 2010 [Naqvi (2010)]

Nasu, Hitoshi, "Status of Rebels in Non-International Armed Conflict" in: Doswald-Beck, Louise; Chowdhury, Azizur Rahman and Bhuiyan, Jahid Hossain (eds.), *International Humanitarian Law: An Anthology*, Nagpur, LexisNexis & Butterworths Wadhwa, 2009, pp. 239-260 [Nasu in Doswald-Beck et al. (2009)]

Neff, Stephen C., *The Rights and Duties of Neutrals: A General History*, Manchester, Manchester University Press, 2000 [Neff (2000)]

Ngyuen, Quoc Dinh; Daillier, Patrick and Pellet, Alain, *Droit international public*, 6th ed., Paris, Librairie générale de droit et de jurisprudence, 1999 [Nguyen, Daillier & Pellet (1999)]

Nowak, Manfred, *U.N. Covenant on Civil and Political Rights. CCPR Commentary*, Kehl am Rhein/Strasbourg/Arlington, N.P. Engel, 2005 [Nowak (2005)]

Nwogugu, E.I., "The Nigerian Civil War: A Case Study in the Law of War", *Indian Journal of International Law*, Vol. 14, 1974, pp. 13-53 [Nwogugu (*IJIL* 1974)]

O'Boyle, Michael P., "Emergency Situations and the Protection of Human Rights: A Model Derogation Provision for a Northern Ireland Bill of Rights", *Northern Ireland Legal Quarterly*, Vol. 28, No. 2, 1977, pp. 160-187 [O'Boyle (*NILQ* 1977)]

O'Rourke, Vernon A., "Recognition of Belligerency in the Spanish Civil War", *American Journal of International Law*, Vol. 31, No. 3, 1937, pp. 398-413 [O'Rourke (*AJIL* 1937)]

Ojeda, Stéphane, "US Detention of Taliban Fighters: Some Legal Considerations" in: Schmitt, Michael N. (ed.), *The War in Afghanistan: A Legal Analysis*, Newport, Naval War College, *International Law Studies*, Vol. 85, 2009, pp. 357-370 [Ojeda in Schmitt (2009)]

Olson, Laura, "Practical Challenges of Implementing the Complementarity between International Humanitarian and Human Rights Law - Demonstrated by the Procedural Regulation of Internment in Non-International Armed Conflict", *Case Western Reserve Journal of International Law*, Vol. 40, No. 3, 2009, pp. 437-461 [Olson (*CWRJIL* 2009)]

Oppenheim, Lassa F.L., *International Law*, London, Longmans/Green, 1905 (Vol. I), 1906 (Vol. II) [Oppenheim (1906)]

Orakhelashvili, Alexander, "The Interaction between Human Rights and Humanitarian Law: Fragmentation, Conflict, Parallelism, or Convergence?", *European Journal of International Law*, Vol. 19, No. 1, 2008, pp. 161-182 [Orakhelashvili (*EJIL* 2008)]

Oswald, Bruce, "Detention in Military Operations: Some Military, Political and Legal Aspects", *Military Law and Law of War Review*, Vol. 46, No. 2, 2007, pp. 341-362 [Oswald, *MLLWR* 2007]

___, "The Law on Military Occupation: Answering the Challenges of Detention during Contemporary Peace Operations?", *Melbourne Journal of International Law*, Vol. 8, No. 2, 2007, pp. 311-326 [Oswald (*Melb.JIL* 2007)]

Ozerden, Kemal, *Le sort des militaires belligérants, victimes de la guerre, débarqués dans un port neutre, d'après la Convention de Genève*, Paris, Pedone, 1971 [Ozerden (1971)]

Pak, Chi Young, *Korea and the United Nations*, The Hague, Kluwer Law International, 2000 [Pak (2000)]

Patel, Faiza, "Who Can Be Detained in 'The War on Terror'? The Emerging Answer", *ASIL Insights*, Vol. 13, No. 18, 2009, available at http://www.asil.org/insights091020.cfm [Patel (*ASIL Insights* 2009)]

Paust, Jordan J., "The Common Plan to Violate the Geneva Conventions", *Jurist*, 25 May 2004, available at http://jurist.law.pitt.edu/forum/paust2.php [Paust (*Jurist* 2004)]

Pautsch, Ilse Dorothee, "Prisoners of War and Internees in the Second World War: A Survey of Some Recent Publications", *Contemporary European History*, Vol. 12, No. 2, 2003, pp. 225-238 [Pautsch (*CEH* 2003)]

Pauwelyn, Joost, *Conflict of Norms in Public International Law: How WTO Law Relates to Other Rules of International Law*, Cambridge, Cambridge University Press, 2003 [Pauwelyn (2003)]

Pejic, Jelena, "Terrorist Acts and Groups: A Role for International Law?", *British Year Book of International Law*, Vol. 57, 2004, pp. 71-100 [Pejic (*BYIL* 2004)]

___, "Procedural Principles and Safeguards for Internment/Administrative Detention in Armed Conflict Other Situations of Violence", *International Review of the Red Cross*, Vol. 87, No. 858, 2005, pp. 375-391 [Pejic (*IRRC* 2005)]

___, "Status of Armed Conflicts" in: Wilmshurst, Elizabeth and Breau, Susan (eds.), *Perspectives on the ICRC Study on Customary International Humanitarian Law*, Cambridge, Cambridge University Press, 2007, pp. 77-100 [Pejic in Wilmshurst & Breau (2007]

Perna, Laura, *The Formation of the Treaty Law of Non-International Armed Conflict*, Leiden, Martinus Nijhoff Publishers, 2006 [Perna (2006)]

Pfanner, Toni, "Military Uniforms and the Law of War", *International Review of the Red Cross*, Vol. 86, No. 853, 2004, pp. 93-124 [Pfanner (*IRRC* 2004)]

___, "Editorial", *International Review of the Red Cross*, Vol. 87, No. 857, 2005, pp. 5-7 [Pfanner (*IRRC* 2005)]

Pictet, Jean S. (ed.), *Commentary to the First Geneva Convention for the Amelioration of the Condition of the Wounded and Sick in Armed Forces in the Field*, Geneva, International Committee of the Red Cross, 1952 [Pictet, *Commentary GC I* (1952)]

___ (ed.), *Commentary to the Second Geneva Convention for the Amelioration of the Condition of the Wounded and Sick in Armed Forces in the Field*, Geneva, International Committee of the Red Cross, 1952 [Pictet, *Commentary GC II* (1952)]

___ (ed.), *Commentary to the Fourth Geneva Convention relative to the Protection of Civilian Persons in Time of War*, Geneva, International Committee of the Red Cross, 1958 [Pictet, *Commentary GC IV* (1958)]

___ (ed.), *Commentary to the Third Geneva Convention relative to the Treatment of Prisoners of War*, Geneva, International Committee of the Red Cross, 1960 [Pictet, *Commentary GC III* (1960)]

___, *Humanitarian Law and the Protection of War Victims*, Leiden/Geneva, Sijthoff/Henry Dunant Institute, 1975 [Pictet (1975)]

___, "The Medical Profession and International Humanitarian Law", *International Review of the Red Cross*, Vol. 66, No. 247, 1985, pp. 191-209 [Pictet (*IRRC* 1985)]

Pinto, Roger, "Les règles du droit international concernant la guerre civile", *Collected Courses of the Hague Academy of International Law*, Vol. 114, 1965-I, pp. 451-554 [Pinto (*Hague Academy Collected Courses* 1965)]

Plattner, Denise, "La portée juridique des déclarations de respect du droit international humanitaire qui émanent de mouvements en lutte dans un conflit armé", *Revue belge de droit international*, Vol. 18, No. 1, 1984-1985, pp. 298-320 [Plattner (*RBDI* 1984-1985)]

Portmann, Roland, *Legal Personality in International Law*, New York, Cambridge University Press, 2010 [Portmann (2010)]

Prémont, Daniel; Stenersen, Christian and Oseredczuk, Isabelle, *Non-Derogable Rights and States of Emergency*, Brussels, Bruylant, 1996 [Prémont et al. (1996)]

Preux, Jean de, "The Geneva Conventions and Reciprocity", *International Review of the Red Cross*, Vol. 25, No. 244, 1985, pp. 25-29 [de Preux (*IRRC* 1985)]

Provost, René, *International Human Rights and Humanitarian Law*, Cambridge, Cambridge University Press, 2002 [Provost (2002)]

___, "The International Committee of the Red Widget? The Diversity Debate and International Humanitarian Law", *Israel Law Review*, Vol. 40, No. 2, 2007, pp. 614-647 [Provost (*ILR* 2007)]

Prud'homme, Nancie, "*Lex specialis*: Oversimplifying a more Complex and Multifaceted Relationship?", *Israel Law Review*, Vol. 40, No. 2, 2007, pp. 355-395 [Prud'homme (*ILR* 2007)]

Quéguiner, Jean-François, "Dix ans après la création du Tribunal pénal pour l'ex-Yougoslavie : Évaluation de l'apport de sa jurisprudence au droit international humanitaire", *International Review of the Red Cross*, Vol. 85, No. 850, 2003, pp. 271-312 [Quéguiner (*IRRC* 2003)]

Quénivet, Noëlle, "The Right to Life in International Humanitarian Law and Human Rights Law" in: Arnold, Roberta and Quénivet, Noëlle (eds.), *International Humanitarian Law and Human Rights Law: Towards a New Merger in International Law*, Boston, Martinus Nijhoff Publishers, 2008 [Quénivet in Arnold & Quénivet (2008)]

Rauch, Elmar, "Le concept de nécessité militaire dans le droit de la guerre", *Military Law and Law of War Review*, Vol. 19, Nos. 1-2, 1980, pp. 205-237 [Rauch (*MLLWR* 1980)]

Raz, Joseph, *The Authority of Law: Essays on Law and Morality*, 2nd ed., Oxford, Oxford University Press, 2009 [Raz (2009)]

Reidy, Aisling, "The Approach of the European Commission and Court of Human Rights to International Humanitarian Law", *International Review of the Red Cross*, Vol. 79, No. 324, 1998, pp. 513-529 [Reidy (*IRRC* 1998)]

Renz, Bettina, "The Status and Treatment of Detainees in Russia's Chechen Campaigns" in: Scheipers, Sybille (ed.), *Prisoners in War*, Oxford, Oxford University Press, 2009, pp. 205-218 [Renz in Scheipers (2009)]

Rieff, David, "What is Really at Stake in the US Campaign against Terrorism", September 2002, available at www.crimesofwar.org [Rieff (*Crimes of War* 2002)]

___, "When Does the Application of International Humanitarian Law Properly Begin and End in New Conflict Situations such as the 'War on Terror'?", 2003, on file with author

Risius, Gordon, "Prisoners of War in the United Kingdom" in: Rowe, Peter, *The Gulf War 1990-91 in International and English Law*, London, Routledge/Sweet & Maxwell, 1993, pp. 289-303 [Risius in Rowe (1993)]

Roberts, Adam, "What is Military Occupation?", *British Year Book of International Law*, Vol. 55, 1984, pp. 249-305 [Roberts (*BYIL* 1984)]

___, "Prolonged Military Occupation: The Israeli-Occupied Territories since 1967", *American Journal of International Law*, Vol. 84, No. 1, 1990, pp. 44-103 [Roberts (*AJIL* 1990)]

___ **and Guelff, Richard** (eds.), *Documents on the Laws of War*, Oxford, Oxford University Press, 2000 [Roberts & Guelff (2000)]

Roberts, Adam, "The Laws of War in the War on Terror", *Israel Yearbook on Human Rights*, Vol. 32, 2002, pp. 193-245 [Roberts (*Isr.YHR* 2002)]

___, "Role of Law in the 'War on Terror': A Tragic Clash", *ASIL Proceedings*, Vol. 97, 2003, pp. 19-23 [Roberts (*ASIL Proceedings* 2003)]

___, "Military Occupations and the Problem of Transformation: Applying the Laws of War and of Human Rights", paper for the University of Tehran's *Colloquium on the Interplay between International Humanitarian Law and International Human Rights Law: Global and Regional Perspectives*, Tehran, 13-14 April 2004 [Roberts (*Tehran Conference Paper* 2004)]

___, "Transformative Military Occupation: Applying the Laws of War and Human Rights", *American Journal of International Law*, Vol. 100, No. 3, 2006, pp. 580-622 [Roberts (*AJIL* 2006)]

Rodley, Nigel S., "Can Armed Opposition Groups Violate Human Rights Standards?" in: Mahoney, Kathleen E. and Mahoney, Paul (eds.), *Human Rights in the Twenty-First Century: A Global Challenge*, The Hague, Martinus Nijhoff Publishers, 1993 [Rodley in Mahoney et al. (1993)]

___ **and Pollard, Matt**, *The Treatment of Prisoners under International Law*, 3rd ed., Oxford, Oxford University Press, 2009 [Rodley & Pollard (2009)]

Rogers, Anthony P.V., *Law on the Battlefield*, Manchester/New York, Manchester University Press, 1996 [Rogers (1996)]

___, "Combatant Status" in: Wilmshurst, Elizabeth and Breau, Susan (eds.), *Perspectives on the ICRC Study on Customary International Humanitarian Law*, Cambridge, Cambridge University Press, 2007, pp. 101-128 [Rogers in Wilmshurst & Breau (2007)]

Rona, Gabor, "Interesting Times for International Humanitarian Law: Challenges from the 'War on Terror'", *The Fletcher Forum of World Affairs*, Vol. 27, No. 2, 2003, pp. 55-74 [Rona (*FFWA* 2003)]

___, "Observations on U.S. Practice Relating to 'Enemy Combatants'", New York, Human Rights First, 12 March 2008, on file with author [Rona (*Human Rights First paper* 2008)]

Rosas, Allan, *The Legal Status of Prisoners of War*, Helsinki, Suomalainen Tiedeakatemia, 1976, reprinted as *The Legal Status of Prisoners of War: A Study in International Humanitarian Law Applicable in Armed Conflicts*, Turku/Åbo, Institute for Human Rights, Åbo Akademi University, 2005 [Rosas (1976)]

___, "Human Rights at Risk in Situations of Internal Violence and Public Emergency: Towards Common Minimum Standards" in: Eide, Asbjørn and Helgesen, Jan (eds.), *The Future of Human Rights Protection in a Changing World: Fifty Years since the Four Freedoms Address. Essays in Honour of Torkel Opsahl*, Oslo, Norwegian University Press, 1991, pp. 165–181 [Rosas in *Liber Amoricum Opsahl* (1991)]

Rosenblad, Esbjorn, "Guerilla Warfare and International Law", *Military Law and Law of War Review*, Vol. 12, No. 1, 1973, pp. 91-136 [Rosenblad (*MLLWR* (1973)]

Roth, Kenneth, "The Law of War in the War on Terror", *Foreign Affairs*, Vol. 83, 2004, pp. 2-7 [Roth (*FA* (2004)]

Rousseau, Charles, *Le droit des conflits armés*, Paris, Pedone, 1983 [Rousseau (1983)]

Rowe, Peter, "Prisoners of War in the Gulf Area" in: Rowe, Peter (ed.), *The Gulf War 1990-91 in International and English Law*, London, Routledge/Sweet & Maxwell, 1993, pp. 188-204 [Rowe in Rowe (1993)]

___, *The Impact of Human Rights Law on Armed Forces*, Cambridge, Cambridge University Press, 2006 [Rowe (2006)]

Rudman, Mara and Qupty, Mazen, "The Emergency Powers (Detention) Law: Israel's Courts Have a Mission – Should they Choose to Accept it?", *Columbia Human Rights Law Review*, Vol. 21, No. 2, 1989-1990, pp. 469-513 [Rudman & Qupty (*CHRLR* 1989-1990)]

Samuels, Kirsti, "*Jus ad Bellum* and Civil Conflicts: A Case Study of the International Community's Approach to Violence in the Conflict in Sierra Leone", *Journal of Conflict and Security Law*, Vol. 8, 2003, pp. 315-338 [Samuels (*JCSL* 2003)]

Sandoz, Yves; Swinarski, Christophe and Zimmerman, Bruno (eds.), *Commentary on the Additional Protocols of 8 June 1977 to the Geneva Conventions of 12 August 1949*, Geneva/The Hague, International Committee of the Red Cross/Martinus Nijhoff Publishers, 1987 [Sandoz et al., *Commentary AP I and II* (1987)]

Sassòli, Marco, "The Status, Treatment and Repatriation of Deserters under International Humanitarian Law", *Yearbook of the International Institute of Humanitarian Law*, 1985, pp. 9-36 [Sassòli (*YIIHL* 1985)]

___ **and Olson, Laura M.**, "The Judgment of the ICTY Appeals Chamber on the Merits in the Tadić Case", *International Review of the Red Cross*, Vol. 81, No. 839, 2000, pp. 733-769 [Sassòli & Olson (*IRRC* 2000)]

Sassòli, Marco, "La 'guerre contre le terrorisme', le droit international humanitaire et le statut de prisonnier de guerre", *Annuaire canadien de droit international*, Vol. 39, 2001, pp. 211-252 [Sassòli (*ACDI* 2001)]

___, "The Legal Qualification of the Conflicts in the Former Yugoslavia: Double Standards or New Horizons for International Humanitarian Law?" in: Yee, Sienho and

Tieya, Wang (eds.), *International Law in the Post-Cold War World: Essays in Honour of Li Haopei*, London/New York, Routledge, 2001, pp. 307-333 [Sassòli in *Liber Amoricum Li Haopei* (2001)]

___, "State Responsibility for Violations of International Humanitarian Law", *International Review of the Red Cross*, No. 846, 2002, pp. 401-434 [Sassòli (*IRRC* 2002)]

___, "'Unlawful Combatants': The Law and whether it Needs to Be Revised", *ASIL Proceedings*, Vol. 97, 2003, pp. 196-200 [Sassòli (*ASIL Proceedings* 2003)]

___, "The Status of Persons Held in Guantánamo under International Humanitarian Law", *Journal of International Criminal Justice*, Symposium on the Guantánamo Entanglement, Vol. 2, 2004, pp. 96-106 [Sassòli (*JICJ* 2004)]

___, "Legislation and Maintenance of Public Order and Civil Life by Occupying Powers", *European Journal of International Law*, Vol. 16, No. 4, 2005, pp. 661-694 [Sassòli (*EJIL* 2005)]

___ **and Bouvier, Antoine A.**, *How Does Law Protect in War? Cases, Documents, Teaching Materials on Contemporary Practice in International Humanitarian Law*, Geneva, International Committee of the Red Cross, 2006 [Sassòli & Bouvier (2006)]

Sassòli, Marco, "Transnational Armed Groups and International Humanitarian Law" in: Harvard University, Program on Humanitarian Policy and Conflict Research, *HPCR Occasional Paper Series*, No. 6, 2006, available at http://www.hpcr.org/pdfs/OccasionalPaper6.pdf [Sassòli (*HPCR Series* 2006)]

___, "*Ius ad Bellum* and *Jus in Bello*: The Separation between the Legality of the Use of Force and Humanitarian Rules to Be Respected in Warfare: Crucial or Outdated?" in: Schmitt, Michael N. and Pejic, Jelena (eds.), *International Law and Armed Conflict: Exploring the Faultlines. Essays in Honour of Yoram Dinstein*, Martinus Nijhoff Publishers, Leiden 2007, pp. 241-264 [Sassòli in *Liber Amoricum Dinstein* (2007]

___, "Le droit international humanitaire, une *lex specialis* par rapport aux droits humains?" in: Auer, Andreas; Flückiger, Alexandre and Hottelier, Michel (eds.), *Les droits de l'homme et la constitution : Études en l'honneur du Professeur Giorgio Malinverni*, Geneva, Schulthess, 2007, pp. 375-395 [Sassòli in *Liber Amoricum Malinverni* (2007)]

___ **and Olson, Laura**, "The Relationship between International Humanitarian and Human Rights Law where it Matters: Admissible Killing and Internment of Fighters in Non-International Armed Conflicts", *International Review of the Red Cross*, Vol. 90, No. 871, 2008, pp. 599-627 [Sassòli & Olson (*IRRC* 2008)]

Sassòli, Marco, "The International Legal Framework for Stability Operations: When May International Forces Attack or Detain Someone in Afghanistan ?" in: Schmitt, Michael N. (ed.), *The War in Afghanistan: A Legal Analysis*, Newport, Naval War College, *International Law Studies*, Vol. 85, 2009, pp. 431-464 [Sassòli in Schmitt (2009)]

___, "Taking Armed Groups Seriously: Ways to Improve their Compliance with International Humanitarian Law", *Journal of International Humanitarian Legal Studies*, Vol. 1, 2010 (forthcoming), on file with author [Sassòli (*JIHLS* 2010)]

Schabas, William, "*Lex specialis*? Belt and Suspenders? The Parallel Operation of Human Rights Law and the Law of Armed Conflict, and the Conundrum of *Jus ad Bellum*", *Israel Law Review*, Vol. 40, No. 2, 2007, pp. 592-613 [Schabas (*ILR* 2007)]

Schachter, Oscar, "The Decline of the Nation-State and Implications for International Law", *Columbia Journal of Transnational Law*, Vol. 36, Nos. 1-2, 1998, pp. 7-24 [Schachter (*CJTL*1997)]

Schamis, Gerardo Jorge, *War and Terrorism in International Affairs*, New Brunswick NJ, Transaction Books, 1980 [Schamis (1980)]

Scheipers, Sybil, *Prisoners in War*, Oxford, Oxford University Press, 2010 [Scheipers (2010)]

Schindler, Dietrich, "The Different Types of Armed Conflicts according to the Geneva Conventions and Protocols", *Collected Courses of the Hague Academy of International Law*, Vol. 163, 1979-II, pp. 117-163 [Schindler (*Hague Academy Collected Courses* 1979)]

___, "The International Committee of the Red Cross and Human Rights", *International Review of the Red Cross*, Vol. 60, No. 208, 1979, pp. 3-14 [Schindler (*IRRC* 1979)]

___, "Human Rights and Humanitarian Law: Interrelationship of the Laws", *American University Law Review*, Vol. 31, No. 4, 1981-1982, pp. 935-978 [Schindler (*AULR* 1981-1982)]

Schmid, Jürg, H., *Die Völkerrechtliche Stellung der Partisanen im Kriege*, Zürich, Polygraphischer Verlag A.G., 1956 [Schmid (1956)]

Schmitt, Michael N., "Humanitarian Law and Direct Participation in Hostilities by Private Contractors or Civilian Employees", *Chicago Journal of International Law*, Vol. 5, No. 2, 2004-2005, pp. 511-546 [Schmitt (*Ch.JIL* 2005]

___, "Deconstructing Direct Participation in Hostilities: The Constitutive Elements", *New York University Journal of International Law and Policy*, Vol. 42, No. 3, 2010, pp. 697-739 [Schmitt (*NYUJILP* 2010)]

___, "Military Necessity and Humanity in International Humanitarian Law: Preserving the Delicate Balance", *Virginia Journal of International Law*, Vol. 50, No. 4, 2010, pp. 795-839 [Schmitt (*Virg.JIL* 2010)]

Schreuer, Christoph, "The Waning of the Sovereign State: Towards a New Paradigm for International Law?", *European Journal of International Law*, Vol. 4, No. 4, 1993, pp. 447-471 [Schreuer (*EJIL* 1993)]

Schwab, Herbert, *Irreguläre Kombattanten als Kriegsgefangene*, Ph.D. thesis, Bayerischen Julius-Maximilians-Universität, 1978 [Schwab (1978)]

Schwarzenberger, Georg, *International Law*, London, Stevens & Sons, 1968 [Schwarzenberger (1968)]

___, "Privileged Belligerency in Guerrilla Warfare: An Implied Test of Legitimacy", *Revue des droits de l'homme*, Vol. 4, 1971, pp. 535-553 [Schwarzenberger (*RDH* 1971)]

Schwenk, Edmund H., "Legislative Power of the Military Occupant under Article 43, Hague Regulations", *Yale Law Journal*, Vol. 54, No. 2, 1944-1945, pp. 393-416 [Schwenk (*YLJ* 1944-1945)]

Scobbie, Ian, "Principle or Pragmatics? The Relationship between Human Rights Law and the Law of Armed Conflict", *Journal of Conflict & Security Law*, Vol. 14, No. 3, 2009, pp. 449-457 [Scobbie (*JCSL* 2009)]

Seeger, Roland, *Le statut personnel des étrangers ennemis et la Convention de Genève du 12 août 1949 relative à la protection des civils*, Zofingue, Éditions Ringier, 1958 [Seeger (1958)]

Shamgar, Meir, "*The Observance of International Law in the Administered Territories*", *Israel Yearbook on Human Rights*, Vol. 1, 1971, p. 262-277 [Shamgar (*Isr.YHR* 1971)]

Shany, Yuval, "Human Rights and Humanitarian Law as Competing Legal Paradigms for Fighting Terror", The Hebrew University of Jerusalem, Faculty of Law, *Research paper*

No. 23-09, 9 November 2009, available at http://ssrn.com/abstract=1504106 [Shany (*Hebrew University of Jerusalem Research Papers* 2009)]

Shapiro, L.B., "Repatriation of Deserters", *British Year Book of International Law*, Vol. 29, 1952, pp. 310-324 [Shapiro (*BYIL* 1952)]

Shaw, Malcolm N., *International Law*, 4th ed., Cambridge, Cambridge University Press, 1997 [Shaw (1997)]

Shelton, Dinah, "The Legal Status of the Detainees at Guantánamo Bay: Innovative Elements in the Decision of the Inter-American Commission on Human Rights of 12 March 2002", *Human Rights Law Journal*, Vol. 23, 2002, pp. 13-14 [Shelton (*HRLJ* 2002)]

Shields-Delessert, Christiane, *Release and Repatriation of Prisoners of War at the End of Active Hostilities: A Study of Article 118, Paragraph 1, of the Third Geneva Convention relative to the Treatment of Prisoners of War* (PhD thesis No. 291 on file with the Graduate Institute of International Studies), 1977; published as: *Release and Repatriation of Prisoners of War at the End of Active Hostilities*, Zurich, Schulthess Verlag, 1977 [Shields-Delessert (1977)]

Shraga, Daphna, "The UN as an Actor Bound by International Humanitarian Law" in: Condorelli, Luigi et al. (eds.), *The United Nations and International Humanitarian Law*, Paris, Pedone, 1996, pp. 317-338 [Shraga in Condorelli et al. (*1996*)]

___, "UN Peacekeeping Operations: Applicability of International Humanitarian Law and Responsibility for Operations-Related Damage", *American Journal of International Law*, Vol. 94, No. 2, 2000, pp. 406-412 [Shraga (*AJIL* 2000)]

Simma, Bruno and Alston, Philip, "The Sources of Human Rights Law: Custom, *Jus Cogens*, and General Principles", *Australian Yearbook of International Law*, Vol. 12, 1988-1989, pp. 82-108 [Simma & Alston (*Austr.YIL* 1988-1989)]

Simma, Bruno, "From Bilateralism to Community Interest in International Law", *Collected Courses of the Hague Academy of International Law*, Vol. 250, 1994, pp. 217-384 [Simma (*Hague Academy Collected Courses* 1994)]

Siordet, Frédéric, "The Geneva Conventions and Civil War", *International Review of the Red Cross (supp.)*, Vol. 3, Nos. 8, 9 and 11, Geneva, 1950 [Siordet (1950)]

Siotis, Jean, *Le droit de la guerre et les conflits armés d'un caractère non international*, Paris, Librairie Générale de Droit et de Jurisprudence, 1958 [Siotis (1958)]

Simmonds, Robert, *Legal Problems Arising from the United Nations Military Operations in the Congo*, The Hague, Martinus Nijhoff Publishers, 1968 [Simmonds (1968)]

Sivakumaran, Sandesh, "Courts of Armed Opposition Groups: Fair Trials or Summary Justice?", *Journal of International Criminal Justice*, Vol. 7, No. 3, 2009, pp. 489-513 [Sivakumaran (*JICJ* 2009)]

Sloane, Robert D., "The Cost of Conflation: Preserving the Dualism of *Jus ad Bellum* and *Jus in Bello* in the Contemporary Law of War", *Yale Journal of International Law*, Vol. 34, No. 1, 2009, pp. 47-112 [Sloane (*YJIL* 2009)]

Smith, Herbert A., "Some Problems of the Spanish Civil War", *British Year Book of International Law*, Vol. 18, 1937, pp. 17-31 [Smith (*BYIL* 1937)]

Solf, Waldemar A., "Problems with the Application of Norms Governing Interstate Armed Conflict to Non-International Armed Conflict", *Georgia Journal of International and Comparative Law*, Vol. 13, No. 1, 1983, pp. 291-301 [Solf (*GJICL* 1983)]

___, "The Status of Combatants in Non-International Armed Conflicts under Domestic Law and Transnational Practice", *American University Law Review*, Vol. 33, No. 1, 1983, pp. 53-66 [Solf (*AULR* 1983)]

Somer, Jonathan, "Jungle Justice: Passing Sentence on the Equality of Belligerents in Non-International Armed Conflict", *International Review of the Red Cross*, Vol. 89, No. 867, 2007, pp. 655-690 [Somer (*IRRC* 2007)]

Steiner, Max, *Die Internierung von Armeeangehörigen Kriegführender Mächte in neutralen Staate, insbesondere in der Schweiz während des Weltkrieges 1939/45*, Zürich, Ernst Lang, 1947 [Steiner (1947)]

Steiner, Henry J. and Alston, Philip, *International Human Rights in Context. Law, Politics, Morals*, 2nd ed., Oxford, Oxford University Press, 2000 [Steiner & Alston (2000)]

Stewart, James G., "Towards a Single Definition of Armed Conflict in International Humanitarian Law: A Critique of Internationalized Armed Conflict", *International Review of the Red Cross*, Vol. 85, No. 850, 2003, pp. 313-350 [Stewart (*IRRC* 2003)]

___, "Rethinking Guantánamo: Unlawful Confinement as Applied in International Criminal Law", *Journal of International Criminal Justice*, Vol. 4, No. 1, 2006, pp. 12-30 [Stewart (*JICJ* 2006)]

Steyn, Johan, "Guantánamo Bay: The Legal Black Hole", *International and Comparative Law Quarterly*, Vol. 53, No. 1, 2004, pp. 1-15 [Steyn (*ICLQ* 2004)]

Stibbe, Matthew, "The Internment of Civilians by Belligerent States during the First World War and the Response of the International Committee of the Red Cross", *Journal of Contemporary History*, Vol. 41, No. 1, 2006, pp. 5-19 [Stibbe (*JCH* 2006)]

Svensson-McCarthy, Anna-Lena, *The International Law of Human Rights and States of Exception. With Special Reference to the Preparatory Works and the Case-Law of the International Monitoring Organs*, Geneva, Graduate Institute for International Studies, 1996 [Svensson-McCarthy (1996)]

Swinarski, Christophe (ed.), *Studies and Essays on International Humanitarian Law and Red Cross Principles in Honour of Jean Pictet*, Geneva/The Hague, International Committee of the Red Cross/Martinus Nijhoff Publishers, 1984 [Swinarski (1984)]

Taft, William H., "The Law of Armed Conflict after 9/11: Some Salient Features. Remarks at the Symposium on Current Pressures on International Humanitarian Law", *Yale Journal of International Law*, Vol. 28, No. 2, 2003, pp. 319-323 [Taft (*YJIL* 2003)]

Tahzib-Lie, Bahia and Swaak-Goldman, Olivia, "Determining the Threshold for the Application of International Humanitarian Law" in: Lijnzaad, Liesbeth; Sambeek, Johana van and Tahzib-Lie, Bahia (eds.), *Making the Voice of Humanity Heard: Essays on Humanitarian Assistance and International Humanitarian Law in Honour of HRH Princess Margriet of the Netherlands*, Leiden, Nijhoff, 2004, pp. 239-253 [Tahzib-Lie & Swaak-Goldman in Lijnzaad et al.(2004)]

Tamanaha, Brian Z., *On the Rule of Law: History, Politics, Theory*, Cambridge, Cambridge University Press, 2004 [Tamanaha (2004)]

Tavernier, Paul, "Combattants et non-combattants : L'expérience de la guerre entre l'Irak et l'Iran", *Revue belge de droit international*, Vol. 23, 1990-1991, pp. 74-92 [Tavernier *(RBDI* 1990-1991)]

Tittemore, Brian, "Belligerents in Blue Helmets: Applying International Humanitarian Law to United Nations Peace Operations", *Stanford Journal of International Law*, Vol. 33, 1997, pp. 61-118 [Tittemore (*SJIL* 1997)]

Tomuschat, Christian, "The Applicability of Human Rights Law to Insurgent Movements" in: Fischer, Horst; Froissart, Ulrike; Heintschel von Heinegg, Wolff and Raap, Christian (eds.), *Krisensicherung und humanitärer Schutz/Crisis Management and Humanitarian Protection: Festschrift für Dieter Fleck*, Berlin, Berliner Wissenschaftsverlag, 2004, pp. 573-591 [Tomuschat in *Liber Amoricum Fleck* (2004)]

___, *Human Rights: Between Idealism and Realism*, 2nd ed., Oxford, Oxford University Press, 2008 [Tomuschat (2008)]

___, "Human Rights and International Humanitarian Law", *European Journal of International Law*, Vol. 21, No. 1, 2010, pp. 15-23 [Tomuschat (*EJIL* 2010)]

Tracy, Jonathan, "Detention and Prosecution of Alleged Terrorists and Combatants", *Human Rights Brief*, Vol. 16, No. 3, 2009, pp. 15-18 [Tracy (*HRB* 2009)]

Tse, Ka Ho, "The Relevancy of Nationality to the Right to Prisoner of War Status", *Chinese Journal of International Law*, Vol. 8, No. 2, 2009, pp. 395-421 [Tse (*CJIL* 2009)]

Tully, Stephen, "Australian Court Permits Damages Claim for Torture by Former Guantanamo Bay Detainee to Proceed", *ASIL Insights*, Vol. 14, No. 27, 16 September 2010, available at http://www.asil.org/insights100916.cfm [Tully (*ASIL Insights* 2010)]

Vance, Jonathan F. (ed.), *Encyclopedia of Prisoners of War and Internment*, New York, Grey House Publishing, 2006 [Vance (2006)]

(Various authors), "Symposium on Limitation and Derogation Provisions in the International Covenant on Civil and Political Rights", Siracusa, April/May 1984, *Human Rights Quarterly*, Vol. 7, No. 1, 1985, pp. 1-131

(Various authors), "AGORA: The U.S. Decision not to Ratify Protocol I to the Geneva Conventions on the Protection of War Victims", *American Journal of International Law*, Vol. 81, No. 4, 1987, pp. 910-925

(Various authors), "Focus Section: The Non-International Armed Conflict", *German Yearbook of International Law*, Vol. 45, 2002, pp. 55-165

(Various authors), Issue on Legal Aspects of Emergency Regimes: International and Comparative Perspectives", *Israel Yearbook on Human Rights*, Vol. 33, 2003

(Various authors), "Symposium: 'A War against Terrorism': What Role for International Law? US and European Perspectives, *European Journal of International Law*, Vol. 14, No. 2, 2003, pp. 209-378

(Various authors), Symposium: Post-ILC Debate on Fragmentation of International law, *Finnish Yearbook of International Law*, Vol. 17, 2006, pp. 39-90

Vattel, Emer de, *Le droit des gens ou principes du droit naturel* (1758), Washington, Carnegie Institution of Washington, 1916 [de Vattel (1758)]

Verri, Pietro, *Dictionary of the International Law of Armed Conflict*, Geneva, International Committee of the Red Cross, 1992 [Verri (1992)]

Veuthey, Michel, "Les conflits armés de caractère non international et le droit humanitaire", reprinted from Cassese, Antonio (ed.), *Current Problems of International Law. Essays on U.N. Law and on the Law of Armed Conflict*, Milan, Giuffrè, 1975, pp. 179-266 [Veuthey in Cassese (1975)]

___, *Guérilla et droit humanitaire*, Geneva, Institut Henry Dunant/International Committee of the Red Cross, 1983 [Veuthey (1983)]

Vierucci, Luisa, "Prisoners of War or Protected Persons *qua* Unlawful Combatants? The Judicial Safeguards to which Guantánamo Bay Detainees Are Entitled", *Journal of International Criminal Justice*, Vol. 1, 2003, pp. 284-314 [Vierruci (*JICJ* 2003)]

___, "Is the Geneva Convention on Prisoners of War Obsolete? The Views of the Counsel to the US President on the Application of International Law to the Afghan Conflict", *Journal of International Criminal Justice*, Vol. 2, 2004, pp. 866-871 [Vierucci (*JICJ* 2004)]

Villiger, Mark E., *Customary International Law and Treaties: A Study of their Interactions and Interrelations with Special Consideration of the 1969 Vienna Convention on the Law of Treaties*, Dordrecht, Martinus Nijhoff Publishers, 1985 [Villiger (1985)]

___, *Commentary on the 1969 Vienna Convention on the Law of Treaties*, Leiden/Boston, Martinus Nijhoff Publishers, 2009 [Villiger (2009)]

Vité, Sylvain, "Typology of Armed Conflicts in International Humanitarian Law: Legal Concepts and Actual Situations", *International Review of the Red Cross*, Vol. 91, No. 873, 2009, pp. 69-94 [Vité (*IRRC* 2009)]

Vöneky, Silja, "The Fight against Terrorism and the Rules of the Law of Warfare" in: Walter, Christian; Vöneky, Silja; Rüben, Volker and Schorkopf, Frank (eds.), *Terrorism as a Challenge for National and International Law: Security versus Liberty?*, Berlin/Heidelberg, Springer, 2004 [Vöneky (2004)]

Walen, Alex and Venzke, Ingo, "Unconstitutional Detention of Nonresident Aliens: Revisiting the Supreme Court's Treatment of the Law of War in *Hamdi v. Rumsfeld*", *Zeitschrift für ausländisches öffentliches Recht und Völkerrecht*, Vol. 67, No. 3, 2007, pp. 843-885 [Walen & Venzke (*ZaöRV* 2007)]

Walsh, Bernadette, "Detention and Deportation of Foreign Nationals in the United Kingdom during the Gulf Conflict" in: Rowe, Peter, *The Gulf War 1990-91 in International and English Law*, London, Routledge/Sweet & Maxwell, 1993, pp. 304-332 [Walsh in Rowe (1993)]

Walzer, Michael, *Just and Unjust Wars*, 3rd ed., New York, Basic Books, 2000 [Walzer (2000)]

___, *Arguing about War*, New Haven, Yale University Press, 2006 [Walzer (2006)]

Watkin, Kenneth W., "Combatants, Unprivileged Belligerents and Conflicts in the 21st Century", background paper for the Informal High-Level Expert Meeting on the Reaffirmation and Development of International Law, organized by the Program on Humanitarian Policy and Conflict Research at Harvard University Cambridge, 27-29 June 2003, on file with author [Watkin (*HPCR Background Paper* 2003)]

___, "Controlling the Use of Force: A Role for Human Rights Norms in Contemporary Armed Conflict", *American Journal of International Law*, Vol. 98, 2004, pp. 1-34 [Watkin (*AJIL* 2004)]

___, "Warriors without Rights? Combatants, Unprivileged Belligerents, and the Struggle over Legitimacy", Harvard University, Program on Humanitarian Policy and Conflict Research, *HPCR Occasional Paper Series*, No. 2, Winter 2005, available at http://www.hpcr.org/pdfs/OccasionalPaper2.pdf[Watkin (*HPCR Series* 2005)]

___, "Opportunity Lost: Organized Armed Groups and the ICRC 'Direct Participation in Hostilities' Interpretative Guidance", *New York University Journal of International Law and Policy*, Vol. 42, No. 3, 2010, pp. 641-695 [Watkin (*NYUJILP* 2010)]

Waxman, Matthew C., "Detention as Targeting: Standards of Certainty and Detention of Suspected Terrorists", *Columbia Law Review*, Vol. 108, No. 6, 2008, pp. 1365-1430 [Waxman (*CLR* 2008)]

___, "Administrative Detention: The Integration of Strategy and Legal Process", working paper of the *Series on Counterterrorism and American Statutory Law*, joint project of the Brookings Institution, the Georgetown University Law Center, and the Hoover Institution, 24 July 2008, available at http://www.brookings.edu/papers/2008/0724_detention_waxman.aspx [Waxman (*Counterterrorism and American Statutory Law Series* 2008)]

Wayne, Elliot H., "Hostages or Prisoners of War: War Crimes at Dinner", *Military Law Review*, Vol. 149, 1995, pp. 241-274 [Wayne (*MLR* 1995)]

Weis, Peter, *Nationality and Statelessness in International Law*, Alphen aan den Rijn, Sijthoff & Noordhoff, 1979 [Weis (1979)]

Wellens, Karel and Huesa Vinaixa, Rosario (eds.), *L'influence des sources sur l'unité et la fragmentation du droit international*, Brussels, Bruylant, 2006 [Wellens & Huesa Vinaixa (2006)]

Weller, Marc, *Escaping the Self-Determination Trap*, Leiden, Martinus Nijhoff Publishers, 2009 [Weller (2009)]

Wilde, Ralph, "Triggering State Obligations Extraterritorially: The Spatial Test in Certain Human Rights Treaties", *Israel Law Review*, Vol. 40, No. 2, 2007, pp. 503-526 [Wilde (*ILR* 2007)]

___, "Compliance with Human Rights Norms Extraterritorially: "Human Rights Imperialism"?" in: Boisson de Chazournes, Laurence, and Kohen, Marcelo G., *International Law and the Quest for its Implementation/Le droit international et la quête de sa mise en oeuvre. Liber Amicorum Vera Gowlland-Debbas*, Leiden, Brill, 2010, pp. 319-348 [Wilde in *Liber Amoricum Gowlland-Debbas* (2010)]

Wilhelm, René-Jean, "Problèmes relatifs à la protection de la personne humaine par le droit international dans les conflits armés ne présentant pas un caractère international", *Collected Courses of the Hague Academy of International Law*, Vol. 137, 1972-III, pp. 317-417 [Wilhelm (*Hague Academy Collected Courses* 1972)]

Wilmshurst, Elizabeth and Breau, Susan (eds.), *Perspectives on the ICRC Study on Customary International Humanitarian Law*, Cambridge, Cambridge University Press, 2007 [Wilmshurst & Breau (2007)]

Wilson, Heather A., *International Law and the Use of Force by National Liberation Movements*, Oxford, Clarendon Press, 1988 [Wilson (1988)]

Wilson, Robert R., "Treatment of Civilian Alien Enemies", *American Journal of International Law*, Vol. 37, No. 1, 1943, pp. 30-45 [Wilson (*AJIL* 1943)]

Winkler, Thomas, "The Copenhagen Process on Detainees: A Necessity", *Nordic Journal of International Law*, Vol. 78, No. 4, 2009, pp. 489-498 [Winkler (*Nordic JIL* 2010)]

Wittes, Benjamin and Peppard, Colleen A., "Designing Detention: A Model Law for Terrorist Incapacitation", research paper, Washington, Brookings Institution, 26 June 2009 [Wittes & Peppard (*Brookings Institution Research Paper* 2009)]

Wood, Michael, Detention during International Military Operations: Article 103 of the Charter and the *Al-Jedda* Case", *Military Law and Law of War Review*, Vol. 47, Nos. 1-2, 2008, pp. 139-166 [Wood (*MLLWR* 2009)]

Zegveld, Liesbeth, "The Inter-American Commission on Human Rights and International Humanitarian Law: A Comment on the *Tablada Case*", *International Review of the Red Cross*, Vol. 79, No. 324, 1998, pp. 505-511 [Zegveld (*IRRC* 1998)]

___, *Accountability of Armed Opposition Groups under International Law*, Cambridge, Cambridge University Press, 2002 [Zegveld (2002)]

Zemmali, Ameur, *Combattants et prisonniers de guerre en droit islamique et en droit international humanitaire*, Paris, Pedone, 1997 [Zemmali (1997)]

Zimmerman, Andreas; Hofmann, Rainer and Goeters, Hanna (eds.), *Unity and Diversity of International Law: Proceedings of an International Symposium of the Kiel Walther Schücking Institute of International Law*, Berlin, Duncker und Humblot, 2006 [Zimmerman, Hoffman & Goeters (2006)]

Zorgbibe, Charles, *La guerre civile*, Paris, PUF, 1975 [Zorgbibe (1958)]

REPORTS OF EXPERT MEETINGS

- Expert meeting organized by the Institute for Human Rights, Åbo Akademi University, Turku/Åbo, 30 November - 2 December 1990, resulting in a *Declaration of Minimum Humanitarian Standards*, available at http://web.abo.fi/instut/imr/publications/publications_online_text.htm, and reprinted with an introduction by Theodor Meron and Allan Rosas in *American Journal of International Law*, Vol. 85, No. 2, 1991, pp. 375-381 [*Turku Declaration* (1990)]
- Expert Meeting on Multinational Peace Operations: Applicability of International Humanitarian Law and International Human Rights Law to UN Mandated Forces, organized by the International Committee of the Red Cross and the University Centre for International Humanitarian Law, Geneva, 11-12 December 2003, available at http://www.icrc.org/web/eng/siteeng0.nsf/html/p0912 [*Report of the Expert Meeting on Multinational Peace Operations* (2003)]
- Expert Meeting on the Supervision of the Lawfulness of Detention during Armed Conflict, organized by the University Centre for International Humanitarian Law, Geneva, 24-25 July 2004, available at http://www.adh-geneva.ch/events/pdf/expert-meetings/2004/4rapport_detention.pdf [*Report of the Expert Meeting on the Supervision of Lawfulness of Detention* (2004)]
- Expert Meeting on Private Military Contractors: Status and State Responsibility for their Actions, organized by the University Centre for International Humanitarian Law, Geneva, 29-30 August 2005, available at http://www.adh-geneva.ch/events/pdf/expert-meetings/2005/2report_private_companies.pdf [*Report of the Expert Meeting on Private Military Contractors* (2005)]
- Expert Meeting on the Right to Life in Armed Conflicts and Situations of Occupation, organized by the University Centre for International Humanitarian Law, Geneva, 1-2 September 2005, available at http://www.adh-geneva.ch/events/pdf/expert-meetings/2005/3report_right_life.pdf [*Report of the Expert Meeting on the Right to Life* (2005)]
- Expert Meeting on Security Detention, organized by the International Committee of the Red Cross and Frederick K. Cox International Law Center, Cleveland, 14-15 September 2007, *Case Western Reserve Journal of International Law*, Vol. 40, No. 3, 2009, pp. 323-381 [*Report of the Expert Meeting on Security Detention* (2007)]
- Expert Meeting on Procedural Safeguards for Security Detention in Non-International Armed Conflict, organized by the International Committee of the Red Cross and Chatham House, London, 22-23 September 2008, *International Review of the Red Cross*, Vol. 91, No. 876, 2009, pp. 859-881 [*Report of the Expert Meeting on Security Detention in NIAC* (2008)]

NGO REPORTS AND PUBLICATIONS

Amnesty International, *Sri Lanka: Security Measures Violate Human rights*, London, 30 June 1995, available at http://www.amnesty.org/en/library/info/ASA37/012/1995/en [AI, *Sri Lanka Report* (1995)]

___, *Rights at Risk*, London, 18 January 2002, available at http://www.amnesty.org/en/library/info/ACT30/001/2002/en [AI, *Rights at Risk* (2002)]

___, *Syria: 41 Years of the State of Emergency*, London, 8 March 2004, available at http://www.amnesty.org/en/library/info/MDE24/016/2004/en [AI, *Syria Report* (2004)]

___, *Egypt: Systematic Abuses in the Name of Security*, London, 11 April 2007, available at http://www.amnesty.org/en/library/info/MDE12/001/2007/en [AI, *Egypt Report* (2007)]

B'Tselem and Hamoked, *Without Trial: Administrative Detention of Palestinians by Israel and the Internment of Unlawful Combatants Law*, Jerusalem, October 2009, available at http://www.btselem.org/Download/200910_Without_Trial_Eng.pdf [B'Tselem, *Without Trial* (2009)]

Egyptian Organization of Human Rights, *The Effects of the Emergency Law on the Human Rights Situation in Egypt: 1992-2002*, Cairo, February 2003, available at http://www.eohr.org/report/2003/emergency.HTM [EOHR, *Emergency Legislation Report* (2003)]

Human Rights First, *Behind the Wire*, New York, May 2005, available at http://www.humanrightsfirst.org/us_law/PDF/behind-the-wire-033005.pdf [HRF, *Behind the Wire* (2005)]

___, *Fixing Bagram: Strengthening Detention Reforms to Align with U.S. Strategic Priorities*, New York, November 2009, available at http://www.humanrightsfirst.info/pdf/Fixing-Bagram-110409.pdf [HRF, *Fixing Bagram* (2009)]

Human Rights Watch, *In the Name of Counter-Terrorism: Human Rights Abuses Worldwide*, briefing paper for the 59th session of the UN Commission on Human Rights, Geneva, 25 March 2003, on file with author

___, *World Report 2004: Human Rights and Armed Conflict*, New York, 2004

___, *Genocide, War Crimes and Crimes against Humanity. A Topical Digest of the Case Law of the International Criminal Tribunal for the Former Yugoslavia*, New York, 1 July 2006, available at http://www.hrw.org/node/11277 [HRW, *Digest of the Case Law of the ICTY* (2006)]

___, *An Analysis of Ethiopia's Draft Anti-Terrorism Law*, New York, 30 June 2009, available at http://www.hrw.org/node/84132

___, *Genocide, War Crimes and Crimes against Humanity. A Digest of the Case Law of the International Criminal Tribunal for Rwanda*, New York, 15 January 2010, available at http://www.hrw.org/node/87652 [HRW, *Digest of the Case Law of the ICTR* (2010)]

International Commission of Jurists, *Conference Report: Human Rights and the Administration of Justice through Military Tribunals*, Geneva, 26-28 January 2004, available at http://www.jurahominis.it/docs/ICJ%20conference%20report.pdf

___, *Sri Lanka Briefing Paper: Emergency Laws and International Standards*, Geneva, March 2009, available at http://www.icj.org/IMG/SriLanka-BriefingPaper-Mar09-FINAL.pdf

International Council on Human Rights Policy, *Ends & Means: Human Rights Approaches to Armed Groups*, Versoix, September 2000, available at http://www.ichrp.org/files/reports/6/105_report_en.pdf

___, *Human Rights after September 11*, Versoix, 2002, available at http://www.ichrp.org/files/reports/29/118_report_en.pdf

International Crisis Group, *Southern Thailand: Moving Towards Political Solutions?*, Asia Report No. 181, Bangkok/Brussels, 8 December 2009, available at http://www.crisisgroup.org/~/media/Files/asia/south-east-asia/thailand/181%20 Southern%20Thailand%20Moving%20towards%20Political%20Solutions.ashx

PRESS ARTICLES AND BLOGPOSTS

Anon., "Martitegi adiestraba desde Francia a un nuevo comando", *El País*, 19 April 2009, available at http://www.elpais.com/articulo/espana7Martitegi/adiestraba/Francia/nuevo/comando/el pepuesp/20090419elpepunac_4/Tes?print=1

BBC, "Israel to Release Lebanese Prisoners", 18 April 2000, available at http://news.bbc.co.uk/2/hi/middle_east/718295.stm

___, "Profile: ECOMOG", last updated on 17 June 2004, available at http://news.bbc.co.uk/2/hi/africa/country_profiles/2364029.stm

___, "Timeline: Iraq after Saddam", 20 March 2007, available at http://news.bbc.co.uk/2/hi/middle_east/4192189.stm

___, "Timeline: UK-Iran Stand-Off", last updated on 3 April 2007, available at http://news.bbc.co.uk/2/hi/uk_news/6502801.stm

___, "David Hicks: 'Australian Taleban'", last updated on 20 May 2007, available at http://news.bbc.co.uk/2/hi/asia-pacific/3044386.stm

___, "UK Troops in Iraq Moved to Kuwait", 28 July 2009, available at http://news.bbc.co.uk/2/hi/uk_news/8172893.stm

Carmella, Jay, "Spain Court Sentences Former Basque Separatist Leader for Promoting Terrorism", 3 March 2010, available at http://jurist.law.pitt.edu/paperchase/2010/03/spain-court-sentences-former-basque.php

CNN, "Walker Lindh Sentenced to 20 years", 4 October 2002, available at http://archives.cnn.com/2002/LAW/10/04/lindh.statement

Ehret, Christian, "Ethiopia Lawmakers Pass Controversial New Anti-Terrorism Law", *Jurist*, 9 July 2009, available at http://jurist.law.pitt.edu/paperchase/2009/07/ethiopia-lawmakers-pass-controversial.php

Fawkes, Helen, "Prisoner Swap at Russian Checkpoint", 19 August 2008, available at http://news.bbc.co.uk/2/hi/7570949.stm

Frieden, Terry, "U.S. Grilled over Terror Policies", *CNN International*, 2 December 2004, available at http://edition.cnn.com/2004/LAW/12/01/justice.gitmo.court/index.html

Goldsmith, Jack L. and Katyal, Neal, "The Terrorists' Court", *New York Times*, 11 July 2007

Heller, Kevin Jon, "Detention in NIAC – A Response to Wittes and Chesney (and a Defense of Vladeck)", *Opinio Juris*, 20 September 2010, available at http://opiniojuris.org/2010/09/20/detention-in-niac-a-reply-to-wittes-and-chesney-and-a-defense-of-vladeck/ [Heller (*Opinio Juris* 2010)]

Stemple, Hillary, "Federal Judge Allows Indefinite Detention of Guantanamo Detainee", *Jurist*, 7 September 2010, available at http://jurist.org/paperchase/2010/09/federal-judge-allows-indefinite-detention-of-guantanamo-detainee.php

Unknown, "New Yorker in London Gets Prison for al-Qaida Help", *Miami Herald Online*, June 2010, summary by Valentina Spiga available at http://legalift.wordpress.com/2010/06/14/new-yorker-in-london-gets-prison-for-al-qaida-help/

Wright, Lawrence, "The Master Plan: For the New Theorists of Jihad, Al Qaeda is just the Beginning", *The New Yorker*, 11 September 2006, available at http://www.newyorker.com/archive/2006/09/11/060911fa_fact3

Wedgewood, Ruth, "Personal View: Prisoners of a Different War: The Geneva Convention Applies to Conventional Soldiers, not to the Terrorists Being Held at Camp X-Ray", *Financial Times*, 30 January 2002, available at http://www.globalarchive.ft.com/globalarchive/article.html?id=020130001411&query=camp+x

ONLINE DATABASES AND WEBPORTALS

African Union
- AMISOM:
  http://www.africa-union.org/root/au/auc/departments/psc/amisom/amisom.htm
- African Standby Force:
  http://www.africa-union.org/root/au/AUC/Departments/PSC/Asf/ asf.htm

American University Washington College of Law
- War Crimes Research Office: http://www.wcl.american.edu/warcrimes

Amnesty International, webportal on the death penalty: http://www.amnesty.org/en/death-penalty

Australian National Archives webportal on wartime internment: http://www.naa.gov.au/whats-on/online/feature-exhibits/internment-camps/introduction.aspx

Crimes of War Project: http://www.crimesofwar.org

Eurocorps: http://www.eurocorps.org

EULEX: http://www.eulex-kosovo.eu

Geneva Academy of International Humanitarian Law and Human Rights, *Rule of Law in Armed Conflicts*, database available at http://www.adh-geneva.ch/RULAC/

Global Security, Webportal on the Korean War (1950-1953): http://www.globalsecurity.org/military/ops/korea.htm

International Committee of the Red Cross
- Treaty Database: http://www.icrc.org/ihl
- Customary IHL Database: http://www.icrc.org/customary-ihl/eng/docs/home
- Direct Participation in Hostilities webportal:
  http://www.icrc.org/web/eng/siteeng0.nsf/html/direct-participation-article-020709

International Labour Organization, National Legislation Database: http://www.ilo.org/dyn/natlex/natlex_browse.details?p_lang=en&p_country=SDN&p_classification=02&p_origin=COUNTRY&p_sortby=SORTBY_COUNTRY

INTERFET, online archives:
http://pandora.nla.gov.au/parchive/2000/S2000-Nov-7/easttimor.defence.gov.au/index.html

MNF-I, online archives:
http://webarchive.nationalarchives.gov.uk/+/http://www.mod.uk/DefenceInternet/FactSheets/OperationsInIraqKeyFactsFigures.htm

North Atlantic Treaty Organization (NATO)

- KFOR: http://www.nato.int/kfor/
- ISAF: http://www.isaf.nato.int/

Oxford English Dictionary: http://dictionary.oed.com/entrance.dtl

Petit Robert: http://pr2010.bvdep.com/

United Nations

- United Nations Office on Drugs and Crime, *Electronic Legal Resources on International Terrorism*, database available at https://www.unodc.org/tldb/
- United Nations Terrorism webportal: http://www.un.org/terrorism/
- United Nations Rule of Law webportal: http://www.unrol.org
- MONUC: http://monuc.unmissions.org/

Achevé d'imprimer par Corlet Numérique - 14110 Condé-sur-Noireau
N° d'Imprimeur : 96421 - Dépôt légal : mars 2013 - *Imprimé en France*

www.ingramcontent.com/pod-product-compliance
Ingram Content Group UK Ltd.
Pitfield, Milton Keynes, MK11 3LW, UK
UKHW020129290926
15471UKWH00003B/377

9 781849 465304